Financial Accounting

INFORMATION FOR DECISIONS

8th edition

John J. Wild

University of Wisconsin at Madison

Mc
Graw
Hill
Education

To my students and family, especially **Kimberly, Jonathan, Stephanie,** and **Trevor.**

FINANCIAL ACCOUNTING: INFORMATION FOR DECISIONS, EIGHTH EDITION

Published by McGraw-Hill Education, 2 Penn Plaza, New York, NY 10121. Copyright © 2017 by McGraw-Hill Education. All rights reserved. Printed in the United States of America. Previous editions © 2015, 2013, and 2011. No part of this publication may be reproduced or distributed in any form or by any means, or stored in a database or retrieval system, without the prior written consent of McGraw-Hill Education, including, but not limited to, in any network or other electronic storage or transmission, or broadcast for distance learning.

Some ancillaries, including electronic and print components, may not be available to customers outside the United States.

This book is printed on acid-free paper.

2 3 4 5 6 7 8 9 DOW 21 20 19 18 17 16

ISBN 978-1-259-53300-6

MHID 1-259-53300-X

Senior Vice President, Products & Markets: *Kurt L. Strand*
Vice President, General Manager, Products & Markets: *Marty Lange*
Vice President, Content Design & Delivery: *Kimberly Meriwether David*
Managing Director: *Tim Vertovec*
Brand Manager: *Steve Schuetz*
Director, Product Development: *Rose Koos*
Director of Digital Content: *Patricia Plumb*
Lead Product Developer: *Ann Torbert*
Product Developer: *Michael McCormick*
Marketing Manager: *Kyle Burdette*
Digital Product Analyst: *Xin Lin*
Director, Content Design & Delivery: *Linda Avenarius*
Program Manager: *Daryl Horrocks*
Content Project Managers: *Lori Koetters, Brian Nacik*
Buyer: *Sandy Ludovissy*
Design: *Debra Kubiak*
Content Licensing Specialists: *Shawntel Schmitt, Beth Thole*
Cover Images: **Google**: © *Bloomberg/Getty Images;* **Tesla**: © *Bloomberg/Getty Images;*
  Bull: © *xPACIFICA/Getty Images*
Compositor: *Aptara®, Inc.*
Printer: *R.R. Donnelley*

All credits appearing on page or at the end of the book are considered to be an extension of the copyright page.

Library of Congress Cataloging-in-Publication Data

Wild, John J., author.
    Financial accounting : information for decisions / John J. Wild.—8th edition.
      pages cm
    ISBN 978-1-259-53300-6 (alk. paper) — ISBN 1-259-53300-X (alk. paper)
    1. Accounting. I. Title.
  HF5635.W695 2017
  657—dc23

                                                            2015033848

The Internet addresses listed in the text were accurate at the time of publication. The inclusion of a website does not indicate an endorsement by the authors or McGraw-Hill Education, and McGraw-Hill Education does not guarantee the accuracy of the information presented at these sites.

mheducation.com/highered

Adapting to Today's Students

Financial Accounting, 8e

Enhancements in technology have changed how we live and learn. Working with learning resources across devices, whether smartphones, tablets, or laptop computers, empowers students to drive their own learning by putting increasingly intelligent technology into their hands.

Whether the goal is to become an accountant, a businessperson, or simply an informed consumer of accounting information, *Financial Accounting (FA)* has helped generations of students succeed. Its leading-edge accounting content, paired with state-of-the-art technology, supports student learning and elevates understanding of key accounting principles.

FA excels at **engaging students** with content that will help them see the relevance of accounting. Its chapter-opening vignettes showcase dynamic, successful entrepreneurial individuals and companies and **highlight the usefulness of accounting.** This edition's featured companies—**Apple, Google,** and **Samsung**—capture student interest with their products, and their annual reports serve as a pathway for learning financial statements. Need-to-Know illustrations in each chapter demonstrate how to apply key accounting concepts and procedures. The illustrations are supported by guided video presentations.

FA also delivers innovative technology to help student performance. **Connect** provides students with a media-rich eBook version of the textbook and offers instant grading and feedback for assignments that are completed online. Our system for completing exercise and problem material takes accounting content to the next level, delivering assessment material in a **more intuitive, less restrictive** format that adapts to the needs of today's students.

This technology features:

- **a general journal interface** that looks and feels more like that found in practice.
- **an auto-calculation** feature that allows students to focus on concepts rather than rote tasks.
- **a smart (auto-fill) drop-down design.**

The end result is content that better prepares students for the real world.

Connect also includes digitally based, interactive, adaptive learning tools that provide an opportunity to engage students more effectively by offering varied instructional methods and more personalized learning paths that build on different learning styles, interests, and abilities.

The revolutionary technology of **SmartBook®** is available only from McGraw-Hill Education. Based on an intelligent learning system, Smartbook uses a series of adaptive questions to pinpoint each student's knowledge gaps and then provides an optimal learning path. Students spend less time in areas they already know and more time in areas they don't. The result: Students study more efficiently, learn faster, and retain more knowledge. Valuable reports provide insights into how students are progressing through textbook content and information useful for shaping in-class time or assessment.

Interactive Presentations teach each chapter's core learning objectives in a rich, multimedia format, bringing the content to life. Your students will come to class prepared when you assign Interactive Presentations. Students can also review the Interactive Presentations as they study. Further, **Guided Examples** provide students with narrated, animated, step-by-step walk-throughs of algorithmic versions of assigned exercises. Students appreciate the Guided Examples, which help them learn accounting and complete assignments outside of class.

A **General Ledger (GL) application** offers students the ability to see how transactions post from the general journal all the way through the financial statements. It uses the intuitive, less restrictive format used for other homework, and it adds critical thinking components to each GL question, to ensure understanding of the entire process.

The first and only analytics tool of its kind, **Connect Insight®** is a series of visual data displays—each framed by an intuitive question—to provide at-a-glance information about how your class is doing. Connect Insight provides a quick analysis on five key dimensions, available at a moment's notice from a tablet device.

> "A great enhancement! I love the fact that GL makes the student choose from an entire chart of accounts."
>
> —**TAMMY METZKE, Milwaukee Area Technical College**

About the Author

JOHN J. WILD is a distinguished professor of accounting at the University of Wisconsin at Madison. He previously held appointments at Michigan State University and the University of Manchester in England. He received his BBA, MS, and PhD from the University of Wisconsin.

Professor Wild teaches accounting courses at both the undergraduate and graduate levels. He has received numerous teaching honors, including the Mabel W. Chipman Excellence-in-Teaching Award, the departmental Excellence-in-Teaching Award, and the Teaching Excellence Award (multiple times) from the business graduates at the University of Wisconsin. He also received the Beta Alpha Psi and Roland F. Salmonson Excellence-in-Teaching Award from Michigan State University. Professor Wild has received several research honors, is a past KPMG Peat Marwick National Fellow, and is a recipient of fellowships from the American Accounting Association and the Ernst and Young Foundation.

Professor Wild is an active member of the American Accounting Association and its sections. He has served on several committees of these organizations, including the Outstanding Accounting Educator Award, Wildman Award, National Program Advisory, Publications, and Research Committees. Professor Wild is author of *Fundamental Accounting Principles, Financial and Managerial Accounting,* and *College Accounting,* each published by McGraw-Hill Education. His research articles on accounting and analysis appear in *The Accounting Review; Journal of Accounting Research; Journal of Accounting and Economics; Contemporary Accounting Research; Journal of Accounting, Auditing and Finance; Journal of Accounting and Public Policy;* and other journals. He is past associate editor of *Contemporary Accounting Research* and has served on several editorial boards including *The Accounting Review.* Professor Wild is a recognized expert in accounting and financial analysis, and is known for his teaching innovations within an active learning classroom environment.

In his leisure time, Professor Wild enjoys hiking, sports, travel, people, and spending time with family and friends.

Dear Colleagues and Friends,

As I roll out the new edition of *Financial Accounting,* I thank each of you who provided suggestions to improve the textbook and its teaching resources. This new edition reflects the advice and wisdom of many dedicated reviewers, symposium and workshop participants, students, and instructors. Throughout the revision process, I steered this textbook and its teaching tools in the manner you directed. As you'll find, the new edition offers a rich set of features—especially digital features—to improve student learning and assist instructor teaching and grading. I believe you and your students will like what you find in this new edition.

Many talented educators and professionals have worked hard to create the materials for this textbook, and for their efforts, I'm grateful. **I extend a special thank-you to our contributing and technology supplement authors,** who have worked so diligently to support this textbook and its teaching aids:

Contributing Author: Kathleen O'Donnell, *Onondaga Community College*

Accuracy Checkers: Dave Krug, *Johnson County Community College;* and Beth Woods

LearnSmart Author: April Mohr, *Jefferson Community and Technical College, SW*

Interactive Presentations: Jeannie Folk, *College of DuPage*

PowerPoint Presentations: April Mohr, *Jefferson Community and Technical College, SW*

Instructor Resource Manual: April Mohr, *Jefferson Community and Technical College, SW*

Test Bank Contributor: Brenda J. McVey, *University of Mississippi*

Digital Contributor, Connect Content, General Ledger Problems, and Exercise PowerPoints: Kathleen O'Donnell, *Onondaga Community College*

In addition to the invaluable help from the colleagues listed above, I thank the entire *FA,* 8e, team at McGraw-Hill Education: Tim Vertovec, Steve Schuetz, Kyle Burdette, Michael McCormick, Lori Koetters, Ann Torbert, Patricia Plumb, Xin Lin, Kevin Moran, Debra Kubiak, Sandy Ludovissy, Shawntel Schmitt, Beth Thole, Brian Nacik, and Daryl Horrocks. I could not have completed this new edition without your efforts.

John J. Wild

Innovative Textbook Features . . .

Using Accounting for Decisions

Whether we prepare, analyze, or apply accounting information, one skill remains essential: decision making. To help develop good decision-making habits and to illustrate the relevance of accounting, we use a learning framework we call the Decision Center. This framework encompasses a variety of approaches and subject areas, giving students insight into every aspect of business decision making; see the four nearby examples for the different types of decision boxes, including those that relate to fraud. Answers to Decision Maker and Ethics boxes are at the end of each chapter.

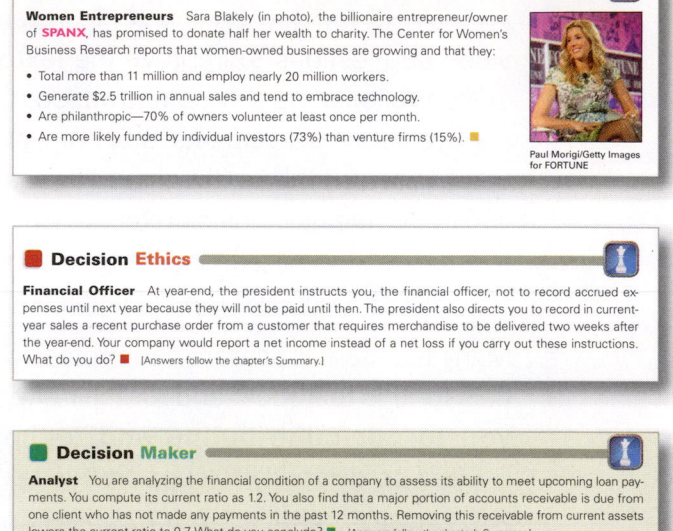

Decision Insight

Women Entrepreneurs Sara Blakely (in photo), the billionaire entrepreneur/owner of **SPANX**, has promised to donate half her wealth to charity. The Center for Women's Business Research reports that women-owned businesses are growing and that they:

- Total more than 11 million and employ nearly 20 million workers.
- Generate $2.5 trillion in annual sales and tend to embrace technology.
- Are philanthropic—70% of owners volunteer at least once per month.
- Are more likely funded by individual investors (73%) than venture firms (15%). ■

Paul Morigi/Getty Images for FORTUNE

Decision Ethics

Financial Officer At year-end, the president instructs you, the financial officer, not to record accrued expenses until next year because they will not be paid until then. The president also directs you to record in current-year sales a recent purchase order from a customer that requires merchandise to be delivered two weeks after the year-end. Your company would report a net income instead of a net loss if you carry out these instructions. What do you do? ■ [Answers follow the chapter's Summary.]

Decision Maker

Analyst You are analyzing the financial condition of a company to assess its ability to meet upcoming loan payments. You compute its current ratio as 1.2. You also find that a major portion of accounts receivable is due from one client who has not made any payments in the past 12 months. Removing this receivable from current assets lowers the current ratio to 0.7. What do you conclude? ■ [Answers follow the chapter's Summary.]

Profit margin and current ratio **Decision Analysis**

Profit Margin

A useful measure of a company's operating results is the ratio of its net income to net sales. This ratio is called **profit margin**, or *return on sales*, and is computed as in Exhibit 3.22.

$$\text{Profit margin} = \frac{\text{Net income}}{\text{Net sales}}$$

EXHIBIT 3.22

Profit Margin

A1

Compute profit margin and describe its use in analyzing company performance.

This ratio is interpreted as reflecting the percent of profit in each dollar of sales. To illustrate how we compute and use profit margin, let's look at the results of **Limited Brands, Inc.**, in Exhibit 3.23 for its fiscal years 2010 through 2014.

> *"This textbook does address many learning styles and at the same time allows for many teaching styles . . . our faculty have been very pleased with the continued revisions and supplements. I'm a 'Wild' fan!"*
>
> **—RITA HAYS, Southwestern Oklahoma State University**

Chapter Preview

Each chapter opens with a visual chapter preview. Students can begin their reading with a clear understanding of what they will learn and when, allowing them to stay more focused and organized along the way. Learning objective numbers highlight the location of related content.

Chapter Preview

BASICS OF ANALYSIS	HORIZONTAL ANALYSIS	VERTICAL ANALYSIS	RATIO ANALYSIS AND REPORTING
C1 Analysis: Its purpose, building blocks, and information needs	**P1** Application of:	**P2** Application of:	**P3** Liquidity and efficiency
C2 Standards for comparisons, and analysis tools	Comparative balance sheets	Common-size balance sheet	Solvency
	Comparative income statements	Common-size income statement	Profitability
	Trend analysis	Common-size graphics	Market prospects
			A1 Analysis reports

CAP Model

The Conceptual/Analytical/Procedural (CAP) model allows courses to be specially designed to meet the teaching needs of a diverse faculty. This model identifies learning objectives, textual materials, assignments, and test items by C, A, or P, allowing different instructors to teach from the same materials, yet easily customize their courses toward a conceptual, analytical, or procedural approach (or a combination thereof) based on personal preferences.

Learning Objectives

CONCEPTUAL

C1 Explain the purpose and identify the building blocks of analysis.

C2 Describe standards for comparisons in analysis.

ANALYTICAL

A1 Summarize and report results of analysis.

A2 *Appendix 13A*—Explain the form and assess the content of a complete income statement.

PROCEDURAL

P1 Explain and apply methods of horizontal analysis.

P2 Describe and apply methods of vertical analysis.

P3 Define and apply ratio analysis.

Bring Accounting to Life

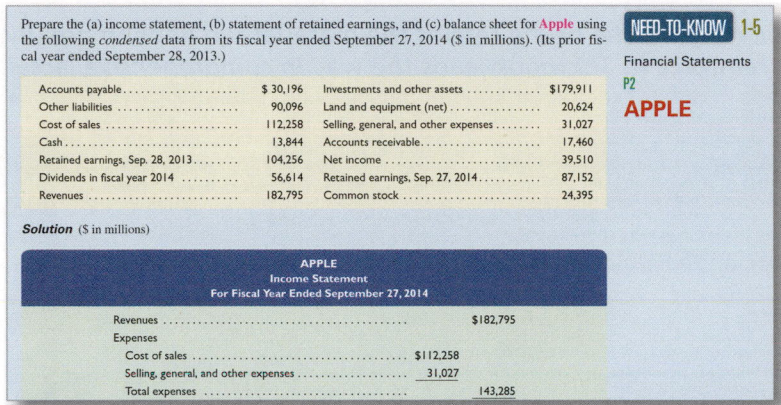

Need-to-Know Illustrations

Need-to-Know illustrations are located at key junctures in each chapter. These illustrations pose questions about the material just presented—content that students "need to know" to successfully learn accounting. Accompanying solutions walk students through key procedures and analysis necessary to be successful with homework and test materials. Need-to-Know illustrations are supplemented with narrated, animated, step-by-step walk-through videos led by an instructor and available via *Connect*.

Global View

The Global View section explains international accounting practices relating to the material covered in that chapter. The aim of this section is to describe accounting practices and to identify the similarities and differences in international accounting practices versus those in the United States. As we move toward global convergence in accounting practices, and as we witness the likely convergence of U.S. GAAP to IFRS, the importance of student familiarity with international accounting grows. This innovative section helps us begin down that path. This section is purposefully located at the end of each chapter so that each instructor can decide what emphasis, if at all, is to be assigned to it.

GLOBAL VIEW

Financial accounting according to U.S. GAAP is similar, but not identical, to IFRS. This section discusses differences in analyzing and recording transactions, and with the preparation of financial statements.

Analyzing and Recording Transactions Both U.S. GAAP and IFRS include broad and similar guidance for financial accounting. Further, both U.S. GAAP and IFRS apply transaction analysis and recording as shown in this chapter—using the same debit and credit system and accrual accounting. Although some variations exist in revenue and expense recognition and other accounting principles, all of the transactions in this chapter are accounted for identically under these two systems.

Financial Statements Both U.S. GAAP and IFRS prepare the same four basic financial statements. A few differences within each statement do exist and we will discuss those throughout the book. For example, both U.S. GAAP and IFRS require balance sheets to separate current items from noncurrent items. However, while U.S. GAAP balance sheets report current items first, IFRS balance sheets normally (but are not required to) present noncurrent items first, and equity before liabilities. To illustrate, a condensed version of **Piaggio**'s balance sheet follows. Piaggio is an Italian manufacturer of scooters and compact vehicles.

PIAGGIO

PIAGGIO Balance Sheet (in thousands of euros) December 31, 2014			
Assets		**Equity and Liabilities**	
Noncurrent assets	€1,079,117	Total equity	€ 413,069
Current assets	477,491	Noncurrent liabilities	581,366
		Current liabilities	562,173
Total assets	€1,556,608	Total equity and liabilities	€1,556,608

Sustainability and Accounting

Sustainability and Accounting The **Sustainability Accounting Standards Board (SASB)** is a nonprofit entity engaged in creating and disseminating sustainability accounting standards for use by companies. Sustainability refers to *environmental, social*, and *governance (ESG)* aspects of a company. A company's social aspects include donations to hospitals, colleges, community programs, and law enforcement. Environmental aspects include programs to reduce pollution, increase product safety, improve worker conditions, and support "green" activities. Governance aspects include social responsibility programs, community relations, and use of sustainable materials. Sustainability accounting standards are intended to complement financial accounting standards. The SASB has its own *Conceptual Framework* to guide the development of sustainability standards. It has also developed a set of *principles*, which serve as a set of minimum criteria.

Apple, as introduced in this chapter's opening feature, focuses on sustainability. Apple hired a Vice President of Environmental Initiatives, Lisa Jackson (in photo), to oversee its sustainability initiative. Lisa has set high goals for Apple, including powering all of its facilities with 100% renewable energy and making its products 100% recyclable. "We are swinging for the fences [on sustainability]," proclaims Lisa, which has resulted in some home runs for Apple. In Apple's sustainability report, Lisa points out that it powers data centers with 100% renewable energy and relies solely on renewable energy to power 80% of its corporate facilities and 50% of its retail stores. As Lisa stresses, "[Sustainability] is really important at Apple." Apple is also committed to reducing carbon emissions. "We would like to eliminate certain toxins," explains Lisa. Apple's sustainability report asserts that it has markedly improved its carbon efficiency and reduced the amount of carbon dioxide produced per dollar of revenue—see graphic. Lisa insists, "Leave the world better than how we found it . . . this is what really inspires people at Apple."

© Xinhua/Alamy

Source: *Greenbiz*, October 2014; Apple Sustainability Report, January 2015

New in this edition are brief sections that highlight the importance of sustainability within the broader context of global accounting (and accountability). Companies increasingly address sustainability in their public reporting and consider the sustainability accounting standards (from the Sustainability Accounting Standards Board) and the expectations of our global society. These boxes, located near the end of the Global View section, cover different aspects of sustainability, often within the context of the chapter's featured entrepreneurial company.

Outstanding Assignment Material . . .

Once a student has finished reading the chapter, how well he or she retains the material can depend greatly on the questions, exercises, and problems that reinforce it. This book leads the way in comprehensive, accurate assignments.

Comprehensive Need-to-Know Problems present both a problem and a complete solution, allowing students to review the entire problem-solving process and achieve success. The problems draw on material from the entire chapter.

NEED-TO-KNOW 10-4

COMPREHENSIVE

Water Sports Company (WSC) patented and successfully test-marketed a new product. To expand its ability to produce and market the new product, WSC needs to raise $800,000 of financing. On January 1, 2016, the company obtained the money in two ways:

a. WSC signed a $400,000, 10% installment note to be repaid with five equal annual installments to be made on December 31 of 2016 through 2020.

b. WSC issued five-year bonds with a par value of $400,000. The bonds have a 12% annual contract rate and pay interest on June 30 and December 31. The bonds' annual market rate is 10% as of January 1, 2016.

Required

1. For the installment note, (*a*) compute the size of each annual payment, (*b*) prepare an amortization table similar to Exhibit 10.14, and (*c*) prepare the journal entry for the first payment.

2. For the bonds, (*a*) compute their issue price; (*b*) prepare the January 1, 2016, journal entry to record their issuance; (*c*) prepare an amortization table using the straight-line method; (*d*) prepare the June 30, 2016, journal entry to record the first interest payment; and (*e*) prepare a journal entry to record retiring the bonds at a $416,000 call price on January 1, 2018.

3.[B] Redo parts 2(*c*), 2(*d*), and 2(*e*) assuming the bonds are amortized using the effective interest method.

PLANNING THE SOLUTION

- For the installment note, divide the borrowed amount by the annuity factor (from Table B.3) using the 10% rate and five payments to compute the amount of each payment. Prepare a table similar to Exhibit 10.14 and use the numbers in the table's first line for the journal entry.

- Compute the bonds' issue price by using the market rate to find the present value of their cash flows (use tables found in Appendix B). Then use this result to record the bonds' issuance. Next, prepare an amortization table like Exhibit 10.11 (and Exhibit 10B.2) and use it to get the numbers needed for the journal entry. Also use the table to find the carrying value as of the date of the bonds' retirement that you need for the journal entry.

SOLUTION

Part 1: Installment Note

a. Annual payment = Note balance/PV annuity factor = $400,000/3.7908 = $105,519 (The present value annuity factor is for five payments and a rate of 10%.)

Summary

C1 **Explain the importance of periodic reporting and the role of accrual accounting.** The value of information is often linked to its timeliness. To provide timely information, accounting systems prepare periodic reports at regular intervals. The time period assumption presumes that an organization's activities can be divided into specific time periods for periodic reporting. Accrual accounting recognizes revenue when earned and expenses when incurred—not necessarily when cash inflows and outflows occur.

C2 **Identify steps in the accounting cycle.** The accounting cycle consists of 10 steps: (1) analyze transactions, (2) journalize, (3) post, (4) prepare an unadjusted trial balance, (5) adjust accounts, (6) prepare an adjusted trial balance, (7) prepare statements, (8) close, (9) prepare a post-closing trial balance, and (10) prepare (optional) reversing entries.

C3 **Explain and prepare a classified balance sheet.** Classified balance sheets report assets and liabilities in two categories: current and noncurrent. Noncurrent assets often include long-term investments, plant assets, and intangible assets. A corporation separates equity into common stock and retained earnings.

accounts. *Prepaid expenses* refer to items paid for in advance of receiving their benefits. Prepaid expenses are assets. Adjusting entries for prepaids involve increasing (debiting) expenses and decreasing (crediting) assets. *Unearned* (or *prepaid*) *revenues* refer to cash received in advance of providing products and services. Unearned revenues are liabilities. Adjusting entries for unearned revenues involve increasing (crediting) revenues and decreasing (debiting) unearned revenues. *Accrued expenses* refer to costs incurred in a period that are both unpaid and unrecorded. Adjusting entries for recording accrued expenses involve increasing (debiting) expenses and increasing (crediting) liabilities. *Accrued revenues* refer to revenues earned in a period that are both unrecorded and not yet received in cash. Adjusting entries for recording accrued revenues involve increasing (debiting) assets and increasing (crediting) revenues.

P2 **Explain and prepare an adjusted trial balance.** An adjusted trial balance is a list of accounts and balances prepared after recording and posting adjusting entries. Financial statements are often prepared from the adjusted trial balance.

P3 **Prepare financial statements from an adjusted trial balance.** Revenue and expense balances are reported on

Chapter Summaries provide students with a review organized by learning objectives. Chapter Summaries are a component of the CAP model (as discussed in the "Innovative Textbook Features" section), which recaps each conceptual, analytical, and procedural objective.

Key Terms are bolded in the text and repeated at the end of the chapter. A complete glossary of key terms is available online through *Connect*.

Key Terms

Annuity	Debt-to-equity ratio	Pension plan
Bearer bonds	Discount on bonds payable	Premium on bonds
Bond	Effective interest method	Registered bonds
Bond certificate	Fair value option	Secured bonds
Bond indenture	Installment note	Serial bonds
Callable bonds	Lease	Sinking fund bonds
Capital leases	Market rate	Straight-line bond amortization
Carrying (book) value of bonds	Mortgage	Term bonds
Contract rate	Off-balance-sheet financing	Unsecured bonds
Convertible bonds	Operating leases	
Coupon bonds	Par value of a bond	

Helps Students Master Key Concepts

Multiple Choice Quiz questions quickly test chapter knowledge before a student moves on to complete Quick Studies, Exercises, and Problems.

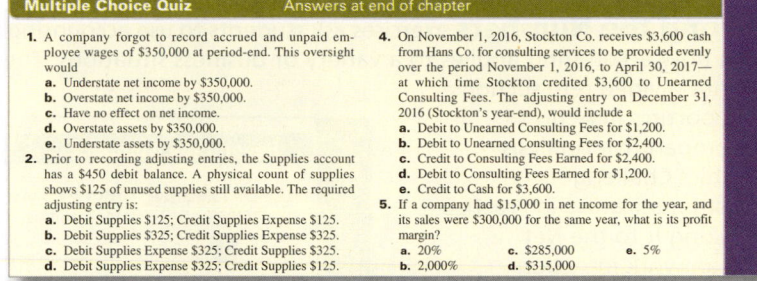

Multiple Choice Quiz   Answers at end of chapter

1. A company forgot to record accrued and unpaid employee wages of $350,000 at period-end. This oversight would
   a. Understate net income by $350,000.
   b. Overstate net income by $350,000.
   c. Have no effect on net income.
   d. Overstate assets by $350,000.
   e. Understate assets by $350,000.
2. Prior to recording adjusting entries, the Supplies account has a $450 debit balance. A physical count of supplies shows $125 of unused supplies still available. The required adjusting entry is:
   a. Debit Supplies $125; Credit Supplies Expense $125.
   b. Debit Supplies $325; Credit Supplies Expense $325.
   c. Debit Supplies Expense $325; Credit Supplies $325.
   d. Debit Supplies Expense $325; Credit Supplies $125.
4. On November 1, 2016, Stockton Co. receives $3,600 cash from Hans Co. for consulting services to be provided evenly over the period November 1, 2016, to April 30, 2017—at which time Stockton credited $3,600 to Unearned Consulting Fees. The adjusting entry on December 31, 2016 (Stockton's year-end), would include a
   a. Debit to Unearned Consulting Fees for $1,200.
   b. Debit to Unearned Consulting Fees for $2,400.
   c. Credit to Consulting Fees Earned for $2,400.
   d. Debit to Consulting Fees Earned for $1,200.
   e. Credit to Cash for $3,600.
5. If a company had $15,000 in net income for the year, and its sales were $300,000 for the same year, what is its profit margin?
   a. 20%   c. $285,000   e. 5%
   b. 2,000%   d. $315,000

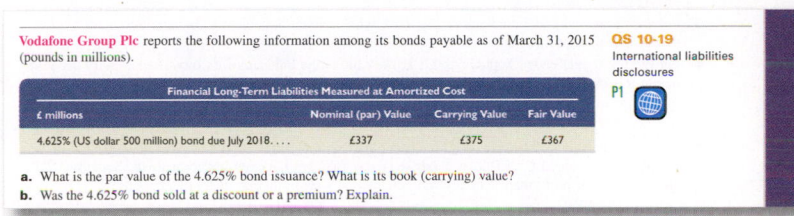

Vodafone Group Plc reports the following information among its bonds payable as of March 31, 2015 (pounds in millions).

QS 10-19
International liabilities disclosures
P1

Financial Long-Term Liabilities Measured at Amortized Cost

£ millions	Nominal (par) Value	Carrying Value	Fair Value
4.625% (US dollar 500 million) bond due July 2018....	£337	£375	£367

a. What is the par value of the 4.625% bond issuance? What is its book (carrying) value?
b. Was the 4.625% bond sold at a discount or a premium? Explain.

Quick Study assignments are short exercises that often focus on one learning objective. Most are included in *Connect*. There are at least 10–15 Quick Study assignments per chapter.

Exercises are one of this book's many strengths and a competitive advantage. There are at least 10–15 per chapter, and most are included in *Connect*.

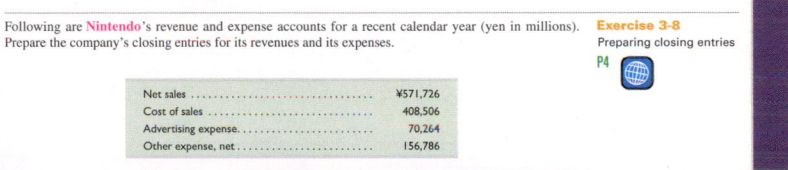

Following are **Nintendo**'s revenue and expense accounts for a recent calendar year (yen in millions). Prepare the company's closing entries for its revenues and its expenses.

Exercise 3-8
Preparing closing entries
P4

Net sales	¥571,726
Cost of sales	408,506
Advertising expense	70,264
Other expense, net	156,786

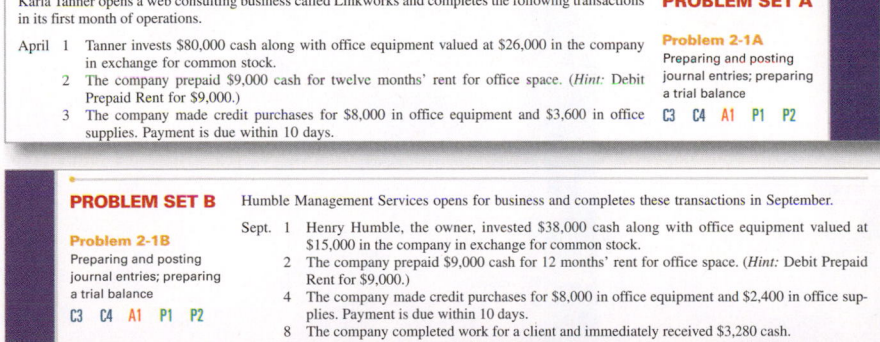

connect

Karla Tanner opens a web consulting business called Linkworks and completes the following transactions in its first month of operations.

PROBLEM SET A

April 1 Tanner invests $80,000 cash along with office equipment valued at $26,000 in the company in exchange for common stock.
       2 The company prepaid $9,000 cash for twelve months' rent for office space. (*Hint:* Debit Prepaid Rent for $9,000.)
       3 The company made credit purchases for $8,000 in office equipment and $3,600 in office supplies. Payment is due within 10 days.

Problem 2-1A
Preparing and posting journal entries; preparing a trial balance
C3 C4 A1 P1 P2

Problem Sets A & B are proven problems that can be assigned as homework or for in-class projects. All problems are coded according to the CAP model (see the "Innovative Textbook Features" section), and Set A is included in *Connect*.

PROBLEM SET B

Problem 2-1B
Preparing and posting journal entries; preparing a trial balance
C3 C4 A1 P1 P2

Humble Management Services opens for business and completes these transactions in September.

Sept. 1 Henry Humble, the owner, invested $38,000 cash along with office equipment valued at $15,000 in the company in exchange for common stock.
       2 The company prepaid $9,000 cash for 12 months' rent for office space. (*Hint:* Debit Prepaid Rent for $9,000.)
       4 The company made credit purchases for $8,000 in office equipment and $2,400 in office supplies. Payment is due within 10 days.
       8 The company completed work for a client and immediately received $3,280 cash.
      12 The company completed a $15,400 project for a client, who must pay within 30 days.

Outstanding Assignment Material . . .

Beyond the Numbers exercises ask students to use accounting figures and understand their meaning. Students also learn how accounting applies to a variety of business situations. These creative and fun exercises are all new or updated and are divided into sections:

- Reporting in Action
- Comparative Analysis
- Ethics Challenge
- Communicating in Practice
- Taking It to the Net
- Teamwork in Action
- Hitting the Road
- Entrepreneurial Decision
- Global Decision

Beyond the Numbers

REPORTING IN ACTION

A1 P4

APPLE

BTN 3-1 Refer to Apple's financial statements in Appendix A to answer the following.

1. Identify and write down the revenue recognition principle as explained in the chapter.
2. Review Apple's footnotes (in Appendix A and/or from its 10-K on its website) to discover how it applies the revenue recognition principle and when it recognizes revenue. Report what you discover.
3. What is Apple's profit margin for fiscal years ended September 27, 2014, and September 28, 2013?
4. For the fiscal year ended September 27, 2014, what amount is credited to Income Summary to summarize its revenues earned?
5. For the fiscal year ended September 27, 2014, what amount is debited to Income Summary to summarize its expenses incurred?
6. For the fiscal year ended September 27, 2014, what is the balance of its Income Summary account before it is closed?

Fast Forward

7. Access Apple's annual report (10-K) for fiscal years ending after September 27, 2014, at its website (Apple.com) or the SEC's EDGAR database (www.SEC.gov). Assess and compare the September 27, 2014, fiscal year profit margin to any subsequent year's profit margin that you compute.

Serial Problems use a continuous running case study to illustrate chapter concepts in a familiar context. The Serial Problem can be followed continuously from the first chapter or picked up at any later point in the book; enough information is provided to ensure students can get right to work.

This serial problem began in Chapter 1 and continues through most of the book. If previous chapter segments were not completed, the serial problem can still begin at this point. It is helpful, but not necessary, to use the Working Papers that accompany the book.

SERIAL PROBLEM
Business Solutions
P1 P2 P3 P4 P5

SP 3 After the success of the company's first two months, Santana Rey continues to operate Business Solutions. (Transactions for the first two months are described in the Chapter 2 serial problem.) The November 30, 2016, unadjusted trial balance of Business Solutions (reflecting its transactions for October and November of 2016) follows.

No.	Account Title	Debit	Credit
101	Cash.	$38,264	
106	Accounts receivable	12,618	
126	Computer supplies	2,545	
128	Prepaid insurance	2,220	
131	Prepaid rent.	3,300	
163	Office equipment.	8,000	
164	Accumulated depreciation—Office equipment		$ 0
167	Computer equipment	20,000	
168	Accumulated depreciation—Computer equipment.		0
201	Accounts payable.		0
210	Wages payable.		0
236	Unearned computer services revenue		0
307	Common stock.		73,000
318	Retained earnings		0
319	Dividends	5,600	
403	Computer services revenue		25,659
612	Depreciation expense—Office equipment.	0	
613	Depreciation expense—Computer equipment	0	
623	Wages expense.	2,625	
637	Insurance expense.	0	
640	Rent expense.	0	
652	Computer supplies expense	0	
655	Advertising expense	1,728	
676	Mileage expense	704	
677	Miscellaneous expenses.	250	
684	Repairs expense—Computer	805	
	Totals.	$98,659	$98,659

Helps Students Master Key Concepts

General Ledger Problems enable students to see how transactions post. Students can track an amount in any financial statement all the way back to the original journal entry. Critical thinking components then challenge students to analyze the business activities in the problem.

GENERAL LEDGER PROBLEMS

Available in Connect

The **General Ledger** tool in *Connect* allows students to immediately see the financial statements as of a specific date. Each of the following questions begins with an unadjusted trial balance. Using transactions from the following assignment, prepare the necessary adjustments and determine the impact each adjustment has on net income. The financial statements are automatically populated.

GL 3-1 Based on the FastForward illustration in this chapter

Using transactions from the following assignments, prepare the necessary adjustments, create the financial statements, and determine the impact each adjustment has on net income.

GL 3-2 Based on Problem 3-3A   **GL 3-5** Based on Problem 3-6A

GL 3-3 Extension of Problem 2-1A   **GL 3-6** Based on Serial Problem SP 3

GL 3-4 Extension of Problem 2-2A

The End of the Chapter Is Only the Beginning Our valuable and proven assignments aren't just confined to the book. From problems that require technological solutions to materials found exclusively online, this book's end-of-chapter material is fully integrated with its technology package.

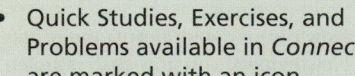

- Quick Studies, Exercises, and Problems available in *Connect* are marked with an icon.

- Assignments that focus on global accounting practices and companies are often identified with an icon.

- Assignments that involve decision analysis are identified with an icon.

Content Revisions Enhance Learning

This edition's revisions are driven by feedback from instructors and students. They include the following:

- Many new, revised, and updated assignments throughout, including serial problem and entrepreneurial assignments.
- Many Need-to-Know demonstrations added to each chapter at key junctures to reinforce key topics.
- New Sustainability section for each chapter, with examples linked to the company featured in the chapter opener.
- New annual reports and comparative (BTN) assignments: Apple, Google, and Samsung.
- Revised opening layout for each chapter.

- Revised art program, visual infographics, and text layout.
- Updated ratio/tool analysis, using data from well-known firms.
- Revised General Ledger assignments for most chapters.
- Revised material on International Financial Reporting Standards (IFRS).
- New and revised entrepreneurial examples and elements.
- New technology content integrated and referenced in the book.

Chapter 1

Updated opener—Apple.
Updated salary info for accountants and for those with higher degrees.
Streamlined "Fraud Triangle" section.
Updated "Cooking the Books" Fraud box.
Streamlined the "Fundamentals of Accounting" section, including the conceptual framework.
Removed the "Principles and Scruples" box.
Removed the "Economic Downturn" box.
New graphic to launch "Communicating with Users" section on financial statements.
New margin point to highlight layout of income statement.
Streamlined Global View section by removing world map of IFRS coverage.
New discussion of FASB and IASB convergence.
New Sustainability section for Apple's environmental efforts, including SASB.
Updated Decision Insights box on sustainability returns.
New company, Verizon, for Decision Analysis section.
Streamlined Appendix 1B.

Chapter 2

NEW opener—Twitter.
Simplified discussion on analyzing and recording process.
Streamlined discussion of classified vs. unclassified balance sheet.
Updated SPANX Decision Insight box.
Enhanced Exhibit 2.2 on expanded accounting equation.
Changed selected numbers for FastForward transactions.
Enhanced Exhibit 2.15 on financial links across time.
New layout for Exhibit 2.16 showing financial statements drawn from trial balance.

Updated Piaggio's (IFRS) balance sheet.
Updated "Data Quality" Fraud box with new information from KPMG.
New Sustainability section on Twitter's environmental efforts.
Updated Skechers's ratio analyses.

Chapter 3

NEW opener—GoPro.
Added partial income statement to margins of Exhibits 3.2 and 3.3.
New box on Saba accounting fraud and clawbacks.
Enhanced Exhibit 3.4 with added entries and financial statement effects.
Simplified depreciation illustration under "Prepaid Expenses."
New art added to introduce accrued revenues.
Changed selected numbers for FastForward in Exhibits 3.13 through 3.18.
Updated Piaggio's classified balance sheet.
New Sustainability section on GoPro's environmental efforts.
Updated Limited Brands's ratio analyses.
Enhanced Exhibit 3B.1 with explanatory notes at bottom of Excel screen to aid learning.

Chapter 4

NEW opener—Chipotle.
Added T-account to Exhibit 4.4 to aid student understanding.
Enhanced explanation, including entries, for cash and credit purchases.
Simplified purchase returns illustration.
Enhanced explanation to section on transportation costs.
New column added to Exhibit 4.7 to show who owns goods in transit.
Sales entries reflect new revenue recognition rules.
New adjusting entries for future sales discounts and sales returns and allowances.
New Decision Insight box highlights three new accounts.

New NTK 4-2, Part 1 to illustrate sales transactions.
New NTK 4-2, Part 2 to illustrate new adjusting entries.
Revised Exhibit 4.12 covers new revenue recognition rules.
Updated "Merchandising Shenanigans" Fraud box with new data from KPMG.
New Sustainability section for Chipotle's four keys.
Updated gross margin and quick ratios using JCPenney.
New Appendix 4C showing entries for gross (and net) method.
Numerous revised and new assignments.
Revised assignments for new revenue recognition rules for sales discounts and sales returns and allowances.

Chapter 5

NEW opener—Tesla Motors.
Updated box on wireless inventory scans.
Updated box on employees receiving kickbacks or gifts from suppliers.
Updated global accounting to remove convergence project reference.
New Sustainability section on Tesla's new-age manufacturing.
Updated inventory ratios section using Toys "R" Us.
Appendix 5A: Simplified by deleting detailed review of entries with each method.
Appendix 5B: Revised to be consistent with new revenue recognition rules.

Chapter 6

UPDATED opener—Google.
New image included for bonding certificate.
New discussion of controls over social media with reference to Facebook's "mood" posts.
New discussion of how fraud is detected.
New evidence on how cash is stolen from companies.

Added T-account in margin of bank statement to aid learning.
New table to identify five common items for bank reconciliation.
New discussion of control weaknesses contributing to fraud.
New section on cash spent for **Google's** sustainable initiatives.
Updated receivables analysis using **Hasbro** and **Mattel**.
New learning notes added to bank reconciliation.
New chart for timing differences for bank reconciliation.
Deleted Appendix 6B (now Appendix 4C).
Added several new Quick Study assignments.

Chapter 7

NEW opener—**GrubHub**.
Updated data in Exhibit 7.1.
Updated credit card processing explanation, including links to more explanations.
New list on pros/cons of allowance vs. direct write-off.
New three-step process to estimate bad debts.
New marginal T-accounts to show impact of estimating bad debts.
Expanded Exhibit 7.13 to include the adjusting entry amount.
New Sustainability section on **GrubHub's** efforts.
Revised analysis section with new companies: **IBM** and **Oracle**.

Chapter 8

NEW opener—**Kate Spade**.
Updated data in Exhibit 8.1.
Added info boxes to Exhibits 8.8, 8.10, and 8.12.
New margin notes added for SL and DDB rates.
Updated **Dale Jarrett Racing Adventure** asset listing.
Revised "In Control" Fraud box with new information from KPMG.
New goodwill references to **Facebook** and **WhatsApp**.
New Sustainability section on **Kate Spade's** efforts.
Updated analysis section for **Molson Coors** and **Boston Beer**.

Chapter 9

NEW opener—**Noodles & Co.**
Updated data in Exhibit 9.2.

Clarified bonus explanation and computations.
Updated payroll rates to 2015.
New explanation of *Additional Medicare Tax*.
Updated FUTA rate.
Updated "False Move" Fraud box using new information.
Enhanced payroll reports and related exhibits.
New Sustainability section on **Noodles & Co.'s** environmental initiatives.

Chapter 10

NEW opener—**Box**.
Simplified Exhibit 10.1 for ease of learning.
Reported largest bond offerings in history—**Verizon** and **Apple**.
New bond image from the **Minnesota Vikings**.
Added T-accounts for bond payable and related discounts and premiums to demonstrate pattern over bond life.
New Point explaining what determines bond payments and interest expense.
Updated "Missing Debt" Fraud box using new data from KPMG.
Added T-accounts for bond discounts and premium over bond life in Appendix 10B.
New Decision Insight box on equivalent payments concept to aid learning.
Updated learning notes for bond interest computations.
New Decision Insight box on junk bonds and investment strategy.
New color highlighting for learning amortization.
New Sustainability section on **Box's** nonprofit activities.
Revised analysis section with new company: **Amazon**.

Chapter 11

NEW opener—**Alibaba**.
Updated dividend tax rates.
Updated the **Target** stock quote data.
New five-step process for help in learning accounting for dividends.
Enhanced Exhibit 11.8 to include *declaration* and *issuance* effects.
New reference to **Apple's** 7-for-1 split.
Updated the **Apple** statement of equity.
New Sustainability section on **Alibaba's** program.

Updated learning notes for computations.
Updated PE and dividend yield ratios for **Amazon** and **Altria**.

Chapter 12

NEW opener—**Amazon**.
New infographics for operating, investing, and financing activities.
New Exhibit 12.4 linking cash flow classifications to balance sheet.
Simplified discussion of noncash investing and financing.
New, simplified five-step process for preparing the statement of cash flows.
Streamlined the categories from *three* to *two* for adjustment to income to get operating cash flow.
Simplified cash flows from investing presentation.
New summary T-account for learning statement of cash flows.
New *reconstruction entries* to aid student learning.
New Sustainability section on **Amazon's** initiatives.
Updated cash flow analysis using Nike.
Three new Quick Studies and three new Exercises.

Chapter 13

Revised opener—**Morgan Stanley**.
Updated data for analysis of **Apple** throughout using horizontal, vertical, and ratio analysis.
Updated comparative analysis with **Google** and **Samsung**.
New evidence on accounting ruses by CFOs.
Revised "All Else Being Equal" Fraud box to incorporate new data.
Revised Appendix 13A to reflect new rules that eliminate the separate disclosure of *extraordinary items*.
New Sustainability section on Morgan Stanley's initiatives.
Revised assignments for new standard on extraordinary items.

Appendix C

New three-step process for fair value adjustment.
New learning note for investee vs. investor securities.
Updated Google example for comprehensive income.
Updated returns analysis using Gap.

Required=Results

McGraw-Hill Connect®
Learn Without Limits

Connect is a teaching and learning platform that is proven to deliver better results for students and instructors.

Connect empowers students by continually adapting to deliver precisely what they need, when they need it, and how they need it, so your class time is more engaging and effective.

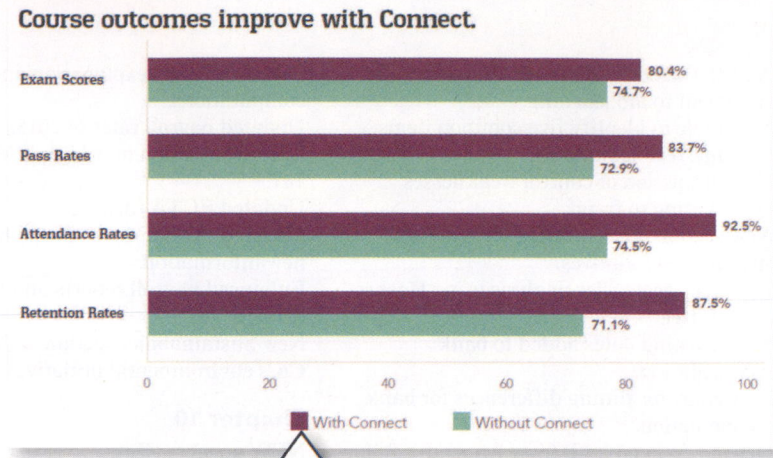

Course outcomes improve with Connect.

	With Connect	Without Connect
Exam Scores	80.4%	74.7%
Pass Rates	83.7%	72.9%
Attendance Rates	92.5%	74.5%
Retention Rates	87.5%	71.1%

Using **Connect** improves passing rates by **10.8%** and retention by **16.4%**.

88% of instructors who use Connect require it; instructor satisfaction increases by 38% when Connect is required.

Analytics

Connect Insight®

Connect Insight is Connect's new one-of-a-kind visual analytics dashboard that provides at-a-glance information regarding student performance, which is immediately actionable. By presenting assignment, assessment, and topical performance results together with a time metric that is easily visible for aggregate or individual results, Connect Insight gives the user the ability to take a just-in-time approach to teaching and learning, which was never before available. Connect Insight presents data that helps instructors improve class performance in a way that is efficient and effective.

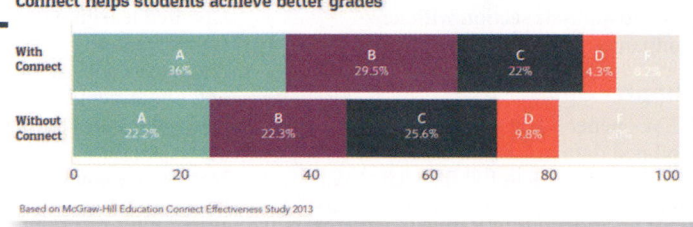

Connect helps students achieve better grades

	A	B	C	D	F
With Connect	36%	29.5%	22%	4.3%	
Without Connect	22.2%	22.3%	25.6%	9.8%	

Based on McGraw-Hill Education Connect Effectiveness Study 2013

Adaptive

THE FIRST AND ONLY ADAPTIVE READING EXPERIENCE DESIGNED TO TRANSFORM THE WAY STUDENTS READ

More students earn **A's** and **B's** when they use McGraw-Hill Education **Adaptive** products.

SmartBook®

Proven to help students improve grades and study more efficiently, SmartBook contains the same content within the print book, but actively tailors that content to the needs of the individual. SmartBook's adaptive technology provides precise, personalized instruction on what the student should do next, guiding the student to master and remember key concepts, targeting gaps in knowledge and offering customized feedback, and driving the student toward comprehension and retention of the subject matter. Available on smartphones and tablets, SmartBook puts learning at the student's fingertips—anywhere, anytime.

Over **4 billion questions** have been answered, making McGraw-Hill Education products more intelligent, reliable, and precise.

STUDENTS WANT

SMARTBOOK®

95% of students reported **SmartBook** to be a more effective way of reading material

100% of students want to use the Practice Quiz feature available within **SmartBook** to help them study

100% of students reported having reliable access to off-campus wifi

90% of students say they would purchase **SmartBook** over print alone

95% reported that **SmartBook** would impact their study skills in a positive way

*Findings based on a 2015 focus group survey at Pellissippi State Community College administered by McGraw-Hill Education

www.learnsmartadvantage.com

Acknowledgments

John J. Wild and McGraw-Hill Education recognize the following instructors for their valuable feedback and involvement in the development of *Financial Accounting,* 8e. We are thankful for their suggestions, counsel, and encouragement

Thomas Arcuri, Florida State University
Sidney Askew, Borough of Manhattan Community College
Richard Barnhart, Grand Rapids Community College
Jaswinder Bhangal, Chabot College
Patrick Borja, Citrus College
Anna Boulware, St. Charles Community College
Bruce Bradford, Fairfield University
Billy Brewster, University of Texas at Arlington
Marci Butterfield, University of Utah
Lawrence Chui, University of Saint Thomas
Colleen Chung, Miami Dade College–Kendall
Kwang-Hyun Chung, Pace University
Robert Churchman, Harding University
Marilyn Ciolino, Delgado Community College
Robin Clement, University of Oregon
Ken Couvillion, Delta College
Karen Crisonino, County College of Morris
Stan Davis, University of Tennessee at Chattanooga
Walter DeAguero, Saddleback College
Stephanie and Mike Derr, Derr Properties
Mike Deschamps, MiraCosta College
Ron Dustin, Fresno City College
David Emerson, Salisbury University
Magdy Farag, California State Polytechnic University–Pomona
Albert Fisher, College of Southern Nevada
Linda Flowers, Houston Community College
Jeannie Folk, College of DuPage
Ernesto Gonzalez, Florida National College
Ann Gregory, South Plains College
Rebecca Hancock, El Paso Community College–Valley Verde
Laurie Hays, Western Michigan University
Rita Hays, Southwestern Oklahoma State University
Bambi Hora, University of Central Oklahoma
Constance Hylton, George Mason University
Todd Jensen, Sierra College
Gina M. Jones, Aims Community College
Jeff Jones, College of Southern Nevada
Sandra Jordan, Florida State College at Jacksonville
Dmitriy Kalyagin, Chabot College
Thomas Kam, Hawaii Pacific University
Ann Kelley, Providence College
Shirly A. Kleiner, Johnson County Community College
Jo Koehn, University of Central Missouri
Sudha Krishnan, California State University–Long Beach
Anita Kroll, University of Wisconsin–Madison
David Krug, Johnson County Community College
Christopher Kwak, DeAnza College
David Laurel, South Texas College

Joan Lee, Fairfield University
Charles Lewis, Houston Community College
Jeannie Liu, Chaffey College
Thomas S. Marsh, Northern Virginia Community College–Annandale
Stacie Mayes, Rose State College
Brenda McVey, University of Mississippi
Donald McWilliams, Jackson State University
Jeanine Metzler, Northampton Community College
Edna C. Mitchell, Polk State College
April Mohr, Jefferson Community and Technical College, SW
Kathleen O'Donnell, Onondaga Community College
Yvonne Phang, Borough of Manhattan Community College
M. Jeff Quinlan, Madison College
James Racic, Lakeland Community College
Ruthie Reynolds, Howard University
Helen Roybark, Radford University
Richard Sarkisian, Camden County College
Linda Schain, Hofstra University
Tracy Schmeltzer, Wayne Community College
Debbie Schmidt, Cerritos College
Raymond Shaffer, Youngstown State University
Geeta Shankhar, University of Dayton
Ken W. Shaw, University of Missouri
Regina Shea, Community College of Baltimore County–Essex
Jaye Simpson, Tarrant County College
Erik Slayter, California Polytechnic State University–San Luis Obispo
Gerald Smith, University of Northern Iowa
Kevin Smith, Utah Valley University
Dominique Svarc, William Rainey Harper College
Ulysses Taylor, Fayetteville State University
Anthony Teng, Saddleback College
Teresa Thompson, Chaffey Community College
Tom Thompson, Madison College
Jerri Tittle, Rose State College
Bob Urell, Irvine Valley College
Patricia Walczak, Lansing Community College
Dave Welch, Franklin University
Jean Wells-Jessup, Howard University
Christopher Widmer, Tidewater Community College
Jonathan M. Wild, University of Wisconsin
Kenneth L. Wild, University of London
Gayle Williams, Sacramento City College
Wanda Wong, Chabot College
John Woodward, Polk State College
Qiang Wu, Rensselaer Polytechnic Institute
Judy Zander, Grossmont College

Brief Contents

*Appendix D is available in McGraw-Hill Connect and as a print copy from a McGraw-Hill Education representative.

Contents

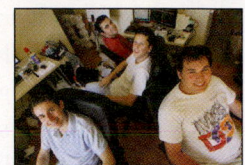

10 Reporting and Analyzing Long-Term Liabilities 442

11 Reporting and Analyzing Equity 488

12 Reporting and Analyzing Cash Flows 534

*Appendix D is available in McGraw-Hill Connect and as a print copy from a McGraw-Hill Education representative.

Financial Accounting

chapter 1

Introducing Financial Statements

Chapter Preview

IMPORTANCE OF ACCOUNTING

C1 Purpose of accounting

C2 Accounting information users

Opportunities in accounting

FUNDAMENTALS OF ACCOUNTING

C3 Ethics—Key concept

C4 Generally accepted accounting principles

Conceptual framework

Regulatory setting

BUSINESS TRANSACTIONS

A1 Accounting equation and its components

Key financial measures

P1 Transaction analysis—Illustrated

FINANCIAL COMMUNICATIONS

P2 Income statement

Statement of retained earnings

Balance sheet

Statement of cash flows

A2 Financial analysis

Chapter Preview is organized by key topics and includes learning objectives
Learning Objectives are classified as conceptual, analytical, or procedural

Learning Objectives

CONCEPTUAL

C1 Explain the purpose and importance of accounting.

C2 Identify users and uses of, and opportunities in, accounting.

C3 Explain why ethics are crucial to accounting.

C4 Explain generally accepted accounting principles and define and apply several accounting principles.

C5 *Appendix 1B*—Identify and describe the three major activities of organizations.

ANALYTICAL

A1 Define and interpret the accounting equation and each of its components.

A2 Compute and interpret return on assets.

A3 *Appendix 1A*—Explain the relation between return and risk.

PROCEDURAL

P1 Analyze business transactions using the accounting equation.

P2 Identify and prepare basic financial statements and explain how they interrelate.

One Smart Apple

A **Decision Feature** launches each chapter showing the relevance of accounting for a real entrepreneur. An **Entrepreneurial Decision** assignment returns to this feature with a mini-case

"Wherever smart people work, doors are unlocked"—STEVE WOZNIAK

CUPERTINO, CA—"When I designed the Apple stuff," says Steve Wozniak (a.k.a. the *Wizard of Woz*), "I never thought in my life I would have enough money to fly to Hawaii or make a down payment on a house." But some dreams do come true. Woz, along with Steve Jobs and Ron Wayne, founded Apple. Today, **Apple** (**Apple.com**) boasts a value of over $700 billion and revenues of over $180 billion—recent revenues and income follow.

($ billions)	2011	2012	2013	2014
Revenues	$108.2	$156.5	$170.9	$182.8
Net income . . .	25.9	41.7	37.0	39.5

Along the way, the young entrepreneurs faced many challenges, including accounting issues such as how to properly read and interpret accounting data. The first challenge was how to finance the new company, which they did by selling some of their prized possessions, such as Woz's Hewlett-Packard scientific calculator and Jobs's Volkswagen van. The $1,300 they raised helped them purchase the electronic equipment Woz used to build the first Apple computer.

Apple Inc.
NASDAQ: AAPL

$231,839 mil. assets
93,000 **employees**

Revenue Sources

In setting up their company, the two young entrepreneurs had to decide what type of entity to form—a partnership or a corporation. They decided on a partnership, and Ron Wayne "sat down at a typewriter and typed our partnership contract right out of his head," recalls Woz. "He did an etching of Newton under the apple tree for the cover of our Apple I manual [and] he wrote the manual." The original partnership agreement included Wayne as a third partner with 10% ownership. However, a few days later, Wayne had a change of heart when he considered the unlimited liability of a partnership. He pulled out, leaving Woz and Jobs holding 50% each. Within nine months, Woz and Jobs identified some advantages to the corporate form of business organization, and they converted Apple to a corporation.

As their company grew, Woz and Jobs had to learn more accounting, along with details of preparing and interpreting financial statements. Important questions involving transaction analysis and financial reporting arose, and the owners took care to do things right. "Everything we did," asserts Woz, "we were setting the tone for the world." Still, there were doubters, including Woz's father, who worried about his son's cash controls. "A person like him shouldn't have that much money," said his father after finding $250,000 worth of uncashed checks in Woz's Porsche.

Woz and Jobs enhanced their accounting system and focused it on providing information for business decisions. Today, Woz believes that Apple is integral to the language of technology, just as accounting is the language of business. In retrospect, Woz says, "Every dream I have ever had in life has come true ten times over." He adds: "In the end, I hope there's a little note somewhere that says I designed a good computer."

Sources: *Woz website,* Woz.org, January 2016; *iWoz: From Computer Geek to Cult Icon,* W.W. Norton & Co., 2006; *Founders at Work,* Apress, 2007; *Apple website,* January 2016

IMPORTANCE OF ACCOUNTING

C1

Explain the purpose and importance of accounting.

Why is accounting so popular on campus? Why are there so many openings for accounting jobs? Why is accounting so important to companies? Why do politicians and business leaders focus on accounting regulations? The answer is that we live in an information age in which accounting information impacts us all.

Accounting is an information and measurement system that identifies, records, and communicates relevant, reliable, and comparable information about an organization's business activities. Exhibit 1.1 portrays these accounting functions.

EXHIBIT 1.1

Accounting Functions

Identifying	Recording	Communicating
Select transactions and events	Input, measure, and log	Prepare, analyze, and interpret
Examples are Apple's sale of iPhones and TicketMaster's receipt of ticket money.	Examples are chronological logs of transactions measured in dollars.	Examples are reports such as financial statements that we analyze and interpret.

Accounting is part of our everyday lives. Our most common contact with accounting is through credit approvals, checking accounts, tax forms, and payroll. These experiences tend to focus on the recordkeeping parts of accounting. **Recordkeeping,** or **bookkeeping,** is the recording of transactions and events, either manually or electronically. This is just one part of accounting. Accounting also includes the analysis and interpretation of information.

Technology is a key part of modern business and plays a major role in accounting. Technology reduces the time, effort, and cost of recordkeeping while improving clerical accuracy. Some small organizations perform various accounting tasks manually, but even they are impacted by technology. As technology makes more information available, the demand for accounting knowledge increases. Consulting, planning, and other financial services are now closely linked to accounting.

Point: Technology is only as useful as the accounting data available, and users' decisions are only as good as their understanding of accounting. The best software and recordkeeping cannot make up for lack of accounting knowledge.

Users of Accounting Information

C2

Identify users and uses of, and opportunities in, accounting.

Accounting is called the *language of business* because all organizations set up an accounting system to communicate data that help people make better decisions. Exhibit 1.2 divides these people into two user groups, *external users* and *internal users,* and provides examples of each.

EXHIBIT 1.2

Users of Accounting Information

External users

Infographics reinforce key concepts through visual learning

- Lenders
- Shareholders
- Governments
- Consumer groups
- External auditors
- Customers

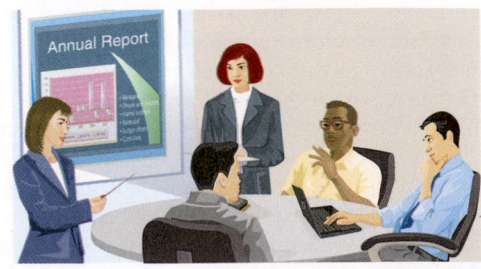

Internal users

- Officers
- Managers
- Internal auditors
- Sales staff
- Budget officers
- Controllers

External Information Users **External users** of accounting information do *not* directly run the organization and have limited access to its accounting information. They include shareholders (investors), lenders, directors, customers, suppliers, regulators, lawyers, brokers, and the press. Their business decisions depend on information that is reliable, relevant, and comparable. **Financial accounting** is the area of accounting aimed at serving external users by providing them with *general-purpose financial statements*. The term *general-purpose* refers to the broad range of purposes for which external users rely on these statements. Following is a partial list of external users and some decisions they make with accounting information.

- *Lenders* (creditors) loan money or other resources to an organization. Banks, savings and loans, co-ops, and mortgage and finance companies are lenders. Lenders use information to assess whether an organization will repay its loans with interest.
- *Shareholders* (*investors*) are the owners of a corporation. They use accounting reports in deciding whether to buy, hold, or sell stock.
- *Directors* are elected to a *board of directors* that oversees an organization. Directors report to shareholders and they hire top executive management.
- *External* (independent) *auditors* examine financial statements to verify that they are prepared according to generally accepted accounting principles.
- *Nonexecutive employees* and *labor unions* use financial statements to judge the fairness of wages, assess job prospects, and bargain for better wages.
- *Regulators* have legal authority over certain activities of organizations. For example, the Internal Revenue Service (IRS) requires accounting reports in computing taxes. Other regulators include utility boards that use accounting to set utility rates and securities regulators that require reports for companies that sell their stock to the public.
- *Voters, legislators,* and *government officials* use accounting information to monitor and evaluate government receipts and expenses.
- *Contributors* to nonprofit organizations use accounting information to evaluate the use and impact of their donations.
- *Suppliers* use accounting information to judge the soundness of a customer before making sales on credit.
- *Customers* use financial reports to assess the staying power of potential suppliers.

Internal Information Users **Internal users** of accounting information directly manage and operate the organization such as the chief executive officer (CEO), chief financial officer (CFO), chief audit executive (CAE), treasurer, and other executive or managerial-level employees. **Managerial accounting** is the area of accounting that serves the decision-making needs of internal users. Internal reports are not subject to the same rules as external reports and instead are designed with the unique needs of internal users in mind. Following is a partial list of internal users and some decisions they make with accounting information.

- *Research and development managers* need information about projected costs and revenues of innovations.
- *Purchasing managers* need to know what, when, and how much to purchase.
- *Human resource managers* need information about employees' payroll, benefits, performance, and compensation.
- *Production managers* depend on information to monitor costs and ensure quality.
- *Distribution managers* need reports for timely, accurate, and efficient delivery of products and services.
- *Marketing managers* use reports about sales and costs to target consumers, set prices, and monitor consumer needs, tastes, and price concerns.
- *Service managers* require information on the costs and benefits of looking after products and services.

Opportunities in Accounting

Accounting has four broad areas of opportunities: financial, managerial, taxation, and accounting-related. Exhibit 1.3 lists selected opportunities in each area.

EXHIBIT 1.3

Accounting Opportunities

Exhibit 1.4 shows that the majority of opportunities are in *private accounting,* which are employees working for businesses. *Public accounting* offers the next largest number of opportunities, which involve accounting services such as auditing and taxation. Opportunities also exist in government and not-for-profit agencies, including business regulation and investigation of law violations.

EXHIBIT 1.4

Accounting Jobs by Area

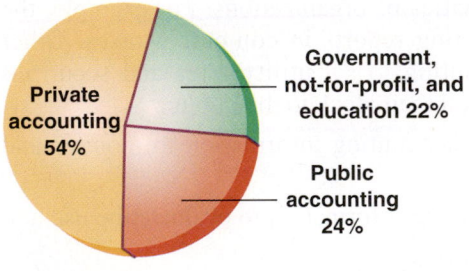

Point: The largest accounting firms are EY, KPMG, PwC, and Deloitte.

Margin notes further enhance textual material

Point: Census Bureau reports that for workers 18 and over, higher education yields higher average pay:

Master's degree	$73,738
Bachelor's degree	56,665
Associate's degree	39,771
High school degree	30,627
No high school degree	20,241

Accounting specialists are highly regarded and their professional standing is often denoted by a certificate. Certified public accountants (CPAs) must meet education and experience requirements, pass an examination, and exhibit ethical character. Many accounting specialists hold certificates in addition to or instead of the CPA. Two of the most common are the certificate in management accounting (CMA) and the certified internal auditor (CIA). Employers also look for specialists with designations such as certified bookkeeper (CB), certified payroll professional (CPP), personal financial specialist (PFS), certified fraud examiner (CFE), and certified forensic accountant (CrFA).

Demand for accounting specialists is strong. Exhibit 1.5 reports average annual salaries for several accounting positions. Salary variation depends on location, company size, professional designation, experience, and other factors. For example, salaries for chief financial officers (CFOs) range from under $100,000 to more than $1 million per year. Likewise, salaries for bookkeepers range from under $30,000 to more than $80,000.

EXHIBIT 1.5

Accounting Salaries for Selected Positions

Point: U.S. Bureau of Labor reports higher education is linked to a lower unemployment rate:

Bachelor's degree or more	3.2%
Associate's degree	4.5%
High school degree	6.0%
No high school degree	9.0%

Point: For updated salary info: Abbott-Langer.com www.AICPA.org Kforce.com

Field	Title (experience)	2015 Salary	2020 Estimate*
Public Accounting	Partner	$240,000	$265,000
	Manager (6–8 years)	109,500	121,000
	Senior (3–5 years)	88,000	97,000
	Junior (0–2 years)	60,500	67,000
Private Accounting	CFO	290,000	320,000
	Controller/Treasurer	180,000	199,000
	Manager (6–8 years)	98,500	109,000
	Senior (3–5 years)	81,500	90,000
	Junior (0–2 years)	58,000	64,000
Recordkeeping	Full-charge bookkeeper	60,500	67,000
	Accounts manager	58,000	64,000
	Payroll manager	59,500	65,500
	Accounting clerk (0–2 years)	39,500	43,500

* Estimates assume a 2% compounded annual increase over current levels (rounded to nearest $500).

NEED-TO-KNOWs *highlight key procedures and concepts in learning accounting*

Identify the following users of accounting information as either an (a) external or (b) internal user.

1. ____ Regulator
2. ____ CEO
3. ____ Shareholder
4. ____ Controller
5. ____ Executive employee
6. ____ External auditor
7. ____ Production manager
8. ____ Nonexecutive employee

NEED-TO-KNOW 1-1

Accounting Users

C1 **C2**

Do More: QS 1-1, QS 1-2, E 1-1, E 1-2, E 1-3

Solution

1. a 2. b 3. a 4. b 5. b 6. a 7. b 8. a

FUNDAMENTALS OF ACCOUNTING

Accounting is guided by principles, standards, concepts, and assumptions. This section describes several of these key fundamentals of accounting.

Ethics—A Key Concept

For information to be useful, it must be trusted. This demands ethics in accounting. **Ethics** are beliefs that distinguish right from wrong. They are accepted standards of good and bad behavior.

Identifying the ethical path is a course of action that avoids casting doubt on one's decisions. For example, accounting users are less likely to trust an auditor's report if the auditor's pay depends on that client's success. To avoid such concerns, ethics rules are often set. For example, auditors are banned from direct investment in their client and cannot accept pay that depends on figures in the client's reports. Exhibit 1.6 gives a three-step process for making ethical decisions.

C3 ____
Explain why ethics are crucial to accounting.

Point: Sarbanes-Oxley Act requires each issuer of securities to disclose whether it has adopted a code of ethics for its officers and the contents of that code.

 1. Identify ethical concerns

Use personal ethics to recognize an ethical concern.

 2. Analyze options

Consider all good and bad consequences.

 3. Make ethical decision

Choose best option after weighing all consequences.

EXHIBIT 1.6
Ethical Decision Making

Accountants face ethical choices as they prepare financial reports. These choices can affect the price a buyer pays and the wages paid to workers. They can even affect the success of products and services. Misleading information can lead to a wrongful closing of a division that harms workers, customers, and suppliers. There is an old saying: *Good ethics are good business.*

Point: A *Code of Professional Conduct* is available at **www.AICPA.org.**

Fraud Triangle

The fraud triangle asserts that *three* factors must exist for a person to commit fraud: opportunity, pressure, and rationalization.

- *Opportunity.* A person must envision a way to commit fraud with a low risk of getting caught.
- *Pressure,* or incentive. A person must feel pressure to commit fraud.
- *Rationalization,* or attitude. A person rationalizes the fraud and fails to see its criminal nature or justifies the fraud.

The key to dealing with fraud is to focus on prevention. It is less expensive and more effective to prevent fraud from happening than it is to detect it. By the time a fraud is discovered, the money is often gone and chances for recovery are slim.

Both internal and external users rely on internal controls to reduce the likelihood of fraud. *Internal controls* are procedures set up to protect company property and equipment, ensure reliable accounting, promote efficiency, and encourage adherence to policies. Examples are good records, physical controls (locks, passwords, guards), and independent reviews.

Fraud

Cooking the Books Our economic and social welfare depends on reliable accounting. Some individuals forgot that and are now paying their dues. They include Hisao Tanaka (in photo) of **Toshiba**, guilty of inflating income by $1.2 billion over five years; Tsuyoshi Kikukawa of **Olympus**, guilty of hiding $1.7 billion in losses; Bernard Ebbers of **WorldCom**, convicted of an $11 billion accounting scandal; Andrew Fastow of **Enron**, guilty of hiding debt and inflating income; and Ramalinga Raju of **Satyam Computers**, accused of overstating assets by $1.5 billion.

KAZUHIRO NOGI/AFP/ Getty Images

Generally Accepted Accounting Principles

Financial accounting is governed by concepts and rules known as **generally accepted accounting principles (GAAP).** We must understand these principles when using accounting data. GAAP aims to make information *relevant, reliable,* and *comparable.* Relevant information affects decisions of users. Reliable information is trusted by users. Comparable information aids in contrasting organizations.

In the United States, the **Securities and Exchange Commission (SEC),** a government agency, has the legal authority to set GAAP. The SEC oversees proper use of GAAP by companies that raise money from the public through issuance of stock and debt. The SEC has largely delegated the task of setting U.S. GAAP to the **Financial Accounting Standards Board (FASB),** which is a private-sector group that sets both broad and specific principles.

International Standards

Our global economy creates demand by external users for comparability in accounting reports. To that end, the **International Accounting Standards Board (IASB),** an independent group (consisting of individuals from many countries), issues **International Financial Reporting Standards (IFRS)** that identify preferred accounting practices. If global standards were harmonized, one company could potentially use a single set of financial statements across financial markets.

Differences between U.S. GAAP and IFRS have been decreasing in recent years as the FASB and IASB pursued a *convergence* process aimed at reducing inconsistencies. Further, more than 115 countries now require or permit companies to follow IFRS. However, it is clear that convergence will not be achieved anytime soon. More recently, the FASB said it will work on global accounting issues with the IASB through its membership in the Accounting Standards Advisory Forum (ASAF).

The SEC encourages the FASB, when possible, to converge U.S. GAAP to IFRS by endorsing, and thereby incorporating, individual IFRS standards into U.S. GAAP. This process still permits the FASB to modify IFRS when necessary. The SEC maintains its oversight of the FASB, including authority to prescribe accounting principles and standards for U.S. issuers. The SEC also has a role in oversight and governance of the IASB through its involvement on the IFRS Foundation Monitoring Board. For updates on global accounting issues, we can check with the AICPA (**IFRS.com**), FASB (**FASB.org**), and IASB (**ifrs.org**).

 IFRS

Like the FASB, the IASB uses a conceptual framework to aid in revising or drafting new standards. However, unlike the FASB, the IASB's conceptual framework is used as a reference when specific guidance is lacking. The IASB also requires that transactions be accounted for according to their substance (not only their legal form) and that financial statements give a fair presentation, whereas the FASB narrows that scope to fair presentation *in accordance with U.S. GAAP.* ◼

Conceptual Framework and Convergence

The FASB and IASB are attempting to converge and enhance the **conceptual framework** that guides standard setting. The FASB framework consists broadly of the following:

- **Objectives**—to provide information useful to investors, creditors, and others.
- **Qualitative Characteristics**—to require information that is *relevant, reliable,* and *comparable.*
- **Elements**—to define items that financial statements can contain.
- **Recognition and Measurement**—to set criteria that an item must meet for it to be recognized as an element and how to measure that element.

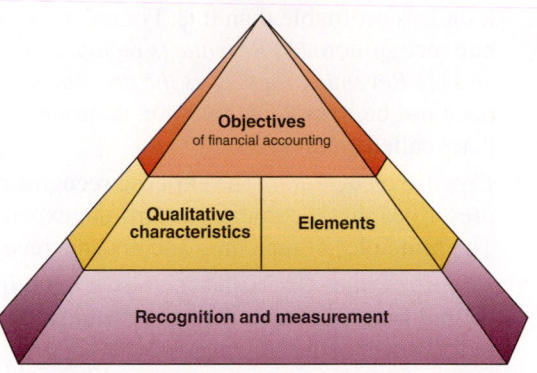

For updates on this joint FASB and IASB conceptual framework convergence we can check the **FASB.org** or **ifrs.org** websites. We must remember that U.S. GAAP and IFRS are two similar, but not identical, systems. However, their similarities greatly outweigh differences. The remainder of this section describes key principles and assumptions of accounting.

Principles and Assumptions of Accounting   Accounting principles (and assumptions) are of two types. *General principles* are the basic assumptions, concepts, and guidelines for preparing financial statements. *Specific principles* are detailed rules used in reporting business transactions and events. General principles stem from long-used accounting practices. Specific principles arise more often from the rulings of authoritative groups.

We need to understand both general and specific principles to effectively use accounting information. Several general principles are described in this section that are relied on in later chapters. General principles (in purple font with white shading) and assumptions (in red font with white shading) are portrayed as building blocks of GAAP in Exhibit 1.7. The specific principles are described as we encounter them in the book.

EXHIBIT 1.7

Building Blocks for GAAP

Accounting Principles   General principles consist of at least four basic principles, four assumptions, and two constraints.

- *Measurement* The **measurement principle,** also called the **cost principle,** prescribes that accounting information is based on actual cost (with a potential for subsequent adjustments to market). Cost is measured on a cash or equal-to-cash basis. This means if cash is given for a service, its cost is measured by the cash paid. If something besides cash is exchanged (such as a car traded for a truck), cost is measured as the cash value of what is given up or received. The cost principle emphasizes reliability and verifiability, and information based on cost is considered objective. *Objectivity* means that information is supported by independent, unbiased evidence; it demands more than a person's opinion. To illustrate, suppose a company pays $5,000 for equipment. The cost principle requires that this purchase be recorded at $5,000. It makes no difference if the owner thinks this equipment is worth $7,000. Later in the book we introduce *fair value* measures.

Point: The cost principle is also called the *historical cost principle.*

- *Revenue recognition* Revenue (sales) is the amount received from selling products and services. The **revenue recognition principle** provides guidance on when a company must recognize revenue. To *recognize* means to record it. If revenue is recognized too early, a company would look more profitable than it is. If revenue is recognized too late, a company would look less profitable than it is. For our purposes, two simple points can help understand revenue recognition: (1) *Revenue is recognized when goods or services are provided to customers* and (2) *Revenue proceeds is the amount expected to be received from the customer*. Proceeds need not be in cash. A common noncash proceed is a customer's promise to pay at a future date, called credit sales.

- *Expense recognition* The **expense recognition principle,** also called the **matching principle,** prescribes that a company record the expenses it incurred to generate the revenue reported. The principles of matching and revenue recognition are key to modern accounting.

- *Full disclosure* The **full disclosure principle** prescribes that a company report the details behind financial statements that would impact users' decisions. Those disclosures are often in footnotes to the statements.

Decision Insight

Revenues for the **Seattle Seahawks**, **Green Bay Packers**, and other professional football teams include ticket sales, television and cable broadcasts, radio rights, concessions, and advertising. Revenues from ticket sales are earned when the NFL team plays each game. Advance ticket sales are not revenues; instead, they represent a liability until the NFL team plays the game for which the ticket was sold. At that point, the liability is removed and revenues are reported. ■

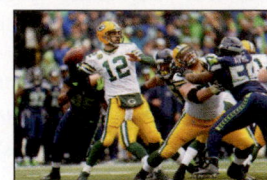

Christian Petersen/Getty Images

Accounting Assumptions There are four accounting assumptions: the going-concern assumption, the monetary unit assumption, the time period assumption, and the business entity assumption.

- *Going concern* The **going-concern assumption** means that accounting information reflects a presumption that the business will continue operating instead of being closed or sold. This implies, for example, that property is reported at cost instead of, say, liquidation value, which assumes closure.

- *Monetary unit* The **monetary unit assumption** means that we can express transactions and events in monetary, or money, units. Money is the common denominator in business. Examples of monetary units are the dollar in the United States, Canada, Australia, and Singapore; and the peso in Mexico, the Philippines, and Chile. The monetary unit a company uses in its accounting reports usually depends on the country where it operates, but many companies today are expressing reports in more than one monetary unit.

- *Time period* The **time period assumption** presumes that the life of a company can be divided into time periods, such as months and years, and that useful reports can be prepared for those periods.

- *Business entity* The **business entity assumption** means that a business is accounted for separately from other business entities, including its owner. The reason for this assumption is that separate information about each business is necessary for good decisions. A business entity can take one of three legal forms: *proprietorship, partnership,* or *corporation.*

  1. A **sole proprietorship,** or simply **proprietorship,** is a business owned by one person. The business is a separate entity for accounting purposes. However, a proprietorship is *not* a separate legal entity from its owner. This means, for example, that a court can order an owner to sell personal belongings to pay a proprietorship's debt. This *unlimited liability* of a proprietorship is a disadvantage. However, an advantage is that a proprietorship's income is not subject to a business income tax but is instead reported and taxed on the owner's personal income tax return. Proprietorship attributes are summarized in Exhibit 1.8, as well as those for partnerships and corporations.

Attribute Present	Proprietorship	Partnership	Corporation
One owner allowed.............	yes	no	yes
Business taxed	no	no	yes
Limited liability................	no*	no*	yes
Business entity	yes	yes	yes
Legal entity...................	no	no	yes
Unlimited life	no	no	yes

EXHIBIT 1.8

Attributes of Businesses

* Proprietorships and partnerships that are set up as LLCs provide limited liability.

2. A **partnership** is a business owned by two or more people, called *partners,* who are jointly liable for tax and other obligations. Like a proprietorship, no special legal requirements must be met in starting a partnership. The only requirement is an agreement between partners to run a business together. The agreement can be either oral or written and usually indicates how income and losses are to be shared. A partnership, like a proprietorship, is *not* legally separate from its owners. This means that each partner's share of profits is reported and taxed on that partner's tax return. It also means *unlimited liability* for its partners. However, at least three types of partnerships limit liability. A *limited partnership (LP)* includes a general partner(s) with unlimited liability and a limited partner(s) with liability restricted to the amount invested. A *limited liability partnership (LLP)* restricts partners' liabilities to their own acts and the acts of individuals under their control. This protects an innocent partner from the negligence of another partner, yet all partners remain responsible for partnership debts. A *limited liability company (LLC)* offers the limited liability of a corporation and the tax treatment of a partnership (and proprietorship). Most proprietorships and partnerships are now organized as LLCs.

3. A **corporation,** also called a *C corporation,* is a business legally separate from its owner or owners, meaning it is responsible for its own acts and its own debts. Separate legal status means that a corporation can conduct business with the rights, duties, and responsibilities of a person. A corporation acts through its managers, who are its legal agents. Separate legal status also means that its owners, who are called **shareholders** (or **stockholders**), are not personally liable for corporate acts and debts. This limited liability is its main advantage. A main disadvantage is what's called *double taxation*—meaning that (1) the corporation income is taxed and (2) any distribution of income to its owners through dividends is taxed as part of the owners' personal income, usually at the individual's income tax rate. (For "qualified" dividends, the tax rate is 0%, 15%, or 20%, depending on the individual's tax bracket.) An *S corporation,* a corporation with special attributes, does not owe corporate income tax. Owners of S corporations report their share of corporate income with their personal income. Ownership of all corporations is divided into units called **shares** or **stock.** When a corporation issues only one class of stock, we call it **common stock** (or *capital stock*).

Point: Proprietorships and partnerships are usually managed by their owners. In a corporation, the owners (shareholders) elect a board of directors who appoint managers to run the business.

Decision Ethics boxes are role-playing exercises that stress ethics in accounting

■ **Decision Ethics** ━━━━━━━━━━━━━━━━━━━

Entrepreneur   You and a friend develop a new design for in-line skates that improves speed by 25% to 30%. You plan to form a business to manufacture and market the skates. You and your friend want to minimize taxes, but your prime concern is potential lawsuits from individuals who might be injured on these skates. What form of organization do you set up? ■   [Answers follow the chapter's Summary.]

Accounting Constraints   There are two basic constraints on financial reporting.

- *Materiality* The **materiality constraint** prescribes that only information that would influence the decisions of a reasonable person need be disclosed. This constraint looks at both the importance and relative size of an amount.
- *Benefit exceeds cost* The **cost-benefit constraint** prescribes that only information with benefits of disclosure greater than the costs of providing it need be disclosed.

Conservatism and *industry practices* are also sometimes referred to as accounting constraints.

Sarbanes-Oxley (SOX)

Congress passed the **Sarbanes-Oxley Act,** also called *SOX,* to help curb financial abuses at companies that issue their stock to the public. SOX requires that these public companies apply both accounting oversight and stringent internal controls. The desired results include more transparency, accountability, and truthfulness in reporting transactions.

Compliance with SOX requires documentation and verification of internal controls and increased emphasis on internal control effectiveness. Failure to comply can yield financial penalties, stock market delisting, and criminal prosecution of executives. Management must issue a report stating that internal controls are effective. CEOs and CFOs who knowingly sign off on bogus accounting reports risk millions of dollars in fines and years in prison. **Auditors** also must verify the effectiveness of internal controls.

A listing of some of the more publicized accounting scandals in recent years follows.

Company	Alleged Accounting Abuses
Tesco, Plc.	Inflated revenues and income, and deferred expenses
WorldCom	Understated expenses to inflate income and hid debt
AOL Time Warner	Inflated revenues and income
Fannie Mae	Inflated income
Xerox.	Inflated income
Bristol-Myers Squibb	Inflated revenues and income
Global Crossing.	Inflated revenues and income
Tyco	Hid debt and CEO evaded taxes
Nortel Networks	Understated expenses to inflate income
Enron	Inflated income, hid debt, and bribed officials

To reduce the risk of accounting fraud, companies set up *governance systems.* A company's governance system includes its owners, managers, employees, board of directors, and other important stakeholders, who work together to reduce the risk of accounting fraud and increase confidence in accounting reports.

Dodd-Frank

Congress passed the **Dodd-Frank Wall Street Reform and Consumer Protection Act,** or *Dodd-Frank,* to (1) promote accountability and transparency in the financial system, (2) put an end to the notion of "too big to fail," (3) protect the taxpayer by ending bailouts, and (4) protect consumers from abusive financial services. A few of its notable provisions follow:

- *Exemption* Exemption from Section 404(b) of SOX for smaller public entities from the requirement to obtain an external audit on effectiveness of internal control over financial reporting.
- *Independence* Independence for all members of the compensation committee (including additional disclosures); in the event of an accounting restatement, an entity must set policies mandating recovery ("clawback") of excess incentive compensation.
- *Whistleblower* Requires the SEC, when sanctions exceed $1 million, to pay whistleblowers between 10% and 30% of the sanction.

NEED-TO-KNOW 1-2

Accounting Guidance

C3 C4

Part 1: Identify each of the following terms/phrases as either an accounting (a) principle, (b) assumption, or (c) constraint.

1. ___ Materiality
2. ___ Measurement
3. ___ Business entity
4. ___ Going concern
5. ___ Full disclosure
6. ___ Time period
7. ___ Expense recognition
8. ___ Revenue recognition

Solution

1. c   **2.** a   **3.** b   **4.** b   **5.** a   **6.** b   **7.** a   **8.** a

Part 2: Complete the following table with either a yes or a no regarding the attributes of a partnership and a corporation.

Attribute Present	Partnership	Corporation
Business taxed..........	a. ___	e. ___
Limited liability	b. ___	f. ___
Legal entity	c. ___	g. ___
Unlimited life...........	d. ___	h. ___

Solution

a. no   **b.** no   **c.** no   **d.** no   **e.** yes   **f.** yes   **g.** yes   **h.** yes

Do More: QS 1-3, QS 1-4, QS 1-5, QS 1-6, E 1-4, E 1-5, E 1-6, E 1-7

BUSINESS TRANSACTIONS AND ACCOUNTING

To understand accounting information, we need to know how an accounting system captures relevant data about transactions and then classifies, records, and reports data.

A1

Define and interpret the accounting equation and each of its components.

Accounting Equation

The accounting system reflects two basic aspects of a company: what it owns and what it owes. *Assets* are resources a company owns or controls. Examples are cash, supplies, equipment, and land, where each carries expected benefits. The claims on a company's assets—what it owes—are separated into owner and nonowner claims. *Liabilities* are what a company owes its nonowners (creditors) in future payments, products, or services. *Equity* (also called stockholders' equity or capital) refers to the claims of its owner(s). Together, liabilities and equity are the source of funds to acquire assets. The relation of assets, liabilities, and equity is reflected in the following **accounting equation:**

$$\text{Assets} = \text{Liabilities} + \text{Equity}$$

Liabilities are usually shown before equity in this equation because creditors' claims must be paid before the claims of owners. (The terms in this equation can be rearranged; for example, Assets − Liabilities = Equity.) The accounting equation applies to all transactions and events, to all companies and forms of organization, and to all points in time. Using **Apple** as an example, its assets equal $231,839, its liabilities equal $120,292, and its equity equals $111,547 ($ in millions). Let's now look at the accounting equation in more detail.

Real company names are printed in bold magenta

Assets   Assets are resources a company owns or controls. These resources are expected to yield future benefits. Examples are web servers for an online services company, musical instruments for a rock band, and land for a vegetable grower. The term *receivable* is used to refer to an asset that promises a future inflow of resources. A company that provides a service or product on credit is said to have an account receivable from that customer.

Point: The phrases "on credit" and "on account" imply that cash payment will occur at a future date.

Liabilities   Liabilities are creditors' claims on assets. These claims reflect company obligations to provide assets, products, or services to others. The term *payable* refers to a liability that promises a future outflow of resources. Examples are wages payable to workers, accounts payable to suppliers, notes payable to banks, and taxes payable to the government.

Equity   Equity is the owner's claim on assets, and is equal to assets minus liabilities. Equity is also called *net assets* or *residual equity*.

Equity increases from owner investments, called stock issuances, and from revenues. It decreases from dividends and expenses. A corporation's equity—also called *stockholders'* or *shareholders' equity*—consists of four elements.

● *Common Stock* **Common stock,** which is part of contributed capital, reflects inflows of resources such as cash and other net assets from stockholders in exchange for stock (later chapters identify other parts of contributed capital).

Contributed capital

- *Dividends* The outflow of resources such as cash and other assets to stockholders is called **dividends,** which reduce equity.
- *Revenues* **Revenues** increase equity (via net income) from sales of products and services to customers; examples are sales of produce, consulting services provided, facilities rented to others, and commissions from services.
- *Expenses* **Expenses** decrease equity (via net income) from costs of providing products and services to customers; examples are costs of employee time, use of supplies, advertising, utilities, and insurance fees.

More generally, **contributed capital** refers to the amount stockholders invest in the company, whereas **retained earnings** is the accumulated revenues *less* the accumulated expenses and dividends since the company began. This breakdown of equity yields the following **expanded accounting equation:**

$$\text{Assets} = \text{Liabilities} + \overbrace{\text{Contributed Capital} + \text{Retained Earnings}}^{\text{Equity}}$$
$$= \text{Liabilities} + \text{Common Stock} - \text{Dividends} + \text{Revenues} - \text{Expenses}$$

Net income occurs when revenues exceed expenses. Equity increases from net income. A **net loss** occurs when expenses exceed revenues, which decreases equity.

▉ Decision Insight

APPLE **Big Data** Most organizations offer access to accounting databases—see **Apple** (**Apple.com**) as an example. The SEC keeps an online database called **EDGAR (www.SEC.gov/edgar.shtml),** which has accounting information for thousands of companies that issue stock to the public. The annual report filing for most publicly traded U.S. companies is known as Form 10-K, and the quarterly filing is Form 10-Q. Information services such as **Finance.Google.com** and **Finance. Yahoo.com** offer online data and analysis. ■

Yasuyoshi Chiba/AFP/Getty Images

NEED-TO-KNOW 1-3

Accounting Equation
A1

Part 1: Use the *accounting equation* to compute the missing financial statement amounts.

Company	Assets	Liabilities	Equity
Bose	$150	$ 30	$_(a)_
Vogue	$_(b)_	$100	$300

Solution

a. $120   **b.** $400

Part 2: Use the *expanded accounting equation* to compute the missing financial statement amounts.

Company	Assets	Liabilities	Common Stock	Dividends	Revenues	Expenses
Tesla	$200	$ 85	$100	$5	_(a)_	$40
YouTube	$400	$160	$220	_(b)_	$120	$90

Do More: QS 1-7, QS 1-8, E 1-8, E 1-9

Solution

a. $60   **b.** $10

Transaction Analysis

P1

Analyze business transactions using the accounting equation.

Business activities can be described in terms of transactions and events. **External transactions** are exchanges of value between two entities, which yield changes in the accounting equation. An example is the sale of the *AppleCare Protection Plan* by **Apple**. **Internal transactions** are exchanges within an entity, which may or may not affect the accounting equation. An example is **Twitter**'s use of its supplies, which are reported as expenses when used. **Events** refer to happenings that affect the accounting equation *and* are reliably measured. They include business events such as changes in the market value of certain assets and liabilities and natural events such as floods and fires that destroy assets and create losses. They do not include, for example, the signing of service or product contracts, which by themselves do not impact the accounting equation.

This section uses the accounting equation to analyze 11 selected transactions and events of FastForward, a start-up consulting (service) business, in its first month of operations. Remember that each transaction and event leaves the equation in balance and that assets *always* equal the sum of liabilities and equity.

Transaction 1: Investment by Owner On December 1, Chas Taylor forms a consulting business, named FastForward and set up as a corporation, that focuses on assessing the performance of footwear and accessories. Taylor owns and manages the business. The marketing plan for the business is to focus primarily on publishing online reviews and consulting with clubs, athletes, and others who place orders for footwear and accessories with manufacturers. Taylor personally invests $30,000 cash in the new company and deposits the cash in a bank account opened under the name of FastForward. After this transaction, the cash (an asset) and the stockholders' equity each equals $30,000. The source of increase in equity is the owner's investment (stock issuance), which is included in the column titled Common Stock. The effect of this transaction on FastForward is reflected in the accounting equation as follows (we label the equity entries):

FASTForward

Point: There are three basic types of company operations: (1) **Services**—providing customer services for profit, (2) **Merchandisers**—buying products and reselling them for profit, and (3) **Manufacturers**—creating products and selling them for profit.

	Assets	=	Liabilities	+	Equity
	Cash	=			**Common Stock**
(1)	**+$30,000**	=			**+$30,000** Owner investment

Transaction 2: Purchase Supplies for Cash FastForward uses $2,500 of its cash to buy supplies of brand name footwear for performance testing over the next few months. This transaction is an exchange of cash, an asset, for another kind of asset, supplies. It merely changes the form of assets from cash to supplies. The decrease in cash is exactly equal to the increase in supplies. The supplies of footwear are assets because of the expected future benefits from the test results of their performance. This transaction is reflected in the accounting equation as follows:

	Assets			=	Liabilities	+	Equity
	Cash	+	**Supplies**	=			**Common Stock**
Old Bal.	$30,000			=			$30,000
(2)	**−2,500**	+	**$2,500**				
New Bal.	$27,500	+	$ 2,500	=			$30,000
		$30,000				$30,000	

Transaction 3: Purchase Equipment for Cash FastForward spends $26,000 to acquire equipment for testing footwear. Like transaction 2, transaction 3 is an exchange of one asset, cash, for another asset, equipment. The equipment is an asset because of its expected future benefits from testing footwear. This purchase changes the makeup of assets but does not change the asset total. The accounting equation remains in balance.

	Assets					=	Liabilities	+	Equity
	Cash	+	**Supplies**	+	**Equipment**	=			**Common Stock**
Old Bal.	$27,500	+	$2,500			=			$30,000
(3)	**−26,000**			+	**$26,000**				
New Bal.	$ 1,500	+	$2,500	+	$ 26,000	=			$30,000
		$30,000						$30,000	

Example: If FastForward pays $500 cash in transaction 4, how does this partial payment affect the liability to CalTech? *Answer:* The liability to CalTech would be reduced to $6,600 and the cash balance would be reduced to $1,000.

Transaction 4: Purchase Supplies on Credit

Taylor decides more supplies of footwear and accessories are needed. These additional supplies total $7,100, but as we see from the accounting equation in transaction 3, FastForward has only $1,500 in cash. Taylor arranges to purchase them on credit from CalTech Supply Company. Thus, FastForward acquires supplies in exchange for a promise to pay for them later. This purchase increases assets by $7,100 in supplies, and liabilities (called *accounts payable* to CalTech Supply) increase by the same amount. The effects of this purchase follow:

| | | Assets | | | | | = | Liabilities | + | Equity |
	Cash	+	Supplies	+	Equipment	=	Accounts Payable	+	Common Stock
Old Bal.	$1,500	+	$2,500	+	$26,000	=			$30,000
(4)		+	7,100				+$7,100		
New Bal.	$1,500	+	$9,600	+	$26,000	=	$ 7,100	+	$30,000
			$37,100					$37,100	

Transaction 5: Provide Services for Cash

FastForward plans to earn revenues by selling online ad space to manufacturers and by consulting with clients about test results on footwear and accessories. It earns net income only if its revenues are greater than its expenses incurred in earning them. In one of its first jobs, FastForward provides consulting services to a power-walking club and immediately collects $4,200 cash. The accounting equation reflects this increase in cash of $4,200 and in equity of $4,200. This increase in equity is identified in the far right column under Revenues because the cash received is earned by providing consulting services.

Point: Revenue recognition principle requires that revenue is recognized when work is performed.

| | | Assets | | | | | = | Liabilities | + | | Equity | |
	Cash	+	Supplies	+	Equipment	=	Accounts Payable	+	Common Stock	+	Revenues
Old Bal.	$1,500	+	$9,600	+	$26,000	=	$7,100	+	$30,000		
(5)	+4,200									+	$4,200 Consulting
New Bal.	$5,700	+	$9,600	+	$26,000	=	$7,100	+	$30,000	+	$ 4,200
			$41,300						$41,300		

Transactions 6 and 7: Payment of Expenses in Cash

FastForward pays $1,000 rent to the landlord of the building where its facilities are located. Paying this amount allows FastForward to occupy the space for the month of December. The rental payment is reflected in the following accounting equation as transaction 6. FastForward also pays the biweekly $700 salary of the company's only employee. This is reflected in the accounting equation as transaction 7. Both transactions 6 and 7 are December expenses for FastForward. The costs of both rent and salary are expenses, as opposed to assets, because their benefits are used in December (they have no future benefits after December). These transactions also use up an asset (cash) in carrying out FastForward's operations. The accounting equation shows that both transactions reduce cash and equity. The far right column identifies these decreases as Expenses.

Point: Expense recognition principle requires that expenses are recognized when the revenue they help generate is recorded. Expenses are outflows of net assets, which decrease equity.

By definition, increases in expenses yield decreases in equity.

| | | Assets | | | | | = | Liabilities | + | | Equity | | | |
	Cash	+	Supplies	+	Equipment	=	Accounts Payable	+	Common Stock	+	Revenues	−	Expenses
Old Bal.	$5,700	+	$9,600	+	$26,000	=	$7,100	+	$30,000	+	$4,200		
(6)	−1,000											−	$1,000 Rent
Bal.	4,700	+	9,600	+	26,000	=	7,100	+	30,000	+	4,200	−	1,000
(7)	− 700											−	700 Salaries
New Bal.	$4,000	+	$9,600	+	$26,000	=	$7,100	+	$30,000	+	$4,200	−	$ 1,700
			$39,600						$39,600				

Transaction 8: Provide Services and Facilities for Credit   FastForward provides consulting services of $1,600 and rents its test facilities for $300 to a podiatric services center. The rental involves allowing members to try recommended footwear and accessories at FastForward's testing area. The center is billed for the $1,900 total. This transaction results in a new asset, called *accounts receivable,* from this client. It also yields an increase in equity from the two revenue components reflected in the Revenues column of the accounting equation:

Point: Transaction 8, like 5, records revenue when work is performed, not necessarily when cash is received.

	Cash	+	Accounts Receivable	+	Supplies	+	Equipment	=	Accounts Payable	+	Common Stock	+	Revenues	−	Expenses
					Assets			=	**Liabilities**	+			**Equity**		
Old Bal.	$4,000	+		+	$9,600	+	$26,000	=	$7,100	+	$30,000	+	$4,200	−	$1,700
(8)		+	**$1,900**									+	**1,600** Consulting		
												+	**300** Rental		
New Bal.	$4,000	+	$ 1,900	+	$9,600	+	$26,000	=	$7,100	+	$30,000	+	$6,100	−	$1,700
			$41,500								$41,500				

Transaction 9: Receipt of Cash from Accounts Receivable   The client in transaction 8 (the podiatric center) pays $1,900 to FastForward 10 days after it is billed for consulting services. This transaction 9 does not change the total amount of assets and does not affect liabilities or equity. It converts the receivable (an asset) to cash (another asset). It does not create new revenue. Revenue was recognized when FastForward rendered the services in transaction 8, not when the cash is now collected. This emphasis on when products or services are provided instead of on cash flows is a key part of revenue recognition. The new balances follow:

Point: Transaction 9 involved no added client work, so no added revenue is recorded.

Point: Receipt of cash is not always a revenue.

	Cash	+	Accounts Receivable	+	Supplies	+	Equipment	=	Accounts Payable	+	Common Stock	+	Revenues	−	Expenses
					Assets			=	**Liabilities**	+			**Equity**		
Old Bal.	$4,000	+	$1,900	+	$9,600	+	$26,000	=	$7,100	+	$30,000	+	$6,100	−	$1,700
(9)	+1,900	−	1,900												
New Bal.	$5,900	+	$ 0	+	$9,600	+	$26,000	=	$7,100	+	$30,000	+	$6,100	−	$1,700
			$41,500								$41,500				

Transaction 10: Payment of Accounts Payable   FastForward pays CalTech Supply $900 cash as partial payment for its earlier $7,100 purchase of supplies (transaction 4), leaving $6,200 unpaid. The accounting equation shows that this transaction decreases FastForward's cash by $900 and decreases its liability to CalTech Supply by $900. Equity does not change. This event does not create an expense even though cash flows out of FastForward (instead the expense is recorded when FastForward derives the benefits from these supplies).

	Cash	+	Accounts Receivable	+	Supplies	+	Equipment	=	Accounts Payable	+	Common Stock	+	Revenues	−	Expenses
					Assets			=	**Liabilities**	+			**Equity**		
Old Bal.	$5,900	+	$ 0	+	$9,600	+	$26,000	=	$7,100	+	$30,000	+	$6,100	−	$1,700
(10)	− 900								−900						
New Bal.	$5,000	+	$ 0	+	$9,600	+	$26,000	=	$6,200	+	$30,000	+	$6,100	−	$1,700
			$40,600								$40,600				

Transaction 11: Payment of Cash Dividend   FastForward declares and pays a $200 cash dividend to its owner (the sole shareholder). Dividends (decreases in equity) are not reported as expenses because they are not part of the earnings process. Dividends are not company expenses, and they are not used in computing net income.

By definition, increases in dividends yield decreases in equity.

	Assets			=	Liabilities	+				Equity		
	Cash	+ Accounts Receivable	+ Supplies	+ Equipment	=	Accounts Payable	+	Common Stock	− Dividends	+ Revenues	− Expenses
Old Bal.	$5,000	+ $ 0	+ $9,600	+ $26,000	=	$6,200	+	$30,000		+ $6,100	− $1,700
(11)	− 200								− $200 Dividends		
New Bal.	$4,800	+ $ 0	+ $9,600	+ $26,000	=	$6,200	+	$30,000	− $200	+ $6,100	− $1,700
			$40,400						$40,400		

Summary of Transactions

Point: Knowing how financial statements are prepared improves our analysis of them.

EXHIBIT 1.9

Summary of Transactions Using the Accounting Equation

We summarize in Exhibit 1.9 the effects of these 11 transactions of FastForward using the accounting equation. We see that the accounting equation remains in balance after each transaction. Transactions can be analyzed by their effects on components of the accounting equation. Transaction analysis is key to modern financial analysis, which often adjusts financial measures based on footnote or other data.

	Assets				=	Liabilities	+		Equity			
	Cash	+ Accounts Receivable	+ Supplies	+ Equipment	=	Accounts Payable	+	Common Stock	− Dividends	+ Revenues	− Expenses
(1)	$30,000				=			$30,000			
(2)	− 2,500		+ $2,500								
Bal.	27,500		+ 2,500		=			30,000			
(3)	−26,000			+ $26,000							
Bal.	1,500		+ 2,500	+ 26,000	=			30,000			
(4)			+ 7,100			+$7,100					
Bal.	1,500		+ 9,600	+ 26,000	=	7,100	+	30,000			
(5)	+ 4,200									+ $4,200	
Bal.	5,700		+ 9,600	+ 26,000	=	7,100	+	30,000		+ 4,200	
(6)	− 1,000										− $1,000
Bal.	4,700		+ 9,600	+ 26,000	=	7,100	+	30,000		+ 4,200	− 1,000
(7)	− 700									+	− 700
Bal.	4,000		+ 9,600	+ 26,000	=	7,100	+	30,000		+ 4,200	− 1,700
(8)		+ $1,900								+ 1,600	
										+ 300	
Bal.	4,000	+ 1,900	+ 9,600	+ 26,000	=	7,100	+	30,000		+ 6,100	− 1,700
(9)	+ 1,900	− 1,900									
Bal.	5,900	+ 0	+ 9,600	+ 26,000	=	7,100	+	30,000		+ 6,100	− 1,700
(10)	− 900					− 900					
Bal.	5,000	+ 0	+ 9,600	+ 26,000	=	6,200	+	30,000		+ 6,100	− 1,700
(11)	− 200								− $200		
Bal.	$ 4,800	+ $ 0	+ $9,600	+ $ 26,000	=	$ 6,200	+	$ 30,000	− $ 200	+ $6,100	− $ 1,700

NEED-TO-KNOW 1-4

Transaction Analysis

P1

Do More: QS 1-10, QS 1-11, E 1-10, E 1-11, E 1-13

Assume Tata Company began operations on January 1 and completed the following transactions during its first month of operations. Arrange the following asset, liability, and equity titles in a table like Exhibit 1.9: Cash; Accounts Receivable; Equipment; Accounts Payable; Common Stock; Dividends; Revenues; and Expenses.

Jan. 1 Jamsetji Tata invested $4,000 cash in Tata Company in exchange for its common stock.

     5 The company purchased $2,000 of equipment on credit.

    14 The company provided $540 of services for a client on credit.

    21 The company paid $250 cash for an employee's salary.

Solution

	Assets					=	Liabilities	+			Equity				
	Cash	+	Accounts Receivable	+	Equipment	=	Accounts Payable	+	Common Stock	−	Dividends	+	Revenues	−	Expenses
Jan. 1	$4,000					=			$4,000						
Jan. 5				+	$2,000		+$2,000								
Bal.	4,000			+	2,000	=	2,000	+	4,000						
Jan. 14		+	$540									+	$540		
Bal.	4,000	+	540	+	2,000	=	2,000	+	4,000			+	540		
Jan. 21	− 250													−	$250
Bal.	3,750	+	540	+	2,000	=	2,000	+	4,000			+	540	−	250

$6,290 = $6,290

COMMUNICATING WITH USERS

This section introduces us to how financial statements are prepared from the analysis of business transactions. The four financial statements and their purposes are:

P2

Identify and prepare basic financial statements and explain how they interrelate.

1. **Income statement**—describes a company's revenues and expenses along with the resulting net income or loss over a period of time.
2. **Statement of retained earnings**—explains changes in equity from net income (or loss) and from any dividends over a period of time.
3. **Balance sheet**—describes a company's financial position (types and amounts of assets, liabilities, and equity) at a point in time.
4. **Statement of cash flows**—identifies cash inflows (receipts) and cash outflows (payments) over a period of time.

We prepare these financial statements, in the order above, using the 11 selected transactions of FastForward. (These statements are called *unadjusted*—we explain this in Chapters 2 and 3.) The graphic to the side shows that financial statements reflect different parts of the expanded accounting equation.

Assets = Liabilities + Equity	} Balance Sheet
+ Revenues	
− Expenses	⎭ Income Statement
− Dividends	⎫ Statement of Retained Earnings
+ Common Stock	

Income Statement

FastForward's income statement for December is shown at the top of Exhibit 1.10. Information about revenues and expenses is conveniently taken from the Equity columns of Exhibit 1.9. Revenues are reported first on the income statement. They include consulting revenues of $5,800 from transactions 5 and 8 and rental revenue of $300 from transaction 8. Expenses are reported after revenues. (For convenience in this chapter, we list larger amounts first, but we can sort expenses in different ways.) Rent and salary expenses are from transactions 6 and 7. Expenses reflect the costs to generate the revenues reported. Net income (or loss) is reported at the bottom of the statement and is the amount earned in December. Stockholders' investments and dividends are *not* part of income.

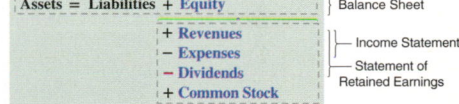

Point: Total revenues
  − Total expenses
  = Net income (or loss)

Point: Net income is sometimes called *earnings* or *profit*.

Statement of Retained Earnings

The statement of retained earnings reports information about how retained earnings changes over the reporting period. This statement shows beginning retained earnings, events that increase it (net income), and events that decrease it (dividends and net loss). Ending retained earnings is computed in this statement and is carried over and reported on the balance sheet. FastForward's statement of retained earnings is the second report in Exhibit 1.10. The beginning balance is measured as of the start of business on December 1. It is zero because FastForward did not exist before then. An existing business reports the beginning balance equal to that as of the end of the prior reporting period (such as from November 30). FastForward's statement shows the $4,400 of net income earned during the period. This links the income statement to the statement of retained earnings (see line ①). The statement reports the $200 cash dividend and FastForward's end-of-period retained earnings balance.

Point: The statement of retained earnings is also called the *statement of changes in retained earnings*. Note: Beg. Retained Earnings + Net Income − Dividends = End. Retained Earnings

EXHIBIT 1.10

Financial Statements and
Their Links

Point: A statement's heading
identifies the company, the
statement title, and the date or
time period.

Point: Arrow lines show how
the statements are linked.
① Net income is used to
compute equity. ② Retained
earnings is used to prepare the
balance sheet. ③ Cash from
the balance sheet is used to
reconcile the statement of
cash flows.

Point: The income statement,
the statement of retained earnings, and the statement of cash
flows are prepared for a *period*
of time. The balance sheet is
prepared as of a *point* in time.

Point: A single ruled line denotes an addition or subtraction.
Final totals are double under-
lined. Negative amounts may or
may not be in parentheses.

FASTFORWARD
Income Statement
For Month Ended December 31, 2016

Revenues		
Consulting revenue ($4,200 + $1,600)	$ 5,800	
Rental revenue	300	
Total revenues		$ 6,100
Expenses		
Rent expense	1,000	
Salaries expense	700	
Total expenses		1,700
Net income		$ 4,400

FASTFORWARD
Statement of Retained Earnings
For Month Ended December 31, 2016

Retained earnings, December 1, 2016		$ 0
Plus: Net income		4,400
		4,400
Less: Dividends		200
Retained earnings, December 31, 2016		$ 4,200

FASTFORWARD
Balance Sheet
December 31, 2016

Assets		Liabilities	
Cash	$ 4,800	Accounts payable	$ 6,200
Supplies	9,600	Total liabilities	6,200
Equipment	26,000	**Equity**	
		Common stock	30,000
		Retained earnings	4,200
		Total equity	34,200
Total assets	$ 40,400	Total liabilities and equity	$ 40,400

FASTFORWARD
Statement of Cash Flows
For Month Ended December 31, 2016

Cash flows from operating activities		
Cash received from clients ($4,200 + $1,900)	$ 6,100	
Cash paid for supplies ($2,500 + $900)	(3,400)	
Cash paid for rent	(1,000)	
Cash paid to employee	(700)	
Net cash provided by operating activities		$ 1,000
Cash flows from investing activities		
Purchase of equipment	(26,000)	
Net cash used by investing activities		(26,000)
Cash flows from financing activities		
Investments from stockholder	30,000	
Dividends to stockholder	(200)	
Net cash provided by financing activities		29,800
Net increase in cash		$ 4,800
Cash balance, December 1, 2016		0
Cash balance, December 31, 2016		$ 4,800

Balance Sheet

FastForward's balance sheet is the third report in Exhibit 1.10. This statement refers to FastForward's financial condition at the close of business on December 31. The left side of the balance sheet lists FastForward's assets: cash, supplies, and equipment. The upper right side of the balance sheet shows that FastForward owes $6,200 to creditors. Any other liabilities (such as a bank loan) would be listed here. The equity balance is $34,200. Line ② shows the link between the ending balance of the statement of retained earnings and the retained earnings balance on the balance sheet. (This presentation of the balance sheet is called the *account form:* assets on the left and liabilities and equity on the right. Another presentation is the *report form:* assets on top, followed by liabilities and then equity at the bottom. Either presentation is acceptable.) As always, we see the accounting equation applies: Assets of $40,400 = Liabilities of $6,200 + Equity of $34,200.

Statement of Cash Flows

FastForward's statement of cash flows is the final report in Exhibit 1.10. The first section reports cash flows from *operating activities*. It shows the $6,100 cash received from clients and the $5,100 cash paid for supplies, rent, and employee salaries. Outflows are in parentheses to denote subtraction. Net cash provided by operating activities for December is $1,000. If cash paid exceeded the $5,100 cash received, we would call it "cash used by operating activities." The second section reports *investing activities,* which involve buying and selling assets such as land and equipment that are held for *long-term use* (typically more than one year). The only investing activity is the $26,000 purchase of equipment. The third section shows cash flows from *financing activities,* which include the *long-term* borrowing and repaying of cash from lenders and the cash investments from, and dividends to, stockholders. FastForward reports $30,000 from the owner's initial investment and the $200 cash dividend. The net cash effect of all financing transactions is a $29,800 cash inflow. The final part of the statement shows FastForward increased its cash balance by $4,800 in December. Since it started with no cash, the ending balance is also $4,800—see line ③. We see that its cash flow numbers are different from income statement (*accrual*) numbers, which is common.

Point: Statement of cash flows has three main sections: operating, investing, and financing.

Point: Payment for supplies is an operating activity because supplies are expected to be used up in short-term operations (typically less than one year).

Point: Investing activities refer to long-term asset investments by the company, *not* to owner investments.

Prepare the (a) income statement, (b) statement of retained earnings, and (c) balance sheet for **Apple** using the following *condensed* data from its fiscal year ended September 27, 2014 ($ in millions). (Its prior fiscal year ended September 28, 2013.)

NEED-TO-KNOW 1-5

Financial Statements

P2

APPLE

Accounts payable	$ 30,196	Investments and other assets	$179,911
Other liabilities	90,096	Land and equipment (net)	20,624
Cost of sales	112,258	Selling, general, and other expenses	31,027
Cash	13,844	Accounts receivable	17,460
Retained earnings, Sep. 28, 2013	104,256	Net income	39,510
Dividends in fiscal year 2014	56,614	Retained earnings, Sep. 27, 2014	87,152
Revenues	182,795	Common stock	24,395

Solution ($ in millions)

APPLE
Income Statement
For Fiscal Year Ended September 27, 2014

Revenues		$182,795
Expenses		
Cost of sales	$112,258	
Selling, general, and other expenses	31,027	
Total expenses		143,285
Net income		$ 39,510

To next page statement of retained earnings

APPLE

APPLE
Statement of Retained Earnings
For Fiscal Year Ended September 27, 2014

Retained earnings, Sep. 28, 2013		$104,256
Plus: Net income		39,510
		143,766
Less: Dividends		56,614
Retained earnings, Sep. 27, 2014		$ 87,152

From prior page income statement

APPLE
Balance Sheet
September 27, 2014

Assets		Liabilities	
Cash	$ 13,844	Accounts payable	$ 30,196
Accounts receivable	17,460	Other liabilities	90,096
Land and equipment (net)	20,624	Total liabilities	120,292
Investments and other assets	179,911	**Equity**	
		Common stock	24,395
		Retained earnings	87,152
		Total equity	111,547
Total assets	$231,839	Total liabilities and equity	$231,839

Do More: QS 1-12, QS 1-13, QS 1-14, E 1-15, E 1-16, E 1-17

GLOBAL VIEW

Accounting according to U.S. GAAP is similar, but not identical, to IFRS. We use the last section of each chapter to identify major similarities and differences between IFRS and U.S. GAAP.

Basic Principles   Both U.S. GAAP and IFRS include broad and similar guidance. However, neither system specifies particular account names nor the detail required. (A typical *chart of accounts* is shown near the end of this book.) IFRS does require certain minimum line items be reported in the balance sheet along with other minimum disclosures that U.S. GAAP does not. On the other hand, U.S. GAAP requires disclosures for the current and prior two years for the income statement, statement of cash flows, and statement of retained earnings (equity), while IFRS requires disclosures for the current and prior year only. Still, the basic principles behind these two systems are similar.[†]

Transaction Analysis   Both U.S. GAAP and IFRS apply transaction analysis identically as shown in this chapter. Although some variations exist in revenue and expense recognition and other principles, all of the transactions in this chapter are accounted for identically under these two systems. It is often said that U.S. GAAP is more *rules-based* whereas IFRS is more *principles-based*. Under U.S. GAAP, the approach is said to be more focused on following the accounting rules; under IFRS, the approach is more focused on a review of the situation and how accounting can best reflect it. This difference typically impacts advanced topics beyond the introductory course.

Financial Statements   Both U.S. GAAP and IFRS prepare the same four basic financial statements. To illustrate, a condensed version of **Samsung**'s income statement follows using Korean IFRS (numbers are in thousands of U.S. dollars). Appendix A to the book has a full set of financial statements for **Samsung** along with those for **Apple** and **Google**.

[†] The FASB and the IASB completed a joint project in 2014 to clarify the principles for recognizing revenue and to develop a common revenue standard for U.S. GAAP and IFRS. The FASB amended the FASB Accounting Standards Codification® and created a new Topic 606, *Revenue from Contracts with Customers,* and the IASB issued IFRS 15, *Revenue from Contracts with Customers.* The core principle is that "an entity should recognize revenue to depict the transfer of promised goods or services to customers in an amount that reflects the consideration to which the entity expects to be entitled in exchange for those goods or services." All discussions and presentations in this book are consistent with this new standard.

SAMSUNG Income Statement ($ thousands) For Year Ended December 31, 2014	
Revenues	$195,882,955
Cost of sales	121,856,939
Cost of selling, wages, depreciation, and other expenses, net	47,546,456
Tax expense	4,256,366
Net income (profit)	$ 22,223,194

Status of IFRS IFRS is now adopted or accepted in over 115 countries, including over 30 member-states of the EU. The FASB and IASB continue to work on the convergence of IFRS and U.S. GAAP.

Sustainability and Accounting The **Sustainability Accounting Standards Board (SASB)** is a nonprofit entity engaged in creating and disseminating sustainability accounting standards for use by companies. Sustainability refers to *environmental*, *social*, and *governance (ESG)* aspects of a company. A company's social aspects include donations to hospitals, colleges, community programs, and law enforcement. Environmental aspects include programs to reduce pollution, increase product safety, improve worker conditions, and support "green" activities. Governance aspects include social responsibility programs, community relations, and use of sustainable materials. Sustainability accounting standards are intended to complement financial accounting standards. The SASB has its own *Conceptual Framework* to guide the development of sustainability standards. It has also developed a set of *principles,* which serve as a set of minimum criteria.

© Xinhua/Alamy

Apple, as introduced in this chapter's opening feature, focuses on sustainability. Apple hired a Vice President of Environmental Initiatives, Lisa Jackson (in photo), to oversee its sustainability initiative. Lisa has set high goals for Apple, including powering all of its facilities with 100% renewable energy and making its products 100% recyclable. "We are swinging for the fences [on sustainability]," proclaims Lisa, which has resulted in some home runs for Apple. In Apple's sustainability report, Lisa points out that it powers data centers with 100% renewable energy and relies solely on renewable energy to power 80% of its corporate facilities and 50% of its retail stores. As Lisa stresses, "[Sustainability] is really important at Apple." Apple is also committed to reducing carbon emissions. "We would like to eliminate certain toxins," explains Lisa. Apple's sustainability report asserts that it has markedly improved its carbon efficiency and reduced the amount of carbon dioxide produced per dollar of revenue—see graphic. Lisa insists, "Leave the world better than how we found it . . . this is what really inspires people at Apple."

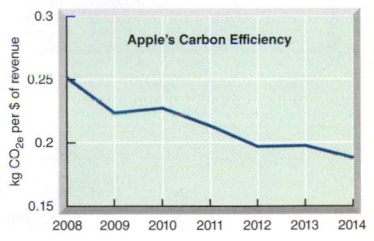

Source: Greenbiz, October 2014; Apple Sustainability Report, January 2015

Decision Insight

Sustainability Returns Virtue is not always its own reward. Compare the S&P 500 with the Domini Social Index (DSEFX), which covers 400 companies that have especially good records for sustainability. We see that returns for companies with sustainable behavior are roughly on par with, or better than, those of the S&P 500 for the recent five-year period. Varying, but similar, results are evident over several recent time periods. ■

Decision Analysis (a section at the end of each chapter) introduces and explains ratios for decision making using real company data. All ratios are covered in Chapter 13

Return on Assets   **Decision Analysis**

A *Decision Analysis* section at the end of each chapter is devoted to financial statement analysis. We organize financial statement analysis into four areas: (1) liquidity and efficiency, (2) solvency, (3) profitability, and (4) market prospects—Chapter 13 has a ratio listing with definitions and groupings by area. When analyzing ratios, we need benchmarks to identify good, bad, or average levels. Common benchmarks include the company's prior levels and those of its competitors.

A2

Compute and interpret return on assets.

This chapter presents a profitability measure: return on assets. Return on assets is useful in evaluating management, analyzing and forecasting profits, and planning activities. **Dell** has its marketing department compute return on assets for *each* order. **Return on assets (ROA),** also called *return on investment (ROI),* is defined in Exhibit 1.11.

EXHIBIT 1.11

Return on Assets

$$\text{Return on assets} = \frac{\text{Net income}}{\text{Average total assets}}$$

Net income is from the annual income statement, and average total assets is computed by adding the beginning and ending amounts for that same period and dividing by 2. To illustrate, **Verizon** reports total net income of $11,956 million for 2014. At the beginning of 2014, its total assets are $274,098 million and at the end of 2014, they total $232,708 million. Verizon's return on assets for 2014 is:

$$\text{Return on assets} = \frac{\$11,956 \text{ million}}{(\$274,098 \text{ million} + \$232,708 \text{ million})/2} = 4.7\%$$

Is a 4.7% return on assets good or bad for Verizon? To help answer this question, we compare (benchmark) Verizon's return with its prior performance, the returns of competitors (such as **AT&T**, **T-Mobile**, and **Sprint**), and the returns from alternative investments. Verizon's return for each of the prior five years is in the middle column of Exhibit 1.12, which ranges from 4.5% to 9.4%.

EXHIBIT 1.12

Verizon and Industry Returns

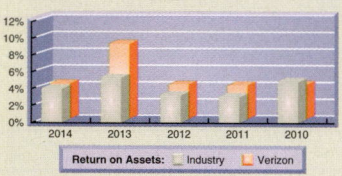

	Return on Assets	
Fiscal Year	**Verizon**	**Industry**
2014	4.7%	4.1%
2013	9.4	5.4
2012	4.6	3.3
2011	4.5	3.1
2010	4.6	4.9

Verizon shows a fairly stable pattern of good returns that reflect its productive use of assets. There is a higher than usual return in 2013 reflecting some nonrecurring items. We also compare Verizon's return to the normal return from its competitors (third column). We compute industry norms, which are sometimes available from services such as **Dun & Bradstreet**'s *Industry Norms and Key Ratios* and **The Risk Management Association**'s *Annual Statement Studies*. When compared to the industry, Verizon often performs slightly better.

*Each **Decision Analysis** section ends with a role-playing scenario to show the usefulness of ratios*

■ **Decision Maker** ━━━━━━━━━━━━━━━━━━━━━━━━

Business Owner　You own a winter ski resort that earns a 21% return on its assets. An opportunity to purchase a winter ski equipment manufacturer is offered to you. This manufacturer earns a 14% return on its assets. The industry return for this manufacturer is 9%. Do you purchase this manufacturer? ■ 　[Answers follow the chapter's Summary.]

The **Comprehensive Need-to-Know** *is a review of key chapter content. The Planning the Solution section offers strategies in solving it*

 1-6

COMPREHENSIVE

After several months of planning, Jasmine Worthy started a haircutting business called Expressions. The following events occurred during its first month of business.

a. On August 1, Worthy invested $3,000 cash and $15,000 of equipment in Expressions in exchange for its common stock.
b. On August 2, Expressions paid $600 cash for furniture for the shop.
c. On August 3, Expressions paid $500 cash to rent space in a strip mall for August.
d. On August 4, it purchased $1,200 of equipment on credit for the shop (using a long-term note payable).
e. On August 5, Expressions opened for business. Cash received from haircutting services in the first week and a half of business (ended August 15) was $825.
f. On August 15, it provided $100 of haircutting services on account.
g. On August 17, it received a $100 check for services previously rendered on account.

h. On August 17, it paid $125 cash to an assistant for hours worked during the grand opening.
i. Cash received from services provided during the second half of August was $930.
j. On August 31, it paid a $400 installment toward principal on the note payable entered into on August 4.
k. On August 31, it paid $900 cash in dividends to Worthy (sole shareholder).

Required

1. Arrange the following asset, liability, and equity titles in a table similar to the one in Exhibit 1.9: Cash; Accounts Receivable; Furniture; Store Equipment; Note Payable; Common Stock; Dividends; Revenues; and Expenses. Show the effects of each transaction using the accounting equation.

2. Prepare an income statement for August.

3. Prepare a statement of retained earnings for August.

4. Prepare a balance sheet as of August 31.

5. Prepare a statement of cash flows for August.

6. Determine the return on assets ratio for August.

PLANNING THE SOLUTION

- Set up a table like Exhibit 1.9 with the appropriate columns for accounts.
- Analyze each transaction and show its effects as increases or decreases in the appropriate columns. Be sure the accounting equation remains in balance after each transaction.
- Prepare the income statement, and identify revenues and expenses. List those items on the statement, compute the difference, and label the result as *net income* or *net loss*.
- Use information in the Equity columns to prepare the statement of retained earnings.
- Use information in the last row of the transactions table to prepare the balance sheet.
- Prepare the statement of cash flows; include all events listed in the Cash column of the transactions table. Classify each cash flow as operating, investing, or financing.
- Calculate return on assets by dividing net income by average assets.

SOLUTION

1.

	Assets				=	Liabilities +		Equity				
	Cash +	Accounts Receivable +	Furniture +	Store Equipment =		Note Payable +	Common Stock −	Dividends +	Revenues −	Expenses		
a.	$3,000			$15,000			$18,000					
b.	− 600		+ $600									
Bal.	2,400 +		+ 600 +	15,000 =			18,000					
c.	− 500									− $500		
Bal.	1,900 +		+ 600 +	15,000 =			18,000			− 500		
d.				+ 1,200		+$1,200						
Bal.	1,900 +		+ 600 +	16,200 =		1,200 +	18,000			− 500		
e.	+ 825								+ $ 825			
Bal.	2,725 +		+ 600 +	16,200 =		1,200 +	18,000		+ 825	− 500		
f.		+ $100							+ 100			
Bal.	2,725 +	100	+ 600 +	16,200 =		1,200 +	18,000		+ 925	− 500		
g.	+ 100 −	100										
Bal.	2,825 +	0	+ 600 +	16,200 =		1,200 +	18,000		+ 925	− 500		
h.	− 125									− 125		
Bal.	2,700 +	0	+ 600 +	16,200 =		1,200 +	18,000		+ 925	− 625		
i.	+ 930								+ 930			
Bal.	3,630 +	0	+ 600 +	16,200 =		1,200 +	18,000		+ 1,855	− 625		
j.	− 400						− 400					
Bal.	3,230 +	0	+ 600 +	16,200 =		800 +	18,000		+ 1,855	− 625		
k.	− 900								− $900			
Bal.	$ 2,330 +	0	+ $600 +	$ 16,200 =		$ 800 +	$ 18,000 −	$900 +	$1,855	− $625		

2.

EXPRESSIONS
Income Statement
For Month Ended August 31

Revenues		
Haircutting services revenue		$1,855
Expenses		
Rent expense	$500	
Wages expense	125	
Total expenses		625
Net income		$1,230

3.

EXPRESSIONS
Statement of Retained Earnings
For Month Ended August 31

Retained earnings, August 1*	$ 0
Plus: Net income	1,230
	1,230
Less: Dividend to owner	900
Retained earnings, August 31	$ 330

* If Expressions had been an existing business from a prior period, the beginning retained earnings balance would equal the retained earnings balance from the end of the prior period.

4.

EXPRESSIONS
Balance Sheet
August 31

Assets		**Liabilities**	
Cash	$ 2,330	Note payable	$ 800
Furniture	600	**Equity**	
Store equipment	16,200	Common stock	18,000
		Retained earnings	330
		Total equity	18,330
Total assets	$19,130	Total liabilities and equity	$19,130

5.

EXPRESSIONS
Statement of Cash Flows
For Month Ended August 31

Cash flows from operating activities		
Cash received from customers	$1,855	
Cash paid for rent	(500)	
Cash paid for wages	(125)	
Net cash provided by operating activities		$1,230
Cash flows from investing activities		
Cash paid for furniture		(600)
Cash flows from financing activities		
Cash investments from stockholders	3,000	
Cash dividends to stockholders	(900)	
Partial repayment of (long-term) note payable	(400)	
Net cash provided by financing activities		1,700
Net increase in cash		$2,330
Cash balance, August 1		0
Cash balance, August 31		$2,330

6. Return on assets $= \dfrac{\text{Net income}}{\text{Average assets}} = \dfrac{\$1{,}230}{(\$18{,}000^* + \$19{,}130)/2} = \dfrac{\$1{,}230}{\$18{,}565} = \underline{\underline{\mathbf{6.63\%}}}$

* Uses the initial \$18,000 investment as the beginning balance for the *start-up period only*.

Return and Risk

1A

A3

Explain the relation between return and risk.

This appendix explains return and risk analysis and its role in business and accounting.

Net income is often linked to **return.** Return on assets (ROA) is stated in ratio form as income divided by assets invested. For example, banks report return from a savings account in the form of an interest return such as 4%. If we invest in a savings account or in U.S. Treasury bills, we expect a return of around 1% to 5%. We could also invest in a company's stock, or even start our own business. How do we decide among these options? The answer depends on our trade-off between return and risk.

Risk is the uncertainty about the return we will earn. All business investments involve risk, but some investments involve more risk than others. The lower the risk of an investment, the lower is our expected return. The reason that savings accounts pay such a low return is the low risk of not being repaid with interest (the government guarantees most savings accounts). If we buy a share of **eBay** or any other company, we might obtain a large return. However, we have no guarantee of any return; there is even the risk of loss.

The bar graph in Exhibit 1A.1 shows recent returns for 10-year bonds with different risks. *Bonds* are written promises by organizations to repay amounts loaned with interest. U.S. Treasury bonds provide a low expected return, but they also offer low risk since they are backed by the U.S. government. High-risk corporate bonds offer a much larger potential return but with much higher risk.

The trade-off between return and risk is a normal part of business. Higher risk implies higher, but riskier, expected returns. To help us make better decisions, we use accounting information to assess both return and risk.

EXHIBIT 1A.1

Average Returns for Bonds with Different Risks

Business Activities

1B

C5

Identify and describe the three major activities of organizations.

This appendix explains how the accounting equation is linked to business activities.

Financing   *Financing activities* provide the means organizations use to pay for resources such as land, buildings, and equipment. The two sources of financing are owner and nonowner. *Owner financing* refers to resources contributed by the owner along with any income the owner leaves in the organization. *Nonowner* (or *creditor*) *financing* refers to resources contributed by creditors (lenders).

Investing   *Investing activities* are the acquiring and disposing of resources (assets) that an organization uses to acquire and sell its products or services. Assets are funded by an organization's financing. Some organizations require land and factories to operate. Others need only an office. Invested amounts are referred to as *assets*. Creditor and owner financing hold claims on assets. Creditors' claims are

Point: Management must understand accounting data to set financial goals, make financing and investing decisions, and evaluate operating performance.

Point: Investing (assets) and financing (liabilities plus equity) totals are *always* equal.

called *liabilities,* and the owner's claim is called *equity.* This yields the *accounting equation:* Assets = Liabilities + Equity.

EXHIBIT 1B.1

Activities of Organizations

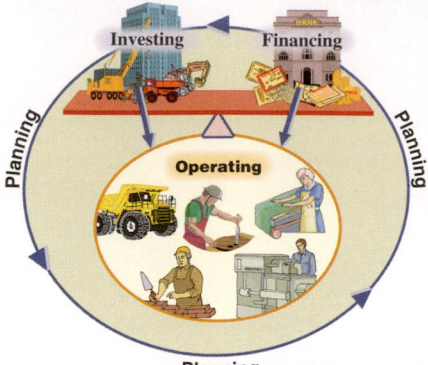

Operating   *Operating activities* involve using resources to research, develop, purchase, produce, distribute, and market products and services. Sales and revenues are the inflow of assets from selling products and services. Costs and expenses are the outflow of assets to support operating activities.

Exhibit 1B.1 summarizes business activities. Planning is part of each activity and gives them meaning and focus. Investing (assets) and financing (liabilities and equity) are set opposite each other to stress their balance. Operating activities are below investing and financing activities to show that operating activities are the result of investing and financing.

Summary

*A **Summary** organized by learning objectives concludes each chapter*

C1 **Explain the purpose and importance of accounting.** Accounting is an information and measurement system that aims to identify, record, and communicate relevant, reliable, and comparable information about business activities. It helps assess opportunities, products, investments, and social and community responsibilities.

C2 **Identify users and uses of, and opportunities in, accounting.** Users of accounting are both internal and external. Some users and uses of accounting include (a) managers in controlling, monitoring, and planning; (b) lenders for measuring the risk and return of loans; (c) shareholders for assessing the return and risk of stock; (d) directors for overseeing management; and (e) employees for judging employment opportunities. Opportunities in accounting include financial, managerial, and tax accounting.

C3 **Explain why ethics are crucial to accounting.** The goal of accounting is to provide useful information for decision making. For information to be useful, it must be trusted. This demands ethical behavior in accounting.

C4 **Explain generally accepted accounting principles and define and apply several accounting principles.** Generally accepted accounting principles are a common set of standards applied by accountants. Accounting principles aid in producing relevant, reliable, and comparable information. Four principles underlying financial statements were introduced: cost, revenue recognition, expense recognition, and full disclosure. Financial statements reflect four assumptions: going-concern, monetary unit, time period, and business entity.

C5^B **Identify and describe the three major activities of organizations.** Organizations carry out three major activities: financing, investing, and operating. Financing is the means

used to pay for resources such as land, buildings, and machines. Investing refers to the buying and selling of resources used in acquiring and selling products and services. Operating activities are those necessary for carrying out the organization's plans.

A1 **Define and interpret the accounting equation and each of its components.** The accounting equation is: Assets = Liabilities + Equity. Assets are resources owned by a company. Liabilities are creditors' claims on assets. Equity is the owner's claim on assets (*the residual*). The expanded accounting equation is: Assets = Liabilities + [Common Stock − Dividends + Revenues − Expenses].

A2 **Compute and interpret return on assets.** Return on assets is computed as net income divided by average assets. For example, if we have an average balance of $100 in a savings account and it earns $5 interest for the year, the return on assets is $5/$100, or 5%.

A3^A **Explain the relation between return and risk.** *Return* refers to income, and *risk* is the uncertainty about the return we hope to make. All investments involve risk. The lower the risk of an investment, the lower is its expected return. Higher risk implies higher, but riskier, expected return.

P1 **Analyze business transactions using the accounting equation.** A *transaction* is an exchange of economic consideration between two parties. Examples include exchanges of products, services, money, and rights to collect money. Transactions always have at least two effects on one or more components of the accounting equation. This equation is always in balance.

P2 **Identify and prepare basic financial statements and explain how they interrelate.** Four financial statements report on an organization's activities: balance sheet, income statement, statement of retained earnings, and statement of cash flows.

Guidance Answers to Decision Maker and Decision Ethics

Entrepreneur   You should probably form the business as a corporation if potential lawsuits are of prime concern. The corporate form helps protect personal property from lawsuits di-

rected at the business and places only the corporation's resources at risk. A downside of the corporate form is double taxation: The corporation must pay taxes on its income, and you normally must pay taxes on any money distributed to you (even though the corporation already paid taxes on this money). Formation as an LLC or S corp. can also be explored. You should also examine the ethical and socially responsible aspects of starting a business in which you anticipate injuries to others.

Business Owner   The 14% return on assets for the manufacturer exceeds the 9% industry return (and many others). This is a positive factor for a potential purchase. Also, the purchase of this manufacturer is an opportunity to spread your risk over two businesses as opposed to one. Still, you should hesitate to purchase a business whose return of 14% is lower than your current resort's return of 21%. You are probably better off directing efforts to increase investment in your resort, assuming you can continue to earn a 21% return.

A list of key terms concludes each chapter (a complete glossary is also available)

Key Terms

Accounting
Accounting equation
Assets
Audit
Auditors
Balance sheet
Bookkeeping
Business entity assumption
Common stock
Conceptual framework
Contributed capital
Corporation
Cost-benefit constraint
Cost principle
Dividends
Dodd-Frank Wall Street Reform and
 Consumer Protection Act
Equity
Ethics
Events
Expanded accounting equation
Expense recognition principle
Expenses
External transactions

External users
Financial accounting
Financial Accounting Standards Board
 (FASB)
Full disclosure principle
Generally accepted accounting principles
 (GAAP)
Going-concern assumption
Income statement
Internal transactions
Internal users
International Accounting Standards
 Board (IASB)
International Financial Reporting
 Standards (IFRS)
Liabilities
Managerial accounting
Manufacturer
Matching principle
Materiality constraint
Measurement principle
Merchandiser
Monetary unit assumption
Net income

Net loss
Partnership
Proprietorship
Recordkeeping
Retained earnings
Return
Return on assets (ROA)
Revenue recognition principle
Revenues
Risk
Sarbanes-Oxley Act (SOX)
Securities and Exchange Commission
 (SEC)
Shareholders
Shares
Sole proprietorship
Statement of cash flows
Statement of retained earnings
Stock
Stockholders
Sustainability Accounting Standards
 Board (SASB)
Time period assumption

Multiple Choice Quiz   Answers at end of chapter

1. A building is offered for sale at $500,000 but is currently assessed at $400,000. The purchaser of the building believes the building is worth $475,000, but ultimately purchases the building for $450,000. The purchaser records the building at:
 a. $50,000   d. $475,000
 b. $400,000   e. $500,000
 c. $450,000

2. On December 30, 2015, KPMG signs a $150,000 contract to provide accounting services to one of its clients in 2016. KPMG has a December 31 year-end. Which accounting principle or assumption requires KPMG to record the accounting services revenue from this client in 2016 and not 2015?
 a. Business entity assumption
 b. Revenue recognition principle

 c. Monetary unit assumption
 d. Cost principle
 e. Going-concern assumption

3. If the assets of a company increase by $100,000 during the year and its liabilities increase by $35,000 during the same year, then the change in equity of the company during the year must have been:
 a. An increase of $135,000.
 b. A decrease of $135,000.
 c. A decrease of $65,000.
 d. An increase of $65,000.
 e. An increase of $100,000.

4. **Brunswick** borrows $50,000 cash from Third National Bank. How does this transaction affect the accounting equation for Brunswick?
   a. Assets increase by $50,000; liabilities increase by $50,000; no effect on equity.
   b. Assets increase by $50,000; no effect on liabilities; equity increases by $50,000.
   c. Assets increase by $50,000; liabilities decrease by $50,000; no effect on equity.
   d. No effect on assets; liabilities increase by $50,000; equity increases by $50,000.
   e. No effect on assets; liabilities increase by $50,000; equity decreases by $50,000.

5. **Geek Squad** performs services for a customer and bills the customer for $500. How would Geek Squad record this transaction?
   a. Accounts receivable increase by $500; revenues increase by $500.
   b. Cash increases by $500; revenues increase by $500.
   c. Accounts receivable increase by $500; revenues decrease by $500.
   d. Accounts receivable increase by $500; accounts payable increase by $500.
   e. Accounts payable increase by $500; revenues increase by $500.

A(B) *Superscript letter A (B) denotes assignments based on Appendix 1A (1B).*
♟ Icon denotes assignments that involve decision making.

Discussion Questions

1. What is the purpose of accounting in society?
2. Technology is increasingly used to process accounting data. Why then must we study and understand accounting?
3. ♟ Identify four kinds of external users and describe how they use accounting information.
4. ♟ What are at least three questions business owners and managers might be able to answer by looking at accounting information?
5. Identify three actual businesses that offer services and three actual businesses that offer products.
6. ♟ Describe the internal role of accounting for organizations.
7. Identify three types of services typically offered by accounting professionals.
8. ♟ What type of accounting information might be useful to the marketing managers of a business?
9. Why is accounting described as a service activity?
10. What are some accounting-related professions?
11. How do ethics rules affect auditors' choice of clients?
12. What work do tax accounting professionals perform in addition to preparing tax returns?
13. What does the concept of *objectivity* imply for information reported in financial statements? Why?
14. A business reports its own office stationery on the balance sheet at its $400 cost, although it cannot be sold for more than $10 as scrap paper. Which accounting principle and/or assumption justifies this treatment?
15. Why is the revenue recognition principle needed? What does it demand?
16. Describe the three basic forms of business organization and their key attributes.
17. Define (*a*) *assets,* (*b*) *liabilities,* (*c*) *equity,* and (*d*) *net assets.*
18. What events or transactions change equity?

19. Identify the two main categories of accounting principles.
20. What do accountants mean by the term *revenue*?
21. Define *net income* and explain its computation.
22. Identify the four basic financial statements of a business.
23. ♟ What information is reported in an income statement?
24. Give two examples of expenses a business might incur.
25. What is the purpose of the statement of retained earnings?
26. ♟ What information is reported in a balance sheet?
27. The statement of cash flows reports on what major activities?
28. ♟ Define and explain return on assets.
29.^A ♟ Define return and risk. Discuss the trade-off between them.
30.^B Describe the three major business activities in organizations.
31.^B Explain why investing (assets) and financing (liabilities and equity) totals are always equal.
32. ♟ Refer to the financial statements of **Apple** in Appendix A near the end of the book. To **APPLE** what level of significance are dollar amounts rounded? What time period does its income statement cover?
33. Identify the dollar amounts of **Google**'s **GOOGLE** 2014 assets, liabilities, and equity as reported in its statements in Appendix A near the end of the book.
34. Refer to **Samsung**'s 2014 balance **Samsung** sheet in Appendix A near the end of the book. Confirm that its total assets equal its total liabilities plus total equity.
35. ♟ Access the SEC EDGAR database (www. **APPLE** SEC.gov) and retrieve **Apple**'s 2014 10-K (filed October 27, 2014). Identify its auditor. What responsibility does its independent auditor claim regarding Apple's financial statements?

Quick Study *exercises offer a brief test of key elements*

![McGraw-Hill Education] **connect**

Choose from the following list of terms/phrases to best complete the following statements.

QUICK STUDY

a. Accounting	**c.** Recording	**e.** Governmental	**g.** Language of business
b. Identifying	**d.** Communicating	**f.** Technology	**h.** Recordkeeping (bookkeeping)

1. _____ reduces the time, effort, and cost of recordkeeping while improving clerical accuracy.

2. _____ business activities requires that we keep a chronological log of transactions and events measured in dollars.

3. _____ is the recording of transactions and events, either manually or electronically.

QS 1-1
Understanding accounting
C1

Identify the following users as either external users (E) or internal users (I).

_____ **a.** Customers	_____ **e.** Managers	_____ **i.** Controllers
_____ **b.** Suppliers	_____ **f.** District attorney	_____ **j.** FBI and IRS
_____ **c.** Brokers	_____ **g.** Shareholders	_____ **k.** Consumer group
_____ **d.** Business press	_____ **h.** Lenders	_____ **l.** Janitors

QS 1-2
Identifying accounting users
C2

---

a. Accounting professionals must sometimes choose between two or more acceptable methods of accounting for business transactions and events. Explain why these situations can involve difficult matters of ethical concern.

b. An important responsibility of many accounting professionals is to design and implement internal control procedures for organizations. Explain the purpose of internal control procedures. Provide two examples of internal controls applied by companies.

QS 1-3
Identifying ethical concerns   **C3**

Icon highlights assignments that enhance decision-making skills

---

Identify each of the following terms/phrases as either an accounting: (a) principle, (b) assumption, or (c) constraint.

_____ **1.** Materiality	_____ **3.** Benefit exceeds cost
_____ **2.** Time period	_____ **4.** Revenue recognition

QS 1-4
Identifying principles, assumptions, and constraints   **C4**

Complete the following table with either a yes or no regarding the attributes of a proprietorship, partnership, and corporation.

Attribute Present	Proprietorship	Partnership	Corporation
1. Business taxed.	_____	_____	_____
2. Business entity.	_____	_____	_____
3. Legal entity	_____	_____	_____

QS 1-5
Identifying attributes of businesses
C4

Identify which accounting principle or assumption best describes each of the following practices:

a. In December 2015, Liz Landscaping received a customer's order and cash prepayment for sod installation at a house in March 2016. Liz should record the revenue from the customer order in March 2016, not in December 2015.

b. If $51,000 cash is paid to buy land, the land is reported on the buyer's balance sheet at $51,000.

c. Mike Derr owns both Sailing Supplies and Dockside Digs. In preparing financial statements for Dockside Digs, Mike makes sure that the expense transactions of Sailing Supplies are kept separate from Dockside Digs's transactions and financial statements.

QS 1-6
Identifying accounting principles
C4

---

a. Total assets of Celia Company equal $700,000 and its equity is $420,000. What is the amount of its liabilities?

b. Total assets of Ming Marine equal $500,000 and its liabilities and equity amounts are equal to each other. What is the amount of its liabilities? What is the amount of its equity?

QS 1-7
Applying the accounting equation
A1

QS 1-8

Applying the accounting equation

A1

1. Use the accounting equation to compute the missing financial statement amounts (a), (b), and (c).

	A	B		C		D
1	Company	Assets	=	Liabilities	+	Equity
2	1	$ 75,000		$ (a)		$ 40,000
3	2	(b)		25,000		70,000
4	3	85,000		20,000		(c)
5						

2. Use the expanded accounting equation to compute the missing financial statement amounts (a) and (b).

	A	B	C	D	E	F	G
1				Common			
2	Company	Assets	Liabilities	Stock	Dividends	Revenues	Expenses
3	1	$ 40,000	$ 16,000	$ 20,000	$ 0	(a)	$ 8,000
4	2	$ 80,000	$ 32,000	$ 44,000	(b)	$ 24,000	$ 18,000
5							

QS 1-9

Identifying and computing assets, liabilities, and equity A1

Samsung

Use **Samsung**'s December 31, 2014, financial statements, in Appendix A near the end of the book, to answer the following:

a. Identify the amounts (in millions of Korean won) of its 2014 (1) assets, (2) liabilities, and (3) equity.

b. Using amounts from part a, verify that Assets = Liabilities + Equity.

QS 1-10

Identifying effects of transactions using accounting equation— Revenues and Expenses

P1

Create a table like the one in Exhibit 1.9, using the following headings for columns: Cash; Accounts Receivable; Accounts Payable; Common Stock; Dividends; Revenues; and Expenses. Then use additions and subtractions to show the effects of each transaction on individual items of the accounting equation (identify each revenue and expense type, such as commissions revenue or rent expense).

a. The company completed consulting work for a client and immediately collected $5,500 cash earned.

b. The company completed commission work for a client and sent a bill for $4,000 to be received within 30 days.

c. The company paid an assistant $1,400 cash as wages for the period.

d. The company collected $1,000 cash as a partial payment for the amount owed by the client in transaction b.

e. The company paid $700 cash for this period's cleaning services.

QS 1-11

Identifying effects of transactions using accounting equation— Assets and Liabilities

P1

Create a table like the one in Exhibit 1.9, using the following headings for columns: Cash; Supplies; Equipment; Land; Accounts Payable; Notes Payable; Common Stock; Dividends; Revenues; and Expenses. Then use additions and subtractions to show the effects of each transaction on individual items of the accounting equation.

a. The owner (Alex Carr) invested $15,000 cash in the company in exchange for its common stock.

b. The company purchased supplies for $500 cash.

c. The company purchased $10,000 in equipment on credit (record liability as Note Payable).

d. The company purchased $200 of additional supplies on credit.

e. The company purchased land for $9,000 cash.

QS 1-12

Identifying items with financial statements

P2

Indicate in which financial statement each item would most likely appear: income statement (I), balance sheet (B), statement of retained earnings (E), or statement of cash flows (CF).

_____ **a.** Assets

_____ **b.** Cash from operating activities

_____ **c.** Dividends

_____ **d.** Equipment

_____ **e.** Expenses

_____ **f.** Liabilities

_____ **g.** Net decrease (or increase) in cash

_____ **h.** Revenues

_____ **i.** Total liabilities and equity

Classify each of the following items as revenues (R), expenses (EX), or dividends (D).

_____ **1.** Cost of sales (expense)   _____ **3.** Wages expense

_____ **2.** Service revenue   _____ **4.** Dividends

QS 1-13
Identifying income and equity accounts **P2**

Classify each of the following items as assets (A), liabilities (L), or equity (EQ).

_____ **1.** Land   _____ **3.** Equipment   _____ **5.** Accounts receivable

_____ **2.** Common stock   _____ **4.** Accounts payable

QS 1-14
Identifying assets, liabilities, and equity **P2**

In a recent year's financial statements, **Home Depot** reported the following results. Compute and interpret Home Depot's return on assets (assume competitors average an 11.0% return on assets).

Sales	$83 billion
Net income	6 billion
Average total assets	40 billion

QS 1-15
Computing and interpreting return on assets **A2**

Answer each of the following questions related to international accounting standards.

a. The International Accounting Standards Board (IASB) issues preferred accounting practices that are referred to as what?

b. The FASB and IASB are working on a convergence process for what purpose?

QS 1-16
International accounting standards **C4**

Icon highlights assignments that focus on IFRS-related content

---

Match each of the numbered descriptions with the term or phrase it best reflects. Indicate your answer by writing the letter for the term or phrase in the blank provided.

A. SASB   **D.** Company sustainability   **G.** Sustainability standards

B. Principles   **E.** SASB conceptual framework   **H.** Domini Social Index

C. Social aspect   **F.** Environmental aspect

_____ **1.** Refers to the set of environmental, social, and governance aspects of a company.

_____ **2.** A structure to help guide development of sustainability standards.

_____ **3.** An entity that creates and publishes sustainability accounting standards.

_____ **4.** Aspect of company sustainability involved with donations to hospitals, colleges, and community programs.

QS 1-17
Sustainability accounting

---

connect

Accounting is an information and measurement system that identifies, records, and communicates relevant, reliable, and comparable information about an organization's business activities. Classify the following activities as part of the identifying (I), recording (R), or communicating (C) aspects of accounting.

_____ **1.** Analyzing and interpreting reports.   _____ **5.** Preparing financial statements.

_____ **2.** Presenting financial information.   _____ **6.** Seeing revenues generated from a service.

_____ **3.** Keeping a log of service costs.   _____ **7.** Observing employee tasks behind a product.

_____ **4.** Measuring the costs of a product.   _____ **8.** Registering cash sales of products sold.

EXERCISES

Exercise 1-1
Classifying activities reflected in the accounting system
C1

Part A. Identify the following questions as most likely to be asked by an internal (I) or an external (E) user of accounting information.

_____ **1.** What are reasonable payroll benefits and wages?

_____ **2.** Should we make a five-year loan to that business?

_____ **3.** What are the costs of our product's ingredients?

_____ **4.** Do income levels justify the current stock price?

_____ **5.** Should we spend additional money for redesign of our product?

_____ **6.** Which firm reports the highest sales and income?

_____ **7.** What are the costs of our service to customers?

Exercise 1-2
Identifying accounting users and uses
C2

Continued on next page . . .

Part B. Identify the following users of accounting information as either an internal (I) or an external (E) user.

_____ **1.** Research and development director	_____ **5.** Distribution managers
_____ **2.** Human resources director	_____ **6.** Creditors
_____ **3.** Nonexecutive employee	_____ **7.** Production manager
_____ **4.** Shareholders	_____ **8.** Purchasing manager

Exercise 1-3
Describing accounting responsibilities
C2

Many accounting professionals work in one of the following three areas:

A. Financial accounting

B. Managerial accounting

C. Tax accounting

Identify the area of accounting that is most involved in each of the following responsibilities:

_____ **1.** Internal auditing	_____ **5.** Investigating violations of tax laws
_____ **2.** External auditing	_____ **6.** Planning transactions to minimize taxes
_____ **3.** Cost accounting	_____ **7.** Preparing external financial statements
_____ **4.** Budgeting	_____ **8.** Reviewing reports for SEC compliance

---

Exercise 1-4
Learning the language of business
C1   C2   C3

Match each of the numbered descriptions with the term or phrase it best reflects. Indicate your answer by writing the letter for the term or phrase in the blank provided.

A. Audit	**C.** Ethics	**E.** SEC	**G.** Net income
B. GAAP	**D.** Tax accounting	**F.** Public accountants	**H.** IASB

_____ **1.** An examination of an organization's accounting system and records that adds credibility to financial statements.

_____ **2.** Amount a business earns in excess of all expenses and costs associated with its sales and revenues.

_____ **3.** An accounting area that includes planning future transactions to minimize taxes paid.

_____ **4.** Accounting professionals who provide services to many clients.

_____ **5.** Principles that determine whether an action is right or wrong.

Exercise 1-5
Identifying ethical concerns
C3

Assume the following role and describe a situation in which ethical considerations play an important part in guiding your decisions and actions:

a. You are an accounting professional with audit clients that are competitors in business.

b. You are an accounting professional preparing tax returns for clients.

c. You are a manager with responsibility for several employees.

d. You are a student in an introductory accounting course.

Exercise 1-6
Distinguishing business organizations
C4

The following describe several different business organizations. Determine whether the description refers to a sole proprietorship (SP), partnership (P), or corporation (C).

_____ **a.** Douglas and Logan own Financial Services, a financial services provider. Neither Douglas nor Logan has personal responsibility for the debts of Financial Services.

_____ **b.** Riley and Kay own Speedy Packages, a courier service. Both are personally liable for the debts of the business.

_____ **c.** Derr Company does not have separate legal existence apart from the one person who owns it.

_____ **d.** Trent Company is owned by Trent Topaz, who is personally liable for the company's debts.

_____ **e.** Ownership of Zander Company is divided into 1,000 shares of stock.

_____ **f.** Puma Products does not pay income taxes and has one owner.

_____ **g.** Celia Company pays its own income taxes and has two owners.

Match each of the numbered descriptions with the principle or assumption it best reflects. Enter the letter for the appropriate principle or assumption in the blank space next to each description.

A. General accounting principle
B. Cost principle
C. Business entity assumption
D. Revenue recognition principle
E. Specific accounting principle
F. Matching (expense recognition) principle
G. Going-concern assumption
H. Full disclosure principle

_____ **1.** A company reports details behind financial statements that would impact users' decisions.
_____ **2.** Financial statements reflect the assumption that the business continues operating.
_____ **3.** A company records the expenses incurred to generate the revenues reported.
_____ **4.** Derived from long-used and generally accepted accounting practices.
_____ **5.** Every business is accounted for separately from its owner or owners.
_____ **6.** Revenue is recorded when products or services are delivered.
_____ **7.** Usually created by a pronouncement from an authoritative body.
_____ **8.** Information is based on actual costs incurred in transactions.

Exercise 1-7
Identifying accounting principles and assumptions
C4

Determine the missing amount from each of the separate situations *a*, *b*, and *c* below.

Exercise 1-8
Using the accounting equation
A1

	A		B		C
1	**Assets**	=	**Liabilities**	+	**Equity**
2	(a) $?		$ 20,000		$ 45,000
3	(b) 100,000		34,000		?
4	(c) 154,000		?		40,000
5					

Answer the following questions. (*Hint:* Use the accounting equation.)

a. At the beginning of the year, Chan Company's assets are $300,000 and its equity is $100,000. During the year, assets increase $80,000 and liabilities increase $50,000. What is the equity at year-end?

b. Twitter has assets equal to $123,000 and liabilities equal to $47,000 at year-end. What is the equity for Twitter at year-end?

c. At the beginning of the year, Pandora's liabilities equal $70,000. During the year, assets increase by $60,000, and at year-end assets equal $190,000. Liabilities decrease $5,000 during the year. What are the beginning and ending amounts of equity?

Exercise 1-9
Using the accounting equation
A1

Check (c) Beg. equity, $60,000

Zen began a new consulting firm on January 5. The accounting equation showed the following balances after each of the company's first five transactions. Analyze the accounting equation for each transaction and describe each of the five transactions with their amounts.

Exercise 1-10
Analysis using the accounting equation
P1

			Assets				=	**Liabilities**	+		**Equity**	
Trans-action	Cash	+	Accounts Receiv-able	+	Office Sup-plies	+	Office Furni-ture	=	Accounts Payable	+	Common Stock	+	Revenues
a.	$40,000	+	$ 0	+	$ 0	+	$ 0	=	$ 0	+	$40,000	+	$ 0
b.	38,000	+	0	+	3,000	+	0	=	1,000	+	40,000	+	0
c.	30,000	+	0	+	3,000	+	8,000	=	1,000	+	40,000	+	0
d.	30,000	+	6,000	+	3,000	+	8,000	=	1,000	+	40,000	+	6,000
e.	31,000	+	6,000	+	3,000	+	8,000	=	1,000	+	40,000	+	7,000

Exercise 1-11
Identifying effects of transactions on the accounting equation
P1

The following table shows the effects of five transactions (*a* through *e*) on the assets, liabilities, and equity of Mulan's Boutique. Write short descriptions of the probable nature of each transaction.

		Assets				=	Liabilities	+		Equity	
	Cash	+	Accounts Receivable	+	Office Supplies	+ Land	=	Accounts Payable	+	Common Stock	+ Revenues
	$21,000	+ $ 0		+ $3,000	+ $19,000	= $ 0		+ $43,000		+ $ 0
a.	−4,000				+ 4,000					
b.				+ 1,000			+1,000			
c.		+ 1,900								+ 1,900
d.	−1,000						−1,000			
e.	+1,900	− 1,900								
	$17,900	+ $ 0		+ $4,000	+ $23,000	= $ 0		+ $43,000		+ $1,900

Exercise 1-12
Identifying effects of transactions on the accounting equation
P1

Provide an example of a transaction that creates the described effects for the separate cases *a* through *g*.

a. Decreases an asset and decreases equity.
b. Increases an asset and increases a liability.
c. Decreases a liability and increases a liability.
d. Decreases an asset and decreases a liability.

e. Increases an asset and decreases an asset.
f. Increases a liability and decreases equity.
g. Increases an asset and increases equity.

Exercise 1-13
Identifying effects of transactions using the accounting equation
P1

Ming Chen began a professional practice on June 1 and plans to prepare financial statements at the end of each month. During June, Ming Chen (the owner) completed these transactions:

a. Owner invested $60,000 cash in the company along with equipment that had a $15,000 market value in exchange for its common stock.
b. The company paid $1,500 cash for rent of office space for the month.
c. The company purchased $10,000 of additional equipment on credit (payment due within 30 days).
d. The company completed work for a client and immediately collected the $2,500 cash earned.
e. The company completed work for a client and sent a bill for $8,000 to be received within 30 days.
f. The company purchased additional equipment for $6,000 cash.
g. The company paid an assistant $3,000 cash as wages for the month.
h. The company collected $5,000 cash as a partial payment for the amount owed by the client in transaction *e*.
i. The company paid $10,000 cash to settle the liability created in transaction *c*.
j. The company paid $1,000 cash in dividends to the owner (sole shareholder).

Required

Check   Net income, $6,000

Create a table like the one in Exhibit 1.9, using the following headings for columns: Cash; Accounts Receivable; Equipment; Accounts Payable; Common Stock; Dividends; Revenues; and Expenses. Then use additions and subtractions to show the effects of the transactions on individual items of the accounting equation. Show new balances after each transaction.

Exercise 1-14
Analysis of return on assets   A2

Swiss Group reports net income of $40,000 for 2016. At the beginning of 2016, Swiss Group had $200,000 in assets. By the end of 2016, assets had grown to $300,000. What is Swiss Group's 2016 return on assets? How would you assess its performance if competitors average an 11% return on assets?

Exercise 1-15
Preparing an income statement   P2

On October 1, Ebony Ernst organized Ernst Consulting; on October 3, the owner contributed $84,000 in assets to launch the business. On October 31, the company's records show the following items and amounts. Use this information to prepare an October income statement for the business.

Cash.....................	$11,360	Cash dividends	$ 2,000
Accounts receivable	14,000	Consulting revenues	14,000
Office supplies	3,250	Rent expense	3,550
Land.....................	46,000	Salaries expense	7,000
Office equipment	18,000	Telephone expense.............	760
Accounts payable...........	8,500	Miscellaneous expenses	580
Common stock	84,000		

Check   Net income, $2,110

Use the information in Exercise 1-15 to prepare an October statement of retained earnings for Ernst Consulting.

Exercise 1-16
Preparing a statement of retained earnings
P2

Use the information in Exercise 1-15 (if completed, you can also use your solution to Exercise 1-16) to prepare an October 31 balance sheet for Ernst Consulting.

Exercise 1-17
Preparing a balance sheet
P2

Use the information in Exercise 1-15 to prepare an October 31 statement of cash flows for Ernst Consulting. Also assume the following:

a. The owner's initial investment consists of $38,000 cash and $46,000 in land in exchange for its common stock.

b. The company's $18,000 equipment purchase is paid in cash.

c. The accounts payable balance of $8,500 consists of the $3,250 office supplies purchase and $5,250 in employee salaries yet to be paid.

d. The company's rent, telephone, and miscellaneous expenses are paid in cash.

e. No cash has been collected on the $14,000 consulting revenues.

Exercise 1-18
Preparing a statement of cash flows
P2

Check   Net increase in cash, $11,360

Indicate the section where each of the following would appear on the statement of cash flows.

O. Cash flows from operating activity
I. Cash flows from investing activity
F. Cash flows from financing activity

_____	**1.** Cash purchase of equipment	_____	**5.** Cash paid on account payable to supplier
_____	**2.** Cash paid for dividends	_____	**6.** Cash received from clients
_____	**3.** Cash paid for advertising	_____	**7.** Cash investment from stockholders
_____	**4.** Cash paid for wages	_____	**8.** Cash paid for rent

Exercise 1-19
Identifying sections of the statement of cash flows
P2

BMW Group, one of Europe's largest manufacturers, reports the following income statement accounts for the year ended December 31, 2014 (euros in millions).

Exercise 1-20
Preparing an income statement for a global company
P2

Revenues	€80,401
Cost of sales	63,396
Sales and administrative costs	7,892
Other expenses	3,296

Use this information to prepare BMW's income statement for the year ended December 31, 2014.

Exercise 1-21^B

Identifying business activities

C5

Match each transaction or event to one of the following activities of an organization: financing activities (F), investing activities (I), or operating activities (O).

_____ **a.** An owner contributes resources to the business in exchange for its common stock.

_____ **b.** An organization borrows money from a bank.

_____ **c.** An organization advertises a new product.

_____ **d.** An organization sells some of its land.

_____ **e.** An organization purchases equipment.

Problem Set B located at the end of Problem Set A is provided for each problem to reinforce the learning process

PROBLEM SET A

Problem 1-1A

Identifying effects of transactions on financial statements

A1　P1　

Identify how each of the following separate transactions affects financial statements. For the balance sheet, identify how each transaction affects total assets, total liabilities, and total equity. For the income statement, identify how each transaction affects net income. For the statement of cash flows, identify how each transaction affects cash flows from operating activities, cash flows from investing activities, and cash flows from financing activities. For increases, place a "+" in the column or columns. For decreases, place a "−" in the column or columns. If both an increase and a decrease occur, place a "+/−" in the column or columns. The first transaction is completed as an example.

	Transaction	Balance Sheet			Income Statement	Statement of Cash Flows		
		Total Assets	Total Liab.	Total Equity	Net Income	Operating Activities	Investing Activities	Financing Activities
1	Owner invests cash for its stock	+		+				+
2	Receives cash for services provided							
3	Pays cash for employee wages							
4	Incurs legal costs on credit							
5	Borrows cash by signing long-term note payable							
6	Buys office equipment for cash							
7	Buys land by signing note payable							
8	Provides services on credit							
9	Pays cash dividend							
10	Collects cash on receivable from (8)							

Problem 1-2A

Computing missing information using accounting knowledge

A1　P1　

The following financial statement information is from five separate companies:

	Company A	Company B	Company C	Company D	Company E
December 31, 2015					
Assets........................	$55,000	$34,000	$24,000	$60,000	$119,000
Liabilities	24,500	21,500	9,000	40,000	?
December 31, 2016					
Assets........................	58,000	40,000	?	85,000	113,000
Liabilities	?	26,500	29,000	24,000	70,000
During year 2016					
Stock issuances	6,000	1,400	9,750	?	6,500
Net income (loss)	8,500	?	8,000	14,000	20,000
Cash dividends	3,500	2,000	5,875	0	11,000

Required

1. Answer the following questions about Company A:
   a. What is the amount of equity on December 31, 2015?
   b. What is the amount of equity on December 31, 2016?
   c. What is the amount of liabilities on December 31, 2016?

2. Answer the following questions about Company B:
   a. What is the amount of equity on December 31, 2015?
   b. What is the amount of equity on December 31, 2016?
   c. What is net income for year 2016?

3. Calculate the amount of assets for Company C on December 31, 2016.

4. Calculate the amount of stock issuances for Company D during year 2016.

5. Calculate the amount of liabilities for Company E on December 31, 2015.

Check   (1b) $41,500

(2c) $1,600

(3) $55,875

The following is selected financial information for Armani Company as of December 31, 2016: liabilities, $44,000; equity, $46,000; assets, $90,000.

Required

Prepare the balance sheet for Armani Company as of December 31, 2016.

Problem 1-3A
Preparing a balance sheet
P2

The following is selected financial information for Edison Energy Company for the year ended December 31, 2016: revenues, $55,000; expenses, $40,000; net income, $15,000.

Required

Prepare the 2016 calendar-year income statement for Edison Energy Company.

Problem 1-4A
Preparing an income statement
P2

Following is selected financial information for Kojo Company for the year ended December 31, 2016.

Retained earnings, Dec. 31, 2016	$14,000	Cash dividends	$1,000
Net income	8,000	Retained earnings, Dec. 31, 2015	7,000

Required

Prepare the 2016 statement of retained earnings for Kojo Company.

Problem 1-5A
Preparing a statement of retained earnings
P2

Following is selected financial information of Kia Company for the year ended December 31, 2016.

Cash used by investing activities	$(2,000)
Net increase in cash	1,200
Cash used by financing activities	(2,800)
Cash from operating activities	6,000
Cash, December 31, 2015	2,300

Required

Prepare the 2016 statement of cash flows for Kia Company.

Problem 1-6A
Preparing a statement of cash flows
P2

Check   Cash balance, Dec. 31, 2016, $3,500

Gabi Gram started The Gram Co., a new business that began operations on May 1. The Gram Co. completed the following transactions during its first month of operations.

May 1 G. Gram invested $40,000 cash in the company in exchange for its common stock.
     1 The company rented a furnished office and paid $2,200 cash for May's rent.
     3 The company purchased $1,890 of office equipment on credit.
     5 The company paid $750 cash for this month's cleaning services.
     8 The company provided consulting services for a client and immediately collected $5,400 cash.
     12 The company provided $2,500 of consulting services for a client on credit.
     15 The company paid $750 cash for an assistant's salary for the first half of this month.
     20 The company received $2,500 cash payment for the services provided on May 12.
     22 The company provided $3,200 of consulting services on credit.

Problem 1-7A
Analyzing transactions and preparing financial statements
C4   P1   P2

25   The company received $3,200 cash payment for the services provided on May 22.
26   The company paid $1,890 cash for the office equipment purchased on May 3.
27   The company purchased $80 of advertising in this month's (May) local paper on credit; cash payment is due June 1.
28   The company paid $750 cash for an assistant's salary for the second half of this month.
30   The company paid $300 cash for this month's telephone bill.
30   The company paid $280 cash for this month's utilities.
31   The company paid $1,400 cash in dividends to the owner (sole shareholder).

Required

Check (2) Ending balances: Cash, $42,780; Expenses, $5,110

1. Arrange the following asset, liability, and equity titles in a table like Exhibit 1.9: Cash; Accounts Receivable; Office Equipment; Accounts Payable; Common Stock; Dividends; Revenues; and Expenses.

2. Show effects of the transactions on the accounts of the accounting equation by recording increases and decreases in the appropriate columns. Do not determine new account balances after each transaction. Determine the final total for each account and verify that the equation is in balance.

(3) Net income, $5,990; Total assets, $44,670

3. Prepare an income statement for May, a statement of retained earnings for May, a May 31 balance sheet, and a statement of cash flows for May.

Problem 1-8A
Analyzing effects of transactions

C4 P1 P2 A1

Lita Lopez started Biz Consulting, a new business, and completed the following transactions during its first year of operations.

a. Lita Lopez invested $70,000 cash and office equipment valued at $10,000 in the company in exchange for its common stock.

b. The company purchased a $150,000 building to use as an office. Biz Consulting paid $20,000 in cash and signed a note payable promising to pay the $130,000 balance over the next 10 years.

c. The company purchased office equipment for $15,000 cash.

d. The company purchased $1,200 of office supplies and $1,700 of office equipment on credit.

e. The company paid a local newspaper $500 cash for printing an announcement of the office's opening.

f. The company completed a financial plan for a client and billed that client $2,800 for the service.

g. The company designed a financial plan for another client and immediately collected a $4,000 cash fee.

h. The company paid $3,275 cash in dividends to the owner (sole shareholder).

i. The company received $1,800 cash as partial payment from the client described in transaction f.

j. The company made a partial payment of $700 cash on the equipment purchased in transaction d.

k. The company paid $1,800 cash for the office secretary's wages for this period.

Required

Check (2) Ending balances: Cash, $34,525; Expenses, $2,300; Notes Payable, $130,000

1. Create a table like the one in Exhibit 1.9, using the following headings for the columns: Cash; Accounts Receivable; Office Supplies; Office Equipment; Building; Accounts Payable; Notes Payable; Common Stock; Dividends; Revenues; and Expenses.

2. Use additions and subtractions within the table created in part 1 to show the dollar effects of each transaction on individual items of the accounting equation. Show new balances after each transaction.

(3) Net income, $4,500

3. Once you have completed the table, determine the company's net income.

Problem 1-9A
Analyzing transactions and preparing financial statements

C4 P1 P2

Sanyu Sony started a new business and completed these transactions during December.

Dec. 1   Sanyu Sony transferred $65,000 cash from a personal savings account to a checking account in the name of Sony Electric in exchange for its common stock.
2   The company rented office space and paid $1,000 cash for the December rent.
3   The company purchased $13,000 of electrical equipment by paying $4,800 cash and agreeing to pay the $8,200 balance in 30 days.
5   The company purchased office supplies by paying $800 cash.
6   The company completed electrical work and immediately collected $1,200 cash for these services.
8   The company purchased $2,530 of office equipment on credit.
15   The company completed electrical work on credit in the amount of $5,000.
18   The company purchased $350 of office supplies on credit.
20   The company paid $2,530 cash for the office equipment purchased on December 8.
24   The company billed a client $900 for electrical work completed; the balance is due in 30 days.

28   The company received $5,000 cash for the work completed on December 15.
29   The company paid the assistant's salary of $1,400 cash for this month.
30   The company paid $540 cash for this month's utility bill.
31   The company paid $950 cash in dividends to the owner (sole shareholder).

Required

1. Arrange the following asset, liability, and equity titles in a table like Exhibit 1.9: Cash; Accounts Receivable; Office Supplies; Office Equipment; Electrical Equipment; Accounts Payable; Common Stock; Dividends; Revenues; and Expenses.

2. Use additions and subtractions to show the effects of each transaction on the accounts in the accounting equation. Show new balances after each transaction.

3. Use the increases and decreases in the columns of the table from part 2 to prepare an income statement, a statement of retained earnings, and a statement of cash flows—each of these for the current month. Also prepare a balance sheet as of the end of the month.

Analysis Component

4. Assume that the owner investment transaction on December 1 was $49,000 cash instead of $65,000 and that Sony Electric obtained another $16,000 in cash by borrowing it from a bank. Explain the effect of this change on total assets, total liabilities, and total equity.

Check (2) Ending balances: Cash, $59,180, Accounts Payable, $8,550

(3) Net income, $4,160; Total assets, $76,760

Kyzera manufactures, markets, and sells cellular accessories. The average total assets for Kyzera is $250,000. In its most recent year, Kyzera reported net income of $65,000 on revenues of $475,000.

Required

1. What is Kyzera's return on assets?

2. Does return on assets seem satisfactory for Kyzera given that its competitors average a 12% return on assets?

3. What are total expenses for Kyzera in its most recent year?

4. What is the average total amount of liabilities plus equity for Kyzera?

Problem 1-10A
Determining expenses, liabilities, equity, and return on assets

A1   A2

Check (3) $410,000

(4) $250,000

Coca-Cola and PepsiCo both produce and market beverages that are direct competitors. Key financial figures (in $ millions) for these businesses for a recent year follow.

Key Figures ($ millions)	Coca-Cola	PepsiCo
Sales	$46,542	$66,504
Net income	8,634	6,462
Average assets	76,448	70,518

Problem 1-11A
Computing and interpreting return on assets

A2

Required

1. Compute return on assets for (*a*) Coca-Cola and (*b*) PepsiCo.

2. Which company is more successful in its total amount of sales to consumers?

3. Which company is more successful in returning net income from its assets invested?

Check (1a) 11.3%; (1b) 9.2%

Analysis Component

4. Write a one-paragraph memorandum explaining which company you would invest your money in and why. (Limit your explanation to the information provided.)

All business decisions involve aspects of risk and return.

Required

Identify both the risk and the return in each of the following activities:

1. Investing $2,000 in a 5% savings account.
2. Placing a $2,500 bet on your favorite sports team.
3. Investing $10,000 in **Yahoo!** stock.
4. Taking out a $15,000 college loan toward earning an accounting degree.

Problem 1-12A[A]
Identifying risk and return

A3

Problem 1-13A^B
Describing organizational activities
C5

A start-up company often engages in the following transactions in its first year of operations. Classify those transactions in one of the three major categories of an organization's business activities.

F. Financing   **I.** Investing   **O.** Operating

_____ **1.** Owner investing land in business.   _____ **5.** Purchasing equipment.
_____ **2.** Purchasing a building.   _____ **6.** Selling and distributing products.
_____ **3.** Purchasing land.   _____ **7.** Paying for advertising.
_____ **4.** Borrowing cash from a bank.   _____ **8.** Paying employee wages.

Problem 1-14A^B
Describing organizational activities   **C5**

An organization undertakes various activities in pursuit of business success. Identify an organization's three major business activities, and describe each activity.

PROBLEM SET B

Problem 1-1B
Identifying effects of transactions on financial statements

A1   P1

Identify how each of the following separate transactions affects financial statements. For the balance sheet, identify how each transaction affects total assets, total liabilities, and total equity. For the income statement, identify how each transaction affects net income. For the statement of cash flows, identify how each transaction affects cash flows from operating activities, cash flows from investing activities, and cash flows from financing activities. For increases, place a "+" in the column or columns. For decreases, place a "−" in the column or columns. If both an increase and a decrease occur, place "+/−" in the column or columns. The first transaction is completed as an example.

		Balance Sheet			Income Statement	Statement of Cash Flows		
	Transaction	Total Assets	Total Liab.	Total Equity	Net Income	Operating Activities	Investing Activities	Financing Activities
1	Owner invests cash for its stock	+		+				+
2	Buys building by signing note payable							
3	Buys store equipment for cash							
4	Provides services for cash							
5	Pays cash for rent incurred							
6	Incurs utilities costs on credit							
7	Pays cash for salaries incurred							
8	Pays cash dividend							
9	Provides services on credit							
10	Collects cash on receivable from (9)							

Problem 1-2B
Computing missing information using accounting knowledge

A1   P1

The following financial statement information is from five separate companies.

	Company V	Company W	Company X	Company Y	Company Z
December 31, 2015					
Assets	$54,000	$80,000	$141,500	$92,500	$144,000
Liabilities	25,000	60,000	68,500	51,500	?
December 31, 2016					
Assets	59,000	100,000	186,500	?	170,000
Liabilities	36,000	?	65,800	42,000	42,000
During year 2016					
Stock issuances	5,000	20,000	?	48,100	60,000
Net income or (loss)	?	40,000	18,500	24,000	32,000
Cash dividends	5,500	2,000	0	20,000	8,000

Required

1. Answer the following questions about Company V:
   a. What is the amount of equity on December 31, 2015?
   b. What is the amount of equity on December 31, 2016?
   c. What is the net income or loss for the year 2016?
2. Answer the following questions about Company W:
   a. What is the amount of equity on December 31, 2015?
   b. What is the amount of equity on December 31, 2016?
   c. What is the amount of liabilities on December 31, 2016?
3. Calculate the amount of stock issuances for Company X during 2016.
4. Calculate the amount of assets for Company Y on December 31, 2016.
5. Calculate the amount of liabilities for Company Z on December 31, 2015.

Check   (1b) $23,000

(2c) $22,000

(4) $135,100

The following is selected financial information for Safari Company as of December 31, 2016.

Problem 1-3B
Preparing a balance sheet

P2

| Liabilities .... | $64,000 | Equity .... | $50,000 | Assets .... | $114,000 |

Required

Prepare the balance sheet for Safari Company as of December 31, 2016.

Selected financial information for Solar Company for the year ended December 31, 2016, follows.

Problem 1-4B
Preparing an income statement

P2

| Revenues .... | $68,000 | Expenses........ | $40,000 | Net income .... | $28,000 |

Required

Prepare the 2016 income statement for Solar Company.

Following is selected financial information of Audi Company for the year ended December 31, 2016.

Problem 1-5B
Preparing a statement of retained earnings

P2

| Retained earnings, Dec. 31, 2016 .... | $47,000 | Cash dividends .... | $ 7,000 |
| Net income .... | 5,000 | Retained earnings, Dec. 31, 2015........ | 49,000 |

Required

Prepare the 2016 statement of retained earnings for Audi Company.

Selected financial information of Banji Company for the year ended December 31, 2016, follows.

Problem 1-6B
Preparing a statement of cash flows

P2

Cash from investing activities	$1,600
Net increase in cash	400
Cash from financing activities	1,800
Cash used by operating activities	(3,000)
Cash, December 31, 2015	1,300

Required

Prepare the 2016 statement of cash flows for Banji Company.

Problem 1-7B
Analyzing transactions and preparing financial statements

C4   P1   P2

Nina Niko launched a new business, Niko's Maintenance Co., that began operations on June 1. The following transactions were completed by the company during that first month.

June 1   Nina Niko invested $130,000 cash in the company in exchange for its common stock.
2   The company rented a furnished office and paid $6,000 cash for June's rent.
4   The company purchased $2,400 of equipment on credit.
6   The company paid $1,150 cash for this month's advertising of the opening of the business.
8   The company completed maintenance services for a customer and immediately collected $850 cash.
14   The company completed $7,500 of maintenance services for City Center on credit.
16   The company paid $800 cash for an assistant's salary for the first half of the month.
20   The company received $7,500 cash payment for services completed for City Center on June 14.
21   The company completed $7,900 of maintenance services for Paula's Beauty Shop on credit.
24   The company completed $675 of maintenance services for Build-It Coop on credit.
25   The company received $7,900 cash payment from Paula's Beauty Shop for the work completed on June 21.
26   The company made payment of $2,400 cash for equipment purchased on June 4.
28   The company paid $800 cash for an assistant's salary for the second half of this month.
29   The company paid $4,000 cash in dividends to the owner (sole shareholder).
30   The company paid $150 cash for this month's telephone bill.
30   The company paid $890 cash for this month's utilities.

Required

1. Arrange the following asset, liability, and equity titles in a table like Exhibit 1.9: Cash; Accounts Receivable; Equipment; Accounts Payable; Common Stock; Dividends; Revenues; and Expenses.
2. Show the effects of the transactions on the accounts of the accounting equation by recording increases and decreases in the appropriate columns. Do not determine new account balances after each transaction. Determine the final total for each account and verify that the equation is in balance.
3. Prepare a June income statement, a June statement of retained earnings, a June 30 balance sheet, and a June statement of cash flows.

Check   (2) Ending balances: Cash, $130,060; Expenses, $9,790

(3) Net income, $7,135; Total assets, $133,135

Problem 1-8B
Analyzing effects of transactions

C4   P1   P2   A1

Neva Nadal started a new business, Nadal Computing, and completed the following transactions during its first year of operations.

a. Neva Nadal invested $90,000 cash and office equipment valued at $10,000 in the company in exchange for its common stock.
b. The company purchased a $150,000 building to use as an office. It paid $40,000 in cash and signed a note payable promising to pay the $110,000 balance over the next 10 years.
c. The company purchased office equipment for $25,000 cash.
d. The company purchased $1,200 of office supplies and $1,700 of office equipment on credit.
e. The company paid a local newspaper $750 cash for printing an announcement of the office's opening.
f. The company completed a financial plan for a client and billed that client $2,800 for the service.
g. The company designed a financial plan for another client and immediately collected a $4,000 cash fee.
h. The company paid $11,500 cash in dividends to the owner (sole shareholder).
i. The company received $1,800 cash from the client described in transaction f.
j. The company made a payment of $700 cash on the equipment purchased in transaction d.
k. The company paid $2,500 cash for the office secretary's wages.

Required

1. Create a table like the one in Exhibit 1.9, using the following headings for the columns: Cash; Accounts Receivable; Office Supplies; Office Equipment; Building; Accounts Payable; Notes Payable; Common Stock; Dividends; Revenues; and Expenses.
2. Use additions and subtractions within the table created in part 1 to show the dollar effects of each transaction on individual items of the accounting equation. Show new balances after each transaction.
3. Once you have completed the table, determine the company's net income.

Check   (2) Ending balances: Cash, $15,350; Expenses, $3,250; Notes Payable, $110,000

(3) Net income, $3,550

Rivera Roofing Company, owned by Reyna Rivera, began operations in July and completed these transactions during that first month of operations.

July 1   Reyna Rivera invested $80,000 cash in the company in exchange for its common stock.
      2   The company rented office space and paid $700 cash for the July rent.
      3   The company purchased roofing equipment for $5,000 by paying $1,000 cash and agreeing to pay the $4,000 balance in 30 days.
      6   The company purchased office supplies for $600 cash.
      8   The company completed work for a customer and immediately collected $7,600 cash for the work.
     10   The company purchased $2,300 of office equipment on credit.
     15   The company completed work for a customer on credit in the amount of $8,200.
     17   The company purchased $3,100 of office supplies on credit.
     23   The company paid $2,300 cash for the office equipment purchased on July 10.
     25   The company billed a customer $5,000 for work completed; the balance is due in 30 days.
     28   The company received $8,200 cash for the work completed on July 15.
     30   The company paid an assistant's salary of $1,560 cash for this month.
     31   The company paid $295 cash for this month's utility bill.
     31   The company paid $1,800 cash in dividends to the owner (sole shareholder).

Required

1. Arrange the following asset, liability, and equity titles in a table like Exhibit 1.9: Cash; Accounts Receivable; Office Supplies; Office Equipment; Roofing Equipment; Accounts Payable; Common Stock; Dividends; Revenues; and Expenses.
2. Use additions and subtractions to show the effects of each transaction on the accounts in the accounting equation. Show new balances after each transaction.
3. Use the increases and decreases in the columns of the table from part 2 to prepare an income statement, a statement of retained earnings, and a statement of cash flows—each of these for the current month. Also prepare a balance sheet as of the end of the month.

Analysis Component

4. Assume that the $5,000 purchase of roofing equipment on July 3 was financed from an owner investment of another $5,000 cash in the business in exchange for more common stock (instead of the purchase conditions described in the transaction). Explain the effect of this change on total assets, total liabilities, and total equity.

Problem 1-9B
Analyzing transactions and preparing financial statements

C4   P1   P2

Check   (2) Ending balances: Cash, $87,545; Accounts Payable, $7,100

(3) Net income, $18,245; Total assets, $103,545

Ski-Doo Company manufactures, markets, and sells snowmobiles and snowmobile equipment and accessories. The average total assets for Ski-Doo is $3,000,000. In its most recent year, Ski-Doo reported net income of $201,000 on revenues of $1,400,000.

Required

1. What is Ski-Doo Company's return on assets?
2. Does return on assets seem satisfactory for Ski-Doo given that its competitors average a 9.5% return on assets?
3. What are the total expenses for Ski-Doo Company in its most recent year?
4. What is the average total amount of liabilities plus equity for Ski-Doo Company?

Problem 1-10B
Determining expenses, liabilities, equity, and return on assets

A1   A2

Check   (3) $1,199,000
(4) $3,000,000

AT&T and **Verizon** produce and market telecommunications products and are competitors. Key financial figures (in $ millions) for these businesses for a recent year follow.

Key Figures ($ millions)	AT&T	Verizon
Sales	$126,723	$110,875
Net income	4,184	10,198
Average assets	269,868	225,233

Problem 1-11B
Computing and interpreting return on assets

A2

Required

1. Compute return on assets for (*a*) AT&T and (*b*) Verizon.

2. Which company is more successful in the total amount of sales to consumers?

3. Which company is more successful in returning net income from its assets invested?

Analysis Component

4. Write a one-paragraph memorandum explaining which company you would invest your money in and why. (Limit your explanation to the information provided.)

Problem 1-12B[A]

Identifying risk and return

A3

All business decisions involve aspects of risk and return.

Required

Identify both the risk and the return in each of the following activities:

1. Stashing $500 cash under your mattress.

2. Placing a $250 bet on a horse running in the Kentucky Derby.

3. Investing $20,000 in **Nike** stock.

4. Investing $35,000 in U.S. Savings Bonds.

Problem 1-13B[B]

Describing organizational activities

C5

A start-up company often engages in the following activities during its first year of operations. Classify each of the following activities into one of the three major activities of an organization.

F. Financing   **I.** Investing   **O.** Operating

_____ **1.** Providing client services.   _____ **5.** Supervising workers.

_____ **2.** Obtaining a bank loan.   _____ **6.** Owner investing money in business.

_____ **3.** Purchasing machinery.   _____ **7.** Renting office space.

_____ **4.** Research for its products.   _____ **8.** Paying utilities expenses.

Problem 1-14B[B]

Describing organizational activities   C5

Identify in outline format the three major business activities of an organization. For each of these activities, identify at least two specific transactions or events normally undertaken by the business's owners or its managers.

This serial problem starts here and continues throughout the book. It is most readily solved if you use the Working Papers that accompany this book (but working papers are not required)

SERIAL PROBLEM

Business Solutions

C4   P1

SP 1   On October 1, 2016, Santana Rey launched a computer services company, **Business Solutions,** that is organized as a corporation and provides consulting services, computer system installations, and custom program development. Rey adopts the calendar year for reporting purposes and expects to prepare the company's first set of financial statements on December 31, 2016.

Required

Create a table like the one in Exhibit 1.9 using the following headings for columns: Cash; Accounts Receivable; Computer Supplies; Computer System; Office Equipment; Accounts Payable; Common Stock; Dividends; Revenues; and Expenses. Then use additions and subtractions within the table created to show the dollar effects for each of the following October transactions for Business Solutions on the individual items of the accounting equation. Show new balances after each transaction.

Oct.   1   S. Rey invested $45,000 cash, a $20,000 computer system, and $8,000 of office equipment in the company in exchange for its common stock.

     3   The company purchased $1,420 of computer supplies on credit from Harris Office Products.

     6   The company billed Easy Leasing $4,800 for services performed in installing a new web server.

     8   The company paid $1,420 cash for the computer supplies purchased from Harris Office Products on October 3.

   10   The company hired Lyn Addie as a part-time assistant for $125 per day, as needed.

Continued on next page . . .

12   The company billed Easy Leasing another $1,400 for services performed.

15   The company received $4,800 cash from Easy Leasing as partial payment toward its account.

17   The company paid $805 cash to repair computer equipment damaged when moving it.

20   The company paid $1,728 cash for advertisements published in the local newspaper.

22   The company received $1,400 cash from Easy Leasing toward its account.

28   The company billed IFM Company $5,208 for services performed.

31   The company paid $875 cash for Lyn Addie's wages for seven days of work this month.

31   The company paid $3,600 cash in dividends to the owner (sole shareholder).

Check   Ending balances: Cash, $42,772; Revenues, $11,408; Expenses, $3,408

Accounting professionals apply many technology tools to aid them in their everyday tasks and decision making. The **General Ledger** tool in *Connect* automates several of the procedural steps in the accounting cycle so that the accounting professional can focus on the impacts of each transaction on the full set of financial statements. Chapter 2 is the first chapter to exploit this tool in helping students see the advantages of technology and, in particular, the power of the General Ledger tool in accounting practice, including financial analysis and "what if" scenarios.

GENERAL LEDGER PROBLEM

Available in Connect

*→**Beyond the Numbers (BTN)** is a special problem section aimed to refine communication, conceptual, analysis, and research skills. It includes many activities helpful in developing an active learning environment*

Beyond the Numbers

BTN 1-1   Key financial figures for **Apple**'s fiscal year ended September 27, 2014, follow.

Key Figure	$ Millions
Liabilities + Equity	$231,839
Net income	39,510
Revenues	182,795

REPORTING IN ACTION

A1   A2   A3

APPLE

Required

1.   What is the total amount of assets invested in Apple?

2.   What is Apple's return on assets for fiscal year 2014? Its assets at September 28, 2013, equal $207,000 (in $ millions).

3.   How much are total expenses for Apple for the year ended September 27, 2014?

4.   Does Apple's return on assets for fiscal 2014 seem satisfactory if competitors average an 11% return?

Fast Forward

5.   Access Apple's financial statements (Form 10-K) for years ending after September 27, 2014, from its website (**Apple.com**) or from the SEC website (**www.SEC.gov**) and compute its return on assets for those years. Compare the September 27, 2014, year-end return on assets to any subsequent years' returns you are able to compute, and interpret the results.

BTN 1-2   Key comparative figures ($ millions) for both **Apple** and **Google** follow.

Key Figure ($ millions)	Apple	Google
Liabilities + Equity	$231,839	$131,133
Net income	39,510	14,444
Revenues and sales	182,795	66,001

COMPARATIVE ANALYSIS

A1   A2   A3

APPLE

GOOGLE

Required

1. What is the total amount of assets invested in (*a*) Apple and (*b*) Google?
2. What is the return on assets for (*a*) Apple and (*b*) Google? Apple's beginning-year assets equal $207,000 (in millions) and Google's beginning-year assets equal $110,920 (in millions).
3. How much are expenses for (*a*) Apple and (*b*) Google?
4. Is return on assets satisfactory for (*a*) Apple and (*b*) Google? (Assume competitors average an 11% return.)
5. What can you conclude about Apple and Google from these computations?

Check   (2b) 11.9%

ETHICS CHALLENGE

C3 C4

BTN 1-3 Tana Thorne works in a public accounting firm and hopes to eventually be a partner. The management of Allnet Company invites Thorne to prepare a bid to audit Allnet's financial statements. In discussing the audit fee, Allnet's management suggests a fee range in which the amount depends on the reported profit of Allnet. The higher its profit, the higher will be the audit fee paid to Thorne's firm.

Required

1. Identify the parties potentially affected by this audit and the fee plan proposed.
2. What are the ethical factors in this situation? Explain.
3. Would you recommend that Thorne accept this audit fee arrangement? Why or why not?
4. Describe some ethical considerations guiding your recommendation.

COMMUNICATING IN PRACTICE

A1 C2

APPLE

BTN 1-4 Refer to this chapter's opening feature about **Apple**. Assume that the owners, sometime during their first five years of business, desire to expand their computer product services to meet people's demands regarding technical support. They eventually decide to meet with their banker to discuss a loan to allow Apple to expand and offer computing services.

Required

1. Prepare a half-page report outlining the information you would request from the owners if you were the loan officer.
2. Indicate whether the information you request and your loan decision are affected by the form of business organization for Apple.

TAKING IT TO THE NET

A2

BTN 1-5 Visit the EDGAR database at **www.SEC.gov**. Access the Form 10-K report of **Rocky Mountain Chocolate Factory** (ticker RMCF) filed on May 27, 2015, covering its 2015 fiscal year.

Required

1. Item 6 of the 10-K report provides comparative financial highlights of RMCF for the years 2011–2015. How would you describe the revenue trend for RMCF over this five-year period?
2. Has RMCF been profitable (see net income) over this five-year period? Support your answer.

TEAMWORK IN ACTION

C1

BTN 1-6 Teamwork is important in today's business world. Successful teams schedule convenient meetings, maintain regular communications, and cooperate with and support their members. This assignment aims to establish support/learning teams, initiate discussions, and set meeting times.

Required

1. Form teams and open a team discussion to determine a regular time and place for your team to meet between each scheduled class meeting. Notify your instructor via a memorandum or e-mail message as to when and where your team will hold regularly scheduled meetings.
2. Develop a list of telephone numbers and/or e-mail addresses of your teammates.

BTN 1-7   Refer to this chapter's opening feature about Apple. Assume that the owners decide to open a new company with an innovative mobile app devoted to microblogging for accountants and those learning accounting. This new company will be called AccountApp.

Required

1. AccountApp obtains a $500,000 loan and the two owners contribute $250,000 in total from their own savings in exchange for common stock in the new company.
    a. What is the new company's total amount of liabilities plus equity?
    b. What is the new company's total amount of assets?
2. If the new company earns $80,250 in net income in the first year of operation, compute its return on assets (assume average assets equal $750,000). Assess its performance if competitors average a 10% return.

ENTREPRENEURIAL DECISION

A1   P1

APPLE

Check   (2) 10.7%

BTN 1-8   You are to interview a local business owner. (This can be a friend or relative.) Opening lines of communication with members of the business community can provide personal benefits of business networking. If you do not know the owner, you should call ahead to introduce yourself and explain your position as a student and your assignment requirements. You should request a 30-minute appointment for a face-to-face or phone interview to discuss the form of organization and operations of the business. Be prepared to make a good impression.

Required

1. Identify and describe the main operating activities and the form of organization for this business.
2. Determine and explain why the owner(s) chose this particular form of organization.
3. Identify any special advantages and/or disadvantages the owner(s) experiences in operating with this form of business organization.

HITTING THE ROAD

C2

BTN 1-9   Samsung (Samsung.com) is a leading global manufacturer, and it competes to varying degrees with both Apple and Google. Key financial figures for Samsung follow.

Key Figures*	Korean Won in Millions
Average assets...........	₩222,248,988
Net income	₩ 23,394,358
Revenue	₩206,205,987
Return on assets	10.5%

* Figures prepared in accordance with International Financial Reporting Standards as adopted by the Republic of Korea.

GLOBAL DECISION

A1 A2 A3

Samsung

APPLE

GOOGLE

Required

1. Identify any concerns you have in comparing Samsung's income and revenue figures to those of Apple and Google (in BTN 1-2) for purposes of making business decisions.
2. Identify any concerns you have in comparing Samsung's return on assets ratio to those of Apple and Google (computed for BTN 1-2) for purposes of making business decisions.

ANSWERS TO MULTIPLE CHOICE QUIZ

1. c; $450,000 is the actual cost incurred.
2. b; revenue is recorded when earned.
3. d;

4. a
5. a

Assets	=	Liabilities	+	Equity
+$100,000	=	+$35,000	+	?

Change in equity = $100,000 − $35,000 = $65,000

Financial Statements and the Accounting System

Chapter Preview

FINANCIAL STATEMENT ACCOUNTS AND ANALYSIS

Using financial statements

C1 Source documents

C2 The account and its analysis

Types of accounts

Unclassified vs. classified

ANALYZING AND PROCESSING TRANSACTIONS

C3 General ledger

C4 Double-entry accounting

P1 Journalizing transactions

A1 Processing transactions— An illustration

TRIAL BALANCE AND THE FINANCIAL STATEMENTS

P2 Trial balance preparation and use

P3 Financial statement preparation

Reading an annual report

A2 Analysis of financing sources

Learning Objectives

CONCEPTUAL

C1 Explain the steps in processing transactions and the role of source documents.

C2 Describe an account and its use in recording transactions.

C3 Describe a ledger and a chart of accounts.

C4 Define *debits* and *credits* and explain double-entry accounting.

ANALYTICAL

A1 Analyze the impact of transactions on accounts and financial statements.

A2 Compute the debt ratio and describe its use in analyzing financial condition.

PROCEDURAL

P1 Record transactions in a journal and post entries to a ledger.

P2 Prepare and explain the use of a trial balance.

P3 Prepare financial statements from business transactions.

#accounting

"Success is never accidental"—JACK DORSEY

SAN FRANCISCO—"We came across the word 'twitter,' and it was just perfect," recalls Jack Dorsey. "The definition was 'a short burst of inconsequential information,' and 'chirps from birds,' and that's exactly what the product was." Today, Twitter boasts over 300 million active users. Founded by Jack, along with Biz Stone and Evan Williams, **Twitter** (**Twitter.com**) is "facilitating connections between businesses and individuals in meaningful and relevant ways," says Jack. Along the way, the young entrepreneurs had to learn accounting and the details of preparing and interpreting financial statements.

"There is so much going on here," explains Biz when describing Twitter's business model. However, admits Evan, "We did a poor job of communicating." To address this concern, the group studied entrepreneurial activities and learned the value of accounting information. They established recordkeeping processes, transaction analysis, control procedures, and financial statement reporting. "If you stand pat," says Evan, "you risk being stagnant." To this day, the three entrepreneurs have had many entrepreneurial successes and have a reliable accounting system to help them make good business decisions.

Twitter Inc.
NYSE: TWTR

4,100 employees
320 mil. members
2007 founded

Revenue Sources

- Desktop ads 13%
- Mobile ads 76%
- Data licensing & other 11%

Information is the focus within Twitter's accounting records and systems. Jack recalls that when they launched Twitter there were many reasons for them not to succeed, but they applied their familiar "can-do" approach to accounting information. "My whole philosophy is making tech [and accounting] more accessible and human," says Jack. This includes using accounting information to make key business decisions. Biz recalls how his team had to account and control for numerous expenses and then obtain sufficient revenues to survive. Biz adds that Twitter had to explore "interesting ways to generate revenue" because very few users were willing to pay for the service. Today, Twitter believes mobile advertising is the way to generate sustainable revenue. Roughly 90% of Twitter's total advertising revenue now comes from mobile advertising. This

commitment to mobile advertising has coincided with a very positive trend in revenue over the past three years:

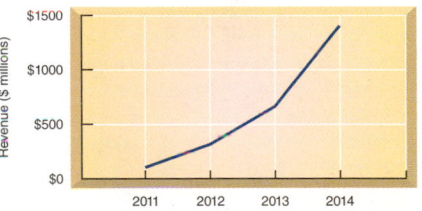

The three entrepreneurs emphasize that accounting records must be in order for Twitter to realize its full potential. Although Twitter has already achieved a market value of over $20 billion, many experts believe Twitter still has considerable room for growth. Still, Evan recognizes that "so many people here [at Twitter] contribute to that success." He also emphasizes that learning is a key to their business success. "I realized," insists Evan, "I could buy books and learn something that people spent years learning."

Sources: *Twitter website,* January 2016; *The Guardian,* April 2014; *Washington Post,* December 2013; *Entrepreneur,* December 2010; *The Wall Street Journal,* February 2011; *Twitter 10-K Report,* April 2015

USING FINANCIAL STATEMENTS

We introduced the four financial statements in Chapter 1. This chapter extends that discussion to analysis of financial statements and the underlying transactions. Our approach is to gradually develop both skills. The basics of transaction analysis are slowly introduced over Chapters 1, 2, and 3. The basics of financial statement analysis are introduced throughout Chapters 1 through 13. We begin this chapter with *financial statement analysis,* which refers to applying analytical tools to financial statements for making business decisions.

Analyzing Financial Statements   Financial statement analysis is used by both internal and external users of accounting. Internal users use it to improve company efficiency and effectiveness in providing products and services. External users use financial analysis for investing, lending, and monitoring management. For example, analysts such as **Moody's** and **Standard & Poor's** use financial statements in making buy/sell stock advice and in setting credit ratings. The common goal of all users is to evaluate company performance and its financial condition.

Assessing Company Results   When interpreting measures of analysis, we must decide whether the measures indicate good, bad, or average performance. To make such judgments, we need standards (benchmarks) for comparisons that include the following:

APPLE

- *Intracompany*—comparing company results across two or more periods; an example is comparing **Apple**'s current income to its prior-year income.
- *Intercompany*—comparing results across competitors; an example is comparing **Nike**'s profit margin to that of **Adidas**.
- *Industry*—comparing results to industry norms; an example is comparing a company's debt level to the industry average.
- *Guidelines (rules of thumb)*—comparing results to standards based on experience; an example is the 2:1 level for the current ratio.

Using Ratios to Analyze Financial Statements

Ratio analysis is the most widely used tool of financial analysis. A ratio, which expresses a mathematical relation between two quantities, can help uncover a condition or trend. It can be expressed as a percent, rate, or proportion. For instance, a change in an account balance from $100 to $250 can be expressed as (1) 150% increase, (2) 2.5 times, or (3) 2.5 to 1 (or 2.5:1). To be meaningful, a ratio must refer to an economically important relation. For example, an important relation exists between a product's sales price and its cost. Accordingly, the ratio of cost of goods sold to sales is meaningful. However, no useful relation exists between delivery expense and cleaning costs.

Building Blocks of Analysis
Financial statement analysis focuses on one or more of four basic *building blocks* of analysis:

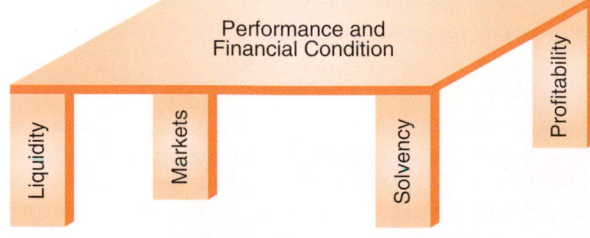

- **Liquidity**—ability to meet short-term obligations and generate revenues.
- **Solvency**—ability to generate future revenues and meet long-term obligations.
- **Profitability**—ability to provide financial rewards sufficient to attract and retain financing.
- **Market prospects**—ability to generate positive market expectations.

The four building blocks focus on different, but interrelated, aspects of a company's financial condition or performance. We can view these blocks as making up the four legs of a table, where the four must work for the table to perform properly.

Liquidity (and Efficiency)

Liquidity refers to the availability of resources to meet short-term cash requirements. (*Efficiency* refers to how productive a company is in using its assets.) Liquidity and efficiency are important and complementary. If a company fails to meet its current obligations, its continued existence is doubtful. Moreover, inefficient use of assets can cause liquidity problems. One measure of liquidity is the current ratio, defined as current assets divided by current liabilities (where "current" is defined in the next section). For **Apple**'s statements in Appendix A, its current ratio follows:

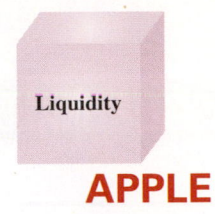

APPLE

$$\textbf{Current ratio} = \textbf{Current assets/Current liabilities}$$
$$1.08 \qquad = \$68,531/\$63,448$$

For comparison, **Google**'s current ratio is 4.80, which is higher (implying greater liquidity, which is better in meeting short run cash needs).

GOOGLE

Solvency

Solvency refers to a company's long-run financial viability and its ability to cover long-term obligations. Solvency analysis focuses on a company's ability to both meet its obligations and provide security to its creditors *over the long run*. One measure of solvency is the debt ratio, defined as total liabilities divided by total assets. For Apple's statements in Appendix A, its debt ratio follows:

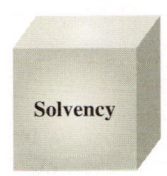

$$\textbf{Debt ratio} = \textbf{Total liabilities/Total assets}$$
$$0.52 \qquad = \$120,292/\$231,839$$

For comparison, Google's debt ratio is 0.20, which is lower (implying greater solvency, which is better). To better understand, the larger the debt, the larger the contractual obligations to outsiders.

Profitability

Profitability refers to a company's ability to use its assets to produce profits (and positive cash flows). It is commonly assessed by comparing income to sales or to the amount invested. One such measure is the profit margin ratio, defined as net income divided by net sales. For Apple's statements in Appendix A, its profit margin follows:

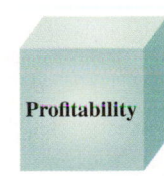

$$\textbf{Profit margin} = \textbf{Net income/Net sales}$$
$$0.22 \qquad = \$39,510/\$182,795$$

For comparison, Google's profit margin ratio is 0.22, which is the same as Apple's (for reference, the higher the profit margin, the better).

Market Prospects

Market measures are useful for analyzing companies with publicly traded stock. Market measures use stock price, which reflects the market's expectations for the company. This includes expectations of both company return and risk. One measure of market performance is the price-to-earnings ratio, defined as price per share divided by earnings per share. For Apple's statements in Appendix A, its price-to-earnings follows:

$$\textbf{Price-to-earnings} = \textbf{Price per share/Earnings per share}$$
$$15.52 \qquad = \$100.75/\$6.49$$

For comparison, Google's price-to-earnings ratio is 24.6, which is higher (implying greater market expectations for Google's future performance).

Summarizing Ratios

Exhibit 13.16 in Chapter 13 lists additional measures of liquidity, solvency, profitability, and market prospects. This summary includes each ratio's title, its formula, and the purpose for which it is commonly used. The final section of each chapter includes one or more of these ratios relevant to that chapter.

BASIS OF FINANCIAL STATEMENTS

C1
Explain the steps in processing transactions and the role of source documents.

Point: Accounting records are informally referred to as the *accounting books,* or simply the *books.*

Business transactions and events are the starting points of financial statements. The process to get from transactions and events to financial statements follows:

- Identify each transaction and event from source documents.
- Analyze each transaction and event using the accounting equation.
- Record relevant transactions and events in a journal.
- Post journal information to ledger accounts.
- Prepare and analyze the trial balance and financial statements.

Source Documents

Source documents identify and describe transactions and events entering the accounting process. They can be in either hard copy or electronic form. Examples are sales tickets, checks, purchase orders, bills from suppliers, employee earnings records, and bank statements. To illustrate, many cash registers record information for each sale on a tape or electronic file locked inside the register. This record can be used as a source document for recording sales in the accounting records. Source documents, especially if obtained from outside the organization, provide objective and reliable evidence about transactions and events and their amounts.

Point: To ensure that all sales are rung up on the register, most sellers require customers to have their receipts to exchange or return purchased items.

The "Account" Underlying Financial Statements

C2
Describe an account and its use in recording transactions.

An **account** is a record of increases and decreases in a specific asset, liability, equity, revenue, or expense item. Information from an account is analyzed, summarized, and presented in reports and financial statements. The **general ledger,** or simply **ledger,** is a record containing all accounts used by a company. The ledger is often in electronic form. While most companies' ledgers contain similar accounts, a company often uses one or more unique accounts because of its type of operations. An *unclassified balance sheet* broadly groups accounts into assets, liabilities, and equity. Exhibit 2.1 shows typical asset, liability, and equity accounts.

EXHIBIT 2.1

Accounts Organized by the Accounting Equation

Asset Accounts   Assets are resources owned or controlled by a company, and those resources have expected future benefits. Most accounting systems include (at a minimum) separate accounts for the assets described here.

Cash   A *Cash* account reflects a company's cash balance. All increases and decreases in cash are recorded in the Cash account. It includes money and any medium of exchange that a bank accepts for deposit (coins, checks, money orders, and checking account balances).

Point: Customers and others who owe a company are called its **debtors.**

Accounts Receivable   *Accounts receivable* are held by a seller and refer to promises of payment from customers to sellers. These transactions are often called *credit sales* or *sales on account* (or *on credit*). Accounts receivable are increased by credit sales and billings to customers, but are decreased by customer payments. We record all increases and decreases in receivables in the Accounts Receivable account. When there are multiple customers, separate records are kept for each, titled Accounts Receivable—'Customer Name'.

Note Receivable   A *note receivable,* or promissory note, is a written promise of another entity to pay a definite sum of money on a specified future date to the holder of the note. A company holding a promissory note signed by another entity has an asset that is recorded in a Note (or Notes) Receivable account.

Prepaid Accounts   *Prepaid accounts* (also called *prepaid expenses*) are assets that represent prepayments of future expenses (expenses expected to be incurred in one or more future accounting periods). When the expenses are later incurred, the amounts in prepaid accounts are transferred to expense accounts. Common examples of prepaid accounts include prepaid insurance, prepaid rent, and prepaid services (such as club memberships). Prepaid accounts expire with the passage of time (such as with rent) or through use (such as with prepaid meal tickets). When financial statements are prepared, prepaid accounts are adjusted so that (1) all expired and used prepaid accounts are recorded as expenses and (2) all unexpired and unused prepaid accounts are recorded as assets (reflecting future use in future periods). To illustrate, when an insurance fee, called a *premium,* is paid in advance, the cost is typically recorded in the asset account titled Prepaid Insurance. Over time, the expiring portion of the insurance cost is removed from this asset account and reported in expenses on the income statement. Any unexpired portion remains in Prepaid Insurance and is reported on the balance sheet as an asset.

Supplies Accounts   *Supplies* are assets until they are used. When they are used up, their costs are reported as expenses. The costs of unused supplies are recorded in a Supplies asset account. Supplies are often grouped by purpose—for example, office supplies and store supplies. *Office supplies* include stationery, paper, toner, and pens. *Store supplies* include packaging materials, plastic and paper bags, gift boxes and cartons, and cleaning materials. The costs of these unused supplies can be recorded in an Office Supplies or a Store Supplies asset account. When supplies are used, their costs are transferred from the asset accounts to expense accounts.

Equipment Accounts   *Equipment* is an asset. When equipment is used and gets worn down, its cost is gradually reported as an expense (called depreciation). Equipment is often grouped by its purpose—for example, office equipment and store equipment. *Office equipment* includes computers, printers, desks, chairs, and shelves. Costs incurred for these items are recorded in an Office Equipment asset account. The *Store Equipment* account includes the costs of assets used in a store, such as counters, showcases, ladders, hoists, and cash registers.

Buildings Accounts   *Buildings* such as stores, offices, warehouses, and factories are assets because they provide expected future benefits to those who control or own them. Their costs are recorded in a Buildings asset account. When several buildings are owned, separate accounts are sometimes kept for each of them.

Land   The cost of *land* owned by a business is recorded in a Land account. The cost of buildings located on the land is separately recorded in one or more building accounts.

Point: A college parking fee is a prepaid account from the student's standpoint. At the beginning of the term, it is an asset that entitles a student to park on or near campus. The benefits of the parking fee expire as the term progresses. At term-end, prepaid parking (asset) equals zero as it has been entirely recorded as parking expense.

Point: Prepaid accounts that apply to current and future periods are assets. These assets are adjusted at the end of each period to reflect only those amounts that have not yet expired, and to record as expenses those amounts that have expired.

Point: Some assets are described as *intangible* because they do not have physical existence or their benefits are highly uncertain. A recent balance sheet for **Coca-Cola Company** shows nearly $15 billion in intangible assets.

🟨 Decision Insight

Women Entrepreneurs   Sara Blakely (in photo), the billionaire entrepreneur/owner of **SPANX**, has promised to donate half her wealth to charity. The Center for Women's Business Research reports that women-owned businesses are growing and that they:

- Total more than 11 million and employ nearly 20 million workers.
- Generate $2.5 trillion in annual sales and tend to embrace technology.
- Are philanthropic—70% of owners volunteer at least once per month.
- Are more likely funded by individual investors (73%) than venture firms (15%). 🟨

Paul Morigi/Getty Images for FORTUNE

Liability Accounts   Liabilities are claims (by creditors) against assets, which means they are obligations to transfer assets or provide products or services to others. **Creditors** are individuals and organizations that have rights to receive payments from a company. If a company fails to pay its obligations, the law gives creditors a right to force the sale of that company's assets to obtain the money to meet creditors' claims. When assets are sold under these conditions, creditors are paid first, but only up to the amount of their claims. Any remaining money, the residual, goes to the owners of the company. Creditors often use a balance sheet to help decide whether to loan money to a company. A loan is less risky if the borrower's liabilities are small in comparison to assets because this means there are more resources than claims on resources. Common liability accounts are described here.

Point: Accounts payable are also called *trade payables*.

Accounts Payable   *Accounts payable* refer to oral or implied promises to pay later, which usually arise from purchases of merchandise. Payables can also arise from purchases of supplies, equipment, and services. We record all increases and decreases in payables in the Accounts Payable account. When there are multiple suppliers, separate records are kept for each, titled Accounts Payable—'Supplier Name'.

Note Payable   A *note payable* refers to a formal promise, usually denoted by the signing of a promissory note, to pay a future amount. It is recorded in either a short-term Note Payable account or a long-term Note Payable account, depending on when it must be repaid. We explain details of short- and long-term classification in the next two chapters.

Point: Two words that almost always identify liability accounts: "Payable," meaning liabilities that must be paid, and "Unearned," meaning liabilities that must be fulfilled.

Unearned Revenue Accounts   *Unearned revenue* refers to a liability that is settled in the future when a company delivers its products or services. When customers pay in advance for products or services (before revenue is earned), the revenue recognition principle requires that the seller consider this receipt as unearned revenue. Examples of unearned revenue include magazine subscriptions collected in advance by a publisher, rent collected in advance by a landlord, and season ticket sales by sports teams. The seller would record these in liability accounts such as Unearned Subscriptions, Unearned Rent, and Unearned Ticket Revenue. When products and services are later delivered, the earned portion of the unearned revenue is transferred to revenue accounts such as Subscription Fees Revenue, Rent Revenue, and Ticket Revenue.[1]

Point: If a subscription is canceled, the publisher is expected to refund the unused portion to the subscriber.

Accrued Liabilities   *Accrued liabilities* are amounts owed that are not yet paid. Examples are wages payable, taxes payable, and interest payable. These are often recorded in separate liability accounts by the same title. If they are not large in amount, one or more ledger accounts can be added and reported as a single amount on the balance sheet. (Financial statements often have amounts reported that are a summation of several ledger accounts.)

 Decision Insight

NFL Revenues   The **Seattle Seahawks**, **New England Patriots**, and most of the NFL teams have *Unearned Revenues* of over $100 million in advance ticket sales. When a team plays its home games, it settles this liability to its ticket holders and then transfers the amount earned to *Ticket Revenues*. Other teams in other major sports have similar unearned revenues. ■

Jeff Gross/Getty Images

Point: Equity is also called *net assets*.

Equity Accounts   The owner's claim on a company's assets is called *equity, stockholders' equity,* or *shareholders' equity.* Equity is the owner's *residual interest* in the assets of a business after deducting liabilities. In its simple form, equity is impacted by four types of accounts as follows: **Equity = Common stock − Dividends + Revenues − Expenses**. We show this

---

[1] In practice, account titles vary. As one example, Subscription Fees Revenue is sometimes called Subscription Fees, Subscription Fees Earned, or Earned Subscription Fees. As another example, Rent Revenue is sometimes called Rent Earned, Rental Revenue, or Earned Rent Revenue. We must use good judgment when reading financial statements because titles can differ even within the same industry. For example, product sales are called *net sales* at **Apple**, *revenues* at **Google**, and *revenue* at **Samsung**. Generally, the term *revenues* or *fees* is more commonly used with service businesses, and *net sales* or *sales* with product businesses.

visually in Exhibit 2.2 by expanding the accounting equation. We also organize assets and liabilities into subgroups that have similar attributes. An important subgroup for both assets and liabilities is the *current* items. Current items are usually those expected to come due (either collected or owed) within the next year. The next chapter explains this in detail. At this point, know that a *classified balance sheet* reports current assets before noncurrent assets and current liabilities before noncurrent liabilities.

EXHIBIT 2.2

Expanded Accounting Equation

Owner Investments   When an owner invests in a company in exchange for its common stock, it increases both assets and equity of the company. The increase to equity is recorded in an account titled Common Stock. Any further owner investments are also recorded in this account.

Owner Distributions   When a corporation distributes assets to its owner, it decreases both company assets and total equity. The decrease to equity is recorded in an account titled Dividends. Dividends are not expenses of the business; they are simply the opposite of owner investments.

Point: The Dividends account is sometimes referred to as a *contra equity* account because it reduces the normal balance of equity.

Revenue Accounts   The inflow of net assets from providing products and services to customers increases equity through increases in revenue accounts. Examples of revenue accounts are Sales, Commissions Earned, Professional Fees Earned, Rent Revenue, and Interest Revenue. *Revenues always increase equity.*

Point: The withdrawal of assets by the owners of a corporation is called a *dividend.*

Expense Accounts   The outflow of net assets in helping generate revenues decreases equity through increases in expense accounts. Examples of expense accounts are Advertising Expense, Store Supplies Expense, Office Salaries Expense, Office Supplies Expense, Rent Expense, Utilities Expense, and Insurance Expense. *Expenses always decrease equity.*

   The variety of revenues and expenses can be seen by looking at the *chart of accounts* at the end of this book. (Different companies sometimes use different account titles than those in this book's chart of accounts. For example, some might use Interest Revenue instead of Interest Earned, or Rental Expense instead of Rent Expense. It is important only that an account title describe the item it represents.)

▨ Decision Insight

Sporting Accounts   The **Cleveland Cavaliers**, **Boston Celtics**, **San Antonio Spurs**, **Golden State Warriors**, **Los Angeles Clippers**, and other NBA teams have the following major revenue and expense accounts:

Revenues	Expenses
Basketball ticket sales	Team salaries
TV & radio broadcast fees	Game costs
Advertising revenues	NBA franchise costs
Basketball playoff receipts	Promotional costs ■

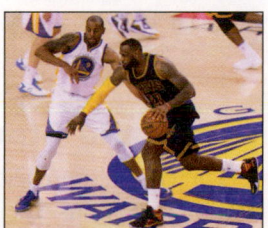

FREDERIC J. BROWN/AFP/
Getty Images

Classify each of the following accounts as either an asset (A), liability (L), or equity (EQ).

1. ____ Prepaid Rent
2. ____ Common Stock
3. ____ Note Receivable
4. ____ Accounts Payable
5. ____ Accounts Receivable
6. ____ Equipment
7. ____ Interest Payable
8. ____ Unearned Revenue
9. ____ Land
10. ____ Prepaid Insurance
11. ____ Wages Payable
12. ____ Taxes Payable

Solution

1. A 2. EQ 3. A 4. L 5. A 6. A 7. L 8. L 9. A 10. A 11. L 12. L

ANALYZING AND PROCESSING TRANSACTIONS

This section explains several tools and processes that comprise an accounting system. These include a ledger, T-account, debits and credits, double-entry accounting, journalizing, and posting.

Ledger and Chart of Accounts

C3 Describe a ledger and a chart of accounts.

The collection of all accounts and their balances for an accounting system is called a *ledger* (or *general ledger*). If accounts are in files on a hard drive, the sum of those files is the ledger. If the accounts are pages in a file, that file is the ledger. A company's size and diversity of operations affect the number of accounts needed. A small company can get by with as few as 20 or 30 accounts; a large company can require several thousand. The **chart of accounts** is a list of all ledger accounts and includes an identification number assigned to each account. Exhibit 2.3 shows a common numbering system of accounts for a smaller business.

EXHIBIT 2.3

Typical Chart of Accounts for a Smaller Business

Chart of Accounts	
101–199	Asset accounts
201–299	Liability accounts
301–399	Equity accounts
401–499	Revenue accounts
501–699	Expense accounts

These account numbers provide a three-digit code that is useful in recordkeeping. In this case, the first digit assigned to asset accounts is a 1, the first digit assigned to liability accounts is a 2, and so on. The second and third digits relate to the accounts' subcategories. Exhibit 2.4 shows a partial chart of accounts for FastForward, the focus company of Chapter 1. (Please review the more complete chart of accounts that follows the index at the end of this book.)

EXHIBIT 2.4

Partial Chart of Accounts for FastForward

Chart of Accounts					
Acct. No.	Account Name	Acct. No.	Account Name	Acct. No.	Account Name
101	Cash	236	Unearned consulting revenue	406	Rental revenue
106	Accounts receivable	307	Common stock	622	Salaries expense
126	Supplies	318	Retained earnings	637	Insurance expense
128	Prepaid insurance	319	Dividends	640	Rent expense
167	Equipment	403	Consulting revenue	652	Supplies expense
201	Accounts payable			690	Utilities expense

Debits and Credits

C4 Define *debits* and *credits* and explain double-entry accounting.

A **T-account** represents a ledger account and is a tool used to depict the effects of one or more transactions. Its name comes from its shape like the letter **T**. The layout of a T-account, shown in Exhibit 2.5, is (1) the account title on top; (2) a left, or debit, side; and (3) a right, or credit, side.

The left side of an account is called the **debit** side, often abbreviated *Dr.* The right side is called the **credit** side, abbreviated *Cr.*² To enter amounts on the left side of an account is to *debit* the account. To enter amounts on the

Account Title	
(Left side)	(Right side)
Debit	*Credit*

EXHIBIT 2.5
The T-Account

right side is to *credit* the account. The term *debit* or *credit*, by itself, does not mean increase or decrease. Whether a debit or a credit is an increase or decrease depends on the account. The difference between total debits and total credits for an account, including any beginning balance, is the **account balance.** When the sum of debits exceeds the sum of credits, the account has a *debit balance*. It has a *credit balance* when the sum of credits exceeds the sum of debits. When the sum of debits equals the sum of credits, the account has a *zero balance*.

Point: Think of *debit* and *credit* as accounting directions for left and right.

Double-Entry Accounting

Double-entry accounting demands the accounting equation remain in balance. This implies that for each transaction:

- At least two accounts are involved, with at least one debit and one credit.
- The total amount debited must equal the total amount credited.

"Total debits equal total credits for each entry."

This also means that the sum of the debits for all entries must equal the sum of the credits for all entries, and the sum of debit account balances in the ledger must equal the sum of credit account balances.

The system for recording debits and credits follows from the accounting equation—see Exhibit 2.6. First, like any simple mathematical relation, net increases or decreases on one side have equal net effects on the other side. For example, a net increase in assets must be accompanied by an identical net increase on the liabilities and equity side. Recall that some transactions affect only one side of the equation, such as acquiring a land asset by giving up a cash asset, but their net effect on this one side is zero. Second, the left side is the *normal balance* side for assets, and the right side is the *normal balance* side for liabilities and equity. This matches their layout in the accounting equation where assets are on the left side of this equation, and liabilities and equity are on the right.

Point: Assets are on the left-hand side of the equation and thus increase on the left. Liabilities and Equity are on the right-hand side of the equation and thus increase on the right.

Assets		=	Liabilities		+	Equity	
Debit for increases	Credit for decreases		Debit for decreases	Credit for increases		Debit for decreases	Credit for increases
+	−		−	+		−	+
Normal				Normal			Normal

EXHIBIT 2.6
Debits and Credits in the Accounting Equation

Point: Equity increases from owner investments and revenues; it decreases from dividends and expenses.

Recall that equity increases from revenues and owner investments (stock issuances); it decreases from expenses and dividends. These important equity relations are conveyed by expanding the accounting equation to include debits and credits in double-entry form as shown in Exhibit 2.7.

EXHIBIT 2.7
Debit and Credit Effects for Component Accounts

		Equity				
Assets =	Liabilities +	Common Stock −	Dividends +	Revenues −	Expenses
Dr. for increases / Cr. for decreases	Dr. for decreases / Cr. for increases	Dr. for decreases / Cr. for increases	Dr. for increases / Cr. for decreases	Dr. for decreases / Cr. for increases	Dr. for increases / Cr. for decreases
+ Normal / −	− / + Normal	− / + Normal	+ Normal / −	− / + Normal	+ Normal / −

² These abbreviations are remnants of 18th-century English recordkeeping practices where the terms *debitor* and *creditor* were used instead of *debit* and *credit.* The abbreviations use the first and last letters of these terms, just as we still do for Saint (St.) and Doctor (Dr.).

Point: Debits and credits do not mean favorable or unfavorable. A debit to an asset increases it, as does a debit to an expense. A credit to a liability increases it, as does a credit to a revenue.

Increases (credits) to common stock and to revenues *increase* equity; increases (debits) to dividends and to expenses *decrease* equity. The *normal balance* of each account (asset, liability, common stock, dividends, revenue, or expense) refers to the side where *increases* are recorded. Understanding these diagrams is required to fully prepare, analyze, and interpret financial statements.

The T-account for FastForward's Cash account, reflecting its first 11 transactions (from Exhibit 1.9), is shown in Exhibit 2.8. The total increases (debits) in its Cash account are $36,100; the total decreases (credits) are $31,300. Total debits exceed total credits by $4,800—resulting in its ending debit balance of $4,800.

EXHIBIT 2.8

Computing the Balance for a T-Account

Cash			
Receive investment by owner for stock	30,000	Purchase of supplies	2,500
Consulting services revenue earned	4,200	Purchase of equipment	26,000
Collection of account receivable	1,900	Payment of rent	1,000
		Payment of salary	700
		Payment of account payable	900
		Payment of cash dividend	200
Balance	**4,800**		

Point: The ending balance is on the side with the larger dollar amount. Also, a plus (+) and minus (−) are *not* used in a T-account.

NEED-TO-KNOW **2-2**

Normal Account Balance

C3 C4

Do More: QS 2-4, QS 2-5, QS 2-7, E 2-4

Identify the normal balance (debit [Dr] or credit [Cr]) for each of the following accounts.

1. ____ Prepaid Rent   **5.** ____ Accounts Receivable   **9.** ____ Land

2. ____ Common Stock   **6.** ____ Equipment   **10.** ____ Prepaid Insurance

3. ____ Note Receivable   **7.** ____ Interest Payable   **11.** ____ Dividends

4. ____ Accounts Payable   **8.** ____ Unearned Revenue

Solution

1. Dr. **2.** Cr. **3.** Dr. **4.** Cr. **5.** Dr. **6.** Dr. **7.** Cr. **8.** Cr. **9.** Dr. **10.** Dr. **11.** Dr.

Journalizing and Posting Transactions

P1

Record transactions in a journal and post entries to a ledger.

Processing transactions is a key part of accounting. The four usual steps of this process are depicted in Exhibit 2.9. Steps 1 and 2—involving transaction analysis and the accounting equation—were already discussed. This section extends that discussion and focuses on steps 3 and 4 of the accounting process. Step 3 is to record each transaction chronologically in a journal. A **journal** gives a complete record of each transaction in one place. It also shows debits and credits for each transaction. The process of recording transactions in a journal is called **journalizing**. Step 4 is to transfer (or *post*) entries from the journal to the ledger. The process of transferring journal entry information to the ledger is called **posting.**

Journalizing Transactions   The process of journalizing transactions requires an understanding of a journal. While companies can use various journals, every company uses a **general journal.** It can be used to record any transaction and includes the following information about each transaction: ⓐ date of transaction, ⓑ titles of affected accounts, ⓒ dollar amount of each debit and credit, and ⓓ explanation of the transaction. Exhibit 2.10 shows how the first two transactions of FastForward are recorded in a general journal. This process is similar for manual and computerized systems. Computerized journals are often designed to look like a manual journal page, and include error-checking routines that ensure debits equal credits for each entry. Shortcuts allow recordkeepers to select account names and numbers from pull-down menus.

EXHIBIT 2.9

Steps in Processing Transactions

Step 1: Identify transactions and source documents.

Step 2: Analyze transactions using the accounting equation.

Step 3: Record journal entry.

Step 4: Post entry to ledger.

To record entries in a general journal, apply these steps; refer to the entries in Exhibit 2.10 when reviewing these steps.

a. Date the transaction: Enter the year at the top of the first column and the month and day on the first line of each journal entry.

b. Enter titles of accounts debited and then enter amounts in the Debit column on the same line. Account titles are taken from the chart of accounts and are aligned with the left margin of the Account Titles and Explanation column.

c. Enter titles of accounts credited and then enter amounts in the Credit column on the same line. Account titles are from the chart of accounts and are indented from the left margin of the Account Titles and Explanation column to distinguish them from debited accounts.

d. Enter a brief explanation of the transaction on the line below the entry (it often references a source document). This explanation is indented about half as far as the credited account titles to avoid confusing it with accounts, and it is italicized.

A blank line is left between each journal entry for clarity. When a transaction is first recorded, the **posting reference (PR) column** is left blank (in a manual system). Later, when posting entries to the ledger, the identification numbers of the individual ledger accounts are entered in the PR column.

Point: There are no exact rules for writing journal entry explanations. An explanation should be short yet describe why an entry is made.

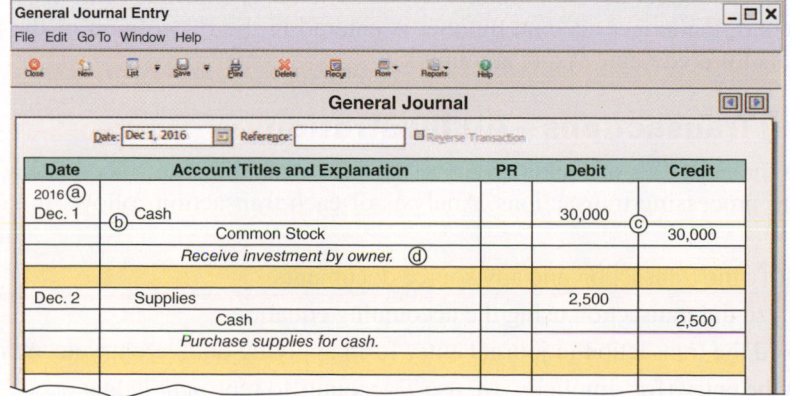

EXHIBIT 2.10

Partial General Journal for FastForward

IFRS

IFRS requires that companies report the following four basic financial statements with explanatory notes:

- Balance sheet
- Income statement
- Statement of changes in equity (or statement of recognized revenue and expense)
- Statement of cash flows

IFRS does not prescribe specific formats, and comparative information is required for the preceding period only. ■

Balance Column Account   T-accounts are simple and direct means to show how the accounting process works. However, actual accounting systems need more structure and therefore use **balance column accounts,** such as that in Exhibit 2.11.

EXHIBIT 2.11

Cash Account in Balance Column Format

General Ledger					
Cash					Account No. 101
Date	Explanation	PR	Debit	Credit	Balance
2016 Dec. 1		G1	30,000		30,000
Dec. 2		G1		2,500	27,500
Dec. 3		G1		26,000	1,500
Dec. 10		G1	4,200		5,700

The balance column account format is similar to a T-account in having columns for debits and credits. It is different in including transaction date and explanation columns. It also has a column with the balance of the account after each entry is recorded. To illustrate, FastForward's Cash account in Exhibit 2.11 is debited on December 1 for the $30,000 owner investment, yielding a $30,000 debit balance. The account is credited on December 2 for $2,500, yielding a $27,500 debit balance. On December 3, it is credited again, this time for $26,000, and its debit balance is reduced to $1,500. The Cash account is debited for $4,200 on December 10, and its debit balance increases to $5,700; and so on.

The heading of the Balance column does not show whether it is a debit or credit balance. Instead, an account is assumed to have a *normal balance*. Unusual events can sometimes temporarily give an account an abnormal balance. An *abnormal balance* refers to a balance on the side where decreases are recorded. For example, a customer might mistakenly overpay a bill. This gives that customer's account receivable an abnormal (credit) balance. An abnormal balance is often identified by highlighting it, setting it in brackets, or entering it in red or some other unusual color. A zero balance for an account is usually shown by writing zeros or a dash in the Balance column to avoid confusion between a zero balance and one omitted in error.

Point: Explanations are typically included in ledger accounts only for unusual transactions or events.

Point: Computerized systems often provide a code beside a balance such as *dr.* or *cr.* to identify its balance. Posting is automatic and immediate with accounting software.

Point: A journal is often referred to as the *book of original entry.* The ledger is referred to as the *book of final entry* because financial statements are prepared from it.

Posting Journal Entries   Step 4 of processing transactions is to post journal entries to ledger accounts (see Exhibit 2.9). All entries must be posted to the ledger before financial statements are prepared to ensure that account balances are up to date. When entries are posted to the ledger, the debits in journal entries are transferred into ledger accounts as debits, and credits are transferred into ledger accounts as credits. Exhibit 2.12 shows the *four parts to the process of posting a journal entry.* First, the ledger account that is debited in the entry is identified; then, in the ledger, the entry date, the journal and page from the journal, the debit amount, and the new balance of the ledger account are entered. (The letter *G* shows it came from the General Journal.) Second, the ledger account number is entered in the PR column of the journal. The process repeats for credit entries and amounts.

Analyzing Transactions—An Illustration

A1

Analyze the impact of transactions on accounts and financial statements.

We return to the activities of FastForward to show how double-entry accounting is useful in analyzing and processing transactions. Analysis of each transaction follows the four steps of Exhibit 2.9.

Step 1 Identify the transaction and any source documents.

Step 2 Analyze the transaction using the accounting equation.

Step 3 Record the transaction in journal entry form applying double-entry accounting.

Step 4 Post the entry (for simplicity, we use T-accounts to represent ledger accounts).

EXHIBIT 2.12

Process of Posting an Entry to the Ledger

Key: ① Identify debit account in Ledger: enter date, journal page, amount, and balance.
② Enter the debit account number from the Ledger in the PR column of the journal.
③ Identify credit account in Ledger: enter date, journal page, amount, and balance.
④ Enter the credit account number from the Ledger in the PR column of the journal.

Point: The fundamental concepts of a manual (pencil-and-paper) system are identical to those of a computerized information system.

Study each transaction thoroughly before proceeding to the next. The first 11 transactions are from Chapter 1, and we analyze five additional December transactions of FastForward (numbered 12 through 16) that were omitted earlier.

Point: In this chapter's Comprehensive Need-To-Know we show how to use "balance column accounts" for the ledger.

*FAST*Forward

1. Receive Investment by Owner

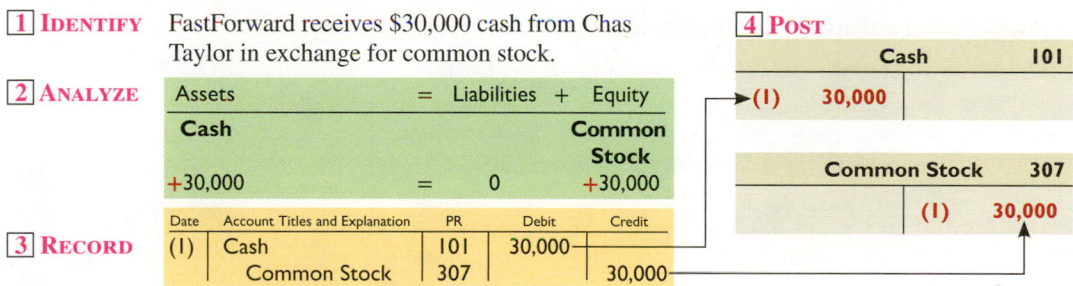

2. Purchase Supplies for Cash

3. Purchase Equipment for Cash

1 IDENTIFY   FastForward pays $26,000 cash for equipment.

2 ANALYZE

Assets		=	Liabilities	+	Equity
Cash	**Equipment**				
−26,000	+26,000	=	0	+	0

Changes the composition of assets but not the total.

3 RECORD

Date	Account Titles and Explanation	PR	Debit	Credit
(3)	Equipment	167	26,000	
	Cash	101		26,000

4 POST

Equipment		167
(3)	26,000	

Cash		101	
(1)	30,000	(2)	2,500
		(3)	26,000

4. Purchase Supplies on Credit

1 IDENTIFY   FastForward purchases $7,100 of supplies on credit from a supplier.

2 ANALYZE

Assets	=	Liabilities	+	Equity
Supplies		**Accounts Payable**		
+7,100	=	+7,100	+	0

3 RECORD

Date	Account Titles and Explanation	PR	Debit	Credit
(4)	Supplies	126	7,100	
	Accounts Payable	201		7,100

4 POST

Supplies		126
(2)	2,500	
(4)	7,100	

Accounts Payable		201
	(4)	7,100

5. Provide Services for Cash

1 IDENTIFY   FastForward provides consulting services and immediately collects $4,200 cash.

2 ANALYZE

Assets	=	Liabilities	+	Equity
Cash				**Consulting Revenue**
+4,200	=	0		+4,200

3 RECORD

Date	Account Titles and Explanation	PR	Debit	Credit
(5)	Cash	101	4,200	
	Consulting Revenue	403		4,200

4 POST

Cash		101	
(1)	30,000	(2)	2,500
(5)	4,200	(3)	26,000

Consulting Revenue		403
	(5)	4,200

6. Payment of Expense in Cash

1 IDENTIFY   FastForward pays $1,000 cash for December rent.

2 ANALYZE

Assets	=	Liabilities	+	Equity
Cash				**Rent Expense**
−1,000	=	0		−1,000

3 RECORD

Date	Account Titles and Explanation	PR	Debit	Credit
(6)	Rent Expense	640	1,000	
	Cash	101		1,000

4 POST

Rent Expense		640
(6)	1,000	

Cash		101	
(1)	30,000	(2)	2,500
(5)	4,200	(3)	26,000
		(6)	1,000

7. Payment of Expense in Cash

1 IDENTIFY   FastForward pays $700 cash for employee salary.

2 ANALYZE

Assets	=	Liabilities	+	Equity
Cash				**Salaries Expense**
−700	=	0		−700

3 RECORD

Date	Account Titles and Explanation	PR	Debit	Credit
(7)	Salaries Expense	622	700	
	Cash	101		700

4 POST

Salaries Expense		622
(7)	700	

Cash		101	
(1)	30,000	(2)	2,500
(5)	4,200	(3)	26,000
		(6)	1,000
		(7)	700

Point: *Salary* usually refers to compensation for an employee who receives a fixed amount for a given time period, whereas *wages* usually refers to compensation based on time worked.

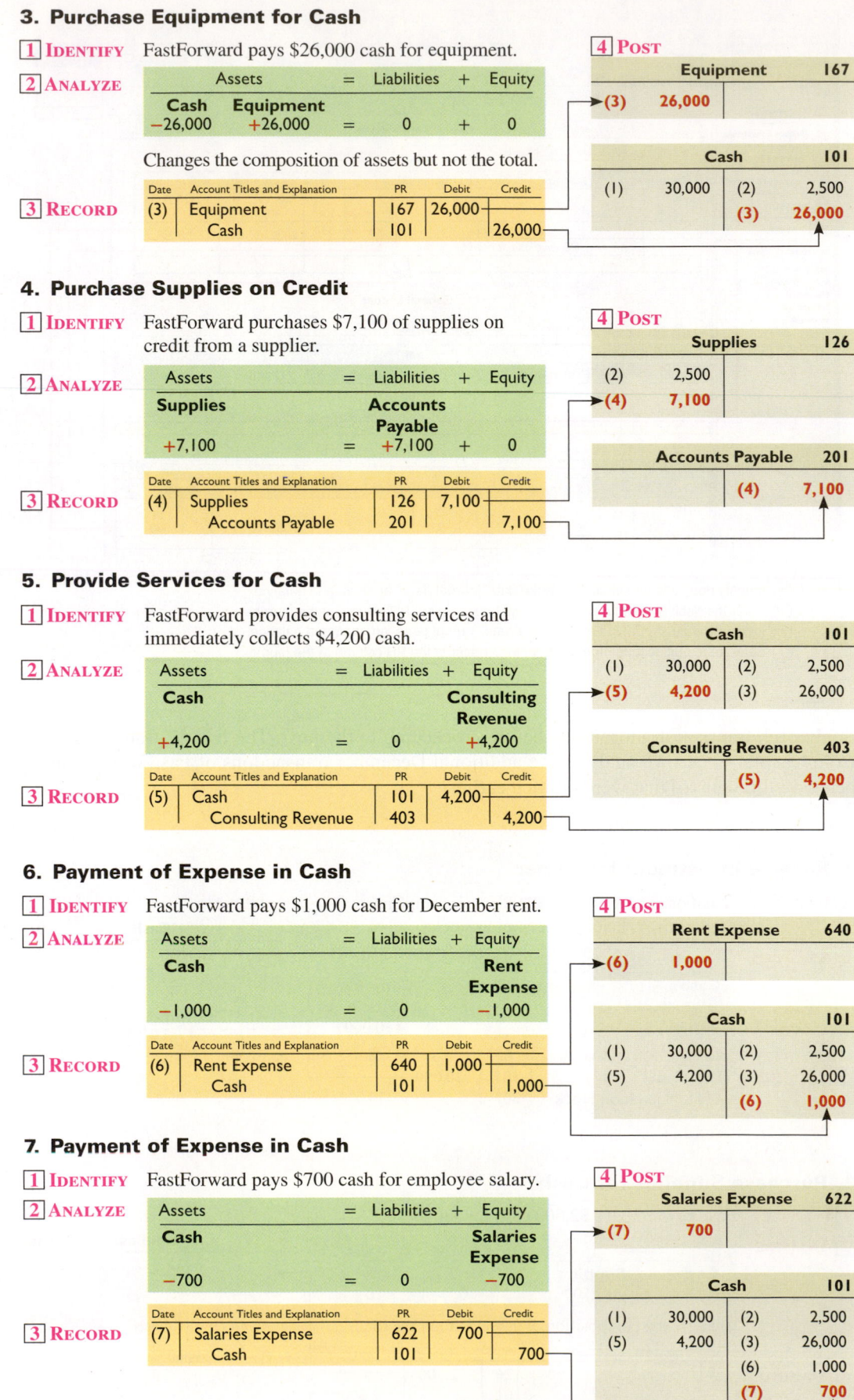

8. Provide Consulting and Rental Services on Credit

1 IDENTIFY FastForward provides consulting services of $1,600 and rents its test facilities for $300. The customer is billed $1,900 for these services.

2 ANALYZE

3 RECORD

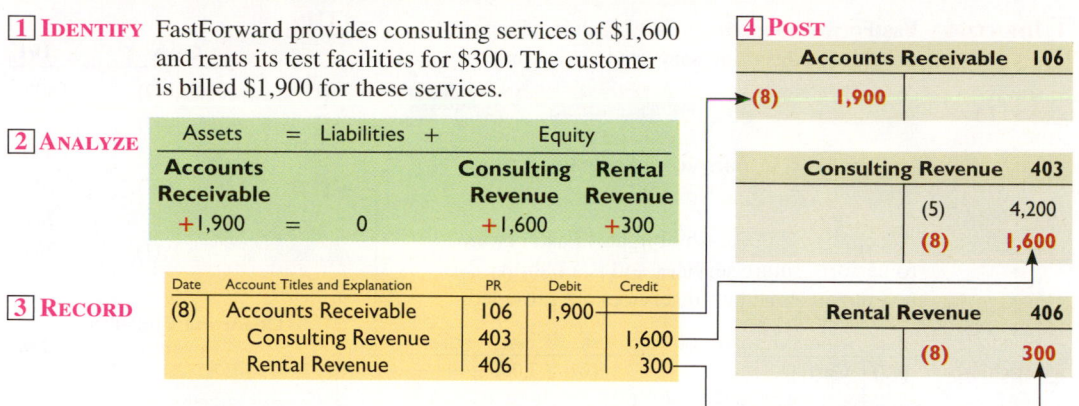

4 POST

Point: The *revenue recognition principle* requires revenue to be recognized when the company provides products and services to a customer. This is not necessarily the same time that the customer pays. A customer can pay before or after products or services are provided.

Point: Transaction 8 is a **compound journal entry**, which affects three or more accounts.

9. Receipt of Cash on Account

1 IDENTIFY FastForward receives $1,900 cash from the client billed in transaction 8.

2 ANALYZE

3 RECORD

4 POST

10. Partial Payment of Accounts Payable

1 IDENTIFY FastForward pays CalTech Supply $900 cash toward the payable of transaction 4.

2 ANALYZE

3 RECORD

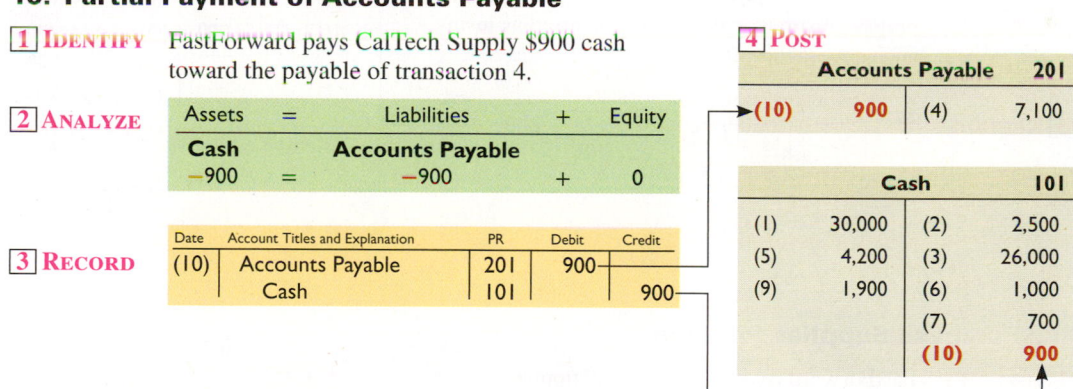

4 POST

11. Payment of Cash Dividend

1 IDENTIFY FastForward pays $200 cash for dividends.

2 ANALYZE

3 RECORD

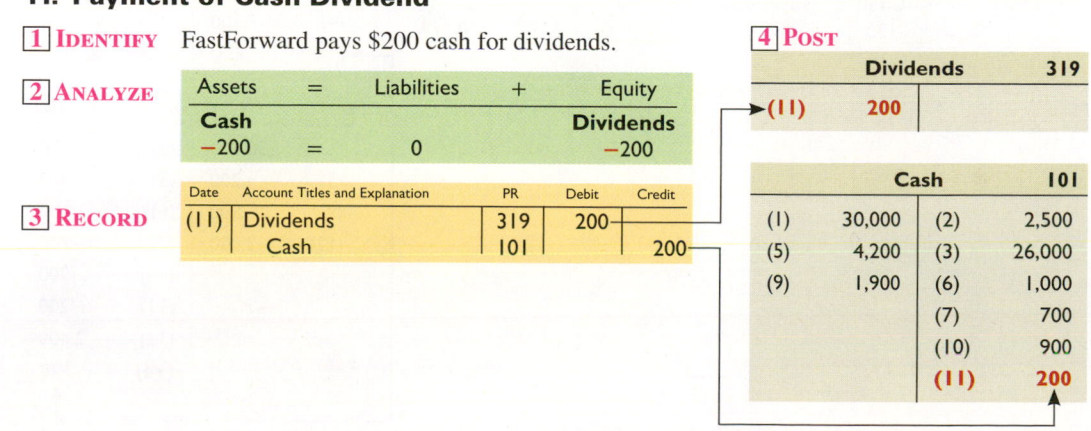

4 POST

Point: Dividends always decrease equity.

12. Receipt of Cash for Future Services

1 IDENTIFY   FastForward receives $3,000 cash in advance of providing consulting services to a customer.

2 ANALYZE

Assets	=	Liabilities	+	Equity
Cash		**Unearned Consulting Revenue**		
+3,000	=	+3,000	+	0

Accepting $3,000 cash obligates FastForward to perform future services and is a liability. No revenue is earned until services are provided.

3 RECORD

Date	Account Titles and Explanation	PR	Debit	Credit
(12)	Cash	101	3,000	
	Unearned Consulting Revenue	236		3,000

4 POST

Cash			101
(1)	30,000	(2)	2,500
(5)	4,200	(3)	26,000
(9)	1,900	(6)	1,000
(12)	**3,000**	(7)	700
		(10)	900
		(11)	200

Unearned Consulting Revenue			236
		(12)	**3,000**

13. Pay Cash for Future Insurance Coverage

1 IDENTIFY   FastForward pays $2,400 cash (insurance premium) for a 24-month insurance policy. Coverage begins on December 1.

2 ANALYZE

Assets		=	Liabilities	+	Equity
Cash	**Prepaid Insurance**				
−2,400	+2,400	=	0	+	0

Changes the composition of assets from cash to prepaid insurance. Expense is incurred as insurance coverage expires.

3 RECORD

Date	Account Titles and Explanation	PR	Debit	Credit
(13)	Prepaid Insurance	128	2,400	
	Cash	101		2,400

4 POST

Prepaid Insurance		128
(13)	**2,400**	

Cash			101
(1)	30,000	(2)	2,500
(5)	4,200	(3)	26,000
(9)	1,900	(6)	1,000
(12)	3,000	(7)	700
		(10)	900
		(11)	200
		(13)	**2,400**

14. Purchase Supplies for Cash

1 IDENTIFY   FastForward pays $120 cash for supplies.

2 ANALYZE

Assets		=	Liabilities	+	Equity
Cash	**Supplies**				
−120	+120	=	0	+	0

3 RECORD

Date	Account Titles and Explanation	PR	Debit	Credit
(14)	Supplies	126	120	
	Cash	101		120

4 POST

Supplies		126
(2)	2,500	
(4)	7,100	
(14)	**120**	

Cash			101
(1)	30,000	(2)	2,500
(5)	4,200	(3)	26,000
(9)	1,900	(6)	1,000
(12)	3,000	(7)	700
		(10)	900
		(11)	200
		(13)	2,400
		(14)	**120**

15. Payment of Expense in Cash

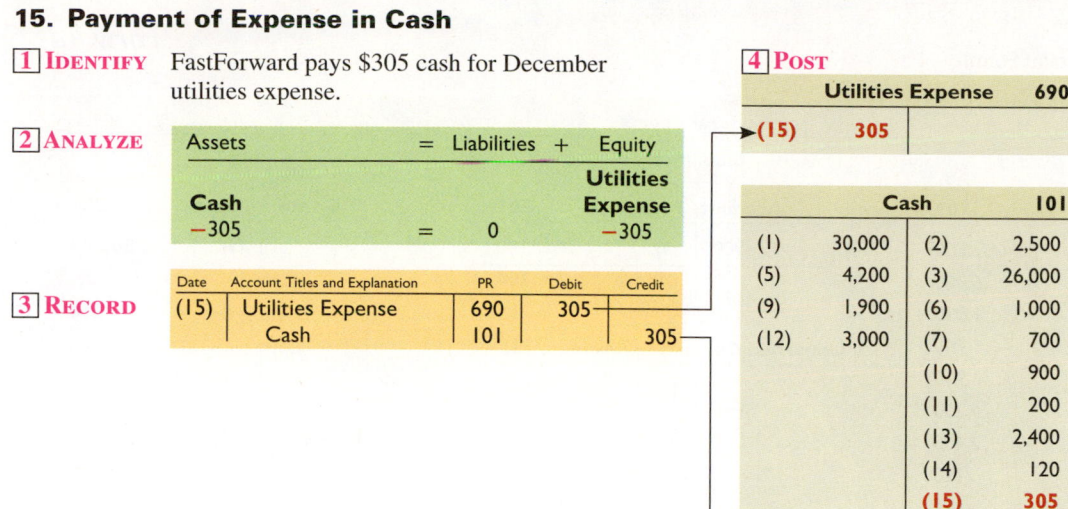

1 IDENTIFY   FastForward pays $305 cash for December utilities expense.

2 ANALYZE

Assets	= Liabilities	+	Equity
Cash			**Utilities Expense**
−305	=	0	−305

3 RECORD

Date	Account Titles and Explanation	PR	Debit	Credit
(15)	Utilities Expense	690	305	
	Cash	101		305

4 POST

Utilities Expense	690
(15) 305	

Cash		101	
(1)	30,000	(2)	2,500
(5)	4,200	(3)	26,000
(9)	1,900	(6)	1,000
(12)	3,000	(7)	700
		(10)	900
		(11)	200
		(13)	2,400
		(14)	120
		(15)	**305**

Point: Expenses always decrease equity.

16. Payment of Expense in Cash

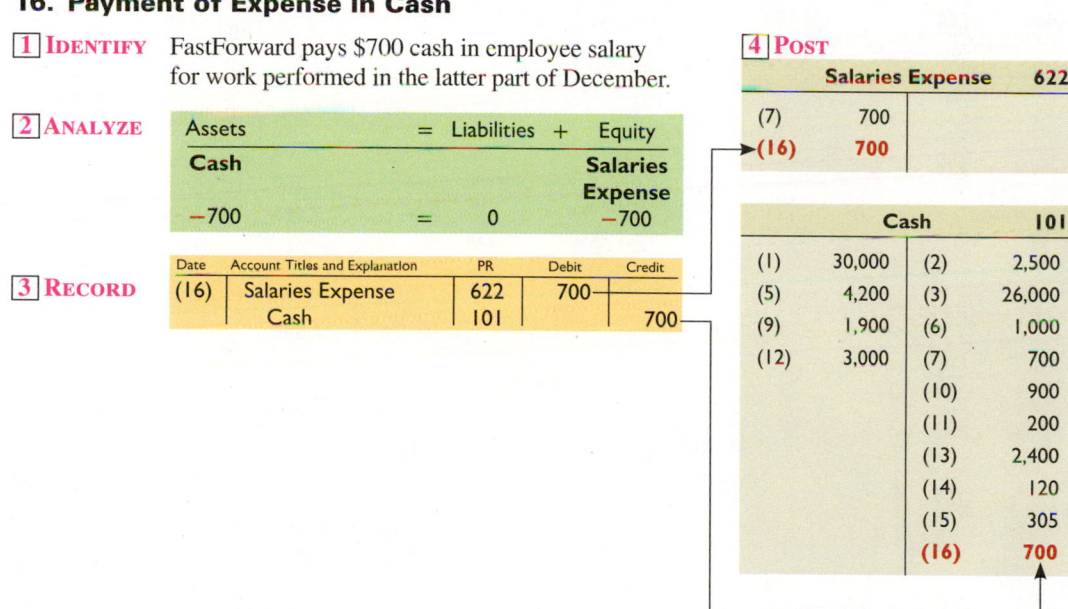

1 IDENTIFY   FastForward pays $700 cash in employee salary for work performed in the latter part of December.

2 ANALYZE

Assets	= Liabilities	+	Equity
Cash			**Salaries Expense**
−700	=	0	−700

3 RECORD

Date	Account Titles and Explanation	PR	Debit	Credit
(16)	Salaries Expense	622	700	
	Cash	101		700

4 POST

Salaries Expense	622
(7) 700	
(16) 700	

Cash		101	
(1)	30,000	(2)	2,500
(5)	4,200	(3)	26,000
(9)	1,900	(6)	1,000
(12)	3,000	(7)	700
		(10)	900
		(11)	200
		(13)	2,400
		(14)	120
		(15)	305
		(16)	**700**

Point: We could merge transactions 15 and 16 into one *compound entry*.

Accounting Equation Analysis

Exhibit 2.13 shows the ledger accounts (in T-account form) of FastForward after all 16 transactions are recorded and posted and the balances computed. The accounts are grouped into three major columns corresponding to the accounting equation: assets, liabilities, and equity. Note several important points. First, as with each transaction, the totals for the three columns must obey the accounting equation. Specifically, assets equal **$42,395** ($4,275 + $0 + $9,720 + $2,400 + $26,000); liabilities equal **$9,200** ($6,200 + $3,000); and equity equals **$33,195** ($30,000 − $200 + $5,800 + $300 − $1,400 − $1,000 − $305). These numbers prove the accounting equation: Assets of $42,395 = Liabilities of $9,200 + Equity of $33,195. Second, the common stock, dividends, revenue, and expense accounts reflect the transactions that change equity. These account categories underlie the statement of retained earnings. Third, the revenue and expense account balances will be summarized and reported in the income statement. Fourth, increases and decreases in the Cash account make up the elements reported in the statement of cash flows.

Point: Technology does not provide the judgment required to analyze most business transactions. Analysis requires the expertise of skilled and ethical professionals.

Debit and Credit Rules		
Accounts	**Increase (normal bal.)**	**Decrease**
Asset	Debit	Credit
Liability	Credit	Debit
Common Stock	Credit	Debit
Dividends	Debit	Credit
Revenue	Credit	Debit
Expense	Debit	Credit

EXHIBIT 2.13

Ledger for FastForward (in T-Account Form)

General Ledger

Assets	=	Liabilities	+	Equity

Assets

Cash   101

(1)	30,000	(2)	2,500
(5)	4,200	(3)	26,000
(9)	1,900	(6)	1,000
(12)	3,000	(7)	700
		(10)	900
		(11)	200
		(13)	2,400
		(14)	120
		(15)	305
		(16)	700
Balance	4,275		

Accounts Receivable   106

| (8) | 1,900 | (9) | 1,900 |
| Balance | 0 | | |

Supplies   126

(2)	2,500		
(4)	7,100		
(14)	120		
Balance	9,720		

Prepaid Insurance   128

| (13) | 2,400 | | |

Equipment   167

| (3) | 26,000 | | |

Liabilities

Accounts Payable   201

| (10) | 900 | (4) | 7,100 |
| | | Balance | 6,200 |

Unearned Consulting Revenue 236

| | | (12) | 3,000 |

Equity

Common Stock   307

| | | (1) | 30,000 |

Dividends   319

| (11) | 200 | | |

Consulting Revenue   403

		(5)	4,200
		(8)	1,600
		Balance	5,800

Rental Revenue   406

| | | (8) | 300 |

Salaries Expense   622

(7)	700		
(16)	700		
Balance	1,400		

Rent Expense   640

| (6) | 1,000 | | |

Utilities Expense   690

| (15) | 305 | | |

Accounts in this white area reflect those reported on the income statement.

$42,395	=	$9,200	+	$33,195

NEED-TO-KNOW 2-3

Recording Transactions

P1   A1

Assume Tata Company began operations on January 1 and completed the following transactions during its first month of operations. For each transaction, (a) analyze the transaction using the accounting equation, (b) record the transaction in journal entry form, and (c) post the entry using T-accounts to represent ledger accounts. Tata Company has the following (partial) chart of accounts—account numbers in parentheses: Cash (101); Accounts Receivable (106); Equipment (167); Accounts Payable (201); Common Stock (307); Dividends (319); Services Revenue (403); and Wages Expense (601).

Jan. 1 Jamsetji Tata invested $4,000 cash in the Tata Company in exchange for common stock.

     5 Tata Company purchased $2,000 of equipment on credit.

    14 Tata Company provided $540 of services for a client on credit.

Solution

Jan. 1 Receive Investment by Owner

Jan. 5 Purchase Equipment on Credit

Jan. 14 Provide Services on Credit

Do More: QS 2-6, E 2-7, E 2-9, E 2-11, E 2-12

TRIAL BALANCE

Double-entry accounting requires the sum of debit account balances to equal the sum of credit account balances. A trial balance is used to confirm this. A **trial balance** is a list of ledger accounts and their balances (either debit or credit) at a point in time. Exhibit 2.14 shows the trial balance for FastForward after its 16 entries have been posted to the ledger. (This is an *unadjusted* trial balance—Chapter 3 explains the necessary adjustments.)

P2
Prepare and explain the use of a trial balance.

Preparing a Trial Balance

Preparing a trial balance involves three steps:

1. List each account title and its amount (from ledger) in the trial balance. If an account has a zero balance, list it with a zero in its normal balance column (or omit it entirely).
2. Compute the total of debit balances and the total of credit balances.
3. Verify (*prove*) total debit balances equal total credit balances.

The total of debit balances equals the total of credit balances for the trial balance in Exhibit 2.14. Equality of these two totals does not guarantee that no errors were made. For example, the column totals will be equal when a debit or credit of a correct amount is made to a

Point: A trial balance is *not* a financial statement but a mechanism for checking equality of debits and credits in the ledger. Financial statements do not have debit and credit columns.

EXHIBIT 2.14

Trial Balance (Unadjusted)

File Edit Lists Maintain Tasks Analysis Options Reports & Forms Services Window Help			
Company	**FASTFORWARD** **Trial Balance** **December 31, 2016**		
		Debit	**Credit**
Cash		$ 4,275	
Accounts receivable		0	
Supplies		9,720	
Prepaid insurance		2,400	
Equipment		26,000	
Accounts payable			$ 6,200
Unearned consulting revenue			3,000
Common stock			30,000
Dividends		200	
Consulting revenue			5,800
Rental revenue			300
Salaries expense		1,400	
Rent expense		1,000	
Utilities expense		305	
Totals		$ 45,300	$ 45,300

Sidebar shortcuts: Business Status, Customers & Sales, Vendors & Purchases, Inventory & Services, Employees & Payroll, Banking, Company

Shortcuts Customize
Sales Invoice
Receive Money from Customer
Bills - Pay Bill
Customer List
Vendor List
Find Transactions
General Journal Entry

Point: The ordering of accounts in a trial balance follows their identification number from the chart of accounts: asset, liability, equity, revenue, and expense accounts.

Point: IRS requires companies to keep records that can be audited.

Example: If a credit to Unearned Revenue was incorrectly posted from the journal as a credit to the Revenue ledger account, would the ledger still balance? Would the financial statements be correct? *Answers:* The ledger would balance, but liabilities would be understated, equity would be overstated, and income would be overstated (all because of overstated revenues).

wrong account. Another error not identified with a trial balance is when equal debits and credits of an incorrect amount are entered.

Searching for and Correcting Errors   If the trial balance does not balance (when its columns are not equal), the error(s) must be found and corrected. An efficient way to search for an error is to check the journalizing, posting, and trial balance preparation in *reverse order*. Step 1 is to verify that the trial balance columns are correctly added. If step 1 fails to find the error, step 2 is to verify that account balances are accurately entered from the ledger. Step 3 is to see whether a debit (or credit) balance is mistakenly listed in the trial balance as a credit (or debit). A clue to this error is when the difference between total debits and total credits equals twice the amount of the incorrect account balance. If the error is still undiscovered, step 4 is to recompute each account balance in the ledger. Step 5 is to verify that each journal entry is properly posted. Step 6 is to verify that the original journal entry has equal debits and credits. At this point, the errors should be uncovered.[3]

Using a Trial Balance to Prepare Financial Statements

This section shows how to prepare *financial statements* from the trial balance.

Financial Statements and Time   How financial statements are linked in time is illustrated in Exhibit 2.15. A balance sheet reports on an organization's financial position at a *point in*

P3

Prepare financial statements from business transactions.

---

[3] *Transposition* occurs when two digits are switched, or transposed, within a number. If transposition is the only error, it yields a difference between the two trial balance totals that is evenly divisible by 9. For example, assume that a $691 debit in an entry is incorrectly posted to the ledger as $619. Total credits in the trial balance are then larger than total debits by $72 ($691 − $619). The $72 error is *evenly* divisible by 9 (72/9 = 8). The first digit of the quotient (in our example it is 8) equals the difference between the digits of the two transposed numbers (the 9 and the 1). The number of digits in the quotient also tells the location of the transposition, starting from the right. The quotient in our example had only one digit (8), so it tells us the transposition is in the first digit. Consider another example where a transposition error involves posting $961 instead of the correct $691. The difference in these numbers is $270, and its quotient is 30 (270/9). The quotient has two digits, so it tells us to check the second digit from the right for a transposition of two numbers that have a difference of 3.

time. The income statement, statement of retained earnings, and statement of cash flows report on financial performance over a *period of time*. The three statements in the middle column of Exhibit 2.15 link balance sheets from the beginning to the end of a reporting period. They explain how financial position changes from one point to another.

Preparers and users (including regulatory agencies) determine the length of the reporting period. A one-year, or annual, reporting period is common, as are semi-annual, quarterly, and monthly periods. The one-year reporting period is known as the *accounting*, or *fiscal, year*. Businesses whose accounting year begins on January 1 and ends on December 31 are known as *calendar-year* companies. Google is a calendar-year company. Many companies choose a fiscal year ending on a date other than December 31. Apple is a *noncalendar-year* company as reflected in the headings of its September 27, 2014, year-end financial statements in Appendix A near the end of the book.

EXHIBIT 2.15

Links between Financial Statements across Time

Point: A statement's heading lists the 3 W's: **W**ho—name of organization, **W**hat—name of statement, **W**hen—statement's point in time or period of time.

Financial Statements from Trial Balance   The FastForward financial statements differ from those in Chapter 1 because of several additional transactions. These statements are also more precisely called *unadjusted statements* because we need to make some further accounting adjustments (described in Chapter 3).

Income Statement   An income statement reports the revenues earned less the expenses incurred by a business over a period of time. FastForward's income statement for December is shown at the top of Exhibit 2.16. Information about revenues and expenses is taken from the trial balance in Exhibit 2.14. Net income of $3,395 is reported at the bottom of the statement. Owner investments and dividends are *not* part of income.

Point: An income statement is also called an *earnings statement*, a *statement of operations*, or a *P&L* (profit and loss) *statement*. A balance sheet is also called a *statement of financial position*.

Statement of Retained Earnings   The statement of retained earnings conveys how retained earnings change over the reporting period. FastForward's statement of retained earnings is the second report in Exhibit 2.16. It shows the $3,395 of net income, the $200 dividend, and the $3,195 end-of-period balance. (The beginning balance in the statement of retained earnings is rarely zero; an exception is for the first period of operations. The beginning balance in January 2017 is $3,195, which is December 2016's ending balance.)

Point: While revenues increase equity, and expenses decrease equity, the amounts are not reported in detail in the statement of retained earnings. Instead, their effects are reflected through net income.

Balance Sheet   The balance sheet shows the financial position of a company at a point in time, usually at the end of a month, quarter, or year. FastForward's balance sheet is the third report in Exhibit 2.16. This statement refers to financial condition at the close of business on December 31. The left side of the balance sheet lists its assets: cash, supplies, prepaid insurance, and equipment. The upper right side of the balance sheet shows that it owes $6,200 to creditors and $3,000 in services to customers who paid in advance. The equity section shows an ending balance of $33,195. Notice the link between the ending balance of the statement of retained earnings and the retained earnings balance. (Recall that this presentation of the balance sheet is called the *account form*: assets on the left and liabilities and equity on the right. Another presentation is the *report form*: assets on top, followed by liabilities and then equity. Either presentation is acceptable.)

Point: Knowing how financial statements are prepared improves our analysis of them.

■ **Decision Maker**

Entrepreneur   You open a wholesale business selling entertainment equipment to retail outlets. You find that most of your customers demand to buy on credit. How can you use the balance sheets of customers to decide which ones to extend credit to? ■ [Answers follow the chapter's Summary.]

EXHIBIT 2.16

Financial Statements Prepared from Trial Balance

FASTFORWARD
Trial Balance
December 31, 2016

	Debit	Credit
Cash	$ 4,275	
Accounts receivable.	0	
Supplies.	9,720	
Prepaid insurance.	2,400	
Equipment	26,000	
Accounts payable.		$ 6,200
Unearned consulting revenue . . .		3,000
Common stock		30,000
Dividends	200	
Consulting revenue		5,800
Rental revenue.		300
Salaries expense.	1,400	
Rent expense	1,000	
Utilities expense.	305	
Totals	$45,300	$45,300

Each account on the trial balance is either an asset (to balance sheet), liability (to balance sheet), or equity (to income statement or to statement of retained earnings).

FASTFORWARD
Income Statement
For Month Ended December 31, 2016

Revenues		
Consulting revenue ($4,200 + $1,600)	$5,800	
Rental revenue	300	
Total revenues		$ 6,100
Expenses		
Salaries expense	1,400	
Rent expense	1,000	
Utilities expense	305	
Total expenses		2,705
Net income		$ 3,395

FASTFORWARD
Statement of Retained Earnings
For Month Ended December 31, 2016

Retained earnings, December 1, 2016	$	0
Plus: Net income		3,395
		3,395
Less: Cash dividends		200
Retained earnings, December 31, 2016		$ 3,195

FASTFORWARD
Balance Sheet
December 31, 2016

Assets		Liabilities	
Cash	$ 4,275	Accounts payable	$ 6,200
Supplies	9,720	Unearned consult. revenue . . .	3,000
Prepaid insurance . .	2,400	Total liabilities	9,200
Equipment	26,000	**Equity**	
		Common stock	30,000
		Retained earnings	3,195
		Total equity	33,195
Total assets	$42,395	Total liabilities and equity	$42,395

Point: Arrow lines show how the statements are linked.

Point: To *foot* a column of numbers is to add them.

Point: The terms "Debit" and "Credit" do not appear on financial statements.

Presentation Issues   Dollar signs are not used in journals and ledgers. They do appear in financial statements and other reports such as trial balances. The usual practice is to put dollar signs beside only the first and last numbers in a column. **Apple**'s financial statements in Appendix A show this. When amounts are entered in a journal, ledger, or trial balance, commas are optional to indicate thousands, millions, and so forth. However, commas are always used in financial statements. Companies also commonly round amounts in reports to the nearest dollar, or even to a higher level. Apple is typical of many companies in that it rounds its financial statement amounts to the nearest million. This decision is based on the perceived impact of rounding for users' business decisions.

Reading and Using an Annual Report   An *annual report* is required of more than 10,000 corporations in the United States that trade their stock publicly. This requirement is imposed by the SEC. Another nearly 5 million corporations in the United States do not trade their shares publicly and are called private or closely held corporations, which are not subject to SEC oversight. Appendix A, near the end of this book, shows key excerpts from the annual report of **Apple**. This appendix also reproduces financial statements from the annual reports of **Google** and **Samsung**. The key excerpts are identified and explained on page A-1. We review and use the annual report for many business decisions, especially for valuing corporate stock and assessing a company's ability to pay off its debts.

Prepare a trial balance for **Apple** using the following *condensed* data from its fiscal year ended September 27, 2014 ($ in millions).

NEED-TO-KNOW 2-4

Preparing Trial Balance

P2

APPLE

Common stock	$ 23,313	Dividends	$ 11,215
Accounts payable	30,196	Securities investments and other assets	179,911
Other liabilities	90,096	Land and equipment (net)	20,624
Cost of sales (and other expenses)	126,231	Selling and other expense	17,054
Cash	13,844	Accounts receivable	17,460
Revenues	182,795	Retained earnings	59,939

Solution ($ in millions)

APPLE
Trial Balance
September 27, 2014

	Debit	Credit
Cash	$ 13,844	
Accounts receivable	17,460	
Land and equipment (net)	20,624	
Securities investments and other assets	179,911	
Accounts payable		$ 30,196
Other liabilities		90,096
Common stock		23,313
Retained earnings		59,939
Dividends	11,215	
Revenues		182,795
Cost of sales and other expenses	126,231	
Selling and other expense	17,054	
Totals	$386,339	$386,339

Do More: E 2-8, E 2-10

GLOBAL VIEW

Financial accounting according to U.S. GAAP is similar, but not identical, to IFRS. This section discusses differences in analyzing and recording transactions, and with the preparation of financial statements.

Analyzing and Recording Transactions   Both U.S. GAAP and IFRS include broad and similar guidance for financial accounting. Further, both U.S. GAAP and IFRS apply transaction analysis and recording as shown in this chapter—using the same debit and credit system and accrual accounting. Although some variations exist in revenue and expense recognition and other accounting principles, all of the transactions in this chapter are accounted for identically under these two systems.

PIAGGIO

Financial Statements   Both U.S. GAAP and IFRS prepare the same four basic financial statements. A few differences within each statement do exist and we will discuss those throughout the book. For example, both U.S. GAAP and IFRS require balance sheets to separate current items from noncurrent items. However, while U.S. GAAP balance sheets report current items first, IFRS balance sheets normally (but are not required to) present noncurrent items first, and equity before liabilities. To illustrate, a condensed version of **Piaggio**'s balance sheet follows. Piaggio is an Italian manufacturer of scooters and compact vehicles.

PIAGGIO Balance Sheet (in thousands of euros) December 31, 2014			
Assets		**Equity and Liabilities**	
Noncurrent assets	€1,079,117	Total equity	€ 413,069
Current assets	477,491	Noncurrent liabilities	581,366
		Current liabilities...............	562,173
Total assets	€1,556,608	Total equity and liabilities	€1,556,608

Accounting Controls and Assurance   Accounting systems depend on control procedures that assure proper principles were applied. The passage of SOX legislation strengthened U.S. controls. However, global standards for controls are diverse and so are enforcement activities. Consequently, while global accounting standards are converging, their application in different countries can yield different outcomes depending on the quality of their auditing standards and enforcement.

 Fraud

Data Quality Recording valid and accurate transactions enhances the quality of financial statements. The graph here shows the percentage of employees in information technology who report observing specific types of misconduct *and* the increased risk of such misconduct in recent years (Source: KPMG 2013).

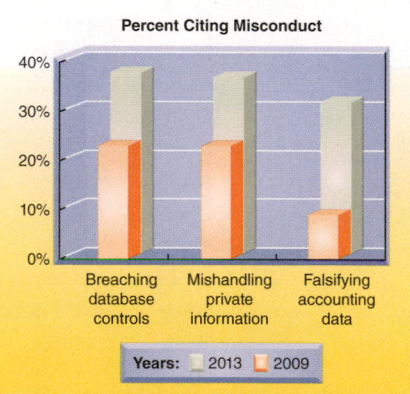

Percent Citing Misconduct

Sustainability and Accounting   **Twitter**, as introduced in this chapter's opening feature, is committed to connecting people interested in sustainability and saving the earth. Twitter co-founder Biz Stone insists that, "to be judged successful, a company needs to make money, make the world a better place and bring joy to the people who work there." Twitter has made the world a better place by providing a space for people with similar interests in sustainability to connect with one another. Sustainability gatherings like cleaning up the park and planting trees are organized on Twitter. The Twitter website has also become a source of news for individuals interested in sustainability. For example, when a new U.S. law was in-process that requires companies to report their use of minerals from conflict regions in the Congo, the director of corporate responsibility at **AMD**, Tim Mohin, learned about it through Twitter.

In addition to believing the earth deserves respect, Twitter believes in treating employees with respect. **Glassdoor** ranked Twitter as one of best places to work. Glassdoor chief executive Robert Hohman explains, "What people say [at Twitter] is that their work has a global impact." Biz Stone responded by asserting that, "If you don't set the bar high, you're never going to get there."

Gabriela Hasbrun/Redux Pictures

Debt Ratio   **Decision Analysis**

An important business objective is gathering information to help assess a company's risk of failing to pay its debts. Companies finance their assets with either liabilities or equity. A company that finances a relatively larger portion of its assets with liabilities is said to have higher *financial leverage*. Higher financial leverage involves greater risk because liabilities must be repaid and often require regular interest payments (equity financing does not). One measure to assess the risk associated with liabilities is the **debt ratio**, seen in Exhibit 2.17.

A2

Compute the debt ratio and describe its use in analyzing financial condition.

$$\text{Debt ratio} = \frac{\text{Total liabilities}}{\text{Total assets}}$$

EXHIBIT 2.17

Debt Ratio

To apply the debt ratio, let's look at **Skechers**'s liabilities and assets. Skechers designs, markets, and sells footwear for men, women, and children. Exhibit 2.18 reports its debt ratio at each year-end from 2010 to 2014.

Point: Compare the equity amount to the liability amount to assess the extent of owner versus nonowner financing.

EXHIBIT 2.18

Computation and Analysis of Debt Ratio

$ in millions	2014	2013	2012	2011	2010
Total liabilities	$ 541	$ 429	$ 421	$ 389	$ 359
Total assets.	$1,675	$1,409	$1,340	$1,282	$1,305
Debt ratio	**0.32**	**0.30**	**0.31**	**0.30**	**0.28**
Industry debt ratio.	0.49	0.47	0.46	0.47	0.49

Skechers's debt ratio ranges from a low of 0.28 to a high of 0.32—also, see graph in margin. Its ratio is lower than the industry norm, suggesting a lower than average risk from financial leverage. So, is financial leverage good or bad for Skechers? The answer: If Skechers is making more money with this debt than it is paying the lenders, then it is successfully borrowing money to make more money. A company's use of debt can quickly turn unprofitable if its return from that money drops below the rate it is paying lenders.

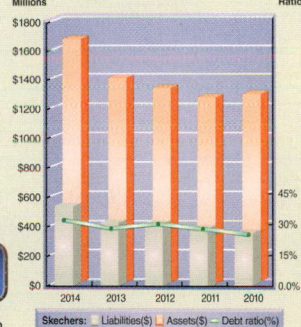

■ **Decision Maker**

Investor   You consider buying stock in **Converse**. As part of your analysis, you compute its debt ratio for 2013, 2014, and 2015 as: 0.35, 0.74, and 0.94, respectively. Based on the debt ratio, is Converse a low-risk investment? Has the risk of buying Converse stock changed over this period? (The industry debt ratio averages 0.40.)
■   [Answers follow the chapter's Summary.]

(This problem extends the Comprehensive Need-To-Know of Chapter 1.) After several months of planning, Jasmine Worthy started a haircutting business called Expressions. The following events occurred during its first month.

NEED-TO-KNOW 2-5

COMPREHENSIVE

a. On August 1, Worthy invested $3,000 cash and $15,000 of equipment in Expressions in exchange for common stock.
b. On August 2, Expressions paid $600 cash for furniture for the shop.
c. On August 3, Expressions paid $500 cash to rent space in a strip mall for August.
d. On August 4, it purchased $1,200 of equipment on credit for the shop (using a long-term note payable).
e. On August 5, Expressions opened for business. Cash received from haircutting services in the first week and a half of business (ended August 15) was $825.
f. On August 15, it provided $100 of haircutting services on account.
g. On August 17, it received a $100 check for services previously rendered on account.
h. On August 17, it paid $125 to an assistant for hours worked during the grand opening.
i. Cash received from services provided during the second half of August was $930.

j. On August 31, it paid a $400 installment toward principal on the note payable entered into on August 4.

k. On August 31, it paid $900 cash in dividends to Worthy (sole shareholder).

Required

1. Open the following ledger accounts in balance column format (account numbers are in parentheses): Cash (101); Accounts Receivable (102); Furniture (161); Store Equipment (165); Note Payable (240); Common Stock (307); Dividends (319); Haircutting Services Revenue (403); Wages Expense (623); and Rent Expense (640). Prepare general journal entries for the transactions.

2. Post the journal entries from part 1 to the ledger accounts.

3. Prepare a trial balance as of August 31.

4. Prepare an income statement for August.

5. Prepare a statement of retained earnings for August.

6. Prepare a balance sheet as of August 31.

7. Determine the debt ratio as of August 31.

Extended Analysis

8. In the coming months, Expressions will experience a greater variety of business transactions. Identify which accounts are debited and which are credited for the following transactions. (*Hint:* We must use some accounts not opened in part 1.)

   a. Purchase supplies with cash.

   b. Pay cash for future insurance coverage.

   c. Receive cash for services to be provided in the future.

   d. Purchase supplies on account.

PLANNING THE SOLUTION

- Analyze each transaction and use the debit and credit rules to prepare a journal entry for each.
- Post each debit and each credit from journal entries to their ledger accounts and cross-reference each amount in the posting reference (PR) columns of the journal and ledger.
- Compute each account balance and list the accounts with their balances on a trial balance.
- Verify that total debits in the trial balance equal total credits.
- To prepare the income statement, identify revenues and expenses. List those items on the statement, compute the difference, and label the result as *net income* or *net loss*.
- Use information in the ledger to prepare the statement of retained earnings.
- Use information in the ledger to prepare the balance sheet.
- Compute the debt ratio by dividing total liabilities by total assets.
- Analyze the future transactions to identify the accounts affected and apply debit and credit rules.

SOLUTION

1. General journal entries:

General Journal   _ □ X

Page 1

Date	Account Titles and Explanation	PR	Debit	Credit
Aug. 1	Cash	101	3,000	
	Store Equipment	165	15,000	
	Common Stock	307		18,000
	Owner's investment in exchange for stock.			
2	Furniture	161	600	
	Cash	101		600
	Purchased furniture for cash.			
3	Rent Expense	640	500	
	Cash	101		500
	Paid rent for August.			
4	Store Equipment	165	1,200	
	Note Payable	240		1,200
	Purchased additional equipment on credit.			

[continued on next page]

[continued from previous page]

15	Cash	101	825	
	Haircutting Services Revenue	403		825
	Cash receipts from first half of August.			
15	Accounts Receivable	102	100	
	Haircutting Services Revenue	403		100
	To record revenue for services provided on account.			
17	Cash	101	100	
	Accounts Receivable	102		100
	To record cash received as payment on account.			
17	Wages Expense	623	125	
	Cash	101		125
	Paid wages to assistant.			
31	Cash	101	930	
	Haircutting Services Revenue	403		930
	Cash receipts from second half of August.			
31	Note Payable	240	400	
	Cash	101		400
	Paid an installment on the note payable.			
31	Dividends	319	900	
	Cash	101		900
	Paid cash for dividends.			

2. Post journal entries from part 1 to the ledger accounts:

General Ledger

Cash   Account No. 101

Date	PR	Debit	Credit	Balance
Aug. 1	G1	3,000		3,000
2	G1		600	2,400
3	G1		500	1,900
15	G1	825		2,725
17	G1	100		2,825
17	G1		125	2,700
31	G1	930		3,630
31	G1		400	3,230
31	G1		900	2,330

Accounts Receivable   Account No. 102

Date	PR	Debit	Credit	Balance
Aug. 15	G1	100		100
17	G1		100	0

Furniture   Account No. 161

Date	PR	Debit	Credit	Balance
Aug. 2	G1	600		600

Store Equipment   Account No. 165

Date	PR	Debit	Credit	Balance
Aug. 1	G1	15,000		15,000
4	G1	1,200		16,200

Note Payable   Account No. 240

Date	PR	Debit	Credit	Balance
Aug. 4	G1		1,200	1,200
31	G1	400		800

Common Stock   Account No. 307

Date	PR	Debit	Credit	Balance
Aug. 1	G1		18,000	18,000

Dividends   Account No. 319

Date	PR	Debit	Credit	Balance
Aug. 31	G1	900		900

Haircutting Services Revenue   Account No. 403

Date	PR	Debit	Credit	Balance
Aug. 15	G1		825	825
15	G1		100	925
31	G1		930	1,855

Wages Expense   Account No. 623

Date	PR	Debit	Credit	Balance
Aug. 17	G1	125		125

Rent Expense   Account No. 640

Date	PR	Debit	Credit	Balance
Aug. 3	G1	500		500

3. Prepare a trial balance from the ledger:

EXPRESSIONS
Trial Balance
August 31

	Debit	Credit
Cash	$ 2,330	
Accounts receivable	0	
Furniture	600	
Store equipment	16,200	
Note payable		$ 800
Common stock		18,000
Dividends	900	
Haircutting services revenue		1,855
Wages expense	125	
Rent expense	500	
Totals	$20,655	$20,655

4.

EXPRESSIONS
Income Statement
For Month Ended August 31

Revenues		
Haircutting services revenue		$1,855
Operating expenses		
Rent expense	$500	
Wages expense	125	
Total operating expenses		625
Net income		$1,230

5.

EXPRESSIONS
Statement of Retained Earnings
For Month Ended August 31

Retained earnings, August 1................	$ 0
Plus: Net income......................	1,230
	1,230
Less: Cash dividends	900
Retained earnings, August 31..............	$ 330

6.

EXPRESSIONS
Balance Sheet
August 31

Assets		Liabilities	
Cash	$ 2,330	Note payable	$ 800
Furniture	600	**Equity**	
Store equipment	16,200	Common stock	18,000
		Retained earnings	330
		Total equity....................	18,330
Total assets	$19,130	Total liabilities and equity	$19,130

7. Debt ratio $= \dfrac{\text{Total liabilities}}{\text{Total assets}} = \dfrac{\$800}{\$19{,}130} = \underline{\underline{\textbf{4.18\%}}}$

8a. Supplies *debited*
      Cash *credited*

8b. Prepaid Insurance *debited*
      Cash *credited*

8c. Cash *debited*
      Unearned Services Revenue *credited*

8d. Supplies *debited*
      Accounts Payable *credited*

Summary

C1 **Explain the steps in processing transactions and the role of source documents.** The accounting process identifies business transactions and events, analyzes and records their effects, and summarizes and prepares information useful in making decisions. Transactions and events are the starting points in the accounting process. Source documents identify and describe transactions and events, and provide objective and reliable evidence. Examples are sales tickets, checks, purchase orders, bills, and bank statements. The effects of transactions and events are recorded in journals. Posting along with a trial balance helps summarize and classify these effects.

C2 **Describe an account and its use in recording transactions.** An account is a detailed record of increases and decreases in a specific asset, liability, equity, revenue, or expense. Information from accounts is analyzed, summarized, and presented in reports and financial statements.

C3 **Describe a ledger and a chart of accounts.** The ledger (or general ledger) is a record containing all accounts used by a company and their balances. It is referred to as the *books*. The chart of accounts is a list of all accounts and usually includes an identification number assigned to each account.

C4 **Define *debits* and *credits* and explain double-entry accounting.** *Debit* refers to left, and *credit* refers to right. Debits increase assets, expenses, and dividends, while credits decrease them. Credits increase liabilities, common stock, and revenues; debits decrease them. Double-entry accounting means each transaction affects at least two accounts and has at least one debit and one credit. The system for recording debits and credits follows from the accounting equation. The left side of an account is the normal balance for assets, dividends, and expenses, and the right side is the normal balance for liabilities, common stock, and revenues.

A1 **Analyze the impact of transactions on accounts and financial statements.** We analyze transactions using concepts of double-entry accounting. This analysis is performed by determining a transaction's effects on accounts. These effects are recorded in journals and posted to ledgers.

A2 **Compute the debt ratio and describe its use in analyzing financial condition.** A company's debt ratio is computed as total liabilities divided by total assets. It reveals how much of the assets are financed by creditor (nonowner) financing. The higher this ratio, the more risk a company faces because liabilities must be repaid at specific dates.

P1 **Record transactions in a journal and post entries to a ledger.** Transactions are recorded in a journal. Each entry in a journal is posted to the accounts in the ledger. This provides information that is used to produce financial statements. Balance column accounts are widely used and include columns for debits, credits, and the account balance.

P2 **Prepare and explain the use of a trial balance.** A trial balance is a list of accounts from the ledger showing their debit or credit balances in separate columns. The trial balance is a summary of the ledger's contents and is useful in preparing financial statements and in revealing recordkeeping errors.

P3 **Prepare financial statements from business transactions.** The balance sheet, the statement of retained earnings, the income statement, and the statement of cash flows use data from the trial balance (and other financial statements) for their preparation.

Guidance Answers to Decision Maker and Decision Ethics

Entrepreneur We can use the accounting equation (Assets = Liabilities + Equity) to help us identify risky customers to whom we would likely not want to extend credit. A balance sheet provides amounts for each of these key components. The lower a customer's equity is relative to liabilities, the less likely you would extend credit. A low equity means the business has little value that does not already have creditor claims to it.

Investor The debt ratio suggests the stock of **Converse** is of higher risk than normal and that this risk is rising. The average industry ratio of 0.40 further supports this conclusion. The 2015 debt ratio for Converse is twice the industry norm. Also, a debt ratio approaching 1.0 indicates little to no equity.

Key Terms

Account	Debtors	Posting
Account balance	Double-entry accounting	Posting reference (PR) column
Balance column account	General journal	Profitability
Chart of accounts	General ledger	Solvency
Compound journal entry	Journal	Source documents
Credit	Journalizing	T-account
Creditors	Ledger	Trial balance
Debit	Liquidity	Unearned revenue
Debt ratio	Market Prospects	

Multiple Choice Quiz   Answers at end of chapter

1. Amalia Company received its utility bill for the current period of $700 and immediately paid it. Its journal entry to record this transaction includes a
   a. Credit to Utility Expense for $700.
   b. Debit to Utility Expense for $700.
   c. Debit to Accounts Payable for $700.
   d. Debit to Cash for $700.
   e. Credit to Common Stock for $700.

2. On May 1, Mattingly Lawn Service collected $2,500 cash from a customer in advance of five months of lawn service. Mattingly's journal entry to record this transaction includes a
   a. Credit to Unearned Lawn Service Fees for $2,500.
   b. Debit to Lawn Service Fees Earned for $2,500.
   c. Credit to Cash for $2,500.
   d. Debit to Unearned Lawn Service Fees for $2,500.
   e. Credit to Common Stock for $2,500.

3. Liang Shue contributed $250,000 cash and land worth $500,000 to open her new business, Shue Consulting Corporation. Which of the following journal entries does Shue Consulting make to record this transaction?
   a. Cash Assets 750,000
          Common Stock   750,000
   b. Common Stock 750,000
          Assets   750,000

   c. Cash 250,000
      Land 500,000
          Common Stock   750,000
   d. Common Stock 750,000
          Cash   250,000
          Land   500,000

4. A trial balance prepared at year-end shows total credits exceed total debits by $765. This discrepancy could have been caused by
   a. An error in the general journal where a $765 increase in Accounts Payable was recorded as a $765 decrease in Accounts Payable.
   b. The ledger balance for Accounts Payable of $7,650 being entered in the trial balance as $765.
   c. A general journal error where a $765 increase in Accounts Receivable was recorded as a $765 increase in Cash.
   d. The ledger balance of $850 in Accounts Receivable was entered in the trial balance as $85.
   e. An error in recording a $765 increase in Cash as a credit.

5. Bain Company has total assets of $1,000,000, liabilities of $400,000, and equity of $600,000. What is its debt ratio (rounded to a whole percent)?
   a. 250%   c. 67%   e. 40%
   b. 167%   d. 150%

Icon denotes assignments that involve decision making.

Discussion Questions

1. Provide the names of two (a) asset accounts, (b) liability accounts, and (c) equity accounts.
2. What is the difference between a note payable and an account payable?
3. Discuss the steps in processing business transactions.
4. What kinds of transactions can be recorded in a general journal?
5. Are debits or credits typically listed first in general journal entries? Are the debits or the credits indented?
6. Should a transaction be recorded first in a journal or the ledger? Why?

7. If assets are valuable resources and asset accounts have debit balances, why do expense accounts also have debit balances?
8. Why does the recordkeeper prepare a trial balance?
9. If an incorrect amount is journalized and posted to the accounts, how should the error be corrected?
10. Identify the four financial statements of a business.
11. What information is reported in a balance sheet?
12. What information is reported in an income statement?
13. Why does the user of an income statement need to know the time period that it covers?

14. Define (*a*) *assets,* (*b*) *liabilities,* (*c*) *equity,* and (*d*) *net assets.*

15. Which financial statement is sometimes called the *statement of financial position?*

16. Review the **Apple** balance sheet in Appendix A. Identify three accounts on its **APPLE** balance sheet that carry debit balances and three accounts on its balance sheet that carry credit balances.

17. Review the **Google** balance sheet in Appendix A. Identify an asset with the **GOOGLE** word *receivable* in its account title and a liability with the word *payable* in its account title.

18. Review the **Samsung** balance sheet in Appendix A. Identify three current **Samsung** liabilities and three noncurrent liabilities in its balance sheet.

connect

QUICK STUDY

Identify the items from the following list that are likely to serve as source documents.

a. Sales ticket
b. Trial balance
c. Balance sheet
d. Telephone bill
e. Invoice from supplier
f. Company revenue account
g. Income statement
h. Bank statement
i. Prepaid insurance

QS 2-1
Identifying source documents   C1

Classify each of the following accounts as an asset (A), liability (L), or equity (EQ) account.

a. Cash
b. Prepaid Rent
c. Office Supplies
d. Prepaid Insurance
e. Office Equipment
f. Common Stock
g. Accounts Payable
h. Unearned Rent Revenue
i. Dividends

QS 2-2
Identifying financial statement accounts
C2

A chart of accounts is a list of all ledger accounts and an identification number for each. One example of a chart of accounts is near the end of the book. Using that chart, identify the following accounts as either an asset (A), liability (L), equity (EQ), revenue (R), or expense (E) account, along with its identification number.

a. Advertising Expense
b. Rent Revenue
c. Rent Receivable
d. Patents
e. Rent Payable
f. Furniture
g. Notes Payable
h. Common Stock
i. Utilities Expense

QS 2-3
Reading a chart of accounts
C3

Identify the normal balance (debit or credit) for each of the following accounts.

a. Fees Earned (Revenues)
b. Office Supplies
c. Dividends
d. Wages Expense
e. Accounts Receivable
f. Prepaid Rent
g. Wages Payable
h. Building
i. Common Stock

QS 2-4
Identifying normal balance
C4

Indicate whether a debit or credit *decreases* the normal balance of each of the following accounts.

a. Interest Payable
b. Service Revenue
c. Salaries Expense
d. Accounts Receivable
e. Common Stock
f. Prepaid Insurance
g. Buildings
h. Interest Revenue
i. Dividends
j. Unearned Revenue
k. Accounts Payable
l. Land

QS 2-5
Linking debit or credit with normal balance
C4

For each transaction, (1) analyze the transaction using the accounting equation, (2) record the transaction in journal entry form, and (3) post the entry using T-accounts to represent ledger accounts. Use the following (partial) chart of accounts—account numbers in parentheses: Cash (101); Accounts Receivable (106); Office Supplies (124); Trucks (153); Equipment (167); Accounts Payable (201); Unearned Landscaping Revenue (236); Common Stock (307); Dividends (319); Landscaping Revenue (403); Wages Expense (601), and Landscaping Expense (696).

a. On May 15, DeShawn Tyler opens a landscaping company called Elegant Lawns by investing $7,000 in cash along with equipment having a $3,000 value in exchange for common stock.

b. On May 21, Elegant Lawns purchases office supplies on credit for $500.

c. On May 25, Elegant Lawns receives $4,000 cash for performing landscaping services.

d. On May 30, Elegant Lawns receives $1,000 cash in advance of providing landscaping services to a customer.

QS 2-6
Analyzing transactions and preparing journal entries
P1

QS 2-7

Analyzing debit or credit by account

A1

Identify whether a debit or credit yields the indicated change for each of the following accounts.

a. To increase Land

b. To decrease Cash

c. To increase Fees Earned (Revenues)

d. To increase Office Expense

e. To decrease Unearned Revenue

f. To decrease Prepaid Rent

g. To increase Notes Payable

h. To decrease Accounts Receivable

i. To increase Common Stock

j. To increase Store Equipment

QS 2-8

Identifying a posting error

P2

A trial balance has total debits of $20,000 and total credits of $24,500. Which one of the following errors would create this imbalance? Explain.

a. A $2,250 debit to Utilities Expense in a journal entry is incorrectly posted to the ledger as a $2,250 credit, leaving the Utilities Expense account with a $3,000 debit balance.

b. A $4,500 debit to Salaries Expense in a journal entry is incorrectly posted to the ledger as a $4,500 credit, leaving the Salaries Expense account with a $750 debit balance.

c. A $2,250 credit to Consulting Fees Earned (Revenues) in a journal entry is incorrectly posted to the ledger as a $2,250 debit, leaving the Consulting Fees Earned account with a $6,300 credit balance.

d. A $2,250 debit posting to Accounts Receivable was posted mistakenly to Land.

e. A $4,500 debit posting to Equipment was posted mistakenly to Cash.

f. An entry debiting Cash and crediting Accounts Payable for $4,500 was mistakenly not posted.

QS 2-9

Classifying accounts in financial statements

P3

Indicate the financial statement on which each of the following items appears. Use I for income statement, E for statement of retained earnings, and B for balance sheet.

a. Services Revenue

b. Interest Payable

c. Accounts Receivable

d. Salaries Expense

e. Equipment

f. Prepaid Insurance

g. Buildings

h. Rental Revenue

i. Dividends

j. Office Supplies

k. Interest Expense

l. Insurance Expense

QS 2-10

International accounting standards   **C4**

Answer each of the following questions related to international accounting standards.

a. What type of journal entry system is applied when accounting follows IFRS?

b. Identify the number and usual titles of the financial statements prepared under IFRS.

c. How do differences in accounting controls and enforcement impact accounting reports prepared across different countries?

QS 2-11

Computing and using the debt ratio   **A2**

In a recent year's financial statements, **Home Depot** reported the following: Total liabilities = $30,624 million and Total assets = $39,946 million. Compute and interpret Home Depot's debt ratio (assume competitors average a 60.0% debt ratio).

EXERCISES

Exercise 2-1

Steps in analyzing and recording transactions

C1

Order the following steps in the accounting process that focus on analyzing and recording transactions.

_____ **a.** Prepare and analyze the trial balance.

_____ **b.** Analyze each transaction from source documents.

_____ **c.** Record relevant transactions in a journal.

_____ **d.** Post journal information to ledger accounts.

Exercise 2-2

Identifying and classifying accounts

C2

Enter the number for the item that best completes each of the descriptions below.

1. Asset   **3.** Account   **5.** Three

2. Equity   **4.** Liability

a. Balance sheet accounts are arranged into _____ general categories.

b. Common Stock and Dividends are examples of _____ accounts.

c. Accounts Payable, Unearned Revenue, and Note Payable are examples of _____ accounts.

d. Accounts Receivable, Prepaid Accounts, Supplies, and Land are examples of _____ accounts.

e. A(n) _____ is a record of increases and decreases in a specific asset, liability, equity, revenue, or expense item.

Enter the number for the item that best completes each of the descriptions below.

1. Chart   **2.** General ledger

a. A _____ of accounts is a list of all accounts a company uses.

b. The _____ is a record containing all accounts used by a company.

Exercise 2-3
Identifying a ledger and chart of accounts
C3

For each of the following (1) identify the type of account as an asset, liability, equity, revenue, or expense; (2) identify the normal balance of the account; and (3) enter *debit* (*Dr.*) or *credit* (*Cr.*) to identify the kind of entry that would increase the account balance.

a. Land
b. Cash
c. Legal Expense
d. Prepaid Insurance
e. Accounts Receivable
f. Dividends
g. License Fee Revenue
h. Unearned Revenue
i. Fees Earned
j. Equipment
k. Notes Payable
l. Common Stock

Exercise 2-4
Identifying type and normal balances of accounts
C4

GrowPro Co. bills a client $62,000 for services provided and agrees to accept the following three items in full payment: (1) $10,000 cash, (2) computer equipment worth $80,000, and (3) to assume responsibility for a $28,000 note payable related to the computer equipment. The entry GrowPro makes to record this transaction includes which one or more of the following?

a. $28,000 increase in a liability account
b. $10,000 increase in the Cash account
c. $10,000 increase in a revenue account
d. $62,000 increase in an asset account
e. $62,000 increase in a revenue account
f. $62,000 increase in an equity account

Exercise 2-5
Analyzing effects of transactions on accounts
A1

Use the information in each of the following separate cases to calculate the unknown amount.

a. Corentine Co. had $152,000 of accounts payable on September 30 and $132,500 on October 31. Total purchases on account during October were $281,000. Determine how much cash was paid on accounts payable during October.

b. On September 30, Valerian Co. had a $102,500 balance in Accounts Receivable. During October, the company collected $102,890 from its credit customers. The October 31 balance in Accounts Receivable was $89,000. Determine the amount of sales on account that occurred in October.

c. During October, Alameda Company had $102,500 of cash receipts and $103,150 of cash disbursements. The October 31 Cash balance was $18,600. Determine how much cash the company had at the close of business on September 30.

Exercise 2-6
Analyzing account entries and balances
A1

Prepare general journal entries for the following transactions of a new company called Pose-for-Pics. Use the following (partial) chart of accounts: Cash; Office Supplies; Prepaid Insurance; Photography Equipment; Common Stock; Photography Fees Earned; and Utilities Expense.

Aug. 1 Madison Harris, the owner, invested $6,500 cash and $33,500 of photography equipment in the company in exchange for common stock.
      2 The company paid $2,100 cash for an insurance policy covering the next 24 months.
      5 The company purchased office supplies for $880 cash.
     20 The company received $3,331 cash in photography fees earned.
     31 The company paid $675 cash for August utilities.

Exercise 2-7
Preparing general journal entries
P1

Use the information in Exercise 2-7 to prepare an August 31 trial balance for Pose-for-Pics. Begin by opening these T-accounts: Cash; Office Supplies; Prepaid Insurance; Photography Equipment; Common Stock; Photography Fees Earned; and Utilities Expense. Then, post the general journal entries to these T-accounts (which will serve as the ledger), and prepare the trial balance.

Exercise 2-8
Preparing T-accounts (ledger) and a trial balance P2

Prepare general journal entries to record the transactions below for Spade Company by using the following accounts: Cash; Accounts Receivable; Office Supplies; Office Equipment; Accounts Payable; Common Stock; Dividends; Fees Earned; and Rent Expense. Use the letters beside each transaction to identify entries. After recording the transactions, post them to T-accounts, which serves as the general ledger for this assignment. Determine the ending balance of each T-account.

a. Kacy Spade, owner, invested $100,750 cash in the company in exchange for common stock.
b. The company purchased office supplies for $1,250 cash.
c. The company purchased $10,050 of office equipment on credit.

Exercise 2-9
Recording effects of transactions in T-accounts
A1

Continued on next page . . .

d. The company received $15,500 cash as fees for services provided to a customer.

e. The company paid $10,050 cash to settle the payable for the office equipment purchased in transaction *c*.

f. The company billed a customer $2,700 as fees for services provided.

g. The company paid $1,225 cash for the monthly rent.

Check Cash ending balance, $94,850

h. The company collected $1,125 cash as partial payment for the account receivable created in transaction *f*.

i. The company paid $10,000 cash in dividends to the owner (sole shareholder).

Exercise 2-10
Preparing a trial balance
P2

After recording the transactions of Exercise 2-9 in T-accounts and calculating the balance of each account, prepare a trial balance. Use May 31, 2016, as its report date.

Exercise 2-11
Analyzing and journalizing expense transactions

A1 P1

Examine the following transactions and identify those that create expenses for Valdez Services. Prepare general journal entries to record those expense transactions and explain why the other transactions did not create expenses.

a. The company paid $12,200 cash for payment on a 16-month-old liability for office supplies.

b. The company paid $1,233 cash for the just-completed two-week salary of the receptionist.

c. The company paid $39,200 cash for equipment purchased.

d. The company paid $870 cash for this month's utilities.

e. The company paid $4,500 cash in dividends to the owner (sole shareholder).

Exercise 2-12
Analyzing and journalizing revenue transactions

A1 P1

Examine the following transactions and identify those that create revenues for Valdez Services, a company owned by Brina Valdez. Prepare general journal entries to record those revenue transactions and explain why the other transactions did not create revenues.

a. Brina Valdez invested $39,350 cash in the company in exchange for common stock.

b. The company provided $2,300 of services on credit.

c. The company provided services to a client and immediately received $875 cash.

d. The company received $10,200 cash from a client in payment for services to be provided next year.

e. The company received $3,500 cash from a client in partial payment of an account receivable.

f. The company borrowed $120,000 cash from the bank by signing a promissory note.

Exercise 2-13
Interpreting and describing transactions from T-accounts

A1

Assume the following T-accounts reflect Belle Co.'s general ledger and that seven transactions *a* through *g* are posted to them. Provide a short description of each transaction. Include the amounts in your descriptions.

Cash			
(a)	6,000	(b)	4,800
(e)	4,500	(c)	900
		(f)	1,600
		(g)	820

Office Supplies	
(c)	900
(d)	300

Prepaid Insurance	
(b)	4,800

Equipment	
(a)	7,600
(d)	9,700

Automobiles	
(a)	12,000

Accounts Payable			
(f)	1,600	(d)	10,000

Common Stock			
		(a)	25,600

Delivery Services Revenue			
		(e)	4,500

Gas and Oil Expense	
(g)	820

Exercise 2-14
Preparing general journal entries **P1**

Use information from the T-accounts in Exercise 2-13 to prepare general journal entries for each of the seven transactions *a* through *g*.

A corporation had the following assets and liabilities at the beginning and end of this year.

	Assets	Liabilities
Beginning of the year	$ 60,000	$20,000
End of the year	105,000	36,000

Determine the net income earned or net loss incurred by the business during the year for each of the following *separate* cases:

a. Owner made no investments in the business, and no dividends were paid during the year.

b. Owner made no investments in the business, but dividends were $1,250 cash per month.

c. No dividends were paid during the year, but the owner did invest an additional $55,000 cash in exchange for common stock.

d. Dividends were $1,250 cash per month, and the owner invested an additional $35,000 cash in exchange for common stock.

Carmen Camry operates a consulting firm called Help Today, which began operations on August 1. On August 31, the company's records show the following accounts and amounts for the month of August. Use this information to prepare an August income statement for the business.

Cash	$25,360	Consulting fees earned	$ 27,000
Accounts receivable.	22,360	Rent expense.	9,550
Office supplies	5,250	Salaries expense.	5,600
Land	44,000	Telephone expense	860
Office equipment.	20,000	Miscellaneous expenses.	520
Accounts payable.	10,500	Common stock	102,000
Dividends	6,000		

Use the information in Exercise 2-16 to prepare an August statement of retained earnings for Help Today. (The owner invested $102,000 cash in the company on August 1 in exchange for common stock.)

Use the information in Exercise 2-16 (if completed, use the solution to Exercise 2-17) to prepare an August 31 balance sheet for Help Today.

Compute the missing amount for each of the following separate companies *a* through *d*.

A	B (a)	C (b)	D (c)	E (d)
1				
2 Equity, December 31, 2015	$ 0	$ 0	$ 0	$ 0
3 Owner investments for stock during the year	110,000	?	87,000	210,000
4 Dividends during the year	?	(47,000)	(10,000)	(55,000)
5 Net income (loss) for the year	22,000	90,000	(4,000)	?
6 Equity, December 31, 2016	104,000	85,000	?	110,000
7				

Exercise 2-15
Computing net income
A1

Exercise 2-16
Preparing an income statement
C3 P3

Check Net income, $10,470

Exercise 2-17
Preparing a statement of retained earnings P3

Check End. Ret. Earnings, $4,470

Exercise 2-18
Preparing a balance sheet P3

Exercise 2-19
Analyzing changes in a company's equity
P3

Exercise 2-20

Identifying effects of posting errors on the trial balance

A1   P2

Posting errors are identified in the following table. In column (1), enter the amount of the difference between the two trial balance columns (debit and credit) due to the error. In column (2), identify the trial balance column (debit or credit) with the larger amount if they are not equal. In column (3), identify the account(s) affected by the error. In column (4), indicate the amount by which the account(s) in column (3) is under- or overstated. Item (a) is completed as an example.

	Description of Posting Error	(1) Difference between Debit and Credit Columns	(2) Column with the Larger Total	(3) Identify Account(s) Incorrectly Stated	(4) Amount that Account(s) Is Over- or Understated
a.	$3,600 debit to Rent Expense is posted as a $1,340 debit.	$2,260	Credit	Rent Expense	Rent Expense understated $2,260
b.	$6,500 credit to Cash is posted twice as two credits to Cash.				
c.	$10,900 debit to the Dividends account is debited to Common Stock.				
d.	$2,050 debit to Prepaid Insurance is posted as a debit to Insurance Expense.				
e.	$38,000 debit to Machinery is posted as a debit to Accounts Payable.				
f.	$5,850 credit to Services Revenue is posted as a $585 credit.				
g.	$1,390 debit to Store Supplies is not posted.				

Exercise 2-21

Analyzing a trial balance error

A1   P2

You are told the column totals in a trial balance are not equal. After careful analysis, you discover only one error. Specifically, a correctly journalized credit purchase of an automobile for $18,950 is posted from the journal to the ledger with an $18,950 debit to Automobiles and another $18,950 debit to Accounts Payable. The Automobiles account has a debit balance of $37,100 on the trial balance. Answer each of the following questions and compute the dollar amount of any misstatement.

a. Is the Debit column total of the trial balance overstated, understated, or correctly stated?

b. Is the Credit column total of the trial balance overstated, understated, or correctly stated?

c. Is the Automobiles account balance overstated, understated, or correctly stated in the trial balance?

d. Is the Accounts Payable account balance overstated, understated, or correctly stated in the trial balance?

e. If the Debit column total of the trial balance is $200,000 before correcting the error, what is the total of the Credit column before correction?

Exercise 2-22

Preparing a balance sheet following IFRS

P3

Heineken N.V., a global brewer domiciled in the Netherlands, reports the following balance sheet accounts for the year ended December 31, 2014 (euro in millions). Prepare the balance sheet for this company as of December 31, 2014, following the usual IFRS format.

Current liabilities	€ 8,532	Noncurrent liabilities	€12,846
Current assets	6,086	Noncurrent assets	28,744
Total equity	13,452		

Exercise 2-23

Interpreting the debt ratio and return on assets

A2

a. Calculate the debt ratio and the return on assets using the year-end information for each of the following six separate companies ($ in thousands).

Case	Assets	Liabilities	Average Assets	Net Income
Company 1	$90,500	$11,765	$100,000	$20,000
Company 2	64,000	46,720	40,000	3,800
Company 3	32,500	26,650	50,000	650
Company 4	147,000	55,860	200,000	21,000
Company 5	92,000	31,280	40,000	7,520
Company 6	104,500	52,250	80,000	12,000

Continued on next page . . .

b. Of the six companies, which business relies most heavily on creditor financing?

c. Of the six companies, which business relies most heavily on equity financing?

d. Which two companies indicate the greatest risk?

e. Which two companies earn the highest return on assets?

f. Which one company would investors likely prefer based on the risk-return relation?

connect

Karla Tanner opens a web consulting business called Linkworks and completes the following transactions in its first month of operations.

April	1	Tanner invests $80,000 cash along with office equipment valued at $26,000 in the company in exchange for common stock.
	2	The company prepaid $9,000 cash for twelve months' rent for office space. (*Hint:* Debit Prepaid Rent for $9,000.)
	3	The company made credit purchases for $8,000 in office equipment and $3,600 in office supplies. Payment is due within 10 days.
	6	The company completed services for a client and immediately received $4,000 cash.
	9	The company completed a $6,000 project for a client, who must pay within 30 days.
	13	The company paid $11,600 cash to settle the account payable created on April 3.
	19	The company paid $2,400 cash for the premium on a 12-month insurance policy. (*Hint:* Debit Prepaid Insurance for $2,400.)
	22	The company received $4,400 cash as partial payment for the work completed on April 9.
	25	The company completed work for another client for $2,890 on credit.
	28	The company paid $5,500 cash in dividends.
	29	The company purchased $600 of additional office supplies on credit.
	30	The company paid $435 cash for this month's utility bill.

Required

1. Prepare general journal entries to record these transactions (use account titles listed in part 2).

2. Open the following ledger accounts—their account numbers are in parentheses (use the balance column format): Cash (101); Accounts Receivable (106); Office Supplies (124); Prepaid Insurance (128); Prepaid Rent (131); Office Equipment (163); Accounts Payable (201); Common Stock (307); Dividends (319); Services Revenue (403); and Utilities Expense (690). Post journal entries from part 1 to the ledger accounts and enter the balance after each posting.

3. Prepare a trial balance as of April 30.

PROBLEM SET A

Problem 2-1A
Preparing and posting journal entries; preparing a trial balance

C3   C4   A1   P1   P2

Check   (2) Ending balances: Cash, $59,465; Accounts Receivable, $4,490; Accounts Payable, $600

(3) Total debits, $119,490

Aracel Engineering completed the following transactions in the month of June.

a. Jenna Aracel, the owner, invested $100,000 cash, office equipment with a value of $5,000, and $60,000 of drafting equipment to launch the company in exchange for common stock.

b. The company purchased land worth $49,000 for an office by paying $6,300 cash and signing a long-term note payable for $42,700.

c. The company purchased a portable building with $55,000 cash and moved it onto the land acquired in *b*.

d. The company paid $3,000 cash for the premium on an 18-month insurance policy.

e. The company completed and delivered a set of plans for a client and collected $6,200 cash.

f. The company purchased $20,000 of additional drafting equipment by paying $9,500 cash and signing a long-term note payable for $10,500.

g. The company completed $14,000 of engineering services for a client. This amount is to be received in 30 days.

h. The company purchased $1,150 of additional office equipment on credit.

i. The company completed engineering services for $22,000 on credit.

j. The company received a bill for rent of equipment that was used on a recently completed job. The $1,333 rent cost must be paid within 30 days.

k. The company collected $7,000 cash in partial payment from the client described in transaction *g*.

l. The company paid $1,200 cash for wages to a drafting assistant.

m. The company paid $1,150 cash to settle the account payable created in transaction *h*.

n. The company paid $925 cash for minor maintenance of its drafting equipment.

Problem 2-2A
Preparing and posting journal entries; preparing a trial balance

C3   C4   A1   P1   P2

o. The company paid $9,480 cash in dividends.

p. The company paid $1,200 cash for wages to a drafting assistant.

q. The company paid $2,500 cash for advertisements on the web during June.

Required

1. Prepare general journal entries to record these transactions (use the account titles listed in part 2).

2. Open the following ledger accounts—their account numbers are in parentheses (use the balance column format): Cash (101); Accounts Receivable (106); Prepaid Insurance (108); Office Equipment (163); Drafting Equipment (164); Building (170); Land (172); Accounts Payable (201); Notes Payable (250); Common Stock (307); Dividends (319); Engineering Fees Earned (402); Wages Expense (601); Equipment Rental Expense (602); Advertising Expense (603); and Repairs Expense (604). Post the journal entries from part 1 to the accounts and enter the balance after each posting.

3. Prepare a trial balance as of the end of June.

Problem 2-3A

Preparing and posting journal entries; preparing a trial balance

C3   C4   A1   P1   P2

Denzel Brooks opens a web consulting business called Venture Consultants and completes the following transactions in March.

March	1	Brooks invested $150,000 cash along with $22,000 in office equipment in the company in exchange for common stock.
	2	The company prepaid $6,000 cash for six months' rent for an office. (*Hint:* Debit Prepaid Rent for $6,000.)
	3	The company made credit purchases of office equipment for $3,000 and office supplies for $1,200. Payment is due within 10 days.
	6	The company completed services for a client and immediately received $4,000 cash.
	9	The company completed a $7,500 project for a client, who must pay within 30 days.
	12	The company paid $4,200 cash to settle the account payable created on March 3.
	19	The company paid $5,000 cash for the premium on a 12-month insurance policy. (*Hint:* Debit Prepaid Insurance for $5,000.)
	22	The company received $3,500 cash as partial payment for the work completed on March 9.
	25	The company completed work for another client for $3,820 on credit.
	29	The company paid $5,100 cash in dividends.
	30	The company purchased $600 of additional office supplies on credit.
	31	The company paid $500 cash for this month's utility bill.

Required

1. Prepare general journal entries to record these transactions (use the account titles listed in part 2).

2. Open the following ledger accounts—their account numbers are in parentheses (use the balance column format): Cash (101); Accounts Receivable (106); Office Supplies (124); Prepaid Insurance (128); Prepaid Rent (131); Office Equipment (163); Accounts Payable (201); Common Stock (307); Dividends (319); Services Revenue (403); and Utilities Expense (690). Post the journal entries from part 1 to the ledger accounts and enter the balance after each posting.

3. Prepare a trial balance as of the end of March.

Problem 2-4A

Recording transactions; posting to ledger; preparing a trial balance

C3   A1   P1   P2

Business transactions completed by Hannah Venedict during the month of September are as follows.

a. Venedict invested $60,000 cash along with office equipment valued at $25,000 in exchange for common stock of a new company named HV Consulting.

b. The company purchased land valued at $40,000 and a building valued at $160,000. The purchase is paid with $30,000 cash and a long-term note payable for $170,000.

c. The company purchased $2,000 of office supplies on credit.

d. Venedict invested her personal automobile in the company in exchange for more common stock. The automobile has a value of $16,500 and is to be used exclusively in the business.

e. The company purchased $5,600 of additional office equipment on credit.

f. The company paid $1,800 cash salary to an assistant.

g. The company provided services to a client and collected $8,000 cash.

h. The company paid $635 cash for this month's utilities.

i. The company paid $2,000 cash to settle the account payable created in transaction *c*.

j. The company purchased $20,300 of new office equipment by paying $20,300 cash.

k. The company completed $6,250 of services for a client, who must pay within 30 days.

l. The company paid $1,800 cash salary to an assistant.

m. The company received $4,000 cash in partial payment on the receivable created in transaction *k*.

n. The company paid $2,800 cash in dividends.

Required

1. Prepare general journal entries to record these transactions (use account titles listed in part 2).
2. Open the following ledger accounts—their account numbers are in parentheses (use the balance column format): Cash (101); Accounts Receivable (106); Office Supplies (108); Office Equipment (163); Automobiles (164); Building (170); Land (172); Accounts Payable (201); Notes Payable (250); Common Stock (307); Dividends (319); Fees Earned (402); Salaries Expense (601); and Utilities Expense (602). Post the journal entries from part 1 to the ledger accounts and enter the balance after each posting.
3. Prepare a trial balance as of the end of September.

Check (2) Ending balances: Cash, $12,665; Office Equipment, $50,900

(3) Trial balance totals, $291,350

The accounting records of Nettle Distribution show the following assets and liabilities as of December 31, 2015 and 2016.

Problem 2-5A
Computing net income from equity analysis, preparing a balance sheet, and computing the debt ratio

C2   A1   A2   P3

December 31	2015	2016
Cash.....................	$ 64,300	$ 15,640
Accounts receivable.........	26,240	19,390
Office supplies	3,160	1,960
Office equipment...........	44,000	44,000
Trucks....................	148,000	157,000
Building...................	0	80,000
Land	0	60,000
Accounts payable...........	3,500	33,500
Note payable	0	40,000

During 2016, Mr. Nettle, the owner, invested $35,000 additional cash in the business (in exchange for more common stock). Late in December 2016, the business purchased a small building and land valued at $140,000. This purchase required $100,000 cash plus a $40,000 note payable. Also, the business pays $3,000 cash per month for dividends.

Required

1. Prepare balance sheets for the business as of December 31, 2015 and 2016. (*Hint:* Report only total equity on the balance sheet and remember that total equity equals the difference between assets and liabilities.)
2. By comparing equity amounts from the balance sheets and using the additional information presented in this problem, compute the net income earned by the business in 2016.
3. Compute the 2016 year-end debt ratio (in percent and rounded to one decimal).

Check (2) Net income, $23,290

(3) Debt ratio, 19.4%

Yi Min started an engineering firm called Min Engineering. He began operations and completed seven transactions in May, which included his initial investment of $18,000 cash. After those seven transactions, the ledger included the following accounts with normal balances.

Problem 2-6A
Analyzing account balances and reconstructing transactions

C1   C3   A1   P2

Cash........................	$37,641
Office supplies	890
Prepaid insurance.............	4,600
Office equipment..............	12,900
Accounts payable..............	12,900
Common stock	18,000
Dividends....................	3,329
Engineering fees earned........	36,000
Rent expense	7,540

Required

1. Prepare a trial balance for this business as of the end of May.

Analysis Components

2. Analyze the accounts and their balances and prepare a list that describes each of the seven most likely transactions and their amounts.

3. Prepare a report of cash received and cash paid showing how the seven transactions in part 2 yield the $37,641 ending Cash balance.

PROBLEM SET B

Problem 2-1B

Preparing and posting journal entries; preparing a trial balance

Humble Management Services opens for business and completes these transactions in September.

Sept. 1   Henry Humble, the owner, invested $38,000 cash along with office equipment valued at $15,000 in the company in exchange for common stock.

2   The company prepaid $9,000 cash for 12 months' rent for office space. (*Hint:* Debit Prepaid Rent for $9,000.)

4   The company made credit purchases for $8,000 in office equipment and $2,400 in office supplies. Payment is due within 10 days.

8   The company completed work for a client and immediately received $3,280 cash.

12   The company completed a $15,400 project for a client, who must pay within 30 days.

13   The company paid $10,400 cash to settle the payable created on September 4.

19   The company paid $1,900 cash for the premium on an 18-month insurance policy. (*Hint:* Debit Prepaid Insurance for $1,900.)

22   The company received $7,700 cash as partial payment for the work completed on September 12.

24   The company completed work for another client for $2,100 on credit.

28   The company paid $5,300 cash in dividends.

29   The company purchased $550 of additional office supplies on credit.

30   The company paid $860 cash for this month's utility bill.

Required

1. Prepare general journal entries to record these transactions (use account titles listed in part 2).

2. Open the following ledger accounts—their account numbers are in parentheses (use the balance column format): Cash (101); Accounts Receivable (106); Office Supplies (124); Prepaid Insurance (128); Prepaid Rent (131); Office Equipment (163); Accounts Payable (201); Common Stock (307); Dividends (319); Services Revenue (401); and Utilities Expense (690). Post journal entries from part 1 to the ledger accounts and enter the balance after each posting.

3. Prepare a trial balance as of the end of September.

Problem 2-2B

Preparing and posting journal entries; preparing a trial balance

At the beginning of April, Bernadette Grechus launched a custom computer solutions company called Softworks. The company had the following transactions during April.

a. Bernadette Grechus invested $65,000 cash, office equipment with a value of $5,750, and $30,000 of computer equipment in the company in exchange for common stock.

b. The company purchased land worth $22,000 for an office by paying $5,000 cash and signing a long-term note payable for $17,000.

c. The company purchased a portable building with $34,500 cash and moved it onto the land acquired in *b*.

d. The company paid $5,000 cash for the premium on a two-year insurance policy.

e. The company provided services to a client and immediately collected $4,600 cash.

f. The company purchased $4,500 of additional computer equipment by paying $800 cash and signing a long-term note payable for $3,700.

g. The company completed $4,250 of services for a client. This amount is to be received within 30 days.

h. The company purchased $950 of additional office equipment on credit.

i. The company completed client services for $10,200 on credit.

j. The company received a bill for rent of a computer testing device that was used on a recently completed job. The $580 rent cost must be paid within 30 days.

k. The company collected $5,100 cash in partial payment from the client described in transaction *i*.

l. The company paid $1,800 cash for wages to an assistant.

m. The company paid $950 cash to settle the payable created in transaction *h*.

n. The company paid $608 cash for minor maintenance of the company's computer equipment.

o. The company paid $6,230 cash in dividends.

p. The company paid $1,800 cash for wages to an assistant.

q. The company paid $750 cash for advertisements on the web during April.

Required

1. Prepare general journal entries to record these transactions (use account titles listed in part 2).
2. Open the following ledger accounts—their account numbers are in parentheses (use the balance column format): Cash (101); Accounts Receivable (106); Prepaid Insurance (108); Office Equipment (163); Computer Equipment (164); Building (170); Land (172); Accounts Payable (201); Notes Payable (250); Common Stock (307); Dividends (319); Fees Earned (402); Wages Expense (601); Computer Rental Expense (602); Advertising Expense (603); and Repairs Expense (604). Post the journal entries from part 1 to the accounts and enter the balance after each posting.
3. Prepare a trial balance as of the end of April.

Check (2) Ending balances: Cash, $17,262; Accounts Receivable, $9,350; Accounts Payable, $580

(3) Trial balance totals, $141,080

Zucker Management Services opens for business and completes these transactions in November.

Problem 2-3B
Preparing and posting journal entries; preparing a trial balance

Nov. 1 Matt Zucker, the owner, invested $30,000 cash along with $15,000 of office equipment in the company in exchange for common stock.
2 The company prepaid $4,500 cash for six months' rent for an office. (*Hint:* Debit Prepaid Rent for $4,500.)
4 The company made credit purchases of office equipment for $2,500 and of office supplies for $600. Payment is due within 10 days.
8 The company completed work for a client and immediately received $3,400 cash.
12 The company completed a $10,200 project for a client, who must pay within 30 days.
13 The company paid $3,100 cash to settle the payable created on November 4.
19 The company paid $1,800 cash for the premium on a 24-month insurance policy.
22 The company received $5,200 cash as partial payment for the work completed on November 12.
24 The company completed work for another client for $1,750 on credit.
28 The company paid $5,300 cash in dividends.
29 The company purchased $249 of additional office supplies on credit.
30 The company paid $831 cash for this month's utility bill.

Required

1. Prepare general journal entries to record these transactions (use account titles listed in part 2).
2. Open the following ledger accounts—their account numbers are in parentheses (use the balance column format): Cash (101); Accounts Receivable (106); Office Supplies (124); Prepaid Insurance (128); Prepaid Rent (131); Office Equipment (163); Accounts Payable (201); Common Stock (307); Dividends (319); Services Revenue (403); and Utilities Expense (690). Post the journal entries from part 1 to the ledger accounts and enter the balance after each posting.
3. Prepare a trial balance as of the end of November.

Check (2) Ending balances: Cash, $23,069; Accounts Receivable, $6,750; Accounts Payable, $249

(3) Total debits, $60,599

Nuncio Consulting completed the following transactions during June.

Problem 2-4B
Recording transactions; posting to ledger; preparing a trial balance

a. Armand Nuncio, the owner, invested $35,000 cash along with office equipment valued at $11,000 in the new company in exchange for common stock.

b. The company purchased land valued at $7,500 and a building valued at $40,000. The purchase is paid with $15,000 cash and a long-term note payable for $32,500.

c. The company purchased $500 of office supplies on credit.

d. A. Nuncio invested his personal automobile in the company in exchange for more common stock. The automobile has a value of $8,000 and is to be used exclusively in the business.

e. The company purchased $1,200 of additional office equipment on credit.

f. The company paid $1,000 cash salary to an assistant.

g. The company provided services to a client and collected $3,200 cash.

h. The company paid $540 cash for this month's utilities.

i. The company paid $500 cash to settle the payable created in transaction *c*.

j. The company purchased $3,400 of new office equipment by paying $3,400 cash.

k. The company completed $4,200 of services for a client, who must pay within 30 days.

l. The company paid $1,000 cash salary to an assistant.

m. The company received $2,200 cash in partial payment on the receivable created in transaction *k*.

n. The company paid $1,100 cash in dividends.

Required

1. Prepare general journal entries to record these transactions (use account titles listed in part 2).

Check   (2) Ending balances: Cash, $17,860; Office Equipment, $15,600

2. Open the following ledger accounts—their account numbers are in parentheses (use the balance column format): Cash (101); Accounts Receivable (106); Office Supplies (108); Office Equipment (163); Automobiles (164); Building (170); Land (172); Accounts Payable (201); Notes Payable (250); Common Stock (307); Dividends (319); Fees Earned (402); Salaries Expense (601); and Utilities Expense (602). Post the journal entries from part 1 to the ledger accounts and enter the balance after each posting.

(3) Trial balance totals, $95,100

3. Prepare a trial balance as of the end of June.

Problem 2-5B

Computing net income from equity analysis, preparing a balance sheet, and computing the debt ratio

C2   A1   A2   P3

The accounting records of Tama Co. show the following assets and liabilities as of December 31, 2015 and 2016.

December 31	2015	2016
Cash	$20,000	$ 5,000
Accounts receivable.	35,000	25,000
Office supplies	8,000	13,500
Office equipment.	40,000	40,000
Machinery.	28,500	28,500
Building.	0	250,000
Land	0	50,000
Accounts payable.	4,000	12,000
Note payable	0	250,000

During 2016, Joe Tama, the owner, invested $15,000 additional cash in the business (in exchange for more common stock). Late in December 2016, the business purchased a small building and land valued at $300,000. This purchase required $50,000 cash plus a $250,000 note payable. Also, the business pays $250 cash per month for dividends.

Required

1. Prepare balance sheets for the business as of December 31, 2015 and 2016. (*Hint:* Report only total equity on the balance sheet and remember that total equity equals the difference between assets and liabilities.)

Check   (2) Net income, $10,500

2. By comparing equity amounts from the balance sheets and using the additional information from the problem, compute the net income earned by the business in 2016.

(3) Debt ratio, 63.6%

3. Compute the December 31, 2016, debt ratio (in percent and rounded to one decimal).

Problem 2-6B

Analyzing account balances and reconstructing transactions

C1   C3   A1   P2

Roshaun Gould started a web consulting firm called Gould Solutions. He began operations and completed seven transactions in April that resulted in the following accounts, which all have normal balances.

Cash	$19,982
Office supplies	760
Prepaid rent	1,800
Office equipment.	12,250
Accounts payable.	12,250
Common stock	15,000
Dividends	5,200
Consulting fees earned	20,400
Operating expenses.	7,658

Required

1. Prepare a trial balance for this business as of the end of April.

Check (1) Trial balance totals, $47,650

Analysis Components

2. Analyze the accounts and their balances and prepare a list that describes each of the seven most likely transactions and their amounts.

3. Prepare a report of cash received and cash paid showing how the seven transactions in part 2 yield the $19,982 ending Cash balance.

(3) Cash paid, $15,418

(This serial problem started in Chapter 1 and continues through most of the chapters. If the Chapter 1 segment was not completed, the problem can begin at this point. It is helpful, but not necessary, to use the Working Papers that accompany this book.)

SERIAL PROBLEM
Business Solutions
A1 P1 P2

SP 2 On October 1, 2016, Santana Rey launched a computer services company called **Business Solutions,** which provides consulting services, computer system installations, and custom program development. Rey adopts the calendar year for reporting purposes and expects to prepare the company's first set of financial statements on December 31, 2016. The company's initial chart of accounts follows.

Account	No.	Account	No.
Cash	101	Common Stock	307
Accounts Receivable	106	Dividends	319
Computer Supplies	126	Computer Services Revenue	403
Prepaid Insurance	128	Wages Expense	623
Prepaid Rent	131	Advertising Expense	655
Office Equipment	163	Mileage Expense	676
Computer Equipment	167	Miscellaneous Expenses	677
Accounts Payable	201	Repairs Expense—Computer	684

Required

1. Prepare journal entries to record each of the following transactions for Business Solutions.

Oct. 1 S. Rey invested $45,000 cash, a $20,000 computer system, and $8,000 of office equipment in the company in exchange for its common stock.
   2 The company paid $3,300 cash for four months' rent. (*Hint:* Debit Prepaid Rent for $3,300.)
   3 The company purchased $1,420 of computer supplies on credit from Harris Office Products.
   5 The company paid $2,220 cash for one year's premium on a property and liability insurance policy. (*Hint:* Debit Prepaid Insurance for $2,220.)
   6 The company billed Easy Leasing $4,800 for services performed in installing a new web server.
   8 The company paid $1,420 cash for the computer supplies purchased from Harris Office Products on October 3.
   10 The company hired Lyn Addie as a part-time assistant for $125 per day, as needed.
   12 The company billed Easy Leasing another $1,400 for services performed.
   15 The company received $4,800 cash from Easy Leasing as partial payment on its account.
   17 The company paid $805 cash to repair computer equipment that was damaged when moving it.
   20 The company paid $1,728 cash for advertisements published in the local newspaper.
   22 The company received $1,400 cash from Easy Leasing on its account.
   28 The company billed IFM Company $5,208 for services performed.
   31 The company paid $875 cash for Lyn Addie's wages for seven days' work.
   31 The company paid $3,600 cash in dividends.
Nov. 1 The company reimbursed S. Rey in cash for business automobile mileage allowance (Rey logged 1,000 miles at $0.32 per mile).
   2 The company received $4,633 cash from Liu Corporation for computer services performed.
   5 The company purchased computer supplies for $1,125 cash from Harris Office Products.
   8 The company billed Gomez Co. $5,668 for services performed.
   13 The company received notification from Alex's Engineering Co. that Business Solutions's bid of $3,950 for an upcoming project was accepted.
   18 The company received $2,208 cash from IFM Company as partial payment of the October 28 bill.
   22 The company donated $250 cash to the United Way in the company's name.

Continued on next page . . .

24   The company completed work for Alex's Engineering Co. and sent Alex's a bill for $3,950.

25   The company sent another bill to IFM Company for the past-due amount of $3,000.

28   The company reimbursed S. Rey in cash for business automobile mileage (1,200 miles at $0.32 per mile).

30   The company paid $1,750 cash for Lyn Addie's wages for 14 days' work.

30   The company paid $2,000 cash in dividends.

Check   (2) Cash, Nov. 30 bal., $38,264

       (3) Trial bal. totals, $98,659

2. Open ledger accounts (in balance column format) and post the journal entries from part 1 to them.

3. Prepare a trial balance as of the end of November.

GENERAL LEDGER PROBLEMS

Available in Connect

Using transactions from the following assignments, prepare journal entries for each transaction and identify the financial statement impact of each entry. The financial statements are automatically generated based on the journal entries recorded.

GL 2-1 Transactions from the FastForward illustration in this chapter

GL 2-2 Based on Exercise 2-9

GL 2-3 Based on Exercise 2-12

GL 2-4 Based on Problem 2-1A

Using transactions from the following assignments, record journal entries, create financial statements, and assess the impact of each transaction on financial statements.

GL 2-5 Based on Problem 2-2A

GL 2-6 Based on Problem 2-3A

GL 2-7 Based on Problem 2-4A

GL 2-8 Based on the Serial Problem SP 2

Beyond the Numbers

REPORTING IN ACTION

A1   A2

APPLE

BTN 2-1   Refer to **Apple**'s financial statements in Appendix A for the following questions.

Required

1. What amount of total liabilities does it report for each of the fiscal years ended September 27, 2014, and September 28, 2013?

2. What amount of total assets does it report for each of the fiscal years ended September 27, 2014, and September 28, 2013?

3. Compute its debt ratio for each of the fiscal years ended September 27, 2014, and September 28, 2013. (Report ratio in percent and round it to one decimal.)

4. In which fiscal year did it employ more financial leverage (September 27, 2014, or September 28, 2013)? Explain.

Fast Forward

5. Access its financial statements (10-K report) for a fiscal year ending after September 27, 2014, from its website (**Apple.com**) or the SEC's EDGAR database (**www.SEC.gov**). Recompute its debt ratio for any subsequent year's data and compare it with the debt ratio for 2014 and 2013.

COMPARATIVE ANALYSIS

A1   A2

APPLE
GOOGLE

BTN 2-2   Key comparative figures for **Apple** and **Google** follow.

$ millions	Apple Current Year	Apple Prior Year	Google Current Year	Google Prior Year
Total liabilities	$120,292	$ 83,451	$ 26,633	$ 23,611
Total assets	231,839	207,000	131,133	110,920

1. What is the debt ratio for Apple in the current year and for the prior year?
2. What is the debt ratio for Google in the current year and for the prior year?
3. Which of the two companies has the higher degree of financial leverage? What does this imply?

BTN 2-3   Assume that you are a cashier and your manager requires that you immediately enter each sale when it occurs. Recently, lunch hour traffic has increased and the assistant manager asks you to avoid delays by taking customers' cash and making change without entering sales. The assistant manager says she will add up cash and enter sales after lunch. She says that, in this way, customers will be happy and the register record will always match the cash amount when the manager arrives at three o'clock.

The advantage to the process proposed by the assistant manager includes improved customer service, fewer delays, and less work for you. The disadvantage is that the assistant manager could steal cash by simply recording less sales than the cash received and then pocketing the excess cash. You decide to reject her suggestion without the manager's approval and you decide to confront her on the ethics of her suggestion.

Required

Propose and evaluate two other courses of action you might consider, and explain why.

ETHICS CHALLENGE

C1

BTN 2-4   Lila Corentine is an aspiring entrepreneur and your friend. She is having difficulty understanding the purposes of financial statements and how they fit together across time.

Required

Write a one-page memorandum to Corentine explaining the purposes of the four financial statements and how they are linked across time.

COMMUNICATING IN PRACTICE

C1   C2   A1   P3

BTN 2-5   Access EDGAR online (www.SEC.gov) and locate the 2014 10-K report of Amazon.com (ticker AMZN) filed on January 30, 2015. Review its financial statements reported for years ended 2014, 2013, and 2012 to answer the following questions.

Required

1. What are the amounts of its net income or net loss reported for each of these three years?
2. Do Amazon's operating activities provide cash or use cash for each of these three years?
3. If Amazon has a 2014 net loss of $(241) million and 2014 operating cash flows of $6,842 million, how is it possible that its cash balance at December 31, 2014, increases by only $5,899 million relative to its balance at December 31, 2013?

TAKING IT TO THE NET

A1

BTN 2-6   The expanded accounting equation consists of assets, liabilities, common stock, dividends, revenues, and expenses. It can be used to reveal insights into changes in a company's financial position.

Required

1. Form *learning teams* of six (or more) members. Each team member must select one of the six components and each team must have at least one expert on each component: (*a*) assets, (*b*) liabilities, (*c*) common stock, (*d*) dividends, (*e*) revenues, and (*f*) expenses.
2. Form *expert teams* of individuals who selected the same component in part 1. Expert teams are to draft a report that each expert will present to his or her learning team addressing the following:
   a. Identify for its component the (i) increase and decrease side of the account and (ii) normal balance side of the account.
   b. Describe a transaction, with amounts, that increases its component.
   c. Using the transaction and amounts in (b), verify the equality of the accounting equation and then explain any effects on the income statement and statement of cash flows.
   d. Describe a transaction, with amounts, that decreases its component.
   e. Using the transaction and amounts in (d), verify the equality of the accounting equation and then explain any effects on the income statement and statement of cash flows.
3. Each expert should return to his/her learning team. In rotation, each member presents his/her expert team's report to the learning team. Team discussion is encouraged.

TEAMWORK IN ACTION

C1   C2   C4   A1

ENTREPRENEURIAL DECISION

A1   A2   P3

BTN 2-7   Assume Jack Dorsey of Twitter (twitter.com) plans on expanding his business to accommodate more specialized lines of professional listings. He is considering financing the expansion in one of two ways: (1) contributing more of his own funds to the business or (2) borrowing the funds from a bank.

Required

Identify at least two issues that Jack should consider when trying to decide on the method for financing the expansion.

ENTREPRENEURIAL DECISION

A1   A2   P3

BTN 2-8   Angel Martin is a young entrepreneur who operates Martin Music Services, offering singing lessons and instruction on musical instruments. Martin wishes to expand but needs a $30,000 loan. The bank requests that Martin prepare a balance sheet and key financial ratios. Martin has not kept formal records but is able to provide the following accounts and their amounts as of December 31, 2016.

Cash	$ 3,600	Accounts Receivable	$ 9,600	Prepaid Insurance.	$ 1,500
Prepaid Rent.	9,400	Store Supplies	6,600	Equipment	50,000
Accounts Payable.	2,200	Unearned Lesson Fees. . .	15,600	Total Equity*	62,900
Annual Net Income . . .	40,000				

* The total equity amount reflects all owner investments, dividends, revenues, and expenses as of December 31, 2016.

Required

1. Prepare a balance sheet as of December 31, 2016, for Martin Music Services. (Report only the total equity amount on the balance sheet.)
2. Compute Martin's debt ratio and its return on assets (the latter ratio is defined in Chapter 1). Assume average assets equal its ending balance.
3. Do you believe the prospects of a $30,000 bank loan are good? Why or why not?

HITTING THE ROAD

C1

BTN 2-9   Obtain a recent copy of the most prominent newspaper distributed in your area. Research the classified section and prepare a report answering the following questions (attach relevant classified clippings to your report). Alternatively, you may want to search the web for the required information. One suitable website is CareerOneStop (www.CareerOneStop.org). For documentation, you should print copies of websites accessed.

1. Identify the number of listings for accounting positions and the various accounting job titles.
2. Identify the number of listings for other job titles, with examples, that require or prefer accounting knowledge/experience but are not specifically accounting positions.
3. Specify the salary range for the accounting and accounting-related positions if provided.
4. Indicate the job that appeals to you, the reason for its appeal, and its requirements.

GLOBAL DECISION

A2

Samsung
APPLE
GOOGLE

BTN 2-10   Samsung (www.Samsung.com) is a market leader in high-tech electronics manufacturing and digital media, and it competes to some extent with both Apple and Google. Key financial ratios for the current fiscal year follow.

Key Figure	Samsung	Apple	Google
Return on assets	10.5%	18.0%	11.9%
Debt ratio	27.1%	51.9%	20.3%

Required

1. Which company is most profitable according to its return on assets?
2. Which company is most risky according to the debt ratio?
3. Which company deserves increased investment based on a joint analysis of return on assets and the debt ratio? Explain.

ANSWERS TO MULTIPLE CHOICE QUIZ

1. b; debit Utility Expense for $700 and credit Cash for $700.

2. a; debit Cash for $2,500 and credit Unearned Lawn Service Fees for $2,500.

3. c; debit Cash for $250,000, debit Land for $500,000, and credit Common Stock for $750,000.

4. d

5. e; Debt ratio = $400,000/$1,000,000 = 40%

0.19   18.94   1.1   2.33%   +0.45
0.28   19.44   0.5   -5.22%   -1.56
0.62   24.87   2.   6.13%   12.33

chapter 3

Adjusting Accounts for Financial Statements

Chapter Preview

PERIODIC REPORTING AND ADJUSTING ACCOUNTS

C1 Timing and accruals

P1 Accounting adjustments

Prepaid expenses

Unearned revenues

Accrued expenses

Accrued revenues

P2 Adjusted trial balance

FINANCIAL STATEMENTS AND CLOSING PROCESS

P3 Preparing financial statements

P4 Closing entries

P5 Post-closing trial balance

C2 Accounting cycle

CLASSIFIED BALANCE SHEET AND ANALYSIS

C3 Classified balance sheet— Structure and categories

A1 Profit margin analysis

A2 Current ratio analysis

Learning Objectives

CONCEPTUAL

C1 Explain the importance of periodic reporting and the role of accrual accounting.

C2 Identify steps in the accounting cycle.

C3 Explain and prepare a classified balance sheet.

ANALYTICAL

A1 Compute profit margin and describe its use in analyzing company performance.

A2 Compute the current ratio and describe what it reveals about a company's financial condition.

PROCEDURAL

P1 Prepare and explain adjusting entries.

P2 Explain and prepare an adjusted trial balance.

P3 Prepare financial statements from an adjusted trial balance.

P4 Describe and prepare closing entries.

P5 Explain and prepare a post-closing trial balance.

P6 *Appendix 3A*—Explain the alternatives in accounting for prepaids.

P7 *Appendix 3B*—Prepare a work sheet and explain its usefulness.

P8 *Appendix 3C*—Prepare reversing entries and explain their purpose.

From the Get GoPro

"We make it easy for passionate people around the world to capture and share life experiences" — **NICK WOODMAN**

SAN MATEO, CA—"Think it. See it. Do it. This is your life. . . GoPro." These words of advice are from Nick Woodman, founder and CEO of **GoPro, Inc.** (**GoPro.com**). Nick developed the first GoPro camera while he was planning a 5-month surfing trip to Indonesia and Australia. He explained that he developed the first GoPro camera, a simple waterproof wrist camera, because there are so many "people in the world that want to capture themselves doing what they want, what they love to do, their passions and interests." The simple wrist camera evolved into the best-selling "action camera" used by skydivers, snowboarders, surfers, skateboarders, deep-sea divers, and other adventure seekers.

In the process of growing his company, Nick learned the details of preparing and interpreting financial statements. Nick explains that he set up an accounting system shortly after launching his business and beginning to sell his GoPro cameras. He recognized the importance of accounting for all business activities including cash, revenue, receivables, and payables. Further, he had to learn about the deferral and accrual of revenues and expenses as his business grew and he became less involved in

GoPro, Inc.
NASDAQ: GPRO

$7 billion valuation
Founded 2002
$1.4 bil. annual sales

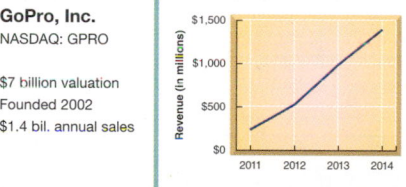

day-to-day transactions. GoPro reported $1,394 million of revenue and $128 million of income in 2014.

($ millions)	2012	2013	2014
Net income	$ 36	$ 61	$128
Research & development....	36	74	152
Total assests	247	440	918

Nick is "stoked" about the prospect of further enhancements to his business and his GoPro cameras. Each year, Nick says it is his goal to make "sizable investments in R&D (research and development) for GoPro's future." This includes positioning his company for the future of "virtual reality" cameras. Nick understands that he cannot position GoPro for the future if he cannot accurately account for and manage

expenses. Thus, he stresses the importance of managing costs by making smart "strategic investments."

In addition to making smart investments, Nick controls costs by using free social media whenever he can. Nick says the company's "**Facebook** followers now total more than 8 million and on **YouTube** GoPro subscribers are up . . . to roughly 3 million. **Twitter** followers are up . . . to 1.4 million and [we are] on **Instagram** with more than 4.5 million followers." Although Facebook friends and Twitter followers are not recorded on financial statements, the cost savings are real and so are the potential revenue streams.

Nick emphasizes that his financial house must be in order for GoPro to continue to do what it does best. Moreover, properly managing his revenues and expenses, both current and deferrals, will help ensure GoPro can continue to provide, insists Nick, the "world's most versatile cameras . . . that enable you to share your life through incredible photos and videos."

Sources: *GoPro website,* January 2016; *SeekingAlpha,* April 2015; *Yahoo!,* January 2016; *CNBC,* June 2014; *Fortune,* October 2014; *GoPro 10-K Report,* April 2015

TIMING AND REPORTING

C1

Explain the importance of periodic reporting and the role of accrual accounting.

This section explains the reporting of accounting information at regular intervals and its impact for recording revenues and expenses.

The Accounting Period

The value of information is often linked to its timeliness. Useful information must reach decision makers frequently and promptly. To provide timely information, accounting systems prepare reports at regular intervals. This results in an accounting process impacted by the time

"Apple announces annual income of . . ."

period (or periodicity) assumption. The **time period assumption** presumes that an organization's activities can be divided into specific time periods such as a month, a three-month quarter, a six-month interval, or a year. Exhibit 3.1 shows various **accounting,** or *reporting,* **periods**. Most organizations use a year as their primary accounting period. Reports covering a one-year period are known as **annual financial statements**. Many organizations also prepare **interim financial statements** covering one, three, or six months.

EXHIBIT 3.1

Accounting Periods

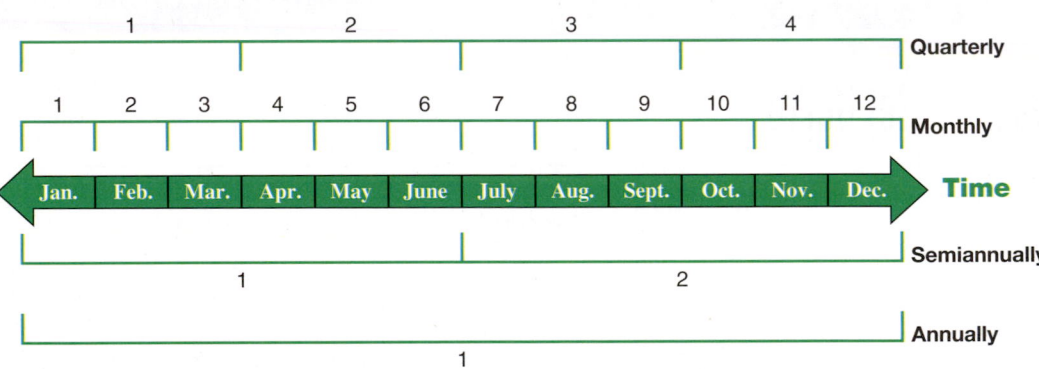

The annual reporting period is not always a calendar year ending on December 31. An organization can adopt a **fiscal year** consisting of any 12 consecutive months. It is also acceptable to adopt an annual reporting period of 52 weeks. For example, Gap's fiscal year consistently ends the final week of January or the first week of February each year.

Companies with little seasonal variation in sales often choose the calendar year as their fiscal year. **Facebook, Inc.,** uses calendar year reporting. However, the financial statements of **The Kellogg Company** (the company that controls characters such as Tony the Tiger, Snap! Crackle! Pop!, and Keebler Elf) reflect a fiscal year that ends on the Saturday nearest December 31. Companies experiencing seasonal variations in sales often choose a **natural business year** end, which is when sales activities are at their lowest level for the year. The natural business year for retailers such as **Walmart**, **Target**, and **Macy's** usually ends around January 31, after the holiday season.

C Flanigan/WireImage/Getty Images

Accrual Basis versus Cash Basis

After external transactions and events are recorded, several accounts require adjustments before their balances appear in financial statements. This need arises because internal transactions and events remain unrecorded.

Accrual basis accounting applies adjustments so that revenues are recognized when services and products are delivered, and expenses when incurred (matched with revenues). **Cash basis accounting** recognizes revenues when cash is received and records expenses when cash is paid. This means that cash basis net income is the difference between cash receipts and cash payments.

Cash basis accounting is *not* consistent with generally accepted accounting principles (neither U.S. GAAP nor IFRS). It is commonly held that accrual accounting better reflects business performance than information about cash receipts and payments. Accrual accounting also increases the *comparability* of financial statements from period to period. Yet, financial statements include both accrual-based and cash-based information.

To see the difference between these two systems, let's consider FastForward's Prepaid Insurance account. FastForward paid $2,400 for 24 months of insurance coverage that began on December 1, 2016. Accrual accounting requires that $100 of insurance expense be reported each month, from December 2016 through November 2018. (This means expenses are $100 in 2016, $1,200 in 2017, and $1,100 in 2018.) Exhibit 3.2 illustrates this allocation of insurance cost across these three years. Any unexpired premium is reported as a Prepaid Insurance asset on the accrual basis balance sheet.

EXHIBIT 3.2

Accrual Accounting for Allocating Prepaid Insurance to Expense

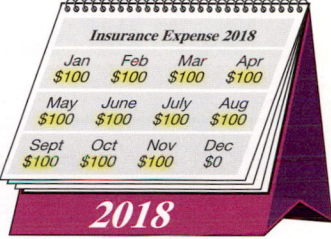

Point: Annual income statements for Exhibit 3.2 follow:

Accrual Basis	2016	2017	2018
Revenues	$ #	$ #	$ #
Insur. exp.....	$100	$1,200	$1,100

Alternatively, a cash basis income statement for December 2016 reports insurance expense of $2,400, as shown in Exhibit 3.3. The cash basis income statements for years 2017 and 2018 report no insurance expense. The cash basis balance sheet never reports an insurance asset because it is immediately expensed. This shows that cash basis income for 2016–2018 fails to match the cost of insurance with the insurance benefits received for those years and months.

EXHIBIT 3.3

Cash Accounting for Allocating Prepaid Insurance to Expense

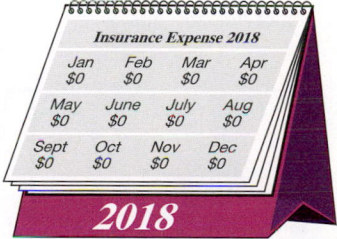

Point: Annual income statements for Exhibit 3.3 follow:

Cash Basis	2016	2017	2018
Revenues	$ #	$#	$#
Insur. exp.	$2,400	$0	$0

Recognizing Revenues and Expenses

We use the time period assumption to divide a company's activities into specific time periods, but not all activities are complete when financial statements are prepared. Thus, adjustments are required to get proper account balances.

We rely on two principles in the adjusting process: revenue recognition and expense recognition (the latter is often referred to as *matching*). Chapter 1 explained that the *revenue recognition principle* requires that revenue be recorded when a company provides services and products to customers. A major goal of the adjusting process is to have revenue recognized (reported) in the time period when those services and products are delivered. The **expense recognition (or matching) principle** aims to record expenses in the same accounting period as the revenues that are recognized as a result of those expenses.

Matching expenses with revenues often requires us to predict certain events. When we use financial statements, we must understand that they require estimates. **Walt Disney**'s annual report explains that its production costs from movies, such as *Star Wars: Episode VII* and *Frozen*, are matched to revenues based on a ratio of current revenues from the movie divided by its predicted total revenues.

Point: Recording revenue early overstates current-period revenue and income; recording it late understates current-period revenue and income.

Point: Recording expense early overstates current-period expense and understates current-period income; recording it late understates current-period expense and overstates current-period income.

Fraud

Clawbacks from Accounting Fraud Former key executives at **Saba Software**, a cloud-based talent management system used by clients to hire, develop, and inspire workers, were charged with accounting fraud by the SEC when they falsified the company's revenue recognition to boost income. This alleged overstatement of income led to the reimbursement of millions of dollars to the company by the former CEO and former CFO. (For more details, see SEC release 2015-28.)

Marco Marchi/Getty Images

ADJUSTING ACCOUNTS

P1

Prepare and explain adjusting entries.

Adjusting accounts is a three-step process:

> **Step 1:** Determine what the current account balance *equals.*
>
> **Step 2:** Determine what the current account balance *should equal.*
>
> **Step 3:** Record an adjusting entry to get from step *1* to step *2*.

Framework for Adjustments

Adjustments are necessary for transactions and events that extend over more than one period. It is helpful to group adjustments by the timing of cash receipt or cash payment in relation to the recognition of the related revenues or expenses. Exhibit 3.4 identifies four types of adjustments.

EXHIBIT 3.4

Types of Adjustments

*For depreciation, the credit is to Accumulated Depreciation (contra asset).
†Exhibit assumes that prepaid expenses are initially recorded as assets and that unearned revenues are initially recorded as liabilities.

Point: Source documents provide information for most daily transactions, and in many businesses the recordkeepers record them. Adjustments require more knowledge and are usually handled by senior accounting professionals.

The upper half of this exhibit shows prepaid expenses (including depreciation) and unearned revenues, which reflect transactions when cash is paid or received *before* a related expense or revenue is recognized. They are also called *deferrals* because the recognition of an expense (or revenue) is *deferred* until after the related cash is paid (or received). The lower half of this exhibit shows accrued expenses and accrued revenues, which reflect transactions when cash is paid or received *after* a related expense or revenue is recognized. Adjusting entries are necessary for each of these so that revenues, expenses, assets, and liabilities are correctly reported. Specifically, an **adjusting entry** is made at the end of an accounting period to reflect a transaction or event that is not yet recorded. Each adjusting entry affects one or more income statement accounts *and* one or more balance sheet accounts (but never the Cash account). The four types of adjusting entries, and the financial statements impacted, are shown in the two right-most columns of Exhibit 3.4.

Prepaid (Deferred) Expenses

Prepaid expenses refer to items *paid for* in advance of receiving their benefits. Prepaid expenses are assets. When these assets are used, their costs become expenses. Adjusting entries for prepaids increase expenses and decrease assets as shown in the T-accounts of Exhibit 3.5. Such adjustments reflect transactions and events that use up prepaid expenses (including passage of time). To illustrate the accounting for prepaid expenses, we look at prepaid insurance, supplies, and depreciation. In each case we decrease an asset (balance sheet) account, and increase an expense (income statement) account.

EXHIBIT 3.5

Adjusting for Prepaid Expenses (decrease an asset and record an expense)

Prepaid Insurance   We use our three-step process for this and all accounting adjustments.

Step 1:   We determine that the current balance of FastForward's prepaid insurance is equal to its $2,400 payment for 24 months of insurance benefits that began on December 1, 2016.

Step 2:   With the passage of time, the benefits of the insurance gradually expire and a portion of the Prepaid Insurance asset becomes expense. For instance, one month's insurance coverage expires by December 31, 2016. This expense is $100, or 1/24 of $2,400, which leaves $2,300.

Step 3:   The adjusting entry to record this expense and reduce the asset, along with T-account postings, follows:

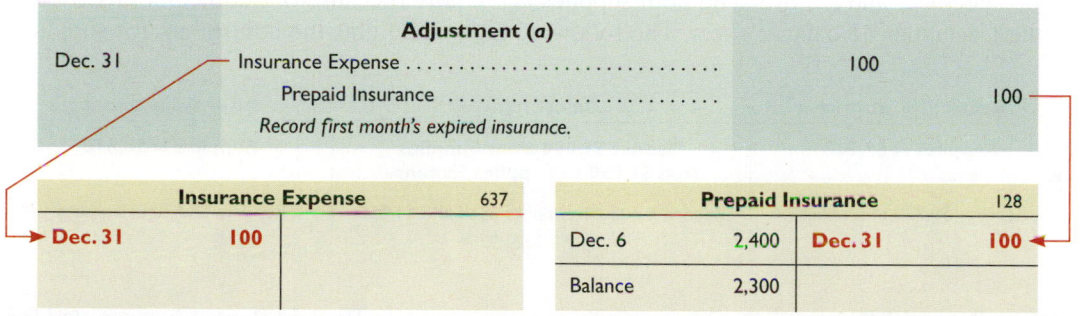

Assets = Liabilities + Equity
−100   −100

Explanation   After adjusting and posting, the $100 balance in Insurance Expense and the $2,300 balance in Prepaid Insurance are ready for reporting in financial statements. *Not* making the adjustment on or before December 31 would (1) understate expenses by $100 and overstate net income by $100 for the December income statement and (2) overstate both prepaid insurance (assets) and equity (because of net income) by $100 in the December 31 balance sheet. (Exhibit 3.2 showed that 2017's adjustments must transfer a total of $1,200 from Prepaid Insurance to Insurance Expense, and 2018's adjustments must transfer the remaining $1,100 to Insurance Expense.) The following table highlights the December 31, 2016, adjustment for prepaid insurance.

Point: Many companies record adjusting entries only at the end of each year because of the time and cost necessary.

Before Adjustment	Adjustment	After Adjustment
Prepaid Insurance = $2,400	**Deduct $100 from Prepaid Insurance Add $100 to Insurance Expense**	**Prepaid Insurance = $2,300**
Reports $2,400 policy for 24 months' coverage.	Record current month's $100 insurance expense and $100 reduction in prepaid amount.	Reports $2,300 in coverage for remaining 23 months.

Supplies   Supplies are a prepaid expense requiring adjustment.

Step 1:   FastForward purchased $9,720 of supplies in December and some of them were used during that same month. When financial statements are prepared at December 31, the cost of supplies used during December must be recognized.

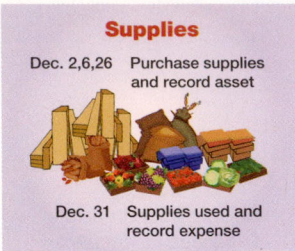

Supplies

Dec. 2,6,26   Purchase supplies
and record asset

Dec. 31   Supplies used and
record expense

Assets = Liabilities + Equity
−1,050   −1,050

Step 2:   When FastForward computes (takes physical count of) its remaining unused supplies at December 31, it finds $8,670 of supplies remaining of the $9,720 total supplies. The $1,050 difference between these two amounts is December's supplies expense.

Step 3:   The adjusting entry to record this expense and reduce the Supplies asset account, along with T-account postings, follows:

	Adjustment (b)	
Dec. 31	Supplies Expense	1,050
	Supplies	1,050
	Record supplies used.	

Supplies Expense		652
Dec. 31	**1,050**	

Supplies				126
Dec. 2	2,500	**Dec. 31**	**1,050**
6	7,100		
26	120		
Balance	8,670		

Explanation   The balance of the Supplies account is $8,670 after posting—equaling the cost of the remaining supplies. *Not* making the adjustment on or before December 31 would (1) understate expenses by $1,050 and overstate net income by $1,050 for the December income statement and (2) overstate both supplies and equity (because of net income) by $1,050 in the December 31 balance sheet. The following table highlights the adjustment for supplies.

Before Adjustment	Adjustment	After Adjustment
Supplies = $9,720	Deduct $1,050 from Supplies Add $1,050 to Supplies Expense	Supplies = $8,670
Reports $9,720 in supplies.	Record $1,050 in supplies used and $1,050 as supplies expense.	Reports $8,670 in supplies.

Point: We assume that prepaid and unearned items are recorded in balance sheet accounts. An alternative is to record them in income statement accounts; Appendix 3A discusses this alternative. The adjusted financial statements are identical.

Other Prepaid Expenses   Other prepaid expenses, such as Prepaid Rent, are accounted for exactly as Insurance and Supplies are. Some prepaid expenses are both paid for and fully used up within a single accounting period. One example is when a company pays monthly rent on the first day of each month. This payment creates a prepaid expense on the first day of each month that fully expires by the end of the month. In these special cases, we can record the cash paid with a debit to an expense account instead of an asset account. This practice is described more completely later in the chapter.

 Decision Maker

Investor   A small publishing company signs an aspiring Olympic gymnast to write a book. The company pays the gymnast $500,000 to sign plus future book royalties. A note to the company's financial statements says that "prepaid expenses include $500,000 in author signing fees to be matched against future expected sales." Is this accounting for the signing bonus acceptable? How does it affect your analysis? ■   [Answers follow the chapter's Summary.]

Point: Plant assets are also called *Plant & Equipment,* or *Property, Plant & Equipment.*

Point: Depreciation does not necessarily measure decline in market value.

Point: An asset's expected value at the end of its useful life is called *salvage value.*

Depreciation   A special category of prepaid expenses is **plant assets,** which refers to long-term tangible assets used to produce and sell products and services. Plant assets are expected to provide benefits for more than one period. Examples of plant assets are buildings, machines, vehicles, and fixtures. All plant assets, with a general exception for land, eventually wear out or decline in usefulness. The costs of these assets are deferred but are gradually reported as expenses in the income statement over the assets' useful lives (benefit periods). **Depreciation** is the process of allocating the costs of these assets over their expected useful lives. Depreciation expense is recorded with an adjusting entry similar to that for other prepaid expenses.

Step 1: Recall that FastForward purchased equipment for $26,000 in early December to use in earning revenue. This equipment's cost must be depreciated.

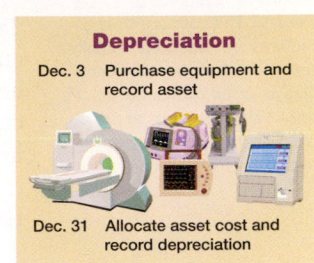

Step 2: The equipment is expected to have a useful life (benefit period) of five years and to be worth about $8,000 at the end of five years. This means the *net* cost of this equipment over its useful life is $18,000 ($26,000 − $8,000). We can use any of several methods to allocate this $18,000 net cost to expense. FastForward uses a method called **straight-line depreciation,** which allocates equal amounts of the asset's net cost to depreciation during its useful life. Dividing the $18,000 net cost by the 60 months (5 years) in the asset's useful life gives a monthly cost of $300 ($18,000/60).

Step 3: The adjusting entry to record monthly depreciation expense, along with T-account postings, follows:

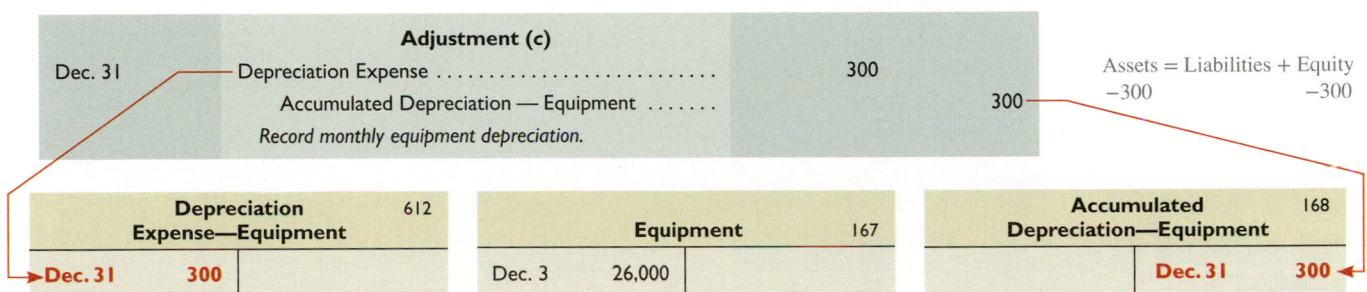

Explanation After posting the adjustment, the Equipment account ($26,000) less its Accumulated Depreciation ($300) account equals the $25,700 net cost (made up of $17,700 for the 59 remaining months in the benefit period plus the $8,000 value at the end of that time). The $300 balance in the Depreciation Expense account is reported in the December income statement. *Not* making the adjustment at December 31 would (1) understate expenses by $300 and overstate net income by $300 for the December income statement and (2) overstate both assets and equity (because of income) by $300 in the December 31 balance sheet. The following table highlights the adjustment for depreciation.

Before Adjustment	Adjustment	After Adjustment
Equipment, net = $26,000	Deduct $300 from Equipment, net Add $300 to Depreciation Expense	Equipment, net = $25,700
Reports $26,000 in equipment.	Record $300 in depreciation and $300 as accumulated depreciation, which is deducted from equipment.	Reports $25,700 in equipment, net of accumulated depreciation.

Accumulated depreciation is kept in a separate contra account. A **contra account** is an account linked with another account, it has an opposite normal balance, and it is reported as a subtraction from that other account's balance. For instance, FastForward's contra account of Accumulated Depreciation—Equipment is subtracted from the Equipment account in the balance sheet (see Exhibit 3.7). This contra account allows balance sheet readers to know both the full costs of assets and the total depreciation.

Point: Accumulated Depreciation has a normal credit balance; it decreases the asset's reported value.

The title of the contra account, *Accumulated Depreciation,* reveals that this account includes total depreciation expense for all prior periods for which the asset was used. To illustrate, the Equipment and the Accumulated Depreciation accounts appear as in Exhibit 3.6 on February

	Equipment	167		Accumulated Depreciation—Equipment	168
Dec. 3	26,000			Dec. 31	300
				Jan. 31	300
				Feb. 28	300
				Balance	**900**

EXHIBIT 3.6

Accounts after Three Months of Depreciation Adjustments

28, 2017, after three months of adjusting entries. The $900 balance in the Accumulated Depreciation account can be subtracted from its related $26,000 asset cost. The difference ($25,100) between these two balances is the cost of the asset that has not yet been depreciated. This difference is called the **book value,** or the *net amount,* which equals the asset's cost less its accumulated depreciation.

These account balances are reported in the assets section of the February 28 balance sheet in Exhibit 3.7.

EXHIBIT 3.7

Equipment and Accumulated Depreciation on February 28 Balance Sheet

Assets (at February 28, 2017)		
Cash		$
⋮		
Equipment	**$26,000**	
Less accumulated depreciation	**900**	**25,100**
Total Assets		$

Commonly titled *Equipment, net*

NEED-TO-KNOW 3-1

Prepaid Expenses

P1

For each separate case below, follow the three-step process for adjusting the prepaid asset account at December 31. Step 1: Determine what the current account balance equals. Step 2: Determine what the current account balance should equal. Step 3: Record the December 31 adjusting entry to get from step 1 to step 2. *Assume no other adjusting entries are made during the year.*

1. **Prepaid Insurance.** The Prepaid Insurance account has a $5,000 debit balance to start the year, and no insurance payments were made during the year. A review of insurance policies and payments shows that $1,000 of unexpired insurance remains at its December 31 year-end.

2. **Prepaid Rent.** On October 1 of the current year, the company prepaid $12,000 for one year of rent for facilities being occupied from that day forward. The company debited Prepaid Rent and credited Cash for $12,000. December 31 year-end statements must be prepared.

3. **Supplies.** The Supplies account has a $1,000 debit balance to start the year. Supplies of $2,000 were purchased during the current year and debited to the Supplies account. A December 31 physical count shows $500 of supplies remaining.

4. **Accumulated Depreciation.** The company has only one fixed asset (equipment) that it purchased at the start of this year. That asset had cost $38,000, had an estimated life of 10 years, and is expected to be valued at $8,000 at the end of the 10-year life. December 31 year-end statements must be prepared.

Solution

1. Step 1: Prepaid Insurance equals $5,000 (before adjustment)
   Step 2: Prepaid Insurance should equal $1,000 (the unexpired part)
   Step 3: Adjusting entry to get from step 1 to step 2

Dec. 31	Insurance Expense	4,000	
	Prepaid Insurance.....................................		4,000
	Record expired insurance coverage ($5,000 – $1,000).		

2. Step 1: Prepaid Rent equals $12,000 (before adjustment)
   Step 2: Prepaid Rent should equal $9,000 (the unexpired part)*
   Step 3: Adjusting entry to get from step 1 to step 2

Dec. 31	Rent Expense	3,000	
	Prepaid Rent...		3,000
	*Record expired prepaid rent. *$12,000 – $3,000 = $9,000, where $3,000 is from: ($12,000/12 months) × 3 months*		

3. Step 1: Supplies equal $3,000 (from $1,000 + $2,000; before adjustment)

Step 2: Supplies should equal $500 (what's left)

Step 3: Adjusting entry to get from step 1 to step 2*

Dec. 31	Supplies Expense	2,500	
	Supplies...		2,500
	*Record supplies used. *$1,000 + $2,000 purchased −*		
	$___ supplies used = $500 remaining		

4. Step 1: Accumulated Depreciation equals $0 (before adjustment)

Step 2: Accumulated Depreciation should equal $3,000 (after current period depreciation of $3,000)*

Step 3: Adjusting entry to get from step 1 to step 2

Dec. 31	Depreciation Expense—Equipment..........................	3,000	
	Accumulated Depreciation—Equipment....................		3,000
	*Record depreciation for period. *($38,000 − $8,000)/10 years*		

Do More: QS 3-5, QS 3-6, QS 3-7, QS 3-8, QS 3-9

Unearned (Deferred) Revenues

The term **unearned revenues** refers to cash received in advance of providing products and services. Unearned revenues, also called *deferred revenues,* are liabilities. When cash is accepted, an obligation to provide products or services is accepted. As products or services are provided, the liability decreases, and the unearned revenues become *earned* revenues. Adjusting entries for unearned items decrease the unearned (balance sheet) account, and increase the revenue (income statement) account, as shown in Exhibit 3.8.

Point: To *defer* is to postpone. We postpone reporting amounts received as revenues until they are earned.

EXHIBIT 3.8

Adjusting for Unearned Revenues (decrease a liability and record revenue)

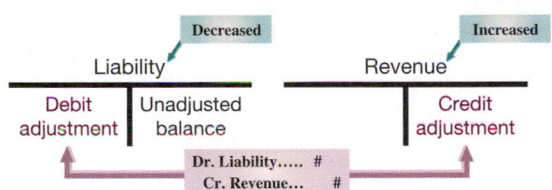

An example of unearned revenues is from **Gannett Co., Inc.**, publisher of *USA TODAY*, which reports unexpired (unearned subscriptions) of $217 million: "Revenue is recognized in the period in which it is earned (as newspapers are delivered)." Unearned revenues are nearly 20% of the current liabilities for Gannett. Another example comes from the **Boston Celtics**. When the Celtics receive cash from advance ticket sales and broadcast fees, they record it in an unearned revenue account called *Deferred Game Revenues.* The Celtics recognize this unearned revenue with adjusting entries on a game-by-game basis. Since the NBA regular season begins in October and ends in April, revenue recognition is mainly limited to this period. For a recent season, the Celtics' quarterly revenues were $0 million for July–September; $34 million for October–December; $48 million for January–March; and $17 million for April–June.

Returning to FastForward, it also has unearned revenues. It agreed on December 26 to provide consulting services to a client for a fixed fee of $3,000 for 60 days.

Step 1: On December 26, the client paid the 60-day fee in advance, covering the period December 27 to February 24. The entry to record the cash received in advance is

Assets = Liabilities + Equity
+3,000   +3,000

Dec. 26	Cash	3,000	
	Unearned Consulting Revenue		3,000
	Received advance payment for services over the		
	next 60 days.		

This advance payment increases cash and creates an obligation to do consulting work over the next 60 days (5 days this year and 55 days next year).

Step 2: As time passes, FastForward earns this payment through consulting. By December 31, it has provided five days' service and earned 5/60 of the $3,000 unearned revenue. This amounts to $250 ($3,000 × 5/60). The *revenue recognition principle* implies that $250 of unearned revenue must be reported as revenue on the December income statement.

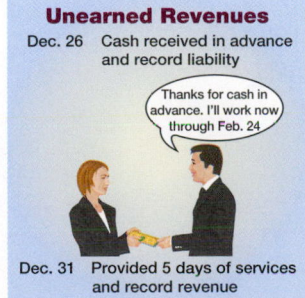

Unearned Revenues

Dec. 26 Cash received in advance and record liability

Thanks for cash in advance. I'll work now through Feb. 24

Dec. 31 Provided 5 days of services and record revenue

Step 3: The adjusting entry to reduce the liability account and recognize earned revenue, along with T-account postings, follows:

$Assets = Liabilities + Equity$
$-250 \qquad +250$

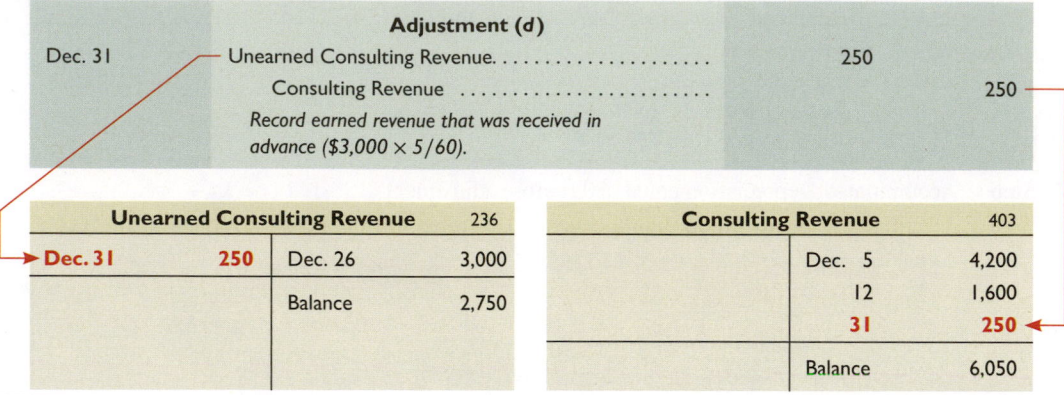

Explanation The adjusting entry transfers $250 from unearned revenue (a liability account) to a revenue account. *Not* making the adjustment (1) understates revenue and net income by $250 in the December income statement and (2) overstates unearned revenue and understates equity by $250 on the December 31 balance sheet. The following highlights the adjustment for unearned revenue.

Before Adjustment	Adjustment	After Adjustment
Unearned Consulting Revenue = $3,000	**Deduct $250 from Unearned Consulting Revenue** **Add $250 to Consulting Revenue**	**Unearned Consulting Revenue = $2,750**
Reports $3,000 in unearned revenue for consulting services promised for 60 days ($50 per day).	Record 5 days of earned consulting revenue, which is 5/60 of unearned amount.	Reports $2,750 in unearned revenue for consulting services owed over next 55 days (55 days × $50 = $2,750).

Accounting for unearned revenues is crucial to many companies. For example, the **National Retail Federation** reports that gift card sales, which are unearned revenues for sellers, exceed $20 billion annually. Gift cards are now the top-selling holiday gift; roughly 60% of all gift givers planned to give at least one gift card within the next year (source: NRF website).

  3-2

Unearned Revenues

P1

For each separate case below, follow the three-step process for adjusting the unearned revenue liability account at December 31. Step 1: Determine what the current account balance equals. Step 2: Determine what the current account balance should equal. Step 3: Record the December 31 adjusting entry to get from step 1 to step 2. *Assume no other adjusting entries are made during the year.*

a. Unearned Rent Revenue. The company collected $24,000 rent in advance on September 1, debiting Cash and crediting Unearned Rent Revenue. The tenant was paying 12 months' rent in advance and occupancy began September 1.

b. Unearned Services Revenue. The company charges $100 per month to spray a house for insects. A customer paid $600 on November 1 in advance for six treatments, which was recorded with a debit to Cash and a credit to Unearned Services Revenue. At year-end, the company has applied two treatments for the customer.

Solution

a. Step 1: Unearned Rent Revenue equals $24,000 (before adjustment)
Step 2: Unearned Rent Revenue should equal $16,000 (current period earned revenue is $8,000*)
Step 3: Adjusting entry to get from step 1 to step 2

Dec. 31	Unearned Rent Revenue	8,000	
	Rent Revenue		8,000
	Record earned portion of rent received in advance.		
	*($24,000/12 months) × 4 months' rental usage		

b. Step 1: Unearned Services Revenue equals $600 (before adjustment)
Step 2: Unearned Services Revenue should equal $400 (current period earned revenue is $200*)
Step 3: Adjusting entry to get from step 1 to step 2

Dec. 31	Unearned Services Revenue..........................	200	
	Services Revenue		200
	Record earned portion of revenue received in advance.		
	*$100 × 2 treatments = Services revenue		

Do More: QS 3-10, QS 3-11

Accrued Expenses

Accrued expenses refer to costs that are incurred in a period but are both unpaid and unrecorded. Accrued expenses must be reported on the income statement for the period when incurred. Adjusting entries for recording accrued expenses increase the expense (income statement) account, and increase a liability (balance sheet) account, as shown in Exhibit 3.9. This adjustment recognizes expenses incurred in a period but not yet paid. Common examples of accrued expenses are salaries, interest, rent, and taxes. We use salaries and interest to show how to adjust accounts for accrued expenses.

Point: Accrued expenses are also called *accrued liabilities.*

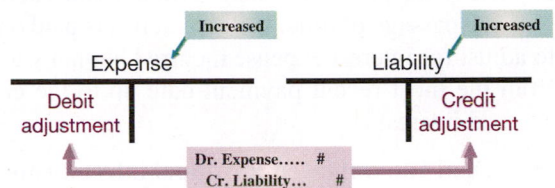

EXHIBIT 3.9

Adjusting for Accrued Expenses (increase a liability and record an expense)

Accrued Salaries Expense   FastForward's employee earns $70 per day, or $350 for a five-day workweek beginning on Monday and ending on Friday.

Step 1: Its employee is paid every two weeks on Friday. On December 12 and 26, the wages are paid, recorded in the journal, and posted to the ledger.

Step 2: The calendar in Exhibit 3.10 shows three working days after the December 26 payday (29, 30, and 31). This means the employee has earned three days' salary by the close of business on Wednesday, December 31, yet this salary cost has not been paid or recorded. The financial statements would be incomplete if FastForward failed to report the added expense and liability to the employee for unpaid salary from December 29, 30, and 31.

Point: An employer records salaries expense and a vacation pay liability when employees earn vacation pay.

EXHIBIT 3.10

Salary Accrual and Paydays

Step 3: The adjusting entry to account for accrued salaries, along with T-account postings, follows:

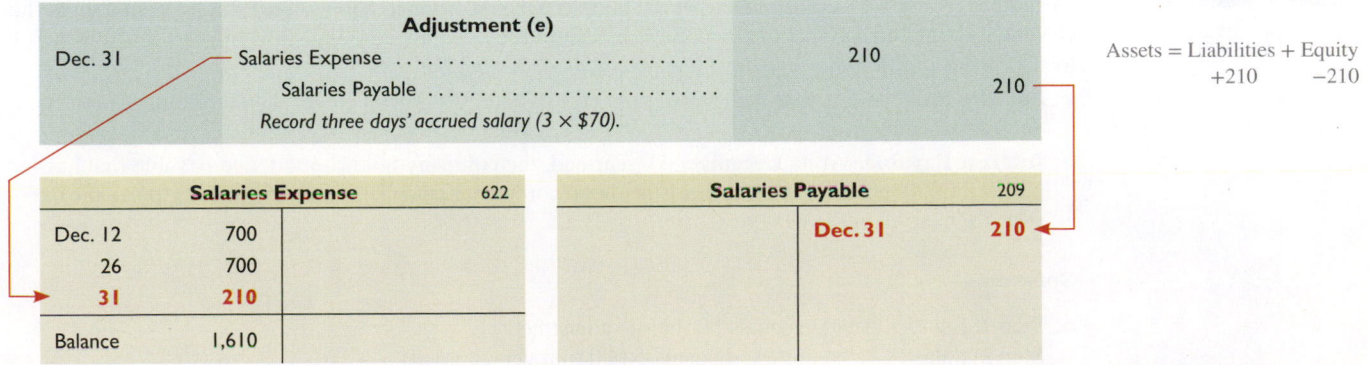

	Adjustment (e)		
Dec. 31	Salaries Expense	210	
	Salaries Payable		210
	Record three days' accrued salary (3 × $70).		

Assets = Liabilities + Equity
                    +210   −210

Salaries Expense		622
Dec. 12	700	
26	700	
31	210	
Balance	1,610	

| **Salaries Payable** | | 209 |
| | Dec. 31 | 210 |

Explanation   Salaries expense of $1,610 is reported on the December income statement, and $210 of salaries payable (liability) is reported in the balance sheet. *Not* making the adjustment (1) understates salaries expense and overstates net income by $210 in the December income statement and (2) understates salaries payable (liabilities) and overstates equity by $210 on the December 31 balance sheet. The following highlights the adjustment for salaries incurred.

Before Adjustment	Adjustment	After Adjustment
Salaries Payable = $0	**Add $210 to Salaries Payable** **Add $210 to Salaries Expense**	**Salaries Payable = $210**
Reports $0 from employee salaries incurred but not yet paid in cash.	Record 3 days' salaries owed to employee, but not yet paid, at $70 per day.	Reports $210 salaries payable to employee but not yet paid.

Accrued Interest Expense   Companies commonly have accrued interest expense on notes payable (loans) and other long-term liabilities at the end of a period. Interest expense is incurred with the passage of time. Unless interest is paid on the last day of an accounting period, we need to adjust for interest expense incurred but not yet paid. This means we must accrue interest cost from the most recent payment date up to the end of the period. The formula for computing accrued interest is:

Principal amount owed × Annual interest rate × Fraction of year since last payment date.

Point: Interest computations assume a 360-day year; known as the *bankers' rule.*

To illustrate, if a company has a $6,000 loan from a bank at 6% annual interest, then 30 days' accrued interest expense is $30—computed as $6,000 × 0.06 × 30/360. The adjusting entry would be to debit Interest Expense for $30 and credit Interest Payable for $30.

Future Payment of Accrued Expenses   Adjusting entries for accrued expenses foretell cash transactions in future periods. Specifically, accrued expenses at the end of one accounting period result in *cash payment* in a *future period*(s). To illustrate, recall that FastForward recorded accrued salaries of $210. On January 9, the first payday of the next period, the following entry settles the accrued liability (salaries payable) and records salaries expense for seven days of work in January:

Assets = Liabilities + Equity
−700   −210   −490

Jan. 9	Salaries Payable (3 days at $70 per day)	210	
	Salaries Expense (7 days at $70 per day)	490	
	Cash		700
	Paid two weeks' salary including three days accrued.		

The $210 debit reflects the payment of the liability for the three days' salary accrued on December 31. The $490 debit records the salary for January's first seven working days (including the New Year's Day holiday) as an expense of the new accounting period. The $700 credit records the total amount of cash paid to the employee.

Accrued Expenses

P1

For each separate case below, follow the three-step process for adjusting the accrued expense account at December 31. Step 1: Determine what the current account balance equals. Step 2: Determine what the current account balance should equal. Step 3: Record the December 31 adjusting entry to get from step 1 to step 2. *Assume no other adjusting entries are made during the year.*

a. Salaries Payable. At year-end, salaries expense of $5,000 has been incurred by the company but is not yet paid to employees.

b. Interest Payable. At its December 31 year-end, the company holds a mortgage payable that has incurred $1,000 in annual interest that is neither recorded nor paid. The company intends to pay the interest on January 3 of the next year.

Solution

a. Step 1: Salaries Payable equals $0 (before adjustment)
   Step 2: Salaries Payable should equal $5,000 (not yet recorded)
   Step 3: Adjusting entry to get from step 1 to step 2

Dec. 31	Salaries Expense	5,000	
	Salaries Payable		5,000
	Record employee salaries earned but not yet paid.		

b. Step 1: Interest Payable equals $0 (before adjustment)

Step 2: Interest Payable should equal $1,000 (not yet recorded)

Step 3: Adjusting entry to get from step 1 to step 2

Dec. 31	Interest Expense..............................	1,000	
	Interest Payable		1,000
	Record interest incurred but not yet paid.		

Do More: QS 3-12, QS 3-13, E 3-1, E 3-2

Accrued Revenues

The term **accrued revenues** refers to revenues earned in a period that are both unrecorded and not yet received in cash (or other assets). An example is a technician who bills customers only when the job is done. If one-third of a job is complete by the end of a period, then the technician must record one-third of the expected billing as revenue in that period—even though there is no billing or collection. The adjusting entries for accrued revenues increase a revenue (income statement) account, and increase an asset (balance sheet) account, as shown in Exhibit 3.11. Accrued revenues commonly arise from services, products, interest, and rent. We use service fees and interest to show how to adjust for accrued revenues.

Point: Accrued revenues are also called *accrued assets.*

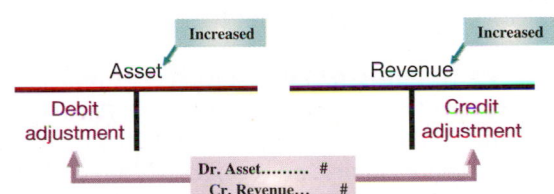

EXHIBIT 3.11

Adjusting for Accrued Revenues (increase an asset and record revenue)

Accrued Services Revenue Accrued revenues are not recorded until adjusting entries are made at the end of the accounting period. These accrued revenues are earned but unrecorded because either the buyer has not yet paid for them or the seller has not yet billed the buyer. FastForward provides an example.

Step 1: In the second week of December, it agreed to provide 30 days of consulting services to a local fitness club for a fixed fee of $2,700 (or $90 per day). The terms of the initial agreement call for FastForward to provide services from December 12, 2016, through January 10, 2017, or 30 days of service. The club agrees to pay FastForward $2,700 on January 10, 2017, when the service period is complete.

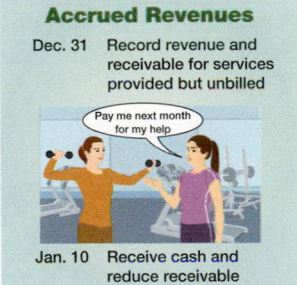

Accrued Revenues

Dec. 31 Record revenue and receivable for services provided but unbilled

Jan. 10 Receive cash and reduce receivable

Step 2: At December 31, 2016, 20 days of services have already been provided. Since the contracted services have not yet been entirely provided, FastForward has neither billed the club nor recorded the services already provided. Still, FastForward has earned two-thirds of the 30-day fee, or $1,800 ($2,700 × 20/30). The *revenue recognition principle* prescribes that it report the $1,800 on the December income statement. The balance sheet also must report that the club owes FastForward $1,800.

Step 3: The year-end adjusting entry to account for accrued services revenue is

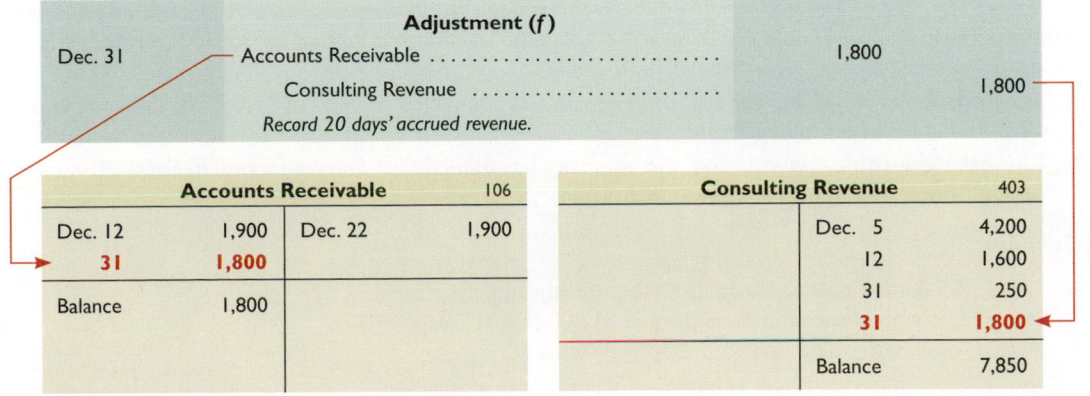

	Adjustment (f)		
Dec. 31	Accounts Receivable	1,800	
	Consulting Revenue		1,800
	Record 20 days' accrued revenue.		

Assets = Liabilities + Equity
+1,800   +1,800

Accounts Receivable			106
Dec. 12	1,900	Dec. 22	1,900
31	**1,800**		
Balance	1,800		

Consulting Revenue			403
		Dec. 5	4,200
		12	1,600
		31	250
		31	**1,800**
		Balance	7,850

Example: What is the adjusting entry if the 30-day consulting period began on December 22? *Answer:* One-third of the fee is earned:
Accounts Receivable . . 900
   Consulting Rev.   900

Explanation   Accounts receivable are reported on the balance sheet at $1,800, and the $7,850 total of consulting revenue is reported on the income statement. *Not* making the adjustment would understate (1) both consulting revenue and net income by $1,800 in the December income statement and (2) both accounts receivable (assets) and equity by $1,800 on the December 31 balance sheet. The following table highlights the adjustment for accrued revenue.

Before Adjustment	Adjustment	After Adjustment
Accounts Receivable = $0	Add $1,800 to Accounts Receivable Add $1,800 to Consulting Revenue	Accounts Receivable = $1,800
Reports $0 from revenue earned but not yet received in cash.	Record 20 days of earned consulting revenue, which is 20/30 of total contract amount.	Reports $1,800 in accounts receivable from consulting services provided.

Accrued Interest Revenue   In addition to the accrued interest expense we described earlier, interest can yield an accrued revenue when a debtor owes money (or other assets) to a company. If a company is holding notes or accounts receivable that produce interest revenue, we must adjust the accounts to record any earned and yet uncollected interest revenue. The adjusting entry is similar to the one for accruing services revenue. Specifically, we debit Interest Receivable (asset) and credit Interest Revenue.

Future Receipt of Accrued Revenues   Accrued revenues at the end of one accounting period result in *cash receipts* in a *future period*(s). To illustrate, recall that FastForward made an adjusting entry for $1,800 to record 20 days' accrued revenue earned from its consulting contract. When FastForward receives $2,700 cash on January 10 for the entire contract amount, it makes the following entry to remove the accrued asset (accounts receivable) and recognize the revenue earned in January. The $2,700 debit reflects the cash received. The $1,800 credit reflects the removal of the receivable, and the $900 credit records the revenue earned in January.

Assets = Liabilities + Equity
+2,700   +900
−1,800

Jan. 10	Cash	2,700	
	Accounts Receivable (20 days at $90 per day)		1,800
	Consulting Revenue (10 days at $90 per day)		900
	Received cash for accrued asset and recorded earned consulting revenue for January.		

■ Decision Maker

Loan Officer   The owner of a custom audio, video, and home theater store applies for a business loan. The store's financial statements reveal large increases in current-year revenues and income. Analysis shows that these increases are due to a promotion that let consumers buy now and pay nothing until January 1 of next year. The store recorded these sales as accrued revenue. Does your analysis raise any concerns? ■ [Answers follow the chapter's Summary.]

NEED-TO-KNOW 3-4

Accrued Revenues

P1

For each separate case below, follow the three-step process for adjusting the accrued revenue account at December 31. Step 1: Determine what the current account balance equals. Step 2: Determine what the current account balance should equal. Step 3: Record the December 31 adjusting entry to get from step 1 to step 2. *Assume no other adjusting entries are made during the year.*

a. Accounts Receivable. At year-end, the company has completed services of $1,000 for a client, but the client has not yet been billed for those services.

b. Interest Receivable. At year-end, the company has earned, but not yet recorded, $500 of interest earned from its investments in government bonds.

Solution

a. Step 1: Accounts Receivable equals $0 (before adjustment)
    Step 2: Accounts Receivable should equal $1,000 (not yet recorded)
    Step 3: Adjusting entry to get from step 1 to step 2

Dec. 31	Accounts Receivable	1,000	
	Services Revenue		1,000
	Record services revenue earned but not yet received.		

b. Step 1: Interest Receivable equals $0 (before adjustment)
Step 2: Interest Receivable should equal $500 (not yet recorded)
Step 3: Adjusting entry to get from step 1 to step 2

Dec. 31	Interest Receivable............................	500	
	Interest Revenue		500
	Record interest earned but not yet received.		

Do More: QS 3-3, QS 3-14

Links to Financial Statements

The process of adjusting accounts is intended to bring an asset or liability account balance to its correct amount. It also updates a related expense or revenue account. These adjustments are necessary for transactions and events that extend over more than one period. (Adjusting entries are posted like any other entry.)

Exhibit 3.12 summarizes the four types of transactions requiring adjustment. Understanding this exhibit is important to understanding the adjusting process and its importance to financial statements. Remember that each adjusting entry affects one or more income statement accounts *and* one or more balance sheet accounts (but never the Cash account).

EXHIBIT 3.12

Summary of Adjustments and Financial Statement Links

	BEFORE Adjusting		
Category	**Balance Sheet**	**Income Statement**	**Adjusting Entry**
Prepaid expenses[†]	Asset overstated	Expense understated	**Dr. Expense**
	Equity overstated		**Cr. Asset***
Unearned revenues[†]	Liability overstated	Revenue understated	**Dr. Liability**
	Equity understated		**Cr. Revenue**
Accrued expenses	Liability understated	Expense understated	**Dr. Expense**
	Equity overstated		**Cr. Liability**
Accrued revenues	Asset understated	Revenue understated	**Dr. Asset**
	Equity understated		**Cr. Revenue**

* For depreciation, the credit is to Accumulated Depreciation (contra asset).

[†] Exhibit assumes that prepaid expenses are initially recorded as assets and that unearned revenues are initially recorded as liabilities.

Information about some adjustments is not always available until several days or even weeks after the period-end. This means that some adjusting and closing entries are recorded later than, but dated as of, the last day of the period. One example is a company that receives a utility bill on January 10 for costs incurred for the month of December. When it receives the bill, the company records the expense and the payable as of December 31. Other examples include long-distance phone usage and costs of many web billings. The December income statement reflects these additional expenses incurred, and the December 31 balance sheet includes these payables, although the amounts were not actually known on December 31.

Point: CFOs often feel compelled to pursue fraudulent accounting due to pressure applied by their superiors, such as overbearing CEOs or aggressive boards.

 Decision Ethics

Financial Officer At year-end, the president instructs you, the financial officer, not to record accrued expenses until next year because they will not be paid until then. The president also directs you to record in current-year sales a recent purchase order from a customer that requires merchandise to be delivered two weeks after the year-end. Your company would report a net income instead of a net loss if you carry out these instructions. What do you do? ■ [Answers follow the chapter's Summary.]

Adjusted Trial Balance

P2

Explain and prepare an adjusted trial balance.

An **unadjusted trial balance** is a list of accounts and balances prepared *before* adjustments are recorded. An **adjusted trial balance** is a list of accounts and balances prepared *after* adjusting entries have been recorded and posted to the ledger.

Exhibit 3.13 shows both the unadjusted and the adjusted trial balances for FastForward at December 31, 2016. The order of accounts in the trial balance usually matches the order in the chart of accounts. Several new accounts commonly arise from adjusting entries.

EXHIBIT 3.13

Unadjusted and Adjusted Trial Balances

FASTFORWARD
Trial Balances
December 31, 2016

Acct. No.	Account Title	Unadjusted Trial Balance Dr.	Cr.	Adjustments Dr.	Cr.	Adjusted Trial Balance Dr.	Cr.
101	Cash	$ 4,275				$ 4,275	
106	Accounts receivable	0		(f) $1,800		1,800	
126	Supplies	9,720			(b) $1,050	8,670	
128	Prepaid insurance	2,400			(a) 100	2,300	
167	Equipment	26,000				26,000	
168	Accumulated depreciation—Equip.		$ 0		(c) 300		$ 300
201	Accounts payable		6,200				6,200
209	Salaries payable		0		(e) 210		210
236	Unearned consulting revenue		3,000	(d) 250			2,750
307	Common stock		30,000				30,000
318	Retained earnings		0				0
319	Dividends	200				200	
403	Consulting revenue		5,800		(d) 250		7,850
					(f) 1,800		
406	Rental revenue		300				300
612	Depreciation expense—Equip.	0		(c) 300		300	
622	Salaries expense	1,400		(e) 210		1,610	
637	Insurance expense	0		(a) 100		100	
640	Rent expense	1,000				1,000	
652	Supplies expense	0		(b) 1,050		1,050	
690	Utilities expense	305				305	
	Totals	$45,300	$45,300	$3,710	$3,710	$47,610	$47,610

Each adjustment (see middle columns) is identified by a letter in parentheses that links it to an adjusting entry explained earlier. Each amount in the Adjusted Trial Balance columns is computed by taking that account's amount from the Unadjusted Trial Balance columns and adding or subtracting any adjustment(s). To illustrate, Supplies has a $9,720 Dr. balance in the unadjusted columns. Subtracting the $1,050 Cr. amount shown in the Adjustments columns yields an adjusted $8,670 Dr. balance for Supplies. An account can have more than one adjustment, such as for Consulting Revenue. Also, some accounts might not require adjustment for this period, such as Accounts Payable.

PREPARING FINANCIAL STATEMENTS

P3

Prepare financial statements from an adjusted trial balance.

We can prepare financial statements directly from information in the *adjusted* trial balance. An adjusted trial balance (see the right-most columns in Exhibit 3.13) includes all accounts and balances appearing in financial statements, and is easier to work from than the entire ledger when preparing financial statements.

Exhibit 3.14 shows how revenue and expense balances are transferred from the adjusted trial balance to the income statement (red lines). The net income and the dividends amount are then used to prepare the statement of retained earnings (black lines). Asset and liability balances on the adjusted trial balance are then transferred to the balance sheet (blue lines). The ending retained earnings is determined on the statement of retained earnings and transferred to the balance sheet (green line).

EXHIBIT 3.14

Preparing Financial Statements (Adjusted Trial Balance from Exhibit 3.13)

Steps to Prepare Financial Statements

Step 1	Prepare income statement using revenue and expense accounts from trial balance
Step 2	Prepare statement of retained earnings using retained earnings and dividends from trial balance; and pull net income from step 1
Step 3	Prepare balance sheet using asset and liability accounts and common stock from trial balance; and pull updated retained earnings from step 2
Step 4	Prepare statement of cash flows from changes in cash flows for the period (illustrated later in the book)

We prepare financial statements in the following order: income statement, statement of retained earnings, and balance sheet. This order makes sense because the balance sheet uses information from the statement of retained earnings, which in turn uses information from the income statement. The statement of cash flows is usually the final statement prepared.

Point: Each trial balance amount is used in only *one* financial statement and, when financial statements are completed, each account will have been used once.

NEED-TO-KNOW   3-5

Preparing Financial
Statements from a Trial
Balance

P3

Use the following adjusted trial balance of Magic Company to prepare its (1) income statement, (2) statement of retained earnings, and (3) balance sheet (unclassified) for the year ended, or date of, December 31, 2016. The Retained Earnings account balance is $45,000 at December 31, 2015.

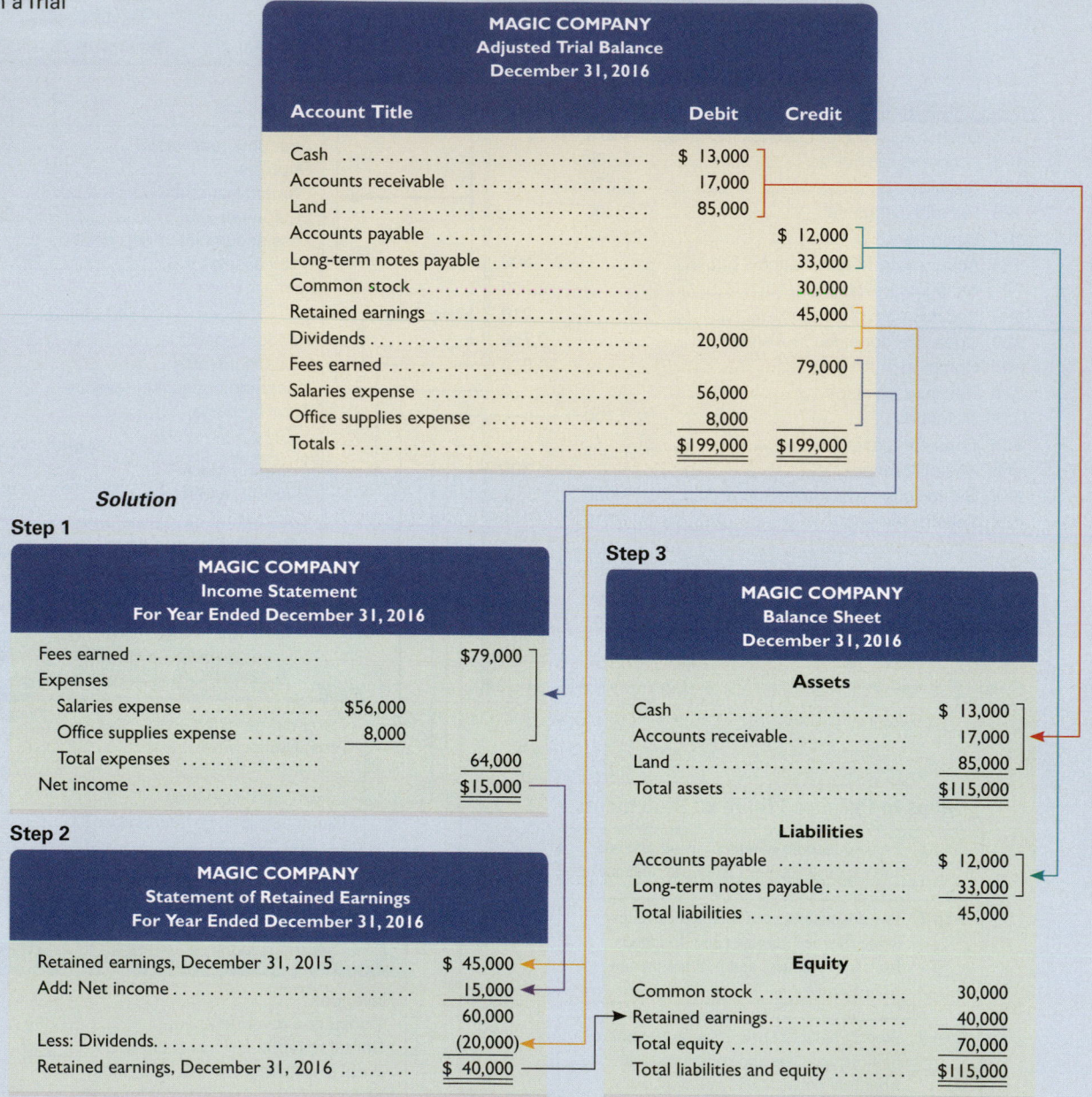

Solution

Do More:
E 3-7, P 3-5, P 3-8

CLOSING PROCESS

P4

Describe and prepare
closing entries.

After financial statements are prepared, the **closing process** readies accounts for recording the transactions and events of the *next* period. In the closing process we must (1) identify accounts for closing, (2) record and post the closing entries, and (3) prepare a post-closing trial balance. The purpose of the closing process is twofold. First, it resets revenue, expense, and dividends account balances to zero at the end of each period (which also updates the Retained Earnings account for inclusion on the balance sheet). This is done so that these accounts can properly measure income and dividends for the next period. Second, it helps in summarizing a period's revenues and expenses. This section explains the closing process.

Temporary and Permanent Accounts

Temporary (or *nominal*) **accounts** accumulate data related to one accounting period. They include all income statement accounts, the Dividends account, and the Income Summary account. They are temporary because the accounts are opened at the beginning of a period, used to record transactions and events for that period, and then closed at the end of the period. *The closing process applies only to temporary accounts.* **Permanent** (or *real*) **accounts** report on activities related to one or more future accounting periods. They carry their ending balances into the next period and generally consist of all balance sheet accounts. These asset, liability, and equity accounts are not closed (balance sheet accounts are permanent).

Temporary Accounts
(closed at period-end)
Revenues
Expenses
Dividends
Income Summary

Permanent Accounts
(not closed at period-end)
Assets
Liabilities
Common Stock
Retained Earnings

Recording Closing Entries

To record and post **closing entries** is to transfer the end-of-period balances in revenue, expense, and dividends accounts to the permanent Retained Earnings account. Closing entries are necessary at the end of each period after financial statements are prepared because

- Revenue, expense, and dividends accounts must begin each period with zero balances.
- Retained earnings must reflect prior periods' revenues, expenses, and dividends.

An income statement aims to report revenues and expenses for a *specific accounting period*. The statement of retained earnings reports similar information, including dividends. Since revenue, expense, and dividends accounts must accumulate information separately for each period, they must start each period with zero balances. To close these accounts, we transfer their balances first to an account called *Income Summary*. **Income Summary** is a temporary account (only used for the closing process) that contains a credit for the sum of all revenues (and gains) and a debit for the sum of all expenses (and losses). Its balance equals net income or net loss and is transferred to retained earnings. Next the Dividends account balance is transferred to retained earnings. After these closing entries are posted, the revenue, expense, dividends, and Income Summary accounts have zero balances. These accounts are then said to be *closed* or *cleared*.

Exhibit 3.15 uses the adjusted account balances of FastForward (from the left side of Exhibit 3.14) to show the four steps necessary to close its temporary accounts. We explain each step.

Point: To understand the closing process, focus on its *outcomes—updating* the Retained Earnings account balance to its proper ending balance and getting *temporary accounts to show zero balances* for purposes of accumulating data for the next period.

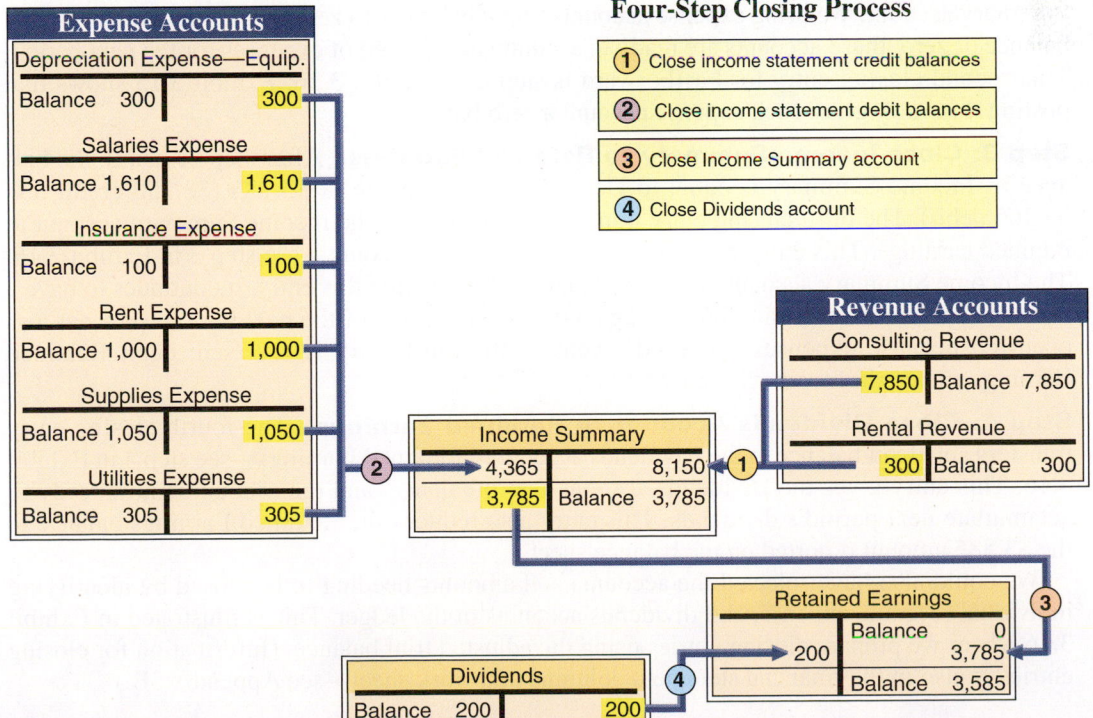

Four-Step Closing Process

1. Close income statement credit balances
2. Close income statement debit balances
3. Close Income Summary account
4. Close Dividends account

EXHIBIT 3.15

Four-Step Closing Process

Point: Retained Earnings is the only *permanent account* in Exhibit 3.15.

Step 1: Close Credit Balances in Revenue Accounts to Income Summary The first closing entry transfers credit balances in revenue (and gain) accounts to the Income Summary account. We bring accounts with credit balances to zero by debiting them. For FastForward, this

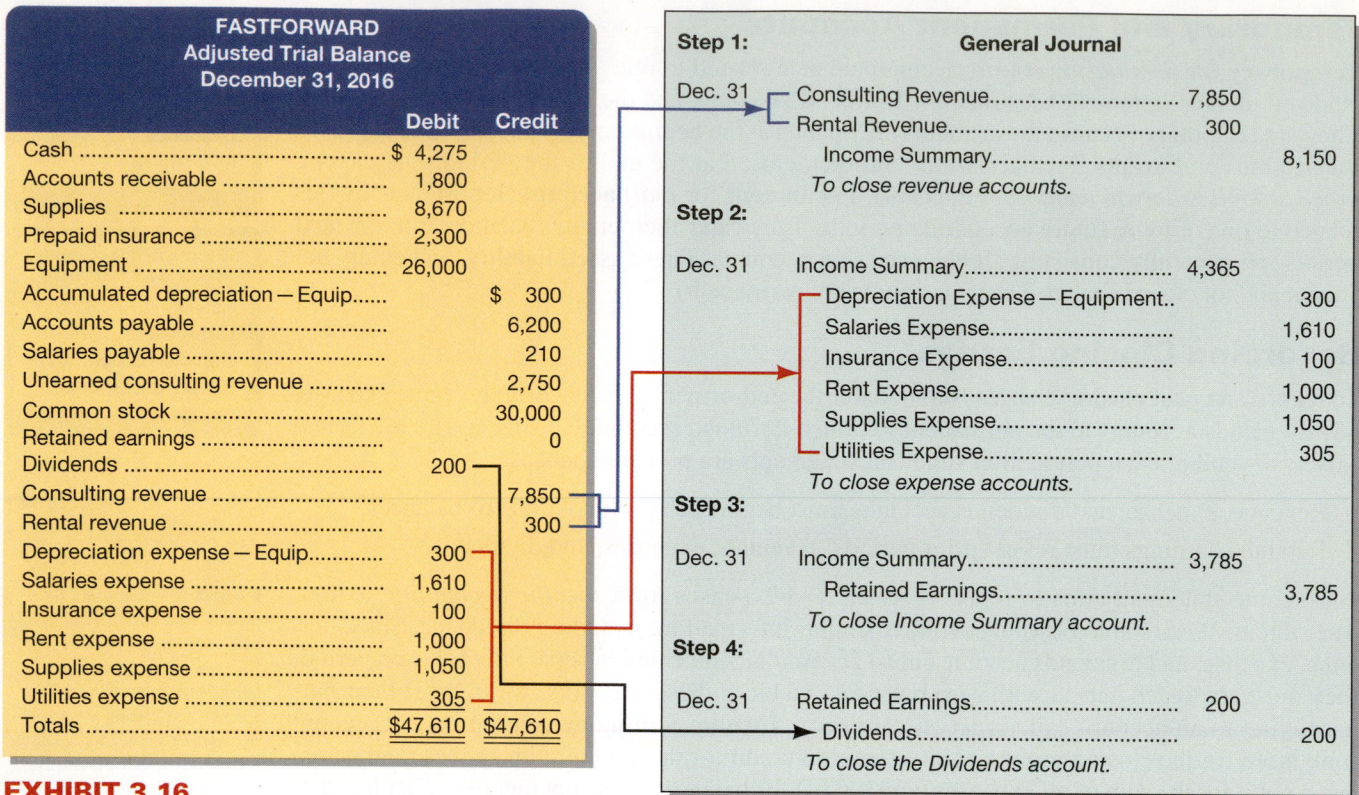

EXHIBIT 3.16

Preparing Closing Entries

Point: It is possible to close revenue and expense accounts directly to Retained Earnings. Computerized accounting systems do this.

journal entry is step 1 in Exhibit 3.16. This entry closes revenue accounts and leaves them with zero balances. The accounts are now ready to record revenues when they occur in the next period. The $8,150 credit entry to Income Summary equals total revenues for the period.

Step 2: Close Debit Balances in Expense Accounts to Income Summary The second closing entry transfers debit balances in expense (and loss) accounts to the Income Summary account. We bring expense accounts' debit balances to zero by crediting them. With a balance of zero, these accounts are ready to accumulate a record of expenses for the next period. This second closing entry for FastForward is step 2 in Exhibit 3.16. Exhibit 3.15 shows that posting this entry gives each expense account a zero balance.

Step 3: Close Income Summary to Retained Earnings After steps 1 and 2, the balance of Income Summary is equal to December's net income of $3,785 ($8,150 credit less $4,365 debit). The third closing entry transfers the balance of the Income Summary account to retained earnings. This entry closes the Income Summary account—see step 3 in Exhibit 3.16. The Income Summary account has a zero balance after posting this entry. It continues to have a zero balance until the closing process again occurs at the end of the next period. (If a net loss occurred because expenses exceeded revenues, the third entry is reversed: debit Retained Earnings and credit Income Summary.)

Step 4: Close Dividends Account to Retained Earnings The fourth closing entry transfers any debit balance in the Dividends account to Retained Earnings—see step 4 in Exhibit 3.16. This entry gives the Dividends account a zero balance, and the account is now ready to accumulate next period's dividends. This entry also reduces the Retained Earnings balance to the $3,585 amount reported on the balance sheet.

We could also have selected the accounts and amounts needing to be closed by identifying individual revenue, expense, and dividends accounts in the ledger. This is illustrated in Exhibit 3.16 where we prepare closing entries using the adjusted trial balance. (Information for closing entries is also in the financial statement columns of a work sheet—see Appendix 3B.)

Post-Closing Trial Balance

P5 _____

Explain and prepare a post-closing trial balance.

Exhibit 3.17 shows the entire ledger of FastForward as of December 31 after adjusting and closing entries are posted. (The transaction entries are in Chapter 2.) The temporary accounts (revenues, expenses, and dividends) have ending balances equal to zero.

EXHIBIT 3.17

General Ledger after the Closing Process for FastForward

Asset Accounts

Cash Acct. No. 101

Date	Explan.	PR	Debit	Credit	Balance
2016					
Dec. 1	(1)	G1	30,000		30,000
2	(2)	G1		2,500	27,500
3	(3)	G1		26,000	1,500
5	(5)	G1	4,200		5,700
6	(13)	G1		2,400	3,300
12	(6)	G1		1,000	2,300
12	(7)	G1		700	1,600
22	(9)	G1	1,900		3,500
24	(10)	G1		900	2,600
24	(11)	G1		200	2,400
26	(12)	G1	3,000		5,400
26	(14)	G1		120	5,280
26	(15)	G1		305	4,975
26	(16)	G1		700	4,275

Accounts Receivable Acct. No. 106

Date	Explan.	PR	Debit	Credit	Balance
2016					
Dec. 12	(8)	G1	1,900		1,900
22	(9)	G1		1,900	0
31	Adj.(f)	G1	1,800		1,800

Supplies Acct. No. 126

Date	Explan.	PR	Debit	Credit	Balance
2016					
Dec. 2	(2)	G1	2,500		2,500
6	(4)	G1	7,100		9,600
26	(14)	G1	120		9,720
31	Adj.(b)	G1		1,050	8,670

Prepaid Insurance Acct. No. 128

Date	Explan.	PR	Debit	Credit	Balance
2016					
Dec. 6	(13)	G1	2,400		2,400
31	Adj.(a)	G1		100	2,300

Equipment Acct. No. 167

Date	Explan.	PR	Debit	Credit	Balance
2016					
Dec. 3	(3)	G1	26,000		26,000

Accumulated Depreciation— Equipment Acct. No. 168

Date	Explan.	PR	Debit	Credit	Balance
2016					
Dec. 31	Adj.(c)	G1		300	300

Liability and Equity Accounts

Accounts Payable Acct. No. 201

Date	Explan.	PR	Debit	Credit	Balance
2016					
Dec. 6	(4)	G1		7,100	7,100
24	(10)	G1	900		6,200

Salaries Payable Acct. No. 209

Date	Explan.	PR	Debit	Credit	Balance
2016					
Dec. 31	Adj.(e)	G1		210	210

Unearned Consulting Revenue Acct. No. 236

Date	Explan.	PR	Debit	Credit	Balance
2016					
Dec. 26	(12)	G1		3,000	3,000
31	Adj.(d)	G1	250		2,750

Common Stock Acct. No. 307

Date	Explan.	PR	Debit	Credit	Balance
2016					
Dec. 1	(1)	G1		30,000	30,000

Retained Earnings Acct. No. 318

Date	Explan.	PR	Debit	Credit	Balance
2016					
Dec. 31	Clos.(3)	G1		3,785	3,785
31	Clos.(4)	G1	200		3,585

Dividends Acct. No. 319

Date	Explan.	PR	Debit	Credit	Balance
2016					
Dec. 24	(11)	G1	200		200
31	Clos.(4)	G1		200	0

Revenue and Expense Accounts (Including Income Summary)

Consulting Revenue Acct. No. 403

Date	Explan.	PR	Debit	Credit	Balance
2016					
Dec. 5	(5)	G1		4,200	4,200
12	(8)	G1		1,600	5,800
31	Adj.(d)	G1		250	6,050
31	Adj.(f)	G1		1,800	7,850
31	Clos.(1)	G1	7,850		0

Rental Revenue Acct. No. 406

Date	Explan.	PR	Debit	Credit	Balance
2016					
Dec. 12	(8)	G1		300	300
31	Clos.(1)	G1	300		0

Depreciation Expense— Equipment Acct. No. 612

Date	Explan.	PR	Debit	Credit	Balance
2016					
Dec. 31	Adj.(c)	G1	300		300
31	Clos.(2)	G1		300	0

Salaries Expense Acct. No. 622

Date	Explan.	PR	Debit	Credit	Balance
2016					
Dec. 12	(7)	G1	700		700
26	(16)	G1	700		1,400
31	Adj.(e)	G1	210		1,610
31	Clos.(2)	G1		1,610	0

Insurance Expense Acct. No. 637

Date	Explan.	PR	Debit	Credit	Balance
2016					
Dec. 31	Adj.(a)	G1	100		100
31	Clos.(2)	G1		100	0

Rent Expense Acct. No. 640

Date	Explan.	PR	Debit	Credit	Balance
2016					
Dec. 12	(6)	G1	1,000		1,000
31	Clos.(2)	G1		1,000	0

Supplies Expense Acct. No. 652

Date	Explan.	PR	Debit	Credit	Balance
2016					
Dec. 31	Adj.(b)	G1	1,050		1,050
31	Clos.(2)	G1		1,050	0

Utilities Expense Acct. No. 690

Date	Explan.	PR	Debit	Credit	Balance
2016					
Dec. 26	(15)	G1	305		305
31	Clos.(2)	G1		305	0

Income Summary Acct. No. 901

Date	Explan.	PR	Debit	Credit	Balance
2016					
Dec. 31	Clos.(1)	G1		8,150	8,150
31	Clos.(2)	G1	4,365		3,785
31	Clos.(3)	G1	3,785		0

A **post-closing trial balance** is a list of permanent accounts and their balances from the ledger after all closing entries have been journalized and posted. It lists the balances for all accounts not closed. These accounts comprise a company's assets, liabilities, and equity, which are identical to those in the balance sheet. The aim of a post-closing trial balance is to verify that (1) total debits equal total credits for permanent accounts and (2) all temporary accounts have zero balances. FastForward's post-closing trial balance is shown in Exhibit 3.18. The post-closing trial balance usually is the last step in the accounting process.

EXHIBIT 3.18

Post-Closing Trial Balance

FASTFORWARD Post-Closing Trial Balance December 31, 2016		
	Debit	Credit
Cash	$ 4,275	
Accounts receivable	1,800	
Supplies	8,670	
Prepaid insurance	2,300	
Equipment	26,000	
Accumulated depreciation—Equipment		$ 300
Accounts payable		6,200
Salaries payable		210
Unearned consulting revenue		2,750
Common stock		30,000
Retained earnings		3,585
Totals	$43,045	$43,045

Point: Only balance sheet (permanent) accounts are on a post-closing trial balance.

Accounting Cycle

C2

Identify steps in the accounting cycle.

The term **accounting cycle** refers to the steps in preparing financial statements. It is called a *cycle* because the steps are repeated each reporting period. Exhibit 3.19 shows the 10 steps in the cycle, beginning with analyzing transactions and ending with a post-closing trial balance or

EXHIBIT 3.19

Steps in the Accounting Cycle*

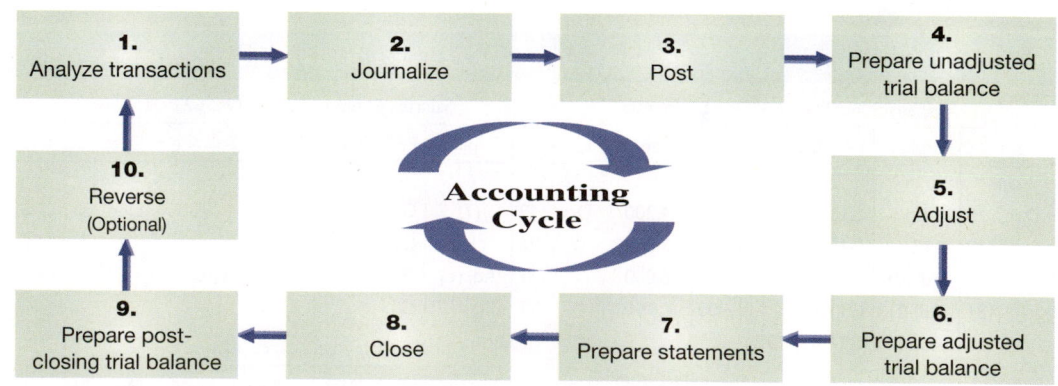

Explanations

1. Analyze transactions	Analyze transactions to prepare for journalizing.
2. Journalize	Record accounts, including debits and credits, in a journal.
3. Post	Transfer debits and credits from the journal to the ledger.
4. Prepare unadjusted trial balance	Summarize unadjusted ledger accounts and amounts.
5. Adjust	Record adjustments to bring account balances up to date; journalize and post adjustments.
6. Prepare adjusted trial balance	Summarize adjusted ledger accounts and amounts.
7. Prepare statements	Use adjusted trial balance to prepare financial statements.
8. Close	Journalize and post entries to close temporary accounts.
9. Prepare post-closing trial balance	Test clerical accuracy of the closing procedures.
10. Reverse (optional)	Reverse certain adjustments in the next period—optional step; see Appendix 3C.

* Steps 4, 6, and 9 can be done on a work sheet. A work sheet is useful in planning adjustments, but adjustments (step 5) must always be journalized and posted. Steps 3, 4, 6, and 9 are automatic with a computerized system.

reversing entries. Steps 1 through 3 usually occur regularly as a company enters into transactions. Steps 4 through 9 are done at the end of a period. *Reversing entries* in step 10 are optional and are explained in Appendix 3C.

Use the adjusted trial balance solution for Magic Company from Need-To-Know 3-5 to prepare its closing entries.

NEED-TO-KNOW 3-6

Closing Entries

P4

Dec. 31	Fees Earned	79,000	
	Income Summary		79,000
	Close revenue account.		
Dec. 31	Income Summary	64,000	
	Salaries Expense		56,000
	Office Supplies Expense		8,000
	Close expense accounts.		
Dec. 31	Income Summary	15,000	
	Retained Earnings		15,000
	Close Income Summary.		
Dec. 31	Retained Earnings	20,000	
	Dividends		20,000
	Close Dividends account.		

Do More: QS 3-21, E 3-8

CLASSIFIED BALANCE SHEET

Our discussion to this point has been limited to unclassified financial statements. This section describes a classified balance sheet. The next chapter describes a classified income statement. An **unclassified balance sheet** is one whose items are broadly grouped into assets, liabilities, and equity. One example is FastForward's balance sheet in Exhibit 3.14. A **classified balance sheet** organizes assets and liabilities into important subgroups that provide more information to decision makers.

C3

Explain and prepare a classified balance sheet.

Classification Structure

A classified balance sheet normally contains the categories in Exhibit 3.20. One of the more important classifications is the separation between current and noncurrent items for both assets and liabilities. Current items are those expected to come due (either collected or owed) within one year or the company's operating cycle, whichever is longer. The **operating cycle** is the time span from when *cash is used* to acquire goods and services until *cash is received* from the sale of goods and services. "Operating" refers to company operations and "cycle" refers to the circular flow of cash used for company inputs and then cash received from its outputs. The length of a company's operating cycle depends on its activities. For a service company, the operating cycle is the time span between (1) paying employees who perform the services and (2) receiving cash from customers. For a merchandiser selling products, the operating cycle is the time span between (1) paying suppliers for merchandise and (2) receiving cash from customers.

Point: Current and noncurrent are also referred to as short-term and long-term, respectively.

Assets	Liabilities and Equity
Current assets	Current liabilities
Noncurrent assets	Noncurrent liabilities
Long-term investments	Equity
Plant assets	
Intangible assets	

EXHIBIT 3.20

Typical Categories in a Classified Balance Sheet

Most operating cycles are less than one year. This means most companies use a one-year period in deciding which assets and liabilities are current. A few companies have an operating cycle

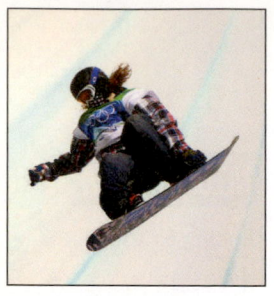

Cameron Spencer/Getty Images

longer than one year. For instance, producers of certain beverages (wine) and products (ginseng) that require aging for several years have operating cycles longer than one year. A balance sheet lists current assets before noncurrent assets and current liabilities before noncurrent liabilities. This consistency in presentation allows users to quickly identify current assets that are most easily converted to cash and current liabilities that are shortly coming due. Items in current assets and current liabilities are listed in the order of how quickly they will be converted to, or paid in, cash.

Classification Categories

This section describes the most common categories in a classified balance sheet. The balance sheet for Snowboarding Components in Exhibit 3.21 shows the typical categories. Its assets are classified as either current or noncurrent. Its noncurrent assets include three main categories: long-term investments, plant assets, and intangible assets. Its liabilities are classified as either current or long-term. Not all companies use the same categories of assets and liabilities for their balance sheets. Jarden, a producer of snowboards and many other goods, reported a balance sheet with five asset classes: current assets; property, plant and equipment; goodwill; intangibles; and other assets.

EXHIBIT 3.21

Example of a Classified Balance Sheet

SNOWBOARDING COMPONENTS
Balance Sheet
January 31, 2016

Assets

Current assets		
Cash	$ 6,500	
Short-term investments	2,100	
Accounts receivable, net	4,400	
Merchandise inventory	27,500	
Prepaid expenses	2,400	
Total current assets		$ 42,900
Long-term investments		
Notes receivable	1,500	
Investments in stocks and bonds	18,000	
Land held for future expansion	48,000	
Total long-term investments		67,500
Plant assets		
Equipment and buildings	203,200	
Less accumulated depreciation	53,000	
Equipment and buildings, net		150,200
Land		73,200
Total plant assets		223,400
Intangible assets		10,000
Total assets		$343,800

Liabilities

Current liabilities		
Accounts payable	$ 15,300	
Wages payable	3,200	
Notes payable	3,000	
Current portion of long-term liabilities	7,500	
Total current liabilities		$ 29,000
Long-term liabilities (net of current portion)		150,000
Total liabilities		179,000

Equity

Common stock		50,000
Retained earnings		114,800
Total equity		164,800
Total liabilities and equity		$343,800

Current Assets   Current assets are cash and other resources that are expected to be sold, collected, or used within one year or the company's operating cycle, whichever is longer. Examples are cash, short-term investments, accounts receivable, short-term notes receivable, goods for sale (called *merchandise* or *inventory*), and prepaid expenses. The individual prepaid expenses of a company are usually small in amount compared to many other assets and are often combined and shown as a single item. The prepaid expenses likely include items such as prepaid insurance, prepaid rent, office supplies, and store supplies. Prepaid expenses are usually listed last because they will not be converted to cash (instead, they are used).

Long-Term Investments   A second major balance sheet classification is **long-term** (or *non-current*) **investments.** Notes receivable and investments in stocks and bonds are long-term assets when they are expected to be held for more than the longer of one year or the operating cycle. Land held for future expansion is a long-term investment because it is *not* used in operations.

Plant Assets   Plant assets are tangible assets that are both *long-lived* and *used to produce or sell products and services*. Examples are equipment, machinery, buildings, and land that are used to produce or sell products and services. The order listing for plant assets is usually from most liquid to least liquid such as equipment and machinery to buildings and land.

Intangible Assets   **Intangible assets** are long-term resources that benefit business operations, usually lack physical form, and have uncertain benefits. Examples are patents, trademarks, copyrights, franchises, and goodwill. Their value comes from the privileges or rights granted to or held by the owner. **Jarden** reports intangible assets of $2,599 million, which is nearly 25 percent of its total assets. Its intangibles include trademarks, patents, and licensing agreements.

Current Liabilities   **Current liabilities** are obligations due to be paid or settled within one year or the operating cycle, whichever is longer. They are usually settled by paying out current assets such as cash. Current liabilities often include accounts payable, notes payable, wages payable, taxes payable, interest payable, and unearned revenues. Also, any portion of a long-term liability due to be paid within one year or the operating cycle, whichever is longer, is a current liability. Unearned revenues are current liabilities when they will be settled by delivering products or services within one year or the operating cycle, whichever is longer. Current liabilities are reported in the order of those to be settled first.

Long-Term Liabilities   **Long-term liabilities** are obligations *not* due within one year or the operating cycle, whichever is longer. Notes payable, mortgages payable, bonds payable, and lease obligations are common long-term liabilities. If a company has both short- and long-term items in each of these categories, they are commonly separated into two accounts in the ledger.

Equity   Equity is the owner's claim on assets. The equity section for a corporation is divided into two main subsections, common stock (contributed capital) and retained earnings.

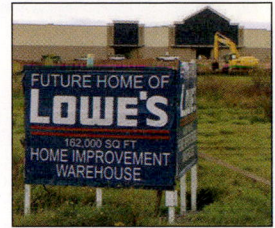

©Stephen D. Cannerelli/Syracuse Newspapers/The Image Works

Point: Plant assets are also called *fixed assets; property, plant and equipment; or long-lived assets.*

Point: Furniture and fixtures are referred to as F&F, which are classified as noncurrent assets.

Point: Many financial ratios are distorted if accounts are not classified correctly.

Point: Only assets and liabilities (not equity) are classified as current or noncurrent.

Use the adjusted trial balance solution for Magic Company from Need-To-Know 3-5 to prepare its classified balance sheet as of December 31, 2016. (*Hint:* The Retained Earnings account balance is $40,000 at December 31, 2016.)

NEED-TO-KNOW 3-7

Classified Balance Sheet

C3

MAGIC COMPANY				
Balance Sheet				
December 31, 2016				
Assets		**Liabilities**		
Current assets		Current liabilities		
Cash....................	$ 13,000	Accounts payable		$ 12,000
Accounts receivable	17,000	Total current liabilities		12,000
Total current assets	30,000	Long-term notes payable		33,000
Plant assets		Total liabilities		45,000
Land.....................	85,000	**Equity**		
Total plant assets	85,000			
		Common stock		30,000
		Retained earnings		40,000
		Total equity		70,000
Total assets	$115,000	Total liabilities and equity		$115,000

Do More: QS 3-24, E 3-9, P 3-7

GLOBAL VIEW

We explained that accounting under U.S. GAAP is similar, but not identical, to that under IFRS. This section discusses differences in adjusting accounts, preparing financial statements, and reporting assets and liabilities on a balance sheet.

Adjusting Accounts   Both U.S. GAAP and IFRS include broad and similar guidance for adjusting accounts. Although some variations exist in revenue and expense recognition and other principles, all of the adjustments in this chapter are accounted for identically under the two systems. In later chapters we describe how certain assets and liabilities can result in different adjusted amounts using fair value measurements.

Preparing Financial Statements   Both U.S. GAAP and IFRS prepare the same four basic financial statements following the same process discussed in this chapter. Chapter 2 explained how both U.S. GAAP and IFRS require current items to be separated from noncurrent items on the balance sheet (yielding a classified balance sheet). U.S. GAAP balance sheets report current items first. Assets are listed from most liquid to least liquid, where liquid refers to the ease of converting an asset to cash. Liabilities are listed from nearest to maturity to furthest from maturity, where maturity refers to the nearness of paying off the liability. IFRS balance sheets normally present noncurrent items first (and equity before liabilities), but this is not a requirement. Other differences with financial statements exist, which we identify in later chapters. **Piaggio** provides the following example of IFRS reporting for its assets, liabilities, and equity within the balance sheet:

PIAGGIO

PIAGGIO
Balance Sheet (in thousands of euros)
December 31, 2014

Assets		Equity and Liabilities	
Noncurrent assets		Total equity.	€ 413,069
Intangible assets	€ 668,354	Noncurrent liabilities	
Property, plant and equipment . . .	307,561	Financial liabilities falling due after one year	506,463
Other noncurrent assets	103,202	Other long-term liabilities	74,903
Total noncurrent assets	1,079,117	Total noncurrent liabilities	581,366
Current assets		Current liabilities	
Trade, tax and other receivables . .	146,887	Financial liabilities falling due within one year	102,474
Inventories	232,398	Trade, tax and other payables	449,881
Cash and cash equivalents	98,206	Current portion of other long-term provisions . .	9,818
Total current assets	477,491	Total current liabilities	562,173
Total assets.	€1,556,608	Total equity and liabilities.	€1,556,608

Point: IASB and FASB are working to improve financial statements. One proposal would reorganize the balance sheet to show assets and liabilities classified as operating, investing, or financing.

IFRS: New revenue recognition rules by the FASB and the IASB reduce variation between U.S. GAAP and IFRS.

Closing Process   The closing process is identical under U.S. GAAP and IFRS. Although unique accounts can arise under either system, the closing process remains the same.

 IFRS ───

Revenue and expense recognition are key to recording accounting adjustments. IFRS tends to be more *principles-based* relative to U.S. GAAP, which is viewed as more *rules-based*. A principles-based system depends heavily on control procedures to reduce the potential for fraud or misconduct. Failure in judgment led to improper accounting adjustments at **Fannie Mae**, **WorldCom**, and others. A KPMG survey of accounting and finance employees found that more than 10% of them had witnessed falsification or manipulation of accounting data within the past year. Internal controls and governance processes are directed at curtailing such behavior. Yet, a 2011 KPMG fraud survey found that one in seven frauds was uncovered by chance, which emphasizes our need to improve internal controls and governance. ■

Sustainability and Accounting   **GoPro**, as introduced in this chapter's opening feature, emphasizes a reduced environmental footprint as part of its sustainability plan. Specifically, GoPro, in partnership with **Goal Zero**, has reduced its environmental impact through the use of renewable energy. Together, the two companies offered solar panel charging stations for spectators at the GoPro Mountain Games. Further, the company powered its product display stations using the renewable solar panel energy. "We've seen strong interest since announcing this exciting new solution," says Nick Woodman, founder of GoPro. "Helping the world . . . is one of the most satisfying aspects of our business and we believe it instills our brand with an invaluable degree of goodwill and good karma."

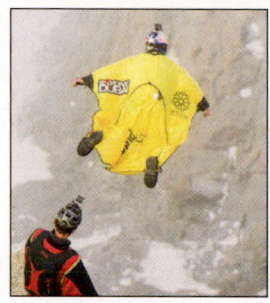
© Ashley Cooper/Corbis

Profit Margin and Current Ratio   **Decision Analysis**

Profit Margin

A useful measure of a company's operating results is the ratio of its net income to net sales. This ratio is called **profit margin,** or *return on sales,* and is computed as in Exhibit 3.22.

$$\text{Profit margin} = \frac{\text{Net income}}{\text{Net sales}}$$

This ratio is interpreted as reflecting the percent of profit in each dollar of sales. To illustrate how we compute and use profit margin, let's look at the results of **Limited Brands, Inc.**, in Exhibit 3.23 for its fiscal years 2010 through 2014.

$ millions	2014	2013	2012	2011	2010
Net income	$ 903	$ 753	$ 850	$ 805	$ 448
Net sales	$10,773	$10,459	$10,364	$9,613	$8,632
Profit margin	8.4%	7.2%	8.2%	8.4%	5.2%
Industry profit margin	2.5%	2.0%	2.2%	2.1%	1.2%

Limited's average profit margin is 7.5% during this five-year period. This favorably compares to the average industry profit margin of 2.0%. Moreover, we see that Limited's profit margin has rebounded from the recent recessionary period and is at the 7% to 8% margin for the past four years (see margin graph). Future success depends on Limited maintaining its market share and increasing its profit margin.

Current Ratio

An important use of financial statements is to help assess a company's ability to pay its debts in the near future. Such analysis affects decisions by suppliers when allowing a company to buy on credit. It also affects decisions by creditors when lending money to a company, including loan terms such as interest rate, due date, and collateral requirements. It can also affect a manager's decisions about using cash to pay debts when they come due. The **current ratio** is one measure of a company's ability to pay its short-term obligations. It is defined in Exhibit 3.24 as current assets divided by current liabilities.

$$\text{Current ratio} = \frac{\text{Current assets}}{\text{Current liabilities}}$$

Using financial information from **Limited Brands, Inc.**, we compute its current ratio for the recent six-year period. The results are in Exhibit 3.25.

$ millions	2014	2013	2012	2011	2010	2009
Current assets	$3,150	$2,205	$2,368	$2,592	$3,250	$2,867
Current liabilities	$1,826	$1,538	$1,526	$1,504	$1,322	$1,255
Current ratio	1.7	1.4	1.6	1.7	2.5	2.3
Industry current ratio	1.7	1.5	1.6	1.7	1.9	2.0

EXHIBIT 3.22
Profit Margin

A1
Compute profit margin and describe its use in analyzing company performance.

EXHIBIT 3.23
Limited Brands's Profit Margin

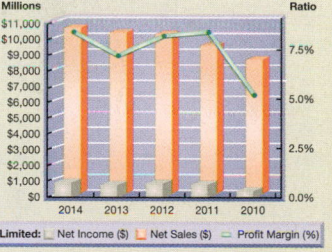

A2
Compute the current ratio and describe what it reveals about a company's financial condition.

EXHIBIT 3.24
Current Ratio

EXHIBIT 3.25
Limited Brands's Current Ratio

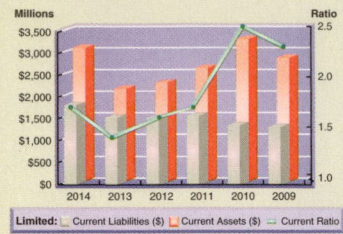

Limited Brands's current ratio averaged 1.9 for its fiscal years 2009 through 2014. The current ratio for each of these years suggests that the company's short-term obligations can be covered with its short-term assets. However, if its ratio would approach 1.0, Limited would expect to face challenges in covering liabilities. If the ratio were *less* than 1.0, current liabilities would exceed current assets, and the company's ability to pay short-term obligations could be in doubt. Limited Brands's liquidity, as evidenced by its current ratio, declined in 2011, 2012, and 2013, which roughly matches the industry decline; but it rose to the norm in 2014.

■ Decision Maker

Analyst   You are analyzing the financial condition of a company to assess its ability to meet upcoming loan payments. You compute its current ratio as 1.2. You also find that a major portion of accounts receivable is due from one client who has not made any payments in the past 12 months. Removing this receivable from current assets lowers the current ratio to 0.7. What do you conclude? ■   [Answers follow the chapter's Summary.]

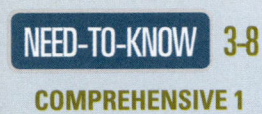

COMPREHENSIVE 1

The following information relates to Fanning's Electronics on December 31, 2016. The company, which uses the calendar year as its annual reporting period, initially records prepaid and unearned items in balance sheet accounts (assets and liabilities, respectively).

a. The company's weekly payroll is $8,750, paid each Friday for a five-day workweek. Assume December 31, 2016, falls on a Monday, but the employees will not be paid their wages until Friday, January 4, 2017.

b. Eighteen months earlier, on July 1, 2015, the company purchased equipment that cost $20,000. Its useful life is predicted to be five years, at which time the equipment is expected to be worthless (zero salvage value).

c. On October 1, 2016, the company agreed to work on a new housing development. The company is paid $120,000 on October 1 in advance of future installation of similar alarm systems in 24 new homes. That amount was credited to the Unearned Services Revenue account. Between October 1 and December 31, work on 20 homes was completed.

d. On September 1, 2016, the company purchased a 12-month insurance policy for $1,800. The transaction was recorded with an $1,800 debit to Prepaid Insurance.

e. On December 29, 2016, the company completed a $7,000 service that has not been billed or recorded as of December 31, 2016.

Required

1. Prepare any necessary adjusting entries on December 31, 2016, in relation to transactions and events *a* through *e*.

2. Prepare T-accounts for the accounts affected by adjusting entries, and post the adjusting entries. Determine the adjusted balances for the Unearned Revenue and the Prepaid Insurance accounts.

3. Complete the following table and determine the amounts and effects of your adjusting entries on the year 2016 income statement and the December 31, 2016, balance sheet. Use up (down) arrows to indicate an increase (decrease) in the Effect columns.

Entry	Amount in the Entry	Effect on Net Income	Effect on Total Assets	Effect on Total Liabilities	Effect on Total Equity

PLANNING THE SOLUTION

- Analyze each situation to determine which accounts need to be updated with an adjustment.
- Calculate the amount of each adjustment and prepare the necessary journal entries.
- Show the amount of each adjustment in the designated accounts, determine the adjusted balance, and identify the balance sheet classification of the account.
- Determine each entry's effect on net income for the year and on total assets, total liabilities, and total equity at the end of the year.

SOLUTION

1. Adjusting journal entries.

(a) Dec. 31	Wages Expense	1,750	
	Wages Payable		1,750
	Accrue wages for last day of the year *($8,750 × 1/5).*		
(b) Dec. 31	Depreciation Expense—Equipment.	4,000	
	Accumulated Depreciation—Equipment.		4,000
	Record depreciation expense for year *($20,000/5 years = $4,000 per year).*		
(c) Dec. 31	Unearned Services Revenue.	100,000	
	Services Revenue		100,000
	Record services revenue earned *($120,000 × 20/24).*		
(d) Dec. 31	Insurance Expense	600	
	Prepaid Insurance.		600
	Adjust for expired portion of insurance *($1,800 × 4/12).*		
(e) Dec. 31	Accounts Receivable	7,000	
	Services Revenue		7,000
	Record services revenue earned.		

2. T-accounts for adjusting journal entries *a* through *e*.

Wages Expense		
(a)	1,750	

Wages Payable		
	(a)	1,750

Depreciation Expense—Equipment		
(b)	4,000	

Accumulated Depreciation— Equipment		
	(b)	4,000

Unearned Services Revenue		
	Unadj. Bal.	120,000
(c)	100,000	
	Adj. Bal.	20,000

Services Revenue		
	(c)	100,000
	(e)	7,000
	Adj. Bal.	107,000

Insurance Expense		
(d)	600	

Prepaid Insurance		
Unadj. Bal.	1,800	
	(d)	600
Adj. Bal.	1,200	

Accounts Receivable		
(e)	7,000	

3. Financial statement effects of adjusting journal entries.

Entry	Amount in the Entry	Effect on Net Income	Effect on Total Assets	Effect on Total Liabilities	Effect on Total Equity
a	$ 1,750	$ 1,750 ↓	No effect	$ 1,750 ↑	$ 1,750 ↓
b	4,000	4,000 ↓	$4,000 ↓	No effect	4,000 ↓
c	100,000	100,000 ↑	No effect	$100,000 ↓	100,000 ↑
d	600	600 ↓	$ 600 ↓	No effect	600 ↓
e	7,000	7,000 ↑	$7,000 ↑	No effect	7,000 ↑

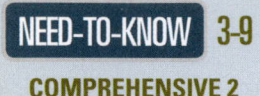

Use the following adjusted trial balance to answer questions 1–3.

CHOI COMPANY Adjusted Trial Balance December 31	Debit	Credit
Cash	$ 3,050	
Accounts receivable	400	
Prepaid insurance.........................	830	
Supplies...................................	80	
Equipment	217,200	
Accumulated depreciation—Equipment		$ 29,100
Wages payable		880
Interest payable		3,600
Unearned rent		460
Long-term notes payable....................		150,000
Common stock.............................		10,000
Retained earnings..........................		30,340
Dividends	21,000	
Rent earned		57,500
Wages expense............................	25,000	
Utilities expense...........................	1,900	
Insurance expense	3,200	
Supplies expense	250	
Depreciation expense—Equipment.............	5,970	
Interest expense...........................	3,000	
Totals	$281,880	$281,880

1. Prepare the annual income statement from the adjusted trial balance of Choi Company.

Answer:

CHOI COMPANY Income Statement For Year Ended December 31		
Revenues		
Rent earned		$57,500
Expenses		
Wages expense..........................	$25,000	
Utilities expense..........................	1,900	
Insurance expense	3,200	
Supplies expense	250	
Depreciation expense—Equipment...........	5,970	
Interest expense..........................	3,000	
Total expenses		39,320
Net income		$18,180

2. Prepare a statement of retained earnings from the adjusted trial balance of Choi Company.

Answer:

CHOI COMPANY Statement of Retained Earnings For Year Ended December 31	
Retained earnings, December 31 prior year-end	$30,340
Plus: Net income	18,180
	48,520
Less: Dividends....................................	21,000
Retained earnings, December 31 current year-end	$27,520

3. Prepare a balance sheet (unclassified) from the adjusted trial balance of Choi Company.

Answer:

CHOI COMPANY		
Balance Sheet		
December 31		
Assets		
Cash		$ 3,050
Accounts receivable..................		400
Prepaid insurance....................		830
Supplies............................		80
Equipment	$217,200	
Less accumulated depreciation	29,100	188,100
Total assets.........................		$192,460
Liabilities		
Wages payable		$ 880
Interest payable		3,600
Unearned rent		460
Long-term notes payable..............		150,000
Total liabilities		154,940
Equity		
Common stock		10,000
Retained earnings...................		27,520
Total equity		37,520
Total liabilities and equity		$192,460

Alternative Accounting for Prepayments

This appendix explains an alternative in accounting for prepaid expenses and unearned revenues.

RECORDING PREPAYMENT OF EXPENSES IN EXPENSE ACCOUNTS

An alternative method is to record *all* prepaid expenses with debits to expense accounts. If any prepaids remain unused or unexpired at the end of an accounting period, then adjusting entries must transfer the cost of the unused portions from expense accounts to prepaid expense (asset) accounts. This alternative method is acceptable. The financial statements are identical under either method, but the adjusting entries are different. To illustrate the differences between these two methods, let's look at FastForward's cash payment of December 6 for 24 months of insurance coverage beginning on December 1. FastForward recorded that payment with a debit to an asset account, but it could have recorded a debit to an expense account. These alternatives are shown in Exhibit 3A.1.

P6

Explain the alternatives in accounting for prepaids.

		Payment Recorded as Asset	Payment Recorded as Expense
Dec. 6	Prepaid Insurance	2,400	
	Cash	2,400	
Dec. 6	Insurance Expense		2,400
	Cash		2,400

EXHIBIT 3A.1

Alternative Initial Entries for Prepaid Expenses

At the end of its accounting period on December 31, insurance protection for one month has expired. This means $100 ($2,400/24) of insurance coverage expired and is an expense for December. The adjusting entry depends on how the original payment was recorded. This is shown in Exhibit 3A.2.

EXHIBIT 3A.2

Adjusting Entry for Prepaid Expenses for the Two Alternatives

			Payment Recorded as Asset	Payment Recorded as Expense
Dec. 31	Insurance Expense		100	
	Prepaid Insurance		100	
Dec. 31	Prepaid Insurance			2,300
	Insurance Expense			2,300

When these entries are posted to the accounts in the ledger, we can see that these two methods give identical results. The December 31 adjusted account balances in Exhibit 3A.3 show Prepaid Insurance of $2,300 and Insurance Expense of $100 for both methods.

EXHIBIT 3A.3

Account Balances under Two Alternatives for Recording Prepaid Expenses

Payment Recorded as Asset				Payment Recorded as Expense			
Prepaid Insurance			128	**Prepaid Insurance**			128
Dec. 6	2,400	Dec. 31	100	Dec. 31	2,300		
Balance	2,300						

Insurance Expense			637	Insurance Expense			637
Dec. 31	100			Dec. 6	2,400	Dec. 31	2,300
				Balance	100		

RECORDING PREPAYMENT OF REVENUES IN REVENUE ACCOUNTS

As with prepaid expenses, an alternative method is to record *all* unearned revenues with credits to revenue accounts. If any revenues are unearned at the end of an accounting period, then adjusting entries must transfer the unearned portions from revenue accounts to unearned revenue (liability) accounts. This alternative method is acceptable. The adjusting entries are different for these two alternatives, but the financial statements are identical. To illustrate the accounting differences between these two methods, let's look at FastForward's December 26 receipt of $3,000 for consulting services covering the period December 27 to February 24. FastForward recorded this transaction with a credit to a liability account. The alternative is to record it with a credit to a revenue account, as shown in Exhibit 3A.4.

EXHIBIT 3A.4

Alternative Initial Entries for Unearned Revenues

			Receipt Recorded as Liability	Receipt Recorded as Revenue
Dec. 26	Cash		3,000	
	Unearned Consulting Revenue		3,000	
Dec. 26	Cash			3,000
	Consulting Revenue			3,000

By the end of its accounting period on December 31, FastForward has earned $250 of this revenue. This means $250 of the liability has been satisfied. Depending on how the initial receipt is recorded, the adjusting entry is as shown in Exhibit 3A.5.

EXHIBIT 3A.5

Adjusting Entry for Unearned Revenues for the Two Alternatives

			Receipt Recorded as Liability	Receipt Recorded as Revenue
Dec. 31	Unearned Consulting Revenue		250	
	Consulting Revenue		250	
Dec. 31	Consulting Revenue			2,750
	Unearned Consulting Revenue			2,750

After adjusting entries are posted, the two alternatives give identical results. The December 31 adjusted account balances in Exhibit 3A.6 show unearned consulting revenue of $2,750 and consulting revenue of $250 for both methods.

Receipt Recorded as Liability		
Unearned Consulting Revenue		236
Dec. 31	250	Dec. 26 3,000
		Balance **2,750**

Receipt Recorded as Revenue		
Unearned Consulting Revenue		236
	Dec. 31	**2,750**

Consulting Revenue		403
	Dec. 31	**250**

Consulting Revenue		403
Dec. 31 2,750	Dec. 26	3,000
	Balance	**250**

EXHIBIT 3A.6

Account Balances under Two Alternatives for Recording Unearned Revenues

---

APPENDIX

Work Sheet as a Tool

3B

Information preparers use various analyses and internal documents when organizing information for internal and external decision makers. Internal documents are often called **working papers.** One widely used working paper is the **work sheet,** which is a useful tool for preparers in working with accounting information. It is usually not available to external decision makers such as investors.

P7 _____

Prepare a work sheet and explain its usefulness.

BENEFITS OF A WORK SHEET (SPREADSHEET)

A work sheet is *not* a required report, yet using a manual or electronic work sheet has several potential benefits. Specifically, a work sheet

- Aids the preparation of financial statements.
- Reduces the risk of errors when working with many accounts and adjustments.
- Links accounts and adjustments to their impacts in financial statements.
- Assists in planning and organizing an audit of financial statements—as it can be used to reflect any adjustments necessary.
- Helps in preparing interim (monthly and quarterly) financial statements when the journalizing and posting of adjusting entries are postponed until year-end.
- Shows the effects of proposed or "what-if" transactions.

USE OF A WORK SHEET

When a work sheet is used to prepare financial statements, it is constructed at the end of a period before the adjusting process. The complete work sheet includes a list of the accounts, their balances and adjustments, and their sorting into financial statement columns. It provides two columns each for the unadjusted trial balance, the adjustments, the adjusted trial balance, the income statement, and the balance sheet. To describe and interpret the work sheet, we use the information from FastForward. Preparing the work sheet has five important steps. Each step, 1 through 5, is color-coded and explained with reference to Exhibit 3B.1.

Point: Since a work sheet is *not* a required report or an accounting record, its format is flexible and can be modified by its user to fit his/her preferences.

① **Step 1. Enter Unadjusted Trial Balance**

Refer to Exhibit 3B.1—green section. The first step in preparing a work sheet is to list the title of every account and its account number that is expected to appear on its financial statements. This includes all accounts in the ledger plus any new ones from adjusting entries. Most adjusting entries—including expenses from salaries, supplies, depreciation, and insurance—are predictable and recurring. The unadjusted balance for each account is then entered in the appropriate Debit or Credit column of the unadjusted trial balance columns. The totals of these two columns must be equal. The light green section of Exhibit 3B.1 shows FastForward's work sheet after completing this first step (dark green rows reflect accounts expected to arise as part of the adjustments). Sometimes blank lines are left on the work sheet based on past experience to indicate where lines will be needed for adjustments to certain accounts. Exhibit 3B.1 shows Consulting Revenue as one example. An alternative is to squeeze adjustments on one line or to combine the effects of two or more adjustments in one amount. In the unusual case when an account is not predicted, we can add a new line for such an account following the *Totals* line.

② Step 2. Enter Adjustments

Refer to Exhibit 3B.1—yellow section. The second step in preparing a work sheet is to enter adjustments in the Adjustments columns. The adjustments shown are the same ones shown in Exhibit 3.13. An identifying letter links the debit and credit of each adjustment. This is called *keying* the adjustments. After preparing a work sheet, adjustments must still be entered in the journal and posted to the ledger. The Adjustments columns provide the information for adjusting entries in the journal.

③ Step 3. Prepare Adjusted Trial Balance

Refer to Exhibit 3B.1—blue section. The adjusted trial balance is prepared by combining the adjustments with the unadjusted balances for each account. As an example, the Prepaid Insurance account has a $2,400 debit balance in the Unadjusted Trial Balance columns. This $2,400 debit is combined with the $100 credit in the Adjustments columns to give Prepaid Insurance a $2,300 debit in the Adjusted Trial Balance columns. The totals of the Adjusted Trial Balance columns confirm the equality of debits and credits.

④ Step 4. Sort Adjusted Trial Balance Amounts to Financial Statements

Refer to Exhibit 3B.1—orange section. This step involves sorting account balances from the adjusted trial balance to their proper financial statement columns. Expenses go to the Income Statement Debit column and revenues to the Income Statement Credit column. Assets and dividends go to the Balance Sheet Debit column. Liabilities, retained earnings, and common stock go to the Balance Sheet Credit column.

⑤ Step 5. Total Statement Columns, Compute Income or Loss, and Balance Columns

Refer to Exhibit 3B.1—purple section. Each financial statement column (from step 4) is totaled. The difference between the totals of the Income Statement columns is net income or net loss. This occurs because revenues are entered in the Credit column and expenses in the Debit column. If the Credit total exceeds the Debit total, there is net income. If the Debit total exceeds the Credit total, there is a net loss. For FastForward, the Credit total exceeds the Debit total, giving a $3,785 net income.

The net income from the Income Statement columns is then entered in the Balance Sheet Credit column. Adding net income to the last Credit column implies that it is to be added to retained earnings. If a loss occurs, it is added to the Debit column. This implies that it is to be subtracted from retained earnings. The ending balance of retained earnings does not appear in the last two columns as a single amount, but it is computed in the statement of retained earnings using these account balances. When net income or net loss is added to the proper Balance Sheet column, the totals of the last two columns must balance. If they do not, one or more errors have been made. The error can either be mathematical or involve sorting one or more amounts to incorrect columns.

WORK SHEET APPLICATIONS AND ANALYSIS

A work sheet does not substitute for financial statements. It is a tool we can use at the end of an accounting period to help organize data and prepare financial statements. FastForward's financial statements are shown in Exhibit 3.14. Its income statement amounts are taken from the Income Statement columns of the work sheet. Similarly, amounts for its balance sheet and its statement of retained earnings are taken from the Balance Sheet columns of the work sheet.

Information from the Adjustments columns of a work sheet can be used to journalize adjusting entries. It is important to remember that a work sheet is not a journal. This means that even when a work sheet is prepared, it is necessary to both journalize adjustments and post them to the ledger.

EXHIBIT 3B.1

Work Sheet with Five-Step Process for Completion

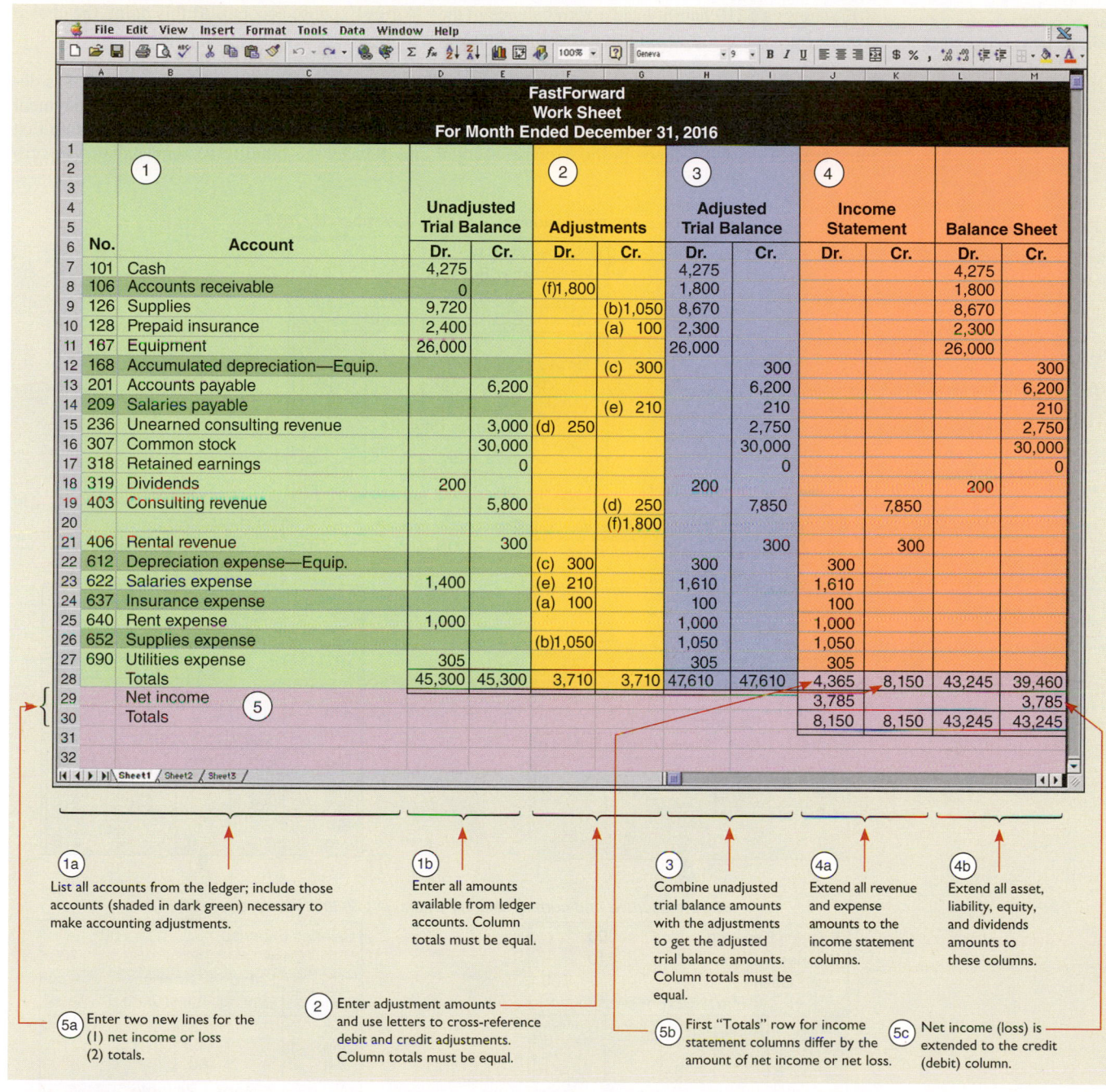

Reversing Entries

APPENDIX

3C

P8

Prepare reversing entries and explain their purpose.

Reversing entries are optional. They are recorded in response to accrued assets and accrued liabilities that were created by adjusting entries at the end of a reporting period. The purpose of reversing entries is to simplify a company's recordkeeping. Exhibit 3C.1 shows an example of FastForward's reversing entries. The top of the exhibit shows the adjusting entry FastForward recorded on December 31 for its employee's earned but unpaid salary. The entry recorded three days' salary of $210, which increased December's total salary expense to $1,610. The entry also recognized a liability of $210. The expense is reported on December's income statement. The expense account is then closed. The ledger on January 1, 2017, shows a $210 liability and a zero balance in the Salaries Expense account. At this point, the choice is made between using or not using reversing entries.

Accounting *without* Reversing Entries   The path down the left side of Exhibit 3C.1 is described in the chapter. To summarize here, when the next payday occurs on January 9, we record payment with a compound entry that debits both the expense and liability accounts and credits Cash. Posting that entry creates a $490 balance in the expense account and reduces the liability account balance to zero

EXHIBIT 3C.1

Reversing Entries for an Accrued Expense

Under both approaches, the expense and liability accounts have identical balances after the cash payment on January 9.

Salaries Expense	$490
Salaries Payable	$ 0

*Circled numbers in the *Balance* column indicate abnormal balances.

because the debt has been settled. The disadvantage of this approach is the slightly more complex entry required on January 9. Paying the accrued liability means that this entry differs from the routine entries made on all other paydays. To construct the proper entry on January 9, we must recall the effect of the December 31 adjusting entry. Reversing entries overcome this disadvantage.

Point: Firms that use reversing entries hope that this simplification will reduce errors.

Accounting *with* Reversing Entries   The right side of Exhibit 3C.1 shows how a reversing entry on January 1 overcomes the disadvantage of the January 9 entry when not using reversing entries. A reversing entry is the exact opposite of an adjusting entry. For FastForward, the Salaries Payable liability account is debited for $210, meaning that this account now has a zero balance after the entry is posted. The Salaries Payable account temporarily understates the liability, but this is not a problem since financial statements are not prepared before the liability is settled on January 9. The credit to the Salaries Expense account is unusual because it gives the account an *abnormal credit balance.* We highlight an abnormal balance by circling it. Because of the reversing entry, the January 9 entry to record payment is straightforward. This entry debits the Salaries Expense account and credits Cash for the full $700 paid. It is the same as all other entries made to record 10 days' salary for the employee. Notice that after the payment entry is posted, the Salaries Expense account has a $490 balance that reflects seven days' salary of $70 per day (see the lower right side of Exhibit 3C.1). The zero balance in the Salaries Payable account is now correct. The lower section of Exhibit 3C.1 shows that the expense and liability accounts have exactly the same balances whether reversing entries are used or not. This means that both approaches yield identical results.

Summary

C1   Explain the importance of periodic reporting and the role of accrual accounting. The value of information is often linked to its timeliness. To provide timely information, accounting systems prepare periodic reports at regular intervals. The time period assumption presumes that an organization's activities can be divided into specific time periods for periodic reporting. Accrual accounting recognizes revenue when earned and expenses when incurred—not necessarily when cash inflows and outflows occur.

C2   Identify steps in the accounting cycle. The accounting cycle consists of 10 steps: (1) analyze transactions, (2) journalize, (3) post, (4) prepare an unadjusted trial balance, (5) adjust accounts, (6) prepare an adjusted trial balance, (7) prepare statements, (8) close, (9) prepare a post-closing trial balance, and (10) prepare (optional) reversing entries.

C3   Explain and prepare a classified balance sheet. Classified balance sheets report assets and liabilities in two categories: current and noncurrent. Noncurrent assets often include long-term investments, plant assets, and intangible assets. A corporation separates equity into common stock and retained earnings.

A1   Compute profit margin and describe its use in analyzing company performance. *Profit margin* is defined as the reporting period's net income divided by its net sales. Profit margin reflects on a company's earnings activities by showing how much income is in each dollar of sales.

A2   Compute the current ratio and describe what it reveals about a company's financial condition. A company's current ratio is defined as current assets divided by current liabilities. We use it to evaluate a company's ability to pay its current liabilities out of current assets.

P1   Prepare and explain adjusting entries. Accounting adjustments bring an asset or liability account balance to its correct amount. They also update related expense or revenue

accounts. *Prepaid expenses* refer to items paid for in advance of receiving their benefits. Prepaid expenses are assets. Adjusting entries for prepaids involve increasing (debiting) expenses and decreasing (crediting) assets. *Unearned* (or *prepaid*) *revenues* refer to cash received in advance of providing products and services. Unearned revenues are liabilities. Adjusting entries for unearned revenues involve increasing (crediting) revenues and decreasing (debiting) unearned revenues. *Accrued expenses* refer to costs incurred in a period that are both unpaid and unrecorded. Adjusting entries for recording accrued expenses involve increasing (debiting) expenses and increasing (crediting) liabilities. *Accrued revenues* refer to revenues earned in a period that are both unrecorded and not yet received in cash. Adjusting entries for recording accrued revenues involve increasing (debiting) assets and increasing (crediting) revenues.

P2   Explain and prepare an adjusted trial balance. An adjusted trial balance is a list of accounts and balances prepared after recording and posting adjusting entries. Financial statements are often prepared from the adjusted trial balance.

P3   Prepare financial statements from an adjusted trial balance. Revenue and expense balances are reported on the income statement. Asset, liability, and equity balances are reported on the balance sheet. We usually prepare statements in the following order: income statement, statement of retained earnings, balance sheet, and statement of cash flows.

P4   Describe and prepare closing entries. Closing entries involve four steps: (1) close credit balances in revenue (and gain) accounts to Income Summary, (2) close debit balances in expense (and loss) accounts to Income Summary, (3) close Income Summary to the Retained Earnings account, and (4) close the Dividends account to Retained Earnings.

P5   Explain and prepare a post-closing trial balance. A post-closing trial balance is a list of permanent accounts and their balances after all closing entries have been journalized and posted. Its purpose is to verify that (1) total debits equal total credits for permanent accounts and (2) all temporary accounts have zero balances.

P6^A Explain the alternatives in accounting for prepaids. Charging all prepaid expenses to expense accounts when they are purchased is acceptable. When this is done, adjusting entries must transfer any unexpired amounts from expense accounts to asset accounts. Crediting all unearned revenues to revenue accounts when cash is received is also acceptable. In this case, the adjusting entries must transfer any unearned amounts from revenue accounts to unearned revenue accounts.

P7^B Prepare a work sheet and explain its usefulness. A work sheet can be a useful tool in preparing and analyzing financial statements. It is helpful at the end of a period in preparing adjusting entries, an adjusted trial balance, and financial statements. A work sheet usually contains five pairs of columns: Unadjusted Trial Balance, Adjustments, Adjusted Trial Balance, Income Statement, and Balance Sheet.

P8^C Prepare reversing entries and explain their purpose. Reversing entries are an optional step. They are applied to accrued expenses and revenues. The purpose of reversing entries is to simplify subsequent journal entries. Financial statements are unaffected by the choice to use or not use reversing entries.

Guidance Answers to Decision Maker and Decision Ethics

Investor Prepaid expenses are items paid for in advance of receiving their benefits. They are assets and are expensed as they are used up. The publishing company's treatment of the signing bonus is acceptable provided future book sales can at least match the $500,000 expense. As an investor, you are concerned about the risk of future book sales. The riskier the likelihood of future book sales is, the more likely your analysis is to treat the $500,000, or a portion of it, as an expense, not a prepaid expense (asset).

Loan Officer Your concern in lending to this store arises from analysis of current-year sales. While increased revenues and income are fine, your concern is with collectibility of these promotional sales. If the owner sold products to customers with poor records of paying bills, then collectibility of these sales is low. Your analysis must assess this possibility and recognize any expected losses.

Financial Officer Omitting accrued expenses and recognizing revenue early can mislead financial statement users. One action is to request a second meeting with the president so you can explain that accruing expenses when incurred and recognizing revenue when earned are required practices. If the president persists, you might discuss the situation with legal counsel and any auditors involved. Your ethical action might cost you this job, but the potential pitfalls for falsification of statements, reputation and personal integrity loss, and other costs are too great.

Analyst A current ratio of 1.2 suggests that current assets are sufficient to cover current liabilities, but it implies a minimal buffer in case of errors in measuring current assets or current liabilities. Removing the past-due receivable reduces the current ratio to 0.7. Your assessment is that the company will have some difficulty meeting its loan payments.

Key Terms

Accounting cycle	Current assets	Plant assets
Accounting periods	Current liabilities	Post-closing trial balance
Accrual basis accounting	Current ratio	Prepaid expenses
Accrued expenses	Depreciation	Profit margin
Accrued revenues	Expense recognition (or matching) principle	Reversing entries
Accumulated depreciation		Sarbanes-Oxley Act (SOX)
Adjusted trial balance	Fiscal year	Straight-line depreciation method
Adjusting entry	Income Summary	Temporary accounts
Annual financial statements	Intangible assets	Time period assumption
Book value	Interim financial statements	Unadjusted trial balance
Cash basis accounting	Long-term investments	Unclassified balance sheet
Classified balance sheet	Long-term liabilities	Unearned revenues
Closing entries	Natural business year	Work sheet
Closing process	Operating cycle	Working papers
Contra account	Permanent accounts	

Multiple Choice Quiz   Answers at end of chapter

1. A company forgot to record accrued and unpaid employee wages of $350,000 at period-end. This oversight would
   a. Understate net income by $350,000.
   b. Overstate net income by $350,000.
   c. Have no effect on net income.
   d. Overstate assets by $350,000.
   e. Understate assets by $350,000.

2. Prior to recording adjusting entries, the Supplies account has a $450 debit balance. A physical count of supplies shows $125 of unused supplies still available. The required adjusting entry is:
   a. Debit Supplies $125; Credit Supplies Expense $125.
   b. Debit Supplies $325; Credit Supplies Expense $325.
   c. Debit Supplies Expense $325; Credit Supplies $325.
   d. Debit Supplies Expense $325; Credit Supplies $125.
   e. Debit Supplies Expense $125; Credit Supplies $125.

3. On May 1, 2016, a two-year insurance policy was purchased for $24,000 with coverage to begin immediately. What is the amount of insurance expense that appears on the company's income statement for the year ended December 31, 2016?
   a. $4,000   c. $12,000   e. $24,000
   b. $8,000   d. $20,000

4. On November 1, 2016, Stockton Co. receives $3,600 cash from Hans Co. for consulting services to be provided evenly over the period November 1, 2016, to April 30, 2017—at which time Stockton credited $3,600 to Unearned Consulting Fees. The adjusting entry on December 31, 2016 (Stockton's year-end), would include a
   a. Debit to Unearned Consulting Fees for $1,200.
   b. Debit to Unearned Consulting Fees for $2,400.
   c. Credit to Consulting Fees Earned for $2,400.
   d. Debit to Consulting Fees Earned for $1,200.
   e. Credit to Cash for $3,600.

5. If a company had $15,000 in net income for the year, and its sales were $300,000 for the same year, what is its profit margin?
   a. 20%   c. $285,000   e. 5%
   b. 2,000%   d. $315,000

6. Based on the following information from Repicor Company's balance sheet, what is Repicor Company's current ratio?

Current assets . . .	$ 75,000	Current liabilities	$ 50,000
Investments	30,000	Long-term liabilities . . .	60,000
Plant assets	300,000	Common stock	295,000

   a. 2.10   c. 1.00   e. 0.67
   b. 1.50   d. 0.95

A(B, C)   *Superscript letter A(B, C) denotes assignments based on Appendix 3A (3B, 3C).*

📖 Icon denotes assignments that involve decision making.

Discussion Questions

1. What is the difference between the cash basis and the accrual basis of accounting?

2. 📖 Why is the accrual basis of accounting generally preferred over the cash basis?

3. What type of business is most likely to select a fiscal year that corresponds to its natural business year instead of the calendar year?

4. What is a prepaid expense and where is it reported in the financial statements?

5. 📖 What type of assets requires adjusting entries to record depreciation?

6. 📖 What contra account is used when recording and reporting the effects of depreciation? Why is it used?

7. 🌐 Assume **Samsung** has unearned revenue. What is unearned revenue and where is it reported in financial statements? **Samsung**

8. What is an accrued revenue? Give an example.

9.ᴬ If a company initially records prepaid expenses with debits to expense accounts, what type of account is debited in the adjusting entries for those prepaid expenses?

10. 📖 Review the balance sheet of **Apple** in Appendix A. Identify one asset account that **APPLE**

requires adjustment before annual financial statements can be prepared. What would be the effect on the income statement if this asset account were not adjusted? (Number not required, but comment on over- or understating of net income.)

11. 📖 Review the balance sheet of **Google** in Appendix A. Identify the amount for **GOOGLE** property and equipment. What adjusting entry is necessary (no numbers required) for this account when preparing financial statements?

12. 📖 Refer to **Samsung**'s balance sheet in Appendix A. If it made an adjustment for unpaid wages at year-end, where would the accrued wages be reported on its balance sheet? **Samsung**

13. What are the steps in recording closing entries?

14. What accounts are affected by closing entries? What accounts are not affected?

15. 📖 What two purposes are accomplished by recording closing entries?

16. What is the purpose of the Income Summary account?

17. 📖 Explain whether an error has occurred if a post-closing trial balance includes a Depreciation Expense account.

18. What tasks are aided by a work sheet?

19. Why are the debit and credit entries in the Adjustments columns of the work sheet identified with letters?

20. What is a company's operating cycle?

21. What classes of assets and liabilities are shown on a typical classified balance sheet?

22. How is unearned revenue classified on the balance sheet?

23. What are the characteristics of plant assets?

24.C How do reversing entries simplify recordkeeping?

25.C If a company recorded accrued salaries expense of $500 at the end of its fiscal year, what reversing entry could be made? When would it be made?

26. 🅘 Refer to the most recent balance sheet for Apple in Appendix A. What five main noncurrent asset categories are used on its classified balance sheet? **APPLE**

27. Refer to Samsung's most recent balance sheet in Appendix A. Identify and list its ten current assets. **Samsung**

28. 🅘 Refer to Google's most recent balance sheet in Appendix A. Identify the eight accounts listed as current liabilities. **GOOGLE**

29. 🅘 Refer to Samsung's financial statements in Appendix A. What journal entry was likely recorded as of December 31, 2014, to close its Income Summary account? **Samsung**

---

connect

QUICK STUDY

QS 3-1
Periodic reporting
C1

Choose from the following list of terms/phrases to best complete the statements below.

a. Fiscal year	**d.** Accounting period	**g.** Natural business year
b. Timeliness	**e.** Annual financial statements	**h.** Time period assumption
c. Calendar year	**f.** Interim financial statements	**i.** Quarterly statements

1. _____ presumes that an organization's activities can be divided into specific time periods.

2. Financial reports covering a one-year period are known as _____.

3. A(n) _____ consists of any 12 consecutive months.

4. A(n) _____ consists of 12 consecutive months ending on December 31.

5. The value of information is often linked to its _____.

QS 3-2
Computing accrual and cash income   C1 🅘

In its first year of operations, Roma Company reports the following:

- Earned revenues of $45,000 ($37,000 cash received from customers)
- Incurred expenses of $25,500 ($20,250 cash paid toward them)
- Prepaid $6,750 cash for costs that will not be expensed until next year.

Compute the company's first-year net income under both the cash basis and the accrual basis of accounting.

QS 3-3
Identifying accounting adjustments

P1

Classify the following adjusting entries as involving prepaid expenses (PE), unearned revenues (UR), accrued expenses (AE), or accrued revenues (AR).

_____ **a.** To record revenue earned that was previously received as cash in advance.

_____ **b.** To record wages expense incurred but not yet paid (nor recorded).

_____ **c.** To record revenue earned but not yet billed (nor recorded).

_____ **d.** To record expiration of prepaid insurance.

_____ **e.** To record annual depreciation expense.

QS 3-4
Concepts of adjusting entries

P1

During the year, a company recorded prepayments of expenses in asset accounts and cash receipts of unearned revenues in liability accounts. At the end of its annual accounting period, the company must make three adjusting entries: (1) accrue salaries expense, (2) adjust the Unearned Services Revenue account to recognize earned revenue, and (3) record services revenue earned for which cash will be received the following period. Indicate the account to be debited and the account to be credited—from a through i below—for each of the adjusting entries (1), (2), and (3).

a. Prepaid Salaries	**d.** Unearned Services Revenue	**g.** Accounts Receivable
b. Cash	**e.** Salaries Expense	**h.** Accounts Payable
c. Salaries Payable	**f.** Services Revenue	**i.** Equipment

For each separate case below, follow the three-step process for adjusting the prepaid asset account at December 31. Step 1: Determine what the current account balance equals. Step 2: Determine what the current account balance should equal. Step 3: Record the December 31 adjusting entry to get from step 1 to step 2. *Assume no other adjusting entries are made during the year.*

QS 3-5
Prepaid (deferred) expenses adjustments
P1

a. **Prepaid Insurance.** The Prepaid Insurance account has a $4,700 debit balance to start the year. A review of insurance policies and payments shows that $900 of unexpired insurance remains at year-end.

b. **Prepaid Insurance.** The Prepaid Insurance account has a $5,890 debit balance at the start of the year. A review of insurance policies and payments shows $1,040 of insurance has expired by year-end.

c. **Prepaid Rent.** On September 1 of the current year, the company prepaid $24,000 for two years of rent for facilities being occupied that day. The company debited Prepaid Rent and credited Cash for $24,000.

For each separate case below, follow the three-step process for adjusting the supplies asset account at December 31. Step 1: Determine what the current account balance equals. Step 2: Determine what the current account balance should equal. Step 3: Record the December 31 adjusting entry to get from step 1 to step 2. *Assume no other adjusting entries are made during the year.*

QS 3-6
Prepaid (deferred) expenses adjustments
P1

a. **Supplies.** The Supplies account has a $300 debit balance to start the year. No supplies were purchased during the current year. A December 31 physical count shows $110 of supplies remaining.

b. **Supplies.** The Supplies account has an $800 debit balance to start the year. Supplies of $2,100 were purchased during the current year and debited to the Supplies account. A December 31 physical count shows $650 of supplies remaining.

c. **Supplies.** The Supplies account has a $4,000 debit balance to start the year. During the current year, supplies of $9,400 were purchased and debited to the Supplies account. The inventory of supplies available at December 31 totaled $2,660.

a. On July 1, 2016, Lopez Company paid $1,200 for six months of insurance coverage. No adjustments have been made to the Prepaid Insurance account, and it is now December 31, 2016. Prepare the journal entry to reflect expiration of the insurance as of December 31, 2016.

QS 3-7
Adjusting prepaid expenses
P1

b. Zim Company has a Supplies account balance of $5,000 on January 1, 2016. During 2016, it purchased $2,000 of supplies. As of December 31, 2016, a supplies inventory shows $800 of supplies available. Prepare the adjusting journal entry to correctly report the balance of the Supplies account and the Supplies Expense account as of December 31, 2016.

For each separate case below, follow the three-step process for adjusting the accumulated depreciation account at December 31. Step 1: Determine what the current account balance equals. Step 2: Determine what the current account balance should equal. Step 3: Record the December 31 adjusting entry to get from step 1 to step 2. *Assume no other adjusting entries are made during the year.*

QS 3-8
Accumulated depreciation adjustments
P1

a. **Accumulated Depreciation.** The Krug Company's Accumulated Depreciation account has a $13,500 balance to start the year. A review of depreciation schedules reveals that $14,600 of depreciation expense must be recorded for the year.

b. **Accumulated Depreciation.** The company has only one fixed asset (truck) that it purchased at the start of this year. That asset had cost $44,000, had an estimated life of five years, and is expected to have zero value at the end of the five years.

c. **Accumulated Depreciation.** The company has only one fixed asset (equipment) that it purchased at the start of this year. That asset had cost $32,000, had an estimated life of seven years, and is expected to be valued at $4,000 at the end of the seven years.

a. Barga Company purchases $20,000 of equipment on January 1, 2016. The equipment is expected to last five years and be worth $2,000 at the end of that time. Prepare the entry to record one year's depreciation expense of $3,600 for the equipment as of December 31, 2016.

QS 3-9
Adjusting for depreciation
P1

b. Welch Company purchases $10,000 of land on January 1, 2016. The land is expected to last indefinitely. What depreciation adjustment, if any, should be made with respect to the Land account as of December 31, 2016?

For each separate case below, follow the three-step process for adjusting the unearned revenue liability account at December 31. Step 1: Determine what the current account balance equals. Step 2: Determine what the current account balance should equal. Step 3: Record the December 31 adjusting entry to get from step 1 to step 2. *Assume no other adjusting entries are made during the year.*

QS 3-10
Unearned (deferred) revenues adjustments
P1

a. **Unearned Rent Revenue.** The Krug Company collected $6,000 rent in advance on November 1, debiting Cash and crediting Unearned Rent Revenue. The tenant was paying 12 months' rent in advance and occupancy began November 1.

b. Unearned Services Revenue. The company charges $75 per month to spray a house for insects. A customer paid $300 on October 1 in advance for four treatments, which was recorded with a debit to Cash and a credit to Unearned Services Revenue. At year-end, the company has applied three treatments for the customer.

c. Unearned Rent Revenue. On September 1, a client paid the company $24,000 cash for six months of rent in advance (the client leased a building and took occupancy immediately). The company recorded the cash as Unearned Rent Revenue.

QS 3-11
Adjusting for unearned revenues

P1

a. Tao Co. receives $10,000 cash in advance for four months of legal services on October 1, 2016, and records it by debiting Cash and crediting Unearned Revenue both for $10,000. It is now December 31, 2016, and Tao has provided legal services as planned. What adjusting entry should Tao make to account for the work performed from October 1 through December 31, 2016?

b. A. Caden started a new publication called *Contest News*. Its subscribers pay $24 to receive 12 monthly issues. With every new subscriber, Caden debits Cash and credits Unearned Subscription Revenue for the amounts received. The company has 100 new subscribers as of July 1, 2016. It sends *Contest News* to each of these subscribers every month from July through December. Assuming no changes in subscribers, prepare the journal entry that Caden must make as of December 31, 2016, to adjust the Subscription Revenue account and the Unearned Subscription Revenue account.

QS 3-12
Accrued expenses adjustments

P1

For each separate case below, follow the three-step process for adjusting the accrued expense account at December 31. Step 1: Determine what the current account balance equals. Step 2: Determine what the current account balance should equal. Step 3: Record the December 31 adjusting entry to get from step 1 to step 2. *Assume no other adjusting entries are made during the year.*

a. Salaries Payable. At year-end, salaries expense of $15,500 has been incurred by the company, but is not yet paid to employees.

b. Interest Payable. At its December 31 year-end, the company owes $250 of interest on a line-of-credit loan. That interest will not be paid until sometime in January of the next year.

c. Interest Payable. At its December 31 year-end, the company holds a mortgage payable that has incurred $875 in annual interest that is neither recorded nor paid. The company intends to pay the interest on January 7 of the next year.

QS 3-13
Accruing salaries

P1

Molly Mocha employs one college student every summer in her coffee shop. The student works the five weekdays and is paid on the following Monday. (For example, a student who works Monday through Friday, June 1 through June 5, is paid for that work on Monday, June 8.) The coffee shop adjusts its books *monthly,* if needed, to show salaries earned but unpaid at month-end.

The student works the last week of July—which is Monday, July 28 through Friday, August 1. If the student earns $100 per day, what adjusting entry must the coffee shop make on July 31 to correctly record accrued salaries expense for July?

QS 3-14
Accrued revenues adjustments

P1

For each separate case below, follow the three-step process for adjusting the accrued revenue account at December 31. Step 1: Determine what the current account balance equals. Step 2: Determine what the current account balance should equal. Step 3: Record the December 31 adjusting entry to get from step 1 to step 2. *Assume no other adjusting entries are made during the year.*

a. Accounts Receivable. At year-end, the Krug Company has completed services of $19,000 for a client, but the client has not yet been billed for those services.

b. Interest Receivable. At year-end, the company has earned, but not yet recorded, $390 of interest earned from its investments in government bonds.

c. Accounts Receivable. A painting company collects fees when jobs are complete. The work for one customer, whose job was bid at $1,300, has been completed, but the customer has not yet been billed.

QS 3-15
Recording and analyzing adjusting entries

P1

Adjusting entries affect at least one balance sheet account and at least one income statement account. For the following entries, identify the account to be debited and the account to be credited. Indicate which of the accounts is the income statement account and which is the balance sheet account.

a. Entry to record revenue earned that was previously received as cash in advance.

b. Entry to record wage expenses incurred but not yet paid (nor recorded).

c. Entry to record revenue earned but not yet billed (nor recorded).

d. Entry to record expiration of prepaid insurance.

e. Entry to record annual depreciation expense.

In making adjusting entries at the end of its accounting period, Chao Consulting mistakenly forgot to record:

- $3,200 of insurance coverage that had expired (this $3,200 cost had been initially debited to the Prepaid Insurance account).
- $2,000 of accrued salaries expense.

As a result of these oversights, the financial statements for the reporting period will [choose one] (1) understate assets by $3,200; (2) understate expenses by $5,200; (3) understate net income by $2,000; or (4) overstate liabilities by $2,000.

QS 3-16
Determining effects of adjusting entries

P1

The following information is taken from Camara Company's unadjusted and adjusted trial balances.

	Unadjusted		Adjusted	
	Debit	Credit	Debit	Credit
Prepaid insurance.........	$4,100		$3,700	
Interest payable		$0		$800

Given this information, which of the following is likely included among its adjusting entries?

a. A $400 debit to Insurance Expense and an $800 debit to Interest Payable.

b. A $400 debit to Insurance Expense and an $800 debit to Interest Expense.

c. A $400 credit to Prepaid Insurance and an $800 debit to Interest Payable.

QS 3-17
Interpreting adjusting entries

P2

Answer each of the following questions related to international accounting standards.

a. Do financial statements prepared under IFRS normally present assets from least liquid to most liquid or vice versa?

b. Do financial statements prepared under IFRS normally present liabilities from furthest from maturity to nearest to maturity or vice versa?

QS 3-18
International accounting standards

P3

Damita Company reported net income of $48,025 and net sales of $425,000 for the current year. Calculate the company's profit margin and interpret the result. Assume that its competitors earn an average profit margin of 15%.

QS 3-19
Analyzing profit margin

A1

Cal Consulting initially records prepaid and unearned items in income statement accounts. Given this company's accounting practices, which of the following applies to the preparation of adjusting entries at the end of its first accounting period?

a. Unearned fees (on which cash was received in advance earlier in the period) are recorded with a debit to Consulting Fees Earned of $500 and a credit to Unearned Consulting Fees of $500.

b. Unpaid salaries of $400 are recorded with a debit to Prepaid Salaries of $400 and a credit to Salaries Expense of $400.

c. Office supplies purchased for the period were $1,000. The cost of unused office supplies of $650 is recorded with a debit to Supplies Expense of $650 and a credit to Office Supplies of $650.

d. Earned but unbilled (and unrecorded) consulting fees for the period were $1,200, which are recorded with a debit to Unearned Consulting Fees of $1,200 and a credit to Consulting Fees Earned of $1,200.

QS 3-20^A
Preparing adjusting entries

P6

The ledger of Mai Company includes the following accounts with normal balances. Prepare the necessary closing entries from this December 31 year-end information.

Common Stock	$ 9,000	Wages Expense	$8,400
Dividends................	800	Rent Expense....................	1,600
Services Revenue	13,000		

QS 3-21
Preparing closing entries from the ledger

P4

QS 3-22
Identifying post-closing accounts   **P5**

Identify which of the following accounts would be included in a post-closing trial balance.

_____ **a.** Accounts Receivable   _____ **c.** Goodwill   _____ **e.** Income Tax Expense
_____ **b.** Salaries Expense   _____ **d.** Land   _____ **f.** Salaries Payable

---

QS 3-23
Identifying the accounting cycle

C2

List the following steps of the accounting cycle in their proper order.

_____ **a.** Posting the journal entries.   _____ **f.** Preparing the financial statements.
_____ **b.** Journalizing and posting adjusting entries.   _____ **g.** Preparing the unadjusted trial balance.
_____ **c.** Preparing the adjusted trial balance.   _____ **h.** Journalizing transactions and events.
_____ **d.** Journalizing and posting closing entries.   _____ **i.** Preparing the post-closing trial balance.
_____ **e.** Analyzing transactions and events.

QS 3-24
Classifying balance sheet items

C3

The following are common categories on a classified balance sheet.

A. Current assets   **D.** Intangible assets
B. Long-term investments   **E.** Current liabilities
C. Plant assets   **F.** Long-term liabilities

For each of the following items, select the letter that identifies the balance sheet category where the item typically would best appear.

_____ **1.** Land not currently used in operations   _____ **5.** Accounts payable
_____ **2.** Notes payable (due in five years)   _____ **6.** Store equipment
_____ **3.** Accounts receivable   _____ **7.** Wages payable
_____ **4.** Trademarks   _____ **8.** Cash

QS 3-25
Identifying current accounts and computing the current ratio

A2

Compute Chavez Company's current ratio using the following information.

Accounts receivable	$18,000	Long-term notes payable	$21,000
Accounts payable	11,000	Office supplies	2,800
Buildings	45,000	Prepaid insurance	3,560
Cash	7,000	Unearned services revenue	3,000

QS 3-26[B]
Extending accounts in a work sheet   **P7**

Check Net income, $17,800

The Adjusted Trial Balance columns of a 10-column work sheet for Planta Company follow. Complete the work sheet by extending the account balances into the appropriate financial statement columns and by entering the amount of net income for the reporting period.

	A	B	C	D	E	F	G	H	I	J	K	L
1			**Unadjusted**				**Adjusted**		**Income**			
2			**Trial Balance**		**Adjustments**		**Trial Balance**		**Statement**		**Balance Sheet**	
3	**No.**	**Account Title**	**Dr.**	**Cr.**	**Dr.**	**Cr.**	**Dr.**	**Cr.**	**Dr.**	**Cr.**	**Dr.**	**Cr.**
4	101	Cash					$ 7,000					
5	106	Accounts receivable					27,200					
6	153	Trucks					42,000					
7	154	Accumulated depreciation—Trucks						$ 17,500				
8	183	Land					32,000					
9	201	Accounts payable						15,000				
10	209	Salaries payable						4,200				
11	233	Unearned fees						3,600				
12	307	Common stock						20,000				
13	318	Retained earnings						45,500				
14	319	Dividends					15,400					
15	401	Plumbing fees earned						84,000				
16	611	Depreciation expense—Trucks					6,500					
17	622	Salaries expense					38,000					
18	640	Rent expense					13,000					
19	677	Miscellaneous expenses					8,700					
20		Totals					$189,800	$189,800				
21												

On December 31, 2015, Yates Co. prepared an adjusting entry for $12,000 of earned but unrecorded consulting fees. On January 16, 2016, Yates received $26,700 cash in consulting fees, which included the accrued fees earned in 2015. (Assume the company uses reversing entries.)

a. Prepare the December 31, 2015, adjusting entry.

b. Prepare the January 1, 2016, reversing entry.

c. Prepare the January 16, 2016, cash receipt entry.

QS 3-27^c
Reversing entries
P8

Mc Graw Hill Education **connect**

Pablo Management has five part-time employees, each of whom earns $250 per day. They are normally paid on Fridays for work completed Monday through Friday of the same week. Assume that December 28, 2016, was a Friday and that they were paid in full on that day. The next week, the five employees worked only four days because New Year's Day was an unpaid holiday.

a. Assuming that December 31, 2016, was a Monday, prepare the adjusting entry that would be recorded at the close of that day.

b. Assuming that January 4, 2017, was a Friday, prepare the journal entry that would be made to record payment of the employees' wages.

EXERCISES

Exercise 3-1
Adjusting and paying accrued wages
P1

The following three separate situations require adjusting journal entries to prepare financial statements as of April 30. For each situation, present both the April 30 adjusting entry and the subsequent entry during May to record the payment of the accrued expenses.

a. On April 1, the company retained an attorney for a flat monthly fee of $3,500. Payment for April legal services was made by the company on May 12.

b. A $900,000 note payable requires 12% annual interest, or $9,000, to be paid at the 20th day of each month. The interest was last paid on April 20 and the next payment is due on May 20. As of April 30, $3,000 of interest expense has accrued.

c. Total weekly salaries expense for all employees is $10,000. This amount is paid at the end of the day on Friday of each five-day workweek. April 30 falls on a Tuesday, which means that the employees had worked two days since the last payday. The next payday is May 3.

Exercise 3-2
Adjusting and paying accrued expenses
P1

Check (b) May 20 Dr. Interest Expense, $6,000

Prepare adjusting journal entries for the year ended (date of) December 31, 2016, for each of these separate situations. Assume that prepaid expenses are initially recorded in asset accounts. Also assume that fees collected in advance of work are initially recorded as liabilities.

a. Depreciation on the company's equipment for 2016 is computed to be $18,000.

b. The Prepaid Insurance account had a $6,000 debit balance at December 31, 2016, before adjusting for the costs of any expired coverage. An analysis of the company's insurance policies showed that $1,100 of unexpired insurance coverage remains.

c. The Office Supplies account had a $700 debit balance on December 31, 2015; and $3,480 of office supplies were purchased during the year. The December 31, 2016, physical count showed $300 of supplies available.

d. Two-thirds of the work related to $15,000 of cash received in advance was performed this period.

e. The Prepaid Insurance account had a $6,800 debit balance at December 31, 2016, before adjusting for the costs of any expired coverage. An analysis of insurance policies showed that $5,800 of coverage had expired.

f. Wage expenses of $3,200 have been incurred but are not paid as of December 31, 2016.

Exercise 3-3
Preparing adjusting entries
P1

Check (c) Dr. Office Supplies Expense, $3,880

(e) Dr. Insurance Expense, $5,800

For each of the following separate cases, prepare adjusting entries required for financial statements for the year ended (date of) December 31, 2016. (Assume that prepaid expenses are initially recorded in asset accounts and that fees collected in advance of work are initially recorded as liabilities.)

a. One-third of the work related to $15,000 cash received in advance is performed this period.

b. Wages of $8,000 are earned by workers but not paid as of December 31, 2016.

c. Depreciation on the company's equipment for 2016 is $18,000.

Continued on next page . . .

Exercise 3-4
Preparing adjusting entries
P1

d. The Office Supplies account had a $240 debit balance on December 31, 2015. During 2016, $5,200 of office supplies are purchased. A physical count of supplies at December 31, 2016, shows $440 of supplies available.

Check   (e) Dr. Insurance
Expense, $2,800

       (f) Cr. Interest
Revenue, $1,050

e. The Prepaid Insurance account had a $4,000 balance on December 31, 2015. An analysis of insurance policies shows that $1,200 of unexpired insurance benefits remain at December 31, 2016.

f. The company has earned (but not recorded) $1,050 of interest from investments in CDs for the year ended December 31, 2016. The interest revenue will be received on January 10, 2017.

g. The company has a bank loan and has incurred (but not recorded) interest expense of $2,500 for the year ended December 31, 2016. The company must pay the interest on January 2, 2017.

Exercise 3-5

Analyzing and preparing adjusting entries

P1   P3

Following are two income statements for Alexis Co. for the year ended December 31. The left column is prepared before any adjusting entries are recorded and the right column includes the effects of adjusting entries. The company records cash receipts and payments related to unearned and prepaid items in balance sheet accounts. Analyze the statements and prepare the eight adjusting entries that likely were recorded. (*Note:* 30% of the $7,000 adjustment for Fees Earned has been earned but not billed, and the other 70% has been earned by performing services that were paid for in advance.)

ALEXIS CO.
Income Statements
For Year Ended December 31

	Unadjusted	Adjusted
Revenues		
Fees earned	$18,000	$25,000
Commissions earned	36,500	36,500
Total revenues	54,500	61,500
Expenses		
Depreciation expense—Computers	0	1,600
Depreciation expense—Office furniture	0	1,850
Salaries expense	13,500	15,750
Insurance expense	0	1,400
Rent expense	3,800	3,800
Office supplies expense	0	580
Advertising expense	2,500	2,500
Utilities expense	1,245	1,335
Total expenses	21,045	28,815
Net income	$33,455	$32,685

Exercise 3-6

Preparing a balance sheet following IFRS

P3

adidas Group reports the following balance sheet accounts for the year ended December 31, 2014 (euros in millions). Prepare the balance sheet for this company as of December 31, 2014, following usual IFRS practices.

Property, plant and equipment	€1,454	Intangible assets	€2,763
Total equity	5,617	Total current liabilities	4,378
Accounts receivable	1,946	Inventories	2,526
Total noncurrent liabilities	2,422	Total liabilities	6,800
Cash and cash equivalents	1,683	Other current assets	1,192
Total current assets	7,347	Total noncurrent assets	5,070
Other noncurrent assets	853		

Use the following adjusted trial balance of Wilson Trucking Company to prepare the (1) income statement and (2) statement of retained earnings for the year ended December 31, 2016. The Retained Earnings account balance is $155,000 at December 31, 2015.

Exercise 3-7
Preparing financial statements
P3

Account Title	Debit	Credit
Cash	$ 8,000	
Accounts receivable	17,500	
Office supplies	3,000	
Trucks	172,000	
Accumulated depreciation—Trucks		$ 36,000
Land	85,000	
Accounts payable		12,000
Interest payable		4,000
Long-term notes payable		53,000
Common stock		20,000
Retained earnings		155,000
Dividends	20,000	
Trucking fees earned		130,000
Depreciation expense—Trucks	23,500	
Salaries expense	61,000	
Office supplies expense	8,000	
Repairs expense—Trucks	12,000	
Totals	$410,000	$410,000

Following are **Nintendo**'s revenue and expense accounts for a recent calendar year (yen in millions). Prepare the company's closing entries for its revenues and its expenses.

Exercise 3-8
Preparing closing entries
P4

Net sales	¥571,726
Cost of sales	408,506
Advertising expense	70,264
Other expense, net	156,786

Use the information in the adjusted trial balance reported in Exercise 3-7 to prepare Wilson Trucking Company's classified balance sheet as of December 31, 2016.

Exercise 3-9
Preparing a classified balance sheet
C3

Check Total assets, $249,500

Use the following information to compute profit margin for each separate company *a* through *e*.

Exercise 3-10
Computing and interpreting profit margin
A1

	Net Income	*Net Sales*		*Net Income*	*Net Sales*
a.	$ 4,361	$ 44,500	**d.**	$65,646	$1,458,800
b.	97,706	398,800	**e.**	80,132	435,500
c.	111,281	257,000			

Which of the five companies is the most profitable according to the profit margin ratio? Interpret that company's profit margin ratio.

Exercise 3-11
Computing and analyzing the current ratio

A2

Calculate the current ratio in each of the following separate cases (round the ratio to two decimals). Identify the company case with the strongest liquidity position. (These cases represent competing companies in the same industry.)

	Current Assets	Current Liabilities
Case 1	$ 79,040	$ 32,000
Case 2	104,880	76,000
Case 3	45,080	49,000
Case 4	85,680	81,600
Case 5	61,000	100,000

Exercise 3-12^A

Exercise 3-12^A
Adjusting for prepaids recorded as expenses and unearned revenues recorded as revenues

P6

Ricardo Construction began operations on December 1. In setting up its accounting procedures, the company decided to debit expense accounts when it prepays its expenses and to credit revenue accounts when customers pay for services in advance. Prepare journal entries for items *a* through *d* and the adjusting entries as of its December 31 period-end for items *e* through *g*.

a. Supplies are purchased on December 1 for $2,000 cash.

b. The company prepays its insurance premiums for $1,540 cash on December 2.

c. On December 15, the company receives an advance payment of $13,000 cash from a customer for remodeling work.

d. On December 28, the company receives $3,700 cash from another customer for remodeling work to be performed in January.

e. A physical count on December 31 indicates that the Company has $1,840 of supplies available.

Check (f) Cr. Insurance Expense, $1,200

f. An analysis of the insurance policies in effect on December 31 shows that $340 of insurance coverage has expired.

(g) Dr. Remodeling Fees Earned, $11,130

g. As of December 31, only one remodeling project has been worked on and completed. The $5,570 fee for this project had been received in advance and recorded as remodeling fees earned.

Exercise 3-13^A

Exercise 3-13^A
Recording and reporting revenues received in advance

P6

Costanza Company experienced the following events and transactions during July.

July	1	Received $3,000 cash in advance of performing work for Vivian Solana.
	6	Received $7,500 cash in advance of performing work for Iris Haru.
	12	Completed the job for Solana.
	18	Received $8,500 cash in advance of performing work for Amina Jordan.
	27	Completed the job for Haru.
	31	None of the work for Jordan has been performed.

a. Prepare journal entries (including any adjusting entries as of the end of the month) to record these events using the procedure of initially crediting the Unearned Fees account when payment is received from a customer in advance of performing services.

b. Prepare journal entries (including any adjusting entries as of the end of the month) to record these events using the procedure of initially crediting the Fees Earned account when payment is received from a customer in advance of performing services.

Check (c) Fees Earned—using entries from part *b*, $10,500

c. Under each method, determine the amount of earned fees reported on the income statement for July and the amount of unearned fees reported on the balance sheet as of July 31.

Exercise 3-14^B

Exercise 3-14^B
Completing a work sheet

P7

The following data are taken from the unadjusted trial balance of the Westcott Company at December 31, 2016. Each account carries a normal balance and the accounts are shown here.

Accounts Payable	$ 6	Prepaid Insurance.......	$18	Retained earnings	$32
Accounts Receivable	12	Revenue	75	Dividends	6
Accumulated Depreciation—Equip.	15	Salaries Expense........	18	Unearned Revenue	12
Cash	21	Supplies..............	24	Utilities Expense	12
Equipment	39	Common Stock	10		

1. Use the data above to prepare a work sheet. Enter the accounts in proper order and enter their balances in the correct Debit or Credit column.
2. Use the following adjustment information to complete the work sheet.
   a. Depreciation on equipment, $3
   b. Accrued salaries, $6
   c. The $12 of unearned revenue has been earned
   d. Supplies available at December 31, 2016, $15
   e. Expired insurance, $15

The following two events occurred for Trey Co. on October 31, 2016, the end of its fiscal year.

a. Trey rents a building from its owner for $2,800 per month. By prearrangement, the company delayed paying October's rent until November 5. On this date, the company paid the rent for both October and November.
b. Trey rents space in a building it owns to a tenant for $850 per month. By prearrangement, the tenant delayed paying the October rent until November 8. On this date, the tenant paid the rent for both October and November.

Exercise 3-15^C

Preparing reversing entries

P8

Required

1. Prepare adjusting entries that the company must record for these events as of October 31.
2. Assuming Trey does *not* use reversing entries, prepare journal entries to record Trey's payment of rent on November 5 and the collection of the tenant's rent on November 8.
3. Assuming that the company uses reversing entries, prepare reversing entries on November 1 and the journal entries to record Trey's payment of rent on November 5 and the collection of the tenant's rent on November 8.

connect

For each of the following entries, enter the letter of the explanation that most closely describes it in the space beside each entry. (You can use letters more than once.)

A. To record receipt of unearned revenue.
B. To record this period's earning of prior unearned revenue.
C. To record payment of an accrued expense.
D. To record receipt of an accrued revenue.
E. To record an accrued expense.

F. To record an accrued revenue.
G. To record this period's use of a prepaid expense.
H. To record payment of a prepaid expense.
I. To record this period's depreciation expense.

PROBLEM SET A

Problem 3-1A
Identifying adjusting entries with explanations

P1

___	1.	Interest Expense..............................	1,000	
		Interest Payable		1,000
___	2.	Depreciation Expense	4,000	
		Accumulated Depreciation		4,000
___	3.	Unearned Professional Fees....................	3,000	
		Professional Fees Earned		3,000
___	4.	Insurance Expense	4,200	
		Prepaid Insurance............................		4,200
___	5.	Salaries Payable	1,400	
		Cash		1,400
___	6.	Prepaid Rent................................	4,500	
		Cash		4,500
___	7.	Salaries Expense............................	6,000	
		Salaries Payable............................		6,000
___	8.	Interest Receivable..........................	5,000	
		Interest Revenue............................		5,000
___	9.	Cash	9,000	
		Accounts Receivable (from consulting)...........		9,000
___	10.	Cash	7,500	
		Unearned Professional Fees....................		7,500
___	11.	Cash	2,000	
		Interest Receivable..........................		2,000
___	12.	Rent Expense	2,000	
		Prepaid Rent................................		2,000

Problem 3-2A

Preparing adjusting and subsequent journal entries

A1   P1

Arnez Co. follows the practice of recording prepaid expenses and unearned revenues in balance sheet accounts. The company's annual accounting period ends on December 31, 2016. The following information concerns the adjusting entries to be recorded as of that date.

a. The Office Supplies account started the year with a $4,000 balance. During 2016, the company purchased supplies for $13,400, which was added to the Office Supplies account. The inventory of supplies available at December 31, 2016, totaled $2,554.

b. An analysis of the company's insurance policies provided the following facts.

Policy	Date of Purchase	Months of Coverage	Cost
A	April 1, 2014	24	$14,400
B	April 1, 2015	36	12,960
C	August 1, 2016	12	2,400

The total premium for each policy was paid in full (for all months) at the purchase date, and the Prepaid Insurance account was debited for the full cost. (Year-end adjusting entries for Prepaid Insurance were properly recorded in all prior years.)

c. The company has 15 employees, who earn a total of $1,960 in salaries each working day. They are paid each Monday for their work in the five-day workweek ending on the previous Friday. Assume that December 31, 2016, is a Tuesday, and all 15 employees worked the first two days of that week. Because New Year's Day is a paid holiday, they will be paid salaries for five full days on Monday, January 6, 2017.

d. The company purchased a building on January 1, 2016. It cost $960,000 and is expected to have a $45,000 salvage value at the end of its predicted 30-year life. Annual depreciation is $30,500.

e. Since the company is not large enough to occupy the entire building it owns, it rented space to a tenant at $3,000 per month, starting on November 1, 2016. The rent was paid on time on November 1, and the amount received was credited to the Rent Earned account. However, the tenant has not paid the December rent. The company has worked out an agreement with the tenant, who has promised to pay both December and January rent in full on January 15. The tenant has agreed not to fall behind again.

f. On November 1, the company rented space to another tenant for $2,800 per month. The tenant paid five months' rent in advance on that date. The payment was recorded with a credit to the Unearned Rent account.

Check   (1b) Dr. Insurance Expense, $7,120

(1d) Dr. Depreciation Expense, $30,500

Required

1. Use the information to prepare adjusting entries as of December 31, 2016.

2. Prepare journal entries to record the first subsequent cash transaction in 2017 for parts *c* and *e*.

Problem 3-3A

Preparing adjusting entries, adjusted trial balance, and financial statements

P1   P2   P3

Wells Technical Institute (WTI), a school owned by Tristana Wells, provides training to individuals who pay tuition directly to the school. WTI also offers training to groups in off-site locations. Its unadjusted trial balance as of December 31, 2016, follows. WTI initially records prepaid expenses and unearned revenues in balance sheet accounts. Descriptions of items *a* through *h* that require adjusting entries on December 31, 2016, follow.

Additional Information Items

a. An analysis of WTI's insurance policies shows that $2,400 of coverage has expired.

b. An inventory count shows that teaching supplies costing $2,800 are available at year-end 2016.

c. Annual depreciation on the equipment is $13,200.

d. Annual depreciation on the professional library is $7,200.

e. On November 1, WTI agreed to do a special six-month course (starting immediately) for a client. The contract calls for a monthly fee of $2,500, and the client paid the first five months' fees in advance. When the cash was received, the Unearned Training Fees account was credited. The fee for the sixth month will be recorded when it is collected in 2016.

f. On October 15, WTI agreed to teach a four-month class (beginning immediately) for an individual for $3,000 tuition per month payable at the end of the class. The class started on October 15, but no payment has yet been received. (WTI's accruals are applied to the nearest half-month; for example, October recognizes one-half month accrual.)

g. WTI's two employees are paid weekly. As of the end of the year, two days' salaries have accrued at the rate of $100 per day for each employee.

h. The balance in the Prepaid Rent account represents rent for December.

	WELLS TECHNICAL INSTITUTE Unadjusted Trial Balance December 31, 2016	Debit	Credit
3	Cash	$ 34,000	
4	Accounts receivable	0	
5	Teaching supplies	8,000	
6	Prepaid insurance	12,000	
7	Prepaid rent	3,000	
8	Professional library	35,000	
9	Accumulated depreciation—Professional library		$ 10,000
10	Equipment	80,000	
11	Accumulated depreciation—Equipment		15,000
12	Accounts payable		26,000
13	Salaries payable		0
14	Unearned training fees		12,500
15	Common stock		10,000
16	Retained earnings		80,000
17	Dividends	50,000	
18	Tuition fees earned		123,900
19	Training fees earned		40,000
20	Depreciation expense—Professional library	0	
21	Depreciation expense—Equipment	0	
22	Salaries expense	50,000	
23	Insurance expense	0	
24	Rent expense	33,000	
25	Teaching supplies expense	0	
26	Advertising expense	6,000	
27	Utilities expense	6,400	
28	Totals	$ 317,400	$ 317,400

Required

1. Prepare T-accounts (representing the ledger) with balances from the unadjusted trial balance.

2. Prepare the necessary adjusting journal entries for items *a* through *h* and post them to the T-accounts. Assume that adjusting entries are made only at year-end.

3. Update balances in the T-accounts for the adjusting entries and prepare an adjusted trial balance.

4. Prepare Wells Technical Institute's income statement and statement of retained earnings for the year 2016 and prepare its balance sheet as of December 31, 2016.

Check   (2c) Cr. Training Fees Earned, $5,000
(2f) Cr. Tuition Fees Earned, $7,500
(3) Adj. trial balance totals, $345,700
(4) Net income, $49,600

A six-column table for JKL Company follows. The first two columns contain the unadjusted trial balance for the company as of July 31, 2016. The last two columns contain the adjusted trial balance as of the same date.

Required

Analysis Component

1. Analyze the differences between the unadjusted and adjusted trial balances to determine the eight adjustments that likely were made. Show the results of your analysis by inserting these adjustment amounts in the table's two middle columns. Label each adjustment with a letter *a* through *h* and provide a short description of it at the bottom of the table.

Preparation Component

2. Use the information in the adjusted trial balance to prepare the company's (*a*) income statement and its statement of retained earnings for the year ended July 31, 2016 (*Note:* Retained earnings at July 31, 2015, was $25,000, and the current-year dividends were $5,000), and (*b*) the balance sheet as of July 31, 2016.

Problem 3-4A
Interpreting unadjusted and adjusted trial balances, and preparing financial statements

P1   P2   P3

Check   (2) Net income, $4,960; Total assets, $124,960

	Unadjusted Trial Balance		Adjustments		Adjusted Trial Balance	
Cash	$ 34,000				$ 34,000	
Accounts receivable	14,000				22,000	
Office supplies	16,000				2,000	
Prepaid insurance	8,540				2,960	
Office equipment	84,000				84,000	
Accum. depreciation—						
Office equip.		$ 14,000				$ 20,000
Accounts payable		9,100				10,000
Interest payable		0				1,000
Salaries payable		0				7,000
Unearned consulting fees		18,000				15,000
Long-term notes payable		52,000				52,000
Common stock..............		15,000				15,000
Retained earnings		25,000				25,000
Dividends	5,000				5,000	
Consulting fees earned		123,240				134,240
Depreciation expense—						
Office equip.	0				6,000	
Salaries expense	67,000				74,000	
Interest expense	1,200				2,200	
Insurance expense	0				5,580	
Rent expense	14,500				14,500	
Office supplies expense	0				14,000	
Advertising expense	12,100				13,000	
Totals	$256,340	$256,340			$279,240	$279,240

Problem 3-5A
Preparing financial statements from the adjusted trial balance and calculating profit margin

P3   A1

The adjusted trial balance for Chiara Company as of December 31, 2016, follows.

	Debit	Credit
Cash.......................................	$ 30,000	
Accounts receivable	52,000	
Interest receivable............................	18,000	
Notes receivable (due in 90 days)	168,000	
Office supplies................................	16,000	
Automobiles	168,000	
Accumulated depreciation—Automobiles		$ 50,000
Equipment...................................	138,000	
Accumulated depreciation—Equipment............		18,000
Land.......................................	78,000	
Accounts payable..............................		96,000
Interest payable		20,000
Salaries payable		19,000
Unearned fees................................		30,000
Long-term notes payable........................		138,000
Common stock		20,000
Retained earnings		235,800
Dividends....................................	46,000	
Fees earned..................................		484,000
Interest earned		24,000
Depreciation expense—Automobiles	26,000	
Depreciation expense—Equipment	18,000	
Salaries expense	188,000	
Wages expense	40,000	
Interest expense	32,000	
Office supplies expense.........................	34,000	
Advertising expense	58,000	
Repairs expense—Automobiles	24,800	
Totals......................................	$1,134,800	$1,134,800

Required

1. Use the information in the adjusted trial balance to prepare (*a*) the income statement for the year ended December 31, 2016; (*b*) the statement of retained earnings for the year ended December 31, 2016; and (*c*) the balance sheet as of December 31, 2016.
2. Compute the profit margin for year 2016 (use total revenues as the denominator).

Check (1) Total assets, $600,000

On April 1, 2016, Jiro Nozomi created a new travel agency, Adventure Travel. The following transactions occurred during the company's first month.

Problem 3-6A
Applying the accounting cycle
P1 P2 P3 P4 P5

April	1	Nozomi invested $30,000 cash and computer equipment worth $20,000 in the company in exchange for common stock.
	2	The company rented furnished office space by paying $1,800 cash for the first month's (April) rent.
	3	The company purchased $1,000 of office supplies for cash.
	10	The company paid $2,400 cash for the premium on a 12-month insurance policy. Coverage begins on April 11.
	14	The company paid $1,600 cash for two weeks' salaries earned by employees.
	24	The company collected $8,000 cash on commissions from airlines on tickets obtained for customers.
	28	The company paid $1,600 cash for two weeks' salaries earned by employees.
	29	The company paid $350 cash for minor repairs to the company's computer.
	30	The company paid $750 cash for this month's telephone bill.
	30	The company paid $1,500 cash in dividends.

The company's chart of accounts follows:

101	Cash		405	Commissions Earned
106	Accounts Receivable		612	Depreciation Expense — Computer Equip.
124	Office Supplies		622	Salaries Expense
128	Prepaid Insurance		637	Insurance Expense
167	Computer Equipment		640	Rent Expense
168	Accumulated Depreciation—Computer Equip.		650	Office Supplies Expense
209	Salaries Payable		684	Repairs Expense
307	Common Stock		688	Telephone Expense
318	Retained Earnings		901	Income Summary
319	Dividends			

Required

1. Use the balance column format to set up each ledger account listed in its chart of accounts.
2. Prepare journal entries to record the transactions for April and post them to the ledger accounts. The company records prepaid and unearned items in balance sheet accounts.
3. Prepare an unadjusted trial balance as of April 30.
4. Use the following information to journalize and post adjusting entries for the month:
   a. Two-thirds (or $133) of one month's insurance coverage has expired.
   b. At the end of the month, $600 of office supplies are still available.
   c. This month's depreciation on the computer equipment is $500.
   d. Employees earned $420 of unpaid and unrecorded salaries as of month-end.
   e. The company earned $1,750 of commissions that are not yet billed at month-end.
5. Prepare the adjusted trial balance as of April 30. Prepare the income statement and the statement of retained earnings for the month of April and the balance sheet at April 30, 2016.
6. Prepare journal entries to close the temporary accounts and post these entries to the ledger.
7. Prepare a post-closing trial balance.

Check (3) Unadj. trial balance totals, $58,000

(4a) Dr. Insurance Expense, $133

(5) Net income, $2,197; Total assets, $51,117

(7) P-C trial balance totals, $51,617

Problem 3-7A
Determining balance
sheet classifications

C3

In the blank space beside each numbered balance sheet item, enter the letter of its balance sheet classification. If the item should not appear on the balance sheet, enter a Z in the blank.

A. Current assets   **E.** Current liabilities
B. Long-term investments   **F.** Long-term liabilities
C. Plant assets   **G.** Equity
D. Intangible assets

_____ **1.** Long-term investment in stock   _____ **12.** Accumulated depreciation—Trucks
_____ **2.** Depreciation expense—Building   _____ **13.** Cash
_____ **3.** Prepaid rent   _____ **14.** Buildings
_____ **4.** Interest receivable   _____ **15.** Store supplies
_____ **5.** Taxes payable   _____ **16.** Office equipment
_____ **6.** Automobiles   _____ **17.** Land (used in operations)
_____ **7.** Notes payable (due in 3 years)   _____ **18.** Repairs expense
_____ **8.** Accounts payable   _____ **19.** Office supplies
_____ **9.** Prepaid insurance   _____ **20.** Current portion of long-term note
_____ **10.** Common stock   payable
_____ **11.** Unearned services revenue

Problem 3-8A
Preparing closing entries,
financial statements, and
ratios

A1   A2   P3   P4

The adjusted trial balance for Tybalt Construction as of December 31, 2016, follows.

No.	Account Title	Debit	Credit
	TYBALT CONSTRUCTION		
	Adjusted Trial Balance		
	December 31, 2016		
101	Cash	$ 5,000	
104	Short-term investments	23,000	
126	Supplies	8,100	
128	Prepaid insurance	7,000	
167	Equipment	40,000	
168	Accumulated depreciation—Equipment		$ 20,000
173	Building	150,000	
174	Accumulated depreciation—Building		50,000
183	Land	55,000	
201	Accounts payable		16,500
203	Interest payable		2,500
208	Rent payable		3,500
210	Wages payable		2,500
213	Property taxes payable		900
233	Unearned professional fees		7,500
251	Long-term notes payable		67,000
307	Common stock..............................		5,000
318	Retained earnings		121,400
319	Dividends	13,000	
401	Professional fees earned		97,000
406	Rent earned		14,000
407	Dividends earned		2,000
409	Interest earned		2,100
606	Depreciation expense—Building	11,000	
612	Depreciation expense—Equipment	6,000	
623	Wages expense	32,000	
633	Interest expense	5,100	
637	Insurance expense	10,000	
640	Rent expense	13,400	
652	Supplies expense	7,400	
682	Postage expense	4,200	
683	Property taxes expense	5,000	
684	Repairs expense	8,900	
688	Telephone expense	3,200	
690	Utilities expense	4,600	
	Totals	$411,900	$411,900

The December 31, 2015, credit balance of the Retained Earnings account was $121,400. Tybalt Construction is required to make a $7,000 payment on its long-term notes payable during 2017.

Required

1. Prepare the income statement and the statement of retained earnings for the calendar year 2016 and the classified balance sheet at December 31, 2016.

2. Prepare the necessary closing entries at December 31, 2016.

3. Use the information in the financial statements to compute these ratios: (*a*) return on assets (total assets at December 31, 2015, was $200,000), (*b*) debt ratio, (*c*) profit margin ratio (use total revenues as the denominator), and (*d*) current ratio. Round ratios to three decimals for parts *a* and *c*, and to two decimals for parts *b* and *d*.

Check (1) Total assets (12/31/2016), $218,100; Net income, $4,300

For each of the following entries, enter the letter of the explanation that most closely describes it in the space beside each entry. (You can use letters more than once.)

PROBLEM SET B

A. To record payment of a prepaid expense.

B. To record this period's use of a prepaid expense.

C. To record this period's depreciation expense.

D. To record receipt of unearned revenue.

E. To record this period's earning of prior unearned revenue.

F. To record an accrued expense.

G. To record payment of an accrued expense.

H. To record an accrued revenue.

I. To record receipt of an accrued revenue.

Problem 3-1B
Identifying adjusting entries with explanations

P1

_____	1.	Interest Receivable...........................	3,500
		Interest Revenue	3,500
_____	2.	Salaries Payable	9,000
		Cash	9,000
_____	3.	Depreciation Expense	8,000
		Accumulated Depreciation	8,000
_____	4.	Cash	9,000
		Unearned Professional Fees.............	9,000
_____	5.	Insurance Expense	4,000
		Prepaid Insurance......................	4,000
_____	6.	Interest Expense	5,000
		Interest Payable	5,000
_____	7.	Cash	1,500
		Accounts Receivable (from services) ...	1,500
_____	8.	Salaries Expense	7,000
		Salaries Payable.......................	7,000
_____	9.	Cash	1,000
		Interest Receivable	1,000
_____	10.	Prepaid Rent	3,000
		Cash	3,000
_____	11.	Rent Expense	7,500
		Prepaid Rent..........................	7,500
_____	12.	Unearned Professional Fees...............	6,000
		Professional Fees Earned	6,000

Natsu Co. follows the practice of recording prepaid expenses and unearned revenues in balance sheet accounts. The company's annual accounting period ends on October 31, 2016. The following information concerns the adjusting entries that need to be recorded as of that date.

a. The Office Supplies account started the fiscal year with a $600 balance. During the fiscal year, the company purchased supplies for $4,570, which was added to the Office Supplies account. The supplies available at October 31, 2016, totaled $800.

b. An analysis of the company's insurance policies provided the following facts.

Problem 3-2B
Preparing adjusting and subsequent journal entries

P1

Policy	Date of Purchase	Months of Coverage	Cost
A	April 1, 2015	24	$6,000
B	April 1, 2016	36	7,200
C	August 1, 2016	12	1,320

The total premium for each policy was paid in full (for all months) at the purchase date, and the Prepaid Insurance account was debited for the full cost. (Year-end adjusting entries for Prepaid Insurance were properly recorded in all prior fiscal years.)

c. The company has four employees, who earn a total of $1,000 for each workday. They are paid each Monday for their work in the five-day workweek ending on the previous Friday. Assume that October 31, 2016, is a Monday, and all four employees worked the first day of that week. They will be paid salaries for five full days on Monday, November 7, 2016.

d. The company purchased a building on November 1, 2013, that cost $175,000 and is expected to have a $40,000 salvage value at the end of its predicted 25-year life. Annual depreciation is $5,400.

e. Since the company does not occupy the entire building it owns, it rented space to a tenant at $1,000 per month, starting on September 1, 2016. The rent was paid on time on September 1, and the amount received was credited to the Rent Earned account. However, the October rent has not been paid. The company has worked out an agreement with the tenant, who has promised to pay both October and November rent in full on November 15. The tenant has agreed not to fall behind again.

f. On September 1, the company rented space to another tenant for $725 per month. The tenant paid five months' rent in advance on that date. The payment was recorded with a credit to the Unearned Rent account.

Required

1. Use the information to prepare adjusting entries as of October 31, 2016.

2. Prepare journal entries to record the first subsequent cash transaction in November 2016 for parts c and e.

Problem 3-3B

Preparing adjusting entries, adjusted trial balance, and financial statements

P1   P2   P3

Following is the unadjusted trial balance for Alonzo Institute as of December 31, 2016, which initially records prepaid expenses and unearned revenues in balance sheet accounts. The Institute provides one-on-one training to individuals who pay tuition directly to the business and offers extension training to groups in off-site locations. Shown after the trial balance are items *a* through *h* that require adjusting entries as of December 31, 2016.

ALONZO INSTITUTE Unadjusted Trial Balance December 31, 2016		
	Debit	**Credit**
Cash	$ 60,000	
Accounts receivable	0	
Teaching supplies	70,000	
Prepaid insurance	19,000	
Prepaid rent	3,800	
Professional library	12,000	
Accumulated depreciation—Professional library		$ 2,500
Equipment	40,000	
Accumulated depreciation—Equipment		20,000
Accounts payable		11,200
Salaries payable		0
Unearned training fees		28,600
Common stock		11,000
Retained earnings		60,500
Dividends	20,000	
Tuition fees earned		129,200
Training fees earned		68,000
Depreciation expense—Professional library	0	
Depreciation expense—Equipment	0	
Salaries expense	44,200	
Insurance expense	0	
Rent expense	29,600	
Teaching supplies expense	0	
Advertising expense	19,000	
Utilities expense	13,400	
Totals	$331,000	$331,000

Additional Information Items

a. An analysis of the Institute's insurance policies shows that $9,500 of coverage has expired.

b. An inventory count shows that teaching supplies costing $20,000 are available at year-end 2016.

c. Annual depreciation on the equipment is $5,000.

d. Annual depreciation on the professional library is $2,400.

e. On November 1, the Institute agreed to do a special five-month course (starting immediately) for a client. The contract calls for a $14,300 monthly fee, and the client paid the first two months' fees in advance. When the cash was received, the Unearned Training Fees account was credited. The last two months' fees will be recorded when collected in 2017.

f. On October 15, the Institute agreed to teach a four-month class (beginning immediately) to an individual for $2,300 tuition per month payable at the end of the class. The class started on October 15, but no payment has yet been received. (The Institute's accruals are applied to the nearest half-month; for example, October recognizes one-half month accrual.)

g. The Institute's only employee is paid weekly. As of the end of the year, three days' salaries have accrued at the rate of $150 per day.

h. The balance in the Prepaid Rent account represents rent for December.

Required

1. Prepare T-accounts (representing the ledger) with balances from the unadjusted trial balance.

2. Prepare the necessary adjusting journal entries for items *a* through *h*, and post them to the T-accounts. Assume that adjusting entries are made only at year-end.

3. Update balances in the T-accounts for the adjusting entries and prepare an adjusted trial balance.

4. Prepare the company's income statement and statement of retained earnings for the year 2016, and prepare its balance sheet as of December 31, 2016.

Check (2e) Cr. Training Fees Earned, $28,600; (2f) Cr. Tuition Fees Earned, $5,750; (3) Adj. trial balance totals, $344,600; (4) Net income, $54,200

A six-column table for Yan Consulting Company follows. The first two columns contain the unadjusted trial balance for the company as of December 31, 2016, and the last two columns contain the adjusted trial balance as of the same date.

Problem 3-4B
Interpreting unadjusted and adjusted trial balances, and preparing financial statements

P1 P2 P3

	Unadjusted Trial Balance		Adjustments		Adjusted Trial Balance	
Cash	$ 45,000				$ 45,000	
Accounts receivable	60,000				66,660	
Office supplies	40,000				17,000	
Prepaid insurance	8,200				3,600	
Office equipment	120,000				120,000	
Accumulated depreciation— Office equip.		$ 20,000				$ 30,000
Accounts payable		26,000				32,000
Interest payable		0				2,150
Salaries payable		0				16,000
Unearned consulting fees		40,000				27,800
Long-term notes payable		75,000				75,000
Common stock		4,000				4,000
Retained earnings		76,200				76,200
Dividends...................	20,000				20,000	
Consulting fees earned		234,600				253,460
Depreciation expense— Office equip.	0				10,000	
Salaries expense	112,000				128,000	
Interest expense	8,600				10,750	
Insurance expense	0				4,600	
Rent expense	20,000				20,000	
Office supplies expense	0				23,000	
Advertising expense	42,000				48,000	
Totals.....................	$475,800	$475,800			$516,610	$516,610

Required

Analysis Component

1. Analyze the differences between the unadjusted and adjusted trial balances to determine the eight adjustments that likely were made. Show the results of your analysis by inserting these adjustment amounts in the table's two middle columns. Label each adjustment with a letter *a* through *h* and provide a short description of it at the bottom of the table.

Preparation Component

Check   (2) Net income, $9,110; Total assets, $222,260

2. Use the information in the adjusted trial balance to prepare this company's (*a*) income statement and its statement of retained earnings for the year ended December 31, 2016 (*Note:* Retained earnings at December 31, 2015, was $76,200, and the current-year dividends were $20,000), and (*b*) the balance sheet as of December 31, 2016.

Problem 3-5B
Preparing financial statements from the adjusted trial balance and calculating profit margin

P3   A1

The adjusted trial balance for Speedy Courier as of December 31, 2016, follows.

	Debit	Credit
Cash.	$ 58,000	
Accounts receivable	120,000	
Interest receivable.	7,000	
Notes receivable (due in 90 days)	210,000	
Office supplies.	22,000	
Trucks	134,000	
Accumulated depreciation—Trucks		$ 58,000
Equipment	270,000	
Accumulated depreciation—Equipment.		200,000
Land.	100,000	
Accounts payable.		134,000
Interest payable		20,000
Salaries payable		28,000
Unearned delivery fees		120,000
Long-term notes payable.		200,000
Common stock		15,000
Retained earnings		110,000
Dividends.	50,000	
Delivery fees earned		611,800
Interest earned		34,000
Depreciation expense—Trucks	29,000	
Depreciation expense—Equipment	48,000	
Salaries expense	74,000	
Wages expense	300,000	
Interest expense	15,000	
Office supplies expense.	31,000	
Advertising expense	27,200	
Repairs expense—Trucks	35,600	
Totals.	$1,530,800	$1,530,800

Required

Check   (1) Total assets, $663,000

1. Use the information in the adjusted trial balance to prepare (*a*) the income statement for the year ended December 31, 2016; (*b*) the statement of retained earnings for the year ended December 31, 2016; and (*c*) the balance sheet as of December 31, 2016.

2. Compute the profit margin for year 2016 (use total revenues as the denominator).

Problem 3-6B
Applying the accounting cycle

P1   P2   P3   P4   P5

On July 1, 2016, Lula Plume created a new self-storage business, Safe Storage Co. The following transactions occurred during the company's first month.

July 1   Plume invested $30,000 cash and buildings worth $150,000 in the company in exchange for common stock.
     2   The company rented equipment by paying $2,000 cash for the first month's (July) rent.
     5   The company purchased $2,400 of office supplies for cash.
    10   The company paid $7,200 cash for the premium on a 12-month insurance policy. Coverage begins on July 11.

14   The company paid an employee $1,000 cash for two weeks' salary earned.
24   The company collected $9,800 cash for storage fees from customers.
28   The company paid $1,000 cash for two weeks' salary earned by an employee.
29   The company paid $950 cash for minor repairs to a leaking roof.
30   The company paid $400 cash for this month's telephone bill.
31   The company paid $2,000 cash in dividends.

The company's chart of accounts follows:

101	Cash	401	Storage Fees Earned
106	Accounts Receivable	606	Depreciation Expense—Buildings
124	Office Supplies	622	Salaries Expense
128	Prepaid Insurance	637	Insurance Expense
173	Buildings	640	Rent Expense
174	Accumulated Depreciation—Buildings	650	Office Supplies Expense
209	Salaries Payable	684	Repairs Expense
307	Common Stock	688	Telephone Expense
318	Retained Earnings	901	Income Summary
319	Dividends		

Required

1. Use the balance column format to set up each ledger account listed in its chart of accounts.
2. Prepare journal entries to record the transactions for July and post them to the ledger accounts. Record prepaid and unearned items in balance sheet accounts.
3. Prepare an unadjusted trial balance as of July 31.
4. Use the following information to journalize and post adjusting entries for the month:
    a. Two-thirds of one month's insurance coverage has expired.
    b. At the end of the month, $1,525 of office supplies are still available.
    c. This month's depreciation on the buildings is $1,500.
    d. An employee earned $100 of unpaid and unrecorded salary as of month-end.
    e. The company earned $1,150 of storage fees that are not yet billed at month-end.
5. Prepare the adjusted trial balance as of July 31. Prepare the income statement and the statement of retained earnings for the month of July and the balance sheet at July 31, 2016.
6. Prepare journal entries to close the temporary accounts and post these entries to the ledger.
7. Prepare a post-closing trial balance.

Check   (3) Unadj. trial balance totals, $189,800

(4a) Dr. Insurance Expense, $400

(5) Net income, $2,725; Total assets, $180,825

(7) P-C trial balance totals, $182,325

In the blank space beside each numbered balance sheet item, enter the letter of its balance sheet classification. If the item should not appear on the balance sheet, enter a Z in the blank.

A. Current assets
B. Long-term investments
C. Plant assets
D. Intangible assets

E. Current liabilities
F. Long-term liabilities
G. Equity

Problem 3-7B
Determining balance sheet classifications

C3

_____   **1.** Commissions earned
_____   **2.** Interest receivable
_____   **3.** Long-term investment in stock
_____   **4.** Prepaid insurance
_____   **5.** Machinery
_____   **6.** Notes payable (due in 15 years)
_____   **7.** Copyrights
_____   **8.** Current portion of long-term note payable
_____   **9.** Accumulated depreciation—Trucks
_____ **10.** Office equipment

_____ **11.** Rent receivable
_____ **12.** Salaries payable
_____ **13.** Income taxes payable
_____ **14.** Common stock
_____ **15.** Office supplies
_____ **16.** Interest payable
_____ **17.** Rent revenue
_____ **18.** Notes receivable (due in 120 days)
_____ **19.** Land (used in operations)
_____ **20.** Depreciation expense—Trucks

Problem 3-8B
Preparing closing entries,
financial statements, and
ratios

A1   A2   P3   P4

The adjusted trial balance for Anara Co. as of December 31, 2016, follows.

No.	Account Title	Debit	Credit
	ANARA COMPANY		
	Adjusted Trial Balance		
	December 31, 2016		
101	Cash.	$ 7,400	
104	Short-term investments	11,200	
126	Supplies	4,600	
128	Prepaid insurance	1,000	
167	Equipment.	24,000	
168	Accumulated depreciation—Equipment.		$ 4,000
173	Building	100,000	
174	Accumulated depreciation—Building		10,000
183	Land.	30,500	
201	Accounts payable		3,500
203	Interest payable.		1,750
208	Rent payable		400
210	Wages payable.		1,280
213	Property taxes payable		3,330
233	Unearned professional fees.		750
251	Long-term notes payable		40,000
307	Common stock.		30,000
318	Retained earnings		62,800
319	Dividends.	8,000	
401	Professional fees earned		59,600
406	Rent earned.		4,500
407	Dividends earned		1,000
409	Interest earned		1,320
606	Depreciation expense—Building	2,000	
612	Depreciation expense—Equipment	1,000	
623	Wages expense	18,500	
633	Interest expense	1,550	
637	Insurance expense.	1,525	
640	Rent expense.	3,600	
652	Supplies expense	1,000	
682	Postage expense	410	
683	Property taxes expense	4,825	
684	Repairs expense	679	
688	Telephone expense	521	
690	Utilities expense	1,920	
	Totals.	$224,230	$224,230

The December 31, 2015, credit balance of the Retained Earnings account was $62,800. Anara Company is required to make an $8,400 payment on its long-term notes payable during 2017.

Required

Check (1) Total assets (12/31/2016), $164,700; Net income, $28,890

1. Prepare the income statement and the statement of retained earnings for the calendar year 2016 and the classified balance sheet at December 31, 2016.

2. Prepare the necessary closing entries at December 31, 2016.

3. Use the information in the financial statements to calculate these ratios: (a) return on assets (total assets at December 31, 2015, were $160,000), (b) debt ratio, (c) profit margin ratio (use total revenues as the denominator), and (d) current ratio. Round ratios to three decimals for parts a and c, and to two decimals for parts b and d.

This serial problem began in Chapter 1 and continues through most of the book. If previous chapter segments were not completed, the serial problem can still begin at this point. It is helpful, but not necessary, to use the Working Papers that accompany the book.

SERIAL PROBLEM

Business Solutions

P1   P2   P3   P4   P5

SP 3 After the success of the company's first two months, Santana Rey continues to operate Business Solutions. (Transactions for the first two months are described in the Chapter 2 serial problem.) The November 30, 2016, unadjusted trial balance of Business Solutions (reflecting its transactions for October and November of 2016) follows.

No.	Account Title	Debit	Credit
101	Cash..	$38,264	
106	Accounts receivable	12,618	
126	Computer supplies	2,545	
128	Prepaid insurance	2,220	
131	Prepaid rent.................................	3,300	
163	Office equipment............................	8,000	
164	Accumulated depreciation—Office equipment		$ 0
167	Computer equipment	20,000	
168	Accumulated depreciation—Computer equipment.........		0
201	Accounts payable............................		0
210	Wages payable..............................		0
236	Unearned computer services revenue		0
307	Common stock		73,000
318	Retained earnings		0
319	Dividends...................................	5,600	
403	Computer services revenue		25,659
612	Depreciation expense—Office equipment................	0	
613	Depreciation expense—Computer equipment	0	
623	Wages expense	2,625	
637	Insurance expense..........................	0	
640	Rent expense...............................	0	
652	Computer supplies expense	0	
655	Advertising expense	1,728	
676	Mileage expense	704	
677	Miscellaneous expenses....................	250	
684	Repairs expense—Computer	805	
	Totals......................................	$98,659	$98,659

Business Solutions had the following transactions and events in December 2016.

Dec. 2 Paid $1,025 cash to Hillside Mall for Business Solutions's share of mall advertising costs.
    3 Paid $500 cash for minor repairs to the company's computer.
    4 Received $3,950 cash from Alex's Engineering Co. for the receivable from November.
   10 Paid cash to Lyn Addie for six days of work at the rate of $125 per day.
   14 Notified by Alex's Engineering Co. that Business Solutions's bid of $7,000 on a proposed project has been accepted. Alex's paid a $1,500 cash advance to Business Solutions.
   15 Purchased $1,100 of computer supplies on credit from Harris Office Products.
   16 Sent a reminder to Gomez Co. to pay the fee for services recorded on November 8.
   20 Completed a project for Liu Corporation and received $5,625 cash.
22–26 Took the week off for the holidays.
   28 Received $3,000 cash from Gomez Co. on its receivable.
   29 Reimbursed S. Rey for business automobile mileage (600 miles at $0.32 per mile).
   31 The company paid $1,500 cash in dividends.

The following additional facts are collected for use in making adjusting entries prior to preparing financial statements for the company's first three months:

a. The December 31 inventory count of computer supplies shows $580 still available.

b. Three months have expired since the 12-month insurance premium was paid in advance.

c. As of December 31, Lyn Addie has not been paid for four days of work at $125 per day.

d. The computer system, acquired on October 1, is expected to have a four-year life with no salvage value.

e. The office equipment, acquired on October 1, is expected to have a five-year life with no salvage value.

f. Three of the four months' prepaid rent has expired.

Required

1. Prepare journal entries to record each of the December transactions and events for Business Solutions. Post those entries to the accounts in the ledger.

2. Prepare adjusting entries to reflect *a* through *f*. Post those entries to the accounts in the ledger.

Check   (3) Adjusted trial balance totals, $109,034

3. Prepare an adjusted trial balance as of December 31, 2016.

4. Prepare an income statement for the three months ended December 31, 2016.

5. Prepare a statement of retained earnings for the three months ended December 31, 2016.

(6) Total assets, $83,460

6. Prepare a balance sheet as of December 31, 2016.

7. Record and post the necessary closing entries for Business Solutions.

(8) Post-closing trial balance totals, $85,110

8. Prepare a post-closing trial balance as of December 31, 2016.

GENERAL LEDGER PROBLEMS

Available in Connect

The **General Ledger** tool in *Connect* allows students to immediately see the financial statements as of a specific date. Each of the following questions begins with an unadjusted trial balance. Using transactions from the following assignment, prepare the necessary adjustments and determine the impact each adjustment has on net income. The financial statements are automatically populated.

GL 3-1 Based on the FastForward illustration in this chapter

Using transactions from the following assignments, prepare the necessary adjustments, create the financial statements, and determine the impact each adjustment has on net income.

GL 3-2 Based on Problem 3-3A   **GL 3-5** Based on Problem 3-6A

GL 3-3 Extension of Problem 2-1A   **GL 3-6** Based on Serial Problem SP 3

GL 3-4 Extension of Problem 2-2A

Beyond the Numbers

REPORTING IN ACTION

A1   P4

APPLE

BTN 3-1   Refer to **Apple**'s financial statements in Appendix A to answer the following.

1. Identify and write down the revenue recognition principle as explained in the chapter.

2. Review Apple's footnotes (in Appendix A and/or from its 10-K on its website) to discover how it applies the revenue recognition principle and when it recognizes revenue. Report what you discover.

3. What is Apple's profit margin for fiscal years ended September 27, 2014, and September 28, 2013?

4. For the fiscal year ended September 27, 2014, what amount is credited to Income Summary to summarize its revenues earned?

5. For the fiscal year ended September 27, 2014, what amount is debited to Income Summary to summarize its expenses incurred?

6. For the fiscal year ended September 27, 2014, what is the balance of its Income Summary account before it is closed?

Fast Forward

7. Access Apple's annual report (10-K) for fiscal years ending after September 27, 2014, at its website (**Apple.com**) or the SEC's EDGAR database (**www.SEC.gov**). Assess and compare the September 27, 2014, fiscal year profit margin to any subsequent year's profit margin that you compute.

BTN 3-2 Key figures for the recent two years of both **Apple** and **Google** follow.

COMPARATIVE ANALYSIS

A1   A2

APPLE

GOOGLE

$ millions	Apple		Google	
	Current Year	**Prior Year**	**Current Year**	**Prior Year**
Net income.	$ 39,510	$ 37,037	$14,444	$12,920
Net sales.	182,795	170,910	66,001	55,519
Current assets	68,531	73,286	80,685	72,886
Current liabilities	63,448	43,658	16,805	15,908

Required

1. Compute profit margins for (*a*) Apple and (*b*) Google for the two years of data shown.
2. Which company is more successful on the basis of profit margin? Explain.
3. Compute the current ratio for both years for both companies.
4. Which company has the better ability to pay short-term obligations according to the current ratio?
5. Analyze and comment on each company's current ratios for the past two years.
6. How do Apple's and Google's current ratios compare to their industry (assumed) average ratio of 2.0?

BTN 3-3 Jessica Boland works for Sea Biscuit Co. She and Farah Smith, her manager, are preparing adjusting entries for annual financial statements. Boland computes depreciation and records it as

ETHICS CHALLENGE

C1

Depreciation Expense—Equipment	123,000	
Accumulated Depreciation—Equipment		123,000

Smith agrees with her computation but says the credit entry should be directly to the Equipment account. Smith argues that while accumulated depreciation is technically correct, "it is less hassle not to use a contra account and just credit the Equipment account directly. And besides, the balance sheet shows the same amount for total assets under either method."

Required

1. How should depreciation be recorded? Do you support Boland or Smith?
2. Evaluate the strengths and weaknesses of Smith's reasons for preferring her method.
3. Indicate whether the situation Boland faces is an ethical problem. Explain.

BTN 3-4 Assume that one of your classmates states that a company's books should be ongoing and therefore not closed until that business is terminated. Write a half-page memo to this classmate explaining the concept of the closing process by drawing analogies between (1) a scoreboard for an athletic event and the revenue and expense accounts of a business or (2) a sports team's record book and retained earnings. (*Hint:* Think about what would happen if the scoreboard is not cleared before the start of a new game.)

COMMUNICATING IN PRACTICE

P4

BTN 3-5 Access EDGAR online (www.SEC.gov) and locate the 10-K report of **The Gap, Inc.**, (ticker GPS) filed on March 23, 2015. Review its financial statements reported for the year ended January 31, 2015, to answer the following questions.

TAKING IT TO THE NET

A1

Required

1. What are Gap's main brands?
2. What is Gap's fiscal year-end?
3. What is Gap's net sales for the period ended January 31, 2015?
4. What is Gap's net income for the period ended January 31, 2015?
5. Compute Gap's profit margin for the year ended January 31, 2015.
6. Do you believe Gap's decision to use a year-end of late January or early February relates to its natural business year? Explain.

TEAMWORK IN ACTION

P1

BTN 3-6   Four types of adjustments are described in the chapter: (1) prepaid expenses, (2) unearned revenues, (3) accrued expenses, and (4) accrued revenues.

Required

1. Form *learning teams* of four (or more) members. Each team member must select one of the four adjustments as an area of expertise (each team must have at least one expert in each area).

2. Form *expert teams* from the individuals who have selected the same area of expertise. Expert teams are to discuss and write a report that each expert will present to his or her learning team addressing the following:

   a. Description of the adjustment and why it's necessary.

   b. Example of a transaction or event, with dates and amounts, that requires adjustment.

   c. Adjusting entry(ies) for the example in requirement *b*.

   d. Status of the affected account(s) before and after the adjustment in requirement *c*.

   e. Effects on financial statements of not making the adjustment.

3. Each expert should return to his or her learning team. In rotation, each member should present his or her expert team's report to the learning team. Team discussion is encouraged.

ENTREPRENEURIAL DECISION

C1   A1

BTN 3-7   Review the opening feature of this chapter dealing with **GoPro, Inc.**, and its entrepreneurial owner, Nick Woodman.

Required

1. Assume that GoPro sells a $300 gift certificate to a customer, collecting the $300 cash in advance. Prepare the journal entry for the (*a*) collection of the cash for delivery of the gift certificate to the customer and (*b*) revenue from the subsequent delivery of a GoPro Camera when the gift certificate is used.

2. How can keeping less inventory help to improve GoPro's profit margin?

3. Nick Woodman understands that many companies carry considerable inventory, and he is thinking of carrying additional inventory of merchandise for sale. Nick desires your advice on the pros and cons of carrying such inventory. Provide at least one reason for, and one reason against, carrying additional inventory.

HITTING THE ROAD

C1

BTN 3-8   Select a company that you can visit in person or interview on the telephone. Call ahead to the company to arrange a time when you can interview an employee (preferably an accountant) who helps prepare the annual financial statements. Inquire about the following aspects of its *accounting cycle:*

1. Does the company prepare interim financial statements? What time period(s) is used for interim statements?

2. Does the company use the cash or accrual basis of accounting?

3. Does the company use a work sheet in preparing financial statements? Why or why not?

4. Does the company use a spreadsheet program? If so, which software program is used?

5. How long does it take after the end of its reporting period to complete annual statements?

GLOBAL DECISION

A1   C1

Samsung
APPLE
GOOGLE

BTN 3-9   **Samsung** (**Samsung.com**) is a leading manufacturer of consumer electronic products. The following selected information is available from Samsung's financial statements along with that from **Apple** and **Google**.

In millions	Samsung	Apple	Google
Net income	₩ 23,394,358	$ 39,510	$14,444
Net sales	206,205,987	182,795	66,001

Required

1. Compute profit margin for the current year for Samsung, Apple, and Google.

2. Which company has the higher profit margin? For that company, how much net income does it receive for each $1 or ₩1 of sales?

ANSWERS TO MULTIPLE CHOICE QUIZ

1. b; the forgotten adjusting entry is: *dr.* Wages Expense, *cr.* Wages Payable.

2. c; Supplies used = $450 − $125 = $325

3. b; Insurance expense = $24,000 × (8/24) = $8,000; adjusting entry is: *dr.* Insurance Expense for $8,000, *cr.* Prepaid Insurance for $8,000.

4. a; Consulting fees earned = $3,600 × (2/6) = $1,200; adjusting entry is: *dr.* Unearned Consulting Fee for $1,200, *cr.* Consulting Fees Earned for $1,200.

5. e; Profit margin = $15,000/$300,000 = 5%

6. b

chapter 4

Reporting and Analyzing Merchandising Operations

Chapter Preview

MERCHANDISING ACTIVITIES

C1 Reporting income and inventory

C2 Operating cycles and inventory system

MERCHANDISING PURCHASES

P1 Accounting for:

Purchase discounts

Purchase returns and allowances

Transportation costs

MERCHANDISING SALES

P2 Accounting for:

Sales of merchandise

Sales discounts

Sales returns and allowances

MERCHANDISE REPORTING AND ANALYSIS

P3 Adjusting and closing for merchandisers

P4 Multiple- and single-step income statements

A1 Acid-test analysis

A2 Gross margin analysis

Learning Objectives

CONCEPTUAL

C1 Describe merchandising activities and identify income components for a merchandising company.

C2 Identify and explain the inventory asset and cost flows of a merchandising company.

ANALYTICAL

A1 Compute the acid-test ratio and explain its use to assess liquidity.

A2 Compute the gross margin ratio and explain its use to assess profitability.

PROCEDURAL

P1 Analyze and record transactions for merchandise purchases using a perpetual system.

P2 Analyze and record transactions for merchandise sales using a perpetual system.

P3 Prepare adjustments and close accounts for a merchandising company.

P4 Define and prepare multiple-step and single-step income statements.

P5 *Appendix 4A* Record and compare merchandising transactions using both periodic and perpetual inventory systems.

P6 *Appendix 4C* Record and compare merchandising transactions using the gross method and net method.

Food with Integrity

"We'll continue to change the way people think about, and eat, food"—STEVE ELLS

DENVER—**Chipotle Mexican Grill (Chipotle.com)** founder Steve Ells invited friends over for dinner. His friends had become accustomed to elaborate meals prepared by Steve, a chef from a popular San Francisco restaurant. When friends arrived at his house one evening, recalled Steve, they were "extraordinarily disappointed" and wondered, "how good could a burrito be?" However, after Steve served his creation, his friends were hooked on the "absolutely delicious" burritos.

After that dinner, Steve approached his parents with the idea of starting a burrito restaurant. "We were at my parents' house writing out all these different names. And it was just like a light bulb went off: 'I should call it Chipotle'." Everyone told Steve to call it something else. Steve said his friends and family asked, "'How do you pronounce it?' Or, they said, 'No one knows what it is.'" Ignoring their advice, Steve moved ahead with the Chipotle name. Armed with a one-page business plan, Steve secured a $75,000 loan from his father to open the first Chipotle restaurant.

As business grew, Steve quickly focused on getting the company's accounting house in order. "It was making much more money than I had ever anticipated." Even as Chipotle sales were exploding, the business "was beginning to run out of money." In response, Steve set up an accounting

Chipotle Mexican Grill
NYSE: CMG

53,000 employees
1,783 restaurants
$4.1 billion in sales

Restaurant Operating Costs

Other 15%
Occupancy 8%
Labor 30%
Food, beverage & packaging 47%

system to measure, track, summarize, and report on all operations, especially purchases. He also computerized the accounting system, prepared monthly financial statements per restaurant, developed annual budgets, produced financial statements, and managed all bank accounts and payables. "We focused on the value in the future," explains Steve.

That discipline fundamentally altered Chipotle's accounting system and renewed its focus on quality products, including the tracking of purchases, purchase returns, and purchase allowances. Developing an accounting system to capture all aspects of the operations is worth the effort, according to Steve. "I'm pleased with our performance . . . [it] was an extraordinary year for our business," proclaims Steve. Chipotle's revenues, net income, and asset growth for the past four years reflect his optimism:

($ millions)	2011	2012	2013	2014
Revenues	$2,270	$2,731	$3,215	$4,108
Net income	215	278	327	445
Total assets	1,425	1,669	2,009	2,546

"Our performance is the direct result of our continued focus on the things that really drive our business," insists Steve. The financial markets are equally enthused about the accounting discipline and the vision provided by Steve—this is reflected in Chipotle's stock price over the past four years.

The company is flying high with the right accounting for long-run success. The company will open "between 190 and 205 restaurants" this year and plans for further expansion are already "underway."

"The idea was simple: show that food served fast didn't have to be a 'fast-food' experience," explains Steve. "Using high-quality raw ingredients, classic cooking techniques, and distinctive interior design, we brought features from the realm of fine dining to the world of quick-service restaurants."

Sources: *Chipotle website,* January 2016; *Bloomberg,* February 2015; *SeekingAlpha,* April 2015; *Fortune,* March 2015; *CNN,* April 2015; *Nature.org,* April 2011

MERCHANDISING ACTIVITIES

C1

Describe merchandising activities and identify income components for a merchandising company.

Previous chapters emphasized the accounting and reporting activities of service companies. A merchandising company's activities differ from those of a service company. **Merchandise** consists of products, also called *goods,* that a company acquires to resell to customers. A **merchandiser** earns net income by buying and selling merchandise. Merchandisers are often identified as either wholesalers or retailers. A **wholesaler** is an *intermediary* that buys products from manufacturers or other wholesalers and sells them to retailers or other wholesalers. A **retailer** is an intermediary that buys products from manufacturers or wholesalers and sells them to consumers. Many retailers sell both products and services.

Reporting Income for a Merchandiser

Net income for a merchandiser equals revenues from selling merchandise minus both the cost of merchandise sold to customers and the cost of other expenses for the period; see Exhibit 4.1. The usual accounting term for revenues from selling merchandise is *sales,* and the term used for the expense of buying and preparing the merchandise is **cost of goods sold.** (Some service companies use the term *sales* instead of revenues; and cost of goods sold is also called *cost of sales.*)

EXHIBIT 4.1

Computing Income for a Merchandising Company versus a Service Company

Point: Fleming, SuperValu, and SYSCO are wholesalers. **Aeropostale, Coach, Target,** and **Walmart** are retailers.

The income statement for Z-Mart in Exhibit 4.2 illustrates these key components of a merchandiser's net income. The first two lines show that products are acquired at a cost of $230,400 and sold for $314,700. The third line shows an $84,300 **gross profit,** also called **gross margin,** which equals net sales less cost of goods sold. Additional expenses of $71,400 are reported, which leaves $12,900 in net income.

EXHIBIT 4.2

Merchandiser's Income Statement

Z-MART Income Statement For Year Ended December 31, 2016	
Net sales	$ 314,700
Cost of goods sold	**230,400**
Gross profit	**84,300**
Expenses	71,400
Net income	$ 12,900

Reporting Inventory for a Merchandiser

C2

Identify and explain the inventory asset and cost flows of a merchandising company.

A merchandiser's balance sheet includes a current asset called *merchandise inventory,* an item not on a service company's balance sheet. **Merchandise inventory,** or simply *inventory,* refers to products that a company owns and intends to sell. The cost of this asset includes the cost incurred to buy the goods, ship them to the store, and make them ready for sale.

Operating Cycle for a Merchandiser

A merchandising company's operating cycle begins by purchasing merchandise and ends by collecting cash from selling the merchandise. The length of an operating cycle differs across the types of businesses. Department stores often have operating cycles of two to five months. Operating cycles for grocery merchants usually range from two to eight weeks. A grocer has more operating cycles in a year than, say, clothing or electronics retailers.

Exhibit 4.3 illustrates an operating cycle for a merchandiser with credit sales. The cycle moves from (*a*) cash purchases of merchandise to (*b*) inventory for sale to (*c*) credit sales to (*d*) accounts receivable to (*e*) cash. Companies try to keep their operating cycles short because assets tied up in inventory and receivables are not productive. Cash sales shorten operating cycles.

EXHIBIT 4.3

Merchandiser's Operating Cycle

Inventory Systems

Cost of goods sold is the cost of merchandise sold to customers during a period. It is often the largest single expense on a merchandiser's income statement. **Inventory** refers to products a company owns and expects to sell in its normal operations. Exhibit 4.4 shows that a company's merchandise available for sale consists of what it begins with (beginning inventory) and what it purchases (net purchases). The merchandise available is either sold (cost of goods sold) or kept for future sales (ending inventory).

Merchandise Inventory			
Beg. inventory	#		
Net purchases	#		
Merchandise avail. for sale	#		
		COGS	#
End. inventory	#		

EXHIBIT 4.4

Merchandiser's Cost Flow for a Single Time Period

Point: Mathematically, Exhibit 4.4 says

$$BI + NP = MAS,$$

where BI is beginning inventory, NP is net purchases, and MAS is merchandise available for sale. Exhibit 4.4 also says

$$MAS = EI + COGS$$

which can be rewritten as $MAS − EI = COGS$ or $MAS − COGS = EI$, where EI is ending inventory and COGS is cost of goods sold. In both equations above, if we know two of the three values, we can solve for the third.

Two alternative inventory accounting systems can be used to collect information about cost of goods sold and cost of inventory: *perpetual system* or *periodic system*. The **perpetual inventory system** continually updates accounting records for merchandising transactions—specifically, for those records of inventory available for sale and inventory sold. The **periodic inventory system** updates the accounting records for merchandise transactions only at the *end of a period*. Technological advances and competitive pressures have dramatically increased use of the perpetual system. It gives managers immediate access to detailed information on sales and inventory levels, where they can strategically react to sales trends, cost changes, consumer tastes, and so forth, to increase gross profit. (Some companies use a *hybrid* system where the perpetual system is used for tracking units available and the periodic system is used to compute cost of sales.)

Point: Growth of superstores such as **Costco** and **Sam's Club** is fueled by efficient use of perpetual inventory. Such large stores evolved after scannable UPC codes to help control inventory were invented.

*The following sections on purchasing, selling, and adjusting merchandise use the perpetual system (**ending with NTK 4.3**). Appendix 4A uses the periodic system (with the perpetual results on the side). An instructor can choose to cover either one or both inventory systems. If the periodic system only is covered, then read Appendix 4A and return to the section titled "Financial Statement Formats" (after NTK 4.3).*

ACCOUNTING FOR MERCHANDISE PURCHASES

P1

Analyze and record transactions for merchandise purchases using a perpetual system.

The cost of merchandise, also called *goods,* that are purchased for resale is recorded in the Merchandise Inventory asset account. This section explains how we record purchases under different purchase terms.

Purchases <u>without</u> Cash Discounts

Z-Mart would record a $500 cash purchase of merchandise on November 2 as follows:

Assets = Liabilities + Equity
+500
−500

Nov. 2	Merchandise Inventory.	500	
	Cash		500
	Purchased goods for cash.		

If these goods were instead *purchased on credit,* and no discounts were offered for early payment, Z-Mart would make the same entry except that Accounts Payable would be credited instead of Cash.

Point: The Merchandise Inventory account reflects the cost of goods available for resale. Costs recorded in Merchandise Inventory are sometimes called *inventoriable costs.*

Point: **Lowe's** and **Home Depot** offer trade discounts to construction companies and contractors. Trade discounts help create loyalty among customers. Trade discounts are not journalized; purchases are recorded based on the invoice amount.

 Decision Insight

Trade Discounts   When a manufacturer or wholesaler prepares a catalog of items it has for sale, it usually gives each item a **list price,** also called a *catalog price.* However, an item's intended *selling price* equals list price minus a given percent called a **trade discount.** The amount of trade discount usually depends on whether a buyer is a wholesaler, retailer, or final consumer. A wholesaler buying in large quantities is often granted a larger discount than a retailer buying in smaller quantities. A buyer records the net amount of list price minus trade discount. For example, a supplier of Z-Mart lists an item of merchandise in its catalog at $625 and it grants Z-Mart a 20% trade discount. This means that Z-Mart's purchase price for that item is $500, computed as $625 − (20% × $625). ■

Purchases <u>with</u> Cash Discounts

The purchase of goods on credit includes details of expected future payments and dates. **Credit terms** for a purchase include the amounts and timing of payments from a buyer to a seller. Credit terms usually reflect an industry's practices. To illustrate, when sellers require payment within 10 days after the end of the month of the invoice date, the invoice will show credit terms as "n/10 EOM," which stands for net 10 days after end of month (**EOM**). When sellers require payment within 30 days after the invoice date, the invoice shows credit terms of "n/30," which stands for *net 30 days.*

Exhibit 4.5 portrays credit terms. The amount of time allowed before full payment is due is called the **credit period.** Sellers can grant a **cash discount** to encourage buyers to pay earlier. A buyer views a cash discount as a **purchase discount.** A seller views a cash discount as a **sales discount.** Any cash discounts are described in the credit terms on the invoice. For example, credit terms of "2/10, n/60" mean that full payment is due within a 60-day credit period, but the buyer can deduct 2% of the invoice amount if payment is made within 10 days of the invoice date. This reduced payment applies only for the **discount period.**

EXHIBIT 4.5

Credit Terms

Discount refers to a purchase discount for a buyer and a sales discount for a seller.

To illustrate how a buyer accounts for a purchase discount, assume that on November 2, Z-Mart purchases $500 of merchandise **on credit** with terms of 2/10, n/30. The amount due, if paid on or before November 12, is $490, computed as $500 − ($500 × 2%)—or alternatively computed as $500 × (100% − 2%). Many buyers take advantage of a purchase discount because of the usually high interest rate implied by not taking it.[1] If Z-Mart does not pay within the 10-day 2% discount period, it can delay payment by 20 more days, at which point it must pay $500. The *gross method* for recording purchases enters the full invoice (gross) amount for merchandise. If Z-Mart uses the gross method, it makes the following entry dated as of the invoice date:

Point: Appendix 4A repeats journal entries *a* through *g* using a periodic inventory system.

(a) Nov. 2	Merchandise Inventory...........................	500	
	Accounts Payable...........................		500
	Purchased goods, terms 2/10, n/30.		

Assets = Liabilities + Equity
+500   +500

The invoice for this purchase is shown in Exhibit 4.6. The buyer usually receives the original invoice, and the seller keeps a copy. This *source document* serves as the purchase invoice of Z-Mart (buyer) and the sales invoice for Trex (seller). The amount recorded for merchandise inventory includes its purchase cost, shipping fees, taxes, and any other costs necessary to make it ready for sale. (For recording, it can help to add the name to the payable [or receivable], such as Account Payable—Trex.)

EXHIBIT 4.6

Invoice

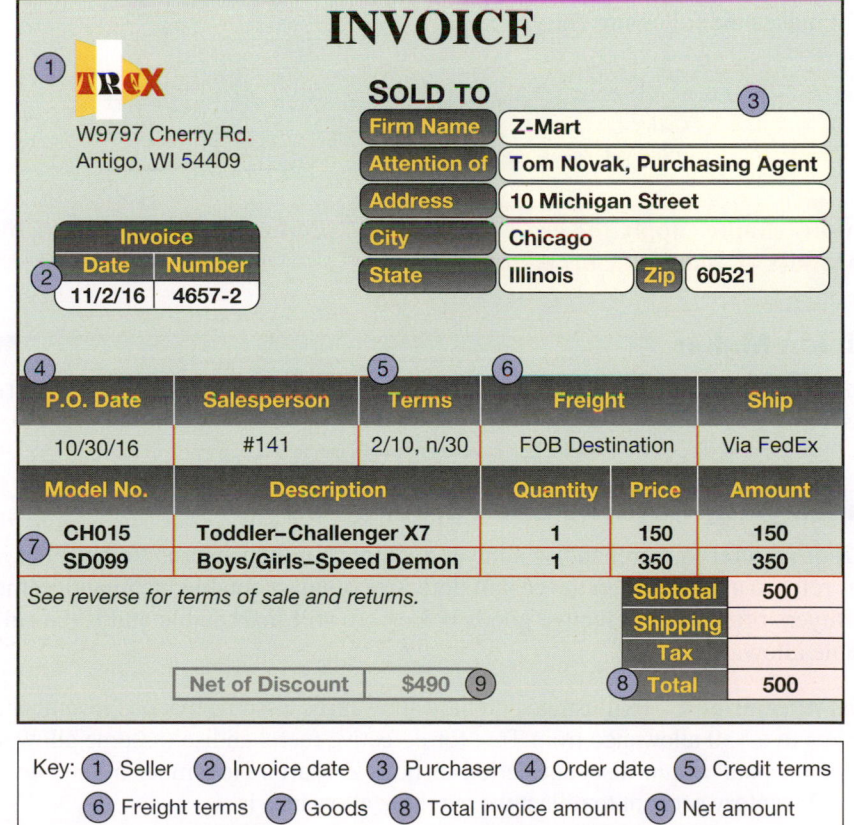

Point: The invoice date is used in setting the discount and credit periods as both buyer and seller know this date.

---

[1] The *implied annual interest rate* formula is:

$$[365 \text{ days} \div (\text{Credit period} - \text{Discount period})] \times \text{Cash discount rate.}$$

For terms of 2/10, n/30, missing the 2% discount for an additional 20 days is equal to an annual interest rate of 36.5%, computed as [365 days/(30 days − 10 days)] × 2% discount rate. *Favorable purchase discounts* are those with implied annual interest rates that exceed the purchaser's annual rate for borrowing money.

Payment within Discount Period   Good cash management means that invoices are not paid until the last day of the discount or credit period. This is because the buyer can use that money until payment is required. If Z-Mart pays the amount due on (or before) November 12, the entry is

Assets = Liabilities + Equity
−490   −500
− 10

(b1) Nov. 12	Accounts Payable	500	
	Merchandise Inventory		10
	Cash*		490
	Paid for goods within discount period.		
	* $500 × (100% − 2%)		

The Merchandise Inventory account reflects the $490 net cost of purchases after these entries, and the Accounts Payable account reveals a zero balance. The relevant ledger accounts, in T-account form, follow:

Merchandise Inventory			Accounts Payable			Cash	
Nov. 2	500				Nov. 2	500	
		Nov. 12	10	Nov. 12	500		
							Nov. 12	**490**
Bal.	**490**				Bal.	0	

Payment after Discount Period   If the amount is paid sometime *after* November 12, the discount is lost. For example, if Z-Mart pays the gross amount due on December 2 (the n/30 due date), it makes the following entry.

Assets = Liabilities + Equity
−500   −500

(b2) Dec. 2	Accounts Payable	500	
	Cash		500
	Paid for goods outside discount period.		

Entries in this chapter apply the *gross method* of accounting for purchases with discount terms. Appendix 4C shows the *net method*.

Point: Buyers sometimes make partial payments toward amounts owed. Assume that credit terms apply to both partial and full payments.

■ Decision Maker

Entrepreneur   You purchase a batch of products on terms of 3/10, n/90, but your company has limited cash and you must borrow funds at an 11% annual rate if you are to pay within the discount period. Is it to your advantage to take the purchase discount? Explain. ■ [Answers follow the chapter's Summary.]

Purchases <u>with</u> Returns and Allowances

Point: When a buyer returns or takes an allowance on merchandise, the buyer issues a **debit memorandum.** This informs the seller of a debit made to the seller's account payable in the buyer's records.

Purchase returns refer to merchandise a buyer acquires but then returns to the seller. *Purchase allowances* refer to a reduction in the cost of defective or unacceptable merchandise that a buyer acquires. Buyers often keep defective goods if they are still marketable and if the seller grants an acceptable allowance.

Purchase Allowances   To illustrate purchase allowances, assume that on November 5, Z-Mart (buyer) agrees to a $30 allowance from Trex for defective merchandise (assume allowance terms are $30 whether paid within discount period or not). Z-Mart's November 5 entry to update its Merchandise Inventory account to reflect the purchase allowance is

Assets = Liabilities + Equity
−30   −30

(c1) Nov. 5	Accounts Payable	30	
	Merchandise Inventory		30
	Allowance for defective goods.		

The buyer's allowance for defective merchandise is usually offset against the buyer's current account payable balance to the seller. If cash is refunded, the Cash account is debited.

Purchase Returns   Returns are recorded at the costs charged to buyers. To illustrate the accounting for returns, suppose on June 1 that Z-Mart purchases $250 of merchandise with terms 2/10, n/60. On June 3, Z-Mart returns $50 of those goods. When Z-Mart pays on June 11, it takes the 2% discount only on the $200 remaining balance ($250 − $50). When goods are returned, a buyer can take a discount on only the remaining balance of the invoice. This means the discount is $4 (computed as $200 × [100% − 2%]) and the cash payment is $196 ($200 − $4). The following entries reflect this illustration.

June 1		Merchandise Inventory...........................	250	
		Accounts Payable........................		250
		Purchased goods, terms 2/10, n/60.		
(c2) June 3		Accounts Payable................................	50	
		Merchandise Inventory.....................		50
		Returned goods to seller.		
June 11		Accounts Payable................................	200	
		Merchandise Inventory.....................		4
		Cash..................................		196
		Paid for $200 goods less $4 discount.		

Assets = Liabilities + Equity
+250   +250

Assets = Liabilities + Equity
−50   −50

Assets = Liabilities + Equity
−196   −200
− 4

For this example, the following ledger accounts, in T-account form, show the $196 in inventory, the zero balance in Accounts Payable, and the $196 cash payment.

Merchandise Inventory			
Jun. 1	250		
		Jun. 3	50
		Jun. 11	4
Bal.	**196**		

Accounts Payable			
		Jun. 1	250
Jun. 3	50		
Jun. 11	200		
		Bal.	0

Cash			
		Jun. 11	**196**

Example: Assume on June 20, Z-Mart returns goods paid for on June 11. The return entry is

Cash 196
  Merch. Inv. 196

 Decision Insight

Point of No Return   Although many companies allow returns, many others do not. Buyers must be especially alert to purchase terms. Companies that often do not permit returns include those selling any of the following items: hair products such as extensions, barrettes, claws, combs, and pins; undergarments including swimsuits, leotards, and shorts; custom products such as tailored suits, pants, and shirts; and beauty and cosmetic items such as lip liners and makeup. Many of these are sold "as is," meaning returns are not allowed. ■

Purchases and Transportation Costs

The buyer and seller must agree on who is responsible for paying any freight costs and who bears the risk of loss during transit for merchandising transactions. This is essentially the same as asking at what point ownership transfers from the seller to the buyer. The point of transfer is called the **FOB** (*free on board*) point, which determines who pays transportation costs (and often other incidental costs of transit such as insurance). Whoever owns the goods in transit takes on the shipping cost.

Exhibit 4.7 identifies two alternative points of transfer. (1) *FOB shipping point,* also called *FOB factory,* means the buyer accepts ownership when the goods depart the seller's place of business. The buyer is then responsible for paying shipping costs and bearing the risk of damage or loss when goods are in transit. The goods are part of the buyer's inventory when they are in transit since ownership has transferred to the buyer. **1-800-Flowers.com**, a floral and gift merchandiser, and **Bare Escentuals**, a cosmetic manufacturer, both use FOB shipping point. (2) *FOB destination* means ownership of goods transfers to the buyer when the goods arrive at the buyer's place of business. The seller is responsible for paying shipping charges and bears the risk of damage or loss in transit. The seller does not record revenue from this sale until the goods arrive at the destination because this transaction is not complete before that point. **Kyocera**, a manufacturer, uses FOB destination.

Kirby Hamilton/istock/Getty Images

Point: When the party not responsible for shipping pays shipping cost, it either bills the other party responsible or, more commonly, adjusts its account payable or account receivable with the other party. For example, a buyer paying shipping cost when terms are FOB destination can decrease its account payable to the seller by the amount of shipping cost. Assume that any freight payments to carriers are *not* applied in computing discounts.

EXHIBIT 4.7

Ownership Transfer and
Transportation Costs

Seller   Buyer

Shipping point   Goods in transit   Destination

Shipping Terms	Ownership Transfers at	Goods in Transit Owned by	Transportation Costs Paid by	
FOB shipping point	Shipping point	Buyer	**Buyer** Merchandise Inventory . . . #	
			Cash	#
FOB destination	Destination	Seller	**Seller** Delivery Expense . . . . #	
			Cash	#

Point: If we place an order online and receive free shipping, we have terms FOB destination.

Z-Mart's $500 purchase on November 2 is on terms of FOB destination. This means Z-Mart is not responsible for paying transportation costs. When a buyer is responsible for paying transportation costs, the payment is made to a carrier or directly to the seller depending on the agreement. The cost principle requires that any necessary transportation costs of a buyer (often called *transportation-in* or *freight-in*) be included as part of the cost of purchased merchandise. To illustrate, Z-Mart's entry to record a $75 freight charge from an independent carrier for merchandise purchased FOB shipping point is

Assets = Liabilities + Equity
+75
−75

(d) Nov. 24	Merchandise Inventory.	75	
	Cash		75
	Paid freight costs on goods.		

Point: **IN**coming freight costs are charged to **IN**ventory. When inventory **EX**its, freight costs are charged to **EX**pense.

A seller records the costs of shipping goods to customers in a Delivery Expense account when the seller is responsible for these costs. Delivery expense, also called *transportation-out* or *freight-out,* is reported as a selling expense in the seller's income statement.

Purchases and Their Itemized Costs   In summary, purchases are recorded as debits to Merchandise Inventory (or Inventory). Any later purchase discounts, returns, and allowances are credited to (deducted from) Merchandise Inventory. Transportation-in is debited (added) to Merchandise Inventory. Z-Mart's itemized costs of merchandise purchases for year 2016 are in Exhibit 4.8.

Point: With *tracking numbers* it is possible to know the exact time shipped goods arrive at their destination.

EXHIBIT 4.8

Itemized Costs of
Merchandise Purchases

Z-MART Itemized Costs of Merchandise Purchases For Year Ended December 31, 2016	
Invoice cost of merchandise purchases.	$ 235,800
Less: Purchase discounts received.	(4,200)
Purchase returns and allowances	(1,500)
Add: Costs of transportation-in	2,300
Total net cost of merchandise purchases	**$232,400**

Point: Some companies have separate accounts for purchase discounts, returns and allowances, and transportation-in. These accounts are then transferred to Merchandise Inventory at period-end. This is a *hybrid system* of perpetual and periodic. That is, Merchandise Inventory is updated on a perpetual basis but only for purchases and cost of goods sold.

The accounting system described here does not provide separate records (accounts) for total purchases, total purchase discounts, total purchase returns and allowances, and total transportation-in. Yet nearly all companies collect this information in supplementary records because managers need this information to evaluate and control each of these cost elements. **Supplementary records,** also called *supplemental records,* refer to information outside the usual general ledger accounts.

■ **Decision Ethics**

Payables Manager   As a new accounts payable manager, you are being trained by the outgoing manager. She explains that the system prepares checks for amounts net of favorable cash discounts, and the checks are dated the last day of the discount period. She also tells you that checks are not mailed until five days later, adding that "the company gets free use of cash for an extra five days, and our department looks better. When a supplier complains, we blame the computer system and the mailroom." Do you continue this payment policy? ■   [Answers follow the chapter's Summary.]

Prepare journal entries to record each of the following purchases transactions of a merchandising company. Assume a perpetual inventory system using the gross method for recording purchases.

Oct. 1   Purchased $1,000 of goods. Terms of the sale are 4/10, n/30, and FOB shipping point; the invoice is dated October 1.
Oct. 3   Paid $30 cash for freight charges from UPS for the October 1 purchase.
Oct. 7   Returned $50 of the $1,000 of goods from the October 1 purchase and received full credit.
Oct. 11   Paid the amount due from the October 1 purchase (less the return on October 7).
Oct. 31   *Assume the October 11 payment was never made* and, instead, payment of the amount due, less the return on October 7, occurred on October 31.

NEED-TO-KNOW 4-1

Merchandise Purchases
P1

Solution

Oct. 1	Merchandise Inventory.............................	1,000	
	Accounts Payable............................		1,000
	Purchased goods, terms 4/10, n/30.		
Oct. 3	Merchandise Inventory.............................	30	
	Cash......................................		30
	Paid freight on purchases FOB shipping point.		
Oct. 7	Accounts Payable.................................	50	
	Merchandise Inventory.......................		50
	Returned goods.		
Oct. 11	Accounts Payable.................................	950	
	Merchandise Inventory*......................		38
	Cash†......................................		912
	Paid for goods within discount period.		
	* $950 × 4%. †$950 − ($950 × 4%).*		
Oct. 31	Accounts Payable*................................	950	
	Cash......................................		950
	Paid for goods outside discount period.		
	* $1,000 − $50.*		

Do More: QS 4-5, QS 4-6, QS 4-7, E 4-3, E 4-5

ACCOUNTING FOR MERCHANDISE SALES

Merchandising companies must account for sales, sales discounts, sales returns and allowances, and cost of goods sold. A merchandising company such as Z-Mart reflects these items in its gross profit computation, as shown in Exhibit 4.9. This shows that customers paid $314,700 for merchandise that cost Z-Mart $230,400, yielding a markup (gross profit) of $84,300.

P2

Analyze and record transactions for merchandise sales using a perpetual system.

EXHIBIT 4.9

Gross Profit Computation

Z-MART	
Computation of Gross Profit	
For Year Ended December 31, 2016	
Net sales (net of discounts, returns, and allowances)................	$314,700
Cost of goods sold.....................................	230,400
Gross profit	**$ 84,300**

Each sale of merchandise has two parts: the revenue side and the cost side.

> 1. **Revenue received (and asset increased) from the customer.**
> 2. **Cost of goods sold incurred (and asset decreased) to the customer.**

Accounting for a sales transaction under the perpetual system requires recording information about both parts. This means that **each sales transaction for a merchandiser, whether for cash or on credit, requires** *two entries:* **one for revenue and one for cost**.

Sales <u>without</u> Cash Discounts

Revenue Side: Inflow of Assets   To illustrate, Z-Mart sold $1,000 of merchandise on credit terms n/60 on November 12. The revenue part of this transaction is recorded as

Assets = Liabilities + Equity
+1,000   +1,000

Nov. 12	Accounts Receivable	1,000	
	Sales		1,000
	Sold goods on credit.		

This entry reflects an increase in Z-Mart's assets in the form of accounts receivable. It also shows the increase in revenue (Sales). If the sale is for cash, the debit is to Cash instead of Accounts Receivable.

Point: Gross profit on Nov. 12 sale:

Net sales	$1,000
Cost of goods sold. . .	300
Gross profit	$ 700

Cost Side: Outflow of Assets   The cost side of each sales transaction ensures that the Merchandise Inventory account decreases for the cost of each sale under a perpetual inventory system. For example, the cost of the merchandise Z-Mart sold on November 12 is $300, and the entry to record the cost part of this sales transaction follows.

Assets = Liabilities + Equity
−300   −300

Nov. 12	Cost of Goods Sold	300	
	Merchandise Inventory.		300
	Record cost of Nov. 12 sale.		

Point: The cost side entry shows the *expense recognition principle* as expense is recorded when sales are. Further, when a UPC code is scanned using point-of-sale software, the sale [increase in cash or receivable] and cost [decrease in inventory] can be recorded at the same time.

🟨 Decision Insight

Suppliers and Demands   Large merchandising companies often bombard suppliers with demands. These include discounts for bar coding and technology support systems, and fines for shipping errors. Merchandisers' goals are to reduce inventories, shorten lead times, and eliminate errors. Many colleges now offer programs in supply chain management and logistics to train future employees to help merchandisers meet such goals. ■

Sales <u>with</u> Cash Discounts

Sales discounts on credit sales can benefit a seller through earlier cash receipts and reduced collection efforts. Many sales discounts are favorable to the buyer, and many buyers will take advantage of them. *New revenue recognition rules* **require that sellers report sales net of expected sales discounts.** *These rules apply to annual periods of public entities beginning after December 15, 2017 (earlier use is permitted for periods beginning after December 15, 2016).*

Either the gross method or net method is used to record sales with cash discounts. The *gross method* records sales at the gross amount and records sales discounts if, and when, they are taken. The gross method requires a period-end adjusting entry to estimate future sales discounts. (The **net method** records sales at the net amount, which assumes that all discounts are taken. If discounts are subsequently lost, the seller records those discounts lost. The net method is described in Appendix 4C.)

Sales on Credit   To illustrate, Z-Mart completes a credit sale for $1,000 on November 12 with terms of 2/10, n/45 (the cost of the merchandise sold is $300). The entry to record the revenue part of this sale given that the seller uses the gross method is

Nov. 12	Accounts Receivable	1,000	
	Sales		1,000
	Sold goods, terms 2/10, n/45.		
	Cost side entry is: Dr. Cost of Goods Sold . . . 300		
	Cr. Merchandise Inventory 300		

Assets = Liabilities + Equity
+1,000   +1,000

This entry records the receivable and the revenue as if the customer will pay the gross amount. The customer has two options, however.

Buyer Pays <u>within</u> Discount Period   One option is for the buyer to pay $980 within the 10-day discount period ending November 22. The $20 sales discount is computed as $1,000 × 2%. Thus, if the customer pays on (or before) November 22, Z-Mart records the cash receipt as

Nov. 22	Cash*	980	
	Sales Discounts	20	
	Accounts Receivable		1,000
	Received payment on Nov. 12 sale less discount.		
	* $1,000 − ($1,000 × 2%)		

Assets = Liabilities + Equity
+   980   −20
−1,000

Sales Discounts is a **contra revenue account,** meaning the Sales Discounts account is deducted from the Sales account when computing a company's net sales. The Sales Discounts account has a *normal debit balance* because it decreases Sales, which has a normal credit balance.

Point: Radio-frequency identification (RFID) tags attach to objects for tracking purposes. Such tags help employees find items in a store, monitor shipments, and check on production progress.

Buyer Pays <u>after</u> Discount Period   The customer's second option is to wait 45 days until December 27 (or at least until after the discount period) and then pay $1,000. Z-Mart records that cash receipt as

Dec. 27	Cash	1,000	
	Accounts Receivable		1,000
	Received payment on Nov. 12 sale after		
	discount period.		

Assets = Liabilities + Equity
+1,000
−1,000

Sales <u>with</u> Returns and Allowances

If a customer is unhappy with a purchase, many sellers allow the customer to either return the merchandise for a full refund (*sales return*) or keep the merchandise along with a partial refund (*sales allowance*). Most sellers can reliably estimate returns and allowances (often abbreviated *R&A*).

Returns Received by Seller   *Seller Issues Refund for Returned Goods.* When returns occur, the seller debits **Sales Returns and Allowances, a contra revenue account** to Sales. For example, assuming that a customer returns merchandise on November 26, and the returned items had sold for $15 and cost $9, the returns entry is

(e1) Nov. 26	Sales Returns and Allowances	15	
	Cash		15
	Goods returned from Nov. 12 sale.		

Assets = Liabilities + Equity
−15   −15

Seller Receives Returned Goods into Inventory. When returns occur, the seller also reduces the cost of sales. Extending the above example where the returned items sold for $15 and cost $9, the entry depends on whether the goods are defective or not.

Returned Goods Not Defective. If the merchandise returned to the seller is not defective and can be resold to another customer, the seller returns these goods to its inventory and records it as follows.

Assets = Liabilities + Equity
+9   +9

(e2) Nov. 26	Merchandise Inventory............................	9	
	Cost of Goods Sold..........................		9
	Returned goods added to inventory.		

Returned Goods Are Defective. If the merchandise returned to the seller is defective, the returned inventory is recorded at its estimated value, not its cost. For example, if the returned goods costing $9 are defective and estimated to be worth $2, the following entry is made

Assets = Liabilities + Equity
+2   −7
                         +9

Point: Some sellers charge buyers a restocking fee for returns.

Nov. 26	Merchandise Inventory............................	2	
	Loss from Defective Merchandise...................	7	
	Cost of Goods Sold..........................		9
	Returned defective goods to inventory and recorded loss.		

Allowances Granted by Seller   To illustrate sales allowances, assume that $40 of merchandise previously sold is defective but the buyer decides to keep it because the seller offers a $10 price reduction paid in cash to the buyer. The seller records this allowance as follows

Assets = Liabilities + Equity
−10   −10

Point: When a seller accepts returns or grants an allowance on merchandise, the seller issues a **credit memorandum**. This informs the buyer of a credit made to the buyer's account receivable in the seller's records.

(f) Nov. 24	Sales Returns and Allowances.....................	10	
	Cash......................................		10
	Sales allowance granted.		

If the seller has *not* yet collected cash for the goods sold, the seller could credit the buyer's Account Receivable. For example, instead of the seller sending $10 cash to the buyer in the entry above, the seller could credit Accounts Receivable for $10.

NEED-TO-KNOW 4-2

Merchandise Sales

P2

Prepare journal entries to record each of the following sales transactions of a merchandising company. Assume a perpetual inventory system and use of the gross method (beginning inventory equals $9,000).

June 1   Sold 50 units of merchandise to a customer for $150 per unit under credit terms of 2/10, n/30, FOB shipping point, and the invoice is dated June 1. The 50 units of merchandise had cost $100 per unit.

June 7   The customer returns 2 units purchased on June 1 because those units did not fit its needs. The seller restores those units to its inventory (as they are not defective) and credits Accounts Receivable from the customer.

June 11   The seller receives the balance due from the June 1 sale to the customer less returns and allowances.

June 14   The customer discovers that 10 units have minor damage but keeps them because the seller sends a $50 cash payment allowance to compensate.

Solution

June 1	Accounts Receivable	7,500	
	Sales		7,500
	Sold goods. 50 units × $150		
June 1	Cost of Goods Sold.............................	5,000	
	Merchandise Inventory.......................		5,000
	Cost of sale. 50 units × $100		
June 7	Sales Returns and Allowances	300	
	Accounts Receivable		300
	Returns accepted. 2 units × $150		
June 7	Merchandise Inventory...........................	200	
	Cost of Goods Sold.........................		200
	Returns added to inventory. 2 units × $100		
June 11	Cash	7,056	
	Sales Discounts*...............................	144	
	Accounts Receivable		7,200
	*Received payment. *($7,500 − $300) × 2%*		
June 14	Sales Returns and Allowances	50	
	Cash		50
	Recorded allowance on goods.		

Do More: QS 4-8, E 4-4

COMPLETING THE ACCOUNTING CYCLE

Exhibit 4.10 shows the flow of merchandising costs during a period and where these costs are reported at period-end. Specifically, beginning inventory plus the net cost of purchases is the merchandise available for sale. As inventory is sold, its cost is recorded in cost of goods sold on the income statement; what remains is ending inventory on the balance sheet. A period's ending inventory is the next period's beginning inventory.

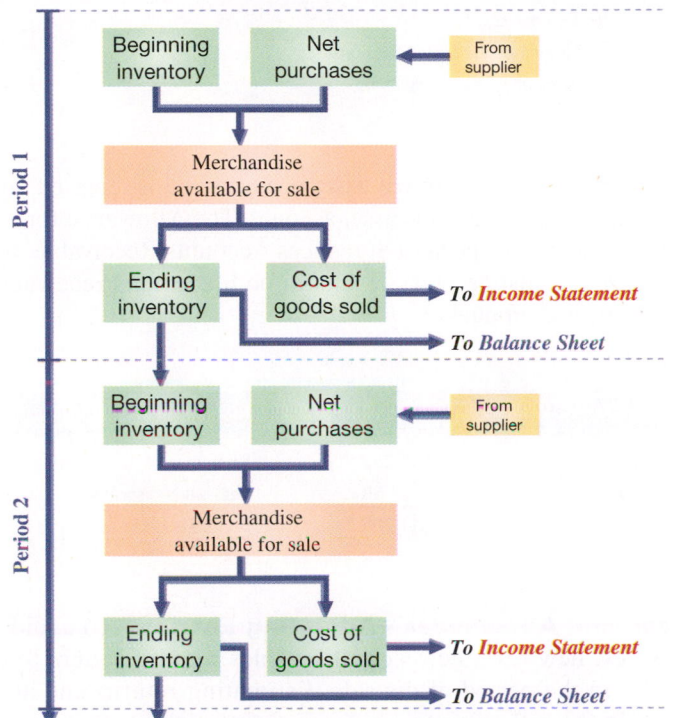

EXHIBIT 4.10

Merchandising Cost Flow in the Accounting Cycle

Adjusting Entries for Merchandisers

Each of the steps in the accounting cycle described in the prior chapter for a service company applies to a merchandiser. This section and the next two expand upon three steps of the accounting cycle for a merchandiser—adjustments, statement preparation, and closing.

Inventory Shrinkage—Adjusting Entry   Adjusting entries are similar for merchandising companies and service companies. However, a merchandiser using a *perpetual* inventory system also makes an adjustment to update the Merchandise Inventory account to reflect any loss of merchandise, including theft and deterioration. **Shrinkage** is the term used to refer to the loss of inventory, and it is computed by comparing a physical count of inventory with recorded amounts. A physical count is usually performed at least once annually.

To illustrate, Z-Mart's Merchandise Inventory account at the end of year 2016 has a balance of $21,250, but a physical count reveals that only $21,000 of inventory exists. The adjusting entry to record this $250 shrinkage is

P3

Prepare adjustments and close accounts for a merchandising company.

Point: About two-thirds of shoplifting losses are thefts by employees.

Dec. 31	Cost of Goods Sold............................	250	
	Merchandise Inventory.....................		250
	Adjust for $250 shrinkage.		

Assets = Liabilities + Equity
−250   −250

Expected Sales Discounts—Adjusting Entry New revenue recognition rules require the reporting of sales at the net amount expected. This means that a period-end adjusting entry is needed to estimate sales discounts for current period's sales that are expected to be taken in future periods. To illustrate, assume Z-Mart has the following unadjusted balances: Accounts Receivable, $11,250; and Allowance for Sales Discounts, $0. Of the $11,250 of receivables, $2,500 of them are within the 2% discount period, and we expect buyers to take $50 in future-period discounts (computed as $2,500 × 2%) arising from this period's sales. The adjusting entry for the $50 update to the allowance for sales discounts is

Assets = Liabilities + Equity
−50   −50

Allow. for Sales Discounts	
Beg. bal.	0
Req. adj.	50
Estim. bal.	50

(g) Dec. 31	Sales Discounts.	50	
	Allowance for Sales Discounts		50
	Adjustment for future discounts.		

Allowance for Sales Discounts is a **contra asset account** and is reported on the balance sheet as a reduction to the Accounts Receivable asset account. The Allowance for Sales Discounts account has a *normal credit balance* because it reduces Accounts Receivable, which has a normal debit balance. The above adjusting entry results in both accounts receivable and sales being reported at their net expected amounts:[2]

Balance Sheet	
Accounts receivable.	$11,250
Less allowance for sales discounts	50
Accounts receivable, net	$11,200

Income Statement	
Sales	$321,000
Less sales discounts	4,300
Net sales	$316,700

Expected Returns and Allowances—Adjusting Entries To avoid overstatement of sales and cost of sales, new revenue recognition rules require sellers to estimate sales returns and allowances in the period of the sale. Estimating returns and allowances requires companies to maintain the following two balance sheet accounts that are set up with adjusting entries:

Current asset: Inventory Returns Estimated
Current liability: Sales Refund Payable

Two adjusting entries are made: one for the revenue (sale) side *and* one for the cost side.

Revenue Side for Expected R&A When returns and allowances are expected, a seller sets up a **Sales Refund Payable** account, which is **a current liability reflecting the amount expected to be refunded to customers.** To illustrate, assume that on December 31 the company estimates future sales refunds to be $1,200. Assume also that the *unadjusted balance*

---

[2] *Next Period Adjustment* The Allowance for Sales Discounts balance remains unchanged during a period except for the period-end adjusting entry. At next period-end, assume that Z-Mart computes an $80 balance for the Allowance for Sales Discounts. Using our 3-step adjusting process from Chapter 3 we get:

Step 1: Current bal. *is* $50 credit in Allowance for Sales Discounts.

Step 2: Current bal. *should be* $80 credit in Allowance for Sales Discounts.

Step 3: Record entry to get from step 1 to step 2.

Sales Discounts   30

Allowance for Sales Discounts   30

in Sales Refund Payable is a $300 credit. The adjusting entry for the $900 update to Sales Refund Payable is

(h1) Dec. 31	Sales Returns and Allowances	900	
	Sales Refund Payable		900
	*Expected refund of sales.**		

Assets = Liabilities + Equity
         +900   −900

Sales Refund Payable

	Beg. bal.	300
	Req. adj.	900
	Estim. bal.	1,200

* This entry uses our 3-step adjusting process from Chapter 3:
Step 1: Current bal. <u>is</u> $300 credit for Sales Refund Payable.
Step 2: Current bal. <u>should be</u> $1,200 credit for Sales Refund Payable.
Step 3: Record entry to get from step 1 to step 2.

The Sales Refund Payable account is updated only during the adjusting entry process. Its balance remains unchanged during the period when actual returns and allowances are recorded.

Cost Side for Expected R&A   On the cost side, the expected returns and allowances implies that some inventory is expected to be returned, which means that cost of goods sold recorded at the time of sale is overstated due to expected returns. A seller sets up an **Inventory Returns Estimated** account, which is **a current asset reflecting the inventory estimated to be returned.** Extending the example above, assume that the company estimates future inventory returns to be $500 (which is the cost-side of the $1,200 expected returns and allowances above). Assume also that the (beginning) *unadjusted balance* in Inventory Returns Estimated is a $200 debit. The adjusting entry for the $300 update to expected returns is

(h2) Dec. 31	**Inventory Returns Estimated**	**300**	
	Cost of Goods Sold.		300
	*Expected return of inventory.**		

Assets = Liabilities + Equity
         +300   +300

Inventory Returns Estim.

Beg. bal.	200	
Req. adj.	300	
Est. bal.	500	

* This entry uses our 3-step adjusting process from Chapter 3:
Step 1: Current bal. <u>is</u> $200 debit for Inventory Returns Estimated.
Step 2: Current bal. <u>should be</u> $500 debit for Inventory Returns Estimated.
Step 3: Record entry to get from step 1 to step 2.

The Inventory Returns Estimated account is updated only during the adjusting entry process. Its balance remains unchanged during the period when actual returns and allowances are recorded.

   Use of expected amounts better recognizes both sales and costs in their proper periods, including the amount of sales and inventory actually sold (net of expected returns and allowances). If estimates of returns and allowances prove too high or too low, we adjust future estimates accordingly. (Advanced courses cover variations in revenue and expense recognition.)

◼ **Decision** Insight ═══════════════════════════════════

Call to Account   It is important we know these accounts:

- **Allowance for Sales Discounts** is a contra asset account and is reported in the balance sheet as a reduction to the Accounts Receivable asset account.
- **Sales Refund Payable** is a current liability account, meaning it is reported in the balance sheet.
- **Inventory Returns Estimated** is a current asset account (often as a subcategory of Inventory), meaning it is reported in the balance sheet—this asset is subject to impairment, which is explained in advanced courses. ◼

Preparing Financial Statements

The financial statements of a merchandiser, and their preparation, are similar to those for a service company. The income statement mainly differs by the inclusion of *cost of goods*

Point: **Staples**'s costs of
shipping merchandise to its
stores are included in its costs
of inventories as required by
the cost principle.

sold and *gross profit*. Also, net sales is affected by discounts, returns, and allowances, and some additional expenses are possible such as delivery expense and loss from defective merchandise. The balance sheet mainly differs by the inclusion of *merchandise inventory* and *inventory returns estimated* as part of current assets, and *sales refund payable* as part of current liabilities. The statement of retained earnings is unchanged. A work sheet can be used to help prepare these statements, and one for Z-Mart is illustrated in Appendix 4B.

Closing Entries for Merchandisers

Point: The Inventory account
is not affected by the closing process under a perpetual system.

Closing entries are similar for service companies and merchandising companies using a perpetual system. The difference is that we must close some new temporary accounts that arise from merchandising activities. Z-Mart has several temporary accounts unique to merchandisers: Sales (of goods), Sales Discounts, Sales Returns and Allowances, and Cost of Goods Sold. Their existence in the ledger means that the first two closing entries for a merchandiser are slightly different from the ones described in the prior chapter for a service company. These differences are set in **red boldface** in the closing entries of Exhibit 4.11.

EXHIBIT 4.11

Closing Entries for a
Merchandiser

Step 1: Close Credit Balances in Temporary Accounts to Income Summary.

Dec. 31	**Sales**..	**321,000**	
	Income Summary		321,000
	Close credit balances in temporary accounts.		

Step 2: Close Debit Balances in Temporary Accounts to Income Summary.

Dec. 31	Income Summary	308,100	
	Sales Discounts..............................		**4,300**
	Sales Returns and Allowances		**2,000**
	Cost of Goods Sold		**230,400**
	Depreciation Expense		3,700
	Salaries Expense.............................		43,800
	Insurance Expense		600
	Rent Expense		9,000
	Supplies Expense		3,000
	Advertising Expense..........................		11,300
	Close debit balances in temporary accounts.		

Step 3: Close Income Summary to Retained Earnings.

The third closing entry is identical for a merchandising company and a service company. The $12,900 amount is net income reported on the income statement.

Dec. 31	Income Summary	12,900	
	Retained Earnings...........................		12,900
	Close Income Summary account.		

Step 4: Close Dividends Account to Retained Earnings.

The fourth closing entry is identical for a merchandising company and a service company. It closes the Dividends account and adjusts the Retained Earnings account to the amount shown on the balance sheet.

Dec. 31	Retained Earnings.............................	4,000	
	Dividends		4,000
	Close the Dividends account.		

Summary of Merchandising Entries

Exhibit 4.12 summarizes key adjusting and closing entries of a merchandiser (using a perpetual inventory system) (**Need-To-Know 4–6** illustrates these entries).

EXHIBIT 4.12

Summary of Key Merchandising Entries (using perpetual system and gross method)

	Merchandising Transactions	Merchandising Entries	Dr.	Cr.
Purchases	Purchasing merchandise for resale.	Merchandise Inventory . . . . Cash or Accounts Payable	# 	 #
	Paying freight costs on purchases; FOB shipping point.	Merchandise Inventory . . . . Cash	# 	 #
	Paying within discount period.	Accounts Payable . . . . Merchandise Inventory . . . . Cash	# 	 # #
	Paying outside discount period.	Accounts Payable . . . . Cash	# 	 #
	Recording purchase returns or allowances.	Cash or Accounts Payable. . . . . Merchandise Inventory	# 	 #
Sales	Selling merchandise.	Cash or Accounts Receivable . . . . Sales	# 	 #
		Cost of Goods Sold . . . . Merchandise Inventory	# 	 #
	Receiving payment within discount period.	Cash . . . . Sales Discounts . . . . Accounts Receivable	# # 	 #
	Receiving payment outside discount period.	Cash . . . . Accounts Receivable	# 	 #
	Receiving sales returns of nondefective inventory.	Sales Returns and Allowances . . . . Cash or Accounts Receivable	# 	 #
		Merchandise Inventory . . . . Cost of Goods Sold	# 	 #
	Recognizing sales allowances.	Sales Returns and Allowances . . . . Cash or Accounts Receivable	# 	 #
	Paying freight costs on sales; FOB destination.	Delivery Expense. Cash	# 	 #

	Merchandising Events	Adjusting and Closing Entries	Dr.	Cr.
Adjusting	Adjustment for shrinkage (occurs when recorded amount larger than physical inventory).	Cost of Goods Sold . . . . Merchandise Inventory	# 	 #
	Period-end adjustment for expected sales discounts.*	Sales Discounts . . . . Allowance for Sales Discounts	# 	 #
	Period-end adjustment for expected returns—both revenue-side and cost-side.*	Sales Returns and Allowances . . . . Sales Refund Payable . . . . Inventory Returns Estimated. . . . . Cost of Goods Sold.	# # 	 # #
Closing	Closing temporary accounts with credit balances.	Sales . . . . Income Summary	# 	 #
	Closing temporary accounts with debit balances.	Income Summary . . . . Sales Returns and Allowances . . . . Sales Discounts . . . . Cost of Goods Sold . . . . Delivery Expense . . . . "Other Expenses"	# 	 # # # # #

Merchandise Inventory	
Beginning inventory	
Purchases	Pur. returns
Freight-in (FOB shp pt)	Pur. allowances
	Pur. discounts
	Shrinkage
Goods avail. for sale	
Customer returns	COGS
Ending inventory	

* Period-end adjustments depend on unadjusted balances, which can reverse the adjusting entries shown.

4-3

Part 1: Recording Shrinkage and Closing Entries

P3

A merchandising company's ledger on May 31, its fiscal year-end, includes the following accounts that have normal balances (it uses the perpetual inventory system). A physical count of its May 31 year-end inventory reveals that the cost of the merchandise inventory still available is $656. (a) Prepare the entry to record any inventory shrinkage. (b) Prepare the four closing entries as of May 31.

Merchandise inventory	$ 756	Other operating expenses	$ 300
Retained earnings	2,300	Cost of goods sold	2,100
Dividends	150	Depreciation expense	400
Sales	4,300	Salaries expense	600
Sales discounts	50	Sales returns and allowances	250

Solution

May 31	Cost of Goods Sold	100	
	Merchandise Inventory		100
	Adjust for shrinkage ($756 − $656).		
May 31	Sales	4,300	
	Income Summary		4,300
	Close temporary accounts with credit balances.		
May 31	Income Summary	3,800	
	Sales Discounts		50
	Sales Returns and Allowances		250
	Cost of Goods Sold*		2,200
	Depreciation Expense		400
	Salaries Expense		600
	Other Operating Expenses		300
	Close temporary accounts with debit balances.		
	*$2,100 (Unadj. bal.) + $100 (Shrinkage)		
May 31	Income Summary	500	
	Retained Earnings		500
	Close Income Summary account.		
May 31	Retained Earnings	150	
	Dividends		150
	Close Dividends account.		

Do More: QS 4-11, E 4-13, E 4-15, P 4-4

Part 2: Estimating Discounts, Returns, and Allowances

P3

At the current year-end, a company shows the following unadjusted balances for selected accounts:

Allowance for Sales Discounts	$ 75 credit	Sales Discounts	$1,850 debit
Sales Refund Payable	800 credit	Sales Returns and Allowances	4,825 debit
Inventory Returns Estimated	450 debit	Cost of Goods Sold	9,875 debit

a. After an analysis of future sales discounts, the company estimates that the Allowance for Sales Discounts account should have a $275 credit balance. Prepare the current year-end adjusting journal entry for future sales discounts.

b. After an analysis of future sales returns and allowances, the company estimates that the Sales Refund Payable account should have an $870 credit balance (revenue side).

c. After an analysis of future inventory returns, the company estimates that the Inventory Returns Estimated account should have a $500 debit balance (cost side).

Solution

Dec. 31	Sales Discounts	200	
	Allowance for Sales Discounts		200
	Adjustment for future discounts.		

Dec. 31	Sales Returns and Allowances	70	
	Sales Refund Payable..........................		70
	Adjustment for future sales refund.		
Dec. 31	Inventory Returns Estimated	50	
	Cost of Goods Sold..........................		50
	Adjustment for future inventory returns.		

> Do More: QS 4-9, QS 4-10, E 4-10, E 4-11, E 4-12

FINANCIAL STATEMENT FORMATS

Generally accepted accounting principles do not require companies to use any one presentation format for financial statements, so we see many different formats in practice. This section describes two common income statement formats: multiple-step and single-step. The classified balance sheet of a merchandiser is also explained.

P4

Define and prepare multiple-step and single-step income statements.

Multiple-Step Income Statement

A **multiple-step income statement** format shows detailed computations of net sales and other costs and expenses, and reports subtotals for various classes of items. Exhibit 4.13 shows a multiple-step income statement for Z-Mart. The statement has three main parts: (1) *gross profit*, determined by net sales less cost of goods sold; (2) *income from operations,* determined by gross profit less operating expenses; and (3) *net income,* determined by income from operations adjusted for nonoperating items.

Point: Z-Mart did not have any nonoperating activities; however, Exhibit 4.13 includes some for illustrative purposes.

EXHIBIT 4.13

Multiple-Step Income Statement

Z-MART
Income Statement
For Year Ended December 31, 2016

Sales			$321,000
Less: Sales discounts	$ 4,300		
Sales returns and allowances	2,000	6,300	
Net sales			314,700
Cost of goods sold*.................................			230,400
Gross profit			84,300
Operating Expenses			
Selling expenses			
Depreciation expense—Store equipment	3,000		
Sales salaries expense	18,500		
Rent expense—Selling space	8,100		
Store supplies expense	1,200		
Advertising expense	11,300		
Total selling expenses	42,100		
General and administrative expenses			
Depreciation expense—Office equipment	700		
Office salaries expense	25,300		
Insurance expense	600		
Rent expense—Office space	900		
Office supplies expense	1,800		
Total general and administrative expenses	29,300		
Total operating expenses		71,400	
Income from operations......................		12,900	
Other revenues and gains (expenses and losses)			
Interest revenue	1,000		
Gain on sale of building	2,500		
Interest expense	(1,500)		
Total other revenue and gains (expenses and losses).........		2,000	
Net income		$ 14,900	

Gross profit computation

Income from operations computation

Nonoperating activities computation

* Cost of goods sold consists of the following:
Beginning inventory..............	$ 19,000
Net cost of purchases	232,400
Goods available for sale...........	251,400
Less ending inventory	21,000
Cost of goods sold	$230,400

Point: Many companies report interest expense and interest revenue in separate categories after operating income and before subtracting income tax expense. As one example, see **Samsung's** income statement in Appendix A.

Example: Sometimes interest revenue and interest expense are reported on the income statement as *interest, net.* To illustrate, if a company has $1,000 of interest expense and $600 of interest revenue, it might report $400 as *interest, net.*

Operating expenses are classified into two sections. **Selling expenses** include the expenses of promoting sales by displaying and advertising merchandise, making sales, and delivering goods to customers. **General and administrative expenses** support a company's overall operations and include expenses related to accounting, human resource management, and financial management. Expenses are allocated between sections when they contribute to more than one. Z-Mart allocates rent expense of $9,000 from its store building between two sections: $8,100 to selling expense and $900 to general and administrative expense.

Nonoperating activities consist of other expenses, revenues, losses, and gains that are unrelated to a company's operations. *Other revenues and gains* commonly include interest revenue, dividend revenue, rent revenue, and gains from asset disposals. *Other expenses and losses* commonly include interest expense, losses from asset disposals, and casualty losses. When a company has no reportable nonoperating activities, its income from operations is simply labeled net income.

Single-Step Income Statement

A **single-step income statement** is another widely used format and is shown in Exhibit 4.14 for Z-Mart. It lists cost of goods sold as another expense and shows only one subtotal for total expenses. Expenses are grouped into very few, if any, categories. Many companies use formats that combine features of both single- and multiple-step statements. Provided that income statement items are shown sensibly, management can choose the format. (In later chapters, we describe some items, such as discontinued operations, that must be reported in certain locations on the income statement.) Similar presentation options are available for the statement of retained earnings and statement of cash flows.

EXHIBIT 4.14

Single-Step Income Statement

Z-MART		
Income Statement		
For Year Ended December 31, 2016		
Revenues		
Net sales		$314,700
Interest revenue		1,000
Gain on sale of building.		2,500
Total revenues.		318,200
Expenses		
Cost of goods sold	$230,400	
Selling expenses.	42,100	
General and administrative expenses.	29,300	
Interest expense	1,500	
Total expenses.		303,300
Net income		$ 14,900

Point: Net income is identical under the single-step and multiple-step formats.

Classified Balance Sheet

The merchandiser's classified balance sheet reports merchandise inventory, and often an inventory returns estimated account, as part of current assets, usually after accounts receivable (net of allowance for sales discounts) according to an asset's nearness to liquidity. Inventory is usually less liquid than accounts receivable because inventory must first be sold before cash can be received; but it is more liquid than supplies and prepaid expenses. Exhibit 4.15 shows the current asset section of

EXHIBIT 4.15

Classified Balance Sheet (partial) of a Merchandiser

Z-MART		
Balance Sheet (partial)		
December 31, 2016		
Current assets		
Cash.		$ 8,200
Accounts receivable	$11,250	
Less: **Allowance for sales discounts**.	50	11,200
Merchandise inventory		**21,000**
Inventory returns estimated		**2,000**
Supplies		800
Prepaid insurance		300
Total current assets.		$43,500

Z-Mart's classified balance sheet. The current liability section includes the Sales Refund Payable account (and other sections are as shown and explained in prior chapters).

Fraud

Merchandising Shenanigans Accurate invoices are important to both sellers and buyers. Merchandisers rely on invoices to make certain they receive all monies for products provided—no more, no less. To achieve this, controls are set up. Still, failures arise. A survey reports that 30% of employees in sales and marketing witnessed false or misleading invoices sent to customers. Another 29% observed employees violating contract terms with customers (KPMG 2013).

Assume Taret's adjusted trial balance on April 30, 2016, its fiscal year-end, follows (data for discounts, returns, and allowances are taken from supplementary records). (a) Prepare a multiple-step income statement that begins with gross sales and includes separate categories for net sales, cost of goods sold, selling expenses, and general and administrative expenses. (b) Prepare a single-step income statement that begins with net sales and includes these expense categories: cost of goods sold, selling expenses, and general and administrative expenses.

NEED-TO-KNOW 4-4

Multiple- and Single-Step Income Statements

P4

Merchandise inventory	$ 800	
Other (noninventory) assets	2,600	
Total liabilities		$ 500
Common stock		400
Retained earnings		1,700
Dividends	300	
Sales		9,467
Sales discounts	227	
Sales returns and allowances	240	
Cost of goods sold	6,500	
Sales salaries expense	450	
Rent expense—Selling space	160	
Store supplies expense	30	
Advertising expense	260	
Office salaries expense	420	
Rent expense—Office space	72	
Office supplies expense	8	
Totals	$12,067	$12,067

Solution

a. Multiple-step income statement

TARET Income Statement For Year Ended April 30, 2016		
Sales		$9,467
Less: Sales discounts	$ 227	
Sales returns and allowances	240	467
Net sales		9,000
Cost of goods sold		6,500
Gross profit		2,500
Operating expenses		
Selling expenses		
Sales salaries expense	450	
Rent expense—Selling space	160	
Store supplies expense	30	
Advertising expense	260	
Total selling expenses		900
General and administrative expenses		
Office salaries expense	420	
Rent expense—Office space	72	
Office supplies expense	8	
Total general and administrative expenses		500
Total operating expenses		1,400
Net income		$1,100

b. Single-step income statement

TARET Income Statement For Year Ended April 30, 2016		
Net sales		$9,000
Expenses		
Cost of goods sold	$6,500	
Selling expenses	900	
General and administrative expenses	500	
Total expenses		7,900
Net income		$1,100

Do More: QS 4-13, E 4-14, P 4-3

GLOBAL VIEW

This section discusses similarities and differences between U.S. GAAP and IFRS in accounting and reporting for merchandise purchases and sales, and for the income statement.

Accounting for Merchandise Purchases and Sales   Both U.S. GAAP and IFRS include broad and similar guidance for the accounting of merchandise purchases and sales. Nearly all of the transactions presented and illustrated in this chapter are accounted for identically under the two systems. The closing process for merchandisers is also similar for U.S. GAAP and IFRS.

Income Statement Presentation   We explained that net income, profit, and earnings refer to the same (*bottom line*) item. However, IFRS tends to use the term *profit* more than any other term, whereas U.S. statements tend to use *net income* more than any other term. Both U.S. GAAP and IFRS income statements begin with the net sales or net revenues (*top line*) item. For merchandisers and manufacturers, this is followed by cost of goods sold. The remaining presentation is similar with the following differences.

- U.S. GAAP offers little guidance about the presentation or order of expenses. IFRS requires separate disclosures for financing costs (interest expense), income tax expense, and some other special items.
- Both systems require separate disclosure of items when their size, nature, or frequency is important.
- IFRS permits expenses to be presented by their function or their nature. U.S. GAAP provides no direction but the SEC requires presentation by function.
- Neither U.S. GAAP nor IFRS defines *operating* income, which results in latitude in reporting.
- IFRS permits alternative income measures on the income statement; U.S. GAAP does not.

VOLKSWAGEN   **Volkswagen Group** provides the following example of income statement reporting. We see the separate disclosure of finance costs, taxes, and other items. We also see the unusual practice of using the minus symbol in an income statement.

VOLKSWAGEN GROUP Income Statement (in euros million) For Year Ended December 31, 2014	
Sales revenue	€ 202,458
Cost of sales	−165,934
Gross profit	36,524
Distribution expenses	−20,292
Administrative expenses	−6,841
Other operating income (net of other expenses)	3,306
Operating profit	12,697
Finance costs	−2,658
Other financial results (including equity investments)	4,755
Profit before tax	14,794
Income tax	−3,726
Profit	€ 11,068

Balance Sheet Presentation   Chapters 2 and 3 explained how both U.S. GAAP and IFRS require current items to be separated from noncurrent items on the balance sheet (yielding a *classified balance sheet*). As discussed, U.S. GAAP balance sheets report current items first. Assets are listed from most liquid to least liquid, whereas liabilities are listed from nearest to maturity to furthest from maturity. IFRS balance sheets normally present noncurrent items first (and equity before liabilities), but this is *not* a requirement as evidenced in **Samsung**'s balance sheet in Appendix A.

Sustainability and Accounting   **Chipotle**'s founder, Steve Ells, makes certain his restaurants are committed to sustainability and the environment by implementing his "Food with Integrity" program, which focuses on four issues—see graphic. Buying food produced under such conditions of sustainability would suggest higher expenses. However, Steve explains that the full financial statement impact of sustainable purchasing is of practical value. "Sustainable food appears to cost more. But, if you look at the cost of industrialized/processed food and then add in the cost of environmental degradation, displaced family farms, the exploitation of animals, the ramifications of the overuse of antibiotics, etc., you come to understand that there's no real value in the industrialized system."

Buying Local
"As I visited various pork producers across the country, I witnessed how family farms have been displaced by industrialized meat production operations ... I wanted a different option and began working with ... a network of independent ranchers who are committed to humanely raising animals outdoors and without the use of antibiotics"
S. Ells, *Nature.com*

Making Space
"We set minimum space requirements for the animals producing the meat and dairy products ... and are always setting the bar higher"
Chipotle.com

Healthy Stock
"We buy meat from farmers and ranchers who raise their animals without antibiotics and synthetic hormones. If animals fall sick, our protocols require that farmers bring them back to health in the most responsible manner possible" *Chipotle.com*

Respecting Land
"When the same crop is planted over and over in the same place (a practice called monoculture), the land suffers. Essential nutrients are depleted from the soil, and crops are more likely to fall prey to diseases and pest infestations, requiring the heavy use of chemical fertilizers and pesticides" *Chipotle.com*

Acid-Test and Gross Margin Ratios 🟩🟨🟥 **Decision Analysis**

Acid-Test Ratio

For many merchandisers, inventory makes up a large portion of current assets. Inventory must be sold and any resulting accounts receivable must be collected before cash is available. Chapter 3 explained that the current ratio, defined as current assets divided by current liabilities, is useful in assessing a company's ability to pay current liabilities. Because it is sometimes unreasonable to assume that inventories are a source of payment for current liabilities, we look to other measures.

A1
Compute the acid-test ratio and explain its use to assess liquidity.

One measure of a merchandiser's ability to pay its current liabilities (referred to as its *liquidity*) is the acid-test ratio. It differs from the current ratio by excluding less liquid current assets such as inventory and prepaid expenses that take longer to be converted to cash. The **acid-test ratio,** also called *quick ratio,* is defined as *quick assets* (cash, short-term investments, and current receivables) divided by current liabilities—see Exhibit 4.16.

$$\text{Acid-test ratio} = \frac{\text{Cash and cash equivalents} + \text{Short-term investments} + \text{Current receivables}}{\text{Current liabilities}}$$

EXHIBIT 4.16
Acid-Test (Quick) Ratio

Exhibit 4.17 shows both the acid-test and current ratios of retailer **JCPenney** for fiscal years 2010 through 2015—also see graph that follows. JCPenney's acid-test ratio reveals an increase in 2014 and

EXHIBIT 4.17
JCPenney's Acid-Test and Current Ratios

$ millions	2015	2014	2013	2012	2011	2010
Total quick assets	$1,318	$1,519	$ 987	$1,920	$2,956	$3,406
Total current assets	$4,331	$4,833	$3,683	$5,081	$6,370	$6,652
Total current liabilities	$2,241	$2,846	$2,568	$2,756	$2,647	$3,249
Acid-test ratio	**0.59**	**0.53**	**0.38**	**0.70**	**1.12**	**1.05**
Current ratio	**1.93**	**1.70**	**1.43**	**1.84**	**2.41**	**2.05**
Industry acid-test ratio	0.55	0.50	0.51	0.54	0.61	0.59
Industry current ratio	2.03	1.99	1.94	2.01	2.27	2.15

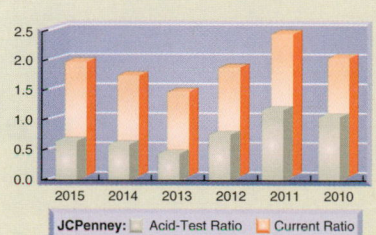

2015 that exceeds the industry average (following a marked decline in 2012 and 2013). Further, JCPenney's current ratio shows an increase in 2014 and 2015 (again, following marked declines in 2012 and 2013). This suggests that its short-term obligations are more confidently covered with short-term assets in recent years as compared with prior years (especially versus 2013).

An acid-test ratio less than 1.0 means that current liabilities exceed quick assets. A rule of thumb is that the acid-test ratio should have a value near, or higher than, 1.0 to conclude that a company is unlikely to face near-term liquidity problems. A value much less than 1.0 raises liquidity concerns unless a company can generate enough cash from inventory sales or if much of its liabilities are not due until late in the next period. Similarly, a value slightly larger than 1.0 can hide a liquidity problem if payables are due shortly and receivables are not collected until late in the next period. Analysis of JCPenney shows some need for concern regarding its liquidity as its acid-test ratio is less than 1.0. However, retailers such as JCPenney pay many current liabilities from inventory sales; moreover, in all years except 2013, JCPenney's acid-test ratios exceed the industry norm (and its inventory is fairly liquid).

■ Decision Maker

Supplier   A retailer requests to purchase supplies on credit from your company. You have no prior experience with this retailer. The retailer's current ratio is 2.1, its acid-test ratio is 0.5, and inventory makes up most of its current assets. Do you extend credit? ■   [Answers follow the chapter's Summary.]

Gross Margin Ratio

The cost of goods sold makes up much of a merchandiser's expenses. Without sufficient gross profit, a merchandiser will likely fail. Users often compute the gross margin ratio to help understand this relation. It differs from the profit margin ratio in that it excludes all costs except cost of goods sold. The **gross margin ratio** (also called *gross profit ratio*) is defined as *gross margin* (net sales minus cost of goods sold) divided by net sales—see Exhibit 4.18.

A2
_____

Compute the gross margin ratio and explain its use to assess profitability.

EXHIBIT 4.18

Gross Margin Ratio

$$\text{Gross margin ratio} = \frac{\text{Net sales} - \text{Cost of goods sold}}{\text{Net sales}}$$

Point: The power of a ratio is often its ability to identify areas for more detailed analysis.

Exhibit 4.19 shows the gross margin ratio of **JCPenney** for fiscal years 2010 through 2015. For JCPenney, each $1 of sales in 2015 yielded about 34.8¢ in gross margin to cover all other expenses and still produce a net income. This 34.8¢ margin is up from 29.4¢ in 2014. This increase is a favorable development. Success for merchandisers such as JCPenney depends on adequate gross margin. For example, the 5.4¢ increase in the gross margin ratio, computed as 34.8¢ − 29.4¢, means that JCPenney has $662 million more in gross margin! (This is computed as net sales of $12,257 million multiplied by the 5.4% increase in gross margin.)

EXHIBIT 4.19

JCPenney's Gross Margin Ratio

$ millions	2015	2014	2013	2012	2011	2010
Gross margin	$ 4,261	$ 3,492	$ 4,066	$ 6,218	$ 6,960	$ 6,910
Net sales	$12,257	$11,859	$12,985	$17,260	$17,759	$17,556
Gross margin ratio	**34.8%**	**29.4%**	**31.3%**	**36.0%**	**39.2%**	**39.4%**

■ Decision Maker

Financial Officer   Your company has a 36% gross margin ratio and a 17% net profit margin ratio. Industry averages are 44% for gross margin and 16% for net profit margin. Do these comparative results concern you? ■   [Answers follow the chapter's Summary.]

Use the following adjusted trial balance and additional information to complete the requirements (data for discounts and returns and allowances are taken from supplementary records).

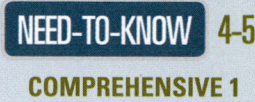

KC Antiques
Adjusted Trial Balance
December 31, 2016

	Debit	Credit
Cash	$ 7,000	
Accounts receivable	13,000	
Merchandise inventory	60,000	
Store supplies	1,500	
Equipment.	45,600	
Accumulated depreciation—Equipment		$ 16,600
Accounts payable		9,000
Salaries payable		2,000
Common stock.		20,000
Retained earnings		59,000
Dividends	10,000	
Sales		343,250
Sales discounts	5,000	
Sales returns and allowances	6,000	
Cost of goods sold.	159,900	
Depreciation expense—Store equipment	4,100	
Depreciation expense—Office equipment	1,600	
Sales salaries expense.	30,000	
Office salaries expense.	34,000	
Insurance expense	11,000	
Rent expense (70% is store, 30% is office)	24,000	
Store supplies expense.	5,750	
Advertising expense	31,400	
Totals.	$449,850	$449,850

KC Antiques's *supplementary records* for 2016 reveal the following itemized costs for merchandising purchases:

Invoice cost of merchandise purchases	$150,000
Purchase discounts received.	2,500
Purchase returns and allowances	2,700
Cost of transportation-in	5,000

Required

1. Use the supplementary records to compute the total cost of merchandise purchases for 2016.

2. Prepare a 2016 multiple-step income statement. (Inventory at December 31, 2015, is $70,100.)

3. Prepare a single-step income statement for 2016.

4. Prepare closing entries for KC Antiques at December 31, 2016. (KC Antiques does not give discount terms on its sales nor does it accept returns.)

5. Compute the acid-test ratio and the gross margin ratio. Explain the meaning of each ratio and interpret them for KC Antiques.

PLANNING THE SOLUTION

● Compute the total cost of merchandise purchases for 2016.

● To prepare the multiple-step statement, first compute net sales. Then, to compute cost of goods sold, add the net cost of merchandise purchases for the year to beginning inventory and subtract the cost of ending inventory. Subtract cost of goods sold from net sales to get gross profit. Then classify expenses as selling expenses or general and administrative expenses.

● To prepare the single-step income statement, begin with net sales. Then list and subtract the expenses.

● The first closing entry debits all temporary accounts with credit balances and opens the Income Summary account. The second closing entry credits all temporary accounts with debit balances. The third entry closes the Income Summary account to the Retained Earnings account, and the fourth entry closes the Dividends account to the Retained Earnings account.

- Identify the quick assets on the adjusted trial balance. Compute the acid-test ratio by dividing quick assets by current liabilities. Compute the gross margin ratio by dividing gross profit by net sales.

SOLUTION

1.

Invoice cost of merchandise purchases	$150,000
Less: Purchases discounts received	2,500
Purchase returns and allowances	2,700
Add: Cost of transportation-in.	5,000
Total cost of merchandise purchases	$149,800

2. Multiple-step income statement

KC ANTIQUES
Income Statement
For Year Ended December 31, 2016

Sales.			$343,250
Less: Sales discounts	$ 5,000		
Sales returns and allowances	6,000	11,000	
Net sales		332,250	
Cost of goods sold*		159,900	
Gross profit.		172,350	
Expenses			
Selling expenses			
Depreciation expense—Store equipment	4,100		
Sales salaries expense	30,000		
Rent expense—Selling space	16,800		
Store supplies expense	5,750		
Advertising expense	31,400		
Total selling expenses	88,050		
General and administrative expenses			
Depreciation expense—Office equipment	1,600		
Office salaries expense	34,000		
Insurance expense.	11,000		
Rent expense—Office space.	7,200		
Total general and administrative expenses.	53,800		
Total operating expenses		141,850	
Net income.		$ 30,500	

> Tax expense for a corporation appears immediately before net income in its own category.

* Cost of goods sold can also be directly computed (applying concepts from Exhibit 4.4):

Merchandise inventory, December 31, 2015	$ 70,100
Total cost of merchandise purchases (from part 1)	149,800
Goods available for sale	219,900
Merchandise inventory, December 31, 2016	60,000
Cost of goods sold	$159,900

3. Single-step income statement

KC ANTIQUES
Income Statement
For Year Ended December 31, 2016

Net sales		$332,250
Expenses		
Cost of goods sold	$159,900	
Selling expenses.	88,050	
General and administrative expenses	53,800	
Total expenses.		301,750
Net income		$ 30,500

4.

Dec. 31	Sales	343,250	
	Income Summary		343,250
	Close credit balances in temporary accounts.		
Dec. 31	Income Summary	312,750	
	Sales Discounts.		5,000
	Sales Returns and Allowances		6,000
	Cost of Goods Sold.		159,900
	Depreciation Expense—Store Equipment		4,100
	Depreciation Expense—Office Equipment		1,600
	Sales Salaries Expense		30,000
	Office Salaries Expense		34,000
	Insurance Expense		11,000
	Rent Expense		24,000
	Store Supplies Expense		5,750
	Advertising Expense.		31,400
	Close debit balances in temporary accounts.		
Dec. 31	Income Summary	30,500	
	Retained Earnings.		30,500
	Close Income Summary account.		
Dec. 31	Retained Earnings.	10,000	
	Dividends		10,000
	Close Dividends account.		

5. Acid-test ratio = (Cash and equivalents + Short-term investments + Current receivables)/
    Current liabilities

= (Cash + Accounts receivable/(Accounts payable + Salaries payable)

= ($7,000 + $13,000)/($9,000 + $2,000) = $20,000/$11,000 = 1.82

Gross margin ratio = Gross profit/Net sales = $172,350/$332,250 = 0.52 (or 52%)

KC Antiques has a healthy acid-test ratio of 1.82. This means it has $1.82 in liquid assets to satisfy each $1.00 in current liabilities. The gross margin of 0.52 shows that KC Antiques spends 48¢ ($1.00 − $0.52) of every dollar of net sales on the costs of acquiring the merchandise it sells. This leaves 52¢ of every dollar of net sales to cover other expenses incurred in the business and to provide a net profit.

Prepare journal entries to record the following merchandising transactions for both the seller (BMX) and buyer (Sanuk).

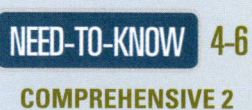

NEED-TO-KNOW 4-6

COMPREHENSIVE 2

May 4	BMX sold $1,500 of merchandise on account to Sanuk, terms FOB shipping point, n/45, invoice dated May 4. The cost of the merchandise was $900. This sale was "as is" with no returns.
May 6	Sanuk paid transportation charges of $30 on the May 4 purchase from BMX.
May 8	BMX sold $1,000 of merchandise on account to Sanuk, terms FOB destination, n/15, invoice dated May 8. The cost of the merchandise was $700. This sale permits returns for 30 days.
May 10	BMX paid transportation costs of $50 for delivery of merchandise sold to Sanuk on May 8.
May 16	BMX issued Sanuk a $200 credit memorandum for merchandise returned. The merchandise was purchased by Sanuk on account on May 8. The cost of the merchandise returned was $140.
May 18	BMX received payment from Sanuk for purchase of May 8.
May 21	BMX sold $2,400 of merchandise on account to Sanuk, terms FOB shipping point, 2/10, n/EOM. The cost of the merchandise was $1,440. This sale permits returns for 90 days.
May 31	BMX received payment from Sanuk for purchase of May 21, less discount.

SOLUTION

BMX (Seller)		
May 4 Accounts Receivable—Sanuk	1,500	
Sales		1,500
Cost of Goods Sold	900	
Merchandise Inventory		900
6 No entry.		
8 Accounts Receivable—Sanuk	1,000	
Sales		1,000
Cost of Goods Sold	700	
Merchandise Inventory		700
10 Delivery Expense	50	
Cash		50
16 Sales Returns and Allowances	200	
Accounts Receivable—Sanuk . . .		200
Merchandise Inventory	140	
Cost of Goods Sold		140
18 Cash	800	
Accounts Receivable—Sanuk		800
21 Accounts Receivable—Sanuk	2,400	
Sales		2,400
Cost of Goods Sold	1,440	
Merchandise Inventory		1,440
31 Cash	2,352	
Sales Discount	48	
Accounts Receivable—Sanuk		2,400

Sanuk (Buyer)		
Merchandise Inventory	1,500	
Accounts Payable—BMX		1,500
Merchandise Inventory	30	
Cash		30
Merchandise Inventory	1,000	
Accounts Payable—BMX		1,000
No entry.		
Accounts Payable—BMX	200	
Merchandise Inventory		200
Accounts Payable—BMX	800	
Cash		800
Merchandise Inventory	2,400	
Accounts Payable—BMX		2,400
Accounts Payable—BMX	2,400	
Merchandise Inventory		48
Cash		2,352

APPENDIX

4A   Recording Transactions under the Periodic System

A periodic inventory system requires updating the inventory account only at the *end of a period* to reflect the cost of both the goods available and the goods sold. Thus, during the period, the Merchandise Inventory balance remains unchanged. It reflects the beginning inventory balance until it is updated at the end of the period. During the period the cost of merchandise is recorded in a temporary *Purchases* account. When a company sells merchandise, it records revenue *but not the cost of the goods sold.* At the end of the period when a company prepares financial statements, it takes a *physical count of inventory* by counting the quantities and costs of merchandise available. The cost of goods sold is then computed by subtracting the ending inventory amount from the cost of merchandise available for sale.

P5

Record and compare merchandising transactions using both periodic and perpetual inventory systems.

Recording Merchandise Purchases   Under a periodic system, the purchases, purchase returns and allowances, purchase discounts, and transportation-in transactions are recorded in separate temporary accounts. At period-end, each of these temporary accounts is closed, which updates the Merchandise Inventory account. To illustrate, journal entries under the periodic inventory system are shown for the most common transactions (codes *a* through *d* link these transactions to those in the chapter, and we drop explanations for simplicity). For comparison, perpetual system journal entries are shown to the right of each periodic entry, where differences are highlighted in yellow.

Credit Purchases with Cash Discounts   The periodic system uses a temporary **Purchases** account that accumulates the cost of all purchase transactions during each period. The Purchases account has a normal debit balance, as it increases the cost of merchandise available for sale. Z-Mart's November 2 entry to record the purchase of merchandise for $500 on credit with terms of 2/10, n/30 is

(a)

Periodic			Perpetual		
Purchases...............	500		Merchandise Inventory	500	
Accounts Payable		500	Accounts Payable		500

Payment of Purchases   The periodic system uses a temporary **Purchase Discounts** account that accumulates discounts taken on purchase transactions during the period. If payment for transaction (a) is made *within the discount period,* the entry is

(b1)

Periodic			Perpetual		
Accounts Payable	500		Accounts Payable..............	500	
Purchases Discounts*..		10	Merchandise Inventory*.....		10
Cash................		490	Cash		490
*$500 × 2%			*$500 × 2%		

If payment for transaction (a) is made *after the discount period expires,* the entry is

(b2)

Periodic			Perpetual		
Accounts Payable	500		Accounts Payable..............	500	
Cash................		500	Cash		500

Purchase Returns and Allowances   *Purchase Allowance.* The buyer and seller agree to a $30 purchase allowance for defective goods (assume allowance terms are $30 whether paid within the discount period or not). In the periodic system, the temporary **Purchase Returns and Allowances** account accumulates the cost of all returns and allowances during a period. The buyer records the $30 allowance as

(c1)

Periodic			Perpetual		
Accounts Payable	30		Accounts Payable..............	30	
Purchase Returns and Allowances		30	Merchandise Inventory		30

Purchase Returns. The buyer returns $50 of merchandise within the discount period. The entry is

(c2)

Periodic			Perpetual		
Accounts Payable	50		Accounts Payable..............	50	
Purchase Returns and Allowances		50	Merchandise Inventory		50

Transportation-In   The buyer paid a $75 freight charge to transport goods with terms FOB destination. In the periodic system, this cost is charged to a temporary **Transportation-In** account, which has a normal debit balance as it increases the cost of merchandise available for sale.

(d)

Periodic			Perpetual		
Transportation-In	75		Merchandise Inventory	75	
Cash................		75	Cash		75

Point: Purchase Discounts _and_ Purchase Returns and Allowances are contra purchases accounts _and_ have normal credit balances, as they both decrease the cost of merchandise available for sale.

Recording Merchandise Sales   Journal entries under the periodic system are shown for the most common transactions (codes *e* through *h* link these transactions to those in the chapter). Perpetual system entries are shown to the right of each periodic entry, where differences are highlighted.

Credit Sales and Receipt of Payments   Both the periodic and perpetual systems record sales entries similarly, using the gross method. The same holds for entries related to payment of receivables from sales both within and after the discount period. However, under the periodic system, the cost of goods sold is *not* recorded at the time of each sale (whereas it is under the perpetual system)—we show later in this appendix how to compute cost of goods sold at period-end under the periodic system. The entries to record $1,000 in credit sales (costing $300) is

Periodic			Perpetual		
Accounts Receivable.......	1,000		Accounts Receivable	1,000	
Sales...............		1,000	Sales		1,000
			Cost of Goods Sold............	300	
No cost-side entry			Merchandise Inventory......		300

Returns Received by Seller   A customer returned merchandise for a cash refund. The goods sell for $15 and cost $9. (*Recall:* The periodic system records only the revenue effect, not the cost effect, for sales transactions.) The entries for the seller to restore the returned items to inventory are

	Periodic				Perpetual		
(e1)	Sales Returns and Allowances . . .	15			Sales Returns and Allowances	15	
	Cash.		15		Cash		15
(e2)					Merchandise Inventory	9	
	No entry				Cost of Goods Sold		9

Allowances Granted by Seller   A customer received an allowance in transaction (*f*) of $10 cash; only the revenue side is impacted as no inventory was returned and cost stays the same. The entry is identical under the periodic and perpetual systems. The seller records this allowance as

	Periodic				Perpetual		
(f)	Sales Returns and Allowances. . .	10			Sales Returns and Allowances	10	
	Cash.		10		Cash		10

EXHIBIT 4A.1

Comparison of Adjusting and Closing Entries— Periodic and Perpetual

Adjusting Entries   *Shrinkage—Adjusting Entry* Adjusting (and closing) entries for the two systems are shown in Exhibit 4A.1. The $250 shrinkage is only recorded under the perpetual system—see entry (*z*) in Exhibit 4A.1. Shrinkage is unknown under the periodic system and is simply included as part of cost of goods sold.

PERIODIC

Adjusting Entries

(z)	None		
(g)	Sales Discounts	50	
	Allowance for Sales Discounts		50
(h1)	Sales Returns and Allowances.	900	
	Sales Refund Payable		900
(h2)	Inventory Returns Estimated.	300	
	Purchases		300

PERPETUAL

Adjusting Entries

(z)	Cost of Goods Sold	250	
	Merchandise Inventory		250
(g)	Sales Discounts	50	
	Allowance for Sales Discounts. . . .		50
(h1)	Sales Returns and Allowances.	900	
	Sales Refund Payable		900
(h2)	Inventory Returns Estimated	300	
	Cost of Goods Sold		300

PERIODIC

Closing Entries

(1)	Sales	321,000	
	Merchandise Inventory (ending)	**21,000**	
	Purchase Discounts	**4,200**	
	Purchase Returns and Allowances	**1,500**	
	Income Summary		347,700
(2)	Income Summary	334,800	
	Sales Discounts		4,300
	Sales Returns and Allowances		2,000
	Merchandise Inventory (beginning). . .	**19,000**	
	Purchases	**235,800**	
	Transportation-In	**2,300**	
	Depreciation Expense		3,700
	Salaries Expense		43,800
	Insurance Expense		600
	Rent Expense		9,000
	Supplies Expense		3,000
	Advertising Expense		11,300
(3)	Income Summary	12,900	
	Retained Earnings		12,900
(4)	Retained Earnings	4,000	
	Dividends		4,000

PERPETUAL

Closing Entries

(1)	Sales	321,000	
	Income Summary		321,000
(2)	Income Summary	308,100	
	Sales Discounts		4,300
	Sales Returns and Allowances		2,000
	Cost of Goods Sold		230,400
	Depreciation Expense		3,700
	Salaries Expense		43,800
	Insurance Expense		600
	Rent Expense		9,000
	Supplies Expense		3,000
	Advertising Expense		11,300
(3)	Income Summary	12,900	
	Retained Earnings		12,900
(4)	Retained Earnings.	4,000	
	Dividends		4,000

Expected Sales Discounts—Adjusting Entry Both the periodic and perpetual methods make a period-end adjusting entry under the gross method to estimate the $50 sales discounts arising from current period's sales that are likely to be taken in future periods. Z-Mart made the period-end adjusting entry (g) in Exhibit 4A.1 for expected sales discounts.

Expected Returns and Allowances—Adjusting Entry Both the periodic and perpetual inventory systems estimate returns and allowances arising from current-period sales that will occur in future periods. The adjusting entry approach for both systems is identical for the sales side, but slightly different for the cost side. The period-end entries (h1) and (h2) in Exhibit 4A.1 are used to record the updates to expected sales refunds of $900 and the cost-side of $300. Under both systems, the seller sets up a **Sales Refund Payable** account, which is a current liability reflecting the amount expected to be refunded to customers, and an **Inventory Returns Estimated** account, which is a current asset reflecting the inventory estimated to be returned.

Closing Entries The periodic and perpetual inventory systems have slight differences in closing entries. The period-end Merchandise Inventory balance (unadjusted) is $19,000 under the periodic system. Since the periodic system does not update the Merchandise Inventory balance during the period, the $19,000 amount is the beginning inventory. A physical count of inventory taken at the end of the period reveals $21,000 of merchandise available. The adjusting and closing entries for the two systems are shown in Exhibit 4A.1. Recording the periodic inventory balance is a two-step process. The ending inventory balance of $21,000 (which includes shrinkage) is entered by debiting the inventory account in the first closing entry. The beginning inventory balance of $19,000 is deleted by crediting the inventory account in the second closing entry.[3]

By updating Merchandise Inventory and closing Purchases, Purchase Discounts, Purchase Returns and Allowances, and Transportation-In, the periodic system transfers the cost of sales amount to Income Summary. Review the periodic side of Exhibit 4A.1 and see that the **red boldface** items affect Income Summary as follows.

Credit to Income Summary in the first closing entry includes amounts from:	
Merchandise inventory (ending)	$ 21,000
Purchase discounts.	4,200
Purchase returns and allowances.	1,500
Debit to Income Summary in the second closing entry includes amounts from:	
Merchandise inventory (beginning)	(19,000)
Purchases	(235,800)
Transportation-in.	(2,300)
Net effect on Income Summary (net debit = cost of goods sold)	**$(230,400)**

This $230,400 effect on Income Summary is the cost of goods sold amount (which is equal to cost of goods sold reported in a perpetual inventory system). The periodic system transfers cost of goods sold to the Income Summary account but without using a Cost of Goods Sold account. Also, the periodic system does not separately measure shrinkage. Instead, it computes cost of goods available for sale, subtracts the cost of ending inventory, and defines the difference as cost of goods sold, which includes shrinkage.

Preparing Financial Statements The financial statements of a merchandiser using the periodic system are similar to those for a service company described in prior chapters. The income statement mainly differs by the inclusion of *cost of goods sold* and *gross profit*—of course, net sales is affected by discounts, returns, and allowances. The cost of goods sold section under the periodic system follows.

---

[3] This approach is called the *closing entry method*. An alternative approach, referred to as the *adjusting entry method,* would not make any entries to Merchandise Inventory in the closing entries of Exhibit 4A.1, but instead would make two adjusting entries. Using Z-Mart data, the two adjusting entries would be: (1) Dr. Income Summary and Cr. Merchandise Inventory for $19,000 each and (2) Dr. Merchandise Inventory and Cr. Income Summary for $21,000 each. The first entry removes the beginning balance of Merchandise Inventory and the second entry records the actual ending balance.

Calculation of Cost of Goods Sold For Year Ended December 31, 2016	
Beginning inventory	$ 19,000
Net cost of purchases	232,400
Cost of goods available for sale	251,400
Less ending inventory	21,000
Cost of goods sold	$230,400

EXHIBIT 4A.2

Work Sheet for Merchandiser (using a periodic system)

The balance sheet mainly differs by the inclusion of *merchandise inventory,* inventory returns estimated, allowance for sales discounts, and sales refund payable. The work sheet in Exhibit 4A.2 can be used to help prepare these statements. The only differences under the periodic system from the work sheet illustrated in Appendix 4B using the perpetual system are highlighted as follows in **blue boldface**.

		Unadjusted Trial Balance		Adjustments		Adjusted Trial Balance		Income Statement		Balance Sheet and Statement of Equity	
No.	Account	Dr.	Cr.	Dr.	Cr.	Dr.	Cr.	Dr.	Cr.	Dr.	Cr.
101	Cash	8,200				8,200				8,200	
106	Accounts receivable	11,250				11,250				11,250	
108	Allowance for sales discounts		0		(e) 50		50				50
119	**Merchandise inventory**	19,000				19,000		19,000	21,000	21,000	
121	Inventory returns estimated	200		(h2) 300		500				500	
126	Supplies	3,800			(2) 3,000	800				800	
128	Prepaid insurance	900			(1) 600	300				300	
167	Equipment	34,200				34,200				34,200	
168	Accumulated depr.—Equip.		3,700		(3) 3,700		7,400				7,400
201	Accounts payable		16,000				16,000				16,000
209	Salaries payable				(4) 800		800				800
227	Sales refund payable		300		(h1) 900		1,200				1,200
307	Common stock		10,000				10,000				10,000
318	Retained earnings		31,900				31,900				31,900
319	Dividends	4,000				4,000				4,000	
413	Sales		321,000				321,000		321,000		
414	Sales returns and allowances	1,100		(h1) 900		2,000		2,000			
415	Sales discounts	4,250		(e) 50		4,300		4,300			
505	**Purchases**	236,100			(h2) 300	235,800		235,800			
506	**Purchases returns & allowances**		1,500				1,500		1,500		
507	**Purchases discounts**		4,200				4,200		4,200		
508	**Transportation-in**	2,300				2,300		2,300			
612	Depreciation expense—Equip.			(3) 3,700		3,700		3,700			
622	Salaries expense	43,000		(4) 800		43,800		43,800			
637	Insurance expense			(1) 600		600		600			
640	Rent expense	9,000				9,000		9,000			
652	Supplies expense			(2) 3,000		3,000		3,000			
655	Advertising expense	11,300				11,300		11,300			
	Totals	388,600	388,600	9,350	9,350	394,050	394,050	334,800	347,700	80,250	67,350
	Net income							12,900			12,900
	Totals							347,700	347,700	80,250	80,250

APPENDIX

4B   Work Sheet—Perpetual System

Exhibit 4B.1 shows the work sheet for preparing financial statements of a merchandiser. It differs slightly from the work sheet layout in Chapter 3—the differences are in **red boldface**. Also, the adjustments in the work sheet reflect the following: (*1*) expiration of $600 of prepaid insurance, (*2*) use of $3,000 of supplies, (*3*) depreciation of $3,700 for equipment, (*4*) accrual of $800 of unpaid salaries, and (*5*) inventory shrinkage of $250. Once the adjusted amounts are extended into the financial statement columns, the information is used to develop financial statements. We also see that the far-right Balance Sheet and Statement of Equity columns are identical under the perpetual and periodic methods.

EXHIBIT 4B.1

Work Sheet for Merchandiser (using a perpetual system)

	No.	Account	Unadjusted Trial Balance Dr.	Cr.	Adjustments Dr.	Cr.	Adjusted Trial Balance Dr.	Cr.	Income Statement Dr.	Cr.	Balance Sheet and Statement of Equity Dr.	Cr.
3	101	Cash	8,200				8,200				8,200	
4	106	Accounts receivable	11,250				11,250				11,250	
5	108	Allowance for sales discounts		0		(e) 50		50				50
6	119	Merchandise inventory	21,250			(5) 250	21,000				21,000	
7	121	Inventory returns estimated	200			(h2) 300	500				500	
8	126	Supplies	3,800			(2) 3,000	800				800	
9	128	Prepaid insurance	900			(1) 600	300				300	
10	167	Equipment	34,200				34,200				34,200	
11	168	Accumulated depr.—Equip.		3,700		(3) 3,700		7,400				7,400
12	201	Accounts payable		16,000				16,000				16,000
13	209	Salaries payable				(4) 800		800				800
14	227	Sales refund payable		300		(h1) 900		1,200				1,200
15	307	Common stock		10,000				10,000				10,000
16	318	Retained earnings		31,900				31,900				31,900
17	319	Dividends	4,000				4,000				4,000	
18	413	Sales		321,000				321,000		321,000		
19	414	Sales returns and allowances	1,100		(h1) 900		2,000		2,000			
20	415	Sales discounts	4,250		(e) 50		4,300		4,300			
21	502	Cost of goods sold	230,450		(5) 250	(h2) 300	230,400		230,400			
22	612	Depreciation expense—Equip.			(3) 3,700		3,700		3,700			
23	622	Salaries expense	43,000		(4) 800		43,800		43,800			
24	637	Insurance expense			(1) 600		600		600			
25	640	Rent expense	9,000				9,000		9,000			
26	652	Supplies expense			(2) 3,000		3,000		3,000			
27	655	Advertising expense	11,300				11,300		11,300			
28		Totals	382,900	382,900	9,600	9,600	388,350	388,350	308,100	321,000	80,250	67,350
29		Net income							12,900			12,900
30		Totals							321,000	321,000	80,250	80,250

APPENDIX

Recording Transactions under the Net Method

4C

P6

Record and compare merchandising transactions using the gross method and net method.

This chapter described entries to record the receipt and payment of an invoice for merchandise with and without cash discount terms. Those entries were prepared under the **gross method,** which initially records an invoice at its *gross* amount. The **net method** is another means of recording invoices, which initially records the invoice at its *net* amount (net of any cash discount). This appendix records merchandising transactions using the net method, where key differences with the gross method are highlighted.

When invoices are recorded at *net* amounts, any cash discounts are deducted from the balance of the Merchandise Inventory account when initially recorded. This assumes that all cash discounts will be taken. If any discounts are later lost, they are recorded in a **Discounts Lost** expense account reported on the income statement.

Perpetual Inventory System

PURCHASES—Perpetual   A company purchases merchandise on November 2 at a $500 invoice price ($490 net) with terms of 2/10, n/30. Its November 2 entries under the gross and net methods are

Gross Method—Perpetual		
Merchandise Inventory	500	
Accounts Payable		500

Net Method—Perpetual		
Merchandise Inventory.	490	
Accounts Payable		490

If the invoice is paid on (or before) November 12 within the discount period, it records

Gross Method—Perpetual		
Accounts Payable	500	
Merchandise Inventory...		10
Cash...............		490

Net Method—Perpetual		
Accounts Payable.............	490	
Cash...................		490

If, instead, the invoice is *not* paid within the discount period, but it is later paid on December 2 (the n/30 due date), *after the discount period,* it records

Gross Method—Perpetual		
Accounts Payable	500	
Cash...............		500

Net Method—Perpetual		
Accounts Payable.............	490	
Discounts Lost*...............	10	
Cash...................		500

*For simplicity, we record Discounts Lost on the *payment date* when that date is after the discount period.

SALES—Perpetual   To illustrate, a company sells merchandise on November 2 at a $500 invoice price ($490 net) with terms of 2/10, n/30. The goods cost $200. Its November 2 entries under the gross and net methods are

Gross Method—Perpetual		
Accounts Receivable.......	500	
Sales...............		500
Cost of Goods Sold	200	
Merchandise Inventory..		200

Net Method—Perpetual		
Accounts Receivable...........	490	
Sales...................		490
Cost of Goods Sold............	200	
Merchandise Inventory......		200

If cash is received on (or before) November 12 within the discount period, it records

Gross Method—Perpetual		
Cash...................	490	
Sales Discounts...........	10	
Accounts Receivable...		500

Net Method—Perpetual		
Cash........................	490	
Accounts Receivable		490

If, instead, cash is *not* received within the discount period, but it is later received on December 2 (the n/30 due date), *after the discount period*, it records

Gross Method—Perpetual*		
Cash...................	500	
Accounts Receivable...		500

Net Method—Perpetual*		
Cash........................	500	
Interest Revenue		10
Accounts Receivable		490

*Two points: (1) An adjusting entry for expected sales discounts is common with the gross method (see in-chapter text); also, an adjusting entry *may* be necessary with the net method if the seller expects that some future sales discounts will *not* be taken (this is explained in advanced courses). (2) Adjusting entries for sales returns and allowances are identical under the gross and net methods.

Periodic Inventory System

PURCHASES—Periodic   Under the periodic system, the balance of the Merchandise Inventory account remains unchanged during the period and is updated at period-end as part of the adjusting process. During the period, three accounts are used to record purchases of inventory: Purchases; Purchase Discounts; and Purchase Returns and Allowances. *It is helpful to see that the entries below are identical to the perpetual system __except__ that Merchandise Inventory is substituted for each of the three purchases accounts.*

To illustrate, we apply the periodic system to purchases transactions. On November 2, a buyer purchases goods ($500 gross; $490 net) with terms of 2/10, n/30. Its November 2 entries under the gross and net methods are

Gross Method—Periodic		
Purchases...............	500	
Accounts Payable		500

Net Method—Periodic		
Purchases	490	
Accounts Payable..........		490

If the invoice is paid on (or before) November 12 within the discount period, it records

Gross Method—Periodic		
Accounts Payable	500	
Purchase Discounts. . . .		10
Cash.		490

Net Method—Periodic		
Accounts Payable	490	
Cash		490

If, instead, the invoice is *not* paid within the discount period, but it is later paid on December 2 (the n/30 due date), *after the discount period*, it records

Gross Method—Periodic		
Accounts Payable	500	
Cash.		500

Net Method—Periodic		
Accounts Payable	490	
Discounts Lost	10	
Cash		500

SALES—Periodic   For the above sales transactions, the **perpetual and periodic entries are identical except** that under the periodic system the cost-side entries are *not* made at the time of each sale nor **for any subsequent returns.** Instead, the cost of goods sold is computed at period-end based on a physical count of inventory. This entry is illustrated in Exhibit 4A.1.

Summary

C1 **Describe merchandising activities and identify income components for a merchandising company.** Merchandisers buy products and resell them. Examples of merchandisers include Walmart, Home Depot, The Limited, and Barnes & Noble. A merchandiser's costs on the income statement include an amount for cost of goods sold. Gross profit, or gross margin, equals sales minus cost of goods sold.

C2 **Identify and explain the inventory asset and cost flows of a merchandising company.** The current asset section of a merchandising company's balance sheet includes the cost of products held for resale as of the balance sheet date. When the merchandise is sold, its cost is transferred from the balance sheet to the income statement, where it is reported as Cost of Goods Sold.

A1 **Compute the acid-test ratio and explain its use to assess liquidity.** The acid-test ratio is computed as quick assets (cash, short-term investments, and current receivables) divided by current liabilities. It indicates a company's ability to pay its current liabilities with its existing quick assets. An acid-test ratio equal to or greater than 1.0 is often adequate.

A2 **Compute the gross margin ratio and explain its use to assess profitability.** The gross margin ratio is computed as gross margin (net sales minus cost of goods sold) divided by net sales. It indicates a company's profitability before considering other expenses.

P1 **Analyze and record transactions for merchandise purchases using a perpetual system.** For a perpetual inventory system, purchases of inventory are added to the Merchandise Inventory account. Discounts, returns, and allowances of purchases are subtracted from Merchandise Inventory, and transportation-in costs are added to Merchandise Inventory.

P2 **Analyze and record transactions for merchandise sales using a perpetual system.** A merchandiser records sales at the invoice price (using the gross method). The cost of items sold is transferred from Merchandise Inventory to Cost of Goods Sold. When cash discounts from the sales price are offered and customers pay within the discount period, the seller records this in Sales Discounts, a contra account to Sales.

Refunds or credits given to customers for unsatisfactory merchandise are recorded in Sales Returns and Allowances, a contra account to Sales.

P3 **Prepare adjustments and close accounts for a merchandising company.** With a perpetual system, it is sometimes necessary to make an adjustment for inventory shrinkage. This is computed by comparing a physical count of inventory with the Merchandise Inventory balance. Shrinkage is normally charged to Cost of Goods Sold. New revenue recognition rules are applied using adjusting entries. Future expected sales discounts arising from current-period sales are recorded using an adjusting entry with a debit to Sales Discounts and a credit to Allowance for Sales Discounts. Estimates of future sales returns and allowances are made with an adjusting entry to debit Sales Returns and Allowances and to credit Sales Refund Payable (a current liability); this means that Sales is recorded net of expected returns and allowances. Similarly, an estimate of future inventory returns is made and recorded in Inventory Returns Estimated (a current asset, debit) with a corresponding credit to Cost of Goods Sold. Finally, temporary accounts closed to Income Summary for a merchandiser include Sales, Sales Discounts, Sales Returns and Allowances, and Cost of Goods Sold.

P4 **Define and prepare multiple-step and single-step income statements.** Multiple-step income statements include greater detail for sales and expenses than do single-step income statements. They often show details of net sales and report expenses in categories reflecting different activities, where some information is taken from supplementary records.

P5A **Record and compare merchandising transactions using both periodic and perpetual inventory systems.** A perpetual inventory system continuously tracks the cost of goods available for sale and the cost of goods sold. A periodic system accumulates the cost of goods purchased during the period but does not tally the cost of goods sold until the end of a period. Transactions involving the sale and purchase of merchandise are recorded and analyzed under both the periodic and perpetual inventory systems. Adjusting and closing entries for both inventory systems are illustrated and explained.

P6C **Record and compare merchandising transactions using the gross method and net method.** When invoices are recorded at gross amounts, the amount of discounts later taken is deducted from the balance of the Inventory account. When purchases are recorded at net amounts, a Discounts Lost account is brought to management's attention as an operating expense.

Guidance Answers to Decision Maker and Decision Ethics

Entrepreneur   For terms of 3/10, n/90, missing the 3% discount for an additional 80 days equals an implied annual interest rate of 13.69%, computed as (365 days ÷ 80 days) × 3%. Since you can borrow funds at 11% (assuming no other processing costs), it is better to borrow and pay within the discount period. You save 2.69% (13.69% − 11%) in interest costs by paying early.

Payables Manager   Your decision is whether to comply with prior policy or to create a new policy and not abuse discounts offered by suppliers. Your first step should be to meet with your superior to find out if the late payment policy is the actual policy and, if so, its rationale. If it is the policy to pay late, you must apply your own sense of ethics. One point of view is that the late payment policy is unethical. A deliberate plan to make late payments means the company lies when it pretends to make payment within the discount period. Another view is that the late payment policy is acceptable. In some markets, attempts to take discounts through late payments are accepted as a continued phase of "price negotiation." Also, your company's suppliers can respond by billing your company for the discounts not accepted because of late payments. However, this is a dubious viewpoint, especially since the prior manager proposes that you dishonestly explain late payments as computer or mail problems and since some suppliers have complained.

Supplier   A current ratio of 2.1 suggests sufficient current assets to cover current liabilities. An acid-test ratio of 0.5 suggests, however, that quick assets can cover only about one-half of current liabilities. This implies that the retailer depends on money from sales of inventory to pay current liabilities. If sales of inventory decline or profit margins decrease, the likelihood that this retailer will default on its payments increases. Your decision is probably not to extend credit. If you do extend credit, you are likely to closely monitor the retailer's financial condition. (It is better to hold unsold inventory than uncollectible receivables.)

Financial Officer   Your company's net profit margin is about equal to the industry average and suggests typical industry performance. However, gross margin reveals that your company is paying far more in cost of goods sold or receiving far less in sales price than competitors. Your attention must be directed to finding the problem with cost of goods sold, sales, or both. One positive note is that your company's expenses make up 19% of sales (36% − 17%). This favorably compares with competitors' expenses that make up 28% of sales (44% − 16%).

Key Terms

Acid-test ratio	Gross margin	Perpetual inventory system
Allowance for Sales Discounts	Gross margin ratio	Purchase discount
Cash discount	Gross method	Retailer
Cost of goods sold	Gross profit	Sales discount
Credit memorandum	Inventory	Sales refund payable
Credit period	Inventory returns estimated	Selling expenses
Credit terms	List price	Shrinkage
Debit memorandum	Merchandise	Single-step income statement
Discount period	Merchandise inventory	Supplementary records
Discounts Lost	Merchandiser	Trade discount
EOM	Multiple-step income statement	Wholesaler
FOB	Net method	
General and administrative expenses	Periodic inventory system	

Multiple Choice Quiz   Answers at end of chapter

1. A company has $550,000 in net sales and $193,000 in gross profit. This means its cost of goods sold equals
   - a. $743,000
   - b. $550,000
   - c. $357,000
   - d. $193,000
   - e. $(193,000)

2. A company purchased $4,500 of merchandise on May 1 with terms of 2/10, n/30. On May 6, it returned $250 of the $4,500 of merchandise. On May 8, it paid the balance owed for merchandise, taking any discount it was entitled to. The cash paid on May 8 is
   - a. $4,500
   - b. $4,250
   - c. $4,160
   - d. $4,165
   - e. $4,410

3. A company has cash sales of $75,000, credit sales of $340,000, sales discounts of $8,000, sales returns and allowances of $12,000, inventory returns estimated of

$13,700, and sales refund payable of $6,000. Its net sales equal

a. $395,000   **c.** $300,300   **e.** $414,700
b. $375,300   **d.** $339,700

4. A company's quick assets are $37,500, its current assets are $80,000, and its current liabilities are $50,000. Its acid-test ratio equals

a. 1.600   **c.** 0.625   **e.** 0.469
b. 0.750   **d.** 1.333

5. A company's net sales are $675,000, its cost of goods sold is $459,000, and its net income is $74,250. Its gross margin ratio equals

a. 32%   **c.** 47%   **e.** 34%
b. 68%   **d.** 11%

A(B,C) *Superscript letter A (B,C) denotes assignments based on Appendix 4A (4B,4C).*

Icon denotes assignments that involve decision making.

Discussion Questions

1. What items appear in financial statements of merchandising companies but not in the statements of service companies?

2. In comparing the accounts of a merchandising company with those of a service company, what additional accounts would the merchandising company likely use, assuming it employs a perpetual inventory system?

3. Explain how a business can earn a positive gross profit on its sales and still have a net loss.

4. Why do companies offer a cash discount?

5. How does a company that uses a perpetual inventory system determine the amount of inventory shrinkage?

6. Distinguish between cash discounts and trade discounts for purchases. Is the amount of a trade discount on purchased merchandise recorded in the accounts?

7. What is the difference between a sales discount and a purchase discount?

8. Why would a company's manager be concerned about the quantity of its purchase returns if its suppliers allow unlimited returns?

9. Does the sender (maker) of a debit memorandum record a debit or a credit in the recipient's account? What entry (debit or credit) does the recipient record?

10. What is the difference between the single-step and multiple-step income statement formats?

11. Refer to the balance sheet and income statement for **Apple** in Appendix A. What **APPLE** does the company title its inventory account? Does the company present a detailed calculation of its cost of goods sold?

12. Refer to **Google**'s income statement in Appendix A. What title does it use for **GOOGLE** cost of goods sold?

13. Refer to the income statement for **Samsung** in Appendix A. What does **Samsung** Samsung title its cost of goods sold account?

14. Refer to the income statement of **Samsung** in Appendix A. Does its **Samsung** income statement report a gross profit figure? If yes, what is the amount?

15. Buyers negotiate purchase contracts with suppliers. What type of shipping terms should a buyer attempt to negotiate to minimize freight-in costs?

connect

Enter the letter for each term in the blank space beside the definition that it most closely matches.

A. Sales discount   **E.** FOB shipping point   **H.** Purchase discount
B. Credit period   **F.** Gross profit   **I.** Cash discount
C. Discount period   **G.** Merchandise inventory   **J.** Trade discount
D. FOB destination

_____ **1.** Goods a company owns and expects to sell to its customers.

_____ **2.** Time period that can pass before a customer's payment is due.

_____ **3.** Seller's description of a cash discount granted to buyers in return for early payment.

_____ **4.** Reduction below list or catalog price that is negotiated in setting the price of goods.

_____ **5.** Ownership of goods is transferred when the seller delivers goods to the carrier.

_____ **6.** Purchaser's description of a cash discount received from a supplier of goods.

_____ **7.** Reduction in a receivable or payable if it is paid within the discount period.

_____ **8.** Difference between net sales and the cost of goods sold.

_____ **9.** Time period in which a cash discount is available.

_____ **10.** Ownership of goods is transferred when delivered to the buyer's place of business.

QUICK STUDY

QS 4-1
Applying merchandising terms
C1

QS 4-2
Identifying inventory costs
C2

Costs of $5,000 were incurred to acquire goods and make them ready for sale. The goods were shipped to the buyer (FOB shipping point) for a cost of $200. Additional necessary costs of $400 were incurred to acquire the goods. No other incentives or discounts were available. What is the buyer's total cost of merchandise inventory?

a. $5,000   **b.** $5,200   **c.** $5,400   **d.** $5,600

QS 4-3
Merchandise equations and flows
C2

Use the following information (in random order) from a service company and from a merchandiser to compute net income. For the merchandiser, also compute gross profit, the goods available for sale, and the cost of goods sold. *Hint:* Not all information may be necessary and some is taken from supplemental records.

Krug Service Company		Kleiner Merchandising Company	
Expenses	$ 8,500	Accumulated depreciation.	$ 700
Revenues	14,000	Beginning inventory	5,000
Dividends	1,600	Common stock	50
Cash.	700	Retained earnings	900
Prepaid rent	800	Ending inventory	1,700
Accounts payable	200	Operating expenses.	1,450
Common stock	500	Purchases	3,900
Retained earnings.	2,500	Sales	9,500
Equipment	1,300	Dividends	1,600

QS 4-4
Computing net invoice amounts
P1

Compute the amount to be paid for each of the four separate invoices assuming that all invoices are paid *within* the discount period.

	Merchandise (gross)	**Terms**		**Merchandise (gross)**	**Terms**
a.	$5,000	2/10, n/60	**c.**	$75,000	1/10, n/30
b.	$20,000	1/15, EOM	**d.**	$10,000	3/15, n/45

QS 4-5
Recording purchases, returns and discounts taken
P1

Prepare journal entries to record each of the following transactions of a merchandising company. The company records purchases using the gross method and a perpetual inventory system.

Nov. 5   Purchased 600 units of product at a cost of $10 per unit. Terms of the sale are 2/10, n/60; the invoice is dated November 5.
Nov. 7   Returned 25 defective units from the November 5 purchase and received full credit.
Nov. 15   Paid the amount due from the November 5 purchase, less the return on November 7.

QS 4-6
Recording purchases and discounts taken
P1

Prepare journal entries to record each of the following transactions. The company records purchases using the gross method and a perpetual inventory system.

Aug. 1   Purchased merchandise with an invoice price of $60,000 and credit terms of 3/10, n/30.
Aug. 11   Paid supplier the amount owed from the August 1 purchase.

QS 4-7
Recording purchases and discounts missed
P1

Prepare journal entries to record each of the following transactions. The company records purchases using the gross method and a perpetual inventory system.

Sept. 15   Purchased merchandise with an invoice price of $35,000 and credit terms of 2/5, n/15.
Sept. 29   Paid supplier the amount owed on the September 15 purchase.

QS 4-8
Recording sales, returns and discounts taken
P2

Prepare journal entries to record each of the following sales transactions of a merchandising company. The company uses a perpetual inventory system and the gross method.

Apr. 1   Sold merchandise for $3,000, with credit terms n/30; invoice dated April 1. The cost of the merchandise is $1,800.
Apr. 4   The customer in the April 1 sale returned $300 of merchandise for full credit. The merchandise, which had cost $180, is returned to inventory.
Apr. 8   Sold merchandise for $1,000, with credit terms of 1/10, n/30; invoice dated April 8. Cost of the merchandise is $700.
Apr. 11   Received payment for the amount due from the April 1 sale less the return on April 4.

ProBuilder has the following June 30, 2016, fiscal-year-end unadjusted balances: Allowance for Sales Discounts, $0; and Accounts Receivable, $10,000. Of the $10,000 of receivables, $2,000 are within a 3% discount period, meaning that it expects buyers to take $60 in future discounts arising from this period's sales.

a. Prepare the June 30, 2016, fiscal-year-end adjusting journal entry for future sales discounts.

b. Assume the same facts above *and* that there is a $10 fiscal-year-end unadjusted credit balance in the Allowance for Sales Discounts. Prepare the June 30, 2016, fiscal-year-end adjusting journal entry for future sales discounts.

QS 4-9
Recording estimated sales discounts
P3

ProBuilder reports merchandise sales of $50,000 and cost of merchandise sales of $20,000 in its first year of operations ending June 30, 2016. It makes fiscal-year-end adjusting entries for estimated future returns and allowances equal to 2% of sales, or $1,000, and 2% of cost of sales, or $400.

a. Prepare the June 30, 2016, fiscal-year-end adjusting journal entry for future returns and allowances related to sales.

b. Prepare the June 30, 2016, fiscal-year-end adjusting journal entry for future returns and allowances related to cost of sales.

QS 4-10
Recording estimated sales returns
P3

Nix'It Company's ledger on July 31, its fiscal year-end, includes the following selected accounts that have normal balances (Nix'It uses the perpetual inventory system).

QS 4-11
Accounting for shrinkage—perpetual system
P3

Merchandise inventory	$ 37,800	Inventory returns estimated.........	$ 9,500
Retained earnings	115,300	Cost of goods sold	105,000
Dividends....................	7,000	Depreciation expense	10,300
Sales	149,000	Salaries expense	32,500
Sales refund payable...........	8,700	Miscellaneous expenses	5,000

A physical count of its July 31 year-end inventory discloses that the cost of the merchandise inventory available is $35,900. Prepare the entry to record any inventory shrinkage.

Refer to QS 4-11 and prepare journal entries to close the balances in temporary revenue and expense accounts. Remember to consider the entry for shrinkage that is made to solve QS 4-11.

QS 4-12
Closing entries   **P3**

For each item below indicate whether the statement describes a multiple-step income statement or a single-step income statement.

a. Multiple-step income statement   **b.** Single-step income statement

_____ **1.** Typically shows detailed computations of net sales and other costs and expenses.

_____ **2.** Statement limited to two main categories (revenues and expenses).

_____ **3.** Reports gross profit as a separate line item.

_____ **4.** Reports net income equal to income from operations adjusted for any nonoperating items.

QS 4-13
Multiple-step income statement
P4

Use the following information on current assets and current liabilities to compute and interpret the acid-test ratio. Explain what the acid-test ratio of a company measures.

QS 4-14
Computing and interpreting acid-test ratio
A1

Cash........................	$1,490	Prepaid expenses	$ 700
Accounts receivable............	2,800	Accounts payable	5,750
Inventory	6,000	Other current liabilities	850

Identify similarities and differences between the acid-test ratio and the current ratio. Compare and describe how the two ratios reflect a company's ability to meet its current obligations.

QS 4-15
Contrasting liquidity ratios   **A1**

Compute gross profit and the gross margin ratio for each separate case *a* through *d*. Interpret the gross margin ratio for case *a*.

QS 4-16
Computing and analyzing gross margin
A2

	a	b	c	d
Net sales	$125,000	$526,500	$33,000	$250,000
Cost of goods sold...............	79,750	329,589	24,453	126,500

QS 4-17

IFRS income statement
presentation

P4

Income statement information for **adidas Group**, a German footwear, apparel, and accessories manufacturer, for the year ended December 31, 2014, follows. The company applies IFRS, as adopted by the European Union, and reports its results in millions of euros. Prepare its calendar-year 2014 (1) multiple-step income statement and (2) single-step income statement.

Net income	€ 564
Financial income	19
Financial expenses	67
Operating profit	883
Cost of sales	7,610
Income taxes	271
Income before taxes	835
Gross profit	6,924
Royalty and commission income	102
Other operating income	138
Other operating expenses.............	6,281
Net sales	14,534

QS 4-18ᴬ

Contrasting periodic and
perpetual systems

P5

Identify whether each description best applies to a periodic or a perpetual inventory system.

_____ **a.** Updates the inventory account only at period-end.

_____ **b.** Requires an adjusting entry to record inventory shrinkage.

_____ **c.** Markedly increased in frequency and popularity in business within the past decade.

_____ **d.** Records cost of goods sold each time a sales transaction occurs.

_____ **e.** Provides more timely information to managers.

QS 4-19ᴬ

Recording purchases,
returns and discounts—
periodic & gross
methods **P5**

Refer to QS 4-5 and prepare journal entries to record each of the merchandising transactions assuming that the company records purchases using the gross method and a *periodic* inventory system.

QS 4-20ᴬ

Recording sales, returns
and discounts—periodic &
gross methods **P5**

Refer to QS 4-8 and prepare journal entries to record each of the merchandising transactions assuming that the company records purchases using the gross method and a *periodic* inventory system.

QS 4-21ᶜ

Recording purchases,
returns and discounts—
net & perpetual methods

P5

Refer to QS 4-5 and prepare journal entries to record each of the merchandising transactions assuming that the company records purchases using the *net* method and a *perpetual* inventory system.

QS 4-22ᶜ

Recording sales, returns
and discounts—net &
perpetual methods **P5**

Refer to QS 4-8 and prepare journal entries to record each of the merchandising transactions assuming that the company records purchases using the *net* method and a *perpetual* inventory system.

QS 4-23

International accounting
standards

C1

Answer each of the following questions related to international accounting standards.

a. Explain how the accounting for merchandise purchases and sales is different between accounting under IFRS versus U.S. GAAP.

b. Income statements prepared under IFRS usually report an item titled *finance costs*. What do finance costs refer to?

c. U.S. GAAP prohibits alternative measures of income reported on the income statement. Does IFRS permit such alternative measures on the income statement?

■ connect

Using your accounting knowledge, fill in the blanks in the following separate income statements *a* through *e*. Identify any negative amount by putting it in parentheses.

EXERCISES

Exercise 4-1
Computing revenues, expenses, and income
C1

	a	b	c	d	e
Sales	$62,000	$43,500	$46,000	$?	$25,600
Cost of goods sold					
Merchandise inventory (beginning)	8,000	17,050	7,500	8,000	4,560
Total cost of merchandise purchases	38,000	?	?	32,000	6,600
Merchandise inventory (ending)	?	(3,000)	(9,000)	(6,600)	?
Cost of goods sold	34,050	16,000	?	?	7,000
Gross profit	?	?	3,750	45,600	?
Expenses	10,000	10,650	12,150	3,600	6,000
Net income (loss)	$?	$16,850	$ (8,400)	$42,000	$?

The operating cycle of a merchandiser with credit sales includes the following five activities. Starting with merchandise acquisition, identify the chronological order of these five activities.

_____ **a.** Prepare merchandise for sale.

_____ **b.** Collect cash from customers on account.

_____ **c.** Make credit sales to customers.

_____ **d.** Purchase merchandise.

_____ **e.** Monitor and service accounts receivable.

Exercise 4-2
Operating cycle for merchandiser
C2

Prepare journal entries to record the following transactions for a retail store. The company uses a perpetual inventory system and the gross method.

Apr. 2 Purchased $4,600 of merchandise from Lyon Company with credit terms of 2/15, n/60, invoice dated April 2, and FOB shipping point.
 3 Paid $300 cash for shipping charges on the April 2 purchase.
 4 Returned to Lyon Company unacceptable merchandise that had an invoice price of $600.
 17 Sent a check to Lyon Company for the April 2 purchase, net of the discount and the returned merchandise.
 18 Purchased $8,500 of merchandise from Frist Corp. with credit terms of 1/10, n/30, invoice dated April 18, and FOB destination.
 21 After negotiations, received from Frist a $500 allowance toward the $8,500 owed on the April 18 purchase.
 28 Sent check to Frist paying for the April 18 purchase, net of the allowance and the discount.

Exercise 4-3
Recording purchases, purchase returns, and purchase allowances
P1

Check April 28, Cr. Cash $7,920

Allied Merchandisers was organized on May 1. Macy Co. is a major customer (buyer) of Allied (seller) products. Prepare journal entries to record the following transactions for Allied assuming it uses a perpetual inventory system and the gross method. (Allied estimates returns using an adjusting entry at each year-end.)

May 3 Allied made its first and only purchase of inventory for the period on May 3 for 2,000 units at a price of $10 cash per unit (for a total cost of $20,000).
 5 Allied sold 1,500 of the units in inventory for $14 per unit (invoice total: $21,000) to Macy Co. under credit terms 2/10, n/60. The goods cost $15,000 to Allied.
 7 Macy returns 125 units because they did not fit the customer's needs (invoice amount: $1,750). Allied restores the units, which cost $1,250, to its inventory.
 8 Macy discovers that 200 units are scuffed but are still of use and, therefore, keeps the units. Allied sends Macy a credit memorandum for $300 toward the original invoice amount to compensate for the damage.
 15 Allied receives payment from Macy for the amount owed on the May 5 purchase; payment is net of returns, allowances, and any cash discount.

Exercise 4-4
Recording sales, sales returns, and sales allowances
P2

Refer to Exercise 4-4 and prepare journal entries for Macy Co. to record each of the May transactions. Macy is a retailer that uses the gross method and a perpetual inventory system, and purchases these units for resale.

Exercise 4-5
Recording purchases, purchase returns, and purchase allowances P1

Exercise 4-6
Recording sales,
purchases, and cash
discounts—buyer *and*
seller P1 P2

Santa Fe Retailing purchased merchandise "as is" (with no returns) from Mesa Wholesalers with credit terms of 3/10, n/60 and an invoice price of $24,000. The merchandise had cost Mesa $16,000. Assume that both buyer and seller use a perpetual inventory system and the gross method.

1. Prepare entries that the *buyer* records for the (*a*) purchase, (*b*) cash payment *within* the discount period, and (*c*) cash payment *after* the discount period.

2. Prepare entries that the *seller* records for the (*a*) sale, (*b*) cash collection *within* the discount period, and (*c*) cash collection *after* the discount period.

Exercise 4-7
Recording sales,
purchases, shipping and
returns—buyer *and* seller

P1 P2

Sydney Retailing (buyer) and Troy Wholesalers (seller) enter into the following transactions. Both Sydney and Troy use a perpetual inventory system and the gross method.

May 11   Sydney accepts delivery of $40,000 of merchandise it purchases for resale from Troy: invoice dated May 11; terms 3/10, n/90; FOB shipping point. The goods cost Troy $30,000. Sydney pays $345 cash to Express Shipping for delivery charges on the merchandise.

May 12   Sydney returns $1,400 of the $40,000 of goods to Troy, who receives them the same day and restores them to its inventory. The returned goods had cost Troy $1,050.

May 20   Sydney pays Troy for the amount owed. Troy receives the cash immediately.

Check (1) May 20, Cr.
Cash $37,442

1. Prepare journal entries that Sydney Retailing (buyer) records for these three transactions.

2. Prepare journal entries that Troy Wholesalers (seller) records for these three transactions.

Exercise 4-8
Inventory and cost of
sales transactions in
T-accounts

P1 P2

The following *supplementary records* summarize Tesla Company's merchandising activities for year 2016 (it uses a perpetual inventory system). Set up T-accounts for Merchandise Inventory and Cost of Goods Sold. Then record the summarized activities in those T-accounts and compute account balances.

Cost of merchandise sold to customers in sales transactions	$196,000
Merchandise inventory, December 31, 2015.	25,000
Invoice cost of merchandise purchases, gross amount.	192,500
Shrinkage determined on December 31, 2016.	800
Cost of transportation-in	2,900
Cost of merchandise returned by customers and restored to inventory	2,100
Purchase discounts received	1,700
Purchase returns and allowances.	4,000

Check Year-end Merch.
Inventory, Dec. 31, $20,000

Exercise 4-9
Recording purchases,
sales, returns and
shipping

P1 P2

Prepare journal entries for the following merchandising transactions of the Dollar Store assuming it uses a perpetual inventory system and the gross method.

Nov. 1   Dollar Store purchases merchandise for $1,500 on terms of 2/5, n/30, FOB shipping point, invoice dated November 1.

5   Dollar Store pays cash for the November 1 purchase.

7   Dollar Store discovers and returns $200 of defective merchandise purchased on November 1, and paid for on November 5, for a cash refund.

10   Dollar Store pays $90 cash for transportation costs for the November 1 purchase.

13   Dollar Store sells merchandise for $1,600 with terms n/30. The cost of the merchandise is $800.

16   Merchandise is returned to the Dollar Store from the November 13 transaction. The returned items are priced at $160 and cost $80; the items were not damaged and were returned to inventory.

Exercise 4-10
Recording estimated
sales discounts

P3

Med Labs has the following December 31, 2016, year-end unadjusted balances: Allowance for Sales Discounts, $0; and Accounts Receivable, $5,000. Of the $5,000 of receivables, $1,000 are within a 2% discount period, meaning that it expects buyers to take $20 in future-period discounts arising from this period's sales.

a. Prepare the December 31, 2016, year-end adjusting journal entry for future sales discounts.

b. Assume the same facts above *and* that there is a $5 year-end unadjusted credit balance in the Allowance for Sales Discounts. Prepare the December 31, 2016, year-end adjusting journal entry for future sales discounts.

c. Is the Allowance for Sales Discounts a contra asset or a contra liability account?

Chico Company allows its customers to return merchandise within 30 days of purchase.

- At December 31, 2016, the end of its first year of operations, Chico estimates future period merchandise returns of $60,000 (cost of $22,500) related to its 2016 sales.
- On January 3, 2017, a customer returns merchandise with a selling price of $2,000 for a cash refund; the returned merchandise cost $750 and is returned to inventory as it is not defective.

a. Prepare the December 31, 2016, year-end adjusting journal entry for estimated future sales returns and allowances (revenue side).

b. Prepare the December 31, 2016, year-end adjusting journal entry for estimated future inventory returns and allowances (cost side).

c. Prepare the January 3, 2017, journal entry(ies) to record the merchandise returned.

Exercise 4-11
Recording estimates of future returns
P3

Lopez Company reports unadjusted first-year merchandise sales of $100,000 and cost of merchandise sales of $30,000.

a. Compute gross profit (using the unadjusted numbers above).

b. The company expects future returns and allowances equal to 5% of sales and 5% of cost of sales.

   1. Prepare the year-end adjusting entry to record the sales expected to be refunded.

   2. Prepare the year-end adjusting entry to record the cost side of sales returns and allowances.

   3. Recompute gross profit (using the adjusted numbers from parts *1* and *2*).

c. Is the Sales Refund Payable an asset, liability, or equity account?

d. Is the Inventory Returns Estimated an asset, liability, or equity account?

Exercise 4-12
Recording estimates of future returns
P3

The following list includes selected permanent accounts and all of the temporary accounts from the December 31, 2016, unadjusted trial balance of Emiko Co., a business owned by Kumi Emiko. Use these account balances along with the additional information to journalize (*a*) adjusting entries and (*b*) closing entries. Emiko Co. uses a perpetual inventory system.

Exercise 4-13
Preparing adjusting and closing entries for a merchandiser
P3

	Debit	Credit
Merchandise inventory.	$ 30,000	
Prepaid selling expenses	5,600	
Dividends	33,000	
Sales		$529,000
Sales returns and allowances	17,000	
Sales discounts	5,000	
Cost of goods sold.	212,000	
Sales salaries expense	48,000	
Utilities expense.	15,000	
Selling expenses	36,000	
Administrative expenses	105,000	

Additional Information

Accrued sales salaries amount to $1,700. Prepaid selling expenses of $3,000 have expired. A physical count of year-end merchandise inventory shows $28,700 of goods still available.

Check   Entry to close Income Summary: Cr. Retained Earnings $85,000

A company reports the following sales-related information. Compute and prepare the net sales portion only of this company's multiple-step income statement.

Exercise 4-14
Net sales computation for multiple-step income statement
P4

Sales, gross.	$200,000	Sales returns and allowances	$16,000
Sales discounts	4,000	Sales salaries expense.	10,000

A retail company recently completed a physical count of ending merchandise inventory to use in preparing adjusting entries. In determining the cost of the counted inventory, company employees failed to consider that $3,000 of incoming goods had been shipped by a supplier on December 31 under an FOB shipping point agreement. These goods had been recorded in Merchandise Inventory as a purchase, but *they were not included in the physical count because they were in transit.*

a. Explain how this overlooked fact impacts its balance sheet and income statement.

b. Indicate whether this overlooked fact results in an overstatement, understatement, or no effect on the following separate ratios: return on assets, debt ratio, current ratio, and acid-test ratio.

Exercise 4-15
Interpreting a physical count error as inventory shrinkage
A1

Exercise 4-16
Physical count error and profits **A2**

Refer to the information in Exercise 4-15 and indicate whether the failure to include in-transit inventory as part of the physical count results in an overstatement, understatement, or no effect on the following separate ratios: (*a*) gross margin ratio and (*b*) profit margin ratio.

Exercise 4-17
Computing and analyzing acid-test and current ratios

A1

Compute the current ratio and acid-test ratio for each of the following separate cases. (Round ratios to two decimals.) Which company situation is in the best position to meet short-term obligations? Explain.

	Case X	Case Y	Case Z
Cash	$2,000	$ 110	$1,000
Short-term investments	50	0	580
Current receivables	350	470	700
Inventory	2,600	2,420	4,230
Prepaid expenses	200	500	900
Total current assets	$5,200	$3,500	$7,410
Current liabilities	$2,000	$1,000	$3,800

Exercise 4-18^A
Recording purchases, returns and allowances—periodic **P5**

Refer to Exercise 4-3 and prepare journal entries to record each of the merchandising transactions assuming that the buyer uses the *periodic inventory system and the gross method.*

Exercise 4-19^A
Recording sales, purchases and discounts: buyer and seller—periodic **P5**

Refer to Exercise 4-6 and prepare journal entries to record each of the merchandising transactions assuming that the *periodic inventory system and the gross method* are used by both the buyer and the seller.

Exercise 4-20^A
Recording sales, purchases, shipping and returns: buyer and seller—periodic **P5**

Refer to Exercise 4-7 and prepare journal entries to record each of the merchandising transactions assuming that the *periodic inventory system and the gross method* are used by both the buyer and the seller.

Exercise 4-21
Preparing an income statement under IFRS

P4

L'Oréal reports the following income statement accounts for the year ended December 31, 2014 (euros in millions). Prepare the income statement for this company for the year ended December 31, 2014, following usual IFRS practices.

Net profit.............	€ 4,908.6	Income tax expense	€1,111.0
Finance costs	31.4	Profit before tax expense	6,019.6
Net sales	22,532.0	Research and development expense.........	760.6
Gross profit	16,031.3	Selling, general and administrative expense	4,821.1
Other income	2,118.0	Advertising and promotion expense.........	6,558.9
Cost of sales	6,500.7	Finance income	42.3

Exercise 4-22^C
Recording sales, purchases, shipping and returns: buyer and seller—perpetual and net method **P5**

Refer to Exercise 4-7 and prepare journal entries to record each of the merchandising transactions assuming that the *perpetual inventory system and the net method* are used by both the buyer and the seller.

Exercise 4-23^C
Recording purchases, sales, returns and discounts: buyer *and* seller—perpetual and both net & gross methods **P6**

Piere Imports uses the perpetual system in accounting for merchandise inventory and had the following transactions during the month of October. Prepare entries to record these transactions assuming that Piere Imports records invoices (*a*) at gross amounts and (*b*) at net amounts.

Oct. 2   Purchased merchandise at a $3,000 price ($2,940 net), invoice dated October 2, terms 2/10, n/30.
     10   Received a credit memorandum toward the return of $500 ($490 net) of merchandise that it purchased on October 2.
     17   Purchased merchandise at a $5,400 price ($5,292 net), invoice dated October 17, terms 2/10, n/30.

Continued on next page . . .

27 Paid for the merchandise purchased on October 17, less the discount.
31 Paid for the merchandise purchased on October 2. (Payment was mistakenly delayed, which caused the discount to be lost.)

connect

Prepare journal entries to record the following merchandising transactions of Cabela's, which uses the perpetual inventory system and the gross method. (*Hint:* It will help to identify each receivable and payable; for example, record the purchase on July 1 in Accounts Payable—Boden.)

July 1 Purchased merchandise from Boden Company for $6,000 under credit terms of 1/15, n/30, FOB shipping point, invoice dated July 1.
2 Sold merchandise to Creek Co. for $900 under credit terms of 2/10, n/60, FOB shipping point, invoice dated July 2. The merchandise had cost $500.
3 Paid $125 cash for freight charges on the purchase of July 1.
8 Sold merchandise that had cost $1,300 for $1,700 cash.
9 Purchased merchandise from Leight Co. for $2,200 under credit terms of 2/15, n/60, FOB destination, invoice dated July 9.
11 Received a $200 credit memorandum from Leight Co. for the return of part of the merchandise purchased on July 9.
12 Received the balance due from Creek Co. for the invoice dated July 2, net of the discount.
16 Paid the balance due to Boden Company within the discount period.
19 Sold merchandise that cost $800 to Art Co. for $1,200 under credit terms of 2/15, n/60, FOB shipping point, invoice dated July 19.
21 Issued a $100 credit memorandum to Art Co. for an allowance on goods sold on July 19.
24 Paid Leight Co. the balance due, net of discount.
30 Received the balance due from Art Co. for the invoice dated July 19, net of discount.
31 Sold merchandise that cost $4,800 to Creek Co. for $7,000 under credit terms of 2/10, n/60, FOB shipping point, invoice dated July 31.

PROBLEM SET A

Problem 4-1A
Preparing journal entries for merchandising activities—perpetual system
P1 P2

Check July 12, Dr. Cash $882

July 16, Cr. Cash $5,940

July 24, Cr. Cash $1,960

July 30, Dr. Cash $1,078

Prepare journal entries to record the following merchandising transactions of Lowe's, which uses the perpetual inventory system and the gross method. (*Hint:* It will help to identify each receivable and payable; for example, record the purchase on August 1 in Accounts Payable—Aron.)

Aug. 1 Purchased merchandise from Aron Company for $7,500 under credit terms of 1/10, n/30, FOB destination, invoice dated August 1.
5 Sold merchandise to Baird Corp. for $5,200 under credit terms of 2/10, n/60, FOB destination, invoice dated August 5. The merchandise had cost $4,000.
8 Purchased merchandise from Waters Corporation for $5,400 under credit terms of 1/10, n/45, FOB shipping point, invoice dated August 8.
9 Paid $125 cash for shipping charges related to the August 5 sale to Baird Corp.
10 Baird returned merchandise from the August 5 sale that had cost Lowe's $400 and was sold for $600. The merchandise was restored to inventory.
12 After negotiations with Waters Corporation concerning problems with the purchases on August 8, Lowe's received a credit memorandum from Waters granting a price reduction of $400 off the $5,400 of goods purchased.
14 At Aron's request, Lowe's paid $200 cash for freight charges on the August 1 purchase, reducing the amount owed to Aron.
15 Received balance due from Baird Corp. for the August 5 sale less the return on August 10.
18 Paid the amount due Waters Corporation for the August 8 purchase less the price allowance from August 12.
19 Sold merchandise to Tux Co. for $4,800 under credit terms of n/10, FOB shipping point, invoice dated August 19. The merchandise had cost $2,400.
22 Tux requested a price reduction on the August 19 sale because the merchandise did not meet specifications. Lowe's sent Tux a $500 credit memorandum toward the $4,800 invoice to resolve the issue.
29 Received Tux's cash payment for the amount due from the August 19 sale less the price allowance from August 22.
30 Paid Aron Company the amount due from the August 1 purchase.

Problem 4-2A
Preparing journal entries for merchandising activities—perpetual system
P1 P2

Check Aug. 9, Dr. Delivery Expense, $125

Aug. 18, Cr. Cash $4,950

Aug. 29, Dr. Cash $4,300

Problem 4-3A
Computing merchandising amounts and formatting income statements

C2   P4

Valley Company's adjusted trial balance on August 31, 2016, its fiscal year-end, follows.

	Debit	Credit
Merchandise inventory	$ 41,000	
Other (noninventory) assets	130,400	
Total liabilities......................		$ 25,000
Common stock		10,000
Retained earnings....................		94,550
Dividends.........................	8,000	
Sales............................		225,600
Sales discounts.....................	2,250	
Sales returns and allowances..........	12,000	
Cost of goods sold	74,500	
Sales salaries expense	32,000	
Rent expense—Selling space..........	8,000	
Store supplies expense	1,500	
Advertising expense..................	13,000	
Office salaries expense	28,500	
Rent expense—Office space..........	3,600	
Office supplies expense..............	400	
Totals	$355,150	$355,150

On August 31, 2015, merchandise inventory was $25,400. Supplementary records of merchandising activities for the year ended August 31, 2016, reveal the following itemized costs.

Invoice cost of merchandise purchases.........	$92,000
Purchase discounts received	2,000
Purchase returns and allowances..............	4,500
Costs of transportation-in...................	4,600

Required

1. Compute the company's net sales for the year.
2. Compute the company's total cost of merchandise purchased for the year.
3. Prepare a multiple-step income statement that includes separate categories for net sales, cost of goods sold, selling expenses, and general and administrative expenses.
4. Prepare a single-step income statement that includes these expense categories: cost of goods sold, selling expenses, and general and administrative expenses.

Check   (2) $90,100
   (3) Gross profit,
$136,850; Net income,
$49,850
   (4) Total expenses,
$161,500

Problem 4-4A
Preparing closing entries and interpreting information about discounts and returns

C2   P3

Check   (1) $49,850 Dr. to
close Income Summary
   (2) Current-year
ratio, 5.3%

Use the data for Valley Company in Problem 4-3A to complete the following requirements.

Required

1. Prepare closing entries as of August 31, 2016 (the perpetual inventory system is used).

Analysis Component

2. In prior years, the company experienced a 4% returns and allowance rate on its sales, which means approximately 4% of its gross sales were eventually returned outright or caused the company to grant allowances to customers. Compute the ratio of sales returns and allowances divided by gross sales. How does this year's ratio compare to the 4% ratio in prior years?

The following unadjusted trial balance is prepared at fiscal year-end for Nelson Company.

	A	B	C
	NELSON COMPANY **Unadjusted Trial Balance** **January 31, 2016**		
1		**Debit**	**Credit**
2	Cash	$ 1,000	
3	Merchandise inventory	12,500	
4	Store supplies	5,800	
5	Prepaid insurance	2,400	
6	Store equipment	42,900	
7	Accumulated depreciation—Store equipment		$ 15,250
8	Accounts payable		10,000
9	Common stock		5,000
10	Retained earnings		27,000
11	Dividends	2,200	
12	Sales		111,950
13	Sales discounts	2,000	
14	Sales returns and allowances	2,200	
15	Cost of goods sold	38,400	
16	Depreciation expense—Store equipment	0	
17	Salaries expense	35,000	
18	Insurance expense	0	
19	Rent expense	15,000	
20	Store supplies expense	0	
21	Advertising expense	9,800	
22	Totals	$169,200	$169,200
23			

Rent expense and salaries expense are equally divided between selling activities and general and administrative activities. Nelson Company uses a perpetual inventory system.

Required

1. Prepare adjusting journal entries to reflect each of the following:

   a. Store supplies still available at fiscal year-end amount to $1,750.

   b. Expired insurance, an administrative expense, for the fiscal year is $1,400.

   c. Depreciation expense on store equipment, a selling expense, is $1,525 for the fiscal year.

   d. To estimate shrinkage, a physical count of ending merchandise inventory is taken. It shows $10,900 of inventory is still available at fiscal year-end.

2. Prepare a multiple-step income statement for fiscal year 2016 that begins with gross sales and includes separate categories for net sales, cost of goods sold, selling expenses, and general and administrative expenses.

3. Prepare a single-step income statement for fiscal year 2016.

4. Compute the current ratio, acid-test ratio, and gross margin ratio as of January 31, 2016. (Round ratios to two decimals.)

Problem 4-5A
Preparing adjusting entries and income statements; and computing gross margin, acid-test, and current ratios
A1   A2   P3   P4

Check   (2) Gross profit, $67,750

(3) Total expenses, $106,775; Net income, $975

Refer to the data and information in Problem 4-5A.

Required

Prepare and complete the entire 10-column work sheet for Nelson Company. Follow the structure of Exhibit 4B.1 in Appendix 4B.

Problem 4-6A^B
Preparing a work sheet for a merchandiser
P3

PROBLEM SET B

Problem 4-1B
Preparing journal entries for merchandising activities—perpetual system

P1 P2

Prepare journal entries to record the following merchandising transactions of IKEA, which uses the perpetual inventory system and gross method. (*Hint:* It will help to identify each receivable and payable; for example, record the purchase on May 2 in Accounts Payable—Havel.)

May 2 Purchased merchandise from Havel Co. for $10,000 under credit terms of 1/15, n/30, FOB shipping point, invoice dated May 2.

4 Sold merchandise to Rath Co. for $11,000 under credit terms of 2/10, n/60, FOB shipping point, invoice dated May 4. The merchandise had cost $5,600.

5 Paid $250 cash for freight charges on the purchase of May 2.

9 Sold merchandise that had cost $2,000 for $2,500 cash.

10 Purchased merchandise from Duke Co. for $3,650 under credit terms of 2/15, n/60, FOB destination, invoice dated May 10.

12 Received a $650 credit memorandum from Duke Co. for the return of a portion of the merchandise purchased on May 10.

Check May 14, Dr. Cash $10,780

14 Received the balance due from Rath Co. for the invoice dated May 4, net of the discount.

17 Paid the balance due to Havel Co. within the discount period.

May 17, Cr. Cash $9,900

20 Sold merchandise that cost $1,450 to Tamer Co. for $2,800 under credit terms of 2/15, n/60, FOB shipping point, invoice dated May 20.

22 Issued a $300 credit memorandum to Tamer Co. for an allowance on goods sold on May 20.

25 Paid Duke Co. the balance due, net of the discount.

May 30, Dr. Cash $2,450

30 Received the balance due from Tamer Co. for the invoice dated May 20, net of discount and allowance.

31 Sold merchandise that cost $3,600 to Rath Co. for $7,200 under credit terms of 2/10, n/60, FOB shipping point, invoice dated May 31.

Problem 4-2B
Preparing journal entries for merchandising activities—perpetual system

P1 P2

Prepare journal entries to record the following merchandising transactions of Menards, which applies the perpetual inventory system and gross method. (*Hint:* It will help to identify each receivable and payable; for example, record the purchase on July 3 in Accounts Payable—OLB.)

July 3 Purchased merchandise from OLB Corp. for $15,000 under credit terms of 1/10, n/30, FOB destination, invoice dated July 3.

7 Sold merchandise to Brill Co. for $11,500 under credit terms of 2/10, n/60, FOB destination, invoice dated July 7. The merchandise had cost $7,750.

10 Purchased merchandise from Rupert Co. for $14,200 under credit terms of 1/10, n/45, FOB shipping point, invoice dated July 10.

11 Paid $300 cash for shipping charges related to the July 7 sale to Brill Co.

12 Brill returned merchandise from the July 7 sale that had cost Menards $1,450 and been sold for $2,000. The merchandise was restored to inventory.

14 After negotiations with Rupert Co. concerning problems with the merchandise purchased on July 10, Menards received a credit memorandum from Rupert granting a price reduction of $1,200.

15 At OLB's request, Menards paid $200 cash for freight charges on the July 3 purchase, reducing the amount owed to OLB.

Check July 17, Dr. Cash $9,310

17 Received balance due from Brill Co. for the July 7 sale less the return on July 12.

20 Paid the amount due Rupert Co. for the July 10 purchase less the price reduction granted on July 14.

21 Sold merchandise to Brown for $11,000 under credit terms of 1/10, n/30, FOB shipping point, invoice dated July 21. The merchandise had cost $7,000.

24 Brown requested a price reduction on the July 21 sale because the merchandise did not meet specifications. Menards sent Brown a credit memorandum for $1,000 toward the $11,000 invoice to resolve the issue.

July 30, Dr. Cash $9,800

30 Received Brown's cash payment for the amount due from the July 21 sale less the price allowance from August 24.

July 31, Cr. Cash $14,800

31 Paid OLB Corp. the amount due from the July 3 purchase.

Barkley Company's adjusted trial balance on March 31, 2016, its fiscal year-end, follows.

Problem 4-3B
Computing merchandising
amounts and formatting
income statements

C1   C2   P4

	Debit	Credit
Merchandise inventory..............	$ 56,500	
Other (noninventory) assets.........	202,600	
Total liabilities		$ 42,500
Common stock		10,000
Retained earnings..................		154,425
Dividends	3,000	
Sales		332,650
Sales discounts....................	5,875	
Sales returns and allowances.........	20,000	
Cost of goods sold.................	115,600	
Sales salaries expense	44,500	
Rent expense—Selling space.........	16,000	
Store supplies expense	3,850	
Advertising expense................	26,000	
Office salaries expense	40,750	
Rent expense—Office space	3,800	
Office supplies expense.............	1,100	
Totals	$539,575	$539,575

On March 31, 2015, merchandise inventory was $37,500. Supplementary records of merchandising activities for the year ended March 31, 2016, reveal the following itemized costs.

Invoice cost of merchandise purchases.........	$138,500
Purchase discounts received	2,950
Purchase returns and allowances..............	6,700
Costs of transportation-in...................	5,750

Required

1. Compute the company's net sales for the year.
2. Compute the company's total cost of merchandise purchased for the year.
3. Prepare a multiple-step income statement that includes separate categories for net sales, cost of goods sold, selling expenses, and general and administrative expenses.
4. Prepare a single-step income statement that includes these expense categories: cost of goods sold, selling expenses, and general and administrative expenses.

Check   (2) $134,600
(3) Gross profit,
$191,175; Net income,
$55,175
(4) Total expenses,
$251,600

Use the data for Barkley Company in Problem 4-3B to complete the following requirements.

Problem 4-4B
Preparing closing entries
and interpreting
information about
discounts and returns

C2   P3

Required

1. Prepare closing entries as of March 31, 2016 (the perpetual inventory system is used).

Analysis Component

2. In prior years, the company experienced a 5% returns and allowance rate on its sales, which means approximately 5% of its gross sales were eventually returned outright or caused the company to grant allowances to customers. Compute the ratio of sales returns and allowances divided by gross sales. How does this year's ratio compare to the 5% ratio in prior years?

Check   (1) $55,175 Dr. to
close Income Summary

(2) Current-year
ratio, 6.0%

Problem 4-5B
Preparing adjusting
entries and income
statements; and
computing gross margin,
acid-test, and current
ratios

A1   A2   P3   P4

The following unadjusted trial balance is prepared at fiscal year-end for Foster Products Company.

	A	B	C
	FOSTER PRODUCTS COMPANY Unadjusted Trial Balance October 31, 2016		
1		**Debit**	**Credit**
2	Cash	$ 7,400	
3	Merchandise inventory	24,000	
4	Store supplies	9,700	
5	Prepaid insurance	6,600	
6	Store equipment	81,800	
7	Accumulated depreciation—Store equipment		$ 32,000
8	Accounts payable		18,000
9	Common stock		3,000
10	Retained earnings		40,000
11	Dividends	2,000	
12	Sales		227,100
13	Sales discounts	1,000	
14	Sales returns and allowances	5,000	
15	Cost of goods sold	75,800	
16	Depreciation expense—Store equipment	0	
17	Salaries expense	63,000	
18	Insurance expense	0	
19	Rent expense	26,000	
20	Store supplies expense	0	
21	Advertising expense	17,800	
22	Totals	$320,100	$320,100
23			

Rent expense and salaries expense are equally divided between selling activities and general and administrative activities. Foster Products Company uses a perpetual inventory system.

Required

1. Prepare adjusting journal entries to reflect each of the following:
   a. Store supplies still available at fiscal year-end amount to $3,700.
   b. Expired insurance, an administrative expense, for the fiscal year is $2,800.
   c. Depreciation expense on store equipment, a selling expense, is $3,000 for the fiscal year.
   d. To estimate shrinkage, a physical count of ending merchandise inventory is taken. It shows $21,300 of inventory is still available at fiscal year-end.

Check   (2) Gross profit, $142,600

2. Prepare a multiple-step income statement for fiscal year 2016 that begins with gross sales and includes separate categories for net sales, cost of goods sold, selling expenses, and general and administrative expenses.

(3) Total expenses, $197,100; Net income, $24,000

3. Prepare a single-step income statement for fiscal year 2016.
4. Compute the current ratio, acid-test ratio, and gross margin ratio as of October 31, 2016. (Round ratios to two decimals.)

Problem 4-6Bᴮ
Preparing a work sheet
for a merchandiser

P3

Refer to the data and information in Problem 4-5B.

Required

Prepare and complete the entire 10-column work sheet for Foster Products Company. Follow the structure of Exhibit 4B.1 in Appendix 4B.

(This serial problem began in Chapter 1 and continues through most of the book. If previous chapter segments were not completed, the serial problem can begin at this point. It is helpful, but not necessary, to use the Working Papers that accompany the book.)

SERIAL PROBLEM
Business Solutions
P1 P2 P3 P4

SP 4   Santana Rey created Business Solutions on October 1, 2016. The company has been successful, and its list of customers has grown. To accommodate the growth, the accounting system is modified to set up separate accounts for each customer. The following chart of accounts includes the account number used for each account and any balance as of December 31, 2016. Santana Rey decided to add a fourth digit with a decimal point to the 106 account number that had been used for the single Accounts Receivable account. This change allows the company to continue using the existing chart of accounts.

No.	Account Title	Dr.	Cr.
101	Cash	$48,372	
106.1	Alex's Engineering Co.	0	
106.2	Wildcat Services	0	
106.3	Easy Leasing	0	
106.4	IFM Co.	3,000	
106.5	Liu Corp.	0	
106.6	Gomez Co.	2,668	
106.7	Delta Co.	0	
106.8	KC, Inc.	0	
106.9	Dream, Inc.	0	
108	Allowance for Sales Discounts		$ 0
119	Merchandise inventory.	0	
121	Inventory returns estimated	0	
126	Computer supplies.	580	
128	Prepaid insurance.	1,665	
131	Prepaid rent	825	
163	Office equipment.	8,000	
164	Accumulated depreciation— Office equipment.		400
167	Computer equipment	20,000	
168	Accumulated depreciation— Computer equipment		1,250

No.	Account Title	Dr.	Cr.
201	Accounts payable		1,100
210	Wages payable.		500
227	Sales refund payable		0
236	Unearned computer services revenue		1,500
307	Common stock.		73,000
318	Retained earnings		7,360
319	Dividends.	0	
403	Computer services revenue		0
413	Sales.		0
414	Sales returns and allowances	0	
415	Sales discounts	0	
502	Cost of goods sold	0	
612	Depreciation expense—Office equipment.	0	
613	Depreciation expense—Computer equipment . . .	0	
623	Wages expense	0	
637	Insurance expense.	0	
640	Rent expense.	0	
652	Computer supplies expense	0	
655	Advertising expense	0	
676	Mileage expense	0	
677	Miscellaneous expenses	0	
684	Repairs expense—Computer	0	

In response to requests from customers, S. Rey will begin selling computer software. The company will extend credit terms of 1/10, n/30, FOB shipping point, to all customers who purchase this merchandise; and it applies perpetual inventory and the gross method. However, no cash discount is available on consulting fees. Additional accounts (Nos. 108, 119, 121, 227, 413, 414, 415, and 502) are added to its general ledger to accommodate the company's new merchandising activities. Business Solutions does not use reversing entries and, therefore, all revenue and expense accounts have zero beginning balances as of January 1, 2017. Its transactions for January through March follow:

Jan. 4   The company paid cash to Lyn Addie for five days' work at the rate of $125 per day. Four of the five days relate to wages payable that were accrued in the prior year.
  5   Santana Rey invested an additional $25,000 cash in the company in exchange for more common stock.
  7   The company purchased $5,800 of merchandise from Kansas Corp. with terms of 1/10, n/30, FOB shipping point, invoice dated January 7.
  9   The company received $2,668 cash from Gomez Co. as full payment on its account.
  11   The company completed a five-day project for Alex's Engineering Co. and billed it $5,500, which is the total price of $7,000 less the advance payment of $1,500.
  13   The company sold merchandise with a retail value of $5,200 and a cost of $3,560 to Liu Corp., invoice dated January 13.
  15   The company paid $600 cash for freight charges on the merchandise purchased on January 7.
  16   The company received $4,000 cash from Delta Co. for computer services provided.
  17   The company paid Kansas Corp. for the invoice dated January 7, net of the discount.

Check   Jan. 11, Dr. Unearned Computer Services Revenue $1,500

Continued on next page . . .

Check   Jan. 20, No entry
to Cost of Goods Sold

20   Liu Corp. returned $500 of defective merchandise from its invoice dated January 13. The returned merchandise, which had a $320 cost, is discarded. (For materiality reasons, this company's policy is to leave the cost of defective products in Cost of Goods Sold.)

22   The company received the balance due from Liu Corp., net of both the discount and the credit for the returned merchandise.

24   The company returned defective merchandise to Kansas Corp. and accepted a credit against future purchases. The defective merchandise invoice amount was $496, which is the price net of the discount.

26   The company purchased $9,000 of merchandise from Kansas Corp. with terms of 1/10, n/30, FOB destination, invoice dated January 26.

26   The company sold merchandise with a $4,640 cost for $5,800 on credit to KC, Inc., invoice dated January 26.

31   The company paid cash to Lyn Addie for 10 days' work at $125 per day.

Feb.   1   The company paid $2,475 cash to Hillside Mall for another three months' rent in advance.

3   The company paid Kansas Corp. for the balance due, net of the cash discount, less the $496 in the credit memorandum of January 24.

5   The company paid $600 cash to the local newspaper for an advertising insert in today's paper.

11   The company received the balance due from Alex's Engineering Co. for fees billed on January 11.

15   The company paid $4,800 cash for dividends.

23   The company sold merchandise with a $2,660 cost for $3,220 on credit to Delta Co., invoice dated February 23.

26   The company paid cash to Lyn Addie for eight days' work at $125 per day.

27   The company reimbursed Santana Rey for business automobile mileage (600 miles at $0.32 per mile).

Mar.   8   The company purchased $2,730 of computer supplies from Harris Office Products on credit with terms n/15, invoice dated March 8.

9   The company received the balance due from Delta Co. for merchandise sold on February 23.

11   The company paid $960 cash for minor repair costs on the company's computer.

16   The company received $5,260 cash from Dream, Inc., for computing services provided.

19   The company paid the full amount due to Harris Office Products, consisting of amounts created on December 15 (of $1,100) and March 8.

24   The company billed Easy Leasing for $9,047 of computing services provided.

25   The company sold merchandise with a $2,002 cost for $2,800 on credit to Wildcat Services, invoice dated March 25.

30   The company sold merchandise with a $1,048 cost for $2,220 on credit to IFM Company, invoice dated March 30.

31   The company reimbursed Santana Rey for business automobile mileage (400 miles at $0.32 per mile).

The following additional facts are available for preparing adjustments on March 31 prior to financial statement preparation:

a. The March 31 amount of computer supplies still available totals $2,005.

b. Three more months have expired since the company purchased its annual insurance policy at a $2,220 cost for 12 months of coverage.

c. Lyn Addie has not been paid for seven days of work at the rate of $125 per day.

d. Three months have passed since any prepaid rent has been transferred to expense. The monthly rent expense is $825.

e. Depreciation on the computer equipment for January 1 through March 31 is $1,250.

f. Depreciation on the office equipment for January 1 through March 31 is $400.

g. After a March 31 physical count of inventory, it is determined that shrinkage occurred and the amount of merchandise inventory still available totals $704.

h. On March 31, Rey estimates future-period returns and allowances will be a small percent of sales, or roughly $1,100, and similarly a small percent of cost of sales, or roughly $400.

i. On March 31, Rey estimates future-period discounts arising from this period's sales to be roughly $0.

Required

1. Prepare journal entries to record each of the January through March transactions.

Check   (2) Ending balances
at March 31: Cash, $68,057
        (3) Unadj. TB totals,
$151,557; Adj. TB totals,
$154,082

2. Post the journal entries in part 1 to the accounts in the company's general ledger. (*Note:* Begin with the ledger's post-closing adjusted balances as of December 31, 2016.)

3. Prepare a partial work sheet consisting of the first six columns (similar to the one shown in Exhibit 4B.1) that includes the unadjusted trial balance, the March 31 adjustments (*a*) through (*h*), and the adjusted trial balance. To make it easier, *do not prepare closing entries and do not journalize the adjustments or post them to the ledger.*

4. Prepare an income statement (from the adjusted trial balance in part 3) for the three months ended March 31, 2017. Use a single-step format. List all expenses without differentiating between selling expenses and general and administrative expenses.

5. Prepare a statement of retained earnings (from the adjusted trial balance in part 3) for the three months ended March 31, 2017.

6. Prepare a classified balance sheet (from the adjusted trial balance) as of March 31, 2017.

(4) Net income, $18,133

(6) Total assets, $120,668

The **General Ledger** tool in *Connect Plus* automates several of the procedural steps in the accounting cycle so the accounting professional can focus on the impacts of each transaction on the various financial reports. The following General Ledger questions highlight the operating cycle of a merchandising company. In each case, the trial balance is automatically updated from the journal entries recorded.

GL 4-1 Based on Problem 4-1A

GL 4-2 Based on Problem 4-2A

GL 4-3 Based on Problem 4-5A

GENERAL LEDGER PROBLEMS

Available in Connect

connect

Beyond the Numbers

BTN 4-1   Refer to **Apple**'s financial statements in Appendix A to answer the following.

Required

1. Assume that the amounts reported for inventories and cost of sales reflect items purchased in a form ready for resale. Compute the net cost of goods purchased for the year ended September 27, 2014.

2. Compute the current ratio and acid-test ratio as of September 27, 2014, and September 28, 2013. Interpret and comment on the ratio results. How does Apple compare to the industry average of 1.5 for the current ratio and 1.25 for the acid-test ratio?

Fast Forward

3. Access Apple's financial statements (10-K report) for fiscal years ending after September 27, 2014, from its website (**Apple.com**) or the SEC's EDGAR database (**www.SEC.gov**). Recompute and interpret the current ratio and acid-test ratio for these current fiscal years.

REPORTING IN ACTION

A1

APPLE

BTN 4-2   Key comparative figures for both **Apple** and **Google** follow.

$ millions	Apple		Google	
	Current Year	Prior Year	Current Year	Prior Year
Net sales	$182,795	$170,910	$66,001	$55,519
Cost of sales	112,258	106,606	25,691	21,993

COMPARATIVE ANALYSIS

A2

APPLE

GOOGLE

Required

1. Compute the dollar amount of gross margin and the gross margin ratio for the two years shown for each of these companies.

2. Which company earns more in gross margin for each dollar of net sales? How do they compare to the industry average of 45.0%?

3. Did the gross margin ratio improve or decline for these companies?

ETHICS CHALLENGE

C1 P2

BTN 4-3 Amy Martin is a student who plans to attend approximately four professional events a year at her college. Each event necessitates a financial outlay of $100 to $200 for a new suit and accessories. After incurring a major hit to her savings for the first event, Amy developed a different approach. She buys the suit on credit the week before the event, wears it to the event, and returns it the next week to the store for a full refund on her charge card.

Required

1. Comment on the ethics exhibited by Amy and possible consequences of her actions.
2. How does the merchandising company account for the suits that Amy returns?

COMMUNICATING IN PRACTICE

C2 P3 P5

BTN 4-4 You are the financial officer for Music Plus, a retailer that sells goods for home entertainment needs. The business owner, Vic Velakturi, recently reviewed the annual financial statements you prepared and sent you an e-mail stating that he thinks you overstated net income. He explains that although he has invested a great deal in security, he is sure shoplifting and other forms of inventory shrinkage have occurred, but he does not see any deduction for shrinkage on the income statement. The store uses a perpetual inventory system.

Required

Prepare a brief memorandum that responds to the owner's concerns.

TAKING IT TO THE NET

A2 C1

BTN 4-5 Access the SEC's EDGAR database (www.SEC.gov) and obtain the March 17, 2015, filing of its fiscal 2014 10-K report (for year ended January 31, 2014) for **J. Crew Group, Inc.** (ticker: JCG).

Required

Prepare a table that reports the gross margin ratios for J. Crew using the revenues and cost of goods sold data from J. Crew's income statement for each of its most recent three years. Analyze and comment on the trend in its gross margin ratio.

TEAMWORK IN ACTION

C1 C2

BTN 4-6 Official Brands's general ledger *and supplementary records* at the end of its current period reveal the following.

Sales, gross	$600,000		Merchandise inventory (beginning of period)	$ 98,000
Sales returns & allowances	20,000		Invoice cost of merchandise purchases	360,000
Sales discounts	13,000		Purchase discounts received	9,000
Cost of transportation-in	22,000		Purchase returns & allowances	11,000
Operating expenses	50,000		Merchandise inventory (end of period)	84,000

Required

1. *Each* member of the team is to assume responsibility for computing *one* of the following items. You are not to duplicate your teammates' work. Get any necessary amounts to compute your item from the appropriate teammate. Each member is to explain his or her computation to the team in preparation for reporting to the class.

Point: In teams of four, assign the same student *a* and *e*. Rotate teams for reporting on a different computation and the analysis in step 3.

    a. Net sales   **d.** Gross profit
    b. Total cost of merchandise purchases   **e.** Net income
    c. Cost of goods sold

2. Check your net income with the instructor. If correct, proceed to step 3.
3. Assume that a physical inventory count finds that actual ending inventory is $76,000. Discuss how this affects previously computed amounts in step 1.

ENTREPRENEURIAL DECISION

C1 C2 P4

BTN 4-7 Refer to the opening feature about **Chipotle**. Chipotle has a small segment of its business devoted to merchandising shirts, mugs, hats, and other related items tied to its branding strategy. Assume that its merchandising segment has current annual sales of approximately $1 million and it prepares the following income statement.

CHIPOTLE	
Income Statement	
For Year Ended January 31, 2015	
Net sales	$1,000,000
Cost of sales	610,000
Expenses (other than cost of sales)	200,000
Net income	$ 190,000

This segment sells to individuals and retailers, ranging from small shops to large chains. Assume that it currently offers credit terms of 1/15, n/60, and ships FOB destination. To improve cash flow, it is considering changing credit terms to 3/10, n/30. In addition, it proposes to change shipping terms to FOB shipping point. The segment's manager expects that the increase in discount rate will increase net sales by 9%, but the gross margin ratio (and ratio of cost of sales divided by net sales) is expected to remain unchanged. The segment's manager also expects that delivery expenses will be zero under this proposal; thus, expenses other than cost of sales are expected to increase only 6%.

Required

1. Prepare a forecasted income statement for the year ended January 31, 2016, based on the proposal.

2. Based on the forecasted income statement alone (from your part 1 solution), do you recommend that Chipotle implement the new sales policies? Explain.

3. What else should Chipotle consider before deciding whether or not to implement the new policies? Explain.

BTN 4-8   Arrange an interview (in person or by phone) with the manager of a retail shop in a mall or in the downtown area of your community. Explain to the manager that you are a student studying merchandising activities and the accounting for sales returns and sales allowances. Ask the manager what the store policy is regarding returns. Also find out if sales allowances are ever negotiated with customers. Inquire whether management perceives that customers are abusing return policies and what actions management takes to counter potential abuses. Be prepared to discuss your findings in class.

HITTING THE ROAD

C1

Point: This activity complements the Ethics Challenge assignment.

BTN 4-9   **Samsung** (www.Samsung.com), **Apple**, and **Google** are competitors in the global marketplace. Key comparative figures for each company follow.

	Net Sales	Cost of Sales
Samsung*	₩206,205,987	₩128,278,800
Apple†	$ 182,795	$ 112,258
Google†	$ 66,001	$ 25,691

* Millions of Korean won for Samsung.
† Millions of dollars for Apple and Google.

GLOBAL DECISION

A2   P4

Samsung
APPLE
GOOGLE

Required

1. Rank the three companies (highest to lowest) based on the gross margin ratio.

2. Which of the companies uses a multiple-step income statement format? (These companies' income statements are in Appendix A.)

ANSWERS TO MULTIPLE CHOICE QUIZ

1. c; Gross profit = $550,000 − $193,000 = $357,000

2. d; ($4,500 − $250) × (100% − 2%) = $4,165

3. a; Net sales = $75,000 + $340,000 − $8,000 − $12,000 = $395,000

4. b; Acid-test ratio = $37,500/$50,000 = 0.750

5. a; Gross margin ratio = ($675,000 − $459,000)/$675,000 = 32%

chapter 5

Reporting and Analyzing Inventories

Chapter Preview

INVENTORY BASICS

C1 Determining inventory items

C2 Determining inventory costs

Control of inventory

INVENTORY COSTING

P1 Cost flow assumptions:

Specific identification

First-in, first-out

Last-in, first-out

Weighted average

A1 Effects on financial statements

INVENTORY VALUATION, ERRORS, AND ANALYSIS

P2 Inventory valuation at lower of cost or market

A2 Financial statement effects of inventory errors

A3 Inventory management

P3 Perpetual system

P4 Inventory estimation

Learning Objectives

CONCEPTUAL

C1 Identify the items making up merchandise inventory.

C2 Identify the costs of merchandise inventory.

ANALYTICAL

A1 Analyze the effects of inventory methods for both financial and tax reporting.

A2 Analyze the effects of inventory errors on current and future financial statements.

A3 Assess inventory management using both inventory turnover and days' sales in inventory.

PROCEDURAL

P1 Compute inventory in a periodic system using the methods of specific identification, FIFO, LIFO, and weighted average.

P2 Compute the lower of cost or market amount of inventory.

P3 *Appendix 5A*—Compute inventory in a perpetual system using the methods of specific identification, FIFO, LIFO, and weighted average.

P4 *Appendix 5B*—Apply both the retail inventory and gross profit methods to estimate inventory.

One for the Road

"When something is important enough, you do it even if the odds are not in your favor" — **ELON MUSK**

PALO ALTO, CA—During college, when he would go on a first date, Elon Musk would ask, "Do you ever think about electric cars?" This was roughly 20 years ago, when there was little interest in electric cars. Elon admits today that his talking about dreams of electric cars "was not a winning combination!" But today, Elon's dreams have evolved into **Tesla Motors, Inc. (TeslaMotors.com)**, which is a $31 billion business.

When Elon and a group of investors founded Tesla Motors, their plan was to introduce a high-end electric sports car and later an electric sedan for the masses. "We really wanted to break the mold," insists Elon. The first Tesla sports car, the Roadster, traveled almost 250 miles on a single charge and earned terrific reviews. "Great companies are built on great products," explains Elon. Next, Tesla hopes to launch an affordable electric sedan, the Model 3, which has the potential to exponentially increase sales in 2017.

Elon insists that inventory management is one key to his company's success. "I don't spend my time pontificating about high-concept things," explains Elon. "I spend my time solving manufacturing [and inventory] problems." To ensure Tesla's cars are of the highest quality, Elon locates his

Tesla Motors, Inc.
Nasdaq: TSLA

6,000 workers
$31 bil. value
59,500 cars sold

Electric Car Market Share
Other 13%
Nissan 25%
Toyota 11%
Ford 19%
Tesla 15%
GM 17%

desk "in the middle of the factory." This attention to inventory quality and inventory management separates Tesla Motors from its competitors, which is reflected in its sales, income, inventory, and asset growth over the past few years.

($ millions)	2011	2012	2013	2014
Revenues	$204	$ 413	$2,014	$3,198
Cost of sales.....	143	383	1,557	2,317
Inventories	50	269	340	954
Total assets	713	1,114	2,417	5,849

Getting inventory to market when customers demand it is a challenge. "Some companies out there quote a start of production that is substantially in advance of when customers get their cars," explains Elon. "I don't think that's a good idea." Instead, to ensure customers receive their cars when promised, Tesla carefully tracks

inventory. Elon set up an inventory system, learned to prepare and read inventory reports, and applied inventory management tools. His inventory system tracks all transactions, and he regularly reviews inventory reports when making decisions.

The financial markets seem equally enthused about the inventory practices of Tesla Motors, as reflected in its stock price over the past few years.

Although Tesla has already achieved considerable success, Elon is not satisfied. He wants to revolutionize the automobile industry much like Henry Ford did with the Model T. "When Henry Ford made cheap, reliable cars, people said, 'Nah, what's wrong with a horse?' That was a huge bet he made, and it worked."

Sources: *Tesla Motors website,* January 2016; *Bloomberg,* July 2013; *CNN Money,* September 2014; *Ted,* March 2013; *Biography.com,* January 2016; *Los Angeles Times,* April 2003; *CBS,* March 2012; *CleanTechnica,* December 2014

INVENTORY BASICS

C1

Identify the items making up merchandise inventory.

This section identifies the items and costs making up merchandise inventory. It also describes the importance of internal controls in taking a physical count of inventory.

Determining Inventory Items

Merchandise inventory includes all goods that a company owns and holds for sale. This rule holds regardless of where the goods are located when inventory is counted. Certain inventory items require special attention, including goods in transit, goods on consignment, and goods that are damaged or obsolete.

Point: FOB shipping point is also called *FOB origin* or *FOB supplier's warehouse*.

Goods in Transit   Does a purchaser's inventory include goods in transit from a supplier? The answer is that if ownership has passed to the purchaser, the goods are included in the purchaser's inventory. We determine this by reviewing the shipping terms: *FOB destination* or *FOB shipping point*. Goods purchased FOB shipping point are included in the buyer's inventory when the items are shipped. Goods purchased FOB destination are not included in the buyer's inventory until they arrive at their destination.

Goods on Consignment   Goods on consignment are goods shipped by the owner, called the **consignor,** to another party, the **consignee.** A consignee sells goods for the owner. The consignor continues to own the consigned goods and reports them in its inventory. **Upper Deck**, for instance, pays sports celebrities such as Aaron Rodgers of the Green Bay Packers to sign memorabilia, which are offered to shopping networks on consignment. Upper Deck, the consignor, must report these items in its inventory until sold. The consignee never includes consigned goods in inventory.

Goods Damaged or Obsolete   Damaged and obsolete (and deteriorated) goods are not counted in inventory if they cannot be sold. If these goods can be sold at a reduced price, they are included in inventory at a conservative estimate of their **net realizable value.** Net realizable value is sales price minus the cost of making the sale. The period when damage or obsolescence (or deterioration) occurs is the period when the loss in value is reported.

◼ Decision **Insight**

Gunning for Inventory   A wireless portable device with a two-way radio allows clerks to quickly record inventory by scanning bar codes and to instantly send and receive inventory data. It gives managers access to up-to-date information on inventory and its location. Bar codes have influenced nearly all aspects of inventory control and management. The use of bar codes makes accounting for inventory simpler, more accurate, and more efficient. ◼

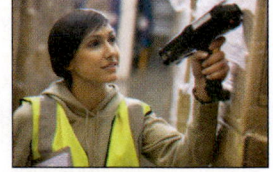

Clerkenwell/Getty Images

C2

Identify the costs of merchandise inventory.

Determining Inventory Costs

Merchandise inventory includes costs of expenditures necessary, directly or indirectly, to bring an item to a salable condition and location. This means that the cost of an inventory item includes its invoice cost minus any discount, plus any incidental costs necessary to put it in a place and condition for sale. Incidental costs can include import tariffs, freight, storage, insurance, and costs incurred in an aging process (for example, aging wine or cheese). The *expense recognition (matching) principle* states that inventory costs should be recorded as cost of goods sold in the period when inventory is sold.

Point: Some use the *materiality constraint (cost-to-benefit constraint)* to avoid assigning some incidental costs of acquiring merchandise to inventory. Instead, they expense those costs to cost of goods sold when incurred as they argue those costs are immaterial or the cost in assigning them outweighs the benefit.

Internal Controls and Taking a Physical Count

Events can cause the Inventory account balance to differ from the actual inventory available. Such events include theft, loss, damage, and errors. Thus, nearly all companies take a *physical count of inventory* at least once each year—informally called *taking an inventory.* This often occurs at the end of a fiscal year or when inventory amounts are low. This physical count is used to adjust the Inventory account balance to the actual inventory available.

Fraud

In Control A company applies internal controls when taking a physical count of inventory that usually include the following to minimize fraud and to increase reliability:

- *Prenumbered inventory tickets* are distributed to *counters*—each ticket must be accounted for.
- Counters of inventory are assigned and do not include those responsible for inventory.
- Counters confirm the validity of inventory, including its existence, amount, and quality.
- A second count is taken by a different counter.
- A manager confirms that all inventories are ticketed once, and only once.

Fraud: Auditors commonly observe employees as they take a physical inventory. Auditors take their own test counts to monitor the accuracy of a company's count.

Point: The Inventory account is a controlling account for the inventory subsidiary ledger. This *subsidiary ledger* contains a separate record (units and costs) for each separate product, and it can be in electronic or paper form. Subsidiary records assist managers in planning and monitoring inventory.

1. A master carver of wooden birds operates her business out of a garage. At the end of the current period, the carver has 17 units (carvings) in her garage, 3 of which were damaged by water and cannot be sold. The distributor also has another 5 units in her truck, ready to deliver per a customer order, terms FOB destination, and another 11 units out on consignment at several small retail stores. How many units does the carver include in the business's period-end inventory?

2. A distributor of artistic iron-based fixtures acquires a piece for $1,000, terms FOB shipping point. Additional costs in obtaining it and offering it for sale include $150 for transportation-in, $300 for import duties, $100 for insurance during shipment, $200 for advertising, a $50 voluntary gratuity to the delivery person, $75 for enhanced store lighting, and $250 for sales staff salaries. For computing inventory, what cost is assigned to this artistic piece?

NEED-TO-KNOW 5-1

Inventory Items and Costs

C1 C2

Solutions

1.

Units in ending inventory	
Units in storage	17 units
Less damaged (unsalable) units	(3)
Plus units in transit	5
Plus units on consignment	11
Total units in ending inventory	30 units

2.

Merchandise cost.	$1,000
Plus:	
Transportation-in.	150
Import duties	300
Insurance	100
Total inventory cost	$1,550

Do More: QS 5-1, QS 5-2, E 5-1, E 5-2

INVENTORY COSTING UNDER A PERIODIC SYSTEM

Accounting for inventory affects both the balance sheet and the income statement. A major goal in accounting for inventory is to properly match costs with sales. We use the *expense recognition* (or *matching*) *principle* to decide how much of the cost of the goods available for sale is deducted from sales and how much is carried forward as inventory and matched against future sales.

Management decisions in accounting for inventory involve the following:

- Items included in inventory and their costs.
- Costing method (specific identification, FIFO, LIFO, or weighted average).
- Inventory system (perpetual or periodic).
- Use of market values or other estimates.

The first point was explained in the prior section. The second and third points will be addressed now. The fourth point is the focus at the end of this chapter. Decisions on these points affect the reported amounts for inventory, cost of goods sold, gross profit, income, current assets, and other accounts.

One of the most important issues in accounting for inventory is determining the per unit costs assigned to inventory items. When all units are purchased at the same unit cost, this process is simple. When identical items are purchased at different costs, however, a question arises as to which amounts to record in cost of goods sold and which amounts remain in inventory.

EXHIBIT 5.1

Frequency in Use of Inventory Methods

*Includes specific identification.

Four methods are commonly used to assign costs to inventory and to cost of goods sold: (1) specific identification; (2) first-in, first-out (FIFO); (3) last-in, first-out (LIFO); and (4) weighted average. Exhibit 5.1 shows the frequency in the use of these methods.

Each method assumes a particular pattern for how costs flow through inventory. Each of these four methods is acceptable whether or not the actual physical flow of goods follows the cost flow assumption. Physical flow of goods depends on the type of product and the way it is stored. (Perishable goods such as fresh fruit demand that a business attempt to sell them in a first-in, first-out physical flow. Other products such as crude oil and minerals such as coal, gold, and decorative stone can be sold in a last-in, first-out physical flow.) With the exception of specific identification, the **physical flow and cost flow need not be the same**.

Inventory Cost Flow Assumptions

Point: Cost of goods sold is abbreviated COGS.

This section introduces inventory cost flow assumptions. For this purpose, assume that three identical units are purchased separately at the following three dates and costs: May 1 at $45, May 3 at $65, and May 6 at $70. One unit is then sold on May 7 for $100. Exhibit 5.2 gives a visual layout of the flow of costs to either the gross profit section of the income statement or the inventory reported on the balance sheet for FIFO, LIFO, and weighted average.

(1) *FIFO assumes costs flow in the order incurred.* The unit purchased on May 1 for $45 is the earliest cost incurred—it is sent to cost of goods sold on the income statement first. The remaining two units ($65 and $70) are reported in inventory on the balance sheet.

EXHIBIT 5.2

Cost Flow Assumptions

(2) *LIFO assumes costs flow in the reverse order incurred*. The unit purchased on May 6 for $70 is the most recent cost incurred—it is sent to cost of goods sold on the income statement. The remaining two units ($45 and $65) are reported in inventory on the balance sheet.

(3) *Weighted average assumes costs flow at an average of the costs available*. The units available at the May 7 sale average $60 in cost, computed as ($45 + $65 + $70)/3. One unit's $60 average cost is sent to cost of goods sold on the income statement. The remaining two units' average costs are reported in inventory at $120 on the balance sheet.

Cost flow assumptions can markedly impact gross profit and inventory numbers. Exhibit 5.2 shows that gross profit as a percent of net sales ranges from 30% to 55% due to nothing else but the cost flow assumption.

Point: It is helpful to recall the cost flow of inventory.

The following sections on inventory costing use the periodic system. Appendix 5A uses the perpetual system. An instructor can choose to cover either one or both systems. If the periodic system is skipped, then read Appendix 5A and return to the Decision Maker box (ahead) titled "Cost Analyst."

Most companies use a perpetual system to track sales and units (see Chapter 4). However, many fewer companies use a perpetual system to track costs. The reasons extend to use of standard costs by some companies, dollar-value LIFO by others, and so forth. Still, we see both systems in practice for recording inventory costs. Further, the two methods of specific identification and FIFO, which make up a majority of companies in the world today, give the same result under the periodic and the perpetual systems. Also, LIFO is rarely applied outside the U.S. In light of this mix, we show the periodic method here with the perpetual method in the appendix. As an aside, the perpetual system is akin to the periodic system applied at the point of each purchase and sale.

Inventory Costing Illustration

This section provides a comprehensive illustration of inventory costing methods. We use information from Trekking, a sporting goods store. Among its many products, Trekking carries one type of mountain bike whose sales are directed at resorts that provide inexpensive mountain bikes for complimentary guest use. We use Trekking's data from August. Its mountain bike (unit) inventory at the beginning of August and its purchases and sales during August are shown in Exhibit 5.3. It ends August with 12 bikes remaining in inventory.

P1

Compute inventory in a periodic system using the methods of specific identification, FIFO, LIFO, and weighted average.

EXHIBIT 5.3

Purchases and Sales of Goods

Date	Activity	Units Acquired at Cost	Units Sold at Retail	Unit Inventory
Aug. 1	Beginning inventory	10 units @ $ 91 = $ 910		10 units
Aug. 3	Purchases	15 units @ $106 = $ 1,590		25 units
Aug. 14	Sales		20 units @ $130	5 units
Aug. 17	Purchases	20 units @ $115 = $ 2,300		25 units
Aug. 28	Purchases	10 units @ $119 = $ 1,190		35 units
Aug. 31	Sales		23 units @ $150	**12 units**
	Totals	**55 units** **$5,990**	**43 units**	
		Units available for sale Goods available for sale	Units sold Units left	

Trekking uses the periodic inventory system, which means that its Merchandise Inventory account is updated at the end of each period (monthly for Trekking) to reflect purchases and sales. **(Appendix 5A describes the assignment of costs to inventory using a perpetual system.)** Regardless of what inventory method or system is used, cost of goods available for sale must be allocated between cost of goods sold and ending inventory.

Point: Three key variables determine the value assigned to ending inventory: (1) inventory quantity, (2) unit costs of inventory, and (3) cost flow assumption.

Specific Identification

When each item in inventory can be identified with a specific purchase and invoice, we can use **specific identification** or **SI** (also called *specific invoice inventory pricing*) to assign costs. We also need sales records that identify exactly which items were sold and when. Trekking's internal documents reveal the following specific unit sales:

August 14   Sold 8 bikes costing $91 each and 12 bikes costing $106 each

August 31   Sold 2 bikes costing $91 each, 3 bikes costing $106 each, 15 bikes costing $115 each, and 3 bikes costing $119 each

Applying specific identification, and using the information above and from Exhibit 5.3, we prepare Exhibit 5.4. This exhibit begins with the $5,990 in total units available for sale—this is from Exhibit 5.3. Applying specific identification, we know that for the 20 units sold on August 14, the company specifically identified that 8 of them had cost $91 each and 12 had cost $106 each, resulting in an August 14 cost of sales of $2,000. Next, for the 23 units sold on August 31, the company specifically identified that 2 of them had cost $91 each, 3 had cost $106 each, 15 had cost $115 each, and 3 had cost $119 each, resulting in an August 31 cost of sales of $2,582. This yields a total cost of sales for the period of $4,582. We then subtract this $4,582 in cost of goods sold from the $5,990 in cost of goods available to get $1,408 in ending inventory. Carefully study this exhibit and the explanations to see the flow of costs. Each unit, whether sold or remaining in inventory, has its own specific cost attached to it.

EXHIBIT 5.4

Specific Identification Computations

Total cost of 55 units available for sale (from Exhibit 5.3)		$5,990
Cost of goods sold*		
Aug. 14 (8 @ $91) + (12 @ $106).................................	$2,000	
Aug. 31 (2 @ $91) + (3 @ $106) + (15 @ $115) + (3 @ $119)	2,582	4,582
Ending inventory		$1,408

* Identification of items sold (and their costs) is obtained from internal documents that track each unit from its purchase to its sale.

Point: Specific identification is usually practical for companies with expensive or custom-made inventory. Examples include car dealerships, implement dealers, jewelers, and fashion designers.

When using specific identification, Trekking's cost of goods sold reported on the income statement totals **$4,582**, the sum of $2,000 and $2,582 from the cost of goods sold section of Exhibit 5.4. Trekking's ending inventory reported on the balance sheet is **$1,408**, which is the final inventory balance from Exhibit 5.4. The following graphic visually reflects the computations under specific identification.

First-In, First-Out

The **first-in, first-out (FIFO)** method of assigning costs to both inventory and cost of goods sold assumes that inventory items are sold in the order acquired. When sales occur, the costs of the earliest units acquired are charged to cost of goods sold. This leaves the costs from the most recent purchases in ending inventory. Use of FIFO for computing the cost of inventory and cost of goods sold is shown in Exhibit 5.5.

This exhibit starts with computing $5,990 in total units available for sale—this is from Exhibit 5.3. Applying FIFO, we know that the 12 units in ending inventory will be reported at the cost of the most recent 12 purchases. Reviewing purchases in reverse order, we assign costs to the 12 bikes in ending inventory as follows: $119 cost to 10 bikes and $115 cost to 2 bikes. This yields 12 bikes costing $1,420 in ending inventory. We then subtract this $1,420 in ending inventory from $5,990 in cost of goods available to get $4,570 in cost of goods sold.

Point: Under FIFO, a unit sold is assigned the earliest (oldest) cost from inventory. This leaves the most recent costs in ending inventory.

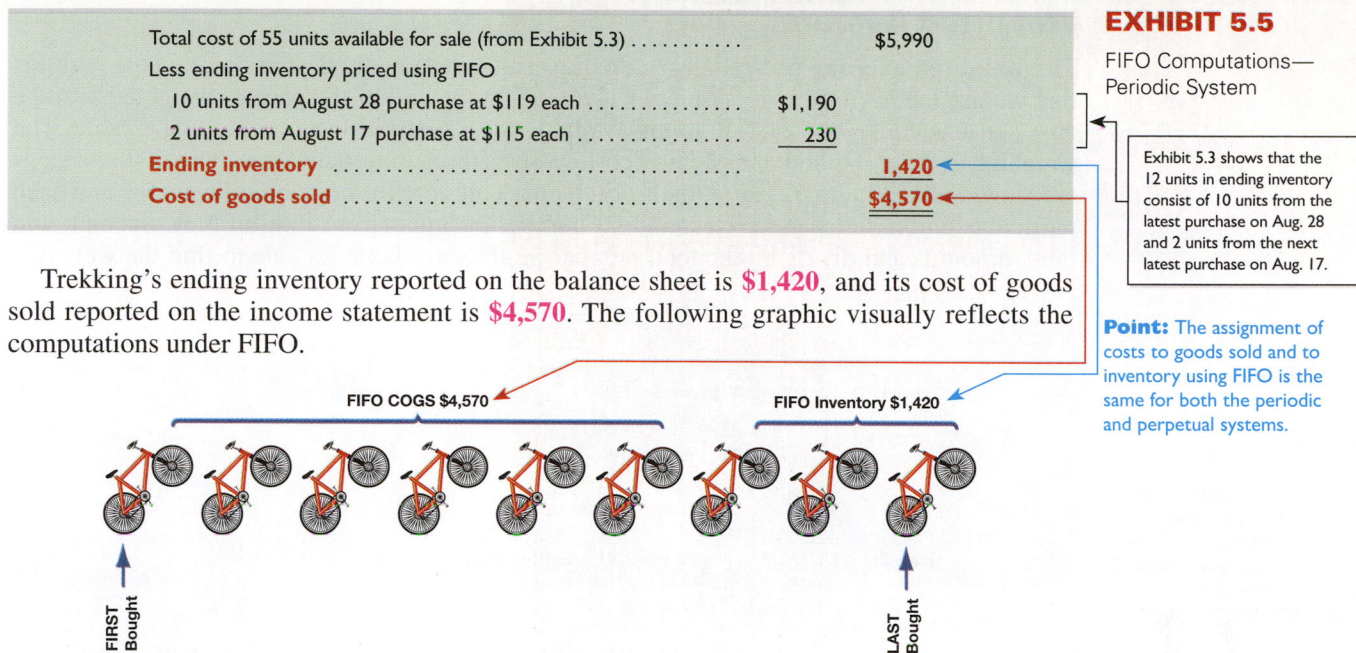

EXHIBIT 5.5

FIFO Computations—
Periodic System

> Exhibit 5.3 shows that the 12 units in ending inventory consist of 10 units from the latest purchase on Aug. 28 and 2 units from the next latest purchase on Aug. 17.

Trekking's ending inventory reported on the balance sheet is **$1,420**, and its cost of goods sold reported on the income statement is **$4,570**. The following graphic visually reflects the computations under FIFO.

Point: The assignment of costs to goods sold and to inventory using FIFO is the same for both the periodic and perpetual systems.

Last-In, First-Out

The **last-in, first-out (LIFO)** method of assigning costs assumes that the most recent purchases are sold first. These more recent costs are charged to goods sold, and the costs of the earliest purchases are assigned to inventory. LIFO results in costs of the most recent purchases being assigned to cost of goods sold, which means that LIFO comes close to matching current costs of goods sold with revenues. Use of LIFO for computing cost of inventory and cost of goods sold is shown in Exhibit 5.6.

This exhibit starts with computing $5,990 in total units available for sale—this is from Exhibit 5.3. Applying LIFO, we know that the 12 units in ending inventory will be reported at the cost of the earliest 12 purchases. Reviewing the earliest purchases in order, we assign costs to the 12 bikes in ending inventory as follows: $91 cost to 10 bikes and $106 cost to 2 bikes. This yields 12 bikes costing $1,122 in ending inventory. We then subtract this $1,122 in ending inventory from $5,990 in cost of goods available to get $4,868 in cost of goods sold.

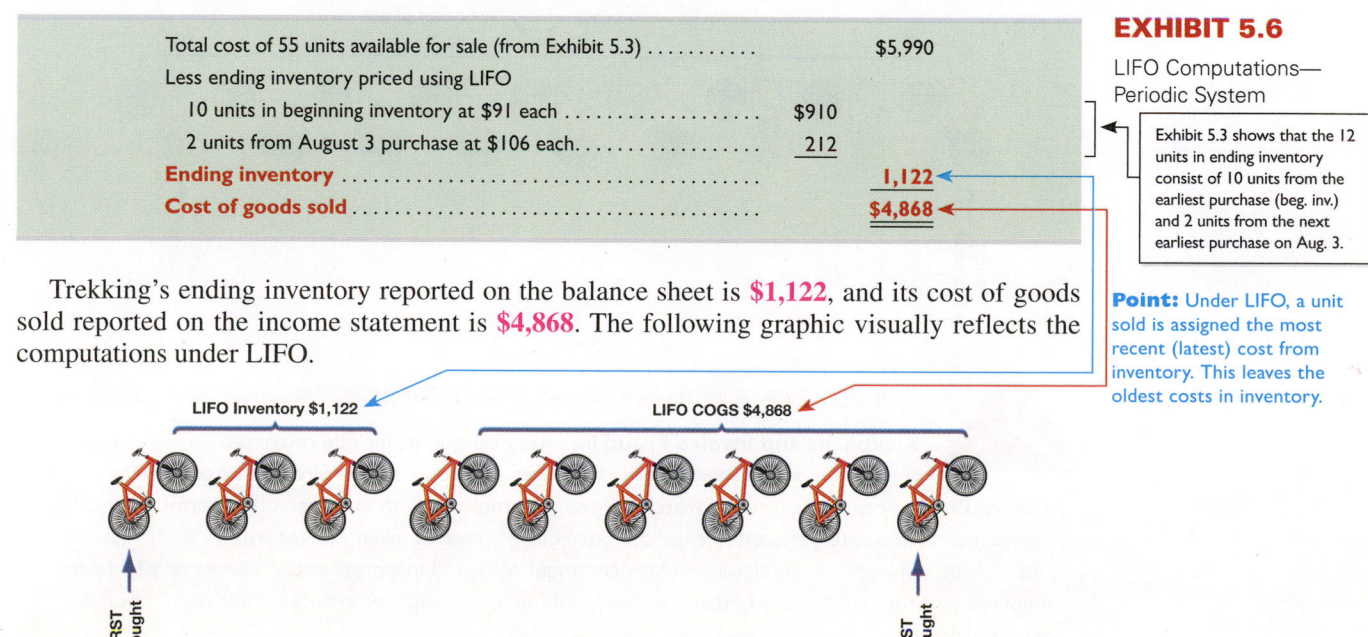

EXHIBIT 5.6

LIFO Computations—
Periodic System

> Exhibit 5.3 shows that the 12 units in ending inventory consist of 10 units from the earliest purchase (beg. inv.) and 2 units from the next earliest purchase on Aug. 3.

Trekking's ending inventory reported on the balance sheet is **$1,122**, and its cost of goods sold reported on the income statement is **$4,868**. The following graphic visually reflects the computations under LIFO.

Point: Under LIFO, a unit sold is assigned the most recent (latest) cost from inventory. This leaves the oldest costs in inventory.

Weighted Average

The **weighted average** or **WA** (also called **average cost**) method of assigning cost requires that we use the average cost per unit of inventory at the end of the period. Weighted average cost per unit equals the cost of goods available for sale divided by the units available. The weighted average method of assigning cost involves three important steps. The first two steps are shown in Exhibit 5.7a. First, multiply the per unit cost for beginning inventory and each particular purchase by the corresponding number of units (from Exhibit 5.3). Second, add these amounts and divide by the total number of units available for sale to find the weighted average cost per unit.

EXHIBIT 5.7a

Weighted Average Cost per Unit

Example: In Exhibit 5.7a, if 5 more units had been purchased at $120 each, what would be the weighted average cost per unit?
Answer: $109.83 ($6,590/60)

Step 1:	10 units @ $ 91 =	$ 910	
	15 units @ $106 =	1,590	
	20 units @ $115 =	2,300	
	10 units @ $119 =	1,190	
	55	$5,990	
Step 2:	$5,990/55 units =	$108.91 weighted average cost per unit	

The third step is to use the weighted average cost per unit to assign costs to inventory and to the units sold, as shown in Exhibit 5.7b.

EXHIBIT 5.7b

Weighted Average Computations—Periodic

Step 3: Total cost of 55 units available for sale (from Exhibit 5.3).	$5,990
Less **ending inventory** priced on a weighted average cost basis: 12 units at $108.91 each (from Exhibit 5.7a).	1,307
Cost of goods sold (43 units at $108.91 each).	**$4,683**

Trekking's ending inventory reported on the balance sheet is **$1,307**, and its cost of goods sold reported on the income statement is **$4,683** when using the weighted average (periodic) method. The following graphic visually reflects the computations under weighted average.

Fraud

Kickbacks and Invoice Fraud Inventory safeguards include restricted access, use of authorized requisitions, security measures, and controlled environments to prevent damage. Proper accounting includes matching inventory received with purchase order terms and quality requirements, preventing misstatements, and controlling access to inventory records. A study reports that 35% of employees in purchasing and procurement observed inappropriate kickbacks or gifts from suppliers. Another study reports that submission of fraudulent supplier invoices is not uncommon, and perpetrators are often employees (Source: KPMG 2013).

Financial Statement Effects of Costing Methods

When purchase prices do not change, each inventory costing method assigns the same cost amounts to inventory and to cost of goods sold. When purchase prices are different, however, the methods nearly always assign different cost amounts. We show these differences in Exhibit 5.8 using Trekking's data.

A1
Analyze the effects of inventory methods for both financial and tax reporting.

EXHIBIT 5.8

Financial Statement Effects of Inventory Costing Methods

TREKKING COMPANY For Month Ended August 31				
	Specific Identification	FIFO	LIFO	Weighted Average
Income Statement				
Sales	$ 6,050	$ 6,050	$ 6,050	$ 6,050
Cost of goods sold	4,582	4,570	4,868	4,683
Gross profit	1,468	1,480	1,182	1,367
Expenses.......................	450	450	450	450
Income before taxes.............	1,018	1,030	732	917
Income tax expense (30%)	305	309	220	275
Net income	$ 713	$ 721	$ 512	$ 642
Balance Sheet				
Inventory	$1,408	$1,420	$1,122	$1,307

This exhibit reveals two important results. First, when purchase costs *regularly rise,* as in Trekking's case, observe the following:

- FIFO assigns the lowest amount to cost of goods sold—yielding the highest gross profit and net income.
- LIFO assigns the highest amount to cost of goods sold—yielding the lowest gross profit and net income, which also yields a temporary tax advantage by postponing payment of some income tax.
- Weighted average yields results between FIFO and LIFO.
- Specific identification always yields results that depend on which units are sold.

Point: Managers prefer FIFO when costs are rising *and* incentives exist to report higher income for reasons such as bonus plans, job security, and reputation.

Second, when costs *regularly decline,* the reverse occurs for FIFO and LIFO. FIFO gives the highest cost of goods sold—yielding the lowest gross profit and income. And LIFO gives the lowest cost of goods sold—yielding the highest gross profit and income.

All four inventory costing methods are acceptable in practice. A company must disclose the inventory method it uses. Each method offers certain advantages as follows:

- FIFO assigns an amount to inventory on the balance sheet that approximates its current cost; it also mimics the actual flow of goods for most businesses.
- LIFO assigns an amount to cost of goods sold on the income statement that approximates its current cost; it also better matches current costs with revenues in computing gross profit.
- Weighted average tends to smooth out erratic changes in costs.
- Specific identification exactly matches the costs of items with the revenues they generate.

Point: LIFO inventory is often less than the inventory's replacement cost because LIFO inventory is valued using the oldest inventory purchase costs.

Decision Maker

Cost Analyst   Your supervisor says she finds managing product costs easier if the balance sheet reflects inventory values that closely reflect replacement cost. Which inventory costing method do you advise adopting? ■ [Answers follow the chapter's Summary.]

Tax Effects of Costing Methods   Trekking's segment income statement in Exhibit 5.8 includes income tax expense (at a rate of 30%) because it was formed as a corporation. Since inventory costs affect net income, they have potential tax effects. Trekking gains a temporary tax advantage by using LIFO. Many companies use LIFO for this reason.

Point: *LIFO conformity rule may be revised if IFRS is adopted for U.S. companies as IFRS currently does not permit LIFO (see Global View).*

Companies can and often do use different costing methods for financial reporting and tax reporting. *The only exception is when LIFO is used for tax reporting; in this case, the IRS requires that it also be used in financial statements*—called the LIFO conformity rule.

Consistency in Using Costing Methods

The **consistency concept** prescribes that a company use the same accounting methods period after period so that financial statements are comparable across periods—the only exception is when a change from one method to another will improve its financial reporting. The *full-disclosure principle* prescribes that the notes to the statements report this type of change, its justification, and its effect on income.

The consistency concept does *not* require a company to use one method exclusively. For example, it can use different methods to value different categories of inventory.

 Decision Ethics

Inventory Manager   Your compensation as inventory manager includes a bonus plan based on gross profit. Your superior asks your opinion on changing the inventory costing method from FIFO to LIFO. Since costs are expected to continue to rise, your superior predicts that LIFO would match higher current costs against sales, thereby lowering taxable income (and gross profit). What do you recommend? ■   [Answers follow the chapter's Summary.]

 5-2

Periodic SI, FIFO, LIFO, and WA

P1

A company reported the following December purchases and sales data for its only product.

Date	Activities	Units Acquired at Cost	Units Sold at Retail
Dec. 1	Beginning inventory.........	5 units @ $3.00 = $ 15.00	
Dec. 8	Purchase	10 units @ $4.50 = 45.00	
Dec. 9	Sales.....................		8 units @ $7.00
Dec. 19	Purchase	13 units @ $5.00 = 65.00	
Dec. 24	Sales		18 units @ $8.00
Dec. 30	Purchase	8 units @ $5.30 = 42.40	
Totals	....	36 units $167.40	26 units

The company uses a *periodic inventory system*. Determine the cost assigned to ending inventory and to cost of goods sold using (*a*) specific identification, (*b*) FIFO, (*c*) LIFO, and (*d*) weighted average. (Round per unit costs and inventory amounts to cents.) For specific identification, ending inventory consists of 10 units, where 8 are from the December 30 purchase and 2 are from the December 8 purchase.

Solutions

a. Specific identification: Ending inventory—eight units from December 30 purchase and two units from December 8 purchase

Specific Identification	Ending Inventory	Cost of Goods Sold
(8 × $5.30) + (2 × $4.50)	$51.40	
(5 × $3.00) + (8 × $4.50) + (13 × $5.00) + (0 × $5.30)...................		$116.00
or $167.40 [Total Goods Available] − $51.40 [Ending Inventory].........		$116.00

b. FIFO—Periodic

FIFO	Ending Inventory	Cost of Goods Sold
(8 × $5.30) + (2 × $5.00)	$52.40	
(5 × $3.00) + (10 × $4.50) + (11 × $5.00)		$115.00
or $167.40 [Total Goods Available] − $52.40 [Ending Inventory]		$115.00

c. LIFO—Periodic

LIFO	Ending Inventory	Cost of Goods Sold
(5 × $3.00) + (5 × $4.50)	$37.50	
(8 × $5.30) + (13 × $5.00) + (5 × $4.50)		$129.90
or $167.40 [Total Goods Available] − $37.50 [Ending Inventory]		$129.90

d. WA—Periodic

WA	Ending Inventory	Cost of Goods Sold
10 × $4.65 (computed from $167.40/36)	$46.50	
26 × $4.65 (computed from $167.40/36)		$120.90
or $167.40 [Total Goods Available] − $46.50 [Ending Inventory]		$120.90

> Do More: QS 5-4, QS 5-5, QS 5-6, QS 5-10, QS 5-11, QS 5-12, QS 5-13

VALUING INVENTORY AT LCM AND THE EFFECTS OF INVENTORY ERRORS

This section examines the role of market costs in determining inventory on the balance sheet and also the financial statement effects of inventory errors.

Lower of Cost or Market

We explained how to assign costs to ending inventory and cost of goods sold using one of four costing methods (FIFO, LIFO, weighted average, or specific identification). However, *accounting principles require that inventory be reported at the market value (cost) of replacing inventory when market value is lower than cost.* Merchandise inventory is then said to be reported on the balance sheet at the **lower of cost or market (LCM).**

P2

Compute the lower of cost or market amount of inventory.

Computing the Lower of Cost or Market   *Market* in the term *LCM* is defined as the current replacement cost of purchasing the same inventory items in the usual manner. A decline in replacement cost reflects a loss of value in inventory. When the recorded cost of inventory is higher than the replacement cost, a loss is recognized. When the recorded cost is lower, no adjustment is made.

LCM is applied in one of three ways: (1) to each individual item separately, (2) to major categories of items, or (3) to the whole of inventory. The less similar the items that make up inventory, the more likely companies are to apply LCM to individual items or categories. With the increasing application of technology and inventory tracking, companies increasingly apply LCM to each individual item separately. Accordingly, we show that method only; however, advanced courses cover the other two methods. To illustrate LCM, we apply it to the ending inventory of a motorsports retailer in Exhibit 5.9.

Point: LCM applied to each individual item always yields the lowest inventory.

Inventory Items	Units	Per Unit Cost	Per Unit Market	Total Cost	Total Market	LCM Applied to Items
Cycles						
Roadster	20	$8,000	$7,000	$160,000	$140,000	$ 140,000
Sprint	10	5,000	6,000	50,000	60,000	50,000
Off-Road						
Trax-4	8	5,000	6,500	40,000	52,000	40,000
Blazer	5	9,000	7,000	45,000	35,000	35,000
Totals				$295,000	$265,000	$265,000

EXHIBIT 5.9

Lower of Cost or Market Computations

$140,000 is the lower of $160,000 or $140,000.

Market amount of $265,000 is lower than the $295,000 recorded cost.

LCM Applied to Individual Items   When LCM is applied to individual *items* of inventory, the number of comparisons equals the number of items. For Roadster, $140,000 is the lower of the $160,000 cost and the $140,000 market. For Sprint, $50,000 is the lower of the $50,000 cost and the $60,000 market. For Trax-4, $40,000 is the lower of the $40,000 cost and the $52,000 market. For Blazer, $35,000 is the lower of the $45,000 cost and the $35,000 market. This yields a $265,000 reported inventory, computed from $140,000 for Roadster plus $50,000 for Sprint plus $40,000 for Trax-4 plus $35,000 for Blazer.

The retailer **The Buckle** applies LCM and reports that its "inventory is stated at the lower of cost or market. Cost is determined using the average cost method."

Recording the Lower of Cost or Market   Inventory must be adjusted downward when market is less than cost. To illustrate, if LCM is applied to the individual items of inventory in Exhibit 5.9, the Merchandise Inventory account must be adjusted from the $295,000 recorded cost down to the $265,000 market amount as follows.

Cost of Goods Sold	30,000	
Merchandise Inventory		30,000
Adjust inventory cost to market.		

Accounting rules require that inventory be adjusted to market when market is less than cost, but inventory normally cannot be written up to market when market exceeds cost. If recording inventory down to market is acceptable, why are companies not allowed to record inventory up to market? One view is that a gain from a market increase should not be realized until a sales transaction verifies the gain. However, this view also applies when market is less than cost. A second and primary reason is the **conservatism constraint,** which prescribes the use of the less optimistic amount when more than one estimate of the amount to be received or paid exists and these estimates are about equally likely.

NEED-TO-KNOW 5-3

LCM Method

P2

A company has the following products in its ending inventory, along with cost and market values. (a) Compute the lower of cost or market for its inventory when applied *separately to each product.* (b) If the market amount is less than the recorded cost of the inventory, then record the December 31 LCM adjustment to the Merchandise Inventory account.

		Per Unit	
	Units	**Cost**	**Market**
Road bikes	5	$1,000	$800
Mountain bikes.	4	500	600
Town bikes	10	400	450

Solution

a.

		Per Unit		Total	Total	
Inventory Items	**Units**	**Cost**	**Market**	**Cost**	**Market**	**LCM Items**
Road bikes	5	$1,000	$800	$ 5,000	$4,000	$ 4,000
Mountain bikes.	4	500	600	2,000	2,400	2,000
Town bikes	10	400	450	4,000	4,500	4,000
				$11,000		$ 10,000
LCM applied to each product						**$10,000**

b.

Dec. 31	Cost of Goods Sold.	1,000	
	Merchandise Inventory		1,000
	Adjust inventory cost to market ($11,000 − $10,000).		

Do More: QS 5-19, E 5-10

Financial Statement Effects of Inventory Errors

Companies must take care both in taking a physical count of inventory and in assigning a cost to it. An inventory error causes misstatements in cost of goods sold, gross profit, net income, current assets, and equity. It also causes misstatements in the next period's statements because ending inventory of one period is the beginning inventory of the next. As we consider the financial statement effects in this section, it is helpful if we recall the following *inventory relation*.

A2

Analyze the effects of inventory errors on current and future financial statements.

 Beginning inventory **+** Net purchases **−** Ending inventory **=** Cost of goods sold

Income Statement Effects   Exhibit 5.10 shows the effects of inventory errors on key amounts in the current and next periods' income statements. Let's look at row 1 and year 1. We see that understating ending inventory overstates cost of goods sold. This can be seen from the above inventory relation where we subtract a smaller ending inventory amount in computing cost of goods sold. Then a higher cost of goods sold yields a lower income.

To understand year 2 of row 1, remember that an understated ending inventory for year 1 becomes an understated beginning inventory for year 2. Using the above inventory relation, we see that if beginning inventory is understated, then cost of goods sold is understated (because we are starting with a smaller amount). A lower cost of goods sold yields a higher income.

Turning to overstatements, let's look at row 2 and year 1. If ending inventory is overstated, we use the inventory relation to see that cost of goods sold is understated. A lower cost of goods sold yields a higher income.

For year 2 of row 2, we again recall that an overstated ending inventory for year 1 becomes an overstated beginning inventory for year 2. If beginning inventory is overstated, we use the inventory relation to see that cost of goods sold is overstated. A higher cost of goods sold yields a lower income.

EXHIBIT 5.10

Effects of Inventory Errors on the Income Statement

	Year 1		Year 2	
Ending Inventory	Cost of Goods Sold	Net Income	Cost of Goods Sold	Net Income
Understated ⬇	Overstated ⬆	Understated ⬇	Understated ⬇	Overstated ⬆
Overstated* ⬆	Understated ⬇	Overstated ⬆	Overstated ⬆	Understated ⬇

* This error is less likely under a perpetual system versus a periodic system because it implies more inventory than is recorded (or less shrinkage than expected). Management will normally follow up and discover and correct this error before it impacts any accounts.

To illustrate, consider an inventory error for a company with $100,000 in sales for each of the years 2014, 2015, and 2016. If this company maintains a steady $20,000 inventory level during this period and makes $60,000 in purchases in each of these years, its cost of goods sold is $60,000 and its gross profit is $40,000 each year.

Ending Inventory Understated—Year 1   Assume that this company errs in computing its 2014 ending inventory and reports $16,000 instead of the correct amount of $20,000. The effects of this error are shown in Exhibit 5.11. The $4,000 understatement of 2014 ending inventory causes a $4,000 overstatement in 2014 cost of goods sold and a $4,000 understatement in both gross profit and net income for 2014. We see that these effects match the effects predicted in Exhibit 5.10.

Ending Inventory Understated—Year 2   The 2014 understated ending inventory becomes the 2015 understated beginning inventory. We see in Exhibit 5.11 that this error causes an understatement in 2015 cost of goods sold and a $4,000 overstatement in both gross profit and net income for 2015.

Ending Inventory Understated—Year 3   Exhibit 5.11 shows that the 2014 ending inventory error affects only that period and the next. It does not affect 2016 results or any period thereafter. An inventory error is said to be self-correcting because it always yields an offsetting error

Example: If 2014 ending inventory in Exhibit 5.11 is overstated by $3,000 (not understated by $4,000), what is the effect on cost of goods sold, gross profit, assets, and equity? *Answer:* Cost of goods sold is understated by $3,000 in 2014 and overstated by $3,000 in 2015. Gross profit and net income are overstated in 2014 and understated in 2015. Assets and equity are overstated in 2014.

EXHIBIT 5.11

Effects of Inventory Errors
on Three Periods' Income
Statements

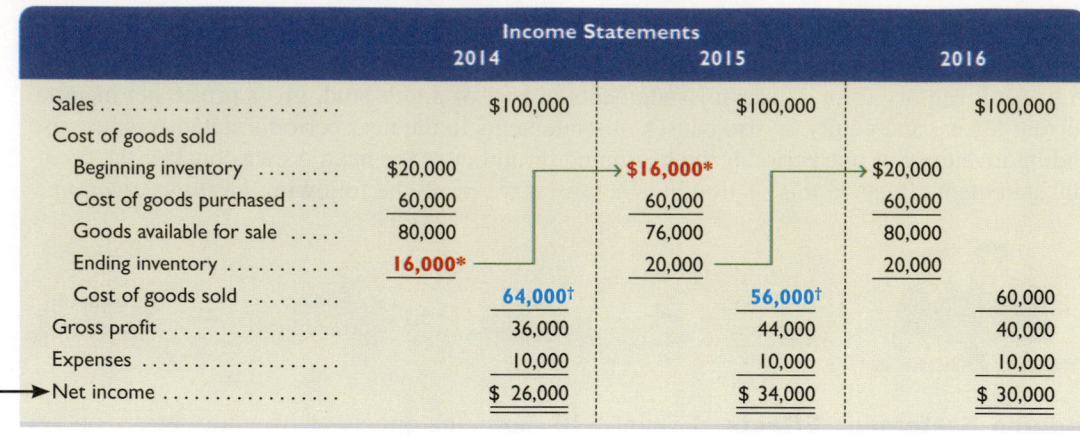

Income Statements	2014	2015	2016
Sales	$100,000	$100,000	$100,000
Cost of goods sold			
Beginning inventory	$20,000	→$16,000*	→$20,000
Cost of goods purchased	60,000	60,000	60,000
Goods available for sale	80,000	76,000	80,000
Ending inventory	16,000*	20,000	20,000
Cost of goods sold	64,000†	56,000†	60,000
Gross profit	36,000	44,000	40,000
Expenses	10,000	10,000	10,000
Net income	$ 26,000	$ 34,000	$ 30,000

Correct income is $30,000
for each year.

* Correct amount is $20,000.   † Correct amount is $60,000.

Point: A former internal auditor at **Coca-Cola** alleges that just before midnight at a prior calendar year-end, fully loaded Coke trucks were ordered to drive about 2 feet away from the loading dock so that Coke could record millions of dollars in extra sales.

in the next period. This does not reduce the severity of inventory errors. Managers, lenders, owners, and others make important decisions from analysis of income and costs.

We can also do an analysis of beginning inventory errors. The income statement effects are the opposite of those for ending inventory.

Balance Sheet Effects   Balance sheet effects of an inventory error can be seen by considering the accounting equation: Assets = Liabilities + Equity. For example, understating ending inventory understates both current and total assets. An understatement in ending inventory also yields an understatement in equity because of the understatement in net income. Exhibit 5.12 shows the effects of inventory errors on the current period's balance sheet amounts. Errors in beginning inventory do not yield misstatements in the end-of-period balance sheet, but they do affect that current period's income statement.

EXHIBIT 5.12

Effects of Inventory Errors
on Current Period's
Balance Sheet

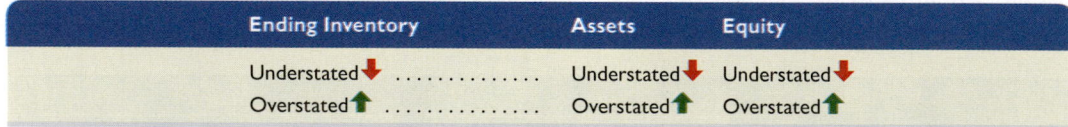

Ending Inventory	Assets	Equity
Understated ↓	Understated ↓	Understated ↓
Overstated ↑	Overstated ↑	Overstated ↑

NEED-TO-KNOW   **5-4**

Effects of Inventory
Errors

A2

A company had $10,000 of sales in each of three consecutive years, 2014–2016, and it purchased merchandise costing $7,000 in each of those years. It also maintained a $2,000 physical inventory from the beginning to the end of that three-year period. In accounting for inventory, it made an error at the end of year 2014 that caused its year-end 2014 inventory to appear on its statements as $1,600 rather than the correct $2,000. (a) Determine the correct amount of the company's gross profit in each of the years 2014–2016. (b) Prepare comparative income statements as in Exhibit 5.11 to show the effect of this error on the company's cost of goods sold and gross profit for each of the years 2014–2016.

Solution

a. Correct gross profit = $10,000 − $7,000 = $3,000 (for each year).

b. Cost of goods sold and gross profit figures follow:

	Year 2014	Year 2015	Year 2016
Sales	$10,000	$10,000	$10,000
Cost of goods sold			
Beginning inventory	$2,000	→$1,600	→$2,000
Cost of purchases	7,000	7,000	7,000
Goods available for sale	9,000	8,600	9,000
Ending inventory	1,600	2,000	2,000
Cost of goods sold..........	7,400	6,600	7,000
Gross profit	$ 2,600	$ 3,400	$ 3,000

Do More: QS 5-20, E 5-12

See that combined income for the 3 years is $9,000 ($2,600 + $3,400 + $3,000), which is correct, meaning the inventory error is "self-correcting" (even though individual years' inventory amounts are in error).

GLOBAL VIEW

This section discusses differences between U.S. GAAP and IFRS in the items and costs making up merchandise inventory, in the methods to assign costs to inventory, and in the methods to estimate inventory values.

Items and Costs Making Up Inventory   Both U.S. GAAP and IFRS include broad and similar guidance for the items and costs making up merchandise inventory. Specifically, under both accounting systems, merchandise inventory includes all items that a company owns and holds for sale. Further, merchandise inventory includes costs of expenditures necessary, directly or indirectly, to bring those items to a salable condition and location.

Assigning Costs to Inventory   Both U.S. GAAP and IFRS allow companies to use specific identification in assigning costs to inventory. Further, both systems allow companies to apply a *cost flow assumption*. The usual cost flow assumptions are FIFO, weighted average, and LIFO. However, IFRS does not allow use of LIFO.

Estimating Inventory Costs   Inventory value can decrease or increase as it awaits sale.

Decreases in Inventory Value   Both U.S. GAAP and IFRS require companies to write down (reduce the cost recorded for) inventory when its value falls below the cost recorded. This is referred to as the *lower of cost or market* method explained in this chapter. U.S. GAAP prohibits any later increase in the recorded value of that inventory even if that decline in value is reversed through value increases in later periods. However, IFRS allows reversals of those write-downs up to the original acquisition cost. For example, if Apple wrote down its 2014 inventory from $2,111 million to $2,100 million, it could not reverse this in future periods even if its value increased to more than $2,111 million. However, if Apple applied IFRS, it could reverse that previous loss. (Another difference is that value refers to *replacement cost* under U.S. GAAP, but *net realizable value* under IFRS.)

APPLE

Increases in Inventory Value   Neither U.S. GAAP nor IFRS allow inventory to be adjusted upward beyond the original cost. (One exception is that IFRS requires agricultural assets such as animals, forests, and plants to be measured at fair value less point-of-sale costs.)

Nokia provides the following description of its inventory valuation procedures:

> Inventories are stated at the lower of cost or net realizable value. Cost approximates actual cost on a FIFO (first-in first-out) basis. Net realizable value is the amount that can be realized from the sale of the inventory in the normal course of business after allowing for the costs of realization.

Sustainability and Accounting   Tesla Motors, as introduced in this chapter's opening feature, is built around the idea of sustainability and preserving the environment. Tesla produces sustainable electric vehicles that are not powered by gasoline or diesel fossil fuels. The Tesla vehicles do not emit harmful toxins and create no greenhouse gases. "When I was in college, I wanted to be involved in things that would change the world," Elon Musk, co-founder and CEO of Tesla, proclaims. "I think the biggest problem that humanity faces is one of sustainable energy. If we don't solve that problem this century, independent of any environmental concerns, we will face economic collapse."

In addition to producing vehicles that are powered by sustainable energy, Elon believes that vehicles should be produced with sustainable materials. Elon carefully considers what the cars are made of and where the materials come from. "In our cars we do not use any rare earth [materials] originating from doubtful countries. Our engine mainly consists of copper and steel. Our batteries only contain materials such as synthesized graphite and nickel."

Construction now is under way on Tesla's Gigafactory battery plant. When completed, it will be one of the largest battery plants in the world and will run exclusively on renewable energy sources. The roof of the Gigafactory is to be lined with solar panels, the building surrounded by wind turbines, and all ready to capture geothermal power. It is to be one of the largest "net zero" energy factories in the world. Elon explains, "The Gigafactory is an important step in advancing the cause of sustainable transportation and will enable the mass production of compelling electric vehicles for decades to come."

Justin Sullivan/Getty Images

Decision Analysis   Inventory Turnover and Days' Sales in Inventory

A3
_____

Assess inventory management using both inventory turnover and days' sales in inventory.

Inventory Turnover

Earlier chapters described two important ratios useful in evaluating a company's short-term liquidity: current ratio and acid-test ratio. A merchandiser's ability to pay its short-term obligations also depends on how quickly it sells its merchandise inventory. **Inventory turnover,** also called *merchandise inventory turnover* or, simply, *turns,* is one ratio used to assess this and is defined in Exhibit 5.13.

EXHIBIT 5.13

Inventory Turnover

$$\text{Inventory turnover} = \frac{\text{Cost of goods sold}}{\text{Average inventory}}$$

Point: We must take care when comparing turnover ratios across companies that use different costing methods (such as FIFO and LIFO).

Point: Companies with low inventory turnover can be susceptible to losses due to obsolescence and trend changes.

This ratio reveals how many *times* a company turns over (sells) its inventory during a period. If a company's inventory greatly varies within a year, average inventory amounts can be computed from interim periods such as quarters or months.

Users apply inventory turnover to help analyze short-term liquidity and to assess whether management is doing a good job controlling the amount of inventory available. A low ratio compared to that of competitors suggests inefficient use of assets. The company may be holding more inventory than it needs to support its sales volume. Similarly, a very high ratio compared to that of competitors suggests inventory might be too low. This can cause lost sales if customers must back-order merchandise. Inventory turnover has no simple rule except to say *a high ratio is preferable provided inventory is adequate to meet demand.*

Days' Sales in Inventory

Point: Inventory turnover is higher and days' sales in inventory is lower for industries such as foods and other perishable products. The reverse holds for nonperishable product industries.

To better interpret inventory turnover, many users measure the adequacy of inventory to meet sales demand. **Days' sales in inventory,** also called *days' stock on hand,* is a ratio that reveals how much inventory is available in terms of the number of days' sales. It can be interpreted as the number of days one can sell from inventory if no new items are purchased. This ratio is often viewed as a measure of the buffer against out-of-stock inventory and is useful in evaluating liquidity of inventory. It is defined in Exhibit 5.14.

EXHIBIT 5.14

Days' Sales in Inventory

$$\text{Days' sales in inventory} = \frac{\text{Ending inventory}}{\text{Cost of goods sold}} \times 365$$

Days' sales in inventory focuses on ending inventory and it estimates how many days it will take to convert inventory at the end of a period into accounts receivable or cash. Days' sales in inventory focuses on *ending* inventory whereas inventory turnover focuses on *average* inventory.

Analysis of Inventory Management

Inventory management is a major emphasis for merchandisers. They must both plan and control inventory purchases and sales. **Toys "R" Us** is one of those merchandisers. Its inventory at fiscal year-end 2015 was $2,064 million. This inventory constituted 67% of its current assets and 29% of its total assets. We apply the analysis tools in this section to Toys "R" Us, as shown in Exhibit 5.15—also see margin graph.

EXHIBIT 5.15

Inventory Turnover and Days' Sales in Inventory for Toys "R" Us

$ millions	2015	2014	2013	2012	2011	2010
Cost of goods sold	$7,931	$8,154	$8,592	$8,939	$8,939	$8,790
Ending inventory	$2,064	$2,171	$2,229	$2,232	$2,104	$1,810
Inventory turnover	**3.7** times	**3.7** times	**3.9** times	**4.1** times	**4.6** times	**4.9** times
Industry inventory turnover	3.3 times	3.4 times	3.2 times	3.4 times	3.3 times	3.5 times
Days' sales in inventory	**95** days	**97** days	**95** days	**91** days	**86** days	**75** days
Industry days' sales in inventory	126 days	129 days	132 days	128 days	132 days	129 days

Its 2015 inventory turnover of 3.7 times means that Toys "R" Us turns over its inventory 3.7 times per year, or once every 99 days (365 days ÷ 3.7). We prefer inventory turnover to be high provided inventory is not out of stock and the company is not losing customers. The second metric computed, the 2015 days' sales in inventory of 95 days, reveals that it is carrying 95 days of sales in inventory. This inventory buffer seems more than adequate. The slight decrease in days' sales in inventory suggests that Toys "R" Us would benefit from management efforts to increase inventory turnover and to especially reduce inventory levels.

▪ Decision Maker

Entrepreneur   Analysis of your retail store yields an inventory turnover of 5.0 and a days' sales in inventory of 73 days. The industry norm for inventory turnover is 4.4 and for days' sales in inventory is 74 days. What is your assessment of inventory management? ▪ [Answers follow the chapter's Summary.]

Craig Company buys and sells one product. Its beginning inventory, purchases, and sales during calendar year 2016 follow:

NEED-TO-KNOW 5-7

COMPREHENSIVE 1

Periodic Method

Date		Activity	Units Acquired at Cost	Units Sold at Retail	Unit Inventory
Jan.	1	Beg. inventory....	400 units @ $14 = $ 5,600		400 units
Jan.	15	Sale............		200 units @ $30	200 units
March	10	Purchase........	200 units @ $15 = $ 3,000		400 units
April	1	Sale............		200 units @ $30	200 units
May	9	Purchase........	300 units @ $16 = $ 4,800		500 units
Sept.	22	Purchase........	250 units @ $20 = $ 5,000		750 units
Nov.	1	Sale............		300 units @ $35	450 units
Nov.	28	Purchase........	100 units @ $21 = $ 2,100		550 units
		Totals.........	1,250 units $20,500	700 units	

Additional tracking data for specific identification: (1) January 15 sale—200 units @ $14, (2) April 1 sale—200 units @ $15, and (3) November 1 sale—200 units @ $14 and 100 units @ $20.

Required

1. Compute the cost of goods available for sale.
2. Apply the four different methods of inventory costing (FIFO, LIFO, weighted average, and specific identification) to compute ending inventory and cost of goods sold under each method using the periodic system.
3. Compute gross profit earned by the company for each of the four costing methods in part 2. Also, report the inventory amount reported on the balance sheet for each of the four methods.

4. In preparing financial statements for year 2016, the financial officer was instructed to use FIFO but failed to do so and instead computed cost of goods sold according to LIFO. Determine the impact of the error on year 2016's income. Also determine the effect of this error on year 2017's income. Assume no income taxes.

PLANNING THE SOLUTION

- Compute cost of goods available for sale by multiplying the units of beginning inventory and each purchase by their unit costs to determine the total cost of goods available for sale.
- Prepare a periodic FIFO computation starting with cost of units available and subtracting FIFO ending inventory amounts to obtain FIFO cost of goods sold (see Exhibit 5.5).
- Prepare a periodic LIFO computation starting with cost of units available and subtracting LIFO ending inventory amounts to obtain LIFO cost of goods sold (see Exhibit 5.6).
- Compute weighted average ending inventory and cost of goods sold using the three-step process illustrated in Exhibits 5.7a and 5.7b.
- Prepare a table showing the computation of cost of goods sold and ending inventory using the specific identification method (see Exhibit 5.4).
- Compare the year-end 2016 inventory amounts under FIFO and LIFO to determine the misstatement of year 2016 income that results from using LIFO. The errors for year 2016 and 2017 are equal in amount but opposite in effect.

SOLUTION

1. Cost of goods available for sale (this amount is the same for all methods).

Date			Units	Unit Cost	Cost
Jan.	1	Beg. inventory	400	$14	$ 5,600
March 10		Purchase	200	15	3,000
May	9	Purchase	300	16	4,800
Sept.	22	Purchase	250	20	5,000
Nov.	28	Purchase	100	21	2,100
		Total goods available for sale	1,250		$20,500

2a. FIFO periodic method (FIFO under periodic and perpetual yields identical results).

Hint: Students may mistakenly assume that the costing acronym refers to what remains in inventory. It is important to realize, for example, that FIFO refers to costs that are assumed to flow into COGS; namely, the first units purchased are assumed to be the first ones to flow out to cost of goods sold. For FIFO, this means that the goods purchased most recently are assumed to be in ending inventory.

Cost of goods available for sale (from part 1)		$20,500
Ending inventory*		
Nov. 28 Purchase (100 @ $21)...............	$2,100	
Sept. 22 Purchase (250 @ $20)...............	5,000	
May 9 Purchase (200 @ $16)...............	3,200	
Ending inventory		**10,300**
Cost of goods sold		**$10,200**

* Since FIFO assumes that the earlier costs are the first to flow out, we determine ending inventory by assigning the most recent costs to the remaining items.

2b. LIFO periodic method.

Cost of goods available for sale (from part 1)		$20,500
Ending inventory*		
January 1 Beg. inventory (400 @ $14)..........	$5,600	
March 10 Purchase (150 @ $15)..............	2,250	
Ending inventory...............................		**7,850**
Cost of goods sold		**$12,650**

* Since LIFO assumes that the most recent (newest) costs are the first to flow out, we determine ending inventory by assigning the earliest (oldest) costs to the remaining items.

2c. Weighted average periodic method.

Step 1:	400 units @ $14 = $ 5,600
	200 units @ $15 = 3,000
	300 units @ $16 = 4,800
	250 units @ $20 = 5,000
	100 units @ $21 = 2,100
	1,250 units **$20,500**
Step 2:	$20,500/1,250 units = **$16.40** weighted average cost per unit
Step 3:	Total cost of 1,250 units available for sale $20,500
	Less **ending inventory** priced on a weighted average
	cost basis: 550 units at $16.40 each **9,020**
	Cost of goods sold (700 units at $16.40 each) **$11,480**

2d. Specific identification method.

Date	Goods Purchased	Cost of Goods Sold	Inventory Balance	
Jan. 1	Beginning balance		400 @ $14	= $ 5,600
Jan. 15		200 @ $14 = $2,800	200 @ $14	= $ 2,800
Mar. 10	200 @ $15 = $3,000		200 @ $14 ⎱ 200 @ $15 ⎰	= $ 5,800
April 1		200 @ $15 = $3,000	200 @ $14	= $ 2,800
May 9	300 @ $16 = $4,800		200 @ $14 ⎱ 300 @ $16 ⎰	= $ 7,600
Sept. 22	250 @ $20 = $5,000		200 @ $14 ⎱ 300 @ $16 ⎬ 250 @ $20 ⎰	= $ 12,600
Nov. 1		200 @ $14 = $2,800 ⎱ 100 @ $20 = $2,000 ⎰	300 @ $16 ⎱ 150 @ $20 ⎰	= $ 7,800
Nov. 28	100 @ $21 = $2,100		300 @ $16 ⎱ 150 @ $20 ⎬ 100 @ $21 ⎰	= **$ 9,900**
Total cost of goods sold		**$10,600**		

3.

	FIFO	LIFO	Weighted Average	Specific Identification
Income Statement				
Sales*	$ 22,500	$22,500	$ 22,500	$22,500
Cost of goods sold	10,200	12,650	11,480	10,600
Gross profit	$ 12,300	$ 9,850	$ 11,020	$11,900
Balance Sheet				
Inventory	$10,300	$ 7,850	$ 9,020	$ 9,900

* Sales = (200 units × $30) + (200 units × $30) + (300 units × $35) = $22,500

4. Mistakenly using LIFO, when FIFO should have been used, overstates cost of goods sold in year 2016 by $2,450, which is the difference between the FIFO and LIFO amounts of ending inventory. It understates income in 2016 by $2,450. In year 2017, income is overstated by $2,450 because of the understatement in beginning inventory.

COMPREHENSIVE 2

Perpetual Method

Craig Company buys and sells one product. Its beginning inventory, purchases, and sales during calendar year 2016 follow:

Date	Activity	Units Acquired at Cost	Units Sold at Retail	Unit Inventory
Jan. 1	Beg. inventory....	400 units @ $14 = $ 5,600		400 units
Jan. 15	Sale............		200 units @ $30	200 units
March 10	Purchase........	200 units @ $15 = $ 3,000		400 units
April 1	Sale............		200 units @ $30	200 units
May 9	Purchase........	300 units @ $16 = $ 4,800		500 units
Sept. 22	Purchase........	250 units @ $20 = $ 5,000		750 units
Nov. 1	Sale		300 units @ $35	450 units
Nov. 28	Purchase........	100 units @ $21 = $ 2,100		550 units
	Totals	1,250 units $20,500	700 units	

Additional tracking data for specific identification: (1) January 15 sale—200 units @ $14, (2) April 1 sale—200 units @ $15, and (3) November 1 sale—200 units @ $14 and 100 units @ $20.

Required

1. Calculate the cost of goods available for sale.
2. Apply the four different methods of inventory costing (FIFO, LIFO, weighted average, and specific identification) to calculate ending inventory and cost of goods sold under each method using the perpetual system.
3. Compute gross profit earned by the company for each of the four costing methods in part 2. Also, report the inventory amount reported on the balance sheet for each of the four methods.
4. In preparing financial statements for year 2016, the financial officer was instructed to use FIFO but failed to do so and instead computed cost of goods sold according to LIFO, which led to a $1,400 overstatement in cost of goods sold from using LIFO. Determine the impact on year 2016's income from the error. Also determine the effect of this error on year 2017's income. Assume no income taxes.
5. Management wants a report that shows how changing from FIFO to another method would change net income. Prepare a table showing (1) the cost of goods sold amount under each of the four methods, (2) the amount by which each cost of goods sold total is different from the FIFO cost of goods sold, and (3) the effect on net income if another method is used instead of FIFO.

PLANNING THE SOLUTION

- Compute cost of goods available for sale by multiplying the units of beginning inventory and each purchase by their unit costs to determine the total cost of goods available for sale.
- Prepare a perpetual FIFO table starting with beginning inventory and showing how inventory changes after each purchase and after each sale (see Exhibit 5A.3).
- Prepare a perpetual LIFO table starting with beginning inventory and showing how inventory changes after each purchase and after each sale (see Exhibit 5A.4).
- Make a table of purchases and sales recalculating the average cost of inventory prior to each sale to arrive at the weighted average cost of ending inventory. Total the average costs associated with each sale to determine cost of goods sold (see Exhibit 5A.5).
- Prepare a table showing the computation of cost of goods sold and ending inventory using the specific identification method (see Exhibit 5.4).
- Compare the year-end 2016 inventory amounts under FIFO and LIFO to determine the misstatement of year 2016 income that results from using LIFO. The errors for year 2016 and 2017 are equal in amount but opposite in effect.
- Create a table showing cost of goods sold under each method and how net income would differ from FIFO net income if an alternate method were adopted.

SOLUTION

1. The solution is identical to the solution for part 1 of **Need-To-Know Comprehensive 1.**

2a. FIFO perpetual method.

Date	Goods Purchased	Cost of Goods Sold	Inventory Balance
Jan. 1	Beginning balance		400 @ $14 = $ 5,600
Jan. 15		200 @ $14 = $2,800	200 @ $14 = $ 2,800
Mar. 10	200 @ $15 = $3,000		200 @ $14 200 @ $15 } = $ 5,800
April 1		200 @ $14 = $2,800	200 @ $15 = $ 3,000
May 9	300 @ $16 = $4,800		200 @ $15 300 @ $16 } = $ 7,800
Sept. 22	250 @ $20 = $5,000		200 @ $15 300 @ $16 250 @ $20 } = $ 12,800
Nov. 1		200 @ $15 = $3,000 100 @ $16 = $1,600	200 @ $16 250 @ $20 } = $ 8,200
Nov. 28	100 @ $21 = $2,100		200 @ $16 250 @ $20 100 @ $21 } = **$10,300**
Total cost of goods sold		**$10,200**	

Note to students: **In a classroom situation,** once we compute cost of goods available for sale, we can compute the amount for either cost of goods sold or ending inventory—it is a matter of preference. **In practice,** the costs of items sold are identified as sales are made and immediately transferred from the Inventory account to the Cost of Goods Sold account. The previous solution showing the line-by-line approach illustrates actual application in practice. The following alternate solutions illustrate that, once the concepts are understood, other solution approaches are available. Although this is only shown for FIFO, it could be shown for all methods.

Alternate Methods to Compute FIFO Perpetual Numbers

[FIFO Alternate No. 1: Computing cost of goods sold first]

Cost of goods available for sale (from part 1)			$20,500
Cost of goods sold			
Jan. 15	Sold (200 @ $14)	$2,800	
April 1	Sold (200 @ $14)	2,800	
Nov. 1	Sold (200 @ $15 and 100 @ $16)	4,600	10,200
Ending inventory			$10,300

[FIFO Alternate No. 2: Computing ending inventory first]

Cost of goods available for sale (from part 1)			$20,500
Ending inventory*			
Nov. 28	Purchase (100 @ $21)	$2,100	
Sept. 22	Purchase (250 @ $20)	5,000	
May 9	Purchase (200 @ $16)	3,200	
Ending inventory			10,300
Cost of goods sold			$10,200

* Since FIFO assumes that the earlier costs are the first to flow out, we determine ending inventory by assigning the most recent costs to the remaining items.

2b. LIFO perpetual method.

Date	Goods Purchased	Cost of Goods Sold	Inventory Balance
Jan. 1	Beginning balance		400 @ $14 = $ 5,600
Jan. 15		200 @ $14 = $2,800	200 @ $14 = $ 2,800
Mar. 10	200 @ $15 = $3,000		200 @ $14 200 @ $15 } = $ 5,800
April 1		200 @ $15 = $3,000	200 @ $14 = $ 2,800
May 9	300 @ $16 = $4,800		200 @ $14 300 @ $16 } = $ 7,600
Sept. 22	250 @ $20 = $5,000		200 @ $14 300 @ $16 250 @ $20 } = $12,600
Nov. 1		250 @ $20 = $5,000 50 @ $16 = $ 800	200 @ $14 250 @ $16 } = $ 6,800
Nov. 28	100 @ $21 = $2,100		200 @ $14 250 @ $16 100 @ $21 } = **$ 8,900**
Total cost of goods sold		**$11,600**	

2c. Weighted average perpetual method.

Date	Goods Purchased	Cost of Goods Sold	Inventory Balance
Jan. 1	Beginning balance		400 @ $14.00 = $ 5,600 ($5,600/400 units = $14.00 avg. cost)
Jan. 15		200 @ $14.00 = $2,800	200 @ $14.00 = $ 2,800
Mar. 10	200 @ $15.00 = $3,000		200 @ $14.00 200 @ $15.00 } = $ 5,800 ($5,800/400 units = $14.50 avg. cost)
April 1		200 @ $14.50 = $2,900	200 @ $14.50 = $ 2,900
May 9	300 @ $16.00 = $4,800		200 @ $14.50 300 @ $16.00 } = $ 7,700 ($7,700/500 units = $15.40 avg. cost)
Sept. 22	250 @ $20.00 = $5,000		500 @ $15.40 250 @ $20.00 } = $ 12,700 ($12,700/750 units = $16.93[†] avg. cost)
Nov. 1		300 @ $16.93 = $5,079	450 @ $16.93 = $ 7,618.5
Nov. 28	100 @ $21.00 = $2,100		450 @ $16.93 100 @ $21.00 } = **$9,718.5** ($9,718.50/550 units = $17.67 avg. cost)
Total cost of goods sold*		**$10,779**	

* Cost of goods sold ($10,779) plus ending inventory ($9,718.5) is $2.5 less than the cost of goods available for sale ($20,500) due to rounding.

[†] Rounded to 2 decimal places.

2d. Specific identification method.

The solution is identical to the solution shown in part 2d of **Need-To-Know Comprehensive 1.** This is because specific identification is *not* a cost flow assumption; instead, this method specifically identifies each item in inventory and each item that is sold.

3.

	FIFO	LIFO	Weighted Average	Specific Identification
Income Statement				
Sales*	$ 22,500	$22,500	$ 22,500	$22,500
Cost of goods sold	10,200	11,600	10,779	10,600
Gross profit	$ 12,300	$10,900	$ 11,721	$11,900
Balance Sheet				
Inventory	$10,300	$ 8,900	$9,718.5	$ 9,900

* Sales = (200 units × $30) + (200 units × $30) + (300 units × $35) = $22,500

4. Mistakenly using LIFO when FIFO should have been used overstates cost of goods sold in year 2016 by $1,400, which is the difference between the FIFO and LIFO amounts of ending inventory. It understates income in 2016 by $1,400. In year 2017, income is overstated by $1,400 because of the understatement in beginning inventory.

5. Analysis of the effects of alternative inventory methods.

	Cost of Goods Sold	Difference from FIFO Cost of Goods Sold	Effect on Net Income If Adopted Instead of FIFO
FIFO	$10,200	—	—
LIFO	11,600	+$1,400	$1,400 lower
Weighted average	10,779	+ 579	579 lower
Specific identification	10,600	+ 400	400 lower

APPENDIX

Inventory Costing under a Perpetual System

5A

P3

Compute inventory in a perpetual system using the methods of specific identification, FIFO, LIFO, and weighted average.

This section illustrates inventory costing methods. We use information from Trekking, a sporting goods store. Among its products, Trekking carries one type of mountain bike whose sales are directed at resorts that provide inexpensive mountain bikes for complimentary guest use. These resorts usually purchase in amounts of 10 or more bikes. We use Trekking's data from August. Its mountain bike (unit) inventory at the beginning of August and its purchases and sales during August are in Exhibit 5A.1. It ends August with 12 bikes in inventory.

EXHIBIT 5A.1

Purchases and Sales of Goods

Date	Activity	Units Acquired at Cost	Units Sold at Retail	Unit Inventory
Aug. 1	Beginning inventory	10 units @ $ 91 = $ 910		10 units
Aug. 3	Purchases	15 units @ $106 = $ 1,590		25 units
Aug. 14	Sales		20 units @ $130	5 units
Aug. 17	Purchases	20 units @ $115 = $ 2,300		25 units
Aug. 28	Purchases	10 units @ $119 = $ 1,190		35 units
Aug. 31	Sales		23 units @ $150	12 units
	Totals	55 units $5,990	43 units	

Units available for sale

Goods available for sale

Units sold

Units left

Trekking uses the **perpetual inventory system**, which means that its Merchandise Inventory account is continually updated to reflect purchases and sales. Regardless of what inventory method or system is used, cost of goods available for sale must be allocated between cost of goods sold and ending inventory.

Specific Identification

Specific Identification   When each item in inventory can be identified with a specific purchase and invoice, we can use **specific identification** or **SI** (also called *specific invoice inventory pricing*) to assign costs. We also need sales records that identify exactly which items were sold and when. For example, each bike's serial number could be used to track costs and compute cost of goods sold. Trekking's internal documents reveal the following specific unit sales:

August 14   Sold 8 bikes costing $91 each and 12 bikes costing $106 each

August 31   Sold 2 bikes costing $91 each, 3 bikes costing $106 each, 15 bikes costing $115 each, and 3 bikes costing $119 each

Applying specific identification and using the information above, we prepare Exhibit 5A.2. This exhibit begins with the $5,990 in total units available for sale—this is from Exhibit 5A.1. Applying specific identification, we know that for the 20 units sold on August 14, the company specifically identified that 8 of them had cost $91 each and 12 had cost $106 each, resulting in an August 14 cost of sales of $2,000. Next, for the 23 units sold on August 31, the company specifically identified that 2 of them had cost $91 each, that 3 had cost $106 each, that 15 had cost $115 each, and 3 had cost $119 each, resulting in an August 31 cost of sales of $2,582. This yields a total cost of sales for the period of $4,582. We then subtract this $4,582 in cost of goods sold from the $5,990 in cost of goods available to get $1,408 in ending inventory. Carefully study Exhibit 5A.2 to see the flow of costs. Each unit, whether sold or remaining in inventory, has its own specific cost attached to it.

EXHIBIT 5A.2

Specific Identification Computations

Merchandise Inventory (SI)		
Aug. 1 910		
Aug. 3 1,590		
	Aug. 14 2,000	
Aug. 17 2,300		
Aug. 28 1,190		
	Aug. 31 2,582	
Aug. 31 1,408		

Total cost of 55 units available for sale (from Exhibit 5A.1)		$5,990
Cost of goods sold*		
Aug. 14 (8 @ $91) + (12 @ $106)......................................	$2,000	
Aug. 31 (2 @ $91) + (3 @ $106) + (15 @ $115) + (3 @ $119)...........	2,582	4,582
Ending inventory		$1,408

* Identification of items sold (and their costs) is obtained from internal documents that track each unit from its purchase to its sale.

Point: Specific identification is usually practical for companies with expensive or custom-made inventory. Examples include car dealerships, implement dealers, jewelers, and fashion designers.

Point: SI yields identical results under both periodic and perpetual.

Point: The "Goods Purchased" column is identical for all methods. Data are taken from Exhibit 5A.1.

Point: Under FIFO, a unit sold is assigned the earliest (oldest) cost from inventory. This leaves the most recent costs in ending inventory.

When using specific identification, Trekking's cost of goods sold reported on the income statement totals **$4,582**, the sum of $2,000 and $2,582 from the cost of goods sold section of Exhibit 5A.2. Trekking's ending inventory reported on the balance sheet is **$1,408**, which is the final inventory balance from Exhibit 5A.2.

First-In, First-Out

First-In, First-Out   The **first-in, first-out (FIFO)** method of assigning costs to both inventory and cost of goods sold assumes that inventory items are sold in the order acquired. When sales occur, the costs of the earliest units acquired are charged to cost of goods sold. This leaves the costs from the most recent purchases in ending inventory. Use of FIFO for computing the cost of inventory and cost of goods sold is shown in Exhibit 5A.3.

This exhibit starts with beginning inventory of 10 bikes at $91 each. On August 3, 15 more bikes costing $106 each are bought for $1,590. Inventory now consists of 10 bikes at $91 each and 15 bikes at $106 each, for a total of $2,500. On August 14, 20 bikes are sold—applying FIFO, the first 10 sold cost $91 each and the next 10 sold cost $106 each, for a total cost of $1,970. This leaves 5 bikes costing $106 each, or $530, in inventory. On August 17, 20 bikes costing $2,300 are purchased, and on August 28, another 10 bikes costing $1,190 are purchased, for a total of 35 bikes costing $4,020 in inventory. On August 31, 23 bikes are sold—applying FIFO, the first 5 bikes sold cost $530 and the next 18 sold cost $2,070, which leaves 12 bikes costing $1,420 in ending inventory.

Trekking's FIFO cost of goods sold reported on its income statement (reflecting the 43 units sold) is **$4,570** ($1,970 + $2,600), and its ending inventory reported on the balance sheet (reflecting the 12 units unsold) is **$1,420**.

EXHIBIT 5A.3

FIFO Computations— Perpetual System

Date	Goods Purchased	Cost of Goods Sold	Inventory Balance
Aug. 1	Beginning balance		10 @ $ 91 = $ 910
Aug. 3	15 @ $106 = $1,590		10 @ $ 91 ⎫ 15 @ $106 ⎬ = $2,500
Aug. 14		10 @ $ 91 = $ 910 ⎫ 10 @ $106 = $1,060 ⎬ = **$1,970**	5 @ $106 = $ 530
Aug. 17	20 @ $115 = $2,300		5 @ $106 ⎫ 20 @ $115 ⎬ = $2,830
Aug. 28	10 @ $119 = $1,190		5 @ $106 ⎫ 20 @ $115 ⎬ = $4,020 10 @ $119 ⎭
Aug. 31		5 @ $106 = $ 530 ⎫ 18 @ $115 = $2,070 ⎬ = **$2,600** **$4,570**	2 @ $115 ⎫ 10 @ $119 ⎬ = **$1,420**

For the 20 units sold on Aug. 14, the first 10 sold are assigned the earliest cost of $91 (from beg. bal.). The next 10 sold are assigned the next earliest cost of $106.

For the 23 units sold on Aug. 31, the first 5 sold are assigned the earliest available cost of $106 (from Aug. 3 purchase). The next 18 sold are assigned the next earliest cost of $115 (from Aug. 17 purchase).

Merchandise Inventory (FIFO)

Aug. 1	910		
Aug. 3	1,590		
		Aug. 14	1,970
Aug. 17	2,300		
Aug. 28	1,190		
		Aug. 31	2,600
Aug. 31	1,420		

Last-In, First-Out   The **last-in, first-out (LIFO)** method of assigning costs assumes that the most recent purchases are sold first. These more recent costs are charged to the goods sold, and the costs of the earliest purchases are assigned to inventory. As with other methods, LIFO is acceptable even when the physical flow of goods does not follow a last-in, first-out pattern. One appeal of LIFO is that by assigning costs from the most recent purchases to cost of goods sold, LIFO comes closest to matching current costs of goods sold with revenues (compared to FIFO or weighted average).

Exhibit 5A.4 shows the LIFO computations. It starts with beginning inventory of 10 bikes at $91 each. On August 3, 15 more bikes costing $106 each are bought for $1,590. Inventory now consists of 10 bikes at $91 each and 15 bikes at $106 each, for a total of $2,500. On August 14, 20 bikes are sold—applying LIFO, the first 15 sold are from the most recent purchase costing $106 each, and the next 5 sold are from the next most recent purchase costing $91 each, for a total cost of $2,045. This leaves 5 bikes costing $91 each, or $455, in inventory. On August 17, 20 bikes costing $2,300 are purchased, and on August 28, another 10 bikes costing $1,190 are purchased, for a total of 35 bikes costing $3,945 in inventory. On August 31, 23 bikes are sold—applying LIFO, the first 10 bikes sold are from the most recent purchase costing

Point: Under LIFO, a unit sold is assigned the most recent (latest) cost from inventory. This leaves the oldest costs in inventory.

EXHIBIT 5A.4

LIFO Computations— Perpetual System

Date	Goods Purchased	Cost of Goods Sold	Inventory Balance
Aug. 1	Beginning balance		10 @ $ 91 = $ 910
Aug. 3	15 @ $106 = $1,590		10 @ $ 91 ⎫ 15 @ $106 ⎬ = $ 2,500
Aug. 14		15 @ $106 = $1,590 ⎫ 5 @ $ 91 = $ 455 ⎬ = **$2,045**	5 @ $ 91 = $ 455
Aug. 17	20 @ $115 = $2,300		5 @ $ 91 ⎫ 20 @ $115 ⎬ = $ 2,755
Aug. 28	10 @ $119 = $1,190		5 @ $ 91 ⎫ 20 @ $115 ⎬ = $ 3,945 10 @ $119 ⎭
Aug. 31		10 @ $119 = $1,190 ⎫ 13 @ $115 = $1,495 ⎬ = **$2,685** **$4,730**	5 @ $ 91 ⎫ 7 @ $115 ⎬ = **$1,260**

For the 20 units sold on Aug. 14, the first 15 sold are assigned the most recent cost of $106. The next 5 sold are assigned the next most recent cost of $91.

For the 23 units sold on Aug. 31, the first 10 sold are assigned the most recent cost of $119. The next 13 sold are assigned the next most recent cost of $115.

Merchandise Inventory (LIFO)

Aug. 1	910		
Aug. 3	1,590		
		Aug. 14	2,045
Aug. 17	2,300		
Aug. 28	1,190		
		Aug. 31	2,685
Aug. 31	1,260		

$1,190, and the next 13 sold are from the next most recent purchase costing $1,495, which leaves 12 bikes costing $1,260 in ending inventory.

Trekking's LIFO of goods sold reported on the income statement is **$4,730** ($2,045 + $2,685), and its ending inventory reported on the balance sheet is **$1,260**.

Weighted Average   The **weighted average** (also called **average cost**) method of assigning cost requires that we use the weighted average cost per unit of inventory at the time of each sale. Weighted average cost per unit at the time of each sale equals the cost of goods available for sale divided by the units available. The results using weighted average (WA) for Trekking are shown in Exhibit 5A.5.

EXHIBIT 5A.5

Weighted Average Computations—Perpetual System

For the 20 units sold on Aug. 14, the cost assigned is the $100 *average cost* per unit from the Inventory Balance column at the time of sale.

For the 23 units sold on Aug. 31, the cost assigned is the $114 *average cost* per unit from the Inventory Balance column at the time of sale.

Date	Goods Purchased	Cost of Goods Sold	Inventory Balance
Aug. 1	Beginning balance		10 @ $ 91 = $ 910 (10 @ $ 91 per unit)
Aug. 3	15 @ $106 = $1,590		10 @ $ 91 } = $2,500 (25 @ $100 per unit)ᵃ 15 @ $106 }
Aug. 14		20 @ $100 = **$2,000**	5 @ $100 = $ 500 (5 @ $100 per unit)ᵇ
Aug. 17	20 @ $115 = $2,300		5 @ $100 } = $2,800 (25 @ $112 per unit)ᶜ 20 @ $115 }
Aug. 28	10 @ $119 = $1,190		25 @ $112 } = $3,990 (35 @ $114 per unit)ᵈ 10 @ $119 }
Aug. 31		23 @ $114 = **$2,622**	12 @ $114 = **$1,368** (12 @ $114 per unit)ᵉ
		$4,622	

ᵃ $100 per unit = ($2,500 inventory balance ÷ 25 units in inventory).
ᵇ $100 per unit = ($500 inventory balance ÷ 5 units in inventory).
ᶜ $112 per unit = ($2,800 inventory balance ÷ 25 units in inventory).
ᵈ $114 per unit = ($3,990 inventory balance ÷ 35 units in inventory).
ᵉ $114 per unit = ($1,368 inventory balance ÷ 12 units in inventory).

Merchandise Inventory (WA)

Aug. 1	910		
Aug. 3	1,590		
		Aug. 14	2,000
Aug. 17	2,300		
Aug. 28	1,190		
		Aug. 31	2,622
Aug. 31	1,368		

This exhibit starts with beginning inventory of 10 bikes at $91 each. On August 3, 15 more bikes costing $106 each are bought for $1,590. Inventory now consists of 10 bikes at $91 each and 15 bikes at $106 each, for a total of $2,500. The average cost per bike for that inventory is $100, computed as $2,500/(10 bikes + 15 bikes). On August 14, 20 bikes are sold—applying WA, the 20 sold are assigned the $100 average cost, for a total cost of $2,000. This leaves 5 bikes with an average cost of $100 each, or $500, in inventory. On August 17, 20 bikes costing $2,300 are purchased, and on August 28, another 10 bikes costing $1,190 are purchased, for a total of 35 bikes costing $3,990 in inventory at August 28. The average cost per bike for the August 28 inventory is $114, computed as $3,990/(5 bikes + 20 bikes + 10 bikes). On August 31, 23 bikes are sold—applying WA, the 23 sold are assigned the $114 average cost, for a total cost of $2,622. This leaves 12 bikes costing $1,368 in ending inventory.

Trekking's cost of goods sold reported on the income statement (reflecting the 43 units sold) is **$4,622** ($2,000 + $2,622), and its ending inventory reported on the balance sheet (reflecting the 12 units unsold) is **$1,368**.

This completes computations under the four most common perpetual inventory costing methods. Advances in technology have greatly reduced the cost of a perpetual inventory system. Many companies now ask whether they can afford *not* to have a perpetual inventory system because timely access to inventory information is a competitive advantage and it can help reduce the amount of inventory, which reduces costs.

Point: Under weighted average, a unit sold is assigned the average cost of all items currently available for sale at the date of each sale. This means a new average cost is computed after each purchase.

Point: Cost of goods available for sale, units available for sale, and units in ending inventory are identical for all methods.

A1

Analyze the effects of inventory methods for both financial and tax reporting.

Financial Statement Effects of Costing Methods   When purchase prices do not change, each inventory costing method assigns the same cost amounts to inventory and to cost of goods sold. When purchase prices are different, however, the methods nearly always assign different cost amounts. We show these differences in Exhibit 5A.6 using Trekking's data.

EXHIBIT 5A.6

Financial Statement
Effects of Inventory
Costing Methods

TREKKING COMPANY For Month Ended August 31	Specific Identification	FIFO	LIFO	Weighted Average
Income Statement				
Sales	$ 6,050	$ 6,050	$ 6,050	$ 6,050
Cost of goods sold	4,582	4,570	4,730	4,622
Gross profit	1,468	1,480	1,320	1,428
Expenses	450	450	450	450
Income before taxes	1,018	1,030	870	978
Income tax expense (30%)	305	309	261	293
Net income	$ 713	$ 721	$ 609	$ 685
Balance Sheet				
Inventory	$1,408	$1,420	$1,260	$1,368

This exhibit reveals two important results. First, when purchase costs *regularly rise,* as in Trekking's case, the following occurs:

- FIFO assigns the lowest amount to cost of goods sold—yielding the highest gross profit and net income.
- LIFO assigns the highest amount to cost of goods sold—yielding the lowest gross profit and net income, which also yields a temporary tax advantage by postponing payment of some income tax.
- Weighted average yields results between FIFO and LIFO.
- Specific identification always yields results that depend on which units are sold.

Second, when costs *regularly decline,* the reverse occurs for FIFO and LIFO. Namely, FIFO gives the highest cost of goods sold—yielding the lowest gross profit and income. However, LIFO then gives the lowest cost of goods sold—yielding the highest gross profit and income.

All four inventory costing methods are acceptable. However, a company must disclose the inventory method it uses in its financial statements or notes. Each method offers certain advantages as follows:

- FIFO assigns an amount to inventory on the balance sheet that approximates its current cost; it also mimics the actual flow of goods for most businesses.
- LIFO assigns an amount to cost of goods sold on the income statement that approximates its current cost; it also better matches current costs with revenues in computing gross profit.
- Weighted average tends to smooth out erratic changes in costs.
- Specific identification exactly matches the costs of items with the revenues they generate.

Point: Managers prefer FIFO when costs are rising *and* incentives exist to report higher income for reasons such as bonus plans, job security, and reputation.

Point: LIFO inventory is often less than the inventory's replacement cost because LIFO inventory is valued using the oldest inventory purchase costs.

A company reported the following December purchases and sales data for its only product.

NEED-TO-KNOW 5-5

Perpetual SI, FIFO,
LIFO, and WA

P3

Date	Activities	Units Acquired at Cost	Units Sold at Retail
Dec. 1	Beginning inventory.........	5 units @ $3.00 = $ 15.00	
Dec. 8	Purchase	10 units @ $4.50 = 45.00	
Dec. 9	Sales.....................		8 units @ $7.00
Dec. 19	Purchase	13 units @ $5.00 = 65.00	
Dec. 24	Sales.....................		18 units @ $8.00
Dec. 30	Purchase	8 units @ $5.30 = 42.40	
Totals	....	36 units $167.40	26 units

The company uses a *perpetual inventory system.* Determine the cost assigned to ending inventory and to cost of goods sold using (*a*) specific identification, (*b*) FIFO, (*c*) LIFO, and (*d*) weighted average. (Round per unit costs and inventory amounts to cents.) For specific identification, ending inventory consists of 10 units, where 8 are from the December 30 purchase and 2 are from the December 8 purchase.

Solutions

a. Specific identification: Ending inventory—eight units from December 30 purchase and two units from December 8 purchase.

Merchandise Inventory (SI)

Beg. inventory	15.00		
Net purchases	152.40		
Avail. for sale	167.40		
		COGS	116.00
End. inventory	51.40		

Specific Identification	Ending Inventory	Cost of Goods Sold
(8 × $5.30) + (2 × $4.50)	$51.40	
(5 × $3.00) + (8 × $4.50) + (13 × $5.00) + (0 × $5.30)		$116.00
or $167.40 [Total Goods Available] − $51.40 [Ending Inventory]		$116.00

b. FIFO—Perpetual

Date	Goods Purchased	Cost of Goods Sold	Inventory Balance
12/1			5 @ $3.00 = $15.00
12/8	10 @ $4.50		5 @ $3.00 10 @ $4.50 } = $60.00
12/9		5 @ $3.00 3 @ $4.50 } = $ 28.50	7 @ $4.50 = $31.50
12/19	13 @ $5.00		7 @ $4.50 13 @ $5.00 } = $96.50
12/24		7 @ $4.50 11 @ $5.00 } = $ 86.50	2 @ $5.00 = $10.00
12/30	8 @ $5.30	 $115.00	2 @ $5.00 8 @ $5.30 } = $52.40

Merchandise Inventory (FIFO)

Beg. inventory	15.00		
Net purchases	152.40		
Avail. for sale	167.40		
		COGS	115.00
End. inventory	52.40		

OR "short-cut" FIFO—Perpetual

FIFO	Ending Inventory	Cost of Goods Sold
(8 × $5.30) + (2 × $5.00)	$52.40	
(5 × $3.00) + (10 × $4.50) + (11 × $5.00)		$115.00
or $167.40 [Total Goods Available] − $52.40 [Ending Inventory]		$115.00

c. LIFO—Perpetual

Date	Goods Purchased	Cost of Goods Sold	Inventory Balance
12/1			5 @ $3.00 = $15.00
12/8	10 @ $4.50		5 @ $3.00 10 @ $4.50 } = $60.00
12/9		8 @ $4.50 = $ 36.00	5 @ $3.00 2 @ $4.50 } = $24.00
12/19	13 @ $5.00		5 @ $3.00 2 @ $4.50 13 @ $5.00 } = $89.00
12/24		13 @ $5.00 2 @ $4.50 3 @ $3.00 } = $ 83.00	2 @ $3.00 = $ 6.00
12/30	8 @ $5.30	 $119.00	2 @ $3.00 8 @ $5.30 } = $48.40

Merchandise Inventory (LIFO)

Beg. inventory	15.00		
Net purchases	152.40		
Avail. for sale	167.40		
		COGS	119.00
End. inventory	48.40		

d. Weighted Average—Perpetual

Date	Goods Purchased	Cost of Goods Sold	Inventory Balance
12/1			5 @ $3.00 = $15.00 (5 @ $3.00 per unit)
12/8	10 @ $4.50		5 @ $3.00 } = $60.00 10 @ $4.50 ($60.00/15 units = $4.00 avg. cost)
12/9		8 @ $4.00 = $ 32.00	7 @ $4.00 = $28.00 (7 @ $4.00 per unit)
12/19	13 @ $5.00		7 @ $4.00 } = $93.00 13 @ $5.00 ($93.00/20 units = $4.65 avg. cost)
12/24		18 @ $4.65 = $ 83.70	2 @ $4.65 = $ 9.30 (2 @ $4.65 per unit)
12/30	8 @ $5.30	$115.70	2 @ $4.65 } = $51.70 8 @ $5.30 ($51.70/10 units = $5.17 avg. cost)

Merchandise Inventory (WA)

Beg. inventory	15.00		
Net purchases	152.40		
Avail. for sale	167.40		
		COGS	115.70
End. inventory	51.70		

Do More: QS 5-7, QS 5-8,
QS 5-9, QS 5-14, QS 5-15,
QS 5-16, QS 5-17

Inventory Estimation Methods

5B

P4

Apply both the retail inventory and gross profit methods to estimate inventory.

Inventory sometimes requires estimation for two reasons. First, companies often require **interim statements** (financial statements prepared for periods of less than one year), but they only annually take a physical count of inventory. Second, companies may require an inventory estimate if some casualty such as fire or flood makes taking a physical count impossible. Estimates are usually only required for companies that use the periodic system. Companies using a perpetual system would presumably have updated inventory data.

This appendix describes two methods to estimate inventory.

Retail Inventory Method   To avoid the time-consuming and expensive process of taking a physical inventory each month or quarter, some companies use the **retail inventory method** to estimate cost of goods sold and ending inventory. Some companies even use the retail inventory method to prepare the annual statements. **Home Depot**, for instance, says in its annual report: "Inventories are stated at the lower of cost (first-in, first-out) or market, as determined by the retail inventory method." A company may also estimate inventory for audit purposes or when inventory is damaged or destroyed.

The retail inventory method uses a three-step process to estimate ending inventory. We need to know the amount of inventory a company had at the beginning of the period in both *cost* and *retail* amounts. We already explained how to compute the cost of inventory. The *retail amount of inventory* refers to its dollar amount measured using selling prices of inventory items. We also need to know the net amount of goods purchased (minus returns, allowances, and discounts) in the period, both at cost and at retail. The amount of net sales at retail is also needed. The process is shown in Exhibit 5B.1.

The reasoning behind the retail inventory method is that if we can get a good estimate of the cost-to-retail ratio, we can multiply ending inventory at retail by

Point: When a retailer takes a physical inventory, it can restate the retail value of inventory to a cost basis by applying the cost-to-retail ratio. It can also estimate the amount of shrinkage by comparing the inventory computed with the amount from a physical inventory.

EXHIBIT 5B.1

Retail Inventory Method of Inventory Estimation

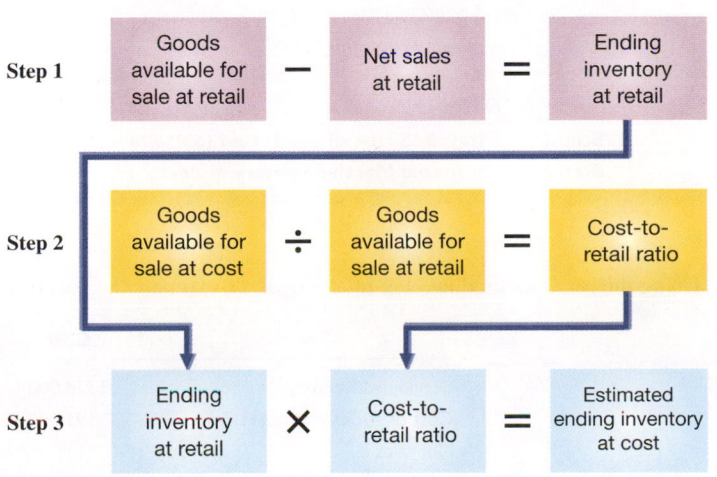

this ratio to estimate ending inventory at cost. We show in Exhibit 5B.2 how these steps are applied to esti-mate ending inventory for a typical company. First, we find that $100,000 of goods (at retail selling prices) were available for sale. We see that $70,000 of these goods were sold, leaving $30,000 (retail value) of merchandise in ending inventory. Second, the cost of these goods is 60% of the $100,000 retail value. Third, since cost for these goods is 60% of retail, the estimated cost of ending inventory is $18,000.

EXHIBIT 5B.2

Estimated Inventory Using the Retail Inventory Method

			At Cost	At Retail
Goods available for sale				
Beginning inventory			$ 20,500	$ 34,500
Cost of goods purchased			39,500	65,500
Goods available for sale			60,000	100,000
Step 1:	Deduct net sales at retail			70,000
	Ending inventory at retail			$ 30,000
Step 2:	Cost-to-retail ratio: ($60,000 ÷ $100,000) = 60%			
Step 3:	Estimated ending inventory at cost ($30,000 × 60%)		$18,000	

Point: A retailer such as **Target** can speed up its year-end physical count by using the retail inventory method. Inventory counters can record the item's retail price without having to look up the cost of each item.

Gross Profit Method

The **gross profit method** estimates the cost of ending inventory by applying the gross profit ratio to net sales (at retail). This type of estimate often is needed when inventory is destroyed, lost, or stolen. These cases require an inventory estimate so that a company can file a claim with its insurer. Users also apply this method to see whether inventory amounts from a physical count are reasonable. This method uses the historical relation between cost of goods sold and net sales to estimate the proportion of cost of goods sold making up current sales. This cost of goods sold estimate is then subtracted from cost of goods available for sale to estimate the ending inventory at cost. These two steps are shown in Exhibit 5B.3.

EXHIBIT 5B.3

Gross Profit Method of Inventory Estimation

Step 1: Net sales at retail × (1.0 – Gross profit ratio) = Estimated cost of goods sold

Step 2: Goods available for sale at cost − Estimated cost of goods sold = Estimated ending inventory at cost

Point: Reliability of the gross profit method depends on an accurate and stable estimate of the gross profit ratio.

Point: A fire or other catas-trophe can result in an insur-ance claim for lost inventory or income. Backup and off-site storage of data help ensure coverage for such losses.

To illustrate, assume that a company's inventory is destroyed by fire in March 2016. When the fire occurs, the company's accounts show the following balances for January through March: Net Sales, $30,000; Inventory, $12,000 (at January 1, 2016); and Cost of Goods Purchased, $20,500. If this company's gross profit ratio is 30%, then 30% of each net sales dollar is gross profit and 70% is cost of goods sold. We show in Exhibit 5B.4 how this 70% is used to estimate lost inventory of $11,500. To understand this exhibit, think of subtracting the cost of goods sold from the goods available for sale to get the ending inventory.

EXHIBIT 5B.4

Estimated Inventory Using the Gross Profit Method

Goods available for sale		
Inventory, January 1, 2016		$ 12,000
Cost of goods purchased		20,500
Goods available for sale (at cost)		32,500
Net sales at retail		$30,000
Step 1:	Estimated cost of goods sold ($30,000 × 70%)	(21,000) × 0.70
Step 2:	Estimated March inventory at cost	$11,500

NEED-TO-KNOW 5-6

Retail Inventory Estimation

P4

Using the retail method and the following data, estimate the cost of ending inventory.

	Cost	Retail
Beginning inventory	$324,000	$530,000
Cost of goods purchased	195,000	335,000
Net sales		320,000

Solution

Estimated ending inventory (at cost) is $327,000. It is computed as follows:

Step 1: ($530,000 + $335,000) − $320,000 = $545,000

Step 2: $\dfrac{\$324,000 + \$195,000}{\$530,000 + \$335,000} = 60\%$

Step 3: $545,000 × 60\% = \underline{\$327,000}$

Do More: QS 5-22, E 5-16, E 5-17

Summary

C1 **Identify the items making up merchandise inventory.** Merchandise inventory refers to goods owned by a company and held for resale. Three special cases merit our attention. Goods in transit are reported in inventory of the company that holds ownership rights. Goods on consignment are reported in the consignor's inventory. Goods damaged or obsolete are reported in inventory at their net realizable value.

C2 **Identify the costs of merchandise inventory.** Costs of merchandise inventory include expenditures necessary to bring an item to a salable condition and location. This includes its invoice cost minus any discount plus any added or incidental costs necessary to put it in a place and condition for sale.

A1 **Analyze the effects of inventory methods for both financial and tax reporting.** When purchase costs are rising or falling, the inventory costing methods are likely to assign different costs to inventory. Specific identification exactly matches costs and revenues. Weighted average smooths out cost changes. FIFO assigns an amount to inventory closely approximating current replacement cost. LIFO assigns the most recent costs incurred to cost of goods sold and likely better matches current costs with revenues.

A2 **Analyze the effects of inventory errors on current and future financial statements.** An error in the amount of ending inventory affects assets (inventory), net income (cost of goods sold), and equity for that period. Since ending inventory is next period's beginning inventory, an error in ending inventory affects next period's cost of goods sold and net income. Inventory errors in one period are offset in the next period.

A3 **Assess inventory management using both inventory turnover and days' sales in inventory.** We prefer a high inventory turnover, provided that goods are not out of stock and customers are not turned away. We use days' sales in inventory to assess the likelihood of goods being out of stock. We prefer a small number of days' sales in inventory if we can serve customer needs and provide a buffer for uncertainties.

P1 **Compute inventory in a periodic system using the methods of specific identification, FIFO, LIFO, and weighted average.** Periodic inventory systems allocate the cost of goods available for sale between cost of goods sold and ending inventory *at the end of a period*. Specific identification and FIFO give identical results whether the periodic or perpetual system is used. LIFO assigns costs to cost of goods sold assuming the last units purchased for the period are the first units sold. The weighted average cost per unit is computed by dividing the total cost of beginning inventory and net purchases for the period by the total number of units available. Then, it multiplies cost per unit by the number of units sold to give cost of goods sold.

P2 **Compute the lower of cost or market amount of inventory.** Inventory is reported at market cost when market is *lower* than recorded cost, called the *lower of cost or market (LCM) inventory*. Market is typically measured as replacement cost. Lower of cost or market can be applied separately to each item, to major categories of items, or to the entire inventory.

P3A **Compute inventory in a perpetual system using the methods of specific identification, FIFO, LIFO, and weighted average.** Costs are assigned to the Cost of Goods Sold account *each time* a sale occurs in a perpetual system. Specific identification assigns a cost to each item sold by referring to its actual cost (for example, its net invoice cost). Weighted average assigns a cost to items sold by dividing the current balance in the Inventory account by the total items available for sale to determine cost per unit. We then multiply the number of units sold by this cost per unit to get the cost of each sale. FIFO assigns cost to items sold assuming that the earliest units purchased are the first units sold. LIFO assigns cost to items sold assuming that the most recent units purchased are the first units sold.

P4B **Apply both the retail inventory and gross profit methods to estimate inventory.** The retail inventory method involves three steps: (1) goods available at retail minus net sales at retail equals ending inventory at retail, (2) goods available at cost divided by goods available at retail equals the cost-to-retail ratio, and (3) ending inventory at retail multiplied by the cost-to-retail ratio equals estimated ending inventory at cost. The gross profit method involves two steps: (1) net sales at retail multiplied by 1 minus the gross profit ratio equals estimated cost of goods sold and (2) goods available at cost minus estimated cost of goods sold equals estimated ending inventory at cost.

Guidance Answers to Decision Maker and Decision Ethics

Cost Analyst   Explain to your supervisor that when inventory costs are increasing, FIFO results in an inventory valuation that approximates replacement cost. The most recently purchased goods are assigned to ending inventory under FIFO and are likely closer to replacement values than earlier costs that would be assigned to inventory if LIFO were used.

Inventory Manager   It seems your company can save (or at least postpone) taxes by switching to LIFO, but the switch is likely to reduce bonus money that you think you have earned and deserve. Since the U.S. tax code requires companies that use LIFO for tax reporting also to use it for financial reporting, your options are further constrained. Your best decision is to tell your superior about the tax savings with LIFO. You also should

discuss your bonus plan and how this is likely to hurt you unfairly. You might propose to compute inventory under the LIFO method for reporting purposes but use the FIFO method for your bonus calculations. Another solution is to revise the bonus plan to reflect the company's use of the LIFO method.

Entrepreneur   Your inventory turnover is markedly higher than the norm, whereas days' sales in inventory approximates the norm. Since your turnover is already 14% better than average, you are probably best served by directing attention to days' sales in inventory. You should see whether you can reduce the level of inventory while maintaining service to customers. Given your higher turnover, you should be able to hold less inventory.

Key Terms

Average cost

Conservatism constraint

Consignee

Consignor

Consistency concept

Days' sales in inventory

First-in, first-out (FIFO)

Gross profit method

Interim statements (interim financial statements)

Inventory turnover

Last-in, first-out (LIFO)

Lower of cost or market (LCM)

Net realizable value

Retail inventory method

Specific identification

Weighted average

Multiple Choice Quiz   Answers at end of chapter

Use the following information from Marvel Company for the month of July to answer questions 1 through 4.

July 1	Beginning inventory	75 units @ $25 each
July 3	Purchase	348 units @ $27 each
July 8	Sale	300 units
July 15	Purchase	257 units @ $28 each
July 23	Sale	275 units

1. **Periodic:** Assume that Marvel uses a *periodic* FIFO inventory system. What is the dollar value of its ending inventory?
   a. $2,940   **d.** $2,852
   b. $2,685   **e.** $2,705
   c. $2,625

2. **Periodic and Perpetual:** Assume that Marvel uses a specific identification inventory system. Its ending inventory consists of 20 units from beginning inventory, 40 units from the July 3 purchase, and 45 units from the July 15 purchase. What is the dollar value of its ending inventory?
   a. $2,940   **d.** $2,852
   b. $2,685   **e.** $2,840
   c. $2,625

3. **Perpetual:** Assume that Marvel uses a *perpetual* FIFO inventory system. What is the dollar value of its ending inventory?
   a. $2,940   **d.** $2,852
   b. $2,685   **e.** $2,705
   c. $2,625

4. **Perpetual:** Assume that Marvel uses a *perpetual* LIFO inventory system. What is the dollar value of its ending inventory?
   a. $2,940   **d.** $2,852
   b. $2,685   **e.** $2,705
   c. $2,625

5. **Periodic:** A company reports the following beginning inventory and purchases, and it ends the period with 30 units in inventory.

Beginning inventory	100 units at $10 cost per unit
Purchase 1..............	40 units at $12 cost per unit
Purchase 2..............	20 units at $14 cost per unit

   i) Compute ending inventory using the FIFO *periodic* system.
   a. $400   **b.** $1,460   **c.** $1,360   **d.** $300
   ii) Compute cost of goods sold using the LIFO *periodic* system.
   a. $400   **b.** $1,460   **c.** $1,360   **d.** $300

6. A company has cost of goods sold of $85,000 and ending inventory of $18,000. Its days' sales in inventory equals:
   a. 49.32 days   **d.** 77.29 days
   b. 0.21 day   **e.** 1,723.61 days
   c. 4.72 days

$^{A(B)}$ *Superscript letter A(B) denotes assignments based on Appendix 5A (5B).*
🛈 Icon denotes assignments that involve decision making.

Discussion Questions

1. Describe how costs flow from inventory to cost of goods sold for the following methods: (*a*) FIFO and (*b*) LIFO.

2. Where is the amount of merchandise inventory disclosed in the financial statements?

3. Why are incidental costs sometimes ignored in inventory costing? Under what accounting constraint is this permitted?

4. 🛈 If costs are declining, will the LIFO or FIFO method of inventory valuation yield the lower cost of goods sold? Why?

5. What does the full-disclosure principle prescribe if a company changes from one acceptable accounting method to another?

6. Can a company change its inventory method each accounting period? Explain.

7. 🛈 Does the accounting concept of consistency preclude any changes from one accounting method to another?

8. 🛈 If inventory errors are said to correct themselves, why are accounting users concerned when such errors are made?

9. Explain the following statement: "Inventory errors correct themselves."

10. What is the meaning of *market* as it is used in determining the lower of cost or market for inventory?

11. 🛈 What guidance does the accounting constraint of conservatism offer?

12. What factors contribute to (or cause) inventory shrinkage?

13.^{B} When preparing interim financial statements, what two methods can companies utilize to estimate cost of goods sold and ending inventory?

14. Refer to **Google**'s financial statements in Appendix A. On December 31, 2014, what percent of current assets is represented by inventory?   **GOOGLE**

15. Refer to **Apple**'s financial statements in Appendix A and compute its cost of goods available for sale for the year ended September 27, 2014.   **APPLE**

16. Refer to **Samsung**'s financial statements in Appendix A. Compute its cost of goods available for sale for the year ended December 31, 2014.   **Samsung**

17. Refer to **Samsung**'s financial statements in Appendix A. What percent of its current assets is inventory as of December 31, 2014 and 2013?   **Samsung**

---

connect

Homestead Crafts, a distributor of handmade gifts, operates out of owner Emma Finn's house. At the end of the current period, Emma reports she has:

- 1,300 units (products) in her basement, 20 of which were damaged by water and cannot be sold.
- 350 units in her van, ready to deliver per a customer order, terms FOB destination.
- 80 units out on consignment to a friend who owns a retail store.

How many units should Emma include in her company's period-end inventory?

QUICK STUDY

QS 5-1
Inventory ownership
C1

A car dealer acquires a used car for $14,000, terms FOB shipping point. Additional costs in obtaining and offering the car for sale include:

- $250 for transportation-in.
- $300 for insurance during shipment.
- $900 for import duties.
- $150 for advertising.
- $1,250 for sales staff salaries.

For computing inventory, what cost is assigned to the used car?

QS 5-2
Inventory costs
C2

Wattan Company reports beginning inventory of 10 units at $60 each. Every week for four weeks it purchases an additional 10 units at respective costs of $61, $62, $65, and $70 per unit for weeks 1 through 4. Compute the cost of goods available for sale and the units available for sale for this four-week period. Assume that no sales occur during those four weeks.

QS 5-3
Computing goods available for sale   **P1**

QS 5-4
Periodic: Inventory costing with FIFO
P1

A company reports the following beginning inventory and two purchases for the month of January. Also, on January 26, the company sells 350 units. Ending inventory at January 31 totals 150 units.

	Units	Unit Cost
Beginning inventory on January 1	320	$3.00
Purchase on January 9	80	3.20
Purchase on January 25	100	3.34

Required

Assume the periodic inventory system is used and then determine the costs assigned to ending inventory when costs are assigned based on the FIFO method. (Round per unit costs and inventory amounts to cents.)

QS 5-5
Periodic: Inventory costing with LIFO **P1**

Refer to the information in QS 5-4 and assume the periodic inventory system is used. Determine the costs assigned to ending inventory when costs are assigned based on LIFO. (Round per unit costs and inventory amounts to cents.)

QS 5-6
Periodic: Inventory costing with weighted average **P1**

Refer to the information in QS 5-4 and assume the periodic inventory system is used. Determine the costs assigned to ending inventory when costs are assigned based on the weighted average method. (Round per unit costs and inventory amounts to cents.)

QS 5-7[A]
Perpetual: Inventory costing with FIFO **P3**

Refer to the information in QS 5-4 and assume the perpetual inventory system is used. Determine the costs assigned to ending inventory when costs are assigned based on the FIFO method. (Round per unit costs and inventory amounts to cents.)

QS 5-8[A]
Perpetual: Inventory costing with LIFO **P3**

Refer to the information in QS 5-4 and assume the perpetual inventory system is used. Determine the costs assigned to ending inventory when costs are assigned based on the LIFO method. (Round per unit costs and inventory amounts to cents.)

QS 5-9[A]
Perpetual: Inventory costing with weighted average **P3**
Check End. inv., $465

Refer to the information in QS 5-4 and assume the perpetual inventory system is used. Determine the costs assigned to ending inventory when costs are assigned based on the weighted average method. (Round per unit costs and inventory amounts to cents.)

QS 5-10
Periodic: Assigning costs with FIFO
P1

Trey Monson starts a merchandising business on December 1 and enters into the following three inventory purchases. Also, on December 15, Monson sells 15 units for $20 each.

Purchases on December 7	10 units @ $ 6.00 cost
Purchases on December 14	20 units @ $12.00 cost
Purchases on December 21	15 units @ $14.00 cost

Required

Monson uses a periodic inventory system. Determine the costs assigned to the December 31 ending inventory based on the FIFO method. (Round per unit costs and inventory amounts to cents.)

QS 5-11
Periodic: Inventory costing with LIFO **P1**

Refer to the information in QS 5-10 and assume the periodic inventory system is used. Determine the costs assigned to ending inventory when costs are assigned based on the LIFO method. (Round per unit costs and inventory amounts to cents.)

QS 5-12
Periodic: Inventory costing with weighted average **P1**

Refer to the information in QS 5-10 and assume the periodic inventory system is used. Determine the costs assigned to ending inventory when costs are assigned based on the weighted average method. (Round per unit costs and inventory amounts to cents.)

Refer to the information in QS 5-10 and assume the periodic inventory system is used. Determine the costs assigned to ending inventory when costs are assigned based on specific identification. Of the units sold, eight are from the December 7 purchase and seven are from the December 14 purchase. (Round per unit costs and inventory amounts to cents.)

QS 5-13
Periodic: Inventory costing with specific identification **P1**

Refer to the information in QS 5-10 and assume the perpetual inventory system is used. Determine the costs assigned to ending inventory when costs are assigned based on the FIFO method. (Round per unit costs and inventory amounts to cents.)

QS 5-14^A
Perpetual: Inventory costing with FIFO **P3**

Refer to the information in QS 5-10 and assume the perpetual inventory system is used. Determine the costs assigned to ending inventory when costs are assigned based on the LIFO method. (Round per unit costs and inventory amounts to cents.)

QS 5-15^A
Perpetual: Inventory costing with LIFO **P3**

Refer to the information in QS 5-10 and assume the perpetual inventory system is used. Determine the costs assigned to ending inventory when costs are assigned based on the weighted average method. (Round per unit costs and inventory amounts to cents.)

QS 5-16^A
Perpetual: Inventory costing with weighted average **P3**
Check End. inv., $360

Refer to the information in QS 5-10 and assume the perpetual inventory system is used. Determine the costs assigned to ending inventory when costs are assigned based on specific identification. Of the units sold, eight are from the December 7 purchase and seven are from the December 14 purchase. (Round per unit costs and inventory amounts to cents.)

QS 5-17^A
Perpetual: Inventory costing with specific identification **P3**

Identify the inventory costing method best described by each of the following separate statements. Assume a period of increasing costs.

_____ **1.** Yields a balance sheet inventory amount often markedly less than its replacement cost.
_____ **2.** Results in a balance sheet inventory amount approximating replacement cost.
_____ **3.** Provides a tax advantage (deferral) to a corporation when costs are rising.
_____ **4.** Recognizes (matches) recent costs against net sales.
_____ **5.** The preferred method when each unit of product has unique features that markedly affect cost.

QS 5-18
Contrasting inventory costing methods
A1

Ames Trading Co. has the following products in its ending inventory. Compute lower of cost or market for inventory applied separately to each product.

Product	Quantity	Cost per Unit	Market per Unit
Mountain bikes.........	11	$600	$550
Skateboards	13	350	425
Gliders	26	800	700

QS 5-19
Applying LCM to inventories
P2

In taking a physical inventory at the end of year 2016, Grant Company forgot to count certain units. Explain how this error affects the following: (*a*) 2016 cost of goods sold, (*b*) 2016 gross profit, (*c*) 2016 net income, (*d*) 2017 net income, (*e*) the combined two-year income, and (*f*) income for years after 2017.

QS 5-20
Inventory errors
A2

Endor Company begins the year with $140,000 of goods in inventory. At year-end, the amount in inventory has increased to $180,000. Cost of goods sold for the year is $1,200,000. Compute Endor's inventory turnover and days' sales in inventory. Assume that there are 365 days in the year.

QS 5-21
Analyzing inventory **A3**

QS 5-22ᴮ
Estimating inventories—
gross profit method
P4

Confucius Bookstore's inventory is destroyed by a fire on September 5, 2016. The following data for year 2016 are available from the accounting records. Estimate the cost of the inventory destroyed.

Jan. 1 inventory	$190,000
Jan. 1 through Sept. 5 purchases (net)	$352,000
Jan. 1 through Sept. 5 sales (net)..............	$685,000
Year 2016 estimated gross profit rate..........	44%

QS 5-23
International accounting
standards

C1   C2   P2

Answer each of the following questions related to international accounting standards.

a. Explain how the accounting for items and costs making up merchandise inventory is different between IFRS and U.S. GAAP.

b. Can companies reporting under IFRS apply a cost flow assumption in assigning costs to inventory? If yes, identify at least two acceptable cost flow assumptions.

c. Both IFRS and U.S. GAAP apply the lower of cost or market method for reporting inventory values. If inventory is written down from applying the lower of cost or market method, explain in general terms how IFRS and U.S. GAAP differ in accounting for any subsequent period reversal of that reported decline in inventory value.

EXERCISES

Exercise 5-1
Inventory ownership
C1

1. At year-end, Harris Company had shipped $12,500 of merchandise FOB destination to Harlow Co. Which company should include the $12,500 of merchandise in transit as part of its year-end inventory?

2. Harris Company has shipped $20,000 of goods to Harlow Co., and Harlow Co. has arranged to sell the goods for Harris. Identify the consignor and the consignee. Which company should include any unsold goods as part of its inventory?

Exercise 5-2
Inventory costs
C2

Walberg Associates, antique dealers, purchased the contents of an estate for $75,000. Terms of the purchase were FOB shipping point, and the cost of transporting the goods to Walberg Associates' warehouse was $2,400. Walberg Associates insured the shipment at a cost of $300. Prior to putting the goods up for sale, they cleaned and refurbished them at a cost of $980. Determine the cost of the inventory acquired from the estate.

Exercise 5-3
Periodic: Inventory
costing methods
P1

Laker Company reported the following January purchases and sales data for its only product.

Date	Activities	Units Acquired at Cost	Units Sold at Retail
Jan. 1	Beginning inventory	140 units @ $6.00 = $ 840	
Jan. 10	Sales		100 units @ $15
Jan. 20	Purchase	60 units @ $5.00 = 300	
Jan. 25	Sales		80 units @ $15
Jan. 30	Purchase	180 units @ $4.50 = 810	
	Totals	380 units $1,950	180 units

Required

The company uses a periodic inventory system. Determine the cost assigned to ending inventory and to cost of goods sold using (*a*) specific identification, (*b*) weighted average, (*c*) FIFO, and (*d*) LIFO. (Round per unit costs and inventory amounts to cents.) For specific identification, ending inventory consists of 200 units, where 180 are from the January 30 purchase, 5 are from the January 20 purchase, and 15 are from beginning inventory.

Exercise 5-4
Periodic: Income
effects of inventory
methods

A1

Use the data in Exercise 5-3 to prepare comparative income statements for the month of January for Laker Company similar to those shown in Exhibit 5.8 for the four inventory methods. Assume expenses are $1,250, and that the applicable income tax rate is 40%. (Round amounts to cents.)

1. Which method yields the highest net income?

2. Does net income using weighted average fall between that using FIFO and LIFO?

3. If costs were rising instead of falling, which method would yield the highest net income?

Refer to the information in Exercise 5-3 and assume the perpetual inventory system is used. Determine the costs assigned to ending inventory and to cost of goods sold using (*a*) specific identification, (*b*) weighted average, (*c*) FIFO, and (*d*) LIFO. (Round per unit costs and inventory amounts to cents.) For specific identification, ending inventory consists of 200 units, where 180 are from the January 30 purchase, 5 are from the January 20 purchase, and 15 are from beginning inventory.

Exercise 5-5[A]
Perpetual: Inventory costing   **P3**

Check   Ending inventory: WA, $918; LIFO, $930

Use the data and results from Exercise 5-5 to prepare comparative income statements for the month of January for the company similar to those shown in Exhibit 5.8 for the four inventory methods. Assume expenses are $1,250, and that the applicable income tax rate is 40%. (Round amounts to cents.)

Required

1. Which method yields the highest net income?
2. Does net income using weighted average fall between that using FIFO and LIFO?
3. If costs were rising instead of falling, which method would yield the highest net income?

Exercise 5-6[A]
Perpetual: Income effects of inventory methods

A1

Hemming Co. reported the following current-year purchases and sales for its only product.

Exercise 5-7
Periodic: Inventory costing methods—FIFO and LIFO

P1

Date	Activities	Units Acquired at Cost		Units Sold at Retail
Jan. 1	Beginning inventory	200 units @ $10 =	$ 2,000	
Jan. 10	Sales			150 units @ $40
Mar. 14	Purchase	350 units @ $15 =	5,250	
Mar. 15	Sales			300 units @ $40
July 30	Purchase	450 units @ $20 =	9,000	
Oct. 5	Sales			430 units @ $40
Oct. 26	Purchase	100 units @ $25 =	2,500	
	Totals	1,100 units	$18,750	880 units

Required

Hemming uses a periodic inventory system. Determine the costs assigned to ending inventory and to cost of goods sold using (*a*) FIFO and (*b*) LIFO. Compute the gross margin for each method. (Round amounts to cents.)

Refer to the information in Exercise 5-7. Ending inventory consists of 45 units from the March 14 purchase, 75 units from the July 30 purchase, and all 100 units from the October 26 purchase. Using the specific identification method, compute (*a*) the cost of goods sold and (*b*) the gross profit. (Round amounts to cents.)

Exercise 5-8
Specific identification

P1

Refer to the information in Exercise 5-7 and assume the perpetual inventory system is used. Determine the costs assigned to ending inventory and to cost of goods sold using (*a*) FIFO and (*b*) LIFO. Then (*c*) compute the gross margin for each method.

Exercise 5-9[A]
Perpetual: Inventory costing   **P3**

Check   Ending inventory: LIFO, $4,150

Martinez Company's ending inventory includes the following items. Compute the lower of cost or market for ending inventory applied separately to each product.

Exercise 5-10
Lower of cost or market

P2

Product	Units	Cost per Unit	Market per Unit
Helmets	24	$50	$54
Bats	17	78	72
Shoes	38	95	91
Uniforms	42	36	36

Check   LCM = $7,394

Exercise 5-11
Comparing LIFO
numbers to FIFO
numbers; ratio analysis

A1   A3

Cruz Company uses LIFO for inventory costing and reports the following financial data. It also recomputed inventory and cost of goods sold using FIFO for comparison purposes.

	2016	2015
LIFO inventory..............	$160	$110
LIFO cost of goods sold	740	680
FIFO inventory..............	240	110
FIFO cost of goods sold	660	645
Current assets (using LIFO) .	220	180
Current liabilities.........	200	170

Check   (1b) FIFO: Current
ratio, 1.5; Inventory turnover,
3.8 times

1. Compute its current ratio, inventory turnover, and days' sales in inventory for 2016 using (*a*) LIFO numbers and (*b*) FIFO numbers. (Round answers to one decimal.)
2. Comment on and interpret the results of part 1.

Exercise 5-12
Analysis of inventory
errors

A2

Vibrant Company had $850,000 of sales in each of three consecutive years 2015–2017, and it purchased merchandise costing $500,000 in each of those years. It also maintained a $250,000 physical inventory from the beginning to the end of that three-year period. In accounting for inventory, it made an error at the end of year 2015 that caused its year-end 2015 inventory to appear on its statements as $230,000 rather than the correct $250,000.

Check   2015 reported
gross profit, $330,000

1. Determine the correct amount of the company's gross profit in each of the years 2015–2017.
2. Prepare comparative income statements as in Exhibit 5.11 to show the effect of this error on the company's cost of goods sold and gross profit for each of the years 2015–2017.

Exercise 5-13
Inventory turnover and
days' sales in inventory

A3

Use the following information for Palmer Co. to compute inventory turnover for 2016 and 2015, and its days' sales in inventory at December 31, 2016 and 2015. (Round answers to one decimal.) Comment on Palmer's efficiency in using its assets to increase sales from 2015 to 2016.

	2016	2015	2014
Cost of goods sold	$643,825	$426,650	$391,300
Ending inventory	97,400	87,750	92,500

Exercise 5-14
Periodic: Cost flow
assumptions

P1

Lopez Company reported the following current-year data for its only product. The company uses a periodic inventory system, and its ending inventory consists of 150 units—50 from each of the last three purchases. Determine the cost assigned to ending inventory and to cost of goods sold using (*a*) specific identification, (*b*) weighted average, (*c*) FIFO, and (*d*) LIFO. (Round per unit costs and inventory amounts to cents.) Which method yields the highest net income?

Jan. 1	Beginning inventory	96 units @ $2.00 =	$ 192
Mar. 7	Purchase	220 units @ $2.25 =	495
July 28	Purchase	544 units @ $2.50 =	1,360
Oct. 3	Purchase	480 units @ $2.80 =	1,344
Dec. 19	Purchase	160 units @ $2.90 =	464
	Totals	1,500 units	$3,855

Check   Inventory: FIFO,
$435.00; LIFO, $313.50

Exercise 5-15
Periodic: Cost flow
assumptions

P1

Flora's Gifts reported the following current-month data for its only product. The company uses a periodic inventory system, and its ending inventory consists of 60 units—50 units from the January 6 purchase and 10 units from the January 25 purchase. Determine the cost assigned to ending inventory and to cost of goods sold using (*a*) specific identification, (*b*) weighted average, (*c*) FIFO, and (*d*) LIFO. (Round per unit costs and inventory amounts to cents.) Which method yields the lowest net income?

Jan.	1	Beginning inventory	138 units @ $3.00 =	$ 414
Jan.	6	Purchase	300 units @ $2.80 =	840
Jan.	17	Purchase	540 units @ $2.30 =	1,242
Jan.	25	Purchase	22 units @ $2.00 =	44
		Totals	1,000 units	$2,540

Check   Inventory: FIFO, $131.40; LIFO, $180.00

In 2016, Dakota Company had net sales (at retail) of $260,000. The following additional information is available from its records at the end of 2016. Use the retail inventory method to estimate Dakota's 2016 ending inventory at cost.

	At Cost	At Retail
Beginning inventory	$ 63,800	$128,400
Cost of goods purchased.........	115,060	196,800

Exercise 5-16ᴮ
Estimating ending inventory—retail method
P4

Check   End. inventory at cost, $35,860

On January 1, JKR Shop had $225,000 of inventory at cost. In the first quarter of the year, it purchased $795,000 of merchandise, returned $11,550, and paid freight charges of $18,800 on purchased merchandise, terms FOB shipping point. The company's gross profit averages 30%, and the store had $1,000,000 of net sales (at retail) in the first quarter of the year. Use the gross profit method to estimate its cost of inventory at the end of the first quarter.

Exercise 5-17ᴮ
Estimating ending inventory—gross profit method **P4**

Samsung Electronics reports the following regarding its accounting for inventories.

> Inventories are stated at the lower of cost or net realizable value. Cost is determined using the average cost method, except for materials-in-transit. Inventories are reduced for the estimated losses arising from excess, obsolescence, and the decline in value. This reduction is determined by estimating market value based on future customer demand. The losses on inventory obsolescence are recorded as a part of cost of sales.

Exercise 5-18
Accounting for inventory following IFRS
P2

Samsung

1. What cost flow assumption(s) does Samsung apply in assigning costs to its inventories?
2. If at year-end 2015 there was an increase in the value of its inventories such that there was a reversal of ₩550 (₩ is Korean won) million for the 2014 write-down, how would Samsung account for this under IFRS? Would Samsung's accounting be different for this reversal if it reported under U.S. GAAP? Explain.

🄼ᴳᴴ connect˙

Warnerwoods Company uses a periodic inventory system. It entered into the following purchases and sales transactions for March. (For specific identification, the March 9 sale consisted of 80 units from beginning inventory and 340 units from the March 5 purchase and the March 29 sale consisted of 40 units from the March 18 purchase and 120 units from the March 25 purchase.)

PROBLEM SET A

Problem 5-1A
Periodic: Alternative cost flows
P1

Date	Activities	Units Acquired at Cost	Units Sold at Retail
Mar. 1	Beginning inventory	100 units @ $50.00 per unit	
Mar. 5	Purchase...................	400 units @ $55.00 per unit	
Mar. 9	Sales		420 units @ $85.00 per unit
Mar. 18	Purchase...................	120 units @ $60.00 per unit	
Mar. 25	Purchase...................	200 units @ $62.00 per unit	
Mar. 29	Sales		160 units @ $95.00 per unit
	Totals	820 units	580 units

Required

1. Compute cost of goods available for sale and the number of units available for sale.
2. Compute the number of units in ending inventory.
3. Compute the cost assigned to ending inventory using (*a*) FIFO, (*b*) LIFO, (*c*) weighted average, and (*d*) specific identification. (Round all amounts to cents.)
4. Compute gross profit earned by the company for each of the four costing methods in part 3.

Check (3) Ending inventory: FIFO, $14,800; LIFO, $12,700, WA, $13,639.20
(4) LIFO gross profit, $17,000

Problem 5-2A^A

Perpetual: Alternative cost flows

P3

Refer to the information in Problem 5-1A and assume the perpetual inventory system is used.

Required

1. Compute cost of goods available for sale and the number of units available for sale.
2. Compute the number of units in ending inventory.
3. Compute the cost assigned to ending inventory using (*a*) FIFO, (*b*) LIFO, (*c*) weighted average, and (*d*) specific identification. (Round all amounts to cents.)
4. Compute gross profit earned by the company for each of the four costing methods in part 3.

Check (3) Ending inventory: FIFO, $14,800; WA, $14,352
(4) LIFO gross profit, $17,980

Problem 5-3A

Periodic: Alternative cost flows

P1

Montoure Company uses a periodic inventory system. It entered into the following calendar-year 2016 purchases and sales transactions. (For specific identification, units sold consist of 600 units from beginning inventory, 300 from the February 10 purchase, 200 from the March 13 purchase, 50 from the August 21 purchase, and 250 from the September 5 purchase.)

Date	Activities	Units Acquired at Cost	Units Sold at Retail
Jan. 1	Beginning inventory	600 units @ $45.00 per unit	
Feb. 10	Purchase...................	400 units @ $42.00 per unit	
Mar. 13	Purchase..................	200 units @ $27.00 per unit	
Mar. 15	Sales		800 units @ $75.00 per unit
Aug. 21	Purchase.................	100 units @ $50.00 per unit	
Sept. 5	Purchase..................	500 units @ $46.00 per unit	
Sept. 10	Sales		600 units @ $75.00 per unit
	Totals	1,800 units	1,400 units

Required

1. Compute cost of goods available for sale and the number of units available for sale.
2. Compute the number of units in ending inventory.
3. Compute the cost assigned to ending inventory using (*a*) FIFO, (*b*) LIFO, (*c*) weighted average, and (*d*) specific identification. (Round all amounts to cents.)
4. Compute gross profit earned by the company for each of the four costing methods in part 3.

Check (3) Ending inventory: FIFO, $18,400; LIFO, $18,000; WA, $17,156
(4) LIFO gross profit, $45,800

Analysis Component

5. If the company's manager earns a bonus based on a percent of gross profit, which method of inventory costing will the manager likely prefer?

Problem 5-4A^A

Perpetual: Alternative cost flows

P3

Refer to the information in Problem 5-3A and assume the perpetual inventory system is used.

Required

1. Compute cost of goods available for sale and the number of units available for sale.
2. Compute the number of units in ending inventory.
3. Compute the cost assigned to ending inventory using (*a*) FIFO, (*b*) LIFO, (*c*) weighted average, and (*d*) specific identification. (Round all amounts to cents.)
4. Compute gross profit earned by the company for each of the four costing methods in part 3.

Check (3) Ending inventory: FIFO, $18,400; WA, $17,760
(4) LIFO gross profit, $45,800

Analysis Component

5. If the company's manager earns a bonus based on a percentage of gross profit, which method of inventory costing will the manager likely prefer?

A physical inventory of Liverpool Company taken at December 31 reveals the following.

	A	B	C	D
1, 2	**Item**	**Units**	**Cost per Unit**	**Market per Unit**
3	Audio equipment			
4	Receivers	345	$ 90	$ 98
5	CD players	260	111	100
6	MP3 players	326	86	95
7	Speakers	204	52	41
8	Video equipment			
9	Handheld LCDs	480	150	125
10	VCRs	291	93	84
11	Camcorders	212	310	322
12	Car audio equipment			
13	Satellite radios	185	70	84
14	CD/MP3 radios	170	97	105
15				

Required

1. Compute the lower of cost or market for the inventory applied separately to each item.
2. If the market amount is less than the recorded cost of the inventory, then record the LCM adjustment to the Merchandise Inventory account.

Navajo Company's financial statements show the following. The company recently discovered that in making physical counts of inventory, it had made the following errors: Inventory on December 31, 2015, is understated by $56,000, and inventory on December 31, 2016, is overstated by $20,000.

For Year Ended December 31		2015	2016	2017
(a)	Cost of goods sold	$ 615,000	$ 957,000	$ 780,000
(b)	Net income	230,000	285,000	241,000
(c)	Total current assets	1,255,000	1,365,000	1,200,000
(d)	Total equity	1,387,000	1,530,000	1,242,000

Required

1. For each key financial statement figure—(a), (b), (c), and (d) above—prepare a table similar to the following to show the adjustments necessary to correct the reported amounts.

Figure: _____	2015	2016	2017
Reported amount			
Adjustments for: 12/31/2015 error			
12/31/2016 error			
Corrected amount			

Analysis Component

2. What is the error in total net income for the combined three-year period resulting from the inventory errors? Explain.
3. Explain why the understatement of inventory by $56,000 at the end of 2015 results in an understatement of equity by the same amount in that year.

Seminole Company began year 2016 with 23,000 units of product in its January 1 inventory costing $15 each. It made successive purchases of its product in year 2016 as follows. The company uses a periodic inventory system. On December 31, 2016, a physical count reveals that 40,000 units of its product remain in inventory.

Mar. 7	30,000 units @ $18.00 each
May 25	39,000 units @ $20.00 each
Aug. 1	23,000 units @ $25.00 each
Nov. 10	35,000 units @ $26.00 each

Required

Check (2) Cost of goods sold: FIFO, $2,115,000; LIFO, $2,499,000; WA, $2,310,000

1. Compute the number and total cost of the units available for sale in year 2016.
2. Compute the amounts assigned to the 2016 ending inventory and the cost of goods sold using (*a*) FIFO, (*b*) LIFO, and (*c*) weighted average. (Round all amounts to cents.)

Problem 5-8A
Periodic: Income comparisons and cost flows

A1   P1

QP Corp. sold 4,000 units of its product at $50 per unit in year 2016 and incurred operating expenses of $5 per unit in selling the units. It began the year with 700 units in inventory and made successive purchases of its product as follows.

Jan. 1	Beginning inventory.........	700 units @ $18.00 per unit
Feb. 20	Purchase	1,700 units @ $19.00 per unit
May 16	Purchase	800 units @ $20.00 per unit
Oct. 3	Purchase	500 units @ $21.00 per unit
Dec. 11	Purchase	2,300 units @ $22.00 per unit
	Total	6,000 units

Required

Check (1) Net income: FIFO, $61,200; LIFO, $57,180; WA, $59,196

1. Prepare comparative income statements similar to Exhibit 5.8 for the three inventory costing methods of FIFO, LIFO, and weighted average. (Round all amounts to cents.) Include a detailed cost of goods sold section as part of each statement. The company uses a periodic inventory system, and its income tax rate is 40%.
2. How would the financial results from using the three alternative inventory costing methods change if the company had been experiencing declining costs in its purchases of inventory?
3. What advantages and disadvantages are offered by using (*a*) LIFO and (*b*) FIFO? Assume the continuing trend of increasing costs.

Problem 5-9A[B]
Retail inventory method

P4

The records of Alaska Company provide the following information for the year ended December 31.

	At Cost	At Retail
January 1 beginning inventory........	$ 469,010	$ 928,950
Cost of goods purchased	3,376,050	6,381,050
Net sales		5,553,000

Required

Check (1) Inventory, $924,182 cost

(2) Inventory shortage at cost, $36,873

1. Use the retail inventory method to estimate the company's year-end inventory at cost.
2. A year-end physical inventory at retail prices yields a total inventory of $1,686,900. Prepare a calculation showing the company's loss from shrinkage at cost and at retail.

Problem 5-10A[B]
Gross profit method

P4

Wayward Company wants to prepare interim financial statements for the first quarter. The company wishes to avoid making a physical count of inventory. Wayward's gross profit rate averages 34%. The following information for the first quarter is available from its records.

January 1 beginning inventory	$ 302,580
Cost of goods purchased	941,040
Net sales	1,202,750

Required

Check Estim. ending inv., $449,805

Use the gross profit method to estimate the company's first-quarter ending inventory.

Ming Company uses a periodic inventory system. It entered into the following purchases and sales transactions for April. (For specific identification, the April 9 sale consisted of 8 units from beginning inventory and 27 units from the April 6 purchase; the April 30 sale consisted of 12 units from beginning inventory, 3 units from the April 6 purchase, and 10 units from the April 25 purchase.)

PROBLEM SET B

Problem 5-1B
Periodic: Alternative
cost flows
P1

Date	Activities	Units Acquired at Cost	Units Sold at Retail
Apr. 1	Beginning inventory	20 units @ $3,000.00 per unit	
Apr. 6	Purchase	30 units @ $3,500.00 per unit	
Apr. 9	Sales		35 units @ $12,000.00 per unit
Apr. 17	Purchase	5 units @ $4,500.00 per unit	
Apr. 25	Purchase	10 units @ $4,800.00 per unit	
Apr. 30	Sales		25 units @ $14,000.00 per unit
	Total	65 units	60 units

Required

1. Compute cost of goods available for sale and the number of units available for sale.
2. Compute the number of units in ending inventory.
3. Compute the cost assigned to ending inventory using (*a*) FIFO, (*b*) LIFO, (*c*) weighted average, and (*d*) specific identification. (Round all amounts to cents.)
4. Compute gross profit earned by the company for each of the four costing methods in part 3.

Check   (3) Ending inventory:
FIFO, $24,000; LIFO, $15,000;
WA, $18,115.40
         (4) LIFO gross
profit, $549,500

Refer to the information in Problem 5-1B and assume the perpetual inventory system is used.

Problem 5-2B^A
Perpetual: Alternative
cost flows   **P3**

Required

1. Compute cost of goods available for sale and the number of units available for sale.
2. Compute the number of units in ending inventory.
3. Compute the cost assigned to ending inventory using (*a*) FIFO, (*b*) LIFO, (*c*) weighted average, and (*d*) specific identification. (Round all amounts to cents.)
4. Compute gross profit earned by the company for each of the four costing methods in part 3.

Check   (3) Ending
inventory: FIFO, $24,000;
WA, $20,000
         (4) LIFO gross
profit, $549,500

Aloha Company uses a periodic inventory system. It entered into the following calendar-year 2016 purchases and sales transactions. (For specific identification, the May 9 sale consisted of 80 units from beginning inventory and 100 units from the May 6 purchase and the May 30 sale consisted of 200 units from the May 6 purchase and 100 units from the May 25 purchase.)

Problem 5-3B
Periodic: Alternative
cost flows

P1

Date	Activities	Units Acquired at Cost	Units Sold at Retail
May 1	Beginning inventory	150 units @ $300.00 per unit	
May 6	Purchase	350 units @ $350.00 per unit	
May 9	Sales		180 units @ $1,200.00 per unit
May 17	Purchase	80 units @ $450.00 per unit	
May 25	Purchase	100 units @ $458.00 per unit	
May 30	Sales		300 units @ $1,400.00 per unit
	Total	680 units	480 units

Required

1. Compute cost of goods available for sale and the number of units available for sale.
2. Compute the number of units in ending inventory.
3. Compute the cost assigned to ending inventory using (*a*) FIFO, (*b*) LIFO, (*c*) weighted average, and (*d*) specific identification. (Round all amounts to cents.)
4. Compute gross profit earned by the company for each of the four costing methods in part 3.

Check   (3) Ending
inventory: FIFO, $88,800;
LIFO, $62,500; WA, $73,324
         (4) LIFO gross
profit, $449,200

Analysis Component

5. If the company's manager earns a bonus based on a percent of gross profit, which method of inventory costing will the manager likely prefer?

Problem 5-4B[A]
Perpetual: Alternative cost flows

P3

Check   (3) Ending inventory: FIFO, $88,800; WA, $75,600
        (4) LIFO gross profit, $449,200

Refer to the information in Problem 5-3B and assume the perpetual inventory system is used.

Required

1. Compute cost of goods available for sale and the number of units available for sale.
2. Compute the number of units in ending inventory.
3. Compute the cost assigned to ending inventory using (*a*) FIFO, (*b*) LIFO, (*c*) weighted average, and (*d*) specific identification. (Round all amounts to cents.)
4. Compute gross profit earned by the company for each of the four costing methods in part 3.

Analysis Component

5. If the company's manager earns a bonus based on a percentage of gross profit, which method of inventory costing will the manager likely prefer?

Problem 5-5B
Lower of cost or market

P2

A physical inventory of Office Necessities Company taken at December 31 reveals the following.

	A	B	C	D
1	**Item**	**Units**	**Cost per Unit**	**Market per Unit**
2				
3	Office furniture			
4	Desks	536	$261	$305
5	Credenzas	395	227	256
6	Chairs	687	49	43
7	Bookshelves	421	93	82
8	Filing cabinets			
9	Two-drawer	114	81	70
10	Four-drawer	298	135	122
11	Lateral	75	104	118
12	Office equipment			
13	Fax machines	370	168	200
14	Copiers	475	317	288
15	Telephones	302	125	117
16				

Required

Check   (1) $580,054

1. Compute the lower of cost or market for the inventory applied separately to each item.
2. If the market amount is less than the recorded cost of the inventory, then record the LCM adjustment to the Merchandise Inventory account.

Problem 5-6B
Analysis of inventory errors

A2

Hallam Company's financial statements show the following. The company recently discovered that in making physical counts of inventory, it had made the following errors: Inventory on December 31, 2015, is overstated by $18,000, and inventory on December 31, 2016, is understated by $26,000.

For Year Ended December 31	2015	2016	2017
(*a*) Cost of goods sold	$207,200	$213,800	$197,030
(*b*) Net income	175,800	212,270	184,910
(*c*) Total current assets	276,000	277,500	272,950
(*d*) Total equity	314,000	315,000	346,000

Required

1. For each key financial statement figure—(*a*), (*b*), (*c*), and (*d*) above—prepare a table similar to the following to show the adjustments necessary to correct the reported amounts.

Figure: _____	2015	2016	2017
Reported amount	_____	_____	_____
Adjustments for: 12/31/2015 error	_____	_____	_____
12/31/2016 error	_____	_____	_____
Corrected amount	_____	_____	_____

Check (1) Corrected net income: 2015, $157,800; 2016, $256,270; 2017, $158,910

Analysis Component

2. What is the error in total net income for the combined three-year period resulting from the inventory errors? Explain.

3. Explain why the overstatement of inventory by $18,000 at the end of 2015 results in an overstatement of equity by the same amount in that year.

Seneca Co. began year 2016 with 6,500 units of product in its January 1 inventory costing $35 each. It made successive purchases of its product in year 2016 as follows. The company uses a periodic inventory system. On December 31, 2016, a physical count reveals that 8,500 units of its product remain in inventory.

Jan. 4	11,500 units @ $33 each
May 18	13,400 units @ $32 each
July 9	11,000 units @ $29 each
Nov. 21	7,600 units @ $27 each

Problem 5-7B
Periodic: Alternative cost flows

P1

Required

1. Compute the number and total cost of the units available for sale in year 2016.

2. Compute the amounts assigned to the 2016 ending inventory and the cost of goods sold using (*a*) FIFO, (*b*) LIFO, and (*c*) weighted average. (Round all amounts to cents.)

Check (2) Cost of goods sold: FIFO, $1,328,700; LIFO, $1,266,500; WA, $1,294,800

Shepard Company sold 4,000 units of its product at $100 per unit in year 2016 and incurred operating expenses of $15 per unit in selling the units. It began the year with 840 units in inventory and made successive purchases of its product as follows.

Jan. 1	Beginning inventory	840 units @ $58 per unit
April 2	Purchase	600 units @ $59 per unit
June 14	Purchase	1,205 units @ $61 per unit
Aug. 29	Purchase	700 units @ $64 per unit
Nov. 18	Purchase	1,655 units @ $65 per unit
	Total	5,000 units

Problem 5-8B
Periodic: Income comparisons and cost flows

A1 P1

Required

1. Prepare comparative income statements similar to Exhibit 5.8 for the three inventory costing methods of FIFO, LIFO, and weighted average. (Round all amounts to cents.) Include a detailed cost of goods sold section as part of each statement. The company uses a periodic inventory system, and its income tax rate is 40%.

2. How would the financial results from using the three alternative inventory costing methods change if the company had been experiencing decreasing prices in its purchases of inventory?

3. What advantages and disadvantages are offered by using (*a*) LIFO and (*b*) FIFO? Assume the continuing trend of increasing costs.

Check (1) Net income: LIFO, $52,896; FIFO, $57,000; WA, $55,200

Problem 5-9B^B
Retail inventory method
P4

The records of Macklin Co. provide the following information for the year ended December 31.

	At Cost	At Retail
January 1 beginning inventory.......	$ 90,022	$115,610
Cost of goods purchased	502,250	761,830
Net sales		778,840

Check   (1) Inventory,
$66,555 cost
           (2) Inventory
shortage at cost, $12,251.25

Required

1. Use the retail inventory method to estimate the company's year-end inventory.
2. A year-end physical inventory at retail prices yields a total inventory of $80,450. Prepare a calculation showing the company's loss from shrinkage at cost and at retail.

Problem 5-10B^B
Gross profit method
P4

Otingo Equipment Co. wants to prepare interim financial statements for the first quarter. The company wishes to avoid making a physical count of inventory. Otingo's gross profit rate averages 35%. The following information for the first quarter is available from its records.

January 1 beginning inventory.......	$ 802,880
Cost of goods purchased	2,209,636
Net sales	3,680,960

Required

Check   Estim. ending inv.,
$619,892

Use the gross profit method to estimate the company's first-quarter ending inventory.

SERIAL PROBLEM
Business Solutions

P2   A3

(This serial problem began in Chapter 1 and continues through most of the book. If previous chapter segments were not completed, the serial problem can begin at this point.)

SP 5
Part A

Santana Rey of Business Solutions is evaluating her inventory to determine whether it must be adjusted based on lower of cost or market rules. Business Solutions has three different types of software in its inventory, and the following information is available for each.

Inventory Items	Units	Cost per Unit	Market per Unit
Office productivity	3	$ 76	$ 74
Desktop publishing	2	103	100
Accounting	3	90	96

Required

1. Compute the lower of cost or market for ending inventory assuming Rey applies the lower of cost or market rule to inventory as a whole. Must Rey adjust the reported inventory value? Explain.
2. Assume that Rey had instead applied the lower of cost or market rule to each product in inventory. Under this assumption, must Rey adjust the reported inventory value? Explain.

Part B

Selected accounts and balances for the three months ended March 31, 2017, for Business Solutions follow.

January 1 beginning inventory........	$ 0
Cost of goods sold	13,652
March 31 ending inventory..........	704

Required

1. Compute inventory turnover and days' sales in inventory for the three months ended March 31, 2017.
2. Assess the company's performance if competitors average 15 times for inventory turnover and 25 days for days' sales in inventory.

Beyond the Numbers

BTN 5-1 Refer to **Apple**'s financial statements in Appendix A to answer the following.

Required

1. What amount of inventories did Apple report as a current asset on September 27, 2014? On September 28, 2013?
2. Inventories represent what percent of total assets on September 27, 2014? On September 28, 2013?
3. Comment on the relative size of Apple's inventories compared to its other types of assets.
4. What accounting method did Apple use to compute inventory amounts on its balance sheet?
5. Compute inventory turnover for fiscal year ended September 27, 2014, and days' sales in inventory as of September 27, 2014.

Fast Forward

6. Access Apple's financial statements for fiscal years ended after September 27, 2014, from its website (**Apple.com**) or the SEC's EDGAR database (**www.SEC.gov**). Answer questions 1 through 5 using the current Apple information and compare results to those prior years.

REPORTING IN ACTION

C2   A3

APPLE

BTN 5-2 Comparative figures for **Apple** and **Google** follow.

| | Apple | | | Google | | |
$ millions	Current Year	One Year Prior	Two Years Prior	Current Year	One Year Prior	Two Years Prior
Inventory	$ 2,111	$ 1,764	$ 791	$ 0	$ 426	$ 505
Cost of sales	112,258	106,606	87,846	25,691	21,993	17,176

Required

1. Compute inventory turnover for each company for the most recent two years shown.
2. Compute days' sales in inventory for each company for the three years shown.
3. Comment on and interpret your findings from parts 1 and 2. Assume an industry average for inventory turnover of 40.

COMPARATIVE ANALYSIS

A3

APPLE
GOOGLE

BTN 5-3 Golf Challenge Corp. is a retail sports store carrying golf apparel and equipment. The store is at the end of its second year of operation and is struggling. A major problem is that its cost of inventory has continually increased in the past two years. In the first year of operations, the store assigned inventory costs using LIFO. A loan agreement the store has with its bank, its prime source of financing, requires the store to maintain a certain profit margin and current ratio. The store's owner is currently looking over Golf Challenge's preliminary financial statements for its second year. The numbers are not favorable. The only way the store can meet the required financial ratios agreed on with the bank is to change from LIFO to

ETHICS CHALLENGE

A1

FIFO. The store originally decided on LIFO because of its tax advantages. The owner recalculates ending inventory using FIFO and submits those numbers and statements to the loan officer at the bank for the required bank review. The owner thankfully reflects on the available latitude in choosing the inventory costing method.

Required

1. How does Golf Challenge's use of FIFO improve its net profit margin and current ratio?
2. Is the action by Golf Challenge's owner ethical? Explain.

COMMUNICATING IN PRACTICE

A1

BTN 5-4   You are a financial adviser with a client in the wholesale produce business that just completed its first year of operations. Due to weather conditions, the cost of acquiring produce to resell has escalated during the later part of this period. Your client, Javonte Gish, mentions that because her business sells perishable goods, she has striven to maintain a FIFO flow of goods. Although sales are good, the increasing cost of inventory has put the business in a tight cash position. Gish has expressed concern regarding the ability of the business to meet income tax obligations.

Required

Prepare a memorandum that identifies, explains, and justifies the inventory method you recommend your client, Ms. Gish, adopt.

TAKING IT TO THE NET

A3

APPLE

BTN 5-5   Access the September 27, 2014, 10-K report for **Apple, Inc.** (ticker AAPL), filed on October 27, 2014, from the EDGAR filings at **www.SEC.gov**.

Required

1. What products are manufactured by Apple?
2. What inventory method does Apple use? (*Hint:* See Note 1 to its financial statements.)
3. Compute its gross margin and gross margin ratio for the 2014 fiscal year. Comment on your computations—assume an industry average of 40% for the gross margin ratio.
4. Compute its inventory turnover and days' sales in inventory for the year ended September 27, 2014. Comment on your computations—assume an industry average of 40 for inventory turnover and 9 for days' sales in inventory.

TEAMWORK IN ACTION

A1   P3

Hint: Step 1 allows four choices or areas for expertise. Larger teams will have some duplication of choice, but the specific identification method should not be duplicated.

BTN 5-6[A]   Each team member has the responsibility to become an expert on an inventory method. This expertise will be used to facilitate teammates' understanding of the concepts relevant to that method.

1. Each learning team member should select an area for expertise by choosing one of the following inventory methods: specific identification, LIFO, FIFO, or weighted average.
2. Form expert teams made up of students who have selected the same area of expertise. The instructor will identify where each expert team will meet.
3. Using the following data, each expert team must collaborate to develop a presentation that illustrates the relevant concepts and procedures for its inventory method. Each team member must write the presentation in a format that can be shown to the learning team.

Data

The company uses a *perpetual* inventory system. It had the following beginning inventory and current-year purchases of its product.

Jan.	1	Beginning inventory	50 units @ $100 = $ 5,000
Jan.	14	Purchase	150 units @ $120 = 18,000
Apr.	30	Purchase	200 units @ $150 = 30,000
Sept.	26	Purchase	300 units @ $200 = 60,000

The company transacted sales on the following dates at a $350 per unit sales price.

Jan. 10	30 units	(specific cost: 30 @ $100)
Feb. 15	100 units	(specific cost: 100 @ $120)
Oct. 5	350 units	(specific cost: 100 @ $150 and 250 @ $200)

Concepts and Procedures to Illustrate in Expert Presentation

a. Identify and compute the costs to assign to the units sold. (Round per unit costs to three decimals.)

b. Identify and compute the costs to assign to the units in ending inventory. (Round inventory balances to the dollar.)

c. How likely is it that this inventory costing method will reflect the actual physical flow of goods? How relevant is that factor in determining whether this is an acceptable method to use?

d. What is the impact of this method versus others in determining net income and income taxes?

e. How closely does the ending inventory amount reflect replacement cost?

4. Re-form learning teams. In rotation, each expert is to present to the team the presentation developed in part 3. Experts are to encourage and respond to questions.

BTN 5-7   Review the chapter's opening feature highlighting Elon Musk and his company, Tesla Motors. Assume that Tesla consistently maintains an inventory level of $30,000, meaning that its average and ending inventory levels are the same. Also assume its annual cost of sales is $120,000. To cut costs, Elon proposes to slash inventory to a constant level of $15,000 with no impact on cost of sales. He plans to work with suppliers to get quicker deliveries and to order smaller quantities more often.

ENTREPRENEURIAL DECISION

A3

Required

1. Compute the company's inventory turnover and its days' sales in inventory under (*a*) current conditions and (*b*) proposed conditions.

2. Evaluate and comment on the merits of this proposal given your analysis for part 1. Identify any concerns you might have about the proposal.

BTN 5-8   Visit four retail stores with another classmate. In each store, identify whether the store uses a bar coding system to help manage its inventory. Try to find at least one store that does not use bar coding. If a store does not use bar coding, ask the store's manager or clerk whether he or she knows which type of inventory method the store employs. Create a table that shows columns for the name of store visited, type

HITTING THE ROAD

C1 C2

of merchandise sold, use or nonuse of bar coding, and the inventory method used if bar coding is not employed. You might also inquire as to what the store's inventory turnover is and how often physical inventory is taken.

GLOBAL DECISION

A3

Samsung
APPLE
GOOGLE

BTN 5-9   Following are key figures (in millions of Korean won) for **Samsung** (www.Samsung.com), which is a leading manufacturer of consumer electronics products.

₩ in millions	Current Year	One Year Prior	Two Years Prior
Inventory	₩ 17,317,504	₩ 19,134,868	₩ 17,747,413
Cost of sales	128,278,800	137,696,309	126,651,931

1. Use these data and those from BTN 5-2 to compute (a) inventory turnover and (b) days' sales in inventory for the most recent two years shown for **Samsung**, **Apple**, and **Google**.
2. Comment on and interpret your findings from part 1.

ANSWERS TO MULTIPLE CHOICE QUIZ

1. a; FIFO periodic. Ending inventory computation: 105 units @ $28 each = $2,940.

   (*Hint:* FIFO periodic inventory computation is identical to the FIFO perpetual inventory computation—see question 3.)

2. e; Specific identification (perpetual and periodic are identical for specific identification). Ending inventory computation:

20 units @ $25	$ 500
40 units @ $27	1,080
45 units @ $28	1,260
105 units	$2,840

3. a; FIFO perpetual

Date	Goods Purchased	Cost of Goods Sold	Inventory Balance
July 1			75 units @ $25 = $ 1,875
July 3	348 units @ $27 = $9,396		75 units @ $25 } 348 units @ $27 } = $11,271
July 8		75 units @ $25 } 225 units @ $27 } = $ 7,950	123 units @ $27 = $ 3,321
July 15	257 units @ $28 = $7,196		123 units @ $27 } 257 units @ $28 } = $10,517
July 23		123 units @ $27 } 152 units @ $28 } = $ 7,577	105 units @ $28 = **$ 2,940**
		$15,527	

4. b; LIFO perpetual

Date	Goods Purchased	Cost of Goods Sold	Inventory Balance
July 1			75 units @ $25 = $ 1,875
July 3	348 units @ $27 = $9,396		75 units @ $25 348 units @ $27 } = $11,271
July 8		300 units @ $27 = $ 8,100	75 units @ $25 48 units @ $27 } = $ 3,171
July 15	257 units @ $28 = $7,196		75 units @ $25 48 units @ $27 257 units @ $28 } = $10,367
July 23		257 units @ $28 18 units @ $27 } = $ 7,682 $15,782	75 units @ $25 30 units @ $27 } = $ 2,685

5. **i)** a; FIFO periodic inventory = $(20 \times \$14) + (10 \times \$12)$
$= \$400$

   ii) b; LIFO periodic cost of goods sold = $(20 \times \$14) + (40 \times \$12) +$
$(70 \times \$10) = \$1,460$

6. d; Days' sales in inventory = (Ending inventory/Cost of goods sold
$\times \ 365) = (\$18,000/\$85,000)$
$\times \ 365 = \underline{77.29 \text{ days}}$

Reporting and Analyzing Cash, Fraud, and Internal Controls

Chapter Preview

FRAUD AND INTERNAL CONTROL

C1 Purpose and principles of controls

Technology and controls

Limitations of controls

CONTROL OF CASH

C2 Definition and reporting of cash

P1 Control of cash receipts and cash disbursements

TOOLS OF CONTROL AND ANALYSIS

P2 Control of petty cash

P3 Bank reconciliation as a control tool

A1 Assessing liquidity

Learning Objectives

CONCEPTUAL

C1 Define internal control and identify its purpose and principles.

C2 Define cash and cash equivalents and explain how to report them.

ANALYTICAL

A1 Compute the days' sales uncollected ratio and use it to assess liquidity.

PROCEDURAL

P1 Apply internal control to cash receipts and disbursements.

P2 Explain and record petty cash fund transactions.

P3 Prepare a bank reconciliation.

P4 *Appendix 6A*—Describe use of documentation and verification to control cash disbursements.

Google Eyes the Future

"We want Google to be the third half of your brain" —SERGEY BRIN

MOUNTAIN VIEW, CA—You know you've hit it big when you are profiled in a comic book series! Enter Larry Page and Sergey Brin, founders of **Google, Inc. (Google.com)**, who are the focus of Bluewater Productions's business leaders comic book series. Yet, their real life story is just as amazing.

Larry and Sergey met in college, where it is said they disagreed "about most everything." However, a college project on measuring the importance of a website led the two to develop an algorithm for an improved search engine. The duo ran their project out of their dorm rooms but soon were getting 10,000 searches per day. With some angst, they borrowed $15,000, wrote a business plan, and launched Google (Google is based on the word "googol," a mathematical term for the number 1 followed by 100 zeros). Larry recalls a night, at 23 years old, when he woke from a dream, "grabbed a pen and started writing . . . scribbling out the details and convincing myself it would work."

Google is now the dominant search engine, has expanded into several markets, and now competes head-to-head with **Apple** on many fronts. Google's revenues and net income for the past four years follow:

($ billions)	2011	2012	2013	2014
Revenues	$38	$46	$56	$66
Net income	10	11	13	14

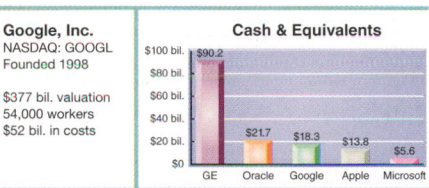

Google, Inc.
NASDAQ: GOOGL
Founded 1998

$377 bil. valuation
54,000 workers
$52 bil. in costs

Cash & Equivalents — GE $90.2, Oracle $21.7, Google $18.3, Apple $13.8, Microsoft $5.6

Financial markets also see Google in a positive light, viewing it as an innovative company with dynamic leaders and creative employees. Its stock price over the past four years reflects that enthusiasm.

An important part of Google's success is setting up systems of internal controls, including controls over cash, to foster future success. Larry explains that proper internal controls are important to Google's future and to the integrity of its systems. This includes establishing control procedures to monitor business activities and safeguard its assets. Both Larry and Sergey claim that such controls and management practices raise productivity, cut expenses, reduce fraud, and enhance the user experience.

Google has established strong internal controls for cash. This is fueled by its growth in the amount of cash, which now makes up nearly 14% of its total assets.

($ billions)	2011	2012	2013	2014
Cash	$10	$15	$ 19	$ 18
Total assets	73	94	111	131

Google's liquid assets, including its current securities of $46 billion, make up nearly one-half of its total assets. This "excess liquidity" concerns investors as the return on liquid assets is low. With such a large amount of liquid assets, Google invests substantial resources into cash management, including controls over cash receipts, disbursements, and petty cash. A bank reconciliation is one of many tools that it uses. It also takes advantage of readily available banking services to enhance cash controls.

Larry and Sergey, however, insist that much of the cash be devoted to R&D. They call it the 70-20-10 rule. "About 70% . . . [spent] on the core efforts of the company," explains Sergey, and "about 20% to adjacent areas and expansion." And, "for the final 10%," admits Sergey, "to anything goes!"

Sources: *Google website,* January 2016; *Google 10-K,* 2016; *Entrepreneur,* October 2008; *Fortune,* April 2012; *The Guardian,* January 2012; *ABC,* February 2004; *CNET,* March 2013

AP Images/Ben Margot

FRAUD AND INTERNAL CONTROL

C1
_____

Define internal control and identify its purpose and principles.

This section describes internal control and its fundamental principles. We also discuss the impact of technology on internal control and the limitations of control procedures.

Purpose of Internal Control

Managers (or owners) of small businesses often control the entire operation. These managers usually purchase all assets, hire and manage employees, negotiate all contracts, and sign all checks. They know from personal contact and observation whether the business is actually receiving the assets and services paid for. Most companies, however, cannot maintain this close personal supervision. They must delegate responsibilities and rely on formal procedures rather than personal contact in controlling business activities.

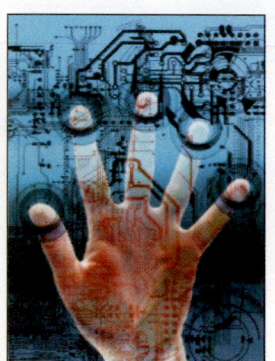

©Victor Habbick Visions/Corbis

Internal Control System   Managers use an internal control system to monitor and control business activities. An **internal control system** consists of the policies and procedures managers use to

- Protect assets.
- Ensure reliable accounting.
- Promote efficient operations.
- Urge adherence to company policies.

A properly designed internal control system is a key part of systems design, analysis, and performance. Managers place a high priority on internal control systems because they can prevent avoidable losses, help managers plan operations, and monitor company and employee performance. For example, internal controls for health care must protect patient records and privacy. Internal controls do not provide guarantees, but they lower the company's risk of loss.

Sarbanes-Oxley Act (SOX)   The **Sarbanes-Oxley Act (SOX)** requires the managers and auditors of companies whose stock is traded on an exchange (called *public companies*) to document and certify the system of internal controls. Following are some of the specific requirements:

- Auditors must evaluate internal controls and issue an internal control report.
- Auditors of a client are restricted as to what consulting services they can provide that client.
- The person leading an audit can serve no more than seven years without a two-year break.
- Auditors' work is overseen by the *Public Company Accounting Oversight Board* (PCAOB).
- Harsh penalties exist for violators—sentences up to 25 years in prison with severe fines.

SOX has markedly impacted companies, and the costs of its implementation are high. Importantly, **Section 404 of SOX** requires that managers document and assess the effectiveness of all internal control processes that can impact financial reporting. The benefits include greater confidence in accounting systems and their related reports. However, the public continues to debate the costs versus the benefits of SOX as nearly all business activities of these companies are impacted by SOX. Section 404 of SOX requires that managers document and assess their internal controls *and* that auditors provide an opinion on managers' documentation and assessment. Costs of complying with Section 404 for companies is reported to average $4 million (Financial Executives Institute).

Principles of Internal Control

Internal control policies and procedures vary from company to company according to such factors as the nature of the business and its size. Certain fundamental internal control principles apply to all companies. The **principles of internal control** are to

1. Establish responsibilities.
2. Maintain adequate records.
3. Insure assets and bond key employees.
4. Separate recordkeeping from custody of assets.
5. Divide responsibility for related transactions.
6. Apply technological controls.
7. Perform regular and independent reviews.

...a control system is only as strong as its weakest link

This section explains these seven principles and describes how internal control procedures minimize the risk of fraud and theft. These procedures also increase the reliability and accuracy of accounting records. A framework for how these seven principles improve the quality of financial reporting is provided by the **Committee of Sponsoring Organizations (COSO)** (**www.COSO.org**). Specifically, these principles link to five aspects of internal control: control activities, control environment, risk assessment, monitoring, and communication.

Establish Responsibilities   Proper internal control means that responsibility for a task is clearly established and assigned to one person. When a problem occurs in a company where responsibility is not identified, determining who is at fault is difficult. For instance, if two sales-clerks share the same cash register and there is a cash shortage, neither clerk can be held accountable. To prevent this problem, one clerk might be given responsibility for handling all cash sales. Alternately, a company can use a register with separate cash drawers for each clerk. Most of us have waited at a retail counter during a shift change while employees swap cash drawers.

Maintain Adequate Records   Good recordkeeping is part of an internal control system. It helps protect assets and ensures that employees use prescribed procedures. Reliable records are also a source of information that managers use to monitor company activities. When detailed records of equipment are kept, for instance, items are unlikely to be lost or stolen without detection. Similarly, transactions are less likely to be entered in wrong accounts if a chart of accounts is set up and carefully used. Many preprinted forms and internal documents are also designed for use in a good internal control system. When sales slips are properly designed, for instance, sales personnel can record needed information efficiently with less chance of errors or delays to customers. When sales slips are prenumbered and controlled, each one issued is the responsibility of one salesperson, preventing the salesperson from pocketing cash by making a sale and destroying the sales slip. Computerized point-of-sale systems achieve the same control results.

Insure Assets and Bond Key Employees   Good internal control means that assets are adequately insured against casualty and that employees handling large amounts of cash and easily transferable assets are bonded. An employee is *bonded* when a company purchases an insurance policy, or a bond, against losses from theft by that employee. Bonding reduces the risk of loss. It also discourages theft because bonded employees know an independent bonding company will be involved when theft is uncovered and is unlikely to be sympathetic to an employee involved in theft. (A common question on job applications is whether you are bonded or bondable.)

Commercial Law League of America
Commercial Collection Agency
Association
Certificate of Bond Coverage

This is to certify that

«Company»

A member of the Commercial Collection Agency Association of the Commercial Law League of America has in place for the benefit of its customer's indemnity bond coverage totaling 500,000. The insurance afforded is subject to all terms, exclusions and conditions of such policies. Copies of the original bonds and the current status of the bonds can be obtained by writing:

Jeff Henderson
Executive Vice President
Commercial Law League of America
1000 N. Rand Rd., Suite 214
Wauconda, IL 60084

Jeff Henderson, EVP

Policy effective dates:
August 1, 2015 - July 31, 2016

Certificate Number: 982

Courtesy of Commercial Collection Agency Association of the Commercial Law League of America

Fraud

Asset Theft Control A novel technique exists for marking physical assets. It involves embedding a less than one-inch-square tag of fibers that creates a unique optical signature recordable by scanners. Manufacturers hope to embed tags in everything from smart phones and credit cards to designer clothes for purposes of internal control and efficiency.

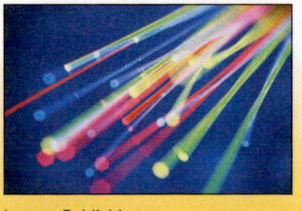

Ingram Publishing

Separate Recordkeeping from Custody of Assets   A person who controls or has access to an asset must not keep that asset's accounting records. This principle reduces the risk of theft or waste of an asset because the person with control over it knows that another person keeps its records. Also, a recordkeeper who does not have access to the asset has no reason to falsify records. This means that to steal an asset and hide the theft from the records, two or more people must *collude*—or agree in secret to commit the fraud. Some payroll cash checking services require fingerprint ID before the payroll check is cashed.

Divide Responsibility for Related Transactions   Good internal control divides responsibility for a transaction or a series of related transactions between two or more individuals or departments. This is to ensure that the work of one individual acts as a check on the other. This principle, often called *separation of duties,* is not a call for duplication of work. Each employee or department should perform unduplicated effort. Examples of transactions with divided responsibility are placing purchase orders, receiving merchandise, and paying vendors. These tasks should not be given to one individual or department. Assigning responsibility for two or more of these tasks to one party increases mistakes and perhaps fraud. Having an independent person, for example, check incoming goods for quality and quantity encourages more care and attention to detail than having the person who placed the order do the checking. Added protection can result from identifying a third person to approve payment of the invoice. A company can even designate a fourth person with authority to write checks as another protective measure.

Apply Technological Controls   Cash registers, check protectors, time clocks, and personal identification scanners are examples of devices that can improve internal control. Technology often improves the effectiveness of controls. A cash register with a locked-in tape or electronic file makes a record of each cash sale. A check protector perforates the amount of a check into its face and makes it difficult to alter the amount. A time clock registers the exact time an employee both arrives at and departs from the job. Mechanical change and currency counters quickly and accurately count amounts, and personal scanners limit access to only authorized individuals. These and other technological controls are an effective part of many internal control systems. Some companies video record workers as they clock in and out, which discourages them from clocking in or out for others.

🟨 Decision Insight

What's-Her-Face   Face-recognition software snaps a digital picture of the face and converts key facial features—say, the distance between the eyes—into a series of numerical values. These can be stored on an ID or ATM card as a simple bar code to prohibit unauthorized access. ◾

Perform Regular and Independent Reviews   Changes in personnel, stress of time pressures, and technological advances present opportunities for shortcuts and lapses. To counter these factors, regular reviews of internal control systems are needed to ensure that procedures are followed. These reviews are preferably done by internal auditors not directly involved in the activities. Their impartial perspective encourages an evaluation of the efficiency as well as the effectiveness of the internal control system. Many companies also pay for audits by independent, external auditors. These external auditors test the company's financial records to give an opinion as to whether its financial statements are presented fairly. Before external auditors decide on how much testing is needed, they evaluate the effectiveness of the internal control system. This evaluation is often helpful to a client. Independent, external audits are usually performed by auditors who work for public accounting firms.

🟩 Decision Maker

Entrepreneur   As owner of a start-up information services company, you hire a systems analyst. The analyst sees that your company employs only two workers. She recommends you improve controls and says that as owner you must serve as a compensating control. What does the analyst mean? ◾ [Answers follow the chapter's Summary.]

Technology, Fraud, and Internal Control

The fundamental principles of internal control are relevant no matter what the technological state of the accounting system, from purely manual to fully automated systems. Technology impacts an internal control system in several important ways. Perhaps the most obvious is that technology allows us quicker access to databases and information. Used effectively, technology greatly improves managers' abilities to monitor and control business activities. This section describes some technological impacts we must be alert to.

Reduced Processing Errors   Technologically advanced systems reduce the number of errors in processing information. Provided the software and data entry are correct, the risk of mechanical and mathematical errors is nearly eliminated. However, we must remember that erroneous software or data entry does exist. Also, less human involvement in data processing can cause data entry errors to go undiscovered. Moreover, errors in software can produce consistent but erroneous processing of transactions. Continually checking and monitoring all types of systems are important.

Point: Evidence of any internal control failure for a company reduces user confidence in its financial statements.

More Extensive Testing of Records   A company's review and audit of electronic records can include more extensive testing when information is easily and rapidly accessed. When accounting records are kept manually, auditors and others likely select only small samples of data to test. When data are accessible with computer technology, however, auditors can quickly analyze large samples or even the entire database.

Limited Evidence of Processing   Many data processing steps are increasingly done by computer. Accordingly, fewer hard-copy items of documentary evidence are available for review. Yet technologically advanced systems can provide new evidence. They can, for instance, record who made the entries, the date and time, the source of the entry, and so on. Technology can also be designed to require the use of passwords or other identification before access to the system is granted. This means that internal control depends more on the design and operation of the information system and less on the analysis of its resulting documents.

Point: We look to several sources when assessing a company's internal controls. Sources include the auditor's report, management report on controls (if available), management discussion and analysis, and financial press.

Crucial Separation of Duties   Technological advances in accounting information systems often yield some job eliminations or consolidations. While those who remain have the special skills necessary to operate advanced programs and equipment, a company with a reduced workforce risks losing its crucial separation of duties. The company must establish ways to control and monitor employees to minimize risk of error and fraud. For instance, the person who designs and programs the information system must not be the one who operates it. The company must also separate control over programs and files from the activities related to cash receipts and disbursements. For instance, a computer operator should not control check-writing activities. Achieving acceptable separation of duties can be especially difficult and costly in small companies with few employees.

Increased E-Commerce   Technology has encouraged the growth of e-commerce. **Amazon.com** and **eBay** are examples of companies that have successfully exploited e-commerce. Most companies have some e-commerce transactions. All such transactions involve at least three risks. (1) *Credit card number theft* is a risk of using, transmitting, and storing such data online. This increases the cost of e-commerce. (2) *Computer viruses* are malicious programs that attach themselves to innocent files for purposes of infecting and harming other files and programs. (3) *Impersonation* online can result in charges of sales to bogus accounts, purchases of inappropriate materials, and the unknowing giving up of confidential information to hackers. Companies use both firewalls and encryption to combat some of these risks—firewalls are points of entry to a system that require passwords to continue and encryption is a mathematical process to rearrange contents that cannot be read without the process code. Nearly 5% of Americans already report being victims of identity theft, and roughly 10 million say their privacy has been compromised.

"Worst case of identity theft I've ever seen!"

Copyright 2004 by Randy Glasbergen. www.glasbergen.com

 Decision Insight

Controls and Social Media   Should controls extend to social media? What controls exist for a company's social media strategy? Controls over social media might have impacted **Facebook**'s decision to experiment with the "mood" of posts to see if it affected the happiness of the content posted by those users. **OKCupid** later acknowledged its own experiments on members. Given the potential financial impacts of such activities, can companies afford not to adopt control systems over social media? ■

Limitations of Internal Control

All internal control policies and procedures have limitations that usually arise from either (1) the human element or (2) the cost-benefit principle.

Internal control policies and procedures are applied by people. This human element creates several potential limitations that we can categorize as either (1) human error or (2) human fraud. *Human error* can occur from negligence, fatigue, misjudgment, or confusion. *Human fraud* involves intent by people to defeat internal controls, such as *management override,* for personal gain. Fraud also includes collusion to thwart the separation of duties. The human element highlights the importance of establishing an *internal control environment* to convey management's commitment to internal control policies and procedures. Human fraud is driven by the *triple-threat* of fraud:

- **Opportunity**—refers to internal control deficiencies in the workplace.
- **Pressure**—refers to financial, family, society, and other stresses to succeed.
- **Rationalization**—refers to employees justifying fraudulent behavior.

Point: Cybercrime.gov pursues computer and intellectual property crimes, including that of e-commerce.

The second major limitation on internal control is the *cost-benefit principle,* which dictates that the costs of internal controls must not exceed their benefits. Analysis of costs and benefits must consider all factors, including the impact on morale. Most companies, for instance, have a legal right to read employees' e-mails, yet companies seldom exercise that right unless they are confronted with evidence of potential harm to the company. The same holds for drug testing, phone tapping, and hidden cameras. The bottom line is that managers must establish internal control policies and procedures with a net benefit to the company.

Hacker's Guide to Cyberspace

Pharming Viruses attached to e-mails and websites load software onto your PC that monitors keystrokes; when you sign on to financial websites, it steals your passwords.

Phishing Hackers send e-mails to you posing as banks; you are asked for information using fake websites where they reel in your passwords and personal data.

Wi-Phishing Cybercrooks set up wireless networks hoping you will use them to connect to the web; your passwords and data are stolen as you use their network.

Bot-Networking Hackers send remote-control programs to your PC that take control to send out spam and viruses; they even rent your bot to other cybercrooks.

Typo-Squatting Hackers set up websites with addresses similar to legit outfits; when you make a typo and hit their sites, they infect your PC with viruses or take them over as bots.

Hackers also have their own self-identification system:
- *Hackers,* or *external attackers,* crack systems and take data for illicit gains (as unauthorized users).
- *Rogue insiders,* or *internal attackers,* crack systems and take data for illicit gains or revenge (as authorized users).
- *Ethical hackers,* or *good-guys* or *white-hat hackers,* crack systems and reveal vulnerabilities to enhance controls.
- *Crackers,* or *criminal hackers,* crack systems illegally for illicit gains, fame, or revenge.

Fraud

Fraud Discovery The Association for Certified Fraud Examiners (ACFE) reports that 42% of frauds are detected from a "tip," which is much higher than the next three detection sources (16% from management review, 14% from internal audit, and 7% by accident). The top source for a tip is an employee, followed by a customer and a vendor—see graph.

Who Detects Fraud?

Source: 2014 Report to the Nations, ACFE (acfe.com).

Identify the following phrases/terms as best associated with the (a) purposes of an internal control system, (b) principles of internal control, or (c) limitations of internal control.

1. ____ Protect assets
2. ____ Establish responsibilities
3. ____ Human error
4. ____ Maintain adequate records
5. ____ Apply technological controls
6. ____ Ensure reliable accounting
7. ____ Insure assets and bond key employees

8. ____ Human fraud
9. ____ Separate recordkeeping from custody of assets
10. ____ Divide responsibility for related transactions
11. ____ Cost-benefit principle
12. ____ Promote efficient operations
13. ____ Perform regular and independent reviews
14. ____ Urge adherence to company policies

Solution

1. a   **2.** b   **3.** c   **4.** b   **5.** b   **6.** a   **7.** b   **8.** c   **9.** b   **10.** b   **11.** c   **12.** a   **13.** b   **14.** a

Do More: QS 6-1, E 6-1, E 6-2, P 6-1

CONTROL OF CASH

Cash is a necessary asset of every company. Most companies also own *cash equivalents* (defined below), which are assets similar to cash. Cash and cash equivalents are the most liquid of all assets and are easily hidden and moved. Cash is also the most desired asset as other assets must be *fenced* (sold in a secondary market). An effective system of internal controls protects cash assets and it should meet three basic guidelines:

1. Handling cash is separate from recordkeeping of cash.
2. Cash receipts are promptly deposited in a bank.
3. Cash disbursements are made by check (or electronic funds transfer, EFT).

The first guideline applies separation of duties to minimize errors and fraud. When duties are separated, two or more people must collude to steal cash and conceal this action in the accounting records. The second guideline uses immediate (say, daily) deposits of all cash receipts to produce a timely independent record of the cash received. It also reduces the likelihood of cash theft (or loss) and the risk that an employee could personally use the money before depositing it. The third guideline uses payments by check to develop an independent bank record of cash disbursements. This guideline also reduces the risk of cash theft (or loss).

This section begins with definitions of cash and cash equivalents. Discussion then focuses on controls and accounting for both cash receipts and disbursements. The exact procedures used to achieve control over cash vary across companies. They depend on factors such as company size, number of employees, volume of cash transactions, and sources of cash.

Cash, Cash Equivalents, and Liquidity

Good accounting systems help in managing the amount of cash and controlling who has access to it. Cash is the usual means of payment when paying for assets, services, or liabilities. **Liquidity** refers to a company's ability to pay for its near-term obligations. Cash and similar assets are called **liquid assets** because they can be readily used to settle such obligations. A company needs liquid assets to effectively operate.

Cash includes currency and coins along with the amounts on deposit in bank accounts, checking accounts (called *demand deposits*), and many savings accounts (called *time deposits*). Cash also includes items that are acceptable for deposit in these accounts such as customer checks, cashier's checks, certified checks, and money orders. **Cash equivalents** are short-term, highly liquid investment assets meeting two criteria: (1) readily convertible to a known cash amount and (2) sufficiently close to their due date so that their market value is not sensitive to interest rate changes. Only investments purchased within three months of their due date usually satisfy these criteria. Examples of cash equivalents are short-term investments in assets such as U.S. Treasury bills and money market funds. To increase their return, many companies invest

C2 _____

Define cash and cash equivalents and explain how to report them.

Point: The most-liquid assets are usually reported first on a balance sheet; the least-liquid assets are reported last.

idle cash in cash equivalents. Most companies combine cash equivalents with cash as a single item on the balance sheet.

Cash Management

When companies fail, one of the most common causes is their inability to manage cash. Companies must plan both cash receipts and cash payments. The goals of cash management are twofold:

1. Plan cash receipts to meet cash payments when due.
2. Keep a minimum level of cash necessary to operate.

The *treasurer* of the company is responsible for cash management. Effective cash management involves applying the following cash management principles.

- **Encourage collection of receivables.** The more quickly customers and others pay the company, the more quickly that company can use the money. Some companies have cash-only sales policies. Others might offer discounts for payments received early.
- **Delay payment of liabilities.** The more delayed a company is in paying others, the more time it has to use the money. Some companies regularly wait to pay their bills until the last possible day allowed, although a company must take care not to hurt its credit standing.
- **Keep only necessary levels of assets.** The less money a company has tied up in idle assets, the more money it has to invest in productive assets. Some companies maintain *just-in-time* inventory, meaning they plan inventory to be available at the same time orders are filled. Others might lease out excess warehouse space or rent equipment instead of buying it.
- **Plan expenditures.** Money should be spent only when it is available. Companies must look at seasonal and business cycles to plan expenditures.
- **Invest excess cash.** Excess cash earns no return and should be invested. Excess cash from seasonal cycles can be placed in a bank account or other short-term investment for income. Excess cash beyond what's needed for regular business should be invested in productive assets like factories and inventories.

 Decision Insight

Days' Cash Expense Coverage   The ratio of *cash (and cash equivalents) to average daily cash expenses* indicates the number of days a company can operate without additional cash inflows. It reflects on company liquidity and on the potential of excess cash. ■

Control of Cash Receipts

P1_____

Apply internal control to cash receipts and disbursements.

Internal control of cash receipts ensures that cash received is properly recorded and deposited. Cash receipts can arise from transactions such as cash sales, collections of customer accounts, receipts of interest earned, bank loans, sales of assets, and owner investments. This section explains internal control over two important types of cash receipts: over-the-counter and by mail.

Over-the-Counter Cash Receipts   For purposes of internal control, over-the-counter cash receipts from sales should be recorded on a cash register at the time of each sale. To help ensure that correct amounts are entered, each register should be located so customers can read the amounts entered. Clerks also should be required to enter each sale before wrapping merchandise and to give the customer a receipt for each sale. The design of each cash register should provide a permanent, locked-in record of each transaction. In many systems, the register is directly linked with computing and accounting services. Less advanced registers simply print a record of each transaction on a paper tape or electronic file locked inside the register.

Proper internal control prescribes that custody over cash should be separate from its record-keeping. For over-the-counter cash receipts, this separation begins with the cash sale. The clerk who has access to cash in the register should not have access to its locked-in record. At the end of the clerk's work period, the clerk should count the cash in the register, record the amount, and turn over the cash and a record of its amount to the company cashier. The cashier, like the clerk, has access to the cash but should not have access to accounting records (or the register tape or file). A third employee, often a supervisor, compares the record of total register transactions (or the register tape or file) with the cash receipts reported by the cashier. This record is the basis for a journal entry recording over-the-counter cash receipts. The third employee has access to the records for cash but not to the actual cash. The clerk and the cashier have access to cash but not to the accounting records. None of them can make a mistake or divert cash without the difference being revealed (see the following diagram).

Point: Convenience stores sometimes display a sign: *Cashier has no access to cash in locked floor (or wall) safe.* Such signs help deter theft and holdups.

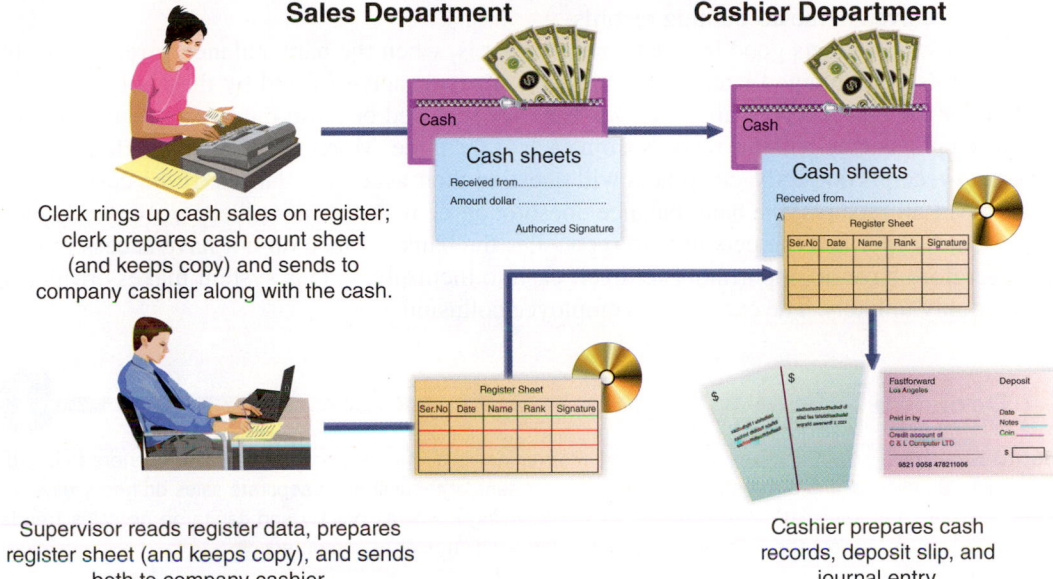

Sales Department / Cashier Department

Clerk rings up cash sales on register; clerk prepares cash count sheet (and keeps copy) and sends to company cashier along with the cash.

Supervisor reads register data, prepares register sheet (and keeps copy), and sends both to company cashier.

Cashier prepares cash records, deposit slip, and journal entry.

Point: Many businesses have signs that read: If you receive no receipt, your purchase is free! This helps ensure that clerks ring up all transactions on registers.

Cash Over and Short Sometimes errors in making change are discovered from differences between the cash in a cash register and the record of the amount of cash receipts. Although a clerk is careful, one or more customers can be given too much or too little change. This means that at the end of a work period, the cash in a cash register might not equal the record of cash receipts. This difference is reported in the **Cash Over and Short** account, also called *Cash Short and Over,* which is an income statement account recording the income effects of cash overages and cash shortages. To illustrate, if a cash register's record shows $550 but the count of cash in the register is $555, the entry to record cash sales and its overage is

Point: Retailers often require cashiers to restrictively endorse checks immediately on receipt by stamping them "For deposit only."

Cash	555	
Cash Over and Short		5
Sales		550
Record cash sales and a cash overage.		

Assets = Liabilities + Equity
+555 .... + 5
.... +550

On the other hand, if a cash register's record shows $625 but the count of cash in the register is $621, the entry to record cash sales and its shortage is

Cash	621	
Cash Over and Short	4	
Sales		625
Record cash sales and a cash shortage.		

Assets = Liabilities + Equity
+621 .... − 4
.... +625

Since customers are more likely to dispute being shortchanged than being given too much change, the Cash Over and Short account usually has a debit balance at the end of an accounting period. A debit balance reflects an expense. It is reported on the income statement as part of selling, general, and administrative expenses. (Since the amount is usually small, it is often combined with other small expenses and reported as part of *miscellaneous expenses*—or as part of *miscellaneous revenues* if it has a credit balance.)

Point: Merchants begin a business day with a *change fund* in their cash register. The accounting for a change fund is similar to that for petty cash, including that for cash shortages or overages.

Point: Collusion implies that two or more individuals are knowledgeable about or involved with the activities of the other(s).

Cash Receipts by Mail   Control of cash receipts that arrive through the mail starts with the person who opens the mail. Preferably, two people are assigned the task of, and are present for, opening the mail. In this case, theft of cash receipts by mail requires collusion between these two employees. Specifically, the person(s) opening the mail enters a list (in triplicate) of money received. This list should contain a record of each sender's name, the amount, and an explanation of why the money is sent. The first copy is sent with the money to the cashier. A second copy is sent to the recordkeeper in the accounting area. A third copy is kept by the clerk(s) who opened the mail. The cashier deposits the money in a bank, and the recordkeeper records the amounts received in the accounting records.

This process reflects good internal control. That is, when the bank balance is reconciled by another person (explained later in the chapter), errors or acts of fraud by the mail clerks, the cashier, or the recordkeeper are revealed. They are revealed because the bank's record of cash deposited must agree with the records from each of the three. Moreover, if the mail clerks do not report all receipts correctly, customers will question their account balances. If the cashier does not deposit all receipts, the bank balance does not agree with the recordkeeper's cash balance. The recordkeeper and the person who reconciles the bank balance do not have access to cash and therefore have no opportunity to divert cash to themselves. This system makes errors and fraud highly unlikely. The exception is employee collusion.

▢ Decision Insight

Rapid Receipts   **Walmart** uses a network of information links with its point-of-sale cash registers to coordinate sales, purchases, and distribution. Its stores ring up tens of thousands of separate sales on heavy days. By using cash register information, the company can fix pricing mistakes quickly and capitalize on sales trends. Interestingly, Sam Walton, the founder, was a self-described distruster of computers. ▪

Control of Cash Disbursements

Control of cash disbursements is especially important as most large thefts occur from payment of fictitious invoices. One key to controlling cash disbursements is to require all expenditures to be made by check. The only exception is small payments made from petty cash. Another key is to deny access to the accounting records to anyone other than the owner who has the authority to sign checks. A small-business owner often signs checks and knows from personal contact that the items being paid for are actually received. This arrangement is impossible in large businesses. Instead, internal control procedures must be substituted for personal contact. Such procedures are designed to assure the check signer that the obligations recorded are properly incurred and should be paid. This section describes these and other internal control procedures, including the voucher system and petty cash system.

Cash Budget   Projected cash receipts and cash disbursements are often summarized in a *cash budget*. Provided that sufficient cash exists for effective operations, companies wish to minimize the cash they hold because of its risk of theft and its low return versus other investment opportunities.

▢ Decision Insight

Lockbox   Some companies do not receive cash in the mail but, instead, elect to have customers send deposits directly to the bank using a *lockbox* system. Bank employees are charged with receipting the cash and depositing it in the correct business bank account. ▪

Voucher System of Control   A **voucher system** is a set of procedures and approvals designed to control cash disbursements and the acceptance of obligations. The voucher system of control establishes procedures for

- Verifying, approving, and recording obligations for eventual cash disbursement.
- Issuing checks for payment of verified, approved, and recorded obligations.

A reliable voucher system follows standard procedures for every transaction. This applies even when multiple purchases are made from the same supplier.

A voucher system's control over cash disbursements begins when a company incurs an obligation that will result in payment of cash. A key factor in this system is that only approved departments and individuals are authorized to incur such obligations. The system often limits the type of obligations that a department or individual can incur. In a large retail store, for instance, only a purchasing department should be authorized to incur obligations for merchandise inventory. Another key factor is that procedures for purchasing, receiving, and paying for merchandise are divided among several departments (or individuals). These departments include the one requesting the purchase, the purchasing department, the receiving department, and the accounting department. To coordinate and control responsibilities of these departments, a company uses several different business documents. Exhibit 6.1 shows how documents are accumulated in a **voucher,** which is an internal document (or file) used to accumulate information to control cash disbursements and to ensure that a transaction is properly recorded. This specific example begins with a *purchase requisition* and concludes with a *check* drawn against cash. Appendix 6A describes the documentation and verification necessary for a voucher system of control. It also describes the internal control objective served by each document.

Point: MCI, formerly **WorldCom,** paid a whopping $500 million in SEC fines for accounting fraud. Among the charges were that it inflated earnings by as much as $10 billion. Its CEO, Bernard Ebbers, was sentenced to 25 years.

Sender

Cashier → Supplier (vendor)
Accounting → Cashier
Receiving → Accounting; Requesting; and Purchasing
Supplier (vendor) → Accounting
Purchasing → Supplier; Requesting; Receiving; and Accounting
Requesting → Purchasing; and Accounting

Receiver(s)

Voucher

EXHIBIT 6.1

Document Flow in a Voucher System

A voucher system should be applied not only to purchases of inventory but to all expenditures. To illustrate, when a company receives a monthly telephone bill, it should review and verify the charges, prepare a voucher (file), and insert the bill. This transaction is then recorded with a journal entry. If the amount is currently due, a check is issued. If not, the voucher is filed for payment on its due date. If no voucher is prepared, verifying the invoice and its amount after several days or weeks can be difficult. Also, without records, a dishonest employee could collude with a dishonest supplier to get more than one payment for an obligation, payment for excessive amounts, or payment for goods and services not received. An effective voucher system helps prevent such frauds.

Point: A *voucher* is an internal document (or file).

Point: The basic purposes of paper and electronic documents are similar. However, the internal control system must change to reflect different risks, including confidential and competitive-sensitive information that is at greater risk in electronic systems.

Fraud

At Risk The Association for Certified Fraud Examiners (ACFE) reports that 85% of fraud is from asset theft. Of those asset thefts, the graph here shows a few that stand out—in both frequency and median loss. Namely, cash is most frequently stolen through billing (22%) and theft (21%). However, losses are largest through check tampering ($120,000) and billing ($100,000).

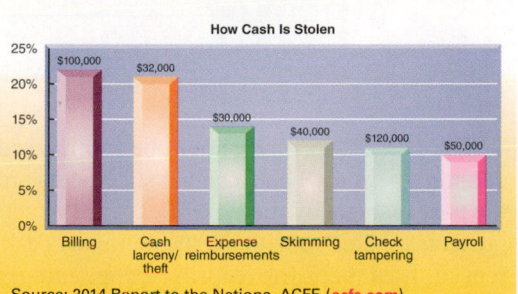

How Cash Is Stolen

Billing	Cash larceny/ theft	Expense reimbursements	Skimming	Check tampering	Payroll
$100,000	$32,000	$30,000	$40,000	$120,000	$50,000

Source: 2014 Report to the Nations, ACFE (acfe.com).

6-2

Control of Cash Receipts and Payments

P1 C2

A good system of internal control for cash provides adequate procedures for protecting both cash receipts and cash disbursements. Which of the following statements is true regarding the control of cash receipts and cash disbursements?

____ **1.** Over-the-counter cash receipts from sales should be recorded on a cash register at the time of each sale.

____ **2.** Custody over cash should be separate from the recordkeeping of cash.

____ **3.** For control of cash receipts that arrive through the mail, two people should be assigned the task of, and be present for, opening that mail.

____ **4.** One key to controlling cash disbursements is to require that no expenditures be made by check; instead, all expenditures should be made from petty cash.

____ **5.** A voucher system of control should be applied only to purchases of inventory and never to other expenditures.

Solution

Do More: QS 6-3, E 6-3, E 6-4

1. True   **2.** True   **3.** True   **4.** False   **5.** False

---

P2

Explain and record petty cash fund transactions.

Petty Cash System of Control   A basic principle for controlling cash disbursements is that all payments must be made by check. An exception to this rule is made for *petty cash disbursements,* which are the small payments required for items such as postage, courier fees, minor repairs, and low-cost supplies. To avoid the time and cost of writing checks for small amounts, a company sets up a petty cash fund to make small payments. (**Petty cash** activities are part of an *imprest system,* which designates advance money to establish the fund, to withdraw from the fund, and to reimburse the fund.)

Operating a Petty Cash Fund   Establishing a petty cash fund requires estimating the total amount of small payments likely to be made during a short period such as a week or month. A check is then drawn by the company cashier for an amount slightly in excess of this estimate. This check is recorded with a debit to the Petty Cash account (an asset) and a credit to Cash. The check is cashed, and the currency is given to an employee designated as the *petty cashier* or *petty cash custodian.* The petty cashier is responsible for keeping this cash safe, making payments from the fund, and keeping records of it in a secure place referred to as the *petty cashbox.*

Point: A petty cash fund is used only for business expenses.

When each cash disbursement is made, the person receiving payment should sign a prenumbered *petty cash receipt,* also called *petty cash ticket*—see Exhibit 6.2. The petty cash receipt is then placed in the petty cashbox with the remaining money. Under this system, the sum of all receipts plus the remaining cash equals the total fund amount. A $100 petty cash fund, for instance, contains any combination of cash and petty cash receipts that totals $100 (examples are $80 cash plus $20 in receipts, or $10 cash plus $90 in receipts). Each disbursement reduces cash and increases the amount of receipts in the petty cashbox.

EXHIBIT 6.2

Petty Cash Receipt

Z-Mart		No. 9
PETTY CASH RECEIPT		
For *Freight charges*		
Date *November 5, 2016*	Approved by *fl Gull*	
Charge to *Merchandise Inventory*		
Amount *$6.75*	Received by *Db Fll*	

Point: Petty cash receipts with either no signature or a forged signature usually indicate misuse of petty cash. Companies respond with surprise petty cash counts for verification.

The petty cash fund should be reimbursed when it is nearing zero and at the end of an accounting period when financial statements are prepared. For this purpose, the petty cashier sorts the paid receipts by the type of expense or account and then totals the receipts. The petty cashier presents all paid receipts to the company cashier, who stamps all receipts *paid* so they cannot be reused, files them for recordkeeping, and gives the petty cashier a check for their sum. When this check is cashed and the money placed in the cashbox, the total money in the cashbox is restored to its original amount. The fund is now ready for a new cycle of petty cash payments.

Illustrating a Petty Cash Fund   To illustrate, assume Z-Mart establishes a petty cash fund on November 1 and designates one of its office employees as the petty cashier. A $75 check is drawn, cashed, and the proceeds given to the petty cashier. The entry to record the setup of this petty cash fund is

Nov. 1	Petty Cash	75	
	Cash		75
	Establish a petty cash fund.		

Assets = Liabilities + Equity
+75
−75

After the petty cash fund is established, the Petty Cash account is not debited or credited again unless the amount of the fund is changed. (A fund should be increased if it requires reimbursement too frequently. On the other hand, if the fund is too large, some of its money should be redeposited in the Cash account.)

Next, assume that Z-Mart's petty cashier makes several November payments from petty cash. Each person who received payment is required to sign a receipt. On November 27, after making a $26.50 cash payment for tile cleaning, only $3.70 cash remains in the fund. The petty cashier then summarizes and totals the petty cash receipts as shown in Exhibit 6.3.

Point: Although *individual* petty cash disbursements are not evidenced by a check, the initial petty cash fund is evidenced by a check, and later petty cash expenditures are evidenced by a check to replenish them *in total.*

Z-MART
Petty Cash Payments Report

Miscellaneous Expenses

Nov. 2	Cleaning of LCD panels	$20.00	
Nov. 27	Tile cleaning	26.50	$ 46.50

Merchandise Inventory (transportation-in)

Nov. 5	Transport of merchandise purchased...............	6.75	
Nov. 20	Transport of merchandise purchased...............	8.30	15.05

Delivery Expense

Nov. 18	Customer's package delivered		5.00

Office Supplies Expense

Nov. 15	Purchase of office supplies immediately used		4.75
Total			**$71.30**

EXHIBIT 6.3

Petty Cash Payments Report

Point: This report can also include receipt number and names of those who approved and received cash payment (see **Need-To-Know 6-3**).

The petty cash payments report and all receipts are given to the company cashier in exchange for a $71.30 check to reimburse the fund. The petty cashier cashes the check and puts the $71.30 cash in the petty cashbox. The company records this reimbursement as follows.

Nov. 27	Miscellaneous Expenses	46.50	
	Merchandise Inventory	15.05	
	Delivery Expense	5.00	
	Office Supplies Expense	4.75	
	Cash*		71.30
	*Reimburse petty cash. *$75 fund bal. − $3.70 cash rem.*		

Assets = Liabilities + Equity
−71.30   −46.50
                              −15.05
                              − 5.00
                              − 4.75

A petty cash fund is usually reimbursed at the end of an accounting period so that expenses are recorded in the proper period, even if the fund is not low on money. If the fund is not reimbursed at the end of a period, the financial statements would show both an overstated cash asset and understated expenses (or assets) that were paid out of petty cash. Some companies do not reimburse the petty cash fund at the end of each period under the notion that this amount is immaterial to users of financial statements.

Point: To avoid errors in recording petty cash reimbursement, follow these steps: (1) prepare payments report, (2) compute cash needed by subtracting cash remaining from total fund amount, (3) record entry, and (4) check "Dr. = Cr." in entry. Any difference is Cash Over and Short.

Increasing or Decreasing a Petty Cash Fund   A decision to increase or decrease a petty cash fund is often made when reimbursing it. To illustrate, assume Z-Mart decides to *increase* its petty cash fund from $75 to $100 on November 27 when it reimburses the fund. The entries required are to (1) reimburse the fund as usual (see the preceding November 27 entry) and (2) increase the fund amount as follows.

Nov. 27	Petty Cash	25	
	Cash		25
	Increase the petty cash fund amount.		

Alternatively, if Z-Mart *decreases* the petty cash fund from $75 to $55 on November 27, the entry is

Nov. 27	Cash	20	
	Petty Cash		20
	Decrease the petty cash fund amount.		

Summary of Petty Cash Accounting			
Event	Petty Cash	Cash	Expenses
Set up fund.......	Dr.	Cr.	—
Reimburse fund....	—	Cr.	Dr.
Increase fund.....	Dr.	Cr.	—
Decrease fund....	Cr.	Dr.	—

Cash Over and Short   Sometimes a petty cashier fails to get a receipt for payment or overpays for the amount due. When this occurs and the fund is later reimbursed, the petty cash payments report plus the cash remaining will not total to the fund balance. This mistake causes the fund to be *short*. This shortage is recorded as an expense in the reimbursing entry with a debit to the Cash Over and Short account. (An overage in the petty cash fund is recorded with a credit to Cash Over and Short in the reimbursing entry.) To illustrate, prepare the June 1 entry to reimburse a $200 petty cash fund when its payments report shows $178 in miscellaneous expenses and $15 cash remains.

$200 Petty Cash Fund

June 1	Miscellaneous Expenses	178	
	Cash Over and Short	**7**	
	Cash*		185
	*Reimburse petty cash. *$200 fund bal. − $15 cash rem.*		

$15 Cash $7 Short $178 Receipts

Fraud

Have a Clue There are clues to fraudulent activities. Clues from accounting include (1) an increase in customer refunds—could be fake, (2) missing documents—could be used for fraud, (3) differences between bank deposits and cash receipts—could be cash embezzled, and (4) delayed recording—could reflect fraudulent records. Clues from employees include (1) lifestyle change—could be embezzlement, (2) too close with suppliers—could signal fraudulent transactions, and (3) failure to leave job, even for vacations—could conceal fraudulent activities.

NEED-TO-KNOW 6-3

Petty Cash System

P2

Bacardi Company established a $150 petty cash fund with Eminem as the petty cashier. When the fund balance reached $19 cash, Eminem prepared a petty cash payments report, which follows.

Petty Cash Payments Report				
Receipt No.	Account Charged		Approved by	Received by
12	Delivery Expense	$ 29	Eminem	A. Smirnoff
13	Merchandise Inventory	18	Eminem	J. Daniels
15	(Omitted)	32	Eminem	C. Carlsberg
16	Miscellaneous Expense	41	(Omitted)	J. Walker
	Total	$120		

Required

1. Identify four internal control weaknesses from the petty cash payments report.
2. Prepare general journal entries to record:
   a. Establishment of the petty cash fund.
   b. Reimbursement of the fund. (Assume for this part only that petty cash receipt no. 15 was issued for miscellaneous expenses.)
3. What is the Petty Cash account balance immediately before reimbursement? Immediately after reimbursement?

Solution

1. Four internal control weaknesses that are apparent from the payments report include:
   a. Petty cash ticket no. 14 is missing. Its omission raises questions about the petty cashier's management of the fund.
   b. The $19 cash balance means that $131 has been withdrawn ($150 − $19 = $131). However, the total amount of the petty cash receipts is only $120 ($29 + $18 + $32 + $41). The fund is $11 short of cash ($131 − $120 = $11). Was petty cash receipt no. 14 issued for $11? Management should investigate.
   c. The petty cashier (Eminem) did not sign petty cash receipt no. 16. This omission could have been an oversight on his part or he might not have authorized the payment. Management should investigate.
   d. Petty cash receipt no. 15 does not indicate which account to charge. This omission could have been an oversight on the petty cashier's part. Management could check with C. Carlsberg and the petty cashier (Eminem) about the transaction. Without further information, debit Miscellaneous Expense.
2. Petty cash general journal entries.
   a. Entry to establish the petty cash fund.   b. Entry to reimburse the fund.

Petty Cash	150	
Cash		150

Delivery Expense	29	
Merchandise Inventory	18	
Miscellaneous Expense ($41 + $32)	73	
Cash Over and Short	11	
Cash ($150 fund bal. − $19 cash rem.) . .		131

3. The Petty Cash account balance *always* equals its fund balance, in this case $150. This account balance does not change unless the fund is increased or decreased.

Do More: QS 6-4, E 6-5, E 6-6, P 6-2

BANKING ACTIVITIES AS CONTROLS

Banks (and other financial institutions) provide many services, including helping companies control cash. Banks safeguard cash, provide detailed and independent records of cash transactions, and are a source of cash financing. This section describes these services and the documents provided by banking activities that increase managers' control over cash.

Basic Bank Services

This section explains basic bank services—such as the bank account, the bank deposit, and checking—that contribute to the control of cash.

Bank Account, Deposit, and Check   A *bank account* is a record set up by a bank for a customer. It permits a customer to deposit money for safekeeping and helps control withdrawals. To limit access to a bank account, all persons authorized to write checks on the account must sign a **signature card,** which bank employees use to verify signatures on checks. Many companies have more than one bank account to serve different needs and to handle special transactions such as payroll.

Point: Online banking services include the ability to stop payment on a check, move money between accounts, get up-to-date balances, and identify cleared checks and deposits.

Each bank deposit is supported by a **deposit ticket,** which lists items such as currency, coins, and checks deposited along with their corresponding dollar amounts. The bank gives the customer a copy of the deposit ticket or a deposit receipt as proof of the deposit. Exhibit 6.4 shows one type of deposit ticket.

EXHIBIT 6.4

Deposit Ticket

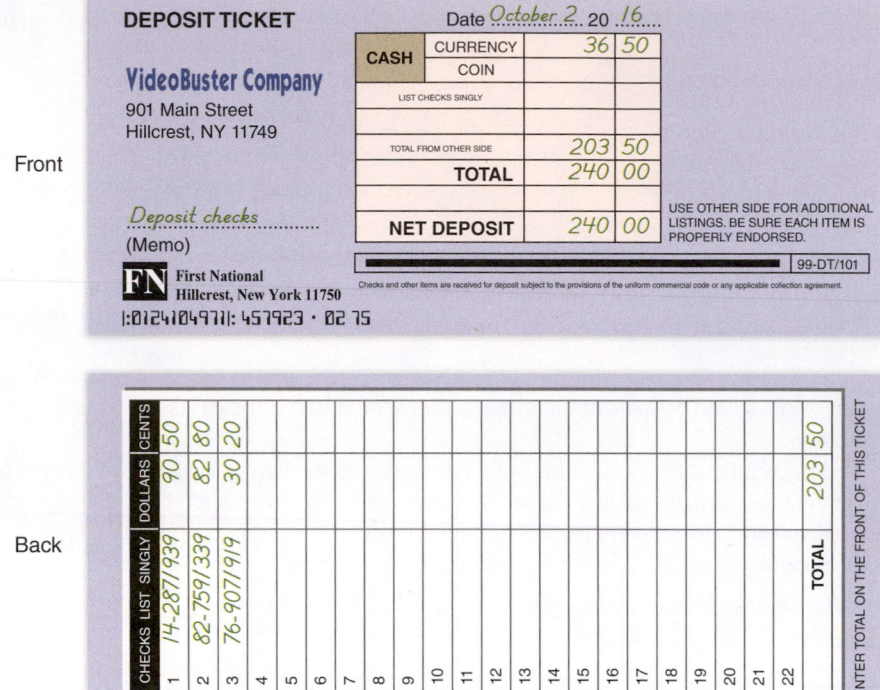

To withdraw money from an account, the depositor can use a **check,** which is a document signed by the depositor instructing the bank to pay a specified amount of money to a designated recipient. A check involves three parties: a *maker* who signs the check, a *payee* who is the recipient, and a *bank* (or *payer*) on which the check is drawn. The bank provides a depositor the checks that are serially numbered and imprinted with the name and address of both the depositor and bank. Both checks and deposit tickets are imprinted with identification codes in magnetic ink for computer processing. Exhibit 6.5 shows one type of check. It is accompanied with an optional *remittance advice* explaining the payment. When a remittance advice is unavailable, the *memo* line is often used for a brief explanation.

Electronic Funds Transfer   Electronic funds transfer (EFT) is the electronic transfer of cash from one party to another. No paper documents are necessary. Banks simply transfer cash from one account to another with a journal entry. Companies are increasingly using EFT because of its convenience and low cost. For instance, it can cost up to 50 cents to process a check through the banking system, whereas EFT cost is near zero. We now commonly see items such as payroll, rent, utilities, insurance, and interest payments being handled by EFT. The bank statement lists cash withdrawals by EFT with the checks and other deductions. Cash receipts by EFT are listed with deposits and other additions. A bank statement is sometimes a depositor's only notice of an EFT.

Bank Statement

Usually once a month, the bank sends each depositor a **bank statement** showing the activity in the account. Although a monthly statement is common, companies often regularly access information on their banking transactions. (Companies can choose to record any accounting adjustments required from the bank statement immediately or later, say, at the end of each day, week,

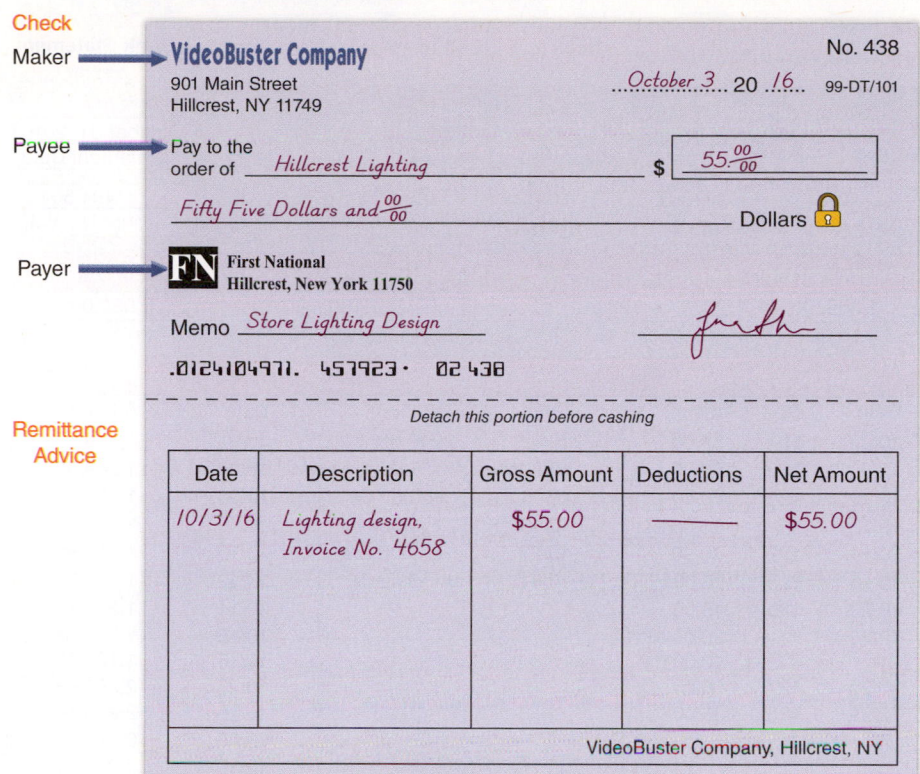

Check
Maker

Payee

Payer

Remittance
Advice

EXHIBIT 6.5

Check with Remittance
Advice

month, or when reconciling a bank statement.) Different banks use different formats for their bank statements, but all of them include the following items of information:

1. Beginning-of-period balance of the depositor's account.
2. Checks and other debits decreasing the account during the period.
3. Deposits and other credits increasing the account during the period.
4. End-of-period balance of the depositor's account.

This information reflects the bank's records. Exhibit 6.6 shows one type of bank statement. Identify each of these four items in that statement. Part Ⓐ of Exhibit 6.6 summarizes changes in the account. Part Ⓑ lists paid checks along with other debits. Part Ⓒ lists deposits and credits to the account, and part Ⓓ shows the daily account balances.

In reading a bank statement note that a depositor's account is a liability on the bank's records. This is because the money belongs to the depositor, not the bank. When a depositor increases the account balance, the bank records it with a *credit* to that liability account. This means that **debit memos from the bank produce *credits* on the depositor's books, and credit memos from the bank produce *debits* on the depositor's books**.

Enclosed with a bank statement is a list of the depositor's canceled checks (or the actual canceled checks) along with any debit or credit memoranda affecting the account. Increasingly, banks are showing canceled checks electronically via online access to accounts. **Canceled checks** are checks the bank has paid and deducted from the customer's account during the period. We say such checks have *cleared the bank*. Other deductions that can appear on a bank statement include (1) service charges and fees assessed by the bank, (2) checks deposited that are uncollectible, (3) corrections of previous errors, (4) withdrawals through automated teller machines (ATMs), and (5) periodic payments arranged in advance by a depositor. (Most company checking accounts do not allow ATM withdrawals because of the company's desire to make all disbursements by check.) Except for service charges, the bank notifies the depositor of each deduction with a debit memorandum when the bank reduces the balance. A copy of each debit memorandum is usually sent with the statement (again, this information is often available earlier via online access and notifications).

Point: Good internal control is to deposit all cash receipts daily and make all payments for goods and services by check. This controls access to cash and creates an independent record of all cash activities. Another good control is to send a copy of the bank statement directly to a party without access to cash or recordkeeping.

Point: Your checking account is a liability from the bank's perspective (but an asset from yours). Credits increase the bank's liability to you. When you make a deposit, they "credit your account." Debits decrease the bank's liability to you. When you write a check, or use your debit card for a purchase, the bank decreases its liability to you; they "debit your account."

Global: If cash is in more than one currency, a company usually translates these amounts into U.S. dollars using the exchange rate as of the balance sheet date. Also, a company must disclose any restrictions on cash accounts located outside the United States.

EXHIBIT 6.6

Bank Statement

FN First National Hillcrest, New York 11750			Bank Statement

Member FDIC

VideoBuster Company
901 Main Street
Hillcrest, NY 11749

October 31, 2016
Statement Date

494 504 2
Account Number

Bank's Liability to Video Buster

9/30 bal.	1,609.58
CRs	1,163.42

DRs 723.00

10/31 bal. 2,050.00

Ⓐ

Previous Balance	Total Checks and Debits	Total Deposits and Credits	Current Balance
1,609.58	723.00	1,163.42	2,050.00

Ⓑ Checks and Debits   Ⓒ Deposits and Credits   Ⓓ Daily Balance

Date	No.	Amount	Date	Amount	Date	Amount
10/03	119	55.00	10/02	240.00	10/01	1,609.58
10/09	120	200.00	10/09	180.00	10/02	1,849.58
10/10	121	120.00	10/15	100.00 EFT	10/03	1,794.58
10/12		23.00 DM	10/16	150.00	10/09	1,774.58
10/14	122	70.00	10/23	485.00 CM	10/10	1,654.58
10/16	123	25.00 EFT	10/31	8.42 IN	10/12	1,631.58
10/23	125	15.00			10/14	1,561.58
10/25		20.00 NSF			10/15	1,661.58
		10.00 DM			10/16	1,786.58
10/26	127	50.00			10/23	2,256.58
10/29	128	135.00			10/25	2,226.58
					10/26	2,176.58
					10/29	2,041.58
					10/31	2,050.00

Debits decrease bank's liability to depositor   Credits increase bank's liability to depositor

Symbols: **CM**–Credit Memo   **EC**–Error Correction   **NSF**–Non-Sufficient Funds   **SC**–Service Charge
DM–Debit Memo   **IN**–Interest Earned   **EFT**–Electronic Funds Transfer   **OD**–Overdraft

< Reconcile the account immediately. >

Point: Many banks separately report other debits and credits apart from checks and deposits.

Transactions that increase the depositor's account include amounts the bank collects on behalf of the depositor and the corrections of previous errors. Credit memoranda notify the depositor of all increases when they are recorded. A copy of each credit memorandum is often sent with the bank statement. Banks that pay interest on checking accounts often compute the amount of interest earned on the average cash balance and credit it to the depositor's account each period. In Exhibit 6.6, the bank credits $8.42 of interest to the account.

Bank Reconciliation

P3

Prepare a bank reconciliation.

When a company deposits all cash receipts and makes all cash payments (except petty cash) by check, it can use the bank statement for proving the accuracy of its cash records. This is done using a **bank reconciliation,** which is a report explaining any differences between the checking account balance according to the depositor's records and the balance reported on the bank statement. The figure below reflects this process, which we describe in the following sections.

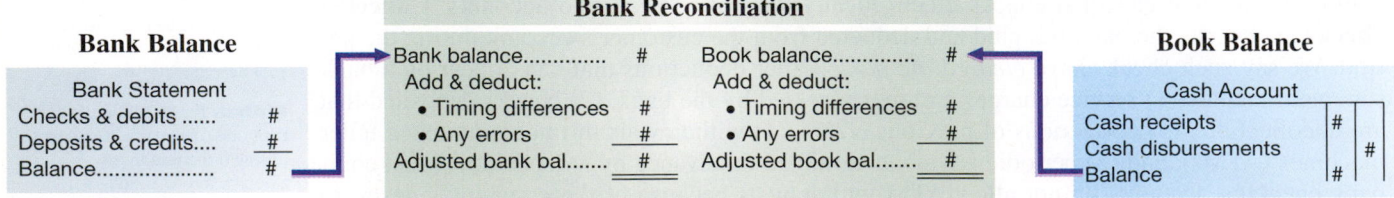

	Bank Reconciliation	
Bank Balance		**Book Balance**
Bank Statement	Bank balance.............. # Book balance.............. #	Cash Account
Checks & debits ...... #	Add & deduct: Add & deduct:	Cash receipts #
Deposits & credits.... #	• Timing differences # • Timing differences #	Cash disbursements #
Balance................... #	• Any errors # • Any errors #	Balance #
	Adjusted bank bal....... # Adjusted book bal....... #	

Purpose of Bank Reconciliation The balance of a checking account reported on the bank statement rarely equals the balance in the depositor's accounting records. This is usually due to information that one party has that the other does not. We must therefore prove the accuracy of both the depositor's records and those of the bank. This means we must *reconcile* the two balances and explain or account for any differences in them. Among the factors causing the bank statement balance to differ from the depositor's book balance are these:

- **Outstanding checks.** [Adjust bank balance.] **Outstanding checks** are checks written (or drawn) by the depositor, deducted on the depositor's records, and sent to the payees but not yet received by the bank for payment at the bank statement date.

- **Deposits in transit** (also called **outstanding deposits**). [Adjust bank balance.] **Deposits in transit** are deposits made and recorded by the depositor but not yet recorded on the bank statement. For example, companies can make deposits (in the night depository) at the end of a business day after the bank is closed. If such a deposit occurred on a bank statement date, it would not appear on this period's statement. The bank would record such a deposit on the next business day, and it would appear on the next period's bank statement. Deposits mailed to the bank near the end of a period also can be in transit and unrecorded when the statement is prepared.

- **Deductions for uncollectible items and for services.** [Adjust book balance.] A company sometimes deposits another party's check that is uncollectible (usually meaning the balance in that party's account is not large enough to cover the check). This check is called a *nonsufficient funds (NSF)* check. The bank would have initially credited the depositor's account for the amount of the check. When the bank learns the check is uncollectible, it debits (reduces) the depositor's account for the amount of that check. The bank may also charge the depositor a fee for processing an uncollectible check and notify the depositor of the deduction by sending a debit memorandum. The depositor should record each deduction when a debit memorandum is received, but an entry is sometimes not made until the bank reconciliation is prepared. Other possible bank charges to a depositor's account that are first reported on a bank statement include printing new checks and service fees.

- **Additions for collections and for interest.** [Adjust book balance.] Banks sometimes act as collection agents for their depositors by collecting notes and other items. Banks can also receive electronic funds transfers to the depositor's account. When a bank collects an item, it is added to the depositor's account, less any service fee. The bank also sends a credit memorandum to notify the depositor of the transaction. When the memorandum is received, the depositor should record it; yet it sometimes remains unrecorded until the bank reconciliation is prepared. The bank statement also includes a credit for any interest earned.

- **Errors.** [Adjust bank or book balance.] Both banks and depositors can make errors. Bank errors might not be discovered until the depositor prepares the bank reconciliation. Also, depositor errors are sometimes discovered when the bank balance is reconciled. Error testing includes: (a) comparing deposits on the bank statement with deposits in the accounting records and (b) comparing canceled checks on the bank statement with checks recorded in the accounting records.

Forms of Check Fraud (CkFraud.org)

- Forged signatures—legitimate blank checks with fake payer signature
- Forged endorsements—stolen check that is endorsed and cashed by someone other than the payee
- Counterfeit checks—fraudulent checks with fake payer signature
- Altered checks—legitimate check altered (such as changed payee or amount) to benefit perpetrator
- Check kiting—deposit check from one bank account (without sufficient funds) into a second bank account.

Point: Small businesses with few employees often allow recordkeepers to both write checks and keep the general ledger. If this is done, it is essential that the owner do the bank reconciliation.

Point: The person preparing the bank reconciliation should not be responsible for processing cash receipts, managing checks, or maintaining cash records.

Timing Differences   The following lists common timing differences. Each of these items has already been recorded by either the bank, or the company, but not both.

Reconciling Item	Is Already:	On Bank Reconciliation Must be:
Outstanding checks	Subtracted from book balance	Subtracted from bank balance
Deposits in transit	Added to book balance	Added to bank balance
Bank fees	Subtracted from bank balance	Subtracted from book balance
NSF checks	Subtracted from bank balance	Subtracted from book balance
Interest earned	Added to bank balance	Added to book balance

Illustration of a Bank Reconciliation   We follow nine steps in preparing the bank reconciliation. It is helpful to refer to the bank reconciliation in Exhibit 6.7 when studying steps ① through ⑨.

EXHIBIT 6.7

Bank Reconciliation

	VIDEOBUSTER Bank Reconciliation October 31, 2016						
①	Bank statement balance		$ 2,050.00	⑤	Book balance		$ 1,404.58
②	Add			⑥	Add		
	Deposit of Oct. 31 in transit		145.00		Collect $500 note less $15 fee	$485.00	
			2,195.00		Interest earned	8.42	493.42
③	Deduct						1,898.00
	Outstanding checks			⑦	Deduct		
	No. 124	$150.00			Check printing charge	23.00	
	No. 126	200.00	350.00		NSF check plus service fee	30.00	53.00
④	**Adjusted bank balance**		**$1,845.00**	⑧	**Adjusted book balance**		**$1,845.00**

⑨ Balances are equal (reconciled)

① Identify the bank statement balance of the Cash account (*balance per bank*). VideoBuster's bank balance is $2,050.

Point: Outstanding checks are identified by comparing canceled checks on the bank statement with checks recorded. This includes identifying any outstanding checks listed on the *previous* period's bank reconciliation that are not included in the canceled checks on this period's bank statement.

② Identify and list any unrecorded deposits and any bank errors understating the bank balance. Add them to the bank balance. VideoBuster's $145 deposit placed in the bank's night depository on October 31 is not recorded on its bank statement.

③ Identify and list any outstanding checks and any bank errors overstating the bank balance. Deduct them from the bank balance. VideoBuster's comparison of canceled checks with its books shows two checks outstanding: No. 124 for $150 and No. 126 for $200.

④ Compute the *adjusted bank balance,* also called the *corrected* or *reconciled balance.*

⑤ Identify the company's book balance of the Cash account (*balance per book*). VideoBuster's book balance is $1,404.58.

⑥ Identify and list any unrecorded credit memoranda from the bank, any interest earned, and errors understating the book balance. Add them to the book balance. VideoBuster's bank statement includes a credit memorandum showing the bank collected a note receivable for the company on October 23. The note's proceeds of $500 (minus a $15 collection fee) are credited to the company's account. VideoBuster's bank statement also shows a credit of $8.42 for interest earned on the average cash balance. There was no prior notification of this item, and it is not yet recorded.

⑦ Identify and list any unrecorded debit memoranda from the bank, any service charges, and errors overstating the book balance. Deduct them from the book balance. Debits on VideoBuster's bank statement that are not yet recorded include (a) a $23 charge for check printing and (b) an NSF check for $20 plus a related $10 processing fee. (The NSF check is dated October 16 and was included in the book balance.)

Point: Adjusting entries can be combined into one compound entry.

⑧ Compute the *adjusted book balance,* also called *corrected* or *reconciled balance.*

⑨ Verify that the two adjusted balances from steps 4 and 8 are equal. If so, they are reconciled. If not, check for accuracy and missing data to achieve reconciliation.

Adjusting Entries from a Bank Reconciliation   A bank reconciliation often identifies unrecorded items that need recording by the company. In VideoBuster's reconciliation, the adjusted balance of $1,845 is the correct balance as of October 31. But the company's accounting records show a $1,404.58 balance. We must prepare journal entries to adjust the book balance to the correct balance. **It is important to remember that only the items reconciling the *book***

balance **require adjustment**. A review of Exhibit 6.7 indicates that four entries are required for VideoBuster.

Collection of Note   The first entry is to record the proceeds of its note receivable collected by the bank less the expense of having the bank perform that service.

Oct. 31	Cash	485	
	Collection Expense	15	
	Notes Receivable		500
	Record collection fee and proceeds		
	for a note collected by the bank.		

Assets = Liabilities + Equity
+485   −15
−500

Interest Earned   The second entry records interest credited to its account by the bank.

Oct. 31	Cash	8.42	
	Interest Revenue.........................		8.42
	Record interest earned on the cash		
	balance in checking account.		

Assets = Liabilities + Equity
+8.42   +8.42

Check Printing   The third entry records expenses for the check printing charge.

Oct. 31	Miscellaneous Expenses........................	23	
	Cash		23
	Check printing charge.		

Assets = Liabilities + Equity
−23   −23

NSF Check   The fourth entry records the NSF check that is returned as uncollectible. The $20 check was originally received from T. Woods in payment of his account and then deposited. The bank charged $10 for handling the NSF check and deducted $30 total from VideoBuster's account. This means the entry must reverse the effects of the original entry made when the check was received and must record (add) the $10 bank fee.

Point: The company will try to collect the entire NSF amount of $30 from the customer.

Oct. 31	Accounts Receivable—T. Woods..................	30	
	Cash		30
	Charge Woods' account for $20 NSF check		
	and $10 bank fee.		

Assets = Liabilities + Equity
+30
−30

After these four entries are recorded, the book balance of cash is adjusted to the correct amount of $1,845 (the adjusted book balance). The Cash T-account to the side shows the same computation, where entries are keyed to the numerical codes in Exhibit 6.7.

Cash			
Unadj. bal.	1,404.58		
⑥	485.00	⑦	23.00
⑥	8.42	⑦	30.00
Adj. bal.	1,845.00		

Point: Need-To-Know 6-4 shows an adjusting entry for an error correction.

Fraud

Weakest Link The Association for Certified Fraud Examiners (ACFE) reports that the primary factor contributing to frauds is the lack of internal controls (33%), including the override of existing controls (19%). Together, this highlights the importance of internal controls (52%), including controls over cash. The chart shows the top five factors contributing to frauds.

Top Contributors to Fraud

Lack of competent oversight, 7%

Poor tone at the top, 8%

Other, 13%

Lack of internal controls, 33%

Override of existing controls, 19%

Lack of management review, 20%

Source: 2014 Report to the Nations, ACFE (acfe.com).

Bank Reconciliation

P3

The following information is available to reconcile Gucci's book balance of cash with its bank statement cash balance as of December 31, 2016.

a. The December 31 cash balance according to the accounting records is $1,610, and the bank statement cash balance for that date is $1,900.

b. Gucci's December 31 daily cash receipts of $800 were placed in the bank's night depository on December 31 but do not appear on the December 31 bank statement.

c. Check No. 6273 for $400 and Check No. 6282 for $100, both written and entered in the accounting records in December, are not among the canceled checks. Two checks, No. 6231 for $2,000 and No. 6242 for $200, were outstanding on the most recent November 30 reconciliation. Check No. 6231 is listed with the December canceled checks, but Check No. 6242 is not.

d. When the December checks are compared with entries in the accounting records, it is found that Check No. 6267 had been correctly drawn for $340 to pay for office supplies but was erroneously entered in the accounting records as $430.

e. A credit memorandum indicates that the bank collected $500 cash on a note receivable for the company, deducted a $30 collection fee, and credited the balance to the company's Cash account. Gucci had not recorded this transaction before receiving the statement.

f. Two debit memoranda are enclosed with the statement and are unrecorded at the time of the reconciliation. One debit memorandum is for $150 and dealt with an NSF check for $140 received from a customer, Prada Inc., in payment of its account. The bank assessed a $10 fee for processing it. The second debit memorandum is a $20 charge for check printing. Gucci had not recorded these transactions before receiving the statement.

Required

1. Prepare the bank reconciliation for this company as of December 31, 2016.

2. Prepare the journal entries necessary to bring Gucci's book balance of cash into conformity with the reconciled cash balance as of December 31, 2016.

Solutions

Part 1

GUCCI Bank Reconciliation December 31, 2016					
Bank statement balance..............		$1,900	Book balance...........		$1,610
Add			Add		
Deposit of Dec. 31		800	Error (Ck 6267)	$ 90	
		2,700	Proceeds of note		
			less $30 fee	470	560
					2,170
Deduct			Deduct		
Outstanding Checks No. 6242....	$200		NSF check	$150	
6273....	400		Printing fee...........	20	
6282....	100	700			170
Adjusted bank balance...............		$2,000	Adjusted book balance ...		$2,000

Part 2

Dec. 31	Cash	90	
	Office Supplies		90
	Correct an entry error.		
Dec. 31	Cash	470	
	Collection Expense	30	
	Notes Receivable		500
	Record note collection less fees.		
Dec. 31	Accounts Receivable—Prada Inc.	150	
	Cash		150
	Charge account for NSF check plus fees.		
Dec. 31	Miscellaneous Expenses...........................	20	
	Cash		20
	Record check printing charge.		

Do More: QS 6-5, QS 6-6, QS 6-7, E 6-8, E 6-9, E 6-10, E 6-11

GLOBAL VIEW

This section discusses similarities and differences between U.S. GAAP and IFRS regarding internal controls and in the accounting and reporting of cash.

Internal Control Purposes, Principles, and Procedures   Both U.S. GAAP and IFRS aim for high-quality financial reporting. The purposes and principles of internal control systems are fundamentally the same across the globe. However, culture and other realities suggest different emphases on the mix of control procedures, and some sensitivity to different customs and environments when establishing that mix. **Nokia** provides the following description of its control activities.

> Nokia has an internal audit function that acts as an independent appraisal function by examining and evaluating the adequacy and effectiveness of the company's system of internal control.

Control of Cash   Accounting definitions for cash are similar for U.S. GAAP and IFRS. The need for control of cash is universal. This means that companies worldwide desire to apply cash management procedures as explained in this chapter and aim to control both cash receipts and disbursements. Accordingly, systems that employ tools such as cash monitoring mechanisms, verification of documents, and petty cash processes are applied worldwide. The basic techniques of this chapter are part of those control procedures.

Banking Activities as Controls   There is a global demand for banking services, bank statements, and bank reconciliations. To the extent feasible, companies utilize banking services as part of their effective control procedures. Further, bank statements are similarly used along with bank reconciliations to control and monitor cash.

 IFRS

Internal controls are crucial to companies that convert from U.S. GAAP to IFRS. Major risks include misstatement of financial information and fraud. Other risks are ineffective communication of the impact of this change for investors, creditors, and others, and management's inability to certify the effectiveness of controls over financial reporting. ■

Sustainability and Accounting   Sergey Brin and Larry Page, founders of **Google**, are committed to sustainability and the environment. Their commitment to reducing Google's environmental imprint has earned the company a net zero carbon footprint. "My job as a leader is to make . . . a meaningful impact," insists Larry. This includes "contributing to the good of society." Google has achieved its net zero footprint by consuming less energy, using a greater percentage of renewable energy, and investing in projects that reduce carbon emissions. At least 35% of Google's total energy consumption is from renewable sources like solar and wind power. Moreover, Google's data centers use 50% less energy than the average data center, and Google invests cash in projects outside of the company to reduce carbon emissions. Yet, Larry and Sergey have greater dreams. Google has made agreements to fund over $1.5 billion in renewable energy projects that will have a capacity of over 2.5 GW, which is equivalent to powering 500,000 homes. Sergey stresses that he and Larry "want to be looked back on as being very innovative, very trusted and ethical, and ultimately making a big difference in the world."

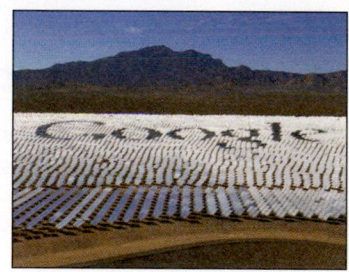

© STEVE MARCUS/Reuters/Corbis

Days' Sales Uncollected **Decision Analysis**

An important part of cash management is monitoring the receipt of cash from receivables. If customers and others who owe money to a company are delayed in payment, then that company can find it difficult to pay its obligations when they are due. A company's customers are crucial partners in its cash management. Many companies attract customers by selling to them on credit. This means that cash receipts from customers are delayed until accounts receivable are collected.

One measure of how quickly a company can convert its accounts receivable into cash is the **days' sales uncollected,** also called *days' sales in receivables.* This measure is computed by dividing the current balance of receivables by net credit sales over the year just completed and then multiplying by 365 (number

A1

Compute the days' sales uncollected ratio and use it to assess liquidity.

of days in a year). Since net credit sales usually are not reported to external users, the net sales (or revenues) figure is commonly used in the computation as in Exhibit 6.8.

EXHIBIT 6.8

Days' Sales Uncollected

$$\text{Days' sales uncollected} = \frac{\text{Accounts receivable}}{\text{Net sales}} \times 365$$

We use days' sales uncollected to estimate how much time is likely to pass before the current amount of
accounts receivable is received in cash. For evaluation purposes, we need to compare this estimate to that
for other companies in the same industry. We also make comparisons between current and prior periods.

To illustrate, we select data from the annual reports of two toy manufacturers, **Hasbro** and **Mattel**.
Their days' sales uncollected figures are shown in Exhibit 6.9.

EXHIBIT 6.9

Analysis Using Days' Sales
Uncollected

Company	Figure ($ millions)	2014	2013	2012	2011	2010
Hasbro	Accounts receivable	$1,095	$1,094	$1,030	$1,035	$961
	Net sales	$4,277	$4,082	$4,089	$4,286	$4,002
	Days' sales uncollected	**93 days**	**98 days**	**92 days**	**88 days**	**88 days**
Mattel	Accounts receivable	$1,093	$1,260	$1,227	$1,247	$1,146
	Net sales	$6,024	$6,485	$6,421	$6,266	$5,856
	Days' sales uncollected	**66 days**	**71 days**	**70 days**	**73 days**	**71 days**

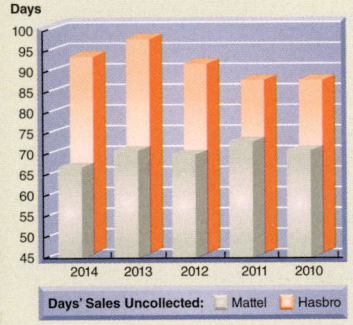

Days' sales uncollected for Hasbro in 2014 is computed as ($1,095/$4,277) × 365 days = 93 days.
This means that it will take about 93 days to collect cash from ending accounts receivable. This
number reflects one or more of the following factors: a company's ability to collect receivables,
customer financial health, customer payment strategies, and discount terms. To further assess
days' sales uncollected for Hasbro, we compare it to its own four prior years and to those of
Mattel. We see that Hasbro's days' sales uncollected has worsened in 2012 and 2013 as it took
longer to collect its receivables relative to prior years; however, 2014 marked an improvement as
the days' sales uncollected was shorter. In comparison, Mattel's performance bounced around
71 days, but markedly improved to only 66 days in 2014. For all years, Mattel is superior to
Hasbro on this measure of cash management. The less time that money is tied up in receivables
often translates into increased profitability.

■ **Decision Maker**

Sales Representative   The sales staff are told to take action to help reduce days' sales uncollected for cash
management purposes. What can you, a salesperson, do to reduce days' sales uncollected? ■ [Answers follow the
chapter's Summary.]

 6-5

COMPREHENSIVE

Prepare a bank reconciliation for Jamboree Enterprises for the month ended November 30, 2016. The following information is available to reconcile Jamboree Enterprises's book balance of cash with its bank
statement balance as of November 30, 2016:

a. After all posting is complete on November 30, the company's book balance of cash has a $16,380 debit
balance, but its bank statement shows a $38,520 balance.

b. Checks No. 2024 for $4,810 and No. 2026 for $5,000 are outstanding.

c. In comparing the canceled checks on the bank statement with the entries in the accounting records,
it is found that Check No. 2025 in payment of rent is correctly drawn for $1,000 but is erroneously
entered in the accounting records as $880.

d. The November 30 deposit of $17,150 was placed in the night depository after banking hours on that
date, and this amount does not appear on the bank statement.

e. In reviewing the bank statement, a check written by Jumbo Enterprises in the amount of $160 was erroneously drawn against Jamboree's account.

f. A credit memorandum enclosed with the bank statement indicates that the bank collected a $30,000 note and $900 of related interest on Jamboree's behalf. This transaction was not recorded by Jamboree prior to receiving the statement.

g. A debit memorandum for $1,100 lists a $1,100 NSF check received from a customer, Marilyn Welch. Jamboree had not recorded the return of this check before receiving the statement.

h. Bank service charges for November total $40. These charges were not recorded by Jamboree before receiving the statement.

Point: Generally, the party that is not the initial recorder of an item, but is later informed, includes that item on its "book" of the bank reconciliation. For example, the bank records an NSF check and then informs the company. The company, as not the initial recorder of the item, reports it on the book side of its reconciliation.

PLANNING THE SOLUTION

● Set up a bank reconciliation with a bank side and a book side (as in Exhibit 6.7). Leave room to both add and deduct items. Each column will result in a reconciled, equal balance.

● Examine each item *a* through *h* to determine whether it affects the book or the bank balance and whether it should be added or deducted from the bank or book balance.

● After all items are analyzed, complete the reconciliation and arrive at a reconciled balance between the bank side and the book side.

● For each reconciling item on the book side, prepare an adjusting entry. Additions to the book side require an adjusting entry that debits Cash. Deductions on the book side require an adjusting entry that credits Cash.

SOLUTION

JAMBOREE ENTERPRISES
Bank Reconciliation
November 30, 2016

Bank statement balance		$ 38,520	Book balance		$ 16,380
Add			Add		
Deposit of Nov. 30	$17,150		Collection of note	$30,000	
Bank error (Jumbo)	160	17,310	Interest earned	900	30,900
		55,830			47,280
Deduct			Deduct		
Outstanding checks			NSF check (M. Welch)	1,100	
No. 2024	4,810		Recording error (# 2025) ...	120	
No. 2026	5,000	9,810	Service charge	40	1,260
Adjusted bank balance ...		**$46,020**	**Adjusted book balance**		**$46,020**

Required Adjusting Entries for Jamboree

Nov. 30	Cash	30,900	
	Notes Receivable		30,000
	Interest Earned		900
	Record collection of note with interest.		
Nov. 30	Accounts Receivable—M. Welch	1,100	
	Cash		1,100
	Reinstate account due from an NSF check.		
Nov. 30	Rent Expense	120	
	Cash		120
	Correct recording error on Check No. 2025.		
Nov. 30	Bank Service Charges	40	
	Cash		40
	Record bank service charges.		

Point: Error correction can alternatively involve (1) reversing the erroneous entry and (2) recording the correct entry. Auditors prefer this alternative.

APPENDIX

6A

Documentation and Verification

P4
_____

Describe use of
documentation and
verification to control cash
disbursements.

This appendix describes the important business documents of a voucher system of control.

Purchase Requisition   Department managers are usually not allowed to place orders directly with suppliers for control purposes. Instead, a department manager must inform the purchasing department of its needs by preparing and signing a **purchase requisition,** which lists the merchandise needed and requests that it be purchased—see Exhibit 6A.1. Two copies of the purchase requisition are sent to the purchasing department, which then sends one copy to the accounting department. When the accounting department receives a purchase requisition, it creates and maintains a voucher for this transaction. The requesting department keeps the third copy.

EXHIBIT 6A.1

Purchase Requisition

Z-Mart

PURCHASE REQUISITION   No. 917

| From | _Sporting Goods Department_ | Date | _October 28, 2016_ |
| To | _Purchasing Department_ | Preferred Vendor | _Trex_ |

Request purchase of the following item(s):

MODEL NO.	DESCRIPTION	QUANTITY
CH 015	Toddler–Challenger X7	1
SD 099	Boys/Girls–Speed Demon	1

Reason for Request _____ _Replenish inventory_

Approval for Request _____ _T.Z._

For Purchasing Department use only: Order Date _10/30/16_   P.O. No. _P98_

Purchase Order   A **purchase order** is a document the purchasing department uses to place an order with a **vendor** (seller or supplier). A purchase order authorizes a vendor to ship ordered merchandise at the stated price and terms—see Exhibit 6A.2. When the purchasing department receives a purchase requisition, it prepares at least five copies of a purchase order. The copies are distributed as follows: *copy 1* to the vendor as a purchase request and as authority to ship merchandise; *copy 2,* along with a copy of the purchase requisition, to the accounting department, where it is entered in the voucher and used in approving payment of the invoice; *copy 3* to the requesting department to inform its manager that action is being taken; *copy 4*

Point: A voucher system is designed to uniquely meet the needs of a specific business. Thus, we should read this appendix as one example of a common voucher system design, but *not* the only design.

EXHIBIT 6A.2

Purchase Order

Point: Shipping terms and credit terms are shown on the purchase order.

to the receiving department without order quantity so it can compare with goods received and provide an independent count of goods received; and *copy 5* retained on file by the purchasing department.

Invoice An **invoice** is an itemized statement of goods prepared by the vendor listing the customer's name, items sold, sales prices, and terms of sale. An invoice is also a bill sent to the buyer from the supplier. From the vendor's point of view, it is a *sales invoice*. The buyer, or **vendee,** treats it as a *purchase invoice*. When receiving a purchase order, the vendor ships the ordered merchandise to the buyer and includes or mails a copy of the invoice covering the shipment to the buyer. The invoice is sent to the buyer's accounting department where it is placed in the voucher. (Refer back to Exhibit 4.6, which shows Z-Mart's purchase invoice.)

Receiving Report Many companies maintain a separate department to receive all merchandise and purchased assets. When each shipment arrives, this receiving department counts the goods and checks them for damage and agreement with the purchase order. It then prepares four or more copies of a **receiving report,** which is used within the company to notify the appropriate persons that ordered goods have been received and to describe the quantities and condition of the goods. One copy is sent to accounting and placed in the voucher. Copies are also sent to the requesting department and the purchasing department to notify them that the goods have arrived. The receiving department retains a copy in its files.

Invoice Approval When a receiving report arrives, the accounting department should have copies of the following documents in the voucher: purchase requisition, purchase order, and invoice. With the information in these documents, the accounting department can record the purchase and approve its payment. In approving an invoice for payment, it checks and compares information across all documents. To facilitate this checking and to ensure that no step is omitted, it often uses an **invoice approval,** also called *check authorization*—see Exhibit 6A.3. An invoice approval is a checklist of steps necessary for approving an invoice for recording and payment. It is a separate document either filed in the voucher or preprinted (or stamped) on the voucher.

EXHIBIT 6A.3

Invoice Approval

INVOICE APPROVAL			
DOCUMENT		**BY**	**DATE**
Purchase requisition	· 917	TZ	10/28/16
Purchase order	P98	JW	10/30/16
Receiving report	R85	SK	11/03/16
Invoice:	4657		11/12/16
Price		JK	11/12/16
Calculations		JK	11/12/16
Terms		JK	11/12/16
Approved for payment		BC	

As each step in the checklist is approved, the person initials the invoice approval and records the current date. Final approval implies the following steps have occurred:

1. **Requisition check:** Items on invoice are requested per purchase requisition.
2. **Purchase order check:** Items on invoice are ordered per purchase order.
3. **Receiving report check:** Items on invoice are received per receiving report.
4. **Invoice check: Price:** Invoice prices are as agreed with the vendor.
   Calculations: Invoice has no mathematical errors.
   Terms: Terms are as agreed with the vendor.

Voucher Once an invoice has been checked and approved, the voucher is complete. A complete voucher is a record summarizing a transaction. Once the voucher certifies a transaction, it authorizes recording an obligation. A voucher also contains approval for paying the obligation on an appropriate date. The physical form of a voucher varies across companies. Many are designed so that the invoice and other related source documents are placed inside the voucher, which can be a folder.

Completion of a voucher usually requires a person to enter certain information on both the inside and outside of the voucher. Typical information required on the inside of a voucher is shown in Exhibit 6A.4, and that for the outside is shown in Exhibit 6A.5. This information is taken from the invoice and the supporting documents filed in the voucher. A complete voucher is sent to an authorized individual (often called an *auditor*). This person performs a final review, approves the accounts and amounts for debiting (called the *accounting distribution*), and authorizes recording of the voucher.

After a voucher is approved and recorded (in a journal called a **voucher register**), it is filed by its due date. A check is then sent on the payment date from the cashier, the voucher is marked "paid," and the voucher is sent to the accounting department and recorded (in a journal called the **check register**). The

Point: Recording a purchase is initiated by an invoice approval, not an invoice. An invoice approval verifies that the amount is consistent with that requested, ordered, and received. This controls and verifies purchases and related liabilities.

Point: Auditors, when auditing inventory, check a sampling of purchases by reviewing the purchase order, receiving report, and invoice.

EXHIBIT 6A.4

Inside of a Voucher

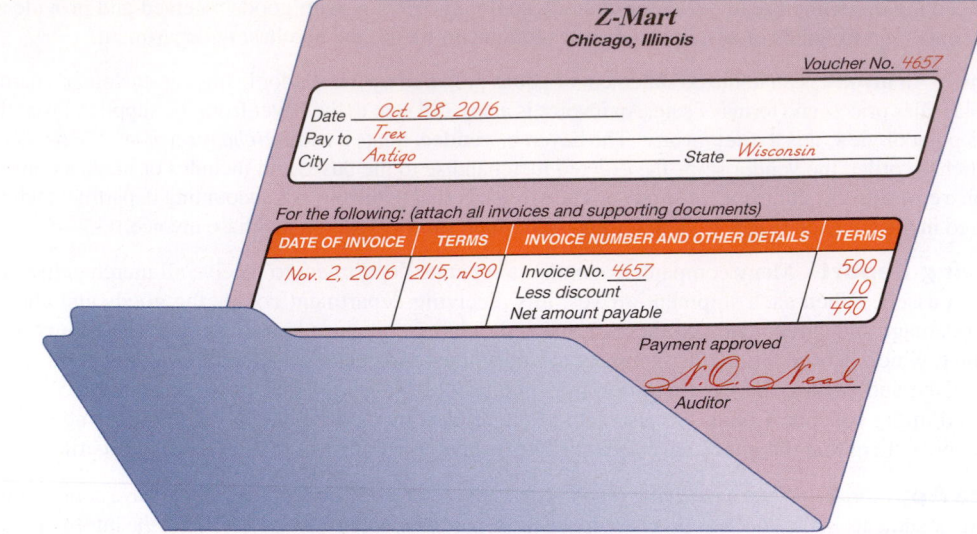

EXHIBIT 6A.5

Outside of a Voucher

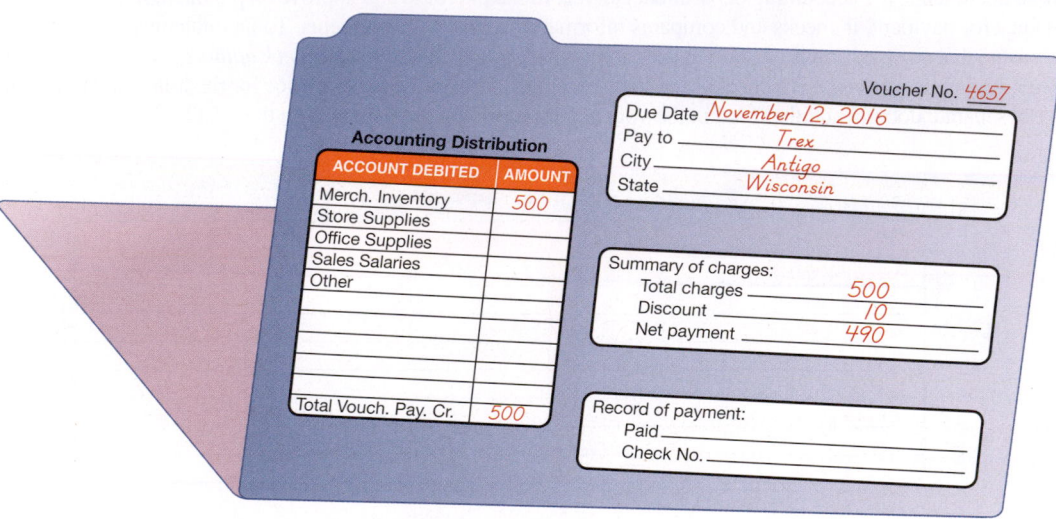

person issuing checks relies on the approved voucher and its signed supporting documents as proof that an obligation has been incurred and must be paid. The purchase requisition and purchase order confirm the purchase was authorized. The receiving report shows that items have been received, and the invoice approval form verifies that the invoice has been checked for errors. There is little chance for error and even less chance for fraud without collusion unless all the documents and signatures are forged.

Summary

C1 **Define internal control and identify its purpose and principles.** An internal control system consists of the policies and procedures managers use to protect assets, ensure reliable accounting, promote efficient operations, and urge adherence to company policies. It can prevent avoidable losses and help managers both plan operations and monitor company and human performance. Principles of good internal control include establishing responsibilities, maintaining adequate records, insuring assets and bonding employees, separating recordkeeping from custody of assets, dividing responsibilities for related transactions, applying technological controls, and performing regular independent reviews.

C2 **Define cash and cash equivalents and explain how to report them.** Cash includes currency, coins, and amounts

on (or acceptable for) deposit in checking and savings accounts. Cash equivalents are short-term, highly liquid investment assets readily convertible to a known cash amount and sufficiently close to their maturity date so that market value is not sensitive to interest rate changes. Cash and cash equivalents are liquid assets because they are readily converted into other assets or can be used to pay for goods, services, or liabilities.

A1 **Compute the days' sales uncollected ratio and use it to assess liquidity.** Many companies attract customers by selling to them on credit. This means that cash receipts from customers are delayed until accounts receivable are collected. Users want to know how quickly a company can convert its accounts receivable into cash. The days' sales uncollected ratio, one measure reflecting company liquidity, is computed by dividing the ending balance of receivables by annual net sales, and then multiplying by 365.

P1 **Apply internal control to cash receipts and disbursements.** Internal control of cash receipts ensures that all cash received is properly recorded and deposited. Attention focuses on two important types of cash receipts: over-the-counter and by mail. Good internal control for over-the-counter cash receipts includes use of a cash register, customer review, use of receipts, a permanent transaction record, and separation of the custody of cash from its recordkeeping. Good internal control for cash receipts by mail includes at least two people assigned to open mail and a listing of each sender's name, amount, and explanation. (Banks offer several services that promote the control and safeguarding of cash.)

P2 **Explain and record petty cash fund transactions.** Petty cash disbursements are payments of small amounts for items such as postage, courier fees, minor repairs, and supplies. A company usually sets up one or more petty cash funds. A petty cash fund cashier is responsible for safekeeping the cash, making payments from this fund, and keeping receipts and

records. A Petty Cash account is debited only when the fund is established or increased in amount. When the fund is replenished, petty cash disbursements are recorded with debits to expense (or asset) accounts and a credit to Cash.

P3 **Prepare a bank reconciliation.** A bank reconciliation proves the accuracy of the depositor's and the bank's records. The bank statement balance is adjusted for items such as outstanding checks and unrecorded deposits made on or before the bank statement date but not reflected on the statement. The book balance is adjusted for items such as service charges, bank collections for the depositor, and interest earned on the account.

P4ᴬ **Describe use of documentation and verification to control cash disbursements.** A voucher system is a set of procedures and approvals designed to control cash disbursements and acceptance of obligations. The voucher system of control relies on several important documents, including the voucher and its supporting files. A key factor in this system is that only approved departments and individuals are authorized to incur certain obligations.

Guidance Answers to Decision Maker

Entrepreneur To achieve proper separation of duties, a minimum of three employees is required. Transaction authorization, recording, and asset custody are ideally handled by three employees. Many small businesses do not employ three workers. In such cases, an owner must exercise more oversight to make sure that the lack of separation of duties does not result in fraudulent transactions.

Sales Representative A salesperson can take several steps to reduce days' sales uncollected. These include (1) decreasing the ratio of sales on account to total sales by encouraging more cash sales, (2) identifying customers most delayed in their payments and encouraging earlier payments or cash sales, and (3) applying stricter credit policies to eliminate credit sales to customers that never pay.

Key Terms

Bank reconciliation	Deposit ticket	Purchase order
Bank statement	Deposits in transit	Purchase requisition
Canceled checks	Electronic funds transfer (EFT)	Receiving report
Cash	Internal control system	Sarbanes-Oxley Act (SOX)
Cash equivalents	Invoice	Section 404 (of SOX)
Cash Over and Short	Invoice approval	Signature card
Check	Liquid assets	Vendee
Check register	Liquidity	Vendor
Committee of Sponsoring Organizations (COSO)	Outstanding checks	Voucher
	Petty cash	Voucher register
Days' sales uncollected	Principles of internal control	Voucher system

Multiple Choice Quiz   Answers at end of chapter

1. A company needs to replenish its $500 petty cash fund. Its petty cashbox has $75 cash and petty cash receipts of $420. The journal entry to replenish the fund includes
   a. A debit to Cash for $75.
   b. A credit to Cash for $75.
   c. A credit to Petty Cash for $420.
   d. A credit to Cash Over and Short for $5.
   e. A debit to Cash Over and Short for $5.

2. The following information is available for Hapley Company:
   • The November 30 bank statement shows a $1,895 balance.
   • The general ledger shows a $1,742 balance at November 30.
   • A $795 deposit placed in the bank's night depository on November 30 does not appear on the November 30 bank statement.
   • Outstanding checks amount to $638 at November 30.

- A customer's $335 note was collected by the bank in November. A collection fee of $15 was deducted by the bank and the difference deposited in Hapley's account.
- A bank service charge of $10 is deducted by the bank and appears on the November 30 bank statement.

How will the customer's note appear on Hapley's November 30 bank reconciliation?

   a. $320 appears as an addition to the book balance of cash.

   b. $320 appears as a deduction from the book balance of cash.

   c. $320 appears as an addition to the bank balance of cash.

   d. $320 appears as a deduction from the bank balance of cash.

   e. $335 appears as an addition to the bank balance of cash.

3. Using the information from question 2, what is the reconciled balance on Hapley's November 30 bank reconciliation?

   a. $2,052   **c.** $1,742   **e.** $1,184

   b. $1,895   **d.** $2,201

4. A company had net sales of $84,000 and accounts receivable of $6,720. Its days' sales uncollected is

   a. 3.2 days   **c.** 230.0 days   **e.** 12.5 days

   b. 18.4 days   **d.** 29.2 days

---

^A *Superscript letter A denotes assignments based on Appendix 6A.*

 Icon denotes assignments that involve decision making.

Discussion Questions

1. List the seven broad principles of internal control.

2. 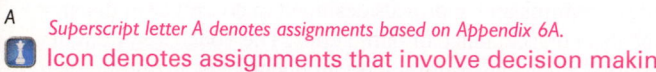 Internal control procedures are important in every business, but at what stage in the development of a business do they become especially critical?

3. Why should responsibility for related transactions be divided among different departments or individuals?

4. Why should the person who keeps the records of an asset not be the person responsible for its custody?

5. When a store purchases merchandise, why are individual departments not allowed to directly deal with suppliers?

6. What are the limitations of internal controls?

7. Which of the following assets—inventory, building, accounts receivable, or cash—is most liquid? Which is least liquid?

8. What is a petty cash receipt? Who should sign it?

9. Why should cash receipts be deposited on the day of receipt?

10. **Apple**'s statement of cash flows in Appendix A describes changes in cash and cash equivalents for the year ended September 27, 2014. What total **APPLE** amount is provided (used) by investing activities? What amount is provided (used) by financing activities?

11. Refer to **Google**'s financial statements in Appendix A. Identify Google's net **GOOGLE** earnings (income) for the year ended December 31, 2014. Is its net earnings equal to the change in cash and cash equivalents for the year? Explain the difference between net earnings and the change in cash and cash equivalents.

12. Refer to **Samsung**'s balance **Samsung** sheet in Appendix A. How does its cash (titled "Cash and cash equivalents") compare with its other current assets (in both amount and percent) as of December 31, 2014? Compare and assess its cash at December 31, 2014, with its cash at December 31, 2013.

13. **Samsung**'s balance sheet in Appendix A reports the change in **Samsung** cash and equivalents for the year ended December 31, 2014. Identify the cash generated (or used) by operating activities, by investing activities, and by financing (funding) activities.

---

^{Mc} **connect**

QUICK STUDY

QS 6-1
Internal control objectives

C1

An internal control system consists of all policies and procedures used to protect assets, ensure reliable accounting, promote efficient operations, and urge adherence to company policies. Evaluate each of the following statements and indicate which are true and which are false regarding the objectives of an internal control system.

_____ **1.** Separation of recordkeeping for assets from the custody over assets is intended to reduce theft and fraud.

_____ **2.** The primary objective of internal control procedures is to safeguard the business against theft from government agencies.

_____ **3.** The main objective of internal control procedures is best accomplished by designing an operational system with managerial policies that protect the assets from waste, fraud, and theft.

_____ **4.** Separating the responsibility for a transaction between two or more individuals or departments will not help prevent someone from creating a fictitious invoice and paying the money to herself or himself.

QS 6-2
Cash and equivalents

C2

Choose from the following list of terms/phrases to best complete the following statements.

   a. Cash   **c.** Outstanding check   **e.** Bank reconciliation

   b. Cash equivalents   **d.** Liquidity   **f.** Current assets

____ **1.** The _____ category includes currency and coins along with amounts on deposit in bank accounts, checking accounts, and savings accounts.

____ **2.** The term _____ refers to a company's ability to pay for its near-term obligations.

____ **3.** The _____ category includes short-term, highly liquid investment assets that are readily convertible to a known cash amount and sufficiently close to their due dates so that their market value is not sensitive to interest rate changes.

A good system of internal control for cash provides adequate procedures for protecting both cash receipts and cash disbursements. Identify each of the following statements as either true or false regarding this protection.

____ **a.** A basic guideline for safeguarding cash is that all cash receipts be deposited weekly or monthly.

____ **b.** A voucher system of control is a control system exclusively for cash receipts.

____ **c.** A basic guideline for safeguarding cash is to separate the duties of those who have custody of cash from those who keep cash records.

____ **d.** A petty cash system is not a control procedure for safeguarding cash.

QS 6-3
Internal control for cash
P1

---

1. The petty cash fund of the Brooks Agency is established at $150. At the end of the current period, the fund contained $28 and had the following receipts: film rentals, $24; refreshments for meetings, $46 (both expenditures to be classified as Entertainment Expense); postage, $30; and printing, $22. Prepare journal entries to record (a) establishment of the fund and (b) reimbursement of the fund at the end of the current period.

2. Identify the two events from the following that cause a Petty Cash account to be credited in a journal entry.

____ **a.** Fund amount is being reduced.   ____ **c.** Fund is being eliminated.

____ **b.** Fund amount is being increased.   ____ **d.** Fund is being established.

QS 6-4
Petty cash accounting
P2

For each of the following items *a* through *g*, indicate whether its amount (1) affects the bank or book side of a bank reconciliation, (2) represents an addition or a subtraction in a bank reconciliation, and (3) requires an adjusting journal entry.

QS 6-5
Bank reconciliation
P3

	Bank or Book Side	Add or Subtract	Adj. Entry or Not
a. Interest on cash balance..........			
b. Bank service charges			
c. Debit memos			
d. Outstanding checks			
e. Credit memos.................			
f. NSF checks..................			
g. Outstanding deposits			

Nolan Company deposits all cash receipts on the day when they are received and it makes all cash payments by check. At the close of business on June 30, 2016, its Cash account shows a $22,352 debit balance. Nolan's June 30 bank statement shows $21,332 on deposit in the bank. Prepare a bank reconciliation for the company using the following information.

a. Outstanding checks as of June 30 total $3,713.

b. The June 30 bank statement included a $41 debit memorandum for bank services; the company has not yet recorded the cost of these services.

c. In reviewing the bank statement, a $90 check written by the company was mistakenly recorded in the company's books at $99.

d. June 30 cash receipts of $4,724 were placed in the bank's night depository after banking hours and were not recorded on the June 30 bank statement.

e. The bank statement included a $23 credit for interest earned on the cash in the bank.

QS 6-6
Bank reconciliation
P3

An entrepreneur commented that a bank reconciliation may not be necessary as she regularly reviews her online bank statement for any unusual items and errors.

a. Describe how a bank reconciliation and an online review (or reading) of the bank statement are not equivalent.

b. Identify and explain at least two frauds or errors that would be uncovered through a bank reconciliation and that would *not* be uncovered through an online review of the bank statement.

QS 6-7
Reviewing bank statements
P3

QS 6-8

Days' sales uncollected

A1

The following annual account balances are taken from Armour Sports at December 31.

	2016	2015
Accounts receivable.........	$ 100,000	$ 85,000
Net sales	2,500,000	2,000,000

What is the change in the number of days' sales uncollected between years 2015 and 2016? (Round the number of days to one decimal.) According to this analysis, is the company's collection of receivables improving? Explain.

QS 6-9ᴬ

Documents in a voucher system   **P4**

Management uses a voucher system to help control and monitor cash disbursements. Which of the four documents listed below are prepared as part of a voucher system of control?

____ **a.** Purchase order   ____ **b.** Outstanding check   ____ **c.** Invoice   ____ **d.** Voucher

---

QS 6-10

International accounting and internal controls

C1   P1

Answer each of the following related to international accounting standards.

a. Explain how the purposes and principles of internal controls are different between accounting systems reporting under IFRS versus U.S. GAAP.

b. Cash presents special internal control challenges. How do internal controls for cash differ for accounting systems reporting under IFRS versus U.S. GAAP? How do the procedures applied differ across those two accounting systems?

EXERCISES

Exercise 6-1

Analyzing internal control

C1

Franco Company is a rapidly growing start-up business. Its recordkeeper, who was hired six months ago, left town after the company's manager discovered that a large sum of money had disappeared over the past three months. An audit disclosed that the recordkeeper had written and signed several checks made payable to her fiancé and then recorded the checks as salaries expense. The fiancé, who cashed the checks but never worked for the company, left town with the recordkeeper. As a result, the company incurred an uninsured loss of $184,000.

Evaluate Franco's internal control system and indicate which principles of internal control appear to have been ignored.

Exercise 6-2

Internal control recommendations

C1

What internal control procedures would you recommend in each of the following situations?

1. A concession company has one employee who sells towels, coolers, and sunglasses at the beach. Each day, the employee is given enough towels, coolers, and sunglasses to last through the day and enough cash to make change. The money is kept in a box at the stand.

2. An antique store has one employee who is given cash and sent to garage sales each weekend. The employee pays cash for any merchandise acquired that the antique store resells.

Exercise 6-3

Cash, liquidity, and return

C2

Good accounting systems help with the management and control of cash and cash equivalents.

1. Define and contrast the terms *liquid asset* and *cash equivalent.*

2. Why would companies invest their idle cash in cash equivalents?

3. Identify five principles of effective cash management.

Exercise 6-4

Control of cash receipts by mail

P1

Some of Crown Company's cash receipts from customers are received by the company with the regular mail. The company's recordkeeper opens these letters and deposits the cash received each day.

a. Identify any internal control problem(s) in this arrangement.

b. What changes to its internal control system do you recommend?

Exercise 6-5

Petty cash fund with a shortage   **P2**

Check   (2) Cr. Cash $246 and (3) Cr. Cash $50

Waupaca Company establishes a $350 petty cash fund on September 9. On September 30, the fund shows $104 in cash along with receipts for the following expenditures: transportation-in, $40; postage expenses, $123; and miscellaneous expenses, $80. The petty cashier could not account for a $3 shortage in the fund.

The company uses the perpetual system in accounting for merchandise inventory. Prepare (1) the September 9 entry to establish the fund, (2) the September 30 entry to reimburse the fund, and (3) an October 1 entry to increase the fund to $400.

Palmona Co. establishes a $200 petty cash fund on January 1. On January 8, the fund shows $38 in cash along with receipts for the following expenditures: postage, $74; transportation-in, $29; delivery expenses, $16; and miscellaneous expenses, $43.

Palmona uses the perpetual system in accounting for merchandise inventory. Prepare journal entries to (1) establish the fund on January 1, (2) reimburse it on January 8, and (3) both reimburse the fund and increase it to $450 on January 8, assuming no entry in part 2. (*Hint:* Make two separate entries for part 3.)

Exercise 6-6
Petty cash fund
accounting   **P2**

Check   (3) Cr. Cash $162 &
$250

The voucher system of control is designed to control cash disbursements and the acceptance of obligations.

1. The voucher system of control establishes procedures for what two processes?

2. What types of expenditures should be overseen by a voucher system of control?

3. When is the voucher initially prepared? Explain.

Exercise 6-7
Voucher system

P1

Prepare a table with the following headings for a monthly bank reconciliation dated September 30.

Exercise 6-8
Bank reconciliation and
adjusting entries

P3

Bank Balance		Book Balance			Not Shown on the Reconciliation
Add	Deduct	Add	Deduct	Adjust	

For each item 1 through 12, place an *x* in the appropriate column to indicate whether the item should be added to or deducted from the book or bank balance, or whether it should not appear on the reconciliation. If the book balance is to be adjusted, place a *Dr.* or *Cr.* in the Adjust column to indicate whether the Cash balance should be debited or credited. At the left side of your table, number the items to correspond to the following list.

1. NSF check from customer is returned on September 25 but not yet recorded by this company.

2. Interest earned on the September cash balance in the bank.

3. Deposit made on September 5 and processed by the bank on September 6.

4. Checks written by another depositor but charged against this company's account.

5. Bank service charge for September.

6. Checks outstanding on August 31 that cleared the bank in September.

7. Check written against the company's account and cleared by the bank; erroneously not recorded by the company's recordkeeper.

8. Principal and interest on a note receivable to this company is collected by the bank but not yet recorded by the company.

9. Checks written and mailed to payees on October 2.

10. Checks written by the company and mailed to payees on September 30.

11. Night deposit made on September 30 after the bank closed.

12. Special bank charge for collection of note in part 8 on this company's behalf.

Del Gato Clinic deposits all cash receipts on the day when they are received and it makes all cash payments by check. At the close of business on June 30, 2016, its Cash account shows an $11,589 debit balance. Del Gato Clinic's June 30 bank statement shows $10,555 on deposit in the bank. Prepare a bank reconciliation for Del Gato Clinic using the following information:

a. Outstanding checks as of June 30 total $1,829.

b. The June 30 bank statement included a $16 debit memorandum for bank services.

c. Check No. 919, listed with the canceled checks, was correctly drawn for $467 in payment of a utility bill on June 15. Del Gato Clinic mistakenly recorded it with a debit to Utilities Expense and a credit to Cash in the amount of $476.

d. The June 30 cash receipts of $2,856 were placed in the bank's night depository after banking hours and were not recorded on the June 30 bank statement.

Exercise 6-9
Bank reconciliation

P3

Check   Reconciled bal.,
$11,582

Prepare the adjusting journal entries that Del Gato Clinic must record as a result of preparing the bank reconciliation in Exercise 6-9.

Exercise 6-10
Adjusting entries from
bank reconciliation   **P3**

Exercise 6-11
Bank reconciliation
P3

Wright Company deposits all cash receipts on the day when they are received and it makes all cash payments by check. At the close of business on May 31, 2016, its Cash account shows a $27,500 debit balance. The company's May 31 bank statement shows $25,800 on deposit in the bank. Prepare a bank reconciliation for the company using the following information.

a. The May 31 bank statement included a $100 debit memorandum for bank services; the company has not yet recorded the cost of these services.

b. Outstanding checks as of May 31 total $5,600.

c. May 31 cash receipts of $6,200 were placed in the bank's night depository after banking hours and were not recorded on the May 31 bank statement.

d. In reviewing the bank statement, a $400 check written by Smith Company was mistakenly drawn against Wright's account.

Check   Reconciled bal.,
$26,800

e. A debit memorandum for $600 refers to a $600 NSF check from a customer; the company has not yet recorded this NSF check.

Exercise 6-12
Liquid assets and
accounts receivable
A1

Barga Co. reported net sales for 2015 and 2016 of $730,000 and $1,095,000, respectively. Its year-end balances of accounts receivable follow: December 31, 2015, $65,000; and December 31, 2016, $123,000.

a. Calculate its days' sales uncollected at the end of each year. Round the number of days to one decimal.

b. Evaluate and comment on any changes in the amount of liquid assets tied up in receivables.

Exercise 6-13^A
Documents in a voucher
system
P4

Match each document in a voucher system in column one with its description in column two.

Document

1. Purchase requisition
2. Purchase order
3. Invoice
4. Receiving report
5. Invoice approval
6. Voucher

Description

_____ **A.** An itemized statement of goods prepared by the vendor listing the customer's name, items sold, sales prices, and terms of sale.

_____ **B.** An internal file used to store documents and information to control cash disbursements and to ensure that a transaction is properly authorized and recorded.

_____ **C.** A document used to place an order with a vendor that authorizes the vendor to ship ordered merchandise at the stated price and terms.

_____ **D.** A checklist of steps necessary for the approval of an invoice for recording and payment; also known as a check authorization.

_____ **E.** A document used by department managers to inform the purchasing department to place an order with a vendor.

_____ **F.** A document used to notify the appropriate persons that ordered goods have arrived, including a description of the quantities and condition of goods.

---

 connect

PROBLEM SET A

Problem 6-1A
Analyzing internal
control
C1

For each of these five separate cases, identify the principle(s) of internal control that is violated. Recommend what the business should do to ensure adherence to principles of internal control.

1. Jen Novinska records all incoming customer cash receipts for her employer and posts the customer payments to their respective accounts.

2. At Tico Company, Julia and Trevor alternate lunch hours. Julia is the petty cash custodian, but if someone needs petty cash when she is at lunch, Trevor fills in as custodian.

3. Nori Nozumi posts all patient charges and payments at the Hopeville Medical Clinic. Each night Nori backs up the computerized accounting system to a tape and stores the tape in a locked file at her desk.

4. Mike Derr prides himself on hiring quality workers who require little supervision. As office manager, Mike gives his employees full discretion over their tasks and for years has seen no reason to perform independent reviews of their work.

5. Carla Farah's manager has told her to reduce costs. Carla decides to raise the deductible on the plant's property insurance from $5,000 to $10,000. This cuts the property insurance premium in half. In a related move, she decides that bonding the plant's employees is a waste of money since the company has not experienced any losses due to employee theft. Carla saves the entire amount of the bonding insurance premium by dropping the bonding insurance.

Kiona Co. set up a petty cash fund for payments of small amounts. The following transactions involving the petty cash fund occurred in May (the last month of the company's fiscal year).

May 1   Prepared a company check for $300 to establish the petty cash fund.
 15   Prepared a company check to replenish the fund for the following expenditures made since May 1.
    a.   Paid $88 for janitorial services.
    b.   Paid $53.68 for miscellaneous expenses.
    c.   Paid postage expenses of $53.50.
    d.   Paid $47.15 to *The County Gazette* (the local newspaper) for an advertisement.
    e.   Counted $62.15 remaining in the petty cashbox.
 16   Prepared a company check for $200 to increase the fund to $500.
 31   The petty cashier reports that $288.20 cash remains in the fund. A company check is drawn to replenish the fund for the following expenditures made since May 15.
    f.   Paid postage expenses of $147.36.
    g.   Reimbursed the office manager for business mileage, $23.50.
    h.   Paid $34.75 to deliver merchandise to a customer, terms FOB destination.
 31   The company decides that the May 16 increase in the fund was too large. It reduces the fund by $100, leaving a total of $400.

Required

1. Prepare journal entries (in dollars and cents) to establish the fund on May 1, to replenish it on May 15 and on May 31, and to reflect any increase or decrease in the fund balance on May 16 and May 31.

Analysis Component

2. Explain how the company's financial statements are affected if the petty cash fund is not replenished and no entry is made on May 31.

Problem 6-2A
Establishing, reimbursing, and adjusting petty cash
P2

Check   (1) Cr. to Cash: May 15, $237.85; May 16, $200.00

Nakashima Gallery had the following petty cash transactions in February of the current year.

Feb. 2   Wrote a $400 check, cashed it, and gave the proceeds and the petty cashbox to Chloe Addison, the petty cashier.
 5   Purchased bond paper for the copier for $14.15 that is immediately used.
 9   Paid $32.50 COD shipping charges on merchandise purchased for resale, terms FOB shipping point. Nakashima uses the perpetual system to account for merchandise inventory.
 12   Paid $7.95 postage to express mail a contract to a client.
 14   Reimbursed Adina Sharon, the manager, $68 for business mileage on her car.
 20   Purchased stationery for $67.77 that is immediately used.
 23   Paid a courier $20 to deliver merchandise sold to a customer, terms FOB destination.
 25   Paid $13.10 COD shipping charges on merchandise purchased for resale, terms FOB shipping point.
 27   Paid $54 for postage expenses.
 28   The fund had $120.42 remaining in the petty cashbox. Sorted the petty cash receipts by accounts affected and exchanged them for a check to reimburse the fund for expenditures.
 28   The petty cash fund amount is increased by $100 to a total of $500.

Required

1. Prepare the journal entry to establish the petty cash fund.

2. Prepare a petty cash payments report for February with these categories: delivery expense, mileage expense, postage expense, merchandise inventory (for transportation-in), and office supplies expense. Sort the payments into the appropriate categories and total the expenditures in each category.

3. Prepare the journal entries (in dollars and cents) for part 2 to both (*a*) reimburse and (*b*) increase the fund amount.

Problem 6-3A
Establishing, reimbursing, and increasing petty cash
P2

Check   Cash credit: (3a) $279.58; (3b) $100.00

The following information is available to reconcile Branch Company's book balance of cash with its bank statement cash balance as of July 31, 2016.

a. On July 31, the company's Cash account has a $27,497 debit balance, but its July bank statement shows a $27,233 cash balance.

b. Check No. 3031 for $1,482 and Check No. 3040 for $558 were outstanding on the June 30 bank reconciliation. Check No. 3040 is listed with the July canceled checks, but Check No. 3031 is not. Also, Check No. 3065 for $382 and Check No. 3069 for $2,281, both written in July, are not among the canceled checks on the July 31 statement.

Problem 6-4A
Preparing a bank reconciliation and recording adjustments
P3

c. In comparing the canceled checks on the bank statement with the entries in the accounting records, it is found that Check No. 3056 for July rent was correctly written and drawn for $1,270 but was erroneously entered in the accounting records as $1,250.

d. A credit memorandum enclosed with the July bank statement indicates the bank collected $8,000 cash on a noninterest-bearing note for Branch, deducted a $45 collection fee, and credited the remainder to its account. Branch had not recorded this event before receiving the statement.

e. A debit memorandum for $805 lists a $795 NSF check plus a $10 NSF charge. The check had been received from a customer, Evan Shaw. Branch has not yet recorded this check as NSF.

f. Enclosed with the July statement is a $25 debit memorandum for bank services. It has not yet been recorded because no previous notification had been received.

g. Branch's July 31 daily cash receipts of $11,514 were placed in the bank's night depository on that date but do not appear on the July 31 bank statement.

Required

Check   (1) Reconciled balance, $34,602; (2) Cr. Notes Receivable $8,000

1. Prepare the bank reconciliation for this company as of July 31, 2016.

2. Prepare the journal entries necessary to bring the company's book balance of cash into conformity with the reconciled cash balance as of July 31, 2016.

Analysis Component

3. Assume that the July 31, 2016, bank reconciliation for this company is prepared and some items are treated incorrectly. For each of the following errors, explain the effect of the error on (i) the adjusted bank statement cash balance and (ii) the adjusted Cash account book balance.

   a. The company's unadjusted Cash account balance of $27,497 is listed on the reconciliation as $27,947.

   b. The bank's collection of the $8,000 note less the $45 collection fee is added to the bank statement cash balance on the reconciliation.

Problem 6-5A
Preparing a bank reconciliation and recording adjustments
P3

Chavez Company most recently reconciled its bank statement and book balances of cash on August 31 and it reported two checks outstanding, No. 5888 for $1,028.05 and No. 5893 for $494.25. The following information is available for its September 30, 2016, reconciliation.

From the September 30 Bank Statement

PREVIOUS BALANCE	TOTAL CHECKS AND DEBITS	TOTAL DEPOSITS AND CREDITS	CURRENT BALANCE
16,800.45	9,620.05	11,272.85	18,453.25

CHECKS AND DEBITS			DEPOSITS AND CREDITS		DAILY BALANCE	
Date	No.	Amount	Date	Amount	Date	Amount
09/03	5888	1,028.05	09/05	1,103.75	08/31	16,800.45
09/04	5902	719.90	09/12	2,226.90	09/03	15,772.40
09/07	5901	1,824.25	09/21	4,093.00	09/04	15,052.50
09/17		600.25 NSF	09/25	2,351.70	09/05	16,156.25
09/20	5905	937.00	09/30	12.50 IN	09/07	14,332.00
09/22	5903	399.10	09/30	1,485.00 CM	09/12	16,558.90
09/22	5904	2,090.00			09/17	15,958.65
09/28	5907	213.85			09/20	15,021.65
09/29	5909	1,807.65			09/21	19,114.65
					09/22	16,625.55
					09/25	18,977.25
					09/28	18,763.40
					09/29	16,955.75
					09/30	18,453.25

From Chavez Company's Accounting Records

Cash Receipts Deposited			Cash Disbursements		
Date		Cash Debit	Check No.		Cash Credit
Sept.	5	1,103.75	5901		1,824.25
	12	2,226.90	5902		719.90
	21	4,093.00	5903		399.10
	25	2,351.70	5904		2,060.00
	30	1,682.75	5905		937.00
		11,458.10	5906		982.30
			5907		213.85
			5908		388.00
			5909		1,807.65
					9,332.05

Cash						Acct. No. 101
Date		Explanation	PR	Debit	Credit	Balance
Aug.	31	Balance				15,278.15
Sept.	30	Total receipts	R12	11,458.10		26,736.25
	30	Total disbursements	D23		9,332.05	17,404.20

Additional Information

Check No. 5904 is correctly drawn for $2,090 to pay for computer equipment; however, the recordkeeper misread the amount and entered it in the accounting records with a debit to Computer Equipment and a credit to Cash of $2,060. The NSF check shown in the statement was originally received from a customer, S. Nilson, in payment of her account. Its return has not yet been recorded by the company. The credit memorandum is from the collection of a $1,500 note for Chavez Company by the bank. The bank deducted a $15 collection fee. The collection and fee are not yet recorded.

Required

1. Prepare the September 30, 2016, bank reconciliation for this company.
2. Prepare the journal entries (in dollars and cents) to adjust the book balance of cash to the reconciled balance.

Check (1) Reconciled balance, $18,271.45; (2) Cr. Notes Receivable $1,500.00

Analysis Component

3. The bank statement reveals that some of the prenumbered checks in the sequence are missing. Describe three situations that could explain this.

For each of these five separate cases, identify the principle(s) of internal control that is violated. Recommend what the business should do to ensure adherence to principles of internal control.

1. Latisha Tally is the company's computer specialist and oversees its computerized payroll system. Her boss recently asked her to put password protection on all office computers. Latisha has put a password in place that allows only the boss access to the file where pay rates are changed and personnel are added or deleted from the payroll.
2. Marker Theater has a computerized order-taking system for its tickets. The system is active all week and backed up every Friday night.
3. Sutton Company has two employees handling acquisitions of inventory. One employee places purchase orders and pays vendors. The second employee receives the merchandise.
4. The owner of Super Pharmacy uses a check protector to perforate checks, making it difficult for anyone to alter the amount of the check. The check protector is on the owner's desk in an office that contains company checks and is normally unlocked.
5. Lavina Company is a small business that has separated the duties of cash receipts and cash disbursements. The employee responsible for cash disbursements reconciles the bank account monthly.

PROBLEM SET B

Problem 6-1B
Analyzing internal control

C1

Problem 6-2B
Establishing, reimbursing, and adjusting petty cash
P2

Moya Co. establishes a petty cash fund for payments of small amounts. The following transactions involving the petty cash fund occurred in January (the last month of the company's fiscal year).

Jan. 3　A company check for $150 is written and made payable to the petty cashier to establish the petty cash fund.

14　A company check is written to replenish the fund for the following expenditures made since January 3.
   a.　Purchased office supplies for $14.29 that are immediately used up.
   b.　Paid $19.60 COD shipping charges on merchandise purchased for resale, terms FOB shipping point. Moya uses the perpetual system to account for inventory.
   c.　Paid $38.57 to All-Tech for minor repairs to a computer.
   d.　Paid $12.82 for items classified as miscellaneous expenses.
   e.　Counted $62.28 remaining in the petty cashbox.

15　Prepared a company check for $50 to increase the fund to $200.

31　The petty cashier reports that $17.35 remains in the fund. A company check is written to replenish the fund for the following expenditures made since January 14.
   f.　Paid $50 to *The Smart Shopper* for an advertisement in January's newsletter.
   g.　Paid $48.19 for postage expenses.
   h.　Paid $78 to Smooth Delivery for delivery of merchandise, terms FOB destination.

31　The company decides that the January 15 increase in the fund was too little. It increases the fund by another $50, leaving a total of $250.

Required

Check　(1) Cr. to Cash: Jan. 14, $87.72; Jan. 31 (total), $232.65

1. Prepare journal entries (in dollars and cents) to establish the fund on January 3, to replenish it on January 14 and January 31, and to reflect any increase or decrease in the fund balance on January 15 and 31.

Analysis Component

2. Explain how the company's financial statements are affected if the petty cash fund is not replenished and no entry is made on January 31.

Problem 6-3B
Establishing, reimbursing, and increasing petty cash
P2

Blues Music Center had the following petty cash transactions in March of the current year.

March 5　Wrote a $250 check, cashed it, and gave the proceeds and the petty cashbox to Jen Rouse, the petty cashier.

6　Paid $12.50 COD shipping charges on merchandise purchased for resale, terms FOB shipping point. Blues uses the perpetual system to account for merchandise inventory.

11　Paid $10.75 delivery charges on merchandise sold to a customer, terms FOB destination.

12　Purchased file folders for $14.13 that are immediately used.

14　Reimbursed Bob Geldof, the manager, $11.65 for office supplies purchased and used.

18　Purchased printer paper for $20.54 that is immediately used.

27　Paid $45.10 COD shipping charges on merchandise purchased for resale, terms FOB shipping point.

28　Paid postage expenses of $18.

30　Reimbursed Geldof $56.80 for business car mileage.

31　Cash of $61.53 remained in the fund. Sorted the petty cash receipts by accounts affected and exchanged them for a check to reimburse the fund for expenditures.

31　The petty cash fund amount is increased by $50 to a total of $300.

Required

1. Prepare the journal entry to establish the petty cash fund.

Check　(2) Total expenses $189.47

2. Prepare a petty cash payments report for March with these categories: delivery expense, mileage expense, postage expense, merchandise inventory (for transportation-in), and office supplies expense. Sort the payments into the appropriate categories and total the expenses in each category.

(3a & 3b) Total Cr. to Cash $238.47

3. Prepare the journal entries (in dollars and cents) for part 2 to both (a) reimburse and (b) increase the fund amount.

The following information is available to reconcile Severino Co.'s book balance of cash with its bank statement cash balance as of December 31, 2016.

a. The December 31 cash balance according to the accounting records is $32,878.30, and the bank statement cash balance for that date is $46,822.40.

b. Check No. 1273 for $4,589.30 and Check No. 1282 for $400, both written and entered in the accounting records in December, are not among the canceled checks. Two checks, No. 1231 for $2,289 and No. 1242 for $410.40, were outstanding on the most recent November 30 reconciliation. Check No. 1231 is listed with the December canceled checks, but Check No. 1242 is not.

c. When the December checks are compared with entries in the accounting records, it is found that Check No. 1267 had been correctly drawn for $3,456 to pay for office supplies but was erroneously entered in the accounting records as $3,465.

d. Two debit memoranda are enclosed with the statement and are unrecorded at the time of the reconciliation. One debit memorandum is for $762.50 and dealt with an NSF check for $745 received from a customer, Titus Industries, in payment of its account. The bank assessed a $17.50 fee for processing it. The second debit memorandum is a $99 charge for check printing. Severino did not record these transactions before receiving the statement.

e. A credit memorandum indicates that the bank collected $19,000 cash on a note receivable for the company, deducted a $20 collection fee, and credited the balance to the company's Cash account. Severino did not record this transaction before receiving the statement.

f. Severino's December 31 daily cash receipts of $9,583.10 were placed in the bank's night depository on that date but do not appear on the December 31 bank statement.

Required

1. Prepare the bank reconciliation for this company as of December 31, 2016.

2. Prepare the journal entries (in dollars and cents) necessary to bring the company's book balance of cash into conformity with the reconciled cash balance as of December 31, 2016.

Analysis Component

3. Explain the nature of the communications conveyed by a bank when the bank sends the depositor (*a*) a debit memorandum and (*b*) a credit memorandum.

Problem 6-4B
Preparing a bank reconciliation and recording adjustments

P3

Check (1) Reconciled balance, $51,005.80; (2) Cr. Notes Receivable $19,000.00

Shamara Systems most recently reconciled its bank balance on April 30 and reported two checks outstanding at that time, No. 1771 for $781 and No. 1780 for $1,425.90. The following information is available for its May 31, 2016, reconciliation.

Problem 6-5B
Preparing a bank reconciliation and recording adjustments

P3

From the May 31 Bank Statement

PREVIOUS BALANCE	TOTAL CHECKS AND DEBITS	TOTAL DEPOSITS AND CREDITS	CURRENT BALANCE
18,290.70	13,094.80	16,566.80	21,762.70

CHECKS AND DEBITS			DEPOSITS AND CREDITS		DAILY BALANCE	
Date	No.	Amount	Date	Amount	Date	Amount
05/01	1771	781.00	05/04	2,438.00	04/30	18,290.70
05/02	1783	382.50	05/14	2,898.00	05/01	17,509.70
05/04	1782	1,285.50	05/22	1,801.80	05/02	17,127.20
05/11	1784	1,449.60	05/25	7,350.00 CM	05/04	18,279.70
05/18		431.80 NSF	05/26	2,079.00	05/11	16,830.10
05/25	1787	8,032.50			05/14	19,728.10
05/26	1785	63.90			05/18	19,296.30
05/29	1788	654.00			05/22	21,098.10
05/31		14.00 SC			05/25	20,415.60
					05/26	22,430.70
					05/29	21,776.70
					05/31	21,762.70

From Shamara Systems's Accounting Records

Cash Receipts Deposited		
Date		**Cash Debit**
May	4	2,438.00
	14	2,898.00
	22	1,801.80
	26	2,079.00
	31	2,727.30
		11,944.10

Cash Disbursements		
Check No.		**Cash Credit**
1782		1,285.50
1783		382.50
1784		1,449.60
1785		63.90
1786		353.10
1787		8,032.50
1788		644.00
1789		639.50
		12,850.60

Cash						Acct. No. 101
Date		**Explanation**	**PR**	**Debit**	**Credit**	**Balance**
Apr.	30	Balance				16,083.80
May	31	Total receipts	R7	11,944.10		28,027.90
	31	Total disbursements	D8		12,850.60	15,177.30

Additional Information

Check No. 1788 is correctly drawn for $654 to pay for May utilities; however, the recordkeeper misread the amount and entered it in the accounting records with a debit to Utilities Expense and a credit to Cash for $644. The bank paid and deducted the correct amount. The NSF check shown in the statement was originally received from a customer, W. Sox, in payment of her account. The company has not yet recorded its return. The credit memorandum is from a $7,400 note that the bank collected for the company. The bank deducted a $50 collection fee and deposited the remainder in the company's account. The collection and fee have not yet been recorded.

Required

Check (1) Reconciled balance, $22,071.50; (2) Cr. Notes Receivable $7,400.00

1. Prepare the May 31, 2016, bank reconciliation for Shamara Systems.
2. Prepare the journal entries (in dollars and cents) to adjust the book balance of cash to the reconciled balance.

Analysis Component

3. The bank statement reveals that some of the prenumbered checks in the sequence are missing. Describe three possible situations to explain this.

SERIAL PROBLEM
Business Solutions

P3

(This serial problem began in Chapter 1 and continues through most of the book. If previous chapter segments were not completed, the serial problem can begin at this point. It is helpful, but not necessary, to use the Working Papers that accompany the book.)

SP 6   Santana Rey receives the March bank statement for Business Solutions on April 11, 2017. The March 31 bank statement shows an ending cash balance of $67,566. A comparison of the bank statement with the general ledger Cash account, No. 101, reveals the following.

a. S. Rey notices that the bank erroneously cleared a $500 check against her account in March that she did not issue. The check documentation included with the bank statement shows that this check was actually issued by a company named Business Systems.

b. On March 25, the bank issued a $50 debit memorandum for the safety deposit box that Business Solutions agreed to rent from the bank beginning March 25.

c. On March 26, the bank issued a $102 debit memorandum for printed checks that Business Solutions ordered from the bank.

d. On March 31, the bank issued a credit memorandum for $33 interest earned on Business Solutions's checking account for the month of March.

e. S. Rey notices that the check she issued for $128 on March 31, 2017, has not yet cleared the bank.

f. S. Rey verifies that all deposits made in March do appear on the March bank statement.

g. The general ledger Cash account, No. 101, shows an ending cash balance per books of $68,057 as of March 31 (prior to any reconciliation).

Required

1. Prepare a bank reconciliation for Business Solutions for the month ended March 31, 2017.

2. Prepare any necessary adjusting entries. Use Miscellaneous Expenses, No. 677, for any bank charges. Use Interest Revenue, No. 404, for any interest earned on the checking account for the month of March.

Check   (1) Adj. bank bal. $67,938

The **General Ledger** tool in *Connect* automates several of the procedural steps in the accounting cycle so that the financial professional can focus on the impacts of each transaction on the various financial reports.

GL 6-1   General Ledger assignment GL 6-1, based on Problem 6-2A, focuses on transactions related to the petty cash fund and highlights the impact each transaction has on net income, if any. Prepare the journal entries related to the petty cash fund and assess the impact of each transaction on the company's net income, if any.

GENERAL LEDGER PROBLEM

Available in Connect

Beyond the Numbers

BTN 6-1   Refer to **Apple**'s financial statements in Appendix A to answer the following.

1. For both fiscal years ended September 27, 2014, and September 28, 2013, identify the total amount of cash and cash equivalents. Determine the percent (rounded to one decimal) that this amount represents of total current assets, total current liabilities, total shareholders' equity, and total assets for both years. Comment on any trends.

2. For fiscal years ended September 27, 2014, and September 28, 2013, use the information in the statement of cash flows to determine the percent change (rounded to one decimal) between the beginning and ending year amounts of cash and cash equivalents.

3. Compute the days' sales uncollected (rounded to two decimals) as of September 27, 2014, and September 28, 2013. Has the collection of receivables improved? Are accounts receivable an important asset for Apple? Explain.

Fast Forward

4. Access Apple's financial statements for fiscal years ending after September 27, 2014, from its website (**Apple.com**) or the SEC's EDGAR database (**www.SEC.gov**). Recompute its days' sales uncollected for years ending after September 27, 2014. Compare this to the days' sales uncollected for fiscal years ended September 27, 2014, and September 28, 2013.

REPORTING IN ACTION

C2   A1

APPLE

BTN 6-2   Key comparative figures for **Apple** and **Google** follow.

$ millions	Apple Current Year	Apple Prior Year	Google Current Year	Google Prior Year
Accounts receivable	$ 17,460	$ 13,102	$ 9,383	$ 8,882
Net sales	182,975	170,910	66,001	55,519

COMPARATIVE ANALYSIS

A1

APPLE
GOOGLE

Required

Compute days' sales uncollected (rounded to two decimals) for these companies for each of the two years shown. Comment on any trends for the companies. Which company has the larger percent change (rounded to two decimals) in days' sales uncollected?

ETHICS CHALLENGE

C1

BTN 6-3 Harriet Knox, Ralph Patton, and Marcia Diamond work for a family physician, Dr. Gwen Conrad, who is in private practice. Dr. Conrad is knowledgeable about office management practices and has segregated the cash receipt duties as follows. Knox opens the mail and prepares a triplicate list of money received. She sends one copy of the list to Patton, the cashier, who deposits the receipts daily in the bank. Diamond, the recordkeeper, receives a copy of the list and posts payments to patients' accounts. About once a month the office clerks have an expensive lunch they pay for as follows. First, Patton endorses a patient's check in Dr. Conrad's name and cashes it at the bank. Knox then destroys the remittance advice accompanying the check. Finally, Diamond posts payment to the customer's account as a miscellaneous credit. The three justify their actions by their relatively low pay and knowledge that Dr. Conrad will likely never miss the money.

Required

1. Who is the best person in Dr. Conrad's office to reconcile the bank statement?
2. Would a bank reconciliation uncover this office fraud?
3. What are some procedures to detect this type of fraud?
4. Suggest additional internal controls that Dr. Conrad could implement.

COMMUNICATING IN PRACTICE

C1 P1

BTN 6-4 Assume you are a business consultant. The owner of a company sends you an e-mail expressing concern that the company is not taking advantage of its discounts offered by vendors. The company currently uses the gross method of recording purchases. The owner is considering a review of all invoices and payments from the previous period. Due to the volume of purchases, however, the owner recognizes that this is time-consuming and costly. The owner *seeks your advice about monitoring purchase discounts* in the future. Provide a response in memorandum form. (*Hint:* It will help to review the recording of purchase discounts in Appendix 4C.)

TAKING IT TO THE NET

C1 P1

BTN 6-5 Visit the Association of Certified Fraud Examiners website at acfe.com. Find and open the file "2014 Report to the Nations." Read the two-page Executive Summary and fill in the following blanks. (The report is under its *Fraud Resources* tab or use the *Search* tab.)

1. The median loss caused by the frauds in our study was _____. Additionally, _____ of the cases involved losses of at least $1 million.
2. The typical organization loses _____ of revenues each year to fraud; this translates to a potential projected global fraud loss of nearly _____.
3. The median duration—the amount of time from when the fraud commenced until it was detected—for the fraud cases reported to us was _____.
4. Asset misappropriations are the most common fraud, occurring in _____ of the cases in our study, as well as the least costly, causing a median loss of _____.
5. Only _____ of cases involved financial statement fraud, but those cases had the greatest financial impact, with a median loss of _____. Corruption schemes fell in the middle in terms of both frequency (_____ of cases) and median loss (_____).
6. Over _____ of all cases were detected by a tip—more than twice the rate of any other detection method.
7. Owners/executives only accounted for _____ of all cases, but they caused a median loss of _____. Employees committed _____ of occupational frauds but only caused a median loss of _____. Managers ranked in the middle, committing _____ of frauds with a median loss of _____.
8. Approximately _____ of the frauds in our study were committed by individuals working in one of seven departments: accounting, operations, sales, executive/upper management, customer service, purchasing, and finance.
9. The vast majority of occupational fraudsters are first-time offenders; only _____ had been convicted of a fraud-related offense prior to committing the crimes in our study. Furthermore, _____of fraudsters had never previously been punished or terminated by an employer for fraud-related conduct.

BTN 6-6   Organize the class into teams. Each team must prepare a list of 10 internal controls a consumer could observe in a typical retail department store. When called upon, the team's spokesperson must be prepared to share controls identified by the team that have not been shared by another team's spokesperson.

TEAMWORK IN ACTION
C1

BTN 6-7   Review the opening feature of this chapter that highlights Larry Page and Sergey Brin and their company, **Google, Inc.** Assume that Google is considering opening up retail outlets to sell its portable mobile, gaming, and communication products to consumers.

ENTREPRENEURIAL DECISION
C1   P1

GOOGLE

Required

1. List the seven principles of internal control and explain how a retail outlet might implement each of the principles in its store.
2. Do you believe that a retail outlet will need to add controls to the business as it expands? Explain.

BTN 6-8   Visit an area of your college that serves the student community with either products or services. Some examples are food services, libraries, and bookstores. Identify and describe between four and eight internal controls being implemented.

HITTING THE ROAD
C1

BTN 6-9   The following information is from **Samsung** (**www.Samsung.com** or its financial statements in Appendix A), which is a leading manufacturer of consumer electronic products.

GLOBAL DECISION
C2   A1

Samsung

₩ in millions	Current Year	Prior Year
Cash	₩ 16,840,766	₩ 16,284,780
Accounts receivable	28,234,485	27,875,934
Current assets	115,146,026	110,760,271
Total assets	230,422,958	214,075,018
Current liabilities	52,013,913	51,315,409
Shareholders' equity	168,088,188	150,016,010
Net sales	206,205,987	228,692,667

Required

1. For each year, compute the percentage (rounded to one decimal) that cash represents of current assets, total assets, current liabilities, and shareholders' equity. Comment on any trends in these percentages.
2. Determine the percentage change (rounded to one decimal) between the current and prior year cash balances.
3. Compute the days' sales uncollected (rounded to one decimal) at the end of both the current year and the prior year. Has the collection of receivables improved? Explain.

ANSWERS TO MULTIPLE CHOICE QUIZ

1. e; The entry follows.

Debits to expenses (or assets)	420	
Cash Over and Short	5	
Cash		425

4. d; ($6,720/$84,000) × 365 = 29.2 days

2. a; recognizes cash collection of note by bank.

3. a; the bank reconciliation follows.

Bank Reconciliation November 30			
Balance per bank statement	$1,895	Balance per books	$1,742
Add: Deposit in transit	795	Add: Note collected less fee	320
Deduct: Outstanding checks	(638)	Deduct: Service charge	(10)
Reconciled balance	$2,052	Reconciled balance	$2,052

Reporting and Analyzing Receivables

Chapter Preview

ACCOUNTS RECEIVABLE

C1 Recognizing accounts receivable

P1 Valuing accounts receivable

P2 Estimating and recording bad debts

NOTES RECEIVABLE

C2 Computing maturity and interest

Recognizing notes receivable

P3 Valuing and settling notes receivable

DISPOSAL AND ANALYSIS OF RECEIVABLES

C3 Selling and pledging receivables

A1 Assessing accounts receivable turnover

Learning Objectives

CONCEPTUAL

C1 Describe accounts receivable and how they occur and are recorded.

C2 Describe a note receivable, the computation of its maturity date, and the recording of its existence.

C3 Explain how receivables can be converted to cash before maturity.

ANALYTICAL

A1 Compute accounts receivable turnover and use it to help assess financial condition.

PROCEDURAL

P1 Apply the direct write-off method to account for accounts receivable.

P2 Apply the allowance method and estimate uncollectibles based on sales and accounts receivable.

P3 Record the honoring and dishonoring of a note and adjustments for interest.

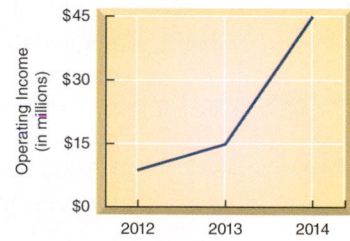

Love That Grub

"Hunger drives the entrepreneur—hunger for the next great idea, validation, challenge, competition, success"—**MATT MALONEY**

CHICAGO—Mike Evans and Matt Maloney were working late. "We were hungry, and sick of ordering the same pizza all the time," recalls Matt. "We were frustrated by the lack of dinner options as well as the pain in the a** of calling restaurants and reading our credit cards." This is when Mike and Matt had the idea to create **GrubHub** (**GrubHub.com**), a website that allows customers to order food delivery from their favorite restaurants. "It's kind of funny that [GrubHub] really was hunger inspired," jokes Matt.

Matt began by amassing "hundreds of menus" from restaurants in Chicago, and Mike "wrote some code" for the website. After a few months, the GrubHub website was up and running. However, Mike and Matt ran into issues with collecting payment from restaurants. "We thought restaurants would pay for the ability to capture the attention of hungry people . . . but when we started asking restaurants for money, most of them didn't see the value." Mike and Matt reevaluated their strategy and decided that restaurants could pay GrubHub "a 10 percent commission" for sales made through GrubHub.com *at a later date*. According to Matt, "Restaurants loved that!"

GrubHub's strategy to allow restaurants to pay later led Matt and Mike to closely monitor their receivables. As shown here,

GrubHub, Inc.
NYSE: GRUB

$3.4 bil. valuation
30,000 restaurants
800 cities serviced

Revenue Sources

Mobile orders 51%
Desktop orders 49%

GrubHub manages receivables to roughly 25 percent of net sales.

($ millions)	2012	2013	2014
Accounts receivable........	$19	$ 33	$ 37
Net sales	$82	$137	$254
Accts. rec./Net sales	23%	24%	15%

Matt and Mike quickly saw that decisions on credit sales and the policies for extending credit could make or break their start-up. To combat this risk, the pair ensured that credit sales were extended to customers in good credit standing. Further, Matt and Mike study cash payment patterns that allow them to estimate uncollectibles and minimize bad debts.

A commitment to a high-quality customer base is propelling GrubHub's growth and shattering Matt and Mike's most optimistic goals. "It's something that I never

imagined when we started," admits Matt. Matt and Mike have also issued notes receivable to select employees. Both accounts and notes receivable receive their regular attention. Moreover, GrubHub's financial report states that its "allowance [for doubtful accounts] is based on historical loss experience."

GrubHub's effective management of accounts receivable has improved its sales and limited its costs. The benefits are seen in the rise of operating income:

Although Matt and Mike have had financial success and built a $3 billion business, they still insist that running GrubHub is about a love of entrepreneurship. "If there are financial rewards in the future, we're going to welcome them," insists Matt. "And hell, that's fantastic!"

Sources: *GrubHub website,* January 2016; *GrubHub 10-K,* March 2015; *Inc.com,* November 2014; *Business Insider,* February 2012; *Yahoo Finance,* January 2016; *BizJournals,* April 2010

ACCOUNTS RECEIVABLE

C1

Describe accounts receivable and how they occur and are recorded.

A *receivable* is an amount due from another party. The two most common receivables are accounts receivable and notes receivable. Other receivables include interest receivable, rent receivable, tax refund receivable, and receivables from employees. **Accounts receivable** are amounts due from customers for credit sales. This section begins by describing how accounts receivable occur. It includes receivables that occur when customers use credit cards issued by third parties and when a company gives credit directly to customers. When a company does extend credit directly to customers, it (1) maintains a separate account receivable for each customer and (2) accounts for bad debts from credit sales.

Recognizing Accounts Receivable

Accounts receivable arise from credit sales to customers. Retailers such as **Costco** and **Best Buy** hold millions of dollars in accounts receivable. Similar amounts are held by wholesalers such as **SUPERVALU** and **SYSCO**. Exhibit 7.1 shows recent dollar amounts of receivables and their percent of total assets for four well-known companies.

EXHIBIT 7.1

Accounts Receivable for Selected Companies

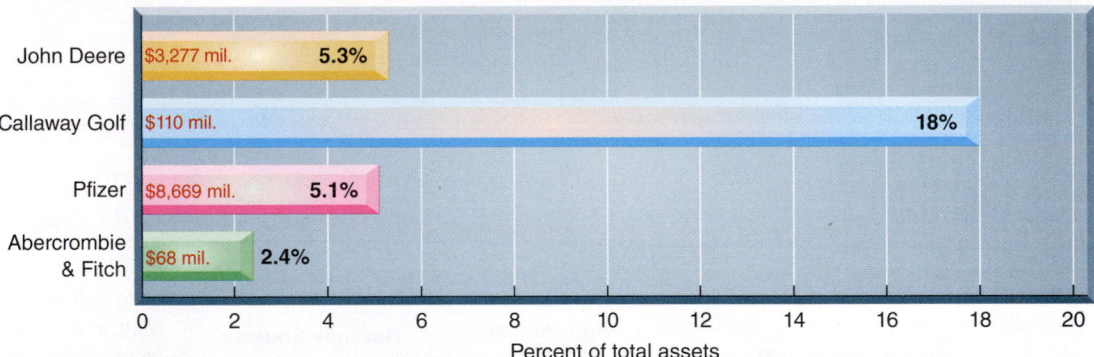

Sales on Credit   Credit sales are recorded by increasing (debiting) Accounts Receivable. A company must also maintain a separate account for each customer that tracks how much that customer purchases, has already paid, and still owes. The general ledger continues to have a single Accounts Receivable account (called a *control* account) along with the other financial statement accounts, but a supplementary record is created to maintain a separate account for each customer. This supplementary record is called the *accounts receivable ledger* (or *accounts receivable subsidiary ledger*).

Exhibit 7.2 shows the relation between the Accounts Receivable account in the general ledger and its individual customer accounts in the accounts receivable ledger for TechCom, a small electronics wholesaler. This exhibit reports a $3,000 ending balance of TechCom's accounts receivable for June 30. TechCom's transactions are mainly in cash, but it has two major credit customers: CompStore and RDA Electronics. Its *schedule of accounts receivable* shows that the $3,000 balance of the Accounts Receivable account in the general ledger equals the total of its two customers' balances in the accounts receivable ledger.

EXHIBIT 7.2

General Ledger and the Accounts Receivable Ledger (before July 1 transactions)

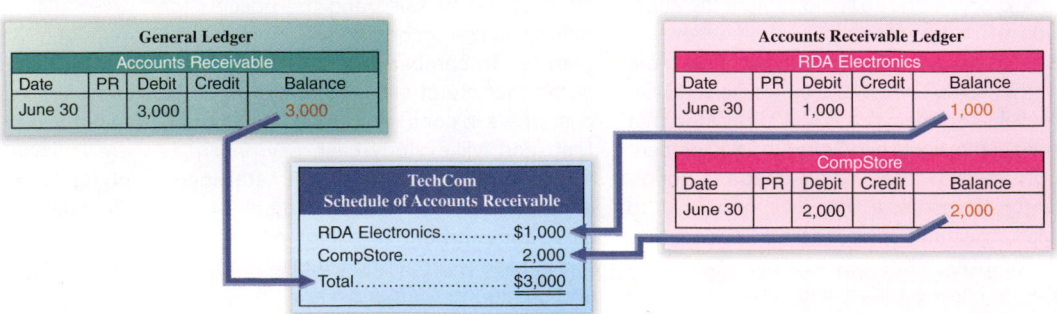

To see how accounts receivable from credit sales are recognized in the accounting records, we look at two transactions on July 1 between TechCom and its credit customers—see Exhibit 7.3. The first is a credit sale of $950 to CompStore. A credit sale is posted with both a debit to the Accounts Receivable account in the general ledger and a debit to the customer account in the accounts receivable ledger. The second transaction is a collection of $720 from RDA Electronics from a prior credit sale. Cash receipts from a credit customer are posted with a credit to the Accounts Receivable account in the general ledger and flow through to credit the customer account in the accounts receivable ledger. (Posting debits or credits to Accounts Receivable in two separate ledgers does not violate the requirement that debits equal credits. The equality of debits and credits is maintained in the general ledger. The accounts receivable ledger is a *supplementary* record providing information on each customer.)

EXHIBIT 7.3

Accounts Receivable Transactions

July 1	Accounts Receivable —CompStore	950	
	Sales		950
	*Record credit sales.**		
July 1	Cash	720	
	Accounts Receivable—RDA Electronics		720
	Record collection of credit sales.		

Assets = Liabilities + Equity
+950   +950

Assets = Liabilities + Equity
+720
−720

* We omit the entry to Dr. Cost of Sales and Cr. Merchandise Inventory to focus on sales and receivables; no sales returns and allowances are expected.

Exhibit 7.4 shows the general ledger and the accounts receivable ledger after recording the two July 1 transactions. The general ledger shows the effects of the sale, the collection, and the resulting balance of $3,230. These events are also reflected in the individual customer accounts: RDA Electronics has an ending balance of $280, and CompStore's ending balance is $2,950. The $3,230 sum of the individual accounts equals the debit balance of the Accounts Receivable account in the general ledger.

EXHIBIT 7.4

General Ledger and the Accounts Receivable Ledger (after July 1 transactions)

Like TechCom, many large retailers such as **Home Depot** and **True Value** sell on credit. Many also maintain their own credit cards to grant credit to approved customers and to earn interest on any balance not paid within a specified period of time. This allows them to avoid the fee charged by credit card companies. The entries in this case are the same as those for TechCom except for the possibility of added interest revenue. If a customer owes interest on a bill, we debit Interest Receivable and credit Interest Revenue for that amount. (Many retailers require clerks to ask customers during checkout if they wish to apply for a store credit card— sweeteners are often used such as: *save 10% off today's purchases if you apply now.*)

Credit Card Sales   Many companies allow their customers to pay for products and services using third-party credit cards such as **Visa**, **MasterCard**, or **American Express**, and debit cards (also called ATM or bank cards). This gives customers the ability to make purchases without cash or checks. Customers using these cards can make single monthly payments instead of several payments to different creditors and can defer their payments.

Many sellers allow customers to use third-party credit cards and debit cards instead of granting credit directly for several reasons. First, the seller does not have to evaluate each customer's

Ken Reid/Photographer's Choice/ Getty Images

Point: Visa USA now transacts more than $1 trillion from its credit, debit, and prepaid cards.

credit standing or make decisions about who gets credit and how much. Second, the seller avoids the risk of extending credit to customers who cannot or do not pay (this risk is transferred to the card company). Third, the seller typically receives cash from the card company sooner than had it granted credit directly to customers. Fourth, a variety of credit options for customers offer a potential increase in sales volume. **Sears** historically offered credit only to customers using a Sears card but later changed its policy to permit customers to charge purchases to third-party credit card companies in a desire to increase sales. It reported: "SearsCharge increased its share of Sears retail sales even as the company expanded the payment options available to its customers with the acceptance . . . of Visa, MasterCard, and American Express in addition to the [Sears] Card."

There are guidelines for how companies account for credit card and debit card sales. Some credit cards, but nearly all debit cards, credit a seller's Cash account immediately upon deposit, via electronic funds transfer. The majority of credit cards, however, remit electronically the details of the card and the proposed transaction to the card company, but receipt of cash usually takes 2 to 5 business days. Until payment is received, the seller has an account receivable from the card company. In both cases, the seller pays a fee for services provided by the card company, often ranging from 1% to 5% of card sales. This charge is deducted from the credit to the seller's account or the cash payment to the seller. (Many retailers accept MasterCard and Visa, but not American Express. The reason is that American Express usually charges retailers a higher percentage fee than other credit card companies.)

Point: Enter a web search with "how debit (or credit) card processing works" for diagrams and explanations, including YouTube videos.

Decision Insight

Debit Card vs. Credit Card   A buyer's debit card purchase reduces the buyer's cash account balance at the card company, which is often a bank. Since the buyer's cash account balance is a liability (with a credit balance) for the card company to the buyer, the card company would debit that account for a buyer's purchase—hence, the term *debit card*. A credit card reflects authorization by the card company of a line of credit for the buyer with pre-set interest rates and payment terms—hence, the term *credit card*. Most card companies waive interest charges if the buyer pays its balance each month. ■

The procedures used in accounting for credit card sales depend on whether cash is received immediately on deposit or cash receipt is delayed until payment is received by the seller.

Point: Web merchants often pay twice as much in credit card association fees as other retailers because they suffer 10 times as much fraud.

Cash Received Immediately on Deposit   To illustrate, if TechCom has $100 of credit card sales with a 4% fee, and its $96 cash is received immediately on deposit, the entry is

Assets = Liabilities + Equity
+96   +100
                          −4

July 15	Cash	96	
	Credit Card Expense	4	
	Sales		100
	*Record credit card sales less a 4% credit card expense.**		

* We omit the entry to Dr. Cost of Sales and Cr. Merchandise Inventory to focus on credit card expense.

Point: *Expense recognition principle* requires that we record credit card expense when we record sales.

Cash Received Sometime after Deposit   However, if instead TechCom remits electronically the credit card sales details to the credit card company and must wait for the $96 cash payment, the entry on the date of sale is

Assets = Liabilities + Equity
+96   +100
                          −4

July 15	**Accounts Receivable—Credit Card Co.**	96	
	Credit Card Expense	4	
	Sales		100
	*Record credit card sales less 4% credit card expense.**		

* We omit the entry to Dr. Cost of Sales and Cr. Merchandise Inventory to focus on credit card expense.

When cash is later received for the credit card sales, usually through electronic funds transfer, the entry is

Assets = Liabilities + Equity
+96
−96

July 20	Cash	96	
	Accounts Receivable—Credit Card Co.		96
	Record cash receipt.		

Some firms report credit card expense in the income statement as a type of discount deducted from sales to get net sales. Other companies classify it as a selling expense or even as an administrative expense. Arguments can be made for each approach. In this book we classify credit card expense as a selling expense.

Point: Third-party credit card costs can be large. **JCPenney** reported third-party credit card costs exceeding $10 million.

Installment Sales and Receivables   Many companies allow their credit customers to make periodic payments over several months. For example, **Ford Motor Company** reports more than $80 billion in installment receivables. The seller refers to such assets as *installment accounts* (or *finance) receivable,* which are amounts owed by customers from credit sales for which payment is required in periodic amounts over an extended time period. Source documents for installment accounts receivable include sales slips or invoices describing the sales transactions. The customer is usually charged interest. Although installment accounts receivable can have credit periods of more than one year, they are classified as current assets if the seller regularly offers customers such terms.

Robert Laberge/NASCAR via Getty Images

■ **Decision** Maker

Entrepreneur   As a small retailer, you are considering allowing customers to buy merchandise using credit cards. Until now, your store accepted only cash and checks. What analysis do you use to make this decision? ■   [Answers follow the chapter's Summary.]

A small retailer allows customers to use two different credit cards in charging purchases. With the AA Bank Card, the retailer receives an immediate credit to its account when it deposits sales receipts. AA Bank assesses a 5% service charge for credit card sales. The second credit card that the retailer accepts is the VIZA Card. The retailer sends (batches) its credit card data to VIZA on a daily basis and is paid by VIZA about 5 business days later. VIZA assesses a 3% charge on sales for using its card. Prepare journal entries to record the following selected credit card transactions for the retailer. (The retailer uses the perpetual inventory system for recording sales.)

NEED-TO-KNOW 7-1

Credit Card Sales

C1

Jan. 2   Sold merchandise for $1,000 (that had cost $600) and accepted the customer's AA Bank Card. AA Bank immediately transferred funds to the retailer's bank account.

Jan. 6   Sold merchandise for $400 (that had cost $300) and accepted the customer's VIZA Card. Transferred $400 of credit card data to VIZA, requesting payment.

Jan. 12   Received VIZA's transfer of funds for the January 6 billing, less the service charge.

Solution

Jan. 2	Cash	950	
	Credit Card Expense*	50	
	Sales		1,000
	*Record credit card sales less 5% fee. *($1,000 × 0.05)*		
Jan. 2	Cost of Goods Sold	600	
	Merchandise Inventory		600
	Record cost of sales.		
Jan. 6	Accounts Receivable—VIZA	388	
	Credit Card Expense*	12	
	Sales		400
	*Record credit card sales less 3% fee. *($400 × 0.03)*		
Jan. 6	Cost of Goods Sold	300	
	Merchandise Inventory..........................		300
	Record cost of sales.		
Jan. 12	Cash	388	
	Accounts Receivable—VIZA		388
	Record cash received on credit sales less fees.		

Do More: QS 7-1, E 7-2

P1

Apply the direct write-off
method to account for
accounts receivable.

Valuing Accounts Receivable—Direct Write-Off Method

When a company directly grants credit to its customers, it expects that some customers will not pay what they promised. The accounts of these customers are *uncollectible accounts,* commonly called **bad debts.** The total amount of uncollectible accounts is an expense of selling on credit. Why do companies sell on credit if they expect some accounts to be uncollectible? The answer is that companies believe that granting credit will increase total sales and net income enough to offset bad debts. Companies use two methods to account for uncollectible accounts: (1) direct write-off method and (2) allowance method.

Point: Managers realize that some portion of credit sales will be uncollectible, but which credit sales are uncollectible is unknown.

Recording and Writing Off Bad Debts   The **direct write-off method** of accounting for bad debts records the loss from an uncollectible account receivable when it is determined to be uncollectible. No attempt is made to predict bad debts expense. To illustrate, if TechCom determines on January 23 that it cannot collect $520 owed to it by its customer J. Kent, it recognizes the loss using the direct write-off method as follows:

Assets = Liabilities + Equity
−520   −520

Jan. 23	Bad Debts Expense	520	
	Accounts Receivable—J. Kent		520
	Write off an uncollectible account.		

The debit in this entry charges the uncollectible amount directly to the current period's Bad Debts Expense account. The credit removes its balance from the Accounts Receivable account in the general ledger (and its subsidiary ledger).

Point: If a customer fails to pay within the credit period, most companies send out repeated billings and make other efforts to collect.

Point: Recovery of a bad debt always requires two journal entries.

Recovering a Bad Debt   Although uncommon, sometimes an account written off is later collected. This can be due to factors such as continual collection efforts or a customer's good fortune. If the account of J. Kent that was written off directly to Bad Debts Expense is later collected in full, the following two entries record this recovery:

Assets = Liabilities + Equity
+520   +520

Mar. 11	Accounts Receivable—J. Kent	520	
	Bad Debts Expense		520
	Reinstate account previously written off.		

Assets = Liabilities + Equity
+520   +520
−520

Mar. 11	Cash	520	
	Accounts Receivable—J. Kent		520
	Record full payment of account.		

Direct write-off method

Advantages:
• Simple
• No estimates required

Disadvantages:
• Receivables and income temporarily overstated
• Bad debts expense often not matched with sales

Assessing the Direct Write-Off Method   Many publicly-traded companies and thousands of privately-held companies use the direct write-off method; they include **Rand Medical Billing**, **Gateway Distributors**, **Microwave Satellite Technologies**, **First Industrial Realty**, **New Frontier Energy**, **Globalink**, **Solar3D**, and **Sub Surface Waste Management**. The following disclosure by **Pharma-Bio Serv** is typical of the justification for this method: Bad debts are accounted for using the direct write-off method whereby an expense is recognized only when a specific account is determined to be uncollectible. The effect of using this method approximates that of the allowance method. Companies weigh at least two concepts when considering use of the direct write-off method: (1) expense recognition (matching) principle and (2) materiality constraint.

Matching Principle Applied to Bad Debts   The **expense recognition (matching) principle** requires expenses to be reported in the same period as the sales they helped produce. This means that if extending credit to customers helped produce sales, the bad debts expense linked to those sales is matched and reported in the same period. The direct write-off method usually does *not* best match sales and expenses because bad debts expense is not recorded until an account becomes uncollectible, which often occurs in a period after that of the credit sale.

Point: Under direct write-off, expense is recorded each time an account is written off. Under the allowance method, expense is recorded with an adjusting entry equal to the total estimated uncollectibles for that period's sales.

Materiality Constraint Applied to Bad Debts   The **materiality constraint** states that an amount can be ignored if its effect on the financial statements is unimportant to users' business decisions. The materiality constraint permits the use of the direct write-off method when bad debts expenses are not significant.

A retailer applies the direct write-off method in accounting for uncollectible accounts. Prepare journal entries to record the following selected transactions.

Feb. 14   The retailer determines that it cannot collect $400 of its accounts receivable from a customer named ZZZ Company.

Apr. 1   ZZZ Company unexpectedly pays its account in full to the retailer, which then records its recovery of this bad debt.

NEED-TO-KNOW 7-2

Entries under Direct Write-Off Method

P1

Solution

Feb. 14	Bad Debts Expense	400	
	Accounts Receivable—ZZZ Co.		400
	To write off an account.		
Apr. 1	Accounts Receivable—ZZZ Co.	400	
	Bad Debts Expense		400
	To reinstate an account previously written off.		
Apr. 1	Cash	400	
	Accounts Receivable—ZZZ Co.		400
	To record cash received on account.		

Do More: QS 7-2, QS 7-3, E 7-3

Valuing Accounts Receivable—Allowance Method

The **allowance method** of accounting for bad debts matches the *estimated* loss from uncollectible accounts receivable against the sales they helped produce. We must use estimated losses because when sales occur, management does not know which customers will not pay their bills. This means that at the end of each period, the allowance method requires an estimate of the total bad debts expected to result from that period's sales. This method has two advantages over the direct write-off method: (1) it records estimated bad debts expense in the period when the related sales are recorded and (2) it reports accounts receivable on the balance sheet at the estimated amount of cash to be collected.

P2

Apply the allowance method and estimate uncollectibles based on sales and accounts receivable.

Recording Bad Debts Expense   The allowance method estimates bad debts expense at the end of each accounting period and records it with an adjusting entry. TechCom, for instance, had credit sales of $300,000 during its first year of operations. At the end of the first year, $20,000 of credit sales remained uncollected. Based on the experience of similar businesses, TechCom estimated that $1,500 of its accounts receivable would be uncollectible. This estimated expense is recorded with the following adjusting entry:

Method	Bad Debts Expense Recognized
Direct write-off..........	*In future* when account deemed uncollectible.
Allowance..............	*Currently,* yielding realizable Accts. Rec. bal.

Dec. 31	Bad Debts Expense	1,500	
	Allowance for Doubtful Accounts		1,500
	Record estimated bad debts.		

Assets = Liabilities + Equity
−1,500   −1,500

The estimated bad debts expense of $1,500 is reported on the income statement (as either a selling expense or an administrative expense) and offsets the $300,000 credit sales it helped produce. The **Allowance for Doubtful Accounts** is a contra asset account. A contra account is used instead of reducing accounts receivable directly because at the time of the adjusting entry, the company does not know which customers will not pay. After the bad debts adjusting entry is posted, TechCom's account balances (in T-account form) for Accounts Receivable and its Allowance for Doubtful Accounts are as shown in Exhibit 7.5.

Allowance method

Advantages:
- Receivables fairly stated
- Bad debts expense matched with sales
- Writing off bad debt does not affect net receivables or income

Disadvantages:
- Estimates required

EXHIBIT 7.5

Ledger after Bad Debts Adjusting Entry

Accounts Receivable			Allowance for Doubtful Accounts		
Dec. 31	20,000			Dec. 31	1,500

The Allowance for Doubtful Accounts credit balance of $1,500 has the effect of reducing accounts receivable to its estimated realizable value. **Realizable value** refers to the expected proceeds from converting an asset into cash. Although credit customers owe $20,000 to Tech-Com, only $18,500 is expected to be realized in cash collections from these customers. (Tech-Com continues to bill its customers a total of $20,000, the amounts from the subsidiary ledger.) In the balance sheet, the Allowance for Doubtful Accounts is subtracted from Accounts Receivable and is often reported as shown in Exhibit 7.6.

EXHIBIT 7.6

Balance Sheet for the Allowance for Doubtful Accounts

Current assets		
Accounts receivable.............................	$20,000	
Less allowance for doubtful accounts	1,500	$18,500

Sometimes the Allowance for Doubtful Accounts is not reported separately. This alternative presentation is shown in Exhibit 7.7 (also see Appendix A).

EXHIBIT 7.7

Alternative Presentation of the Allowance for Doubtful Accounts

Current assets	
Accounts receivable (net of $1,500 doubtful accounts)	$18,500

Writing Off a Bad Debt   When specific accounts are identified as uncollectible, they are written off against the Allowance for Doubtful Accounts. To illustrate, TechCom decides that J. Kent's $520 account is uncollectible and makes the following entry to write it off.

Assets = Liabilities + Equity
+520
−520

Jan. 23	Allowance for Doubtful Accounts	520	
	Accounts Receivable—J. Kent		520
	Write off an uncollectible account.		

Point: The Bad Debts Expense is not debited in the write-off because it was re-corded in the period when sales occurred.

Posting this write-off entry to the Accounts Receivable account removes the amount of the bad debt from the general ledger (it is also posted to the accounts receivable subsidiary ledger). The general ledger accounts now appear as in Exhibit 7.8 (assuming no other transactions affecting these accounts).

EXHIBIT 7.8

Ledger after Write-Off

Accounts Receivable				
Dec. 31	20,000			
		Jan. 23	520	

Allowance for Doubtful Accounts		
	Dec. 31	1,500
Jan. 23	520	

Point: In posting a write-off, the ledger's Explanation column indicates the reason for this credit so it is not misinter-preted as payment in full.

The write-off does *not* affect the realizable value of accounts receivable as shown in Exhibit 7.9. Neither total assets nor net income is affected by the write-off of a specific account. Instead, both assets and net income are affected in the period when bad debts expense is predicted and recorded with an adjusting entry.

EXHIBIT 7.9

Realizable Value before and after Write-Off of a Bad Debt

	Before Write-Off	After Write-Off
Accounts receivable	$ 20,000	$ 19,480
Less allowance for doubtful accounts	1,500	980
Estimated realizable accounts receivable	**$18,500**	**$18,500**

Recovering a Bad Debt   When a customer fails to pay and the account is written off as uncol-lectible, his or her credit standing is jeopardized. To help restore credit standing, a customer some-times volunteers to pay all or part of the amount owed. A company makes two entries when collecting an account previously written off by the allowance method. The first is to reverse the write-off and reinstate the customer's account. The second entry records the collection of the reinstated account. To illustrate, if on March 11 Kent pays in full his account previously written off, the entries are

Point: Recovery of a bad debt always requires two journal entries.

Assets = Liabilities + Equity
+520
−520

Mar. 11	Accounts Receivable—J. Kent	520	
	Allowance for Doubtful Accounts..............		520
	Reinstate account previously written off.		

Assets = Liabilities + Equity
+520
−520

Mar. 11	Cash	520	
	Accounts Receivable—J. Kent		520
	Record full payment of account.		

In this illustration, Kent paid the entire amount previously written off, but sometimes a customer pays only a portion of the amount owed. A question then arises as to whether the entire balance of the account or just the amount paid is returned to accounts receivable. This is a matter of judgment. If we believe this customer will later pay in full, we return the entire amount owed to accounts receivable, but if we expect no further collection, we return only the amount paid.

Example: If TechCom used a collection agency and paid a 35% commission on $520 collected from Kent, how is this recorded? *Answer:*

Cash   338
Collection Expense   182
   Accts. Rec.—J. Kent   520

Point: Bad Debts Expense is also called *Uncollectible Accounts Expense.* The Allowance for Doubtful Accounts is also called *Allowance for Uncollectible Accounts.*

▢ Decision Insight ♟

On the Money   **PayPal** is legally just a money transfer agent, but it is increasingly challenging big credit card brands—see chart. PayPal is successful because: (1) online credit card processing fees can exceed $0.15 per dollar, but PayPal's fees are under $0.10 per dollar; (2) PayPal's merchant fraud losses are under 0.2% of revenues, which compares to nearly 2% for online merchants using credit cards. ▪

A retailer applies the allowance method in accounting for uncollectible accounts. Prepare journal entries to record the following selected transactions.

2015
Dec. 31   The retailer estimates $3,000 of its accounts receivable are uncollectible.

2016
Feb. 14   The retailer determines that it cannot collect $400 of its accounts receivable from a customer named ZZZ Company.

Apr. 1   ZZZ Company unexpectedly pays its account in full to the retailer, which then records its recovery of this bad debt.

NEED-TO-KNOW 7-3

Entries under Allowance Method

P2

Solution

2015			
Dec. 31	Bad Debts Expense	3,000	
	Allowance for Doubtful Accounts.................		3,000
	Record estimated bad debts.		
2016			
Feb. 14	Allowance for Doubtful Accounts......................	400	
	Accounts Receivable—ZZZ Co.		400
	Write off an account.		
Apr. 1	Accounts Receivable—ZZZ Co.	400	
	Allowance for Doubtful Accounts.................		400
	Reinstate an account previously written off.		
Apr. 1	Cash	400	
	Accounts Receivable—ZZZ Co.		400
	Record cash received on account.		

Do More: QS 7-5

Estimating Bad Debts—Percent of Sales Method

The allowance method requires an estimate of bad debts expense to prepare an adjusting entry at the end of each accounting period. There are two common methods. One is based on the income statement relation between bad debts expense and sales. The second is based on the balance sheet relation between accounts receivable and the allowance for doubtful accounts.

The *percent of sales method,* also referred to as the *income statement method,* is based on the idea that a given percent of a company's credit sales for the period is uncollectible. To illustrate, assume that Musicland has credit sales of $400,000 in year 2016. Based on past experience, Musicland estimates 0.6% of credit sales to be uncollectible. This implies that Musicland

Point: Focus is on *credit* sales because cash sales do not produce bad debts. If cash sales are a small or stable percent of credit sales, total sales can be used.

expects $2,400 of bad debts expense from its sales (computed as $400,000 × 0.006). The adjusting entry to record this estimated expense is

Assets = Liabilities + Equity
−2,400   −2,400

Dec. 31*	Bad Debts Expense	2,400	
	Allowance for Doubtful Accounts		2,400
	Record estimated bad debts.		

Bad Debts Expense	
Unadj.	0
Adj. (% Sales)	**2,400**
Est. bal.	2,400

* The adjusting entry above applies our 3-step adjusting entry process from Chapter 3:
Step 1: Current balance for Bad Debts Expense <u>is</u> $0 debit (as the expense account was closed in prior period).
Step 2: Current balance for Bad Debts Expense <u>should be</u> $2,400 debit.
Step 3: Record entry to get from step 1 to step 2.

Point: When using the *percent of sales method* for estimating uncollectibles, and because the "Unadj. bal." in Bad Debts Expense is always $0, the adjusting entry amount always equals the % of sales.

The allowance account ending balance on the balance sheet for this method would rarely equal the bad debts expense on the income statement. This is because unless a company is in its first period of operations, its allowance account has a zero balance only if the prior amounts written off as uncollectible *exactly* equal the prior estimated bad debts expenses. (When computing bad debts expense as a percent of sales, managers monitor and adjust the percent so it is not too high or too low.)

Estimating Bad Debts—Percent of Receivables Method

The *accounts receivable methods,* also referred to as *balance sheet methods,* use balance sheet relations to estimate bad debts—mainly the relation between accounts receivable and the allowance amount. The goal of the bad debts adjusting entry for these methods is to make the Allowance for Doubtful Accounts balance equal to the portion of accounts receivable that is estimated to be uncollectible. The estimated balance for the allowance account is obtained in one of two ways: (1) computing the percent uncollectible from the total accounts receivable or (2) aging accounts receivable.

The *percent of accounts receivable method* assumes that a given percent of a company's receivables is uncollectible. This percent is based on past experience and is impacted by current conditions such as economic trends and customer difficulties. The total dollar amount of all receivables is multiplied by this percent to get the estimated dollar amount of uncollectible accounts—reported in the balance sheet as the Allowance for Doubtful Accounts.

Point: When using an accounts receivable method for estimating uncollectibles, the allowance account balance is adjusted to equal the estimate of uncollectibles.

To illustrate, assume that Musicland has $50,000 of accounts receivable on December 31, 2016. Experience suggests 5% of its receivables is uncollectible. This means that *after* the adjusting entry is posted, we want the Allowance for Doubtful Accounts to show a $2,500 credit balance (5% of $50,000). We are also told that its beginning balance is $2,200, which is 5% of the $44,000 accounts receivable on December 31, 2015—see Exhibit 7.10.

EXHIBIT 7.10

Allowance for Doubtful Accounts after Bad Debts Adjusting Entry

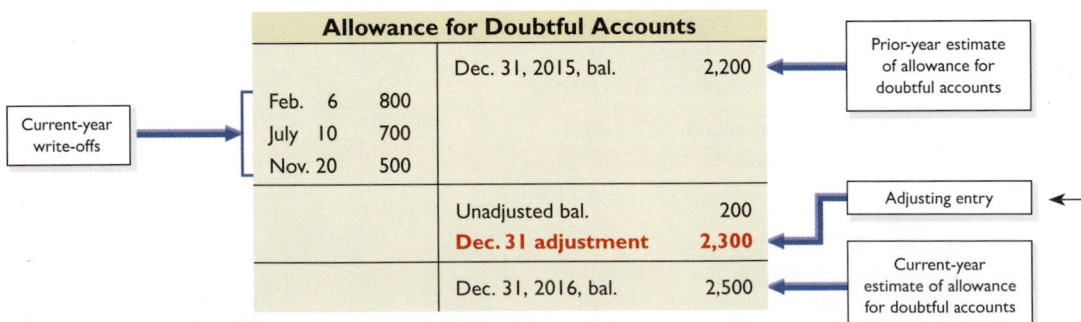

During 2016, accounts of customers are written off on February 6, July 10, and November 20. Thus, the account has a $200 credit balance *before* the December 31, 2016, adjustment. The adjusting entry to give the allowance account the estimated $2,500 balance is

Assets = Liabilities + Equity
−2,300   −2,300

Dec. 31*	Bad Debts Expense	2,300	
	Allowance for Doubtful Accounts		2,300
	Record estimated bad debts.		

* The adjusting entry above applies our 3-step adjusting entry process from Chapter 3:
Step 1: Current balance for Allowance account <u>is</u> $200 credit.
Step 2: Current balance for Allowance account <u>should be</u> $2,500 credit.
Step 3: Record entry to get from Step 1 to Step 2.

Decision Insight

Come of Age   Unlike wine, accounts receivable do not improve with age. Experience shows that the longer a receivable is past due, the less likely it is to be collected. An *aging schedule* uses this knowledge to estimate bad debts. The chart here is from a survey that reported estimates of bad debts for receivables grouped by how long they were past their due dates. Each company sets its own estimates based on its customers and its experiences with those customers' payment patterns. ■

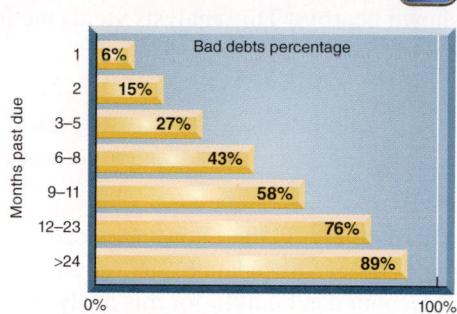

Estimating Bad Debts—Aging of Receivables Method

The **aging of accounts receivable** method uses both past and current receivables information to estimate the allowance amount. Specifically, each receivable is classified by how long it is past its due date. Then estimates of uncollectible amounts are made assuming that the longer an amount is past due, the more likely it is to be uncollectible. Classifications are often based on 30-day periods. After the amounts are classified (or aged), experience is used to estimate the percent of each uncollectible class. These percents are applied to the amounts in each class and then totaled to get the estimated balance of the Allowance for Doubtful Accounts. This computation is performed by setting up a schedule such as Exhibit 7.11.

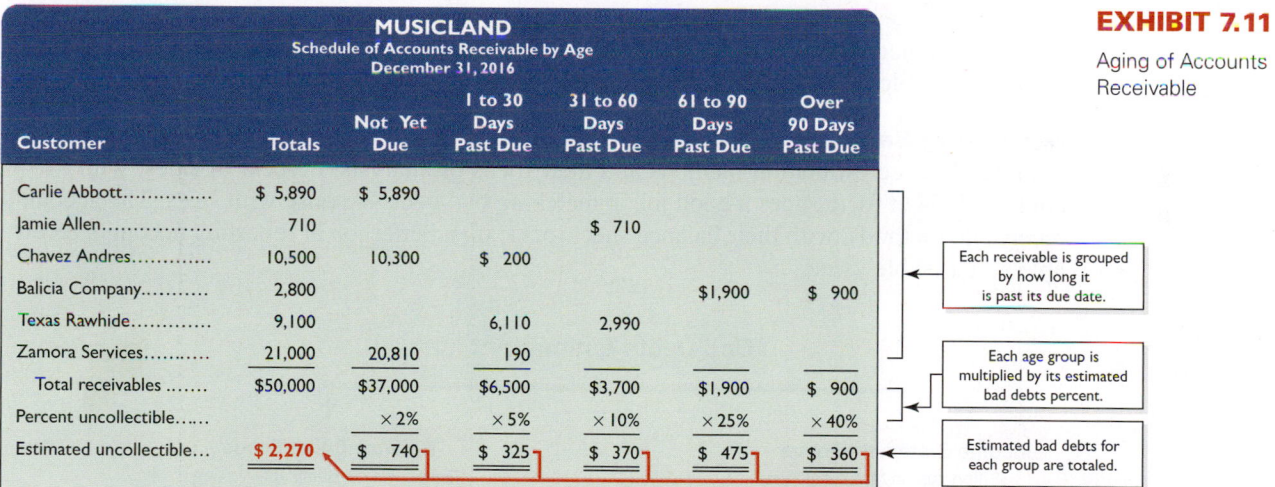

MUSICLAND
Schedule of Accounts Receivable by Age
December 31, 2016

Customer	Totals	Not Yet Due	1 to 30 Days Past Due	31 to 60 Days Past Due	61 to 90 Days Past Due	Over 90 Days Past Due
Carlie Abbott..............	$ 5,890	$ 5,890				
Jamie Allen..................	710			$ 710		
Chavez Andres.............	10,500	10,300	$ 200			
Balicia Company...........	2,800				$1,900	$ 900
Texas Rawhide.............	9,100		6,110	2,990		
Zamora Services...........	21,000	20,810	190			
Total receivables	$50,000	$37,000	$6,500	$3,700	$1,900	$ 900
Percent uncollectible......		× 2%	× 5%	× 10%	× 25%	× 40%
Estimated uncollectible...	$ 2,270	$ 740	$ 325	$ 370	$ 475	$ 360

Each receivable is grouped by how long it is past its due date.

Each age group is multiplied by its estimated bad debts percent.

Estimated bad debts for each group are totaled.

EXHIBIT 7.11

Aging of Accounts Receivable

Exhibit 7.11 lists each customer's individual balances assigned to one of five classes based on its days past due. The amounts in each class are totaled and multiplied by the estimated percent of uncollectible accounts for each class. The percents used are regularly reviewed to reflect changes in the company and economy.

   To explain, Musicland has $3,700 in accounts receivable that are 31 to 60 days past due. Its management estimates 10% of the amounts in this age class are uncollectible, or a total of $370 (computed as $3,700 × 10%). Similar analysis is done for each of the other four classes. The final total of $2,270 ($740 + $325 + $370 + $475 + $360) shown in the first column is the estimated balance for the Allowance for Doubtful Accounts. Exhibit 7.12 shows that since the

Step 1: Current account balance equals	Unadjusted balance	$ 200 credit
Step 2: Determine what account balance should be	Estimated balance	2,270 credit
Step 3: Make adjustment to get from step 1 to step 2	**Required adjustment**	**$2,070 credit**

EXHIBIT 7.12

Computation of the Required Adjustment for the Accounts Receivable Method

Allowance for Doubtful Accounts

	Unadj. bal.	200
	Req. adj.	**2,070**
	Estim. bal.	2,270

Assets = Liabilities + Equity
−2,070   −2,070

Point: A debit balance implies that write-offs for that period exceed the total allowance.

Allowance for Doubtful Accounts

Unadj. bal. 500		
	Req. adj.	**2,770**
	Estim. bal.	2,270

Assets = Liabilities + Equity
−2,770   −2,770

Point: Credit approval is usually not assigned to the selling dept. because its goal is to increase sales, and it may approve customers at the cost of increased bad debts. Instead, approval is assigned to a separate credit-granting or administrative dept.

allowance account has an unadjusted credit balance of $200, the required adjustment to the Allowance for Doubtful Accounts is $2,070. (We could also use a T-account for this analysis as shown nearby.) This analysis yields the following end-of-period adjusting entry:

Dec. 31	Bad Debts Expense	2,070	
	Allowance for Doubtful Accounts..............		2,070
	Record estimated bad debts.		

Alternatively, if the allowance account had an unadjusted *debit* balance of $500 (instead of the $200 credit balance), its required adjustment would be computed as follows. (Again, a T-account can be used for this analysis as shown nearby.)

Step 1: Current account balance equals

Step 2: Determine what account balance should be

Step 3: Make adjustment to get from step 1 to step 2

Unadjusted balance	$ 500 debit
Estimated balance	2,270 credit
Required adjustment	**$ 2,770 credit**

Current-year estimate of allowance for doubtful accounts

Adjusting entry amount

The entry to record the end-of-period adjustment for this alternative case is

Dec. 31	Bad Debts Expense	2,770	
	Allowance for Doubtful Accounts		2,770
	Record estimated bad debts.		

The aging of accounts receivable method is an examination of specific accounts and is usually the most reliable of the estimation methods.

Estimating Bad Debts—Summary of Methods   Exhibit 7.13 summarizes the principles guiding all three estimation methods and their focus of analysis. Percent of sales, with its income statement focus, does a good job at matching bad debts expense with sales. The accounts receivable methods, with their balance sheet focus, do a better job at reporting accounts receivable at realizable value.

EXHIBIT 7.13

Methods to Estimate Bad Debts

Decision Maker

Point: Some companies use an Allowance for Returns, which is a contra account to receivables. Accounting for this is covered in advanced courses.

Labor Union Chief   One week prior to labor contract negotiations, financial statements are released showing no income growth. A 10% growth was predicted. Your analysis finds that the company increased its allowance for uncollectibles from 1.5% to 4.5% of receivables. Without this change, income would show a 9% growth. Does this analysis impact negotiations? ■   [Answers follow the chapter's Summary.]

At its December 31 year-end, a company estimates uncollectible accounts using the allowance method.

1. It prepared the following aging of receivables analysis. (a) Estimate the balance of the Allowance for Doubtful Accounts using the aging of accounts receivable method. (b) Prepare the adjusting entry to record bad debts expense using the estimate from part *a*. Assume the unadjusted balance in the Allowance for Doubtful Accounts is a $10 debit.

NEED-TO-KNOW 7-4

Estimating Bad Debts

P2

		Days Past Due				
	Total	**0**	**I to 30**	**31 to 60**	**61 to 90**	**Over 90**
Accounts receivable..........	$2,600	$2,000	$300	$80	$100	$120
Percent uncollectible.........		1%	2%	5%	7%	10%

2. (a) Estimate the balance of the Allowance for Doubtful Accounts assuming the company uses 2% of total accounts receivable to estimate uncollectibles instead of the aging of receivables method in question 1. (b) Prepare the adjusting entry to record bad debts expense using the estimate from part *a*. Assume the unadjusted balance in the Allowance for Doubtful Accounts is a $4 credit.

3. (a) Estimate the balance of the uncollectibles assuming the company uses 0.5% of annual credit sales (annual credit sales were $10,000). (b) Prepare the adjusting entry to record bad debts expense using the estimate from part *a*. Assume the unadjusted balance in the Allowance for Doubtful Accounts is a $4 credit.

Solutions

1a. Computation of the estimated balance of the allowance for uncollectibles:

Not due:	$2,000 × 0.01 =	$20
I to 30:	300 × 0.02 =	6
31 to 60:	80 × 0.05 =	4
61 to 90:	100 × 0.07 =	7
Over 90:	120 × 0.10 =	12
		$49 credit

Do More: QS 7-6, E 7-4, E 7-5, E 7-6, E 7-7, E 7-8, E 7-9

1b.

Dec. 31	Bad Debts Expense	59	
	Allowance for Doubtful Accounts...........		59
	*Record estimated bad debts.**		

Allowance for Doubtful Accounts	
Unadj. Dec. 31 10	
	Adj. Dec. 31 59
	Est. bal. Dec. 31 49

Step 1: Current account balance equals	*Unadjusted balance	$10 debit
Step 2: Determine what account balance should be	Estimated balance	49 credit
Step 3: Make adjustment to get from step 1 to step 2	Required adjustment	$59 credit

2a. Computation of the estimated balance of the allowance for uncollectibles:

$$\$2{,}600 \times 0.02 = \underline{\$52}\ \text{credit}$$

2b.

Dec. 31	Bad Debts Expense	48	
	Allowance for Doubtful Accounts		48
	*Record estimated bad debts.**		

Allowance for Doubtful Accounts	
	Unadj. Dec. 31 4
	Adj. Dec. 31 48
	Est. bal. Dec. 31 52

Step 1: Current account balance equals	*Unadjusted balance	$ 4 credit
Step 2: Determine what account balance should be	Estimated balance	52 credit
Step 3: Make adjustment to get from step 1 to step 2	Required adjustment	$48 credit

3a. Computation of the estimated balance of the bad debts expense:

$$\$10{,}000 \times 0.005 = \underline{\$50}\ \text{credit}$$

3b.

Dec. 31	Bad Debts Expense	50	
	Allowance for Doubtful Accounts		50
	Record estimated bad debts.		

Bad Debts Expense	
Unadj. Dec. 31 0	
Adj. Dec. 31 50	
Est. bal. Dec. 31 50	

NOTES RECEIVABLE

C2
Describe a note receivable, the computation of its maturity date, and the recording of its existence.

A **promissory note** is a written promise to pay a specified amount of money, usually with interest, either on demand or at a definite future date. Promissory notes are used in many transactions, including paying for products and services, and lending and borrowing money. Sellers sometimes ask for a note to replace an account receivable when a customer requests additional time to pay a past-due account. For legal reasons, sellers generally prefer to receive notes when the credit period is long and when the receivable is for a large amount. If a lawsuit is needed to collect from a customer, a note is the buyer's written acknowledgment of the debt, its amount, and its terms.

Exhibit 7.14 shows a simple promissory note dated July 10, 2016. For this note, Julia Browne promises to pay TechCom or to its order (according to TechCom's instructions) a specified amount of money ($1,000), called the **principal of a note,** at a definite future date (October 8, 2016). As the one who signed the note and promised to pay it at maturity, Browne is the **maker of the note.** As the person to whom the note is payable, TechCom is the **payee of the note.** To Browne, the note is a liability called a *note payable*. To TechCom, the same note is an asset called a *note receivable*. This note bears interest at 12%, as written on the note. **Interest** is the charge for using the money until its due date. To a borrower, interest is an expense. To a lender, it is revenue.

EXHIBIT 7.14

Promissory Note

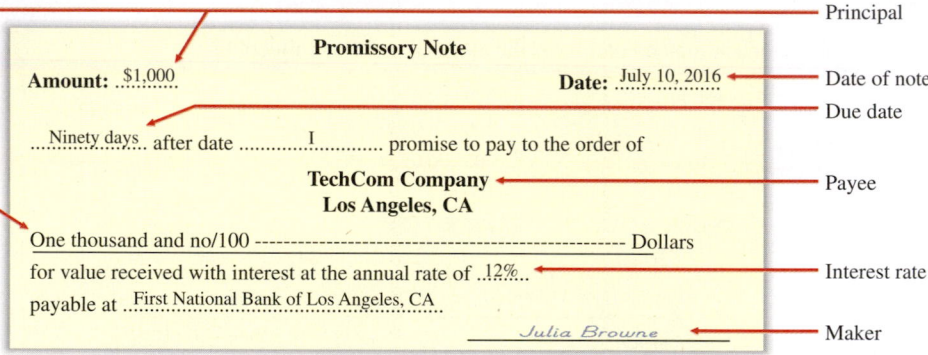

Computing Maturity and Interest

This section describes key computations for notes including the determination of maturity date, period covered, and interest computation.

Maturity Date and Period   The **maturity date of a note** is the day the note (principal and interest) must be repaid. The *period* of a note is the time from the note's (contract) date to its maturity date. Many notes mature in less than a full year, and the period they cover is often expressed in days. When the time of a note is expressed in days, its maturity date is the specified number of days after the note's date. As an example, a five-day note dated June 15 matures and is due on June 20. A 90-day note dated July 10 matures on October 8. This October 8 due date is computed as shown in Exhibit 7.15. The period of a note is sometimes expressed in months or years. When months are used, the note matures and is payable in the month of its maturity on the *same day of the month* as its original date. A nine-month note dated July 10, for instance, is payable on April 10. The same analysis applies when years are used.

EXHIBIT 7.15

Maturity Date Computation

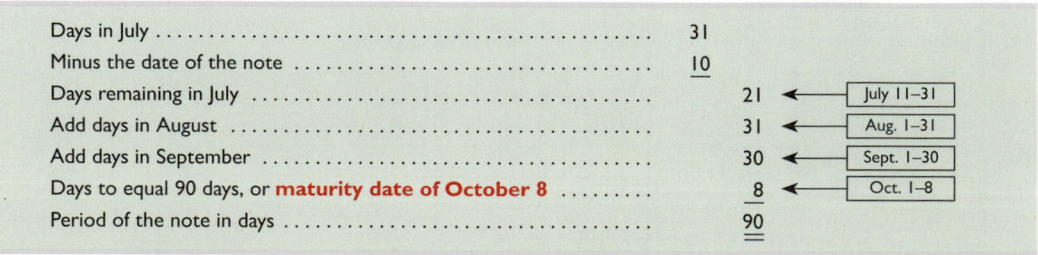

Interest Computation   *Interest* is the cost of borrowing money for the borrower or, alternatively, the profit from lending money for the lender. Unless otherwise stated, the rate of interest on a note is the rate charged for the use of the principal for one year. The formula for computing interest on a note is shown in Exhibit 7.16.

$$\begin{array}{ccccccc} \text{Principal} & \times & \text{Annual} & \times & \text{Time expressed} & = & \text{Interest} \\ \text{of the note} & & \text{interest rate} & & \text{in fraction of year} & & \end{array}$$

EXHIBIT 7.16

Computation of Interest Formula

To simplify interest computations, a year is commonly treated as having 360 days (called the *banker's rule* in the business world and widely used in commercial transactions). **We treat a year as having 360 days for interest computations in the examples and assignments.** Using the promissory note in Exhibit 7.14 where we have a 90-day, 12%, $1,000 note, the total interest is computed as follows:

$$\$1,000 \times 12\% \times \frac{90}{360} = \$1,000 \times 0.12 \times 0.25 = \$30$$

Point: If the *banker's rule* is <u>not</u> followed, interest is computed as:

\$1,000 × 12% × 90/365 = \$29.589041

The *banker's rule* would yield \$30, which is easier to account for than \$29.589041.

Recognizing Notes Receivable

Notes receivable are usually recorded in a single Notes Receivable account to simplify record-keeping. The original notes are kept on file, including information on the maker, rate of interest, and due date. (When a company holds a large number of notes, it sometimes sets up a controlling account and a subsidiary ledger for notes. This is similar to the handling of accounts receivable.) To illustrate the recording for the receipt of a note, we use the $1,000, 90-day, 12% promissory note in Exhibit 7.14. TechCom received this note at the time of a product sale to Julia Browne. This transaction is recorded as follows:

July 10*	Notes Receivable	1,000	
	Sales		1,000
	Sold goods in exchange for a 90-day, 12% note.		

Assets = Liabilities + Equity
+1,000   +1,000

* We omit the entry to Dr. Cost of Sales and Cr. Merchandise Inventory to focus on sales and receivables.

When a seller accepts a note from an overdue customer as a way to grant a time extension on a past-due account receivable, it will often collect part of the past-due balance in cash. This partial payment forces a concession from the customer, reduces the customer's debt (and the seller's risk), and produces a note for a smaller amount. To illustrate, assume that TechCom agreed to accept $232 in cash along with a $600, 60-day, 15% note from Jo Cook to settle her $832 past-due account. TechCom made the following entry to record receipt of this cash and note:

Oct. 5	Cash	232	
	Notes Receivable	600	
	Accounts Receivable—J. Cook		832
	Received cash and note to settle account.		

Assets = Liabilities + Equity
+232
+600
−832

Valuing and Settling Notes

Recording an Honored Note   The principal and interest of a note are due on its maturity date. The maker of the note usually *honors* the note and pays it in full. To illustrate, when J. Cook pays the note above on its due date, TechCom records it as follows:

Dec. 4	Cash	615	
	Notes Receivable		600
	Interest Revenue		15
	Collect note with interest of $600 × 15% × 60/360.		

P3

Record the honoring and dishonoring of a note and adjustments for interest.

Assets = Liabilities + Equity
+615   +15
−600

Interest revenue, also called *interest earned,* is reported on the income statement.

Recording a Dishonored Note   When a note's maker is unable or refuses to pay at maturity, the note is *dishonored*. The act of dishonoring a note does not relieve the maker of the obligation to pay. The payee should use every legitimate means to collect. How do companies report this event? The balance of the Notes Receivable account should include only those notes that have not matured. Thus, when a note is dishonored, we remove the amount of this note from the Notes Receivable account and charge it back to an account receivable from its maker. To illustrate, assume that J. Cook dishonors the note above at maturity. The journal entry to record the dishonoring of the note follows:

Point: When posting a dishonored note to a customer's account, an explanation is included so as not to misinterpret the debit as a sale on account.

Assets = Liabilities + Equity
+615   +15
−600

Dec. 4	Accounts Receivable—J. Cook	615	
	Interest Revenue		15
	Notes Receivable		600
	Charge account of J. Cook for a dishonored note		
	and interest of $600 × 15% × 60/360.		

Point: Reporting the details of notes is consistent with the **full disclosure principle,** which requires financial statements (including footnotes) to report all relevant information.

Charging a dishonored note back to the account of its maker serves two purposes. First, it removes the amount of the note from the Notes Receivable account and records the dishonored note in the maker's account. Second, and more important, if the maker of the dishonored note applies for credit in the future, his or her account will reveal all past dealings, including the dishonored note. Restoring the account also reminds the company to continue collection efforts from Cook for both principal and interest. The entry records the full amount, including interest, to ensure that it is included in collection efforts.

Recording End-of-Period Interest Adjustment   When notes receivable are outstanding at the end of a period, any accrued interest earned is computed and recorded. To illustrate, on December 16, TechCom accepts a $3,000, 60-day, 12% note from a customer in granting an extension on a past-due account. When TechCom's accounting period ends on December 31, $15 of interest has accrued on this note ($3,000 × 12% × 15/360). The following adjusting entry records this revenue:

Assets = Liabilities + Equity
+15   +15

Dec. 31	Interest Receivable	15	
	Interest Revenue		15
	Record accrued interest earned.		

Point: Assume reversing entries are not made unless otherwise stated.

Interest revenue appears on the income statement, and interest receivable appears on the balance sheet as a current asset. When the December 16 note is collected on February 14, TechCom's entry to record the cash receipt is

Assets = Liabilities + Equity
+3,060   +45
   −15
−3,000

Feb. 14	Cash	3,060	
	Interest Revenue		45
	Interest Receivable		15
	Notes Receivable		3,000
	Received payment of note and its interest.		

Total interest earned on the 60-day note is $60. The $15 credit to Interest Receivable on February 14 reflects the collection of the interest accrued from the December 31 adjusting entry. The $45 interest earned reflects TechCom's revenue from holding the note from January 1 to February 14 of the current period.

a. AA Company purchases $1,400 of merchandise from ZZ on December 16, 2015. ZZ accepts AA's $1,400, 90-day, 12% note as payment. ZZ's accounting period ends on December 31, and it does not make reversing entries. Prepare entries for ZZ on December 16, 2015, and December 31, 2015. (Assume reversing entries are not made.)

b. Using the information in part *a*, prepare ZZ's March 16, 2016, entry if AA dishonors the note.

c. Instead of the facts in part *b*, prepare ZZ's March 16, 2016, entry if AA honors the note.

d. Assume the facts in part *b* above (AA dishonors the note). Then, on March 31, ZZ decides to write off the receivable from AA Company. Prepare that write-off entry assuming that ZZ uses the allowance method.

NEED-TO-KNOW 7-5

Honoring and Dishonoring Notes

C2 P3

Solution

a.

Dec. 16	Note Receivable—AA	1,400	
	Sales		1,400
Dec. 31	Interest Receivable	7	
	Interest Revenue		7
	($1,400 × 12% × 15/360)		

b.

Mar. 16	Accounts Receivable—AA	1,442	
	Interest Revenue		35
	Interest Receivable		7
	Notes Receivable—AA		1,400

c.

Mar. 16	Cash	1,442	
	Interest Revenue		35
	Interest Receivable		7
	Notes Receivable—AA		1,400

d.

| Mar. 31 | Allowance for Doubtful Accounts .... | 1,442 | |
| | Accounts Receivable—AA Company .... | | 1,442 |

Do More: QS 7-8, QS 7-9, QS 7-10, E 7-10, E 7-11, E 7-12, E 7-13

DISPOSAL OF RECEIVABLES

Companies can convert receivables to cash before they are due. Reasons for this include the need for cash or the desire not to be involved in collection activities. Converting receivables is usually done either by (1) selling them or (2) using them as security for a loan. A recent survey shows that about 20% of companies obtain cash from either selling receivables or pledging them as security. In some industries such as textiles, apparel, and furniture, this is common practice.

C3

Explain how receivables can be converted to cash before maturity.

Selling Receivables

A company can sell all or a portion of its receivables to a finance company or bank. The buyer, called a *factor,* charges the seller a *factoring fee,* and then the buyer takes ownership of the receivables and receives cash when they come due. By incurring a factoring fee, the seller receives cash earlier and can pass the risk of bad debts to the factor. The seller can also choose to avoid costs of billing and accounting for the receivables. To illustrate, if TechCom sells $20,000 of its accounts receivable and is charged a 4% factoring fee, it records this sale as follows:

Aug. 15	Cash	19,200	
	Factoring Fee Expense.........................	800	
	Accounts Receivable		20,000
	Sold accounts receivable for cash, less 4% fee.		

Assets = Liabilities + Equity
+19,200   −800
−20,000

Global: Firms in export sales increasingly sell their receivables to factors.

The accounting for sales of notes receivable is similar to that for accounts receivable. The detailed entries are covered in advanced courses. *Remember:* When factoring receivables, the company selling receivables always receives less cash than the amount of receivables sold due to factoring fees.

Pledging Receivables

A company can raise cash by borrowing money and *pledging* its receivables as security for the loan. Pledging receivables does not transfer the risk of bad debts to the lender because the borrower retains ownership of the receivables. If the borrower defaults on the loan, the lender has a right to be paid from the cash receipts of the receivable when collected. To illustrate, when Tech-Com borrows $35,000 and pledges its receivables as security, it records this transaction as follows:

Assets = Liabilities + Equity
+35,000   +35,000

Aug. 20	Cash	35,000	
	Notes Payable.............................		35,000
	Borrow with a note secured by pledging receivables.		

Since pledged receivables are committed as security for a specific loan, the borrower's financial statements disclose the pledging of them. TechCom, for instance, includes the following note with its statements: Accounts receivable of $40,000 are pledged as security for a $35,000 note payable. Inventory and accounts receivable are two assets commonly demanded by bankers as collateral when making business loans.

■ **Decision Maker**

Analyst/Auditor   You are reviewing accounts receivable. Over the past five years, the allowance account as a percentage of gross accounts receivable shows a steady downward trend. What does this finding suggest? ■
[Answers follow the chapter's Summary.]

GLOBAL VIEW

This section discusses similarities and differences between U.S. GAAP and IFRS regarding the recognition, measurement, and disposition of receivables.

Recognition of Receivables   Both U.S. GAAP and IFRS have similar asset criteria that apply to recognition of receivables. Further, receivables that arise from revenue-generating activities are subject to broadly similar criteria for U.S. GAAP and IFRS. Specifically, both refer to the realization principle and an earnings process. The realization principle under U.S. GAAP implies an *arm's-length transaction* occurs, whereas under IFRS this notion is applied in terms of reliable measurement and likelihood of economic benefits. Regarding U.S. GAAP's reference to an earnings process, IFRS instead refers to risk transfer and ownership reward. While these criteria are broadly similar, differences do exist, and they arise mainly from industry-specific guidance under U.S. GAAP, which is very limited under IFRS.

Valuation of Receivables   Both U.S. GAAP and IFRS require that receivables be reported net of estimated uncollectibles. Further, both systems require that the expense for estimated uncollectibles be recorded in the same period when any revenues from those receivables are recorded. This means that for accounts receivable, both U.S. GAAP and IFRS require the allowance method for uncollectibles (unless uncollectibles are immaterial). The allowance method using percent of sales, percent of receivables, and aging was explained in this chapter. **Nokia** reports the following for its allowance for uncollectibles:

> Management specifically analyzes accounts receivables and historical bad debt, customer concentrations, customer creditworthiness, current economic trends and changes in our customer payment terms when evaluating the adequacy of the allowance.

Disposition of Receivables   Both U.S. GAAP and IFRS apply broadly similar rules in recording dispositions of receivables. Those rules are discussed in this chapter. We should be aware of an important difference in terminology. Companies reporting under U.S. GAAP disclose Bad Debts Expense, which is also referred to as *Provision for Bad Debts* or the *Provision for Uncollectible Accounts*. For U.S. GAAP, *provision* here refers to expense. Under IFRS, the term *provision* usually refers to a liability whose amount or timing (or both) is uncertain.

Sustainability and Accounting   Matt Maloney, CEO and co-founder of **GrubHub**, strives to reduce his company's impact on the environment and help end childhood hunger. When ordering food on GrubHub's website, customers can opt not to receive plastic utensils. This initiative reduces the amount of trash in landfills and lessens the company's impact on the environment. "Climate change is one of the most challenging problems of our time," says Matt. "By taking these steps, we are helping to build a framework that will reduce the impact of restaurant deliveries on our environment."

AP Images/Richard Drew

GrubHub also partners with charities like *No Kid Hungry* to end childhood hunger in the U.S. To support *No Kid Hungry*, GrubHub donates $1 to the charity when customers check out using a special code. "As a food technology company . . . we understand the importance of supporting our local communities," explains Matt. "Our [partnership] allows GrubHub's more than five million active diners a simple yet impactful opportunity to support *No Kid Hungry*'s numerous local initiatives—improving school breakfast programs, teaching families how to prepare healthy meals on a budget, and recruiting summer meal sites."

Accounts Receivable Turnover 🟩🟨🟥 **Decision Analysis**

For a company selling on credit, we want to assess both the quality and liquidity of its accounts receivable. *Quality* of receivables refers to the likelihood of collection without loss. Experience shows that the longer receivables are outstanding beyond their due date, the lower the likelihood of collection. *Liquidity* of receivables refers to the speed of collection. **Accounts receivable turnover** is a measure of both the quality and liquidity of accounts receivable. It indicates how often, on average, receivables are received and collected during the period. The formula for this ratio is shown in Exhibit 7.17.

A1
Compute accounts receivable turnover and use it to help assess financial condition.

$$\text{Accounts receivable turnover} = \frac{\text{Net sales}}{\text{Average accounts receivable, net}}$$

EXHIBIT 7.17

Accounts Receivable Turnover

We prefer to use net *credit* sales in the numerator because cash sales do not create receivables. However, because financial statements rarely report net credit sales, our analysis uses net sales. The denominator is the *average* accounts receivable balance, computed as (Beginning balance + Ending balance) ÷ 2. TechCom has an accounts receivable turnover of 5.1. This indicates its average accounts receivable balance is converted into cash 5.1 times during the period. Exhibit 7.18 shows graphically this turnover activity for TechCom.

5.1 times per year

| Jan. | Feb. | March | Apr. | May | June | July | Aug. | Sept. | Oct. | Nov. | Dec. |

EXHIBIT 7.18

Rate of Accounts Receivable Turnover for TechCom

Accounts receivable turnover also reflects how well management is doing in granting credit to customers in a desire to increase sales. A high turnover in comparison with competitors suggests that management should consider using more liberal credit terms to increase sales. A low turnover suggests management should consider stricter credit terms and more aggressive collection efforts to avoid having its resources tied up in accounts receivable.

Point: Credit risk ratio is computed by dividing the Allowance for Doubtful Accounts by Accounts Receivable. The higher this ratio, the higher is credit risk.

To illustrate, we take fiscal year data from two competitors: **IBM** and **Oracle** (ORCL). Exhibit 7.19 shows accounts receivable turnover for both companies.

EXHIBIT 7.19

Analysis Using Accounts Receivable Turnover

Company	Figure ($ millions)	2014	2013	2012	2011
IBM	Net sales	$92,793	$98,367	$102,874	$105,056
	Average accounts receivable, net	$ 9,778	$10,566	$ 10,923	$ 11,007
	Accounts receivable turnover ...	**9.5**	**9.3**	**9.6**	**9.5**
Oracle	Net sales	$38,275	$37,180	$ 37,121	$ 35,622
	Average accounts receivable, net	$ 6,068	$ 6,213	$ 6,503	$ 6,107
	Accounts receivable turnover ...	**6.3**	**6.0**	**5.7**	**5.8**

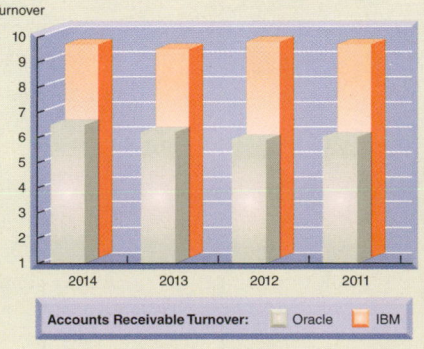

IBM's 2014 turnover is 9.5, computed as $92,793/$9,778 ($ millions). This means that IBM's average accounts receivable balance was converted into cash 9.5 times in 2014. Its turnover increased in 2014 (9.5) compared with 2013 (9.3) and declined compared to

2012 (9.6). However, IBM's turnover exceeds that for Oracle in each of the years shown here. Is either company's turnover too high? Because sales are relatively flat over this time period, neither company's turnover rate appears to be too high. Instead, both IBM and Oracle seem to be doing an adequate job of managing receivables.[1]

■ **Decision Maker**

Family Physician   Your medical practice is barely profitable, so you hire a health care analyst. The analyst highlights several points including the following: *"Accounts receivable turnover is too low. Tighter credit policies are recommended along with discontinuing service to those most delayed in payments."* How do you interpret these recommendations? What actions do you take? ■   [Answers follow the chapter's Summary.]

Clayco Company completes the following selected transactions during year 2016.

July 14   Writes off a $750 account receivable arising from a sale to Briggs Company that dates to 10 months ago. (Clayco Company uses the allowance method.)

      30   Clayco Company receives a $1,000, 90-day, 10% note in exchange for merchandise sold to Sumrell Company (the merchandise cost $600).

Aug. 15   Receives $2,000 cash plus a $10,000 note from JT Co. in exchange for merchandise that sells for $12,000 (its cost is $8,000). The note is dated August 15, bears 12% interest, and matures in 120 days.

Nov.   1   Completes a $200 credit card sale with a 4% fee (the cost of sales is $150). The cash is transferred immediately from the credit card company.

       3   Sumrell Company refuses to pay the note that was due to Clayco Company on October 28. Prepare the journal entry to charge the dishonored note plus accrued interest to Sumrell Company's accounts receivable.

       5   Completes a $500 credit card sale with a 5% fee (the cost of sales is $300). The money transfer from the credit card company is received on Nov. 9.

     15   Receives the full amount of $750 from Briggs Company that was previously written off on July 14. Record the bad debts recovery.

Dec. 13   Receives payment of principal plus interest from JT for the August 15 note.

Required

1. Prepare journal entries to record these transactions on Clayco Company's books.

2. Prepare an adjusting journal entry as of December 31, 2016, assuming the following:

    a. Bad debts are estimated to be $20,400 by aging accounts receivable. The unadjusted balance of the Allowance for Doubtful Accounts is a $1,000 debit.

    b. Alternatively, assume that bad debts are estimated using the percent of sales method. The Allowance for Doubtful Accounts had a $1,000 debit balance before adjustment, and the company estimates bad debts to be 1% of its credit sales of $2,000,000.

PLANNING THE SOLUTION

- Examine each transaction to determine the accounts affected, and then record the entries.
- For the year-end adjustment, record the bad debts expense for the two approaches.

---

[1] As an estimate of *average days' sales uncollected,* we compute how many days (*on average*) it takes to collect receivables as follows: 365 days ÷ accounts receivable turnover. An increase in this *average collection period* can signal a decline in customers' financial condition.

SOLUTION

1.

July 14	Allowance for Doubtful Accounts...................	750	
	Accounts Receivable—Briggs Co.		750
	Wrote off an uncollectible account.		
July 30	Notes Receivable—Sumrell Co.	1,000	
	Sales		1,000
	Sold merchandise for a 90-day, 10% note.		
July 30	Cost of Goods Sold............................	600	
	Merchandise Inventory		600
	Record the cost of July 30 sale.		
Aug. 15	Cash	2,000	
	Notes Receivable—JT Co.	10,000	
	Sales		12,000
	Sold merchandise to customer for		
	$2,000 cash and $10,000 note.		
Aug. 15	Cost of Goods Sold	8,000	
	Merchandise Inventory......................		8,000
	Record the cost of Aug. 15 sale.		
Nov. 1	Cash	192	
	Credit Card Expense	8	
	Sales		200
	Record credit card sale less a 4% credit card expense.		
Nov. 1	Cost of Goods Sold...........................	150	
	Merchandise Inventory......................		150
	Record the cost of Nov. 1 sale.		
Nov. 3	Accounts Receivable—Sumrell Co.	1,025	
	Interest Revenue...........................		25
	Notes Receivable—Sumrell Co.		1,000
	Charge account of Sumrell Company		
	for a $1,000 dishonored note and		
	interest of $1,000 × 10% × 90/360.		
Nov. 5	Accounts Receivable—Credit Card Co.	475	
	Credit Card Expense	25	
	Sales		500
	Record credit card sale less a 5% credit card expense.		
Nov. 5	Cost of Goods Sold	300	
	Merchandise Inventory		300
	Record the cost of Nov. 5 sale.		
Nov. 9	Cash	475	
	Accounts Receivable—Credit Card Co.		475
	Record cash receipt from Nov. 5 sale.		
Nov. 15	Accounts Receivable—Briggs Co..................	750	
	Allowance for Doubtful Accounts		750
	Reinstate account of Briggs Company previously		
	written off.		
Nov. 15	Cash	750	
	Accounts Receivable—Briggs Co.		750
	Cash received in full payment of account.		
Dec. 13	Cash	10,400	
	Interest Revenue		400
	Note Receivable—JT Co.		10,000
	Collect note with interest of $10,000 × 12% × 120/360.		

2a. Aging of accounts receivable method.

Dec. 31	Bad Debts Expense	21,400	
	Allowance for Doubtful Accounts		21,400
	Adjust allowance account from a $1,000		
	debit balance to a $20,400 credit balance.		

2b. Percent of sales method.*

Dec. 31	Bad Debts Expense	20,000	
	Allowance for Doubtful Accounts		20,000
	Record bad debts expense as 1% × $2,000,000		
	of credit sales.		

* For the income statement approach, which requires estimating bad debts as a percent of sales or credit sales, the Allowance account balance is *not* considered when making the adjusting entry.

Summary

C1 **Describe accounts receivable and how they occur and are recorded.** Accounts receivable are amounts due from customers for credit sales. A subsidiary ledger lists amounts owed by each customer. Credit sales arise from at least two sources: (1) sales on credit and (2) credit card sales. *Sales on credit* refers to a company's granting credit directly to customers. Credit card sales involve customers' use of third-party credit cards.

C2 **Describe a note receivable, the computation of its maturity date, and the recording of its existence.** A note receivable is a written promise to pay a specified amount of money at a definite future date. The maturity date is the day the note (principal and interest) must be repaid. Interest rates are normally stated in annual terms. The amount of interest on the note is computed by expressing time as a fraction of one year and multiplying the note's principal by this fraction and the annual interest rate. A note received is recorded at its principal amount by debiting the Notes Receivable account. The credit amount is to the asset, product, or service provided in return for the note.

C3 **Explain how receivables can be converted to cash before maturity.** Receivables can be converted to cash before maturity in at least two ways. First, a company can sell accounts receivable to a factor, who charges a factoring fee. Second, a company can borrow money by signing a note payable that is secured by pledging the accounts receivable.

A1 **Compute accounts receivable turnover and use it to help assess financial condition.** Accounts receivable turnover is a measure of both the quality and liquidity of accounts receivable. The accounts receivable turnover measure indicates how often, on average, receivables are received and collected during the period. Accounts receivable turnover is computed as net sales divided by average accounts receivable.

P1 **Apply the direct write-off method to account for accounts receivable.** The direct write-off method charges Bad Debts Expense when accounts are written off as uncollectible. This method is acceptable only when the amount of bad debts expense is immaterial.

P2 **Apply the allowance method and estimate uncollectibles based on sales and accounts receivable.** Under the allowance method, bad debts expense is recorded with an adjustment at the end of each accounting period that debits the Bad Debts Expense account and credits the Allowance for Doubtful Accounts. The uncollectible accounts are later written off with a debit to the Allowance for Doubtful Accounts. Uncollectibles are estimated by focusing on either (1) the income statement relation between bad debts expense and credit sales or (2) the balance sheet relation between accounts receivable and the allowance for doubtful accounts. The first approach emphasizes the matching principle using the income statement. The second approach emphasizes realizable value of accounts receivable using the balance sheet.

P3 **Record the honoring and dishonoring of a note and adjustments for interest.** When a note is honored, the payee debits the money received and credits both Notes Receivable and Interest Revenue. Dishonored notes are credited to Notes Receivable and debited to Accounts Receivable (to the account of the maker in an attempt to collect), and Interest Revenue is recorded for interest earned for the time the note is held.

Guidance Answers to Decision Maker

Entrepreneur Analysis of credit card sales should weigh the benefits against the costs. The primary benefit is the potential to increase sales by attracting customers who prefer the convenience of credit cards. The primary cost is the fee charged by the credit card company for providing this service. Analysis should therefore estimate the expected increase in dollar sales from allowing credit card sales and then subtract (1) the normal costs and expenses and (2) the credit card fees associated with this expected increase in dollar sales. If your analysis shows an increase in profit from allowing credit card sales, your store should probably accept them.

Labor Union Chief Yes, this information is likely to impact your negotiations. The obvious question is why the company markedly increased this allowance. The large increase in this allowance means a substantial increase in bad debts expense *and* a decrease in earnings. This change (coming immediately prior to labor contract discussions) also raises concerns since it reduces the union's bargaining power for increased compensation. You want to ask management for supporting documentation justifying this increase. You also want data for two or three prior years and similar data from competitors. These data should give you some sense of whether the change in the allowance for uncollectibles is justified.

Analyst/Auditor The downward trend suggests the company is reducing the relative amount charged to bad debts expense each year. This may reflect the company's desire to increase net income.

On the other hand, it might be that collections have improved and the lower provision for bad debts is justified. If this is not the case, the lower allowances might be insufficient for bad debts.

Family Physician The recommendations are twofold. First, the analyst suggests more stringent screening of patients' credit standing. Second, the analyst suggests dropping patients who are most overdue in payments. You are likely bothered by both suggestions. They are probably financially wise recommendations, but you are troubled by eliminating services to those less able to pay. One alternative is to follow the recommendations while implementing a care program directed at patients less able to pay for services. This allows you to continue services to patients less able to pay and lets you discontinue services to patients able but unwilling to pay.

Key Terms

Accounts receivable	Direct write-off method	Maturity date of a note
Accounts receivable turnover	Interest	Payee of the note
Aging of accounts receivable	Maker of the note	Principal of a note
Allowance for Doubtful Accounts	Matching (expense recognition) principle	Promissory note (or note)
Allowance method	Materiality constraint	Realizable value
Bad debts		

Multiple Choice Quiz   Answers at end of chapter

1. A company's Accounts Receivable balance at its December 31 year-end is $125,650, and its Allowance for Doubtful Accounts has a credit balance of $328 before year-end adjustment. Its net sales are $572,300. It estimates that 4% of outstanding accounts receivable are uncollectible. What amount of bad debts expense is recorded at December 31?
   - **a.** $5,354
   - **b.** $328
   - **c.** $5,026
   - **d.** $4,698
   - **e.** $34,338

2. A company's Accounts Receivable balance at its December 31 year-end is $489,300, and its Allowance for Doubtful Accounts has a debit balance of $554 before year-end adjustment. Its net sales are $1,300,000. It estimates that 6% of outstanding accounts receivable are uncollectible. What amount of bad debts expense is recorded at December 31?
   - **a.** $29,912
   - **b.** $28,804
   - **c.** $78,000
   - **d.** $29,358
   - **e.** $554

3. Total interest to be earned on a $7,500, 5%, 90-day note is
   - **a.** $93.75
   - **b.** $375.00
   - **c.** $1,125.00
   - **d.** $31.25
   - **e.** $125.00

4. A company receives a $9,000, 8%, 60-day note. The maturity value of the note is
   - **a.** $120
   - **b.** $9,000
   - **c.** $9,120
   - **d.** $720
   - **e.** $9,720

5. A company has net sales of $489,600 and average accounts receivable of $40,800. What is its accounts receivable turnover?
   - **a.** 0.08
   - **b.** 30.41
   - **c.** 1,341.00
   - **d.** 12.00
   - **e.** 111.78

Icon denotes assignments that involve decision making.

Discussion Questions

1. How do sellers benefit from allowing their customers to use credit cards?

2. Why does the direct write-off method of accounting for bad debts usually fail to match revenues and expenses?

3. Explain the accounting constraint of materiality.

4. Why might a business prefer a note receivable to an account receivable?

5. Explain why writing off a bad debt against the Allowance for Doubtful Accounts does not reduce the estimated realizable value of a company's accounts receivable.

6. ♟ Why does the Bad Debts Expense account usually not have the same adjusted balance as the Allowance for Doubtful Accounts?

7. ♟ Refer to the financial statements and notes of **Apple** in Appendix A. In its presentation of accounts receivable on the balance sheet, how does it title accounts receivable? What does it report for its allowance as of September 27, 2014?

APPLE

8. ♟ Refer to the balance sheet of **Google** in Appendix A. Does it use the

GOOGLE

direct write-off method or allowance method in accounting for its accounts receivable? What is the realizable value of its receivables balance as of December 31, 2014?

9. Refer to the financial statements of **Samsung** in Appendix A. What does Samsung title its accounts receivable on its consolidated balance sheet? What are Samsung's accounts receivable at December 31, 2014?

Samsung

10. Refer to the December 31, 2014, financial statements of **Samsung** in Appendix A. Does Samsung report its accounts receivable as a current or noncurrent asset? Does Samsung report its accounts receivable net of an allowance?

Samsung

---

connect

QUICK STUDY

QS 7-1
Credit card sales
C1

Prepare journal entries for the following credit card sales transactions (the company uses the perpetual inventory system).

1. Sold $20,000 of merchandise, that cost $15,000, on **MasterCard** credit cards. The net cash receipts from sales are immediately transferred to the seller's bank account. MasterCard charges a 5% fee.

2. Sold $5,000 of merchandise, that cost $3,000, on an assortment of credit cards. Net cash receipts are received 5 days later, and a 4% fee is charged.

QS 7-2
Direct write-off method
P1

Solstice Company determines on October 1 that it cannot collect $50,000 of its accounts receivable from its customer P. Moore. Apply the direct write-off method to record this loss as of October 1.

QS 7-3
Recovering a bad debt
P1

Solstice Company determines on October 1 that it cannot collect $50,000 of its accounts receivable from its customer P. Moore. It uses the direct write-off method to record this loss as of October 1. On October 30, P. Moore unexpectedly pays his account in full to Solstice Company. Record Solstice's entry(ies) to reflect recovery of this bad debt.

QS 7-4
Distinguishing between the allowance method and direct write-off method
P1   P2

The following list describes aspects of either the allowance method or the direct write-off method to account for bad debts. For each item listed, indicate if the statement best describes either the allowance (A) method or the direct write-off (DW) method.

____ **1.** No attempt is made to predict bad debts expense.

____ **2.** Accounts receivable on the balance sheet is reported at net realizable value.

____ **3.** The write-off of a specific account does not affect net income.

____ **4.** When an account is written off, the debit is to Bad Debts Expense.

____ **5.** Sales and any bad debts expense are usually not recorded in the same period; thus proper matching (of revenue and expense recognition) does not consistently occur.

____ **6.** Requires a company to estimate bad debts expense related to the sales recorded in that period.

QS 7-5
Allowance method for bad debts
P2

Gomez Corp. uses the allowance method to account for uncollectibles. On January 31, it wrote off an $800 account of a customer, C. Green. On March 9, it receives a $300 payment from Green.

1. Prepare the journal entry or entries for January 31.

2. Prepare the journal entry or entries for March 9; assume no additional money is expected from Green.

QS 7-6
Percent of accounts receivable method
P2

Warner Company's year-end unadjusted trial balance shows accounts receivable of $99,000, allowance for doubtful accounts of $600 (credit), and sales of $280,000. Uncollectibles are estimated to be 1.5% of accounts receivable.

1. Prepare the December 31 year-end adjusting entry for uncollectibles.

2. What amount would have been used in the year-end adjusting entry if the allowance account had a year-end unadjusted debit balance of $300?

Warner Company's year-end unadjusted trial balance shows accounts receivable of $99,000, allowance for doubtful accounts of $600 (credit), and sales of $280,000. Uncollectibles are estimated to be 0.5% of sales. Prepare the December 31 year-end adjusting entry for uncollectibles.

QS 7-7
Percent of sales method
P2

On August 2, 2016, Jun Co. receives a $6,000, 90-day, 12% note from customer Ryan Albany as payment on his $6,000 account. (1) Compute the maturity date for this note. (2) Prepare Jun's journal entry for August 2.

QS 7-8
Note receivable   **C2**

On August 2, 2016, Jun Co. receives a $6,000, 90-day, 12% note from customer Ryan Albany as payment on his $6,000 account. Prepare Jun's journal entry assuming the note is honored by the customer on October 31, 2016.

QS 7-9
Note receivable honored   **P3**

Daw Company's December 31 year-end unadjusted trial balance shows a $10,000 balance in Notes Receivable. This balance is from one 6% note dated December 1, with a period of 45 days. Prepare any necessary journal entries for December 31 and for the note's maturity date assuming it is honored.

QS 7-10
Note receivable   **P3**

Record the sale by Balus Company of $125,000 in accounts receivable on May 1. Balus is charged a 2.5% factoring fee.

QS 7-11
Disposing of receivables   **C3**

The following data are taken from the comparative balance sheets of Ruggers Company. Compute and interpret its accounts receivable turnover for year 2016 (competitors average a turnover of 7.5).

QS 7-12
Accounts receivable turnover

A1

	2016	2015
Accounts receivable, net	$153,400	$138,500
Net sales	861,105	910,600

Answer each of the following related to international accounting standards.

a. Explain (in general terms) how the accounting for recognition of receivables is different between IFRS and U.S. GAAP.

b. Explain (in general terms) how the accounting for valuation of receivables is different between IFRS and U.S. GAAP.

QS 7-13
International accounting standards

C1

 connect

Vail Company recorded the following selected transactions during November 2016.

EXERCISES

Exercise 7-1
Accounts receivable subsidiary ledger; schedule of accounts receivable

C1

Nov. 5	Accounts Receivable—Ski Shop	4,615	
	Sales		4,615
10	Accounts Receivable—Welcome Enterprises	1,350	
	Sales		1,350
13	Accounts Receivable—Zia Natara	832	
	Sales		832
21	Sales Returns and Allowances	209	
	Accounts Receivable—Zia Natara		209
30	Accounts Receivable—Ski Shop	2,713	
	Sales		2,713

1. Open a general ledger having T-accounts for Accounts Receivable, Sales, and Sales Returns and Allowances. Also open an accounts receivable subsidiary ledger having a T-account for each customer. Post these entries to both the general ledger and the accounts receivable ledger.

2. Prepare a schedule of accounts receivable (see Exhibit 7.4) and compare its total with the balance of the Accounts Receivable controlling account as of November 30.

Check (2) Accounts Receivable ending balance, $9,301

Exercise 7-2

Accounting for credit card sales

C1

Levine Company uses the perpetual inventory system and allows customers to use two credit cards in charging purchases. With the Suntrust Bank Card, Levine receives an immediate money transfer to its account when it processes sales receipts. Suntrust assesses a 4% service charge for credit card sales. The second credit card that Levine accepts is the Continental Card. Levine batches its credit sales data to Continental on a daily basis, and the money is transferred to its account about 4 to 7 business days later. Continental assesses a 2.5% charge on sales for using its card. Prepare journal entries to record the following selected credit card transactions of Levine Company.

Apr. 8   Sold merchandise for $8,400 (that had cost $6,000) and accepted the customer's Suntrust Bank Card. Suntrust immediately transfers funds from the credit sales to Levine's bank account.

     12   Sold merchandise for $5,600 (that had cost $3,500) and accepted the customer's Continental Card. Levine batches $5,600 of credit card sales data to Continental, requesting payment.

     20   Received Continental's check for the April 12 billing, less the service charge.

Exercise 7-3

Direct write-off method

P1

Dexter Company applies the direct write-off method in accounting for uncollectible accounts. Prepare journal entries to record the following selected transactions of Dexter.

March 11   Dexter determines that it cannot collect $45,000 of its accounts receivable from its customer Lester Company.

       29   Lester Company unexpectedly pays its account in full to Dexter Company. Dexter records its recovery of this bad debt.

Exercise 7-4

Percent of sales method; write-off

P2

At year-end (December 31), Chan Company estimates its bad debts as 0.5% of its annual credit sales of $975,000. Chan records its bad debts expense for that estimate. On the following February 1, Chan decides that the $580 account of P. Park is uncollectible and writes it off as a bad debt. On June 5, Park unexpectedly pays the amount previously written off.

    Prepare the journal entries of Chan to record these transactions and events of December 31, February 1, and June 5.

Exercise 7-5

Percent of accounts receivable method

P2

At each calendar year-end, Mazie Supply Co. uses the percent of accounts receivable method to estimate bad debts. On December 31, 2016, it has outstanding accounts receivable of $55,000, and it estimates that 2% will be uncollectible.

    Prepare the adjusting entry to record bad debts expense for year 2016 under the assumption that the Allowance for Doubtful Accounts has (a) a $415 credit balance before the adjustment and (b) a $291 debit balance before the adjustment.

Exercise 7-6

Aging of receivables method

P2

Daley Company estimates uncollectible accounts using the allowance method at December 31. It prepared the following aging of receivables analysis.

				Days Past Due		
	Total	0	1 to 30	31 to 60	61 to 90	Over 90
Accounts receivable..........	$570,000	$396,000	$90,000	$36,000	$18,000	$30,000
Percent uncollectible.........		1%	2%	5%	7%	10%

a. Estimate the balance of the Allowance for Doubtful Accounts using the aging of accounts receivable method.

b. Prepare the adjusting entry to record bad debts expense using the estimate from part a. Assume the unadjusted balance in the Allowance for Doubtful Accounts is a $3,600 credit.

c. Prepare the adjusting entry to record bad debts expense using the estimate from part a. Assume the unadjusted balance in the Allowance for Doubtful Accounts is a $100 debit.

Exercise 7-7

Percent of receivables method

P2

Refer to the information in Exercise 7-6 to complete the following requirements.

a. Estimate the balance of the Allowance for Doubtful Accounts assuming the company uses 4.5% of total accounts receivable to estimate uncollectibles, instead of the aging of receivables method.

b. Prepare the adjusting entry to record bad debts expense using the estimate from part a. Assume the unadjusted balance in the Allowance for Doubtful Accounts is a $12,000 credit.

c. Prepare the adjusting entry to record bad debts expense using the estimate from part a. Assume the unadjusted balance in the Allowance for Doubtful Accounts is a $1,000 debit.

Refer to the information in Exercise 7-6 to complete the following requirements.

a. On February 1 of the next period, the company determined that $6,800 in customer accounts is uncollectible; specifically, $900 for Oakley Co. and $5,900 for Brookes Co. Prepare the journal entry to write off those accounts.

b. On June 5 of that next period, the company unexpectedly received a $900 payment on a customer account, Oakley Company, that had previously been written off in part *a*. Prepare the entries necessary to reinstate the account and to record the cash received.

At December 31, Folgeys Coffee Company reports the following results for its calendar year.

Cash sales	$900,000
Credit sales	300,000

Its year-end unadjusted trial balance includes the following items.

Accounts receivable	$125,000 debit
Allowance for doubtful accounts	5,000 debit

a. Prepare the adjusting entry to record bad debts expense assuming uncollectibles are estimated to be 3% of credit sales.

b. Prepare the adjusting entry to record bad debts expense assuming uncollectibles are estimated to be 1% of total sales.

c. Prepare the adjusting entry to record bad debts expense assuming uncollectibles are estimated to be 6% of year-end accounts receivable.

Prepare journal entries for the following selected transactions of Danica Company for 2015.

2015

Dec. 13 Accepted a $9,500, 45-day, 8% note dated December 13 in granting Miranda Lee a time extension on her past-due account receivable.

   31 Prepared an adjusting entry to record the accrued interest on the Lee note.

Refer to the information in Exercise 7-10 and prepare the journal entries for the following selected transactions of Danica Company for 2016.

2016

Jan. 27 Received Lee's payment for principal and interest on the note dated December 13.

Mar. 3 Accepted a $5,000, 10%, 90-day note dated March 3 in granting a time extension on the past-due account receivable of Tomas Company.

   17 Accepted a $2,000, 30-day, 9% note dated March 17 in granting H. Cheng a time extension on his past-due account receivable.

Apr. 16 Cheng dishonors his note when presented for payment.

May 1 Wrote off the Cheng account against the Allowance for Doubtful Accounts.

June 1 Received the Tomas payment for principal and interest on the note dated March 3.

Exercise 7-11
Notes receivable
transactions P3

Check Jan. 27, Dr. Cash
$9,595

June 1, Dr. Cash
$5,125

Prepare journal entries to record these selected transactions for Vitalo Company (assume that no reversing entries are recorded).

Nov. 1 Accepted a $6,000, 180-day, 8% note dated November 1 from Kelly White in granting a time extension on her past-due account receivable.

Dec. 31 Adjusted the year-end accounts for the accrued interest earned on the White note.

Apr. 30 White honors her note when presented for payment; February has 28 days for the current year.

Exercise 7-13

Dishonoring a note

P3

Prepare journal entries to record the following selected transactions of Ridge Company.

Mar. 21   Accepted a $9,500, 180-day, 8% note dated March 21 from Tamara Jackson in granting a time extension on her past-due account receivable.

Sept. 17   Jackson dishonors her note when it is presented for payment.

Dec. 31   After exhausting all legal means of collection, Ridge Company writes off Jackson's account against the Allowance for Doubtful Accounts.

Exercise 7-14

Selling and pledging accounts receivable

C3

On June 30, Petrov Co. has $128,700 of accounts receivable. Prepare journal entries to record the following selected July transactions. Also prepare any footnotes to the July 31 financial statements that result from these transactions. (The company uses the perpetual inventory system.)

July   4   Sold $7,245 of merchandise (that had cost $5,000) to customers on credit.

9   Sold $20,000 of accounts receivable to Main Bank. Main charges a 4% factoring fee.

17   Received $5,859 cash from customers in payment on their accounts.

27   Borrowed $10,000 cash from Main Bank, pledging $12,500 of accounts receivable as security for the loan.

Exercise 7-15

Accounts receivable turnover

A1

The following information is from the annual financial statements of Raheem Company. Compute its accounts receivable turnover for 2015 and 2016. Compare the two years' results and give a possible explanation for any change (competitors average a turnover of 11).

	2016	2015	2014
Net sales	$405,140	$335,280	$388,000
Accounts receivable, net (year-end)	44,800	41,400	34,800

Exercise 7-16

Accounting for bad debts following IFRS

P2

Hitachi, Ltd., reports total revenues of ¥9,616,202 million for its fiscal year ending March 31, 2014; and its March 31, 2014, unadjusted trial balance reports a debit balance for trade receivables (gross) of ¥2,797,935 million.

a. Prepare the adjusting entry to record its bad debts expense assuming uncollectibles are estimated to be 0.4% of total revenues and its unadjusted trial balance reports a credit balance of ¥10,000 million for the allowance for doubtful accounts.

b. Prepare the adjusting entry to record bad debts expense assuming uncollectibles are estimated to be 2.0% of year-end trade receivables (gross) and its unadjusted trial balance reports a credit balance of ¥10,000 million for the allowance for doubtful accounts.

---

connect

PROBLEM SET A

Problem 7-1A

Sales on account and credit card sales

C1

Mayfair Co. allows select customers to make purchases on credit. Its other customers can use either of two credit cards: Zisa or Barclay. Zisa deducts a 3% service charge for sales on its credit card and transfers funds to the bank account of Mayfair *immediately* upon receiving the credit card sales data. Barclay deducts a 2% service charge and transfers the funds to Mayfair within 4 to 8 business days. Mayfair batches the Zisa and the Barclay credit card sales data daily to the card companies. Mayfair completes the following transactions in June.

June   4   Sold $650 of merchandise (that had cost $400) on credit to Natara Morris.

5   Sold $6,900 of merchandise (that had cost $4,200) to customers who used their Zisa cards.

6   Sold $5,850 of merchandise (that had cost $3,800) to customers who used their Barclay cards.

8   Sold $4,350 of merchandise (that had cost $2,900) to customers who used their Barclay cards.

13   Wrote off the account of Abigail McKee against the Allowance for Doubtful Accounts. The $429 balance in McKee's account stemmed from a credit sale in October of last year.

17   Received the transferred funds owed from Barclay for the June 6 and June 8 transactions.

18   Received Morris's check in full payment for the purchase of June 4.

Check   June 17, Dr. Cash $9,996

Required

Prepare journal entries to record the preceding transactions and events. (The company uses the perpetual inventory system. Round amounts to the nearest dollar.)

At December 31, 2016, Hawke Company reports the following results for its calendar year.

Cash sales	$1,905,000
Credit sales	5,682,000

In addition, its unadjusted trial balance includes the following items.

Accounts receivable	$1,270,100 debit
Allowance for doubtful accounts	16,580 debit

Problem 7-2A
Estimating and reporting bad debts

P2

Required

1. Prepare the adjusting entry for this company to recognize bad debts under each of the following independent assumptions.
   a. Bad debts are estimated to be 1.5% of credit sales.
   b. Bad debts are estimated to be 1% of total sales.
   c. An aging analysis estimates that 5% of year-end accounts receivable are uncollectible.
2. Show how Accounts Receivable and the Allowance for Doubtful Accounts appear on its December 31, 2016, balance sheet given the facts in part 1a.
3. Show how Accounts Receivable and the Allowance for Doubtful Accounts appear on its December 31, 2016, balance sheet given the facts in part 1c.

Check Bad Debts Expense: (1a) $85,230, (1c) $80,085

Jarden Company has credit sales of $3,600,000 for year 2016. On December 31, 2016, the company's Allowance for Doubtful Accounts has an unadjusted credit balance of $14,500. Jarden prepares a schedule of its December 31, 2016, accounts receivable by age. On the basis of past experience, it estimates the percent of receivables in each age category that will become uncollectible. This information is summarized here.

Problem 7-3A
Aging accounts receivable and accounting for bad debts

P2

	A	B	C
1	**December 31, 2016**	**Age of**	**Expected Percent**
2	**Accounts Receivable**	**Accounts Receivable**	**Uncollectible**
3	$830,000	Not yet due	1.25%
4	254,000	1 to 30 days past due	2.00
5	86,000	31 to 60 days past due	6.50
6	38,000	61 to 90 days past due	32.75
7	12,000	Over 90 days past due	68.00
8			

Required

1. Estimate the required balance of the Allowance for Doubtful Accounts at December 31, 2016, using the aging of accounts receivable method.
2. Prepare the adjusting entry to record bad debts expense at December 31, 2016.

Check (2) Dr. Bad Debts Expense $27,150

Analysis Component

3. On June 30, 2017, Jarden Company concludes that a customer's $4,750 receivable (created in 2016) is uncollectible and that the account should be written off. What effect will this action have on Jarden's 2017 net income? Explain.

Liang Company began operations on January 1, 2015. During its first two years, the company completed a number of transactions involving sales on credit, accounts receivable collections, and bad debts. These transactions are summarized as follows:

Problem 7-4A
Accounts receivable transactions and bad debts adjustments

C1   P2

2015

a. Sold $1,345,434 of merchandise (that had cost $975,000) on credit, terms n/30.
b. Wrote off $18,300 of uncollectible accounts receivable.
c. Received $669,200 cash in payment of accounts receivable.
d. In adjusting the accounts on December 31, the company estimated that 1.5% of accounts receivable will be uncollectible.

Check (d) Dr. Bad Debts Expense $28,169

2016

e. Sold $1,525,634 of merchandise (that had cost $1,250,000) on credit, terms n/30.

f. Wrote off $27,800 of uncollectible accounts receivable.

g. Received $1,204,600 cash in payment of accounts receivable.

(h) Dr. Bad Debts Expense $32,199

h. In adjusting the accounts on December 31, the company estimated that 1.5% of accounts receivable will be uncollectible.

Required

Prepare journal entries to record Liang's 2015 and 2016 summarized transactions and its year-end adjustments to record bad debts expense. (The company uses the perpetual inventory system and it applies the allowance method for its accounts receivable. Round amounts to the nearest dollar.)

Problem 7-5A

Analyzing and journalizing notes receivable transactions

C2 C3 P3

Check Feb. 14, Cr. Interest Revenue $108

May 31, Cr. Interest Revenue $122

Nov. 2, Cr. Interest Revenue $35

The following selected transactions are from Ohlm Company.

2015

Dec. 16 Accepted a $10,800, 60-day, 8% note dated this day in granting Danny Todd a time extension on his past-due account receivable.

31 Made an adjusting entry to record the accrued interest on the Todd note.

2016

Feb. 14 Received Todd's payment of principal and interest on the note dated December 16.

Mar. 2 Accepted a $6,100, 8%, 90-day note dated this day in granting a time extension on the past-due account receivable from Midnight Co.

17 Accepted a $2,400, 30-day, 7% note dated this day in granting Ava Privet a time extension on her past-due account receivable.

Apr. 16 Privet dishonored her note when presented for payment.

May 31 Midnight Co. refuses to pay the note that was due to Ohlm Co. on May 31. Prepare the journal entry to charge the dishonored note plus accrued interest to Midnight Co.'s accounts receivable.

July 16 Received payment from Midnight Co. for the maturity value of its dishonored note plus interest for 46 days beyond maturity at 8%.

Aug. 7 Accepted a $7,450, 90-day, 10% note dated this day in granting a time extension on the past-due account receivable of Mulan Co.

Sept. 3 Accepted a $2,100, 60-day, 10% note dated this day in granting Noah Carson a time extension on his past-due account receivable.

Nov. 2 Received payment of principal plus interest from Carson for the September 3 note.

Nov. 5 Received payment of principal plus interest from Mulan for the August 7 note.

Dec. 1 Wrote off the Privet account against Allowance for Doubtful Accounts.

Required

1. Prepare journal entries to record these transactions and events. (Round amounts to the nearest dollar.)

Analysis Component

2. What reporting is necessary when a business pledges receivables as security for a loan and the loan is still outstanding at the end of the period? Explain the reason for this requirement and the accounting principle being satisfied.

PROBLEM SET B

Problem 7-1B

Sales on account and credit card sales

C1

Archer Co. allows select customers to make purchases on credit. Its other customers can use either of two credit cards: Commerce Bank or Goldman. Commerce Bank deducts a 3% service charge for sales on its credit card and transfers funds to the bank account of Archer *immediately* upon receiving the credit card sales data. Goldman deducts a 2% service charge and transfers the funds to Archer within 4 to 8 business days. Archer batches the Commerce Bank and Goldman credit card sales data daily to the card companies. Archer completes the following transactions in August.

Aug. 4 Sold $3,700 of merchandise (that had cost $2,000) on credit to McKenzie Carpenter.

10 Sold $5,200 of merchandise (that had cost $2,800) to customers who used their Commerce Bank credit cards.

11 Sold $1,250 of merchandise (that had cost $900) to customers who used their Goldman cards.

14   Received Carpenter's check in full payment for the purchase of August 4.
15   Sold $3,250 of merchandise (that had cost $1,758) to customers who used their Goldman cards.
22   Wrote off the account of Craw Co. against the Allowance for Doubtful Accounts. The $498 balance in Craw Co.'s account stemmed from a credit sale in November of last year.
25   Received the transferred funds owed from Goldman for the August 11 and August 15 transactions.

Check Aug. 25, Dr. Cash $4,410

Required

Prepare journal entries to record the preceding transactions and events. (The company uses the perpetual inventory system. Round amounts to the nearest dollar.)

At December 31, 2016, Ingleton Company reports the following results for the year:

Cash sales	$1,025,000
Credit sales	1,342,000

In addition, its unadjusted trial balance includes the following items:

Accounts receivable	$575,000 debit
Allowance for doubtful accounts	7,500 credit

Problem 7-2B
Estimating and reporting bad debts

P2

Required

1. Prepare the adjusting entry for Ingleton Co. to recognize bad debts under each of the following independent assumptions.
    a. Bad debts are estimated to be 2.5% of credit sales.
    b. Bad debts are estimated to be 1.5% of total sales.
    c. An aging analysis estimates that 6% of year-end accounts receivable are uncollectible.
2. Show how Accounts Receivable and the Allowance for Doubtful Accounts appear on its December 31, 2016, balance sheet given the facts in part 1a.
3. Show how Accounts Receivable and the Allowance for Doubtful Accounts appear on its December 31, 2016, balance sheet given the facts in part 1c.

Check Dr. Bad debts expense: (1b) $35,505, (1c) $27,000

Hovak Company has credit sales of $4,500,000 for year 2016. At December 31, 2016, the company's Allowance for Doubtful Accounts has an unadjusted debit balance of $3,400. Hovak prepares a schedule of its December 31, 2016, accounts receivable by age. On the basis of past experience, it estimates the percent of receivables in each age category that will become uncollectible. This information is summarized here.

Problem 7-3B
Aging accounts receivable and accounting for bad debts

P2

	A	B	C
1	**December 31, 2016**	**Age of**	**Expected Percent**
2	**Accounts Receivable**	**Accounts Receivable**	**Uncollectible**
3	$396,400	Not yet due	2.0%
4	277,800	1 to 30 days past due	4.0
5	48,000	31 to 60 days past due	8.5
6	6,600	61 to 90 days past due	39.0
7	2,800	Over 90 days past due	82.0
8			

Required

1. Compute the required balance of the Allowance for Doubtful Accounts at December 31, 2016, using the aging of accounts receivable method.
2. Prepare the adjusting entry to record bad debts expense at December 31, 2016.

Check (2) Dr. Bad Debts Expense $31,390

Continued on next page . . .

Analysis Component

3. On July 31, 2017, Hovak concludes that a customer's $3,455 receivable (created in 2016) is uncollectible and that the account should be written off. What effect will this action have on Hovak's 2017 net income? Explain.

Problem 7-4B
Accounts receivable transactions and bad debts adjustments
C1   P2

Check (d) Dr. Bad Debts Expense $11,287

(h) Dr. Bad Debts Expense $9,773

Sherman Co. began operations on January 1, 2015, and completed several transactions during 2015 and 2016 that involved sales on credit, accounts receivable collections, and bad debts. These transactions are summarized as follows.

2015

a. Sold $685,350 of merchandise (that had cost $500,000) on credit, terms n/30.

b. Received $482,300 cash in payment of accounts receivable.

c. Wrote off $9,350 of uncollectible accounts receivable.

d. In adjusting the accounts on December 31, the company estimated that 1% of accounts receivable will be uncollectible.

2016

e. Sold $870,220 of merchandise (that had cost $650,000) on credit, terms n/30.

f. Received $990,800 cash in payment of accounts receivable.

g. Wrote off $11,090 of uncollectible accounts receivable.

h. In adjusting the accounts on December 31, the company estimated that 1% of accounts receivable will be uncollectible.

Required

Prepare journal entries to record Sherman's 2015 and 2016 summarized transactions and its year-end adjusting entry to record bad debts expense. (The company uses the perpetual inventory system and it applies the allowance method for its accounts receivable. Round amounts to the nearest dollar.)

Problem 7-5B
Analyzing and journalizing notes receivable transactions
C2   C3   P3

Check Jan. 30, Cr. Interest Revenue $32

April 30, Cr. Interest Revenue $124

Sep. 19, Cr. Interest Revenue $190

The following selected transactions are from Springer Company.

2015

| Nov. | 1 | Accepted a $4,800, 90-day, 8% note dated this day in granting Steve Julian a time extension on his past-due account receivable. |
| Dec. | 31 | Made an adjusting entry to record the accrued interest on the Julian note. |

2016

Jan.	30	Received Julian's payment for principal and interest on the note dated November 1.
Feb.	28	Accepted a $12,600, 30-day, 8% note dated this day in granting a time extension on the past-due account receivable from King Co.
Mar.	1	Accepted a $6,200, 60-day, 12% note dated this day in granting Myron Shelley a time extension on his past-due account receivable.
	30	The King Co. dishonored its note when presented for payment.
Apr.	30	Received payment of principal plus interest from M. Shelley for the March 1 note.
June	15	Accepted a $2,000, 72-day, 8% note dated this day in granting a time extension on the past-due account receivable of Ryder Solon.
	21	Accepted a $9,500, 90-day, 8% note dated this day in granting J. Felton a time extension on his past-due account receivable.
Aug.	26	Received payment of principal plus interest from R. Solon for the note of June 15.
Sep.	19	Received payment of principal plus interest from J. Felton for the June 21 note.
Nov.	30	Wrote off King Co.'s account against Allowance for Doubtful Accounts.

Required

1. Prepare journal entries to record these transactions and events. (Round amounts to the nearest dollar.)

Analysis Component

2. What reporting is necessary when a business pledges receivables as security for a loan and the loan is still outstanding at the end of the period? Explain the reason for this requirement and the accounting principle being satisfied.

(This serial problem began in Chapter 1 and continues through most of the book. If previous chapter segments were not completed, the serial problem can begin at this point. It is helpful, but not necessary, to use the Working Papers that accompany the book.)

SERIAL PROBLEM
Business Solutions

P1   P2

SP 7   Santana Rey, owner of Business Solutions, realizes that she needs to begin accounting for bad debts expense. Assume that Business Solutions has total revenues of $44,000 during the first three months of 2017, and that the Accounts Receivable balance on March 31, 2017, is $22,867.

Required

1. Prepare the adjusting entry needed for Business Solutions to recognize bad debts expense on March 31, 2017, under each of the following independent assumptions (assume a zero unadjusted balance in the Allowance for Doubtful Accounts at March 31).

    a. Bad debts are estimated to be 1% of total revenues. (Round amounts to the dollar.)

    b. Bad debts are estimated to be 2% of accounts receivable. (Round amounts to the dollar.)

2. Assume that Business Solutions's Accounts Receivable balance at June 30, 2017, is $20,250 and that one account of $100 has been written off against the Allowance for Doubtful Accounts since March 31, 2017. If S. Rey uses the method prescribed in part 1*b*, what adjusting journal entry must be made to recognize bad debts expense on June 30, 2017?

Check   (2) Dr. Bad Debts Expense, $48

3. Should S. Rey consider adopting the direct write-off method of accounting for bad debts expense rather than one of the allowance methods considered in part 1? Explain.

The **General Ledger** tool in *Connect* automates several of the procedural steps in accounting so that the financial professional can focus on the impacts of each transaction on various financial reports and performance measures.

GENERAL LEDGER PROBLEM

Available in Connect

GL 7-1   General Ledger assignment GL 7-1, based on Problem 7-5A, focuses on transactions related to accounts and notes receivable and highlights the impact each transaction has on interest revenue, if any. Prepare the journal entries related to accounts and notes receivable; the schedules of accounts receivable and notes receivable are automatically completed using the General Ledger tool. Next, compute both the amount and timing of interest revenue for each note receivable.

Beyond the Numbers

BTN 7-1   Refer to **Apple**'s financial statements in Appendix A to answer the following.

1. What is the amount of Apple's accounts receivable as of September 27, 2014?
2. Compute Apple's accounts receivable turnover as of September 27, 2014.
3. How long does it take, *on average,* for the company to collect receivables?
4. Apple's most liquid assets include (*a*) cash and cash equivalents, (*b*) short-term marketable securities, (*c*) receivables, and (*d*) inventory. Compute the percentage that these liquid assets make up of current liabilities as of September 27, 2014. Do the same computations for September 28, 2013. Comment on the company's ability to satisfy its current liabilities as of its fiscal 2014 year-end compared to its fiscal 2013 year-end.
5. What criteria did Apple use to classify items as cash equivalents? (*Hint:* Refer to Apple's footnotes describing cash equivalents in Appendix A.)

REPORTING IN ACTION

A1

APPLE

Fast Forward

6. Access Apple's financial statements for fiscal years after September 27, 2014, at its website (www.Apple.com) or the SEC's EDGAR database (www.SEC.gov). Recompute parts 2 and 4 and comment on any changes since September 27, 2014.

COMPARATIVE ANALYSIS

A1 P2

APPLE
GOOGLE

BTN 7-2   Comparative figures for **Apple** and **Google** follow.

$ millions	Apple			Google		
	Current Year	One Year Prior	Two Years Prior	Current Year	One Year Prior	Two Years Prior
Accounts receivable, net . .	$ 17,460	$ 13,102	$ 10,930	$ 9,383	$ 8,882	$ 7,885
Net sales	182,795	170,910	156,508	66,001	55,519	46,039

Required

Hint: Average collection period equals 365 divided by the accounts receivable turnover.

1. Compute the accounts receivable turnover for Apple and Google for each of the two most recent years using the data shown.

2. Using results from part 1, compute how many days it takes each company, *on average,* to collect receivables. Compare the collection periods for Apple and Google, and suggest at least one explanation for the difference.

3. Which company is more efficient in collecting its accounts receivable? Explain.

ETHICS CHALLENGE

P2

BTN 7-3   Anton Blair is the manager of a medium-size company. A few years ago, Blair persuaded the owner to base a part of his compensation on the net income the company earns each year. Each December he estimates year-end financial figures in anticipation of the bonus he will receive. If the bonus is not as high as he would like, he offers several recommendations to the accountant for year-end adjustments. One of his favorite recommendations is for the controller to reduce the estimate of doubtful accounts.

Required

1. What effect does lowering the estimate for doubtful accounts have on the income statement and balance sheet?

2. Do you believe Blair's recommendation to adjust the allowance for doubtful accounts is within his rights as manager, or do you believe this action is an ethics violation? Justify your response.

3. What type of internal control(s) might be useful for this company in overseeing the manager's recommendations for accounting changes?

COMMUNICATING IN PRACTICE

P2

BTN 7-4   As the accountant for Pure-Air Distributing, you attend a sales managers' meeting devoted to a discussion of credit policies. At the meeting, you report that bad debts expense is estimated to be $59,000 and accounts receivable at year-end amount to $1,750,000 less a $43,000 allowance for doubtful accounts. Sid Omar, a sales manager, expresses confusion over why bad debts expense and the allowance for doubtful accounts are different amounts. Write a one-page memorandum to him explaining why a difference in bad debts expense and the allowance for doubtful accounts is not unusual. The company estimates bad debts expense as 2% of sales.

TAKING IT TO THE NET

C1

BTN 7-5   Access **eBay**'s February 6, 2015, filing of its 10-K report for the year ended December 31, 2014, at **www.SEC.gov**.

Required

1. What is the amount of eBay's net accounts receivable at December 31, 2014, and at December 31, 2013?

2. "Financial Statement Schedule II" to its financial statements lists eBay's allowance for doubtful accounts (including authorized credits). For the two years ended December 31, 2014 and 2013, compute its allowance for doubtful accounts (including authorized credits) as a percent of gross accounts receivable.

3. Do you believe that these percentages are reasonable based on what you know about eBay? Explain.

TEAMWORK IN ACTION

P2

BTN 7-6   Each member of a team is to participate in estimating uncollectibles using the aging schedule and percents shown in Problem 7-3A. The division of labor is up to the team. Your goal is to accurately complete this task as soon as possible. After estimating uncollectibles, check your estimate with the instructor. If the estimate is correct, the team then should prepare the adjusting entry and the presentation of accounts receivable (net) for the December 31, 2016, balance sheet.

ENTREPRENEURIAL DECISION

C1

BTN 7-7   Matt Maloney of **GrubHub** is introduced in the chapter's opening feature. GrubHub is a website that allows customers to order food delivery from their favorite restaurants. Assume that Matt is considering two new selling options.

Plan A. GrubHub would begin selling packaged foods online directly to customers. The new online customers would use their credit cards. The company currently has the capability of selling packaged foods through its website with no additional investment in hardware or software. Annual credit sales are expected to increase by $250,000. *Costs associated with Plan A:* Cost of these new sales is $135,500; credit card fees will be 4.75% of sales; and additional recordkeeping and shipping costs will be 6% of sales. Packaged food sales will reduce restaurant sales on GrubHub.com by $35,000 annually because some customers will now purchase packaged foods. Assume that restaurant sales on GrubHub.com have a 25% gross margin percentage.

Plan B. GrubHub would expand to more cities. It would make additional annual credit sales of $500,000 to customers in those new cities. *Costs associated with Plan B:* Cost of these new sales is $375,000; additional recordkeeping and shipping costs will be 4% of sales; and uncollectible accounts will be 6.2% of sales.

Required

1. Compute the additional annual net income or loss expected under (a) Plan A and (b) Plan B.
2. Should the company pursue either plan? Discuss both the financial and nonfinancial factors relevant to this decision.

Check   (1b) Additional net income, $74,000

HITTING THE ROAD

C1

BTN 7-8   Many commercials include comments similar to the following: "We accept **VISA**" or "We do not accept **American Express.**" Conduct your own research by contacting at least five companies via interviews, phone calls, or the Internet to determine the reason(s) companies discriminate in their use of credit cards. Collect information on the fees charged by the different cards for the companies contacted. (The instructor can assign this as a team activity.)

GLOBAL DECISION

C1   P2

Samsung
APPLE
GOOGLE

BTN 7-9   Key information from **Samsung** (**www.Samsung.com**), which is a leading manufacturer of consumer electronic products, follows.

₩ in millions	Current Year	One Year Prior	Two Years Prior
Accounts receivable, net*	₩ 28,234,485	₩ 27,875,934	₩ 26,674,596
Sales	206,205,987	228,692,667	201,103,613

* Samsung titles this "Trade and other receivables."

1. Compute the accounts receivable turnover for the current year.
2. How long does it take on average for Samsung to collect receivables?
3. Refer to BTN 7-2. How does Samsung compare to **Apple** and **Google** in terms of its accounts receivable turnover and its collection period?

ANSWERS TO MULTIPLE CHOICE QUIZ

1. d; Desired balance in Allowance for Doubtful Accounts = $ 5,026 cr.
   ($125,650 × 0.04)
   Current balance in Allowance for Doubtful Accounts = ___(328)_ cr.
   Bad Debts Expense to be recorded = $ 4,698

2. a; Desired balance in Allowance for Doubtful Accounts = $29,358 cr.
   ($489,300 × 0.06)
   Current balance in Allowance for Doubtful Accounts = ___554_ dr.
   Bad Debts Expense to be recorded = $29,912

3. a; $7,500 × 0.05 × 90/360 = $93.75

4. c; Principal amount $9,000
   Interest accrued . . . .   _120_ ($9,000 × 0.08 × 60/360)
   Maturity value $9,120

5. d; $489,600/$40,800 = 12

chapter 8

Reporting and Analyzing Long-Term Assets

Chapter Preview

PLANT ASSETS

C1 Cost determination

P1 Depreciation

C2 Partial-years and changes in estimates

C3 Additional expenditures

P2 Disposal

NATURAL RESOURCES

P3 Cost determination

Depletion

Presentation

Plant assets tied into extracting resources

INTANGIBLE ASSETS

P4 Cost determination

Amortization

Types of intangibles

A1 Analyze asset usage

Learning Objectives

CONCEPTUAL

C1 Explain the cost principle for computing the cost of plant assets.

C2 Explain depreciation for partial years and changes in estimates.

C3 Distinguish between revenue and capital expenditures, and account for them.

ANALYTICAL

A1 Compute total asset turnover and apply it to analyze a company's use of assets.

PROCEDURAL

P1 Compute and record depreciation using the straight-line, units-of-production, and declining-balance methods.

P2 Account for asset disposal through discarding or selling an asset.

P3 Account for natural resource assets and their depletion.

P4 Account for intangible assets.

P5 *Appendix 8A*—Account for asset exchanges.

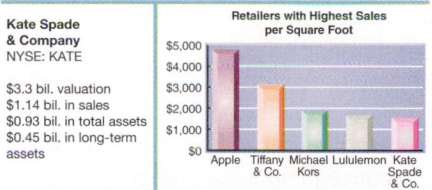

In Spades

"It's a far, far better thing to be overdressed than underdressed" —KATE SPADE

NEW YORK—Most women put their money in their handbags—that is where trendy designer Kate Spade is making hers. Kate's lines of elegant and whimsical bags, which range from pink herringbone carryalls and velvet tiger-print shoppers to simple nylon totes, are among fashion's hottest must-haves. Kate and her husband, Andy, started their business from a New York City loft apartment with $35,000 of his savings. A Kansas City native, Kate has scored by making handbags fashionable as well as functional. Kate's business was merged into Liz Claiborne, Inc., in 2006 for $124 million. Given the success of the Kate Spade brand, Liz Claiborne was renamed **Kate Spade & Company** (**KateSpadeandCompany.com**) in 2014.

While her designs yield bags of money, business is her focus. "It was less about wanting to be a designer and more wanting to start a business," insists Kate. To achieve that level, her company carefully manages its long-term assets, including machinery, equipment, buildings, leasehold improvements, furniture, and fixtures. Her careful management and effective use of property, plant, and equipment have yielded over a 100% increase in sales over the past two years! This dramatic sales growth occurred

Kate Spade & Company
NYSE: KATE

$3.3 bil. valuation
$1.14 bil. in sales
$0.93 bil. in total assets
$0.45 bil. in long-term assets

Retailers with Highest Sales per Square Foot

(bar chart: Apple, Tiffany & Co., Michael Kors, Lululemon, Kate Spade & Co., with values from $0 to $5,000)

without the purchase of additional long-term assets, as shown here:

($ millions)	2012	2013	2014
Total sales	$545	$803	$1,139
Long-term assets	450	326	452
Property, plant & equipment	220	149	174
Intangibles	131	91	90
Goodwill	60	49	65

Her company's efficiency in using its assets, reflected in its asset turnover, has made her company as popular on Wall Street as on Main Street (and malls). The company's stock price has skyrocketed in the past three years.

Kate Spade & Company is on a roll—it now has 150 stores in the United States and 46 stores in foreign countries. It also reports $159 million in net income and a positive cash flow for 2014. The challenge for Kate is to maintain the right kind and amount of assets to meet business demands *and* be profitable and keep growing.

Management at Kate Spade & Company believes that available cash, marketable securities, and the cash generated from operations are sufficient to fund its operations. Management also understands that its success depends on continued monitoring and control of the types and costs of long-term assets. Each of its tangible and intangible assets commands management attention, and the focus is on recovering those costs and returning a profit.

As market analysts predict even greater success for Kate Spade & Company in future years, Kate remains humble, saying, "Luckily, I haven't had to go and get my old job back."

Sources: *Kate Spade website,* January 2016; *Kate Spade & Company 10-K,* January 2015; *Urban Desires,* 1996; *BusinessWeek,* January 2000

Section 1—Plant Assets

Plant assets are tangible assets used in a company's operations that have a useful life of more than one accounting period. Plant assets are also called *plant and equipment; property, plant and equipment;* or *fixed assets.* For many companies, plant assets make up the single largest class of assets they own. Exhibit 8.1 shows plant assets as a percentage of total assets for several companies. Not only do they make up a large percentage of many companies' assets, but their dollar values are large. **McDonald's** plant assets, for instance, are reported at nearly $25 billion, while **Walmart** reports plant assets of more than $115 billion.

EXHIBIT 8.1

Plant Assets of Selected Companies

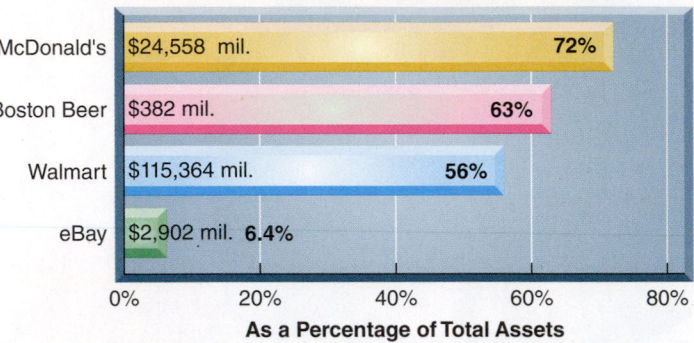

Plant assets are set apart from other assets by two important features. First, *plant assets are used in operations.* This makes them different from, for instance, inventory that is held for sale and not used in operations. The distinctive feature here is use, not type of asset. A company that purchases a computer to resell it reports it on the balance sheet as inventory. If the same company purchases this computer to use in operations, however, it is a plant asset. Another example is land held for future expansion, which is reported as a long-term investment. However, if this land holds a factory used in operations, the land is part of plant assets. Another example is equipment held for use in the event of a breakdown or for peak periods of production, which is reported in plant assets. If this same equipment is removed from use and held for sale, however, it is not reported in plant assets.

The second important feature is that *plant assets have useful lives extending over more than one accounting period.* This makes plant assets different from current assets such as supplies that are normally consumed in a short time period after they are placed in use.

Accordingly, because plant assets are used in operations, we try to match their costs against the revenues they generate. Also, since their useful lives extend over more than one period, our matching of costs and revenues must extend over several periods. Specifically, we value plant assets (balance sheet effect) and then, for many of them, we allocate their costs to periods benefiting from their use (income statement effect). An important exception is land; land cost is not allocated to expense when we expect it to have an indefinite life.

Exhibit 8.2 shows four main issues in accounting for plant assets: (1) computing the costs of plant assets, (2) allocating the costs of most plant assets (less any salvage amounts) against

Point: The phrase *capital-intensive* refers to companies with large amounts invested in plant assets.

Point: It can help to view plant assets as prepaid expenses that benefit several future accounting periods.

EXHIBIT 8.2

Issues in Accounting for Plant Assets

revenues for the periods they benefit, (3) accounting for expenditures such as repairs and improvements to plant assets, and (4) recording the disposal of plant assets. The following sections discuss these issues.

COST DETERMINATION

Plant assets are recorded at cost when acquired. This is consistent with the *cost principle.* **Cost** includes all normal and reasonable expenditures necessary to get the asset in place and ready for its intended use. The cost of a factory machine, for instance, includes its invoice cost less any cash discount for early payment, plus any necessary freight, unpacking, assembling, installing, and testing costs. Examples are the costs of building a base or foundation for a machine, providing electrical hookups, and testing the asset before using it in operations.

C1

Explain the cost principle for computing the cost of plant assets.

To be recorded as part of the cost of a plant asset, an expenditure must be normal, reasonable, and necessary in preparing it for its intended use. If an asset is damaged during unpacking, the repairs are not added to its cost. Instead, they are charged to an expense account. Nor is a paid traffic fine for moving heavy machinery on city streets without a proper permit part of the machinery's cost; but payment for a proper permit is included in the cost of machinery. Charges are sometimes incurred to modify or customize a new plant asset. These charges are added to the asset's cost. We explain in this section how to determine the cost of plant assets for each of its four major classes.

Machinery and Equipment

The costs of machinery and equipment consist of all costs normal and necessary to purchase them and prepare them for their intended use. These include the purchase price, taxes, transportation charges, insurance while in transit, and the installing, assembling, and testing of the machinery and equipment.

Buildings

A Building account is charged for the costs of purchasing or constructing a building that is used in operations. When purchased, a building's costs usually include its purchase price, brokerage fees,

PhotoLink/Getty Images

taxes, title fees, and attorney fees. Its costs also include all expenditures to ready it for its intended use, including any necessary repairs or renovations such as wiring, lighting, flooring, and wall coverings. When a company constructs a building or any plant asset for its own use, its costs include materials and labor plus a reasonable amount of indirect overhead cost. Overhead includes the costs of items such as heat, lighting, power, and depreciation on machinery used to construct the asset. Costs of construction also include design fees, building permits, and insurance during construction. However, costs such as insurance to cover the asset *after* it is placed in use are operating expenses.

Land Improvements

Land improvements are additions to land and have limited useful lives. Examples are parking lot surfaces, driveways, walkways, fences, landscaping, and sprinkling and lighting systems. Costs of land improvements include expenditures necessary to make those improvements ready for their intended use. While the costs of these improvements increase the usefulness of the land, they are charged to a separate Land Improvement account so that their costs can be allocated to the periods they benefit.

Land

Land is the earth's surface and has an indefinite (unlimited) life. Costs of land include expenditures necessary to make that property ready for its intended use. When land is purchased for a building site, its cost includes the total amount paid for the land, including any real estate commissions, title insurance fees, legal fees, and any accrued property taxes paid by the purchaser. Payments for surveying, clearing, grading, and draining also are included in the cost of land. Other costs include government assessments, whether incurred at the time of purchase or later, for items such as public roadways, sewers, and sidewalks. These assessments are included because they permanently add to the land's value. Land purchased as a building site sometimes includes structures that must be removed. In such cases, the total purchase price is charged to the Land account as is the cost of removing the structures, less any amounts recovered through sale of salvaged materials. To illustrate, assume that **Starbucks** paid $167,000 cash to acquire land for a retail store. This land had an old service garage that was removed at a net cost of $13,000 ($15,000 in costs less $2,000 proceeds from salvaged materials). Additional closing costs total $10,000, consisting of brokerage fees ($8,000), legal fees ($1,500), and title costs ($500). The cost of this land to Starbucks is $190,000 and is computed as shown in Exhibit 8.3.

EXHIBIT 8.3

Computing Cost of Land

Cash price of land	$ 167,000
Net cost of garage removal	13,000
Closing costs	10,000
Cost of land	**$190,000**

Example: If appraised values in Exhibit 8.4 are building, $84,000; land improvements, $12,000; and land, $24,000, what cost is assigned to the building? *Answer:*

(1) $84,000 + $12,000 + $24,000 = $120,000 (total appraisal)

(2) $84,000/$120,000 = 70% (building's percent of total)

(3) 70% × $90,000 = $63,000 (building's apportioned cost)

Lump-Sum Purchase

Plant assets sometimes are purchased as a group in a single transaction for a lump-sum price. This transaction is called a *lump-sum purchase,* or *group, bulk,* or *basket purchase.* When this occurs, we allocate the cost of the purchase among the different types of assets acquired based on their *relative market values,* which can be estimated by appraisal or by using the tax-assessed valuations of the assets. To illustrate, assume **CarMax** paid $90,000 cash to acquire a group of items consisting of a building appraised at $60,000, land improvements appraised at $10,000, and land appraised at $30,000. The $90,000 cost is allocated on the basis of these appraised values as shown in Exhibit 8.4.

EXHIBIT 8.4

Computing Costs in a Lump-Sum Purchase

	Appraised Value	Percent of Total	Apportioned Cost
Building	$ 60,000	60% ($60,000/$100,000)	**$54,000** ($90,000 × 60%)
Land improvements	10,000	10 ($10,000/$100,000)	**9,000** ($90,000 × 10%)
Land	30,000	30 ($30,000/$100,000)	**27,000** ($90,000 × 30%)
Totals	$100,000	100%	$90,000

 NEED-TO-KNOW   **8-1**

Cost Determination

C1

Do More: QS 8-1, QS 8-2, E 8-1, E 8-2, E 8-3

Compute the amount recorded as the cost of a new machine given the following payments related to its purchase: gross purchase price, $700,000; sales tax, $49,000; purchase discount taken, $21,000; freight cost—terms FOB shipping point, $3,500; normal assembly costs, $3,000; cost of necessary machine platform, $2,500; cost of parts used in maintaining machine, $4,200.

Solution

$737,000 = $700,000 + $49,000 − $21,000 + $3,500 + $3,000 + $2,500

DEPRECIATION

Depreciation is the process of allocating the cost of a plant asset to expense in the accounting periods benefiting from its use. Depreciation does not measure the decline in the asset's market value each period, nor does it measure the asset's physical deterioration. Since depreciation reflects the cost of using a plant asset, depreciation charges are only recorded when the asset is actually in service. This section describes the factors we must consider in computing

Point: Depreciation is cost allocation, not asset valuation.

depreciation, the depreciation methods used, revisions in depreciation, and depreciation for partial periods.

Factors in Computing Depreciation

Factors that determine depreciation are (1) cost, (2) salvage value, and (3) useful life.

Cost   The cost of a plant asset consists of all necessary and reasonable expenditures to acquire it and to prepare it for its intended use.

Salvage Value   The total amount of depreciation to be charged off over an asset's benefit period equals the asset's cost minus its salvage value. **Salvage value,** also called *residual value* or *scrap value,* is an estimate of the asset's value at the end of its benefit period. This is the amount the owner expects to receive from disposing of the asset at the end of its benefit period. If the asset is expected to be traded in on a new asset, its salvage value is the expected trade-in value.

Useful Life   The **useful life** of a plant asset is the length of time it is productively used in a company's operations. Useful life, also called *service life,* might not be as long as the asset's total productive life. For example, the productive life of a computer can be eight years or more. Some companies, however, trade in old computers for new ones every two years. In this case, these computers have a two-year useful life, meaning the cost of these computers (less their expected trade-in values) is charged to depreciation expense over a two-year period.

Several variables often make the useful life of a plant asset difficult to predict. A major variable is the wear and tear from use in operations. Two other variables, inadequacy and obsolescence, also require consideration. **Inadequacy** refers to the insufficient capacity of a company's plant assets to meet its growing production demands. **Obsolescence** refers to the condition of a plant asset that is no longer useful in producing goods or services with a competitive advantage because of new inventions and improvements. Both inadequacy and obsolescence are difficult to predict because of demand changes, new inventions, and improvements. A company usually disposes of an inadequate or obsolete asset before it wears out.

A company is often able to better predict a new asset's useful life when it has past experience with a similar asset. When it has no such experience, a company relies on the experience of others or on engineering studies and judgment. In note 1 of its annual report, **Tootsie Roll**, a snack food manufacturer, reports the following useful lives:

Buildings	20–35 years
Machinery and Equipment	5–20 years

🟨 Decision **Insight** ♟

Good Life   Life expectancy of plant assets is often in the eye of the beholder. For instance, **Hershey Foods** and **Tootsie Roll** are competitors and apply similar manufacturing processes, yet their equipment's life expectancies are different. Hershey depreciates equipment over 3 to 15 years, but Tootsie Roll depreciates them over 5 to 20 years. Such differences markedly impact financial statements. ◼

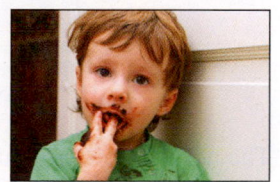

Sergey Lavrentev/iStock/360/
Getty Images

Depreciation Methods

Depreciation methods are used to allocate a plant asset's cost over the accounting periods in its useful life. The most frequently used method of depreciation is the straight-line method. Another common depreciation method is the units-of-production method. We explain both of these methods in this section. This section also describes accelerated depreciation methods, with a focus on the declining-balance method.

The computations in this section use information about a machine that inspects athletic shoes before packaging. Manufacturers such as **Converse**, **Reebok**, **Adidas**, and **Fila** use this machine. Data for this machine are in Exhibit 8.5.

EXHIBIT 8.5

Data for Athletic Shoe–
Inspecting Machine

Cost	$10,000	Useful life:	
Salvage value	1,000	Accounting periods	5 years
Depreciable cost	$ 9,000	Units inspected	36,000 shoes

Straight-Line Method **Straight-line depreciation** charges the same amount of expense to each period of the asset's useful life. A two-step process is used. We first compute the *depreciable cost* of the asset, also called the *cost to be depreciated*. It is computed by subtracting the asset's salvage value from its total cost. Second, depreciable cost is divided by the number of accounting periods in the asset's useful life. The formula for straight-line depreciation, along with its computation for the inspection machine just described, is shown in Exhibit 8.6.

EXHIBIT 8.6

Straight-Line Depreciation
Formula and Example

$$\frac{\text{Cost} - \text{Salvage value}}{\text{Useful life in periods}} = \frac{\$10,000 - \$1,000}{5 \text{ years}} = \$1,800 \text{ per year}$$

If this machine is purchased on December 31, 2015, and used throughout its predicted useful life of five years, the straight-line method allocates an equal amount of depreciation to each of the years 2016 through 2020. We make the following adjusting entry at the end of each of the five years to record straight-line depreciation of this machine.

Assets = Liabilities + Equity
−1,800   −1,800

Dec. 31	Depreciation Expense	1,800	
	Accumulated Depreciation—Machinery		1,800
	Record annual depreciation.		

The $1,800 Depreciation Expense is reported on the income statement among operating expenses. The $1,800 Accumulated Depreciation is a contra asset account to the Machinery account in the balance sheet. The graph on the left in Exhibit 8.7 shows the $1,800 per year expenses reported in each of the five years. The graph on the right shows the amounts reported on each of the six December 31 balance sheets.

EXHIBIT 8.7

Financial Statement
Effects of Straight-Line
Depreciation

Book value = Cost − Accumulated
depreciation

The net balance sheet amount is the **asset book value,** or simply *book value,* and is computed as the asset's total cost less its accumulated depreciation. For example, at the end of year 2 (December 31, 2017), its book value is $6,400, which is $10,000 less $3,600 (2 years × $1,800), and is reported in the balance sheet as follows:

| Machinery .... | $10,000 | |
| Less accumulated depreciation .... | 3,600 | $6,400 ◄── Book value |

The book value of this machine declines by $1,800 each year due to depreciation. The left-side graphic in Exhibit 8.7 reveals why this method is called straight-line.

We also can compute the *straight-line depreciation rate,* defined as 100% divided by the number of periods in the asset's useful life. For the inspection machine, this rate is 20%

Point: Once an asset's book value equals its salvage value, depreciation stops.

(100% ÷ 5 years, or 1/5 per period). We use this rate, along with other information, to compute the machine's *straight-line depreciation schedule* shown in Exhibit 8.8. Note three points in this exhibit. First, depreciation expense is the same each period. Second, accumulated depreciation is the sum of current and prior periods' depreciation expense. Third, book value declines each period until it equals salvage value at the end of the machine's useful life.

Example: If salvage value of the machine is $2,500, what is the annual depreciation? *Answer:* ($10,000 − $2,500)/ 5 years = $1,500

Annual Period	Depreciation for the Period			End of Period	
	Depreciable Cost*	Depreciation Rate	Depreciation Expense	Accumulated Depreciation	Book Value†
2015	—	—	—	—	$10,000
2016	$9,000	20%	**$1,800**	$1,800	8,200
2017	9,000	20	**1,800**	3,600	6,400
2018	9,000	20	**1,800**	5,400	4,600
2019	9,000	20	**1,800**	7,200	2,800
2020	9,000	20	**1,800**	9,000	**1,000** ◄
			$9,000 ◄		

Salvage value is not depreciated

($10,000 cost − $1,000 salvage)

* $10,000 − $1,000.   † Book value is total cost minus accumulated depreciation.

EXHIBIT 8.8

Straight-Line Depreciation Schedule

Units-of-Production Method   The straight-line method charges an equal share of an asset's cost to each period. If plant assets are used up in about equal amounts each accounting period, this method produces a reasonable matching of expenses with revenues. However, the use of some plant assets varies greatly from one period to the next. A builder, for instance, might use a piece of construction equipment for a month and then not use it again for several months. When equipment use varies from period to period, the units-of-production depreciation method can better match expenses with revenues. **Units-of-production depreciation** charges a varying amount to expense for each period of an asset's useful life depending on its *usage*.

A two-step process is used to compute units-of-production depreciation. We first compute *depreciation per unit* by subtracting the asset's salvage value from its total cost and then dividing by the total number of units expected to be produced during its useful life. Units of production can be expressed in product or other units such as hours used or miles driven. The second step is to compute depreciation expense for the period by multiplying the units produced in the period by the depreciation per unit. The formula for units-of-production depreciation, along with its computation for the machine described in Exhibit 8.5, is shown in Exhibit 8.9. (*Note:* 7,000 shoes are inspected and sold in its first year.)

Step 1

$$\text{Depreciation per unit} = \frac{\text{Cost} - \text{Salvage value}}{\text{Total units of production}} = \frac{\$10,000 - \$1,000}{36,000 \text{ shoes}} = \$0.25 \text{ per shoe}$$

Step 2

$$\text{Depreciation expense} = \text{Depreciation per unit} \times \text{Units produced in period}$$
$$\$0.25 \text{ per shoe} \times 7,000 \text{ shoes} = \$1,750$$

EXHIBIT 8.9

Units-of-Production Depreciation Formula and Example

Using data on the number of shoes inspected by the machine, we can compute the *units-of-production depreciation schedule* shown in Exhibit 8.10. For example, depreciation for the first year is $1,750 (7,000 shoes at $0.25 per shoe). Depreciation for the second year is $2,000 (8,000 shoes at $0.25 per shoe). Other years are similarly computed. Exhibit 8.10 shows that (1) depreciation expense depends on unit output, (2) accumulated depreciation is the sum of current and prior periods' depreciation expense, and (3) book value declines each period until it

Example: Refer to Exhibit 8.10. If the number of shoes inspected in 2020 is 5,500, what is depreciation for 2020? *Answer:* $1,250 (never depreciate below salvage value)

EXHIBIT 8.10

Units-of-Production Depreciation Schedule

equals salvage value at the end of the asset's useful life. **Deltic Timber** is one of many companies using the units-of-production depreciation method. It reports that depreciation "is calculated over the estimated useful lives of the assets by using the units of production method for machinery and equipment."

| Annual Period | Depreciation for the Period | | | End of Period | |
	Number of Units	Depreciation per Unit	Depreciation Expense	Accumulated Depreciation	Book Value
2015	—	—	—	—	$10,000
2016	7,000	$0.25	**$1,750**	$1,750	8,250
2017	8,000	0.25	**2,000**	3,750	6,250
2018	9,000	0.25	**2,250**	6,000	4,000
2019	7,000	0.25	**1,750**	7,750	2,250
2020	5,000	0.25	**1,250**	9,000	**1,000**
	36,000 units		**$9,000**		

($10,000 cost − $1,000 salvage)

Salvage value is not depreciated

Declining-Balance Method   An **accelerated depreciation method** yields larger depreciation expenses in the early years of an asset's life and less depreciation in later years. The most common accelerated method is the **declining-balance method** of depreciation, which uses a depreciation rate that is a multiple of the straight-line rate and applies it to the asset's beginning-of-period book value. The amount of depreciation declines each period because book value declines each period.

A common depreciation rate for the declining-balance method is double the straight-line rate. This is called the *double-declining-balance (DDB)* method. This method is applied in three steps: (1) Compute the asset's straight-line depreciation rate, (2) double the straight-line rate, and (3) compute depreciation expense by multiplying this rate by the asset's beginning-of-period book value. To illustrate, let's return to the machine in Exhibit 8.5 and apply the double-declining-balance method to compute depreciation expense. Exhibit 8.11 shows the first-year depreciation computation for the machine. The three-step process is to (1) divide 100% by five years to determine the straight-line rate of 20%, or 1/5, per year; (2) double this 20% rate to get the declining-balance rate of 40%, or 2/5, per year; and (3) compute depreciation expense as 40%, or 2/5, multiplied by the beginning-of-period book value.

Point: In the DDB method, *double* refers to the rate and *declining balance* refers to book value. The rate is applied to beginning book value each period.

EXHIBIT 8.11

Double-Declining-Balance Depreciation Formula*

$$\text{SL rate} = \frac{100\%}{\text{Useful life}}$$

$$\text{DDB rate} = \frac{200\%}{\text{Useful life}}$$

Step 1
Straight-line rate = 100% ÷ Useful life = 100% ÷ 5 years = 20%

Step 2
Double-declining-balance rate = 2 × Straight-line rate = 2 × 20% = 40%

Step 3
Depreciation expense = Double-declining-balance rate × Beginning-period book value
40% × $10,000 = $4,000 (for 2016)

* In simple form: DDB depreciation = (2 × Beginning-period book value)/Useful life.

Example: What is the DDB depreciation in year 2019 if salvage value is $2,000? *Answer:* $2,160 − $2,000 = $160

The *double-declining-balance depreciation schedule* is shown in Exhibit 8.12. The schedule follows the formula except for year 2020, when depreciation expense is $296. This $296 is not equal to 40% × $1,296, or $518.40. If we had used the $518.40 for depreciation expense in 2020, the ending book value would equal $777.60, which is less than the $1,000 salvage value. Instead, the $296 is computed by subtracting the $1,000 salvage value from the $1,296 book value at the beginning of the fifth year (the year when DDB depreciation cuts into salvage value).

EXHIBIT 8.12

Double-Declining-Balance
Depreciation Schedule

Annual Period	Depreciation for the Period			End of Period	
	Beginning of Period Book Value	Depreciation Rate	Depreciation Expense	Accumulated Depreciation	Book Value
2015	—	—	—	—	$10,000
2016	$10,000	40%	**$4,000**	$4,000	6,000
2017	6,000	40	**2,400**	6,400	3,600
2018	3,600	40	**1,440**	7,840	2,160
2019	2,160	40	**864**	8,704	1,296
2020	1,296	40	**296***	9,000	**1,000** ← Salvage value is not depreciated
			$9,000 ← ($10,000 cost − $1,000 salvage)		

* Year 2019 depreciation is $1,296 − $1,000 = $296 (never depreciate book value below salvage value).

Comparing Depreciation Methods

Comparing Depreciation Methods   Exhibit 8.13 shows depreciation expense for each year of the machine's useful life under each of the three depreciation methods. While depreciation expense per period differs for different methods, total depreciation expense of $9,000 is the same over the machine's useful life.

EXHIBIT 8.13

Depreciation Expense for
the Different Methods

	A	B	C	D
1	**Period**	**Straight-Line**	**Units-of-Production**	**Double-Declining-Balance**
2	2016	$1,800	$1,750	$4,000
3	2017	1,800	2,000	2,400
4	2018	1,800	2,250	1,440
5	2019	1,800	1,750	864
6	2020	1,800	1,250	296
7	Totals	**$9,000**	**$9,000**	**$9,000**
8				

Each method starts with a total cost of $10,000 and ends with a salvage value of $1,000. The difference is the pattern in depreciation expense over the useful life. The book value of the asset when using straight-line is always greater than the book value from using double-declining-balance, except at the beginning and end of the asset's useful life, when it is the same. Also, the straight-line method yields a steady pattern of depreciation expense while the units-of-production depreciation depends on the number of units produced. Each of these methods is acceptable because it allocates cost in a systematic and rational manner.

Decision Insight

Survey Says   About 85% of companies use straight-line depreciation for plant assets, 5% use units-of-production, and 4% use declining-balance. Another 6% use an unspecified accelerated method—most likely declining-balance. ■

Depreciation for Tax Reporting

Depreciation for Tax Reporting   The records a company keeps for financial accounting purposes are usually separate from the records it keeps for tax accounting purposes. This is so because financial accounting aims to report useful information on financial performance and position, whereas tax accounting reflects government objectives in raising revenues. Differences between these two accounting systems are normal and expected. Depreciation is a common example of how the records differ. For example, many companies use accelerated depreciation in computing taxable income. Reporting higher depreciation expense in the early years of an asset's life reduces the company's taxable income in those years and increases it in later years, when the depreciation expense is lower. The company's goal here is to *postpone* its tax payments.

The U.S. federal income tax law has rules for depreciating assets. These rules include the **Modified Accelerated Cost Recovery System (MACRS),** which allows straight-line depreciation for some assets but requires accelerated depreciation for most kinds of assets. MACRS separates depreciable assets into different classes and defines the depreciable life and rate for each class. MACRS is *not* acceptable for financial reporting because it often allocates costs over an arbitrary period that is less than the asset's useful life and it fails to estimate salvage value. Details of MACRS are covered in tax accounting courses.

Partial-Year Depreciation

C2
_____

Explain depreciation for partial years and changes in estimates.

Plant assets are purchased and disposed of at various times. When an asset is purchased (or disposed of) at a time other than the beginning or end of an accounting period, depreciation is recorded for part of a year. This is done so that the year of purchase or the year of disposal is charged with its share of the asset's depreciation.

To illustrate, assume that the machine in Exhibit 8.5 is purchased and placed in service on October 8, 2015, and the annual accounting period ends on December 31. Since this machine is purchased and used for nearly three months in 2015, the calendar-year income statement should report depreciation expense on the machine for that part of the year. Normally, depreciation assumes that the asset is purchased on the first day of the month nearest the actual date of purchase. In this case, since the purchase occurred on October 8, we assume an October 1 purchase date. This means that three months' depreciation is recorded in 2015. Using straight-line depreciation, we compute three months' depreciation of $450 as follows.

Point: Assets purchased on days 1 through 15 of a month are usually recorded as purchased on the 1st of that month. Assets purchased on days 16 to the month-end are recorded as if purchased on the 1st of the next month.

Point: Many firms use a "half-year convention," which records 6 months' depreciation in the year of purchase, regardless of the purchase date.

$$\frac{\$10,000 - \$1,000}{5 \text{ years}} \times \frac{3}{12} = \$450$$

A similar computation is necessary when an asset disposal occurs during a period. To illustrate, assume that the machine is sold on June 24, 2020. Depreciation is recorded for the period January 1 through June 24 when it is disposed of. This partial year's depreciation, computed to the nearest whole month, is

Example: If the machine's salvage value is zero and purchase occurs on Oct. 8, 2015, how much depreciation is recorded at Dec. 31, 2015? *Answer:* $10,000/5 × 3/12 = $500

$$\frac{\$10,000 - \$1,000}{5 \text{ years}} \times \frac{6}{12} = \$900$$

Change in Estimates for Depreciation

Depreciation is based on estimates of salvage value and useful life. During the useful life of an asset, new information may indicate that these estimates are inaccurate. If our estimate of an asset's useful life and/or salvage value changes, what should we do? The answer is to use the new estimate to compute depreciation for current and future periods. This means that we revise the depreciation expense computation by spreading the cost yet to be depreciated over the remaining useful life. This approach is used for all depreciation methods.

Point: Remaining depreciable cost equals book value less revised salvage value at the point of revision.

Let's return to the machine described in Exhibit 8.8 using straight-line depreciation. At the beginning of this asset's third year, its book value is $6,400, computed as $10,000 minus $3,600. Assume that at the beginning of its third year, the estimated number of years remaining in its useful life changes from three to four years *and* its estimate of salvage value changes from $1,000 to $400. Straight-line depreciation for each of the four remaining years is computed as shown in Exhibit 8.14.

EXHIBIT 8.14

Computing Revised Straight-Line Depreciation

$$\frac{\text{Book value} - \text{Revised salvage value}}{\text{Revised remaining useful life}} = \frac{\$6,400 - \$400}{4 \text{ years}} = \$1,500 \text{ per year}$$

Example: If at the start of its second year the machine's remaining useful life changes from 4 to 3 years and salvage value from $1,000 to $400, how much straight-line depreciation is recorded in remaining years? *Answer:* Revised depreciation = ($8,200 − $400)/3 = $2,600

Thus, $1,500 of depreciation expense is recorded for the machine at the end of the third through sixth years—each year of its remaining useful life. Since this asset was depreciated at $1,800 per year for the first two years, it is tempting to conclude that depreciation expense was overstated in the first two years. However, these expenses reflected the best information available at that time. We do not go back and restate prior years' financial statements for this type of new information. Instead, we adjust the current and future periods' statements to reflect this new information. Revising an estimate of the useful life or salvage value of a plant asset is referred to as a **change in an accounting estimate** and is reflected in current and future financial statements, not in prior statements.

Reporting Depreciation

Both the cost and accumulated depreciation of plant assets are reported on the balance sheet or in its notes. **Dale Jarrett Racing Adventure**, for instance, reports the following.

Race vehicles and other	$ 778,704
Furniture, software, DJ Graphics, and equipment	105,032
Shop and track equipment	173,739
Property and equipment, gross	1,057,475
Less accumulated depreciation	884,772
Property and equipment, net	$ 172,703

Chris Trotman/NASCAR/Getty Images

Many companies also show plant assets on one line with the net amount of cost less accumulated depreciation. When this is done, the amount of accumulated depreciation is disclosed in a note. **Apple** reports only the net amount of its property, plant, and equipment in its balance sheet. To satisfy the full-disclosure principle, Apple describes its depreciation methods in its Note 1 and the amounts comprising plant assets in its Note 3—see its 10-K at **www.SEC.gov**.

Reporting both the cost and accumulated depreciation of plant assets helps users compare the assets of different companies. For example, a company holding assets costing $50,000 and accumulated depreciation of $40,000 is likely in a situation different from a company with new assets costing $10,000. While the net undepreciated cost of $10,000 is the same in both cases, the first company may have more productive capacity available but likely is facing the need to replace older assets. These insights are not provided if the two balance sheets report only the $10,000 book values.

Users must remember that plant assets are reported on a balance sheet at their undepreciated costs (book value), not at fair (market) values. This emphasis on costs rather than fair values is based on the *going-concern assumption* described in Chapter 1. This assumption states that, unless there is evidence to the contrary, we assume that a company continues in business. This implies that plant assets are held and used long enough to recover their cost through the sale of products and services. Because plant assets are not for sale, their fair values are not reported. An exception is when there is a *permanent decline* in the fair value of an asset relative to its book value, called an asset **impairment.** In this case the company writes the asset down to this fair value (details for the two-step process for assessing and computing the impairment loss are in advanced courses).

Accumulated Depreciation is a contra asset account with a normal credit balance. It does *not* reflect funds accumulated to buy new assets when the assets currently owned are replaced. If a company has funds available to buy assets, the funds are shown on the balance sheet among liquid assets such as cash or investments.

Point: A company usually keeps records for each asset showing its cost and depreciation to date. The combined records for individual assets are a type of *plant asset subsidiary ledger.*

Example: Assume equipment carries a book value of $800 ($900 cost less $100 accumulated depreciation) and a fair (market) value of $750, *and* this $50 decline in value meets the two-step impairment test. The entry to record this impairment is:
Impairment Loss $50
  Accum Depr.–Equip. $50

 ### ■ Decision **Ethics**

Controller You are the controller for a struggling company. Its operations require regular investments in equipment, and depreciation is its largest expense. Its competitors frequently replace equipment—often depreciated over three years. The company president instructs you to revise useful lives of equipment from three to six years and to use a six-year life on all new equipment. What actions do you take? ■ [Answers follow the chapter's Summary.]

Part 1. A machine costing $22,000 with a five-year life and an estimated $2,000 salvage value is installed on January 1. The manager estimates the machine will produce 1,000 units of product during its life. It actually produces the following units: 200 in 1st year, 400 in 2nd year, 300 in 3rd year, 80 in 4th year, 30 in 5th year. The total units produced by the end of year 5 exceed the original estimate—this difference was not predicted. (The machine must not be depreciated below its estimated salvage value.) Prepare a table with the following column headings—Year, Straight-Line, Units-of-Production, Double-Declining-Balance—and then compute depreciation expense for each year (and total depreciation for all years combined) under each method.

Part 2. In early January 2014, a company acquires equipment for $3,800. The company estimates this equipment to have a useful life of three years and a salvage value of $200. Early in 2016, the company

NEED-TO-KNOW **8-2**

Depreciation Computations

P1 C2

changes its estimates to a total four-year useful life and zero salvage value. Using the straight-line method, what is depreciation expense for the year ended 2016?

Solution—Part 1

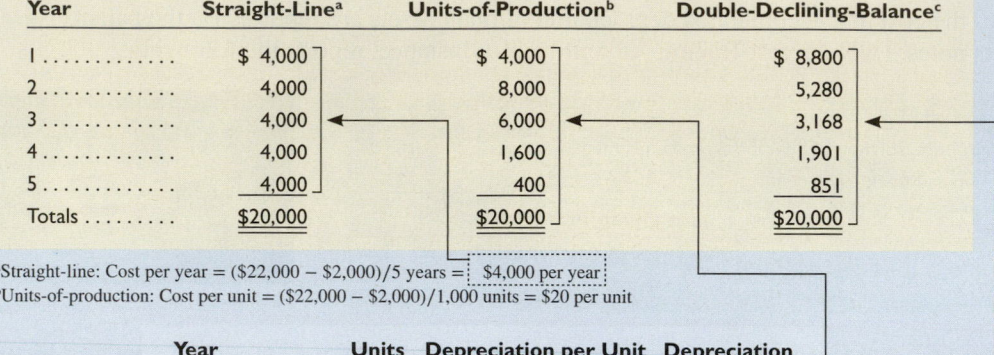

Year	Straight-Line[a]	Units-of-Production[b]	Double-Declining-Balance[c]
1	$ 4,000	$ 4,000	$ 8,800
2	4,000	8,000	5,280
3	4,000	6,000	3,168
4	4,000	1,600	1,901
5	4,000	400	851
Totals	$20,000	$20,000	$20,000

[a]Straight-line: Cost per year = ($22,000 − $2,000)/5 years = $4,000 per year
[b]Units-of-production: Cost per unit = ($22,000 − $2,000)/1,000 units = $20 per unit

Year	Units	Depreciation per Unit	Depreciation
1	200	$20	$ 4,000
2	400	20	8,000
3	300	20	6,000
4	80	20	1,600
5	30	20	400*
Total			$20,000

* Set depreciation in year 5 to reduce book value to the $20,000 salvage value; namely, instead of $600 (30 × $20), we use the maximum of $400 ($20,000 − $19,600 accum depr).

[c]Double-declining-balance: (100%/5) × 2 = 40% depreciation rate

Year	Beginning Book Value	Annual Depreciation (40% of Book Value)	Accumulated Depreciation at the End of the Year	Ending Book Value ($22,000 Cost Less Accumulated Depreciation)
1	$22,000	$ 8,800	$ 8,800	$13,200
2	13,200	5,280	14,080	7,920
3	7,920	3,168	17,248	4,752
4	4,752	1,901*	19,149	2,851
5	2,851	851**	20,000	2,000
Total		$20,000		

* Rounded to the nearest dollar.
** Set depreciation in year 5 to reduce book value to the $20,000 salvage value; namely, instead of $1,140 ($2,851 × 40%), we use the maximum of $851 ($2,851 − $2,000).

Solution—Part 2

($3,800 − $200)/3 years = $1,200 (original depreciation per year)

$1,200 × 2 years = $2,400 (accumulated depreciation at date of change in estimate)

($3,800 − $2,400)/2 years = **$700** (revised depreciation)

 Do More: QS 8-3 through QS 8-7, E 8-4 through E 8-13

ADDITIONAL EXPENDITURES

C3

Distinguish between revenue and capital expenditures, and account for them.

After a company acquires a plant asset and puts it into service, it often makes additional expenditures for that asset's operation, maintenance, repair, and improvement. In recording these expenditures, it must decide whether to capitalize or expense them (to capitalize an expenditure is to debit the asset account). The issue is whether these expenditures are reported as current-period expenses or added to the plant asset's cost and depreciated over its remaining useful life.

Revenue expenditures, also called *income statement expenditures,* are additional costs of plant assets that do not materially increase the asset's life or productive capabilities. They are recorded as expenses and deducted from revenues in the current period's income statement. Examples of revenue expenditures are cleaning, repainting, adjustments, and lubricants. **Capital expenditures,** also called *balance sheet expenditures,* are additional costs of plant assets that provide benefits extending beyond the current period. They are debited to asset accounts and reported on the balance sheet. Capital expenditures increase or improve the type or amount of service an asset provides. Examples are roofing replacement, plant expansion, and major overhauls of machinery and equipment.

Financial Statement Effect		
	Accounting	Expense Timing
Revenue expenditure	Income stmt. account debited	Expensed currently
Capital expenditure	Balance sheet account debited	Expensed in future

Financial statements are affected for several years by the accounting choice of recording costs as either revenue expenditures or capital expenditures. This decision is based on whether the expenditures are identified as ordinary repairs or as betterments and extraordinary repairs.

■ Decision Maker

Entrepreneur   Your start-up Internet services company needs cash, and you are preparing financial statements to apply for a short-term loan. A friend suggests that you treat as many expenses as possible as capital expenditures. What are the impacts on financial statements of this suggestion? What do you think is the aim of this suggestion? ■   [Answers follow the chapter's Summary.]

Ordinary Repairs

Ordinary repairs are expenditures to keep an asset in normal, good operating condition. They are necessary if an asset is to perform to expectations over its useful life. Ordinary repairs do not extend an asset's useful life beyond its original estimate or increase its productivity beyond original expectations. Examples are normal costs of cleaning, lubricating, adjusting, oil changing, and replacing small parts of a machine. Ordinary repairs are treated as *revenue expenditures.* This means their costs are reported as expenses on the current-period income statement. Following this rule, **Brunswick** reports that "maintenance and repair costs are expensed as incurred." If Brunswick's current-year repair costs are $9,500, it makes the following entry.

Point: Many companies apply the *materiality constraint* to treat *low-cost plant assets* (say, less than $500) as revenue expenditures. This practice is referred to as a "capitalization policy."

Dec. 31	Repairs Expense	9,500	
	Cash		9,500
	Record ordinary repairs of equipment.		

Assets = Liabilities + Equity
−9,500   −9,500

Betterments and Extraordinary Repairs

Accounting for betterments and extraordinary repairs is similar—both are treated as *capital expenditures.*

Betterments (Improvements)   **Betterments,** also called *improvements,* are expenditures that make a plant asset more efficient or productive. A betterment often involves adding a component to an asset or replacing one of its old components with a better one and does not always increase an asset's useful life. An example is replacing manual controls on a machine with automatic controls. One special type of betterment is an *addition,* such as adding a new wing or dock to a warehouse. Since a betterment benefits future periods, it is debited to the asset account as a capital expenditure. The new book value (less salvage value) is then depreciated over the asset's remaining useful life. To illustrate, suppose a company pays $8,000 for a machine with an eight-year useful life and no salvage value. After three years and $3,000 of depreciation, it adds an automated control system to the machine at a cost of $1,800. This results in reduced labor costs in future periods. The cost of the betterment is added to the Machinery account with this entry.

Example: Assume a firm owns a web server. Identify each cost as a revenue or capital expenditure: (1) purchase price, (2) necessary wiring, (3) platform for operation, (4) circuits to increase capacity, (5) cleaning after each month of use, (6) repair of a faulty switch, and (7) replacement of a worn fan. *Answer:* Capital expenditures: 1, 2, 3, 4; revenue expenditures: 5, 6, 7.

Jan. 2	Machinery	1,800	
	Cash		1,800
	Record installation of automated system.		

Assets = Liabilities + Equity
+1,800
−1,800

After the betterment is recorded, the remaining cost to be depreciated is $6,800, computed as $8,000 − $3,000 + $1,800. Depreciation expense for the remaining five years is $1,360 per year, computed as $6,800/5 years.

Extraordinary Repairs (Replacements) **Extraordinary repairs** are expenditures extending the asset's useful life beyond its original estimate. Extraordinary repairs are *capital expenditures* because they benefit future periods. Their costs are debited to the asset account (or to accumulated depreciation). For example, **Delta Air Lines** reports, "modifications that . . . extend the useful lives of airframes or engines are capitalized and amortized [depreciated] over the remaining estimated useful life of the asset."

Decision Insight

Far Out If we owned a 20-year-old truck and planned to use it in our work for another 40 years, we would expect some extraordinary repairs in future years. A similar situation confronts Whiteman Air Force Base, home to the B-2 stealth bomber, which rolled out of a **Northrop Grumman** hangar in the 1980s. The plan is to keep those bat-winged bombers flying until 2058. The Pentagon is moving forward with a $2 billion, 10-year effort to modernize the bombers' defensive capabilities. ■

Purestock/Superstock

DISPOSALS OF PLANT ASSETS

P2

Account for asset disposal through discarding or selling an asset.

Plant assets are disposed of for several reasons. Some are discarded because they wear out or become obsolete. Others are sold because of changing business plans. Regardless of the reason, disposal of plant assets occurs in one of three basic ways: discarding, sale, or exchange. The general steps in accounting for a disposal of plant assets are described in Exhibit 8.15.

EXHIBIT 8.15

Accounting for Disposals of Plant Assets

> 1. Record depreciation up to the date of disposal—this also updates Accumulated Depreciation.
> 2. Record the removal of the disposed asset's account balances—including its Accumulated Depreciation.
> 3. Record any cash (and/or other assets) received or paid in the disposal.
> 4. Record any gain or loss—computed by comparing the disposed asset's book value with the market value of any assets received.*

* An exception to step 4 is the case of an exchange that *lacks commercial substance*—see Appendix 8A.

Discarding Plant Assets

A plant asset is *discarded* when it is no longer useful to the company and it has no market value. To illustrate, assume that a machine costing $9,000 with accumulated depreciation of $9,000 is discarded. When accumulated depreciation equals the asset's cost, it is said to be *fully depreciated* (zero book value). The entry to record the discarding of this asset is

Assets = Liabilities + Equity
+9,000
−9,000

June 5	Accumulated Depreciation—Machinery	9,000	
	Machinery		9,000
	Discarding of fully depreciated machinery.		

This entry reflects all four steps of Exhibit 8.15. Step 1 is unnecessary since the machine is fully depreciated. Step 2 is reflected in the debit to Accumulated Depreciation and credit to Machinery. Since no other asset is involved, step 3 is irrelevant. Finally, since book value is zero and no other asset is involved, no gain or loss is recorded in step 4.

How do we account for discarding an asset that is not fully depreciated or one whose depreciation is not up-to-date? To answer this, consider equipment costing $8,000 with accumulated depreciation of $6,000 on December 31 of the prior fiscal year-end. This equipment is being depreciated using the straight-line method over eight years with zero salvage. On July 1 of the current year it is discarded. Step 1 is to bring depreciation up-to-date.

Assets = Liabilities + Equity
−500   −500

July 1	Depreciation Expense	500	
	Accumulated Depreciation—Equipment.		500
	Record 6 months' depreciation ($1,000 × 6/12).		

Point: Both extraordinary repairs and betterments require revising future depreciation.

Point: Recording depreciation expense up-to-date gives an up-to-date book value for determining gain or loss.

Steps 2 through 4 of Exhibit 8.15 are reflected in the second (and final) entry.

July 1	Accumulated Depreciation—Equipment	6,500	
	Loss on Disposal of Equipment	1,500	
	Equipment		8,000
	Discarding equipment with a $1,500 book value.		

Assets = Liabilities + Equity
+6,500   −1,500
−8,000

This loss is computed by comparing the equipment's $1,500 book value ($8,000 − $6,000 − $500) with the zero net cash proceeds. The loss is reported in the Other Expenses and Losses section of the income statement. Discarding an asset can sometimes require a cash payment that would increase the loss.

Point: Gain or loss is determined by comparing "value given" (book value) to "value received."

Selling Plant Assets

Companies often sell plant assets when they restructure or downsize operations. To illustrate the accounting for selling plant assets, we consider BTO's March 31 sale of equipment that cost $16,000 and has accumulated depreciation of $12,000 at December 31 of the prior calendar year-end. Annual depreciation on this equipment is $4,000 computed using straight-line depreciation. Step 1 of this sale is to record depreciation expense and update accumulated depreciation to March 31 of the current year.

March 31	Depreciation Expense	1,000	
	Accumulated Depreciation—Equipment		1,000
	Record 3 months' depreciation ($4,000 × 3/12).		

Assets = Liabilities + Equity
−1,000   −1,000

Steps 2 through 4 of Exhibit 8.15 can be reflected in one final entry that depends on the amount received from the asset's sale. We consider three different possibilities.

Sale at Book Value   If BTO receives $3,000 cash, an amount equal to the equipment's book value as of March 31 (book value = $16,000 − $12,000 − $1,000), no gain or loss occurs on disposal. The entry is

Sale price = Book value → No gain or loss

March 31	Cash	3,000	
	Accumulated Depreciation—Equipment	13,000	
	Equipment		16,000
	Record sale of equipment for no gain or loss.		

Assets   = Liabilities + Equity
+3,000
+13,000
−16,000

Sale above Book Value   If BTO receives $7,000, an amount that is $4,000 above the equipment's $3,000 book value as of March 31, a gain on disposal occurs. The entry is

Sale price > Book value → Gain

March 31	Cash	7,000	
	Accumulated Depreciation—Equipment	13,000	
	Gain on Disposal of Equipment		4,000
	Equipment		16,000
	Record sale of equipment for a $4,000 gain.		

Assets   = Liabilities + Equity
+7,000   +4,000
+13,000
−16,000

Sale below Book Value   If BTO receives $2,500, an amount that is $500 below the equipment's $3,000 book value as of March 31, a loss on disposal occurs. The entry is

Sale price < Book value → Loss

March 31	Cash	2,500	
	Loss on Disposal of Equipment	500	
	Accumulated Depreciation—Equipment.............	13,000	
	Equipment		16,000
	Record sale of equipment for a $500 loss.		

Assets   = Liabilities + Equity
+2,500   −500
+13,000
−16,000

 IFRS _____

Life Changing   Unlike U.S. GAAP, IFRS requires an annual review of useful life and salvage value estimates. IFRS also permits revaluation of plant assets to market if market value is reliably determined. ■

8-3

Additional Expenditures and Asset Disposals

C3   P2

Part 1. A company pays $1,000 for equipment expected to last four years and have a $200 salvage value. Prepare journal entries to record the following costs related to the equipment.

a. During the second year of the equipment's life, $400 cash is paid for a new component expected to increase the equipment's productivity by 20% a year.

b. During the third year, $250 cash is paid for normal repairs necessary to keep the equipment in good working order.

c. During the fourth year, $500 is paid for repairs expected to increase the useful life of the equipment from four to five years.

Part 2. A company owns a machine that cost $500 and has accumulated depreciation of $400. Prepare the entry to record the disposal of the machine on January 2 under each of the following independent situations.

a. The machine needed extensive repairs, and it was not worth repairing. The company disposed of the machine, receiving nothing in return.

b. The company sold the machine for $80 cash.

c. The company sold the machine for $100 cash.

d. The company sold the machine for $110 cash.

Solutions—Part 1

a.

Year 2	Equipment...............................	400	
	Cash...................................		400
	Record betterment.		

b.

Year 3	Repairs Expense	250	
	Cash...................................		250
	Record ordinary repairs.		

c.

Year 4	Equipment	500	
	Cash...................................		500
	Record extraordinary repairs.		

Solutions—Part 2   [Note: Book value of machine = $500 − $400 = $100]

a. Disposed of at no value

Jan. 2	Loss on Disposal of Machine	100	
	Accumulated Depreciation—Machine	400	
	Machine		500
	Record disposal of machine.		

b. Sold for $80 cash

Jan. 2	Cash	80	
	Loss on Sale of Machine	20	
	Accumulated Depreciation—Machine	400	
	Machine		500
	Record cash sale of machine (below book value).		

c. Sold for $100 cash

Jan. 2	Cash	100	
	Accumulated Depreciation—Machine	400	
	Machine		500
	Record cash sale of machine (at book value).		

d. Sold for $110 cash

Jan. 2	Cash	110	
	Accumulated Depreciation—Machine	400	
	Gain on Sale of Machine....................		10
	Machine		500
	Record cash sale of machine (above book value).		

Do More: QS 8-8, QS 8-9, E 8-14, E 8-15, E 8-16, E 8-17

Section 2—Natural Resources

Natural resources are assets that are physically consumed when used. Examples are standing timber, mineral deposits, and oil and gas fields. Since they are consumed when used, they are often called *wasting assets*. These assets represent soon-to-be inventories of raw materials that will be converted into one or more products by cutting, mining, or pumping. Until that conversion takes place, they are noncurrent assets and are shown in a balance sheet using titles such as *Timberlands, Mineral deposits,* or *Oil reserves*. Natural resources are reported under either plant assets or their own separate category. **Alcoa**, for instance, reports its natural resources under the balance sheet title *Properties, plants and equipment*. In a note to its financial statements, Alcoa reports a separate amount for *Land and land rights, including mines*. **Weyerhaeuser**, on the other hand, reports its timber holdings in a separate balance sheet category titled *Timber and timberlands*.

P3

Account for natural resource assets and their depletion.

Cost Determination and Depletion

Natural resources are recorded at cost, which includes all expenditures necessary to acquire the resource and prepare it for its intended use. **Depletion** is the process of allocating the cost of a natural resource to the period when it is consumed. Natural resources are reported on the balance sheet at cost less *accumulated depletion*. The depletion expense per period is usually based on units extracted from cutting, mining, or pumping ExxonMobil. This is similar to units-of-production depreciation. **ExxonMobil** uses this approach to amortize the costs of discovering and operating its oil wells.

Digital Vision/Getty Images

To illustrate depletion of natural resources, let's consider a mineral deposit with an estimated 250,000 tons of available ore. It is purchased for $500,000, and we expect zero salvage value. The depletion charge per ton of ore mined is $2, computed as $500,000 ÷ 250,000 tons. If 85,000 tons are mined and sold in the first year, the depletion charge for that year is $170,000. These computations are detailed in Exhibit 8.16.

EXHIBIT 8.16

Depletion Formula and Example

Step 1

$$\text{Depletion per unit} = \frac{\text{Cost} - \text{Salvage value}}{\text{Total units of capacity}} = \frac{\$500,000 - \$0}{250,000 \text{ tons}} = \$2 \text{ per ton}$$

Step 2

$$\text{Depletion expense} = \text{Depletion per unit} \times \text{Units extracted and sold in period}$$
$$= \$2 \times 85,000 = \$170,000$$

Depletion expense for the first year is recorded as follows.

Dec. 31	Depletion Expense—Mineral Deposit	170,000	
	Accumulated Depletion—Mineral Deposit		170,000
	Record depletion of the mineral deposit.		

Assets = Liabilities + Equity
−170,000   −170,000

The period-end balance sheet reports the mineral deposit as shown in Exhibit 8.17.

| Mineral deposit . . . . | $500,000 | |
| **Less accumulated depletion** . . . . | **170,000** | $330,000 |

EXHIBIT 8.17

Balance Sheet Presentation of Natural Resources

Since all 85,000 tons of the mined ore are sold during the year, the entire $170,000 of depletion is reported on the income statement. If some of the ore remains unsold at year-end, however, the depletion related to the unsold ore is carried forward on the balance sheet and reported as Ore Inventory, a current asset. To illustrate, and continuing with our example, assume that

40,000 tons are mined in the second year, but only 34,000 tons are sold. We record depletion of $68,000 (34,000 tons × $2 depletion per unit) and the remaining Ore Inventory of $12,000 (6,000 tons × $2 depletion per unit) as follows.

Assets = Liabilities + Equity
−80,000   −68,000
+12,000

Dec. 31	Depletion Expense—Mineral Deposit...............	68,000	
	Ore Inventory	12,000	
	Accumulated Depletion—Mineral Deposit.......		80,000
	Record depletion and inventory of mineral deposit.		

Plant Assets Tied into Extracting

The conversion of natural resources by mining, cutting, or pumping usually requires machinery, equipment, and buildings. When the usefulness of these plant assets is directly related to the depletion of a natural resource, their costs are depreciated using the units-of-production method in proportion to the depletion of the natural resource. For example, if a machine is permanently installed in a mine and 10% of the ore is mined and sold in the period, then 10% of the machine's cost (less any salvage value) is allocated to depreciation expense. The same procedure is used when a machine is abandoned once resources have been extracted. If, however, a machine will be moved to and used at another site when extraction is complete, the machine is depreciated over its own useful life.

Fraud

In Control Long-term assets must be safeguarded against theft, misuse, and other damages. Controls take many forms depending on the asset, including use of security tags, the legal monitoring of rights infringements, and approvals of all asset disposals. A study reports that 43% of employees in operations and service areas witnessed the wasting, mismanaging, or abusing of assets in the past year (KPMG 2013).

Depletion Accounting

P3

Do More: QS 8-10, E 8-18

A company acquires a zinc mine at a cost of $750,000 on January 1. At that same time it incurs additional costs of $100,000 to access the mine, which is estimated to hold 200,000 tons of zinc. The estimated value of the land after the zinc is removed is $50,000.

1. Prepare the January 1 entry(ies) to record the cost of the zinc mine.

2. Prepare the December 31 year-end adjusting entry if 50,000 tons of zinc are mined, but only 40,000 tons are sold the first year.

Solution

1.

Jan. 1	Zinc Mine	850,000	
	Cash		850,000
	Record cost of zinc mine.		

2. Depletion per unit = ($750,000 + $100,000 − $50,000)/200,000 tons = $4.00 per ton

Dec. 31	Depletion Expense—Zinc Mine	160,000	
	Zinc Inventory	40,000	
	Accumulated Depletion—Zinc Mine		200,000
	Record depletion of zinc mine (50,000 × $4.00).		

Section 3—Intangible Assets

P4

Account for intangible assets.

Intangible assets are nonphysical assets (used in operations) that confer on their owners long-term rights, privileges, or competitive advantages. Examples are patents, copyrights, licenses, leaseholds, franchises, goodwill, and trademarks. Lack of physical substance does not necessarily imply an intangible asset. Notes and accounts receivable, for instance, lack physical substance, but they are not intangibles. This section identifies the more common types of intangible assets and explains the accounting for them.

Cost Determination and Amortization

An intangible asset is recorded at cost when purchased. Intangibles are then separated into those with limited lives or indefinite lives. If an intangible has a **limited life,** its cost is systematically allocated to expense over its estimated useful life through the process of **amortization.** If an intangible asset has an **indefinite life**—meaning that no legal, regulatory, contractual, competitive, economic, or other factors limit its useful life—it should not be amortized. (If an intangible with an indefinite life is later judged to have a limited life, it is amortized over that limited life.) Amortization of intangible assets is similar to depreciation of plant assets and the depletion of natural resources in that it is a process of cost allocation. However, only the straight-line method is used for amortizing intangibles *unless* the company can show that another method is preferred. The effects of amortization are recorded in a contra account (Accumulated Amortization). The gross acquisition cost of intangible assets is disclosed in the balance sheet along with their accumulated amortization (these disclosures are new). The eventual disposal of an intangible asset involves removing its book value, recording any other asset(s) received or given up, and recognizing any gain or loss for the difference.

 Point: Depreciation, depletion, and amortization are related in that each describes cost allocation.

Many intangibles have limited lives due to laws, contracts, or other asset characteristics. Examples are patents, copyrights, and leaseholds. Other intangibles such as goodwill, trademarks, and trade names have lives that cannot be easily determined. The cost of intangible assets is amortized over the periods expected to benefit by their use, but in no case can this period be longer than the asset's legal existence. The values of some intangible assets such as goodwill continue indefinitely into the future and are not amortized. (An intangible asset that is not amortized is tested annually for **impairment**—if necessary, an impairment loss is recorded. Details for this test are in advanced courses.)

Point: Goodwill is not amortized; instead, it is annually tested for impairment.

Intangible assets are often shown in a separate section of the balance sheet immediately after plant assets. **Callaway Golf,** for instance, follows this approach in reporting nearly $90 million of intangible assets in its balance sheet, plus nearly $30 million in goodwill. Companies usually disclose their amortization periods for intangibles. The remainder of our discussion focuses on accounting for specific types of intangible assets.

Types of Intangibles

Patents The federal government grants patents to encourage the invention of new technology, mechanical devices, and production processes. A **patent** is an exclusive right granted to its owner to manufacture and sell a patented item or to use a process for 20 years. When patent rights are purchased, the cost to acquire the rights is debited to an account called Patents. If the owner engages in lawsuits to successfully defend a patent, the cost of lawsuits is debited to the Patents account; if the defense is unsuccessful, the book value of the patent is expensed. However, the costs of research and development leading to a new patent are expensed when incurred.

Scott Halleran/Getty Images

A patent's cost is amortized over its estimated useful life (not to exceed 20 years). If we purchase a patent costing $25,000 with a useful life of 10 years, we make the following adjusting entry at the end of each of the 10 years to amortize one-tenth of its cost.

Dec. 31	Amortization Expense—Patents	2,500	
	Accumulated Amortization—Patents		2,500
	Amortize patent costs over its useful life.		

Assets = Liabilities + Equity
−2,500   −2,500

The $2,500 debit to Amortization Expense appears on the income statement as a cost of the product or service provided under protection of the patent. The Accumulated Amortization—Patents account is a contra asset account to Patents.

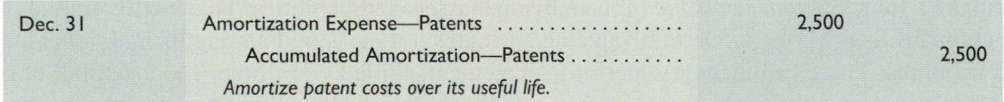

Decision Insight

Meds Mention "drug war" and most people think of illegal drug trade. But another drug war is under way: Brand-name drugmakers are fighting to stop generic copies of their products from hitting the market once patents expire. Delaying a generic rival can yield millions in extra sales. One way drugmakers fight patent expirations is to alter *drug delivery.* The first patent might require a patient to take a pill 4×/day. When that patent expires, the drugmaker can "improve" the drug's delivery release system to 2×/day, and then 1×/day, and so forth. ■

Prescriptions That Specify Generics

Copyrights   A **copyright** gives its owner the exclusive right to publish and sell a musical, literary, or artistic work during the life of the creator plus 70 years, although the useful life of most copyrights is much shorter. The costs of a copyright are amortized over its useful life. The only identifiable cost of many copyrights is the fee paid to the Copyright Office of the federal government or international agency granting the copyright. If this fee is immaterial, it is charged directly to an expense account; but if the identifiable costs of a copyright are material, they are capitalized (recorded in an asset account) and periodically amortized by debiting an account called Amortization Expense—Copyrights.

Decision Insight

Mickey Mouse Protection Act   The Walt Disney Company successfully lobbied Congress to extend copyright protection from the life of the creator plus 50 years to the life of the creator plus 70 years. This extension allows the company to protect its characters for 20 additional years before the right to use them enters the public domain. Mickey Mouse is now protected by copyright law until 2023. The law is officially termed the Copyright Term Extension Act (CTEA), but it is also known as the Mickey Mouse Protection Act. ■

Yoshikazu Tsuno/AFP/Getty Images

Franchises and Licenses   **Franchises** and **licenses** are rights that a company or government grants an entity to deliver a product or service under specified conditions. Many organizations grant franchise and license rights—**Anytime Fitness**, **Firehouse Subs**, and **Major League Baseball** are just a few examples. The costs of franchises and licenses are debited to a Franchises and Licenses asset account and are amortized over the life of the agreement. If an agreement is for an indefinite or perpetual period, those costs are not amortized.

Trademarks and Trade Names   Companies often adopt unique symbols or select unique names and brands in marketing their products. A **trademark** or **trade (brand) name** is a symbol, name, phrase, or jingle identified with a company, product, or service. Examples are Nike swoosh, Marlboro Man, Big Mac, Coca-Cola, and Corvette. Ownership and exclusive right to use a trademark or trade name are often established by showing that one company used it before another. Ownership is best established by registering a trademark or trade name with the government's Patent Office. The cost of developing, maintaining, or enhancing the value of a trademark or trade name (such as advertising) is charged to expense when incurred. If a trademark or trade name is purchased, however, its cost is debited to an asset account and then amortized over its expected life. If the company plans to renew indefinitely its right to the trademark or trade name, the cost is not amortized.

Point: McDonald's "golden arches" are one of the world's most valuable trademarks, yet this asset is not shown on McDonald's balance sheet.

Goodwill   **Goodwill** has a specific meaning in accounting. Goodwill is the amount by which a company's value exceeds the value of its individual assets and liabilities. This usually implies that the company as a whole has certain valuable attributes not measured among its individual assets and liabilities. These can include superior management, skilled workforce, good supplier or customer relations, quality products or services, good location, or other competitive advantages.

Point: Amortization of goodwill is different for financial accounting and tax accounting. The IRS requires the amortization of goodwill over 15 years.

To keep accounting information from being too subjective, goodwill is not recorded unless an entire company or business segment is purchased. Purchased goodwill is measured by taking the purchase price of the company and subtracting the market value of its individual net assets (excluding goodwill). For instance, **Google** paid $1.19 billion to acquire **YouTube**; about $1.13 of the $1.19 billion was for goodwill. Goodwill was also a major portion of the $19 billion that **Facebook** paid to acquire **WhatsApp**.

Example: Assume goodwill carries a book value of $500 and has an implied fair value of $475, *and* this $25 decline in value meets the two-step impairment test. The entry to record this impairment is:
Impairment Loss. . . . $25
  Goodwill. $25

Goodwill is measured as the excess of the cost of an acquired entity over the value of the acquired net assets. Goodwill is recorded as an asset, and it is *not* amortized. Instead, goodwill is annually tested for impairment. If the book value of goodwill does not exceed its fair (market) value, goodwill is not impaired. However, if the book value of goodwill does exceed its fair value, an impairment loss is recorded equal to that excess. (Details of this test are in advanced courses.)

Leaseholds   Property is rented under a contract called a **lease.** The property's owner, called the **lessor,** grants the lease. The one who secures the right to possess and use the property is called the **lessee.** A **leasehold** refers to the rights the lessor grants to the lessee under the terms of the lease. A leasehold is an intangible asset for the lessee.

Certain leases require no advance payment from the lessee but require monthly rent payments. In this case, we do not set up a Leasehold account. Instead, the monthly payments are debited to a Rent Expense account. If a long-term lease requires the lessee to pay the final period's rent in advance when the lease is signed, the lessee records this advance payment with a debit to the Leasehold account. Since the advance payment is not used until the final period, the Leasehold account balance remains intact until that final period, when its balance is transferred to Rent Expense. (Some long-term leases give the lessee essentially the same rights as a purchaser. This results in a tangible asset and a liability reported by the lessee. Chapter 10 describes these so-called *capital leases.*)

A long-term lease can increase in value when current rental rates for similar property rise while the required payments under the lease remain constant. This increase in value of a lease is not reported on the lessee's balance sheet. However, if the property is subleased and the new tenant makes a cash payment to the original lessee for the rights under the old lease, the new tenant debits this payment to a Leasehold account, which is amortized to Rent Expense over the remaining life of the lease.

> **Point:** A Leasehold account implies existence of future benefits that the lessee controls because of a prepayment. It also meets the definition of an asset.

Leasehold Improvements   A lessee sometimes pays for alterations or improvements to the leased property such as partitions, painting, and storefronts. These alterations and improvements are called **leasehold improvements,** and the lessee debits these costs to a Leasehold Improvements account. Since leasehold improvements become part of the property and revert to the lessor at the end of the lease, the lessee amortizes these costs over the life of the lease or the life of the improvements, whichever is shorter. The amortization entry *debits* Amortization Expense—Leasehold Improvements and *credits* Accumulated Amortization—Leasehold Improvements.

Other Intangibles   There are other types of intangible assets such as *software, noncompete covenants, customer lists,* and so forth. Our accounting for them is the same. First, we record the intangible asset's costs. Second, we determine whether the asset has a limited or indefinite life. If limited, we allocate its costs over that period. If indefinite, its costs are not amortized.

Fraud

Into Hiding Most people view fraud involving long-term assets as low risk. Yet, opportunity for fraud in a one-time transaction is a higher risk and requires scrutiny. Theft involving concealment of an asset can include recording it as scrap, obsolete, donated, or destroyed—for example:

- Recording an asset disposal as a customer adjustment, as a no-charge item, or as promotional.
- Recording false counts or altering records after a physical count.
- Recording false receiving reports as to asset quantity.
- Nonbilling of an asset sale.
- Write-off of an asset.

Part 1. A publisher purchases the copyright on a book for $1,000 on January 1 of this year. The copyright legally protects its owner for five more years. The company plans to market and sell prints of the original for seven years. Prepare entries to record the purchase of the copyright on January 1 of this year, and its annual amortization on December 31 of this year.

Part 2. On January 3 of this year, a retailer incurs a $9,000 cost to modernize its store. Improvements include lighting, partitions, and sound system. These improvements are estimated to yield benefits for five years. The retailer leases its store and has three years remaining on its lease. Prepare the entry to record (a) the cost of modernization and (b) amortization at the end of this current year.

NEED-TO-KNOW **8-5**

Accounting for Intangibles

P4

Part 3. On January 6 of this year, a company pays $6,000 for a patent with a remaining 12-year legal life to produce a supplement expected to be marketable for 3 years. Prepare entries to record its acquisition and the December 31 amortization entry for this current year.

Solution—Part 1

Jan. 1	Copyright	1,000	
	Cash		1,000
	Record purchase of copyright.		
Dec. 31	Amortization Expense—Copyright	200	
	Accumulated Amortization—Copyright		200
	Record amortization of copyright [$1,000/5 years].		

Solution—Part 2

a.

Jan. 3	Leasehold Improvements	9,000	
	Cash		9,000
	Record leasehold improvements.		

b.

Dec. 31	Amortization Expense–Leasehold Improvements	3,000	
	Accumulated Amortization—Leasehold Improvements		3,000
	*Record amortization of leasehold over remaining lease life.**		

*Amortization = $9,000/3-year lease term = $3,000 per year

Solution—Part 3

Jan. 6	Patents	6,000	
	Cash...		6,000
	Record purchase of patent.		
Dec. 31	Amortization Expense*	2,000	
	Accumulated Amortization—Patents		2,000
	*Record amortization of patent. *$6,000/3 years = $2,000*		

Do More: QS 8-12, E 8-19, E 8-20

GLOBAL VIEW

This section discusses similarities and differences between U.S. GAAP and IFRS in accounting and reporting for plant assets and intangible assets.

Accounting for Plant Assets   Issues involving cost determination, depreciation, additional expenditures, and disposals of plant assets are subject to broadly similar guidance for both U.S. GAAP and IFRS. Although differences exist, the similarities vastly outweigh the differences. **Nokia** describes its accounting for plant assets as follows:

> Property, plant and equipment are stated at cost less accumulated depreciation. Depreciation is recorded on a straight-line basis over the expected useful lives of the assets. Maintenance, repairs and renewals are generally charged to expense during the financial period in which they are incurred. However, major renovations are capitalized and included in the carrying amount of the asset . . . Major renovations are depreciated over the remaining useful life of the related asset.

One area where notable differences exist is in accounting for changes in the value of plant assets (between the time they are acquired and when they are disposed of). Namely, how do IFRS and U.S. GAAP treat decreases and increases in the value of plant assets subsequent to acquisition?

Decreases in the Value of Plant Assets When the value of plant assets declines after acquisition, but before disposition, both U.S. GAAP and IFRS require companies to record those decreases as *impairment losses*. While the *test for impairment* uses a different base between U.S. GAAP and IFRS, a more fundamental difference is that U.S. GAAP revalues impaired plant assets to *fair value* whereas IFRS revalues them to a *recoverable amount* (defined as fair value less costs to sell).

Increases in the Value of Plant Assets U.S. GAAP prohibits companies from recording increases in the value of plant assets. However, IFRS permits upward *asset revaluations*. Namely, under IFRS, if an impairment was previously recorded, a company would reverse that impairment to the extent necessary and record that increase in income. If the increase is beyond the original cost, that increase is recorded in comprehensive income.

Accounting for Intangible Assets

For intangible assets, the accounting for cost determination, amortization, additional expenditures, and disposals is subject to broadly similar guidance for U.S. GAAP and IFRS. Although differences exist, the similarities vastly outweigh differences. Again, and consistent with the accounting for plant assets, U.S. GAAP and IFRS handle decreases and increases in the value of intangible assets differently. However, IFRS requirements for recording increases in the value of intangible assets are so restrictive that such increases are rare. **Nokia** describes its accounting for intangible assets as follows:

> [Intangible assets] are capitalized and amortized using the straight-line method over their useful lives. Where an indication of impairment exists, the carrying amount of the related intangible asset is assessed for recoverability. Any resulting impairment losses are recognized immediately in the income statement.

Sustainability and Accounting

Kate Spade & Company is committed to sustainable corporate citizenship and giving back to the community. Its charitable foundation has launched many programs geared toward empowerment of women. "Every woman should have the opportunity to reach her full potential and to become financially self-sufficient," says the Kate Spade website. Further, the company matches the donations of its employees up to $10,000 per year, and it encourages employees to volunteer and "meet community needs, specifically those of women and girls" to "make a difference."

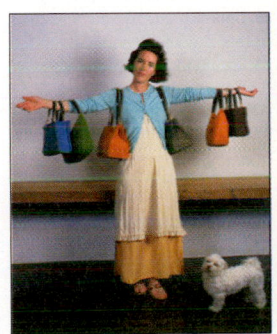

© Jurgen Frank/Corbis

Kate Spade & Company takes several steps to reduce its environmental footprint. When constructing a building, it utilizes energy-saving designs, including high-efficiency metal halide lighting and low-E glass to reduce energy consumption and prevent heat gain in summer. In addition to raising its own standard on sustainability, Kate Spade & Company "insists that suppliers maintain a fair and humane workplace." It now monitors its suppliers to ensure they adhere to all applicable laws and regulations. In 2015, the company hired third-party auditors to evaluate the working conditions in 92 of its 99 active factories. Its website asserts that it desires to "develop direct communication channels with workers" and "ensure [workers] are aware of their rights . . . built around Fair Labor Association best practices."

Total Asset Turnover 🟩🟨🟥 **Decision Analysis**

A company's assets are important in determining its ability to generate sales and earn income. Managers devote much attention to deciding what assets a company acquires, how much it invests in assets, and how to use assets most efficiently and effectively. One important measure of a company's ability to use its assets is **total asset turnover,** defined in Exhibit 8.18.

A1

Compute total asset turnover and apply it to analyze a company's use of assets.

EXHIBIT 8.18

Total Asset Turnover

$$\text{Total asset turnover} = \frac{\text{Net sales}}{\text{Average total assets}}$$

The numerator reflects the net amounts earned from the sale of products and services. The denominator reflects the average total resources devoted to operating the company and generating sales.

To illustrate, let's look at total asset turnover in Exhibit 8.19 for two competing companies: **Molson Coors** and **Boston Beer**.

To show how we use total asset turnover, let's look at Molson Coors. We express Molson Coors's use of assets in generating net sales by saying "it turned its assets over 0.28 times during 2014." This means that each $1.00 of assets produced $0.28 of net sales. Is a total asset turnover of 0.28 good or bad? It is safe to say that all companies desire a high total asset turnover. Like many ratio analyses, however, a company's total asset turnover must be interpreted in comparison with those of prior years and of its competitors. Interpreting the

EXHIBIT 8.19

Analysis Using Total
Asset Turnover

Company	Figure ($ millions)	2014	2013	2012	2011	2010
Molson Coors	Net sales	$ 4,146.3	$ 4,206.1	$ 3,916.5	$ 3,515.7	$ 3,254.4
	Average total assets	$14,788.2	$15,896.2	$14,318.0	$12,560.7	$12,359.4
	Total asset turnover	**0.28**	**0.26**	**0.27**	**0.28**	**0.26**
Boston Beer	Net sales	$ 903.0	$ 739.1	$ 580.2	$ 513.0	$ 463.8
	Average total assets	$ 524.6	$ 401.8	$ 316.0	$ 265.5	$ 260.7
	Total asset turnover	**1.72**	**1.84**	**1.84**	**1.93**	**1.78**

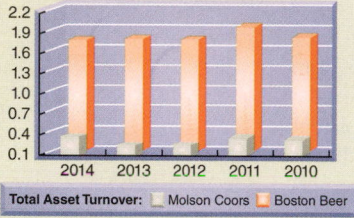

Total Asset Turnover: Molson Coors   Boston Beer

Point: An estimate of **plant asset useful life** equals the plant asset cost divided by depreciation expense.

Point: The **plant asset age** is estimated by dividing accumulated depreciation by depreciation expense. Older plant assets can signal needed asset replacements; they may also signal less efficient assets.

total asset turnover also requires an understanding of the company's operations. Some operations are capital-intensive, meaning that a relatively large amount is invested in assets to generate sales. This suggests a relatively lower total asset turnover. Other companies' operations are labor-intensive, meaning that they generate sales more by the efforts of people than the use of assets. In that case, we expect a higher total asset turnover. Companies with low total asset turnover require higher profit margins (examples are hotels and real estate); companies with high total asset turnover can succeed with lower profit margins (examples are food stores and toy merchandisers). Molson Coors's turnover is much lower than that for Boston Beer and many other competitors. Total asset turnover for Molson Coors's competitors, available in industry publications such as Dun & Bradstreet, is generally in the range of 0.5 to 1.0 over this same period. Overall, Molson Coors must improve relative to its competitors on total asset turnover.

■ Decision **Maker**

Environmentalist   A paper manufacturer claims it cannot afford more environmental controls. It points to its low total asset turnover of 1.9 and argues that it cannot compete with companies whose total asset turnover is much higher. Examples cited are food stores (5.5) and auto dealers (3.8). How do you respond? ■   [Answers follow the chapter's Summary.]

NEED-TO-KNOW **8-7**

COMPREHENSIVE

On July 14, 2015, Tulsa Company pays $600,000 to acquire a fully equipped factory. The purchase involves the following assets and information.

Asset	Appraised Value	Salvage Value	Useful Life	Depreciation Method
Land	$160,000			Not depreciated
Land improvements	80,000	$ 0	10 years	Straight-line
Building	320,000	100,000	10 years	Double-declining-balance
Machinery	240,000	20,000	10,000 units	Units-of-production*
Total	$800,000			

* The machinery is used to produce 700 units in 2015 and 1,800 units in 2016.

Required

1. Allocate the total $600,000 purchase cost among the separate assets.

2. Compute the 2015 (six months) and 2016 depreciation expense for each asset, and compute the company's total depreciation expense for both years.

3. On the last day of calendar year 2017, Tulsa discarded machinery that had been on its books for five years. The machinery's original cost was $12,000 (estimated life of five years) and its salvage value was $2,000. No depreciation had been recorded for the fifth year when the disposal occurred. Journalize the fifth year of depreciation (straight-line method) and the asset's disposal.

4. At the beginning of year 2017, Tulsa purchased a patent for $100,000 cash. The company estimated the patent's useful life to be 10 years. Journalize the patent acquisition and its amortization for the year 2017.

5. Late in the year 2017, Tulsa acquired an ore deposit for $600,000 cash. It added roads and built mine shafts for an additional cost of $80,000. Salvage value of the mine is estimated to be $20,000. The company estimated 330,000 tons of available ore. In year 2017, Tulsa mined and sold 10,000 tons of ore. Journalize the mine's acquisition and its first year's depletion.

6.ᴬ (This question applies this chapter's Appendix coverage.) On the first day of 2017, Tulsa exchanged the machinery that was acquired on July 14, 2015, along with $5,000 cash for machinery with a $210,000 market value. Journalize the exchange of these assets assuming the exchange lacked commercial substance. (Refer to background information in parts 1 and 2.)

PLANNING THE SOLUTION

- Complete a three-column table showing the following amounts for each asset: appraised value, percent of total value, and apportioned cost.
- Using allocated costs, compute depreciation for 2015 (only one-half year) and 2016 (full year) for each asset. Summarize those computations in a table showing total depreciation for each year.
- Depreciation must be recorded up-to-date before discarding an asset. Calculate and record depreciation expense for the fifth year using the straight-line method. Since salvage value is not received at the end of a discarded asset's life, the salvage value becomes a loss on disposal. Record the loss on the disposal as well as the removal of the discarded asset and its related accumulated depreciation.
- Record the patent (an intangible asset) at its purchase price. Use straight-line amortization over its useful life to calculate amortization expense.
- Record the ore deposit (a natural resource asset) at its cost, including any added costs to ready the mine for use. Calculate depletion per ton using the depletion formula. Multiply the depletion per ton by the amount of tons mined and sold to calculate depletion expense for the year.
- Remember that gains and losses on asset exchanges that lack commercial substance are not recognized. Make a journal entry to add the acquired machinery to the books and to remove the old machinery, along with its accumulated depreciation, and to record the cash given in the exchange.

SOLUTION

1. Allocation of the total cost of $600,000 among the separate assets.

Asset	Appraised Value	Percent of Total Value	Apportioned Cost
Land	$160,000	20%	$120,000 ($600,000 × 20%)
Land improvements	80,000	10	60,000 ($600,000 × 10%)
Building	320,000	40	240,000 ($600,000 × 40%)
Machinery	240,000	30	180,000 ($600,000 × 30%)
Total	$800,000	100%	$ 600,000

2. Depreciation for each asset. (Land is not depreciated.)

Land Improvements

Cost	$ 60,000
Salvage value	0
Depreciable cost	$ 60,000
Useful life..	10 years
Annual depreciation expense ($60,000/10 years)	$ 6,000
2015 depreciation ($6,000 × 6/12)	$ 3,000
2016 depreciation	$ 6,000

Building

Straight-line rate = 100%/10 years = 10%
Double-declining-balance rate = 10% × 2 = 20%
2015 depreciation ($240,000 × 20% × 6/12) .... $ 24,000
2016 depreciation [($240,000 − $24,000) × 20%]......... $ 43,200

Machinery

Cost	$180,000
Salvage value	20,000
Depreciable cost	$160,000
Total expected units of production......................	10,000 units
Depreciation per unit ($160,000/10,000 units)	$ 16
2015 depreciation ($16 × 700 units)	$11,200
2016 depreciation ($16 × 1,800 units)	$28,800

Total depreciation expense for each year:

	2015	2016
Land improvements	$ 3,000	$ 6,000
Building	24,000	43,200
Machinery	11,200	28,800
Total	$38,200	$78,000

3. Record the depreciation up-to-date on the discarded asset.

Depreciation Expense—Machinery.	2,000	
Accumulated Depreciation—Machinery		2,000
Record depreciation on date of disposal: ($12,000 − $2,000)/5		

Record the removal of the discarded asset and its loss on disposal.

Accumulated Depreciation—Machinery	10,000	
Loss on Disposal of Machinery	2,000	
Machinery		12,000
Record the discarding of machinery with a $2,000 book value.		

4.

Patent	100,000	
Cash		100,000
Record patent acquisition.		

Amortization Expense—Patent	10,000	
Accumulated Amortization—Patent.		10,000
Record amortization expense: $100,000/10 years = $10,000.		

5.

Ore Deposit	680,000	
Cash		680,000
Record ore deposit acquisition and its related costs.		

Depletion Expense—Ore Deposit	20,000	
Accumulated Depletion—Ore Deposit		20,000
Record depletion expense: ($680,000 − $20,000)/330,000 tons = $2 per ton.		
10,000 tons mined and sold × $2 = $20,000 depletion.		

6. Record the asset exchange: The book value on the exchange date is $180,000 (cost) − $40,000 (accumulated depreciation). The book value of the machinery given up in the exchange ($140,000) plus the $5,000 cash paid is less than the $210,000 value of the machine acquired. The entry to record this exchange of assets that lacks commercial substance does not recognize the $65,000 "gain."

Machinery (new)	145,000*	
Accumulated Depreciation—Machinery (old)	40,000	
Machinery (old)		180,000
Cash		5,000
Record asset exchange that lacks commercial substance.		

* Market value of the acquired asset of $210,000 minus $65,000 "gain."

APPENDIX

Exchanging Plant Assets

P5

Account for asset exchanges.

Many plant assets such as machinery, automobiles, and office equipment are disposed of by exchanging them for newer assets. In a typical exchange of plant assets, a *trade-in allowance* is received on the old asset and the balance is paid in cash. Accounting for the exchange of assets depends on whether the transaction has *commercial substance* (commercial substance implies that it alters the company's future cash flows). If an asset exchange has commercial substance, a gain or loss is recorded based on the difference between the book value of the asset(s) given up and the market value of the asset(s) received. If an asset exchange lacks commercial substance, no gain or loss is recorded, and the asset(s) received is recorded based on the book value of the asset(s) given up. An exchange has commercial substance if the company's future cash flows change as a result of the transaction. This section describes the accounting for the exchange of assets.

Exchange with Commercial Substance: A Loss A company acquires $42,000 in new equipment. In exchange, the company pays $33,000 cash and trades in old equipment. The old equipment originally cost $36,000 and has accumulated depreciation of $20,000, which implies a $16,000 book value at the time of exchange. We are told this exchange has commercial substance and that the old equipment has a trade-in allowance of $9,000. This exchange yields a loss as computed in the middle (Loss) columns of Exhibit 8A.1; the loss is computed as Asset received − Assets given = $42,000 − $49,000 = $(7,000). We can also compute the loss as Trade-in allowance − Book value of assets given = $9,000 − $16,000 = $(7,000).

Asset Exchange Has Commercial Substance	Loss		Gain	
Market value of asset received		$42,000		$52,000
Book value of assets given:				
Equipment ($36,000 − $20,000)	$16,000		$16,000	
Cash	33,000	49,000	33,000	49,000
Gain (loss) on exchange		**$(7,000)**		**$ 3,000**

EXHIBIT 8A.1

Computing Gain or Loss on Asset Exchange with Commercial Substance

The entry to record this asset exchange is

Jan. 3	Equipment (**new**).................................	42,000	
	Loss on Exchange of Assets	7,000	
	Accumulated Depreciation—Equipment (**old**)	20,000	
	Equipment (**old**)		36,000
	Cash		33,000
	Record exchange (with commercial substance) of old equipment and cash for new equipment.		

Assets = Liabilities + Equity
+42,000   −7,000
+20,000
−36,000
−33,000

Point: Parenthetical notes to "new" and "old" equipment are for illustration only. Both the debit and credit are to the same Equipment account.

Exchange with Commercial Substance: A Gain Let's assume the same facts as in the preceding asset exchange *except* that the new equipment received has a market value of $52,000 instead of $42,000. We are told that this exchange has commercial substance and that the old equipment has a trade-in allowance of $19,000. This exchange yields a gain as computed in the right-most (Gain) columns of Exhibit 8A.1; the gain is computed as Asset received − Assets given = $52,000 − $49,000 = $3,000. We can also compute the gain as Trade-in allowance − Book value of assets given = $19,000 − $16,000 = $3,000. The entry to record this asset exchange is

Jan. 3	Equipment (**new**)	52,000	
	Accumulated Depreciation—Equipment (**old**)	20,000	
	Equipment (**old**)		36,000
	Cash		33,000
	Gain on Exchange of Assets		3,000
	Record exchange (with commercial substance) of old equipment and cash for new equipment.		

Assets = Liabilities + Equity
+52,000   +3,000
+20,000
−36,000
−33,000

Exchanges without Commercial Substance   Let's assume the same facts as in the preceding asset exchange involving new equipment received with a market value of $52,000, but let's instead assume the transaction *lacks commercial substance*. The entry to record this asset exchange is

Assets = Liabilities + Equity				
+49,000	Jan. 3	Equipment (**new**)................................	49,000	
+20,000		Accumulated Depreciation—Equipment (**old**)........	20,000	
−36,000		Equipment (**old**)............................		36,000
−33,000		Cash..		33,000
		Record exchange (without commercial substance)		
		of old equipment and cash for new equipment.		

Point: No gain or loss is recorded for exchanges *without commercial substance.*

The $3,000 gain recorded when the transaction has commercial substance is *not* recognized in this entry because of the rule prohibiting recording a gain or loss on asset exchanges without commercial substance. The $49,000 recorded for the new equipment equals its cash price ($52,000) less the unrecognized gain ($3,000) on the exchange. The $49,000 cost recorded is called the *cost basis* of the new machine. This cost basis is the amount we use to compute depreciation and its book value. The cost basis of the new asset also can be computed by summing the book values of the assets given up as shown in Exhibit 8A.2. The same analysis and approach are taken for a loss on an asset exchange without commercial substance.

EXHIBIT 8A.2

Cost Basis of New Asset When Gain Not Recorded on Asset Exchange without Commercial Substance

Cost of old equipment	$ 36,000
Less accumulated depreciation	20,000
Book value of old equipment	16,000
Cash paid in the exchange	33,000
Cost recorded for new	
equipment	**$49,000**

NEED-TO-KNOW 8-6

Asset Exchange

P5

A company acquires $45,000 in new web servers. In exchange, the company trades in old web servers along with a cash payment. The old servers originally cost $30,000 and had accumulated depreciation of $23,400 at the time of the trade. Prepare entries to record the trade under two different assumptions where (*a*) the exchange has commercial substance and the old servers have a trade-in allowance of $3,000 and (*b*) the exchange *lacks* commercial substance and the old servers have a trade-in allowance of $7,000.

Solution

(*a*) Equipment (new)	45,000	
Loss on Exchange of Assets	3,600	
Accumulated Depreciation—Equipment (old).....................	23,400	
Equipment (old)		30,000
Cash ($45,000 − $3,000)		42,000

(*b*) Equipment (new)*	44,600	
Accumulated Depreciation—Equipment (old)	23,400	
Equipment (old)		30,000
Cash ($45,000 − $7,000)		38,000

Do More: QS 8-23

* Includes $400 unrecognized gain.

Summary

C1 Explain the cost principle for computing the cost of plant assets. Plant assets are set apart from other tangible assets by two important features: use in operations and useful lives longer than one period. Plant assets are recorded at cost when purchased. Cost includes all normal and reasonable expenditures necessary to get the asset in place and ready for its intended use. The cost of a lump-sum purchase is allocated among its individual assets.

C2 Explain depreciation for partial years and changes in estimates. Partial-year depreciation is often required because assets are bought and sold throughout the year.

Depreciation is revised when changes in estimates such as salvage value and useful life occur. If the useful life of a plant asset changes, for instance, the remaining cost to be depreciated is spread over the remaining (revised) useful life of the asset.

C3 **Distinguish between revenue and capital expenditures, and account for them.** Revenue expenditures expire in the current period and are debited to expense accounts and matched with current revenues. Ordinary repairs are an example of revenue expenditures. Capital expenditures benefit future periods and are debited to asset accounts. Examples of capital expenditures are extraordinary repairs and betterments.

A1 **Compute total asset turnover and apply it to analyze a company's use of assets.** Total asset turnover measures a company's ability to use its assets to generate sales. It is defined as net sales divided by average total assets. While all companies desire a high total asset turnover, it must be interpreted in comparison with those for prior years and its competitors.

P1 **Compute and record depreciation using the straight-line, units-of-production, and declining-balance methods.** *Depreciation* is the process of allocating to expense the cost of a plant asset over the accounting periods that benefit from its use. Depreciation does not measure the decline in a plant asset's market value or its physical deterioration. Three factors determine depreciation: cost, salvage value, and useful life. Salvage value is an estimate of the asset's value at the end of its benefit period. Useful (service) life is the length of time an asset is productively used. The straight-line method divides cost less salvage value by the asset's useful life to determine depreciation expense per period. The units-of-production method divides cost less salvage value by the estimated number of units

the asset will produce over its life to determine depreciation per unit. The declining-balance method multiplies the asset's beginning-of-period book value by a factor that is often double the straight-line rate.

P2 **Account for asset disposal through discarding or selling an asset.** When a plant asset is discarded or sold, its cost and accumulated depreciation are removed from the accounts. Any cash proceeds from discarding or selling an asset are recorded and compared to the asset's book value to determine gain or loss.

P3 **Account for natural resource assets and their depletion.** The cost of a natural resource is recorded in a noncurrent asset account. Depletion of a natural resource is recorded by allocating its cost to depletion expense using the units-of-production method. Depletion is credited to an Accumulated Depletion account.

P4 **Account for intangible assets.** An intangible asset is recorded at the cost incurred to purchase it. The cost of an intangible asset with a definite useful life is allocated to expense using the straight-line method, and is called *amortization*. Goodwill and intangible assets with an indefinite useful life are not amortized—they are annually tested for impairment. Intangible assets include patents, copyrights, leaseholds, goodwill, and trademarks.

P5^A **Account for asset exchanges.** For an asset exchange with commercial substance, a gain or loss is recorded based on the difference between the book value of the asset given up and the market value of the asset received. For an asset exchange without commercial substance, no gain or loss is recorded, and the asset received is recorded based on the book value of the asset given up.

Guidance Answers to Decision Maker and Decision Ethics

Controller The president's instructions may reflect an honest and reasonable prediction of the future. Since the company is struggling financially, the president may have concluded that the normal pattern of replacing assets every three years cannot continue. Perhaps the strategy is to avoid costs of frequent replacements and stretch use of equipment a few years longer until financial conditions improve. However, if you believe the president's decision is unprincipled, you might confront the president with your opinion that it is unethical to change the estimate to increase income. Another possibility is to wait and see whether the auditor will prohibit this change in estimate. In either case, you should insist that the statements be based on reasonable estimates.

Entrepreneur Treating an expense as a capital expenditure means that reported expenses will be lower and income higher in the short run. This is so because a capital expenditure is not

expensed immediately but is spread over the asset's useful life. Treating an expense as a capital expenditure also means that asset and equity totals are reported at larger amounts in the short run. This continues until the asset is fully depreciated. Your friend is probably trying to help, but the suggestion is misguided. Only an expenditure benefiting future periods is a capital expenditure.

Environmentalist The paper manufacturer's comparison of its total asset turnover with food stores and auto dealers is misdirected. These other industries' turnovers are higher because their profit margins are lower (about 2%). Profit margins for the paper industry are usually 3% to 3.5%. You need to collect data from competitors in the paper industry to show that a 1.9 total asset turnover is about the norm for this industry. You might also want to collect data on this company's revenues and expenses, along with compensation data for its high-ranking officers and employees.

Key Terms

Accelerated depreciation method	Betterments	Copyright
Amortization	Capital expenditures	Cost
Asset book value	Change in an accounting estimate	Declining-balance method

Depletion	Leasehold	Patent
Depreciation	Leasehold improvements	Plant asset age
Extraordinary repairs	Lessee	Plant asset useful life
Franchises	Lessor	Plant assets
Goodwill	Licenses	Revenue expenditures
Impairment	Limited life	Salvage value
Inadequacy	Modified Accelerated Cost Recovery System (MACRS)	Straight-line depreciation
Indefinite life		Total asset turnover
Intangible assets	Natural resources	Trademark or trade (brand) name
Land improvements	Obsolescence	Units-of-production depreciation
Lease	Ordinary repairs	Useful life

Multiple Choice Quiz   Answers at end of chapter

1. A company paid $326,000 for property that included land, land improvements, and a building. The land was appraised at $175,000, the land improvements were appraised at $70,000, and the building was appraised at $105,000. What is the allocation of property costs to the three assets purchased?
   a. Land, $150,000; Land Improvements, $60,000; Building, $90,000
   b. Land, $163,000; Land Improvements, $65,200; Building, $97,800
   c. Land, $150,000; Land Improvements, $61,600; Building, $92,400
   d. Land, $159,000; Land Improvements, $65,200; Building, $95,400
   e. Land, $175,000; Land Improvements, $70,000; Building, $105,000

2. A company purchased a truck for $35,000 on January 1, 2016. The truck is estimated to have a useful life of four years and an estimated salvage value of $1,000. Assuming that the company uses straight-line depreciation, what is the depreciation expense on the truck for the year ended December 31, 2017?
   a. $8,750   **c.** $8,500   **e.** $25,500
   b. $17,500   **d.** $17,000

3. A company purchased machinery for $10,800,000 on January 1, 2016. The machinery has a useful life of 10 years and an estimated salvage value of $800,000. What is the depreciation expense on the machinery for the year ended December 31, 2017, assuming that the double-declining-balance method is used?
   a. $2,160,000   **c.** $1,728,000   **e.** $1,600,000
   b. $3,888,000   **d.** $2,000,000

4. A company sold a machine that originally cost $250,000 for $120,000 when accumulated depreciation on the machine was $100,000. The gain or loss recorded on the sale of this machine is
   a. $0 gain or loss.   **d.** $30,000 gain.
   b. $120,000 gain.   **e.** $150,000 loss.
   c. $30,000 loss.

5. A company had average total assets of $500,000, gross sales of $575,000, and net sales of $550,000. The company's total asset turnover is
   a. 1.15   **d.** 0.87
   b. 1.10   **e.** 1.05
   c. 0.91

A Superscript letter A denotes assignments based on Appendix 8A.
🏛 Icon denotes assignments that involve decision making.

Discussion Questions

1. 🏛 What characteristics of a plant asset make it different from other assets?

2. What is the general rule for cost inclusion for plant assets?

3. What is different between land and land improvements?

4. Why is the cost of a lump-sum purchase allocated to the individual assets acquired?

5. 🏛 Does the balance in the Accumulated Depreciation—Machinery account represent funds to replace the machinery when it wears out? If not, what does it represent?

6. Why is the Modified Accelerated Cost Recovery System not generally accepted for financial accounting purposes?

7. 🏛 What accounting concept justifies charging low-cost plant asset purchases immediately to an expense account?

8. What is the difference between ordinary repairs and extraordinary repairs? How should each be recorded?

9. 🏛 Identify events that might lead to disposal of a plant asset.

10. What is the process of allocating the cost of natural resources to expense as they are used?

11. Is the declining-balance method an acceptable way to compute depletion of natural resources? Explain.

12. What are the characteristics of an intangible asset?

13. What general procedures are applied in accounting for the acquisition and potential cost allocation of intangible assets?

14. When do we know that a company has goodwill? When can goodwill appear in a company's balance sheet?

15. Assume that a company buys another business and pays for its goodwill. If the company plans to incur costs each year to maintain the value of the goodwill, must it also amortize this goodwill?

16. How is total asset turnover computed? Why would a financial statement user be interested in total asset turnover?

17. On its recent balance sheet in Appendix A, **Apple** lists its plant assets as "Property, plant and equipment, net." What does "net" mean in this title? **APPLE**

18. Refer to **Google**'s recent balance sheet in Appendix A. What property, plant, **GOOGLE** and equipment assets does Google list on its balance sheet? What is the book value of its total net property, plant, and equipment assets at December 31, 2014?

19. Refer to **Samsung**'s balance sheet in Appendix A. What does it title its plant assets? What is the book value of its plant assets at December 31, 2014? **Samsung**

20. Refer to the December 31, 2014, balance sheet of **Samsung** in Appendix A. What long-term assets discussed in this chapter are reported by the company? **Samsung**

21. Identify the main difference between (a) plant assets and current assets, (b) plant assets and inventory, and (c) plant assets and long-term investments.

---

connect

Kegler Bowling installs automatic scorekeeping equipment with an invoice cost of $190,000. The electrical work required for the installation costs $20,000. Additional costs are $4,000 for delivery and $13,700 for sales tax. During the installation, a component of the equipment is carelessly left on a lane and hit by the automatic lane-cleaning machine. The cost of repairing the component is $1,850. What is the total recorded cost of the automatic scorekeeping equipment?

QUICK STUDY

QS 8-1

Cost of plant assets

C1

Listed below are certain costs (or discounts) incurred in the purchase or construction of new plant assets. (1) Indicate whether the costs should be *expensed* or *capitalized* (meaning they are included in the cost of the plant assets on the balance sheet). (2) For costs that should be included in plant assets, indicate in which category of plant assets (Equipment, Building, or Land) the related costs should be recorded on the balance sheet.

QS 8-2

Assigning costs to plant assets

C1

Expensed or Capitalized	Asset Category	
————	————	**1.** Charges incurred to train employees to use new equipment
————	————	**2.** Invoice cost to purchase new equipment
————	————	**3.** Deduction for an early payment discount taken on the purchase of new equipment
————	————	**4.** Real estate commissions incurred on land purchased for a new plant
————	————	**5.** Property taxes on land incurred after it was purchased
————	————	**6.** Costs of tune-up for the truck used to deliver new equipment
————	————	**7.** Costs to lay the foundation for a new building
————	————	**8.** Insurance on a new building during the construction phase

---

On January 2, 2016, the Matthews Band acquires sound equipment for concert performances at a cost of $65,800. The band estimates it will use this equipment for four years, during which time it anticipates performing about 200 concerts. It estimates that after four years it can sell the equipment for $2,000. During year 2016, the band performs 45 concerts. Compute the year 2016 depreciation using the straight-line method.

QS 8-3

Straight-line depreciation

P1

On January 2, 2016, the Matthews Band acquires sound equipment for concert performances at a cost of $65,800. The band estimates it will use this equipment for four years, during which time it anticipates performing about 200 concerts. It estimates that after four years it can sell the equipment for $2,000. During year 2016, the band performs 45 concerts. Compute the year 2016 depreciation using the units-of-production method.

QS 8-4

Units-of-production depreciation P1

On January 2, 2016, the Matthews Band acquires sound equipment for concert performances at a cost of $65,800. The band estimates it will use this equipment for four years. It estimates that after four years it can sell the equipment for $2,000. Matthews Band uses straight-line depreciation but realizes at the start of the second year that due to concert bookings beyond expectations, this equipment will last only a total of three years. The salvage value remains unchanged. Compute the revised depreciation for both the second and third years.

QS 8-5

Computing revised depreciation C2

QS 8-6
Double-declining-balance method P1

A fleet of refrigerated delivery trucks is acquired on January 5, 2016, at a cost of $830,000 with an estimated useful life of eight years and an estimated salvage value of $75,000. Compute the depreciation expense for the first three years using the double-declining-balance method.

QS 8-7
Recording plant asset impairment C2

Assume a company's equipment carries a book value of $16,000 ($16,500 cost less $500 accumulated depreciation) and a fair value of $14,750, *and* that the $1,250 decline in fair value in comparison to the book value meets the two-step impairment test. Prepare the entry to record this $1,250 impairment.

QS 8-8
Revenue and capital expenditures

C3

1. Classify the following as either a revenue expenditure or a capital expenditure.
   ____ **a.** Paid $40,000 cash to replace a compressor on a refrigeration system that extends its useful life by four years.
   ____ **b.** Paid $200 cash per truck for the cost of their annual tune-ups.
   ____ **c.** Paid $175 for the monthly cost of replacement filters on an air-conditioning system.
   ____ **d.** Completed an addition to an office building for $225,000 cash.
2. Prepare the journal entries to record transactions *a* and *d* of part 1.

QS 8-9
Disposal of assets P2

Garcia Co. owns equipment that cost $76,800, with accumulated depreciation of $40,800. Garcia sells the equipment for cash. Record the sale of the equipment under the following three separate cases assuming Garcia sells the equipment for (1) $47,000 cash, (2) $36,000 cash, and (3) $31,000 cash.

QS 8-10
Natural resources and depletion

P3

Perez Company acquires an ore mine at a cost of $1,400,000. It incurs additional costs of $400,000 to access the mine, which is estimated to hold 1,000,000 tons of ore. The estimated value of the land after the ore is removed is $200,000.

1. Prepare the entry(ies) to record the cost of the ore mine.
2. Prepare the year-end adjusting entry if 180,000 tons of ore are mined and sold the first year.

QS 8-11
Classifying assets

P3 P4

Identify the following assets *a* through *h* as reported on the balance sheet as intangible assets (IA), natural resources (NR), or other (O).

____ **a.** Oil well   ____ **d.** Gold mine   ____ **g.** Franchise
____ **b.** Trademark   ____ **e.** Building   ____ **h.** Timberland
____ **c.** Leasehold   ____ **f.** Copyright

QS 8-12
Intangible assets and amortization

P4

On January 4 of this year, Diaz Boutique incurs a $105,000 cost to modernize its store. Improvements include new floors, ceilings, wiring, and wall coverings. These improvements are estimated to yield benefits for 10 years. Diaz leases its store and has eight years remaining on the lease. Prepare the entry to record (1) the cost of modernization and (2) amortization at the end of this current year.

QS 8-13
Computing total asset turnover A1

Aneko Company reports the following ($000s): net sales of $14,800 for 2016 and $13,990 for 2015; end-of-year total assets of $19,100 for 2016 and $17,900 for 2015. Compute its total asset turnover for 2016, and assess its level if competitors average a total asset turnover of 2.0 times.

QS 8-14ᴬ
Asset exchange

P5

Caleb Co. owns a machine that costs $42,400 with accumulated depreciation of $18,400. Caleb exchanges the machine for a newer model that has a market value of $52,000. (1) Record the exchange assuming Caleb paid $30,000 cash and the exchange has commercial substance. (2) Record the exchange assuming Caleb pays $22,000 cash and the exchange lacks commercial substance.

QS 8-15
International accounting standards

C1   C3

Answer each of the following related to international accounting standards.
1. Accounting for plant assets involves cost determination, depreciation, additional expenditures, and disposals. Is plant asset accounting broadly similar or dissimilar between IFRS and U.S. GAAP? Identify one notable difference between IFRS and U.S. GAAP in accounting for plant assets.
2. Describe how IFRS and U.S. GAAP treat increases in the value of plant assets subsequent to their acquisition (but before their disposition).

Rizio Co. purchases a machine for $12,500, terms 2/10, n/60, FOB shipping point. The seller prepaid the $360 freight charges, adding the amount to the invoice and bringing its total to $12,860. The machine requires special steel mounting and power connections costing $895. Another $475 is paid to assemble the machine and get it into operation. In moving the machine to its steel mounting, $180 in damages occurred. Materials costing $40 are used in adjusting the machine to produce a satisfactory product. The adjustments are normal for this machine and are not the result of the damages. Compute the cost recorded for this machine. (Rizio pays for this machine within the cash discount period.)

Exercise 8-1
Cost of plant assets
C1

Cala Manufacturing purchases a large lot on which an old building is located as part of its plans to build a new plant. The negotiated purchase price is $280,000 for the lot plus $110,000 for the old building. The company pays $33,500 to tear down the old building and $47,000 to fill and level the lot. It also pays a total of $1,540,000 in construction costs—this amount consists of $1,452,200 for the new building and $87,800 for lighting and paving a parking area next to the building. Prepare a single journal entry to record these costs incurred by Cala, all of which are paid in cash.

Exercise 8-2
Recording costs of assets
C1

Rodriguez Company pays $375,280 for real estate plus $20,100 in closing costs. The real estate consists of land appraised at $157,040; land improvements appraised at $58,890; and a building appraised at $176,670. Allocate the total cost among the three purchased assets and prepare the journal entry to record the purchase.

Exercise 8-3
Lump-sum purchase of plant assets   C1

Ramirez Company installs a computerized manufacturing machine in its factory at the beginning of the year at a cost of $43,500. The machine's useful life is estimated at 10 years, or 385,000 units of product, with a $5,000 salvage value. During its second year, the machine produces 32,500 units of product. Determine the machine's second-year depreciation under the straight-line method.

Exercise 8-4
Straight-line depreciation
P1

Ramirez Company installs a computerized manufacturing machine in its factory at the beginning of the year at a cost of $43,500. The machine's useful life is estimated at 10 years, or 385,000 units of product, with a $5,000 salvage value. During its second year, the machine produces 32,500 units of product. Determine the machine's second-year depreciation using the units-of-production method.

Exercise 8-5
Units-of-production depreciation   P1

Ramirez Company installs a computerized manufacturing machine in its factory at the beginning of the year at a cost of $43,500. The machine's useful life is estimated at 10 years, or 385,000 units of product, with a $5,000 salvage value. During its second year, the machine produces 32,500 units of product. Determine the machine's second-year depreciation using the double-declining-balance method.

Exercise 8-6
Double-declining-balance depreciation   P1

In early January 2016, NewTech purchases computer equipment for $154,000 to use in operating activities for the next four years. It estimates the equipment's salvage value at $25,000. Prepare a table showing depreciation and book value for each of the four years assuming straight-line depreciation.

Exercise 8-7
Straight-line depreciation
P1

In early January 2016, NewTech purchases computer equipment for $154,000 to use in operating activities for the next four years. It estimates the equipment's salvage value at $25,000. Prepare a table showing depreciation and book value for each of the four years assuming double-declining-balance depreciation.

Exercise 8-8
Double-declining-balance depreciation   P1

Tory Enterprises pays $238,400 for equipment that will last five years and have a $43,600 salvage value. By using the equipment in its operations for five years, the company expects to earn $88,500 annually, after deducting all expenses except depreciation. Prepare a table showing income before depreciation, depreciation expense, and net (pretax) income for each year and for the total five-year period, assuming straight-line depreciation.

Exercise 8-9
Straight-line depreciation and income effects

P1

Tory Enterprises pays $238,400 for equipment that will last five years and have a $43,600 salvage value. By using the equipment in its operations for five years, the company expects to earn $88,500 annually, after deducting all expenses except depreciation. Prepare a table showing income before depreciation, depreciation expense, and net (pretax) income for each year and for the total five-year period, assuming double-declining-balance depreciation is used.

Exercise 8-10
Double-declining-balance depreciation   P1

Check   Year 3 NI, $54,170

On April 1, 2015, Cyclone's Backhoe Co. purchases a trencher for $280,000. The machine is expected to last five years and have a salvage value of $40,000. Compute depreciation expense for both 2015 and 2016 assuming the company uses the straight-line method.

Exercise 8-11
Straight-line, partial-year depreciation   C2

Exercise 8-12
Double-declining-balance, partial-year depreciation C2

On April 1, 2015, Cyclone's Backhoe Co. purchases a trencher for $280,000. The machine is expected to last five years and have a salvage value of $40,000. Compute depreciation expense for both 2015 and 2016 assuming the company uses the double-declining-balance method.

Exercise 8-13
Revising depreciation
C2

Check (2) $3,710

Apex Fitness Club uses straight-line depreciation for a machine costing $23,860, with an estimated four-year life and a $2,400 salvage value. At the beginning of the third year, Apex determines that the machine has three more years of remaining useful life, after which it will have an estimated $2,000 salvage value. Compute (1) the machine's book value at the end of its second year and (2) the amount of depreciation for each of the final three years given the revised estimates.

Exercise 8-14
Ordinary repairs, extraordinary repairs, and betterments

C3

Oki Company pays $264,000 for equipment expected to last four years and have a $29,000 salvage value. Prepare journal entries to record the following costs related to the equipment.

1. During the second year of the equipment's life, $22,000 cash is paid for a new component expected to increase the equipment's productivity by 10% a year.

2. During the third year, $6,250 cash is paid for normal repairs necessary to keep the equipment in good working order.

3. During the fourth year, $14,870 is paid for repairs expected to increase the useful life of the equipment from four to five years.

Exercise 8-15
Extraordinary repairs; plant asset age

C3

Check (3) $211,350

Martinez Company owns a building that appears on its prior year-end balance sheet at its original $572,000 cost less $429,000 accumulated depreciation. The building is depreciated on a straight-line basis assuming a 20-year life and no salvage value. During the first week in January of the current calendar year, major structural repairs are completed on the building at a $68,350 cost. The repairs extend its useful life for 5 years beyond the 20 years originally estimated.

1. Determine the building's age (plant asset age) as of the prior year-end balance sheet date.

2. Prepare the entry to record the cost of the structural repairs that are paid in cash.

3. Determine the book value of the building immediately after the repairs are recorded.

4. Prepare the entry to record the current calendar year's depreciation.

Exercise 8-16
Disposal of assets
P2

Diaz Company owns a milling machine that cost $250,000 and has accumulated depreciation of $182,000. Prepare the entry to record the disposal of the milling machine on January 3 under each of the following independent situations.

1. The machine needed extensive repairs, and it was not worth repairing. Diaz disposed of the machine, receiving nothing in return.

2. Diaz sold the machine for $35,000 cash.

3. Diaz sold the machine for $68,000 cash.

4. Diaz sold the machine for $80,000 cash.

Exercise 8-17
Partial-year depreciation; disposal of plant asset
P2

Rayya Co. purchases and installs a machine on January 1, 2016, at a total cost of $105,000. Straight-line depreciation is taken each year for four years assuming a seven-year life and no salvage value. The machine is disposed of on July 1, 2020, during its fifth year of service. Prepare entries to record the partial year's depreciation on July 1, 2020, and to record the disposal under the following separate assumptions:

1. The machine is sold for $45,500 cash.

2. An insurance settlement of $25,000 is received due to the machine's total destruction in a fire.

Exercise 8-18
Depletion of natural resources
P1   P3

On April 2, 2016, Montana Mining Co. pays $3,721,000 for an ore deposit containing 1,525,000 tons. The company installs machinery in the mine costing $213,500, with an estimated seven-year life and no salvage value. The machinery will be abandoned when the ore is completely mined. Montana begins mining on May 1, 2016, and mines and sells 166,200 tons of ore during the remaining eight months of 2016. Prepare the December 31, 2016, entries to record both the ore deposit depletion and the mining machinery depreciation. Mining machinery depreciation should be in proportion to the mine's depletion.

Exercise 8-19
Amortization of intangible assets   P4

Milano Gallery purchases the copyright on an oil painting for $418,000 on January 1, 2016. The copyright legally protects its owner for 10 more years. The company plans to market and sell prints of the original for 11 years. Prepare entries to record the purchase of the copyright on January 1, 2016, and its annual amortization on December 31, 2016.

On January 1, 2016, Robinson Company purchased Franklin Company at a price of $2,500,000. The fair market value of the net assets purchased equals $1,800,000.

1. What is the amount of goodwill that Robinson records at the purchase date?
2. Explain how Robinson would determine the amount of goodwill amortization for the year ended December 31, 2016.
3. Robinson Company believes that its employees provide superior customer service, and through their efforts, Robinson Company believes it has created $900,000 of goodwill. How would Robinson Company record this goodwill?

Exercise 8-20
Goodwill

P4

Refer to the statement of cash flows for **Google** in Appendix A for the fiscal year ended December 31, 2014, to answer the following.

1. What amount of cash is used to purchase property and equipment?
2. How much depreciation and amortization of property and equipment are recorded?
3. What total amount of net cash is used in investing activities?

Exercise 8-21
Cash flows related to assets C1

GOOGLE

Lok Co. reports net sales of $5,856,480 for 2015 and $8,679,690 for 2016. End-of-year balances for total assets are 2014, $1,686,000; 2015, $1,800,000; and 2016, $1,982,000. (*a*) Compute Lok's total asset turnover for 2015 and 2016. (*b*) Comment on Lok's efficiency in using its assets if its competitors average a total asset turnover of 3.0.

Exercise 8-22
Evaluating efficient use of assets A1

Gilly Construction trades in an old tractor for a new tractor, receiving a $29,000 trade-in allowance and paying the remaining $83,000 in cash. The old tractor had cost $96,000, and straight-line accumulated depreciation of $52,500 had been recorded to date under the assumption that it would last eight years and have a $12,000 salvage value. Answer the following questions assuming the exchange has commercial substance.

1. What is the book value of the old tractor at the time of exchange?
2. What is the loss on this asset exchange?
3. What amount should be recorded (debited) in the asset account for the new tractor?

Exercise 8-23^A

Exercise 8-23ᴬ
Exchanging assets

P5

Check (2) $14,500

On January 2, 2016, Bering Co. disposes of a machine costing $44,000 with accumulated depreciation of $24,625. Prepare the entries to record the disposal under each of the following separate assumptions.

1. The machine is sold for $18,250 cash.
2. The machine is traded in for a newer machine having a $60,200 cash price. A $25,000 trade-in allowance is received, and the balance is paid in cash. Assume the asset exchange lacks commercial substance.
3. The machine is traded in for a newer machine having a $60,200 cash price. A $15,000 trade-in allowance is received, and the balance is paid in cash. Assume the asset exchange has commercial substance.

Exercise 8-24ᴬ
Recording plant asset disposals P2   P5

Check (2) Dr. Machinery (new), $54,575

Volkswagen Group reports the following information for property, plant, and equipment as of December 31, 2014, along with additions, disposals, depreciation, and impairments for the year ended December 31, 2014 (euros in millions):

Exercise 8-25
Accounting for plant assets under IFRS

C2   P1   P2

Property, plant, and equipment, net	€46,169
Additions to property, plant, and equipment	11,560
Disposals of property, plant, and equipment	2,430
Depreciation on property, plant, and equipment	7,509
Impairments to property, plant, and equipment	143

1. Prepare Volkswagen's journal entry to record its depreciation for 2014.
2. Prepare Volkswagen's journal entry to record its additions for 2014 assuming they are paid in cash and are treated as "betterments (improvements)" to the assets.
3. Prepare Volkswagen's journal entry to record its €2,430 in disposals for 2014 assuming it receives €720 cash in return and the accumulated depreciation on the disposed assets totals €1,195.
4. Volkswagen reports €143 of impairments. Do these impairments increase or decrease the Property, Plant, and Equipment account? By what amount?

PROBLEM SET A

Problem 8-1A
Plant asset costs;
depreciation methods

C1   P1

Check   (2) $30,000

(3) $10,800

Timberly Construction negotiates a lump-sum purchase of several assets from a company that is going out of business. The purchase is completed on January 1, 2016, at a total cash price of $900,000 for a building, land, land improvements, and four vehicles. The estimated market values of the assets are building, $508,800; land, $297,600; land improvements, $28,800; and four vehicles, $124,800. The company's fiscal year ends on December 31.

Required

1. Prepare a table to allocate the lump-sum purchase price to the separate assets purchased (round percents to the nearest 1%). Prepare the journal entry to record the purchase.

2. Compute the depreciation expense for year 2016 on the building using the straight-line method, assuming a 15-year life and a $27,000 salvage value.

3. Compute the depreciation expense for year 2016 on the land improvements assuming a five-year life and double-declining-balance depreciation.

Analysis Component

4. Defend or refute this statement: Accelerated depreciation results in payment of less taxes over the asset's life.

Problem 8-2A
Depreciation methods

P1

Check   Year 4: units-of-production depreciation, $4,300; DDB depreciation, $12,187

A machine costing $257,500 with a four-year life and an estimated $20,000 salvage value is installed in Luther Company's factory on January 1. The factory manager estimates the machine will produce 475,000 units of product during its life. It actually produces the following units: 220,000 in 1st year; 124,600 in 2nd year; 121,800 in 3rd year; 15,200 in 4th year. The total number of units produced by the end of year 4 exceeds the original estimate—this difference was not predicted. (The machine must not be depreciated below its estimated salvage value.)

Required

Prepare a table with the following column headings and compute depreciation for each year (and total depreciation of all years combined) for the machine under each depreciation method.

Year	Straight-Line	Units-of-Production	Double-Declining-Balance

Problem 8-3A
Asset cost allocation;
straight-line depreciation

C1   P1

Check   (1) Land costs, $2,115,800; Building 2 costs, $598,000

(3) Depr.—Land Improv. 1 and 2, $32,500 and $8,200

In January 2016, Mitzu Co. pays $2,600,000 for a tract of land with two buildings on it. It plans to demolish Building 1 and build a new store in its place. Building 2 will be a company office; it is appraised at $644,000, with a useful life of 20 years and a $60,000 salvage value. A lighted parking lot near Building 1 has improvements (Land Improvements 1) valued at $420,000 that are expected to last another 12 years with no salvage value. Without the buildings and improvements, the tract of land is valued at $1,736,000. The company also incurs the following additional costs:

Cost to demolish Building 1	$ 328,400
Cost of additional land grading	175,400
Cost to construct new building (Building 3), having a useful life of 25 years and a $392,000 salvage value	2,202,000
Cost of new land improvements (Land Improvements 2) near Building 2, having a 20-year useful life and no salvage value	164,000

Required

1. Prepare a table with the following column headings: Land, Building 2, Building 3, Land Improvements 1, and Land Improvements 2. Allocate the costs incurred by Mitzu to the appropriate columns and total each column (round percents to the nearest 1%).

2. Prepare a single journal entry to record all the incurred costs assuming they are paid in cash on January 1, 2016.

3. Using the straight-line method, prepare the December 31 adjusting entries to record depreciation for the 12 months of 2016 when these assets were in use.

Champion Contractors completed the following transactions and events involving the purchase and operation of equipment in its business.

2015

Jan.   1   Paid $287,600 cash plus $11,500 in sales tax and $1,500 in transportation (FOB shipping point) for a new loader. The loader is estimated to have a four-year life and a $20,600 salvage value. Loader costs are recorded in the Equipment account.

Jan.   3   Paid $4,800 to enclose the cab and install air-conditioning in the loader to enable operations under harsher conditions. This increased the estimated salvage value of the loader by another $1,400.

Dec. 31   Recorded annual straight-line depreciation on the loader.

2016

Jan.   1   Paid $5,400 to overhaul the loader's engine, which increased the loader's estimated useful life by two years.

Feb. 17   Paid $820 to repair the loader after the operator backed it into a tree.

Dec. 31   Recorded annual straight-line depreciation on the loader.

Required

Prepare journal entries to record these transactions and events.

Problem 8-4A
Computing and revising depreciation; revenue and capital expenditures
C1   C2   C3

Check   Dec. 31, 2015, Dr. Depr. Expense—Equip., $70,850

Dec. 31, 2016, Dr. Depr. Expense—Equip., $43,590

Yoshi Company completed the following transactions and events involving its delivery trucks.

2015

Jan.   1   Paid $20,515 cash plus $1,485 in sales tax for a new delivery truck estimated to have a five-year life and a $2,000 salvage value. Delivery truck costs are recorded in the Trucks account.

Dec. 31   Recorded annual straight-line depreciation on the truck.

2016

Dec. 31   Due to new information obtained earlier in the year, the truck's estimated useful life was changed from five to four years, and the estimated salvage value was increased to $2,400. Recorded annual straight-line depreciation on the truck.

2017

Dec. 31   Recorded annual straight-line depreciation on the truck.

Dec. 31   Sold the truck for $5,300 cash.

Required

Prepare journal entries to record these transactions and events.

Problem 8-5A
Computing and revising depreciation; selling plant assets
C2   P1   P2

Check   Dec. 31, 2016, Dr. Depr. Expense—Trucks, $5,200

Dec. 31, 2017, Dr. Loss on Disposal of Trucks, $2,300

Onslow Co. purchases a used machine for $178,000 cash on January 2 and readies it for use the next day at a cost of $2,840. On January 3, it is installed on a required operating platform costing $1,160, and it is further readied for operations. The company predicts the machine will be used for six years and have a $14,000 salvage value. Depreciation is to be charged on a straight-line basis. On December 31, at the end of its fifth year in operations, it is disposed of.

Required

1. Prepare journal entries to record the machine's purchase and the costs to ready and install it. Cash is paid for all costs incurred.

2. Prepare journal entries to record depreciation of the machine at December 31 of (*a*) its first year in operations and (*b*) the year of its disposal.

3. Prepare journal entries to record the machine's disposal under each of the following separate assumptions: (*a*) it is sold for $15,000 cash; (*b*) it is sold for $50,000 cash; and (*c*) it is destroyed in a fire and the insurance company pays $30,000 cash to settle the loss claim.

Problem 8-6A
Disposal of plant assets
C1   P1   P2

Check   (2b) Depr. Exp., $28,000

(3c) Dr. Loss from Fire, $12,000

On July 23 of the current year, Dakota Mining Co. pays $4,715,000 for land estimated to contain 5,125,000 tons of recoverable ore. It installs machinery costing $410,000 that has a 10-year life and no salvage value and is capable of mining the ore deposit in eight years. The machinery is paid for on July 25, seven days before mining operations begin. The company removes and sells 480,000 tons of ore during its first five months of operations ending on December 31. Depreciation of the machinery is in proportion to the mine's depletion as the machinery will be abandoned after the ore is mined.

Problem 8-7A
Natural resources
P3

Required

Prepare entries to record (*a*) the purchase of the land, (*b*) the cost and installation of machinery, (*c*) the first five months' depletion assuming the land has a net salvage value of zero after the ore is mined, and (*d*) the first five months' depreciation on the machinery.

Analysis Component

Describe both the similarities and differences in amortization, depletion, and depreciation.

Problem 8-8A
Intangible assets

P4

On July 1, 2011, Falk Company signed a contract to lease space in a building for 15 years. The lease contract calls for annual (prepaid) rental payments of $80,000 on each July 1 throughout the life of the lease and for the lessee to pay for all additions and improvements to the leased property. On June 25, 2016, Falk decides to sublease the space to Ryan & Associates for the remaining 10 years of the lease—Ryan pays $200,000 to Falk for the right to sublease and it agrees to assume the obligation to pay the $80,000 annual rent to the building owner beginning July 1, 2016. After taking possession of the leased space, Ryan pays for improving the office portion of the leased space at a $130,000 cost. The improvements are paid for by Ryan on July 5, 2016, and are estimated to have a useful life equal to the 16 years remaining in the life of the building.

Required

1. Prepare entries for Ryan to record (*a*) its payment to Falk for the right to sublease the building space, (*b*) its payment of the 2016 annual rent to the building owner, and (*c*) its payment for the office improvements.

2. Prepare Ryan's year-end adjusting entries required at December 31, 2016, to (*a*) amortize the $200,000 cost of the sublease, (*b*) amortize the office improvements, and (*c*) record rent expense.

PROBLEM SET B

Problem 8-1B
Plant asset costs;
depreciation methods

C1   P1

Nagy Company negotiates a lump-sum purchase of several assets from a contractor who is relocating. The purchase is completed on January 1, 2016, at a total cash price of $1,800,000 for a building, land, land improvements, and five trucks. The estimated market values of the assets are building, $890,000; land, $427,200; land improvements, $249,200; and five trucks, $213,600. The company's fiscal year ends on December 31.

Required

1. Prepare a table to allocate the lump-sum purchase price to the separate assets purchased (round percents to the nearest 1%). Prepare the journal entry to record the purchase.

2. Compute the depreciation expense for year 2016 on the building using the straight-line method, assuming a 12-year life and a $120,000 salvage value.

3. Compute the depreciation expense for year 2016 on the land improvements assuming a 10-year life and double-declining-balance depreciation.

Analysis Component

4. Defend or refute this statement: Accelerated depreciation results in payment of more taxes over the asset's life.

Problem 8-2B
Depreciation methods

P1

On January 2, Manning Co. purchases and installs a new machine costing $324,000 with a five-year life and an estimated $30,000 salvage value. Management estimates the machine will produce 1,470,000 units of product during its life. Actual production of units is as follows: 355,600 in 1st year; 320,400 in 2nd year; 317,000 in 3rd year; 343,600 in 4th year; 138,500 in 5th year. The total number of units produced by the end of year 5 exceeds the original estimate—this difference was not predicted. (The machine must not be depreciated below its estimated salvage value.)

Required

Prepare a table with the following column headings and compute depreciation for each year (and total depreciation of all years combined) for the machine under each depreciation method.

Year	Straight-Line	Units-of-Production	Double-Declining-Balance

In January 2016, ProTech Co. pays $1,550,000 for a tract of land with two buildings. It plans to demolish Building A and build a new shop in its place. Building B will be a company office; it is appraised at $482,800, with a useful life of 15 years and a $99,500 salvage value. A lighted parking lot near Building B has improvements (Land Improvements B) valued at $142,000 that are expected to last another five years with no salvage value. Without the buildings and improvements, the tract of land is valued at $795,200. The company also incurs the following additional costs.

Problem 8-3B
Asset cost allocation; straight-line depreciation
C1 P1

Cost to demolish Building A	$ 122,000
Cost of additional land grading	174,500
Cost to construct new building (Building C), having a useful life of 20 years and a $258,000 salvage value.	1,458,000
Cost of new land improvements (Land Improvements C) near Building C, having a 10-year useful life and no salvage value.	103,500

Required

1. Prepare a table with the following column headings: Land, Building B, Building C, Land Improvements B, and Land Improvements C. Allocate the costs incurred by ProTech to the appropriate columns and total each column (round percents to the nearest 1%).

2. Prepare a single journal entry to record all incurred costs assuming they are paid in cash on January 1, 2016.

3. Using the straight-line method, prepare the December 31 adjusting entries to record depreciation for the 12 months of 2016 when these assets were in use.

Check (1) Land costs, $1,164,500; Building B costs, $527,000

(3) Depr.—Land Improv. B and C, $31,000 and $10,350

Mercury Delivery Service completed the following transactions and events involving the purchase and operation of equipment for its business.

Problem 8-4B
Computing and revising depreciation; revenue and capital expenditures
C1 C2 C3

2015

Jan. 1   Paid $25,860 cash plus $1,810 in sales tax for a new delivery van that was estimated to have a five-year life and a $3,670 salvage value. Van costs are recorded in the Equipment account.

Jan. 3   Paid $1,850 to install sorting racks in the van for more accurate and quicker delivery of packages. This increases the estimated salvage value of the van by another $230.

Dec. 31   Recorded annual straight-line depreciation on the van.

2016

Jan. 1   Paid $2,064 to overhaul the van's engine, which increased the van's estimated useful life by two years.

May 10   Paid $800 to repair the van after the driver backed it into a loading dock.

Dec. 31   Record annual straight-line depreciation on the van. (Round to the nearest dollar.)

Check Dec. 31, 2015, Dr. Depr. Expense—Equip., $5,124

Dec. 31, 2016, Dr. Depr. Expense—Equip., $3,760

Required

Prepare journal entries to record these transactions and events.

York Instruments completed the following transactions and events involving its machinery.

Problem 8-5B
Computing and revising depreciation; selling plant assets
C2 P1 P2

2015

Jan. 1   Paid $107,800 cash plus $6,470 in sales tax for a new machine. The machine is estimated to have a six-year life and a $9,720 salvage value.

Dec. 31   Recorded annual straight-line depreciation on the machinery.

2016

Dec. 31   Due to new information obtained earlier in the year, the machine's estimated useful life was changed from six to four years, and the estimated salvage value was increased to $14,345. Recorded annual straight-line depreciation on the machinery.

Check Dec. 31, 2016, Dr. Depr. Expense—Machinery, $27,500

2017

Dec. 31   Recorded annual straight-line depreciation on the machinery.

Dec. 31   Sold the machine for $25,240 cash.

Required

Prepare journal entries to record these transactions and events.

Dec. 31, 2017, Dr. Loss on Disposal of Machinery, $16,605

Problem 8-6B
Disposal of plant assets
C1   P1   P2

On January 1, Walker purchases a used machine for $150,000 and readies it for use the next day at a cost of $3,510. On January 4, it is mounted on a required operating platform costing $4,600, and it is further readied for operations. Management estimates the machine will be used for seven years and have an $18,110 salvage value. Depreciation is to be charged on a straight-line basis. On December 31, at the end of its sixth year of use, the machine is disposed of.

Required

1. Prepare journal entries to record the machine's purchase and the costs to ready and install it. Cash is paid for all costs incurred.

Check   (2b) Depr. Exp., $20,000

2. Prepare journal entries to record depreciation of the machine at December 31 of (a) its first year in operations and (b) the year of its disposal.

(3c) Dr. Loss from Fire, $13,110

3. Prepare journal entries to record the machine's disposal under each of the following separate assumptions: (a) it is sold for $28,000 cash; (b) it is sold for $52,000 cash; and (c) it is destroyed in a fire and the insurance company pays $25,000 cash to settle the loss claim.

Problem 8-7B
Natural resources
P3

On February 19 of the current year, Quartzite Co. pays $5,400,000 for land estimated to contain 4 million tons of recoverable ore. It installs machinery costing $400,000 that has a 16-year life and no salvage value and is capable of mining the ore deposit in 12 years. The machinery is paid for on March 21, eleven days before mining operations begin. The company removes and sells 254,000 tons of ore during its first nine months of operations ending on December 31. Depreciation of the machinery is in proportion to the mine's depletion as the machinery will be abandoned after the ore is mined.

Required

Prepare entries to record (a) the purchase of the land, (b) the cost and installation of the machinery, (c) the first nine months' depletion assuming the land has a net salvage value of zero after the ore is mined, and (d) the first nine months' depreciation on the machinery.

Check   (c) Depletion, $342,900;

(d) Depreciation, $25,400

Analysis Component

Describe both the similarities and differences in amortization, depletion, and depreciation.

Problem 8-8B
Intangible assets
P4

On January 1, 2009, Mason Co. entered into a 12-year lease on a building. The lease contract requires (1) annual (prepaid) rental payments of $36,000 each January 1 throughout the life of the lease and (2) for the lessee to pay for all additions and improvements to the leased property. On January 1, 2016, Mason decides to sublease the space to Stewart Co. for the remaining five years of the lease—Stewart pays $40,000 to Mason for the right to sublease and agrees to assume the obligation to pay the $36,000 annual rent to the building owner beginning January 1, 2016. After taking possession of the leased space, Stewart pays for improving the office portion of the leased space at a $20,000 cost. The improvements are paid for by Stewart on January 3, 2016, and are estimated to have a useful life equal to the 13 years remaining in the life of the building.

Required

1. Prepare entries for Stewart to record (a) its payment to Mason for the right to sublease the building space, (b) its payment of the 2016 annual rent to the building owner, and (c) its payment for the office improvements.

Check   Dr. Rent Expense: (2a) $8,000, (2c) $36,000

2. Prepare Stewart's year-end adjusting entries required on December 31, 2016, to (a) amortize the $40,000 cost of the sublease, (b) amortize the office improvements, and (c) record rent expense.

SERIAL PROBLEM

Business Solutions

P1   A1

(This serial problem began in Chapter 1 and continues through most of the book. If previous chapter segments were not completed, the serial problem can begin at this point. It is helpful, but not necessary, to use the Working Papers that accompany the book.)

SP 8   Selected ledger account balances for Business Solutions follow.

	For Three Months Ended December 31, 2016	For Three Months Ended March 31, 2017
Office equipment	$ 8,000	$ 8,000
Accumulated depreciation— Office equipment................	400	800
Computer equipment	20,000	20,000
Accumulated depreciation— Computer equipment	1,250	2,500
Total revenue	31,284	44,000
Total assets	83,460	120,268

Required

1. Assume that Business Solutions does not acquire additional office equipment or computer equipment in 2017. Compute amounts for *the year ended* December 31, 2017, for Depreciation Expense—Office Equipment and for Depreciation Expense—Computer Equipment (assume use of the straight-line method).

2. Given the assumptions in part 1, what is the book value of both the office equipment and the computer equipment as of December 31, 2017?

3. Compute the three-month total asset turnover for Business Solutions as of March 31, 2017. Use total revenue for the numerator and average the December 31, 2016, total assets and the March 31, 2017, total assets for the denominator. Interpret its total asset turnover if competitors average 2.5 for annual periods. (Round turnover to two decimals.)

Check   (3) Three-month (annual) turnover = 0.43 (1.73 annual)

Beyond the Numbers

BTN 8-1   Refer to the financial statements of **Apple** in Appendix A to answer the following.

1. What percent of the original cost of Apple's property and equipment remains to be depreciated as of September 27, 2014, and September 28, 2013? Assume these assets have no salvage value.

2. Over what length(s) of time is Apple depreciating its major categories of property and equipment?

3. What is the change in total property, plant, and equipment (before accumulated depreciation) for the year ended September 27, 2014? What is the amount of cash provided (used) by investing activities for property and equipment for the year ended September 27, 2014? What is one possible explanation for the difference between these two amounts?

4. Compute Apple's total asset turnover for the year ended September 27, 2014, and the year ended September 28, 2013. Assume total assets at September 29, 2012, are $176,064 ($ millions).

REPORTING IN ACTION

A1

APPLE

Fast Forward

5. Access Apple's financial statements for fiscal years ending after September 27, 2014, at its website (**Apple.com**) or the SEC's EDGAR database (**www.SEC.gov**). Recompute Apple's total asset turnover for the additional years' data you collect. Comment on any differences relative to the turnover computed in part 4.

BTN 8-2   Comparative figures for **Apple** and **Google** follow.

COMPARATIVE ANALYSIS

A1

APPLE
GOOGLE

	Apple			Google		
$ millions	Current Year	One Year Prior	Two Years Prior	Current Year	One Year Prior	Two Years Prior
Total assets............	$231,839	$207,000	$176,064	$131,133	$110,920	$93,798
Net sales	182,795	170,910	156,508	66,001	55,519	46,039

Required

1. Compute total asset turnover for the most recent two years for Apple and Google using the data shown.

2. Which company is more efficient in generating net sales given the total assets it employs? Assume an industry average of 1.0 for asset turnover.

ETHICS CHALLENGE

C1

BTN 8-3   Flo Choi owns a small business and manages its accounting. Her company just finished a year in which a large amount of borrowed funds was invested in a new building addition as well as in equipment and fixture additions. Choi's banker requires her to submit semiannual financial statements so he can monitor the financial health of her business. He has warned her that if profit margins erode, he might raise the interest rate on the borrowed funds to reflect the increased loan risk from the bank's point of view. Choi knows profit margin is likely to decline this year. As she prepares year-end adjusting entries, she decides to apply the following depreciation rule: All asset additions are considered to be in use on the first day of the following month. (The previous rule assumed assets are in use on the first day of the month nearest to the purchase date.)

Required

1. Identify decisions that managers like Choi must make in applying depreciation methods.
2. Is Choi's rule an ethical violation, or is it a legitimate decision in computing depreciation?
3. How will Choi's new depreciation rule affect the profit margin of her business?

COMMUNICATING IN PRACTICE

A1

BTN 8-4   Teams are to select an industry, and each team member is to select a different company in that industry. Each team member is to acquire the financial statements (Form 10-K) of the company selected—see the company's website or the SEC's EDGAR database (www.SEC.gov). Use the financial statements to compute total asset turnover. Communicate with teammates via a meeting, e-mail, or telephone to discuss the meaning of this ratio, how different companies compare to each other, and the industry norm. The team must prepare a one-page report that describes the ratios for each company and identifies the conclusions reached during the team's discussion.

TAKING IT TO THE NET

P4

BTN 8-5   Access the **Yahoo!** (ticker YHOO) 10-K report for the year ended December 31, 2014, filed on February 27, 2015, at **www.SEC.gov**.

Required

1. What amount of goodwill is reported on Yahoo!'s balance sheet? What percentage of total assets does its goodwill represent? Is goodwill a major asset for Yahoo!? Explain.
2. Locate Note 5 to its financial statements. Identify the change in goodwill from December 31, 2013, to December 31, 2014. Comment on the change in goodwill over this period.
3. Locate Note 6 to its financial statements. What are the three categories of intangible assets that Yahoo! reports at December 31, 2014? What proportion of total assets do the intangibles represent?
4. What does Yahoo! indicate is the life of "Trade names, trademarks, and domain names" according to its Note 6? Comment on the difference between the estimated useful life and the legal life of Yahoo!'s trademark.

TEAMWORK IN ACTION

P1

BTN 8-6   Each team member is to become an expert on one depreciation method to facilitate teammates' understanding of that method. Follow these procedures:

a. Each team member is to select an area of expertise from one of the following depreciation methods: straight-line, units-of-production, or double-declining-balance.

b. Expert teams are to be formed from those who have selected the same area of expertise. The instructor will identify the location where each expert team meets.

c. Using the following data, expert teams are to collaborate and develop a presentation answering the requirements. Expert team members must write the presentation in a format they can show to their learning teams.

Point: This activity can follow an overview of each method. Step 1 allows for three areas of expertise. Larger teams will have some duplication of areas, but the straight-line choice should not be duplicated. Expert teams can use the book and consult with the instructor.

Data and Requirements   On January 8, 2014, Whitewater Riders purchases a van to transport rafters back to the point of departure at the conclusion of the rafting adventures they operate. The cost of the van is $44,000. It has an estimated salvage value of $2,000 and is expected to be used for four years and driven 60,000 miles. The van is driven 12,000 miles in 2014; 18,000 miles in 2015; 21,000 miles in 2016; and 10,000 in 2017.

1. Compute the annual depreciation expense for each year of the van's estimated useful life.
2. Explain when and how annual depreciation is recorded.
3. Explain the impact on income of this depreciation method versus others over the van's life.
4. Identify the van's book value for each year of its life and illustrate the reporting of this amount for any one year.

d. Re-form original learning teams. In rotation, experts are to present to their teams the results from part c. Experts are to encourage and respond to questions.

BTN 8-7   Review the chapter's opening feature involving Kate Spade and her company, **Kate Spade & Company**. Assume that the company currently has net sales of $8,000,000, and that it is planning an expansion that will increase net sales by $4,000,000. To accomplish this expansion, Kate Spade & Company must increase its average total assets from $2,500,000 to $3,000,000.

ENTREPRENEURIAL DECISION

A1

Required

1. Compute the company's total asset turnover under (*a*) current conditions and (*b*) proposed conditions.
2. Evaluate and comment on the merits of the proposal given your analysis in part 1. Identify any concerns you would express about the proposal.

BTN 8-8   Team up with one or more classmates for this activity. Identify companies in your community or area that must account for at least one of the following assets: natural resource; patent; lease; leasehold improvement; copyright; trademark; or goodwill. You might find a company that has more than one type of asset. Once you identify a company with a specific asset, describe the accounting this company uses to allocate the cost of that asset to the periods that benefit from its use.

HITTING THE ROAD

P3   P4

BTN 8-9   **Samsung** (www.Samsung.com), **Apple**, and **Google** are all competitors in the global marketplace. Comparative figures for these companies' recent annual accounting periods follow.

GLOBAL DECISION

A1

In millions, except turnover	Samsung (₩ millions)			Apple		Google	
	Current Year	Prior Year	Two Years Prior	Current Year	Prior Year	Current Year	Prior Year
Total assets..........	₩230,422,958	₩214,075,018	₩181,071,570	$231,839	$207,000	$131,133	$110,920
Net sales	206,205,987	228,692,667	201,103,613	182,795	170,910	66,001	55,519
Total asset turnover....	?	?	—	0.83	0.89	0.55	0.54

Required

1. Compute total asset turnover for the most recent two years for Samsung using the data shown.
2. Which company is most efficient in generating net sales given the total assets it employs?

Samsung
APPLE
GOOGLE

ANSWERS TO MULTIPLE CHOICE QUIZ

1. b;

	Appraisal Value	%	Total Cost	Allocated
Land	$175,000	50%	$326,000	$163,000
Land improvements	70,000	20	326,000	65,200
Building	105,000	30	326,000	97,800
Totals	$350,000			$326,000

2. c; ($35,000 − $1,000)/4 years = $8,500 per year
3. c; 2016: $10,800,000 × (2 × 10%) = $2,160,000
    2017: ($10,800,000 − $2,160,000) × (2 × 10%) = $1,728,000

4. c;

Cost of machine	$250,000
Accumulated depreciation	100,000
Book value	150,000
Cash received	120,000
Loss on sale	$ 30,000

5. b; $550,000/$500,000 = 1.10

chapter 9

Reporting and Analyzing Current Liabilities

Chapter Preview

CHARACTERISTICS OF LIABILITIES

C1 Reporting liabilities based on:

Definition

Classification

Uncertainty

KNOWN LIABILITIES

C2 Accounts payable, sales taxes payable, and unearned revenues

P1 Short-term notes

P2 Employee deductions

P3 Employer payroll

ESTIMATED LIABILITIES

P4 Reporting for:

Health and pension benefits

Vacation benefits

Bonus plans

Warranty liabilities

CONTINGENCIES AND ANALYSIS

C3 Accounting for contingencies based on notions of probable, possible, remote

A1 Times interest earned ratio

Learning Objectives

CONCEPTUAL

C1 Describe current and long-term liabilities and their characteristics.

C2 Identify and describe known current liabilities.

C3 Explain how to account for contingent liabilities.

ANALYTICAL

A1 Compute the times interest earned ratio and use it to analyze liabilities.

PROCEDURAL

P1 Prepare entries to account for short-term notes payable.

P2 Compute and record *employee* payroll deductions and liabilities.

P3 Compute and record *employer* payroll expenses and liabilities.

P4 Account for estimated liabilities, including warranties and bonuses.

P5 *Appendix 9A*—Identify and describe the details of payroll reports, records, and procedures.

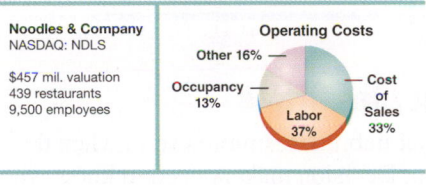

Using His Noodles

"Bring the noodles to the people" — **AARON KENNEDY**

BOULDER, CO—Aaron Kennedy never planned to be an entrepreneur. An evening dinner at a noodle shop in New York's Greenwich Village changed all that. "All of a sudden this idea hit me," explains Aaron. "There are noodle dishes all over the world. I thought, 'What if they were all on one menu? Why not bring all of these influences together and make it affordable and fast.'"

Aaron quickly developed his global noodle concept: "high-quality food made to order." He wanted his noodles "quick and convenient, very affordable, and served in a very appealing dining environment." This led to his launch of **Noodles & Company (Noodles.com).** "We're not fast food—we're casual dining," insists Aaron.

Aaron devoted himself to financial success, including the important task of managing liabilities for payroll, supplies, employee benefits, vacations, training, and taxes. He insists that effective management of liabilities, especially payroll and employee benefits, is crucial to success.

In its recent financial report, Noodles states it has "approximately 9,500 employees, including approximately 900 salaried employees and approximately 8,600 hourly employees." Its labor costs now exceed

Noodles & Company
NASDAQ: NDLS

$457 mil. valuation
439 restaurants
9,500 employees

Operating Costs

Other 16%
Occupancy 13%
Labor 37%
Cost of Sales 33%

$120 million and have grown markedly over the past 5 fiscal years—see graph.

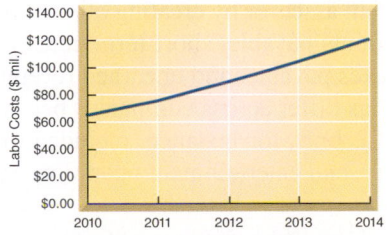

Aaron stresses that monitoring and controlling liabilities are a must. Noodles & Company's balance sheet currently reveals a debt ratio under 42%, meaning that 58% of the business is equity financed.

With grit and determination, Aaron launched the first noodle shop in Denver, followed by a second in Madison, Wisconsin. "The first two restaurants

nearly killed us—physically and fiscally," recalls Aaron. Yet Noodles not only achieved the income to pay the liabilities but also produced revenue growth for expansion. Aaron then took on additional financing, which he successfully predicted would "culminate in accelerating growth."

Aaron's hard work continues to pay off, as revenues for the past three years have substantially risen while liabilities remain in check.

($ millions)	2012	2013	2014
Revenues	$300	$351	$404
Liabilities	143	63	99

Aaron admits he is both surprised and humbled by Noodles & Company's success, but he realizes that simple concepts are often the best. "Noodles are staples," Aaron says. Our task is to "bring the noodles to the people." By all accounts, Aaron has applied his noodles well.

Sources: *Noodles & Company website,* January 2016; *Pinoy Business,* November 2008; *Rocky Mountain News,* February 2002; *Augustana Magazine,* Fall 2002; *Inc.,* January and October 2007; *Food Business Review,* April 2008

CHARACTERISTICS OF LIABILITIES

This section discusses important characteristics of liabilities and how liabilities are classified and reported.

Defining Liabilities

A *liability* is a probable future payment of assets or services that a company is presently obligated to make as a result of past transactions or events. This definition includes three crucial factors:

1. A past transaction or event.
2. A present obligation.
3. A future payment of assets or services.

These three important elements are portrayed visually in Exhibit 9.1. Liabilities reported in financial statements exhibit those characteristics. No liability is reported when one or more of those characteristics is absent. For example, most companies expect to pay wages to their employees in upcoming months and years, but these future payments are *not* liabilities because no past event such as employee work resulted in a present obligation. Instead, such liabilities arise when employees perform their work and earn the wages.

EXHIBIT 9.1

Characteristics of a Liability

Due to a past event ...   Company has a present obligation   ... For future sacrifices

Past   Present   Future

Classifying Liabilities

Point: Account titles using "payable" and "unearned" refer to liabilities. Unearned accounts are liabilities that must be fulfilled rather than repaid.

Information about liabilities is more useful when the balance sheet identifies them as either current or long term. Decision makers need to know when obligations are due so they can plan for them and take appropriate action.

Point: Improper classification of liabilities can distort ratios used in financial statement analysis and business decisions.

Current Liabilities   Current liabilities, also called *short-term liabilities,* are obligations due within one year or the company's operating cycle, whichever is longer. They are expected to be paid using current assets or by creating other current liabilities. Common examples of current liabilities are accounts payable, short-term notes payable, wages payable, warranty liabilities, lease liabilities, taxes payable, and unearned revenues.

Current liabilities differ across companies because they depend on the type of company operations. **MGM Resorts**, for instance, included the following current liabilities related to its gaming, hospitality, and entertainment operations ($000s):

Advance deposits and ticket sales	$103,440
Casino outstanding chip liability	294,466
Casino front money deposits	122,184
Other gaming-related accruals	114,165

Harley-Davidson reports a much different set of current liabilities. It discloses current liabilities made up of items such as warranty, recall, and dealer incentive liabilities.

Long-Term Liabilities   A company's obligations not expected to be paid within the longer of one year or the company's operating cycle are reported as **long-term liabilities.** They can include long-term notes payable, warranty liabilities, lease liabilities, and bonds payable. They are sometimes reported on the balance sheet in a single long-term liabilities total or in multiple categories.

Domino's Pizza, for instance, reports long-term liabilities of $1,573 million. They are reported after current liabilities. A single liability also can be divided between the current and noncurrent sections if a company expects to make payments toward it in both the short and long term. Domino's reports long-term debt, $1,524 million; and current portion of long-term debt, $1 million, which is less than 1%. The second item is reported in current liabilities. We sometimes see liabilities that do not have a fixed due date but instead are payable on the creditor's demand. These are reported as current liabilities because of the possibility of payment in the near term. Exhibit 9.2 shows amounts of current liabilities and as a percentage of total liabilities for selected companies.

Point: The current portion of any long-term debt is a current liability.

	As a percentage of total liabilities
Columbia Sportswear	$373 mil. 85%
Bowl America	$3.0 mil. 55%
Apple	$63,448 mil. 53%
Six Flags	$231 mil. 12%

0%   20%   40%   60%   80%   100%
As a percentage of total liabilities

EXHIBIT 9.2

Current Liabilities of Selected Companies

Uncertainty in Liabilities

Accounting for liabilities involves addressing three important questions: Whom to pay? When to pay? How much to pay? Answers to these questions are often decided when a liability is incurred. For example, if a company has a $100 account payable to a specific individual, payable on March 15, the answers are clear. The company knows whom to pay, when to pay, and how much to pay. However, the answers to one or more of these questions are uncertain for some liabilities.

Uncertainty in Whom to Pay   Liabilities can involve uncertainty in whom to pay. For instance, a company can create a liability with a known amount when issuing a note that is payable to its holder. In this case, a specific amount is payable to the note's holder at a specified date, but the company does not know who the holder is until that date. Despite this uncertainty, the company reports this liability on its balance sheet.

Point: An *accrued expense* is an unpaid expense and is also called an *accrued liability*.

Uncertainty in When to Pay   A company can have an obligation of a known amount to a known creditor but not know when it must be paid. For example, a legal services firm can accept fees in advance from a client who plans to use the firm's services in the future. This means that the firm has a liability that it settles by providing services at an unknown future date. Although this uncertainty exists, the legal firm's balance sheet must report this liability. These types of obligations are reported as current liabilities because they are likely to be settled in the short term.

Uncertainty in How Much to Pay   A company can be aware of an obligation, but not know how much will be required to settle it. For example, a company using electrical power is billed only after the meter has been read. This cost is incurred and the liability created before a bill is received. A liability to the power company is reported as an estimated amount if the balance sheet is prepared before a bill arrives.

🌐 IFRS

IFRS records a contingent liability when an obligation exists from a past event if there is a "probable" outflow of resources and the amount can be estimated reliably. However, IFRS defines probable as "more likely than not" while U.S. GAAP defines it as "likely to occur." ∎

KNOWN LIABILITIES

C2 _____

Identify and describe
known current liabilities.

Most liabilities arise from situations with little uncertainty. They are set by agreements, contracts, or laws and are measurable. These liabilities are **known liabilities,** also called *definitely determinable liabilities*. Known liabilities include accounts payable, notes payable, payroll, sales taxes, unearned revenues, and leases. We describe how to account for these known liabilities in this section.

Accounts Payable

Accounts payable, or trade accounts payable, are amounts owed to suppliers, also called *vendors*, for products or services purchased on credit. Accounting for accounts payable is primarily explained and illustrated in our chapter on merchandising activities.

Sales Taxes Payable

Nearly all states and many cities levy taxes on retail sales. Sales taxes are stated as a percent of selling prices. The seller collects sales taxes from customers when sales occur and remits these collections (often monthly) to the proper government agency. Since sellers currently owe these collections to the government, this amount is a current liability. **Home Depot**, for instance, reports sales taxes payable of $434 million in its recent annual report. To illustrate, if Home Depot sells materials on August 31 for $6,000 cash that are subject to a 5% sales tax, the revenue portion of this transaction is recorded as follows. (The entry for cost of sales is omitted for simplicity.)

Assets = Liabilities + Equity
+6,300   +300   +6,000

Aug. 31	Cash	6,300	
	Sales		6,000
	Sales Taxes Payable ($6,000 × 0.05)		300
	Record cash sales and 5% sales tax.		

Sales Taxes Payable is debited and Cash credited when it remits these collections to the government. Sales Taxes Payable is not an expense. It arises because laws require sellers to collect this cash from customers for the government.[1]

Cameron Spencer/Getty Images

Unearned Revenues

Unearned revenues (also called *deferred revenues, collections in advance,* and *prepayments*) are amounts received in advance from customers for future products or services. Advance ticket sales for sporting events or music concerts are examples. **Rihanna**, for instance, has "deferred revenues" from advance ticket sales. To illustrate, assume that Rihanna sells $5 million in tickets for eight concerts; the entry is:

Point: To *defer* a revenue means to postpone recognition of a revenue collected in advance until it is earned. Sports teams must defer recognition of ticket sales until games are played.

Assets = Liabilities + Equity
+5,000,000   +5,000,000

June 30	Cash	5,000,000	
	Unearned Ticket Revenue		5,000,000
	Record sale of concert tickets.		

---

[1] Sales taxes can be computed from total sales receipts when sales taxes are not separately identified on the register. To illustrate, assume a 5% sales tax and $420 in total sales receipts (which includes sales taxes). Sales are computed as follows:

$$\text{Sales} = \text{Total sales receipts}/(1 + \text{Sales tax percentage}) = \$420/1.05 = \$400$$

Thus, the sales tax amount equals total sales receipts minus sales, or $420 − $400 = $20. Sellers are required to act as "agents" for the government and collect sales tax. This extra work can be offset by the sellers' ability to use or invest that cash until it must be paid to the government.

When a concert is played, Rihanna would record revenue for the portion earned.

Oct. 31	Unearned Ticket Revenue	625,000	
	Ticket Revenue[a]		625,000
	Record concert ticket revenues earned. [a]$5,000,000 × 1/8		

Assets = Liabilities + Equity
−625,000   +625,000

Unearned Ticket Revenue is an unearned revenue account and is reported as a current liability. Unearned revenues also arise with airline ticket sales, magazine subscriptions, construction projects, hotel reservations, gift card sales, and custom orders.

Short-Term Notes Payable

A **short-term note payable** is a written promise to pay a specified amount on a definite future date within one year or the company's operating cycle, whichever is longer. These promissory notes are negotiable (as are checks), meaning they can be transferred from party to party by endorsement. The written documentation provided by notes is helpful in resolving disputes and for pursuing legal actions involving these liabilities. Most notes payable bear interest to compensate for use of the money until payment is made. Short-term notes payable can arise from many transactions. A company that purchases merchandise on credit can sometimes extend the credit period by signing a note to replace an account payable. Such notes also can arise when money is borrowed from a bank. We describe both of these cases.

P1

Prepare entries to account for short-term notes payable.

Point: Required characteristics for negotiability of a note: (1) unconditional promise, (2) in writing, (3) specific amount, and (4) definite due date.

Note Given to Extend Credit Period   A company can replace an account payable with a note payable. A common example is a creditor that requires the substitution of an interest-bearing note for an overdue account payable that does not bear interest. A less common situation occurs when a debtor's weak financial condition motivates the creditor to accept a note, sometimes for a lesser amount, and to close the account to ensure that this customer makes no additional credit purchases.

To illustrate, let's assume that on August 23, Brady Company asks to extend its past-due $600 account payable to McGraw. After some negotiations, McGraw agrees to accept $100 cash and a 60-day, 12%, $500 note payable to replace the account payable. Brady records the transaction with this entry:

Aug. 23	Accounts Payable—McGraw	600	
	Cash		100
	Notes Payable—McGraw.....................		500
	Gave $100 cash and a 60-day, 12% note for payment on account.		

Assets = Liabilities + Equity
−100   −600
          +500

Signing the note does not resolve Brady's debt. Instead, the form of debt is changed from an account payable to a note payable. McGraw prefers the note payable over the account payable because it earns interest and it is written documentation of the debt's existence, term, and amount. When the note comes due, Brady pays the note and interest by giving McGraw a check for $510. Brady records that payment with this entry:

Point: Accounts payable are detailed in a subsidiary ledger, but notes payable sometimes are not. A file with copies of notes can serve as a subsidiary ledger.

Oct. 22	Notes Payable—McGraw	500	
	Interest Expense	10	
	Cash		510
	Paid note with interest ($500 × 12% × 60/360).		

Assets = Liabilities + Equity
−510   −500   −10

Interest expense is computed by multiplying the principal of the note ($500) by the annual interest rate (12%) for the fraction of the year the note is outstanding (60 days/360 days).

Note Given to Borrow from Bank   A bank nearly always requires a borrower to sign a promissory note when making a loan. When the note matures, the borrower repays the note with an amount larger than the amount borrowed. The difference between the amount borrowed and the amount repaid is *interest*. This section considers a type of note whose signer promises to pay

Point: Commercial companies commonly compute interest using a 360-day year. This is known as the *banker's rule*.

principal (the amount borrowed) plus interest. In this case, the *face value* of the note equals the principal. Face value is the value shown on the face (front) of the note. To illustrate, assume that a company needs $2,000 for a project and borrows this money from a bank at 12% annual interest. The loan is made on September 30, 2016, and is due in 60 days. Specifically, the borrowing company signs a note with a face value equal to the amount borrowed. The note includes a statement similar to this: *"I promise to pay $2,000 plus interest at 12% within 60 days after September 30."* This simple note is shown in Exhibit 9.3.

EXHIBIT 9.3

Note with Face Value Equal to Amount Borrowed

The borrower records its receipt of cash and the new liability with this entry:

Assets = Liabilities + Equity
+2,000   +2,000

Sept. 30	Cash	2,000	
	Notes Payable		2,000
	Borrowed $2,000 cash with a 60-day, 12%, $2,000 note.		

When principal and interest are paid, the borrower records payment with this entry:

Assets = Liabilities + Equity
−2,040   −2,000   −40

Nov. 29	Notes Payable.................................	2,000	
	Interest Expense...............................	40	
	Cash		2,040
	Paid note with interest ($2,000 × 12% × 60/360).		

End-of-Period Interest Adjustment When the end of an accounting period occurs between the signing of a note payable and its maturity date, the *expense recognition (matching) principle* requires us to record the accrued but unpaid interest on the note. To illustrate, return to the note in Exhibit 9.3, but assume that the company borrows $2,000 cash on December 16, 2016, instead of September 30. This 60-day note matures on February 14, 2017, and the company's fiscal year ends on December 31. Thus, we need to record interest expense for the final 15 days in December. This means that one-fourth (15 days/60 days) of the $40 total interest is an expense of year 2016. The borrower records this expense (assuming no reversing entries were made) with the following adjusting entry:

Assets = Liabilities + Equity
          +10   −10

2016			
Dec. 31	Interest Expense	10	
	Interest Payable		10
	Record accrued interest ($2,000 × 12% × 15/360).		

When this note matures on February 14, the borrower must recognize 45 days of interest expense for year 2017 and remove the balances of the two liability accounts:

Assets = Liabilities + Equity
−2,040   −10   −30
             −2,000

2017			
Feb. 14	Interest Expense*	30	
	Interest Payable	10	
	Notes Payable	2,000	
	Cash		2,040
	*Paid note with interest. *$2,000 × 12% × 45/360*		

Decision Insight

Sweet Notes   Many franchisors, such as **Baskin-Robbins**, **Planet Smoothie**, and **Cold Stone Creamery**, use notes to help entrepreneurs acquire their own franchises, including using notes to pay for the franchise fee and any equipment. Payments on these notes are usually collected monthly and often are secured by the franchisees' assets. For example, a **McDonald's** franchise can cost from under $200,000 to over $2 million, depending on the type selected; see **FranchiseFoundations.com**. ■

Adam Gault/OJO Images/Getty Images

Part 1. A retailer sells merchandise for $500 cash on June 30 (cost of merchandise is $300). The sales tax law requires the retailer to collect 7% sales tax on every dollar of merchandise sold. Record the entry for the $500 sale and its applicable sales tax. Also record the entry that shows the remittance of the 7% tax on this sale to the state government on July 15.

Part 2. A ticket agency receives $40,000 cash in advance ticket sales for a four-date tour of Haim. Record the advance ticket sales on April 30. Record the revenue earned for the first concert date of May 15, assuming it represents one-fourth of the advance ticket sales.

Part 3. On November 25 of the current year, a company borrows $8,000 cash by signing a 90-day, 5% note payable with a face value of $8,000. (a) Compute the accrued interest payable on December 31 of the current year, (b) prepare the journal entry to record the accrued interest expense at December 31 of the current year, and (c) prepare the journal entry to record payment of the note at maturity.

NEED-TO-KNOW 9-1

Accounting for Known Liabilities

P1   C2

Solution—Part 1

June 30	Cash	535	
	Sales		500
	Sales Taxes Payable		35
	Record cash sales and 7% sales tax.		
June 30	Cost of Goods Sold	300	
	Merchandise Inventory		300
	Record cost of June 30 sales.		
July 15	Sales Taxes Payable	35	
	Cash		35
	Record remittance of sales taxes to govt.		

Solution—Part 2

Apr. 30	Cash	40,000	
	Unearned Ticket Revenue		40,000
	Record sales in advance of concerts.		
May 15	Unearned Ticket Revenue	10,000	
	Earned Ticket Revenue		10,000
	Record concert revenues earned.		

Solution—Part 3

a.

Computation of interest payable at December 31:
Days from November 25 to December 31 .... 36 days
Accrued interest (5% × $8,000 × 36/360) $40

b.

Dec. 31	Interest Expense	40	
	Interest Payable		40
	Record accrued interest (5% × $8,000 × 36/360).		

c.

Feb. 23	Interest Expense	60	
	Interest Payable	40	
	Notes Payable	8,000	
	Cash		8,100
	Record payment of note plus interest		
	(5% × $8,000 × 90/360 = $100 total interest)		
	(5% × $8,000 × 54/360 = $60 interest expense).		

Point: Feb. 23 entry assumes no reversing entry was made.

Do More: QS 9-2, QS 9-3, QS 9-4, E 9-2, E 9-3, E 9-4

Payroll Liabilities

An employer incurs several expenses and liabilities from having employees. These expenses and liabilities are often large and arise from salaries and wages earned, from employee benefits, and from payroll taxes levied on the employer. **Boston Beer**, for instance, reports payroll-related current liabilities of more than $14.528 million from accrued "**employee wages, benefits and reimbursements.**" We discuss payroll liabilities and related accounts in this section. Appendix 9A describes details about payroll reports, records, and procedures.

P2

Compute and record *employee* payroll deductions and liabilities.

Point: Deductions at some companies, such as those for insurance coverage, are "required" under its labor contracts.

Employee **Payroll Deductions**   **Gross pay** is the total compensation an employee earns including wages, salaries, commissions, bonuses, and any compensation earned before deductions such as taxes. (*Wages* usually refer to payments to employees at an hourly rate. *Salaries* usually refer to payments to employees at a monthly or yearly rate.) **Net pay,** also called *take-home pay,* is gross pay less all deductions. **Payroll deductions,** commonly called *withholdings,* are amounts withheld from an employee's gross pay, either required or voluntary. Required deductions result from laws and include income taxes and Social Security taxes. Voluntary deductions, at an employee's option, include pension and health contributions, health and life insurance premiums, union dues, and charitable giving. Exhibit 9.4 shows the typical payroll deductions of an employee. The employer withholds payroll deductions from employees' pay and is obligated to transmit this money to the designated organization. The employer records payroll deductions as current liabilities until these amounts are transmitted. This section discusses the major payroll deductions.

EXHIBIT 9.4

Payroll Deductions

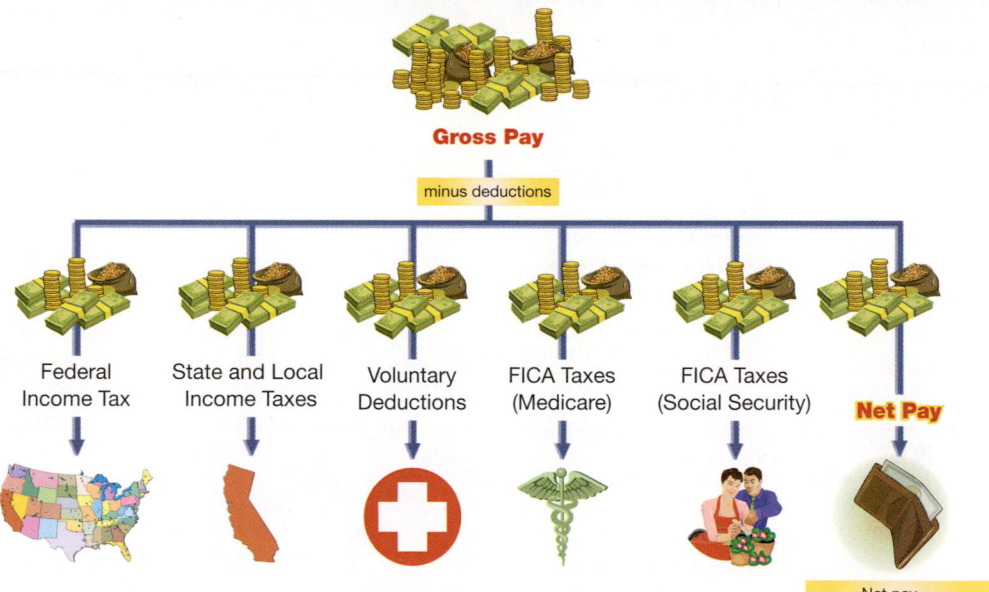

Employee FICA Taxes   The federal Social Security system provides retirement, disability, survivorship, and medical benefits to qualified workers. Laws *require* employers to withhold **Federal Insurance Contributions Act (FICA) taxes** from employees' pay to cover costs of the system. Employers usually separate FICA taxes into two groups: (1) retirement, disability, and survivorship and (2) medical. For the first group, the Social Security system provides monthly cash payments to qualified retired workers for the rest of their lives. These payments are often called *Social Security benefits*. Taxes related to this group are often called *Social Security taxes*. For the second group, the system provides monthly payments to deceased workers' surviving families and to disabled workers who qualify for assistance. These payments are commonly called *Medicare benefits;* like those in the first group, they are paid with *Medicare taxes* (part of FICA taxes).

Law requires employers to withhold FICA taxes from each employee's salary or wages on each payday. The taxes for Social Security and Medicare are computed separately. For 2015 and 2016, the amount scheduled to be withheld from each employee's pay for Social Security tax is 6.2% of the first $118,500 the employee earns in the calendar year. The Medicare tax is 1.45% of *all* amounts the employee earns; there is no maximum limit to Medicare tax. A 0.9% *Additional Medicare Tax* is imposed on the employee for pay in excess of $200,000 (this additional tax is *not* imposed on the employer, whereas the others are).

Employers must pay withheld taxes to the Internal Revenue Service (IRS) on specific filing dates during the year. Employers who fail to send the withheld taxes to the IRS on time can be assessed substantial penalties. Until all the taxes are sent to the IRS, they are included in employers' current liabilities. For any changes in rates or with the maximum earnings level, check the IRS website at **www.IRS.gov** or the SSA website at **www.SSA.gov**.

Employee Income Tax   Most employers are required to withhold federal income tax from each employee's paycheck. The amount withheld is computed using tables published by the IRS. The amount depends on the employee's annual earnings rate and the number of *withholding allowances* the employee claims. Allowances reduce the amount of taxes one owes the government. The more allowances one claims, the less tax the employer will withhold. Employees can claim allowances for themselves and their dependents. They also can claim additional allowances if they expect major declines in their taxable income for medical expenses. (An employee who claims more allowances than appropriate is subject to a fine.) Most states and many local governments require employers to withhold income taxes from employees' pay and to remit them promptly to the proper government agency. Until they are paid, withholdings are reported as a current liability on the employer's balance sheet.

Employee Voluntary Deductions   Beyond Social Security, Medicare, and income taxes, employers often withhold other amounts from employees' earnings. These withholdings arise from employee requests, contracts, unions, or other agreements. They can include amounts for charitable giving, medical and life insurance premiums, pension contributions, and union dues. Until they are paid, such withholdings are reported as part of employers' current liabilities.

Recording Employee Payroll Deductions   Employers must accrue payroll expenses and liabilities at the end of each pay period. To illustrate, assume that an employee earns a salary of $2,000 per month. At the end of January, the employer's entry to accrue payroll expenses and liabilities for this employee is

Jan. 31	Salaries Expense..............................	2,000	
	FICA—Social Security Taxes Payable (6.2%)		124
	FICA—Medicare Taxes Payable (1.45%)		29
	Employee Federal Income Taxes Payable*		213
	Employee Medical Insurance Payable*		85
	Employee Union Dues Payable*		25
	Salaries Payable		1,524
	Record accrued payroll for January.		

Assets = Liabilities + Equity
+124   −2,000
+29
+213
+85
+25
+1,524

* Amounts taken from employer's accounting records.

Salaries Expense (debit) shows that the employee earns a gross salary of $2,000. The first five payables (credits) show the liabilities the employer owes on behalf of this employee to cover FICA taxes, income taxes, medical insurance, and union dues. The Salaries Payable account (credit) records the $1,524 net pay the employee receives from the $2,000 gross pay earned. When the employee is paid, another entry (or a series of entries) is required to record the check written and distributed (or funds transferred). The February 1 entry to record cash payment to this employee is to debit Salaries Payable and credit Cash for $1,524.

Feb. 1	Salaries Payable.................................	1,524	
	Cash		1,524

Fraud

Eyes of the Law "Failure to pay employment taxes is stealing from the employees of the business," alleges former IRS Commissioner Mark W. Everson. "The IRS pursues business owners who don't follow the law, and those who embrace these schemes face civil or criminal sanctions." There are many reasons employers do not withhold or pay employment taxes. Some attempt to use the government as a "bank to borrow money for a short time," some collect the taxes and keep them, and still others object to U.S. tax laws. Regardless, federal law requires employment tax withholding and payment by employers (**IRS.gov/newsroom**).

Point: Sources of U.S. tax receipts follow:
50%   Personal income tax
35   FICA and FUTA taxes
10   Corporate income tax
5   Other taxes

Point: Part-time employees may claim "exempt from withholding" if they did not have any income tax liability in the prior year and do not expect any in the current year.

Point: IRS withholding tables are based on projecting weekly (or other period) pay into an annual figure.

Point: Is there a maximum to the withholding allowances one can claim? Recall, the more allowances, the lower the withholding. However, an employee who claims, say, over 10 allowances on the W-4 is likely to receive an IRS inquiry asking to justify the number of allowances.

P3 ———
Compute and record *employer* payroll expenses and liabilities.

Employer Payroll Taxes   Employers must pay payroll taxes in addition to those required of employees. Employer taxes include FICA and unemployment taxes.

Employer FICA Tax   Employers must pay FICA taxes on their payroll to employees. For 2015 and 2016, the employer must pay Social Security tax of 6.2% on the first $118,500 earned by each employee, and 1.45% Medicare tax on all earnings of each employee. An employer's tax is credited to the same FICA Taxes Payable accounts used to record the Social Security and Medicare taxes withheld from employees. (A self-employed person must pay both the employee and employer FICA taxes.)

Federal and State Unemployment Taxes   The federal government participates with states in a joint federal and state unemployment insurance program. Each state administers its program. These programs provide unemployment benefits to qualified workers. The federal government approves state programs and pays a portion of their administrative expenses.

Federal Unemployment Tax Act (FUTA). Employers are subject to a federal unemployment tax on wages and salaries paid to their employees. For the recent year, employers were required to pay FUTA taxes of as much as 6.0% of the first $7,000 earned by each employee. This federal tax can be reduced by a credit of up to 5.4% for taxes paid to a state program. As a result, the net federal unemployment tax is often only 0.6%.

State Unemployment Tax Act (SUTA). All states support their unemployment insurance programs by placing a payroll tax on employers. (A few states require employees to make a contribution. In the book's assignments, we assume that this tax is only levied on the employer.) In most states, the base rate for SUTA taxes is 5.4% of the first $7,000 paid each employee. This base rate is adjusted according to an employer's merit rating. The state assigns a **merit rating** that reflects a company's stability or instability in employing workers. A good rating reflects stability in employment and means an employer can pay less than the 5.4% base rate. A low rating reflects high turnover or seasonal hirings and layoffs. To illustrate, an employer with 50 employees, each of whom earns $7,000 or more per year, saves $15,400 annually if it has a merit rating of 1.0% versus 5.4%. This is computed by comparing taxes of $18,900 at the 5.4% rate to only $3,500 at the 1.0% rate.

Recording Employer Payroll Taxes   Employer payroll taxes are an added expense beyond the wages and salaries earned by employees. These taxes are often recorded in an entry separate from the one recording payroll expenses and deductions. To illustrate, assume that the $2,000 recorded salaries expense from the previous example is earned by an employee whose earnings have not yet reached $5,000 for the year. This means the entire salaries expense for this period is subject to tax because year-to-date pay is under $7,000. Also assume that the federal unemployment tax rate is 0.6% and the state unemployment tax rate is 5.4%. Consequently, the FICA portion of the employer's tax is $153, computed by multiplying both the 6.2% and 1.45% by the $2,000 gross pay. Moreover, state unemployment (SUTA) taxes are $108 (5.4% of the $2,000 gross pay), and federal unemployment (FUTA) taxes are $12 (0.6% of $2,000). The entry to record the employer's payroll tax expense and related liabilities is

Example: If the employer's merit rating in this example reduces its SUTA rate to 2.9%, what is its SUTA liability?
Answer: SUTA payable = $2,000 × 2.9% = $58

Assets = Liabilities + Equity
    +124   −273
    +29
    +108
    +12

Jan. 31	Payroll Taxes Expense	273	
	FICA—Social Security Taxes Payable (6.2%)......		124
	FICA—Medicare Taxes Payable (1.45%)		29
	State Unemployment Taxes Payable		108
	Federal Unemployment Taxes Payable		12
	Record employer payroll taxes.		

Point: Internal control is important for payroll accounting. Managers must monitor (1) employee hiring, (2) timekeeping, (3) payroll listings, and (4) payroll payments. Poor controls led the U.S. Army to pay nearly $10 million to deserters, fictitious soldiers, and other unauthorized entities.

■ **Decision Ethics** ━━━━━━━━━━━━━━━━━━━━━━━━━━

Web Designer   You take a summer job working for a family friend who runs a small IT service. On your first payday, the owner slaps you on the back, gives you full payment in cash, winks, and adds: "No need to pay those high taxes, eh." What action, if any, do you take? ■ [Answers follow the chapter's Summary.]

Multi-Period Known Liabilities

Many known liabilities extend over multiple periods. These often include unearned revenues and notes payable. For example, if **Sports Illustrated** sells a three-year magazine subscription, it records amounts received for this subscription in an Unearned Subscription Revenues account. Amounts in this account are liabilities, but are they current or long term? They are *both*. The portion of the Unearned Subscription Revenues account that will be fulfilled in the next year is reported as a current liability. The remaining portion is reported as a long-term liability.

The same analysis applies to notes payable. For example, a borrower reports a three-year note payable as a long-term liability in the first two years it is outstanding. In the third year, the borrower reclassifies this note as a current liability since it is due within one year or the operating cycle, whichever is longer. The **current portion of long-term debt** refers to that part of long-term debt due within one year or the operating cycle, whichever is longer. Long-term debt is reported under long-term liabilities, but the *current portion due* is reported under current liabilities. To illustrate, assume that a $7,500 debt is paid in installments of $1,500 per year for five years. The $1,500 due within the year is reported as a current liability. No journal entry is necessary for this reclassification. Instead, we simply classify the amounts for debt as either current or long term when the balance sheet is prepared.

Some known liabilities are rarely reported in long-term liabilities. These include accounts payable, sales taxes, and wages and salaries.

Point: Some accounting systems do make an entry to transfer the current amount due out of Long-Term Debt and into the Current Portion of Long-Term Debt as follows:

Long-Term Debt . . 1,500
    Current Portion
        of L-T Debt . .   1,500

Fraud

False Move Probably the greatest number of frauds involve payroll. Controls include proper approvals and processes for employee additions, deletions, and pay rate changes. A common fraud is a manager adding a fictitious employee to the payroll and then cashing the fictitious employee's check. A study reports that 42% of employees in operations and service areas witnessed violations of employee wage, overtime, or benefit rules in the past year (KPMG 2013). Another 33% observed falsifying of time and expense reports.

Ceridian Connection reports: **8.5%** of fraud is tied to payroll; **$72,000** is the median loss per payroll fraud; and **24 months** is the median time to uncover payroll fraud.

NEED-TO-KNOW 9-2

Payroll Liabilities

P2   P3

A company's first weekly pay period of the year ends on January 8. On that date, the column totals in its payroll register show that sales employees earned $30,000 and office employees earned $20,000 in salaries. The employees are to have withheld from their salaries FICA Social Security taxes at the rate of 6.2%, FICA Medicare taxes at the rate of 1.45%, $9,000 of federal income taxes, $2,000 of medical insurance deductions, and $1,000 of pension contributions. No employee earned more than $7,000 in the first pay period.

Part 1. Compute FICA Social Security taxes payable and FICA Medicare taxes payable. Prepare the journal entry to record the company's January 8 (employee) payroll expenses and liabilities. (Round amounts to cents.)

Part 2. Prepare the journal entry to record the company's (employer) payroll taxes resulting from the January 8 payroll. Its merit rating reduces its state unemployment tax rate to 3.4% of the first $7,000 paid to each employee. The federal unemployment tax rate is 0.6%. (Round amounts to cents.)

Solution—Part 1

Jan. 8			
	Sales Salaries Expense	30,000.00	
	Office Salaries Expense	20,000.00	
	FICA—Social Security Taxes Payable*		3,100.00
	FICA—Medicare Taxes Payable†		725.00
	Employee Fed. Income Taxes Payable		9,000.00
	Employee Med. Insurance Payable		2,000.00
	Employee Pensions Payable		1,000.00
	Salaries Payable		34,175.00
	Record payroll for period.		

* $50,000 × 6.2% = $3,100
† $50,000 × 1.45% = $725

Solution—Part 2

Jan. 8	Payroll Taxes Expense	5,825.00	
	FICA—Social Security Taxes Payable		3,100.00
	FICA—Medicare Taxes Payable		725.00
	State Unemployment Taxes Payable*		1,700.00
	Federal Unemployment Taxes Payable†		300.00
	Record employer payroll taxes.		

Do More: QS 9-5, QS 9-6, E 9-5, E 9-6, E 9-7, E 9-8, E 9-9

* $50,000 × 3.4% = $1,700
† $50,000 × 0.6% = $300

ESTIMATED LIABILITIES

P4
Account for estimated liabilities, including warranties and bonuses.

An **estimated liability** is a known obligation that is of an uncertain amount but that can be reasonably estimated. Common examples are employee benefits such as pensions, health care, and vacation pay, and warranties offered by a seller. We discuss each of these in this section. Other examples of estimated liabilities include property taxes and certain contracts to provide future services.

Health and Pension Benefits

Many companies provide **employee benefits** beyond salaries and wages. An employer often pays all or part of medical, dental, life, and disability insurance. Many employers also contribute to *pension plans,* which are agreements by employers to provide benefits (payments) to employees after retirement. Many companies also provide medical care and insurance benefits to their retirees. When payroll taxes and charges for employee benefits are totaled, payroll cost often exceeds employees' gross earnings by 25% or more.

To illustrate, assume that an employer agrees to (1) pay an amount for medical insurance equal to $8,000 and (2) contribute an additional 10% of the employees' $120,000 gross salaries to a retirement program. The entry to record these accrued benefits is

Assets = Liabilities + Equity
+8,000   −20,000
+12,000

Dec. 31	Employee Benefits Expense.......................	20,000	
	Employee Medical Insurance Payable		8,000
	Employee Retirement Program Payable		12,000
	Record costs of employee benefits.		

 Decision Insight

Win-Win   Baseball was the first pro sport to set up a pension, originally up to $100 per month depending on years played. Many former players now take home six-figure pensions. Cal Ripken Jr.'s pension when he reaches 62 is estimated at $160,000 per year (he played 21 seasons). The requirement is only 43 games for a full pension and just one game for full medical benefits for life. ■

Focus on Sport/Getty Images

Vacation Benefits

Many employers offer paid vacation benefits, also called *paid absences* or *compensated absences.* To illustrate, assume that salaried employees earn 2 weeks' vacation per year. This benefit increases employers' payroll expenses because employees are paid for 52 weeks but work for only 50 weeks. Total annual salary is the same, but the cost per week worked is greater than the amount paid per week. For example, if an employee is paid $20,800 for 52 weeks but works only 50 weeks, the total weekly expense to the employer is $416 ($20,800/50 weeks) instead of the $400 cash paid weekly to the employee ($20,800/52 weeks). The $16 difference between these two amounts is recorded weekly as follows:

Vacation Benefits Expense	16	
Vacation Benefits Payable		16
Record vacation benefits accrued.		

Assets = Liabilities + Equity
　　　　　+16　　　−16

Vacation Benefits Expense is an operating expense, and Vacation Benefits Payable is a current liability. When the employee takes, say, a one-week vacation, the employer reduces (debits) the Vacation Benefits Payable and credits Cash (with no other expense recorded) for the employer's $416 total weekly expense.

Vacation Benefits Payable.........................	416	
Cash		416
Record vacation benefits taken.		

Bonus Plans

Many companies offer bonuses to employees, and many of the bonuses depend on net income. To illustrate, assume that an employer offers a bonus to its employees equal to 5% of the company's annual net income (to be equally shared by all). The company's expected annual *pre-bonus* net income is $210,000. The year-end adjusting entry to record this $10,000 bonus is

Dec. 31	Employee Bonus Expense*	10,000	
	Bonus Payable		10,000
	Record expected bonus costs.		

Assets = Liabilities + Equity
　　　　　+10,000　−10,000

* Bonus Expense (B) equals 5% of net income, where net income equals $210,000 minus the bonus; the bonus is computed as:

$$B = 0.05 (\$210,000 - B)$$
$$B = \$10,500 - 0.05B$$
$$1.05B = \$10,500$$
$$\mathbf{B = \$10,500/1.05 = \$10,000}$$

When the bonus is paid, Bonus Payable is debited and Cash is credited for $10,000.

Warranty Liabilities

A **warranty** is a seller's obligation to replace or correct a product (or service) that fails to perform as expected within a specified period. Most new cars, for instance, are sold with a warranty covering parts for a specified period of time. **Ford Motor Company** reported nearly $11 billion in "dealer and dealers' customer allowances and claims" in its annual report. To comply with the *full disclosure* and *matching principles,* the seller reports the expected warranty expense in the period when revenue from the sale of the product or service is reported. The seller reports this warranty obligation as a liability, although the existence, amount, payee, and date of future sacrifices are uncertain. This is because such warranty costs are probable and the amount can be estimated using, for instance, past experience with warranties.

Point: Fiat, maker of the Ferrari, recently reported about $5 billion in warranty claims.

To illustrate, a dealer sells a used car for $16,000 on December 1, 2016, with a one-year or 12,000-mile warranty covering parts. This dealer's experience shows that warranty expense averages about 4% of a car's selling price, or $640 in this case ($16,000 × 4%). The dealer records the estimated expense and liability related to this sale with this entry:

2016			
Dec. 1	Warranty Expense	640	
	Estimated Warranty Liability		640
	Record estimated warranty expense.		

Assets = Liabilities + Equity
　　　　　+640　　　−640

This entry alternatively could be made as part of end-of-period adjustments. Either way, the estimated warranty expense is reported on the 2016 income statement and the warranty liability on the 2016 balance sheet. To further extend this example, suppose the customer returns the car for warranty repairs on January 9, 2017. The dealer performs this work by

Point: Recognition of warranty liabilities is necessary to comply with the expense recognition (matching) and full disclosure principles.

replacing parts costing $200. The entry to record partial settlement of the estimated warranty liability is

Assets = Liabilities + Equity
−200   −200

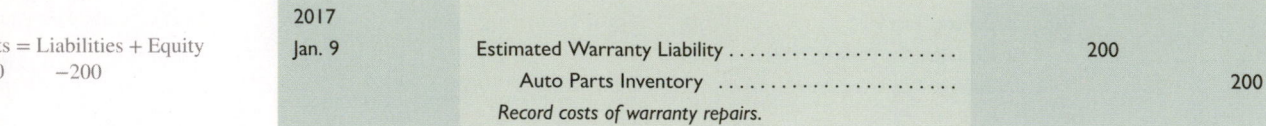

2017			
Jan. 9	Estimated Warranty Liability	200	
	Auto Parts Inventory		200
	Record costs of warranty repairs.		

Point: Both U.S. GAAP and IFRS account for restructuring costs in a manner similar to accounting for warranties.

This entry reduces the balance of the estimated warranty liability. Warranty expense was previously recorded in 2016, the year the car was sold with the warranty. Finally, what happens if total warranty expenses are more or less than the estimated 4%, or $640? The answer is that management should monitor actual warranty expenses to see whether the 4% rate is accurate. If experience reveals a large difference from the estimate, the rate for current and future sales should be changed. Differences are expected, but they should be small.

Decision Insight

Turn a Profit When we purchase a new laptop at **Best Buy**, a sales clerk commonly asks: *"Do you want the Geek Squad Protection Plan?"* Best Buy earns about a 60% profit margin on such warranty contracts, and those contracts are a large part of its profit—see table here (*BusinessWeek*). ■

Warranty contracts as a percentage of sales	4%
Warranty contracts as a percentage of operating profit	45%
Profit margin on warranty contracts	60%

Multi-Period Estimated Liabilities

Estimated liabilities can be both current and long term. For example, pension liabilities to employees are long term to workers who will not retire within the next period. For employees who are retired or will retire within the next period, a portion of pension liabilities is current. Other examples include employee health benefits and warranties. Specifically, many warranties are for 30 or 60 days in length. Estimated costs under these warranties are properly reported in current liabilities. Many other automobile warranties are for three years or 36,000 miles. A portion of these warranties is reported as long term.

CONTINGENT LIABILITIES

C3
_____
Explain how to account for contingent liabilities.

A **contingent liability** is a potential obligation that depends on a future event arising from a past transaction or event. An example is a pending lawsuit. Here, a past transaction or event leads to a lawsuit whose financial outcome depends on the result of the suit. Future payment of a contingent liability depends on whether an uncertain future event occurs.

Accounting for Contingent Liabilities

Accounting for contingent liabilities depends on the likelihood that a future event will occur and the ability to estimate the future amount owed if this event occurs. Three different possibilities are identified in the following chart: record liability, disclose in notes, or no disclosure.

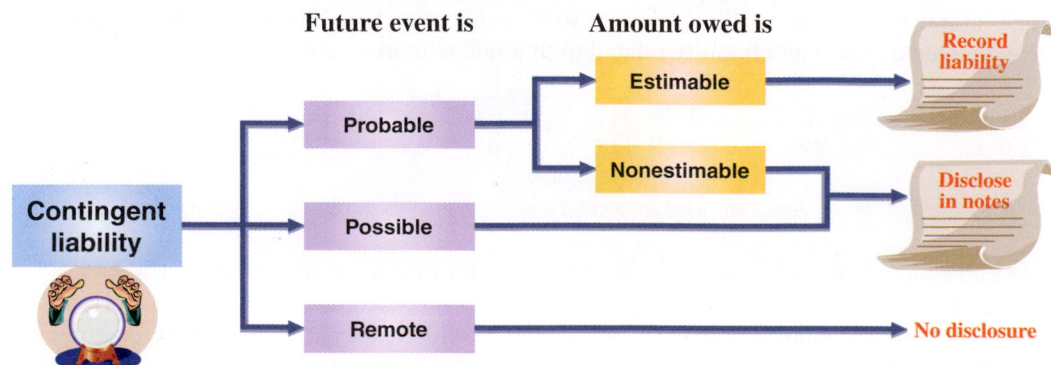

The conditions that determine each of these three possibilities follow:

1. The future event is *probable* (likely) and the amount owed can be *reasonably estimated.* We then record this amount as a liability. Examples are the estimated liabilities described earlier such as warranties, vacation pay, and income taxes.
2. The future event is *reasonably possible* (could occur). We disclose information about this type of contingent liability in notes to the financial statements.
3. The future event is *remote* (unlikely). We do not record or disclose information on remote contingent liabilities.

Point: A contingency is an *if.* Namely, *if* a future event occurs, then financial consequences are likely for the entity.

Reasonably Possible Contingent Liabilities

This section identifies and discusses contingent liabilities that commonly fall in the second category—when the future event is reasonably possible. Disclosing information about contingencies in this category is motivated by the *full disclosure principle,* which requires information relevant to decision makers be reported and not ignored.

Potential Legal Claims   Many companies are sued or at risk of being sued. The accounting issue is whether the defendant should recognize a liability on its balance sheet or disclose a contingent liability in its notes while a lawsuit is outstanding and not yet settled. The answer is that a potential claim is recorded in the accounts *only* if payment for damages is probable and the amount can be reasonably estimated. If the potential claim cannot be reasonably estimated or is less than probable but reasonably possible, it is disclosed. **Ford Motor Company**, for example, includes the following note in its annual report: "Various legal actions, proceedings, and claims are pending . . . arising out of alleged defects in our products."

Point: A sale of a note receivable "with recourse" is a contingent liability. It becomes a liability if the original signer of the note fails to pay it at maturity.

Debt Guarantees   Sometimes a company guarantees the payment of debt owed by a supplier, customer, or another company. The guarantor usually discloses the guarantee in its financial statement notes as a contingent liability. If it is probable that the debtor will default, the guarantor needs to record and report the guarantee in its financial statements as a liability. The **Boston Celtics** report a unique guarantee when it comes to coaches and players: "Certain of the contracts provide for guaranteed payments which must be paid even if the employee [player] is injured or terminated."

Other Contingencies   Other examples of contingencies include environmental damages, possible tax assessments, insurance losses, and government investigations. **Chevron**, for instance, reports that it "is subject to loss contingencies pursuant to laws, regulations, private claims and legal proceedings related to environmental matters that are subject to legal settlements or that in the future may require the company to take action to correct or ameliorate the effects on the environment of prior release of chemicals or petroleum substances. . . . Such contingencies may exist for various sites. . . . These future costs are not fully determinable." Many of Chevron's contingencies are revealed only in notes.

Point: Auditors and managers often have different views about whether a contingency is recorded, disclosed, or omitted.

🟨 **Decision Insight**

At What Price?   What's it worth to see from one side of the Grand Canyon to the other? What's the cost when Gulf Coast beaches are closed due to an oil well disaster? A method to measure environmental liabilities is *contingent valuation,* by which people answer such questions. Regulators use their answers to levy fines and assess punitive damages. ■

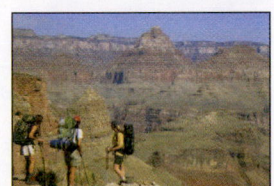

John Burcham/National Geographic/Getty Images

Uncertainties That Are Not Contingencies

All organizations face uncertainties from future events such as natural disasters and the development of new competing products or services. These uncertainties are not contingent liabilities because they are future events *not* arising from past transactions. Accordingly, they are not disclosed.

9-3

Estimated and
Contingent Liabilities

P4   C3

Part 1. A company's salaried employees earn two weeks' vacation per year. It pays $208,000 in total employee salaries for 52 weeks, but its employees work only 50 weeks. This means its total weekly expense is $4,160 ($208,000/50 weeks) instead of the $4,000 cash paid weekly to the employees ($208,000/52 weeks). Record the company's regular weekly vacation benefits expense.

Part 2. For the current year ended December 31, a company has implemented an employee bonus program equal to 5% of its net income, which employees share equally. Its net income (pre-bonus) is expected to be $840,000, and bonus expense is deducted in computing net income. (a) Compute the bonus payable to the employees at year-end using the method described in the chapter and round to the nearest dollar; then prepare the journal entry at December 31 of the current year to record the bonus due. (b) Prepare the journal entry at January 20 of the following year to record payment of that bonus to employees.

Part 3. On June 11 of the current year, a retailer sells a trimmer for $400 with a one-year warranty that covers parts. Warranty expense is estimated at 5% of sales. On March 24 of the next year, the trimmer is brought in for repairs covered under the warranty requiring $15 in materials taken from the Repair Parts Inventory. Prepare the (a) June 11 entry to record the trimmer sale—ignore the cost of sales part of this sales entry—and (b) March 24 entry to record warranty repairs.

Part 4. The following legal claims exist for a company. Identify the accounting treatment for each claim as either (i) a liability that is recorded or (ii) an item described in notes to its financial statements. If an item is to be recorded, prepare the entry (date any entry Dec. 31).

a. The company (defendant) estimates that a pending lawsuit could result in damages of $500,000; it is reasonably possible that the plaintiff will win the case.

b. The company faces a probable loss on a pending lawsuit; the amount is not reasonably estimable.

c. The company estimates environmental damages in a pending case at $900,000 with a high probability of losing the case.

Solution—Part 1

Weekly	Vacation Benefits Expense*	160	
	Vacation Benefits Payable		160
	*Record vacation benefits accrued. *$4,160 − $4,000*		

Solution—Part 2

a. $\text{B} = 0.05(\$840,000 - \text{B})$

$\text{B} = \$42,000 - 0.05\text{B}$

$1.05\text{B} = \$42,000$

$\text{B} = \underline{\$40,000}$

Dec. 31	Employee Bonus Expense	40,000	
	Bonus Payable		40,000
	Record expected bonus costs.		

b.

Jan. 20	Bonus Payable	40,000	
	Cash		40,000
	Record payment of bonus.		

Solution—Part 3

June 11	Cash	400	
	Sales		400
	Record trimmer sales.		
June 11	Warranty Expense	20	
	Estimated Warranty Liability		20
	Record estimated warranty expense ($400 × 5%).		
Mar. 24	Estimated Warranty Liability	15	
	Repair Parts Inventory........................		15
	Record cost of warranty repairs.		

Solution—Part 4

a. (ii); reason—is reasonably estimated but not a probable loss.

b. (ii); reason—probable loss but cannot be reasonably estimated.

c. (i); reason—can be reasonably estimated and loss is probable. The journal entry follows:

Dec. 31	Environmental Contingent Expense	900,000	
	Environmental Contingent Liability		900,000
	Record environmental contingent liability.		

> Do More: QS 9-7, QS 9-8, QS 9-9, QS 9-10, E 9-10, E 9-11, E 9-12, E 9-13

GLOBAL VIEW

This section discusses similarities and differences between U.S. GAAP and IFRS in accounting and reporting for current liabilities.

Characteristics of Liabilities   The definitions and characteristics of current liabilities are broadly similar for both U.S. GAAP and IFRS. Although differences exist, the similarities vastly outweigh any differences. Remembering that "provision" is typically used under IFRS to refer to what is titled "liability" under U.S. GAAP, **Nokia** describes its recognition of liabilities as follows:

> Provisions are recognized when the Group has a present legal or constructive obligation as a result of past events, it is probable that an outflow of resources will be required to settle the obligation and a reliable estimate of the amount can be made.

Known (Determinable) Liabilities   When there is little uncertainty surrounding current liabilities, both U.S. GAAP and IFRS require companies to record them in a similar manner. This correspondence in accounting applies to accounts payable, sales taxes payable, unearned revenues, short-term notes, and payroll liabilities. Of course, tax regulatory systems of countries are different, which implies use of different rates and levels. Still, the basic approach is the same.

Estimated Liabilities   When there is a known current obligation that involves an uncertain amount, but one that can be reasonably estimated, both U.S. GAAP and IFRS require similar treatment. This treatment extends to many obligations such as those arising from vacations, warranties, restructurings, pensions, and health care. Both accounting systems require that companies record estimated expenses related to these obligations when they can reasonably estimate the amounts. **Nokia** reports wages, salaries, and bonuses of €3,215 million. It also reports pension expenses of €207 million.

Sustainability and Accounting   **Noodles & Company**, the focus of this chapter's opener, implements a strategy that is geared toward both sustainability and management of costs. Noodles & Company aims to use a relatively small space to prepare food and serve customers. Its annual report states that its "restaurants are typically 2,600 to 2,700 square feet." Further, it often utilizes space outside of its restaurants for customers to sit and enjoy their meals. Smaller restaurants require much less energy to heat, cool, and provide light. Noodles & Company also strategically locates many of its restaurants in urban areas. This encourages customers to walk to its restaurants rather than drive, resulting in less carbon emissions and a more sustainable planet.

Aaron Ontiveroz/The Denver Post via Getty Images

Times Interest Earned Ratio **Decision Analysis**

A company incurs interest expense on many of its current and long-term liabilities. Examples extend from its short-term notes and the current portion of long-term liabilities to its long-term notes and bonds. Interest expense is often viewed as a *fixed expense* because the amount of these liabilities is likely to remain in one form or another for a substantial period of time. This means that the amount of interest is unlikely to vary due to changes in sales or other operating activities. While fixed expenses can be

A1
Compute the times interest earned ratio and use it to analyze liabilities.

advantageous when a company is growing, they create risk. This risk stems from the possibility that a company might be unable to pay fixed expenses if sales decline. To illustrate, consider Diego Co.'s results for 2016 and two possible outcomes for year 2017 in Exhibit 9.5.

EXHIBIT 9.5

Actual and Projected Results

| $ millions | 2016 | 2017 Projections | |
		Sales Increase	Sales Decrease
Sales	$600	$900	$300
Expenses (75% of sales)	450	675	225
Income before interest..........	150	225	75
Interest expense (fixed)	60	60	60
Net income	$ 90	$165	$ 15

Expenses excluding interest are at, and expected to remain at, 75% of sales. Expenses such as these that change with sales volume are called *variable expenses.* However, interest expense is at, and expected to remain at, $60 million per year due to its fixed nature.

The middle numerical column of Exhibit 9.5 shows that Diego's income increases by 83% to $165 million if sales increase by 50% to $900 million. In contrast, the far right column shows that income decreases by 83% if sales decline by 50%. These results reveal that the amount of fixed interest expense affects a company's risk of its ability to pay interest, which is numerically reflected in the **times interest earned** ratio in Exhibit 9.6.

EXHIBIT 9.6

Times Interest Earned

$$\text{Times interest earned} = \frac{\text{Income before interest expense and income taxes}}{\text{Interest expense}}$$

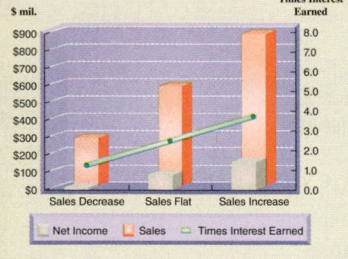

For 2016, Diego's times interest earned is computed as $150 mil./$60 mil., or 2.5 times. This ratio suggests that Diego faces low to moderate risk because its sales must decline sharply before it would be unable to cover its interest expenses. (Diego is an LLC and does not pay income taxes.)

Experience shows that when times interest earned falls below 1.5 to 2.0 and remains at that level or lower for several periods, the default rate on liabilities increases sharply. This reflects increased risk for companies and their creditors. We also must interpret the times interest earned ratio in light of information about the variability of a company's income before interest. If income is stable from year to year or if it is growing, the company can afford to take on added risk by borrowing. If its income greatly varies from year to year, fixed interest expense can increase the risk that it will not earn enough income to pay interest.

■ **Decision Maker**

Entrepreneur You wish to invest in a franchise for either one of two national chains. Each franchise has an expected annual net income *after* interest and taxes of $100,000. Net income for the first franchise includes a regular fixed interest charge of $200,000. The fixed interest charge for the second franchise is $40,000. Which franchise is riskier to you if sales forecasts are not met? Does your decision change if the first franchise has more variability in its income stream? ■ [Answers follow the chapter's Summary.]

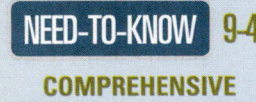

COMPREHENSIVE

The following transactions and events took place at Kern Company during its recent calendar-year reporting period (Kern does *not* use reversing entries).

a. In September 2016, Kern sold $140,000 of merchandise covered by a 180-day warranty. Prior experience shows that costs of the warranty equal 5% of sales. Compute September's warranty expense and prepare the adjusting journal entry for the warranty liability as recorded at September 30. Also prepare the journal entry on October 8 to record a $300 cash expenditure to provide warranty service on an item sold in September.

b. On October 12, 2016, Kern arranged with a supplier to replace Kern's overdue $10,000 account payable by paying $2,500 cash and signing a note for the remainder. The note matures in 90 days and has a 12% interest rate. Prepare the entries recorded on October 12, December 31, and January 10, 2017, related to this transaction.

c. In late December, Kern learns it is facing a product liability suit filed by an unhappy customer. Kern's lawyer advises that although it will probably suffer a loss from the lawsuit, it is not possible to estimate the amount of damages at this time.

d. Sally Bline works for Kern. For the pay period ended November 30, her gross earnings are $3,000. Bline has $800 deducted for federal income taxes and $200 for state income taxes from each paycheck. Additionally, a $35 premium for her health care insurance and a $10 donation to the United Way are deducted. Bline pays FICA Social Security taxes at a rate of 6.2% and FICA Medicare taxes at a rate of 1.45%. She has not earned enough this year to be exempt from any FICA taxes. Journalize the accrual of salaries expense of Bline's wages by Kern.

e. On November 1, Kern borrows $5,000 cash from a bank in return for a 60-day, 12%, $5,000 note. Record the note's issuance on November 1 and its repayment with interest on December 31.

f.[B] *(Part f covers Appendix 9B.)* Kern has estimated and recorded its quarterly income tax payments. In reviewing its year-end tax adjustments, it identifies an additional $5,000 of income tax expense that should be recorded. A portion of this additional expense, $1,000, is deferred to future years. Record this year-end income taxes expense adjusting entry.

g. For this calendar year, Kern's net income is $1,000,000, its interest expense is $275,000, and its income taxes expense is $225,000. Compute Kern's times interest earned ratio.

PLANNING THE SOLUTION

- For *a,* compute the warranty expense for September and record it with an estimated liability. Record the October expenditure as a decrease in the liability.
- For *b,* eliminate the liability for the account payable and create the liability for the note payable. Compute interest expense for the 80 days that the note is outstanding in 2016 and record it as an additional liability. Record the payment of the note, being sure to include the interest for the 10 days in 2017.
- For *c,* decide whether the company's contingent liability needs to be disclosed or accrued (recorded) according to the two necessary criteria: probable loss and reasonably estimable.
- For *d,* set up payable accounts for all items in Bline's paycheck that require deductions. After deducting all necessary items, credit the remaining amount to Salaries Payable.
- For *e,* record the issuance of the note. Compute 60 days' interest due using the 360-day convention in the interest formula.
- For *f,* determine how much of the income taxes expense is payable in the current year and how much needs to be deferred.
- For *g,* apply and compute times interest earned.

SOLUTION

a. Warranty expense = 5% × $140,000 = $7,000

Sept. 30	Warranty Expense	7,000	
	Estimated Warranty Liability		7,000
	Record warranty expense for month.		
Oct. 8	Estimated Warranty Liability	300	
	Cash		300
	Record cost of warranty service.		

b. Interest expense for 2016 = 12% × $7,500 × 80/360 = $200
Interest expense for 2017 = 12% × $7,500 × 10/360 = $25

Oct. 12	Accounts Payable	10,000	
	Notes Payable.		7,500
	Cash		2,500
	Paid $2,500 cash and gave a 90-day, 12% note		
	to extend due date on the account.		
Dec. 31	Interest Expense.	200	
	Interest Payable		200
	Accrue interest on note payable.		
Jan. 10	Interest Expense.	25	
	Interest Payable	200	
	Notes Payable	7,500	
	Cash		7,725
	Paid note with interest, including accrued interest payable.		

c. Disclose the pending lawsuit in the financial statement notes. Although the loss is probable, no liability can be accrued since the loss cannot be reasonably estimated.

d.

Nov. 30	Salaries Expense...............................	3,000.00	
	FICA—Social Security Taxes Payable (6.2%)		186.00
	FICA—Medicare Taxes Payable (1.45%)		43.50
	Employee Federal Income Taxes Payable		800.00
	Employee State Income Taxes Payable		200.00
	Employee Medical Insurance Payable		35.00
	Employee United Way Payable		10.00
	Salaries Payable		1,725.50
	Record Bline's accrued payroll.		

e.

Nov. 1	Cash	5,000	
	Notes Payable.............................		5,000
	Borrowed cash with a 60-day, 12% note.		

When the note and interest are paid 60 days later, Kern Company records this entry:

Dec. 31	Notes Payable	5,000	
	Interest Expense	100	
	Cash		5,100
	Paid note with interest ($5,000 × 12% × 60/360).		

f.

Dec. 31	Income Taxes Expense	5,000	
	Income Taxes Payable		4,000
	Deferred Income Tax Liability		1,000
	Record added income taxes expense and the		
	deferred tax liability.		

g. Times interest earned $= \dfrac{\$1,000,000 + \$275,000 + \$225,000}{\$275,000} = \underline{\underline{5.45 \text{ times}}}$

APPENDIX

9A

Payroll Reports, Records, and Procedures

P5

Identify and describe the details of payroll reports, records, and procedures.

Understanding payroll procedures and keeping adequate payroll reports and records are essential to a company's success. This appendix focuses on payroll accounting and its reports, records, and procedures.

Payroll Reports   Most employees and employers are required to pay local, state, and federal payroll taxes. Payroll expenses involve liabilities to individual employees, to federal and state governments, and to other organizations such as insurance companies. Beyond paying these liabilities, employers are required to prepare and submit reports explaining how they computed these payments.

Reporting FICA Taxes and Income Taxes   The Federal Insurance Contributions Act (FICA) requires each employer to file an Internal Revenue Service (IRS) **Form 941,** the *Employer's Quarterly Federal Tax Return,* within one month after the end of each calendar quarter. A sample Form 941 is shown in Exhibit 9A.1 for Phoenix Sales & Service, a landscape design company. Accounting information and software are helpful in tracking payroll transactions and reporting the accumulated information on Form 941. Specifically, the employer reports total wages subject to income tax withholding on line 2 of Form 941. (For simplicity, this appendix uses *wages* to refer to both wages and salaries.) The income tax withheld is reported on line 3. The combined amount of employee and employer FICA (Social Security) taxes for Phoenix Sales & Service is

Form **941**

Employer's QUARTERLY Federal Tax Return

Department of the Treasury — Internal Revenue Service

(EIN)
Employer identification number 8 6 – 3 2 1 4 5 8 7

Name (not your trade name) Phoenix Sales & Service

Trade name (if any)

Address 1214 Mill Road
Number Street Suite or room number

Phoenix AZ 85621
City State ZIP code

Report for this Quarter ...
(Check one.)

☐ 1: January, February, March
☐ 2: April, May, June
☐ 3: July, August, September
☒ 4: October, November, December

Part 1: Answer these questions for this quarter.

1 Number of employees who received wages, tips, or other compensation for the pay period including: *Mar. 12* (Quarter 1), *June 12* (Quarter 2), *Sept. 12* (Quarter 3), *Dec. 12* (Quarter 4)	1	2
2 Wages, tips, and other compensation	2	36,599.00
3 Total income tax withheld from wages, tips, and other compensation	3	3,056.47

4 If no wages, tips, and other compensation are subject to social security or Medicare tax . ☐ Check and go to line 6.

5 Taxable social security and Medicare wages and tips:

	Column 1		Column 2
5a Taxable social security wages	36,599.00	× .124 =	4,538.28
5b Taxable social security tips	.	× .124 =	.
5c Taxable Medicare wages & tips	36,599.00	× .029 =	1,061.37

5d Total social security and Medicare taxes (*Column 2*, lines 5a + 5b + 5c = line 5d)	5d	5,599.65
6 Total taxes before adjustments (lines 3 + 5d = line 6)	6	8,656.12

7 **TAX ADJUSTMENTS** (Read the instructions for line 7 before completing lines 7a through 7h.):

7a Current quarter's fractions of cents		.
7b Current quarter's sick pay		.
7c Current quarter's adjustments for tips and group-term life insurance		.
7d Current year's income tax withholding (attach Form 941c)		.
7e Prior quarters' social security and Medicare taxes (attach Form 941c)		.
7f Special additions to federal income tax (attach Form 941c)		.
7g Special additions to social security and Medicare (attach Form 941c)		.
7h **TOTAL ADJUSTMENTS** (Combine all amounts: lines 7a through 7g.)	7h	0.00
8 Total taxes after adjustments (Combine lines 6 and 7h.)	8	8,656.12
9 Advance earned income credit (EIC) payments made to employees	9	.
10 Total taxes after adjustment for advance EIC (lines 8 – line 9 = line 10)	10	8,656.12
11 Total deposits for this quarter, including overpayment applied from a prior quarter	11	8,656.12
12 Balance due (If line 10 is more than line 11, write the difference here.) Make checks payable to *United States Treasury*.	12	0.00
13 Overpayment (If line 11 is more than line 10, write the difference here.)		0.00 Check one ☐ Apply to next return. ☐ Send a refund.

Part 2: Tell us about your deposit schedule and tax liability for this quarter.

If you are unsure about whether you are a monthly schedule depositor or a semiweekly schedule depositor, see *Pub. 15 (Circular E)*, section 11.

14 **A Z** Write the state abbreviation for the state where you made your deposits OR write "MU" if you made your deposits in *multiple* states.

15 Check one: ☐ Line 10 is less than $2,500. Go to Part 3.

☒ You were a monthly schedule depositor for the entire quarter. Fill out your tax liability for each month. Then go to Part 3.

Tax liability:	Month 1	3,079.11
	Month 2	2,049.77
	Month 3	3,527.24
	Total liability for quarter	8,656.12 Total must equal line 10.

☐ You were a semiweekly schedule depositor for any part of this quarter. Fill out *Schedule B (Form 941): Report of Tax Liability for Semiweekly Schedule Depositors*, and attach it to this form.

Part 3: Tell us about your business. If a question does NOT apply to your business, leave it blank.

16 If your business has closed or you stopped paying wages . . . . ☐ Check here, and

enter the final date you paid wages / /

17 If you are a seasonal employer and you do not have to file a return for every quarter of the year . ☐ Check here.

Part 4: May we speak with your third-party designee?

Do you want to allow an employee, a paid tax preparer, or another person to discuss this return with the IRS? See the instructions for details.

☐ Yes. Designee's name

Phone ( ) – Personal Identification Number (PIN) ☐ ☐ ☐ ☐ ☐

☒ No.

Part 5: Sign here. You MUST fill out both sides of this form and SIGN it.

Under penalties of perjury, I declare that I have examined this return, including accompanying schedules and statements, and to the best of my knowledge and belief, it is true, correct, and complete.

✗ Sign your name here

Print name and title

Date / / Phone ( ) –

Point: Line 5a shows the matching nature of FICA tax as 6.2% × 2, or 12.4%; which is shown as 0.124.

Point: Auditors rely on the four 941 forms filed during a year when auditing a company's annual wages and salaries expense account.

reported on line 5a (taxable Social Security wages, $36,599 × 12.4% = $4,538.28). The 12.4% is the sum of the Social Security tax withheld, computed as 6.2% tax withheld from the employee wages for the quarter, plus the 6.2% tax levied on the employer. The combined amount of employee Medicare wages is reported on line 5c. The 2.9% is the sum of 1.45% withheld from employee wages for the quarter plus 1.45% tax levied on the employer. Total FICA taxes are reported on line 5d and are added to the total income taxes withheld of $3,056.47 to yield a total of $8,656.12. For this year, assume that income up to $118,500 is subject to Social Security tax. There is no income limit on amounts subject to Medicare tax. Congress sets rates owed for Social Security tax (and it typically changes each year).

Point: Deposits for federal payroll taxes must be made by electronic funds transfer (EFT).

Federal depository banks are authorized to accept deposits of amounts payable to the federal government. Deposit requirements depend on the amount of tax owed. For example, when the sum of FICA taxes plus the employee income taxes is less than $2,500 for a quarter, the taxes can be paid when Form 941 is filed. Companies with large payrolls are often required to pay monthly or even semiweekly.

Reporting FUTA Taxes and SUTA Taxes   An employer's federal unemployment taxes (FUTA) are reported on an annual basis by filing an *Annual Federal Unemployment Tax Return,* IRS **Form 940.** It must be mailed on or before January 31 following the end of each tax year. Ten more days are allowed if all required tax deposits are filed on a timely basis and the full amount of tax is paid on or before January 31. FUTA payments are made quarterly to a federal depository bank if the total amount due exceeds $500. If $500 or less is due, the taxes are remitted annually. Requirements for paying and reporting state unemployment taxes (SUTA) vary depending on the laws of each state. Most states require quarterly payments and reports.

Reporting Wages and Salaries   Employers are required to give each employee an annual report of his or her wages subject to FICA and federal income taxes along with the amounts of these taxes withheld. This report is called a *Wage and Tax Statement,* or **Form W-2.** It must be given to employees before January 31 following the year covered by the report. Exhibit 9A.2 shows Form W-2 for one of the employees at Phoenix Sales & Service. Copies of the W-2 Form must be sent to the Social Security Administration, where the amount of the employee's wages subject to FICA taxes and FICA taxes withheld are posted to each employee's Social Security account. These posted amounts become the basis for determining an employee's retirement and survivors' benefits. The Social Security Administration also transmits to the IRS the amount of each employee's wages subject to federal income taxes and the amount of taxes withheld.

EXHIBIT 9A.2

Form W-2

Form **W-2** Wage and Tax Statement		Department of Treasury—Internal Revenue Service
Copy 1—For State, City, or Local Tax Department		

a Control number AR101	22222	OMB No. 1545-0006	
b Employer identification number (EIN) 86-3214587		1 Wages, tips, other compensation 4,910.00	2 Federal income tax withheld 333.37
c Employer's name, address and ZIP code Phoenix Sales & Service 1214 Mill Road Phoenix, AZ 85621		3 Social security wages 4,910.00	4 Social security tax withheld 304.42
		5 Medicare wages and tips 4,910.00	6 Medicare tax withheld 71.20
		7 Social security tips	8 Allocated tips
d Employee's social security number 333-22-9999		9 Advance EIC payment	10 Dependent care benefits
e Employee's first name and initial Robert J. Last name Austin		11 Nonqualified plans	12a Code
f Employee's address and ZIP code 18 Roosevelt Blvd., Apt. C Tempe, AZ 86322		13 Statutory employee Retirement plan Third-party sick pay	12b Code
		14 Other	12c Code
			12d Code

15 State Employer's state ID number AZ 13-902319	16 State wages, tips, etc. 4,910.00	17 State income tax 26.68	18 Local wages, tips, etc.	19 Local income tax	20 Locality name

Payroll Records   Employers must keep payroll records in addition to reporting and paying taxes. These records usually include a payroll register and an individual earnings report for each employee.

	A	B	C	D	E	F	G	H	I
1					Phoenix Sales & Service				
2					Payroll Register				
3					For Week Ended Jan. 8, 2016				
4	**Employee ID**	**Gross Pay**			**FIT**	**SIT**	**FICA-SS_EE**	**FICA-Med_EE**	
5	**Employee**				**[blank]**	**[blank]**	**[blank]**	**[blank]**	
6	**SS No.**	**Pay**	**Pay**	**Gross**					**Net**
7	**Refer., Date**	**Type**	**Hours**	**Pay**	**FUTA**	**SUTA**	**FICA-SS_ER**	**FICA-Med_ER**	**Pay**
8	AR101	Regular	40.00	400.00	−28.99	−2.32	−24.80	−5.80	338.09
9	Robert Austin	Overtime	0.00	0.00					
10	333-22-9999			400.00	−2.40	−10.80	−24.80	−5.80	
11	9001, 1/8/16								
12	CJ102	Regular	40.00	560.00	−52.97	−4.24	−36.02	−8.42	479.35
13	Judy Cross	Overtime	1.00	21.00					
14	299-11-9201			581.00	−3.49	−15.69	−36.02	−8.42	
15	9002, 1/8/16								
16	DJ103	Regular	40.00	560.00	−48.33	−3.87	−37.32	−8.73	503.75
17	John Diaz	Overtime	2.00	42.00					
18	444-11-9090			602.00	−3.61	−16.25	−37.32	−8.73	
19	9003, 1/8/16								
20	KK104	Regular	40.00	560.00	−68.57	−5.49	−34.72	−8.12	443.10
21	Kay Keife	Overtime	0.00	0.00					
22	909-11-3344			560.00	−3.36	−15.12	−34.72	−8.12	
23	9004, 1/8/16								
24	ML105	Regular	40.00	560.00	−34.24	−2.74	−34.72	−8.12	480.18
25	Lee Miller	Overtime	0.00	0.00					
26	444-56-3211			560.00	−3.36	−15.12	−34.72	−8.12	
27	9005, 1/8/16								
28	SD106	Regular	40.00	560.00	−68.57	−5.49	−34.72	−8.12	443.10
29	Dale Sears	Overtime	0.00	0.00					
30	909-33-1234			560.00	−3.36	−15.12	−34.72	−8.12	
31	9006, 1/8/16								
32	Totals	Regular	240.00	3,200.00	−301.67	−24.15	−202.30	−47.31	2,687.57
33		Overtime	3.00	63.00					
34				3,263.00	−19.58	−88.10	−202.30	−47.31	
35									

Payroll Register A **payroll register** usually shows the pay period dates, hours worked, gross pay, deductions, and net pay of each employee for each pay period. Exhibit 9A.3 shows a payroll register for Phoenix Sales & Service. It is organized into nine columns:

Col. 1   Employee identification (ID); Employee name; Social Security number (SS No.); Reference (check number); and Date (date check issued)
Col. 2   Pay Type (regular and overtime)
Col. 3   Pay Hours (number of hours worked as regular and overtime)
Col. 4   Gross Pay (amount of gross pay)[2]
Col. 5   FIT (federal income taxes withheld); FUTA (federal unemployment taxes)
Col. 6   SIT (state income taxes withheld); SUTA (state unemployment taxes)
Col. 7   FICA-SS_EE (Social Security taxes withheld, employee); FICA-SS_ER (Social Security taxes, employer)
Col. 8   FICA-Med_EE (Medicare tax withheld, employee); FICA-Med_ER (Medicare tax, employer)
Col. 9   Net Pay (Gross pay less amounts withheld from employees)

Net pay for each employee is computed as gross pay minus the items on the first line of columns 5–8. The employer's payroll tax for each employee is computed as the sum of items on the third line of columns 5–8. A payroll register includes all data necessary to record payroll. In some software programs the entries to record payroll are made in a special *payroll journal*.

---

[2] The Gross Pay column shows regular hours worked on the first line multiplied by the regular pay rate—this equals regular pay. Overtime hours multiplied by the overtime premium rate equals overtime premium pay reported on the second line. If employers are engaged in interstate commerce, federal law sets a minimum overtime rate of pay to employees. For this company, workers earn 150% of their regular rate for hours in excess of 40 per week.

Payroll Check   Payment of payroll is usually done by check or electronic funds transfer. Exhibit 9A.4 shows a *payroll check* for a Phoenix employee. This check is accompanied with a detachable *statement of earnings* (at top) showing gross pay, deductions, and net pay.

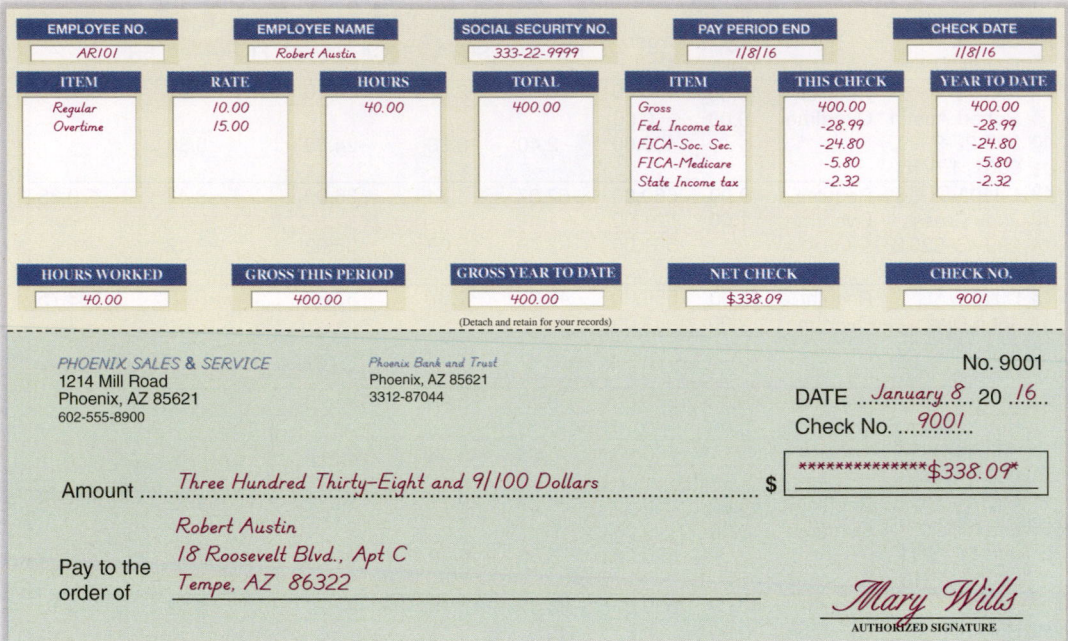

Employee Earnings Report   An **employee earnings report** is a cumulative record of an employee's hours worked, gross earnings, deductions, and net pay. Payroll information on this report is taken from the payroll register. The employee earnings report for R. Austin at Phoenix Sales & Service is shown in Exhibit 9A.5. An employee earnings report accumulates information that can show when an employee's earnings reach the tax-exempt points for FICA, FUTA, and SUTA taxes. It also gives data an employer needs to prepare Form W-2.

Payroll Procedures   Employers must be able to compute federal income tax for payroll purposes. This section explains how we compute this tax and how to use a payroll bank account.

Computing Federal Income Taxes   To compute the amount of taxes withheld from each employee's wages, we need to determine both the employee's wages earned and the employee's number of *withholding allowances*. Each employee records the number of withholding allowances claimed on a withholding allowance certificate, **Form W-4,** filed with the employer. When the number of withholding allowances increases, the amount of income taxes withheld decreases.

Employers often use a **wage bracket withholding table** similar to the one shown in Exhibit 9A.6 to compute the **federal income taxes withheld** from each employee's gross pay. The table in Exhibit 9A.6 is for a single employee paid weekly. Tables are also provided for married employees and for biweekly, semimonthly, and monthly pay periods (most payroll software includes these tables). When using a wage bracket withholding table to compute federal income tax withheld from an employee's gross wages, we need to locate an employee's wage bracket within the first two columns. We then find the amount withheld by looking in the Withholding Allowance column for that employee.

Payroll Bank Account   Companies with few employees often pay them with checks drawn on the company's regular bank account. Companies with many employees often use a special **payroll bank account** to pay employees. When this account is used, a company either (1) draws one check for total payroll on the regular bank account and deposits it in the payroll bank account or (2) executes an *electronic funds transfer* to the payroll bank account. Individual payroll checks are then drawn on this payroll bank account. Since only one check for the total payroll is drawn on the regular bank account each payday, use of a special payroll bank account helps with internal control. It also helps in reconciling the regular bank account. When companies use a payroll bank account, they usually include check numbers in the payroll register. The payroll register in Exhibit 9A.3 shows check numbers in column 1. For

	A	B	C	D	E	F	G	H
1								
2			Phoenix Sales & Service Employee Earnings Report For Month Ended Dec. 31, 2016					
3								
4	**Employee ID**		**Gross Pay**	**FIT** [blank]	**SIT** [blank]	**FICA-SS_EE** [blank]	**FICA-Med_EE** [blank]	**Net Pay**
5	**Employee**	**Date**						
6	**SS No.**	**Reference**		**FUTA**	**SUTA**	**FICA-SS_ER**	**FICA-Med_ER**	
7	Beginning	11/26/16	2,910.00	−188.42	−15.08	−180.42	−42.20	2,483.88
8	Balance for	(balance)						
9	Robert Austin			−17.46	−78.57	−180.42	−42.20	
10	AR101	12/03/16	400.00	−28.99	−2.32	−24.80	−5.80	338.09
11	Robert Austin	9049						
12	333-22-9999			−2.40	−10.80	−24.80	−5.80	
13	AR101	12/10/16	400.00	−28.99	−2.32	−24.80	−5.80	338.09
14	Robert Austin	9055						
15	333-22-9999			−2.40	−10.80	−24.80	−5.80	
16	AR101	12/17/16	400.00	−28.99	−2.32	−24.80	−5.80	338.09
17	Robert Austin	9061						
18	333-22-9999			−2.40	−10.80	−24.80	−5.80	
19	AR101	12/24/16	400.00	−28.99	−2.32	−24.80	−5.80	338.09
20	Robert Austin	9067						
21	333-22-9999			−2.40	−10.80	−24.80	−5.80	
22	AR101	12/31/16	400.00	−28.99	−2.32	−24.80	−5.80	338.09
23	Robert Austin	9073						
24	333-22-9999			−2.40	−10.80	−24.80	−5.80	
25	Total 5-wk month		2,000.00	−144.95	−11.60	−124.00	−29.00	1,690.45
26	thru 12/31/16							
27				−12.00	−54.00	−124.00	−29.00	
28	Year-to-date	12/31/16	4,910.00	−333.37	−26.68	−304.42	−71.20	4,174.33
29	Total for Robert	(balance)						
30	Austin			−29.46	−132.57	−304.42	−71.20	

EXHIBIT 9A.5

Employee Earnings Report

Point: Year-end balances agree with W-2.

instance, Check No. 9001 is issued to Robert Austin. With this information, the payroll register serves as a supplementary record of wages earned by and paid to employees.

Who Pays What Payroll Taxes and Benefits   We conclude this appendix with the following table identifying who pays which payroll taxes and which common employee benefits such as medical, disability, pension, charitable, and union costs. Who pays which employee benefits, and what portion, is subject to agreements between companies and their workers. Also, self-employed workers must pay both the employer and employee FICA taxes for Social Security and Medicare.

EXHIBIT 9A.6

Wage Bracket Withholding Table

SINGLE Persons—WEEKLY Payroll Period												
If the wages are–		And the number of withholding allowances claimed is—										
At least	But less than	0	1	2	3	4	5	6	7	8	9	10
		The amount of income tax to be withheld is—										
$600	$610	$76	$67	$58	$49	$39	$30	$21	$12	$6	$0	$0
610	620	79	69	59	50	41	32	22	13	7	1	0
620	630	81	70	61	52	42	33	24	15	8	2	0
630	640	84	72	62	53	44	35	25	16	9	3	0
640	650	86	73	64	55	45	36	27	18	10	4	0
650	660	89	75	65	56	47	38	28	19	11	5	0
660	670	91	76	67	58	48	39	30	21	12	6	0
670	680	94	78	68	59	50	41	31	22	13	7	1
680	690	96	81	70	61	51	42	33	24	14	8	2
690	700	99	83	71	62	53	44	34	25	16	9	3
700	710	101	86	73	64	54	45	35	27	17	10	4
710	720	104	88	74	65	56	47	37	28	19	11	5
720	730	106	91	76	67	57	48	39	30	20	12	6
730	740	109	93	78	68	59	50	40	31	22	13	7
740	750	111	96	80	70	60	51	42	33	23	14	8

Point: IRS *Statistics of Income Bulletin* (Winter 2012) reports the following average (effective) income tax rate for different categories of U.S. income earners:

Top 1% 24%
Top 5% 20%
Top 10% 18%
Bottom 50% 1.85%

Employer Payroll Taxes and Costs	Employee Payroll Deductions
• FICA—Social Security taxes	• FICA—Social Security taxes
• FICA—Medicare taxes	• FICA—Medicare taxes
• FUTA (federal unemployment taxes)	• Federal income taxes
• SUTA (state unemployment taxes)	• State and local income taxes
• Share of medical coverage, if any	• Share of medical coverage, if any
• Share of pension coverage, if any	• Share of pension coverage, if any
• Share of other benefits, if any	• Share of other benefits, if any

APPENDIX

9B   Corporate Income Taxes

This appendix explains current liabilities involving income taxes for corporations.

Income Tax Liabilities   Corporations are subject to income taxes and must estimate their income tax liability when preparing financial statements. Since income tax expense is created by earning income, a liability is incurred when income is earned. This tax must be paid quarterly under federal regulations. To illustrate, consider a corporation that prepares monthly financial statements. Based on its income in January 2016, this corporation estimates that it owes income taxes of $12,100. The following adjusting entry records this estimate:

Assets = Liabilities + Equity
+12,100   −12,100

Jan. 31	Income Taxes Expense	12,100	
	Income Taxes Payable		12,100
	Accrue January income taxes.		

The tax liability is recorded each month until the first quarterly payment is made. If the company's estimated taxes for this first quarter total $30,000, the entry to record its payment is

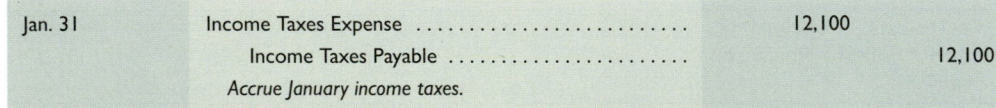

Assets = Liabilities + Equity
−30,000   −30,000

Apr. 10	Income Taxes Payable	30,000	
	Cash		30,000
	Paid estimated quarterly income taxes based on first-quarter income.		

This process of accruing and then paying estimated income taxes continues through the year. When annual financial statements are prepared at year-end, the corporation knows its actual total income and the actual amount of income taxes it must pay. This information allows it to properly record income taxes expense for the fourth quarter so that the total of the four quarters' expense amounts equals the actual taxes paid to the government.

Deferred Income Tax Liabilities   An income tax liability for corporations can arise when the amount of income before taxes that the corporation reports on its income statement is not the same as the amount of income reported on its income tax return. This difference occurs because income tax laws and GAAP measure income differently. (Differences between tax laws and GAAP arise because Congress uses tax laws to generate receipts, stimulate the economy, and influence behavior, whereas GAAP is intended to provide financial information useful for business decisions. Also, tax accounting often follows the cash basis, whereas GAAP follows the accrual basis.)

    Some differences between tax laws and GAAP are temporary. *Temporary differences* arise when the tax return and the income statement report a revenue or expense in different years. As an example, companies are often able to deduct higher amounts of depreciation in the early years of an asset's life and smaller amounts in later years for tax reporting in comparison to GAAP. This means that in the early years, depreciation for tax reporting is often more than depreciation on the income statement. In later years, depreciation for tax reporting is often less than depreciation on the income statement. When temporary differences exist between taxable income on the tax return and the income before taxes on the income statement, corporations compute income taxes expense based on the income reported on the income statement. The result is that income taxes expense reported in the income statement is often different from the amount of income taxes payable to the government. This difference is the **deferred income tax liability.**

To illustrate, assume that in recording its usual quarterly income tax payments, a corporation computes $25,000 of income taxes expense. It also determines that only $21,000 is currently due and $4,000 is deferred to future years (a timing difference). The entry to record this end-of-period adjustment is

Dec. 31	Income Taxes Expense	25,000	
	Income Taxes Payable		21,000
	Deferred Income Tax Liability		4,000
	Record tax expense and deferred tax liability.		

Assets = Liabilities + Equity
          +21,000   −25,000
          +4,000

The credit to Income Taxes Payable reflects the amount currently due to be paid. The credit to Deferred Income Tax Liability reflects tax payments deferred until future years when the temporary difference reverses.

Temporary differences also can cause a company to pay income taxes *before* they are reported on the income statement as expense. If so, the company reports a *Deferred Income Tax Asset* on its balance sheet.

Summary

C1 **Describe current and long-term liabilities and their characteristics.** Liabilities are probable future payments of assets or services that past transactions or events obligate an entity to make. Current liabilities are due within one year or the operating cycle, whichever is longer. All other liabilities are long term.

C2 **Identify and describe known current liabilities.** Known (determinable) current liabilities are set by agreements or laws and are measurable with little uncertainty. They include accounts payable, sales taxes payable, unearned revenues, notes payable, payroll liabilities, and the current portion of long-term debt.

C3 **Explain how to account for contingent liabilities.** If an uncertain future payment depends on a probable future event and the amount can be reasonably estimated, the payment is recorded as a liability. The uncertain future payment is reported as a contingent liability (in the notes) if (*a*) the future event is reasonably possible but not probable or (*b*) the event is probable but the payment amount cannot be reasonably estimated.

A1 **Compute the times interest earned ratio and use it to analyze liabilities.** Times interest earned is computed by dividing a company's net income before interest expense and income taxes by the amount of interest expense. The times interest earned ratio reflects a company's ability to pay interest obligations.

P1 **Prepare entries to account for short-term notes payable.** Short-term notes payable are current liabilities; most bear interest. When a short-term note's face value equals the amount borrowed, it identifies a rate of interest to be paid at maturity.

P2 **Compute and record *employee* payroll deductions and liabilities.** Employee payroll deductions include FICA taxes, income taxes, and voluntary deductions such as for pensions and charities. They make up the difference between gross and net pay.

P3 **Compute and record *employer* payroll expenses and liabilities.** An employer's payroll expenses include employees' gross earnings, any employee benefits, and the payroll taxes levied on the employer. Payroll liabilities include employees' net pay amounts, withholdings from employee wages, any employer-promised benefits, and the employer's payroll taxes.

P4 **Account for estimated liabilities, including warranties and bonuses.** Liabilities for health and pension benefits, warranties, and bonuses are recorded with estimated amounts. These items are recognized as expenses when incurred and matched with revenues generated.

P5^A **Identify and describe the details of payroll reports, records, and procedures.** Employers report FICA taxes and federal income tax withholdings using Form 941. FUTA taxes are reported on Form 940. Earnings and deductions are reported to each employee and the federal government on Form W-2. An employer's payroll records often include a payroll register for each pay period, payroll checks and statements of earnings, and individual employee earnings reports.

Guidance Answers to Decision Maker and Decision Ethics

Web Designer   You need to be concerned about being an accomplice to unlawful payroll activities. Not paying federal and state taxes on wages earned is illegal and unethical. Such payments also will not provide the employee with Social Security and some Medicare credits. The best course of action is to request payment by check. If this fails to change the owner's payment practices, you must consider quitting this job.

Entrepreneur   Risk is partly reflected by the times interest earned ratio. This ratio for the first franchise is 1.5 [($100,000 + $200,000)/$200,000], whereas the ratio for the second franchise is 3.5 [($100,000 + $40,000)/$40,000]. This analysis shows that the first franchise is more at risk of incurring a loss if its sales decline. The second question asks about variability of income. If income greatly varies, this increases the risk an owner will not earn sufficient income to cover interest. Since the first franchise has the greater variability, it is a riskier investment.

Key Terms

Contingent liability	Federal Insurance Contributions Act (FICA) taxes	Merit rating
Current liabilities	Federal Unemployment Tax Act (FUTA)	Net pay
Current portion of long-term debt	Form 940	Payroll bank account
Deferred income tax liability	Form 941	Payroll deductions
Employee benefits	Form W-2	Payroll register
Employee earnings report	Form W-4	Short-term note payable
Estimated liability	Gross pay	State Unemployment Tax Act (SUTA)
Federal depository bank	Known liabilities	Times interest earned
Federal income taxes withheld	Long-term liabilities	Wage bracket withholding table
		Warranty

Multiple Choice Quiz   Answers at end of chapter

1. On December 1, a company signed a $6,000, 90-day, 5% note payable, with principal plus interest due on March 1 of the following year. What amount of interest expense should be accrued at December 31 on the note?
   a. $300   **c.** $100   **e.** $0
   b. $25   **d.** $75

2. An employee earned $50,000 during the year. FICA tax for Social Security is 6.2% and FICA tax for Medicare is 1.45%. The employer's share of FICA taxes is
   a. Zero, since the employee's pay exceeds the FICA limit.
   b. Zero, since FICA is not an employer tax.
   c. $3,100
   d. $725
   e. $3,825

3. Assume the FUTA tax rate is 0.6% and the SUTA tax rate is 5.4%. Both taxes are applied to the first $7,000 of an employee's pay. What is the total unemployment tax an employer must pay on an employee's annual wages of $40,000?
   a. $2,400
   b. $420

   c. $42
   d. $378
   e. Zero; the employee's wages exceed the $7,000 maximum.

4. A company sells big-screen televisions for $3,000 each. Each television has a two-year warranty that covers the replacement of defective parts. It is estimated that 1% of all televisions sold will be returned under warranty at an average cost of $250 each. During July, the company sold 10,000 big-screen televisions, and 80 were serviced under the warranty during July at a total cost of $18,000. The credit balance in the Estimated Warranty Liability account at July 1 was $26,000. What is the company's warranty expense for the month of July?
   a. $51,000   **c.** $25,000   **e.** $18,000
   b. $1,000   **d.** $33,000

5. Employees earn vacation pay at the rate of one day per month. During October, 150 employees qualify for one vacation day each. Their average daily wage is $175 per day. What is the amount of vacation benefit expense for October?
   a. $26,250   **c.** $2,100   **e.** $150
   b. $175   **d.** $63,875

A(B) *Superscript letter A (B) denotes assignments based on Appendix 9A (9B).*
🔵 Icon denotes assignments that involve decision making.

Discussion Questions

1. 🔵 What is the difference between a current and a long-term liability?
2. What is an estimated liability?
3. 🔵 What are the three important questions concerning the uncertainty of liabilities?

4. If $988 is the total of a sale that includes sales tax of 4%, what is the selling price of the item only?
5. What is the combined amount (in percent) of the employee and employer Social Security tax rate? (Assume wages do not exceed $118,500 per year.)

6. What is the current Medicare tax rate? This rate is applied to what maximum level of salary and wages?

7. Which payroll taxes are the employee's responsibility and which are the employer's responsibility?

8. What determines the amount deducted from an employee's wages for federal income taxes?

9. What is an employer's unemployment merit rating? How are these ratings assigned to employers?

10. ♟ Why are warranty liabilities usually recognized on the balance sheet as liabilities even when they are uncertain?

11. ♟ Suppose that a company has a facility located where disastrous weather conditions often occur. Should it report a probable loss from a future disaster as a liability on its balance sheet? Explain.

12.^A What is a wage bracket withholding table?

13.^A What amount of income tax is withheld from the salary of an employee who is single with two withholding allowances and earning $725 per week? What if the employee earns $625 and has no withholding allowances? (Use Exhibit 9A.6.)

14. Refer to **Apple**'s balance sheet in Appendix A. What is the amount of Apple's accounts payable as of September 27, 2014?

APPLE

15. ♟ Refer to **Google**'s balance sheet in Appendix A. What accrued expenses (liabilities) does Google report at December 31, 2014?

GOOGLE

16. ♟ Refer to **Samsung**'s balance sheet in Appendix A. List Samsung's current liabilities as of December 31, 2014.

Samsung

17. ♟ Refer to **Samsung**'s recent balance sheet in Appendix A. What current liabilities related to income taxes are on its balance sheet? Explain the meaning of each income tax account identified.

Samsung

▀ connect

Which of the following items are normally classified as current liabilities for a company that has a 15-month operating cycle?

_____ **1.** Portion of long-term note due in 15 months.

_____ **2.** Note payable maturing in 2 years.

_____ **3.** Note payable due in 18 months.

_____ **4.** Note payable due in 11 months.

_____ **5.** FICA taxes payable.

_____ **6.** Salaries payable.

QUICK STUDY

QS 9-1
Classifying liabilities
C1 ♟

Dextra Computing sells merchandise for $6,000 cash on September 30 (cost of merchandise is $3,900). The sales tax law requires Dextra to collect 5% sales tax on every dollar of merchandise sold. Record the entry for the $6,000 sale and its applicable sales tax. Also record the entry that shows the remittance of the 5% tax on this sale to the state government on October 15.

QS 9-2
Accounting for sales taxes   C2

Ticketsales, Inc., receives $5,000,000 cash in advance ticket sales for a four-date tour of Bon Jovi. Record the advance ticket sales on October 31. Record the revenue earned for the first concert date of November 5, assuming it represents one-fourth of the advance ticket sales.

QS 9-3
Unearned revenue   C2

On November 7, 2016, Mura Company borrows $160,000 cash by signing a 90-day, 8% note payable with a face value of $160,000. (1) Compute the accrued interest payable on December 31, 2016; (2) prepare the journal entry to record the accrued interest expense at December 31, 2016; and (3) prepare the journal entry to record payment of the note at maturity.

QS 9-4
Interest-bearing note transactions   P1

On January 15, the end of the first biweekly pay period of the year, North Company's payroll register showed that its employees earned $35,000 of sales salaries. Withholdings from the employees' salaries include FICA Social Security taxes at the rate of 6.2%, FICA Medicare taxes at the rate of 1.45%, $6,500 of federal income taxes, $772.50 of medical insurance deductions, and $120 of union dues. No employee earned more than $7,000 in this first period. Prepare the journal entry to record North Company's January 15 (employee) payroll expenses and liabilities. (Round amounts to cents.)

QS 9-5
Recording employee payroll taxes
P2

Schmoldt Co. has 10 employees, each of whom earns $2,000 per month and has been employed since January 1. FICA Social Security taxes are 6.2% of the first $118,500 paid to each employee, and FICA Medicare taxes are 1.45% of gross pay. FUTA taxes are 0.6% and SUTA taxes are 5.4% of the first $7,000 paid to each employee. Prepare the March 31 journal entry to record the March payroll taxes expenses. (Round amounts to cents.)

QS 9-6
Recording employer payroll taxes
P3

Quinlan Company offers an annual bonus to employees if the company meets certain net income goals. Prepare the journal entry to record a $15,000 bonus owed to its workers (to be shared equally) at calendar year-end.

QS 9-7
Accounting for bonuses
P4

QS 9-8
Accounting for vacations
P4

Chavez Co.'s salaried employees earn four weeks' vacation per year. It pays $312,000.00 in total employee salaries for 52 weeks, but its employees work only 48 weeks. This means Chavez's total weekly expense is $6,500 ($312,000/48 weeks) instead of the $6,000 cash paid weekly to the employees ($312,000/52 weeks). Record Chavez's weekly vacation benefits expense.

QS 9-9
Recording warranty
repairs   **P4**

On September 11, 2015, Home Store sells a mower for $500 with a one-year warranty that covers parts. Warranty expense is estimated at 8% of sales. On July 24, 2016, the mower is brought in for repairs covered under the warranty requiring $35 in materials taken from the Repair Parts Inventory. Prepare the September 11, 2015, entry to record the mower sale, and the July 24, 2016, entry to record the warranty repairs.

QS 9-10
Accounting for
contingent liabilities

C3

The following legal claims exist for M. Finger Co. Identify the accounting treatment for each claim as either (*a*) a liability that is recorded or (*b*) an item described in notes to its financial statements.

_____ **1.** M. Finger (defendant) estimates that a pending lawsuit could result in damages of $1,250,000; it is reasonably possible that the plaintiff will win the case.

_____ **2.** M. Finger faces a probable loss on a pending lawsuit; the amount is not reasonably estimable.

_____ **3.** M. Finger estimates damages in a case at $3,500,000 with a high probability of losing the case.

QS 9-11
Times interest earned   **A1**

Compute the times interest earned for Park Company, which reports income before interest expense and income taxes of $1,885,000 and interest expense of $145,000. Interpret its times interest earned (assume that its competitors average a times interest earned of 4.0).

QS 9-12ᴬ
Net pay and tax
computations

P5

The payroll records of Speedy Software show the following information about Steffi Derr, an employee, for the weekly pay period ending September 30, 2016. Derr is single and claims one allowance. Compute her Social Security tax (6.2%), Medicare tax (1.45%), federal income tax withholding, state income tax (1.0%), and net pay for the current pay period. (Use the withholding table in Exhibit 9A.6 and round tax amounts to the nearest cent.)

Total (gross) earnings for current pay period	$ 740
Cumulative earnings of previous pay periods	$9,700

Check   Net pay, $579.99

QS 9-13ᴮ
Recording deferred
income tax liability   **P4**

Sera Corporation has made and recorded its quarterly income tax payments. After a final review of taxes for the year, the company identifies an additional $40,000 of income tax expense that should be recorded. A portion of this additional expense, $6,000, is deferred for payment in future years. Record Sera's year-end adjusting entry for income tax expense.

QS 9-14
International accounting
standards

C1   **C2**

Answer each of the following related to international accounting standards.

a. In general, how similar or different are the definitions and characteristics of current liabilities between IFRS and U.S. GAAP?

b. Companies reporting under IFRS often reference a set of current liabilities with the title *financial liabilities*. Identify two current liabilities that would be classified under financial liabilities per IFRS. (*Hint:* **Samsung** lists some in Appendix A.)

EXERCISES

The following items appear on the balance sheet of a company with a two-month operating cycle. Identify the proper classification of each item as follows: *C* if it is a current liability, *L* if it is a long-term liability, or *N* if it is not a liability.

Exercise 9-1
Classifying liabilities

C1

_____ **1.** Notes payable (due in 13 to 24 months)   _____ **6.** FUTA taxes payable
_____ **2.** Notes payable (due in 6 to 12 months)   _____ **7.** Accounts receivable
_____ **3.** Notes payable (mature in five years)   _____ **8.** Sales taxes payable
_____ **4.** Current portion of long-term debt   _____ **9.** Salaries payable
_____ **5.** Notes payable (due in 120 days)   _____ **10.** Wages payable

Exercise 9-2
Recording known current
liabilities

C2

Prepare any necessary entries at December 31, 2016, for Piper Company in preparation for year-end financial statements for each of the following separate transactions and events.

1. Piper Company records a year-end entry for $10,000 of previously unrecorded cash sales (costing $5,000) and its sales taxes at a rate of 4%.

2. The company earned $50,000 of $125,000 previously received in advance and originally recorded as unearned services revenue.

Sylvestor Systems borrows $110,000 cash on May 15, 2016, by signing a 60-day, 12% note.

1. On what date does this note mature?

2. Suppose the face value of the note equals $110,000, the principal of the loan. Prepare the journal entries to record (*a*) issuance of the note and (*b*) payment of the note at maturity.

Exercise 9-3
Accounting for note payable   P1
Check   (2b) Interest expense, $2,200

Keesha Co. borrows $200,000 cash on November 1, 2016, by signing a 90-day, 9% note with a face value of $200,000.

1. On what date does this note mature?

2. How much interest expense results from this note in 2016? (Assume a 360-day year.)

3. How much interest expense results from this note in 2017? (Assume a 360-day year.)

4. Prepare journal entries to record (*a*) issuance of the note, (*b*) accrual of interest at the end of 2016, and (*c*) payment of the note at maturity. (Assume *no* reversing entries are made.)

Exercise 9-4
Interest-bearing notes payable with year-end adjustments   P1
Check   (2) $3,000
Check   (3) $1,500

BMX Company has one employee. FICA Social Security taxes are 6.2% of the first $118,500 paid to its employee, and FICA Medicare taxes are 1.45% of gross pay. For BMX, FUTA taxes are 0.6% and SUTA taxes are 2.9% of the first $7,000 paid to its employee. Compute BMX's amounts for each of these four taxes as applied to the one employee's gross earnings for September under each of three separate situations (*a*), (*b*), and (*c*). (Round amounts to cents.)

Exercise 9-5
Computing payroll taxes
P2   P3

	Gross Pay through August	Gross Pay for September
a.	$ 6,400	$ 800
b.	18,200	2,100
c.	112,200	8,000

Check   (a) FUTA, $3.60; SUTA, $17.40

Using the data in *situation a* of Exercise 9-5, prepare the employer's September 30 journal entries to record salary expense and its related payroll liabilities for this employee. The employee's federal income taxes withheld by the employer are $80 for this pay period. (Round amounts to cents.)

Exercise 9-6
Payroll-related journal entries   P2

Using the data in *situation a* of Exercise 9-5, prepare the employer's September 30 journal entries to record the *employer's* payroll taxes expense and its related liabilities. (Round amounts to cents.)

Exercise 9-7
Payroll-related journal entries   P3

The following monthly data are taken from Ramirez Company at July 31: sales salaries, $200,000; office salaries, $160,000; federal income taxes withheld, $90,000; state income taxes withheld, $20,000; Social Security taxes withheld, $22,320; Medicare taxes withheld, $5,220; medical insurance premiums, $7,000; life insurance premiums, $4,000; union dues deducted, $1,000; and salaries subject to unemployment taxes, $50,000. The employee pays 40% of medical and life insurance premiums.

Prepare journal entries to record: (1) accrued payroll, including employee deductions, for July; (2) cash payment of the net payroll (salaries payable) for July; (3) accrued employer payroll taxes, and other related employment expenses, for July—assume that FICA taxes are identical to those on employees and that SUTA taxes are 5.4% and FUTA taxes are 0.6%; and (4) cash payment of all liabilities related to the July payroll.

Exercise 9-8
Recording payroll
P2   P3

MH Company has 9 employees. FICA Social Security taxes are 6.2% of the first $118,500 paid to each employee, and FICA Medicare taxes are 1.45% of gross pay. FUTA taxes are 0.6% and SUTA taxes are 5.4% of the first $7,000 paid to each employee. Cumulative pay for the current year for each of its employees follows.

Exercise 9-9
Computing payroll taxes
P2   P3

Employee	Cumulative Pay	Employee	Cumulative Pay	Employee	Cumulative Pay
Ken S.	$ 6,000	Michael M.	$143,500	Lori K.	$121,000
Tim V.	60,200	Kyle B.	106,900	Kitty O.	36,900
Steve S.	87,000	Michelle N.	118,500	John W.	4,000

a. Prepare a table with the following six column headings. Compute the amounts in this table for each employee and then total the numerical columns.

Employee	Cumulative Pay	Pay Subject to FICA Social Security	Pay Subject to FICA Medicare	Pay Subject to FUTA Taxes	Pay Subject to SUTA Taxes

Continued on next page . . .

b. For the company, compute each total for: FICA Social Security taxes, FICA Medicare taxes, FUTA taxes, and SUTA taxes. (*Hint:* Remember to include in those totals any employee share of taxes that the company must collect.) (Round amounts to cents.)

Exercise 9-10
Warranty expense and liability computations and entries **P4**

Check (1) $240

(4) $31

Hitzu Co. sold a copier costing $4,800 with a two-year parts warranty to a customer on August 16, 2016, for $6,000 cash. Hitzu uses the perpetual inventory system. On November 22, 2017, the copier requires on-site repairs that are completed the same day. The repairs cost $209 for materials taken from the Repair Parts Inventory. These are the only repairs required in 2017 for this copier. Based on experience, Hitzu expects to incur warranty costs equal to 4% of dollar sales. It records warranty expense with an adjusting entry at the end of each year.

1. How much warranty expense does the company report in 2016 for this copier?
2. How much is the estimated warranty liability for this copier as of December 31, 2016?
3. How much warranty expense does the company report in 2017 for this copier?
4. How much is the estimated warranty liability for this copier as of December 31, 2017?
5. Prepare journal entries to record (*a*) the copier's sale; (*b*) the adjustment on December 31, 2016, to recognize the warranty expense; and (*c*) the repairs that occur in November 2017.

Exercise 9-11
Computing and recording bonuses **P4**

Check (1) $14,563

For the year ended December 31, 2016, Lopez Company has implemented an employee bonus program equal to 3% of Lopez's net income, which employees will share equally. Lopez's net income (pre-bonus) is expected to be $500,000, and bonus expense is deducted in computing net income.

1. Compute the amount of the bonus payable to the employees at year-end (use the method described in the chapter and round to the nearest dollar).
2. Prepare the journal entry at December 31, 2016, to record the bonus due the employees.
3. Prepare the journal entry at January 19, 2017, to record payment of the bonus to employees.

Exercise 9-12
Accounting for estimated liabilities **P4**

Prepare any necessary adjusting entries at December 31, 2016, for Maxum Company's year-end financial statements for each of the following separate transactions and events.

1. Employees earn vacation pay at a rate of one day per month. During December, 20 employees qualify for one vacation day each. Their average daily wage is $160 per employee.
2. During December, Maxum Company sold 12,000 units of a product that carries a 60-day warranty. December sales for this product total $460,000. The company expects 10% of the units to need warranty repairs, and it estimates the average repair cost per unit will be $15.

Exercise 9-13
Accounting for contingent liabilities **C3**

Prepare any necessary adjusting entries at December 31, 2016, for Melbourn Company's year-end financial statements for each of the following separate transactions and events.

1. Melbourn Company guarantees the $100,000 debt of a supplier. It is not probable that the supplier will default on the debt.
2. A disgruntled employee is suing Melbourn Company. Legal advisers believe that the company will probably need to pay damages, but the amount cannot be reasonably estimated.

Exercise 9-14
Computing and interpreting times interest earned **A1**

Check (b) 11.00

Use the following information from separate companies *a* through *f* to compute times interest earned. Which company indicates the strongest ability to pay interest expense as it comes due? (Round ratios to two decimals.)

	Net Income (Loss)	Interest Expense	Income Taxes
a.	$115,000	$44,000	$ 35,000
b.	110,000	16,000	50,000
c.	100,000	12,000	70,000
d.	235,000	14,000	130,000
e.	59,000	14,000	30,000
f.	(5,000)	10,000	0

Exercise 9-15ᴮ
Accounting for income taxes **P4**

Nishi Corporation prepares financial statements for each month-end. As part of its accounting process, estimated income taxes are accrued each month for 30% of the current month's net income. The income taxes are paid in the first month of each quarter for the amount accrued for the prior quarter. The following information is available for the fourth quarter of year 2016. When tax computations are completed on

January 20, 2017, Nishi determines that the quarter's Income Taxes Payable account balance should be $28,300 on December 31, 2016 (its unadjusted balance is $24,690).

October 2016 net income.	$28,600
November 2016 net income	19,100
December 2016 net income	34,600

1. Determine the amount of the accounting adjustment (dated as of December 31, 2016) to produce the proper ending balance in the Income Taxes Payable account.

2. Prepare journal entries to record (*a*) the December 31, 2016, adjustment to the Income Taxes Payable account and (*b*) the January 20, 2017, payment of the fourth-quarter taxes.

Check   (1) $3,610

Lenny Florita, an unmarried employee, works 48 hours in the week ended January 12. His pay rate is $14 per hour, and his wages are subject to no deductions other than FICA Social Security, FICA Medicare, and federal income taxes. He claims two withholding allowances. Compute his regular pay, overtime pay (for this company, workers earn 150% of their regular rate for hours in excess of 40 per week), and gross pay. Then compute his FICA tax deduction (use 6.2% for the Social Security portion and 1.45% for the Medicare portion), income tax deduction (use the wage bracket withholding table from Exhibit 9A.6), total deductions, and net pay. (Round tax amounts to the nearest cent.)

Exercise 9-16[A]
Gross and net pay computation
P5

Check   Net pay, $596.30

Stark Company has five employees. Employees paid by the hour receive a $10 per hour pay rate for the regular 40-hour workweek plus one and one-half times the hourly rate for each overtime hour beyond the 40 hours per week. Hourly employees are paid every two weeks, but salaried employees are paid monthly on the last biweekly payday of each month. FICA Social Security taxes are 6.2% of the first $118,500 paid to each employee, and FICA Medicare taxes are 1.45% of gross pay. FUTA taxes are 0.6% and SUTA taxes are 5.4% of the first $7,000 paid to each employee. The company has a benefits plan that includes medical insurance, life insurance, and retirement funding for employees. Under this plan, employees must contribute 5 percent of their gross income as a payroll withholding, which the company matches with *double* that amount. Following is the partially completed payroll register for the biweekly period ending August 31, which is the last payday of August.

Exercise 9-17
Preparing payroll register and related entries
P5

| Employee | Cumulative Pay (Excludes Current Period) | Current Period Gross Pay | | | FIT | FUTA | FICA-SS_EE | FICA-Med_EE | EE-Ben_Plan Withholding | Employee Net Pay |
		Pay Type	Pay Hours	Gross Pay	SIT	SUTA	FICA-SS_ER	FICA-Med_ER	ER-Ben_Plan Expense	(Current Period)
Kathleen	$116,700.00	Salary	---	$7,000.00	$2,000.00					
					300.00					
Anthony	6,800.00	Salary	---	500.00	80.00				25.00	
					20.00				50.00	
Nichole	15,000.00	Regular	80		110.00					
		Overtime	8		25.00					
Zoey	6,500.00	Regular	80		100.00					
		Overtime	4		22.00					
Gracie	5,000.00	Regular	74	740.00	90.00					
		Overtime	0	0.00	21.00					
Totals	$150,000.00				2,380.00					
					388.00					

a. Complete this payroll register by filling in all cells for the pay period ended August 31. *Hint:* See Exhibit 9A.5 for guidance. (Round amounts to cents.)

b. Prepare the August 31 journal entry to record the accrued biweekly payroll and related liabilities for deductions.

c. Prepare the August 31 journal entry to record the employer's cash payment of the net payroll of part *b*.

d. Prepare the August 31 journal entry to record the employer's payroll taxes including the contribution to the benefits plan.

e. Prepare the August 31 journal entry to pay all liabilities (except for the net payroll in part *c*) for this biweekly period.

Exercise 9-18
Accounting for current liabilities under IFRS

P4

Volvo Group reports the following information for its product warranty costs as of December 31, 2014, along with provisions and utilizations of warranty liabilities for the year ended December 31, 2014 (SEK in millions).

Provision for product warranty   Warranty provisions are estimated with consideration of historical claims statistics, the warranty period, the average time-lag between faults occurring and claims to the company and anticipated changes in quality indexes. Estimated costs for product warranties are recognized as cost of sales when the products are sold . . . Differences between actual warranty claims and the estimated claims generally affect the recognized expense and provisions in future periods. Refunds from suppliers, that decrease the Volvo Group's warranty costs, are recognized to the extent these are considered to be certain. As of December 31, 2014 (2013) warranty cost provisions amount to 10,583 (9,881).

Product warranty liabilities, December 31, 2013	SEK 9,881
Additional provisions to product warranty liabilities	7,836
Utilizations and reductions of product warranty liabilities	(7,134)
Product warranty liabilities, December 31, 2014	10,583

1. Prepare Volvo's journal entry to record its estimated warranty liabilities (provisions) for 2014.
2. Prepare Volvo's journal entry to record its costs (utilizations) related to its warranty program for 2014. Assume those costs involve replacements taken out of Inventory, with no cash involved.
3. How much warranty expense does Volvo report for 2014?

PROBLEM SET A

Problem 9-1A
Short-term notes payable transactions and entries

P1

Tyrell Co. entered into the following transactions involving short-term liabilities in 2015 and 2016.

2015

Apr. 20	Purchased $40,250 of merchandise on credit from Loco, terms n/30. Tyrell uses the perpetual inventory system.
May 19	Replaced the April 20 account payable to Loco with a 90-day, $35,000 note bearing 10% annual interest along with paying $5,250 in cash.
July 8	Borrowed $80,000 cash from NBR Bank by signing a 120-day, 9% interest-bearing note with a face value of $80,000.
___?___	Paid the amount due on the note to Loco at the maturity date.
___?___	Paid the amount due on the note to NBR Bank at the maturity date.
Nov. 28	Borrowed $42,000 cash from Fargo Bank by signing a 60-day, 8% interest-bearing note with a face value of $42,000.
Dec. 31	Recorded an adjusting entry for accrued interest on the note to Fargo Bank.

2016

___?___	Paid the amount due on the note to Fargo Bank at the maturity date.

Required

Check (2) Loco, $875

(3) $308

(4) $252

1. Determine the maturity date for each of the three notes described.
2. Determine the interest due at maturity for each of the three notes. (Assume a 360-day year.)
3. Determine the interest expense to be recorded in the adjusting entry at the end of 2015.
4. Determine the interest expense to be recorded in 2016.
5. Prepare journal entries for all the preceding transactions and events for years 2015 and 2016.

Problem 9-2A
Entries for payroll transactions

P2   P3

On January 8, the end of the first weekly pay period of the year, Regis Company's payroll register showed that its employees earned $22,760 of office salaries and $65,840 of sales salaries. Withholdings from the employees' salaries include FICA Social Security taxes at the rate of 6.2%, FICA Medicare taxes at the rate of 1.45%, $12,860 of federal income taxes, $1,340 of medical insurance deductions, and $840 of union dues. No employee earned more than $7,000 in this first pay period.

Required

Check (1) Cr. Salaries
Payable, $66,782.10

(2) Dr. Payroll Taxes
Expense, $10,853.50

1. Compute FICA Social Security taxes payable and FICA Medicare taxes payable. Prepare the journal entry to record Regis Company's January 8 (employee) payroll expenses and liabilities. (Round amounts to cents.)
2. Prepare the journal entry to record Regis's (employer) payroll taxes resulting from the January 8 payroll. Regis's merit rating reduces its state unemployment tax rate to 4% of the first $7,000 paid each employee. The federal unemployment tax rate is 0.6%. (Round amounts to cents.)

Paloma Co. has four employees. FICA Social Security taxes are 6.2% of the first $118,500 paid to each employee, and FICA Medicare taxes are 1.45% of gross pay. Also, for the first $7,000 paid to each employee, the company's FUTA taxes are 0.6% and SUTA taxes are 2.15%. The company is preparing its payroll calculations for the week ended August 25. Payroll records show the following information for the company's four employees.

Problem 9-3A
Payroll expenses, withholdings, and taxes
P2   P3

	A	B	C	D
1		**Gross Pay**	**Current Week**	
2	**Name**	**through Aug. 18**	**Gross Pay**	**Income Tax Withholding**
3	Dali	$117,400	$2,000	$284
4	Trey	117,600	900	145
5	Kiesha	6,900	450	39
6	Chee	1,250	400	30
7				

In addition to gross pay, the company must pay two-thirds of the $60 per employee weekly health insurance; each employee pays the remaining one-third. The company also contributes an extra 8% of each employee's gross pay (at no cost to employees) to a pension fund.

Required

Compute the following for the week ended August 25 (round amounts to the nearest cent):

1. Each employee's FICA withholdings for Social Security.
2. Each employee's FICA withholdings for Medicare.
3. Employer's FICA taxes for Social Security.
4. Employer's FICA taxes for Medicare.
5. Employer's FUTA taxes.
6. Employer's SUTA taxes.
7. Each employee's net (take-home) pay.
8. Employer's total payroll-related expense for each employee.

Check   (3) $176.70

(4) $54.38

(5) $3.00

(7) Total net pay, $2,940.92

On October 29, 2015, Lobo Co. began operations by purchasing razors for resale. Lobo uses the perpetual inventory method. The razors have a 90-day warranty that requires the company to replace any nonworking razor. When a razor is returned, the company discards it and mails a new one from Merchandise Inventory to the customer. The company's cost per new razor is $20, and its retail selling price is $75 in both 2015 and 2016. The manufacturer has advised the company to expect warranty costs to equal 8% of dollar sales. The following transactions and events occurred.

Problem 9-4A
Warranty expense and liability estimation
P4

2015

Nov. 11	Sold 105 razors for $7,875 cash.
30	Recognized warranty expense related to November sales with an adjusting entry.
Dec. 9	Replaced 15 razors that were returned under the warranty.
16	Sold 220 razors for $16,500 cash.
29	Replaced 30 razors that were returned under the warranty.
31	Recognized warranty expense related to December sales with an adjusting entry.

2016

Jan. 5	Sold 150 razors for $11,250 cash.
17	Replaced 50 razors that were returned under the warranty.
31	Recognized warranty expense related to January sales with an adjusting entry.

Required

1. Prepare journal entries to record these transactions and adjustments for 2015 and 2016.
2. How much warranty expense is reported for November 2015 and for December 2015?
3. How much warranty expense is reported for January 2016?
4. What is the balance of the Estimated Warranty Liability account as of December 31, 2015?
5. What is the balance of the Estimated Warranty Liability account as of January 31, 2016?

Check   (3) $900

(4) $1,050 Cr.

(5) $950 Cr.

Problem 9-5A

Computing and analyzing times interest earned

A1

Shown here are condensed income statements for two different companies (both are organized as LLCs and pay no income taxes).

Miller Company		Weave Company	
Sales	$1,000,000	Sales	$1,000,000
Variable expenses (80%)	800,000	Variable expenses (60%)	600,000
Income before interest	200,000	Income before interest	400,000
Interest expense (fixed)	60,000	Interest expense (fixed)	260,000
Net income	$ 140,000	Net income	$ 140,000

Required

1. Compute times interest earned for Miller Company.
2. Compute times interest earned for Weave Company.

Check (3) Miller net income, $200,000 (43% increase)

3. What happens to each company's net income if sales increase by 30%?
4. What happens to each company's net income if sales increase by 50%?
5. What happens to each company's net income if sales increase by 80%?

(6) Weave net income, $100,000 (29% decrease)

6. What happens to each company's net income if sales decrease by 10%?
7. What happens to each company's net income if sales decrease by 20%?
8. What happens to each company's net income if sales decrease by 40%?

Analysis Component

9. Comment on the results from parts 3 through 8 in relation to the fixed-cost strategies of the two companies and the ratio values you computed in parts 1 and 2.

Problem 9-6A[A]

Entries for payroll transactions

P2   P3   P5

Francisco Company has 10 employees, each of whom earns $2,800 per month and is paid on the last day of each month. All 10 have been employed continuously at this amount since January 1. On March 1, the following accounts and balances exist in its general ledger:

a. FICA—Social Security Taxes Payable, $3,472; FICA—Medicare Taxes Payable, $812. (The balances of these accounts represent total liabilities for *both* the employer's and employees' FICA taxes for the February payroll only.)

b. Employees' Federal Income Taxes Payable, $4,000 (liability for February only).

c. Federal Unemployment Taxes Payable, $336 (liability for January and February together).

d. State Unemployment Taxes Payable, $2,240 (liability for January and February together).

During March and April, the company had the following payroll transactions.

Mar. 15   Issued check payable to Swift Bank, a federal depository bank authorized to accept employers' payments of FICA taxes and employee income tax withholdings. The $8,284 check is in payment of the February FICA and employee income taxes.

Check March 31: Salaries Payable, $21,858

31   Recorded the journal entry for the March salaries payable. Then recorded the cash payment of the March payroll (the company issued checks payable to each employee in payment of the March payroll). The payroll register shows the following summary totals for the March pay period.

Salaries				Federal	
Office Salaries	Shop Salaries	Gross Pay	FICA Taxes*	Income Taxes	Net Pay
$11,200	$16,800	$28,000	$1,736 $ 406	$4,000	$21,858

* FICA taxes are Social Security and Medicare, respectively.

March 31:
Dr. Payroll Taxes Expenses, $2,786

31   Recorded the employer's payroll taxes resulting from the March payroll. The company has a merit rating that reduces its state unemployment tax rate to 4.0% of the first $7,000 paid each employee. The federal rate is 0.6%.

April 15: Cr. Cash, $8,284 (Swift Bank)

Apr. 15   Issued check to Swift Bank in payment of the March FICA and employee income taxes.

15   Issued check to the State Tax Commission for the January, February, and March state unemployment taxes. Filed the check and the first-quarter tax return with the Commission.

30   Issued check payable to Swift Bank in payment of the employer's FUTA taxes for the first quarter of the year.

30   Filed Form 941 with the IRS, reporting the FICA taxes and the employees' federal income tax withholdings for the first quarter.

Required

Prepare journal entries to record the transactions and events for both March and April.

Warner Co. entered into the following transactions involving short-term liabilities in 2015 and 2016.

PROBLEM SET B

Problem 9-1B
Short-term notes payable transactions and entries
P1

2015

Apr. 22   Purchased $5,000 of merchandise on credit from Fox-Pro, terms n/30. Warner uses the perpetual inventory system.

May 23   Replaced the April 22 account payable to Fox-Pro with a 60-day, $4,600 note bearing 15% annual interest along with paying $400 in cash.

July 15   Borrowed $12,000 cash from Spring Bank by signing a 120-day, 10% interest-bearing note with a face value of $12,000.

___?___   Paid the amount due on the note to Fox-Pro at maturity.

___?___   Paid the amount due on the note to Spring Bank at maturity.

Dec. 6   Borrowed $8,000 cash from City Bank by signing a 45-day, 9% interest-bearing note with a face value of $8,000.

   31   Recorded an adjusting entry for accrued interest on the note to City Bank.

2016

___?___   Paid the amount due on the note to City Bank at maturity.

Required

1. Determine the maturity date for each of the three notes described.

2. Determine the interest due at maturity for each of the three notes. (Assume a 360-day year.)

3. Determine the interest expense to be recorded in the adjusting entry at the end of 2015.

4. Determine the interest expense to be recorded in 2016.

5. Prepare journal entries for all the preceding transactions and events for years 2015 and 2016.

Check (2) Fox-Pro, $115
(3) $50
(4) $40

Tavella Company's first weekly pay period of the year ends on January 8. On that date, the column totals in Tavella's payroll register indicate its sales employees earned $34,745, its office employees earned $21,225, and its delivery employees earned $1,030 in salaries. The employees are to have withheld from their salaries FICA Social Security taxes at the rate of 6.2%, FICA Medicare taxes at the rate of 1.45%, $8,625 of federal income taxes, $1,160 of medical insurance deductions, and $138 of union dues. No employee earned more than $7,000 in the first pay period.

Problem 9-2B
Entries for payroll transactions
P2   P3

Required

1. Compute FICA Social Security taxes payable and FICA Medicare taxes payable. Prepare the journal entry to record Tavella Company's January 8 (employee) payroll expenses and liabilities. (Round amounts to cents.)

2. Prepare the journal entry to record Tavella's (employer) payroll taxes resulting from the January 8 payroll. Tavella's merit rating reduces its state unemployment tax rate to 3.4% of the first $7,000 paid each employee. The federal unemployment tax rate is 0.6%. (Round amounts to cents.)

Check (1) Cr. Salaries Payable, $42,716.50

(2) Dr. Payroll Taxes Expense, $6,640.50

Fishing Guides Co. has four employees. FICA Social Security taxes are 6.2% of the first $118,500 paid to each employee, and FICA Medicare taxes are 1.45% of gross pay. Also, for the first $7,000 paid to each employee, the company's FUTA taxes are 0.6% and SUTA taxes are 1.75%. The company is preparing its payroll calculations for the week ended September 30. Payroll records show the following information for the company's four employees.

Problem 9-3B
Payroll expenses, withholdings, and taxes
P2   P3

	A	B	C	D
1		**Gross Pay**	**Current Week**	
2	**Name**	**through Sept. 23**	**Gross Pay**	**Income Tax Withholding**
3	Ahmed	$116,900	$2,500	$198
4	Carlos	116,985	1,515	182
5	Jun	6,650	475	32
6	Marie	23,700	1,000	68
7				

In addition to gross pay, the company must pay 60% of the $50 per employee weekly health insurance; each employee pays the remaining 40%. The company also contributes an extra 5% of each employee's gross pay (at no cost to employees) to a pension fund.

Required

Compute the following for the week ended September 30 (round amounts to the nearest cent):

1. Each employee's FICA withholdings for Social Security.
2. Each employee's FICA withholdings for Medicare.
3. Employer's FICA taxes for Social Security.
4. Employer's FICA taxes for Medicare.
5. Employer's FUTA taxes.
6. Employer's SUTA taxes.
7. Each employee's net (take-home) pay.
8. Employer's total payroll-related expense for each employee.

Check (3) $284.58
(4) $79.61
(5) $2.10

(7) Total net pay, $4,565.81

Problem 9-4B
Warranty expense and liability estimation
P4

On November 10, 2015, Lee Co. began operations by purchasing coffee grinders for resale. Lee uses the perpetual inventory method. The grinders have a 60-day warranty that requires the company to replace any nonworking grinder. When a grinder is returned, the company discards it and mails a new one from Merchandise Inventory to the customer. The company's cost per new grinder is $24, and its retail selling price is $50 in both 2015 and 2016. The manufacturer has advised the company to expect warranty costs to equal 10% of dollar sales. The following transactions and events occurred.

2015

Nov.	16	Sold 50 grinders for $2,500 cash.
	30	Recognized warranty expense related to November sales with an adjusting entry.
Dec.	12	Replaced six grinders that were returned under the warranty.
	18	Sold 200 grinders for $10,000 cash.
	28	Replaced 17 grinders that were returned under the warranty.
	31	Recognized warranty expense related to December sales with an adjusting entry.

2016

Jan.	7	Sold 40 grinders for $2,000 cash.
	21	Replaced 36 grinders that were returned under the warranty.
	31	Recognized warranty expense related to January sales with an adjusting entry.

Required

1. Prepare journal entries to record these transactions and adjustments for 2015 and 2016.
2. How much warranty expense is reported for November 2015 and for December 2015?
3. How much warranty expense is reported for January 2016?
4. What is the balance of the Estimated Warranty Liability account as of December 31, 2015?
5. What is the balance of the Estimated Warranty Liability account as of January 31, 2016?

Check (3) $200
(4) $698 Cr.
(5) $34 Cr.

Problem 9-5B
Computing and analyzing times interest earned
A1

Shown here are condensed income statements for two different companies (both are organized as LLCs and pay no income taxes).

Ellis Company	
Sales	$240,000
Variable expenses (50%)	120,000
Income before interest	120,000
Interest expense (fixed)	90,000
Net income	$ 30,000

Seidel Company	
Sales	$240,000
Variable expenses (75%)	180,000
Income before interest	60,000
Interest expense (fixed)	30,000
Net income	$ 30,000

Required

1. Compute times interest earned for Ellis Company.
2. Compute times interest earned for Seidel Company.
3. What happens to each company's net income if sales increase by 10%?
4. What happens to each company's net income if sales increase by 40%?
5. What happens to each company's net income if sales increase by 90%?
6. What happens to each company's net income if sales decrease by 20%?
7. What happens to each company's net income if sales decrease by 50%?
8. What happens to each company's net income if sales decrease by 80%?

Check   (4) Ellis net income, $78,000 (160% increase)

(6) Seidel net income, $18,000 (40% decrease)

Analysis Component

9. Comment on the results from parts 3 through 8 in relation to the fixed-cost strategies of the two companies and the ratio values you computed in parts 1 and 2.

MLS Company has five employees, each of whom earns $1,600 per month and is paid on the last day of each month. All five have been employed continuously at this amount since January 1. On June 1, the following accounts and balances exist in its general ledger:

Problem 9-6B^A
Entries for payroll transactions

P2 P3 P5

a. FICA—Social Security Taxes Payable, $992; FICA—Medicare Taxes Payable, $232. (The balances of these accounts represent total liabilities for *both* the employer's and employees' FICA taxes for the May payroll only.)
b. Employees' Federal Income Taxes Payable, $1,050 (liability for May only).
c. Federal Unemployment Taxes Payable, $66 (liability for April and May together).
d. State Unemployment Taxes Payable, $440 (liability for April and May together).

During June and July, the company had the following payroll transactions.

June 15   Issued check payable to Security Bank, a federal depository bank authorized to accept employers' payments of FICA taxes and employee income tax withholdings. The $2,274 check is in payment of the May FICA and employee income taxes.
　　30   Recorded the journal entry for the June salaries payable. Then recorded the cash payment of the June payroll (the company issued checks payable to each employee in payment of the June payroll). The payroll register shows the following summary totals for the June pay period.

Check   June 30: Salaries Payable, $6,338

	Salaries		Gross Pay	FICA Taxes*	Federal Income Taxes	Net Pay
	Office Salaries	Shop Salaries				
	$3,800	$4,200	$8,000	$496	$1,050	$6,338
				$116		

* FICA taxes are Social Security and Medicare, respectively.

　　30   Recorded the employer's payroll taxes resulting from the June payroll. The company has a merit rating that reduces its state unemployment tax rate to 4.0% of the first $7,000 paid each employee. The federal rate is 0.6%.
July 15   Issued check payable to Security Bank in payment of the June FICA and employee income taxes.
　　15   Issued check to the State Tax Commission for the April, May, and June state unemployment taxes. Filed the check and the second-quarter tax return with the State Tax Commission.
　　31   Issued check payable to Security Bank in payment of the employer's FUTA taxes for the first quarter of the year.
　　31   Filed Form 941 with the IRS, reporting the FICA taxes and the employees' federal income tax withholdings for the second quarter.

June 30: Dr. Payroll Taxes Expenses, $612

July 15: Cr. Cash $2,274 (Security Bank)

Required

Prepare journal entries to record the transactions and events for both June and July.

SERIAL PROBLEM

Business Solutions

P2 P3 C2

(This serial problem began in Chapter 1 and continues through most of the book. If previous chapter segments were not completed, the serial problem can begin at this point. It is helpful, but not necessary, to use the Working Papers that accompany the book.)

SP 9   Review the February 26 and March 25 transactions for Business Solutions (SP 4) from Chapter 4.

Required

1. Assume that Lyn Addie is an unmarried employee. Her $1,000 of wages are subject to no deductions other than FICA Social Security taxes, FICA Medicare taxes, and federal income taxes. Her federal income taxes for this pay period total $159. Compute her net pay for the eight days' work paid on February 26. (Round amounts to the nearest cent.)

2. Record the journal entry to reflect the payroll payment to Lyn Addie as computed in part 1.

3. Record the journal entry to reflect the (employer) payroll tax expenses for the February 26 payroll payment. Assume Lyn Addie has not met earnings limits for FUTA and SUTA (the FUTA rate is 0.6% and the SUTA rate is 4% for the company). (Round amounts to the nearest cent.)

4. Record the entry(ies) for the merchandise sold on March 25 if a 4% sales tax rate applies.

COMPREHENSIVE PROBLEM

Bug-Off Exterminators
(Review of Chapters 1–9)

CP 9   Bug-Off Exterminators provides pest control services and sells extermination products manufactured by other companies. The following six-column table contains the company's unadjusted trial balance as of December 31, 2016.

BUG-OFF EXTERMINATORS December 31, 2016					
	Unadjusted Trial Balance		Adjustments	Adjusted Trial Balance	
Cash	$ 17,000				
Accounts receivable	4,000				
Allowance for doubtful accounts		$ 828			
Merchandise inventory	11,700				
Trucks	32,000				
Accum. depreciation—Trucks		0			
Equipment	45,000				
Accum. depreciation—Equipment		12,200			
Accounts payable		5,000			
Estimated warranty liability		1,400			
Unearned services revenue		0			
Interest payable		0			
Long-term notes payable		15,000			
Common stock		10,000			
Retained earnings		49,700			
Dividends	10,000				
Extermination services revenue		60,000			
Interest revenue		872			
Sales (of merchandise)		71,026			
Cost of goods sold	46,300				
Depreciation expense—Trucks	0				
Depreciation expense—Equipment	0				
Wages expense	35,000				
Interest expense	0				
Rent expense	9,000				
Bad debts expense	0				
Miscellaneous expense	1,226				
Repairs expense	8,000				
Utilities expense	6,800				
Warranty expense	0				
Totals	$226,026	$226,026			

The following information in *a* through *h* applies to the company at the end of the current year.

a. The bank reconciliation as of December 31, 2016, includes the following facts.

Cash balance per bank	$15,100
Cash balance per books.	17,000
Outstanding checks	1,800
Deposit in transit	2,450
Interest earned (on bank account)	52
Bank service charges (miscellaneous expense)	15

Reported on the bank statement is a canceled check that the company failed to record. (Information from the bank reconciliation allows you to determine the amount of this check, which is a payment on an account payable.)

b. An examination of customers' accounts shows that accounts totaling $679 should be written off as uncollectible. Using an aging of receivables, the company determines that the ending balance of the Allowance for Doubtful Accounts should be $700.

c. A truck is purchased and placed in service on January 1, 2016. Its cost is being depreciated with the straight-line method using the following facts and estimates.

Original cost	$32,000
Expected salvage value	8,000
Useful life (years)	4

d. Two items of equipment (a sprayer and an injector) were purchased and put into service in early January 2014. They are being depreciated with the straight-line method using these facts and estimates.

	Sprayer	Injector
Original cost	$27,000	$18,000
Expected salvage value	3,000	2,500
Useful life (years).	8	5

e. On August 1, 2016, the company is paid $3,840 cash in advance to provide monthly service for an apartment complex for one year. The company began providing the services in August. When the cash was received, the full amount was credited to the Extermination Services Revenue account.

f. The company offers a warranty for the services it sells. The expected cost of providing warranty service is 2.5% of the extermination services revenue of $57,760 for 2016. No warranty expense has been recorded for 2016. All costs of servicing warranties in 2016 were properly debited to the Estimated Warranty Liability account.

g. The $15,000 long-term note is an 8%, five-year, interest-bearing note with interest payable annually on December 31. The note was signed with First National Bank on December 31, 2016.

h. The ending inventory of merchandise is counted and determined to have a cost of $11,700. Bug-Off uses a perpetual inventory system.

Required

1. Use the preceding information to determine amounts for the following items.
   a. Correct (reconciled) ending balance of Cash, and the amount of the omitted check.
   b. Adjustment needed to obtain the correct ending balance of the Allowance for Doubtful Accounts.
   c. Depreciation expense for the truck used during year 2016.
   d. Depreciation expense for the two items of equipment used during year 2016.
   e. The adjusted 2016 ending balances of the Extermination Services Revenue and Unearned Services Revenue accounts.
   f. The adjusted 2016 ending balances of the Warranty Expense and Estimated Warranty Liability accounts.
   g. The adjusted 2016 ending balances of the Interest Expense and Interest Payable accounts. (Round amounts to the nearest whole dollar.)

Continued on next page . . .

Check   (1a) Reconciled cash bal. $15,750
(1b) $551 credit

(1f) Estimated Warranty Liability, $2,844 Cr.

(2) Adjusted trial balance totals, $238,207

2. Use the results of part 1 to complete the six-column table by first entering the appropriate adjustments for items *a* through *g* and then completing the Adjusted Trial Balance columns. (*Hint:* Item *b* requires two adjustments.)

3. Prepare journal entries to record the adjustments entered in the six-column table. Assume Bug-Off's adjusted balance for Merchandise Inventory matches the year-end physical count.

(4) Net income, $9,274; Total assets, $82,771

4. Prepare a single-step income statement, a statement of retained earnings (cash dividends during 2016 were $10,000), and a classified balance sheet.

GENERAL LEDGER PROBLEM

Available in Connect

GL 9-1   General Ledger assignment GL 9-1, based on Problem 9-1A, focuses on transactions related to accounts and notes payable and highlights the impact each transaction has on interest expense, if any. Prepare the journal entries related to accounts and notes payable; the schedules for accounts payable and notes payable are automatically completed using the **General Ledger** tool. Compute both the amount and timing of interest expense for each note. Prepare the subsequent-period journal entries related to accrued interest.

Beyond the Numbers

REPORTING IN ACTION

A1   P4

APPLE

BTN 9-1   Refer to the financial statements of **Apple** in Appendix A to answer the following.

1. Compute times interest earned for the fiscal years ended 2014, 2013, and 2012. Apple reports that in 2014 interest expense was $384 million, in 2013 interest expense was $136 million, and in 2012 it "had no debt outstanding and accordingly did not incur any related interest expense"; however, for purposes of learning from this assignment, assume that Apple had interest expense of $100 million for 2012. Comment on Apple's ability to cover its interest expense for this period. Assume an industry average of 10 for times interest earned.

2. Apple's current liabilities include "Deferred revenue"; assume that this account reflects "Loyalty reward liabilities." Is this a known or an estimated liability? Explain how this liability is created.

3. Identify Apple's total of accrued expenses and search its footnotes to list the six accounts that make up accrued expenses.

Fast Forward

4. Access Apple's financial statements for fiscal years ending after September 27, 2014, at its website (**Apple.com**) or the SEC's EDGAR database (**www.SEC.gov**). Compute its times interest earned for years ending after September 27, 2014, and compare your results to those in part 1. If no interest expense is reported, assume $100 million of interest expense in each year.

COMPARATIVE ANALYSIS

A1

APPLE
GOOGLE

BTN 9-2   Key figures for **Apple** and **Google** follow.

$ millions	Apple			Google		
	Current Year	One Year Prior	Two Years Prior	Current Year	One Year Prior	Two Years Prior
Net income	$39,510	$37,037	$41,773	$14,444	$12,920	$10,737
Income taxes	13,973	13,118	14,030	3,331	2,552	2,916
Interest expense	384	136	100*	101	81	85

* Apple did not report interest expense for this period. Amount included here is assumed for purposes of this analysis.

Required

1. Compute times interest earned for the three years' data shown for each company.
2. Comment on which company appears stronger in its ability to pay interest obligations if income should decline. Assume an industry average of 10.

BTN 9-3   Cameron Bly is a sales manager for an automobile dealership. He earns a bonus each year based on revenue from the number of autos sold in the year less related warranty expenses. Actual warranty expenses have varied over the prior 10 years from a low of 3% of an automobile's selling price to a high of 10%. In the past, Bly has tended to estimate warranty expenses on the high end to be conservative. He must work with the dealership's accountant at year-end to arrive at the warranty expense accrual for cars sold each year.

ETHICS CHALLENGE

P4

1. Does the warranty accrual decision create any ethical dilemma for Bly?
2. Since warranty expenses vary, what percent do you think Bly should choose for the current year? Justify your response.

BTN 9-4   Dusty Johnson is the accounting and finance manager for a manufacturer. At year-end, he must determine how to account for the company's contingencies. His manager, Tom Pretti, objects to Johnson's proposal to recognize an expense and a liability for warranty service on units of a new product introduced in the fourth quarter. Pretti comments, "There's no way we can estimate this warranty cost. We don't owe anyone anything until a product fails and it is returned. Let's report an expense if and when we do any warranty work."

COMMUNICATING IN PRACTICE

C3

Required

Prepare a one-page memorandum for Johnson to send to Pretti defending his proposal.

BTN 9-5   Access the February 24, 2015, filing of the December 31, 2014, annual 10-K report of **McDonald's Corporation** (ticker MCD), which is available from **www.SEC.gov**.

TAKING IT TO THE NET

C1   A1

Required

1. Identify the current liabilities on McDonald's balance sheet as of December 31, 2014.
2. What portion (in percent) of McDonald's long-term debt matures within the next 12 months?
3. Use the consolidated statement of income for the year ended December 31, 2014, to compute McDonald's times interest earned ratio. Comment on the result. Assume an industry average of 15.0.

BTN 9-6   Assume that your team is in business and you must borrow $6,000 cash for short-term needs. You have been shopping banks for a loan, and you have the following two options.

TEAMWORK IN ACTION

C2   P1

A. Sign a $6,000, 90-day, 10% interest-bearing note dated June 1.
B. Sign a $6,000, 120-day, 8% interest-bearing note dated June 1.

Required

1. Discuss these two options and determine the best choice. Ensure that all teammates concur with the decision and understand the rationale.
2. Each member of the team is to prepare *one* of the following journal entries.
   a. Option A—at date of issuance.
   b. Option B—at date of issuance.
   c. Option A—at maturity date.
   d. Option B—at maturity date.
3. In rotation, each member is to explain the entry he or she prepared in part 2 to the team. Ensure that all team members concur with and understand the entries.

Continued on next page . . .

4. Assume that the funds are borrowed on December 1 (instead of June 1) and your business operates on a calendar-year reporting period. Each member of the team is to prepare *one* of the following entries.

     a. Option A—the year-end adjustment.

     b. Option B—the year-end adjustment.

     c. Option A—at maturity date.

     d. Option B—at maturity date.

5. In rotation, each member is to explain the entry he or she prepared in part 4 to the team. Ensure that all team members concur with and understand the entries.

ENTREPRENEURIAL DECISION

A1

BTN 9-7   Review the chapter's opening feature about Aaron Kennedy and the business he founded, **Noodles & Company**. Assume that current management is considering expanding the business to open a location in Europe, and that the current abbreviated income statement appears as follows.

NOODLES & COMPANY Income Statement For Year Ended December 31, 2016	
Sales	$1,000,000
Operating expenses (55%)	550,000
Net income	$ 450,000

Assume also that Noodles & Company currently has no interest-bearing debt. If it expands to open a European location, it will require a $300,000 loan. Noodles & Company has found a bank that will loan it the money on a 7% note payable. The company believes that, at least for the first few years, sales at its European location will equal $250,000, and that all expenses at both locations will continue to equal 55% of sales.

Required

1. Prepare an income statement (showing three separate columns for current operations, European, and total) for the company assuming that it borrows the funds and expands to Europe. Annual revenues for current operations are expected to remain at $1,000,000.

2. Compute the company's times interest earned under the expansion assumptions in part 1.

3. Assume sales at its European location are $400,000. Prepare an income statement (with columns for current operations, European, and total) for the company and compute times interest earned.

4. Assume sales at its European location are $100,000. Prepare an income statement (with columns for current operations, European, and total) for the company and compute times interest earned.

5. Comment on your results from parts 1 through 4.

HITTING THE ROAD

P2

BTN 9-8   Check your phone book or the Social Security Administration website (www.SSA.gov) to locate the Social Security office near you. Visit the office to request a personal earnings and estimate form. Fill out the form and mail according to the instructions. You will receive a statement from the Social Security Administration regarding your earnings history and future Social Security benefits you can receive. (Formerly the request could be made online. The online service has been discontinued and is now under review by the Social Security Administration due to security concerns; however, it might once again be available online.) It is good to request an earnings and benefit statement every 5 to 10 years to make sure you have received credit for all wages earned and for which you and your employer have paid taxes into the system.

GLOBAL DECISION

A1

Samsung

APPLE

GOOGLE

BTN 9-9   **Samsung**, **Apple**, and **Google** are all competitors in the global marketplace. Comparative figures for Samsung (www.Samsung.com), along with selected figures from Apple and Google, follow.

Key Figures	Samsung (₩ millions)		Apple		Google	
	Current Year	Prior Year	Current Year	Prior Year	Current Year	Prior Year
Net income	₩23,394,358	₩30,474,764	—	—	—	—
Income taxes	4,480,676	7,889,515	—	—	—	—
Interest expense	7,294,002	7,754,972	—	—	—	—
Times interest earned	?	?	140.28	369.79	176.99	192.01

Required

1. Compute the times interest earned ratio for the most recent two years for Samsung using the data shown.

2. Which company of the three presented provides the best coverage of interest expense? Explain.

ANSWERS TO MULTIPLE CHOICE QUIZ

1. b; $6,000 \times 0.05 \times 30/360 = \$25$
2. e; $50,000 \times (0.062 + 0.0145) = \$3,825$
3. b; $7,000 \times (0.006 + 0.054) = \$420$

4. c; 10,000 television sets $\times 0.01 \times \$250 = \$25,000$
5. a; 150 employees $\times \$175$ per day $\times 1$ vacation day earned = $26,250

chapter 10

Reporting and Analyzing Long-Term Liabilities

Chapter Preview

BOND BASICS

A1 Fundamentals of:

Bond financing

Bond trading

Bond issuance procedures

BOND ISSUANCES

P1 Issuance at par

P2 Issuance at a discount

P3 Issuance at a premium

Bond pricing

BOND RETIREMENT

P4 Accounting for bond retirement:

At maturity

Before maturity

By conversion

LONG-TERM NOTES

C1 Types of notes

Recording notes

DEBT ANALYSIS

A2 Debt features

A3 Debt-to-equity

Learning Objectives

CONCEPTUAL

C1 Explain the types of notes and prepare entries to account for notes.

C2 *Appendix 10A*—Explain and compute the present value of an amount(s) to be paid at a future date(s).

C3 *Appendix 10C*—Describe interest accrual when bond payment periods differ from accounting periods.

C4 *Appendix 10D*—Describe accounting for leases and pensions.

ANALYTICAL

A1 Compare bond financing with stock financing.

A2 Assess debt features and their implications.

A3 Compute the debt-to-equity ratio and explain its use.

PROCEDURAL

P1 Prepare entries to record bond issuance and interest expense.

P2 Compute and record amortization of bond discount using straight-line method.

P3 Compute and record amortization of bond premium using straight-line method.

P4 Record the retirement of bonds.

P5 *Appendix 10B*—Compute and record amortization of bond discount using effective interest method.

P6 *Appendix 10B*—Compute and record amortization of bond premium using effective interest method.

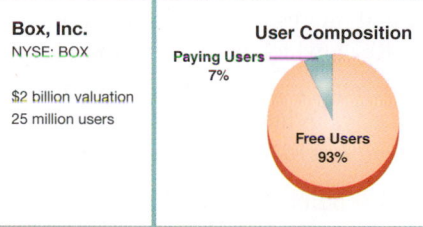

BOX Office Success

"Nothing more exciting than people involved in the creation of great products"—**AARON LEVIE**

LOS ALTOS, CA—Aaron Levie, Dylan Smith, Jeff Queisser, and Sam Ghods met in high school. "[Aaron] was a magician, and I was very much a hard core nerd," recalls Jeff. Beyond magic and nerdiness, the four friends were interested in entrepreneurship. "Aaron and I were always bouncing ideas off of each other just because we were generating them a mile a minute," insists Dylan. The four friends attended different colleges, but Dylan explains that they "stayed in pretty close contact." Then, during their sophomore year, Aaron pitched his idea of a company to Dylan, Jeff, and Sam. Although initially reluctant, the three friends joined Aaron and they launched **Box (Box.com)**, a cloud storage solution for businesses and individuals.

An immediate concern was how to finance the business. "We had a lot of unsuccessful pitches in . . . the venture capital community," explains Dylan. "A couple of 19- and 20-year-olds starting a business isn't that old school." Then a pleasant surprise occurred, and the founders were able to secure financing from a very unlikely source. As a result of a cold e-mail to Mark Cuban, owner of the Dallas Mavericks NBA team and *Shark Tank* TV star, the Box founders received an investment of $350,000. That investment from Mark Cuban helped legitimize and grow the business—see its revenue growth in the nearby chart.

Box, Inc.
NYSE: BOX

$2 billion valuation
25 million users

User Composition

Paying Users 7%

Free Users 93%

Financing comes in two flavors: debt and equity. According to *CrunchBase,* Box has raised over $500 million in 10 rounds of financing since Cuban's investment. After 10 rounds of financing, with much of it equity financing, Aaron had the largest remaining ownership share of the four founders with roughly 4%. The founders, alternatively, could have pursued more debt financing using notes and bonds. This would have had the benefit of greater owner investment and, given the success of Box, generated much more wealth for the founders.

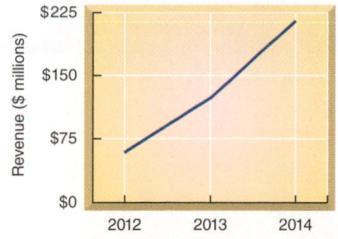

Box's financing preferences, however, might be changing. In 2013, Box secured a $100 million revolving credit facility. It has already drawn on $34 million of this debt financing at a rate of 3.4%. Aaron, now CEO of Box, knows that effective management of those liabilities, especially long-term financing from sources such as notes and bonds, is crucial. Namely, Box must produce sufficient income to pay for interest and principal. Its recent three income statements reveal operating losses and, to meet those obligations, operating results must turn positive for long-run success.

($ millions)	2012	2013	2014
Net income	$(113)	$(169)	$(168)
Interest expense	2	4	2
Long-term debt	30	34	41

The larger message of Box according to Aaron is, "Take the stodgiest, oldest, slowest moving industry you can find. And build amazing software for it . . . that's what we do at Box." Aaron also offers advice to aspiring entrepreneurs: "Take risks. Fail fast . . . [because] if we fail fast, we can correct mistakes quickly."

Sources: *Box website,* January 2016; *Yahoo Finance,* January 2016; *Inc.,* October 2012; *BBC,* May 2013; *TechRepublic,* March 2014; *CrunchBase.com,* 2016

BASICS OF BONDS

This section explains the basics of bonds and a company's motivation for issuing them.

Bond Financing

Projects that demand large amounts of money often are funded from bond issuances. (Both for-profit and nonprofit companies, as well as governmental units, such as nations, states, cities, and school districts, issue bonds.) A **bond** is its issuer's written promise to pay an amount identified as the par value of the bond with interest. The **par value of a bond,** also called the *face amount* or *face value,* is paid at a specified future date known as the bond's *maturity date.* Most bonds also require the issuer to make semiannual interest payments. The amount of interest paid each period is determined by multiplying the par value of the bond by the bond's contract rate of interest for that same period. This section explains both advantages and disadvantages of bond financing.

Advantages of Bonds   There are three main advantages of bond financing:

1. *Bonds do not affect owner control.* Equity financing reflects ownership in a company, whereas bond financing does not. A person who contributes $1,000 of a company's $10,000 equity financing typically controls one-tenth of all owner decisions. A person who owns a $1,000, 11%, 20-year bond has no ownership right. This person, or bond-holder, is to receive from the bond issuer 11% interest, or $110, each year the bond is outstanding and $1,000 when it matures in 20 years.

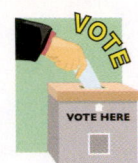

2. *Interest on bonds is tax deductible.* Bond interest payments are tax deductible for the is-suer, but equity payments (distributions) to owners are not. To illustrate, assume that a corporation with no bond financing earns $15,000 in income *before* paying taxes at a 40% tax rate, which amounts to $6,000 ($15,000 × 40%) in taxes. If a portion of its financing is in bonds, however, the resulting bond interest is deducted in computing taxable income. That is, if bond interest expense is $10,000, the taxes owed would be $2,000 ([$15,000 − $10,000] × 40%), which is less than the $6,000 owed with no bond financing.

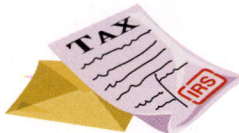

3. *Bonds can increase return on equity.* A company that earns a higher return with borrowed funds than it pays in interest on those funds increases its return on equity. This process is called *financial leverage* or *trading on the equity*.

To illustrate the third point, consider Magnum Co., which has $1,000 million in equity and is planning a $500 million expansion to meet increasing demand for its product. Magnum predicts the $500 million expansion will yield $125 million in additional income before paying any in-terest. It currently earns $100 million per year and has no interest expense. Magnum is consider-ing three plans. Plan A is to not expand. Plan B is to expand and raise $500 million from equity financing. Plan C is to expand and issue $500 million of bonds that pay 10% annual interest ($50 mil.). Exhibit 10.1 shows how these three plans affect Magnum's net income, equity, and return on equity (net income/equity). The owner(s) will earn a higher return on equity if expan-sion occurs. Moreover, the preferred expansion plan is to issue bonds. Projected net income under Plan C ($175 mil.) is smaller than under Plan B ($225 mil.), but the return on equity is larger because of less equity investment. Plan C has another advantage if income is taxable. This illustration reflects a general rule: *Return on equity increases when the expected rate of return from the new assets is higher than the rate of interest expense on the debt financing.*

EXHIBIT 10.1

Financing with Bonds versus Equity

$ millions	Plan A: Do Not Expand	Plan B: Equity Financing	Plan C: Bond Financing
Income before interest expense.........	$ 100	$ 225	$ 225
Interest expense	—	—	(50)
Net income	$ 100	$ 225	$ 175
Equity............................	$1,000	$1,500	$1,000
Return on equity.................	10.0%	15.0%	17.5%

Disadvantages of Bonds   The two main disadvantages of bond financing are these:

1. *Bonds can decrease return on equity.* When a company earns a lower return with the borrowed funds than it pays in interest, it decreases its return on equity. This downside risk of financial leverage is more likely to arise when a company has periods of low income or net losses.
2. *Bonds require payment of both periodic interest and the par value at maturity.* Bond payments can be especially burdensome when income and cash flow are low. Equity financing, in contrast, does not require any payments because cash withdrawals (dividends) are paid at the discretion of the owner (or board).

A company must weigh the advantages and disadvantages of bond financing when deciding whether to issue bonds to finance operations.

Bond Trading

Bonds are securities, and many can be readily bought and sold. A large number of bonds trade on both the New York Exchange and the American Exchange. A bond *issue* consists of a number of bonds, usually in denominations of $1,000 or $5,000, and is sold to many different lenders. After bonds are issued, they often are bought and sold by investors, meaning that any particular bond probably has a number of owners before it matures. Since bonds are exchanged (bought and sold) in the market, they have a market value (price). For convenience, bond market values are expressed as a percent of their par (face) value. For example, a company's bonds might be trading at 103½, meaning they can be bought or sold for 103.5% of their par value. Bonds can also trade below par value. For instance, if a company's bonds are trading at 95, they can be bought or sold at 95% of their par value.

☐ Decision Insight

Quotes   The **IBM** bond quote here is interpreted (left to right) as **Bonds,** issuer name; **Rate,** contract interest rate (5.7%); **Mat,** matures in year 2017 when principal is paid; **Yld,** yield rate (4.7%) of bond at current price; **Vol,** daily dollar worth ($130,000) of trades (in 1,000s); **Close,** closing price (121.18) for the day as percentage of par value; **Chg,** change (+0.24%) in closing price from prior day's close. ■

Bonds	Rate	Mat	Yld	Vol	Close	Chg
IBM	5.7	17	4.7	130	121.18	+0.24%

Bond-Issuing Procedures

State and federal laws govern bond issuances. Bond issuers also want to ensure that they do not violate any of their existing contractual agreements when issuing bonds. Authorization of bond issuances includes the number of bonds authorized, their par value, and the contract interest rate. The legal document identifying the rights and obligations of both the bondholders and the issuer is called the **bond indenture,** which is the legal contract between the issuer and the bondholders (and specifies how often interest is paid). A bondholder may also receive a bond certificate as evidence of the company's debt. A **bond certificate,** such as that shown in Exhibit 10.2, includes specifics such as the issuer's name, the par value, the contract interest rate, and the maturity date. Many companies reduce costs by not issuing paper certificates to bondholders.[1]

Courtesy of RBC Wealth Management

---

[1] The issuing company normally sells its bonds to an investment firm called an *underwriter,* which resells them to the public. An issuing company can also sell bonds directly to investors. When an underwriter sells bonds to a large number of investors, a *trustee* represents and protects the bondholders' interests. The trustee monitors the issuer to ensure that it complies with the obligations in the bond indenture. Most trustees are large banks or trust companies. The trustee writes and accepts the terms of a bond indenture before it is issued. When bonds are offered to the public, called *floating an issue,* they must be registered with the Securities and Exchange Commission (SEC). SEC registration requires the issuer to file certain financial information. Most company bonds are issued in par value units of $1,000 or $5,000. *A baby bond* has a par value of less than $1,000, such as $100.

Point: There are nearly 5 million individual U.S. bond issues, ranging from huge treasuries to tiny municipalities. This compares to about 12,000 individual U.S. stocks that are traded.

Point: Debt financing is desirable when interest is tax deductible, when owner control is preferred, and when return on equity exceeds the debt's interest rate.

Point: The phrase *debt is cheaper than equity* refers in part to interest expense on bonds being tax deductible whereas dividends on stock are not.

Point: Two of the largest bond issuances in history were:
Verizon . . . . $49 billion
Apple . . . . $17 billion

Point: A bond with a par value of $1,000 trading at 103½ sells for $1,035 ($1,000 × 1.035). A bond with a par value of $1,000 trading at 95½ sells for $955 ($1,000 × 0.955).

EXHIBIT 10.2

Bond Certificate

Point: *Indenture* refers to a bond's legal contract; *debenture* refers to an unsecured bond.

Point: The *spread* between the dealer's cost and what buyers pay can be huge. Dealers earn more than $25 billion annually in spread revenue.

Global: In the United Kingdom, government bonds are called *gilts*—short for gilt-edged investments.

BOND ISSUANCES

This section explains accounting for bond issuances at par, below par (discount), and above par (premium). It also describes how to amortize a discount or premium and record bonds issued between interest payment dates.

Issuing Bonds at Par

P1

Prepare entries to record bond issuance and interest expense.

To illustrate an issuance of bonds at par value, suppose a company receives authorization to issue $800,000 of 9%, 20-year bonds dated January 1, 2016, that mature on December 31, 2035, and pay interest semiannually on each June 30 and December 31. After accepting the bond indenture on behalf of the bondholders, the trustee can sell all or a portion of the bonds to an underwriter. If all bonds are sold at par value, the issuer records the sale as follows.

Assets = Liabilities + Equity
+800,000   +800,000

2016			
Jan. 1	Cash	800,000	
	Bonds Payable.............................		800,000
	Sold bonds at par.		

This entry reflects increases in the issuer's cash *and* long-term liabilities.

The issuer records the first semiannual interest payment as follows.

Assets = Liabilities + Equity
−36,000   −36,000

2016			
June 30	Bond Interest Expense...........................	36,000	
	Cash		36,000
	Paid semiannual interest (9% × $800,000 × ½ year).		

The issuer pays and records its semiannual interest obligation every six months until the bonds mature. When they mature, the issuer records its payment of principal as follows.

Assets = Liabilities + Equity
−800,000   −800,000

2035			
Dec. 31	Bonds Payable.................................	800,000	
	Cash		800,000
	Paid bond principal at maturity.		

Bond Discount or Premium

The bond issuer pays the interest rate specified in the indenture, the **contract rate,** also referred to as the *coupon rate, stated rate,* or *nominal rate.* The annual interest paid is determined by multiplying the bond par value by the contract rate. The contract rate is usually stated on an annual basis, even if interest is paid semiannually. For example, if a company issues a $1,000, 8% bond paying interest semiannually, it pays annual interest of $80 (8% × $1,000) in two semiannual payments of $40 each.

The contract rate sets the amount of interest the issuer pays in *cash,* which is not necessarily the *bond interest expense* actually incurred by the issuer. Bond interest expense depends on the bond's market value at issuance, which is determined by market expectations of the risk of lending to the issuer. The bond's **market rate** of interest is the rate that borrowers are willing to pay and lenders are willing to accept for a particular bond and its risk level. As the risk level increases, the rate increases to compensate purchasers for the bonds' increased risk. Also, the market rate is generally higher when the time period until the bond matures is longer due to the risk of adverse events occurring over a longer time period.

Many bond issuers try to set a contract rate of interest equal to the market rate they expect as of the bond issuance date. When the contract rate and market rate are equal, a bond sells at par value, but when they are not equal, a bond does not sell at par value. Instead, it is sold at a *premium* above par value or at a *discount* below par value. Exhibit 10.3 shows the relation between the contract rate, the market rate, and a bond's issue price.

EXHIBIT 10.3

Relation between Bond Issue Price, Contract Rate, and Market Rate

Issuing Bonds at a Discount

A **discount on bonds payable** occurs when a company issues bonds with a contract rate less than the market rate. This means that the issue price is less than par value. To illustrate, assume that **Fila** announces an offer to issue bonds with a $100,000 par value, an 8% annual contract rate (paid semiannually), and a two-year life. Also assume that the market rate for Fila bonds is 10%. These bonds then will sell at a discount since the contract rate is less than the market rate. The exact issue price for these bonds is stated as 96.454 (implying 96.454% of par value, or $96,454); we show how to compute this issue price later in the chapter. These bonds obligate the issuer to pay two separate types of future cash flows:

1. Par value of $100,000 cash at the end of the bonds' two-year life.
2. Cash interest payments of $4,000 ($100,000 × 8% × 1/2 year) at the end of each semiannual period during the bonds' two-year life.

The exact pattern of cash flows for the Fila bonds is shown in Exhibit 10.4.

P2

Compute and record amortization of bond discount using straight-line method.

Point: The difference between the contract rate and the market rate of interest on a new bond issue is usually a fraction of a percent. We use a difference of 2% to emphasize the effects.

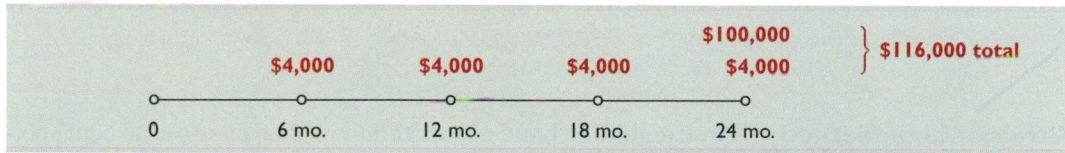

EXHIBIT 10.4

Cash Flows for Fila Bonds

When Fila accepts $96,454 cash for its bonds on the issue date of December 31, 2016, it records the sale as follows.

Dec. 31	Cash	96,454	
	Discount on Bonds Payable	3,546	
	Bonds Payable.............................		100,000
	Sold bonds at a discount on their issue date.		

Assets = Liabilities + Equity
+96,454   +100,000
              −3,546

These bonds are reported in the long-term liability section of the issuer's December 31, 2016, balance sheet as shown in Exhibit 10.5. A discount is deducted from the par value of bonds to yield the **carrying (book) value of bonds.** Discount on Bonds Payable is a contra liability account.

Point: Book value at issuance always equals the issuer's cash borrowed.

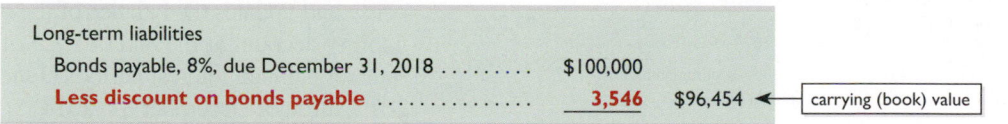

Long-term liabilities		
Bonds payable, 8%, due December 31, 2018	$100,000	
Less discount on bonds payable	3,546	$96,454 ← carrying (book) value

EXHIBIT 10.5

Balance Sheet Presentation of Bond Discount

Amortizing a Bond Discount Fila receives $96,454 for its bonds; in return it must pay bondholders $100,000 after two years (plus semiannual interest payments). The $3,546 discount is paid to bondholders at maturity and is part of the cost of using the $96,454 for two years. The upper portion of panel A in Exhibit 10.6 shows that total bond interest expense of $19,546 is the difference between the total amount repaid to bondholders ($116,000) and the amount borrowed from bondholders ($96,454). Alternatively, we can compute total bond interest expense as the sum of the four interest payments and the bond discount. This alternative computation is shown in the lower portion of panel A.

The total $19,546 bond interest expense must be allocated across the four semiannual periods in the bonds' life, and the bonds' carrying value must be updated at each balance sheet date.

EXHIBIT 10.6

Interest Computation and Entry for Bonds Issued at a Discount

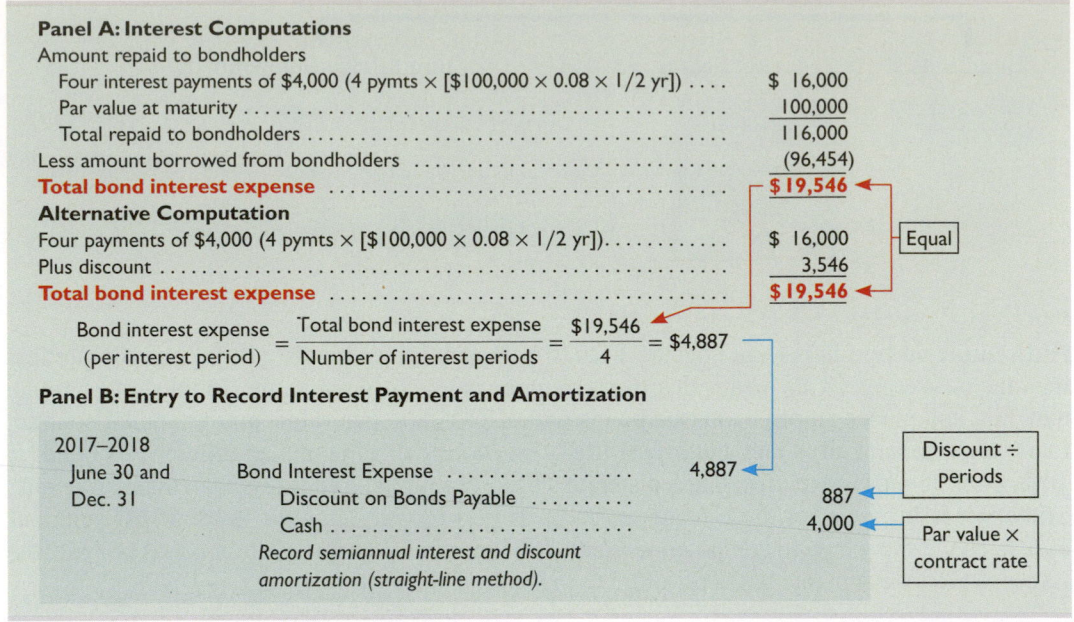

Panel A: Interest Computations

Amount repaid to bondholders

Four interest payments of $4,000 (4 pymts × [$100,000 × 0.08 × 1/2 yr])	$ 16,000
Par value at maturity	100,000
Total repaid to bondholders	116,000
Less amount borrowed from bondholders	(96,454)
Total bond interest expense	**$19,546**

Alternative Computation

Four payments of $4,000 (4 pymts × [$100,000 × 0.08 × 1/2 yr]).	$ 16,000
Plus discount	3,546
Total bond interest expense	**$19,546**

[Equal]

$$\frac{\text{Bond interest expense}}{\text{(per interest period)}} = \frac{\text{Total bond interest expense}}{\text{Number of interest periods}} = \frac{\$19,546}{4} = \$4,887$$

Panel B: Entry to Record Interest Payment and Amortization

2017–2018			
June 30 and	Bond Interest Expense	4,887	
Dec. 31	Discount on Bonds Payable		887
	Cash		4,000
	Record semiannual interest and discount		
	amortization (straight-line method).		

[Discount ÷ periods]

[Par value × contract rate]

This is accomplished using the straight-line method (or the effective interest method in Appendix 10B). Both methods systematically reduce the bond discount to zero over the two-year life. This process is called *amortizing a bond discount*.

> *The following section on discount amortization uses the Straight-Line Method. Appendix 10B uses the effective interest method. An instructor can choose to cover either one or both methods. If the straight-line method is skipped, then move forward to the section titled "Issuing Bonds at a Premium."*

Straight-Line Method   The **straight-line bond amortization** method allocates an equal portion of the total bond interest expense to each interest period. To apply the straight-line method to Fila's bonds, we divide the total bond interest expense of $19,546 by 4 (the number of semiannual periods in the bonds' life). This gives a bond interest expense of $4,887 per period, which is $4,886.5 rounded to the nearest dollar per period (all computations, including those for assignments, are rounded to the nearest whole dollar). Alternatively, we can find this number by first dividing the

Point: Amortization always results in the carrying value of a bond moving closer to its par value.

EXHIBIT 10.7

Straight-Line Amortization of Bond Discount

	Semiannual Period-End	Unamortized Discount*	Carrying Value†
(0)	12/31/2016	$3,546	$ 96,454
(1)	6/30/2017	2,659	97,341
(2)	12/31/2017	1,772	98,228
(3)	6/30/2018	885	99,115
(4)	**12/31/2018**	0‡	100,000

The two columns always sum to par value for a discount bond.

* Total bond discount (of $3,546) less accumulated periodic amortization ($887 per semiannual interest period).

† Bond par value (of $100,000) less unamortized discount.

‡ Adjusted for rounding.

$3,546 discount by 4, which yields the $887 amount of discount to be amortized each interest period. When the $887 is added to the $4,000 cash payment, the bond interest expense for each period is $4,887. Panel B of Exhibit 10.6 shows how the issuer records bond interest expense and updates the balance of the bond liability account at the end of *each* of the four semiannual interest periods (June 30, 2017, through December 31, 2018).

Exhibit 10.7 shows the pattern of decreases in the Discount on Bonds Payable account and the pattern of increases in the bonds' carrying value. The following points summarize the discount bonds' straight-line amortization:

1. At issuance, the $100,000 par value consists of the $96,454 cash received by the issuer plus the $3,546 discount.

2. During the bonds' life, the (unamortized) discount decreases each period by the $887 amortization ($3,546/4), and the carrying value (par value less unamortized discount) increases each period by $887.

3. At maturity, the unamortized discount equals zero, and the carrying value equals the $100,000 par value that the issuer pays the holder.

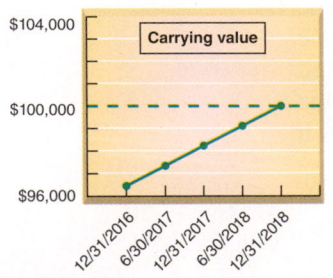

We see that the issuer incurs a $4,887 bond interest expense each period but pays only $4,000 cash. The $887 unpaid portion of this expense is added to the bonds' carrying value. (The total $3,546 unamortized discount is "paid" when the bonds mature; $100,000 is paid at maturity but only $96,454 was received at issuance.)

Bonds Payable

12/31/2016	100,000
6/30/2017	—
12/31/2017	—
6/30/2018	—
12/31/2018	**100,000**

Discount on Bonds Payable

12/31/2016	3,546		
		6/30/2017	887
		12/31/2017	887
		6/30/2018	887
		12/31/2018	885
12/31/2018	**0**		

▨ Decision Insight

Ratings Game   Many bond buyers rely on rating services to assess bond risk. The best known are **Standard & Poor's**, **Moody's**, and **Fitch**. These services focus on the issuer's financial statements and other factors in setting ratings. Standard & Poor's ratings, from best quality to default, are AAA, AA, A, BBB, BB, B, CCC, CC, C, and D. Ratings can include a plus (+) or minus (−) to show relative standing within a category. Bonds rated in the A and B range are referred to as *investment grade;* lower-rated bonds are considered much riskier. ■

A company issues 8%, two-year bonds on December 31, 2016, with a par value of $7,000 and semiannual interest payments. On the issue date, the annual market rate for these bonds is 10%, which implies a selling price of 96.46 or $6,752. (*a*) Prepare an amortization table like the one in Exhibit 10.7 for these bonds; use the straight-line method to amortize the discount. Then, prepare journal entries to record (*b*) the issuance of bonds on December 31, 2016; (*c*) the first through fourth interest payments on each June 30 and December 31; and (*d*) the maturity of the bond on December 31, 2018.

NEED-TO-KNOW 10-1

Recording Discount Bonds

P1   P2

Solution

a.

Semiannual Period-End	Unamortized Discount	Carrying Value
(0) 12/31/2016.	$248	$6,752
(1) 6/30/2017.	186	6,814
(2) 12/31/2017.	124	6,876
(3) 6/30/2018.	62	6,938
(4) 12/31/2018	0	7,000

Interest computations for solutions a, b, and c

Amount repaid to bondholders:	
Four interest payments of $280	
[4 pymts × ($7,000 × 0.08 × 1/2 yr)]	$1,120
Par value at maturity	7,000
Total repaid to bondholders	$8,120
Less amount borrowed from bondholders	
($7,000 × 0.9646)	6,752
Total bond interest expense	$1,368
Divided by number of periods.	÷ 4
Bond interest expense per period.	$ 342

b.

2016			
Dec. 31	Cash	6,752	
	Discount on Bonds Payable	248	
	Bonds Payable.		7,000
	Sold bonds at discount.		

c.

2017			
June 30	Bond Interest Expense	342	
	Discount on Bonds Payable*		62
	Cash†		280
	Pay semiannual interest and record amortization.		
2017			
Dec. 31	Bond Interest Expense	342	
	Discount on Bonds Payable*		62
	Cash†		280
	Pay semiannual interest and record amortization.		
2018			
June 30	Bond Interest Expense	342	
	Discount on Bonds Payable*		62
	Cash†		280
	Pay semiannual interest and record amortization.		
2018			
Dec. 31	Bond Interest Expense	342	
	Discount on Bonds Payable*		62
	Cash†		280
	Pay semiannual interest and record amortization.		

Bonds Payable

	12/31/2016	7,000
	6/30/2017	—
	12/31/2017	—
	6/30/2018	—
	12/31/2018	**7,000**

Discount on Bonds Payable

12/31/2016	248		
		6/30/2017	62
		12/31/2017	62
		6/30/2018	62
		12/31/2018	62
		12/31/2018	**0**

  * $248/4   † $7,000 × 8% × 1/2

d.

2018			
Dec. 31	Bonds Payable.	7,000	
	Cash		7,000
	Record maturity and payment of bonds.		

Do More: QS 10-2, QS 10-6, QS 10-7, E 10-1, E 10-2, E 10-4, E 10-5

P3_____

Compute and record amortization of bond premium using straight-line method.

Issuing Bonds at a Premium

When the contract rate of bonds is higher than the market rate, the bonds sell at a price higher than par value. The amount by which the bond price exceeds par value is the **premium on bonds.** To illustrate, assume that **Adidas** issues bonds with a $100,000 par value, a 12% annual contract rate, semiannual interest payments, and a two-year life. Also assume that the market rate for Adidas bonds is 10% on the issue date. The Adidas bonds will sell at a premium because the contract rate is higher than the market rate. The issue price for these bonds is stated as 103.546 (implying 103.546% of par value, or $103,546); we show how to compute this issue price later in the chapter. These bonds obligate the issuer to pay out two separate future cash flows:

Bond: Contract rate *yields* Cash int. pymt. Market rate *yields* Interest expense. If Cash int. pymt. > Int. expense, *then:*

- Bond sells at premium.
- Carrying value > par value.
- Carrying value declines over time.

1. Par value of $100,000 cash at the end of the bonds' two-year life.
2. Cash interest payments of $6,000 ($100,000 × 12% × 1/2 year) at the end of each semi-annual period during the bonds' two-year life.

The exact pattern of cash flows for the Adidas bonds is shown in Exhibit 10.8.

EXHIBIT 10.8

Cash Flows for Adidas Bonds

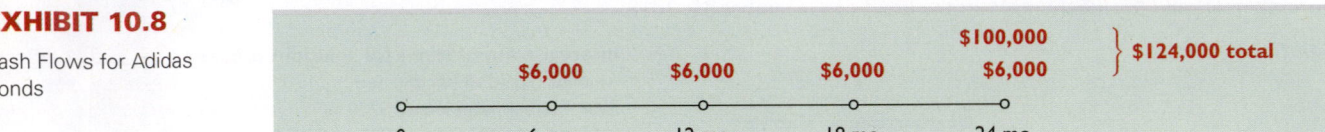

When Adidas accepts $103,546 cash for its bonds on the issue date of December 31, 2016, it records this transaction as follows.

Assets = Liabilities + Equity
+103,546   +100,000
           +3,546

Dec. 31	Cash	103,546	
	Premium on Bonds Payable		3,546
	Bonds Payable		100,000
	Sold bonds at a premium on their issue date.		

These bonds are reported in the long-term liability section of the issuer's December 31, 2016, balance sheet as shown in Exhibit 10.9. A premium is added to par value to yield the carrying (book) value of bonds. Premium on Bonds Payable is an adjunct liability account.

EXHIBIT 10.9

Balance Sheet Presentation of Bond Premium

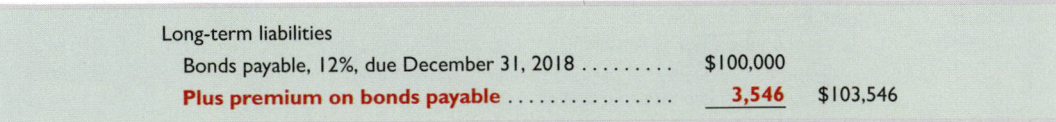

Long-term liabilities		
Bonds payable, 12%, due December 31, 2018	$100,000	
Plus premium on bonds payable	3,546	$103,546

Amortizing a Bond Premium   Adidas receives $103,546 for its bonds; in return, it pays bondholders $100,000 after two years (plus semiannual interest payments). The $3,546 premium not repaid to bondholders at maturity goes to reduce the issuer's expense of using the $103,546 for two years. The upper portion of panel A of Exhibit 10.10 shows that total bond interest expense of $20,454 is the difference between the total amount repaid to bondholders ($124,000) and the amount borrowed from bondholders ($103,546). Alternatively, we can compute total bond interest expense as the sum of the four interest payments less the bond premium. The premium is subtracted because it will not be paid to bondholders when the bonds mature; see the lower portion of panel A. Total bond interest expense must be allocated over the four semiannual periods using the straight-line method (or the effective interest method in Appendix 10B).

Point: The phrase *ability to service debt* refers to making interest and principal payments on time.

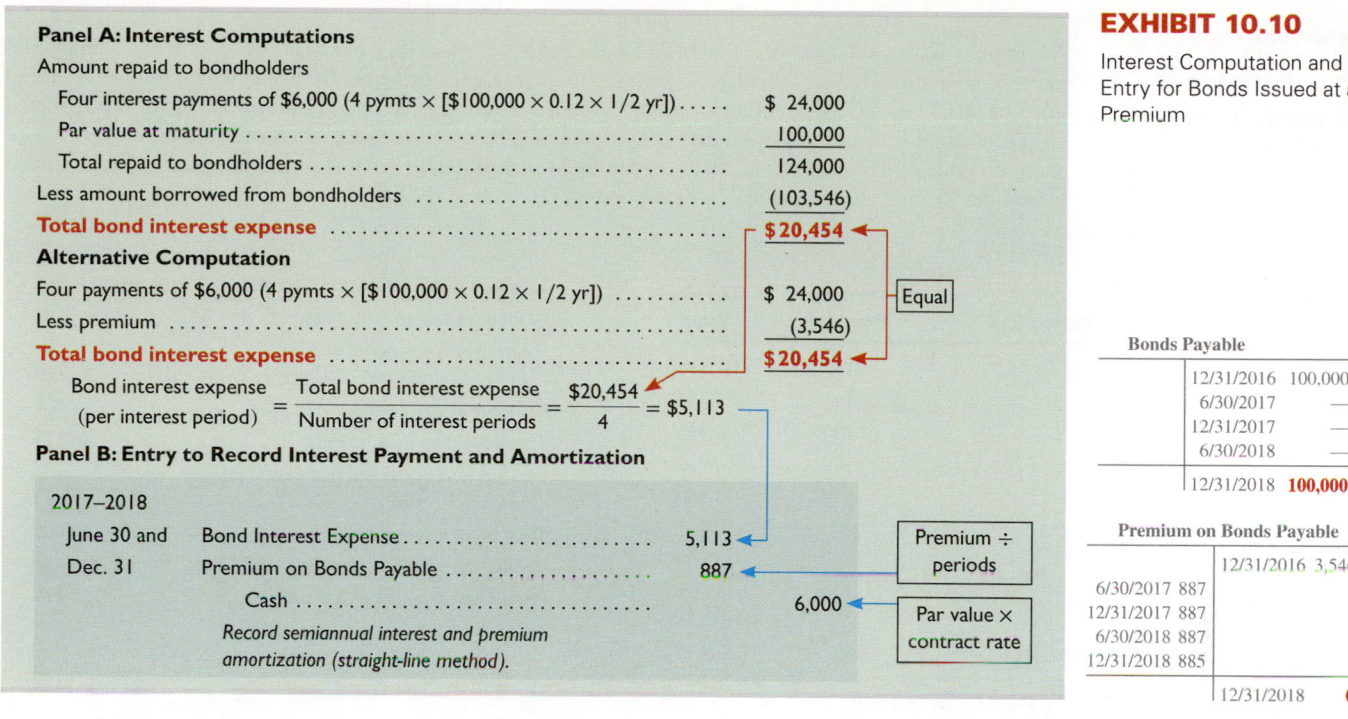

Panel A: Interest Computations

Amount repaid to bondholders

Four interest payments of $6,000 (4 pymts × [$100,000 × 0.12 × 1/2 yr])	$ 24,000
Par value at maturity	100,000
Total repaid to bondholders	124,000
Less amount borrowed from bondholders	(103,546)
Total bond interest expense	**$20,454** ←

Alternative Computation

Four payments of $6,000 (4 pymts × [$100,000 × 0.12 × 1/2 yr])	$ 24,000
Less premium	(3,546)
Total bond interest expense	**$20,454** ←

$$\frac{\text{Bond interest expense}}{\text{(per interest period)}} = \frac{\text{Total bond interest expense}}{\text{Number of interest periods}} = \frac{\$20,454}{4} = \$5,113$$

Panel B: Entry to Record Interest Payment and Amortization

2017–2018			
June 30 and	Bond Interest Expense.	5,113	
Dec. 31	Premium on Bonds Payable	887	
	Cash		6,000
	Record semiannual interest and premium		
	amortization (straight-line method).		

Equal

Premium ÷ periods

Par value × contract rate

EXHIBIT 10.10

Interest Computation and Entry for Bonds Issued at a Premium

Bonds Payable

	12/31/2016	100,000
6/30/2017		—
12/31/2017		—
6/30/2018		—
	12/31/2018	**100,000**

Premium on Bonds Payable

	12/31/2016	3,546
6/30/2017	887	
12/31/2017	887	
6/30/2018	887	
12/31/2018	885	
	12/31/2018	**0**

The following section on premium amortization uses the Straight-Line Method. Appendix 10B uses the effective interest method. An instructor can choose to cover either one or both methods. If the straight-line method is skipped, then move forward to the section titled "Bond Pricing."

Straight-Line Method   The straight-line method allocates an equal portion of total bond interest expense to each of the bonds' semiannual interest periods. To apply this method to Adidas bonds, we divide the two years' total bond interest expense of $20,454 by 4 (the number of semiannual periods in the bonds' life). This gives a total bond interest expense of $5,113 per period, which is $5,113.5 rounded down so that the journal entry balances and for simplicity in presentation (alternatively, one could carry cents). Panel B of Exhibit 10.10 shows how the issuer records bond interest expense and updates the balance of the bond liability account for *each* semiannual period (June 30, 2017, through December 31, 2018).

Exhibit 10.11 shows the pattern of decreases in the unamortized Premium on Bonds Payable account and in the bonds' carrying value. The following points summarize straight-line amortization of the premium bonds:

1. At issuance, the $100,000 par value plus the $3,546 premium equals the $103,546 cash received by the issuer.

2. During the bonds' life, the (unamortized) premium decreases each period by the $887 amortization ($3,546/4), and the carrying value decreases each period by the same $887.

3. At maturity, the unamortized premium equals zero, and the carrying value equals the $100,000 par value that the issuer pays the holder.

Point: A premium decreases Bond Interest Expense; a discount increases it.

EXHIBIT 10.11

Straight-Line Amortization of Bond Premium

Semiannual Period-End	Unamortized Premium*	Carrying Value†
(0) 12/31/2016	$3,546	$103,546
(1) 6/30/2017	2,659	102,659
(2) 12/31/2017	1,772	101,772
(3) 6/30/2018	885	100,885
(4) 12/31/2018	0‡	100,000

* Total bond premium (of $3,546) less accumulated periodic amortization ($887 per semiannual interest period).

† Bond par value (of $100,000) plus unamortized premium.

‡ Adjusted for rounding.

During the bond life, carrying value is adjusted to par and the amortized premium to zero.

Recording Premium Bonds

P3

A company issues 8%, two-year bonds on December 31, 2016, with a par value of $7,000 and semiannual interest payments. On the issue date, the annual market rate for these bonds is 6%, which implies a selling price of 103.71 or $7,260. (*a*) Prepare an amortization table like the one in Exhibit 10.11 for these bonds; use the straight-line method to amortize the premium. Then, prepare journal entries to record (*b*) the issuance of bonds on December 31, 2016; (*c*) the first through fourth interest payments on each June 30 and December 31; and (*d*) the maturity of the bond on December 31, 2018.

Solution

a.

Semiannual Period-End	Unamortized Premium	Carrying Value
(0) 12/31/2016.............	$260	$7,260
(1) 6/30/2017.............	195	7,195
(2) 12/31/2017.............	130	7,130
(3) 6/30/2018.............	65	7,065
(4) 12/31/2018.............	0	7,000

Interest computations for solutions *a*, *b*, and *c*

Amount repaid to bondholders:	
Four interest payments of $280	
[4 pymts × ($7,000 × 0.08 × 1/2 yr)]	$1,120
Par value at maturity	7,000
Total repaid to bondholders	$8,120
Less amount borrowed from bondholders	
($7,000 × 1.0371)	7,260
Total bond interest expense	$ 860
Divided by number of periods.............	÷ 4
Bond interest expense per period...........	$ 215

b.

2016			
Dec. 31	Cash	7,260	
	Premium on Bonds Payable		260
	Bonds Payable.................................		7,000
	Sold bonds at premium.		

c.

2017			
June 30	Bond Interest Expense	215	
	Premium on Bonds Payable*.........................	65	
	Cash†...		280
	Pay semiannual interest and record amortization.		
2017			
Dec. 31	Bond Interest Expense	215	
	Premium on Bonds Payable*.........................	65	
	Cash†...		280
	Pay semiannual interest and record amortization.		
2018			
June 30	Bond Interest Expense	215	
	Premium on Bonds Payable*.........................	65	
	Cash†...		280
	Pay semiannual interest and record amortization.		
2018			
Dec. 31	Bond Interest Expense	215	
	Premium on Bonds Payable*.........................	65	
	Cash†...		280
	Pay semiannual interest and record amortization.		

* $260/4   † $7,000 × 8% × ½

Bonds Payable

12/31/2016 7,000	
6/30/2017 —	
12/31/2017 —	
6/30/2018 —	
12/31/2018 **7,000**	

Discount on Bonds Payable

	12/31/2016 260
6/30/2017 65	
12/31/2017 65	
6/30/2018 65	
12/31/2018 65	
	12/31/2018 **0**

d.

2018			
Dec. 31	Bonds Payable.......................................	7,000	
	Cash		7,000
	Record maturity and payment of bonds.		

Do More: QS 10-8, E 10-6, E 10-7, P 10-3, P 10-4

> *The next section describes bond pricing. An instructor can choose to cover bond pricing or not. Assignments requiring the "Bond Pricing" section are Quick Study 10-3 and 10-5 and Exercises 10-3 and 10-8.*

Bond Pricing

Prices for bonds traded on an organized exchange are commonly published online. This information normally includes the bond price (called *quote*), its contract rate, and its current market (called *yield*) rate. However, only a fraction of bonds are traded on organized exchanges. To compute the price of a bond, we apply present value concepts. This section explains how to use *present value concepts* to price the Fila discount bond and the Adidas premium bond described earlier.

Present Value of a Discount Bond   The issue price of bonds is found by computing the present value of the bonds' cash payments, discounted at the bonds' market rate. When computing the present value of the Fila bonds, we work with *semiannual* compounding periods because this is the time between interest payments; the annual market rate of 10% is considered a semiannual rate of 5%. Also, the two-year bond life is viewed as four semiannual periods. The price computation is twofold: (1) Find the present value of the $100,000 par value paid at maturity and (2) find the present value of the series of four semiannual payments of $4,000 each; see Exhibit 10.4. These present values can be found by using *present value tables*. Appendix B at the end of this book shows present value tables and describes their use. Table B.1 in Appendix B is used for the single $100,000 maturity payment, and Table B.3 in Appendix B is used for the $4,000 series of interest payments. Specifically, we go to Table B.1, row 4, and across to the 5% column to identify the present value factor of 0.8227 for the maturity payment. Next, we go to Table B.3, row 4, and across to the 5% column, where the present value factor is 3.5460 for the series of interest payments. We compute the bond price by multiplying the cash flow payments by their corresponding present value factors and adding them together; see Exhibit 10.12.

Point: *Zero-coupon bonds* do not pay periodic interest (contract rate is zero). These bonds always sell at a discount because their 0% contract rate is always below the market rate.

Point: InvestinginBonds.com is a bond research and learning source.

Point: A bond's market value (price) at issuance equals the present value of its future cash payments, where the interest (discount) rate used is the bond's market rate.

Point: Many calculators have present value functions for computing bond prices.

EXHIBIT 10.12

Computing Issue Price for the Fila Discount Bonds

Cash Flow	Table	Present Value Factor	Amount	Present Value
$100,000 par (maturity) value	B.1 (PV of 1)	0.8227	× $100,000 =	$82,270
$4,000 interest payments.............	B.3 (PV of ann.)	3.5460	× 4,000 =	14,184
Price of bond.....................				**$96,454**

Calculator	
N = 4	PMT = 4,000
I/Yr = 5	FV = 100,000
	PV = 96,454

Present Value of a Premium Bond   We find the issue price of the Adidas bonds by using the market rate to compute the present value of the bonds' future cash flows. When computing the present value of these bonds, we again work with *semiannual* compounding periods because this is the time between interest payments. The annual 10% market rate is applied as a semiannual rate of 5%, and the two-year bond life is viewed as four semiannual periods. The computation is twofold: (1) Find the present value of the $100,000 par value paid at maturity and (2) find the present value of the series of four payments of $6,000 each; see Exhibit 10.8. These present values can be found by using present value tables. First, go to Table B.1, row 4, and across to the 5% column where the present value factor is 0.8227 for the maturity payment. Second, go to Table B.3, row 4, and across to the 5% column, where the present value factor is 3.5460 for the series of interest payments. The bonds' price is computed by multiplying the cash flow payments by their corresponding present value factors and adding them together; see Exhibit 10.13.

Point: Calculator inputs defined:

N   Number of semiannual periods
I/Yr   Market rate per semiannual period
FV   Future (maturity) value
PMT   Payment (interest) per semiannual period
PV   Price (present value)

EXHIBIT 10.13

Computing Issue Price for the Adidas Premium Bonds

Cash Flow	Table	Present Value Factor	Amount	Present Value
$100,000 par (maturity) value	B.1 (PV of 1)	0.8227	× $100,000 =	$ 82,270
$6,000 interest payments.............	B.3 (PV of ann.)	3.5460	× 6,000 =	21,276
Price of bond.....................				**$103,546**

Calculator	
N = 4	PMT = 6,000
I/Yr = 5	FV = 100,000
	PV = 103,546

Decision Insight

Equivalent Payments Concept   Business decisions frequently involve concepts using the time value of money. To help in those decisions, the present value factors can be thought of as *equivalent payments*. For example, using the data in Exhibit 10.12, one payment of $100,000 scheduled two years from today is the *equivalent* of a 0.8227 payment of $100,000 today (assuming a market with 10% return). Similarly, four semiannual payments of $4,000 over the next two years are the equivalent of 3.5460 payments of $4,000 today (again, assuming a 10% return). ■

BOND RETIREMENT

P4
_____

Record the retirement of bonds.

This section describes the retirement of bonds (1) at maturity, (2) before maturity, and (3) by conversion to stock.

Bond Retirement at Maturity

The carrying value of bonds at maturity always equals par value. For example, both Exhibits 10.7 (a discount) and 10.11 (a premium) show that the carrying value of bonds at the end of their lives equals par value ($100,000). The retirement of these bonds at maturity, assuming interest is already paid and entered, is recorded as follows:

Assets = Liabilities + Equity
−100,000   −100,000

2018			
Dec. 31	Bonds Payable.....................................	100,000	
	Cash		100,000
	Record retirement of bonds at maturity.		

Bond Retirement before Maturity

Issuers sometimes wish to retire some or all of their bonds prior to maturity. For instance, if interest rates decline greatly, an issuer may wish to replace high-interest-paying bonds with new low-interest bonds. Two common ways to retire bonds before maturity are to (1) exercise a call option or (2) purchase them on the open market. In the first instance, an issuer can reserve the right to retire bonds early by issuing callable bonds. The bond indenture can give the issuer an option to *call* the bonds before they mature by paying the par value plus a *call premium* to bondholders. In the second case, the issuer retires bonds by repurchasing them on the open market at their current price. Whether bonds are called or repurchased, the issuer is unlikely to pay a price that exactly equals their carrying value. When a difference exists between the bonds' carrying value and the amount paid, the issuer records a gain or loss equal to the difference.

   To illustrate the accounting for retiring callable bonds, assume that a company issued callable bonds with a par value of $100,000. The call option requires the issuer to pay a call premium of $3,000 to bondholders in addition to the par value. Next, assume that after the June 30, 2016, interest payment, the bonds have a carrying value of $104,500. Then on July 1, 2016, the issuer calls these bonds and pays $103,000 to bondholders. The issuer recognizes a $1,500 gain from the difference between the bonds' carrying value of $104,500 and the retirement price of $103,000. The issuer records this bond retirement as follows.

Point: Bond retirement is also referred to as *bond redemption*.

Point: Gains and losses from retiring bonds were *previously* reported as extraordinary items. New standards require that they now be judged by the "unusual and infrequent" criteria for reporting purposes.

Assets   = Liabilities + Equity
−103,000   −100,000   +1,500
                −4,500

July 1	Bonds Payable.....................................	100,000	
	Premium on Bonds Payable	4,500	
	Gain on Bond Retirement		1,500
	Cash		103,000
	Record retirement of bonds before maturity.		

An issuer usually must call all bonds when it exercises a call option. However, to retire as many or as few bonds as it desires, an issuer can purchase them on the open market. If it retires less than the entire class of bonds, it recognizes a gain or loss for the difference between the carrying value of those bonds retired and the amount paid to acquire them.

Bond Retirement by Conversion

Holders of convertible bonds have the right to convert their bonds to stock. When conversion occurs, the bonds' carrying value is transferred to equity accounts and no gain or loss is recorded. (We further describe convertible bonds in the Decision Analysis section of this chapter.)

To illustrate, assume that on January 1 the $100,000 par value bonds of **Converse**, with a carrying value of $100,000, are converted to 15,000 shares of $2 par value common stock. The entry to record this conversion follows (the market prices of the bonds and stock are *not* relevant to this entry; the material in Chapter 11 is helpful in understanding this transaction):

Convertible Bond

Jan. 1	Bonds Payable...........................	100,000	
	Common Stock...........................		30,000
	Paid-In Capital in Excess of Par Value..........		70,000
	Record retirement of bonds by conversion.		

Assets = Liabilities + Equity
−100,000   +30,000
+70,000

Decision Insight

Junk Bonds Junk bonds are company bonds with low credit ratings due to a higher-than-average likelihood of default. On the upside, the high risk of junk bonds can yield high returns if the issuer survives and repays its debt. Investors in junk bonds identify and buy bonds with low credit ratings when they believe those bonds will survive and pay off their obligations. ■

LONG-TERM NOTES PAYABLE

Like bonds, notes are issued to obtain assets such as cash. Unlike bonds, notes are typically transacted with a *single* lender such as a bank. An issuer initially records a note at its selling price—that is, the note's face value minus any discount or plus any premium. Over the note's life, the amount of interest expense allocated to each period is computed by multiplying the market rate (at issuance of the note) by the beginning-of-period note balance. The note's carrying (book) value at any time equals its face value minus any unamortized discount or plus any unamortized premium; carrying value is also computed as the present value of all remaining payments, discounted using the market rate at issuance.

C1

Explain the types of notes and prepare entries to account for notes.

Installment Notes

An **installment note** is an obligation requiring a series of payments to the lender. Installment notes are common for franchises and other businesses when lenders and borrowers agree to spread payments over several periods. To illustrate, assume that Foghog borrows $60,000 from a bank to purchase equipment. It signs an 8% installment note requiring six annual payments of principal plus interest and it records the note's issuance at January 1, 2016, as follows.

Assets = Liabilities + Equity
+60,000   +60,000

Jan. 1	Cash	60,000	
	Notes Payable.		60,000
	Borrowed $60,000 by signing an 8%,		
	six-year note.		

Payments on an installment note normally include the accrued interest expense plus a portion of the amount borrowed (the *principal*). This section describes an installment note with equal payments.

Years

2016 2017 2018 2019 2020 2021

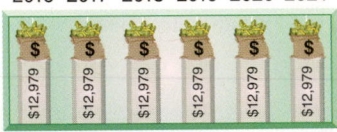

$12,979 $12,979 $12,979 $12,979 $12,979 $12,979

The equal total payments pattern consists of changing amounts of both interest and principal. To illustrate, assume that Foghog borrows $60,000 by signing a $60,000 note that requires six *equal payments* of $12,979 at the end of each year. (The present value of an annuity of six annual payments of $12,979, discounted at 8%, equals $60,000; we show this computation in footnote 2.) The $12,979 includes both interest and principal, the amounts of which change with each payment. Exhibit 10.14 shows the pattern of equal total payments and its two parts, interest and principal. Column A shows the note's beginning balance. Column B shows accrued interest for each year at 8% of the beginning note balance. Column C shows the impact on the note's principal, which equals the difference between the total payment in column D and the interest expense in column B. Column E shows the note's year-end balance.

Point: Most consumer notes are installment notes that require equal total payments.

EXHIBIT 10.14

Installment Note: Equal Total Payments Amortization Schedule

		(A)	(B)		(C)		(D)	(E)
			Debit		Debit		Credit	
Period		Beginning	Interest		Notes		Cash	Ending
Ending		Balance	Expense	+	Payable	=		Balance
Date			8% × (A)		(D) − (B)		(computed)	(A) − (C)
(1) 12/31/2016		$60,000	$ 4,800		$ 8,179		$12,979	$51,821
(2) 12/31/2017		51,821	4,146		8,833		12,979	42,988
(3) 12/31/2018		42,988	3,439		9,540		12,979	33,448
(4) 12/31/2019		33,448	2,676		10,303		12,979	23,145
(5) 12/31/2020		23,145	1,852		11,127		12,979	12,018
(6) 12/31/2021		12,018	961		12,018		12,979	0
			$17,874		$60,000		$77,874	

▢ Interest ▢ Principal

Decreasing Accrued Interest   Increasing Principal Component   Equal Total Payments

End of Year		
2016	$4,800	$8,179
2017	$4,146	$8,833
2018	$3,439	$9,540
2019	$2,676	$10,303
2020	$1,852	$11,127
2021	$961	$12,018

0    $2,500 $5,000 $7,500 $10,000 $12,500 $15,000
Cash Payment Pattern

Although the six cash payments are equal, accrued interest decreases each year because the principal balance of the note declines. As the amount of interest decreases each year, the portion of each payment applied to principal increases. This pattern is graphed in the lower part of Exhibit 10.14. Foghog uses the amounts in Exhibit 10.14 to record its first two payments (for years 2016 and 2017) as follows:

2016			
Dec. 31	Interest Expense...............................	4,800	
	Notes Payable.................................	8,179	
	Cash......................................		12,979
	Record first installment payment.		

Assets = Liabilities + Equity
−12,979   −8,179   −4,800

2017			
Dec. 31	Interest Expense...............................	4,146	
	Notes Payable.................................	8,833	
	Cash......................................		12,979
	Record second installment payment.		

Assets = Liabilities + Equity
−12,979   −8,833   −4,146

Foghog records similar entries but with different amounts for each of the remaining four payments. After six years, the Notes Payable account balance is zero.[2]

Fraud

Missing Debt A study reports that 29% of employees in finance and accounting witnessed the falsifying or manipulating of accounting information in the past year (KPMG 2013). This includes nondisclosure of special concern with long-term liabilities. Another study reports that most people committing fraud (36%) work in the finance function of their firm (KPMG 2011). For example, **Enron** violated GAAP to keep debt off its balance sheet.

Mortgage Notes and Bonds

A **mortgage** is a legal agreement that helps protect a lender if a borrower fails to make required payments on notes or bonds. A mortgage gives the lender a right to be paid from the cash proceeds of the sale of a borrower's assets identified in the mortgage. A legal document, called a *mortgage contract,* describes the mortgage terms.

Mortgage notes carry a mortgage contract pledging title to specific assets as security for the note. Mortgage notes are especially popular in the purchase of homes and the acquisition of plant assets. Less common *mortgage bonds* are backed by the issuer's assets. Accounting for mortgage notes and bonds is similar to that for unsecured notes and bonds, except that the mortgage agreement must be disclosed. For example, **TIBCO Software** reports that its "mortgage note payable . . . is collateralized by the commercial real property acquired [corporate headquarters]."

Point: The Truth in Lending Act requires lenders to provide information about loan costs including finance charges and interest rate.

Global: Countries vary in the preference given to debtholders vs. stockholders when a company is in financial distress. Some countries such as Germany, France, and Japan give preference to stockholders over debtholders.

Decision Maker

Entrepreneur You are a furniture retailer planning a Super Bowl sale on a home theater system that requires no payments for two years. At the end of two years, buyers must pay the full amount. The system's suggested retail price is $4,100, but you are willing to sell it today for $3,000 cash. What is your sale price if payment will not occur for two years and the market interest rate is 10%? ■ [Answers follow the chapter's Summary.]

---

[2] Table B.3 in Appendix B is used to compute the dollar amount of the six payments that equal the initial note balance of $60,000 at 8% interest. We go to Table B.3, row 6, and across to the 8% column, where the present value factor is 4.6229. The dollar amount is then computed by solving this equation:

Table	Present Value Factor		Dollar Amount		Present Value
B.3	4.6229	×	?	=	$60,000

The dollar amount is computed by dividing $60,000 by 4.6229, yielding $12,979.

Example: Suppose the $60,000 installment loan has an 8% interest rate with eight equal annual payments. What is the annual payment? *Answer* (using Table B.3): $60,000/5.7466 = $10,441

10-3

Recording Installment Note

C1   P5

On January 1, 2016, a company borrows $1,000 cash by signing a four-year, 5% installment note. The note requires four equal total payments of accrued interest and principal on December 31 of each year from 2016 through 2019.

1. Compute the amount of each of the four equal total payments.

2. Prepare an amortization table for this installment note like the one in Exhibit 10.14.

3. Prepare journal entries to record the loan on January 1, 2016, and the four payments from December 31, 2016, through December 31, 2019.

Solution

1. Amount of each payment = Initial note balance/PV of annuity (from Table B.3)
$$= \$1,000/3.5460 = \underline{\$282} \text{ (rounded)}$$

2. Amortization table for loan

			Payments		
	(A)	**(B)**	**(C)**	**(D)**	**(E)**
		Debit	*Debit*		
Period Ending Date	**Beginning Balance [Prior (E)]**	**Interest Expense [5% × (A)]** +	**Notes Payable [(D) − (B)]** =	**Credit Cash [computed]**	**Ending Balance [(A) − (C)]**
2016.............	$1,000	$ 50	$ 232	$ 282	$768
2017.............	768	38	244	282	524
2018.............	524	26	256	282	268
2019.............	268	14*	268	282	0
		$128	$1,000	$1,128	

* Adjusted for rounding.

3.

2016				
Jan. 1	Cash	1,000	
	Notes Payable.................................		1,000
	Borrowed $1,000 by signing a 5% note.		
2016				
Dec. 31	Interest Expense.................................	50	
	Notes Payable...................................	232	
	Cash		282
	Record first installment payment.		
2017				
Dec. 31	Interest Expense.................................	38	
	Notes Payable...................................	244	
	Cash		282
	Record second installment payment.		
2018				
Dec. 31	Interest Expense.................................	26	
	Notes Payable...................................	256	
	Cash		282
	Record third installment payment.		
2019				
Dec. 31	Interest Expense.................................	14	
	Notes Payable...................................	268	
	Cash		282
	Record fourth installment payment.		

Do More: QS 10-11, E 10-10, E 10-11

GLOBAL VIEW

This section discusses similarities and differences between U.S. GAAP and IFRS in accounting and reporting for long-term liabilities such as bonds and notes.

Accounting for Bonds and Notes   The definitions and characteristics of bonds and notes are broadly similar for both U.S. GAAP and IFRS. Although slight differences exist, accounting for bonds and notes under U.S. GAAP and IFRS is similar. Specifically, the accounting for issuances (including recording discounts and premiums), market pricing, and retirement of both bonds and notes follows the procedures in this chapter. **Nokia** describes its accounting for bonds, which follows the amortized cost approach explained in this chapter (and in Appendix 10B), as follows: Loans payable [bonds] are recognized initially at fair value, net of transaction costs incurred. In the subsequent periods, loans payable are measured at amortized cost using the effective interest method.

Both U.S. GAAP and IFRS allow companies to account for bonds and notes using fair value (different from the amortized value described in this chapter). This method is referred to as the **fair value option.** This method is similar to that applied in measuring and accounting for debt and equity securities. *Fair value* is the amount a company would receive if it settled a liability (or sold an asset) in an orderly transaction as of the balance sheet date. Companies can use several sources of inputs to determine fair value, and those inputs fall into the following three classes (ranked in order of preference). The procedures for marking liabilities to fair value at each balance sheet date are in advanced courses.

Level 1: Observable quoted market prices in active markets for identical items.
Level 2: Observable inputs other than those in Level 1 such as prices from inactive markets or from similar, but not identical, items.
Level 3: Unobservable inputs reflecting a company's assumptions about value.

Accounting for Leases and Pensions   Both U.S. GAAP and IFRS require companies to distinguish between operating leases and capital leases; the latter are referred to as *finance leases* under IFRS. The accounting and reporting for leases are broadly similar for both U.S. GAAP and IFRS. The main difference is the criteria for identifying a lease as a capital lease are more general under IFRS. However, the basic approach applies.

> **Point:** Lease accounting is expected to change over the next year or so.

For pensions, both U.S. GAAP and IFRS require companies to record costs of retirement benefits as employees work and earn them. The basic methods are similar in accounting and reporting for pensions.

Sustainability and Accounting   **Box**, the company from this chapter's opening feature, provides nonprofit organizations with a way to store content, share files, and collaborate on key ideas. Box runs a special website, **Box.org**, that is solely committed to helping nonprofit organizations be more productive and collaborative in achieving their missions. This is important to Box because 87% of nonprofits are without a dedicated IT department; Box's ease of use lessens the need for an IT department. Over 1,000 nonprofits have teamed with Box and utilize their services. These nonprofits include **Teach for America**, **Boys & Girls Clubs**, and **Livestrong Foundation**. Box reports: "At Box, we believe that those committed to doing good should have the best tools available to them."

Kathryn Scott Osler/The Denver Post via Getty Images

Debt Features and the Debt-to-Equity Ratio   **Decision Analysis**

Collateral agreements can reduce the risk of loss for both bonds and notes. Unsecured bonds and notes are riskier because the issuer's obligation to pay interest and principal has the same priority as all other unsecured liabilities in the event of bankruptcy. If a company is unable to pay its debts in full, the unsecured creditors (including the holders of debentures) lose all or a portion of their balances. These types of legal agreements and other characteristics of long-term liabilities are crucial for effective business decisions. The first part of this section describes the different types of features sometimes included with bonds and notes. The second part explains and applies the debt-to-equity ratio.

A2

Assess debt features and their implications.

Features of Bonds and Notes

This section describes common features of debt securities.

Secured or Unsecured   Secured bonds (and notes) have specific assets of the issuer pledged (or *mortgaged*) as collateral. This arrangement

Secured Debt

Unsecured Debt

Point: More than a million municipal bonds, or "munis," exist, and many are tax exempt. Munis is issued by state, city, town, and county governments to pay for public projects including schools, libraries, roads, bridges, and stadiums.

gives holders added protection against the issuer's default. If the issuer fails to pay interest or par value, the secured holders can demand that the collateral be sold and the proceeds used to pay the obligation. **Unsecured bonds** (and notes), also called *debentures,* are backed by the issuer's general credit standing. Unsecured debt is riskier than secured debt. *Subordinated debentures* are liabilities that are not repaid until the claims of the more senior, unsecured (and secured) liabilities are settled.

Term or Serial   **Term bonds** (and notes) are scheduled for maturity on one specified date. **Serial bonds** (and notes) mature at more than one date (often in series) and thus are usually repaid over a number of periods. For instance, $100,000 of serial bonds might mature at the rate of $10,000 each year from 6 to 15 years after they are issued. Many bonds are **sinking fund bonds,** which, to reduce the holder's risk, require the issuer to create a *sinking fund* of assets set aside at specified amounts and dates to repay the bonds.

Registered or Bearer   Bonds issued in the names and addresses of their holders are **registered bonds.** The issuer makes bond payments by sending checks (or cash transfers) to registered holders. A registered holder must notify the issuer of any ownership change. Registered bonds offer the issuer the practical advantage of not having to actually issue bond certificates. Bonds payable to whoever holds them (the *bearer*) are called **bearer bonds** or *unregistered bonds.* Sales or exchanges might not be recorded, so the holder of a bearer bond is presumed to be its rightful owner. As a result, lost bearer bonds are difficult to replace. Many bearer bonds are also **coupon bonds.** This term reflects interest coupons that are attached to the bonds. When each coupon matures, the holder presents it to a bank or broker for collection. At maturity, the holder follows the same process and presents the bond certificate for collection. Issuers of coupon bonds cannot deduct the related interest expense for taxable income. This is to prevent abuse by taxpayers who own coupon bonds but fail to report interest income on their tax returns.

Convertible Debt

Callable Debt

Convertible and/or Callable   **Convertible bonds** (and notes) can be exchanged for a fixed number of shares of the issuing corporation's common stock. Convertible debt offers holders the potential to participate in future increases in stock price. Holders still receive periodic interest while the debt is held and the par value if they hold the debt to maturity. In most cases, the holders decide whether and when to convert debt to stock. **Callable bonds** (and notes) have an option exercisable by the issuer to retire them at a stated dollar amount before maturity.

 Decision Insight ━━━━━━━━━━━━━━━━━━━━

Collateral   Lenders prefer that more liquid assets serve as collateral for loans. These usually are current assets such as accounts receivable or inventory. The reason is if borrowers default and collateral must be seized, then lenders desire assets that are easily sold to recover losses. ◼

A3 _____

Compute the debt-to-equity ratio and explain its use.

Debt-to-Equity Ratio

Beyond assessing different characteristics of debt as just described, we want to know the level of debt, especially in relation to total equity. Such knowledge helps us assess the risk of a company's financing structure. A company financed mainly with debt is more risky because liabilities must be repaid—usually with periodic interest—whereas equity financing does not. A measure to assess the risk of a company's financing structure is the **debt-to-equity ratio** (see Exhibit 10.15).

EXHIBIT 10.15

Debt-to-Equity Ratio

$$\text{Debt-to-equity} = \frac{\text{Total liabilities}}{\text{Total equity}}$$

The debt-to-equity ratio varies across companies and industries. To apply the debt-to-equity ratio, let's look at this measure for **Amazon.com** in Exhibit 10.16.

EXHIBIT 10.16

Amazon's Debt-to-Equity Ratio

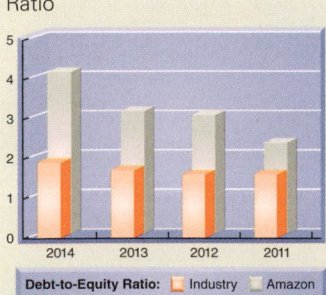

$ millions	2014	2013	2012	2011
Total liabilities	$43,764	$30,413	$24,363	$17,521
Total equity	$10,741	$ 9,746	$ 8,192	$ 7,757
Debt-to-equity	**4.1**	**3.1**	**3.0**	**2.3**
Industry debt-to-equity	1.8	1.6	1.5	1.5

Amazon's 2014 debt-to-equity ratio is 4.1, meaning that debtholders contributed $4.10 for each $1 contributed by equity holders. This implies a riskier-than-usual financing structure for Amazon. A similar interpretation is drawn from a comparison of Amazon with its competitors, where the 2014 industry ratio is 1.8. Analysis across the years shows that Amazon's financing structure has risen to a riskier level in recent years. Given its growth in revenues and innovative past, investors have been patient in waiting for income. However, debtholders will grow increasingly concerned if income fails to rise in the near future.

Decision Maker

Bond Investor   You plan to purchase debenture bonds from one of two companies in the same industry that are similar in size and performance. The first company has $350,000 in total liabilities and $1,750,000 in equity. The second company has $1,200,000 in total liabilities and $1,000,000 in equity. Which company's debenture bonds are less risky based on the debt-to-equity ratio? ■ [Answers follow the chapter's Summary.]

Water Sports Company (WSC) patented and successfully test-marketed a new product. To expand its ability to produce and market the new product, WSC needs to raise $800,000 of financing. On January 1, 2016, the company obtained the money in two ways:

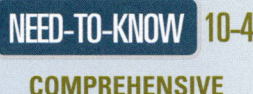

COMPREHENSIVE

a. WSC signed a $400,000, 10% installment note to be repaid with five equal annual installments to be made on December 31 of 2016 through 2020.

b. WSC issued five-year bonds with a par value of $400,000. The bonds have a 12% annual contract rate and pay interest on June 30 and December 31. The bonds' annual market rate is 10% as of January 1, 2016.

Required

1. For the installment note, (*a*) compute the size of each annual payment, (*b*) prepare an amortization table similar to Exhibit 10.14, and (*c*) prepare the journal entry for the first payment.

2. For the bonds, (*a*) compute their issue price; (*b*) prepare the January 1, 2016, journal entry to record their issuance; (*c*) prepare an amortization table using the straight-line method; (*d*) prepare the June 30, 2016, journal entry to record the first interest payment; and (*e*) prepare a journal entry to record retiring the bonds at a $416,000 call price on January 1, 2018.

3.ᴮ Redo parts 2(*c*), 2(*d*), and 2(*e*) assuming the bonds are amortized using the effective interest method.

PLANNING THE SOLUTION

● For the installment note, divide the borrowed amount by the annuity factor (from Table B.3) using the 10% rate and five payments to compute the amount of each payment. Prepare a table similar to Exhibit 10.14 and use the numbers in the table's first line for the journal entry.

● Compute the bonds' issue price by using the market rate to find the present value of their cash flows (use tables found in Appendix B). Then use this result to record the bonds' issuance. Next, prepare an amortization table like Exhibit 10.11 (and Exhibit 10B.2) and use it to get the numbers needed for the journal entry. Also use the table to find the carrying value as of the date of the bonds' retirement that you need for the journal entry.

SOLUTION

Part 1: Installment Note

a. Annual payment = Note balance/PV annuity factor = $400,000/3.7908 = $105,519 (The present value annuity factor is for five payments and a rate of 10%.)

b. An amortization table for the long-term note payable follows.

	A	B	C	D	E	F	G	H
1					**Payments**			
2		**(a)**	**(b)**		**(c)**		**(d)**	**(e)**
3	**Annual**		**Debit**		**Debit**		**Credit**	
4	**Period**	**Beginning**	**Interest**		**Notes**			**Ending**
4	**Ending**	**Balance**	**Expense**	**+**	**Payable**	**=**	**Cash**	**Balance**
5			**10% × (a)**		**(d) − (b)**		**(computed)**	**(a) − (c)**
6	(1) 12/31/2016	$400,000	$ 40,000		$ 65,519		$105,519	$334,481
7	(2) 12/31/2017	334,481	33,448		72,071		105,519	262,410
8	(3) 12/31/2018	262,410	26,241		79,278		105,519	183,132
9	(4) 12/31/2019	183,132	18,313		87,206		105,519	95,926
10	(5) 12/31/2020	95,926	9,593		95,926		105,519	0
11			$127,595		$400,000		$527,595	
12								

c. Journal entry for December 31, 2016, payment.

Dec. 31	Interest Expense..............................	40,000	
	Notes Payable..................................	65,519	
	Cash		105,519
	Record first installment payment.		

Part 2: Bonds (Straight-Line Amortization)

a. Compute the bonds' issue price.

Cash Flow	Table	Present Value Factor*	Amount	Present Value
Par (maturity) value	B.1 in App. B (PV of 1)	0.6139	× 400,000	= $245,560
Interest payments..........	B.3 in App. B (PV of annuity)	7.7217	× 24,000	= 185,321
Price of bond				$430,881

* Present value factors are for 10 payments using a semiannual market rate of 5%.

b. Journal entry for January 1, 2016, issuance.

Jan. 1	Cash	430,881	
	Premium on Bonds Payable		30,881
	Bonds Payable.............................		400,000
	Sold bonds at a premium.		

c. Straight-line amortization table for premium bonds.

	A	B	C
1	**Semiannual**	**Unamortized**	**Carrying**
2	**Period-End**	**Discount**	**Value**
3	(0) 1/1/2016	$ 30,881	$ 430,881
4	(1) 6/30/2016	27,793	427,793
5	(2) 12/31/2016	24,705	424,705
6	(3) 6/30/2017	21,617	421,617
7	(4) 12/31/2017	18,529	418,529
8	(5) 6/30/2018	15,441	415,441
9	(6) 12/31/2018	12,353	412,353
10	(7) 6/30/2019	9,265	409,265
11	(8) 12/31/2019	6,177	406,177
12	(9) 6/30/2020	3,089	403,089
13	(10) 12/31/2020	0*	400,000
14			

* Adjusted for rounding.

d. Journal entry for June 30, 2016, bond payment.

June 30	Bond Interest Expense.........................	20,912	
	Premium on Bonds Payable	3,088	
	Cash		24,000
	Paid semiannual interest on bonds.		

e. Journal entry for January 1, 2018, bond retirement.

Jan. 1	Bonds Payable.................................	400,000	
	Premium on Bonds Payable	18,529	
	Cash		416,000
	Gain on Retirement of Bonds		2,529
	Record bond retirement (carrying value at Dec. 31, 2017).		

Part 3: Bonds (Effective Interest Amortization)—Appendix 10B

c. The effective interest amortization table for premium bonds.

		(A) Cash Interest Paid 6% × $400,000	(B) Interest Expense 5% × Prior (E)	(C) Premium Amortization (A) − (B)	(D) Unamortized Premium Prior (D) − (C)	(E) Carrying Value $400,000 + (D)
	Semiannual Interest Period					
(0)	1/1/2016				$30,881	$430,881
(1)	6/30/2016	$ 24,000	$ 21,544	$ 2,456	28,425	428,425
(2)	12/31/2016	24,000	21,421	2,579	25,846	425,846
(3)	6/30/2017	24,000	21,292	2,708	23,138	423,138
(4)	12/31/2017	24,000	21,157	2,843	20,295	420,295
(5)	6/30/2018	24,000	21,015	2,985	17,310	417,310
(6)	12/31/2018	24,000	20,866	3,134	14,176	414,176
(7)	6/30/2019	24,000	20,709	3,291	10,885	410,885
(8)	12/31/2019	24,000	20,544	3,456	7,429	407,429
(9)	6/30/2020	24,000	20,371	3,629	3,800	403,800
(10)	12/31/2020	24,000	20,200*	3,800	0	400,000
		$240,000	$209,119	$30,881		

* Adjusted for rounding.

d. Journal entry for June 30, 2016, bond payment.

June 30	Bond Interest Expense...........................	21,544	
	Premium on Bonds Payable	2,456	
	Cash		24,000
	Paid semiannual interest on bonds.		

e. Journal entry for January 1, 2018, bond retirement.

Jan. 1	Bonds Payable......................	400,000	
	Premium on Bonds Payable	20,295	
	Cash		416,000
	Gain on Retirement of Bonds		4,295
	Record bond retirement (carrying value at Dec. 31, 2017).		

Present Values of Bonds and Notes

10A

This appendix explains how to apply present value techniques to measure a long-term liability when it is created and to assign interest expense to the periods until it is settled. Appendix B at the end of the book provides additional discussion of present value concepts.

C2

Explain and compute the present value of an amount(s) to be paid at a future date(s).

Present Value Concepts   The basic present value concept is that cash paid (or received) in the future has less value now than the same amount of cash paid (or received) today. To illustrate, if we must pay $1 one year from now, its present value is less than $1. To see this, assume that we borrow $0.9259 today that must be paid back in one year with 8% interest. Our interest expense for this loan is computed as $0.9259 × 8%, or $0.0741. When the $0.0741 interest is added to the $0.9259 borrowed, we get the $1 payment necessary to repay our loan with interest. This is formally computed in Exhibit 10A.1. The

Amount borrowed..............	$0.9259
Interest for one year at 8%	0.0741
Amount owed after 1 year	$ 1.0000

EXHIBIT 10A.1

Components of a One-Year Loan

$0.9259 borrowed is the present value of the $1 future payment. More generally, an amount borrowed equals the present value of the future payment. (This same interpretation applies to an investment. If $0.9259 is invested at 8%, it yields $0.0741 in revenue after one year. This amounts to $1, made up of principal and interest.)

To extend this example, assume that we owe $1 two years from now instead of in one year, and the 8% interest is compounded annually. *Compounded* means that interest during the second period is based on the total of the amount borrowed plus the interest accrued from the first period. The second period's interest is then computed as 8% multiplied by the sum of the amount borrowed plus interest earned in the first period. Exhibit 10A.2 shows how we compute the present value of $1 to be paid in two years. This amount is $0.8573. The first year's interest of $0.0686 is added to the principal so that the second year's interest is based on $0.9259. Total interest for this two-year period is $0.1427, computed as $0.0686 plus $0.0741.

Point: Benjamin Franklin is said to have described compounding as "the money, money makes, makes more money."

EXHIBIT 10A.2

Components of a Two-Year Loan

Amount borrowed..........................	**$0.8573**
Interest for first year ($0.8573 × 8%)	0.0686
Amount owed after 1 year....................	0.9259
Interest for second year ($0.9259 × 8%).........	0.0741
Amount owed after 2 years..................	$ 1.0000

Present Value Tables   The present value of $1 that we must repay at some future date can be computed by using this formula: $1/(1 + i)^n$. The symbol i is the interest rate per period, and n is the number of periods until the future payment must be made. Applying this formula to our two-year loan, we get $1/(1.08)^2$, or $0.8573. This is the same value shown in Exhibit 10A.2. We can use this formula to find any present value. However, a simpler method is to use a *present value table,* which lists present values computed with this formula for various interest rates and time periods. Many people find it helpful in learning present value concepts to first work with the table and then move to using a calculator.

Exhibit 10A.3 shows a present value table for a future payment of 1 for up to 10 periods at three different interest rates. Present values in this table are rounded to four decimal places. This table is drawn from the larger and more complete Table B.1 in Appendix B at the end of the book. Notice that the first value in the 8% column is 0.9259, the value we computed earlier for the present value of a $1 loan for one year at 8% (see Exhibit 10A.1). Go to the second row in the same 8% column and find the present value of 1 discounted at 8% for two years, or 0.8573. This $0.8573 is the present value of our obligation to repay $1 after two periods at 8% interest (see Exhibit 10A.2).

EXHIBIT 10A.3

Present Value of 1

	Rate		
Periods	6%	8%	10%
1	0.9434	**0.9259**	0.9091
2	0.8900	**0.8573**	0.8264
3	0.8396	0.7938	0.7513
4	0.7921	0.7350	0.6830
5	0.7473	0.6806	0.6209
6	0.7050	0.6302	0.5645
7	0.6651	0.5835	0.5132
8	0.6274	0.5403	0.4665
9	0.5919	0.5002	0.4241
10	0.5584	0.4632	0.3855

Example: Use Exhibit 10A.3 to find the present value of $1 discounted for 2 years at 6%. *Answer:* $0.8900

EXHIBIT 10A.4

Present Value of a Series of Unequal Payments

Periods	Payments	Present Value of 1 at 10%	Present Value of Payments
1	$2,000	0.9091	$1,818
2	3,000	0.8264	2,479
3	5,000	0.7513	3,757
Present value of all payments			**$8,054**

Applying a Present Value Table   To illustrate how to measure a liability using a present value table, assume that a company plans to borrow cash and repay it as follows: $2,000 after one year, $3,000 after two years, and $5,000 after three years. How much does this company receive today if the interest rate on this loan is 10%? To answer, we need to compute the present value of the three future payments, discounted at 10%. This computation is shown in Exhibit 10A.4 using present values from Exhibit 10A.3. The company can borrow $8,054 today at 10% interest in exchange for its promise to make these three payments at the scheduled dates.

Present Value of an Annuity   The $8,054 present value for the loan in Exhibit 10A.4 equals the sum of the present values of the three payments. When payments are not equal, their combined present value is best computed by adding the individual present values as shown in Exhibit 10A.4. Sometimes payments follow an **annuity,** which is a series of *equal* payments at equal time intervals. The present value of an annuity is readily computed.

To illustrate, assume that a company must repay a 6% loan with a $5,000 payment at each year-end for the next four years. This loan amount equals the present value of the four payments discounted at 6%. Exhibit 10A.5 shows how to compute this loan's present value of $17,326 by multiplying each payment by its matching present value factor taken from Exhibit 10A.3.

However, the series of $5,000 payments is an annuity, so we can compute its present value with either of two shortcuts. First, the third column of Exhibit 10A.5 shows that the sum of the present values of 1 at 6% for periods 1 through 4 equals 3.4651. One shortcut is to multiply this total of 3.4651 by the $5,000 annual payment to get the combined present value of $17,326. It requires one multiplication instead of four.

The second shortcut uses an *annuity table* such as the one shown in Exhibit 10A.6, which is drawn from the more complete Table B.3 in Appendix B. We go directly to the annuity table to get the present value factor for a specific number of payments and interest rate. We then multiply this factor by the amount of the payment to find the present value of the annuity. Specifically, find the row for four periods and go across to the 6% column, where the factor is 3.4651. This factor equals the present value of an annuity with four payments of 1, discounted at 6%. We then multiply 3.4651 by $5,000 to get the $17,326 present value of the annuity.

Compounding Periods Shorter Than a Year
The present value examples all involved periods of one year. In many situations, however, interest is compounded over shorter periods. For example, the interest rate on bonds is usually stated as an annual rate, but interest is often paid every six months (semiannually). This means that the present value of interest payments from such bonds must be computed using interest periods of six months.

Assume that a borrower wants to know the present value of a series of 10 *semiannual payments* of $4,000 made over five years at an *annual interest rate* of 12%. The interest rate is stated as an annual rate of 12%, but it is actually a rate of 6% per semiannual interest period. To compute the present value of this series of $4,000 payments, go to row 10 of Exhibit 10A.6 and across to the 6% column to find the factor 7.3601. The present value of this annuity is $29,440 (7.3601 × $4,000).

Appendix B further describes present value concepts and includes more complete present value tables and assignments.

EXHIBIT 10A.5

Present Value of a Series of Equal Payments (Annuity) by Discounting Each Payment

Periods	Payments	Present Value of 1 at 6%	Present Value of Payments
1	$5,000	0.9434	$ 4,717
2	5,000	0.8900	4,450
3	5,000	0.8396	4,198
4	5,000	0.7921	3,961
Present value of all payments		3.4651	$17,326

Point: Four payments of $5,000 at the end of each of the next 4 years is the equivalent of 3.4651 payments of $5,000 today.

EXHIBIT 10A.6

Present Value of an Annuity of 1

	Rate		
Periods	6%	8%	10%
1	0.9434	0.9259	0.9091
2	1.8334	1.7833	1.7355
3	2.6730	2.5771	2.4869
4	**3.4651**	3.3121	3.1699
5	4.2124	3.9927	3.7908
6	4.9173	4.6229	4.3553
7	5.5824	5.2064	4.8684
8	6.2098	5.7466	5.3349
9	6.8017	6.2469	5.7590
10	7.3601	6.7101	6.1446

Example: Use Exhibit 10A.6 to find the present value of an annuity of eight $15,000 payments with an 8% interest rate. *Answer:* $15,000 × 5.7466 = $86,199

Example: If this borrower makes five semiannual payments of $8,000, what is the present value of this annuity at a 12% rate? *Answer:* 4.2124 × $8,000 = $33,699

APPENDIX

Effective Interest Amortization

10B

Effective Interest Amortization of a Discount Bond   The straight-line method yields changes in the bonds' carrying value while the amount for bond interest expense remains constant. This gives the impression of a changing interest rate when users divide a constant bond interest expense over a changing carrying value. As a result, accounting standards allow use of the straight-line method only when its results do not differ materially from those obtained using the effective interest method. The **effective interest method,** or simply *interest method,* allocates total bond interest expense over the bonds'

P5

Compute and record amortization of bond discount using effective interest method.

Point: The effective interest method computes bond interest expense using the market rate at issuance. This rate is applied to a changing carrying value.

life in a way that yields a constant rate of interest. This constant rate of interest is the market rate at the issue date. Thus, bond interest expense for a period equals the carrying value of the bond at the beginning of that period multiplied by the market rate when issued.

Exhibit 10B.1 shows an effective interest amortization table for the **Fila** bonds (as described in Exhibit 10.4). The key difference between the effective interest and straight-line methods lies in computing bond interest expense. Instead of assigning an equal amount of bond interest expense to each period, the effective interest method assigns a bond interest expense amount that increases over the life of a discount bond. **Both methods allocate the *same* $19,546 of total bond interest expense to the bonds' life, but in different patterns.** Specifically, the amortization table in Exhibit 10B.1 shows that the balance of the discount (column D) is amortized until it reaches zero. Also, the bonds' carrying value (column E) changes each period until it equals par value at maturity. Compare columns D and E to the corresponding columns in Exhibit 10.7 to see the amortization patterns. Total bond interest expense is $19,546, consisting of $16,000 of semiannual cash payments and $3,546 of the original bond discount, the same for both methods.

Point: Contract rate determines cash interest paid, but the market rate determines the actual interest expense.

EXHIBIT 10B.1

Effective Interest Amortization of Bond Discount

		(A) Cash Interest Paid	(B) Bond Interest Expense	(C) Discount Amortization	(D) Unamortized Discount	(E) Carrying Value
	Semiannual Interest Period-End	4% × $100,000	5% × Prior (E)	(B) – (A)	Prior (D) – (C)	$100,000 – (D)
(0)	12/31/2016				$3,546	$ 96,454
(1)	6/30/2017	$4,000	$4,823	$ 823	2,723	97,277
(2)	12/31/2017	4,000	4,864	864	1,859	98,141
(3)	6/30/2018	4,000	4,907	907	952	99,048
(4)	12/31/2018	4,000	4,952	952	0	100,000
		$16,000	$19,546	$3,546		

Bonds: $100,000 Par Value, Semiannual Interest Payments, Two-Year Life, 4% Semiannual Contract Rate, 5% Semiannual Market Rate

Column **(A)** is the par value ($100,000) multiplied by the semiannual contract rate (4%).
Column **(B)** is the prior period's carrying value multiplied by the semiannual market rate (5%).
Column **(C)** is the difference between interest paid and bond interest expense, or [(B) − (A)].
Column **(D)** is the prior period's unamortized discount less the current period's discount amortization.
Column **(E)** is the par value less unamortized discount, or [$100,000 − (D)].

Bonds Payable

12/31/2016		100,000
6/30/2017	—	
12/31/2017	—	
6/30/2018	—	
12/31/2018		**100,000**

Discount on Bonds Payable

12/31/2016	3,546	
	6/30/2017	823
	12/31/2017	864
	6/30/2018	907
	12/31/2018	952
12/31/2018	**0**	

Except for differences in amounts, journal entries recording the expense and updating the liability balance are the same under the effective interest method and the straight-line method. We can use the numbers in Exhibit 10B.1 to record each semiannual entry during the bonds' two-year life (June 30, 2017, through December 31, 2018). For instance, we record the interest payment at the end of the first semiannual period as follows:

Assets = Liabilities + Equity
−4,000   +823   −4,823

2017		
June 30	Bond Interest Expense	4,823
	Discount on Bonds Payable	823
	Cash	4,000
	Record semiannual interest and discount amortization (effective interest method).	

P6

Compute and record amortization of bond premium using effective interest method.

Effective Interest Amortization of a Premium Bond   Exhibit 10B.2 shows the amortization table using the effective interest method for the **Adidas** bonds (as described in Exhibit 10.8). Column A lists the semiannual cash payments. Column B shows the amount of bond interest expense, computed as the 5% semiannual market rate at issuance multiplied by the beginning-of-period carrying value. The amount of cash paid in column A is larger than the bond interest expense because the cash payment is based on the higher 6% semiannual contract rate. The excess cash payment over the interest expense reduces the principal. These amounts are shown in column C. Column E shows the carrying *(see continu-ing explanation immediately after Exhibit 10B.2)*

EXHIBIT 10B.2

Effective Interest Amortization of Bond Premium

	A	B	C	D	E	F
1	**Bonds: $100,000 Par Value, Semiannual Interest Payments, Two-Year Life,**					
2	**6% Semiannual Contract Rate, 5% Semiannual Market Rate**					
3	**Semiannual Interest Period-End**	**(A) Cash Interest Paid**	**(B) Bond Interest Expense**	**(C) Premium Amortization**	**(D) Unamortized Premium**	**(E) Carrying Value**
4						
5						
6		6% × $100,000	5% × Prior (E)	(A) − (B)	Prior (D) − (C)	$100,000 + (D)
7	(0) **12/31/2016**				**$3,546**	**$103,546**
8	(1) **6/30/2017**	**$6,000**	**$5,177**	**$ 823**	**2,723**	**102,723**
9	(2) 12/31/2017	6,000	5,136	864	1,859	101,859
10	(3) 6/30/2018	6,000	5,093	907	952	100,952
11	(4) 12/31/2018	6,000	5,048	952	**0**	**100,000**
12		$24,000	$20,454	$3,546		
13						

Column (**A**) is the par value ($100,000) multiplied by the semiannual contract rate (6%).
Column (**B**) is the prior period's carrying value multiplied by the semiannual market rate (5%).
Column (**C**) is the difference between interest paid and bond interest expense, or [(A) − (B)].
Column (**D**) is the prior period's unamortized premium less the current period's premium amortization.
Column (**E**) is the par value plus unamortized premium, or [$100,000 + (D)].

value after deducting the amortized premium in column C from the prior period's carrying value. Column D shows the premium's reduction by periodic amortization. When the issuer makes the first semiannual interest payment, the effect of premium amortization on bond interest expense and bond liability is recorded as follows:

2017		
June 30	Bond Interest Expense	5,177	
	Premium on Bonds Payable	823	
	Cash		6,000
	Record semiannual interest and premium amortization (effective interest method).		

Graph: **Carrying value** ($104,000 / $100,000 / $96,000) plotted across 12/31/2016, 6/30/2017, 12/31/2017, 6/30/2018, 12/31/2018.

Bonds Payable

12/31/2016	100,000
6/30/2017	—
12/31/2017	—
6/30/2018	—
12/31/2018	**100,000**

Premium on Bonds Payable

		12/31/2016	3,546
6/30/2017	823		
12/31/2017	864		
6/30/2018	907		
12/31/2018	952		
		12/31/2018	**0**

Assets = Liabilities + Equity
−6,000   −823   −5,177

Similar entries with different amounts are recorded at each payment date until the bond matures at the end of 2018. The effective interest method yields decreasing amounts of bond interest expense and increasing amounts of premium amortization over the bonds' life.

 IFRS ————————————————————————————————

Unlike U.S. GAAP, IFRS requires that interest expense be computed using the effective interest method with *no* exceptions. ■

APPENDIX

Issuing Bonds between Interest Dates

C3 ————

Describe interest accrual when bond payment periods differ from accounting periods.

An issuer can sell bonds at a date other than an interest payment date. When this occurs, the buyers normally pay the issuer the purchase price plus any interest accrued since the prior interest payment date. This accrued interest is then repaid to these buyers on the next interest payment date. To illustrate, suppose Avia sells $100,000 of its 9% bonds at par on March 1, 2016, 60 days after the stated issue date. The interest on Avia bonds is payable semiannually on each June 30 and December 31. Since 60 days have passed, the issuer collects accrued interest from the buyers at the time of issuance. This amount is $1,500 ($100,000 × 9% × $^{60}/_{360}$ year). This case is reflected in Exhibit 10C.1.

EXHIBIT 10C.1

Accruing Interest between Interest Payment Dates

Avia records the issuance of these bonds on March 1, 2016, as follows:

Assets = Liabilities + Equity
+101,500   +100,000
            +1,500

Mar. 1	Cash	101,500	
	Interest Payable		1,500
	Bonds Payable................................		100,000
	Sold bonds at par with accrued interest.		

Example: How much interest is collected from a buyer of $50,000 of Avia bonds sold at par 150 days after the contract issue date? *Answer:* $1,875 (computed as $50,000 × 9% × 150/360 year)

Liabilities for interest payable and bonds payable are recorded in separate accounts. When the June 30, 2016, semiannual interest date arrives, Avia pays the full semiannual interest of $4,500 ($100,000 × 9% × ½ year) to the bondholders. This payment includes the four months' interest of $3,000 earned by the bondholders from March 1 to June 30 *plus* the repayment of the 60 days' accrued interest collected by Avia when the bonds were sold. Avia records this first semiannual interest payment as follows:

Assets = Liabilities + Equity
−4,500   −1,500   −3,000

June 30	Interest Payable	1,500	
	Bond Interest Expense.......................	3,000	
	Cash		4,500
	Paid semiannual interest on the bonds.		

The practice of collecting and then repaying accrued interest with the next interest payment is to simplify the issuer's administrative efforts. To explain, suppose an issuer sells bonds on 15 or 20 different dates between the stated issue date and the first interest payment date. If the issuer does not collect accrued interest from buyers, it needs to pay different amounts of cash to each of them according to the time that passed after purchasing the bonds. The issuer needs to keep detailed records of buyers and the dates they bought bonds. Issuers avoid this recordkeeping by having each buyer pay accrued interest at purchase. Issuers then pay the full semiannual interest to all buyers, regardless of when they bought bonds.

Accruing Bond Interest Expense If a bond's interest period does not coincide with the issuer's accounting period, an adjusting entry is needed to recognize bond interest expense accrued since the most recent interest payment. To illustrate, assume that the stated issue date for **Adidas** bonds described in Exhibit 10.10 is September 1, 2016, instead of December 31, 2016, and that the bonds are sold on September 1, 2016. As a result, four months' interest (and premium amortization) accrue before the end of the 2016 calendar year. Interest for this period equals $3,409, or ⅘ of the first six months' interest of $5,113. Also, the premium amortization is $591, or ⅘ of the first six months' amortization of $887. The sum of the bond interest expense and the amortization is $4,000 ($3,409 + $591), which equals ⅘ of the $6,000 cash payment due on February 28, 2017. Adidas records these effects with an adjusting entry at December 31, 2016.

Point: Computation of accrued bond interest may use months instead of days for simplicity purposes. For example, the accrued interest computation for the Adidas bonds is based on months.

Assets = Liabilities + Equity
          −591   −3,409
          +4,000

Dec. 31	Bond Interest Expense ($5,113 × ⅘)	3,409	
	Premium on Bonds Payable ($887 × ⅘)	591	
	Interest Payable ($6,000 × ⅘)		4,000
	Record four months' accrued interest and premium amortization.		

Similar entries are made on each December 31 throughout the bonds' two-year life. When the $6,000 cash payment occurs on each February 28 interest payment date, Adidas must recognize bond interest expense and amortization for January and February. It must also eliminate the interest payable liability created by the December 31 adjusting entry. For example, Adidas records its payment on February 28, 2017, as follows:

Feb. 28	Interest Payable	4,000	
	Bond Interest Expense ($5,113 × ⅔)...............	1,704	
	Premium on Bonds Payable ($887 × ⅔)	296	
	Cash		6,000
	Record 2 months' interest and amortization,		
	and eliminate accrued interest liability.		

Assets = Liabilities + Equity
−6,000   −4,000   −1,704
          −296

The interest payments made each August 31 are recorded as usual because the entire six-month interest period is included within this company's calendar-year reporting period.

■ Decision **Maker**

Bond Rater   You work for **Moody's** rating service and it's your job to assist in assigning a rating to a bond that reflects its risk to bondholders. Identify factors you consider in assessing bond risk. Indicate the likely levels (relative to the norm) for the factors you identify for a bond that sells at a discount. ■ [Answers follow the chapter's Summary.]

APPENDIX

Leases and Pensions

10D

This appendix briefly explains the accounting and analysis for both leases and pensions.

Lease Liabilities   A **lease** is a contractual agreement between a *lessor* (asset owner) and a *lessee* (asset renter or tenant) that grants the lessee the right to use the asset for a period of time in return for cash (rent) payments. Nearly one-fourth of all equipment purchases are financed with leases. The advantages of lease financing include the lack of an immediate large cash payment and the potential to deduct rental payments in computing taxable income. From an accounting perspective, leases can be classified as either operating or capital leases. (*Lease accounting will change over the next few years, whereby operating leases are likely to be accounted for similar to capital leases . . . stay tuned!*)

C4
Describe accounting for leases and pensions.

Operating Leases   **Operating leases** are short-term (or cancelable) leases in which the lessor retains the risks and rewards of ownership. Examples include most car and apartment rental agreements. The lessee records such lease payments as expenses; the lessor records them as revenue. The lessee does not report the leased item as an asset or a liability (it is the lessor's asset). To illustrate, if an employee of **Amazon** leases a car for $300 at an airport while on company business, Amazon (lessee) records this cost as follows:

Point: Home Depot reports that its rental expenses from operating leases total more than $900 million.

July 4	Rental Expense......................................	300	
	Cash		300
	Record lease rental payment.		

Assets = Liabilities + Equity
−300   −300

Capital Leases   **Capital leases** are long-term (or noncancelable) leases by which the lessor transfers substantially all risks and rewards of ownership to the lessee.[3] Examples include most leases of airplanes and department store buildings. The lessee records the leased item as its own asset along with a lease liability at the start of the lease term; the amount recorded equals the present value of all lease payments. To illustrate, assume that K2 Co. enters into a six-year lease of a building in which it will sell sporting

---

[3] A *capital lease* meets any one or more of four criteria: (1) transfers title of leased asset to lessee, (2) contains a bargain purchase option, (3) has a lease term that is 75% or more of the leased asset's useful life, or (4) has a present value of lease payments that is 90% or more of the leased asset's market value.

equipment. The lease transfers all building ownership risks and rewards to K2 (the present value of its $12,979 annual lease payments is $60,000). K2 records this transaction as follows:

2016				
Jan. 1	Leased Asset—Building..............................	60,000	
	Lease Liability		60,000
	Record leased asset and lease liability.		

K2 reports the leased asset as a plant asset and the lease liability as a long-term liability. The portion of the lease liability expected to be paid in the next year is reported as a current liability.[4] At each year-end, K2 records depreciation on the leased asset (assume straight-line depreciation, six-year lease term, no bargain purchase option, and no salvage value) as follows:

Dec. 31	Depreciation Expense—Leased Asset, Building	10,000	
	Accumulated Depreciation—Leased Asset, Building		10,000
	Record depreciation on leased asset.		

K2 also accrues interest on the lease liability at each year-end. Interest expense is computed by multiplying the remaining lease liability by the interest rate on the lease. Specifically, K2 records its annual interest expense as part of its annual lease payment ($12,979) as follows (for its first year):

2016				
Dec. 31	Interest Expense.....................................	4,800	
	Lease Liability	8,179	
	Cash..		12,979
	*Record first annual lease payment.**		

* These numbers are computed from a *lease payment schedule*. For simplicity, we use the same numbers from Exhibit 10.14 for this lease payment schedule—with different headings as follows:

	(A)	Payments			(E)
		(B) *Debit*	(C) *Debit*	(D) *Credit*	
Period Ending Date	Beginning Balance of Lease Liability	Interest on Lease + Liability 8% × (A)	Lease Liability (D) − (B)	= Cash Lease Payment	Ending Balance of Lease Liability (A) − (C)
12/31/2016	$60,000	$ 4,800	$ 8,179	$12,979	$51,821
12/31/2017	51,821	4,146	8,833	12,979	42,988
12/31/2018	42,988	3,439	9,540	12,979	33,448
12/31/2019	33,448	2,676	10,303	12,979	23,145
12/31/2020	23,145	1,852	11,127	12,979	12,018
12/31/2021	12,018	961	12,018	12,979	0
		$17,874	$60,000	$77,874	

Pension Liabilities   A **pension plan** is a contractual agreement between an employer and its employees for the employer to provide benefits (payments) to employees after they retire. Most employers pay the full cost of the pension, but sometimes employees pay part of the cost. An employer records its payment into a pension plan with a debit to Pension Expense and a credit to Cash. A *plan administrator* receives payments from the employer, invests them in pension assets, and makes benefit payments to *pension recipients* (retired employees). Insurance and trust companies often serve as pension plan administrators.

Many pensions are known as *defined benefit plans* that define future benefits; the employer's contributions vary, depending on assumptions about future pension assets and liabilities. Several disclosures are necessary in this case. Specifically, a pension liability is reported when the accumulated benefit obligation is *more than* the plan assets, a so-called *underfunded plan*. The accumulated benefit obligation is the present value of promised future pension payments to retirees. *Plan assets* refer to the market value of assets

[4] Most lessees try to keep leased assets and lease liabilities off their balance sheets by failing to meet any one of the four criteria of a capital lease. This is because a lease liability increases a company's total liabilities, making it more difficult to obtain additional financing. The acquisition of assets without reporting any related liabilities (or other asset outflows) on the balance sheet is called **off-balance-sheet financing.**

the plan administrator holds. A pension asset is reported when the accumulated benefit obligation is *less than* the plan assets, a so-called *overfunded plan*. An employer reports pension expense when it receives the benefits from the employees' services, which is sometimes decades before it pays pension benefits to employees. (*Other Postretirement Benefits* refer to nonpension benefits such as health care and life insurance benefits. Similar to a pension, costs of these benefits are estimated and liabilities accrued when the employees earn them.)

Summary

C1 **Explain the types of notes and prepare entries to account for notes.** Notes repaid over a period of time are called *installment notes* and usually follow one of two payment patterns: (1) decreasing payments of interest plus equal amounts of principal or (2) equal total payments. Mortgage notes also are common. Interest is allocated to each period in a note's life by multiplying its beginning-period carrying value by its market rate at issuance. If a note is repaid with equal payments, the payment amount is computed by dividing the borrowed amount by the present value of an annuity factor (taken from a present value table) using the market rate and the number of payments.

C2^A **Explain and compute the present value of an amount(s) to be paid at a future date(s).** The basic concept of present value is that an amount of cash to be paid or received in the future is worth less than the same amount of cash to be paid or received today. Another important present value concept is that interest is compounded, meaning interest is added to the balance and used to determine interest for succeeding periods. An annuity is a series of equal payments occurring at equal time intervals. An annuity's present value can be computed using the present value table for an annuity (or a calculator).

C3^C **Describe interest accrual when bond payment periods differ from accounting periods.** Issuers and buyers of debt record the interest accrued when issue dates or accounting periods do not coincide with debt payment dates.

C4^D **Describe accounting for leases and pensions.** A lease is a rental agreement between the lessor and the lessee. When the lessor retains the risks and rewards of asset ownership (an *operating lease*), the lessee debits Rent Expense and credits Cash for its lease payments. When the lessor substantially transfers the risks and rewards of asset ownership to the lessee (a *capital lease*), the lessee capitalizes the leased asset and records a lease liability. Pension agreements can result in either pension assets or pension liabilities.

A1 **Compare bond financing with stock financing.** Bond financing is used to fund business activities. Advantages of bond financing versus stock include (1) no effect on owner control, (2) tax savings, and (3) increased earnings due to financial leverage. Disadvantages include (1) interest and principal payments and (2) amplification of poor performance.

A2 **Assess debt features and their implications.** Certain bonds are secured by the issuer's assets; other bonds, called *debentures,* are unsecured. Serial bonds mature at different points in time; term bonds mature at one time. Registered bonds have each bondholder's name recorded by the issuer; bearer bonds are payable to the holder. Convertible bonds are exchangeable for shares of the issuer's stock. Callable bonds can be retired by the issuer at a set price. Debt features alter the risk of loss for creditors.

A3 **Compute the debt-to-equity ratio and explain its use.** Both creditors and equity holders are concerned about the relation between the amount of liabilities and the amount of equity. A company's financing structure is at less risk when the debt-to-equity ratio is lower, as liabilities must be paid and usually with periodic interest.

P1 **Prepare entries to record bond issuance and interest expense.** When bonds are issued at par, Cash is debited and Bonds Payable is credited for the bonds' par value. At bond interest payment dates (usually semiannual), Bond Interest Expense is debited and Cash credited—the latter for an amount equal to the bond par value multiplied by the bond contract rate.

P2 **Compute and record amortization of bond discount using straight-line method.** Bonds are issued at a discount when the contract rate is less than the market rate, making the issue (selling) price less than par. When this occurs, the issuer records a credit to Bonds Payable (at par) and debits both Discount on Bonds Payable and Cash. The amount of bond interest expense assigned to each period is computed using the straight-line method.

P3 **Compute and record amortization of bond premium using straight-line method.** Bonds are issued at a premium when the contract rate is higher than the market rate, making the issue (selling) price greater than par. When this occurs, the issuer records a debit to Cash and credits both Premium on Bonds Payable and Bonds Payable (at par). The amount of bond interest expense assigned to each period is computed using the straight-line method. The Premium on Bonds Payable is allocated to reduce bond interest expense over the life of the bonds.

P4 **Record the retirement of bonds.** Bonds are retired at maturity with a debit to Bonds Payable and a credit to Cash at par value. The issuer can retire the bonds early by exercising a call option or purchasing them in the market. Bondholders can also retire bonds early by exercising a conversion feature on convertible bonds. The issuer recognizes a gain or loss for the difference between the amount paid and the bond carrying value.

P5^B **Compute and record amortization of bond discount using effective interest method.** Bonds are issued at a discount when the contract rate is less than the market rate, making the issue (selling) price less than par. The amount of bond interest expense assigned to each period, including amortization of the discount, is computed using the effective interest method.

P6^B **Compute and record amortization of bond premium using effective interest method.** Bonds are issued at a premium when the contract rate is higher than the market rate, making the issue (selling) price greater than par. The amount of bond interest expense assigned to each period, including amortization of the premium, is computed using the effective interest method.

Guidance Answers to Decision Maker

Entrepreneur   This is a "present value" question. The market interest rate (10%) and present value ($3,000) are known, but the payment required two years later is unknown. This amount ($3,630) can be computed as $3,000 × 1.10 × 1.10. Thus, the sale price is $3,630 when no payments are received for two years. The $3,630 received two years from today is equivalent to $3,000 cash today.

Bond Investor   The debt-to-equity ratio for the first company is 0.2 ($350,000/$1,750,000) and for the second company is 1.2 ($1,200,000/$1,000,000), suggesting that the financing structure

of the second company is more risky than that of the first company. Consequently, as a buyer of unsecured debenture bonds, you prefer the first company (all else equal).

Bond Rater   Bonds with longer repayment periods (life) have higher risk. Also, bonds issued by companies in financial difficulties or facing higher-than-normal uncertainties have higher risk. Moreover, companies with higher than normal debt and large fluctuations in earnings are considered to be higher risk. Discount bonds are riskier on one or more of these factors.

Key Terms

Annuity	Debt-to-equity ratio	Pension plan
Bearer bonds	Discount on bonds payable	Premium on bonds
Bond	Effective interest method	Registered bonds
Bond certificate	Fair value option	Secured bonds
Bond indenture	Installment note	Serial bonds
Callable bonds	Lease	Sinking fund bonds
Capital leases	Market rate	Straight-line bond amortization
Carrying (book) value of bonds	Mortgage	Term bonds
Contract rate	Off-balance-sheet financing	Unsecured bonds
Convertible bonds	Operating leases	
Coupon bonds	Par value of a bond	

Multiple Choice Quiz   Answers at end of chapter

1. A bond traded at 97½ means that
   a. The bond pays 97½% interest.
   b. The bond trades at $975 per $1,000 bond.
   c. The market rate of interest is below the contract rate of interest for the bond.
   d. The bonds can be retired at $975 each.
   e. The bond's interest rate is 2½%.

2. A bondholder that owns a $1,000, 6%, 15-year (term) bond has
   a. The right to receive $1,000 at maturity.
   b. Ownership rights in the bond-issuing entity.
   c. The right to receive $60 per month until maturity.
   d. The right to receive $1,900 at maturity.
   e. The right to receive $600 per year until maturity.

3. A company issues 8%, 20-year bonds with a par value of $500,000. The current market rate for the bonds is 8%. The amount of interest owed to the bondholders for each semi-annual interest payment is

   a. $40,000   c. $20,000   e. $400,000
   b. $0   d. $800,000

4. A company issued five-year, 5% bonds with a par value of $100,000. The company received $95,735 for the bonds. Using the straight-line method, the company's interest expense for the first semiannual interest period is
   a. $2,926.50   c. $2,500.00   e. $9,573.50
   b. $5,853.00   d. $5,000.00

5. A company issued eight-year, 5% bonds with a par value of $350,000. The company received proceeds of $373,745. Interest is payable semiannually. The amount of premium amortized for the first semiannual interest period, assuming straight-line bond amortization, is
   a. $2,698   c. $8,750   e. $1,484
   b. $23,745   d. $9,344

$^{B(C,D)}$ *Superscript letter B(C, D) denotes assignments based on Appendix 10B(10C, 10D).*

🏛 Icon denotes assignments that involve decision making.

Discussion Questions

1. What is the main difference between notes payable and bonds payable?

2. What is the main difference between a bond and a share of stock?

3. 🏛 What is the advantage of issuing bonds instead of obtaining financing from the company's owners?

4. What is a bond indenture? What provisions are usually included in it?

5. What are the duties of a trustee for bondholders?

6. What are the *contract* rate and the *market* rate for bonds?

7. 🏛 What factors affect the market rates for bonds?

8.^{B} 🏛 Does the straight-line or effective interest method produce an interest expense allocation that yields a constant rate of interest over a bond's life? Explain.

9.^{C} Why does a company that issues bonds between interest dates collect accrued interest from the bonds' purchasers?

10. 🏛 If you know the par value of bonds, the contract rate, and the market rate, how do you compute the bonds' price?

11. What is the issue price of a $2,000 bond sold at 98¼? What is the issue price of a $6,000 bond sold at 101½?

12. Describe the debt-to-equity ratio and explain how creditors and owners would use this ratio to evaluate a company's risk.

13. 🏛 What obligation does an entrepreneur (owner) have to investors that purchase bonds to finance the business?

14. Refer to **Apple**'s annual report in Appendix A. Is there any indication that Apple has issued long-term debt?   **APPLE**

15. By what amount did **Samsung**'s long-term borrowings increase or decrease in 2014?   **Samsung**

16. Refer to the statement of cash flows for **Samsung** in Appendix A. For the year ended December 31, 2014, what was the amount for repayment of long-term borrowings and debentures?   **Samsung**

17. Refer to the statements for **Google** in Appendix A. For the year ended December 31, 2014, what was its debt-to-equity ratio? What does this ratio tell us?   **GOOGLE**

18.^{D} When can a lease create both an asset and a liability for the lessee?

19.^{D} Compare and contrast an operating lease with a capital lease.

20.^{D} Describe the two basic types of pension plans.

---

mc connect

Round dollar amounts to the nearest whole dollar.

Identify the following as either an advantage (A) or a disadvantage (D) of bond financing.

_____ **a.** Bonds do not affect owner control.

_____ **b.** A company earns a lower return with borrowed funds than it pays in interest.

_____ **c.** A company earns a higher return with borrowed funds than it pays in interest.

_____ **d.** Bonds require payment of periodic interest.

_____ **e.** Interest on bonds is tax deductible.

_____ **f.** Bonds require payment of par value at maturity.

QUICK STUDY

QS 10-1
Bond financing

A1

Enviro Company issues 8%, 10-year bonds with a par value of $250,000 and semiannual interest payments. On the issue date, the annual market rate for these bonds is 10%, which implies a selling price of 87½. Prepare the journal entries for the issuance of the bonds. Assume the bonds are issued for cash on January 1, 2016.

QS 10-2
Journalizing bond issuance   **P1**

Using the bond details in QS 10-2, confirm that the bonds' selling price is approximately correct (within $100). Use the present value Tables B.1 and B.3 in Appendix B.

QS 10-3
Computing bond price

P1

Garcia Company issues 10%, 15-year bonds with a par value of $240,000 and semiannual interest payments. On the issue date, the annual market rate for these bonds is 8%, which implies a selling price of 117¼. Prepare the journal entry for the issuance of these bonds. Assume the bonds are issued for cash on January 1, 2016.

QS 10-4
Journalizing bond issuance   **P1**

QS 10-5
Computing bond price
P1

Using the bond details in QS 10-4, confirm that the bonds' selling price is approximately correct (within $100). Use the present value Tables B.1 and B.3 in Appendix B.

QS 10-6
Straight-Line: Bond computations
P2

Enviro Company issues 8%, 10-year bonds with a par value of $250,000 and semiannual interest payments. On the issue date, the annual market rate for these bonds is 10%, which implies a selling price of 87½. The straight-line method is used to allocate interest expense.

1. What are the issuer's cash proceeds from issuance of these bonds?
2. What total amount of bond interest expense will be recognized over the life of these bonds?
3. What is the amount of bond interest expense recorded on the first interest payment date?

QS 10-7
Recording bond issuance and discount amortization
P1 P2

Szmanda Company issues 10%, five-year bonds on December 31, 2015, with a par value of $100,000 and semiannual interest payments. Use the following bond amortization table and prepare journal entries to record (a) the issuance of bonds on December 31, 2015; (b) the first interest payment on June 30, 2016; and (c) the second interest payment on December 31, 2016.

Semiannual Period-End	Unamortized Discount	Carrying Value
(0) 12/31/2015...............	$7,360	$92,640
(1) 6/30/2016...............	6,624	93,376
(2) 12/31/2016...............	5,888	94,112

QS 10-8
Straight-Line: Bond computations
P3

Enviro Company issues 8%, 10-year bonds with a par value of $250,000 and semiannual interest payments. On the issue date, the annual market rate for these bonds is 5%, which implies a selling price of 123⅜. The straight-line method is used to allocate interest expense.

1. What are the issuer's cash proceeds from issuance of these bonds?
2. What total amount of bond interest expense will be recognized over the life of these bonds?
3. What is the amount of bond interest expense recorded on the first interest payment date?

QS 10-9
Bond retirement by call option **P4**

On July 1, 2016, Alvarez Company exercises an $8,000 call option (plus par value) on its outstanding bonds that have a carrying value of $416,000 and par value of $400,000. The company exercises the call option after the semiannual interest is paid on June 30, 2016. Record the entry to retire the bonds.

QS 10-10
Bond retirement by stock conversion **P4**

On January 1, 2016, the $2,000,000 par value bonds of Spitz Company with a carrying value of $2,000,000 are converted to 1,000,000 shares of $1.00 par value common stock. Record the entry for the conversion of the bonds.

QS 10-11
Computing payments for an installment note **C1**

Murray Company borrows $340,000 cash from a bank and in return signs an installment note for five annual payments of equal amount, with the first payment due one year after the note is signed. Use Table B.3 in Appendix B to compute the amount of the annual payment for each of the following annual market rates: (a) 4%, (b) 8%, and (c) 12%.

QS 10-12
Bond features and terminology
A2

Enter the letter of the description A through H that best fits each term or phrase 1 through 8.

A. Records and tracks the bondholders' names.
B. Is unsecured; backed only by the issuer's credit standing.
C. Has varying maturity dates for amounts owed.
D. Identifies rights and responsibilities of the issuer and the bondholders.
E. Can be exchanged for shares of the issuer's stock.
F. Is unregistered; interest is paid to whoever possesses them.
G. Maintains a separate asset account from which bondholders are paid at maturity.
H. Pledges specific assets of the issuer as collateral.

1. _____ Registered bond   **5.** _____ Convertible bond
2. _____ Serial bond   **6.** _____ Bond indenture
3. _____ Secured bond   **7.** _____ Sinking fund bond
4. _____ Bearer bond   **8.** _____ Debenture

Compute the debt-to-equity ratio for each of the following companies. Which company appears to have a riskier financing structure? Explain.

QS 10-13
Debt-to-equity ratio

A3

	Atlanta Company	Spokane Company
Total liabilities	$429,000	$ 549,000
Total equity	572,000	1,830,000

Garcia Company issues 10%, 15-year bonds with a par value of $240,000 and semiannual interest payments. On the issue date, the annual market rate for these bonds is 14%, which implies a selling price of 75¼. The effective interest method is used to allocate interest expense.

1. What are the issuer's cash proceeds from issuance of these bonds?
2. What total amount of bond interest expense will be recognized over the life of these bonds?
3. What amount of bond interest expense is recorded on the first interest payment date?

QS 10-14ᴮ
Effective Interest:
Bond discount computations

P5

Garcia Company issues 10%, 15-year bonds with a par value of $240,000 and semiannual interest payments. On the issue date, the annual market rate for these bonds is 8%, which implies a selling price of 117¼. The effective interest method is used to allocate interest expense.

1. What are the issuer's cash proceeds from issuance of these bonds?
2. What total amount of bond interest expense will be recognized over the life of these bonds?
3. What amount of bond interest expense is recorded on the first interest payment date?

QS 10-15ᴮ
Effective Interest:
Bond premium computations

P6

Madrid Company plans to issue 8% bonds on January 1, 2016, with a par value of $4,000,000. The company sells $3,600,000 of the bonds on January 1, 2016. The remaining $400,000 sells at par on March 1, 2016. The bonds pay interest semiannually as of June 30 and December 31. Record the entry for the March 1 cash sale of bonds.

QS 10-16ᶜ
Issuing bonds between interest dates C3

Jin Li, an employee of ETrain.com, leases a car at O'Hare airport for a three-day business trip. The rental cost is $250. Prepare the entry by ETrain.com to record Jin Li's short-term car lease cost.

QS 10-17ᴰ
Recording operating leases C4

Algoma, Inc., signs a five-year lease for office equipment with Office Solutions. The present value of the lease payments is $15,499. Prepare the journal entry that Algoma records at the inception of this capital lease.

QS 10-18ᴰ
Recording capital leases
C4

Vodafone Group Plc reports the following information among its bonds payable as of March 31, 2015 (pounds in millions).

QS 10-19
International liabilities disclosures

P1

Financial Long-Term Liabilities Measured at Amortized Cost			
£ millions	Nominal (par) Value	Carrying Value	Fair Value
4.625% (US dollar 500 million) bond due July 2018....	£337	£375	£367

a. What is the par value of the 4.625% bond issuance? What is its book (carrying) value?
b. Was the 4.625% bond sold at a discount or a premium? Explain.

Refer to the information in QS 10-19 for **Vodafone Group Plc**. The following price quotes (from Yahoo! Finance Bond Center) relate to its bonds payable. The price quote indicates that the 4.625% bonds have a market price of 111.67 (111.67% of par value), resulting in a yield to maturity of 1.710%.

QS 10-20
International liabilities disclosures and interpretations

P1

Price	Contract Rate (coupon)	Maturity Date	Market Rate (YTM)
111.67........	4.625%	15-Jul-2018	1.710%

a. Assuming that the 4.625% bonds were originally issued at par value, what does the market price reveal about interest rate changes since bond issuance? (Assume that Vodafone's credit rating has remained the same.)

b. Does the change in market rates since the issuance of these bonds affect the amount of interest expense reported on Vodafone's income statement? Explain.

c. How much cash would Vodafone need to pay to repurchase the 4.625% bonds at the quoted market price of 111.67? (Assume no interest is owed when the bonds are repurchased.)

d. Assuming that the 4.625% bonds remain outstanding until maturity, at what market price will the bonds sell on the due date in 2018?

EXERCISES

> Round dollar amounts to the nearest whole dollar. Assume no reversing entries are used.

Exercise 10-1
Recording bond issuance and interest
P1

On January 1, 2016, Boston Enterprises issues bonds that have a $3,400,000 par value, mature in 20 years, and pay 9% interest semiannually on June 30 and December 31. The bonds are sold at par.

1. How much interest will Boston pay (in cash) to the bondholders every six months?
2. Prepare journal entries to record (*a*) the issuance of bonds on January 1, 2016; (*b*) the first interest payment on June 30, 2016; and (*c*) the second interest payment on December 31, 2016.
3. Prepare the journal entry for issuance assuming the bonds are issued at (*a*) 98 and (*b*) 102.

Exercise 10-2
Straight-Line:
Amortization of bond discount
P2

Tano issues bonds with a par value of $180,000 on January 1, 2016. The bonds' annual contract rate is 8%, and interest is paid semiannually on June 30 and December 31. The bonds mature in three years. The annual market rate at the date of issuance is 10%, and the bonds are sold for $170,862.

1. What is the amount of the discount on these bonds at issuance?
2. How much total bond interest expense will be recognized over the life of these bonds?
3. Prepare an amortization table like the one in Exhibit 10.7 for these bonds; use the straight-line method to amortize the discount.

Exercise 10-3
Computing bond interest and price; recording bond issuance
P2

Check (4) $691,287

Bringham Company issues bonds with a par value of $800,000 on their stated issue date. The bonds mature in 10 years and pay 6% annual interest in semiannual payments. On the issue date, the annual market rate for the bonds is 8%.

1. What is the amount of each semiannual interest payment for these bonds?
2. How many semiannual interest payments will be made on these bonds over their life?
3. Use the interest rates given to determine whether the bonds are issued at par, at a discount, or at a premium.
4. Compute the price of the bonds as of their issue date.
5. Prepare the journal entry to record the bonds' issuance.

Exercise 10-4
Straight-Line:
Recording bond issuance and discount amortization
P1   P2

Paulson Company issues 6%, four-year bonds on December 31, 2016, with a par value of $200,000 and semiannual interest payments. Use the following bond amortization table and prepare journal entries to record (*a*) the issuance of bonds on December 31, 2016; (*b*) the first interest payment on June 30, 2017; and (*c*) the second interest payment on December 31, 2017.

Semiannual Period-End	Unamortized Discount	Carrying Value
(0) 12/31/2016	$13,466	$186,534
(1) 6/30/2017	11,782	188,218
(2) 12/31/2017	10,098	189,902

Exercise 10-5
Straight-Line: Recording bond issuance and discount amortization
P1   P2

Dobbs Company issues 5%, two-year bonds on December 31, 2016, with a par value of $200,000 and semiannual interest payments. Use the following bond amortization table and prepare journal entries to record (*a*) the issuance of bonds on December 31, 2016; (*b*) the first through fourth interest payments on each June 30 and December 31; and (*c*) the maturity of the bond on December 31, 2018.

Semiannual Period-End	Unamortized Discount	Carrying Value
(0) 12/31/2016	$12,000	$188,000
(1) 6/30/2017	9,000	191,000
(2) 12/31/2017	6,000	194,000
(3) 6/30/2018	3,000	197,000
(4) 12/31/2018	0	200,000

Woodwick Company issues 10%, five-year bonds on December 31, 2015, with a par value of $200,000 and semiannual interest payments. Use the following bond amortization table and prepare journal entries to record (*a*) the issuance of bonds on December 31, 2015; (*b*) the first interest payment on June 30, 2016; and (*c*) the second interest payment on December 31, 2016.

Exercise 10-6
Straight-Line:
Recording bond issuance and premium amortization
P1 P3

Semiannual Period-End	Unamortized Discount	Carrying Value
(0) 12/31/2015	$16,222	$216,222
(1) 6/30/2016	14,600	214,600
(2) 12/31/2016	12,978	212,978

Quatro Co. issues bonds dated January 1, 2016, with a par value of $400,000. The bonds' annual contract rate is 13%, and interest is paid semiannually on June 30 and December 31. The bonds mature in three years. The annual market rate at the date of issuance is 12%, and the bonds are sold for $409,850.

1. What is the amount of the premium on these bonds at issuance?
2. How much total bond interest expense will be recognized over the life of these bonds?
3. Prepare an amortization table like the one in Exhibit 10.11 for these bonds; use the straight-line method to amortize the premium.

Exercise 10-7
Straight-Line:
Amortization of bond premium
P3

Citywide Company issues bonds with a par value of $150,000 on their stated issue date. The bonds mature in five years and pay 10% annual interest in semiannual payments. On the issue date, the annual market rate for the bonds is 8%.

1. What is the amount of each semiannual interest payment for these bonds?
2. How many semiannual interest payments will be made on these bonds over their life?
3. Use the interest rates given to determine whether the bonds are issued at par, at a discount, or at a premium.
4. Compute the price of the bonds as of their issue date.
5. Prepare the journal entry to record the bonds' issuance.

Exercise 10-8
Computing bond interest and price; recording bond issuance
P3

Check (4) $162,172

On January 1, 2016, Shay issues $700,000 of 10%, 15-year bonds at a price of 97¾. Six years later, on January 1, 2022, Shay retires 20% of these bonds by buying them on the open market at 104½. All interest is accounted for and paid through December 31, 2021, the day before the purchase. The straight-line method is used to amortize any bond discount.

1. How much does the company receive when it issues the bonds on January 1, 2016?
2. What is the amount of the discount on the bonds at January 1, 2016?
3. How much amortization of the discount is recorded on the bonds for the entire period from January 1, 2016, through December 31, 2021?
4. What is the carrying (book) value of the bonds as of the close of business on December 31, 2021? What is the carrying value of the 20% soon-to-be-retired bonds on this same date?
5. How much did the company pay on January 1, 2022, to purchase the bonds that it retired?
6. What is the amount of the recorded gain or loss from retiring the bonds?
7. Prepare the journal entry to record the bond retirement at January 1, 2022.

Exercise 10-9
Straight-Line: Bond computations, amortization, and bond retirement
P2 P4

Check (6) $8,190 loss

On January 1, 2016, Eagle borrows $100,000 cash by signing a four-year, 7% installment note. The note requires four equal total payments of accrued interest and principal on December 31 of each year from 2016 through 2019.

1. Compute the amount of each of the four equal total payments.
2. Prepare an amortization table for this installment note like the one in Exhibit 10.14.

Exercise 10-10
Installment note with equal total payments **C1**

Check (1) $29,523

Exercise 10-11
Installment note entries
C1

Use the information in Exercise 10-10 to prepare the journal entries for Eagle to record the loan on January 1, 2016, and the four payments from December 31, 2016, through December 31, 2019.

Exercise 10-12
Applying debt-to-equity ratio
A3

Montclair Company is considering a project that will require a $500,000 loan. It presently has total liabilities of $220,000 and total assets of $620,000.

1. Compute Montclair's (a) present debt-to-equity ratio and (b) the debt-to-equity ratio assuming it borrows $500,000 to fund the project.
2. Evaluate and discuss the level of risk involved if Montclair borrows the funds to pursue the project.

Exercise 10-13[B]
Effective Interest:
Amortization of bond discount
P5

Stanford issues bonds dated January 1, 2016, with a par value of $500,000. The bonds' annual contract rate is 9%, and interest is paid semiannually on June 30 and December 31. The bonds mature in three years. The annual market rate at the date of issuance is 12%, and the bonds are sold for $463,140.

1. What is the amount of the discount on these bonds at issuance?
2. How much total bond interest expense will be recognized over the life of these bonds?
3. Prepare an amortization table like the one in Exhibit 10B.1 for these bonds; use the effective interest method to amortize the discount.

Exercise 10-14[B]
Effective Interest:
Amortization of bond premium
P6

Quatro Co. issues bonds dated January 1, 2016, with a par value of $400,000. The bonds' annual contract rate is 13%, and interest is paid semiannually on June 30 and December 31. The bonds mature in three years. The annual market rate at the date of issuance is 12%, and the bonds are sold for $409,850.

1. What is the amount of the premium on these bonds at issuance?
2. How much total bond interest expense will be recognized over the life of these bonds?
3. Prepare an amortization table like the one in Exhibit 10B.2 for these bonds; use the effective interest method to amortize the premium.

Exercise 10-15
Straight-Line:
Amortization and accrued bond interest expense
C3   P2

Duval Co. issues four-year bonds with a $100,000 par value on June 1, 2016, at a price of $95,948. The annual contract rate is 7%, and interest is paid semiannually on November 30 and May 31.

1. Prepare an amortization table like the one in Exhibit 10.7 for these bonds. Use the straight-line method of interest amortization.
2. Prepare journal entries to record the first two interest payments and to accrue interest as of December 31, 2016.

Exercise 10-16[C]
Recording bond issuance with accrued interest
C3   P1
Check   (1) $102,000

On May 1, 2016, Brussels Enterprises issues bonds dated January 1, 2016, that have a $3,400,000 par value, mature in 20 years, and pay 9% interest semiannually on June 30 and December 31. The bonds are sold at par plus four months' accrued interest.

1. How much accrued interest do the bond purchasers pay Brussels on May 1, 2016?
2. Prepare Brussels' journal entries to record (a) the issuance of bonds on May 1, 2016; (b) the first interest payment on June 30, 2016; and (c) the second interest payment on December 31, 2016.

Exercise 10-17[D]
Identifying capital and operating leases
C4

Indicate whether the company in each separate case 1 through 3 has entered into an operating lease or a capital lease.

1. The lessor retains title to the asset, and the lease term is three years on an asset that has a five-year useful life.
2. The title is transferred to the lessee, the lessee can purchase the asset for $1 at the end of the lease, and the lease term is five years. The leased asset has an expected useful life of six years.
3. The present value of the lease payments is 95% of the leased asset's market value, and the lease term is 70% of the leased asset's useful life.

Exercise 10-18[D]
Accounting for capital lease
C4

Harbor (lessee) signs a five-year capital lease for office equipment with a $10,000 annual lease payment. The present value of the five annual lease payments is $41,000, based on a 7% interest rate.

1. Prepare the journal entry Harbor will record at inception of the lease.
2. If the leased asset has a five-year useful life with no salvage value, prepare the journal entry Harbor will record each year to recognize depreciation expense related to the leased asset.

General Motors advertised three alternatives for a 25-month lease on a new Tahoe: (1) zero dollars down and a lease payment of $1,750 per month for 25 months, (2) $5,000 down and $1,500 per month for 25 months, or (3) $38,500 down and no payments for 25 months. Use the present value Table B.3 in Appendix B to determine which is the best alternative for the customer (assume you have enough cash to accept any alternative and the annual interest rate is 12% compounded monthly).

Exercise 10-19^D
Analyzing lease options
C4

Heineken N.V. reports the following information for its loans and borrowings as of December 31, 2014, including proceeds and repayments for the year ended December 31, 2014 (euros in millions).

Exercise 10-20
Accounting for long-term liabilities under IFRS
C1

Loans and borrowings (noncurrent liabilities)	
Loans and borrowings, December 31, 2014....................	€ 8,933
Proceeds (cash) from issuances of loans and borrowings..........	858
Repayments (in cash) of loans and borrowings.................	(2,443)

1. Prepare Heineken's journal entry to record its cash proceeds from issuances of its loans and borrowings for 2014. Assume that the par value of these issuances is €900.
2. Prepare Heineken's journal entry to record its cash repayments of its loans and borrowings for 2014. Assume that the par value of these issuances is €2,400, and the premium on them is €24.
3. Compute the discount or premium on its loans and borrowings as of December 31, 2014, assuming that the par value of these liabilities is €8,750.
4. Given the facts in part 3 and viewing the entirety of loans and borrowings as one issuance, was the contract rate on these loans and borrowings higher or lower than the market rate at the time of issuance? Explain. (Assume that Heineken's credit rating has remained the same.)

connect

Round dollar amounts to the nearest whole dollar. Assume no reversing entries are used.

PROBLEM SET A

Hartford Research issues bonds dated January 1, 2016, that pay interest semiannually on June 30 and December 31. The bonds have a $40,000 par value and an annual contract rate of 10%, and they mature in 10 years.

Required

For each of the following three separate situations, (*a*) determine the bonds' issue price on January 1, 2016, and (*b*) prepare the journal entry to record their issuance.
1. The market rate at the date of issuance is 8%.
2. The market rate at the date of issuance is 10%.
3. The market rate at the date of issuance is 12%.

Problem 10-1A
Computing bond price and recording issuance
P1

Check (1) Premium, $5,437

(3) Discount, $4,588

Hillside issues $4,000,000 of 6%, 15-year bonds dated January 1, 2016, that pay interest semiannually on June 30 and December 31. The bonds are issued at a price of $3,456,448.

Required

1. Prepare the January 1, 2016, journal entry to record the bonds' issuance.
2. For each semiannual period, compute (*a*) the cash payment, (*b*) the straight-line discount amortization, and (*c*) the bond interest expense.
3. Determine the total bond interest expense to be recognized over the bonds' life.
4. Prepare the first two years of an amortization table like Exhibit 10.7 using the straight-line method.
5. Prepare the journal entries to record the first two interest payments.

Problem 10-2A
Straight-Line:
Amortization of bond discount
P1 P2

Check (3) $4,143,552
(4) 12/31/2017
carrying value, $3,528,920

Refer to the bond details in Problem 10-2A, *except* assume that the bonds are issued at a price of $4,895,980.

Required

1. Prepare the January 1, 2016, journal entry to record the bonds' issuance.
2. For each semiannual period, compute (*a*) the cash payment, (*b*) the straight-line premium amortization, and (*c*) the bond interest expense.

[continued on next page]

Problem 10-3A
Straight Line:
Amortization of bond premium
P1 P3

3. Determine the total bond interest expense to be recognized over the bonds' life.
4. Prepare the first two years of an amortization table like Exhibit 10.11 using the straight-line method.
5. Prepare the journal entries to record the first two interest payments.

Problem 10-4A

Straight-Line:
Amortization of
bond premium

P1   P3

Ellis issues 6.5%, five-year bonds dated January 1, 2016, with a $250,000 par value. The bonds pay interest on June 30 and December 31 and are issued at a price of $255,333. The annual market rate is 6% on the issue date.

Required

1. Compute the total bond interest expense over the bonds' life.
2. Prepare a straight-line amortization table like Exhibit 10.11 for the bonds' life.
3. Prepare the journal entries to record the first two interest payments.

Problem 10-5A

Straight-Line:
Amortization of bond
premium and discount

P1   P2   P3

Legacy issues $325,000 of 5%, four-year bonds dated January 1, 2016, that pay interest semiannually on June 30 and December 31. They are issued at $292,181 and their market rate is 8% at the issue date.

Required

1. Prepare the January 1, 2016, journal entry to record the bonds' issuance.
2. Determine the total bond interest expense to be recognized over the bonds' life.
3. Prepare a straight-line amortization table like the one in Exhibit 10.7 for the bonds' first two years.
4. Prepare the journal entries to record the first two interest payments.

Analysis Component

5. Assume the market rate on January 1, 2016, is 4% instead of 8%. Without providing numbers, describe how this change affects the amounts reported on Legacy's financial statements.

Problem 10-6A

Installment notes

C1

On November 1, 2016, Norwood borrows $200,000 cash from a bank by signing a five-year installment note bearing 8% interest. The note requires equal total payments each year on October 31.

Required

1. Compute the total amount of each installment payment.
2. Complete an amortization table for this installment note similar to the one in Exhibit 10.14.
3. Prepare the journal entries in which Norwood records (a) accrued interest as of December 31, 2016 (the end of its annual reporting period), and (b) the first annual payment on the note.

Problem 10-7A

Applying the debt-to-
equity ratio

A3

At the end of the current year, the following information is available for both Pulaski Company and Scott Company.

	Pulaski Company	Scott Company
Total assets..........	$860,000	$440,000
Total liabilities	360,000	240,000
Total equity	500,000	200,000

Required

1. Compute the debt-to-equity ratios for both companies.
2. Comment on your results and discuss the riskiness of each company's financing structure.

Problem 10-8A[B]

Effective Interest:
Amortization of bond
discount   **P1   P5**

Refer to the bond details in Problem 10-5A.

Required

1. Prepare the January 1, 2016, journal entry to record the bonds' issuance.
2. Determine the total bond interest expense to be recognized over the bonds' life.
3. Prepare an effective interest amortization table like the one in Exhibit 10B.1 for the bonds' first two years.
4. Prepare the journal entries to record the first two interest payments.

Refer to the bond details in Problem 10-4A.

Required

1. Compute the total bond interest expense over the bonds' life.
2. Prepare an effective interest amortization table like the one in Exhibit 10B.2 for the bonds' life.
3. Prepare the journal entries to record the first two interest payments.
4. Use the market rate at issuance to compute the present value of the remaining cash flows for these bonds as of December 31, 2018. Compare your answer with the amount shown on the amortization table as the balance for that date (from part 2) and explain your findings.

Problem 10-9A[B]
Effective Interest:
Amortization of bond premium; computing bond price   **P1   P6**

Check (2) 6/30/2018 carrying value, $252,865
(4) $252,326

Ike issues $180,000 of 11%, three-year bonds dated January 1, 2016, that pay interest semiannually on June 30 and December 31. They are issued at $184,566. Their market rate is 10% at the issue date.

Required

1. Prepare the January 1, 2016, journal entry to record the bonds' issuance.
2. Determine the total bond interest expense to be recognized over the bonds' life.
3. Prepare an effective interest amortization table like Exhibit 10B.2 for the bonds' first two years.
4. Prepare the journal entries to record the first two interest payments.
5. Prepare the journal entry to record the bonds' retirement on January 1, 2018, at 98.

Analysis Component

6. Assume that the market rate on January 1, 2016, is 12% instead of 10%. Without presenting numbers, describe how this change affects the amounts reported on Ike's financial statements.

Problem 10-10A[B]
Effective Interest:
Amortization of bond; retiring bonds

P1   P4   P5   P6

Check (3) 6/30/2017 carrying value, $182,448

(5) $5,270 gain

Rogers Company signs a five-year capital lease with Packer Company for office equipment. The annual year-end lease payment is $10,000, and the interest rate is 8%.

Required

1. Compute the present value of Rogers's five-year lease payments.
2. Prepare the journal entry to record Rogers's capital lease at its inception.
3. Complete a lease payment schedule for the five years of the lease with the following headings. Assume that the beginning balance of the lease liability (present value of lease payments) is $39,927. (*Hint:* To find the amount allocated to interest in year 1, multiply the interest rate by the beginning-of-year lease liability. The amount of the annual lease payment not allocated to interest is allocated to principal. Reduce the lease liability by the amount allocated to principal to update the lease liability at each year-end.)

Problem 10-11A[D]
Capital lease accounting

C4

Check (1) $39,927

(3) Year 3 ending balance, $17,833

Period Ending Date	Beginning Balance of Lease Liability	Interest on Lease Liability	Reduction of Lease Liability	Cash Lease Payment	Ending Balance of Lease Liability

4. Use straight-line depreciation and prepare the journal entry to depreciate the leased asset at the end of year 1. Assume zero salvage value and a five-year life for the office equipment.

Round dollar amounts to the nearest whole dollar. Assume no reversing entries are used.

Flagstaff Systems issues bonds dated January 1, 2016, that pay interest semiannually on June 30 and December 31. The bonds have a $90,000 par value and an annual contract rate of 12%, and they mature in five years.

Required

For each of the following three separate situations, (a) determine the bonds' issue price on January 1, 2016, and (b) prepare the journal entry to record their issuance.

1. The market rate at the date of issuance is 10%.
2. The market rate at the date of issuance is 12%.
3. The market rate at the date of issuance is 14%.

PROBLEM SET B

Problem 10-1B
Computing bond price and recording issuance

P1

Check (1) Premium, $6,948

(3) Discount, $6,326

Problem 10-2B
Straight-Line:
Amortization of bond
discount

P1   P2

Romero issues $3,400,000 of 10%, 10-year bonds dated January 1, 2016, that pay interest semiannually on June 30 and December 31. The bonds are issued at a price of $3,010,000.

Required

1. Prepare the January 1, 2016, journal entry to record the bonds' issuance.
2. For each semiannual period, compute (*a*) the cash payment, (*b*) the straight-line discount amortization, and (*c*) the bond interest expense.
3. Determine the total bond interest expense to be recognized over the bonds' life.
4. Prepare the first two years of an amortization table like Exhibit 10.7 using the straight-line method.
5. Prepare the journal entries to record the first two interest payments.

Problem 10-3B
Straight-Line:
Amortization of bond
premium

P1   P3

Refer to the bond details in Problem 10-2B, *except* assume that the bonds are issued at a price of $4,192,932.

Required

1. Prepare the January 1, 2016, journal entry to record the bonds' issuance.
2. For each semiannual period, compute (*a*) the cash payment, (*b*) the straight-line premium amortization, and (*c*) the bond interest expense.
3. Determine the total bond interest expense to be recognized over the bonds' life.
4. Prepare the first two years of an amortization table like Exhibit 10.11 using the straight-line method.
5. Prepare the journal entries to record the first two interest payments.

Problem 10-4B
Straight-Line:
Amortization of bond
premium

P1   P3

Ripkin Company issues 9%, five-year bonds dated January 1, 2016, with a $320,000 par value. The bonds pay interest on June 30 and December 31 and are issued at a price of $332,988. Their annual market rate is 8% on the issue date.

Required

1. Compute the total bond interest expense over the bonds' life.
2. Prepare a straight-line amortization table like Exhibit 10.11 for the bonds' life.
3. Prepare the journal entries to record the first two interest payments.

Problem 10-5B
Straight-Line:
Amortization of bond
discount

P1   P2

Gomez issues $240,000 of 6%, 15-year bonds dated January 1, 2016, that pay interest semiannually on June 30 and December 31. They are issued at $198,494, and their market rate is 8% at the issue date.

Required

1. Prepare the January 1, 2016, journal entry to record the bonds' issuance.
2. Determine the total bond interest expense to be recognized over the life of the bonds.
3. Prepare a straight-line amortization table like the one in Exhibit 10.7 for the bonds' first two years.
4. Prepare the journal entries to record the first two interest payments.

Problem 10-6B
Installment notes

C1

On October 1, 2016, Gordon Enterprises borrows $150,000 cash from a bank by signing a three-year installment note bearing 10% interest. The note requires equal total payments each year on September 30.

Required

1. Compute the total amount of each installment payment.
2. Complete an amortization table for this installment note similar to the one in Exhibit 10.14.
3. Prepare the journal entries to record (*a*) accrued interest as of December 31, 2016 (the end of its annual reporting period), and (*b*) the first annual payment on the note.

At the end of the current year, the following information is available for both Atlas Company and Bryan Company.

	Atlas Company	Bryan Company
Total assets.	$180,000	$750,000
Total liabilities	80,000	562,500
Total equity	100,000	187,500

Problem 10-7B
Applying the debt-to-equity ratio

A3

Required

1. Compute the debt-to-equity ratios for both companies.
2. Comment on your results and discuss what they imply about the relative riskiness of these companies.

Refer to the bond details in Problem 10-5B.

Required

1. Prepare the January 1, 2016, journal entry to record the bonds' issuance.
2. Determine the total bond interest expense to be recognized over the bonds' life.
3. Prepare an effective interest amortization table like the one in Exhibit 10B.1 for the bonds' first two years.
4. Prepare the journal entries to record the first two interest payments.

Problem 10-8B[B]
Effective Interest:
Amortization of bond discount   P1   P5

Check   (2) $257,506

(3) 6/30/2017 carrying value, $200,803

Refer to the bond details in Problem 10-4B.

Required

1. Compute the total bond interest expense over the bonds' life.
2. Prepare an effective interest amortization table like the one in Exhibit 10B.2 for the bonds' life.
3. Prepare the journal entries to record the first two interest payments.
4. Use the market rate at issuance to compute the present value of the remaining cash flows for these bonds as of December 31, 2018. Compare your answer with the amount shown on the amortization table as the balance for that date (from part 2) and explain your findings.

Problem 10-9B[B]
Effective Interest:
Amortization of bond premium; computing bond price   P1   P6

Check   (2) 6/30/2018 carrying value, $327,136

(4) $325,807

Valdez issues $450,000 of 13%, four-year bonds dated January 1, 2016, that pay interest semiannually on June 30 and December 31. They are issued at $493,608, and their market rate is 10% at the issue date.

Required

1. Prepare the January 1, 2016, journal entry to record the bonds' issuance.
2. Determine the total bond interest expense to be recognized over the bonds' life.
3. Prepare an effective interest amortization table like the one in Exhibit 10B.2 for the bonds' first two years.
4. Prepare the journal entries to record the first two interest payments.
5. Prepare the journal entry to record the bonds' retirement on January 1, 2018, at 106.

Problem 10-10B[B]
Effective Interest:
Amortization of bond; retiring bonds

P1   P4   P5   P6

Check   (3) 6/30/2017 carrying value, $479,202

(5) $3,088 loss

Analysis Component

6. Assume that the market rate on January 1, 2016, is 14% instead of 10%. Without presenting numbers, describe how this change affects the amounts reported on Valdez's financial statements.

Braun Company signs a five-year capital lease with Verdi Company for office equipment. The annual year-end lease payment is $20,000, and the interest rate is 10%.

Required

1. Compute the present value of Braun's lease payments.
2. Prepare the journal entry to record Braun's capital lease at its inception.
3. Complete a lease payment schedule for the five years of the lease with the following headings. Assume that the beginning balance of the lease liability (present value of lease payments) is $75,816. (*Hint:* To find

Problem 10-11B[D]
Capital lease accounting

C4

Check   (1) $75,816

(3) Year 3 ending balance, $34,712

the amount allocated to interest in year 1, multiply the interest rate by the beginning-of-year lease liability. The amount of the annual lease payment not allocated to interest is allocated to principal. Reduce the lease liability by the amount allocated to principal to update the lease liability at each year-end.)

Period Ending Date	Beginning Balance of Lease Liability	Interest on Lease Liability	Reduction of Lease Liability	Cash Lease Payment	Ending Balance of Lease Liability

4. Use straight-line depreciation and prepare the journal entry to depreciate the leased asset at the end of year 1. Assume zero salvage value and a five-year life for the office equipment.

SERIAL PROBLEM

Business Solutions

A1   A3

(This serial problem began in Chapter 1 and continues through most of the book. If previous chapter segments were not completed, the serial problem can begin at this point. It is helpful, but not necessary, to use the Working Papers that accompany the book.)

SP 10   Santana Rey has consulted with her local banker and is considering financing an expansion of her business by obtaining a long-term bank loan. Assume that selected account balances at March 31, 2017, for Business Solutions follow.

Total assets.........	$120,268	Total liabilities.......	$875	Total equity.......	$119,393

Required

Check   (1) $94,639

1. The bank has offered a long-term secured note to Business Solutions. The bank's loan procedures require that a client's debt-to-equity ratio not exceed 0.8. As of March 31, 2017, what is the maximum amount that Business Solutions could borrow from this bank (rounded to the nearest dollar)?

2. If Business Solutions borrows the maximum amount allowed from the bank, what percentage of assets would be financed (*a*) by debt and (*b*) by equity?

3. What are some factors Santana Rey should consider before borrowing the funds?

Beyond the Numbers

REPORTING IN ACTION

A1   A2

APPLE

BTN 10-1   Refer to **Apple**'s financial statements in Appendix A to answer the following.

1. Identify the items, if any, that make up Apple's long-term debt as reported on its balance sheet at September 27, 2014.

2. Assume that Apple has $100 million in convertible debentures that carry a 4.25% contract rate of interest. How much annual cash interest must be paid on those convertible debentures?

3. Assume that the convertible bonds discussed in part 2 are convertible into 20,000 shares of Apple's stock. If the carrying value of these bonds is $100 million, what is the entry recorded by Apple upon conversion?

Fast Forward

4. Access Apple's financial statements for the years ending after September 27, 2014, from its website (**Apple.com**) or the SEC's EDGAR database (**www.SEC.gov**). Has it issued additional long-term debt since the year-end September 27, 2014? If yes, identify the amount(s).

COMPARATIVE ANALYSIS

A3

APPLE

GOOGLE

BTN 10-2   Key figures for **Apple** and **Google** follow.

$ millions	Apple		Google	
	Current Year	Prior Year	Current Year	Prior Year
Total assets............	$231,839	$207,000	$131,133	$110,920
Total liabilities	120,292	83,451	26,633	23,611
Total equity	111,547	123,549	104,500	87,309

Required

1. Compute the debt-to-equity ratios for Apple and Google for both the current year and the prior year.
2. Use the ratios you computed in part 1 to determine which company's financing structure is least risky. Assume an industry average of 0.44 for debt-to-equity.

BTN 10-3   Traverse County needs a new county government building that would cost $10 million. The politicians feel that voters will not approve a municipal bond issue to fund the building since it would increase taxes. They opt to have a state bank issue $10 million of tax-exempt securities to pay for the building construction. The county then will make yearly lease payments (of principal and interest) to repay the obligation. Unlike conventional municipal bonds, the lease payments are not binding obligations on the county and, therefore, require no voter approval.

ETHICS CHALLENGE
C4 A1

Required

1. Do you think the actions of the politicians and the bankers in this situation are ethical?
2. In terms of risk, how do the tax-exempt securities used to pay for the building compare to a conventional municipal bond issued by Traverse County?

BTN 10-4   Your business associate mentions that she is considering investing in corporate bonds currently selling at a premium. She says that since the bonds are selling at a premium, they are highly valued and her investment will yield more than the going rate of return for the risk involved. Reply with a memorandum to confirm or correct your associate's interpretation of premium bonds.

COMMUNICATING IN PRACTICE
P3

BTN 10-5   Access the March 26, 2015, filing of the 10-K report of **Home Depot** for the year ended February 1, 2015, from **www.SEC.gov** (ticker HD). Refer to Home Depot's balance sheet, including its note 4 (on debt).

TAKING IT TO THE NET
A2

Required

1. Identify Home Depot's long-term liabilities and the amounts for those liabilities from Home Depot's balance sheet at February 1, 2015.
2. Review Home Depot's note 4. The note reports that as of February 1, 2015, it had $2.963 billion of "5.875% Senior Notes; due December 16, 2036; interest payable semiannually on June 16 and December 16." These notes have a face value of $3.0 billion and were originally issued at $2.958 billion.
   a. Why would Home Depot issue $3.0 billion of its notes for only $2.958 billion?
   b. How much cash interest must Home Depot pay each June 16 and December 16 on these notes?

BTN 10-6ᴮ   Break into teams and complete the following requirements related to *effective interest* amortization for a premium bond.

TEAMWORK IN ACTION
P2 P3

1. Each team member is to independently prepare a blank table with proper headings for amortization of a bond premium. When all have finished, compare tables and ensure that all are in agreement.

Parts 2 and 3 require use of these facts: On January 1, 2016, McElroy issues $100,000, 9%, five-year bonds at 104.1. The market rate at issuance is 8%. McElroy pays interest semiannually on June 30 and December 31.

2. In rotation, *each* team member must explain how to complete *one* line of the bond amortization table, including all computations for his or her line. (Round amounts to the nearest dollar.) All members are to fill in their tables during this process. You need not finish the table; stop after all members have explained a line.

3. In rotation, *each* team member is to identify a separate column of the table and indicate what the final number in that column will be and explain the reasoning.

[continued on next page]

Hint: Rotate teams to report on parts 4 and 5. Consider requiring entries for issuance and interest payments.

4. Reach a team consensus as to what the total bond interest expense on this bond issue will be if the bond is not retired before maturity.

5. As a team, prepare a list of similarities and differences between the amortization table just prepared and the amortization table if the bond had been issued at a discount.

ENTREPRENEURIAL DECISION

A1

BTN 10-7   Aaron Levie is the co-founder of **Box**. Assume that his company currently has $250,000 in equity, and he is considering a $100,000 expansion to meet increased demand. The $100,000 expansion would yield $16,000 in additional annual income before interest expense. Assume that the business currently earns $40,000 annual income before interest expense of $10,000, yielding a return on equity of 12% ($30,000/$250,000). To fund the expansion, he is considering the issuance of a 10-year, $100,000 note with annual interest payments (the principal due at the end of 10 years).

Required

1. Using return on equity as the decision criterion, show computations to support or reject the expansion if interest on the $100,000 note is (*a*) 10%, (*b*) 15%, (*c*) 16%, (*d*) 17%, and (*e*) 20%.

2. What general rule do the results in part 1 illustrate?

HITTING THE ROAD

A1

BTN 10-8   Visit your city or county library. Ask the librarian to help you locate the most recent financial records of your city or county government. Examine those records.

Required

1. Determine the amount of long-term bonds and notes currently outstanding.

2. Read the supporting information to your municipality's financial statements and record
   a. The market interest rate(s) when the bonds and/or notes were issued.
   b. The date(s) when the bonds and/or notes will mature.
   c. Any rating(s) on the bonds and/or notes received from **Moody's Investors Service**, **Standard & Poor's Ratings Services**, **Fitch Ratings**, or another rating agency.

GLOBAL DECISION

A3

Samsung
APPLE
GOOGLE

BTN 10-9   **Samsung** (**Samsung.com**), **Apple**, and **Google** are competitors in the global marketplace. Selected results from these companies follow.

Key Figures	Samsung (₩ millions) Current Year	Samsung (₩ millions) Prior Year	Apple ($ millions) Current Year	Apple ($ millions) Prior Year	Google ($ millions) Current Year	Google ($ millions) Prior Year
Total assets.	₩230,422,958	₩214,075,018	$231,839	$207,000	$131,133	$110,920
Total liabilities	62,334,770	64,059,008	120,292	83,451	26,633	23,611
Total equity	168,088,188	150,016,010	111,547	123,549	104,500	87,309
Debt-to-equity ratio	?	?	1.08	0.68	0.25	0.27

Required

1. Compute Samsung's debt-to-equity ratio for the current year and the prior year.

2. Use the data provided and the ratios computed in part 1 to determine which company's financing structure is least risky.

ANSWERS TO MULTIPLE CHOICE QUIZ

1. b

2. a

3. c; $500,000 \times 0.08 \times$ ½ year = $20,000

4. a; Cash interest paid = $100,000 \times 5\% \times$ ½ year = $2,500

Discount amortization = ($100,000 − $95,735)/10 periods = $426.50

Interest expense = $2,500.00 + $426.50 = $2,926.50

5. e; ($373,745 − $350,000)/16 periods = $1,484

Reporting and Analyzing Equity

Chapter Preview

COMMON STOCK

C1 Stock basics

P1 Stock issuance:
   Par value
   No-par value
   Stated value
   Noncash assets

DIVIDENDS

P2 Cash dividends
   Stock dividends
   Stock splits

PREFERRED STOCK

C2 Issuance
   Dividend preferences
   Convertible and callable
   Rationale

TREASURY STOCK

P3 Purchasing treasury stock
   Reissuing treasury stock
   Retiring stock

REPORTING AND ANALYSIS

C3 Statements of retained earnings and equity

A1 EPS
A2 PE ratio
A3 Dividend yield
A4 Book value

Learning Objectives

CONCEPTUAL

C1 Identify characteristics of corporations and their organization.

C2 Explain characteristics of, and distribute dividends between, common and preferred stock.

C3 Explain the items reported in retained earnings.

ANALYTICAL

A1 Compute earnings per share and describe its use.

A2 Compute price-earnings ratio and describe its use in analysis.

A3 Compute dividend yield and explain its use in analysis.

A4 Compute book value and explain its use in analysis.

PROCEDURAL

P1 Record the issuance of corporate stock.

P2 Record transactions involving cash dividends, stock dividends, and stock splits.

P3 Record purchases and sales of treasury stock and the retirement of stock.

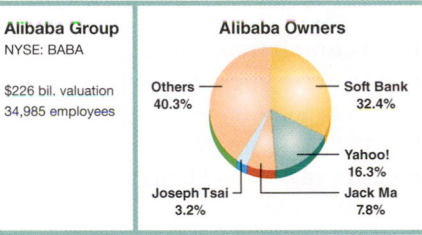

Open Sesame

"Nobody wanted to believe" — **JACK MA**

HANGZHOU, CHINA—"In 1995 a friend showed me the Internet for the first time," recalls Jack Ma. "We searched the word *beer* . . . [then we] discovered that there was no data about China. We decided to launch a website." Jack never looked back. "My dream was to set up my own e-commerce company," explains Jack. "I gathered 17 people in my apartment and spoke to them for two hours about my vision. Everyone put their money on the table."

Jack then needed a company name. "I was in San Francisco in a coffee shop, and I was thinking *Alibaba* is a good name. Then a waitress came, and I said do you know about Alibaba? And she said yes. I said what do you know about Alibaba, and she said 'Open Sesame.' And I said yes, this is the name! Then I went onto the street and found 30 people and asked them, 'Do you know Alibaba?' People from India, people from Germany, people from Tokyo and China . . . They all knew about Alibaba." Thus, the **Alibaba Group (AlibabaGroup.com)** was born.

The success of Alibaba would not have been possible without good decisions regarding creditor vs. equity financing. To make it happen, the new company had to deal with corporate formation, equity

Alibaba Group
NYSE: BABA

$226 bil. valuation
34,985 employees

Alibaba Owners

- Others 40.3%
- Soft Bank 32.4%
- Yahoo! 16.3%
- Jack Ma 7.8%
- Joseph Tsai 3.2%

issuance, stock types, retaining earnings, and dividend policies. Jack eventually set up the Alibaba Group as a corporate-type entity. With his structure in place, Jack was ready to attack the market. Income soon followed, as shown here.

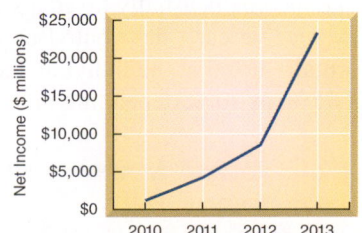

The success of Alibaba's corporate-type structure and its mix of creditor vs. equity financing brought both opportunities and challenges. Jack explains the empowering of consumers. "It's customers number one, employees two, and shareholders three," declares Jack. "It's the shareholders who when the crisis comes . . . ran away. My customers and my people stayed." The challenge is staying the course. "Nobody believed in me," admits Jack. "Do not allow your colleagues and employees to work for you. Instead, let them work for a common goal."

There are new challenges on the horizon for Jack. One is effectively leveraging accounting knowledge to achieve his current task: managing Alibaba stock on the NYSE. This demands knowledge of corporate formation, stock types, and equity transactions. Jack's company recently achieved the largest initial public offering of stock in history. The Alibaba Group's IPO made Jack Ma the richest man in China, with an estimated net worth of $25 billion.

Through it all, Jack remains humble. "I call myself 'blind man riding on the back of a blind tiger.' "

Sources: *Alibaba website,* January 2016; *Wall Street Journal,* September 2014; *Inc.,* January 2008; *Upstart Business Journal,* September 2011; *Talk Asia,* April 2006; *South China Morning Post,* July 2013; *Jungle News,* May 2014; *Vulcan Post,* February 2014

CORPORATE FORM OF ORGANIZATION

C1

Identify characteristics of corporations and their organization.

A **corporation** is an entity created by law that is separate from its owners. It has most of the rights and privileges granted to individuals. Owners of corporations are called *stockholders* or *shareholders*. Corporations can be separated into two types. A *privately held* (or *closely held*) corporation does not offer its stock for public sale and usually has few stockholders. A *publicly held* corporation offers its stock for public sale and can have thousands of stockholders. *Public sale* usually refers to issuance of stock and trading on an organized stock market.

Characteristics of Corporations

Corporations represent an important type of organization. Their unique characteristics offer advantages and disadvantages.

Advantages of Corporate Form

Point: The *business entity assumption* requires a corporation to be accounted for separately from its owners (shareholders).

- **Separate legal entity:** A corporation conducts its affairs with the same rights, duties, and responsibilities of a person. It takes actions through its agents, who are its officers and managers.
- **Limited liability of stockholders:** Stockholders are liable for neither corporate acts nor corporate debt.
- **Transferable ownership rights:** The transfer of shares from one stockholder to another usually has no effect on the corporation or its operations except when this causes a change in the directors who control or manage the corporation.
- **Continuous life:** A corporation's life continues indefinitely because it is not tied to the physical lives of its owners.
- **Lack of mutual agency for stockholders:** A corporation acts through its agents, who are its officers and managers. Stockholders, who are not its officers and managers, do not have the power to bind the corporation to contracts—referred to as *lack of mutual agency*.
- **Ease of capital accumulation:** Buying stock is attractive to investors because (1) stockholders are not liable for the corporation's acts and debts, (2) stocks usually are transferred easily, (3) the life of the corporation is unlimited, and (4) stockholders are not corporate agents. These advantages enable corporations to accumulate large amounts of capital from the combined investments of many stockholders.

Disadvantages of Corporate Form

Point: Proprietorships and partnerships are not subject to income taxes. Their income is taxed as the personal income of their owners.

- **Government regulation:** A corporation must meet requirements of a state's incorporation laws, which subject the corporation to state regulation and control. Proprietorships and partnerships avoid many of these regulations and governmental reports.

Point: Double taxation is less severe when a corporation's owner-manager collects a salary that is taxed only once as part of his or her personal income. At year-end, many small corporations distribute *bonuses* to owner-managers equal to the corporation's income. This reduces corporate income to $0 and avoids double taxation.

- **Corporate taxation:** Corporations are subject to the same property and payroll taxes as proprietorships and partnerships plus *additional* taxes. The most burdensome of these are federal and state income taxes that together can take 40% or more of corporate pretax income. Moreover, corporate income is usually taxed a second time as part of stockholders' personal income when they receive cash distributed as dividends. This is called *double taxation*. (Dividends are normally taxed at the individual's income tax rate; for "qualified" dividends, the tax rate is 0%, 15%, or 20%, depending on the individual's tax bracket.)

■ Decision Insight

Dorm-Corp   Mark Zuckerberg took his company, **Facebook**, public by issuing its first shares on the Nasdaq exchange. The initial public offering (IPO) of Facebook shares raised billions in equity financing. It also raised the importance of accounting reports versus market hype. The IPO of Facebook shares came eight years after the company was founded by Zuckerberg in his college dorm room. Fast-forward to today, Zuckerberg vows to donate 99% of his Facebook shares, worth about $45 billion, toward charitable causes. ■

AP Images/Nasdaq via Facebook, Zef Nikolla

Corporate Organization and Management

This section describes the incorporation, costs, and management of corporate organizations.

Incorporation   A corporation is created by obtaining a charter from a state government. A charter application usually must be signed by the prospective stockholders called *incorporators* or *promoters* and then filed with the proper state official. When the application process is complete and fees paid, the charter is issued and the corporation is formed. Investors then purchase the corporation's stock, meet as stockholders, and elect a board of directors. Directors oversee a corporation's affairs.

Point: A corporation is not required to have an office in its state of incorporation. Delaware is viewed as having favorable corporate laws, and about half of all corporations listed on the NYSE are incorporated there.

Organization Expenses   **Organization expenses** (also called *organization costs*) are the costs to organize a corporation; they include legal fees, promoters' fees, and amounts paid to obtain a charter. The corporation records (debits) these costs to an expense account called *Organization Expenses*. Organization costs are expensed as incurred because it is difficult to determine the amount and timing of their future benefits.

Management of a Corporation   The ultimate control of a corporation rests with stockholders who control a corporation by electing its *board of directors,* or simply, *directors.* Each stockholder usually has one vote for each share of stock owned. This control relation is shown in Exhibit 11.1. Directors are responsible for and have final authority for managing corporate activities. A board can act only as a collective body and usually limits its actions to setting general policy.

A corporation usually holds a stockholder meeting at least once a year to elect directors and transact business as its bylaws require. A group of stockholders owning or controlling votes of more than a 50% share of a corporation's stock can elect the board and control the corporation. Stockholders who do not attend stockholders' meetings must have an opportunity to delegate their voting rights to an agent by signing a **proxy,** a document that gives a designated agent the right to vote the stock.

Day-to-day direction of corporate business is delegated to executive officers appointed by the board. A corporation's chief executive officer (CEO) is often its president. Several vice presidents, who report to the president, are commonly assigned specific areas of management responsibility such as finance, production, and marketing. One person often has the dual role of chairperson of the board of directors and CEO. In this case, the president is usually designated the chief operating officer (COO).

EXHIBIT 11.1

Corporate Structure

Corporate governance is the system by which companies are directed and controlled.

Stockholders → Board of Directors → President, Vice President, and Other Officers → Employees of the Corporation

Point: *Bylaws* are guidelines that govern the behavior of individuals employed by and managing the corporation.

Decision Insight

Angel $s   Sources for start-up money include (1) "angel" investors such as family, friends, or anyone who believes in a company; (2) employees, investors, and even suppliers who can be paid with stock; and (3) venture capitalists (investors) who have a record of entrepreneurial success. See the National Venture Capital Association (**NVCA.org**) for information. ■

Global: Some corporate labels are:

Country	Label
United States	Inc.
France	SA
United Kingdom	
Public	PLC
Private	Ltd.
Germany & Austria . .	
Public	AG
Private	GmbH
Sweden & Finland	AB
Italy	SpA
Netherlands	NV
Australia	AG
Mexico	SA
Bahamas	IBC

Stockholders of Corporations

This section explains stockholder rights, stock purchases and sales, and the role of registrars and transfer agents.

Rights of Stockholders   When investors buy stock, they acquire all *specific* rights the corporation's charter grants to stockholders. They also acquire *general* rights granted stockholders by the laws of the state in which the company is incorporated. When a corporation has only one class of stock, it is identified as **common stock.** State laws vary, but common stockholders usually have the general right to

1. Vote at stockholders' meetings (or register proxy votes electronically).
2. Sell or otherwise dispose of their stock.
3. Purchase their proportional share of any common stock later issued by the corporation. This **preemptive right** protects stockholders' proportionate interest in the corporation. For example, a stockholder who owns 25% of a corporation's common stock has the first opportunity to buy 25% of any new common stock issued.
4. Receive the same dividend, if any, on each common share of the corporation.
5. Share in any assets remaining after creditors and preferred stockholders are paid when, and if, the corporation is liquidated. Each common share receives the same amount.

Stockholders also have the right to receive timely financial reports.

Stock Certificates and Transfer   Investors who buy a corporation's stock sometimes receive a *stock certificate* as proof of share ownership. Many corporations issue only one certificate

Green Bay Packers, Inc.

Courtesy of JJW Images

for each block of stock purchased. A certificate can be for any number of shares. Exhibit 11.2 shows a stock certificate issued by the **Green Bay Packers**. A certificate shows the company name, stockholder name, number of shares, and other crucial information. Issuance of certificates is becoming less common. Instead, many stockholders maintain accounts with the corporation or their stockbrokers and never receive actual certificates.

Registrar and Transfer Agents   If a corporation's stock is traded on a major stock exchange, the corporation must have a registrar and a transfer agent. A *registrar* keeps stockholder records and prepares official lists of stockholders for stockholder meetings and dividend payments. A *transfer agent* assists with purchases and sales of shares by receiving and issuing certificates as necessary. Registrars and transfer agents are usually large banks or trust companies with computer facilities and staff to do this work.

Decision Insight

First Call   A prospectus accompanies a stock's initial public offering (IPO), giving financial information about the company issuing the stock. A prospectus should help answer these questions to price an IPO: (1) Is the underwriter reliable? (2) Is there growth in revenues, profits, and cash flows? (3) What is management's view of operations? (4) Are current owners selling? (5) What are the risks? ■

Basics of Capital Stock

Capital stock is a general term that refers to any shares issued to obtain capital (owner financing). This section introduces terminology and accounting for capital stock.

Authorized Stock   **Authorized stock** is the number of shares that a corporation's charter allows it to sell. The number of authorized shares usually exceeds the number of shares issued (and outstanding), often by a large amount. (*Outstanding stock* refers to issued stock held by stockholders.) No formal journal entry is required for stock authorization. A corporation must apply to the state for a change in its charter if it wishes to issue more shares than previously authorized. A corporation discloses the number of shares authorized in the equity section of its balance sheet or notes. **Apple**'s balance sheet reports 12.6 billion common shares authorized as of the start of its 2015 fiscal year.

Subcategories of Authorized Stock

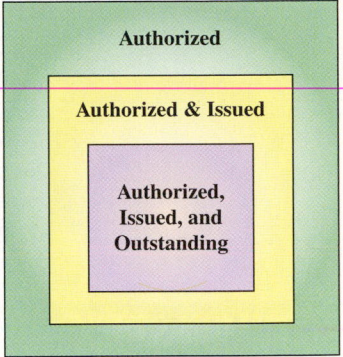

The innermost box shows that shares issued decline if a company buys back its previously issued stock.

Selling (Issuing) Stock A corporation can sell stock directly or indirectly. To *sell directly,* it advertises its stock issuance to potential buyers. This type of issuance is most common with privately held corporations. To *sell indirectly,* a corporation pays a brokerage house (investment banker) to issue its stock. Some brokerage houses *underwrite* an indirect issuance of stock; that is, they buy the stock from the corporation and take all gains or losses from its resale.

Market Value of Stock **Market value per share** is the price at which a stock is bought and sold. Expected future earnings, dividends, growth, and other company and economic factors influence market value. Traded stocks' market values are available daily in newspapers such as the *Wall Street Journal* and online. The current market value of previously issued shares (for example, the price of stock in trades between investors) does not impact the issuing corporation's stockholders' equity.

Classes of Stock When all authorized shares have the same rights and characteristics, the stock is called *common stock*. A corporation is sometimes authorized to issue more than one class of stock, including preferred stock and different classes of common stock. **American Greetings**, for instance, has two types of common stock: Class A stock has 1 vote per share and Class B stock has 10 votes per share.

Par Value Stock **Par value stock** is stock that is assigned a **par value,** which is an amount assigned per share by the corporation in its charter. For example, **Monster Worldwide, Inc.**'s common stock has a par value of $0.001. Other commonly assigned par values are $10, $5, $1 and $0.01. There is no restriction on the assigned par value. In many states, the par value of a stock establishes **minimum legal capital,** which refers to the least amount that the buyers of stock must contribute to the corporation or be subject to paying at a future date. For example, if a corporation issues 1,000 shares of $10 par value stock, the corporation's minimum legal capital in these states would be $10,000. Minimum legal capital is intended to protect a corporation's creditors. Since creditors cannot demand payment from stockholders' personal assets, their claims are limited to the corporation's assets and any minimum legal capital. At liquidation, creditor claims are paid before any amounts are distributed to stockholders.

Point: Managers are motivated to set a low par value when minimum legal capital or state issuance taxes are based on par value.

Point: Minimum legal capital was intended to protect creditors by requiring a minimum level of net assets.

No-Par Value Stock **No-par value stock,** or simply *no-par stock,* is stock *not* assigned a value per share by the corporate charter. Its advantage is that it can be issued at any price without the possibility of a minimum legal capital deficiency.

Point: Par, no-par, and stated value do *not* set the stock's market value.

Stated Value Stock **Stated value stock** is no-par stock to which the directors assign a "stated" value per share. Stated value per share becomes the minimum legal capital per share in this case.

Stockholders' Equity A corporation's equity is known as **stockholders' equity,** also called *shareholders' equity* or *corporate capital*. Stockholders' equity consists of (1) paid-in (or contributed) capital and (2) retained earnings; see Exhibit 11.3. **Paid-in capital** is the total amount of cash and other assets the corporation receives from its stockholders in exchange for its stock. **Retained earnings** is the cumulative net income (and loss) not distributed as dividends to its stockholders.

EXHIBIT 11.3

Equity Composition

Corporation

| Common Stock |
| Normal bal. |

| Paid-In Capital in Excess of Par |
| Normal bal. |

Total Paid-In Capital

| Retained Earnings |
| Normal bal. |

Point: Paid-in capital comes from stock-related transactions, whereas retained earnings come from operations; if Retained Earnings has a debit balance, it is often titled *Accumulated Deficit*.

■ **Decision Insight**

Price Quote   The **Target** stock quote is interpreted as (left to right): **Hi,** highest price in past 52 weeks; **Lo,** lowest price in past 52 weeks; **Sym,** company exchange symbol;

52 Weeks			Yld			Vol				Net
Hi	Lo	Sym	Div	%	PE	mil.	Hi	Lo	Close	Chg
85.81	57.26	TGT	2.24	2.70	16.6	638	58.50	57.84	57.95	−0.14

Div, dividends paid per share in past year; **Yld %,** dividend divided by closing price; **PE,** stock price per share divided by earnings per share; **Vol mil.,** number (in millions) of shares traded; **Hi,** highest price for the day; **Lo,** lowest price for the day; **Close,** closing price for the day; **Net Chg,** change in closing price from prior day. ■

COMMON STOCK

P1
Record the issuance of corporate stock.

Accounting for the issuance of common stock affects only paid-in (contributed) capital accounts; no retained earnings accounts are affected.

Issuing Par Value Stock

Par value stock can be issued at par, at a premium (above par), or at a discount (below par). In each case, stock can be exchanged for either cash or noncash assets.

Issuing Par Value Stock at Par   When common stock is issued at par value, we record amounts for both the asset(s) received and the par value stock issued. To illustrate, the entry to record Dillon Snowboards's issuance of 30,000 shares of $10 par value stock for $300,000 cash on June 5, 2016, follows:

Assets = Liabilities + Equity
+300,000   +300,000

$10 par value × 30,000 shares

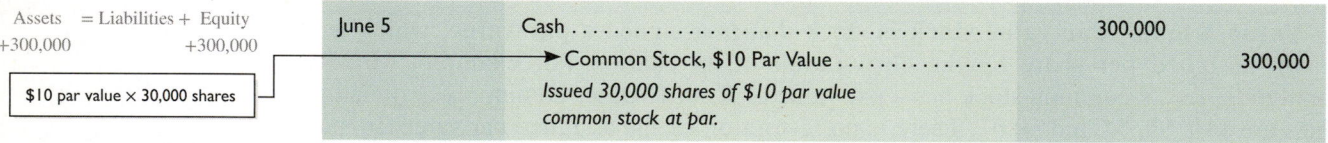

June 5	Cash	300,000	
	► Common Stock, $10 Par Value		300,000
	Issued 30,000 shares of $10 par value		
	common stock at par.		

Exhibit 11.4 shows the stockholders' equity of Dillon Snowboards at year-end 2016 (its first year of operations) after income of $65,000 and no dividend payments.

EXHIBIT 11.4

Stockholders' Equity for Stock Issued at Par

Stockholders' Equity	
Common stock—$10 par value; 50,000 shares authorized;	
30,000 shares issued and outstanding	$300,000
Retained earnings	65,000
Total stockholders' equity	$365,000

Issuing Par Value Stock at a Premium   A **premium on stock** occurs when a corporation sells its stock for more than par (or stated) value. To illustrate, if Dillon Snowboards issues its $10 par value common stock at $12 per share, its stock is sold at a $2 per share premium. The premium, known as **paid-in capital in excess of par value,** is reported as part of equity; it is not revenue and is not listed on the income statement. The entry to record Dillon Snowboards's issuance of 30,000 shares of $10 par value stock for $12 per share on June 5 follows:

Point: A *premium* is the amount by which issue price exceeds par (or stated) value. It is recorded in the Paid-In Capital in Excess of Par Value, Common Stock account; also called *Additional Paid-In Capital, Common Stock.*

Assets = Liabilities + Equity
+360,000   +300,000
                        +60,000

$10 par value × 30,000 shares

[$12 issue price − $10 par value] × 30,000 shares

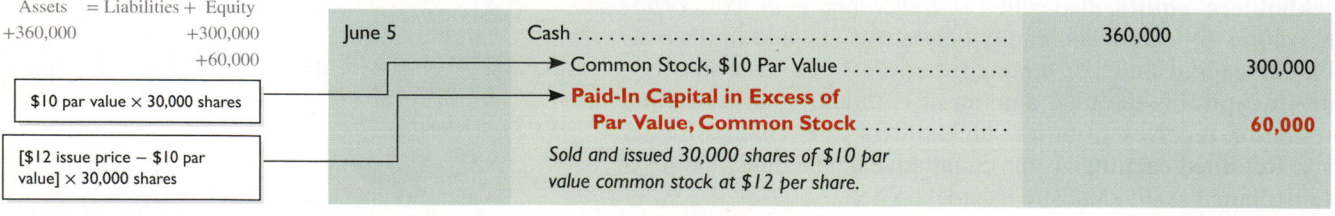

June 5	Cash	360,000	
	► Common Stock, $10 Par Value		300,000
	► **Paid-In Capital in Excess of**		
	Par Value, Common Stock		**60,000**
	Sold and issued 30,000 shares of $10 par		
	value common stock at $12 per share.		

The Paid-In Capital in Excess of Par Value account is added to the par value of the stock in the equity section of the balance sheet as shown in Exhibit 11.5.

Point: The *paid-in capital* terminology is interchangeable with *contributed capital*.

EXHIBIT 11.5

Stockholders' Equity for Stock Issued at a Premium

Stockholders' Equity	
Common stock—$10 par value; 50,000 shares authorized; 30,000 shares issued and outstanding	$300,000
Paid-in capital in excess of par value, common stock	**60,000**
Retained earnings	65,000
Total stockholders' equity	$425,000

Issuing Par Value Stock at a Discount   A **discount on stock** occurs when a corporation sells its stock for less than par (or stated) value. Most states prohibit the issuance of stock at a discount. In states that allow stock to be issued at a discount, its buyers usually become contingently liable to creditors for the discount. If stock is issued at a discount, the amount by which issue price is less than par is debited to a *Discount on Common Stock* account, a contra to the Common Stock account, and its balance is subtracted from the par value of stock in the equity section of the balance sheet. This discount is not an expense and does not appear on the income statement.

Point: Retained earnings can be negative, reflecting accumulated losses. **Pandora Media** had an accumulated deficit of $197 million at the start of 2015.

Issuing No-Par Value Stock

When no-par stock is issued and is not assigned a stated value, the amount the corporation receives becomes legal capital and is recorded as common stock. This means that the entire proceeds are credited to a no-par stock account. To illustrate, a corporation records its October 20 issuance of 1,000 shares of no-par stock for $40 cash per share as follows:

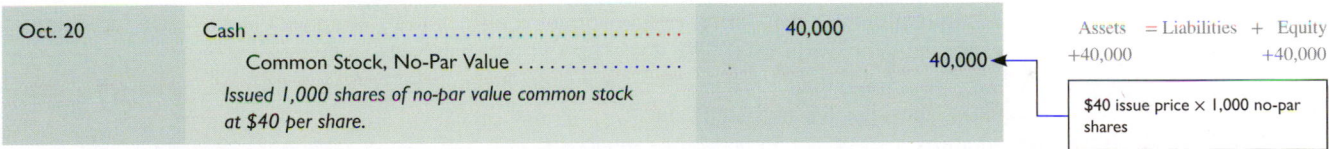

Oct. 20	Cash	40,000	
	Common Stock, No-Par Value		40,000
	Issued 1,000 shares of no-par value common stock at $40 per share.		

Assets = Liabilities + Equity
+40,000   +40,000

$40 issue price × 1,000 no-par shares

Issuing Stated Value Stock

When no-par stock is issued and assigned a stated value, its stated value becomes legal capital and is credited to a stated value stock account. Assuming that stated value stock is issued at an amount in excess of stated value (the usual case), the excess is credited to Paid-In Capital in Excess of Stated Value, Common Stock, which is reported in the stockholders' equity section. To illustrate, a corporation that issues 1,000 shares of no-par common stock having a stated value of $40 per share in return for $50 cash per share records this as follows:

Frequency of Stock Types

Par 88%
Stated 3%
No-Par 9%

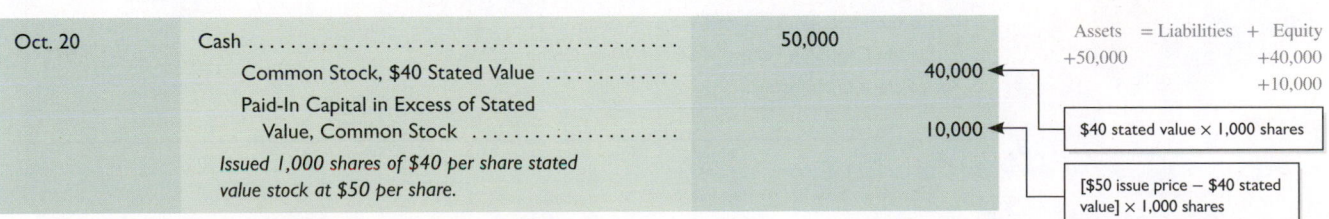

Oct. 20	Cash	50,000	
	Common Stock, $40 Stated Value		40,000
	Paid-In Capital in Excess of Stated Value, Common Stock		10,000
	Issued 1,000 shares of $40 per share stated value stock at $50 per share.		

Assets = Liabilities + Equity
+50,000   +40,000
                             +10,000

$40 stated value × 1,000 shares

[$50 issue price − $40 stated value] × 1,000 shares

Issuing Stock for Noncash Assets

A corporation can receive assets other than cash in exchange for its stock. (It can also assume liabilities on the assets received such as a mortgage on property received.) The corporation records the assets received at their market values as of the date of the transaction. The stock given in exchange is recorded at its par (or stated) value with any excess recorded in the Paid-In Capital in Excess of Par (or Stated) Value account. (If no-par stock is issued, the stock is

Point: Stock issued for noncash assets should be recorded at the market value of either the stock or the noncash assets, whichever is more clearly determinable.

recorded at the assets' market value.) To illustrate, the entry to record receipt of land valued at $105,000 in return for issuance of 4,000 shares of $20 par value common stock on June 10 is

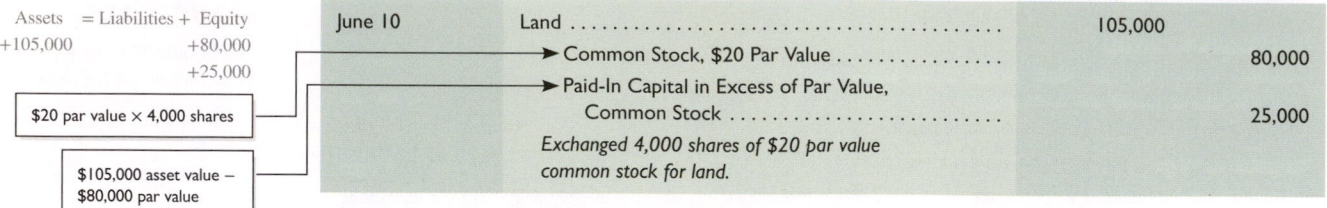

Assets = Liabilities + Equity
+105,000   +80,000
               +25,000

$20 par value × 4,000 shares

$105,000 asset value − $80,000 par value

June 10	Land	105,000	
	➤ Common Stock, $20 Par Value		80,000
	➤ Paid-In Capital in Excess of Par Value, Common Stock		25,000
	Exchanged 4,000 shares of $20 par value common stock for land.		

Point: Any type of stock can be issued for noncash assets.

A corporation sometimes gives shares of its stock to promoters in exchange for their services in organizing the corporation, which the corporation records as organization expenses. The entry to record receipt of services valued at $12,000 in organizing the corporation in return for 600 shares of $15 par value common stock on June 5 is

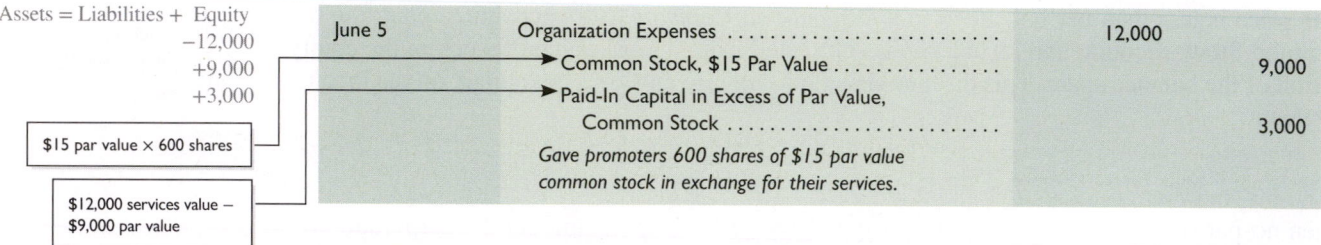

Assets = Liabilities + Equity
           −12,000
           +9,000
           +3,000

$15 par value × 600 shares

$12,000 services value − $9,000 par value

June 5	Organization Expenses	12,000	
	➤ Common Stock, $15 Par Value		9,000
	➤ Paid-In Capital in Excess of Par Value, Common Stock		3,000
	Gave promoters 600 shares of $15 par value common stock in exchange for their services.		

NEED-TO-KNOW 11-1

Recording Stock Issuance

P1

Prepare journal entries to record the following four separate (independent) issuances of stock.

1. A corporation issued 80 shares of $5 par value common stock for $700 cash.

2. A corporation issued 40 shares of no-par common stock to its promoters in exchange for their efforts, estimated to be worth $800. The stock has a $1 per share stated value.

3. A corporation issued 40 shares of no-par common stock in exchange for land, estimated to be worth $800. The stock has no stated value.

4. A corporation issued 20 shares of $30 par value preferred stock for $900 cash.

Solution

1.

Cash	700	
Common Stock, $5 Par Value*		400
Paid-In Capital in Excess of Par Value, Common Stock**		300
Issued common stock for cash.		
*80 shares × $5 per share = $400 **$700 − $400 = $300		

2.

Organization Expenses	800	
Common Stock, $1 Stated Value		40
Paid-In Capital in Excess of Stated Value, Common Stock		760
Issued stock to promoters.		

3.

Land	800	
Common Stock, No-Par Value		800
Issued stock in exchange for land.		

4.

Cash	900	
Preferred Stock, $30 Par Value*		600
Paid-In Capital in Excess of Par Value, Preferred Stock**		300
Issued preferred stock for cash.		
*20 shares × $30 per share = $600 **$900 − $600 = $300		

Do More: QS 11-2, QS 11-3, QS 11-4, QS 11-5, E 11-2, E 11-3, E 11-4

DIVIDENDS

This section describes both cash and stock dividend transactions.

P2

Record transactions involving cash dividends, stock dividends, and stock splits.

Cash Dividends

The decision to pay cash dividends rests with the board of directors and involves more than evaluating the amounts of retained earnings and cash. The directors, for instance, may decide to keep the cash to invest in the corporation's growth, to meet emergencies, to take advantage of unexpected opportunities, or to pay off debt. Alternatively, many corporations pay cash dividends to their stockholders at regular dates. These cash flows provide a return to investors and almost always affect the stock's market value.

Accounting for Cash Dividends Dividend payment involves three important dates: declaration, record, and payment. **Date of declaration** is the date the directors vote to declare and pay a dividend. This creates a legal liability of the corporation to its stockholders. **Date of record** is the future date specified by the directors for identifying those stockholders listed in the corporation's records to receive dividends. The date of record usually follows the date of declaration by at least two weeks. Persons who own stock on the date of record receive dividends. **Date of payment** is the date when the corporation makes payment; it follows the date of record by enough time to allow the corporation to arrange checks, money transfers, or other means to pay dividends.

Percent of Corporations Paying Dividends

Cash Dividend to Common — 75%

Cash Dividend to Preferred — 22%

0% 20% 40% 60% 80% 100%

To illustrate, the entry to record a January 9 declaration of a $1 per share cash dividend by the directors of Z-Tech, Inc., with 5,000 outstanding shares is

Date of Declaration

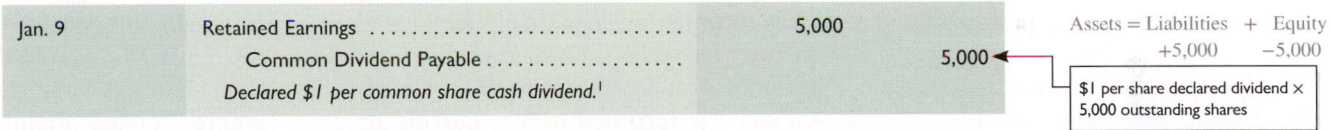

Jan. 9	Retained Earnings	5,000	
	Common Dividend Payable		5,000
	Declared $1 per common share cash dividend.[1]		

Assets = Liabilities + Equity
          +5,000   −5,000

$1 per share declared dividend × 5,000 outstanding shares

Common Dividend Payable is a current liability. The date of record for the Z-Tech dividend is January 22. *No formal journal entry is needed on the date of record.* The February 1 date of payment requires an entry to record both the settlement of the liability and the reduction of the cash balance, as follows:

Date of Payment

Feb. 1	Common Dividend Payable	5,000	
	Cash		5,000
	Paid $1 per common share cash dividend.		

Assets = Liabilities + Equity
−5,000   −5,000

Deficits and Cash Dividends A corporation with a debit (abnormal) balance for Retained Earnings is said to have a **retained earnings deficit,** which arises when a company incurs cumulative losses and/or pays more dividends than total earnings from current and prior years. A deficit is reported as a deduction on the balance sheet, as shown in Exhibit 11.6. Most states prohibit a corporation with a deficit from paying a cash dividend to its stockholders. This legal restriction is designed to protect creditors by preventing distribution of assets to stockholders when the company may be in financial difficulty.

Point: It is often said a dividend is a distribution of retained earnings, but it is more precise to describe a dividend as a distribution of assets to satisfy stockholder claims.

Point: The Retained Earnings Deficit account is also called *Accumulated Deficit.*

---

[1] An alternative entry is to debit Dividends instead of Retained Earnings. The balance in Dividends is then closed to Retained Earnings at the end of the reporting period. The effect is the same: Retained Earnings is decreased and a Dividend Payable is increased. For simplicity, all assignments in this chapter use the Retained Earnings account to record dividend declarations.

EXHIBIT 11.6

Stockholders' Equity with
a Deficit

Common stock—$10 par value, 5,000 shares authorized, issued, and outstanding	$50,000
Retained earnings deficit	**(6,000)**
Total stockholders' equity	$44,000

Point: Amazon.com has
never declared a cash dividend.

Some state laws allow cash dividends to be paid by returning a portion of the capital contributed by stockholders. This type of dividend is called a **liquidating cash dividend,** or simply *liquidating dividend,* because it returns a part of the original investment back to the stockholders. This requires a debit entry to one of the contributed capital accounts instead of Retained Earnings at the declaration date.

Stock Dividends

A **stock dividend,** declared by a corporation's directors, is a distribution of additional shares of the corporation's own stock to its stockholders without the receipt of any payment in return. Stock dividends and cash dividends are different. A stock dividend does not reduce assets and equity but instead transfers a portion of equity from retained earnings to contributed capital.

Reasons for Stock Dividends   Stock dividends exist for at least two reasons. First, directors are said to use stock dividends to keep the market price of the stock affordable. For example, if a corporation continues to earn income but does not issue cash dividends, the price of its common stock likely increases. The price of such a stock may become so high that it discourages some investors from buying the stock (especially in lots of 100 and 1,000). When a corporation has a stock dividend, it increases the number of outstanding shares and lowers the per share stock price. Another reason for a stock dividend is to provide evidence of management's confidence that the company is doing well and will continue to do well.

Accounting for Stock Dividends   A stock dividend affects the components of equity by transferring part of retained earnings to contributed capital accounts, sometimes described as *capitalizing* retained earnings. Accounting for a stock dividend depends on whether it is a small or large stock dividend. A **small stock dividend** is a distribution of 25% or less of previously outstanding shares. It is recorded by capitalizing retained earnings for an amount equal to the

Hint: Five Steps to Record Stock Dividends

Step 1: Identify number of shares outstanding.
Step 2: Identify the stock dividend percentage.
Step 3: Compute number of new shares (step 1 × step 2).
Step 4: Value new shares at market (small stock dividend) or par (large stock dividend).
Step 5: Determine debit (reduction) to Retained Earnings (step 3 × step 4).

market value of the shares to be distributed. A **large stock dividend** is a distribution of more than 25% of previously outstanding shares. A large stock dividend is recorded by capitalizing retained earnings for the minimum amount required by state law governing the corporation. Most states require capitalizing retained earnings equal to the par or stated value of the stock.

To illustrate stock dividends, we use the equity section of Quest's balance sheet shown in Exhibit 11.7 just *before* its declaration of a stock dividend on December 31.

EXHIBIT 11.7

Stockholders' Equity
before a Stock Dividend

Stockholders' Equity	**Before Dividend**
Common stock—$10 par value, 15,000 shares authorized,	
10,000 shares issued and outstanding	$100,000
Paid-in capital in excess of par value, common stock	8,000
Retained earnings	35,000
Total stockholders' equity	$143,000

Point: Small stock dividends
are recorded at market value.

Assets = Liabilities + Equity
                              −15,000
                              +10,000
                              +5,000

Recording a Small Stock Dividend   Assume that Quest's directors declare a 10% stock dividend on December 31. This stock dividend of 1,000 shares, computed as 10% of its 10,000 outstanding shares, is to be distributed on January 20 to the stockholders of record on January 15. Since the market price of Quest's stock on December 31 is $15 per share, this small stock dividend declaration is recorded as follows:

Date of Declaration—Small Stock Dividend

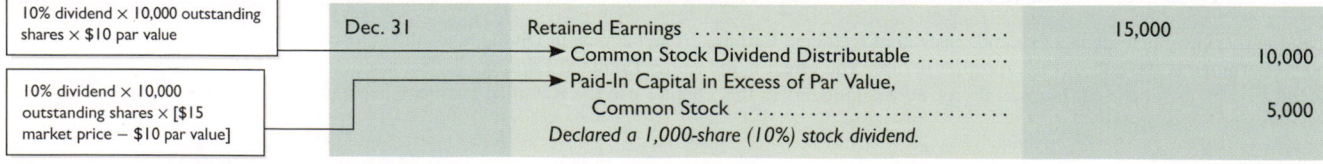

10% dividend × 10,000 outstanding shares × $10 par value

10% dividend × 10,000 outstanding shares × [$15 market price − $10 par value]

Dec. 31	Retained Earnings	15,000	
	Common Stock Dividend Distributable		10,000
	Paid-In Capital in Excess of Par Value,		
	Common Stock		5,000
	Declared a 1,000-share (10%) stock dividend.		

The $10,000 credit in the declaration entry equals the par value of the shares and is recorded in *Common Stock Dividend Distributable,* an equity account. Its balance exists only until the shares are issued. The $5,000 credit equals the amount by which market value exceeds par value. This amount increases the Paid-In Capital in Excess of Par Value account in anticipation of the issuance of shares. In general, the balance sheet changes in three ways when a stock dividend is declared. First, the amount of equity attributed to common stock increases; for Quest, from $100,000 to $110,000 for 1,000 additional declared shares. Second, paid-in capital in excess of par increases by the excess of market value over par value for the declared shares. Third, retained earnings decreases, reflecting the transfer of amounts to both common stock and paid-in capital in excess of par. The impact on stockholders' equity of Quest is shown in Exhibit 11.8 when its 10% stock dividend is declared on December 31—see the Declaration column.

Point: The term *Distributable* (not *Payable*) is used for stock dividends. A stock dividend is never a liability because it never reduces assets.

Point: The credit to Paid-In Capital in Excess of Par Value is recorded when the stock dividend is declared. This account is not affected when stock is later distributed.

EXHIBIT 11.8

Stockholders' Equity before, during, and after a Stock Dividend

Stockholders' Equity	Before Dividend	Declaration	Issuance	After Dividend
Common stock—$10 par value, 15,000 shares authorized, 10,000 shares issued and outstanding	$100,000	$ —	$ 10,000	$110,000
Common stock dividend distributable—1,000 shares	—	10,000	(10,000)	0
Paid-in capital in excess of par value, common stock.	8,000	5,000	—	13,000
Retained earnings.	35,000	(15,000)	—	20,000
Total stockholders' equity.	$143,000	$ 0	$ 0	$143,000

No entry is made on the date of record for a stock dividend. On January 20, the date of payment, Quest distributes the new shares to stockholders and records this entry (this entry is reflected in the Issuance column of Exhibit 11.8):

Date of Payment—Small Stock Dividend

Jan. 20	Common Stock Dividend Distributable	10,000	
	Common Stock, $10 Par Value		10,000
	Record issuance of common stock dividend.		

Assets = Liabilities + Equity
−10,000
+10,000

The combined effect of these stock dividend entries is to transfer (or capitalize) $15,000 of retained earnings to paid-in capital accounts (see far-right column of Exhibit 11.8). The amount of capitalized retained earnings equals the market value of the 1,000 issued shares ($15 × 1,000 shares). A stock dividend has no effect on the ownership percentage of individual stockholders.

Point: A stock dividend does not affect total assets or total equity.

Recording a Large Stock Dividend   A corporation capitalizes retained earnings equal to the minimum amount required by state law for a large stock dividend. For most states, this amount is the par or stated value of the newly issued shares. To illustrate, suppose Quest's board declares a stock dividend of 30% instead of 10% on December 31. Since this dividend is more than 25%, it is treated as a large stock dividend. Thus, the par value of the 3,000 (computed as 10,000 outstanding shares × 30%) dividend shares is capitalized at the date of declaration with this entry:

Point: Large stock dividends are recorded at par or stated value.

Date of Declaration—Large Stock Dividend

Dec. 31	Retained Earnings	30,000	
	Common Stock Dividend Distributable		30,000
	Declared a 3,000-share (30%) stock dividend.		

Assets = Liabilities + Equity
−30,000
+30,000

30% dividend × 10,000 outstanding shares × $10 par value

This transaction decreases retained earnings and increases contributed capital by $30,000. On the date of payment the company debits Common Stock Dividend Distributable and credits Common Stock for $30,000. The effects from a large stock dividend on balance sheet accounts are similar to those for a small stock dividend except for the absence of any effect on paid-in capital in excess of par.

Stock Splits

A **stock split** is the distribution of additional shares to stockholders according to their percent ownership. When a stock split occurs, the corporation "calls in" its outstanding shares and issues more than one new share in exchange for each old share. Splits can be done in any ratio,

Before 5 : 1 Split: 1 share, $50 par

After 5 : 1 Split: 5 shares, $10 par

Point: Berkshire Hathaway has resisted a stock split. Its recent stock price was $200,000 per share.

Point: A reverse stock split is the opposite of a stock split. It increases both the market value per share and the par or stated value per share with a split ratio less than 1-for-1, such as 1-for-2. A reverse split results in fewer shares. Markets often read bad news into reverse splits.

including 2-for-1, 3-for-1, or higher. In 2014, **Apple** directors approved a 7-for-1 stock split. Stock splits reduce the par or stated value per share. The reasons for stock splits are similar to those for stock dividends.

To illustrate, CompTec has 100,000 outstanding shares of $20 par value common stock with a current market value of $88 per share. A 2-for-1 stock split cuts par value in half as it replaces 100,000 shares of $20 par value stock with 200,000 shares of $10 par value stock. Market value is reduced from $88 per share to about $44 per share. The split does not affect any equity amounts reported on the balance sheet or any individual stockholder's percent ownership. Both the Paid-In Capital and Retained Earnings accounts are unchanged by a split, and *no journal entry is made.* The only effect on the accounts is a change in the stock account description. CompTec's 2-for-1 split on its $20 par value stock means that after the split, it changes its stock account title to *Common Stock, $10 Par Value.* This stock's description on the balance sheet also changes to reflect the additional authorized, issued, and outstanding shares and the new par value.

The difference between stock splits and large stock dividends is often blurred. Many companies report stock splits in their financial statements without calling in the original shares by simply changing their par value. This type of "split" is really a large stock dividend and results in additional shares issued to stockholders by capitalizing retained earnings or transferring other paid-in capital to Common Stock. This approach avoids administrative costs of splitting the stock. **Harley-Davidson** declared a 2-for-1 stock split executed in the form of a 100% stock dividend.

■ **Decision Maker**

Entrepreneur   A company you cofounded and own stock in announces a 50% stock dividend. Has the value of your stock investment increased, decreased, or remained the same? Would it make a difference if it was a 3-for-2 stock split executed in the form of a dividend? ■   [Answers follow the chapter's Summary.]

NEED-TO-KNOW 11-2

Recording Dividends

P2

A company began the current year with the following balances in its stockholders' equity accounts.

Common stock—$10 par, 500 shares authorized, 200 shares issued and outstanding	$2,000
Paid-in capital in excess of par, common stock	1,000
Retained earnings	5,000
Total	$8,000

All outstanding common stock was issued for $15 per share when the company was created. Prepare journal entries to account for the following transactions during the current year.

Jan. 10   The board declared a $0.10 cash dividend per share to shareholders of record on January 28.
Feb. 15   Paid the cash dividend declared on January 10.
Mar. 31   Declared a 20% stock dividend. The market value of the stock is $18 per share.
May 1   Distributed the stock dividend declared on March 31.
Dec. 1   Declared a 40% stock dividend. The market value of the stock is $25 per share.
Dec. 31   Distributed the stock dividend declared on December 1.

Jan. 10	Retained Earnings[a]	20	
	Common Dividend Payable		20
	Declared a $0.10 per share cash dividend.		
	[a] 200 outstanding shares × $0.10		
Feb. 15	Common Dividend Payable	20	
	Cash		20
	Paid $0.10 per share cash dividend.		

Mar. 31	Retained Earnings[b]	720	
	Common Stock Dividend Distributable[c]		400
	Paid-In Capital in Excess of Par Value,		
	Common Stock		320

*Declared a small stock dividend of 20% or
40 shares; market value is $18 per share.*

[b] 200 outstanding shares × 20% × $18 market
[c] 40 new shares × $10 par

| May 1 | Common Stock Dividend Distributable .... | 400 | |
| | Common Stock .... | | 400 |

Distributed 40 shares of common stock.

| Dec. 1 | Retained Earnings[d] .... | 960 | |
| | Common Stock Dividend Distributable .... | | 960 |

*Declared a large stock dividend of 40% or 96 shares
(40% × [200 + 40]); par value is $10 per share.*

[d] 240 outstanding shares × 40% × $10 par

| Dec. 31 | Common Stock Dividend Distributable .... | 960 | |
| | Common Stock .... | | 960 |

Distributed 96 shares of common stock.

Do More: QS 11-6, QS 11-7,
QS 11-8, E 11-5, E 11-6

PREFERRED STOCK

A corporation can issue two basic kinds of stock, common and preferred. **Preferred stock** has special rights that give it priority (or senior status) over common stock in one or more areas. Special rights typically include a preference for receiving dividends and for the distribution of assets if the corporation is liquidated. Preferred stock carries all rights of common stock unless the corporate charter nullifies them. Most preferred stock, for instance, does not confer the right to vote. Exhibit 11.9 shows that preferred stock is issued by about one-fourth of corporations. All corporations issue common stock. (While rare, not all common stock carries voting rights; **Google**'s C Class common shares are nonvoting.)

C2

Explain characteristics of, and distribute dividends between, common and preferred stock.

EXHIBIT 11.9

Corporations and Preferred Stock

No Preferred Stock 73%

Issued Preferred Stock 27%

Issuance of Preferred Stock

Preferred stock usually has a par value. Like common stock, it can be sold at a price different from par. Preferred stock is recorded in its own separate capital accounts. To illustrate, if Dillon Snowboards issues 50 shares of $100 par value preferred stock for $6,000 cash on July 1, 2016, the entry is

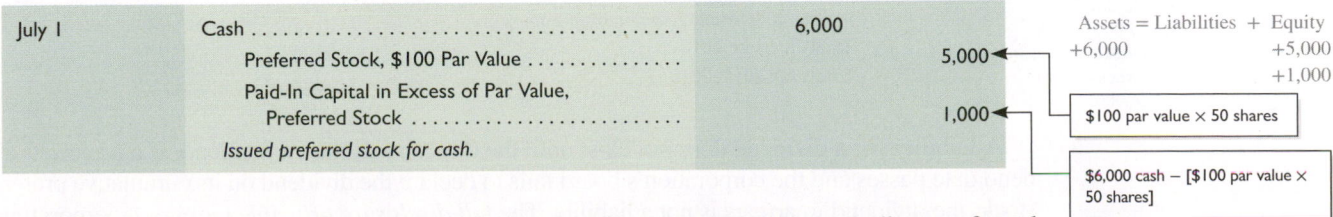

July 1	Cash	6,000	
	Preferred Stock, $100 Par Value		5,000
	Paid-In Capital in Excess of Par Value,		
	Preferred Stock		1,000
	Issued preferred stock for cash.		

Assets = Liabilities + Equity
+6,000   +5,000
                          +1,000

$100 par value × 50 shares

$6,000 cash − [$100 par value × 50 shares]

The equity section of the year-end balance sheet for Dillon Snowboards, including preferred stock, is shown in Exhibit 11.10. (This exhibit assumes that common stock was issued at par.) Issuing no-par preferred stock is similar to issuing no-par common stock. Also, the entries for issuing preferred stock for noncash assets are similar to those for common stock.

EXHIBIT 11.10

Stockholders' Equity with
Common and Preferred
Stock

Stockholders' Equity	
Common stock—$10 par value; 50,000 shares authorized;	
30,000 shares issued and outstanding	$300,000
Preferred stock—$100 par value; 1,000 shares authorized;	
50 shares issued and outstanding	**5,000**
Paid-in capital in excess of par value, preferred stock	**1,000**
Retained earnings	65,000
Total stockholders' equity	$371,000

Dividend Preference of Preferred Stock

Preferred stock usually carries a preference for dividends, meaning that preferred stockholders are allocated their dividends before any dividends are allocated to common stockholders. The dividends allocated to preferred stockholders are usually expressed as a dollar amount per share or a percent applied to par value. A preference for dividends does *not* ensure dividends. If the directors do not declare a dividend, neither the preferred nor the common stockholders receive one.

Point: Dividend preference does not imply that preferred stockholders receive more dividends than common stockholders, nor does it guarantee a dividend.

Cumulative or Noncumulative Dividend   Most preferred stocks carry a cumulative dividend right. **Cumulative preferred stock** gives its owners a right to be paid both the current and all prior periods' unpaid dividends before any dividend is paid to common stockholders. When preferred stock is cumulative and the directors either do not declare a dividend to preferred stockholders or declare one that does not cover the total amount of cumulative dividend, the unpaid dividend amount is called **dividend in arrears.** Accumulation of dividends in arrears on cumulative preferred stock does not guarantee they will be paid. **Noncumulative preferred stock** confers no right to prior periods' unpaid dividends if they were not declared in those prior periods.

To illustrate the difference between cumulative and noncumulative preferred stock, assume that a corporation's outstanding stock includes (1) 1,000 shares of $100 par, 9% preferred stock—yielding $9,000 per year (1,000 shares × $100 par × 9%) in potential dividends—and (2) 4,000 shares of $50 par value common stock. During 2015, the first year of operations, the directors declare cash dividends of $5,000. In year 2016, they declare cash dividends of $42,000. See Exhibit 11.11 for the allocation of dividends for these two years. Allocation of year 2016 dividends depends on whether the preferred stock is noncumulative or cumulative. With noncumulative preferred, the preferred stockholders never receive the $4,000 skipped in 2015. If the preferred stock is cumulative, the $4,000 in arrears is paid in 2016 before any other dividends are paid.

EXHIBIT 11.11

Allocation of Dividends
(noncumulative vs.
cumulative preferred stock)

Example: What dividends do cumulative preferred stockholders receive in 2016 if the corporation paid only $2,000 of dividends in 2015? How does this affect dividends to common stockholders in 2016?
Answers: $16,000 ($7,000 dividends in arrears, plus $9,000 current preferred dividends). Dividends to common stockholders decrease to $26,000.

	Preferred	Common
Preferred Stock Is Noncumulative		
Year 2015	$ 5,000	$ 0
Year 2016		
Step 1: Current year's preferred dividend	$ 9,000	
Step 2: Remainder to common		$33,000
Totals for 2015–2016	$14,000	$33,000
Preferred Stock Is Cumulative		
Year 2015	$ 5,000	$ 0
Year 2016		
Step 1: Dividend in arrears	$ 4,000	
Step 2: Current year's preferred dividend	9,000	
Step 3: Remainder to common		$29,000
Totals for year 2016	$13,000	$29,000
Totals for 2015–2016	$18,000	$29,000

A liability for a dividend does not exist until the directors declare a dividend. If a preferred dividend date passes and the corporation's board fails to declare the dividend on its cumulative preferred stock, the dividend in arrears is not a liability. The *full disclosure principle* requires a corporation to report (usually in a note) the amount of preferred dividends in arrears as of the balance sheet date.

Participating or Nonparticipating Dividend   **Nonparticipating preferred stock** has a feature that limits dividends to a maximum amount each year. This maximum is often stated as a percent of the stock's par value or as a specific dollar amount per share. Once preferred stockholders receive this amount, the common stockholders receive any and all additional dividends. **Participating preferred stock** has a feature allowing preferred stockholders to share with common stockholders any dividends paid in excess of the percent or dollar amount stated on the preferred stock. This participation feature does not apply until common stockholders receive dividends equal to the preferred stock's dividend percent. Many corporations are authorized to issue participating preferred stock but rarely do, and most managers never expect to issue it.[2]

Convertible Preferred Stock

Preferred stock is more attractive to investors if it carries a right to exchange preferred shares for a fixed number of common shares. **Convertible preferred stock** gives holders the option to exchange their preferred shares for common shares at a specified rate. When a company prospers and its common stock increases in value, convertible preferred stockholders can share in this success by converting their preferred stock into more valuable common stock.

Callable Preferred Stock

Callable preferred stock gives the issuing corporation the right to purchase (retire) this stock from its holders at specified future prices and dates. The amount paid to call and retire a preferred share is its **call price,** or *redemption value,* and is set when the stock is issued. The call price normally includes the stock's par value plus a premium giving holders additional return on their investment. When the issuing corporation calls and retires a preferred stock, the terms of the agreement often require it to pay the call price *and* any dividends in arrears.

Point: The issuing corporation has the right, or option, to retire its callable preferred stock.

 IFRS

Like U.S. GAAP, IFRS requires that preferred stocks be classified as debt or equity based on analysis of the stock's contractual terms. However, IFRS uses different criteria for such classification. ■

Reasons for Issuing Preferred Stock

Corporations issue preferred stock for several reasons. One is to raise capital without sacrificing control. For example, suppose a company's organizers have $100,000 cash to invest and organize a corporation that needs $200,000 of capital to start. If they sell $200,000 worth of common stock (with $100,000 to the organizers), they would have only 50% control and would need to negotiate extensively with other stockholders in making policy. However, if they issue $100,000 worth of common stock to themselves and sell outsiders $100,000 of 8%, cumulative preferred stock with no voting rights, they retain control.

A second reason to issue preferred stock is to boost the return earned by common stockholders. To illustrate, suppose a corporation's organizers expect to earn an annual after-tax income of $24,000 on an investment of $200,000. If they sell and issue $200,000 worth of common stock, the $24,000 income produces a 12% return on the $200,000 of common stockholders' equity. However, if they issue $100,000 of 8% preferred stock to outsiders and $100,000 of common stock to themselves, their own return increases to 16% per year, as shown in Exhibit 11.12.

Net (after-tax) income	$24,000
Less preferred dividends at 8%	(8,000)
Balance to common stockholders	$16,000
Return to common stockholders ($16,000/$100,000)	**16%**

EXHIBIT 11.12

Return to Common Stockholders When Preferred Stock Is Issued

---

[2] Participating preferred stock is usually authorized as a defense against a possible corporate *takeover* by an "unfriendly" investor (or a group of investors) who intends to buy enough voting common stock to gain control. Taking a term from spy novels, the financial world refers to this type of plan as a *poison pill* that a company swallows if enemy investors threaten its capture. A poison pill usually works as follows: A corporation's common stockholders on a given date are granted the right to purchase a large amount of participating preferred stock at a very low price. This right to purchase preferred shares is not transferable. If an unfriendly investor buys a large block of common shares (whose right to purchase participating preferred shares does not transfer to this buyer), the board can issue preferred shares at a low price to the remaining common shareholders who retained the right to purchase. Future dividends are then divided between the newly issued participating preferred shares and the common shares. This usually transfers value from common shares to preferred shares, causing the unfriendly investor's common stock to lose much of its value and reducing the potential benefit of a hostile takeover.

Point: Financial leverage also occurs when debt is issued and the interest rate paid on it is less than the rate earned from using the assets the creditors lend the company.

Common stockholders earn 16% instead of 12% because assets contributed by preferred stockholders are invested to earn $12,000 while the preferred dividend is only $8,000. Use of preferred stock to increase return to common stockholders is an example of **financial leverage** (also called *trading on the equity*). As a general rule, when the dividend rate on preferred stock is less than the rate the corporation earns on its assets, the effect of issuing preferred stock is to increase (or *lever*) the rate earned by common stockholders.

Other reasons for issuing preferred stock include its appeal to some investors who believe that the corporation's common stock is too risky or that the expected return on common stock is too low.

■ **Decision Maker** ═══════════════════════════════

Concert Organizer   Assume that you alter your business strategy from organizing concerts targeted at under 1,000 people to those targeted at between 5,000 and 20,000 people. You also incorporate because of an increased risk of lawsuits and a desire to issue stock for financing. It is important that you control the company for decisions on whom to schedule. What types of stock do you offer? ■ [Answers follow the chapter's Summary.]

NEED-TO-KNOW 11-3

Allocating Cash Dividends

C2

A company's outstanding stock consists of 80 shares of *noncumulative* 5% preferred stock with a $5 par value and also 200 shares of common stock with a $1 par value. During its first three years of operation, the corporation declared and paid the following total cash dividends:

2015 total cash dividends	$ 15
2016 total cash dividends	5
2017 total cash dividends	200

Part 1. Determine the amount of dividends paid each year to each of the two classes of stockholders: preferred and common. Also compute the total dividends paid to each class for the three years combined.

Part 2. Determine the amount of dividends paid each year to each of the two classes of stockholders assuming that the preferred stock is *cumulative*. Also determine the total dividends paid to each class for the three years combined.

Solution—Part 1

	Noncumulative Preferred	**Common**
2015 ($15 paid)		
Preferred*.	$15	
Common—remainder		$ 0
Total for the year.	$15	$ 0
2016 ($5 paid)		
Preferred*.	$ 5	
Common—remainder		$ 0
Total for the year.	$ 5	$ 0
2017 ($200 paid)		
Preferred*.	$20	
Common—remainder		$180
Total for the year.	$20	$180
2015–2017 (combined $220 paid)		
Total for three years	$40	$180

* Holders of noncumulative preferred stock are entitled to no more than $20 of dividends in any one year (5% × $5 × 80 shares).

Solution—Part 2

	Cumulative Preferred	Common
2015 ($15 paid)		
Preferred*	$15	
Common—remainder...............................	—	$ 0
Total for the year.......................................	$15	$ 0
(Note: $5 in preferred dividends in arrears; ($20 × 1 yr) − $15 paid.)		
2016 ($5 paid)		
Preferred—arrears from 2015	$ 5	
Preferred*	0	
Common—remainder...............................	—	$ 0
Total for the year.......................................	$ 5	$ 0
(Note: $20 in preferred dividends in arrears; ($20 × 2 yrs) − $15 paid − $5 paid.)		
2017 ($200 paid)		
Preferred—arrears from 2016	$20	
Preferred*	20	
Common—remainder...............................	—	$160
Total for the year.......................................	$40	$160
(Note: $0 in preferred dividends in arrears; ($20 × 3 yrs) − $15 paid − $5 paid − $40 paid.)		
2015–2017 (combined $220 paid)		
Total for three years	$60	$160

* Holders of cumulative preferred stock are entitled to no more than $20 of dividends declared in any year (5% × $5 × 80 shares) plus any dividends in arrears.

Do More: QS 11-9, QS 11-10, E 11-7, E 11-8, E 11-9

TREASURY STOCK

Corporations acquire shares of their own stock for several reasons: (1) to use their shares to acquire another corporation, (2) to purchase shares to avoid a hostile takeover of the company, (3) to reissue them to employees as compensation, and (4) to maintain a strong market for their stock or to show management confidence in the current price.

A corporation's reacquired shares are called **treasury stock,** which is similar to unissued stock in several ways: (1) neither treasury stock nor unissued stock is an asset, (2) neither receives cash dividends or stock dividends, and (3) neither allows the exercise of voting rights. However, treasury stock does differ from unissued stock in one major way: The corporation can resell treasury stock at less than par without having the buyers incur a liability, provided it was originally issued at par value or higher. Treasury stock purchases also require management to exercise ethical sensitivity because funds are being paid to specific stockholders instead of all stockholders. Managers must be sure the purchase is in the best interest of all stockholders. These concerns cause companies to fully disclose treasury stock transactions.

P3

Record purchases and sales of treasury stock and the retirement of stock.

Corporations and Treasury Stock

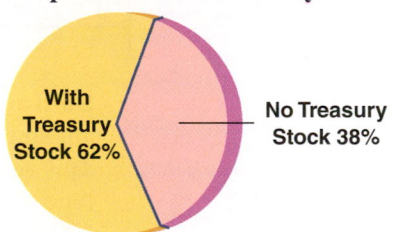

With Treasury Stock 62% · No Treasury Stock 38%

Purchasing Treasury Stock

Purchasing treasury stock reduces the corporation's assets and equity by equal amounts. (We describe the *cost method* of accounting for treasury stock, which is the most widely used method. The *par value* method is another method explained in advanced courses.) To illustrate, Exhibit 11.13 shows Cyber Corporation's account balances *before* any treasury stock purchase (Cyber has no liabilities).

EXHIBIT 11.13

Account Balances *before* Purchasing Treasury Stock

Assets		Stockholders' Equity	
Cash	$ 30,000	Common stock—$10 par; 10,000 shares authorized, issued, and outstanding............	$100,000
Other assets.........	95,000	Retained earnings............................	25,000
Total assets.........	$125,000	Total stockholders' equity	$125,000

Cyber then purchases 1,000 of its own shares for $11,500 on May 1, which is recorded as follows:

Assets = Liabilities + Equity
−11,500   −11,500

$11.50 cost per share ×
1,000 shares

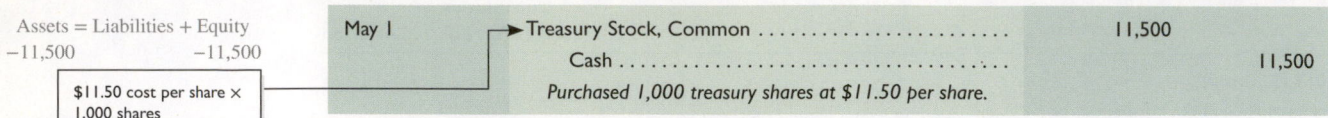

May 1	Treasury Stock, Common	11,500	
	Cash		11,500
	Purchased 1,000 treasury shares at $11.50 per share.		

This entry reduces equity through the debit to the Treasury Stock account, which is a contra equity account. Exhibit 11.14 shows account balances *after* this transaction.

EXHIBIT 11.14

Account Balances *after*
Purchasing Treasury Stock

Assets		Stockholders' Equity	
Cash	$ 18,500	Common stock—$10 par; 10,000 shares authorized and issued; 1,000 shares in treasury.	$100,000
Other assets.	95,000	Retained earnings, $11,500 restricted by treasury stock purchase	25,000
		Less cost of treasury stock.	**(11,500)**
Total assets.	$113,500	Total stockholders' equity	$113,500

Point: The Treasury Stock account is *not* an asset. Treasury stock does not carry voting or dividend rights.

Point: A treasury stock purchase is also called a *stock buyback*.

The treasury stock purchase reduces Cyber's cash, total assets, and total equity by $11,500 but does not reduce the balance of either the Common Stock or the Retained Earnings account. The equity reduction is reported by deducting the cost of treasury stock in the equity section. Also, two disclosures are evident. First, the stock description reveals that 1,000 issued shares are in treasury, leaving only 9,000 shares still outstanding. Second, the description for retained earnings reveals that it is partly restricted.

Reissuing Treasury Stock

Treasury stock can be reissued by selling it at cost, above cost, or below cost.

Point: The phrase *treasury stock* is believed to arise from the fact that reacquired stock is held in a corporation's treasury.

Selling Treasury Stock at Cost   If treasury stock is **reissued at cost**, the entry is the reverse of the one made to record the purchase. For instance, if on May 21 Cyber reissues 100 of the treasury shares purchased on May 1 at the same $11.50 per share cost, the entry is

Assets = Liabilities + Equity
+1,150   +1,150

$11.50 cost per share ×
100 shares

May 21	Cash	1,150	
	Treasury Stock, Common		1,150
	Received $11.50 per share for 100 treasury shares costing $11.50 per share.		

Point: Treasury stock does not represent ownership. A company cannot own a part of itself.

Selling Treasury Stock *above* **Cost**   If treasury stock is **sold for more than cost**, the amount received in excess of cost is credited to the Paid-In Capital, Treasury Stock account. This account is reported as a separate item in the stockholders' equity section. No gain is ever reported from the sale of treasury stock. To illustrate, if Cyber receives $12 cash per share for 400 treasury shares costing $11.50 per share on June 3, the entry is

Assets = Liabilities + Equity
+4,800   +4,600
                        +200

$11.50 cost per share ×
400 shares

[$12 issue price − $11.50 cost per share] × 400 shares

June 3	Cash	4,800	
	Treasury Stock, Common		4,600
	Paid-In Capital, Treasury Stock		**200**
	Received $12 per share for 400 treasury shares costing $11.50 per share.		

Point: The Paid-In Capital, Treasury Stock account can have a zero or credit balance but never a debit balance.

Selling Treasury Stock *below* **Cost**   When treasury stock is **sold below cost**, the entry to record the sale depends on whether the Paid-In Capital, Treasury Stock account has a credit balance. If it has a zero balance, the excess of cost over the sales price is debited to Retained Earnings. If the Paid-In Capital, Treasury Stock account has a credit balance, it is debited for the excess of the cost over the selling price but not to exceed the balance in this account. When the credit balance in this paid-in capital account is eliminated, any remaining difference between the cost and selling price is debited to Retained Earnings. To illustrate, if Cyber sells its remaining 500 shares of treasury stock at $10 per share on July 10, equity is reduced by $750 ($500 shares × $1.50 per share excess of cost over selling price), as shown in this entry:

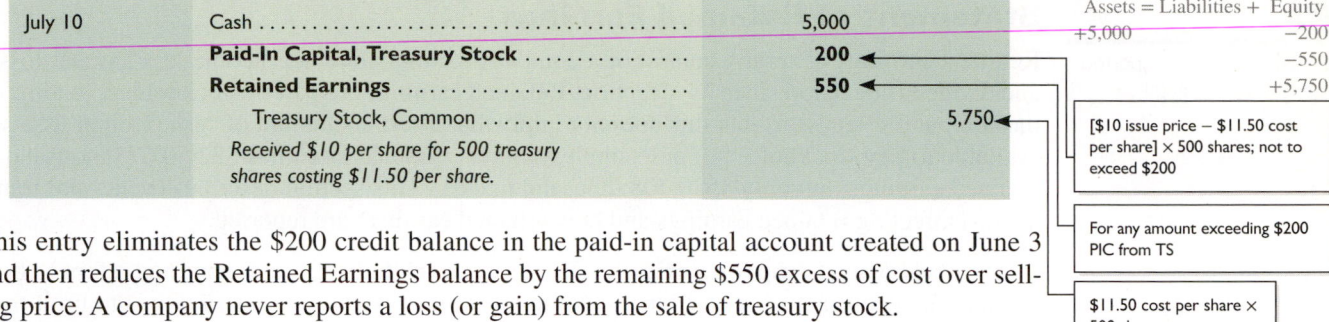

July 10	Cash	5,000	
	Paid-In Capital, Treasury Stock	200	
	Retained Earnings	550	
	Treasury Stock, Common		5,750
	Received $10 per share for 500 treasury shares costing $11.50 per share.		

Assets = Liabilities + Equity
+5,000   −200
                              −550
                              +5,750

[$10 issue price − $11.50 cost per share] × 500 shares; not to exceed $200

For any amount exceeding $200 PIC from TS

$11.50 cost per share × 500 shares

This entry eliminates the $200 credit balance in the paid-in capital account created on June 3 and then reduces the Retained Earnings balance by the remaining $550 excess of cost over selling price. A company never reports a loss (or gain) from the sale of treasury stock.

Retiring Stock

A corporation can purchase its own stock and retire it. Retiring stock reduces the number of issued shares. Retired stock is the same as authorized and unissued shares. Purchases and retirements of stock are permissible under state law only if they do not jeopardize the interests of creditors and stockholders. When stock is purchased for retirement, we remove all capital amounts related to the retired shares. If the purchase price exceeds the net amount removed, this excess is debited to Retained Earnings. If the net amount removed from all capital accounts exceeds the purchase price, this excess is credited to the Paid-In Capital from Retirement of Stock account. A company's assets and equity are always reduced by the amount paid for the retiring stock.

Point: Recording stock retirement results in canceling the equity from the original issuance of the shares.

A company began the current year with the following balances in its stockholders' equity accounts.

NEED-TO-KNOW 11-4

Recording Treasury Stock

P3

Common stock—$10 par, 500 shares authorized, 200 shares issued and outstanding.....................................	$2,000
Paid-in capital in excess of par, common stock....................	1,000
Retained earnings...	5,000
Total..	$8,000

All outstanding common stock was issued for $15 per share when the company was created. Prepare journal entries to account for the following transactions during the current year.

July 1   Purchased 30 shares of treasury stock at $20 per share.
Sept. 1   Sold 20 treasury shares at $26 cash per share.
Dec. 1   Sold the remaining 10 shares of treasury stock at $7 cash per share.

July 1	Treasury Stock, Common[a].........................	600	
	Cash		600
	Purchased 30 common shares at $20 per share.		
	[a]30 shares × $20 cost		
Sept. 1	Cash[b]..	520	
	Treasury Stock, Common[c]....................		400
	Paid-In Capital, Treasury Stock		120
	Sold 20 treasury shares at $26 per share.		
	[b]20 shares × $26 reissue price [c]20 shares × $20 cost		
Dec. 1	Cash[d].......................................	70	
	Paid-In Capital, Treasury Stock[e]....................	120	
	Retained Earnings.............................	10	
	Treasury Stock, Common[f]....................		200
	Sold 10 treasury shares at $7 per share.		
	[d]10 shares × $7 reissue price		
	[e]Not to exceed existing balance [f]10 shares × $20 cost		

Do More: QS 11-11, E 11-10

REPORTING OF EQUITY

C3

Explain the items reported in retained earnings.

Statement of Retained Earnings

Retained earnings generally consist of a company's cumulative net income less any net losses and dividends declared since its inception. Retained earnings are part of stockholders' claims on the company's net assets, but this does *not* imply that a certain amount of cash or other assets is available to pay stockholders. For example, **Abercrombie & Fitch** has $2,550,673 thousand in retained earnings, but only $520,708 thousand in cash. This section describes events and transactions affecting retained earnings and how retained earnings are reported.

Restrictions and Appropriations   The term **restricted retained earnings** refers to both statutory and contractual restrictions. A common *statutory* (or *legal*) *restriction* is to limit treasury stock purchases to the amount of retained earnings. The balance sheet in Exhibit 11.14 provides an example. A common *contractual restriction* involves loan agreements that restrict paying dividends beyond a specified amount or percent of retained earnings. Restrictions are usually described in the notes. The term **appropriated retained earnings** refers to a voluntary transfer of amounts from the Retained Earnings account to the Appropriated Retained Earnings account to inform users of special activities that require funds.

Prior Period Adjustments   **Prior period adjustments** are corrections of material errors in prior period financial statements. These errors include arithmetic mistakes, unacceptable accounting, and missed facts. Prior period adjustments are reported in the *statement of retained earnings* (or the statement of stockholders' equity), net of any income tax effects. Prior period adjustments result in changing the beginning balance of retained earnings for events occurring prior to the earliest period reported in the current set of financial statements. To illustrate, assume that ComUS makes an error in a 2014 journal entry for the purchase of land by incorrectly debiting an expense account. When this is discovered in 2016, the statement of retained earnings includes a prior period adjustment, as shown in Exhibit 11.15. This exhibit also shows the usual format of the statement of retained earnings.

Point: If a year 2014 error is discovered in 2015, the company records the adjustment in 2015. But if the financial statements include 2014 and 2015 figures, the statements report the correct amounts for 2014, and a note describes the correction.

EXHIBIT 11.15

Statement of Retained Earnings with a Prior Period Adjustment

ComUS Statement of Retained Earnings For Year Ended December 31, 2016	
Retained earnings, Dec. 31, 2015, as previously reported	$4,745,000
Prior period adjustment	
Cost of land incorrectly expensed (net of $63,000 of income tax benefit)	147,000
Retained earnings, Dec. 31, 2015, as adjusted.	4,892,000
Plus net income	1,224,300
Less cash dividends declared	(301,800)
Retained earnings, Dec. 31, 2016.	$5,814,500

Point: Accounting for changes in estimates is sometimes criticized as two wrongs to make a right. Consider a change in an asset's life. In this case, the depreciation for the period before the change would not equal the depreciation after the change; nor would they equal the depreciation for the entire period using the actual life of the asset. Regulators chose this approach to avoid restating prior period numbers.

Many items reported in financial statements are based on estimates. Future events are certain to reveal that some of these estimates were inaccurate even when based on the best data available at the time. These inaccuracies are *not* considered errors and are *not* reported as prior period adjustments. Instead, they are identified as **changes in accounting estimates** and are accounted for in current and future periods. To illustrate, we know that depreciation is based on estimated useful lives and salvage values. As time passes and new information becomes available, managers may need to change these estimates and the resulting depreciation expense for current and future periods.

Closing Process   The closing process was explained earlier in the book as (1) close credit balances in revenue accounts to Income Summary, (2) close debit balances in expense accounts to Income Summary, and (3) close Income Summary to Retained Earnings. If dividends are recorded in a Dividends account, and not as an immediate reduction to Retained Earnings (as shown in this chapter), a fourth step is necessary to close the Dividends account to Retained Earnings.

Statement of Stockholders' Equity

Instead of a separate statement of retained earnings, companies commonly report a statement of stockholders' equity that includes changes in retained earnings. A **statement of stockholders' equity** lists the beginning and ending balances of key equity accounts and describes the changes that occur during the period. The companies in Appendix A report such a statement. The usual format is to provide a column for each component of equity and use the rows to describe events occurring in the period. Exhibit 11.16 shows a condensed statement for **Apple**.

APPLE

EXHIBIT 11.16

Statement of Stockholders' Equity

APPLE Statement of Stockholders' Equity					
$ millions, shares in thousands	Common Stock Shares	Common Stock Amount	Retained Earnings	Accum. Other	Total Equity
Balance, Sept. 28, 2013	6,294,494	$19,764	$104,256	$ (471)	$123,549
Net income	—	—	39,510	—	39,510
Issuance of common stock	60,344	(49)	(399)	—	(448)
Repurchase of common stock & other	(488,677)	3,598	(45,000)	1,553	(39,849)
Cash dividends ($11.40 per share)	—	—	(11,215)	—	(11,215)
Balance, Sept. 27, 2014	5,866,161	$23,313	$ 87,152	$1,082	$111,547

Reporting Stock Options

Many corporations whose shares are publicly traded issue **stock options,** which are rights to purchase common stock at a fixed price over a specified period. As the stock's price rises, the option's value increases. **Starbucks** and **Home Depot** offer stock options to both full- and part-time employees. Stock options are said to motivate managers and employees to (1) focus on company performance, (2) take a long-run perspective, and (3) remain with the company. A stock option is like having an investment with no risk ("a carrot with no stick").

To illustrate, Quantum grants each of its employees the option to purchase 100 shares of its $1 par value common stock at its current market price of $50 per share anytime within the next 10 years. If the stock price rises to $70 per share, an employee can exercise the option at a gain of $20 per share (acquire a $70 stock at the $50 option price). With 100 shares, a single employee would have a total gain of $2,000, computed as $20 × 100 shares. Companies report the cost of stock options in the income statement. Measurement of this cost is explained in advanced courses.

Fraud

Pump 'n Dump Fraudulent information can be used by the owners of a company's stock to pump it up and claim it is undervalued, which causes naïve investors to seek to acquire the stock and drive up its price. After that, those behind the release of fraudulent information dump the stock at an inflated price. When later information reveals that the stock is overvalued, its price declines and investors still holding the stock lose value. This scheme is called *pump 'n dump.* Jonathan Lebed, at 15 years old, allegedly made about $1 million in one of the most infamous cases of pump 'n dump.

GLOBAL VIEW

This section discusses similarities and differences between U.S. GAAP and IFRS in accounting and reporting for equity.

Accounting for Common Stock   The accounting for and reporting of common stock under U.S. GAAP and IFRS are similar. Specifically, procedures for issuing common stock at par, at a premium, at a discount, and for noncash assets are similar across the two systems. However, we must be aware of legal

Samsung

and cultural differences across the world that can impact the rights and responsibilities of common shareholders. Samsung's terminology is a bit different as it uses the phrase "share premium" in reference to what U.S. GAAP would title "paid-in capital in excess of par value" (see Appendix A).

Accounting for Dividends   Accounting for and reporting of dividends under U.S. GAAP and IFRS are consistent. This applies to cash dividends, stock dividends, and stock splits. Samsung "declared cash dividends to shareholders of common stock and preferred stock as interim dividends for the six-month periods . . . and as year-end dividends." Samsung, like many other companies, follows a dividend policy set by management and its board.

Accounting for Preferred Stock   Accounting and reporting for preferred stock are similar for U.S. GAAP and IFRS, but there are some important differences. First, preferred stock that is redeemable at the option of the preferred stockholders is reported *between* liabilities and equity in U.S. GAAP balance sheets. However, that same stock is reported as a liability in IFRS balance sheets. Second, the issue price of convertible preferred stock (and bonds) is recorded entirely under preferred stock (or bonds) *and none is assigned to the conversion feature* under U.S. GAAP. However, IFRS requires that a portion of the issue price be allocated to the conversion feature when it exists. Samsung has preferred stock, which is noncumulative and nonvoting.

Accounting for Treasury Stock   Both U.S. GAAP and IFRS apply the principle that companies do not record gains or losses on transactions involving their own stock. This applies to purchases, reissuances, and retirements of treasury stock. Consequently, the accounting for treasury stock explained in this chapter is consistent with that under IFRS. However, IFRS in this area is less detailed than U.S. GAAP.

Sustainability and Accounting   The founder, Jack Ma, of Alibaba Group, as introduced in this chapter's opening feature, explains that sustainability is an important part of his company's mission. Jack explains: "I always believe we shouldn't build an 'empire'; instead, we should build an 'ecosystem.' Every empire will be toppled someday, but an ecosystem is sustainable." Since 2010, Alibaba has donated 0.3% of its annual revenue to fund efforts designed to "encourage environmental awareness and conservation." In 2014, 0.3% of annual revenue was $158 million. Further, products made from endangered species, such as shark fins and ivory, are banned from the Alibaba marketplace.

Alibaba is also dedicated to supporting the community. After earthquakes struck China's Sichuan Province, Alibaba organized several "charity programs to provide postdisaster support to people affected." Moreover, the company created a long-term program in the Sichuan Province to drive development and create jobs. Alibaba continues to provide relief to countries affected by natural disasters, including Japan, Africa, and islands in the Caribbean.

Source: *South China Morning Post,* July 2013

Bloomberg via Getty Images

Decision Analysis   🟩🟨🟥   **Earnings per Share, Price-Earnings Ratio, Dividend Yield, and Book Value per Share**

Earnings per Share

A1

Compute earnings per share and describe its use.

The income statement reports **earnings per share,** also called *EPS* or *net income per share,* which is the amount of income earned per share of a company's outstanding common stock. The **basic earnings per share** formula is shown in Exhibit 11.17. When a company has no preferred stock, then preferred dividends are zero. The weighted-average common shares outstanding is measured over the income reporting period; its computation is explained in advanced courses.

EXHIBIT 11.17

Basic Earnings per Share

$$\text{Basic earnings per share} = \frac{\text{Net income} - \text{Preferred dividends}}{\text{Weighted-average common shares outstanding}}$$

To illustrate, assume that Quantum Co. earns $40,000 net income in 2016 and declares dividends of $7,500 on its noncumulative preferred stock. (If preferred stock is *non*cumulative, the income available [numerator] is the current-period net income less any preferred dividends *declared* in that same period. If preferred stock is cumulative, the income available [numerator] is the current-period net income less the preferred dividends whether declared or not.) Quantum has 5,000 weighted-average common shares outstanding during 2016. Its basic EPS[3] is

$$\text{Basic earnings per share} = \frac{\$40,000 - \$7,500}{5,000 \text{ shares}} = \$6.50$$

Price-Earnings Ratio

A2

Compute price-earnings ratio and describe its use in analysis.

Point: The average PE ratio of stocks in the 1950–2015 period is about 14.

A stock's market value is determined by its *expected* future cash flows. A comparison of a company's EPS and its market value per share reveals information about market expectations. This comparison is traditionally made using a **price-earnings (or PE) ratio,** expressed also as *price earnings, price to earnings,* or *PE*. Some analysts interpret this ratio as what price the market is willing to pay for a company's current earnings stream. Price-earnings ratios can differ across companies that have similar earnings because of either higher or lower expectations of future earnings. The price-earnings ratio is defined in Exhibit 11.18.

EXHIBIT 11.18
Price-Earnings Ratio

$$\text{Price-earnings ratio} = \frac{\text{Market value (price) per share}}{\text{Earnings per share}}$$

This ratio is often computed using EPS from the most recent period. However, many users compute this ratio using *expected* EPS for the next period.

Some analysts view stocks with high PE ratios (higher than 20 to 25) as more likely to be overpriced and stocks with low PE ratios (less than 5 to 8) as more likely to be underpriced. These investors prefer to sell or avoid buying stocks with high PE ratios and to buy or hold stocks with low PE ratios. However, investment decision making is rarely so simple as to rely on a single ratio. For instance, a stock with a high PE ratio can prove to be a good investment if its earnings continue to increase beyond current expectations. Similarly, a stock with a low PE ratio can prove to be a poor investment if its earnings decline below expectations.

Point: Average PE ratios for U.S. stocks increased over the past two decades. Some analysts interpret this as a signal the market is overpriced. But higher ratios can at least partly reflect accounting changes that have reduced reported earnings.

 Decision Maker

Money Manager You plan to invest in one of two companies identified as having identical future prospects. One has a PE of 19 and the other a PE of 25. Which do you invest in? Does it matter if your *estimate* of PE for these two companies is 29 as opposed to 22? ■ [Answers follow the chapter's Summary.]

Dividend Yield

A3

Compute dividend yield and explain its use in analysis.

Investors buy shares of a company's stock in anticipation of receiving a return from either or both cash dividends and stock price increases. Stocks that pay large dividends on a regular basis, called *income stocks,* are attractive to investors who want recurring cash flows from their investments. In contrast, some stocks pay little or no dividends but are still attractive to investors because of their expected stock price increases. The stocks of companies that distribute little or no cash but use their cash to finance expansion are called *growth stocks*. One way to help identify whether a stock is an income stock or a growth stock is to analyze its dividend yield. **Dividend yield,** defined in Exhibit 11.19, shows the annual amount of cash dividends distributed to common shares relative to their market value.

EXHIBIT 11.19
Dividend Yield

$$\text{Dividend yield} = \frac{\text{Annual cash dividends per share}}{\text{Market value per share}}$$

Dividend yield can be computed for current and prior periods using actual dividends and stock prices and for future periods using expected values. Exhibit 11.20 shows recent dividend and stock price data for **Amazon** and **Altria Group** to compute dividend yield.

Dividend yield is zero for Amazon, implying it is a growth stock. An investor in Amazon would look for increases in stock prices (and eventual cash from the sale of stock). Altria has a dividend yield of 4.3%, implying it is an income stock for which dividends are important in assessing its value.

Point: The *payout ratio* equals cash dividends declared on common stock divided by net income. A low payout ratio suggests that a company is retaining earnings for future growth.

---

[3] A corporation can be classified as having either a simple or complex capital structure. The term **simple capital structure** refers to a company with only common stock and nonconvertible preferred stock outstanding. The term **complex capital structure** refers to companies with dilutive securities. **Dilutive securities** include options, rights to purchase common stock, and any bonds and preferred stock that are convertible into common stock. A company with a complex capital structure must often report two EPS figures: basic and diluted. **Diluted earnings per share** is computed by adding all dilutive securities to the denominator of the basic EPS computation. It reflects the decrease in basic EPS *assuming* that all dilutive securities are converted into common shares.

EXHIBIT 11.20

Dividend and Stock Price Information

Company	Cash Dividends per Share	Market Value per Share	Dividend Yield
Amazon	$0.00	$440	0.0%
Altria Group.	$2.08	$ 48	4.3%

Book Value per Share

A4

Compute book value and explain its use in analysis.

Case 1: Common Stock (Only) Outstanding. **Book value per common share,** defined in Exhibit 11.21, reflects the amount of equity applicable to *common* shares on a per share basis. To illustrate, we use Dillon Snowboards's data from Exhibit 11.4. Dillon has 30,000 outstanding common shares, and the stockholders' equity applicable to common shares is $365,000. Dillon's book value per common share is $12.17, computed as $365,000 divided by 30,000 shares.

EXHIBIT 11.21

Book Value per Common Share

$$\text{Book value per common share} = \frac{\text{Stockholders' equity applicable to common shares}}{\text{Number of common shares outstanding}}$$

Point: Book value per share is also referred to as *stockholders' claim to assets on a per share basis.*

Case 2: Common and Preferred Stock Outstanding. To compute book value when both common and preferred shares are outstanding, we allocate total equity between the two types of shares. The **book value per preferred share** is computed first; its computation is shown in Exhibit 11.22.

EXHIBIT 11.22

Book Value per Preferred Share

$$\text{Book value per preferred share} = \frac{\text{Stockholders' equity applicable to preferred shares}}{\text{Number of preferred shares outstanding}}$$

The equity applicable to preferred shares equals the preferred share's call price (or par value if the preferred stock is not callable) plus any cumulative dividends in arrears. The remaining equity is the portion applicable to common shares. To illustrate, consider LTD's equity in Exhibit 11.23. Its preferred stock is callable at $108 per share, and two years of cumulative preferred dividends are in arrears.

EXHIBIT 11.23

Stockholders' Equity with Preferred and Common Stock

Stockholders' Equity	
Preferred stock—$100 par value, 7% cumulative, 2,000 shares authorized, 1,000 shares issued and outstanding.	$100,000
Common stock—$25 par value, 12,000 shares authorized, 10,000 shares issued and outstanding	250,000
Paid-in capital in excess of par value, common stock	15,000
Retained earnings	82,000
Total stockholders' equity	$447,000

The book value computations are in Exhibit 11.24. Equity is first allocated to preferred shares before the book value of common shares is computed.

EXHIBIT 11.24

Computing Book Value per Preferred and Common Share

Total stockholders' equity		$447,000
Less equity applicable to preferred shares		
Call price (1,000 shares × $108)	$108,000	
Dividends in arrears ($100,000 × 7% × 2 years)	14,000	(122,000)
Equity applicable to common shares		$325,000
Book value per preferred share ($122,000/1,000 shares)		**$ 122.00**
Book value per common share ($325,000/10,000 shares)		**$ 32.50**

Book value per share reflects the value per share if a company is liquidated at balance sheet amounts. Book value is also the starting point in many stock valuation models, merger negotiations, price setting for public utilities, and loan contracts. The main limitation in using book value is the potential difference between recorded value and market value for assets and liabilities. Investors often adjust their analysis for estimates of these differences.

■ **Decision Maker** ━━━━━━━━━━━━━━━━━━━━━━━

Investor   You are considering investing in BMX, whose book value per common share is $4 and price per common share on the stock exchange is $7. From this information, are BMX's net assets priced higher or lower than its recorded values? ■   [Answers follow the chapter's Summary.]

Barton Corporation began operations on January 1, 2015. The following transactions relating to stockholders' equity occurred in the first two years of the company's operations.

NEED-TO-KNOW 11-5

COMPREHENSIVE

2015

Jan. 1   Authorized the issuance of 2 million shares of $5 par value common stock and 100,000 shares of $100 par value, 10% cumulative, preferred stock.

Jan. 2   Issued 200,000 shares of common stock for $12 cash per share.

Jan. 3   Issued 100,000 shares of common stock in exchange for a building valued at $820,000 and merchandise inventory valued at $380,000.

Jan. 4   Paid $10,000 cash to the company's founders for organization activities.

Jan. 5   Issued 12,000 shares of preferred stock for $110 cash per share.

2016

June 4   Issued 100,000 shares of common stock for $15 cash per share.

Required

1. Prepare journal entries to record these transactions.

2. Prepare the stockholders' equity section of the balance sheet as of December 31, 2015, and December 31, 2016, based on these transactions.

3. Prepare a table showing dividend allocations and dividends per share for 2015 and 2016 assuming Barton declares the following cash dividends: 2015, $50,000, and 2016, $300,000.

4. Prepare the January 2, 2015, journal entry for Barton's issuance of 200,000 shares of common stock for $12 cash per share assuming

   a. Common stock is no-par stock without a stated value.

   b. Common stock is no-par stock with a stated value of $10 per share.

PLANNING THE SOLUTION

- Record journal entries for the transactions for 2015 and 2016.
- Determine the balances for the 2015 and 2016 equity accounts for the balance sheet.
- Prepare the contributed capital portion of the 2015 and 2016 balance sheets.
- Prepare a table similar to Exhibit 11.11 showing dividend allocations for 2015 and 2016.
- Record the issuance of common stock under both specifications of no-par stock.

SOLUTION

1. Journal entries.

2015			
Jan. 2	Cash	2,400,000	
	Common Stock, $5 Par Value		1,000,000
	Paid-In Capital in Excess of Par Value,		
	Common Stock		1,400,000
	Issued 200,000 shares of common stock.		
Jan. 3	Building	820,000	
	Merchandise Inventory	380,000	
	Common Stock, $5 Par Value		500,000
	Paid-In Capital in Excess of Par Value,		
	Common Stock		700,000
	Issued 100,000 shares of common stock.		
Jan. 4	Organization Expenses	10,000	
	Cash		10,000
	Paid founders for organization costs.		
Jan. 5	Cash	1,320,000	
	Preferred Stock, $100 Par Value		1,200,000
	Paid-In Capital in Excess of Par Value,		
	Preferred Stock		120,000
	Issued 12,000 shares of preferred stock.		
2016			
June 4	Cash	1,500,000	
	Common Stock, $5 Par Value		500,000
	Paid-In Capital in Excess of Par Value,		
	Common Stock		1,000,000
	Issued 100,000 shares of common stock.		

2. Balance sheet presentations (at December 31 year-end).

	2016	2015
Stockholders' Equity		
Preferred stock—$100 par value, 10% cumulative, 100,000 shares authorized, 12,000 shares issued and outstanding	$1,200,000	$1,200,000
Paid-in capital in excess of par value, preferred stock	120,000	120,000
Total paid-in capital by preferred stockholders	1,320,000	1,320,000
Common stock—$5 par value, 2,000,000 shares authorized, 300,000 shares issued and outstanding in 2015, and 400,000 shares issued and outstanding in 2016	2,000,000	1,500,000
Paid-in capital in excess of par value, common stock	3,100,000	2,100,000
Total paid-in capital by common stockholders	5,100,000	3,600,000
Total paid-in capital	$6,420,000	$4,920,000

3. Dividend allocation table.

	Common	Preferred
2015 ($50,000)		
Preferred—current year (12,000 shares × $10 = $120,000)	$ 0	$ 50,000
Common—remainder (300,000 shares outstanding)	0	0
Total for the year	$ 0	$ 50,000
2016 ($300,000)		
Preferred—dividend in arrears from 2015 ($120,000 − $50,000)	$ 0	$ 70,000
Preferred—current year	0	120,000
Common—remainder (400,000 shares outstanding)	110,000	0
Total for the year	$110,000	$190,000
Dividends per share		
2015	$ 0.00	$ 4.17
2016	$ 0.28	$ 15.83

4. Journal entries.

a. For 2015 (no-par stock without a stated value):

Jan. 2	Cash	2,400,000	
	Common Stock, No-Par Value		2,400,000
	Issued 200,000 shares of no-par common		
	stock at $12 per share.		

b. For 2015 (no-par stock with a stated value):

Jan. 2	Cash	2,400,000	
	Common Stock, $10 Stated Value		2,000,000
	Paid-In Capital in Excess of Stated Value, Common Stock		400,000
	Issued 200,000 shares of $10 stated value		
	common stock at $12 per share.		

Summary

C1   **Identify characteristics of corporations and their organization.** Corporations are legal entities whose stockholders are not liable for its debts. Stock is easily transferred, and the life of a corporation does not end with the incapacity of a stockholder. A corporation acts through its agents, who are its officers and managers. Corporations are regulated and subject to income taxes. Authorized stock is the stock that a corporation's charter authorizes it to sell. Issued stock is the portion of authorized shares sold. Par value stock is a value per share assigned by the charter. No-par value stock is stock *not* assigned a value per share by the charter. Stated value stock is no-par stock to which the directors assign a value per share.

C2 Explain characteristics of, and distribute dividends between, common and preferred stock. Preferred stock has a priority (or senior status) relative to common stock in one or more areas, usually (1) dividends and (2) assets in case of liquidation. Preferred stock usually does not carry voting rights and can be convertible or callable. Convertibility permits the holder to convert preferred to common. Callability permits the issuer to buy back preferred stock under specified conditions. Preferred stockholders usually hold the right to dividend distributions before common stockholders. When preferred stock is cumulative and in arrears, the amount in arrears must be distributed to preferred stockholders before any dividends are distributed to common stockholders.

C3 Explain the items reported in retained earnings. Stockholders' equity is made up of (1) paid-in capital and (2) retained earnings. Paid-in capital consists of funds raised by stock issuances. Retained earnings consists of cumulative net income (losses) not distributed. Many companies face statutory and contractual restrictions on retained earnings. Corporations can voluntarily appropriate retained earnings to inform others about their disposition. Prior period adjustments are corrections of errors in prior financial statements.

A1 Compute earnings per share and describe its use. A company with a simple capital structure computes basic EPS by dividing net income less any preferred dividends by the weighted-average number of outstanding common shares. A company with a complex capital structure must usually report both basic and diluted EPS.

A2 Compute price-earnings ratio and describe its use in analysis. A common stock's price-earnings (PE) ratio is computed by dividing the stock's market value (price) per share by its EPS. A stock's PE is based on expectations that can prove to be better or worse than eventual performance.

A3 Compute dividend yield and explain its use in analysis. Dividend yield is the ratio of a stock's annual cash dividends per share to its market value (price) per share. Dividend yield can be compared with the yield of other companies to determine whether the stock is expected to be an income or growth stock.

A4 Compute book value and explain its use in analysis. Book value per common share is equity applicable to common shares divided by the number of outstanding common shares. Book value per preferred share is equity applicable to preferred shares divided by the number of outstanding preferred shares.

P1 Record the issuance of corporate stock. When stock is issued, its par or stated value is credited to the stock account and any excess is credited to a separate contributed capital account. If a stock has neither par nor stated value, the entire proceeds are credited to the stock account. Stockholders must contribute assets equal to minimum legal capital or be potentially liable for the deficiency.

P2 Record transactions involving cash dividends, stock dividends, and stock splits. Cash dividends involve three events. On the date of declaration, the directors bind the company to pay the dividend. A dividend declaration reduces retained earnings and creates a current liability. On the date of record, recipients of the dividend are identified. On the date of payment, cash is paid to stockholders and the current liability is removed. Neither a stock dividend nor a stock split alters the value of the company. However, the value of each share is less due to the distribution of additional shares. The distribution of additional shares is according to individual stockholders' ownership percentage. Small stock dividends ($\leq 25\%$) are recorded by capitalizing retained earnings equal to the market value of distributed shares. Large stock dividends ($>25\%$) are recorded by capitalizing retained earnings equal to the par or stated value of distributed shares. Stock splits do not necessitate journal entries but do necessitate changes in the description of stock.

P3 Record purchases and sales of treasury stock and the retirement of stock. When a corporation purchases its own previously issued stock, it debits the cost of these shares to Treasury Stock. Treasury stock is subtracted from equity in the balance sheet. If treasury stock is reissued, any proceeds in excess of cost are credited to Paid-In Capital, Treasury Stock. If the proceeds are less than cost, they are debited to Paid-In Capital, Treasury Stock to the extent a credit balance exists. Any remaining amount is debited to Retained Earnings. When stock is retired, all accounts related to the stock are removed.

Guidance Answers to Decision Maker

Entrepreneur   The 50% stock dividend provides you no direct income. A stock dividend often reveals management's optimistic expectations about the future and can improve a stock's marketability by making it affordable to more investors. Accordingly, a stock dividend usually reveals "good news" and because of this, it likely increases (slightly) the market value for your stock. The same conclusions apply to the 3-for-2 stock split.

Concert Organizer   You have two basic options: (1) different classes of common stock or (2) common and preferred stock. Your objective is to issue to yourself stock that has all or a majority of the voting power. The other class of stock would carry limited or no voting rights. In this way, you maintain control and are able to raise the necessary funds.

Money Manager   Since one company requires a payment of $19 for each $1 of earnings, and the other requires $25, you would prefer the stock with the PE of 19; it is a better deal given identical prospects. You should make sure these companies' earnings computations are roughly the same, for example, no extraordinary items, unusual events, and so forth. Also, your PE estimates for these companies do matter. If you are willing to pay

$29 for each $1 of earnings for these companies, you obviously expect both to exceed current market expectations.

Investor   Book value reflects recorded values. BMX's book value is $4 per common share. Stock price reflects the market's

expectation of net asset value (both tangible and intangible items). BMX's market value is $7 per common share. Comparing these figures suggests BMX's market value of net assets is higher than its recorded values (by an amount of $7 versus $4 per share).

Key Terms

Appropriated retained earnings	Discount on stock	Preferred stock
Authorized stock	Dividend in arrears	Premium on stock
Basic earnings per share	Dividend yield	Price-earnings (PE) ratio
Book value per common share	Earnings per share (EPS)	Prior period adjustment
Book value per preferred share	Financial leverage	Proxy
Call price	Large stock dividend	Restricted retained earnings
Callable preferred stock	Liquidating cash dividend	Retained earnings
Capital stock	Market value per share	Retained earnings deficit
Changes in an accounting estimate	Minimum legal capital	Reverse stock split
Common stock	Noncumulative preferred stock	Simple capital structure
Complex capital structure	Nonparticipating preferred stock	Small stock dividend
Convertible preferred stock	No-par value stock	Stated value stock
Corporation	Organization expenses (costs)	Statement of stockholders' equity
Cumulative preferred stock	Paid-in capital	Stock dividend
Date of declaration	Paid-in capital in excess of par value	Stock options
Date of payment	Par value	Stock split
Date of record	Par value stock	Stockholders' equity
Diluted earnings per share	Participating preferred stock	Treasury stock
Dilutive securities	Preemptive right	

Multiple Choice Quiz   Answers at end of chapter

1. A corporation issues 6,000 shares of $5 par value common stock for $8 cash per share. The entry to record this transaction includes:
   a. A debit to Paid-In Capital in Excess of Par Value for $18,000.
   b. A credit to Common Stock for $48,000.
   c. A credit to Paid-In Capital in Excess of Par Value for $30,000.
   d. A credit to Cash for $48,000.
   e. A credit to Common Stock for $30,000.

2. A company reports net income of $75,000. Its weighted-average common shares outstanding is 19,000. It has no other stock outstanding. Its earnings per share is:
   a. $4.69   c. $3.75   e. $4.41
   b. $3.95   d. $2.08

3. A company has 5,000 shares of $100 par preferred stock and 50,000 shares of $10 par common stock outstanding.

   Its total stockholders' equity is $2,000,000. Its book value per common share is:
   a. $100.00   c. $40.00   e. $36.36
   b. $10.00   d. $30.00

4. A company paid cash dividends of $0.81 per share. Its earnings per share is $6.95 and its market price per share is $45.00. Its dividend yield is:
   a. 1.8%   c. 15.4%   e. 8.6%
   b. 11.7%   d. 55.6%

5. A company's shares have a market value of $85 per share. Its net income is $3,500,000, and its weighted-average common shares outstanding is 700,000. Its price-earnings ratio is:
   a. 5.9   c. 17.0   e. 41.2
   b. 425.0   d. 10.4

♟ Icon denotes assignments that involve decision making.

Discussion Questions

1. What are organization expenses? Provide examples.
2. How are organization expenses reported?
3. **♟** Who is responsible for directing a corporation's affairs?
4. What is the difference between authorized shares and outstanding shares?
5. What is the preemptive right of common stockholders?
6. List the general rights of common stockholders.
7. What is the difference between the market value per share and the par value per share?
8. What is the difference between the par value and the call price of a share of preferred stock?
9. **♟** Why would an investor find convertible preferred stock attractive?
10. Identify and explain the importance of the three dates relevant to corporate dividends.
11. Why is the term *liquidating dividend* used to describe cash dividends debited against paid-in capital accounts?
12. **♟** How does declaring a stock dividend affect the corporation's assets, liabilities, and total equity? What are the effects of the eventual distribution of that stock?
13. **♟** What is the difference between a stock dividend and a stock split?
14. **♟** Courts have ruled that a stock dividend is not taxable income to stockholders. What justifies this decision?
15. How does the purchase of treasury stock affect the purchaser's assets and total equity?
16. **♟** Why do laws place limits on treasury stock purchases?
17. How are EPS results computed for a corporation with a simple capital structure?
18. What is a stock option?
19. How is book value per share computed for a corporation with no preferred stock? What is the main limitation of using book value per share to value a corporation?
20. Refer to **Apple**'s fiscal 2014 balance sheet in Appendix A. How many shares of common stock are authorized? How many shares of voting common stock are issued? **APPLE**
21. **♟** Refer to the 2014 balance sheet for **Google** in Appendix A. What is the par value per share of its preferred stock? Suggest a rationale for the amount of par value it assigned. **GOOGLE**
22. **♟** Refer to the financial statements for **Samsung** in Appendix A. How much were its cash payments for treasury stock purchases for the year ended December 31, 2014? **Samsung**

Ⓜ connect

Of the following statements, which are true for the corporate form of organization?

_____ 1. Ownership rights cannot be easily transferred.
_____ 2. Owners have unlimited liability for corporate debts.
_____ 3. Capital is more easily accumulated than with most other forms of organization.
_____ 4. Corporate income that is distributed to shareholders is usually taxed twice.
_____ 5. It is a separate legal entity.
_____ 6. It has a limited life.
_____ 7. Owners are not agents of the corporation.

QUICK STUDY

QS 11-1
Characteristics of corporations
C1

Prepare the journal entry to record Zende Company's issuance of 75,000 shares of $5 par value common stock assuming the shares sell for:
a. $5 cash per share.
b. $6 cash per share.

QS 11-2
Issuance of common stock
P1

Prepare the journal entry to record Jevonte Company's issuance of 36,000 shares of its common stock assuming the shares have a:
a. $2 par value and sell for $18 cash per share.
b. $2 stated value and sell for $18 cash per share.

QS 11-3
Issuance of par and stated value common stock **P1**

Prepare the journal entry to record Autumn Company's issuance of 63,000 shares of no-par value common stock assuming the shares:
a. Sell for $29 cash per share.
b. Are exchanged for land valued at $1,827,000.

QS 11-4
Issuance of no-par common stock
P1

QS 11-5

Issuance of common stock   P1

Prepare the issuer's journal entry for each of the following separate transactions.

a. On March 1, Atlantic Co. issues 42,500 shares of $4 par value common stock for $297,500 cash.

b. On April 1, Antigo Company issues no-par value common stock for $70,000 cash.

c. On April 6, MPG issues 2,000 shares of $25 par value common stock for $45,000 of inventory, $145,000 of machinery, and acceptance of a $94,000 note payable.

QS 11-6

Accounting for cash dividends

P2

Prepare journal entries to record the following transactions for Emerson Corporation.

July 15   Declared a cash dividend payable to common stockholders of $165,000.
Aug. 15   Date of record is August 15 for the cash dividend declared on July 15.
Aug. 31   Paid the dividend declared on July 15.

QS 11-7

Accounting for small stock dividend

P2

The stockholders' equity section of Jun Company's balance sheet as of April 1 follows. On April 2, Jun declares and distributes a 10% stock dividend. The stock's per share market value on April 2 is $20 (prior to the dividend). Prepare the stockholders' equity section immediately after the stock dividend.

Common stock—$5 par value, 375,000 shares	
authorized, 200,000 shares issued and outstanding	$1,000,000
Paid-in capital in excess of par value, common stock.	600,000
Retained earnings.	833,000
Total stockholders' equity	$2,433,000

QS 11-8

Accounting for dividends

P2

Which of the following statements are true regarding dividends?

_____ **1.** Cash and stock dividends reduce retained earnings.

_____ **2.** Dividends payable is recorded at the time a cash dividend is declared.

_____ **3.** The date of record refers to the date a cash dividend is paid to stockholders.

_____ **4.** Stock dividends are a mechanism to keep the market price of stock affordable.

QS 11-9

Preferred stock issuance and dividends   C2

1. Prepare the journal entry to record Tamas Company's issuance of 5,000 shares of $100 par value, 7% cumulative preferred stock for $102 cash per share.

2. Assuming the facts in part 1, if Tamas declares a year-end cash dividend, what is the amount of dividend paid to preferred shareholders? (Assume no dividends in arrears.)

QS 11-10

Dividend allocation between classes of shareholders

C2

Stockholders' equity of Ernst Company consists of 80,000 shares of $5 par value, 8% cumulative preferred stock and 250,000 shares of $1 par value common stock. Both classes of stock have been outstanding since the company's inception. Ernst did not declare any dividends in the prior year, but it now declares and pays a $110,000 cash dividend at the current year-end. Determine the amount distributed to each class of stockholders for this two-year-old company.

QS 11-11

Purchase and sale of treasury stock   P3

On May 3, Zirbal Corporation purchased 4,000 shares of its own stock for $36,000 cash. On November 4, Zirbal reissued 850 shares of this treasury stock for $8,500. Prepare the May 3 and November 4 journal entries to record Zirbal's purchase and reissuance of treasury stock.

QS 11-12

Impacts of stock issuances, dividends, splits, and treasury transactions   P2   P3

Listed below are various transactions that a company incurred during the current year. Indicate the impact on total stockholders' equity for each scenario. Specifically state whether stockholders' equity would "Increase," "Decrease," or have "No Effect" as a result of each transaction listed below. Consider each transaction independently.

_____ **1.** A stock dividend equal to 30% of the previously outstanding shares is declared.

_____ **2.** New shares of common stock are issued for cash.

_____ **3.** Treasury shares of common stock are purchased (assume the cost method).

_____ **4.** Cash dividends are paid to shareholders.

Answer the following questions related to a company's activities for the current year:

1. A review of the notes payable files discovers that three years ago the company reported the entire amount of a payment (principal and interest) on an installment note payable as interest expense. This mistake had a material effect on the amount of income in that year. How should the correction be reported in the current-year financial statements?

2. After using an expected useful life of seven years and no salvage value to depreciate its office equipment over the preceding three years, the company decided early this year that the equipment will last only two more years. How should the effects of this decision be reported in the current-year financial statements?

QS 11-13
Accounting for changes in estimates; error adjustments

C3

Murray Company reports net income of $770,000 for the year. It has no preferred stock, and its weighted-average common shares outstanding is 280,000 shares. Compute its basic earnings per share.

QS 11-14
Basic earnings per share

A1

Epic Company earned net income of $900,000 this year. The number of common shares outstanding during the entire year was 400,000, and preferred shareholders received a $20,000 cash dividend. Compute Epic Company's basic earnings per share.

QS 11-15
Basic earnings per share

A1

Compute Topp Company's price-earnings ratio if its common stock has a market value of $20.54 per share and its EPS is $3.95. Would an analyst likely consider this stock potentially overpriced, underpriced, or neither? Explain.

QS 11-16
Price-earnings ratio

A2

Foxburo Company expects to pay a $2.34 per share cash dividend this year on its common stock. The current market value of Foxburo stock is $32.50 per share. Compute the expected dividend yield on the Foxburo stock. Would you classify the Foxburo stock as a growth or an income stock? Explain.

QS 11-17
Dividend yield   A3

The stockholders' equity section of Montel Company's balance sheet follows. The preferred stock's call price is $40. Determine the book value per share of the common stock.

Preferred stock—5% cumulative, $10 par value, 20,000 shares authorized, issued, and outstanding.........	$ 200,000
Common stock—$5 par value, 200,000 shares authorized, 150,000 shares issued and outstanding...................	750,000
Retained earnings.....................................	900,000
Total stockholders' equity.............................	$1,850,000

QS 11-18
Book value per common share

A4

Air France-KLM reports the following equity information for its fiscal year ended December 31, 2014 (euros in millions). Prepare its journal entry, using its account titles, to record the issuance of capital stock assuming that its entire par value stock was issued on December 31, 2014, for cash.

December 31	2014
Issued capital	€ 300
Additional paid-in capital	2,971

QS 11-19
International equity disclosures

P1

---

connect

Describe how each of the following characteristics of organizations applies to a corporation.

1. Owner authority and control	5. Duration of life
2. Ease of formation	6. Owner liability
3. Transferability of ownership	7. Legal status
4. Ability to raise large capital amounts	8. Tax status of income

EXERCISES

Exercise 11-1
Characteristics of corporations

C1

Exercise 11-2
Accounting for par, stated, and no-par stock issuances
P1

Rodriguez Corporation issues 19,000 shares of its common stock for $152,000 cash on February 20. Prepare journal entries to record this event under each of the following separate situations.

1. The stock has a $2 par value.
2. The stock has neither par nor stated value.
3. The stock has a $5 stated value.

Exercise 11-3
Recording stock issuances
P1

Prepare journal entries to record the following four separate issuances of stock.

1. A corporation issued 4,000 shares of $5 par value common stock for $35,000 cash.
2. A corporation issued 2,000 shares of no-par common stock to its promoters in exchange for their efforts, estimated to be worth $40,000. The stock has a $1 per share stated value.
3. A corporation issued 2,000 shares of no-par common stock to its promoters in exchange for their efforts, estimated to be worth $40,000. The stock has no stated value.
4. A corporation issued 1,000 shares of $50 par value preferred stock for $60,000 cash.

Exercise 11-4
Stock issuance for noncash assets   P1

Sudoku Company issues 7,000 shares of $7 par value common stock in exchange for land and a building. The land is valued at $45,000 and the building at $85,000. Prepare the journal entry to record issuance of the stock in exchange for the land and building.

Exercise 11-5
Stock dividends and splits
P2

On June 30, 2016, Sharper Corporation's common stock is priced at $62 per share before any stock dividend or split, and the stockholders' equity section of its balance sheet appears as follows.

Common stock—$10 par value, 120,000 shares authorized, 50,000 shares issued and outstanding	$ 500,000
Paid-in capital in excess of par value, common stock.	200,000
Retained earnings.	660,000
Total stockholders' equity	$1,360,000

1. Assume that the company declares and immediately distributes a 50% stock dividend. This event is recorded by capitalizing retained earnings equal to the stock's par value. Answer these questions about stockholders' equity as it exists *after* issuing the new shares.
   a. What is the retained earnings balance?
   b. What is the amount of total stockholders' equity?
   c. How many shares are outstanding?

Check (1b) $1,360,000

2. Assume that the company implements a 3-for-2 stock split instead of the stock dividend in part 1. Answer these questions about stockholders' equity as it exists *after* issuing the new shares.
   a. What is the retained earnings balance?
   b. What is the amount of total stockholders' equity?
   c. How many shares are outstanding?

(2a) $660,000

3. Explain the difference, if any, to a stockholder of receiving new shares distributed under a large stock dividend versus a stock split.

Exercise 11-6
Stock dividends and per share book values
P2

The stockholders' equity of TVX Company at the beginning of the day on February 5 follows:

Common stock—$10 par value, 150,000 shares authorized, 60,000 shares issued and outstanding	$ 600,000
Paid-in capital in excess of par value, common stock.	425,000
Retained earnings.	550,000
Total stockholders' equity	$1,575,000

On February 5, the directors declare a 20% stock dividend distributable on February 28 to the February 15 stockholders of record. The stock's market value is $40 per share on February 5 before the stock dividend. The stock's market value is $33.40 per share on February 28.

1. Prepare entries to record both the dividend declaration and its distribution.

2. One stockholder owned 800 shares on February 5 before the dividend. Compute the book value per share and total book value of this stockholder's shares immediately before *and* after the stock dividend of February 5.

3. Compute the total market value of the investor's shares in part 2 as of February 5 and February 28.

Check   (2) Book value per share: before, $26.250; after, $21.875

Match each description 1 through 6 with the characteristic of preferred stock that it best describes by writing the letter of that characteristic in the blank next to each description.

A. Callable   **B.** Convertible   **C.** Cumulative

D. Noncumulative   **E.** Nonparticipating   **F.** Participating

_____ **1.** Holders of the stock are entitled to receive current and all past dividends before common stockholders receive any dividends.

_____ **2.** The issuing corporation can retire the stock by paying a prespecified price.

_____ **3.** Holders of the stock can receive dividends exceeding the stated rate under certain conditions.

_____ **4.** Holders of the stock are not entitled to receive dividends in excess of the stated rate.

_____ **5.** Holders of this stock can exchange it for shares of common stock.

_____ **6.** Holders of the stock lose any dividends that are not declared in the current year.

Exercise 11-7
Identifying characteristics of preferred stock
C2

York's outstanding stock consists of 80,000 shares of *noncumulative* 7.5% preferred stock with a $5 par value and also 200,000 shares of common stock with a $1 par value. During its first four years of operation, the corporation declared and paid the following total cash dividends:

2015 total cash dividends	$ 20,000
2016 total cash dividends	28,000
2017 total cash dividends	200,000
2018 total cash dividends	350,000

Determine the amount of dividends paid each year to each of the two classes of stockholders: preferred and common. Also compute the total dividends paid to each class for the four years combined.

Exercise 11-8
Dividends on common and noncumulative preferred stock
C2

Check   4-year total paid to preferred, $108,000

Use the data in Exercise 11-8 to determine the amount of dividends paid each year to each of the two classes of stockholders assuming that the preferred stock is *cumulative*. Also determine the total dividends paid to each class for the four years combined.

Exercise 11-9
Dividends on common and cumulative preferred stock   **C2**

On October 10, the stockholders' equity of Sherm Systems appears as follows:

Common stock—$10 par value, 72,000 shares authorized, issued, and outstanding	$ 720,000
Paid-in capital in excess of par value, common stock.	216,000
Retained earnings.	864,000
Total stockholders' equity.	$1,800,000

1. Prepare journal entries to record the following transactions for Sherm Systems.

  a. Purchased 5,000 shares of its own common stock at $25 per share on October 11.

  b. Sold 1,000 treasury shares on November 1 for $31 cash per share.

  c. Sold all remaining treasury shares on November 25 for $20 cash per share.

2. Explain how the company's equity section changes after the October 11 treasury stock purchase, and prepare the revised equity section of its balance sheet at that date.

Exercise 11-10
Recording and reporting treasury stock transactions

P3

Check   (1c) Dr. Retained Earnings, $14,000

Exercise 11-11
Preparing a statement of retained earnings
C3

The following information is available for Amos Company for the year ended December 31, 2016.
a. Balance of retained earnings, December 31, 2015, prior to discovery of error, $1,375,000.
b. Cash dividends declared and paid during 2016, $43,000.
c. It neglected to record 2014 depreciation expense of $55,500, which is net of $4,500 in tax benefits.
d. The company earned $126,000 in 2016 net income.
Prepare a 2016 statement of retained earnings for Amos Company.

Exercise 11-12
Earnings per share
A1

Check (2) $3.41

Ecker Company reports $2,700,000 of net income for 2016 and declares $388,020 of cash dividends on its preferred stock for 2016. At the end of 2016, the company had 678,000 weighted-average shares of common stock.
1. What amount of net income is available to common stockholders for 2016?
2. What is the company's basic EPS for 2016?

Exercise 11-13
Earnings per share
A1

Check (2) $2.10

Kelley Company reports $960,000 of net income for 2016 and declares $120,000 of cash dividends on its preferred stock for 2016. At the end of 2016, the company had 400,000 weighted-average shares of common stock.
1. What amount of net income is available to common stockholders for 2016?
2. What is the company's basic EPS for 2016? Round your answer to the nearest whole cent.

Exercise 11-14
Price-earnings ratio computation and interpretation
A2

Compute the price-earnings ratio for each of these four separate companies. Which stock might an analyst likely investigate as being potentially undervalued by the market? Explain.

	A	B	C
1		**Earnings**	**Market Value**
2	**Company**	**per Share**	**per Share**
3	1	$12.00	$176.40
4	2	10.00	96.00
5	3	7.50	93.75
6	4	50.00	250.00
7			

Exercise 11-15
Dividend yield computation and interpretation
A3

Compute the dividend yield for each of these four separate companies. Which company's stock would probably *not* be classified as an income stock? Explain.

	A	B	C
1		**Annual Cash**	**Market Value**
2	**Company**	**Dividend per Share**	**per Share**
3	1	$16.06	$220.00
4	2	13.86	132.00
5	3	3.96	72.00
6	4	0.48	80.00
7			

Exercise 11-16
Book value per share
A4

The equity section of Cyril Corporation's balance sheet shows the following:

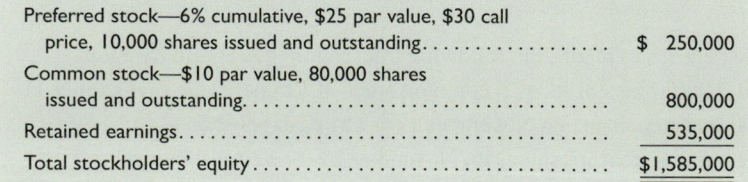

Preferred stock—6% cumulative, $25 par value, $30 call price, 10,000 shares issued and outstanding.	$ 250,000
Common stock—$10 par value, 80,000 shares issued and outstanding.	800,000
Retained earnings.	535,000
Total stockholders' equity.	$1,585,000

Determine the book value per share of the preferred and common stock under two separate situations.

1. No preferred dividends are in arrears.

2. Three years of preferred dividends are in arrears.

Check   (1) Book value of common, $16.06 per share

Unilever Group reports the following equity information for the years ended December 31, 2014 and 2013 (euros in millions).

Exercise 11-17
Accounting for equity under IFRS

C3   P1

December 31	2014	2013
Share capital...............	€ 484	€ 484
Share premium..............	145	138
Other reserves.............	(7,538)	(6,746)
Retained profit.............	20,560	20,468
Shareholders' equity	€13,651	€14,344

1. Match each of the three account titles—*share capital, share premium,* and *retained profit*—with the usual account title applied under U.S. GAAP from the following options:

_____ **a.** Paid-in capital in excess of par value, common stock

_____ **b.** Retained earnings

_____ **c.** Common stock, par value

2. Prepare Unilever's journal entry, using its account titles, to record the issuance of capital stock assuming that its entire par value stock was issued on December 31, 2013, for cash.

3. What were Unilever's 2014 dividends assuming that only dividends and income impacted retained profit for 2014 and that its 2014 income totaled €5,092?

Alexander Corporation reports the following components of stockholders' equity on December 31, 2015:

Exercise 11-18
Cash dividends, treasury stock, and statement of retained earnings

C3   P2   P3

Common stock—$25 par value, 50,000 shares authorized, 30,000 shares issued and outstanding....................	$ 750,000
Paid-in capital in excess of par value, common stock..........	50,000
Retained earnings......................................	340,000
Total stockholders' equity..............................	$1,140,000

In year 2016, the following transactions affected its stockholders' equity accounts.

Jan.   2   Purchased 3,000 shares of its own stock at $25 cash per share.

Jan.   7   Directors declared a $1.50 per share cash dividend payable on Feb. 28 to the Feb. 9 stockholders of record.

Feb. 28   Paid the dividend declared on January 7.

July   9   Sold 1,200 of its treasury shares at $30 cash per share.

Aug. 27   Sold 1,500 of its treasury shares at $20 cash per share.

Sept. 9   Directors declared a $2 per share cash dividend payable on October 22 to the September 23 stockholders of record.

Oct. 22   Paid the dividend declared on September 9.

Dec. 31   Closed the $52,000 credit balance (from net income) in the Income Summary account to Retained Earnings.

Required

1. Prepare journal entries to record each of these transactions for 2016.

2. Prepare a statement of retained earnings for the year ended December 31, 2016.

3. Prepare the stockholders' equity section of the company's balance sheet as of December 31, 2016.

PROBLEM SET A

Problem 11-1A
Stockholders' equity
transactions and analysis

C2   P1

Kinkaid Co. is incorporated at the beginning of this year and engages in a number of transactions. The following journal entries impacted its stockholders' equity during its first year of operations.

a.	Cash	300,000	
	Common Stock, $25 Par Value		250,000
	Paid-In Capital in Excess of		
	Par Value, Common Stock..................		50,000
b.	Organization Expenses.........................	150,000	
	Common Stock, $25 Par Value		125,000
	Paid-In Capital in Excess of		
	Par Value, Common Stock..................		25,000
c.	Cash	43,000	
	Accounts Receivable	15,000	
	Building.......................................	81,500	
	Notes Payable.............................		59,500
	Common Stock, $25 Par Value		50,000
	Paid-In Capital in Excess of		
	Par Value, Common Stock..................		30,000
d.	Cash	120,000	
	Common Stock, $25 Par Value		75,000
	Paid-In Capital in Excess of		
	Par Value, Common Stock..................		45,000

Required

1. Explain the transaction(s) underlying each journal entry (*a*) through (*d*).
2. How many shares of common stock are outstanding at year-end?
3. What is the amount of minimum legal capital (based on par value) at year-end?
4. What is the total paid-in capital at year-end?
5. What is the book value per share of the common stock at year-end if total paid-in capital plus retained earnings equals $695,000?

Problem 11-2A
Cash dividends, treasury
stock, and statement of
retained earnings

C3   P2   P3

Kohler Corporation reports the following components of stockholders' equity on December 31, 2015:

Common stock—$10 par value, 100,000 shares authorized,	
40,000 shares issued and outstanding...........................	$400,000
Paid-in capital in excess of par value, common stock.................	60,000
Retained earnings..	270,000
Total stockholders' equity.....................................	$730,000

In year 2016, the following transactions affected its stockholders' equity accounts.

Jan.   1   Purchased 4,000 shares of its own stock at $20 cash per share.
Jan.   5   Directors declared a $2 per share cash dividend payable on Feb. 28 to the Feb. 5 stockholders of record.
Feb. 28   Paid the dividend declared on January 5.
July   6   Sold 1,500 of its treasury shares at $24 cash per share.
Aug. 22   Sold 2,500 of its treasury shares at $17 cash per share.
Sept. 5   Directors declared a $2 per share cash dividend payable on October 28 to the September 25 stockholders of record.
Oct. 28   Paid the dividend declared on September 5.
Dec. 31   Closed the $388,000 credit balance (from net income) in the Income Summary account to Retained Earnings.

Required

1. Prepare journal entries to record each of these transactions for 2016.
2. Prepare a statement of retained earnings for the year ended December 31, 2016.
3. Prepare the stockholders' equity section of the company's balance sheet as of December 31, 2016.

Check   (2) Retained earnings, Dec. 31, 2016, $504,500

At September 30, the end of Beijing Company's third quarter, the following stockholders' equity accounts are reported.

Problem 11-3A
Equity analysis—journal entries and account balances
P2

Common stock, $12 par value	$360,000
Paid-in capital in excess of par value, common stock..........	90,000
Retained earnings.....................................	320,000

In the fourth quarter, the following entries related to its equity are recorded:

Oct. 2	Retained Earnings................................	60,000	
	Common Dividend Payable		60,000
Oct. 25	Common Dividend Payable	60,000	
	Cash		60,000
Oct. 31	Retained Earnings................................	75,000	
	Common Stock Dividend Distributable		36,000
	Paid-In Capital in Excess of Par Value, Common Stock..................		39,000
Nov. 5	Common Stock Dividend Distributable	36,000	
	Common Stock, $12 Par Value		36,000
Dec. 1	Memo—Change the title of the Common Stock account to reflect the new par value of $4.		
Dec. 31	Income Summary	210,000	
	Retained Earnings............................		210,000

Required

1. Explain the transaction(s) underlying each journal entry.
2. Complete the following table showing the equity account balances at each indicated date (include the balances from September 30).

	Oct. 2	Oct. 25	Oct. 31	Nov. 5	Dec. 1	Dec. 31
Common stock......................	$____	$____	$____	$____	$____	$____
Common stock dividend distributable	____	____	____	____	____	____
Paid-in capital in excess of par, common stock.........	____	____	____	____	____	____
Retained earnings	____	____	____	____	____	____
Total equity........................	$____	$____	$____	$____	$____	$____

Check   Total equity: Oct. 2, $710,000; Dec. 31, $920,000

The equity sections from Atticus Group's 2015 and 2016 year-end balance sheets follow.

Problem 11-4A
Analysis of changes in stockholders' equity accounts

C3   P2   P3

Stockholders' Equity (December 31, 2015)	
Common stock—$4 par value, 100,000 shares authorized, 40,000 shares issued and outstanding	$160,000
Paid-in capital in excess of par value, common stock...............	120,000
Retained earnings.......................................	320,000
Total stockholders' equity..................................	$600,000

Stockholders' Equity (December 31, 2016)	
Common stock—$4 par value, 100,000 shares authorized, 47,400 shares issued, 3,000 shares in treasury	$189,600
Paid-in capital in excess of par value, common stock	179,200
Retained earnings ($30,000 restricted by treasury stock)	400,000
	768,800
Less cost of treasury stock	(30,000)
Total stockholders' equity	$738,800

The following transactions and events affected its equity during year 2016.

Jan.   5   Declared a $0.50 per share cash dividend, date of record January 10.
Mar. 20   Purchased treasury stock for cash.
Apr.   5   Declared a $0.50 per share cash dividend, date of record April 10.
July   5   Declared a $0.50 per share cash dividend, date of record July 10.
July 31   Declared a 20% stock dividend when the stock's market value was $12 per share.
Aug. 14   Issued the stock dividend that was declared on July 31.
Oct.   5   Declared a $0.50 per share cash dividend, date of record October 10.

Required

1. How many common shares are outstanding on each cash dividend date?
2. What is the total dollar amount for each of the four cash dividends?

Check   (3) $88,800

   (4) $10

   (5) $248,000

3. What is the amount of the capitalization of retained earnings for the stock dividend?
4. What is the per share cost of the treasury stock purchased?
5. How much net income did the company earn during year 2016?

Problem 11-5A
Computation of book values and dividend allocations

C2   A4

Raphael Corporation's common stock is currently selling on a stock exchange at $85 per share, and its current balance sheet shows the following stockholders' equity section:

Preferred stock—5% cumulative, $___ par value, 1,000 shares authorized, issued, and outstanding	$ 50,000
Common stock—$___ par value, 4,000 shares authorized, issued, and outstanding	80,000
Retained earnings	150,000
Total stockholders' equity	$280,000

Required (Round per share amounts to cents.)

1. What is the current market value (price) of this corporation's common stock?
2. What are the par values of the corporation's preferred stock and its common stock?
3. If no dividends are in arrears, what are the book values per share of the preferred stock and the common stock?

Check   (4) Book value of common, $56.25

   (5) Book value of common, $55.00

   (6) Dividends per common share, $1.00

4. If two years' preferred dividends are in arrears, what are the book values per share of the preferred stock and the common stock?
5. If two years' preferred dividends are in arrears and the preferred stock is callable at $55 per share, what are the book values per share of the preferred stock and the common stock?
6. If two years' preferred dividends are in arrears and the board of directors declares cash dividends of $11,500, what total amount will be paid to the preferred and to the common shareholders? What is the amount of dividends per share for the common stock?

Analysis Component

7. What are some factors that can contribute to a difference between the book value of common stock and its market value (price)?

Weiss Company is incorporated at the beginning of this year and engages in a number of transactions. The following journal entries impacted its stockholders' equity during its first year of operations.

a.	Cash	120,000	
	Common Stock, $1 Par Value		3,000
	Paid-In Capital in Excess of Par Value, Common Stock		117,000
b.	Organization Expenses.	40,000	
	Common Stock, $1 Par Value		1,000
	Paid-In Capital in Excess of Par Value, Common Stock		39,000
c.	Cash	13,300	
	Accounts Receivable	8,000	
	Building.	37,000	
	Notes Payable.		18,300
	Common Stock, $1 Par Value		800
	Paid-In Capital in Excess of Par Value, Common Stock		39,200
d.	Cash	60,000	
	Common Stock, $1 Par Value		1,200
	Paid-In Capital in Excess of Par Value, Common Stock		58,800

PROBLEM SET B

Problem 11-1B
Stockholders' equity transactions and analysis

C2 P1

Required

1. Explain the transaction(s) underlying each journal entry (*a*) through (*d*).
2. How many shares of common stock are outstanding at year-end?
3. What is the amount of minimum legal capital (based on par value) at year-end?
4. What is the total paid-in capital at year-end?
5. What is the book value per share of the common stock at year-end if total paid-in capital plus retained earnings equals $283,000?

Check   (2) 6,000 shares
(3) $6,000
(4) $260,000

Balthus Corp. reports the following components of stockholders' equity on December 31, 2015:

Common stock—$1 par value, 320,000 shares authorized, 200,000 shares issued and outstanding........................	$ 200,000
Paid-in capital in excess of par value, common stock..............	1,400,000
Retained earnings...	2,160,000
Total stockholders' equity.................................	$3,760,000

Problem 11-2B
Cash dividends, treasury stock, and statement of retained earnings

C3 P2 P3

It completed the following transactions related to stockholders' equity in year 2016:

Jan. 10   Purchased 40,000 shares of its own stock at $12 cash per share.
Mar. 2   Directors declared a $1.50 per share cash dividend payable on March 31 to the March 15 stock-holders of record.
Mar. 31   Paid the dividend declared on March 2.
Nov. 11   Sold 24,000 of its treasury shares at $13 cash per share.
Nov. 25   Sold 16,000 of its treasury shares at $9.50 cash per share.
Dec. 1   Directors declared a $2.50 per share cash dividend payable on January 2 to the December 10 stockholders of record.
Dec. 31   Closed the $1,072,000 credit balance (from net income) in the Income Summary account to Retained Earnings.

Required

1. Prepare journal entries to record each of these transactions for 2016.
2. Prepare a statement of retained earnings for the year ended December 31, 2016.
3. Prepare the stockholders' equity section of the company's balance sheet as of December 31, 2016.

Check   (2) Retained earnings, Dec. 31, 2016, $2,476,000

Problem 11-3B
Equity analysis—journal entries and account balances

P2

At December 31, the end of Chilton Communication's third quarter, the following stockholders' equity accounts are reported:

Common stock, $10 par value	$ 960,000
Paid-in capital in excess of par value, common stock.	384,000
Retained earnings.	1,600,000

In the fourth quarter, the following entries related to its equity are recorded:

Jan. 17	Retained Earnings.	96,000	
	Common Dividend Payable		96,000
Feb. 5	Common Dividend Payable	96,000	
	Cash		96,000
Feb. 28	Retained Earnings.	252,000	
	Common Stock Dividend Distributable		120,000
	Paid-In Capital in Excess of Par Value,		
	Common Stock		132,000
Mar. 14	Common Stock Dividend Distributable	120,000	
	Common Stock, $10 Par Value		120,000
Mar. 25	Memo—Change the title of the Common		
	Stock account to reflect the new par value of $5.		
Mar. 31	Income Summary	720,000	
	Retained Earnings.		720,000

Required

1. Explain the transaction(s) underlying each journal entry.
2. Complete the following table showing the equity account balances at each indicated date (include the balances from December 31).

	Jan. 17	Feb. 5	Feb. 28	Mar. 14	Mar. 25	Mar. 31
Common stock.	$_____	$_____	$_____	$_____	$_____	$_____
Common stock dividend distributable	_____	_____	_____	_____	_____	_____
Paid-in capital in excess of par, common stock	_____	_____	_____	_____	_____	_____
Retained earnings	_____	_____	_____	_____	_____	_____
Total equity.	$_____	$_____	$_____	$_____	$_____	$_____

Check   Total equity:
Jan. 17, $2,848,000; Mar. 31,
$3,568,000

Problem 11-4B
Analysis of changes in stockholders' equity accounts

C3   P2   P3

The equity sections from Hovo Corporation's 2015 and 2016 balance sheets follow.

Stockholders' Equity (December 31, 2015)	
Common stock—$20 par value, 30,000 shares authorized,	
17,000 shares issued and outstanding.	$340,000
Paid-in capital in excess of par value, common stock.	60,000
Retained earnings.	270,000
Total stockholders' equity.	$670,000

Stockholders' Equity (December 31, 2016)

Common stock—$20 par value, 30,000 shares authorized, 19,000 shares issued, 1,000 shares in treasury	$380,000
Paid-in capital in excess of par value, common stock	104,000
Retained earnings ($40,000 restricted by treasury stock)	295,200
	779,200
Less cost of treasury stock	(40,000)
Total stockholders' equity	$739,200

The following transactions and events affected its equity during year 2016.

Feb. 15   Declared a $0.40 per share cash dividend, date of record five days later.
Mar. 2   Purchased treasury stock for cash.
May 15   Declared a $0.40 per share cash dividend, date of record five days later.
Aug. 15   Declared a $0.40 per share cash dividend, date of record five days later.
Oct.   4   Declared a 12.5% stock dividend when the stock's market value is $42 per share.
Oct. 20   Issued the stock dividend that was declared on October 4.
Nov. 15   Declared a $0.40 per share cash dividend, date of record five days later.

Required

1. How many common shares are outstanding on each cash dividend date?
2. What is the total dollar amount for each of the four cash dividends?
3. What is the amount of the capitalization of retained earnings for the stock dividend?
4. What is the per share cost of the treasury stock purchased?
5. How much net income did the company earn during year 2016?

Check   (3) $84,000

(4) $40

(5) $136,000

Soltech Company's common stock is currently selling on a stock exchange at $90 per share, and its current balance sheet shows the following stockholders' equity section.

Problem 11-5B
Computation of book values and dividend allocations

C2   A4

Preferred stock—8% cumulative, $___ par value, 1,500 shares authorized, issued, and outstanding	$ 375,000
Common stock—$___ par value, 18,000 shares authorized, issued, and outstanding	900,000
Retained earnings	1,125,000
Total stockholders' equity	$2,400,000

Required (Round per share amounts to cents.)

1. What is the current market value (price) of this corporation's common stock?
2. What are the par values of the corporation's preferred stock and its common stock?
3. If no dividends are in arrears, what are the book values per share of the preferred stock and the common stock?
4. If two years' preferred dividends are in arrears, what are the book values per share of the preferred stock and the common stock?
5. If two years' preferred dividends are in arrears and the preferred stock is callable at $280 per share, what are the book values per share of the preferred stock and the common stock?
6. If two years' preferred dividends are in arrears and the board of directors declares cash dividends of $100,000, what total amount will be paid to the preferred and to the common shareholders? What is the amount of dividends per share for the common stock?

Check   (4) Book value of common, $109.17

(5) Book value of common, $106.67

(6) Dividends per common share, $0.56

Analysis Component

7. Discuss why the book value of common stock is not always a good estimate of its market value.

SERIAL PROBLEM

Business Solutions

P1 C1 C2

(This serial problem began in Chapter 1 and continues through most of the book. If previous chapter segments were not completed, the serial problem can begin at this point. It is helpful, but not necessary, to use the Working Papers that accompany the book.)

SP 11 Santana Rey created Business Solutions on October 1, 2016. The company has been successful, and Santana plans to expand her business. She believes an additional $86,000 is needed and is investigating three funding sources.

a. Santana's sister Cicely is willing to invest $86,000 in the business as a common shareholder. Since Santana currently has about $129,000 invested in the business, Cicely's investment will mean that Santana will maintain about 60% ownership, and Cicely will have 40% ownership of Business Solutions.

b. Santana's uncle Marcello is willing to invest $86,000 in the business as a preferred shareholder. Marcello would purchase 860 shares of $100 par value, 7% preferred stock.

c. Santana's banker is willing to lend her $86,000 on a 7%, 10-year note payable. She would make payments of $1,000 per month for 10 years.

Required

1. Prepare the journal entry to reflect the initial $86,000 investment under each of the options (*a*), (*b*), and (*c*).

2. Evaluate the three proposals for expansion, providing the pros and cons of each option.

3. Which option do you recommend Santana adopt? Explain.

GENERAL LEDGER PROBLEMS

Available in Connect

The following General Ledger assignments highlight the impact, or lack thereof, on financial statements from equity-based transactions.

GL 11-1 General Ledger assignment 11-1 is adapted from Problem 11-2A, including beginning equity balances. Prepare journal entries related to treasury stock, cash dividends, and net income. Then, prepare the statement of retained earnings and the stockholders' equity section of the balance sheet.

GL 11-2 General Ledger assignment 11-2 is adapted from Problem 11-4A, including beginning and ending equity balances. Prepare journal entries related to cash dividends and stock dividends. Calculate the number of shares outstanding, the amount of net income, and the amount of retained earnings to be capitalized as a result of the stock dividend, if any.

Beyond the Numbers

REPORTING IN ACTION

C2 A1 A4

APPLE

BTN 11-1 Refer to **Apple**'s financial statements in Appendix A to answer the following.

1. How many shares of common stock are issued and outstanding at September 27, 2014, and September 28, 2013? How do these numbers compare with the basic weighted-average common shares outstanding at September 27, 2014, and September 28, 2013?

2. What is the book value of its entire common stock at September 27, 2014?

3. What is the total amount of cash dividends paid to common stockholders for the years ended September 27, 2014, and September 28, 2013?

4. Identify and compare basic EPS amounts across fiscal years 2014, 2013, and 2012. Identify and comment on any notable changes.

5. How many shares does Apple hold in treasury stock, if any, as of September 27, 2014, and September 28, 2013?

Fast Forward

6. Access Apple's financial statements for fiscal years ending after September 27, 2014, from its website (**Apple.com**) or the SEC's EDGAR database (**www.SEC.gov**). Has the number of common shares outstanding increased since that date? Has the company increased the total amount of cash dividends paid compared to the total amount for fiscal year 2014?

BTN 11-2   Key comparative figures for **Apple** and **Google** follow.

Key Figures	Apple	Google
Net income (in millions)	$ 39,510	$ 14,444
Cash dividends declared per common share	$ 1.82	$ —
Common shares outstanding (in millions)	5,866.161	680.172
Weighted-average common shares outstanding (in millions)	6,085.572	675.935
Market value (price) per share	$ 100.75	$ 530.66
Equity applicable to common shares (in millions).................	$ 111,547	$104,500

Required

1. Compute the book value per common share for each company using these data.
2. Compute the basic EPS for each company using these data.
3. Compute the dividend yield for each company using these data. Does the dividend yield of either of the companies characterize it as an income or growth stock? Explain.
4. Compute, compare, and interpret the price-earnings ratio for each company using these data.

BTN 11-3   Harriet Moore is an accountant for New World Pharmaceuticals. Her duties include tracking research and development spending in the new product development division. Over the course of the past six months, Harriet has noticed that a great deal of funds have been spent on a particular project for a new drug. She hears "through the grapevine" that the company is about to patent the drug and expects it to be a major advance in antibiotics. Harriet believes that this new drug will greatly improve company performance and will cause the company's stock to increase in value. Harriet decides to purchase shares of New World in order to benefit from this expected increase.

Required

What are Harriet's ethical responsibilities, if any, with respect to the information she has learned through her duties as an accountant for New World Pharmaceuticals? What are the implications of her planned purchase of New World shares?

BTN 11-4   Teams are to select an industry, and each team member is to select a different company in that industry. Each team member then is to acquire the selected company's financial statements (or Form 10-K) from the SEC site (**www.SEC.gov**). Use these data to identify basic EPS. Use the financial press (or **finance.yahoo.com**) to determine the market price of this stock, and then compute the price-earnings ratio. Communicate with teammates via a meeting, e-mail, or telephone to discuss the meaning of this ratio, how companies compare, and the industry norm. The team must prepare a single memorandum reporting the ratio for each company and identifying the team conclusions or consensus of opinion. The memorandum is to be duplicated and distributed to the instructor and teammates.

BTN 11-5   Access the February 24, 2015, filing of the 2014 calendar-year 10-K report of **McDonald's** (ticker MCD) from **www.SEC.gov**.

Required

1. Review McDonald's balance sheet and identify how many classes of stock it has issued.
2. What are the par values, number of authorized shares, and number of issued shares of the classes of stock you identified in part 1?
3. Review its statement of cash flows and identify what total amount of cash it paid in 2014 to purchase treasury stock.
4. What amount did McDonald's pay out in common stock cash dividends for 2014?

TEAMWORK IN ACTION

P3

Hint: Instructor must be sure each team accurately completes part 1 before proceeding.

BTN 11-6   This activity requires teamwork to reinforce understanding of accounting for treasury stock.

1. Write a brief team statement (*a*) generalizing what happens to a corporation's financial position when it engages in a stock "buyback" and (*b*) identifying reasons why a corporation would engage in this activity.

2. Assume that an entity acquires 100 shares of its $100 par value common stock at a cost of $134 cash per share. Discuss the entry to record this acquisition. Next, assign *each* team member to prepare *one* of the following entries (assume each entry applies to all shares):

   a. Reissue treasury shares at cost.

   b. Reissue treasury shares at $150 per share.

   c. Reissue treasury shares at $120 per share; assume the paid-in capital account from treasury shares has a $1,500 balance.

   d. Reissue treasury shares at $120 per share; assume the paid-in capital account from treasury shares has a $1,000 balance.

   e. Reissue treasury shares at $120 per share; assume the paid-in capital account from treasury shares has a zero balance.

3. In sequence, each member is to present his/her entry to the team and explain the *similarities* and *differences* between that entry and the previous entry.

ENTREPRENEURIAL DECISION

C2   P2

BTN 11-7   Assume that **Alibaba Group** decides to launch a new website to market discount bookkeeping services to consumers. This chain, named Aladin, requires $500,000 of start-up capital. The founder contributes $375,000 of personal assets in return for 15,000 shares of common stock, but he must raise another $125,000 in cash. There are two alternative plans for raising the additional cash.

- *Plan A* is to sell 3,750 shares of common stock to one or more investors for $125,000 cash.
- *Plan B* is to sell 1,250 shares of cumulative preferred stock to one or more investors for $125,000 cash (this preferred stock would have a $100 par value, an annual 8% dividend rate, and be issued at par).

1. If the new business is expected to earn $72,000 of after-tax net income in the first year, what rate of return on beginning equity will the founder earn under each alternative plan? Which plan will provide the higher expected return?

2. If the new business is expected to earn $16,800 of after-tax net income in the first year, what rate of return on beginning equity will the founder earn under each alternative plan? Which plan will provide the higher expected return?

3. Analyze and interpret the differences between the results for parts 1 and 2.

HITTING THE ROAD

A1   A2   A3

BTN 11-8   Review 30 to 60 minutes of financial news programming on television. Take notes on companies that are catching analysts' attention. You might hear reference to over- and undervaluation of firms and to reports about PE ratios, dividend yields, and earnings per share. Be prepared to give a brief description to the class of your observations.

GLOBAL DECISION

A1   C3

Samsung

BTN 11-9   Financial information for **Samsung** (**www.Samsung.com**) follows (drawn from its financial statements and footnotes):

Net income less dividends available to preferred shares (in millions)	₩ 22,686,627
Cash dividends declared for common stock (in millions).	₩ 2,604,100
Cash dividends declared per common share	₩ 20,000
Number of common shares outstanding (in millions)*.	130.205
Weighted average common shares outstanding (in millions)	148.177
Equity applicable to common shares (in millions)†	₩167,968,721

* Computed as 147.299 mil. issued shares less 17.095 mil. treasury shares.
† Computed as ₩168,088,188 total equity less ₩119,467 preferred stock.

Required

1. Compute book value per share for Samsung.
2. Compute earnings per share (EPS) for Samsung.
3. Compare Samsung's dividends per share with its EPS. Is Samsung paying out a large or small amount of its income as dividends? Explain.

ANSWERS TO MULTIPLE CHOICE QUIZ

1. e; Entry to record this stock issuance is:

Cash (6,000 × $8)	48,000	
Common Stock (6,000 × $5)		30,000
Paid-In Capital in Excess of Par Value, Common Stock		18,000

2. b; $75,000/19,000 shares = $3.95 per share

3. d; Preferred stock = 5,000 × $100 = $500,000
   Book value per share = ($2,000,000 − $500,000)/50,000 shares = $30 per common share

4. a; $0.81/$45.00 = 1.8%

5. c; Earnings per share = $3,500,000/700,000 shares = $5 per share; PE ratio = $85/$5 = 17.0

12 chapter

Reporting and Analyzing Cash Flows

Chapter Preview

BASICS OF CASH FLOW REPORTING	CASH FLOWS FROM OPERATING	CASH FLOWS FROM INVESTING	CASH FLOWS FROM FINANCING
C1 Purpose, measurement, and classification	**P2** Indirect and direct methods of reporting	**P3** Three-stage process of analysis	**P3** Three-stage process of analysis
Noncash activities	Illustration of indirect method	Analyzing noncurrent assets	Analyzing noncurrent liabilities
P1 Format and preparation	Summary of indirect method adjustments	Analyzing other assets	Analyzing equity
			Overall summary using T-accounts
			A1 Analyzing cash

Learning Objectives

CONCEPTUAL

C1 Distinguish between operating, investing, and financing activities, and describe how noncash investing and financing activities are disclosed.

ANALYTICAL

A1 Analyze the statement of cash flows and apply the cash flow on total assets ratio.

PROCEDURAL

P1 Prepare a statement of cash flows.

P2 Compute cash flows from operating activities using the indirect method.

P3 Determine cash flows from both investing and financing activities.

P4 *Appendix 12A*—Illustrate use of a spreadsheet to prepare a statement of cash flows.

P5 *Appendix 12B*—Compute cash flows from operating activities using the direct method.

Watching Amazon Flows

"Your margin is my opportunity" — JEFF BEZOS

SEATTLE—Market gurus warn us of companies with losses and rising debt. One of those companies, however, is **Amazon.com** (**Amazon.com**), the largest U.S. Internet retailer. Jeff Bezos, founder and CEO of Amazon, started the company in his garage. "The first initial start-up capital for Amazon.com came primarily from my parents, and they invested a large fraction of their life savings," recalls Jeff. "My dad's first question was, 'What's the Internet?' . . . He wasn't making a bet on this company or this concept. He was making a bet on his son."

Jeff has grown Amazon from an online bookstore into one of the world's largest online retail stores to compete with the likes of **Walmart** and **Target**. Amazon's income and liabilities for the past four years follow:

($ millions)	2011	2012	2013	2014
Net income ..	$ 631	$ (39)	$ 274	$ (241)
Liabilities	17,521	24,363	30,413	43,764

Interestingly, while Amazon reports negative income and rising debt, the market sees the company in a positive light. Financial publications such as *Forbes* named Amazon the 6th "Most Innovative Company in the World" and ranked it as the 13th "World's Most Valuable Brand." The following graphic

Amazon.com, Inc.
NASDAQ: AMZN

$200 bil. valuation
$89 bil. annual sales
250 mil. product offerings

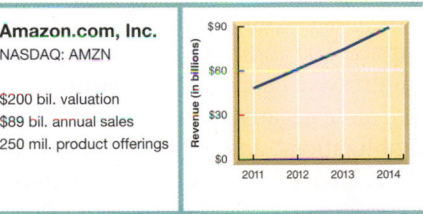

depicts its rising market assessment over the past four years.

Given Amazon's losses and debt levels, is the market failing to incorporate this? Is there something else that the market is focusing on?

Let's dig a bit deeper. Amazon's financial statements reveal rising sales, nearly doubling over the past four years. Although costs exceed sales in two of the recent four years, the growth in revenues foretells a positive future. Further, Amazon has pursued sizeable investments in research and development—to the tune of $9 billion in 2014 alone, which could yield large future

payoffs. Finally, there are its cash flows, which are depicted here:

($ millions)	2011	2012	2013	2014
Operating CF..	$ 3,903	$ 4,180	$ 5,475	$ 6,842
Investing CF...	(1,930)	(3,595)	(4,276)	(5,065)
Financing CF...	(482)	2,259	(539)	4,432

A key here is its operating cash flows, which have increased 75% over the past four years . . . an impressive trend! In addition, its large investing cash outflows are what we expect from a growth company. Also, its relatively small financing cash inflows suggest that much of its expansion is self-funded (a positive finding).

It is clear that analysis of Amazon requires examination and interpretation of its cash flows. Moreover, while there is risk in investing in a company with high research and development outlays, the market often sees such outlays as a precursor to sales and income growth. While only the future can reveal the success or failure of such cash outlays, it is clear that the market utilizes cash flow numbers in predicting the future and for stock valuation. "We earn trust with customers over time," insists Jeff. "And that actually does maximize free cash flow over the long term."

Sources: *Amazon website,* January 2016; *GreenBiz,* August 2014; *Bloomberg,* January 2013; *Wall Street Journal,* October 2011; *Biography.com,* January 2016; *Fundable,* June 2015; *Inc.com,* May 2014

535

BASICS OF CASH FLOW REPORTING

This section describes the basics of cash flow reporting, including its purpose, measurement, classification, format, and preparation.

Purpose of the Statement of Cash Flows

The purpose of the **statement of cash flows** is to report cash receipts (inflows) and cash payments (outflows) during a period. This includes separately identifying the cash flows related to operating, investing, and financing activities. It is the detailed disclosure of individual sources and uses of cash that makes this statement useful to users. Information in this statement helps users answer questions such as these:

Point: Internal users rely on the statement of cash flows to make investing and financing decisions. External users rely on this statement to assess the amount and timing of a company's cash flows.

- What explains the change in the cash balance?
- Where does a company spend its cash?
- How does a company receive its cash?
- Why do income and cash flows differ?
- How much is paid in dividends?
- Is there a cash shortage?

Importance of Cash Flows

Information about cash flows can influence decision makers in important ways. For instance, we look more favorably at a company that is financing its expenditures with cash from operations than one that does it by selling its assets. Information about cash flows helps users decide whether a company has enough cash to pay its existing debts as they mature. It is also relied upon to evaluate a company's ability to meet unexpected obligations and pursue unexpected opportunities. External information users, especially, want to assess a company's ability to take advantage of new business opportunities. Internal users such as managers use cash flow information to plan day-to-day operating activities and make long-term investment decisions.

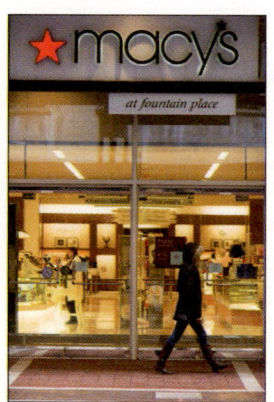

Bloomberg via Getty Images

Macy's striking turnaround is an example of how analysis and management of cash flows can lead to improved financial stability. Several years ago Macy's obtained temporary protection from bankruptcy. The company desperately needed to improve its cash flows, and it did so by engaging in aggressive cost-cutting measures. As a result, Macy's annual cash flow rose to $210 million, up from a negative cash flow of $38.9 million in the prior year. Macy's eventually met its financial obligations, and today its annual operating cash flow is $2,709 million.

The case of **W. T. Grant Co.** is a classic example of the importance of cash flow information in predicting a company's future performance and financial strength. Grant reported net income of more than $40 million per year for three consecutive years. At that same time, it was experiencing an alarming decrease in cash from its operations. For instance, net cash outflow was more than $90 million by the end of that three-year period. Grant soon went bankrupt. Users who relied solely on Grant's income numbers were unpleasantly surprised. This reminds us that cash flows as well as income statement and balance sheet information are crucial in business decisions.

🟨 Decision Insight

Know Cash Flows   "A lender must have a complete understanding of a borrower's cash flows to assess both the borrowing needs and repayment sources. This requires information about the major types of cash inflows and outflows. I have seen many companies, whose financial statements indicate good profitability, experience severe financial problems because the owners or managers lacked a good understanding of cash flows."—Mary E. Garza, **Bank of America** ■

Measurement of Cash Flows

Cash Equivalents

Cash flows are defined to include both *cash* and *cash equivalents*. The statement of cash flows explains the difference between the beginning and ending balances of cash and cash equivalents. We continue to use the phrases *cash flows* and the *statement of cash flows*, but remember that both phrases refer to cash *and* cash equivalents.

Recall that a cash equivalent must satisfy two criteria: (1) be readily convertible to a known amount of cash and (2) be sufficiently close to its maturity so its market value is unaffected by interest rate changes. In most cases, a debt security must be within three months of its maturity to satisfy these criteria. Companies must disclose and follow a clear policy for determining cash and cash equivalents and apply it consistently from period to period. **American Express**, for example, defines its cash equivalents as including "highly liquid investments with original maturities of 90 days or less."

Classification of Cash Flows

C1

Distinguish between operating, investing, and financing activities, and describe how noncash investing and financing activities are disclosed.

Since cash and cash equivalents are combined, the statement of cash flows does not report transactions *between* cash and cash equivalents, such as cash paid to purchase cash equivalents and cash received from selling cash equivalents. However, all other cash receipts and cash payments are classified and reported on the statement in one of three categories—operating, investing, or financing activities. Individual cash receipts and payments for each of these three categories are labeled to identify their originating transactions or events. A net cash inflow (source) occurs when the receipts in a category exceed the payments. A net cash outflow (use) occurs when the payments in a category exceed the receipts.

Operating Activities   **Operating activities** include those transactions and events that determine net income. Examples are the production and purchase of inventory, the sale of goods and services to customers, and the expenditures to operate the business. Not all items in income, such as unusual gains and losses, are operating activities (we discuss these exceptions later). Exhibit 12.1 lists the more common cash inflows and outflows from operating activities.

EXHIBIT 12.1

Cash Flows from Operating Activities

Investing Activities   **Investing activities** generally include those transactions and events that affect long-term assets—namely, the purchase and sale of long-term assets. They also include (1) the purchase and sale of short-term investments in the securities of other entities, *except* trading securities, and (2) lending and collecting money for notes receivable. Exhibit 12.2 lists examples of cash flows from investing activities. Cash from collecting the principal amounts of notes that result from a loan to another party are classified as investing. However, the FASB requires that the collection of interest on notes be reported as an operating activity; also, if a note results from sales to customers, it is classified as operating.

Point: FASB requires that *cash dividends received* and *cash interest received* be reported as operating activities.

EXHIBIT 12.2

Cash Flows from Investing Activities

Financing Activities   **Financing activities** include those transactions and events that affect long-term liabilities and equity. Examples are (1) obtaining cash from issuing debt and repaying the amounts borrowed and (2) receiving cash from or distributing cash to owners. These activities involve transactions with a company's owners and creditors. They also involve borrowing and repaying principal amounts relating to both short- and long-term debt. GAAP requires that payments of interest expense be classified as operating activities. Exhibit 12.3 lists examples of cash flows from financing activities.

EXHIBIT 12.3

Cash Flows from
Financing Activities

Link between Classification of Cash Flows and the Balance Sheet   Operating, investing, and financing activities are loosely linked to different parts of the balance sheet. Operating activities are affected by changes in current assets and current liabilities (and the income statement). Investing activities are affected by changes in long-term assets. Financing activities are affected by changes in long-term liabilities and equity. These links are depicted in Exhibit 12.4. Exceptions to these links are (1) current assets *unrelated* to operations, which are then treated as investing, and (2) current liabilities *unrelated* to operations, which are then treated as financing. Examples of the first exception are short-term notes receivable from noncustomers and marketable (not trading) securities, which are considered investing transactions. Examples of the second exception are short-term notes payable and dividends payable, which are considered financing transactions.

EXHIBIT 12.4

Linkage of Cash Flow
Classifications to the
Balance Sheet

Fraud

Where in the Statement Are Cash Flows? Cash flows can be delayed or accelerated at the end of a period to improve or reduce current period cash flows. Also, cash flows can be misclassified. Cash outflows reported under operating activities are interpreted as expense payments. However, cash outflows reported under investing activities are interpreted as a positive sign of growth potential. Thus, managers face incentives to misclassify cash flows. For these reasons, cash flow reporting warrants scrutiny.

Noncash Investing and Financing

Some important investing and financing activities do not affect cash receipts or payments. One example of such a transaction is the purchase of long-term assets using a long-term note payable (loan). This transaction involves both investing and financing activities but does not affect any (immediate) cash inflow or outflow, so it is not reported in any of the three sections of the statement of cash flows. Such transactions are reported at the bottom of the statement of cash flows or in a note to the statement because of their importance and the *full-disclosure principle.* Exhibit 12.5 lists transactions commonly disclosed as noncash investing and financing activities.

- Retirement of debt by issuing equity stock.
- Conversion of preferred stock to common stock.
- Lease of assets in a capital lease transaction.
- Purchase of long-term assets by issuing a note or bond.
- Exchange of noncash assets for other noncash assets.
- Purchase of noncash assets by issuing equity or debt.

EXHIBIT 12.5

Examples of Noncash Investing and Financing Activities

Format of the Statement of Cash Flows

A statement of cash flows must report information about a company's cash receipts and cash payments during the period. Exhibit 12.6 shows the usual format. A company must report cash flows from three activities: operating, investing, and financing. The statement then shows the net increase or decrease from those activities. Finally, it explains how transactions and events impact the prior period-end cash balance to produce its current period-end balance. Any non-cash investing and financing transactions are disclosed in a note disclosure or separate schedule.

P1_____

Prepare a statement of cash flows.

EXHIBIT 12.6

Format of the Statement of Cash Flows

COMPANY NAME
Statement of Cash Flows
For *period* Ended *date*

Cash flows from operating activities
  [Compute operating cash flows using indirect or direct method]
  Net cash provided (used) by operating activities . . . . $ #
Cash flows from investing activities
  [List of individual inflows and outflows]
  Net cash provided (used) by investing activities . . . . #
Cash flows from financing activities
  [List of individual inflows and outflows]
  Net cash provided (used) by financing activities . . . . #
Net increase (decrease) in cash. . . . . $ #
Cash (and equivalents) balance at prior period-end . . . . #
Cash (and equivalents) balance at current period-end . . . . $ #

Separate schedule or note disclosure of any noncash investing and financing transactions is required.

Point: Positive cash flows for a section are titled net cash "provided by" or "from." Negative cash flows are labeled as net cash "used by."

■ Decision Maker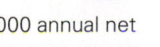

Entrepreneur You are considering purchasing a start-up business that recently reported a $110,000 annual net loss and a $225,000 annual net cash inflow. How are these results possible? ■ [Answers follow the chapter's Summary.]

Preparing the Statement of Cash Flows

Preparing a statement of cash flows involves the following five steps, as also shown in Exhibit 12.7.

1. Compute the net increase or decrease in cash.
2. Compute and report the net cash provided or used by operating activities (using either the direct or indirect method; both are explained).
3. Compute and report the net cash provided or used by investing activities.
4. Compute and report the net cash provided or used by financing activities.
5. Compute the net cash flow by combining net cash provided or used by operating, investing, and financing activities, and then *prove it* by adding it to the beginning cash balance to show that it equals the ending cash balance.

Point: View the change in cash as a *target* number (or check figure) that we will fully explain and prove in the statement of cash flows.

EXHIBIT 12.7

Five Steps in Preparing the
Statement of Cash Flows

Step 1 Compute net increase or decrease in cash.

Step 2 Compute net cash from operating activities.

Step 3 Compute net cash from investing activities.

Step 4 Compute net cash from financing activities.

Step 5 Prove and report beginning and ending cash balances.

Computing the net increase or net decrease in cash is a simple but crucial computation. It equals the current period's cash balance minus the prior period's cash balance. This is the *bottom-line* figure for the statement of cash flows and is a check on accuracy.

Analyzing the Cash Account   A company's cash receipts and cash payments are recorded in the Cash account in its general ledger. The Cash account is therefore a natural place to look for information about cash flows from operating, investing, and financing activities. To illustrate, see the summarized Cash T-account of Genesis, Inc., in Exhibit 12.8. The Cash account increased $5,000, from $12,000 to $17,000. Individual cash transactions are summarized in this Cash account according to the major types of cash receipts and cash payments. For instance, only the total of cash receipts from all customers is listed. Individual cash transactions underlying these totals can number in the thousands. Accounting software is available to provide summarized cash accounts.

EXHIBIT 12.8

Summarized Cash Account

Accounting System:
File   Edit   Maintain   Tasks   Analysis   Options   Reports   Window   Help

Cash			
Balance, Dec. 31, 2015	12,000		
Receipts from customers	570,000	Payments for inventory	319,000
Receipts from asset sales	2,000	Payments for wages and operating expenses	218,000
Receipts from stock issuance ..	15,000	Payments for interest	8,000
		Payments for taxes	5,000
		Payments for notes retirement	18,000
		Payments for dividends	14,000
Balance, Dec. 31, 2016	17,000		

Sales   Purchases   General Ledger   Payroll   Inventory   Company   Analysis

The statement of cash flows summarizes and classifies the transactions that led to the $5,000 increase in the Cash account. Preparing a statement of cash flows from Exhibit 12.8 requires determining whether an individual cash inflow or outflow is an operating, investing, or financing activity, and then listing each by activity. However, preparing the statement of cash flows from an analysis of the summarized Cash account has two limitations. First, most companies have many individual cash receipts and payments, making it difficult to review them all. Accounting software minimizes this burden, but it is still a task requiring professional judgment for many transactions. Second, the Cash account does not usually carry an adequate description of each cash transaction, making assignment of all cash transactions according to activity difficult. (We return to this approach in Exhibit 12.14.)

Analyzing Noncash Accounts   A second approach to preparing the statement of cash flows is analyzing noncash accounts. This approach uses the fact that when a company records cash inflows and outflows with debits and credits to the Cash account (see Exhibit 12.8), it also records credits and debits in noncash accounts (reflecting double-entry accounting). Many of these noncash accounts are balance sheet accounts—for instance, from the sale of land for cash. Others are revenue and expense accounts that are closed to equity. For instance, the sale of services for cash yields a credit to Services Revenue that is closed to Retained Earnings for a corporation. In sum, *all cash transactions eventually affect noncash balance sheet accounts*. Thus, we can determine cash inflows and outflows by analyzing changes in noncash balance sheet accounts.

Exhibit 12.9 uses the accounting equation to show the relation between the Cash account and the noncash balance sheet accounts. This exhibit starts with the accounting equation (at the top). It is then expanded in line (2) to separate cash from noncash asset accounts. To isolate cash on one side of the equation, line (3) shows noncash asset accounts being subtracted from both sides of the equation. Cash now equals the sum of the liability and equity accounts *minus* the noncash asset accounts. Line (4) points out that *changes* on one side of the accounting equation equal *changes* on the other side. It shows that we can explain changes in cash by analyzing changes in the noncash accounts consisting of liability accounts, equity accounts, and noncash asset accounts. By analyzing noncash balance sheet accounts and any related income statement accounts, we can prepare a statement of cash flows.

EXHIBIT 12.9

Relation between Cash and Noncash Accounts

Information to Prepare the Statement   Information to prepare the statement of cash flows usually comes from three sources: (1) comparative balance sheets, (2) the current income statement, and (3) additional information. Comparative balance sheets are used to compute changes in noncash accounts from the beginning to the end of the period. The current income statement is used to help compute cash flows from operating activities. Additional information often includes details on transactions and events that help explain both the cash flows and noncash investing and financing activities.

CASH FLOWS FROM OPERATING

Indirect and Direct Methods of Reporting

Cash flows provided (used) by operating activities are reported in one of two ways: the *direct method* or the *indirect method*. **These two different methods apply only to the operating activities section**.

The **direct method** separately lists each major item of operating cash receipts (such as cash received from customers) and each major item of operating cash payments (such as cash paid for inventory). The cash payments are subtracted from cash receipts to determine the net cash provided (used) by operating activities.

The **indirect method** reports net income and then adjusts it for items necessary to obtain net cash provided or used by operating activities. It does *not* report individual items of cash inflows and cash outflows from operating activities. Instead, the indirect method reports the necessary adjustments to reconcile net income to net cash provided or used by operating activities. **The net cash amount provided by operating activities is *identical* under both the direct and indirect methods.** This equality always exists. The difference in these methods is with the computation and presentation of this amount. The FASB recommends the direct method, but because it is not required and the indirect method is arguably easier to compute, nearly all companies report operating cash flows using the indirect method.

To illustrate, we prepare the operating activities section of the statement of cash flows for Genesis. Exhibit 12.10 shows the December 31, 2015 and 2016, balance sheets of Genesis along with its 2016 income statement. We use this information to prepare a statement of cash flows that explains the $5,000 increase in cash for 2016 as highlighted in its balance sheets. This $5,000 is computed as Cash of $17,000 at the end of 2016 minus Cash of $12,000 at the end of 2015.

EXHIBIT 12.10

Financial Statements

GENESIS Income Statement For Year Ended December 31, 2016		
Sales.........................		$590,000
Cost of goods sold.............	$300,000	
Wages and other operating expenses...........	216,000	
Interest expense..............	7,000	
Depreciation expense...........	24,000	(547,000)
		43,000
Other gains (losses)		
Loss on sale of plant assets.....	(6,000)	
Gain on retirement of notes ...	16,000	10,000
Income before taxes............		53,000
Income taxes expense..........		(15,000)
Net income...................		$ 38,000

GENESIS Balance Sheets December 31, 2016 and 2015			
	2016	**2015**	**Change**
Assets			
Current assets			
Cash.....................	$ 17,000	$ 12,000	$ 5,000 Increase
Accounts receivable	60,000	40,000	20,000 Increase
Inventory.................	84,000	70,000	14,000 Increase
Prepaid expenses...........	6,000	4,000	2,000 Increase
Total current assets.........	167,000	126,000	
Long-term assets			
Plant assets	250,000	210,000	40,000 Increase
Accumulated depreciation...	(60,000)	(48,000)	12,000 Increase
Total assets	$357,000	$288,000	
Liabilities			
Current liabilities			
Accounts payable...........	$ 35,000	$ 40,000	$ 5,000 Decrease
Interest payable............	3,000	4,000	1,000 Decrease
Income taxes payable	22,000	12,000	10,000 Increase
Total current liabilities.......	60,000	56,000	
Long-term notes payable.......	90,000	64,000	26,000 Increase
Total liabilities	150,000	120,000	
Equity			
Common stock, $5 par........	95,000	80,000	15,000 Increase
Retained earnings	112,000	88,000	24,000 Increase
Total equity	207,000	168,000	
Total liabilities and equity	$357,000	$288,000	

Additional information for 2016

a. The accounts payable balances result from inventory purchases.

b. Purchased $60,000 in plant assets by issuing $60,000 of notes payable.

c. Sold plant assets with a book value of $8,000 (original cost of $20,000 and accumulated depreciation of $12,000) for $2,000 cash, yielding a $6,000 loss.

d. Received $15,000 cash from issuing 3,000 shares of common stock.

e. Paid $18,000 cash to retire notes with a $34,000 book value, yielding a $16,000 gain.

f. Declared and paid cash dividends of $14,000.

The next section describes the indirect method. Appendix 12B describes the direct method. An instructor can choose to cover either one or both methods. Neither section depends on the other. If the indirect method is skipped, then read Appendix 12B and return to the section titled "Cash Flows from Investing."

Applying the Indirect Method of Reporting

Net income is computed using accrual accounting, which recognizes revenues when earned and expenses when incurred. Revenues and expenses do not necessarily reflect the receipt and payment of cash. The indirect method of computing and reporting net cash flows from operating activities involves adjusting the net income figure to obtain the net cash provided or used by operating activities. This includes subtracting noncash increases from net income and adding noncash charges back to net income.

To illustrate, the indirect method begins with Genesis's net income of $38,000 and adjusts it to obtain net cash provided by operating activities of $20,000. Exhibit 12.11 shows the results of the indirect method of reporting operating cash flows, which adjusts net income for two types of adjustments. There are ① adjustments to income statement items that neither provide nor use cash and ② adjustments to reflect changes in balance sheet current assets and current liabilities (linked to operating activities). This section describes each of these adjustments.

P2

Compute cash flows from operating activities using the indirect method.

GENESIS		
Statement of Cash Flows—Operating Section under Indirect Method		
For Year Ended December 31, 2016		
Cash flows from operating activities		
Net income	$ 38,000	
Adjustments to reconcile net income to net cash provided by operating activities		
Income statement items not affecting cash		
① Depreciation expense	24,000	
Loss on sale of plant assets	6,000	
Gain on retirement of notes	(16,000)	
Changes in current assets and liabilities		
Increase in accounts receivable	(20,000)	
Increase in inventory	(14,000)	
② Increase in prepaid expenses	(2,000)	
Decrease in accounts payable	(5,000)	
Decrease in interest payable	(1,000)	
Increase in income taxes payable	10,000	
Net cash provided by operating activities		**$20,000**

EXHIBIT 12.11

Operating Activities Section—Indirect Method

① **Adjustments for Income Statement Items Not Affecting Cash**   The income statement usually includes some expenses and losses that do not reflect cash outflows. Examples are depreciation, amortization, depletion, bad debts expense, loss from an asset sale, and loss from retirement of notes payable. When there are expenses and losses that do not reflect cash outflows, the indirect method for reporting operating cash flows requires the following adjustment:

Expenses and losses with no cash outflows are added back to net income.

To see the logic of this adjustment, recall that items such as depreciation, amortization, and depletion have *no* cash effect, and adding them back cancels their deductions. To see the logic for losses, consider that items such as a plant asset sale and a notes retirement are usually recorded by recognizing the cash, removing all plant asset or notes accounts, and recording any loss or gain. The cash received or paid is part of either investing or financing cash flows. Because *no* operating cash flow effect occurs, we add it back to net income to reverse the deduction.

Similarly, when net income includes revenues that do not reflect cash inflows, the indirect method for reporting operating cash flows requires the following adjustment:

Revenues and gains with no cash inflows are subtracted from net income.

We apply these adjustments to the income statement items in Exhibit 12.10 that do not affect cash.

Depreciation   Depreciation expense is Genesis's only operating item that has no effect on cash flows. We must add back the $24,000 depreciation expense to net income when computing cash

Point: An income statement reports revenues, gains, expenses, and losses on an accrual basis. The statement of cash flows reports cash received and cash paid for operating, financing, and investing activities.

provided by operating activities. Adding it back cancels the expense. (We later explain that any cash outflow to acquire a plant asset is reported as an investing activity.)

Loss on Sale of Plant Assets   Genesis reports a $6,000 loss on sale of plant assets as part of net income. This loss is a proper deduction in computing income, but it is *not part of operating activities*. Instead, a sale of plant assets is part of investing activities. Thus, the $6,000 nonoperating loss is added back to net income (see Exhibit 12.11). Adding it back cancels the loss. We later explain how to report the cash inflow from the asset sale in investing activities.

Gain on Retirement of Debt   A $16,000 gain on retirement of debt is properly included in net income, but it is *not part of operating activities*. This means the $16,000 nonoperating gain must be subtracted from net income to obtain net cash provided by operating activities (see Exhibit 12.11). Subtracting it cancels the recorded gain. We later describe how to report the cash outflow to retire debt.

These three adjustments to net income for "items not affecting cash" are shown as follows in the operating section:

Net income	$ 38,000
Adjustments to reconcile net income to net cash provided by operating activities	
Income statement items not affecting cash	
Depreciation expense	24,000
Loss on sale of plant assets	6,000
Gain on retirement of notes	(16,000)

② **Adjustments for Changes in Current Assets and Current Liabilities**   This section describes adjustments for changes in current assets and current liabilities.

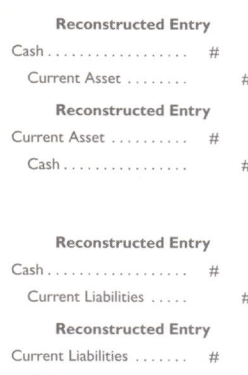

Adjustments for Changes in Current Assets   Decreases in current assets require the following adjustment:

> **Decreases in current assets are added to net income.**

Increases in current assets require the following adjustment:

> **Increases in current assets are subtracted from net income.**

Adjustments for Changes in Current Liabilities   Increases in current liabilities require the following adjustment to net income when computing operating cash flows:

> **Increases in current liabilities are added to net income.**

Conversely, when current liabilities decrease, the following adjustment is required:

> **Decreases in current liabilities are subtracted from net income.**

To illustrate, we apply these adjustment rules to the three noncash current assets and three current liabilities in Exhibit 12.10, which are then reported as follows in the operating section:

Net income	$ 38,000
Adjustments to reconcile net income to net cash provided by operating activities	
Increase in accounts receivable	(20,000)
Increase in inventory	(14,000)
Increase in prepaid expenses	(2,000)
Decrease in accounts payable	(5,000)
Decrease in interest payable	(1,000)
Increase in income taxes payable	10,000

Following is an explanation, including T-account analysis, for how these adjustments result in cash receipts and cash payments.

Accounts receivable. Following the rule above, the $20,000 increase in the current asset of accounts receivable is subtracted from income. This increase implies that Genesis collects less cash than is reported in sales. To see this it is helpful to use *account analysis*. This involves setting up a T-account and reconstructing its major entries to compute cash receipts or payments as follows.

	Accounts Receivable			
Bal., Dec. 31, 2015	40,000			
Sales	590,000	**Cash receipts =**	**570,000**	
Bal., Dec. 31, 2016	60,000			

Numbers in black are taken from Exhibit 12.10. The red number is the computed (plug) figure.

We see that sales are $20,000 greater than cash receipts. This $20,000—reflected in the increase in Accounts Receivable—is subtracted from net income when computing cash provided by operating activities.

Inventory. The $14,000 increase in inventory is subtracted from income. This increase implies that Genesis had greater cash purchases than cost of goods sold, as reflected in the following account analysis:

	Inventory		
Bal., Dec. 31, 2015	70,000		
Purchases =	**314,000**	Cost of goods sold	300,000
Bal., Dec. 31, 2016	84,000		

Prepaid expenses. The $2,000 increase in prepaid expenses is subtracted from income, implying that Genesis's cash payments exceed its recorded prepaid expenses and is reflected in the following T-account:

	Prepaid Expenses		
Bal., Dec. 31, 2015	4,000		
Cash payments =	**218,000**	Wages and other operating exp.	216,000
Bal., Dec. 31, 2016	6,000		

Accounts payable. The $5,000 decrease in the current liability for accounts payable is subtracted from income. This decrease implies that cash payments to suppliers exceed purchases, which is reflected in the following T-account:

	Accounts Payable		
		Bal., Dec. 31, 2015	40,000
Cash payments =	**319,000**	Purchases	314,000
		Bal., Dec. 31, 2016	35,000

Interest payable. The $1,000 decrease in interest payable is subtracted from income. This decrease indicates that cash paid for interest exceeds interest expense, which is reflected in the following T-account:

	Interest Payable		
		Bal., Dec. 31, 2015	4,000
Cash paid for interest =	**8,000**	Interest expense	7,000
		Bal., Dec. 31, 2016	3,000

Point: Operating activities are typically those that determine income, which are often reflected in changes in current assets and current liabilities.

Income taxes payable. The $10,000 increase in income taxes payable is added to income. This increase implies that reported income taxes exceed the cash paid for taxes, which is reflected in the following T-account:

Income Taxes Payable			
		Bal., Dec. 31, 2015	12,000
Cash paid for taxes =	**5,000**	Income taxes expense	15,000
		Bal., Dec. 31, 2016	22,000

Summary Adjustments for Operating Activities—Indirect Method

Exhibit 12.12 summarizes the adjustments to net income when computing net cash provided or used by operating activities under the indirect method.

EXHIBIT 12.12

Summary of Adjustments for Operating Activities— Indirect Method

---

Net Income (or Loss)

① Adjustments for operating items not providing or using cash

    + Noncash expenses and losses

       Examples: Expenses for depreciation, depletion, and amortization; losses from disposal of long-term assets and from retirement of debt

    − Noncash revenues and gains

       Examples: Earnings from equity-method investments; gains from disposal of long-term assets and from retirement of debt

② Adjustments for changes in current assets and current liabilities

    + Decrease in noncash current operating asset

    − Increase in noncash current operating asset

    + Increase in current operating liability

    − Decrease in current operating liability

Net cash provided (used) by operating activities

■ Decision **Insight**

How Much Cash in Income?   The difference between net income and operating cash flows can be large and sometimes reflects on the quality of earnings. This bar chart shows the net income and operating cash flows of three companies. Operating cash flows can be either higher or lower than net income. ■

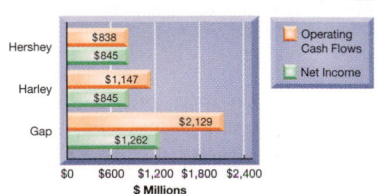

NEED-TO-KNOW 12-2

Reporting Operating Cash Flows (Indirect)

P2

A company's current-year income statement and selected balance sheet data at December 31 of the current and prior years follow. Prepare the cash flows from operating activities section only of its statement of cash flows using the indirect method for the current year.

Income Statement For Current Year Ended December 31	
Sales revenue	$120
Expenses	
Cost of goods sold.	50
Depreciation expense	30
Salaries expense.	17
Interest expense.	3
Net income	$ 20

Selected Balance Sheet Accounts		
At December 31	Current Yr	Prior Yr
Accounts receivable.	$12	$10
Inventory	6	9
Accounts payable.	7	11
Salaries payable.	8	3
Interest payable	1	0

Solution

Cash Flows from Operating Activities—Indirect Method For Current Year Ended December 31		
Cash flows from operating activities		
Net income		$20
Adjustments to reconcile net income to net cash provided by operating activities		
Income statement items not affecting cash		
Depreciation expense	$30	
Changes in current assets and current liabilities		
Increase in accounts receivable	(2)	
Decrease in inventory	3	
Decrease in accounts payable	(4)	
Increase in salaries payable	5	
Increase in interest payable	1	33
Net cash provided by operating activities		$53

> **Do More:** QS 12-3, QS 12-4,
> E 12-4, E 12-5, E 12-6

CASH FLOWS FROM INVESTING

The third major step in preparing the statement of cash flows is to compute and report cash flows from investing activities. We normally do this by identifying changes in (1) all noncurrent asset accounts and (2) the current accounts for both notes receivable and investments in securities (excluding trading securities). We then analyze changes in these accounts to determine their effect, if any, on cash and report the cash flow effects in the investing activities section of the statement of cash flows. **Reporting of investing activities is identical under the direct method and indirect method**.

Three-Stage Process of Analysis

Information to compute cash flows from investing activities is usually taken from beginning and ending balance sheets and the income statement. We use a three-stage process to determine cash provided or used by investing activities: (1) identify changes in investing-related accounts, (2) explain these changes using reconstruction analysis, and (3) report their cash flow effects.

P3_____

Determine cash flows from both investing and financing activities.

Analyzing Noncurrent Assets

Information about the Genesis transactions provided earlier reveals that the company both purchased and sold plant assets during the period. Both transactions are investing activities and are analyzed for their cash flow effects in this section.

Plant Asset Transactions   The *first stage* in analyzing the Plant Assets account and its related Accumulated Depreciation account is to identify any changes in these accounts from comparative balance sheets in Exhibit 12.10. This analysis reveals a $40,000 increase in plant assets from $210,000 to $250,000 and a $12,000 increase in accumulated depreciation from $48,000 to $60,000.

The *second stage* is to explain these changes. Items *b* and *c* of the additional information in Exhibit 12.10 affect plant assets. Recall that the Plant Assets account is affected by both asset purchases and sales; its Accumulated Depreciation account is normally increased from depreciation and decreased from the removal of accumulated depreciation in asset sales. To explain changes in these accounts and to identify their cash flow effects, we prepare *reconstructed entries* from prior transactions; *they are not the actual entries by the preparer*.

Point: Investing activities include (1) purchasing and selling long-term assets, (2) lending and collecting on notes receivable, and (3) purchasing and selling short-term investments other than cash equivalents and trading securities.

Point: Financing and investing info are available in ledger accounts to help explain changes in comparative balance sheets. Post references lead to relevant entries and explanations.

To illustrate, item *b* reports that Genesis purchased plant assets of $60,000 by issuing $60,000 in notes payable to the seller. The reconstructed entry for analysis of item *b* follows.

Reconstruction	Plant Assets	60,000	
	Notes Payable.		60,000

Next, item *c* reports that Genesis sold plant assets costing $20,000 (with $12,000 of accumulated depreciation) for $2,000 cash, resulting in a $6,000 loss. The reconstructed entry for analysis of item *c* follows.

Reconstruction	**Cash**.	**2,000**	
	Accumulated Depreciation	12,000	
	Loss on Sale of Plant Assets	6,000	
	Plant Assets		20,000

We also reconstruct the entry for Depreciation Expense from the income statement. Depreciation expense results in no cash flow effect.

Reconstruction	Depreciation Expense	24,000	
	Accumulated Depreciation		24,000

These three reconstructed entries are reflected in the following plant asset and related T-accounts.

Plant Assets				Accumulated Depreciation—Plant Assets			
Bal., Dec. 31, 2015	210,000					Bal., Dec. 31, 2015	48,000
Purchase	**60,000**	**Sale**	**20,000**	**Sale**	**12,000**	**Depr. expense**	**24,000**
Bal., Dec. 31, 2016	250,000					Bal., Dec. 31, 2016	60,000

Point: T-account analysis helps to reconstruct accounts and amounts.

This reconstruction analysis is complete in that the change in plant assets from $210,000 to $250,000 is fully explained by the $60,000 purchase and the $20,000 sale. Also, the change in accumulated depreciation from $48,000 to $60,000 is fully explained by depreciation expense of $24,000 and the removal of $12,000 in accumulated depreciation from the asset sale.

The *third stage* in analyzing the Plant Assets account looks back at the reconstructed entries to identify any cash flows. The identified cash flow effect is reported in the investing section of the statement as follows:

Cash flows from investing activities	
Cash received from sale of plant assets	$2,000

Example: If a plant asset costing $40,000 with $37,000 of accumulated depreciation is sold at a $1,000 loss, what is the cash flow? What is the cash flow if this asset is sold at a gain of $3,000?
Answers: +$2,000; +$6,000.

The $60,000 purchase described in item *b* and financed by issuing notes is a noncash investing and financing activity. It is reported in a note or in a separate schedule to the statement as follows:

Noncash investing and financing activity	
Purchased plant assets with issuance of notes	$60,000

Analyzing Additional Assets

Genesis did not have any additional noncurrent assets (or nonoperating current assets) and, therefore, we have no additional investing transactions to analyze. If other investing assets did exist, we would identify and report the investing cash flows using the same three-stage process illustrated for plant assets.

Use the following information to determine this company's cash flows from investing activities.

a. A factory with a book value of $100 and an original cost of $800 was sold at a loss of $10.

b. Paid $70 cash for new equipment.

c. Long-term stock investments were sold for $20 cash, yielding a loss of $4.

d. Sold land costing $175 for $160 cash, yielding a loss of $15.

Solution

Cash flows from investing activities	
Cash received from sale of factory*......................	$ 90
Cash paid for new equipment	(70)
Cash received from sale of long-term investments	20
Cash received from sale of land	160
Net cash provided by investing activities	$200

* Cash received from sale of factory = Book value − Loss = $100 − $10 = $90

NEED-TO-KNOW 12-3

Reporting Investing Cash Flows

P3

Do More: QS 12-5, QS 12-6, QS 12-8, E 12-7

CASH FLOWS FROM FINANCING

The fourth major step in preparing the statement of cash flows is to compute and report cash flows from financing activities. We normally do this by identifying changes in all noncurrent liability accounts (including the current portion of any notes and bonds) and the equity accounts. These accounts include long-term debt, notes payable, bonds payable, common stock, and retained earnings. Changes in these accounts are then analyzed using available information to determine their effect, if any, on cash. Results are reported in the financing activities section of the statement. **Reporting of financing activities is identical under the direct method and indirect method.**

Three-Stage Process of Analysis

We again use a three-stage process to determine cash provided or used by financing activities: (1) identify changes in financing-related accounts, (2) explain these changes using reconstruction analysis, and (3) report their cash flow effects.

Analyzing Noncurrent Liabilities

Information about Genesis provided earlier reveals two transactions involving noncurrent liabilities. We analyzed one of those, the $60,000 issuance of notes payable to purchase plant assets. This transaction is reported as a significant noncash investing and financing activity in a footnote or a separate schedule to the statement of cash flows. The other remaining transaction involving noncurrent liabilities is the cash retirement of notes payable.

Point: Financing activities generally refer to changes in the noncurrent liability and the equity accounts. Examples are (1) receiving cash from issuing debt or repaying amounts borrowed and (2) receiving cash from or distributing cash to owners.

Notes Payable Transactions   The *first stage* in analysis of notes is to review the comparative balance sheets from Exhibit 12.10. This analysis reveals an increase in notes payable from $64,000 to $90,000.

The *second stage* explains this change. Item *e* of the additional information in Exhibit 12.10 reports that notes with a carrying value of $34,000 are retired for $18,000 cash, resulting in a $16,000 gain. The reconstructed entry for analysis of item *e* follows:

Reconstruction	Notes Payable................................	34,000	
	Gain on retirement of debt		16,000
	Cash....................................		**18,000**

This entry reveals an $18,000 cash outflow for retirement of notes and a $16,000 gain from comparing the notes payable carrying value to the cash received. This gain does not reflect any cash inflow or outflow. Also, item *b* of the additional information reports that Genesis purchased plant assets costing $60,000 by issuing $60,000 in notes payable to the seller. We reconstructed this entry when analyzing investing activities: It showed a $60,000 increase to notes payable that is reported as a noncash investing and financing transaction. The Notes Payable account is explained by these reconstructed entries as follows:

		Notes Payable	
		Bal., Dec. 31, 2015	64,000
Retired notes	34,000	**Issued notes**	**60,000**
		Bal., Dec. 31, 2016	90,000

The *third stage* is to report the cash flow effect of the notes retirement in the financing section of the statement as follows:

Cash flows from financing activities	
Cash paid to retire notes..................	$(18,000)

Analyzing Equity

The Genesis information reveals two transactions involving equity accounts. The first is the issuance of common stock for cash. The second is the declaration and payment of cash dividends. We analyze both.

Common Stock Transactions   The *first stage* in analyzing common stock is to review the comparative balance sheets from Exhibit 12.10, which reveal an increase in common stock from $80,000 to $95,000.

The *second stage* explains this change. Item *d* of the additional information in Exhibit 12.10 reports that 3,000 shares of common stock are issued at par for $5 per share. The reconstructed entry for analysis of item *d* follows:

Reconstruction	Cash..	**15,000**	
	Common Stock		15,000

This entry reveals a $15,000 cash inflow from stock issuance and is reflected in (and explains) the Common Stock account as follows:

		Common Stock	
		Bal., Dec. 31, 2015	80,000
		Issued stock	**15,000**
		Bal., Dec. 31, 2016	95,000

The *third stage* discloses the cash flow effect from stock issuance in the financing section of the statement as follows:

Cash flows from financing activities	
Cash received from issuing stock	$15,000

Retained Earnings Transactions   The *first stage* in analyzing the Retained Earnings account is to review the comparative balance sheets from Exhibit 12.10. This reveals an increase in retained earnings from $88,000 to $112,000.

The *second stage* explains this change. Item *f* of the additional information in Exhibit 12.10 reports that cash dividends of $14,000 are paid. The reconstructed entry follows:

Reconstruction	Retained Earnings.............................	14,000	
	Cash..		**14,000**

This entry reveals a $14,000 cash outflow for cash dividends. Also see that the Retained Earnings account is impacted by net income of $38,000. (Net income was analyzed under the operating section of the statement of cash flows.) The reconstructed Retained Earnings account follows:

Retained Earnings			
		Bal., Dec. 31, 2015	88,000
Cash dividend	14,000	Net income	38,000
		Bal., Dec. 31, 2016	112,000

The *third stage* reports the cash flow effect from the cash dividend in the financing section of the statement as follows:

Cash flows from financing activities	
Cash paid for dividends	$(14,000)

Point: Financing activities not affecting cash flow include *declaration* of a cash dividend, *declaration* of a stock dividend, issuance of a stock dividend, and a stock split.

We now have identified and explained all of the Genesis cash inflows and cash outflows and one noncash investing and financing transaction.

Proving Cash Balances

The fifth and final step in preparing the statement is to report the beginning and ending cash balances and prove that the *net change in cash* is explained by operating, investing, and financing cash flows. This step is shown here for Genesis.

Net cash provided by operating activities	$ 20,000
Net cash provided by investing activities	2,000
Net cash used in financing activities	(17,000)
Net increase in cash	$ 5,000
Cash balance at 2015 year-end	12,000
Cash balance at 2016 year-end	$ 17,000

The preceding table shows that the $5,000 net increase in cash, from $12,000 at the beginning of the period to $17,000 at the end, is reconciled by net cash flows from operating ($20,000 inflow), investing ($2,000 inflow), and financing ($17,000 outflow) activities. This is formally reported at the bottom of the complete statement of cash flows as shown in Exhibit 12.13.

Global: There are no requirements to separate domestic and international cash flows, leading some users to ask, "Where in the world is cash flow?"

 Decision Maker

Reporter Management is in labor contract negotiations and grants you an interview. It highlights a recent $600,000 net loss that involves a $930,000 extraordinary loss and a total net cash outflow of $550,000 (which includes net cash outflows of $850,000 for investing activities and $350,000 for financing activities). What is your assessment of this company? ■ [Answers follow the chapter's Summary.]

EXHIBIT 12.13

Complete Statement of Cash Flows—Indirect Method

GENESIS Statement of Cash Flows For Year Ended December 31, 2016		
Cash flows from operating activities		
Net income		$ 38,000
Adjustments to reconcile net income to net cash provided by operating activities		
Income statement items not affecting cash		
Depreciation expense	24,000	
Loss on sale of plant assets	6,000	
Gain on retirement of notes	(16,000)	
Changes in current assets and liabilities		
Increase in accounts receivable	(20,000)	
Increase in inventory	(14,000)	
Increase in prepaid expenses..........................	(2,000)	
Decrease in accounts payable	(5,000)	
Decrease in interest payable	(1,000)	
Increase in income taxes payable	10,000	
Net cash provided by operating activities................		$20,000
Cash flows from investing activities		
Cash received from sale of plant assets	2,000	
Net cash provided by investing activities		2,000
Cash flows from financing activities		
Cash received from issuing stock	15,000	
Cash paid to retire notes..............................	(18,000)	
Cash paid for dividends	(14,000)	
Net cash used in financing activities		(17,000)
Net increase in cash...................................		$ 5,000
Cash balance at prior year-end		12,000
Cash balance at current year-end		$17,000

Point: Refer to Exhibit 12.10 and identify the $5,000 change in cash. This change is what the statement of cash flows explains; it serves as a check.

Point: The statement of cash flows is usually the last of the four required financial statements to be prepared.

NEED-TO-KNOW 12-4

Reporting Financing Cash Flows

P3

Use the following information to determine this company's cash flows from financing activities.

a. Issued common stock for $40 cash.

b. Paid $70 cash to retire a note payable at its $70 maturity value.

c. Paid cash dividend of $15.

d. Paid $5 cash to acquire its treasury stock.

Solution

Cash flows from financing activities	
Cash received from issuance of common stock	$ 40
Cash paid to settle note payable.......................	(70)
Cash paid for dividend	(15)
Cash paid to acquire treasury stock	(5)
Net cash used by financing activities	$(50)

Do More: QS 12-9, QS 12-10, QS 12-13, E 12-8

OVERALL SUMMARY USING T-ACCOUNTS

A statement of cash flows is prepared by analyzing changes in noncash balance sheet accounts. Exhibit 12.14 uses T-accounts to summarize how changes in Genesis's noncash balance sheet accounts affect its cash inflows and outflows (dollar amounts in thousands). The top of the exhibit shows the company's Cash T-account, and the lower part shows T-accounts for its remaining balance sheet accounts. We see that the $20,000 net cash provided by operating activities and the $5,000 net increase in cash shown in the Cash T-account agree with the same figures in the statement of cash flows in Exhibit 12.13.

We explain Exhibit 12.14 in five parts (amounts in $ thousands):

a. Entry (1) records $38 net income in the credit side of the Retained Earnings account and the debit side of the Cash account. This $38 net income in the Cash T-account is adjusted until it reflects the $5 net increase in cash.

b. Entries (2) through (4) add the $24 depreciation and $6 loss on asset sale to net income, and subtract the $16 gain on retirement of notes.

c. Entries (5) through (10) adjust net income for changes in current asset and current liability accounts.

d. Entry (11) records the noncash investing and financing transaction involving a $60 purchase of assets by issuing $60 of notes.

e. Entries (12) and (13) record the $15 stock issuance and the $14 dividend.

EXHIBIT 12.14

Balance Sheet T-Accounts to Explain the Change in Cash ($ thousands)

GLOBAL VIEW

The statement of cash flows, which explains changes in cash (including cash equivalents) from period to period, is required under both U.S. GAAP and IFRS. This section discusses similarities and differences between U.S. GAAP and IFRS in reporting that statement.

Samsung

Reporting Cash Flows from Operating   Both U.S. GAAP and IFRS permit the reporting of cash flows from operating activities using either the direct or indirect method. Basic requirements underlying the application of both methods are fairly consistent across U.S. GAAP and IFRS. Appendix A shows that Samsung reports its cash flows from operating activities using the indirect method, and in a manner similar to that explained in this chapter. Further, the definition of cash and cash equivalents is roughly similar for U.S. GAAP and IFRS.

There are some differences between U.S. GAAP and IFRS in reporting operating cash flows. We mention two of the more notable. First, U.S. GAAP requires that cash inflows from interest revenue and dividend revenue be classified as operating, whereas IFRS permits classification under operating or investing provided that this classification is consistently applied. Samsung reports its cash from interest received under operating, consistent with U.S. GAAP (no mention is made of any dividends received). Second, U.S. GAAP requires cash outflows for interest expense be classified as operating, whereas IFRS again permits classification under operating or financing provided that it is consistently applied. (Some believe that interest payments, like dividend payments, are better classified as financing because they represent payments to financiers.) Samsung reports cash outflows for interest under operating, which is consistent with U.S. GAAP and acceptable under IFRS.

Reporting Cash Flows from Investing and Financing   U.S. GAAP and IFRS are broadly similar in computing and classifying cash flows from investing and financing activities. A quick review of these two sections for Samsung's statement of cash flows shows a structure similar to that explained in this chapter. One notable exception is that U.S. GAAP requires that cash outflows for income tax be classified as operating, whereas IFRS permits the splitting of those cash flows among operating, investing, and financing depending on the sources of that tax. Samsung reports its cash outflows for income tax under operating, which is similar to U.S. GAAP.

Sustainability and Accounting   Amazon.com seeks to reduce its environmental impact through a number of sustainability initiatives. One is frustration-free packaging. This multiyear initiative is "designed

Manjunath Kiran/AFP/Getty Images

to make it easier for customers to liberate products from their packages." Not only does this initiative lead to higher customer satisfaction, it also reduces waste and the use of plastic. According to Amazon's website, the frustration-free packaging is "100% recyclable" and eliminates "hard plastic clamshell cases and plastic-coated ties." Moreover, Amazon's packaging is made up of "50% recycled content." Since the program's launch, over 2,000 brands such as Fisher-Price, Garmin, and SanDisk have partnered with Amazon in its sustainability initiatives.

Amazon also supports charitable and nonprofit organizations. Amazon has a program called AmazonSmile. According to its website, "AmazonSmile is a simple and automatic way for you to support your favorite charitable organization every time you shop, at no cost to you." AmazonSmile donates 0.5% of the purchase price of certain products to the charity or nonprofit organization of your choice. Programs such as the American Red Cross and Doctors Without Borders receive thousands in additional donations from AmazonSmile.

Decision Analysis 🟩🟨🟥 **Cash Flow Analysis**

A1_____

Analyze the statement of cash flows and apply the cash flow on total assets ratio.

Analyzing Cash Sources and Uses

Most managers stress the importance of understanding and predicting cash flows for business decisions. Creditors evaluate a company's ability to generate cash before deciding whether to lend money. Investors also assess cash inflows and outflows before buying and selling stock. Information in the statement of cash flows helps address these and other questions such as (1) How much cash is generated from or used in operations? (2) What expenditures are made with cash from operations? (3) What is the source of cash for debt payments? (4) What is the source of cash for distributions to owners? (5) How is the increase in investing activities financed? (6) What is the source of cash for new plant assets? (7) Why is cash flow from operations different from income? (8) How is cash from financing used?

To effectively answer these questions, it is important to separately analyze investing, financing, and operating activities. To illustrate, consider data from three different companies in Exhibit 12.15. These companies operate in the same industry and have been in business for several years.

$ thousands	BMX	ATV	Trex
Cash provided (used) by operating activities	$90,000	$40,000	$(24,000)
Cash provided (used) by investing activities			
Proceeds from sale of plant assets			26,000
Purchase of plant assets	(48,000)	(25,000)	
Cash provided (used) by financing activities			
Proceeds from issuance of debt			13,000
Repayment of debt	(27,000)		
Net increase (decrease) in cash	$15,000	$15,000	$ 15,000

EXHIBIT 12.15

Cash Flows of Competing Companies

Each company generates an identical $15,000 net increase in cash, but its sources and uses of cash flows are very different. BMX's operating activities provide net cash flows of $90,000, allowing it to purchase plant assets of $48,000 and repay $27,000 of its debt. ATV's operating activities provide $40,000 of cash flows, limiting its purchase of plant assets to $25,000. Trex's $15,000 net cash increase is due to selling plant assets and incurring additional debt. Its operating activities yield a net cash outflow of $24,000. Overall, analysis of these cash flows reveals that BMX is more capable of generating future cash flows than is ATV or Trex.

■ **Decision** Insight ━━━━━━━━━━━━━━━━━━━━━━━━━━━━━

Free Cash Flows Many investors use cash flows to value company stock. However, cash-based valuation models often yield different stock values due to differences in measurement of cash flows. Most models require cash flows that are "free" for distribution to shareholders. These *free cash flows* are defined as cash flows available to shareholders after operating asset reinvestments and debt payments. Knowledge of the statement of cash flows is key to proper computation of free cash flows. A company's growth and financial flexibility depend on adequate free cash flows. ■

Point: CFO (Cash flow from operations)
Less: Capital Expenditures
Less: Debt Repayments
= FCF (free cash flows)

Cash Flow on Total Assets

Cash flow information has limitations, but it can help measure a company's ability to meet its obligations, pay dividends, expand operations, and obtain financing. Users often compute and analyze a cash-based ratio similar to return on total assets except that its numerator is net cash flows from operating activities. The **cash flow on total assets** ratio is shown in Exhibit 12.16.

$$\text{Cash flow on total assets} = \frac{\text{Cash flow from operations}}{\text{Average total assets}}$$

EXHIBIT 12.16

Cash Flow on Total Assets

This ratio reflects actual cash flows and is not affected by accounting income recognition and measurement. It can help business decision makers estimate the amount and timing of cash flows when planning and analyzing operating activities.

To illustrate, the 2015 cash flow on total assets ratio for Nike is 23.3%—see Exhibit 12.17. Is a 23.3% ratio good or bad? To answer this question, we compare this ratio with the ratios of prior years (we could also compare its ratio with those of its competitors and the market). Nike's cash flow on total assets ratio

Year	Cash Flow on Total Assets	Return on Total Assets
2015	23.3%	16.3%
2014	16.6	14.9
2013	18.3	15.0
2012	12.5	14.6
2011	12.3	14.5

EXHIBIT 12.17

Nike's Cash Flow on Total Assets

for several prior years is in the second (middle) column of Exhibit 12.17. Results show that its 23.3% return is its highest return over the past five years.

Point: Cash flow ratios are often used by financial analysts.

As an indicator of *earnings quality,* some analysts compare the cash flow on total assets ratio to the return on total assets ratio. Nike's return on total assets is provided in the third column of Exhibit 12.17. Nike's cash flow on total assets ratio exceeds its return on total assets in three of the past five years, leading some analysts to infer that Nike's earnings quality is not as good for that period because much of its earnings are not being realized in the form of cash.

■ Decision Insight

Point: The following ratio helps assess whether operating cash flow is adequate to meet long-term obligations:

Cash coverage of debt =
Cash flow from operations ÷
Noncurrent liabilities.

A low ratio suggests a higher risk of insolvency; a high ratio suggests a greater ability to meet long-term obligations.

Cash Flow Ratios   Analysts use various other cash-based ratios, including the following two:

$$\text{(1)} \qquad \text{Cash coverage of growth} = \frac{\text{Operating cash flow}}{\text{Cash outflow for plant assets}}$$

where a low ratio (less than 1) implies cash inadequacy to meet asset growth, whereas a high ratio implies cash adequacy for asset growth.

$$\text{(2)} \qquad \text{Operating cash flow to sales} = \frac{\text{Operating cash flow}}{\text{Net sales}}$$

When this ratio substantially and consistently differs from the operating income to net sales ratio, the risk of accounting improprieties increases. ■

COMPREHENSIVE

Preparing Statement of Cash Flows—Indirect *and* Direct Methods

Comparative balance sheets, income statement, and additional information follow.

UMA COMPANY Balance Sheets December 31, 2016 and 2015		
	2016	**2015**
Assets		
Cash	$ 43,050	$ 23,925
Accounts receivable	34,125	39,825
Inventory	156,000	146,475
Prepaid expenses	3,600	1,650
Total current assets..................	236,775	211,875
Equipment	135,825	146,700
Accum. depreciation—Equipment.	(61,950)	(47,550)
Total assets	$310,650	$311,025
Liabilities		
Accounts payable	$ 28,800	$ 33,750
Income taxes payable	5,100	4,425
Dividends payable	0	4,500
Total current liabilities................	33,900	42,675
Bonds payable.......................	0	37,500
Total liabilities	33,900	80,175
Equity		
Common stock, $10 par	168,750	168,750
Retained earnings	108,000	62,100
Total liabilities and equity	$310,650	$311,025

UMA COMPANY Income Statement For Year Ended December 31, 2016		
Sales		$446,100
Cost of goods sold	$222,300	
Other operating expenses	120,300	
Depreciation expense	25,500	(368,100)
		78,000
Other gains (losses)		
Loss on sale of equipment.....	3,300	
Loss on retirement of bonds...	825	(4,125)
Income before taxes		73,875
Income taxes expense		(13,725)
Net income		$ 60,150

Additional Information

a. Equipment costing $21,375 with accumulated depreciation of $11,100 is sold for cash.
b. Equipment purchases are for cash.
c. Accumulated Depreciation is affected by depreciation expense and the sale of equipment.
d. The balance of Retained Earnings is affected by dividend declarations and net income.
e. All sales are made on credit.
f. All inventory purchases are on credit.
g. Accounts Payable balances result from inventory purchases.
h. Prepaid expenses relate to "other operating expenses."

Required

1. Prepare a statement of cash flows using the indirect method for year 2016.

2.[B] Prepare a statement of cash flows using the direct method for year 2016.

PLANNING THE SOLUTION

- Prepare two blank statements of cash flows with sections for operating, investing, and financing activities using the (1) indirect method format and (2) direct method format.

- Compute the cash paid for equipment and the cash received from the sale of equipment using the additional information provided along with the amount for depreciation expense and the change in the balances of equipment and accumulated depreciation. Use T-accounts to help chart the effects of the sale and purchase of equipment on the balances of the Equipment account and the Accumulated Depreciation account.

- Compute the effect of net income on the change in the Retained Earnings account balance. Assign the difference between the change in retained earnings and the amount of net income to dividends declared. Adjust the dividends declared amount for the change in the Dividends Payable balance.

- Compute cash received from customers, cash paid for inventory, cash paid for other operating expenses, and cash paid for taxes as illustrated in the chapter.

- Enter the cash effects of reconstruction entries to the appropriate section(s) of the statement.

- Total each section of the statement, determine the total net change in cash, and add it to the beginning balance to get the ending balance of cash.

SOLUTION

Supporting computations for cash receipts and cash payments.

(1)	*Cost of equipment sold	$ 21,375
	Accumulated depreciation of equipment sold............	(11,100)
	Book value of equipment sold	10,275
	Loss on sale of equipment	(3,300)
	Cash received from sale of equipment	**$ 6,975**
	Cost of equipment sold	$ 21,375
	Less decrease in the Equipment account balance.........	(10,875)
	Cash paid for new equipment	**$ 10,500**
(2)	Loss on retirement of bonds	$ 825
	Carrying value of bonds retired......................	37,500
	Cash paid to retire bonds	**$ 38,325**
(3)	Net income.......................................	$ 60,150
	Less increase in retained earnings	45,900
	Dividends declared	14,250
	Plus decrease in dividends payable	4,500
	Cash paid for dividends	**$ 18,750**
(4)[B]	Sales	$ 446,100
	Add decrease in accounts receivable	5,700
	Cash received from customers	**$451,800**
(5)[B]	Cost of goods sold................................	$ 222,300
	Plus increase in inventory..........................	9,525
	Purchases	231,825
	Plus decrease in accounts payable	4,950
	Cash paid for inventory	**$236,775**
(6)[B]	Other operating expenses	$ 120,300
	Plus increase in prepaid expenses	1,950
	Cash paid for other operating expenses	**$122,250**
(7)[B]	Income taxes expense	$ 13,725
	Less increase in income taxes payable	(675)
	Cash paid for income taxes	**$ 13,050**

* Supporting T-account analysis for part 1 follows on top of next page.

Equipment				Accumulated Depreciation—Equipment			
Bal., Dec. 31, 2015	146,700					Bal., Dec. 31, 2015	47,550
Cash purchase	10,500	Sale	21,375	Sale	11,100	Depr. expense	25,500
Bal., Dec. 31, 2016	135,825					Bal., Dec. 31, 2016	61,950

1. Indirect method:

UMA COMPANY
Statement of Cash Flows (Indirect Method)
For Year Ended December 31, 2016

Cash flows from operating activities		
Net income		$ 60,150
Adjustments to reconcile net income to net cash provided by operating activities		
Income statement items not affecting cash		
Depreciation expense	25,500	
Loss on sale of plant assets	3,300	
Loss on retirement of bonds	825	
Changes in current assets and current liabilities		
Decrease in accounts receivable	5,700	
Increase in inventory	(9,525)	
Increase in prepaid expenses	(1,950)	
Decrease in accounts payable	(4,950)	
Increase in income taxes payable	675	
Net cash provided by operating activities		$79,725
Cash flows from investing activities		
Cash received from sale of equipment	6,975	
Cash paid for equipment	(10,500)	
Net cash used in investing activities		(3,525)
Cash flows from financing activities		
Cash paid to retire bonds payable	(38,325)	
Cash paid for dividends	(18,750)	
Net cash used in financing activities		(57,075)
Net increase in cash		$19,125
Cash balance at prior year-end		23,925
Cash balance at current year-end		$43,050

2.[B] Direct method (Appendix 12B):

UMA COMPANY
Statement of Cash Flows (Direct Method)
For Year Ended December 31, 2016

Cash flows from operating activities		
Cash received from customers	$ 451,800	
Cash paid for inventory	(236,775)	
Cash paid for other operating expenses	(122,250)	
Cash paid for income taxes	(13,050)	
Net cash provided by operating activities		$79,725
Cash flows from investing activities		
Cash received from sale of equipment	6,975	
Cash paid for equipment	(10,500)	
Net cash used in investing activities		(3,525)
Cash flows from financing activities		
Cash paid to retire bonds payable	(38,325)	
Cash paid for dividends	(18,750)	
Net cash used in financing activities		(57,075)
Net increase in cash		$19,125
Cash balance at prior year-end		23,925
Cash balance at current year-end		$43,050

Spreadsheet Preparation of the Statement of Cash Flows

12A

This appendix explains how to use a spreadsheet (work sheet) to prepare the statement of cash flows under the indirect method.

Preparing the Indirect Method Spreadsheet   Analyzing noncash accounts can be challenging when a company has a large number of accounts and many operating, investing, and financing transactions. A *spreadsheet,* also called *work sheet* or *working paper,* can help us organize the information needed to prepare a statement of cash flows. A spreadsheet also makes it easier to check the accuracy of our work. To illustrate, we return to the comparative balance sheets and income statement shown in Exhibit 12.10. We use the following identifying letters *a* through *g* to code changes in accounts, and letters *h* through *m* for additional information, to prepare the statement of cash flows:

P4_____

Illustrate use of a spreadsheet to prepare a statement of cash flows.

  a. Net income is $38,000.
  b. Accounts receivable increase by $20,000.
  c. Inventory increases by $14,000.
  d. Prepaid expenses increase by $2,000.
  e. Accounts payable decrease by $5,000.
  f. Interest payable decreases by $1,000.
  g. Income taxes payable increase by $10,000.
  h. Depreciation expense is $24,000.
  i. Plant assets costing $20,000 with accumulated depreciation of $12,000 are sold for $2,000 cash. This yields a loss on sale of assets of $6,000.
  j. Notes with a book value of $34,000 are retired with a cash payment of $18,000, yielding a $16,000 gain on retirement.
  k. Plant assets costing $60,000 are purchased with an issuance of notes payable for $60,000.
  l. Issued 3,000 shares of common stock for $15,000 cash.
  m. Paid cash dividends of $14,000.

Exhibit 12A.1 shows the indirect method spreadsheet for Genesis. We enter both beginning and ending balance sheet amounts on the spreadsheet. We also enter information in the Analysis of Changes columns (keyed to the additional information items *a* through *m*) to explain changes in the accounts and determine the cash flows for operating, investing, and financing activities. Information about noncash investing and financing activities is reported near the bottom.

Entering the Analysis of Changes on the Spreadsheet   The following sequence of procedures is used to complete the spreadsheet after the beginning and ending balances of the balance sheet accounts are entered:

① Enter net income as the first item in the statement of cash flows section for computing operating cash inflow (debit) and as a credit to Retained Earnings.

② In the statement of cash flows section, adjustments to net income are entered as debits if they increase cash flows and as credits if they decrease cash flows. Applying this same rule, adjust net income for the change in each noncash current asset and current liability account related to operating activities. For each adjustment to net income, the offsetting debit or credit must help reconcile the beginning and ending balances of a current asset or current liability account.

③ Enter adjustments to net income for income statement items not providing or using cash in the period. For each adjustment, the offsetting debit or credit must help reconcile a noncash balance sheet account.

④ Adjust net income to eliminate any gains or losses from investing and financing activities. Because the cash from a gain must be excluded from operating activities, the gain is entered as a credit in the operating activities section. Losses are entered as debits. For each adjustment, the related debit and/ or credit must help reconcile balance sheet accounts and involve reconstructed entries to show the cash flow from investing or financing activities.

⑤ After reviewing any unreconciled balance sheet accounts and related information, enter the remaining reconciling entries for investing and financing activities. Examples are purchases of plant assets,

Point: Analysis of the changes on the spreadsheet are summarized here:

1. Cash flows from operating activities generally affect net income, current assets, and current liabilities.

2. Cash flows from investing activities generally affect noncurrent asset accounts.

3. Cash flows from financing activities generally affect noncurrent liability and equity accounts.

EXHIBIT 12A.1

Spreadsheet for Preparing
Statement of Cash
Flows—Indirect Method

	A	B	C	D	E	F	G
1		GENESIS					
2		Spreadsheet for Statement of Cash Flows—Indirect Method					
3		For Year Ended December 31, 2016					
4		Dec. 31,		Analysis of Changes			Dec. 31,
5		2015		Debit		Credit	2016
6	**Balance Sheet—Debit Bal. Accounts**						
7	Cash	$ 12,000					$ 17,000
8	Accounts receivable	40,000	(b)	$ 20,000			60,000
9	Inventory	70,000	(c)	14,000			84,000
10	Prepaid expenses	4,000	(d)	2,000			6,000
11	Plant assets	210,000	(k1)	60,000	(i)	$ 20,000	250,000
12		$336,000					$417,000
13	**Balance Sheet—Credit Bal. Accounts**						
14	Accumulated depreciation	$ 48,000	(i)	12,000	(h)	24,000	$ 60,000
15	Accounts payable	40,000	(e)	5,000			35,000
16	Interest payable	4,000	(f)	1,000			3,000
17	Income taxes payable	12,000			(g)	10,000	22,000
18	Notes payable	64,000	(j)	34,000	(k2)	60,000	90,000
19	Common stock, $5 par value	80,000			(l)	15,000	95,000
20	Retained earnings	88,000	(m)	14,000	(a)	38,000	112,000
21		$336,000					$417,000
22	**Statement of Cash Flows**						
23	Operating activities						
24	Net income		(a)	38,000			
25	Increase in accounts receivable				(b)	20,000	
26	Increase in inventory				(c)	14,000	
27	Increase in prepaid expenses				(d)	2,000	
28	Decrease in accounts payable				(e)	5,000	
29	Decrease in interest payable				(f)	1,000	
30	Increase in income taxes payable		(g)	10,000			
31	Depreciation expense		(h)	24,000			
32	Loss on sale of plant assets		(i)	6,000			
33	Gain on retirement of notes				(j)	16,000	
34	Investing activities						
35	Receipts from sale of plant assets		(i)	2,000			
36	Financing activities						
37	Payment to retire notes				(j)	18,000	
38	Receipts from issuing stock		(l)	15,000			
39	Payment of cash dividends				(m)	14,000	
40							
41	**Noncash Investing and Financing Activities**						
42	Purchase of plant assets with notes		(k2)	60,000	(k1)	60,000	
				$317,000		$317,000	

issuances of long-term debt, stock issuances, and dividend payments. Some of these may require entries in the noncash investing and financing section of the spreadsheet (reconciled).

⑥ Check accuracy by totaling the Analysis of Changes columns and by determining that the change in each balance sheet account has been explained (reconciled).

We illustrate these steps in Exhibit 12A.1 for Genesis:

Step	Entries
①.........	(a)
②.........	(b) through (g)
③.........	(h)
④.........	(i) through (j)
⑤.........	(k) through (m)

Since adjustments *i, j,* and *k* are more challenging, we show them in the following debit and credit format. These entries are for purposes of our understanding; they are *not* the entries actually made in the journals. Changes in the Cash account are identified as sources or uses of cash.

i.	Cash—Receipt from sale of plant assets (**source of cash**)	2,000	
	Loss from sale of plant assets	6,000	
	Accumulated depreciation	12,000	
	Plant assets		20,000
	To describe sale of plant assets.		
j.	Notes payable	34,000	
	Cash—Payments to retire notes (**use of cash**).		18,000
	Gain on retirement of notes		16,000
	To describe retirement of notes.		
k1.	Plant assets	60,000	
	Cash—Purchase of plant assets financed by notes		60,000
	To describe purchase of plant assets.		
k2.	Cash—Purchase of plant assets financed by notes	60,000	
	Notes payable		60,000
	To issue notes for purchase of assets.		

APPENDIX

Direct Method of Reporting Operating Cash Flows   **12B**

P5

Compute cash flows from operating activities using the direct method.

We compute cash flows from operating activities under the direct method by adjusting accrual-based income statement items to the cash basis. The usual approach is to adjust income statement accounts related to operating activities for changes in their related balance sheet accounts as follows:

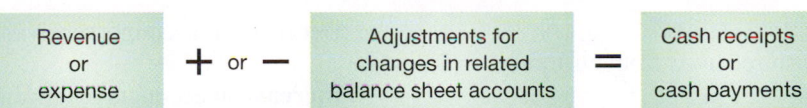

The framework for reporting cash receipts and cash payments for the operating section of the cash flow statement under the direct method is presented in Exhibit 12B.1. We consider cash receipts first and then cash payments.

EXHIBIT 12B.1

Major Classes of Operating Cash Flows

Operating Cash Receipts   A review of Exhibit 12.10 and the additional information reported by Genesis suggests only one potential cash receipt: sales to customers. This section, therefore, starts with sales to customers as reported on the income statement and then adjusts it as necessary to obtain cash received from customers to report on the statement of cash flows.

Cash Received from Customers   If all sales are for cash, the amount received from customers equals the sales reported on the income statement. When some or all sales are on account, however, we must adjust the amount of sales for the change in Accounts Receivable. It is often helpful to use *account analysis* to do this. This usually involves setting up a T-account and reconstructing its major entries, with emphasis on cash receipts and payments.

Point: An accounts receivable increase implies that cash received from customers is less than sales (the converse is also true).

To illustrate, we use a T-account that includes accounts receivable balances for Genesis on December 31, 2015 and 2016. The beginning balance is $40,000 and the ending balance is $60,000. Next, the income statement shows sales of $590,000, which we enter on the debit side of this account. We now can reconstruct the Accounts Receivable account to determine the amount of cash received from customers as follows:

Accounts Receivable			
Bal., Dec. 31, 2015	40,000		
Sales	590,000	**Cash receipts =**	**570,000**
Bal., Dec. 31, 2016	60,000		

Reconstructed Entry

Cash	570,000	
Accts Recble.	20,000	
Sales		590,000

Example: If the ending balance of Accounts Receivable is $20,000 (instead of $60,000), what is cash received from customers? *Answer:* $610,000

This T-account shows that the Accounts Receivable balance begins at $40,000 and increases to $630,000 from sales of $590,000, yet its ending balance is only $60,000. This implies that cash receipts from customers are $570,000, computed as $40,000 + $590,000 − [?] = $60,000. This computation can be rearranged to express cash received as equal to sales of $590,000 minus a $20,000 increase in accounts receivable. This computation is summarized as a general rule in Exhibit 12B.2. Genesis reports the $570,000 cash received from customers as a cash inflow from operating activities.

EXHIBIT 12B.2

Formula to Compute Cash Received from Customers—Direct Method

Cash received from customers = Sales **or**
+ **Decrease** in accounts receivable
− **Increase** in accounts receivable

Other Cash Receipts   While Genesis's cash receipts are limited to collections from customers, we often see other types of cash receipts, most commonly cash receipts involving rent, interest, and dividends. We compute cash received from these items by subtracting an increase in their respective receivable or adding a decrease. For instance, if rent receivable increases in the period, cash received from renters is less than rent revenue reported on the income statement. If rent receivable decreases, cash received is more than reported rent revenue. The same logic applies to interest and dividends. The formulas for these computations are summarized later in this appendix.

Point: Net income is measured using accrual accounting. Cash flows from operations are measured using cash basis accounting.

Operating Cash Payments   A review of Exhibit 12.10 and the additional Genesis information shows four operating expenses: cost of goods sold; wages and other operating expenses; interest expense; and taxes expense. We analyze each expense to compute its cash amounts for the statement of cash flows. (We then examine depreciation and the other losses and gains.)

Cash Paid for Inventory   We compute cash paid for inventory by analyzing both cost of goods sold and inventory. If all inventory purchases are for cash and the ending balance of Inventory is unchanged from the beginning balance, the amount of cash paid for inventory equals cost of goods sold—an uncommon situation. Instead, there normally is some change in the Inventory balance. Also, some or all purchases are often made on credit, and this yields changes in the Accounts Payable balance. When the balances of both Inventory and Accounts Payable change, we must adjust the cost of goods sold for changes in both accounts to compute cash paid for inventory. This is a two-step adjustment.

First, we use the change in the account balance of Inventory, along with the cost of goods sold amount, to compute cost of purchases for the period. An increase in inventory implies that we bought more than we sold, and we add this inventory increase to cost of goods sold to compute cost of purchases. A decrease in inventory implies that we bought less than we sold, and we subtract the inventory decrease from cost of goods sold to compute purchases. We illustrate the *first step* by reconstructing the Inventory account of Genesis:

Inventory			
Bal., Dec. 31, 2015	70,000		
Purchases =	**314,000**	Cost of goods sold	300,000
Bal., Dec. 31, 2016	84,000		

The beginning balance is $70,000, and the ending balance is $84,000. The income statement shows that cost of goods sold is $300,000, which we enter on the credit side of this account. With this information, we determine the amount for cost of purchases to be $314,000. This computation can be rearranged to express cost of purchases as equal to cost of goods sold of $300,000 plus the $14,000 increase in inventory.

The second step uses the change in the balance of Accounts Payable, and the amount of cost of purchases, to compute cash paid for inventory. A decrease in accounts payable implies that we paid for more goods than we acquired this period, and we would then add the accounts payable decrease to cost of purchases to compute cash paid for inventory. An increase in accounts payable implies that we paid for less than the amount of goods acquired, and we would subtract the accounts payable increase from purchases to compute cash paid for inventory. The *second step* is applied to Genesis by reconstructing its Accounts Payable account:

Accounts Payable			
		Bal., Dec. 31, 2015	40,000
Cash payments =	**319,000**	Purchases	314,000
		Bal., Dec. 31, 2016	35,000

Reconstructed Entry

COGS	300,000	
Inventory	14,000	
Accounts Payable	5,000	
Cash		319,000

Its beginning balance of $40,000 plus purchases of $314,000 minus an ending balance of $35,000 yields cash paid of $319,000 (or $40,000 + $314,000 − [?] = $35,000). Alternatively, we can express cash paid for inventory as equal to purchases of $314,000 plus the $5,000 decrease in accounts payable. The $319,000 cash paid for inventory is reported on the statement of cash flows as a cash outflow under operating activities.

We summarize this two-step adjustment to cost of goods sold to compute cash paid for inventory in Exhibit 12B.3.

Example: If the ending balances of Inventory and Accounts Payable are $60,000 and $50,000, respectively (instead of $84,000 and $35,000), what is cash paid for inventory? *Answer:* $280,000

EXHIBIT 12B.3

Two Steps to Compute Cash Paid for Inventory— Direct Method

Step 1

Purchases = Cost of goods sold   **+ Increase** in inventory
                                  or
                                  − Decrease in inventory

Step 2

Cash paid for inventory = Purchases   **+ Decrease** in accounts payable
                                       or
                                       − Increase in accounts payable

Cash Paid for Wages and Operating Expenses (Excluding Depreciation)   The income statement of Genesis shows wages and other operating expenses of $216,000 (see Exhibit 12.10). To compute cash paid for wages and other operating expenses, we adjust this amount for any changes in their related balance sheet accounts. We begin by looking for any prepaid expenses and accrued liabilities related to wages and other operating expenses in the balance sheets of Genesis in Exhibit 12.10. The balance sheets show prepaid expenses but no accrued liabilities. Thus, the adjustment is limited to the change in prepaid expenses. The amount of adjustment is computed by assuming that all cash paid for wages and other operating expenses is initially debited to Prepaid Expenses. This assumption allows us to reconstruct the Prepaid Expenses account:

Prepaid Expenses			
Bal., Dec. 31, 2015	4,000		
Cash payments =	**218,000**	Wages and other operating exp.	216,000
Bal., Dec. 31, 2016	6,000		

Reconstructed Entry

Wages and Other Expenses	216,000	
Prepaid Expenses	2,000	
Cash		218,000

Point: A decrease in prepaid expenses implies that reported expenses include an amount(s) that did not require a cash out-flow in the period.

Prepaid expenses increase by $2,000 in the period, meaning that cash paid for wages and other operating expenses exceeds the reported expense by $2,000. Alternatively, we can express cash paid for wages and other operating expenses as equal to its reported expenses of $216,000 plus the $2,000 increase in prepaid expenses.[1]

Exhibit 12B.4 summarizes the adjustments to wages (including salaries) and other operating expenses. The Genesis balance sheet did not report accrued liabilities, but we include them in the formula to explain the adjustment to cash when they do exist. A decrease in accrued liabilities implies that we paid cash for more goods or services than received this period, so we add the decrease in accrued liabilities to the expense amount to obtain cash paid for these goods or services. An increase in accrued liabilities implies that we paid cash for less than what was acquired, so we subtract this increase in accrued liabilities from the expense amount to get cash paid.

EXHIBIT 12B.4

Formula to Compute Cash Paid for Wages and Operating Expenses— Direct Method

Cash paid for wages and other operating expenses	=	Wages and other operating expenses	+ **Increase** in prepaid expenses or − **Decrease** in prepaid expenses	+ **Decrease** in accrued liabilities or − **Increase** in accrued liabilities

Cash Paid for Interest and Income Taxes   Computing operating cash flows for interest and taxes is similar to that for operating expenses. Both require adjustments to their amounts reported on the income statement for changes in their related balance sheet accounts. We begin with the Genesis income statement showing interest expense of $7,000 and income taxes expense of $15,000. To compute the cash paid, we adjust interest expense for the change in interest payable and then the income taxes expense for the change in income taxes payable. These computations involve reconstructing both liability accounts:

Reconstructed Entry

Int. Expense	7,000	
Int. Payable	1,000	
Cash		8,000

Interest Payable			
		Bal., Dec. 31, 2015	4,000
Cash paid for interest =	**8,000**	Interest expense	7,000
		Bal., Dec. 31, 2016	3,000

Reconstructed Entry

Inc. Tax Exp.	15,000	
Inc. Tax Pay.		10,000
Cash		5,000

Income Taxes Payable			
		Bal., Dec. 31, 2015	12,000
Cash paid for taxes =	**5,000**	Income taxes expense	15,000
		Bal., Dec. 31, 2016	22,000

These T-accounts reveal cash paid for interest of $8,000 and cash paid for income taxes of $5,000. The formulas to compute these amounts are in Exhibit 12B.5. Both of these cash payments are reported as operating cash outflows on the statement of cash flows.

EXHIBIT 12B.5

Formulas to Compute Cash Paid for Both Interest and Taxes—Direct Method

Cash paid for interest	=	Interest expense	+ **Decrease** in interest payable or − **Increase** in interest payable
Cash paid for taxes	=	Income taxes expense	+ **Decrease** in income taxes payable or − **Increase** in income taxes payable

Analyzing Additional Expenses, Gains, and Losses   Genesis has three additional items reported on its income statement: depreciation, loss on sale of assets, and gain on retirement of debt. We must consider each for its potential cash effects.

---

[1] The assumption that all cash payments for wages and operating expenses are initially debited to Prepaid Expenses is not necessary for our analysis to hold. If cash payments are debited directly to the expense account, the total amount of cash paid for wages and other operating expenses still equals the $216,000 expense plus the $2,000 increase in prepaid expenses (which arise from end-of-period adjusting entries).

Depreciation Expense   Depreciation expense is $24,000. It is often called a *noncash expense* because depreciation has no cash flows. Depreciation expense is an allocation of an asset's depreciable cost. The cash outflow with a plant asset is reported as part of investing activities when it is paid for. Thus, depreciation expense is *never* reported on a statement of cash flows using the direct method; nor is depletion or amortization expense.

Loss on Sale of Assets   Sales of assets frequently result in gains and losses reported as part of net income, but the amount of recorded gain or loss does *not* reflect any cash flows in these transactions. Asset sales result in cash inflow equal to the cash amount received, regardless of whether the asset was sold at a gain or a loss. This cash inflow is reported under investing activities. Thus, the loss or gain on a sale of assets is *never* reported on a statement of cash flows using the direct method.

Gain on Retirement of Debt   Retirement of debt usually yields a gain or loss reported as part of net income, but that gain or loss does *not* reflect cash flow in this transaction. Debt retirement results in cash outflow equal to the cash paid to settle the debt, regardless of whether the debt is retired at a gain or loss. This cash outflow is reported under financing activities; the loss or gain from retirement of debt is *never* reported on a statement of cash flows using the direct method.

Point: The direct method is usually viewed as *user friendly* because less accounting knowledge is required to understand and use it.

Summary of Adjustments for Direct Method
Exhibit 12B.6 summarizes common adjustments for net income to yield net cash provided (used) by operating activities under the direct method.

EXHIBIT 12B.6

Summary of Selected Adjustments for Direct Method

Item	From Income Statement	Adjustments to Obtain Cash Flow Numbers
Receipts		
From sales	Sales Revenue	+ Decrease in Accounts Receivable − Increase in Accounts Receivable
From rent	Rent Revenue	+ Decrease in Rent Receivable − Increase in Rent Receivable
From interest	Interest Revenue	+ Decrease in Interest Receivable − Increase in Interest Receivable
From dividends	Dividend Revenue	+ Decrease in Dividends Receivable − Increase in Dividends Receivable
Payments		
To suppliers	Cost of Goods Sold	+ Increase in Inventory + Decrease in Accounts Payable − Decrease in Inventory − Increase in Accounts Payable
For operations	Operating Expense	+ Increase in Prepaids + Decrease in Accrued Liabilities − Decrease in Prepaids − Increase in Accrued Liabilities
To employees	Wages (Salaries) Expense	+ Decrease in Wages (Salaries) Payable − Increase in Wages (Salaries) Payable
For interest	Interest Expense	+ Decrease in Interest Payable − Increase in Interest Payable
For taxes	Income Tax Expense	+ Decrease in Income Tax Payable − Increase in Income Tax Payable

Direct Method Format of Operating Activities Section
Exhibit 12B.7 shows the Genesis statement of cash flows using the direct method. Major items of cash inflows and cash outflows are listed separately in the operating activities section. The format requires that operating cash outflows be subtracted from operating cash inflows to get net cash provided (used) by operating activities.

The FASB recommends that the operating activities section of the statement of cash flows be reported using the direct method, which is considered more useful to financial statement users. *However, the FASB requires a reconciliation of net income to net cash provided (used) by operating activities when the direct method is used* (which can be reported in the notes). This reconciliation follows the preparation of the operating activities section of the statement of cash flows using the indirect method.

Point: Some preparers argue that it is easier to prepare a statement of cash flows using the indirect method. This likely explains its greater frequency in financial statements.

 IFRS

Currently, U.S. GAAP and IFRS allow cash flows from operating activities to be reported using either the indirect method or the direct method. The IASB and FASB are working on joint guidance that would require the direct method for the operating section with the indirect method's operating section disclosed in the footnotes. Stay tuned . . . ■

EXHIBIT 12B.7

Statement of Cash
Flows—Direct Method

GENESIS		
Statement of Cash Flows		
For Year Ended December 31, 2016		
Cash flows from operating activities		
Cash received from customers	$570,000	
Cash paid for inventory	(319,000)	
Cash paid for wages and other operating expenses	(218,000)	
Cash paid for interest	(8,000)	
Cash paid for taxes	(5,000)	
Net cash provided by operating activities		$20,000
Cash flows from investing activities		
Cash received from sale of plant assets	2,000	
Net cash provided by investing activities		2,000
Cash flows from financing activities		
Cash received from issuing stock	15,000	
Cash paid to retire notes	(18,000)	
Cash paid for dividends	(14,000)	
Net cash used in financing activities		(17,000)
Net increase in cash		$ 5,000
Cash balance at prior year-end		12,000
Cash balance at current year-end		$17,000

NEED-TO-KNOW 12-6

Reporting Operating
Cash Flows (Direct)

P5

A company's current-year income statement and selected balance sheet data at December 31 of the current and prior years follow. Prepare the cash flows from operating activities section only of its statement of cash flows using the direct method for the current year.

Income Statement	
For Current Year Ended December 31	
Sales revenue	$120
Expenses	
Cost of goods sold.	50
Depreciation expense	30
Salaries expense.	17
Interest expense.	3
Net income	$ 20

Selected Balance Sheet Accounts		
At December 31	**Current Yr**	**Prior Yr**
Accounts receivable.........	$12	$10
Inventory	6	9
Accounts payable...........	7	11
Salaries payable.	8	3
Interest payable	1	0

Solution

Cash Flows from Operating Activities—Direct Method	
For Current Year Ended December 31	
Cash flows from operating activities*	
Cash received from customers	$118
Cash paid for inventory........................	(51)
Cash paid for salaries........................	(12)
Cash paid for interest	(2)
Net cash provided by operating activities...........	$53

* Supporting computations:
    Cash received from customers = Sales of $120 − Accounts Receivable increase of $2.
    Cash paid for inventory = COGS of $50 − Inventory decrease of $3 + Accounts Payable
                decrease of $4.
    Cash paid for salaries = Salaries Expense of $17 − Salaries Payable increase of $5.
    Cash paid for interest = Interest Expense of $3 − Interest Payable increase of $1.

Do More: QS 12-12, QS 12-13,
QS 12-14, E 12-12, E 12-14,
E 12-15, E 12-16

Summary

C1 **Distinguish between operating, investing, and financing activities, and describe how noncash investing and financing activities are disclosed.** The purpose of the statement of cash flows is to report major cash receipts and cash payments related to operating, investing, or financing activities. Operating activities include transactions and events that determine net income. Investing activities include transactions and events that mainly affect long-term assets. Financing activities include transactions and events that mainly affect long-term liabilities and equity. Noncash investing and financing activities must be disclosed in either a note or a separate schedule to the statement of cash flows. Examples are the retirement of debt by issuing equity and the exchange of a note payable for plant assets.

A1 **Analyze the statement of cash flows and apply the cash flow on total assets ratio.** To understand and predict cash flows, users stress identification of the sources and uses of cash flows by operating, investing, and financing activities. Emphasis is on operating cash flows since they derive from continuing operations. The cash flow on total assets ratio is defined as operating cash flows divided by average total assets. Analysis of current and past values for this ratio can reflect a company's ability to yield regular and positive cash flows. It is also viewed as a measure of earnings quality.

P1 **Prepare a statement of cash flows.** Preparation of a statement of cash flows involves five steps: (1) Compute the net increase or decrease in cash; (2) compute net cash provided or used by operating activities (*using either the direct or indirect method*); (3) compute net cash provided or used by investing activities; (4) compute net cash provided or used by

financing activities; and (5) report the beginning and ending cash balances and prove that the ending cash balance is explained by net cash flows. Noncash investing and financing activities are also disclosed.

P2 **Compute cash flows from operating activities using the indirect method.** The indirect method for reporting net cash provided or used by operating activities starts with net income and then adjusts it for three items: (1) changes in noncash current assets and current liabilities related to operating activities, (2) revenues and expenses not providing or using cash, and (3) gains and losses from investing and financing activities.

P3 **Determine cash flows from both investing and financing activities.** Cash flows from both investing and financing activities are determined by identifying the cash flow effects of transactions and events affecting each balance sheet account related to these activities. All cash flows from these activities are identified when we can explain changes in these accounts from the beginning to the end of the period.

P4A **Illustrate use of a spreadsheet to prepare a statement of cash flows.** A spreadsheet is a useful tool in preparing a statement of cash flows. Six key steps (see Appendix 12A) are applied when using the spreadsheet to prepare the statement.

P5B **Compute cash flows from operating activities using the direct method.** The direct method for reporting net cash provided or used by operating activities lists major operating cash inflows less cash outflows to yield net cash inflow or outflow from operations.

Guidance Answers to Decision Maker

Entrepreneur   Several factors might explain an increase in net cash flows when a net loss is reported, including (1) early recognition of expenses relative to revenues generated (such as research and development), (2) cash advances on long-term sales contracts not yet recognized in income, (3) issuances of debt or equity for cash to finance expansion, (4) cash sale of assets, (5) delay of cash payments, and (6) cash prepayment on sales. Analysis needs to focus on the components of both the net loss and the net cash flows and their implications for future performance.

Reporter   Your initial reaction based on the company's $600,000 loss with a $550,000 decrease in net cash is not positive. However, closer scrutiny reveals a more positive picture of this company's performance. Cash flow from operating activities is $650,000, computed as [?] − $850,000 − $350,000 = $(550,000). You also note that net income *before* the extraordinary loss is $330,000, computed as [?] − $930,000 = $(600,000).

Key Terms

Cash flow on total assets	Indirect method	Operating activities
Direct method	Investing activities	Statement of cash flows
Financing activities		

Multiple Choice Quiz   Answers at end of chapter

1. A company uses the indirect method to determine its cash flows from operating activities. Use the following information to determine its net cash provided or used by operating activities.

Net income	$15,200
Depreciation expense	10,000
Cash payment on note payable	8,000
Gain on sale of land..................	3,000
Increase in inventory	1,500
Increase in accounts payable	2,850

   a. $23,550 used by operating activities
   b. $23,550 provided by operating activities
   c. $15,550 provided by operating activities
   d. $42,400 provided by operating activities
   e. $20,850 provided by operating activities

2. A machine with a cost of $175,000 and accumulated depreciation of $94,000 is sold for $87,000 cash. The amount reported as a source of cash under cash flows from investing activities is
   a. $81,000.
   b. $6,000.
   c. $87,000.
   d. Zero; this is a financing activity.
   e. Zero; this is an operating activity.

3. A company settles a long-term note payable plus interest by paying $68,000 cash toward the principal amount and $5,440 cash for interest. The amount reported as a use of cash under cash flows from financing activities is
   a. Zero; this is an investing activity.
   b. Zero; this is an operating activity.
   c. $73,440.
   d. $68,000.
   e. $5,440.

4. The following information is available regarding a company's annual salaries and wages. What amount of cash is paid for salaries and wages?

Salaries and wages expense..................	$255,000
Salaries and wages payable, prior year-end	8,200
Salaries and wages payable, current year-end	10,900

   a. $252,300   c. $255,000   e. $235,900
   b. $257,700   d. $274,100

5. The following information is available for a company. What amount of cash is paid for inventory for the current year?

Cost of goods sold.	$545,000
Inventory, prior year-end...................	105,000
Inventory, current year-end	112,000
Accounts payable, prior year-end	98,500
Accounts payable, current year-end	101,300

   a. $545,000   c. $540,800   e. $549,200
   b. $554,800   d. $535,200

A(B) *Superscript letter A (B) denotes assignments based on Appendix 12A (12B).*
🛈 Icon denotes assignments that involve decision making.

Discussion Questions

1. What is the reporting purpose of the statement of cash flows? Identify at least two questions that this statement can answer.

2. What are some investing activities reported on the statement of cash flows?

3. What are some financing activities reported on the statement of cash flows?

4.B Describe the direct method of reporting cash flows from operating activities.

5. When a statement of cash flows is prepared using the direct method, what are some of the operating cash flows?

6. Describe the indirect method of reporting cash flows from operating activities.

7. Where on the statement of cash flows is the payment of cash dividends reported?

8. 🛈 Assume that a company purchases land for $1,000,000, paying $400,000 cash and borrowing the remainder with a long-term note payable. How should this transaction be reported on a statement of cash flows?

9. 🛈 On June 3, a company borrows $200,000 cash by giving its bank a 90-day, interest-bearing note. On the statement of cash flows, where should this be reported?

10. 🛈 If a company reports positive net income for the year, can it also show a net cash outflow from operating activities? Explain.

11. 🛈 Is depreciation a source of cash flow?

12. ♟ Refer to **Apple**'s statement of cash flows in Appendix A. (*a*) Which method is used to compute its net cash provided by operating activities? (*b*) Its balance sheet shows an increase in accounts receivable from September 28, 2013, to September 27, 2014; why is this increase in accounts receivable subtracted when computing net cash provided by operating activities for the fiscal year ended September 27, 2014?

APPLE

13. ♟ Refer to **Google**'s statement of cash flows in Appendix A. What are its

GOOGLE

cash flows from financing activities for the year ended December 31, 2014? List the items and amounts.

14. ♟ Refer to **Samsung**'s 2014 statement of cash flows in Appendix A. List its cash flows from operating activities, investing activities, and financing activities.

Samsung

15. ♟ Refer to **Samsung**'s statement of cash flows in Appendix A. What investing activities result in cash outflows for the year ended December 31, 2014? List items and amounts.

Samsung

---

connect

Classify the following cash flows as either operating, investing, or financing activities.

_____ **1.** Sold long-term investments for cash.
_____ **2.** Received cash payments from customers.
_____ **3.** Paid cash for wages and salaries.
_____ **4.** Purchased inventories for cash.
_____ **5.** Paid cash dividends.
_____ **6.** Issued common stock for cash.
_____ **7.** Received cash interest on a note.
_____ **8.** Paid cash interest on outstanding notes.
_____ **9.** Received cash from sale of land at a loss.
_____ **10.** Paid cash for property taxes on a building.

QUICK STUDY

QS 12-1
Transaction classification by activity C1 ♟

Label the following headings, line items, and notes with the numbers *1* through *13* according to their sequential order (from top to bottom) for presentation of the statement of cash flows.

_____ **a.** "Cash flows from investing activities" title
_____ **b.** "For *period* Ended *date*" heading
_____ **c.** "Cash flows from operating activities" title
_____ **d.** Company name
_____ **e.** Schedule or note disclosure of noncash investing and financing transactions
_____ **f.** "Statement of Cash Flows" heading
_____ **g.** Net increase (decrease) in cash . . . . $ #
_____ **h.** Net cash provided (used) by operating activities . . . . $ #
_____ **i.** Cash (and equivalents) balance at prior period-end . . . . $ #
_____ **j.** Net cash provided (used) by financing activities . . . . $ #
_____ **k.** "Cash flows from financing activities" title
_____ **l.** Net cash provided (used) by investing activities . . . . $ #
_____ **m.** Cash (and equivalents) balance at current period-end . . . . $ #

QS 12-2
Statement of cash flows

P1 ♟

For each of the following three separate cases X, Y, and Z, compute cash flows from operations using the indirect method. The list includes all balance sheet accounts related to cash from operating activities.

QS 12-3
Indirect: Computing cash flows from operations

P2

	Case X	Case Y	Case Z
Net income	$ 4,000	$100,000	$72,000
Depreciation expense	30,000	8,000	24,000
Accounts receivable increase (decrease)	40,000	20,000	(4,000)
Inventory increase (decrease)	(20,000)	(10,000)	10,000
Accounts payable increase (decrease)	24,000	(22,000)	14,000
Accrued liabilities increase (decrease)	(44,000)	12,000	(8,000)

QS 12-4

Indirect: Computing cash from operations   **P2**

Use the following information to determine this company's cash flows from operating activities using the indirect method.

MOSS COMPANY Selected Balance Sheet Information December 31, 2016 and 2015		
	2016	**2015**
Current assets		
Cash	$84,650	$26,800
Accounts receivable.	25,000	32,000
Inventory	60,000	54,100
Current liabilities		
Accounts payable.	30,400	25,700
Income taxes payable.	2,050	2,200

MOSS COMPANY Income Statement For Year Ended December 31, 2016		
Sales		$515,000
Cost of goods sold.		331,600
Gross profit		183,400
Operating expenses		
Depreciation expense	$ 36,000	
Other expenses	121,500	157,500
Income before taxes		25,900
Income taxes expense		7,700
Net income		$ 18,200

QS 12-5

Indirect: Computing investing cash flows

P2

The plant assets section of the comparative balance sheets of Anders Company is reported below.

ANDERS COMPANY Comparative Balance Sheets		
	2016	**2015**
Plant assets		
Equipment	$ 180,000	$270,000
Accum. Depr.—Equipment	(100,000)	(210,000)
Equipment, net.	80,000	60,000
Buildings	380,000	400,000
Accum. Depr.—Buildings.	(100,000)	(285,000)
Buildings, net	$ 280,000	$115,000

Refer to the balance sheet data above from Anders Company. During 2016, equipment with a book value of $40,000 and an original cost of $210,000 was sold at a loss of $3,000.

1. How much cash did Anders receive from the sale of equipment?
2. How much depreciation expense was recorded on equipment during 2016?
3. What was the cost of new equipment purchased by Anders during 2016?

QS 12-6

Indirect: Computing investing cash flows

P2

Refer to the balance sheet data in **QS 12-5** from Anders Company. During 2016, a building with a book value of $70,000 and an original cost of $300,000 was sold at a gain of $60,000.

1. How much cash did Anders receive from the sale of the building?
2. How much depreciation expense was recorded on buildings during 2016?
3. What was the cost of buildings purchased by Anders during 2016?

QS 12-7

Computing cash from asset sales

P3

The following selected information is from Eller Company's comparative balance sheets.

At December 31	2016	2015
Furniture.	$132,000	$ 184,500
Accumulated depreciation—Furniture	(88,700)	(110,700)

The income statement reports depreciation expense for the year of $18,000. Also, furniture costing $52,500 was sold for its book value. Compute the cash received from the sale of furniture.

Compute cash flows from investing activities using the following company information.

Sale of short-term investments......................	$ 6,000
Cash collections from customers	16,000
Purchase of used equipment	5,000
Depreciation expense	2,000

QS 12-8
Computing cash flows from investing
P3

The following selected information is from Princeton Company's comparative balance sheets.

At December 31	2016	2015
Common stock, $10 par value	$105,000	$100,000
Paid-in capital in excess of par..........	567,000	342,000
Retained earnings....................	313,500	287,500

QS 12-9
Computing financing cash flows
P3

The company's net income for the year ended December 31, 2016, was $48,000.
1. Compute the cash received from the sale of its common stock during 2016.
2. Compute the cash paid for dividends during 2016.

Compute cash flows from financing activities using the following company information.

Additional short-term borrowings	$20,000
Purchase of short-term investments................	5,000
Cash dividends paid	16,000
Interest paid...................................	8,000

QS 12-10
Computing cash flows from financing
P3

CRUZ, INC.
Comparative Balance Sheets
December 31, 2016

	2016	2015
Assets		
Cash......................................	$ 94,800	$ 24,000
Accounts receivable, net...............	41,000	51,000
Inventory	85,800	95,800
Prepaid expenses.....................	5,400	4,200
Total current assets...................	227,000	175,000
Furniture.............................	109,000	119,000
Accum. depreciation—Furniture.........	(17,000)	(9,000)
Total assets..........................	$319,000	$285,000
Liabilities and Equity		
Accounts payable.....................	$ 15,000	$ 21,000
Wages payable	9,000	5,000
Income taxes payable.................	1,400	2,600
Total current liabilities................	25,400	28,600
Notes payable (long-term).............	29,000	69,000
Total liabilities	54,400	97,600
Equity		
Common stock, $5 par value	229,000	179,000
Retained earnings....................	35,600	8,400
Total liabilities and equity	$319,000	$285,000

QS 12-11
Indirect: Computing cash from operations
P2

CRUZ, INC.
Income Statement
For Year Ended December 31, 2016

Sales		$488,000
Cost of goods sold.............		314,000
Gross profit		174,000
Operating expenses		
Depreciation expense	$37,600	
Other expenses...............	89,100	126,700
Income before taxes		47,300
Income taxes expense..........		17,300
Net income		$ 30,000

Required

Use the indirect method to prepare the cash provided or used from operating activities section only of the statement of cash flows for this company.

QS 12-12
Computing cash from
asset sales

P3

Refer to the financial data in QS 12-11.
Furniture costing $55,000 is sold at its book value in 2016. Acquisitions of furniture total $45,000 cash, on which no depreciation is necessary because it is acquired at year-end. What is the cash inflow related to the sale of furniture?

QS 12-13
Computing financing
cash outflows

P3

Refer to the financial data in QS 12-11.
1. Assume that all common stock is issued for cash. What amount of cash dividends is paid during 2016?
2. Assume that no additional notes payable are issued in 2016. What cash amount is paid to reduce the notes payable balance in 2016?

QS 12-14ᴮ
Direct: Computing cash
received from customers

P5

Refer to the financial data in QS 12-11.
1. How much cash is received from sales to customers for year 2016?
2. What is the net increase or decrease in cash for year 2016?

QS 12-15ᴮ
Direct: Computing
operating cash outflows

P5

Refer to the financial data in QS 12-11.
1. How much cash is paid to acquire inventory during year 2016?
2. How much cash is paid for "other expenses" during year 2016? (*Hint:* Examine prepaid expenses and wages payable.)

QS 12-16ᴮ
Direct: Computing cash
from operations

P5

Refer to the financial data in QS 12-11.
Use the direct method to prepare the cash provided or used from operating activities section only of the statement of cash flows for this company.

QS 12-17
Analyzing sources and
uses of cash

A1

Financial data from three competitors in the same industry follow.
1. Which of the three competitors is in the strongest position as shown by its statement of cash flows?
2. Analyze and compare the strength of Moore's cash flow on total assets ratio to that of Sykes.

	A	B	C	D
1	($ thousands)	Moore	Sykes	Kritch
2	Cash provided (used) by operating activities	$ 70,000	$ 60,000	$ (24,000)
3	Cash provided (used) by investing activities			
4	Proceeds from sale of operating assets			26,000
5	Purchase of operating assets	(28,000)	(34,000)	
6	Cash provided (used) by financing activities			
7	Proceeds from issuance of debt			23,000
8	Repayment of debt	(6,000)		
9	Net increase (decrease) in cash	$ 36,000	$ 26,000	$ 25,000
10				
11	Average total assets	$790,000	$625,000	$300,000

When a spreadsheet for a statement of cash flows is prepared, all changes in noncash balance sheet accounts are fully explained on the spreadsheet. Explain how these noncash balance sheet accounts are used to fully account for cash flows on a spreadsheet.

QS 12-18[A]

Noncash accounts on a spreadsheet

P4

Use the following financial statements and additional information to (1) prepare a statement of cash flows for the year ended December 31, 2016, using the *indirect method* and (2) analyze and briefly discuss the statement prepared in part 1 with special attention to operating activities and to the company's cash level.

QS 12-19

Indirect: Preparation of statement of cash flows

P1   P2   P3

MONTGOMERY INC.
Comparative Balance Sheets
December 31, 2016 and 2015

	2016	2015
Assets		
Cash	$ 30,400	$ 30,550
Accounts receivable, net	10,050	12,150
Inventory	90,100	70,150
Total current assets . . . :	130,550	112,850
Equipment	49,900	41,500
Accum. depreciation—Equipment.	(22,500)	(15,300)
Total assets.	$157,950	$139,050
Liabilities and Equity		
Accounts payable.	$ 23,900	$ 25,400
Salaries payable.	500	600
Total current liabilities.	24,400	26,000
Equity		
Common stock, no par value	110,000	100,000
Retained earnings.	23,550	13,050
Total liabilities and equity	$157,950	$139,050

MONTGOMERY INC.
Income Statement
For Year Ended December 31, 2016

Sales		$45,575
Cost of goods sold.		(18,950)
Gross profit		26,625
Operating expenses		
Depreciation expense	$7,200	
Other expenses	5,550	
Total operating expense		12,750
Income before taxes		13,875
Income tax expense.		3,375
Net income		$10,500

Additional Information

a. No dividends are declared or paid in 2016.

b. Issued additional stock for $10,000 cash in 2016.

c. Purchased equipment for cash in 2016; no equipment was sold in 2016.

Answer each of the following questions related to international accounting standards.

1. Which method, indirect or direct, is acceptable for reporting operating cash flows under IFRS?

2. For each of the following four cash flows, identify whether it is reported under the operating, investing, or financing section (or some combination) within the indirect format of the statement of cash flows reported under IFRS and under U.S. GAAP.

QS 12-20

International cash flow disclosures

C1

Cash Flow Source	US GAAP Reporting	IFRS Reporting
a. Interest paid		
b. Dividends paid		
c. Interest received		
d. Dividends received		

EXERCISES

Exercise 12-1

Indirect: Cash flow
classification C1

The following transactions and events occurred during the year. Assuming that this company uses the *indirect method* to report cash provided by operating activities, indicate where each item would appear on its statement of cash flows by placing an *x* in the appropriate column.

	Statement of Cash Flows			Noncash Investing and Financing Activities	Not Reported on Statement or in Notes
	Operating Activities	Investing Activities	Financing Activities		
a. Declared and paid a cash dividend	___	___	___	___	___
b. Recorded depreciation expense	___	___	___	___	___
c. Paid cash to settle long-term note payable	___	___	___	___	___
d. Prepaid expenses increased in the year	___	___	___	___	___
e. Accounts receivable decreased in the year	___	___	___	___	___
f. Purchased land by issuing common stock	___	___	___	___	___
g. Inventory increased in the year	___	___	___	___	___
h. Sold equipment for cash, yielding a loss	___	___	___	___	___
i. Accounts payable decreased in the year	___	___	___	___	___
j. Income taxes payable increased in the year	___	___	___	___	___

Exercise 12-2

Indirect: Reporting cash
flows from operations

P2

Hampton Company reports the following information for its recent calendar year. Prepare the operating activities section of the statement of cash flows for Hampton Company using the *indirect method*.

Income Statement Data		Selected Year-End Balance Sheet Data	
Sales	$160,000	Accounts receivable increase...........	$10,000
Expenses		Inventory decrease...................	16,000
Cost of goods sold...............	100,000	Salaries payable increase	1,000
Salaries expense.................	24,000		
Depreciation expense	12,000		
Net income	$ 24,000		

Exercise 12-3

Indirect: Reporting and
interpreting cash flows
from operations

P2

Arundel Company disclosed the following information for its recent calendar year.

Income Statement Data		Selected Year-End Balance Sheet Data	
Revenues	$100,000	Accounts receivable decrease..........	$24,000
Expenses		Purchased a machine for cash	10,000
Salaries expense.................	84,000	Salaries payable increase	18,000
Utilities expense.................	14,000	Other accrued liabilities decrease.......	8,000
Depreciation expense	14,600		
Other expenses.................	3,400		
Net loss	$ (16,000)		

Required

1. Prepare the operating activities section of the statement of cash flows using the *indirect method*.
2. What were the major reasons that this company was able to report a net loss but positive cash flow from operations?
3. Of the potential causes of differences between cash flow from operations and net income, which are the most important to investors?

The following income statement and information about changes in noncash current assets and current liabilities are reported.

Exercise 12-4
Indirect: Cash flows from operating activities
P2

SONAD COMPANY
Income Statement
For Year Ended December 31, 2016

Sales		$1,828,000
Cost of goods sold		991,000
Gross profit		837,000
Operating expenses		
Salaries expense	$245,535	
Depreciation expense	44,200	
Rent expense	49,600	
Amortization expenses—Patents	4,200	
Utilities expense	18,125	361,660
		475,340
Gain on sale of equipment		6,200
Net income		$ 481,540

Changes in current asset and current liability accounts for the year that relate to operations follow.

Accounts receivable	$30,500 increase	Accounts payable	$12,500 decrease
Inventory	25,000 increase	Salaries payable	3,500 decrease

Required

Prepare only the cash flows from operating activities section of the statement of cash flows using the *indirect method*.

Fitz Company reports the following information. Use the *indirect method* to prepare only the operating activities section of its statement of cash flows for the year ended December 31, 2016.

Exercise 12-5
Indirect: Cash flows from operating activities
P2

Selected 2016 Income Statement Data		Selected Year-End 2016 Balance Sheet Data	
Net income	$374,000	Accounts receivable decrease	$17,100
Depreciation expense	44,000	Inventory decrease	42,000
Amortization expense	7,200	Prepaid expenses increase	4,700
Gain on sale of plant assets	6,000	Accounts payable decrease	8,200
		Salaries payable increase	1,200

Salud Company reports the following information. Use the *indirect method* to prepare only the operating activities section of its statement of cash flows for the year ended December 31, 2016.

Exercise 12-6
Indirect: Cash flow from operations
P2

Selected 2016 Income Statement Data		Selected Year-End 2016 Balance Sheet Data	
Net income	$400,000	Accounts receivable increase	$40,000
Depreciation expense	80,000	Prepaid expenses decrease	12,000
Gain on sale of machinery	20,000	Accounts payable increase	6,000
		Wages payable decrease	2,000

Use the following information to determine this company's cash flows from investing activities.

Exercise 12-7
Cash flows from investing activities
P3

a. Equipment with a book value of $65,300 and an original cost of $133,000 was sold at a loss of $14,000.
b. Paid $89,000 cash for a new truck.
c. Sold land costing $154,000 for $198,000 cash, yielding a gain of $44,000.
d. Long-term investments in stock were sold for $60,800 cash, yielding a gain of $4,150.

Exercise 12-8

Cash flows from financing activities

P3

Use the following information to determine this company's cash flows from financing activities.

a. Net income was $35,000.

b. Issued common stock for $64,000 cash.

c. Paid cash dividend of $14,600.

d. Paid $50,000 cash to settle a note payable at its $50,000 maturity value.

e. Paid $12,000 cash to acquire its treasury stock.

f. Purchased equipment for $39,000 cash.

Exercise 12-9

Indirect: Statement of cash flows under IFRS

P1

Peugeot S.A. reports the following condensed financial information for the year ended December 31, 2014 (euros in millions). Prepare its statement of cash flows under the *indirect method*. (*Hint:* Each line item below is titled, and any necessary parentheses added, as it is reported in the statement of cash flows.)

Net income (loss)	€ (822)	Cash from issuances of shares	€ 2,961
Depreciation and amortization	2,530	Cash paid for other financing activities	(1,891)
Losses on disposals and other...........	42	Cash from disposal of plant assets & intangibles	206
Net decrease in current operating assets & other......................	2,314	Cash paid for plant assets, intangibles & other.......	(2,542)
Cash paid for dividends	(58)	Cash and cash equivalents, December 31, 2013......	8,162

Exercise 12-10

Analyses of cash flow on total assets   **A1**

A company reported average total assets of $1,240,000 in 2015 and $1,510,000 in 2016. Its net operating cash flow was $102,920 in 2015 and $138,920 in 2016. Calculate its cash flow on total assets ratio for both years. Comment on the results and any change in performance.

Exercise 12-11

Indirect: Preparation of statement of cash flows

P1   P2   P3   A1

The following financial statements and additional information are reported.

IKIBAN INC.
Income Statement
For Year Ended June 30, 2016

Sales		$678,000
Cost of goods sold..................		411,000
Gross profit		267,000
Operating expenses		
Depreciation expense	$58,600	
Other expenses..................	67,000	
Total operating expenses............		125,600
		141,400
Other gains (losses)		
Gain on sale of equipment..........		2,000
Income before taxes		143,400
Income taxes expense...............		43,890
Net income		$ 99,510

IKIBAN INC.
Comparative Balance Sheets
June 30, 2016 and 2015

	2016	2015
Assets		
Cash.....................................	$ 87,500	$ 44,000
Accounts receivable, net.................	65,000	51,000
Inventory	63,800	86,500
Prepaid expenses.......................	4,400	5,400
Total current assets....................	220,700	186,900
Equipment	124,000	115,000
Accum. depreciation—Equipment.........	(27,000)	(9,000)
Total assets............................	$317,700	$292,900
Liabilities and Equity		
Accounts payable.......................	$ 25,000	$ 30,000
Wages payable	6,000	15,000
Income taxes payable...................	3,400	3,800
Total current liabilities.................	34,400	48,800
Notes payable (long term)...............	30,000	60,000
Total liabilities	64,400	108,800
Equity		
Common stock, $5 par value	220,000	160,000
Retained earnings......................	33,300	24,100
Total liabilities and equity	$317,700	$292,900

Additional Information

a. A $30,000 note payable is retired at its $30,000 carrying (book) value in exchange for cash.

b. The only changes affecting retained earnings are net income and cash dividends paid.

c. New equipment is acquired for $57,600 cash.

d. Received cash for the sale of equipment that had cost $48,600, yielding a $2,000 gain.

e. Prepaid Expenses and Wages Payable relate to Other Expenses on the income statement.

f. All purchases and sales of inventory are on credit.

Required

1. Prepare a statement of cash flows for the year ended June 30, 2016, using the *indirect method.*

2. Compute the company's cash flow on total assets ratio for its fiscal year 2016.

Check (1b) Cash paid for dividends, $90,310
(1d) Cash received from equip. sale, $10,000

Refer to the information in Exercise 12-11. Using the *direct method,* prepare the statement of cash flows for the year ended June 30, 2016.

Exercise 12-12[B]
Direct: Preparation of statement of cash flows
P1   P3   P5

Complete the following spreadsheet in preparation of the statement of cash flows. (The statement of cash flows is not required.) Prepare the spreadsheet as in Exhibit 12A.1; report operating activities under the *indirect method.* Identify the debits and credits in the Analysis of Changes columns with letters that correspond to the following transactions and events *a* through *h.*

a. Net income for the year was $100,000.

b. Dividends of $80,000 cash were declared and paid.

c. Scoreteck's only noncash expense was $70,000 of depreciation.

d. The company purchased plant assets for $70,000 cash.

e. Notes payable of $20,000 were issued for $20,000 cash.

f. Change in accounts receivable.

g. Change in inventory.

h. Change in accounts payable.

Exercise 12-13
Indirect: Cash flows spreadsheet
P4

	A	B	C	D	E	F	G
1		SCORETECK CORPORATION					
2		Spreadsheet for Statement of Cash Flows—Indirect Method					
3		For Year Ended December 31, 2016					
4				Analysis of Changes			
5		Dec. 31, 2015		Debit		Credit	Dec. 31, 2016
6	**Balance Sheet—Debit Bal. Accounts**						
7	Cash	$ 80,000					$ 60,000
8	Accounts receivable	120,000					190,000
9	Inventory	250,000					230,000
10	Plant assets	600,000					670,000
11		$1,050,000					$1,150,000
12	**Balance Sheet—Credit Bal. Accounts**						
13	Accumulated depreciation	$ 100,000					$ 170,000
14	Accounts payable	150,000					140,000
15	Notes payable	370,000					390,000
16	Common stock	200,000					200,000
17	Retained earnings	230,000					250,000
18		$1,050,000					$1,150,000
19	**Statement of Cash Flows**						
20	Operating activities						
21	Net income						
22	Increase in accounts receivable						
23	Decrease in inventory						
24	Decrease in accounts payable						
25	Depreciation expense						
26	Investing activities						
27	Cash paid to purchase plant assets						
28	Financing activities						
29	Cash paid for dividends						
30	Cash from issuance of notes						
31							

Exercise 12-14ᴮ
Direct: Cash flow
classification

C1   P5

The following transactions and events occurred during the year. Assuming that this company uses the *direct method* to report cash provided by operating activities, indicate where each item would appear on the statement of cash flows by placing an *x* in the appropriate column.

	Statement of Cash Flows			Noncash Investing and Financing Activities	Not Reported on Statement or in Notes
	Operating Activities	Investing Activities	Financing Activities		
a. Retired long-term notes payable by issuing common stock.........................	___	___	___	___	___
b. Paid cash to acquire inventory	___	___	___	___	___
c. Sold inventory for cash	___	___	___	___	___
d. Paid cash dividend that was declared in a prior period	___	___	___	___	___
e. Accepted six-month note receivable in exchange for plant assets	___	___	___	___	___
f. Recorded depreciation expense...................	___	___	___	___	___
g. Paid cash to acquire treasury stock	___	___	___	___	___
h. Collected cash from sales	___	___	___	___	___
i. Borrowed cash from bank by signing a nine-month note payable	___	___	___	___	___
j. Paid cash to purchase a patent	___	___	___	___	___

Exercise 12-15ᴮ
Direct: Computation of cash flows

P5

For each of the following three separate cases, use the information provided about the calendar-year 2016 operations of Sahim Company to compute the required cash flow information.

Case X: Compute cash received from customers:	
Sales	$515,000
Accounts receivable, December 31, 2015...........	27,200
Accounts receivable, December 31, 2016...........	33,600
Case Y: Compute cash paid for rent:	
Rent expense	$139,800
Rent payable, December 31, 2015.................	7,800
Rent payable, December 31, 2016.................	6,200
Case Z: Compute cash paid for inventory:	
Cost of goods sold..............................	$525,000
Inventory, December 31, 2015	158,600
Accounts payable, December 31, 2015.............	66,700
Inventory, December 31, 2016	130,400
Accounts payable, December 31, 2016.............	82,000

Exercise 12-16ᴮ
Direct: Cash flows from operating activities   P5

Refer to the information about Sonad Company in Exercise 12-4. Use the *direct method* to prepare only the cash provided or used by operating activities section of the statement of cash flows for this company.

Exercise 12-17ᴮ
Direct: Preparation of statement of cash flows and supporting note

P1   P3   P5

Use the following information about the cash flows of Ferron Company to prepare a complete statement of cash flows (*direct method*) for the year ended December 31, 2016. Use a note disclosure for any non-cash investing and financing activities.

Cash and cash equivalents balance, December 31, 2015	$ 40,000
Cash and cash equivalents balance, December 31, 2016	148,000
Cash received as interest...	3,500
Cash paid for salaries..	76,500

[continued on next page]

[continued from previous page]

Bonds payable retired by issuing common stock (no gain or loss on retirement)...	$185,500
Cash paid to retire long-term notes payable...	100,000
Cash received from sale of equipment...	60,250
Cash received in exchange for six-month note payable...	35,000
Land purchased by issuing long-term note payable...	105,250
Cash paid for store equipment...	24,750
Cash dividends paid...	10,000
Cash paid for other expenses...	20,000
Cash received from customers...	495,000
Cash paid for inventory...	254,500

The following summarized Cash T-account reflects the total debits and total credits to the Cash account of Thomas Corporation for calendar-year 2016.

1. Use this information to prepare a complete statement of cash flows for year 2016. The cash provided or used by operating activities should be reported using the *direct method*.

2. Refer to the statement of cash flows prepared for part 1 to answer the following questions *a* through *d*: (*a*) Which section—operating, investing, or financing—shows the largest cash (i) inflow and (ii) outflow? (*b*) What is the largest individual item among the investing cash outflows? (*c*) Are the cash proceeds larger from issuing notes or issuing stock? (*d*) Does the company have a net cash inflow or outflow from borrowing activities?

Exercise 12-18ᴮ
Direct: Preparation of statement of cash flows from Cash T-account
P1   P3   P5

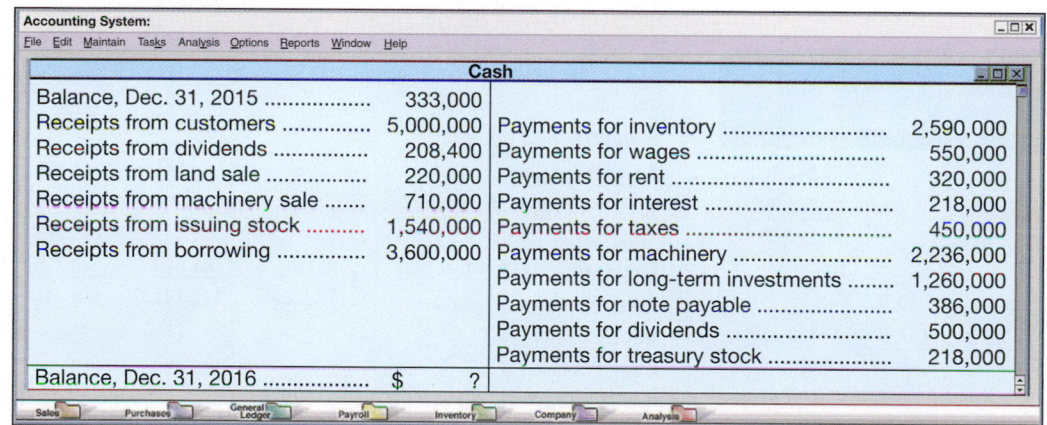

Accounting System:

File Edit Maintain Tasks Analysis Options Reports Window Help

Cash

Balance, Dec. 31, 2015	333,000		
Receipts from customers	5,000,000	Payments for inventory	2,590,000
Receipts from dividends	208,400	Payments for wages	550,000
Receipts from land sale	220,000	Payments for rent	320,000
Receipts from machinery sale	710,000	Payments for interest	218,000
Receipts from issuing stock	1,540,000	Payments for taxes	450,000
Receipts from borrowing	3,600,000	Payments for machinery	2,236,000
		Payments for long-term investments	1,260,000
		Payments for note payable	386,000
		Payments for dividends	500,000
		Payments for treasury stock	218,000
Balance, Dec. 31, 2016	$?		

Sales   Purchases   General Ledger   Payroll   Inventory   Company   Analysis

connect

Lansing Company's 2016 income statement and selected balance sheet data (for current assets and current liabilities) at December 31, 2015 and 2016, follow.

PROBLEM SET A

Problem 12-1A
Indirect: Computing cash flows from operations
P2

LANSING COMPANY
Income Statement
For Year Ended December 31, 2016

Sales revenue	$97,200
Expenses	
Cost of goods sold	42,000
Depreciation expense	12,000
Salaries expense	18,000
Rent expense	9,000
Insurance expense	3,800
Interest expense	3,600
Utilities expense	2,800
Net income	$ 6,000

LANSING COMPANY
Selected Balance Sheet Accounts

At December 31	2016	2015
Accounts receivable	$5,600	$5,800
Inventory	1,980	1,540
Accounts payable	4,400	4,600
Salaries payable	880	700
Utilities payable	220	160
Prepaid insurance	260	280
Prepaid rent	220	180

Required

Prepare the cash flows from operating activities section only of the company's 2016 statement of cash flows using the *indirect method*.

Check   Cash from operating activities, $17,780

Problem 12-2A[B]
Direct: Computing cash flows from operations
P5

Refer to the information in Problem 12-1A.

Required

Prepare the cash flows from operating activities section only of the company's 2016 statement of cash flows using the *direct method*.

Problem 12-3A
Indirect: Statement of cash flows
A1   P1   P2   P3

Forten Company, a merchandiser, recently completed its calendar-year 2016 operations. For the year, (1) all sales are credit sales, (2) all credits to Accounts Receivable reflect cash receipts from customers, (3) all purchases of inventory are on credit, (4) all debits to Accounts Payable reflect cash payments for inventory, and (5) Other Expenses are paid in advance and are initially debited to Prepaid Expenses. The company's income statement and balance sheets follow.

FORTEN COMPANY
Comparative Balance Sheets
December 31, 2016 and 2015

	2016	2015
Assets		
Cash	$ 49,800	$ 73,500
Accounts receivable.	65,810	50,625
Inventory	275,656	251,800
Prepaid expenses	1,250	1,875
Total current assets	392,516	377,800
Equipment	157,500	108,000
Accum. depreciation—Equipment.	(36,625)	(46,000)
Total assets.	$513,391	$439,800
Liabilities and Equity		
Accounts payable.	$ 53,141	$114,675
Short-term notes payable	10,000	6,000
Total current liabilities.	63,141	120,675
Long-term notes payable.	65,000	48,750
Total liabilities	128,141	169,425
Equity		
Common stock, $5 par value	162,750	150,250
Paid-in capital in excess of par, common stock	37,500	0
Retained earnings.	185,000	120,125
Total liabilities and equity	$513,391	$439,800

FORTEN COMPANY
Income Statement
For Year Ended December 31, 2016

Sales		$582,500
Cost of goods sold.		285,000
Gross profit		297,500
Operating expenses		
Depreciation expense	$ 20,750	
Other expenses.	132,400	153,150
Other gains (losses)		
Loss on sale of equipment.		(5,125)
Income before taxes		139,225
Income taxes expense.		24,250
Net income		$114,975

Additional Information on Year 2016 Transactions

a. The loss on the cash sale of equipment was $5,125 (details in *b*).

b. Sold equipment costing $46,875, with accumulated depreciation of $30,125, for $11,625 cash.

c. Purchased equipment costing $96,375 by paying $30,000 cash and signing a long-term note payable for the balance.

d. Borrowed $4,000 cash by signing a short-term note payable.

e. Paid $50,125 cash to reduce the long-term notes payable.

f. Issued 2,500 shares of common stock for $20 cash per share.

g. Declared and paid cash dividends of $50,100.

Required

Check   Cash from operating activities, $40,900

1. Prepare a complete statement of cash flows; report its operating activities using the *indirect method*. Disclose any noncash investing and financing activities in a note.

Analysis Component

2. Analyze and discuss the statement of cash flows prepared in part 1, giving special attention to the wisdom of the cash dividend payment.

Refer to the information reported about Forten Company in Problem 12-3A.

Problem 12-4A[A]
Indirect: Cash flows spreadsheet
P1 P2 P3 P4

Required

Prepare a complete statement of cash flows using a spreadsheet as in Exhibit 12A.1; report its operating activities using the *indirect method*. Identify the debits and credits in the Analysis of Changes columns with letters that correspond to the following list of transactions and events.

a. Net income was $114,975.

b. Accounts receivable increased.

c. Inventory increased.

d. Prepaid expenses decreased.

e. Accounts payable decreased.

f. Depreciation expense was $20,750.

g. Sold equipment costing $46,875, with accumulated depreciation of $30,125, for $11,625 cash. This yielded a loss of $5,125.

h. Purchased equipment costing $96,375 by paying $30,000 cash and **(i.)** by signing a long-term note payable for the balance.

j. Borrowed $4,000 cash by signing a short-term note payable.

k. Paid $50,125 cash to reduce the long-term notes payable.

l. Issued 2,500 shares of common stock for $20 cash per share.

m. Declared and paid cash dividends of $50,100.

Check Analysis of Changes column totals, $600,775

Refer to Forten Company's financial statements and related information in Problem 12-3A.

Problem 12-5A[B]
Direct: Statement of cash flows   P1   P3   P5

Required

Prepare a complete statement of cash flows; report its operating activities according to the *direct method*. Disclose any noncash investing and financing activities in a note.

Check Cash used in financing activities, $(46,225)

Golden Corp., a merchandiser, recently completed its 2016 operations. For the year, (1) all sales are credit sales, (2) all credits to Accounts Receivable reflect cash receipts from customers, (3) all purchases of inventory are on credit, (4) all debits to Accounts Payable reflect cash payments for inventory, (5) Other Expenses are all cash expenses, and (6) any change in Income Taxes Payable reflects the accrual and cash payment of taxes. The company's balance sheets and income statement follow.

Problem 12-6A
Indirect: Statement of cash flows
P1   P2   P3

GOLDEN CORPORATION
Comparative Balance Sheets
December 31, 2016 and 2015

	2016	2015
Assets		
Cash....................................	$ 164,000	$107,000
Accounts receivable	83,000	71,000
Inventory................................	601,000	526,000
Total current assets	848,000	704,000
Equipment.............................	335,000	299,000
Accum. depreciation—Equipment	(158,000)	(104,000)
Total assets	$1,025,000	$899,000
Liabilities and Equity		
Accounts payable	$ 87,000	$ 71,000
Income taxes payable	28,000	25,000
Total current liabilities	115,000	96,000
Equity		
Common stock, $2 par value...........	592,000	568,000
Paid-in capital in excess		
of par value, common stock...........	196,000	160,000
Retained earnings	122,000	75,000
Total liabilities and equity..........	$1,025,000	$899,000

GOLDEN CORPORATION
Income Statement
For Year Ended December 31, 2016

Sales		$1,792,000
Cost of goods sold.............		1,086,000
Gross profit		706,000
Operating expenses		
Depreciation expense	$ 54,000	
Other expenses..............	494,000	548,000
Income before taxes		158,000
Income taxes expense..........		22,000
Net income		$ 136,000

Additional Information on Year 2016 Transactions

   a. Purchased equipment for $36,000 cash.

   b. Issued 12,000 shares of common stock for $5 cash per share.

   c. Declared and paid $89,000 in cash dividends.

Required

Check Cash from operating activities, $122,000

Prepare a complete statement of cash flows; report its cash inflows and cash outflows from operating activities according to the *indirect method*.

Problem 12-7A^A
Indirect: Cash flows spreadsheet

P1   P2   P3   P4

Refer to the information reported about Golden Corporation in Problem 12-6A.

Required

Prepare a complete statement of cash flows using a spreadsheet as in Exhibit 12A.1; report operating activities under the *indirect method*. Identify the debits and credits in the Analysis of Changes columns with letters that correspond to the following list of transactions and events.

   a. Net income was $136,000.

   b. Accounts receivable increased.

   c. Inventory increased.

   d. Accounts payable increased.

   e. Income taxes payable increased.

   f. Depreciation expense was $54,000.

Check Analysis of Changes column totals, $481,000

   g. Purchased equipment for $36,000 cash.

   h. Issued 12,000 shares at $5 cash per share.

   i. Declared and paid $89,000 of cash dividends.

Problem 12-8A^B
Direct: Statement of cash flows

P1   P3   P5

Check Cash used in financing activities, $(29,000)

Refer to Golden Corporation's financial statements and related information in Problem 12-6A.

Required

Prepare a complete statement of cash flows; report its cash flows from operating activities according to the *direct method*.

PROBLEM SET B

Problem 12-1B
Indirect: Computing cash flows from operations

P2

Lake Company's 2016 income statement and selected balance sheet data (for current assets and current liabilities) at December 31, 2015 and 2016, follow.

LAKE COMPANY Income Statement For Year Ended December 31, 2016	
Sales revenue	$156,000
Expenses	
Cost of goods sold	72,000
Depreciation expense	32,000
Salaries expense	20,000
Rent expense	5,000
Insurance expense	2,600
Interest expense	2,400
Utilities expense	2,000
Net income	$ 20,000

LAKE COMPANY Selected Balance Sheet Accounts		
At December 31	**2016**	**2015**
Accounts receivable	$3,600	$3,000
Inventory	860	980
Accounts payable	2,400	2,600
Salaries payable	900	600
Utilities payable	200	0
Prepaid insurance	140	180
Prepaid rent	100	200

Required

Prepare the cash flows from operating activities section only of the company's 2016 statement of cash flows using the *indirect method*.

Check   Cash from operating activities, $51,960

Refer to the information in Problem 12-1B.

Required

Prepare the cash flows from operating activities section only of the company's 2016 statement of cash flows using the *direct method*.

Problem 12-2B[B]

Direct: Computing cash flows from operations

P5

Gazelle Corporation, a merchandiser, recently completed its calendar-year 2016 operations. For the year, (1) all sales are credit sales, (2) all credits to Accounts Receivable reflect cash receipts from customers, (3) all purchases of inventory are on credit, (4) all debits to Accounts Payable reflect cash payments for inventory, and (5) Other Expenses are paid in advance and are initially debited to Prepaid Expenses. The company's balance sheets and income statement follow.

Problem 12-3B

Indirect: Statement of cash flows

A1   P1   P2   P3

GAZELLE CORPORATION
Comparative Balance Sheets
December 31, 2016 and 2015

	2016	2015
Assets		
Cash	$123,450	$ 61,550
Accounts receivable	77,100	80,750
Inventory	240,600	250,700
Prepaid expenses	15,100	17,000
Total current assets	456,250	410,000
Equipment	262,250	200,000
Accum. depreciation—Equipment	(110,750)	(95,000)
Total assets	$607,750	$515,000
Liabilities and Equity		
Accounts payable	$ 17,750	$102,000
Short-term notes payable	15,000	10,000
Total current liabilities	32,750	112,000
Long-term notes payable	100,000	77,500
Total liabilities	132,750	189,500
Equity		
Common stock, $5 par	215,000	200,000
Paid-in capital in excess of par, common stock	30,000	0
Retained earnings	230,000	125,500
Total liabilities and equity	$607,750	$515,000

GAZELLE CORPORATION
Income Statement
For Year Ended December 31, 2016

Sales		$1,185,000
Cost of goods sold		595,000
Gross profit		590,000
Operating expenses		
Depreciation expense	$ 38,600	
Other expenses	362,850	
Total operating expenses		401,450
		188,550
Other gains (losses)		
Loss on sale of equipment		(2,100)
Income before taxes		186,450
Income taxes expense		28,350
Net income		$ 158,100

Additional Information on Year 2016 Transactions

a. The loss on the cash sale of equipment was $2,100 (details in *b*).

b. Sold equipment costing $51,000, with accumulated depreciation of $22,850, for $26,050 cash.

c. Purchased equipment costing $113,250 by paying $43,250 cash and signing a long-term note payable for the balance.

d. Borrowed $5,000 cash by signing a short-term note payable.

e. Paid $47,500 cash to reduce the long-term notes payable.

f. Issued 3,000 shares of common stock for $15 cash per share.

g. Declared and paid cash dividends of $53,600.

Required

1. Prepare a complete statement of cash flows; report its operating activities using the *indirect method*. Disclose any noncash investing and financing activities in a note.

Analysis Component

2. Analyze and discuss the statement of cash flows prepared in part 1, giving special attention to the wisdom of the cash dividend payment.

Problem 12-4B^A
Indirect: Cash flows spreadsheet

P1　P2　P3　P4

Refer to the information reported about Gazelle Corporation in Problem 12-3B.

Required

Prepare a complete statement of cash flows using a spreadsheet as in Exhibit 12A.1; report its operating activities using the *indirect method*. Identify the debits and credits in the Analysis of Changes columns with letters that correspond to the following list of transactions and events.

　a. Net income was $158,100.
　b. Accounts receivable decreased.
　c. Inventory decreased.
　d. Prepaid expenses decreased.
　e. Accounts payable decreased.
　f. Depreciation expense was $38,600.
　g. Sold equipment costing $51,000, with accumulated depreciation of $22,850, for $26,050 cash. This yielded a loss of $2,100.
　h. Purchased equipment costing $113,250 by paying $43,250 cash and **(i.)** by signing a long-term note payable for the balance.
　j. Borrowed $5,000 cash by signing a short-term note payable.
　k. Paid $47,500 cash to reduce the long-term notes payable.
　l. Issued 3,000 shares of common stock for $15 cash per share.
　m. Declared and paid cash dividends of $53,600.

Problem 12-5B^B
Direct: Statement of cash flows

P1　P3　P5

Refer to Gazelle Corporation's financial statements and related information in Problem 12-3B.

Required

Prepare a complete statement of cash flows; report its operating activities according to the *direct method*. Disclose any noncash investing and financing activities in a note.

Problem 12-6B
Indirect: Statement of cash flows

P1　P2　P3

Satu Company, a merchandiser, recently completed its 2016 operations. For the year, (1) all sales are credit sales, (2) all credits to Accounts Receivable reflect cash receipts from customers, (3) all purchases of inventory are on credit, (4) all debits to Accounts Payable reflect cash payments for inventory, (5) Other Expenses are cash expenses, and (6) any change in Income Taxes Payable reflects the accrual and cash payment of taxes. The company's income statement and balance sheets follow.

SATU COMPANY
Comparative Balance Sheets
December 31, 2016 and 2015

	2016	2015
Assets		
Cash	$ 58,750	$ 28,400
Accounts receivable	20,222	25,860
Total current assets	78,972	54,260
Inventory	165,667	140,320
Equipment	107,750	77,500
Accum. depreciation—Equipment	(46,700)	(31,000)
Total assets	$305,689	$241,080
Liabilities and Equity		
Accounts payable	$ 20,372	$157,530
Income taxes payable	2,100	6,100
Total current liabilities	22,472	163,630
Equity		
Common stock, $5 par value	40,000	25,000
Paid-in capital in excess of par,		
common stock	68,000	20,000
Retained earnings	175,217	32,450
Total liabilities and equity	$305,689	$241,080

SATU COMPANY
Income Statement
For Year Ended December 31, 2016

Sales		$750,800
Cost of goods sold		269,200
Gross profit		481,600
Operating expenses		
Depreciation expense	$ 15,700	
Other expenses	173,933	189,633
Income before taxes		291,967
Income taxes expense		89,200
Net income		$202,767

Additional Information on Year 2016 Transactions

a. Purchased equipment for $30,250 cash.

b. Issued 3,000 shares of common stock for $21 cash per share.

c. Declared and paid $60,000 of cash dividends.

Required

Prepare a complete statement of cash flows; report its cash inflows and cash outflows from operating activities according to the *indirect method*.

Check   Cash from operating activities, $57,600

Refer to the information reported about Satu Company in Problem 12-6B.

Required

Prepare a complete statement of cash flows using a spreadsheet as in Exhibit 12A.1; report operating activities under the *indirect method*. Identify the debits and credits in the Analysis of Changes columns with letters that correspond to the following list of transactions and events.

a. Net income was $202,767.

b. Accounts receivable decreased.

c. Inventory increased.

d. Accounts payable decreased.

e. Income taxes payable decreased.

f. Depreciation expense was $15,700.

g. Purchased equipment for $30,250 cash.

h. Issued 3,000 shares at $21 cash per share.

i. Declared and paid $60,000 of cash dividends.

Problem 12-7B[A]
Indirect: Cash flows spreadsheet

P1   P2   P3   P4

Check   Analysis of Changes column totals, $543,860

Refer to Satu Company's financial statements and related information in Problem 12-6B.

Required

Prepare a complete statement of cash flows; report its cash flows from operating activities according to the *direct method*.

Problem 12-8B[B]
Direct: Statement of cash flows

P1   P3   P5

Check   Cash provided by financing activities, $3,000

SERIAL PROBLEM
Business Solutions
(Indirect)
P1 P2 P3

(This serial problem began in Chapter 1 and continues through most of the book. If previous chapter segments were not completed, the serial problem can begin at this point. It is helpful, but not necessary, to use the Working Papers that accompany the book.)

SP 12   Santana Rey, owner of Business Solutions, decides to prepare a statement of cash flows for her business. (Although the serial problem allowed for various ownership changes in earlier chapters, we will prepare the statement of cash flows using the following financial data.)

BUSINESS SOLUTIONS
Income Statement
For Three Months Ended March 31, 2017

Computer services revenue.		$25,307
Net sales		18,693
Total revenue		44,000
Cost of goods sold.	$14,052	
Depreciation expense—Office equipment	400	
Depreciation expense—Computer equipment	1,250	
Wages expense	3,250	
Insurance expense	555	
Rent expense	2,475	
Computer supplies expense	1,305	
Advertising expense.	600	
Mileage expense.	320	
Repairs expense—Computer	960	
Total expenses.		25,167
Net income		$18,833

BUSINESS SOLUTIONS
Comparative Balance Sheets
December 31, 2016, and March 31, 2017

	Mar. 31, 2017	Dec. 31, 2016
Assets		
Cash	$ 68,057	$48,372
Accounts receivable.	22,867	5,668
Inventory	704	0
Computer supplies.	2,005	580
Prepaid insurance.	1,110	1,665
Prepaid rent	825	825
Total current assets	95,568	57,110
Office equipment.	8,000	8,000
Accumulated depreciation—Office equipment	(800)	(400)
Computer equipment	20,000	20,000
Accumulated depreciation—Computer equipment	(2,500)	(1,250)
Total assets.	$120,268	$83,460
Liabilities and Equity		
Accounts payable.	$ 0	$ 1,100
Wages payable	875	500
Unearned computer service revenue	0	1,500
Total current liabilities.	875	3,100
Equity		
Common stock	98,000	73,000
Retained earnings.	21,393	7,360
Total liabilities and equity	$120,268	$83,460

Required

Prepare a statement of cash flows for Business Solutions using the *indirect method* for the three months ended March 31, 2017. Recall that owner Santana Rey contributed $25,000 to the business in exchange for additional stock in the first quarter of 2017 and has received $4,800 in cash dividends.

Check   Cash flows used by operations: $(515)

GENERAL LEDGER PROBLEMS

Available in Connect

The following General Ledger assignments highlight the impact, or lack thereof, on the statement of cash flows from summary journal entries derived from consecutive trial balances. Prepare summary journal entries reflecting changes in consecutive trial balances. Then prepare the statement of cash flows (direct method) from those entries. Finally, prepare the reconciliation to the indirect method for net cash provided (used) by operating activities.

GL 12-1   General Ledger assignment based on Exercise 12-11

GL 12-2   General Ledger assignment based on Problem 12-3

GL 12-3   General Ledger assignment based on Problem 12-6

Beyond the Numbers

BTN 12-1   Refer to **Apple**'s financial statements in Appendix A to answer the following.

1. Is Apple's statement of cash flows prepared under the direct method or the indirect method? How do you know?
2. For each fiscal year 2014, 2013, and 2012, is the amount of cash provided by operating activities more or less than the cash paid for dividends?
3. What is the largest amount in reconciling the difference between net income and cash flow from operating activities in fiscal 2014? In fiscal 2013? In fiscal 2012?
4. Identify the largest cash inflow and cash outflow for investing *and* for financing activities in fiscal 2014 and in fiscal 2013.

Fast Forward

5. Obtain Apple's financial statements for a fiscal year ending after September 27, 2014, from either its website (**Apple.com**) or the SEC's database (**www.SEC.gov**). Since September 27, 2014, what are Apple's largest cash outflows and cash inflows in the investing and in the financing sections of its statement of cash flows?

REPORTING IN ACTION

A1

APPLE

BTN 12-2   Key figures for **Apple** and **Google** follow.

$ millions	Apple			Google		
	Current Year	1 Year Prior	2 Years Prior	Current Year	1 Year Prior	2 Years Prior
Operating cash flows...........	$ 59,713	$ 53,666	$ 50,856	$ 22,376	$ 18,659	$16,619
Total assets..................	231,839	207,000	176,064	131,133	110,920	93,798

COMPARATIVE ANALYSIS

A1

APPLE
GOOGLE

Required

1. Compute the recent two years' cash flow on total assets ratios for Apple and Google.
2. What does the cash flow on total assets ratio measure?
3. Which company has the highest cash flow on total assets ratio for the periods shown?
4. Does the cash flow on total assets ratio reflect on the quality of earnings? Explain.

BTN 12-3   Katie Murphy is preparing for a meeting with her banker. Her business is finishing its fourth year of operations. In the first year, it had negative cash flows from operations. In the second and third years, cash flows from operations were positive. However, inventory costs rose significantly in year 4, and cash flows from operations will probably be down 25%. Murphy wants to secure a line of credit from her banker as a financing buffer. From experience, she knows the banker will scrutinize operating cash flows for years 1 through 4 and will want a projected number for year 5. Murphy knows that a steady progression upward in operating cash flows for years 1 through 4 will help her case. She decides to use her discretion as owner and considers several business actions that will turn her operating cash flow in year 4 from a decrease to an increase.

ETHICS CHALLENGE

C1 A1

Required

1. Identify two business actions Murphy might take to improve cash flows from operations.
2. Comment on the ethics and possible consequences of Murphy's decision to pursue these actions.

BTN 12-4   Your friend, Diana Wood, recently completed the second year of her business and just received annual financial statements from her accountant. Wood finds the income statement and balance sheet informative but does not understand the statement of cash flows. She says the first section is especially confusing because it contains a lot of additions and subtractions that do not make sense to her. Wood adds, "The income statement tells me the business is more profitable than last year and that's most important. If I want to know how cash changes, I can look at comparative balance sheets."

COMMUNICATING IN PRACTICE

C1

Required

Write a half-page memorandum to your friend explaining the purpose of the statement of cash flows. Speculate as to why the first section is so confusing and how it might be rectified.

TAKING IT TO THE NET

A1

BTN 12-5   Access the March 31, 2015, filing of the 10-K report (for year ending December 31, 2014) of **Mendocino Brewing Company, Inc.** (ticker MENB), at **www.SEC.gov**.

Required

1. Does Mendocino Brewing use the direct or indirect method to construct its consolidated statement of cash flows?

2. For the year ended December 31, 2014, what is the largest item in reconciling the net income (or loss) to net cash provided by operating activities?

3. In the recent two years, has the company been more successful in generating operating cash flows or in generating net income? Identify the figures to support the answer.

4. In the year ended December 31, 2014, what was the largest cash outflow for investing activities *and* for financing activities?

5. What item(s) does the company report as supplemental cash flow information?

6. Does the company report any noncash financing activities for 2014? Identify them, if any.

TEAMWORK IN ACTION

C1 A1 P2 P5

BTN 12-6   Team members are to coordinate and independently answer one question within each of the following three sections. Team members should then report to the team and confirm or correct teammates' answers.

1. Answer *one* of the following questions about the statement of cash flows.

   a. What are this statement's reporting objectives?

   b. What two methods are used to prepare it? Identify similarities and differences between them.

   c. What steps are followed to prepare the statement?

   d. What types of analyses are often made from this statement's information?

2. Identify and explain the adjustment from net income to obtain cash flows from operating activities using the indirect method for *one* of the following items.

   a. Noncash operating revenues and expenses.

   b. Nonoperating gains and losses.

   c. Increases and decreases in noncash current assets.

   d. Increases and decreases in current liabilities.

3.^B Identify and explain the formula for computing cash flows from operating activities using the direct method for *one* of the following items.

   a. Cash receipts from sales to customers.

   b. Cash paid for inventory.

   c. Cash paid for wages and operating expenses.

   d. Cash paid for interest and taxes.

Note: For teams of more than four, some pairing within teams is necessary. Use as an in-class activity or as an assignment. If used in class, specify a time limit on each part. Conclude with reports to the entire class, using team rotation. Each team can prepare responses on a transparency.

ENTREPRENEURIAL DECISION

C1 A1

BTN 12-7   Review the chapter's opener involving **Amazon.com** and its founder, Jeff Bezos.

Required

1. In a business such as Amazon, monitoring cash flow is always a priority. Even though Amazon now has billions in annual sales and sometimes earns a positive net income, explain how cash flow can lag behind net income.

2. Amazon is a publicly traded corporation. What are potential sources of financing for its future expansion?

BTN 12-8   Jenna and Matt Wilder are completing their second year operating Mountain High, a downhill ski area and resort. Mountain High reports a net loss of $(10,000) for its second year, which includes an $85,000 extraordinary loss from fire. This past year also involved major purchases of plant assets for renovation and expansion, yielding a year-end total asset amount of $800,000. Mountain High's net cash outflow for its second year is $(5,000); a summarized version of its statement of cash flows follows:

ENTREPRENEURIAL DECISION

C1   A1

Net cash flow provided by operating activities..........	$ 295,000
Net cash flow used by investing activities.............	(310,000)
Net cash flow provided by financing activities	10,000

Required

Write a one-page memorandum to the Wilders evaluating Mountain High's current performance and assessing its future. Give special emphasis to cash flow data and their interpretation.

BTN 12-9   Visit **The Motley Fool**'s website (**Fool.com**). Enter the *Fool's School* (at *Fool.com/School*). Identify and select the link "How to Value Stocks." (This site might ask you to register with your e-mail address; registration had been free and did grant access to articles.)

HITTING THE ROAD

C1

Required

1. Click on "Introduction to Valuation Methods," and then "Cash-Flow-Based Valuations." How does the Fool's school define cash flow? What is the school's reasoning for this definition?
2. Per the school's instruction, why do analysts focus on earnings before interest and taxes (EBIT)?
3. Visit other links at this website that interest you such as "How to Read a Balance Sheet," or find out what the "Fool's Ratio" is. Write a half-page report on what you find.

BTN 12-10   Key comparative information for **Samsung** (**www.Samsung.com**), which is a leading manufacturer of electronic consumer products, follows.

GLOBAL DECISION

C1

Samsung
APPLE
GOOGLE

₩ in millions	Current Year	1 Year Prior	2 Years Prior
Operating cash flows	₩ 36,975,389	₩ 46,707,440	₩ 37,972,809
Total assets	230,422,958	214,075,018	181,071,570

Required

1. Compute the recent two years' cash flow on total assets ratio for Samsung.
2. How does Samsung's ratio compare to **Apple**'s and **Google**'s ratios from BTN 12-2?

ANSWERS TO MULTIPLE CHOICE QUIZ

1. b;

Net income	$15,200
Depreciation expense	10,000
Gain on sale of land....................	(3,000)
Increase in inventory	(1,500)
Increase in accounts payable	2,850
Net cash provided by operations	$23,550

2. c; Cash received from sale of machine is reported as an investing activity.

3. d; FASB requires cash interest paid to be reported under operating.

4. a; Cash paid for salaries and wages = $255,000 + $8,200 − $10,900 = $252,300

5. e; Increase in inventory = $112,000 − $105,000 = $7,000

Increase in accounts payable = $101,300 − $98,500 = $2,800

Cash paid for inventory = $545,000 + $7,000 − $2,800 = $549,200

13 | chapter

Analyzing and Interpreting Financial Statements

Chapter Preview

BASICS OF ANALYSIS	HORIZONTAL ANALYSIS	VERTICAL ANALYSIS	RATIO ANALYSIS AND REPORTING
C1 Analysis: Its purpose, building blocks, and information needs	**P1** Application of:	**P2** Application of:	**P3** Liquidity and efficiency
	Comparative balance sheets	Common-size balance sheet	Solvency
C2 Standards for comparisons, and analysis tools	Comparative income statements	Common-size income statement	Profitability
	Trend analysis	Common-size graphics	Market prospects
			A1 Analysis reports

Learning Objectives

CONCEPTUAL

C1 Explain the purpose and identify the building blocks of analysis.

C2 Describe standards for comparisons in analysis.

ANALYTICAL

A1 Summarize and report results of analysis.

A2 *Appendix 13A*—Explain the form and assess the content of a complete income statement.

PROCEDURAL

P1 Explain and apply methods of horizontal analysis.

P2 Describe and apply methods of vertical analysis.

P3 Define and apply ratio analysis.

Investing In Numbers

"We are in the business of helping people" — JAMES GORMAN

NEW YORK—In preschool, most of the children get trophies. At **Morgan Stanley** (**MorganStanley.com**), the young financiers can earn trophies, or "deal toys," when they complete a deal, according to Nina Godiwalla, who put together a collection of inside stories about life at the firm. Fortunately, work is not always about trophies at Morgan Stanley, which is one of the most respected financial services companies in the world. Morgan Stanley analyzes financial statements for profit. Moreover, based on its stock price over the past few years, the company's analysis techniques are paying off.

One of Morgan Stanley's key tools for company analysis is *ModelWare*. *ModelWare* is a framework to analyze the

Morgan Stanley
NYSE: MS

$77 billion valuation
56,000 employees
$35 billion revenues

Revenue Sources

Asset Mgmt & Other 36%
Commissions & Fees 14%
Investment Banking 18%
Trading & Investments 31%

nuts and bolts of companies' financial statements, and then to compare those companies on the basis of head-to-head performance metrics. One of its key aims is to provide comparable information that focuses on sustainable performance. To do this, it works with the underlying accounting numbers and footnotes.

Specifically, Morgan Stanley draws on the accounting numbers in financial statements to produce comparable metrics using techniques such as horizontal and vertical analysis. It also computes financial ratios for analysis and interpretation. Those ratios include return on equity, return on assets, asset turnover, profit margin, price-to-earnings, and numerous others. The focus is to uncover the drivers of profitability and to predict future levels of those drivers.

The company has experienced decades of success through analyzing financial statements. Despite its best efforts, however, people still do not fully use the information available in financial statements. Accordingly, Morgan Stanley will continue to reap profits from financial statement analysis and interpretation.

Morgan Stanley is also proud to play by the rules. *Fortune* writes, "Five years after the collapse of Lehman Brothers, Morgan Stanley has earned some bragging rights. It's the only major bank that hasn't paid a federal fine related to the financial crisis. [It] hasn't even been accused of breaking the law." James Gorman, its CEO, asserts that the "firm's reputation is our most precious asset." James also offers some advice for budding analysts: "If you [let] your compensation . . . define your overall level of happiness, you have a problem."

Sources: *Morgan Stanley website,* January 2016; *Bloomberg,* January 2012; *Business Insider,* January 2011; *Fortune,* August 2013; *MorganStanleyIQ,* 8 November 2007; *Wall Street Journal,* March 2006

BASICS OF ANALYSIS

Financial statement analysis applies analytical tools to general-purpose financial statements and related data for making business decisions. It involves transforming accounting data into more useful information. Financial statement analysis reduces our reliance on hunches, guesses, and intuition as well as our uncertainty in decision making. It does not lessen the need for expert judgment; instead, it provides us an effective and systematic basis for making business decisions. This section describes the purpose of financial statement analysis, its information sources, the use of comparisons, and some issues in computations.

Purpose of Analysis

Internal users of accounting information are those involved in strategically managing and operating the company. They include managers, officers, internal auditors, consultants, budget directors, and market researchers. The purpose of financial statement analysis for these users is to provide strategic information to improve company efficiency and effectiveness in providing products and services.

External users of accounting information are *not* directly involved in running the company. They include shareholders, lenders, directors, customers, suppliers, regulators, lawyers, brokers, and the press. External users rely on financial statement analysis to make better and more informed decisions in pursuing their own goals.

We can identify other uses of financial statement analysis. Shareholders and creditors assess company prospects to make investing and lending decisions. A board of directors analyzes financial statements in monitoring management's decisions. Employees and unions use financial statements in labor negotiations. Suppliers use financial statement information in establishing credit terms. Customers analyze financial statements in deciding whether to establish supply relationships. Public utilities set customer rates by analyzing financial statements. Auditors use financial statements in assessing the "fair presentation" of their clients' financial results. Analyst services such as **Dun & Bradstreet**, **Moody's**, and **Standard & Poor's** use financial statements in making buy-sell recommendations and in setting credit ratings. The common goal of these users is to evaluate company performance and financial condition. This includes evaluating (1) past and current performance, (2) current financial position, and (3) future performance and risk.

Building Blocks of Analysis

Financial statement analysis focuses on one or more elements of a company's financial condition or performance. Our analysis emphasizes four areas of inquiry—with varying degrees of importance. These four areas are described and illustrated in this chapter and are considered the *building blocks* of financial statement analysis:

- **Liquidity** and **efficiency**—ability to meet short-term obligations and to efficiently generate revenues.
- **Solvency**—ability to generate future revenues and meet long-term obligations.
- **Profitability**—ability to provide financial rewards sufficient to attract and retain financing.
- **Market prospects**—ability to generate positive market expectations.

Applying the building blocks of financial statement analysis involves determining (1) the objectives of analysis and (2) the relative emphasis among the building blocks. We distinguish among these four building blocks to emphasize the different aspects of a company's financial condition or performance, yet we must remember that these areas of analysis are interrelated. For instance, a company's operating performance is affected by the availability of financing and short-term liquidity conditions. Similarly, a company's credit standing is not limited to satisfactory short-term liquidity but depends also on its profitability and efficiency in using assets. Early in our analysis, we need to determine the relative emphasis of each building block. Emphasis and analysis can later change as a result of evidence collected.

Decision Insight

Chips and Brokers   The phrase *blue chips* refers to stock of big, profitable companies. The phrase comes from poker, where the most valuable chips are blue. The term *brokers* refers to those who execute orders to buy or sell stock. The term comes from wine retailers—individuals who broach (break) wine casks. ■

Information for Analysis

Some users, such as managers and regulatory authorities, are able to receive special financial reports prepared to meet their analysis needs. However, most users must rely on **general-purpose financial statements** that include the (1) income statement, (2) balance sheet, (3) statement of stockholders' equity (or statement of retained earnings), (4) statement of cash flows, and (5) notes to these statements.

Financial reporting refers to the communication of financial information useful for making investment, credit, and other business decisions. Financial reporting includes not only general-purpose financial statements but also information from SEC 10-K or other filings, press releases, shareholders' meetings, forecasts, management letters, auditors' reports, and webcasts.

Management's Discussion and Analysis (MD&A) is one example of useful information outside traditional financial statements. **Apple**'s MD&A (available at **Investor.Apple.com** and 'Item 7' in the annual report), for example, begins with an overview, followed by critical accounting policies and estimates. It then discusses operating results followed by financial condition (liquidity, capital resources, and cash flows). The final few parts discuss legal proceedings, market risk of financial instruments, and risks from interest rate and foreign currency fluctuations. The MD&A is an excellent starting point in understanding a company's business activities.

Decision Insight

Reaping Returns   Many websites offer free access and screening of companies by key numbers such as earnings, sales, and book value. For instance, **Investor's Business Daily** has information for more than 10,000 stocks (**www.investors.com**). ■

Standards for Comparisons

When interpreting measures from financial statement analysis, we need to decide whether the measures indicate good, bad, or average performance. To make such judgments, we need standards (benchmarks) for comparisons that include the following:

C2
Describe standards for comparisons in analysis.

- *Intracompany*—The company under analysis can provide standards for comparisons based on its own prior performance and relations between its financial items. Apple's current net income, for instance, can be compared with its prior years' net income and in relation to its revenues or total assets.
- *Competitor*—One or more direct competitors of the company being analyzed can provide standards for comparisons. **Coca-Cola**'s profit margin, for instance, can be compared with **PepsiCo**'s profit margin.
- *Industry*—Industry statistics can provide standards of comparisons. Such statistics are available from services such as Dun & Bradstreet, Standard & Poor's, and Moody's.
- *Guidelines (rules of thumb)*—General standards of comparisons can develop from experience. Examples are the 2:1 level for the current ratio or 1:1 level for the acid-test ratio. Guidelines, or rules of thumb, must be carefully applied because context is crucial.

Point: Each chapter's *Reporting in Action* problems engage students in *intracompany* analysis, whereas *Comparative Analysis* problems require competitor analysis (**Apple** vs. **Google** vs. **Samsung**).

All of these comparison standards are useful when properly applied, yet measures taken from a selected competitor or group of competitors are often best. Intracompany and industry measures are also important. Guidelines or rules of thumb should be applied with care, and then only if they seem reasonable given past experience and industry norms.

Tools of Analysis

Three of the most common tools of financial statement analysis are

1. **Horizontal analysis**—comparison of a company's financial condition and performance across time.
2. **Vertical analysis**—comparison of a company's financial condition and performance to a base amount.
3. **Ratio analysis**—measurement of key relations between financial statement items.

The remainder of this chapter describes these analysis tools and how to apply them.

Fraud

Busting Frauds Horizontal, vertical, and ratio analysis tools can uncover fraud by identifying amounts out of line with expectations. One can then follow up and ask questions that can either identify a logical reason for such results or confirm/raise suspicions of fraud. Many past fraud schemes could have been identified much earlier had people applied these tools and pressured management for explanations.

HORIZONTAL ANALYSIS

P1

Explain and apply methods of horizontal analysis.

Analysis of any single financial number is of limited value. Instead, much of financial statement analysis involves identifying and describing relations between numbers, groups of numbers, and changes in those numbers. Horizontal analysis refers to examination of financial statement data *across time*. (The term *horizontal analysis* arises from the left-to-right [or right-to-left] movement of our eyes as we review comparative financial statements across time.)

Comparative Statements

Comparing amounts for two or more successive periods often helps in analyzing financial statements. **Comparative financial statements** facilitate this comparison by showing financial amounts in side-by-side columns on a single statement, called a *comparative format*. Using figures from **Apple**'s financial statements, this section explains how to compute dollar changes and percent changes for comparative statements.

Computation of Dollar Changes and Percent Changes   Comparing financial statements over relatively short time periods—two to three years—is often done by analyzing changes in line items. A change analysis usually includes analyzing absolute dollar amount changes and percent changes. Both analyses are relevant because dollar changes can yield large percent changes inconsistent with their importance. For instance, a 50% change from a base figure of $100 is less important than the same percent change from a base amount of $100,000 in the same statement. Reference to dollar amounts is necessary to retain a proper perspective and to assess the importance of changes. We compute the *dollar change* for a financial statement item as follows:

Example: Which is a more significant change, a 70% increase on a $1,000 expense or a 30% increase on a $400,000 expense? *Answer:* The 30% increase.

$$\text{Dollar change} = \text{Analysis period amount} - \text{Base period amount}$$

Analysis period is the point or period of time for the financial statements under analysis, and *base period* is the point or period of time for the financial statements used for comparison purposes. The prior year is commonly used as a base period. We compute the *percent change* by dividing the dollar change by the base period amount and then multiplying this quantity by 100 as follows:

$$\text{Percent change (\%)} = \frac{\text{Analysis period amount} - \text{Base period amount}}{\text{Base period amount}} \times 100$$

We can always compute a dollar change, but we must be aware of a few rules in working with percent changes. To illustrate, look at four separate cases in this chart:

Case	Analysis Period	Base Period	Change Analysis Dollar	Change Analysis Percent
A	$ 1,500	$(4,500)	$ 6,000	—
B	(1,000)	2,000	(3,000)	—
C	8,000	—	8,000	—
D	0	10,000	(10,000)	(100%)

- When a negative amount is in the base period and a positive amount in the analysis period (or vice versa), we cannot compute a meaningful percent change; see cases A and B.
- When no value is in the base period, no percent change is computable; see case C.
- When an item has a value in the base period and zero in the analysis period, the decrease is 100 percent; see case D.

Example: When there is a value in the base period and zero in the analysis period, the decrease is 100%. Why isn't the reverse situation an increase of 100%? *Answer:* A 100% increase of zero is still zero.

It is common when using horizontal analysis to compare amounts to either average or median values from prior periods (average and median values smooth out erratic or unusual fluctuations).[1] We also commonly round percents and ratios to one or two decimal places, but practice on this matter is not uniform. Computations are as detailed as necessary, which is judged by whether rounding potentially affects users' decisions. Computations should not be excessively detailed so that important relations are not lost among a mountain of decimal points and digits.

Comparative Balance Sheets   Comparative balance sheets consist of balance sheet amounts from two or more balance sheet dates arranged side by side. The usefulness of this method of analysis is often improved by showing each item's dollar change and percent change to highlight large changes.

Analysis of comparative financial statements begins by focusing on items that show large dollar or percent changes. We then try to identify the reasons for these changes and, if possible, determine whether they are favorable or unfavorable. We also follow up on items with small changes when we expected the changes to be large.

Point: Spreadsheet programs can help with horizontal, vertical, and ratio analyses, including graphical depictions of financial relations.

Exhibit 13.1 shows comparative balance sheets for Apple Inc. (Nasdaq: AAPL). A few items stand out on the asset side. Apple's goodwill shows a substantial 192.7% increase. This increase is likely linked to acquisitions such as that of Beats Music and Beats Electronics. Other notable increases occur with (1) other current assets, partially related to derivatives; (2) accounts receivable, which stands out as it is markedly higher than the sales increase; and (3) vendor non-trade receivables. There is also an apparent shift to more long-term securities (+22.5%) and less short-term (−57.3%). We see an overall total asset growth of 12.0%, which must be accompanied by future income to validate these asset reinvestments. Some Apple shareholders are concerned about the company's growing assets and declining return on assets.

Point: Business consultants use comparative statement analysis to provide management advice.

On Apple's financing side, we see the overall 12.0% increase is driven by a 44.1% increase in liabilities (equity decreased by 9.7%). The largest increase is due to issuance of long-term debt, followed by increases in current liabilities. We also see a 16.4% reduction ($17,104) in retained earnings even though net income is $39,510, which is partly due to its cash dividends and stock repurchases.

Comparative Income Statements   Comparative income statements are prepared similarly to comparative balance sheets. Amounts for two or more periods are placed side by side, with additional columns for dollar and percent changes. Exhibit 13.2 shows Apple's comparative income statements.

Apple reports substantial sales growth of 7.0% in 2014. This finding helps support management's 12.0% growth in assets as reflected in the comparative balance sheets. The 5.3% growth in cost of sales given a larger 7.0% sales increase suggests greater control over its costs of sales. Conversely, the 17.8% increase in operating expenses, which exceeds the 7.0% sales growth, is

Point: Percent change can also be computed by dividing the current period by the prior period and subtracting 1.0. For example, the 7.0% sales increase in Exhibit 13.2 is computed as: ($182,795/$170,910) − 1.

---

[1] *Median* is the middle value in a group of numbers. For instance, if five prior years' incomes are (in 000s) $15, $19, $18, $20, and $22, the median value is $19. When there are two middle numbers, we can take their average. For instance, if four prior years' sales are (in 000s) $84, $91, $96, and $93, the median is $92 (computed as the average of $91 and $93).

EXHIBIT 13.1

Comparative Balance
Sheets

APPLE

APPLE INC. Comparative Balance Sheets September 27, 2014, and September 28, 2013				
$ millions	2014	2013	Dollar Change	Percent Change
Assets				
Cash and cash equivalents	$ 13,844	$ 14,259	$ (415)	(2.9)%
Short-term marketable securities	11,233	26,287	(15,054)	(57.3)
Accounts receivable, net	17,460	13,102	4,358	33.3
Inventories	2,111	1,764	347	19.7
Deferred tax assets	4,318	3,453	865	25.1
Vendor non-trade receivables	9,759	7,539	2,220	29.4
Other current assets	9,806	6,882	2,924	42.5
Total current assets	68,531	73,286	(4,755)	(6.5)
Long-term marketable securities.	130,162	106,215	23,947	22.5
Property, plant and equipment, net.	20,624	16,597	4,027	24.3
Goodwill.	4,616	1,577	3,039	192.7
Acquired intangible assets, net	4,142	4,179	(37)	(0.9)
Other assets.	3,764	5,146	(1,382)	(26.9)
Total assets.	$231,839	$207,000	$ 24,839	12.0
Liabilities				
Accounts payable	$ 30,196	$ 22,367	$ 7,829	35.0%
Accrued expenses	18,453	13,856	4,597	33.2
Deferred revenue.	8,491	7,435	1,056	14.2
Commercial paper	6,308	0	6,308	—
Total current liabilities.	63,448	43,658	19,790	45.3
Deferred revenue—noncurrent.	3,031	2,625	406	15.5
Long-term debt	28,987	16,960	12,027	70.9
Other noncurrent liabilities.	24,826	20,208	4,618	22.9
Total liabilities	120,292	83,451	36,841	44.1
Stockholders' Equity				
Common stock	23,313	19,764	3,549	18.0
Retained earnings.	87,152	104,256	(17,104)	(16.4)
Accumulated other comprehensive income	1,082	(471)	1,553	—
Total stockholders' equity	111,547	123,549	(12,002)	(9.7)
Total liabilities and stockholders' equity	$231,839	$207,000	$ 24,839	12.0

EXHIBIT 13.2

Comparative Income
Statements

APPLE

APPLE INC. Comparative Income Statements For Years Ended September 27, 2014, and September 28, 2013				
$ millions, except per share	2014	2013	Dollar Change	Percent Change
Net sales	$182,795	$170,910	$11,885	7.0%
Cost of sales	112,258	106,606	5,652	5.3
Gross margin	70,537	64,304	6,233	9.7
Research and development	6,041	4,475	1,566	35.0
Selling, general and administrative.	11,993	10,830	1,163	10.7
Total operating expenses.	18,034	15,305	2,729	17.8
Operating income	52,503	48,999	3,504	7.2
Other income, net.	980	1,156	(176)	(15.2)
Income before provision for income taxes	53,483	50,155	3,328	6.6
Provision for income taxes	13,973	13,118	855	6.5
Net income	$ 39,510	$ 37,037	2,473	6.7
Basic earnings per share.	$ 6.49	$ 5.72	$ 0.77	13.5
Diluted earnings per share.	$ 6.45	$ 5.68	$ 0.77	13.6

not good news. Importantly, much of this 17.8% increase is driven by greater research and development costs, from which management/investors hope to reap future rewards. Apple reports an increase of 6.7% in net income, which as mentioned is mainly driven by its $6,233 million growth in gross margin.

Trend Analysis

Trend analysis, also called *trend percent analysis* or *index number trend analysis,* is a form of horizontal analysis that can reveal patterns in data across successive periods. It involves computing trend percents for a series of financial numbers and is a variation on the use of percent changes. The difference is that trend analysis does not subtract the base period amount in the numerator. To compute trend percents, we do the following:

1. Select a *base period* and assign each item in the base period a weight of 100%.
2. Express financial numbers as a percent of their base period number.

Specifically, a *trend percent,* also called an *index number,* is computed as follows:

$$\text{Trend percent (\%)} = \frac{\text{Analysis period amount}}{\text{Base period amount}} \times 100$$

Point: *Index* refers to the comparison of the analysis period to the base period. Percents determined for each period are called *index numbers.*

To illustrate trend analysis, we use the Apple data shown in Exhibit 13.3. These data are from Apple's current and prior financial statements.

EXHIBIT 13.3

Sales and Expenses

$ millions	2014	2013	2012	2011	2010
Net sales	$182,795	$170,910	$156,508	$108,249	$65,226
Cost of sales	112,258	106,606	87,846	64,431	39,541
Operating expenses	18,034	15,305	13,421	10,028	7,299

The trend percents—using the data from Exhibit 13.3—are shown in Exhibit 13.4. The base period is 2010 and the trend percent is computed in each subsequent year by dividing that year's amount by its 2010 amount. For instance, the revenue trend percent for 2014 is 280.3%, computed as $182,795/$65,226.

Point: Trend analysis expresses a percent of base, not a percent of change.

EXHIBIT 13.4

Trend Percents for Sales and Expenses

In trend percent	2014	2013	2012	2011	2010
Net sales	280.3%	262.0%	240.0%	166.0%	100.0%
Cost of sales	283.9	269.6	222.2	162.9	100.0
Operating expenses	247.1	209.7	183.9	137.4	100.0

Graphical depictions often aid analysis of trend percents. Exhibit 13.5 shows the trend percents from Exhibit 13.4 in a *line graph,* which can help us identify trends and detect changes in direction or magnitude. It reveals that the trend line for revenue consistently exceeds that for operating expenses; the same is true for cost of sales, but with a turn for the worse in 2013 and 2014. The marked increase for cost of sales in 2013 is especially noticeable, with a reduction in the difference in trend lines for 2014—long-run profitability will suffer if those costs are not controlled. The trend line for operating expenses is encouraging because it lags revenue growth for each year from 2010–2014.

EXHIBIT 13.5

Trend Percent Lines for Sales and Expenses of Apple

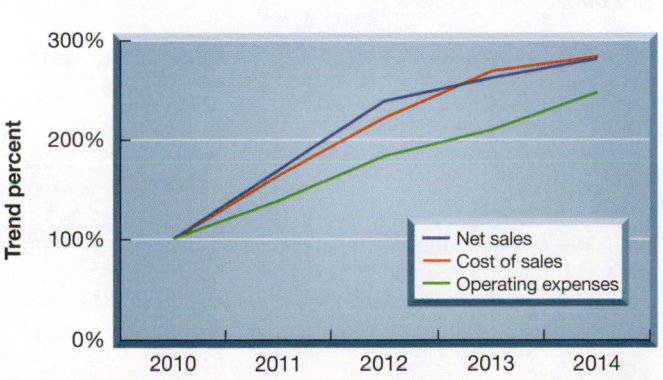

EXHIBIT 13.6

Revenue Trend Percent Lines—Apple, Google, and Samsung

APPLE
GOOGLE
Samsung

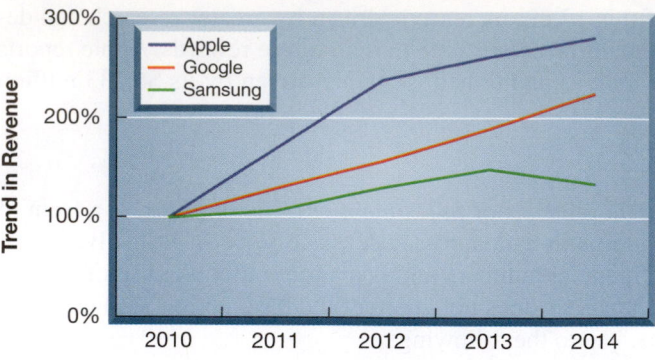

Exhibit 13.6 compares Apple's revenue trend line to that of Google and Samsung for this same period. Apple is able to grow its revenue in each year relative to its base year. In this respect Apple outperforms its competitors, although both Google and Samsung performed well over this same period of time. We can say from these data that Apple products and services have met with consumer acceptance.

Trend analysis of financial statement items can include comparisons of relations between items on different financial statements. For instance, Exhibit 13.7 compares Apple's revenue and total assets. The increase in total assets (208.4%) exceeds the increase in annual revenues (180.3%) since 2010. Is this result favorable or not? One interpretation is that Apple was *less* efficient in using its assets in 2014 versus 2010. This means that management has not generated annual revenues sufficient to compensate for the asset growth.

EXHIBIT 13.7

Sales and Asset Data for Apple

$ millions	2014	2010	Change (2014 vs. 2010)
Net sales..........	$182,795	$65,225	180.3%
Total assets........	231,839	75,183	208.4%

Overall we must remember that an important role of financial statement analysis is identifying questions and areas of interest, which often direct us to important factors bearing on a company's future. Accordingly, financial statement analysis should be seen as a continuous process of refining our understanding and expectations of company performance and financial condition.

■ Decision Maker

Auditor   Your tests reveal a 3% increase in sales from $200,000 to $206,000 and a 4% decrease in expenses from $190,000 to $182,400. Both changes are within your "reasonableness" criterion of ±5%, and thus you don't pursue additional tests. The audit partner in charge questions your lack of follow-up and mentions the *joint relation* between sales and expenses. To what is the partner referring? ■   [Answers follow the chapter's Summary.]

NEED-TO-KNOW 13-1

Horizontal Analysis

P1

Compute trend percents for the following accounts, using 2013 as the base year (round percents to whole numbers). State whether the situation as revealed by the trends appears to be favorable or unfavorable for each account.

$ millions	2016	2015	2014	2013
Sales....................	$500	$350	$250	$200
Cost of goods sold.........	400	175	100	50

Solution

$ millions	2016	2015	2014	2013
Sales....................	250%	175%	125%	100%
	($500/$200)	($350/$200)	($250/$200)	($200/$200)
Cost of goods sold.........	800%	350%	200%	100%
	($400/$50)	($175/$50)	($100/$50)	($50/$50)

Analysis: The trend in sales is favorable; however, we need more information about economic conditions such as inflation rates and competitors' performances to better assess it. Cost of sales is also rising (as expected with increasing sales); however, cost of sales is rising faster than the increase in sales, which is unfavorable and bad news. A quick analysis of the gross margin percentage would highlight this concern.

Do More: QS 13-3, QS 13-4, E 13-3

VERTICAL ANALYSIS

Vertical analysis is a tool to evaluate individual financial statement items or a group of items in terms of a specific base amount. We usually define a key aggregate figure as the base, which for an income statement is usually revenue and for a balance sheet is usually total assets. This section explains vertical analysis and applies it to **Apple**. (The term *vertical analysis* arises from the up-down [or down-up] movement of our eyes as we review common-size financial statements. Vertical analysis is also called *common-size analysis*.)

P2

Describe and apply methods of vertical analysis.

Common-Size Statements

The comparative statements in Exhibits 13.1 and 13.2 show the change in each item over time, but they do not emphasize the relative importance of each item. We use **common-size financial statements** to reveal changes in the relative importance of each financial statement item. All individual amounts in common-size statements are redefined in terms of common-size percents. A *common-size percent* is measured by dividing each individual financial statement amount under analysis by its base amount:

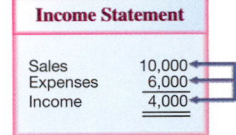

Income Statement	
Sales	10,000
Expenses	6,000
Income	4,000

$$\text{Common-size percent (\%)} = \frac{\text{Analysis amount}}{\text{Base amount}} \times 100$$

Common-Size Balance Sheets Common-size statements express each item as a percent of a *base amount,* which for a common-size balance sheet is usually total assets. The base amount is assigned a value of 100%. (This implies that the total amount of liabilities plus equity equals 100% since this amount equals total assets.) We then compute a common-size percent for each asset, liability, and equity item using total assets as the base amount. When we present a company's successive balance sheets in this way, changes in the mixture of assets, liabilities, and equity are apparent.

Point: The *base* amount in common-size analysis is an *aggregate* amount from that period's financial statement.

Exhibit 13.8 shows common-size comparative balance sheets for Apple. Some relations that stand out on both a magnitude and percentage basis include (1) a 7.9 point decrease in percent of short-term securities, which reflects a $15,054 million decrease; (2) a new issuance of $12,027 million in long-term debt; and (3) a 12.8 point decrease in percent of retained earnings, which reflects a $17,104 million decrease. The absence of substantial changes in Apple's balance sheet suggests a mature company, but with some lack of focus as evidenced by the large and increasing amount of long-term securities. This buildup in securities is a concern as the return on securities is historically smaller than the return on operating assets from successful reinvestment. Time will tell whether Apple can continue to generate sufficient revenue and income from its expanding asset base.

Point: Common-size statements often are used to compare two or more companies in the same industry.

Point: Common-size statements are also useful in comparing firms that report in different currencies.

Common-Size Income Statements Analysis also benefits from use of a common-size income statement. Revenue is usually the base amount, which is assigned a value of 100%. Each common-size income statement item appears as a percent of revenue. If we think of the 100% revenue amount as representing one sales dollar, the remaining items show how each revenue dollar is distributed among costs, expenses, and income.

Exhibit 13.9 shows common-size comparative income statements for each dollar of Apple's revenue. The past two years' common-size numbers are similar with a few exceptions. One item to note is the decrease of 1.0 cent in the cost of sales, which is a positive development. Another is the increase of 0.9 cent in operating expense per each net sales dollar—evidenced by the increase in expense as a percent of net sales from 9.0% to 9.9%. Much of this is attributed to the rising investment in research and development from 2.6% to 3.3% as a percent of net sales. In sum, analysis here shows that common-size percents for successive income statements can uncover important changes in a company's cost management and growth. (Evidence of no changes, especially when changes are expected, is also informative.)

Global: International companies sometimes disclose "convenience" financial statements, which are statements translated in other languages and currencies. However, these statements rarely adjust for differences in accounting principles across countries.

EXHIBIT 13.8

Common-Size Comparative
Balance Sheets

APPLE

$ millions	2014	2013	Common-Size Percents* 2014	Common-Size Percents* 2013
APPLE INC. Common-Size Comparative Balance Sheets September 27, 2014, and September 28, 2013				
Assets				
Cash and cash equivalents	$ 13,844	$ 14,259	6.0%	6.9%
Short-term marketable securities	11,233	26,287	4.8	12.7
Accounts receivable, net	17,460	13,102	7.5	6.3
Inventories	2,111	1,764	0.9	0.9
Deferred tax assets	4,318	3,453	1.9	1.7
Vendor non-trade receivables	9,759	7,539	4.2	3.6
Other current assets	9,806	6,882	4.2	3.3
Total current assets	68,531	73,286	29.6	35.4
Long-term marketable securities	130,162	106,215	56.1	51.3
Property, plant and equipment, net	20,624	16,597	8.9	8.0
Goodwill	4,616	1,577	2.0	0.8
Acquired intangible assets, net	4,142	4,179	1.8	2.0
Other assets	3,764	5,146	1.6	2.5
Total assets	$231,839	$207,000	100.0%	100.0%
Liabilities				
Accounts payable	$ 30,196	$ 22,367	13.0%	10.8%
Accrued expenses	18,453	13,856	8.0	6.7
Deferred revenue	8,491	7,435	3.7	3.6
Commercial paper	6,308	0	2.7	0.0
Total current liabilities	63,448	43,658	27.4	21.1
Deferred revenue—noncurrent	3,031	2,625	1.3	1.3
Long-term debt	28,987	16,960	12.5	8.2
Other noncurrent liabilities	24,826	20,208	10.7	9.8
Total liabilities	120,292	83,451	51.9	40.3
Stockholders' Equity				
Common stock	23,313	19,764	10.1	9.5
Retained earnings	87,152	104,256	37.6	50.4
Accumulated other comprehensive income	1,082	(471)	0.5	(0.2)
Total stockholders' equity	111,547	123,549	48.1	59.7
Total liabilities and stockholders' equity	$231,839	$207,000	100.0%	100.0%

* Percents are rounded to tenths and thus may not exactly sum to totals and subtotals.

EXHIBIT 13.9

Common-Size Comparative
Income Statements

APPLE

$ millions	2014	2013	Common-Size Percents* 2014	Common-Size Percents* 2013
APPLE INC. Common-Size Comparative Income Statements For Years Ended September 27, 2014, and September 28, 2013				
Net sales	$182,795	$170,910	100.0%	100.0%
Cost of sales	112,258	106,606	61.4	62.4
Gross margin	70,537	64,304	38.6	37.6
Research and development	6,041	4,475	3.3	2.6
Selling, general and administrative	11,993	10,830	6.6	6.3
Total operating expenses	18,034	15,305	9.9	9.0
Operating income	52,503	48,999	28.7	28.7
Other income, net	980	1,156	0.5	0.7
Income before provision for income taxes	53,483	50,155	29.3	29.3
Provision for income taxes	13,973	13,118	7.6	7.7
Net income	$ 39,510	$ 37,037	21.6%	21.7%

* Percents are rounded to tenths and thus may not exactly sum to totals and subtotals.

Common-Size Graphics

Two of the most common tools of common-size analysis are trend analysis of common-size statements and graphical analysis. The trend analysis of common-size statements is similar to that of comparative statements discussed under vertical analysis. It is not illustrated here because the only difference is the substitution of common-size percents for trend percents. Instead, this section discusses graphical analysis of common-size statements.

An income statement readily lends itself to common-size graphical analysis. This is so because revenues affect nearly every item in an income statement. Exhibit 13.10 shows Apple's 2014 common-size income statement in graphical form. This pie chart highlights the contribution of each cost component of net sales for net income (for this graph, "other income, net" is included in selling, general, and administrative costs).

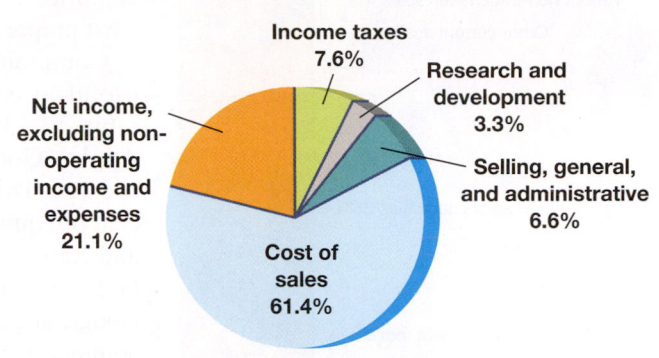

EXHIBIT 13.10

Common-Size Graphic of Income Statement

Exhibit 13.11 previews more complex graphical analyses available and the insights they provide. The data for this exhibit are taken from Apple's *Segments* footnote. Apple reports six operating segments for 2014: (1) Americas, (2) Europe, (3) China, (4) Japan, (5) Asia Pacific, and (6) Retail.

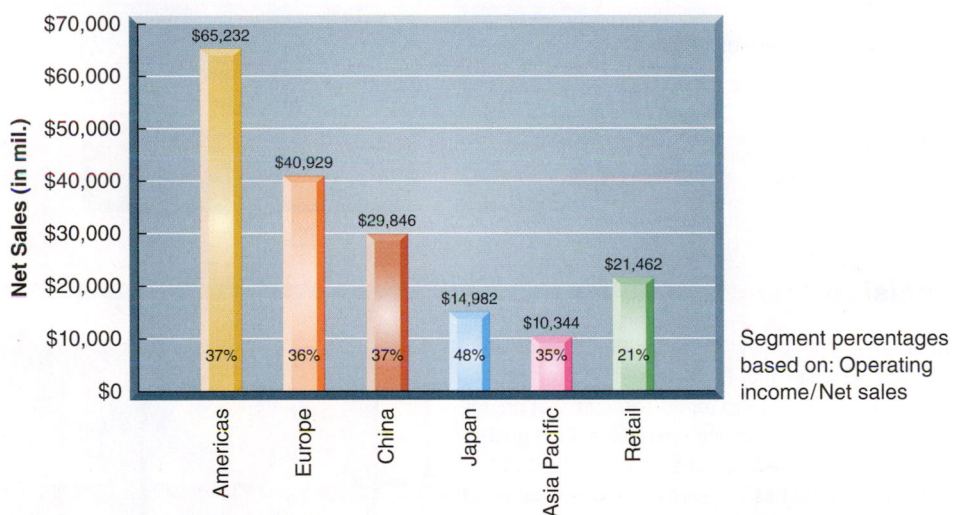

EXHIBIT 13.11

Sales and Operating Income Margin Breakdown by Segment

The bars in Exhibit 13.11 show the level of net sales for each of Apple's six reportable segments. Its Americas segment generates $65,232 million of its total net sales, which is roughly 36% of its total sales. The five other bars show the level of sales generated from each of the other international segments, including its retail segment. Within each bar is that segment's operating income margin, defined as segment operating income divided by segment net sales. The Americas segment yields a 37% operating income margin; margins for the other five segments are shown within each of the other segment bars. This type of graphic presentation can lead to questions about the profitability of each segment and discussion of further expansions into the more lucrative segments. For example, the Japan segment yields an operating margin of 48%. A natural question for management is what potential is there to further expand sales into the Japan segment and maintain a similar operating margin? This type of analysis can help in determining strategic plans and actions.

Graphical analysis is also useful in identifying (1) sources of financing, including the distribution among current liabilities, noncurrent liabilities, and equity capital, and (2) focuses of investing activities, including the distribution among current and noncurrent assets. To illustrate,

EXHIBIT 13.12

Common-Size Graphic of
Asset Components

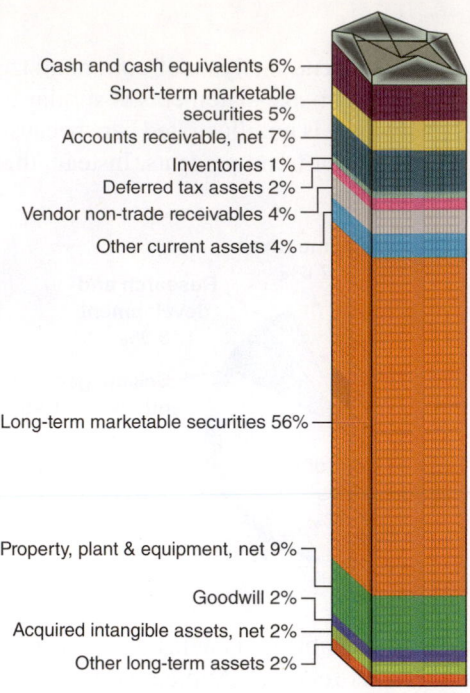

Cash and cash equivalents 6%
Short-term marketable securities 5%
Accounts receivable, net 7%
Inventories 1%
Deferred tax assets 2%
Vendor non-trade receivables 4%
Other current assets 4%

Long-term marketable securities 56%

Property, plant & equipment, net 9%
Goodwill 2%
Acquired intangible assets, net 2%
Other long-term assets 2%

Exhibit 13.12 shows a common-size graphical display of Apple's assets. Common-size balance sheet analysis can be extended to examine the composition of these subgroups. For instance, in assessing liquidity of current assets, knowing what proportion of *current* assets consists of inventories is usually important, and not simply what proportion inventories are of *total* assets.

Common-size financial statements are also useful in comparing different companies. Exhibit 13.13 shows common-size graphics of Apple, Google, and Samsung on financing sources. This graphic highlights the larger percent of equity financing for Google versus Apple and Samsung. It also highlights the somewhat larger noncurrent (debt) financing of Apple versus Google and Samsung. Comparison of a company's common-size statements with competitors' or industry common-size statistics alerts us to differences in the structure or distribution of its financial statements but not to their dollar magnitude.

EXHIBIT 13.13

Common-Size Graphic of
Financing Sources—
Competitor Analysis

APPLE
GOOGLE
Samsung

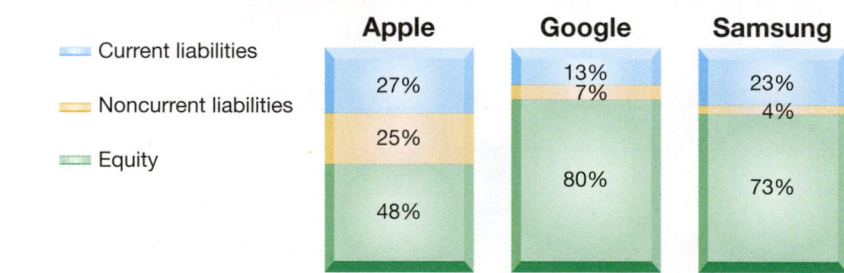

	Apple	Google	Samsung
Current liabilities	27%	13%	23%
Noncurrent liabilities	25%	7%	4%
Equity	48%	80%	73%

Decision Insight

Seeing Truth   In a survey of nearly 200 CFOs of large firms, roughly 20% say that firms, based on their experience, use accounting ruses to report earnings that do not fully reflect the firms' underlying operations. One goal of financial analysis is to see through such ruses. The top five reasons CFOs gave for this behavior are shown here (*Wall Street Journal*, October 2012). ■

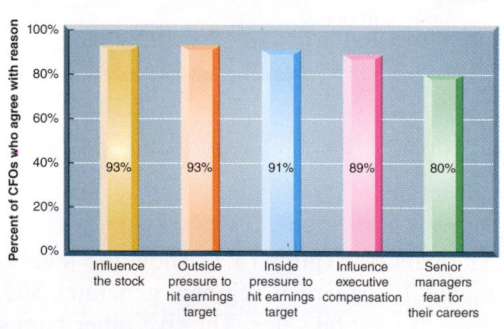

Reason	Percent
Influence the stock	93%
Outside pressure to hit earnings target	93%
Inside pressure to hit earnings target	91%
Influence executive compensation	89%
Senior managers fear for their careers	80%

NEED-TO-KNOW 13-2

Vertical Analysis

P2

Express the following comparative income statements in common-size percents and assess whether or not this company's situation has improved in the most recent year (round percents to whole numbers).

Comparative Income Statements For Years Ended December 31, 2016 and 2015		
	2016	2015
Sales	$800	$500
Total expenses	560	400
Net income	$240	$100

Solution

	2016	**2015**
Sales	100%	100%
	($800/$800)	($500/$500)
Total expenses	70%	80%
	($560/$800)	($400/$500)
Net income	30%	20%

Analysis: This company's situation has improved. This is evident from its substantial increase in net income as a percent of sales for 2016 (30%) relative to 2015 (20%). Further, the company's sales increased from $500 in 2015 to $800 in 2016 (while expenses declined as a percent of sales from 80% to 70%).

Do More: QS 13-5, E 13-4, E 13-6

RATIO ANALYSIS

Ratios are among the more widely used tools of financial analysis because they provide clues to and symptoms of underlying conditions. A ratio can help us uncover conditions and trends difficult to detect by inspecting individual components making up the ratio. Ratios, like other analysis tools, are usually future oriented; that is, they are often adjusted for their probable future trend and magnitude, and their usefulness depends on skillful interpretation.

A ratio expresses a mathematical relation between two quantities. It can be expressed as a percent, rate, or proportion. For instance, a change in an account balance from $100 to $250 can be expressed as (1) 150% increase, (2) 2.5 times, or (3) 2.5 to 1 (or 2.5:1). Computation of a ratio is a simple arithmetic operation, but its interpretation is not. To be meaningful, a ratio must refer to an economically important relation. For example, a direct and crucial relation exists between an item's sales price and its cost. Accordingly, the ratio of cost of goods sold to sales is meaningful. In contrast, no obvious relation exists between freight costs and the balance of long-term investments.

This section describes an important set of financial ratios and their application. The selected ratios are organized into the four building blocks of financial statement analysis: (1) liquidity and efficiency, (2) solvency, (3) profitability, and (4) market prospects. All of these ratios were explained at relevant points in prior chapters. The purpose here is to organize and apply them under a summary framework. We use four common standards, in varying degrees, for comparisons: intracompany, competitor, industry, and guidelines.

P3
Define and apply ratio analysis.

Point: Some sources for industry norms are *Annual Statement Studies* by Robert Morris Associates, *Industry Norms & Key Business Ratios* by Dun & Bradstreet, *Standard & Poor's Industry Surveys,* and Reuters.com/finance.

Liquidity and Efficiency

Liquidity refers to the availability of resources to meet short-term cash requirements. It is affected by the timing of cash inflows and outflows along with prospects for future performance. Analysis of liquidity is aimed at a company's funding requirements. *Efficiency* refers to how productive a company is in using its assets. Efficiency is usually measured relative to how much revenue is generated from a certain level of assets.

Both liquidity and efficiency are important and complementary. If a company fails to meet its current obligations, its continued existence is doubtful. Viewed in this light, all other measures of analysis are of secondary importance. Although accounting measurements assume the company's continued existence, our analysis must always assess the validity of this assumption using liquidity measures. Moreover, inefficient use of assets can cause liquidity problems. A lack of liquidity often precedes lower profitability and fewer opportunities. It can foretell a loss of owner control. To a company's creditors, lack of liquidity can yield delays in collecting interest and principal payments or the loss of amounts due them. A company's customers and suppliers of goods and services also are affected by short-term liquidity problems. Implications include a company's inability to execute contracts and potential damage to important customer and supplier relationships. This section describes and illustrates key ratios relevant to assessing liquidity and efficiency.

Working Capital and Current Ratio   The amount of current assets less current liabilities is called **working capital,** or *net working capital.* A company needs adequate working capital to meet current debts, to carry sufficient inventories, and to take advantage of cash discounts. A company that runs low on working capital is less likely to meet current obligations or to continue operating. When evaluating a company's working capital, we must not only look at the dollar amount of current assets less current liabilities, but also at their ratio. The *current ratio* is defined as follows (see Chapter 3 for additional explanation):

$$\text{Current ratio} = \frac{\text{Current assets}}{\text{Current liabilities}}$$

EXHIBIT 13.14

Apple's Working Capital and Current Ratio

Current ratio
Google = 4.80
Samsung = 2.21
Industry = 2.5

$ millions	2014	2013
Current assets	$68,531	$ 73,286
Current liabilities	63,448	43,658
Working capital	**$ 5,083**	**$29,628**
Current ratio		
$68,531/$63,448 =	1.08 to 1	
$73,286/$43,568 =		1.68 to 1

Drawing on information in Exhibit 13.1, **Apple**'s working capital and current ratio for both 2014 and 2013 are shown in Exhibit 13.14. Also, **Google** (4.80), **Samsung** (2.21), and the industry's current ratio (2.5) are shown in the margin. Apple's 2014 ratio (1.08) is lower than competitors' ratios, but it is not in danger of defaulting on loan payments. A high current ratio suggests a strong liquidity position and an ability to meet current obligations. A company can, however, have a current ratio that is too high. An excessively high current ratio means that the company has invested too much in current assets compared to its current obligations. An excessive investment in current assets is not an efficient use of funds because current assets normally generate a low return on investment (compared with long-term assets).

Many users apply a guideline of 2:1 (or 1.5:1) for the current ratio in helping evaluate a company's debt-paying ability. A company with a 2:1 or higher current ratio is generally thought to be a good credit risk in the short run. Such a guideline or any analysis of the current ratio must recognize at least three additional factors: (1) type of business, (2) composition of current assets, and (3) turnover rate of current asset components.

Type of Business   A service company that grants little or no credit and carries few inventories can probably operate on a current ratio of less than 1:1 if its revenues generate enough cash to pay its current liabilities. On the other hand, a company selling high-priced clothing or furniture requires a higher ratio because of difficulties in judging customer demand and cash receipts. For instance, if demand falls, inventory may not generate as much cash as expected. Accordingly, analysis of the current ratio should include a comparison with ratios from successful companies in the same industry and from prior periods. We must also recognize that a company's accounting methods, especially choice of inventory method, affect the current ratio. For instance, when costs are rising, a company using LIFO tends to report a smaller amount of current assets than when using FIFO.

Point: When a firm uses LIFO in a period of rising costs, the standard for an adequate current ratio usually is lower than if it used FIFO.

Composition of Current Assets   The composition of a company's current assets is important to an evaluation of short-term liquidity. For instance, cash, cash equivalents, and short-term investments are more liquid than accounts and notes receivable. Also, short-term receivables normally are more liquid than inventory. Cash, of course, can be used to immediately pay current debts. Items such as accounts receivable and inventory, however, normally must be converted into cash before payment is made. An excessive amount of receivables and inventory weakens a company's ability to pay current liabilities. The acid-test ratio (see below) can help with this assessment.

Turnover Rate of Assets   Asset turnover measures a company's efficiency in using its assets. One relevant measure of asset efficiency is the revenue generated. A measure of total asset turnover is revenues divided by total assets, but evaluation of turnover for individual assets is also useful. We discuss both receivables turnover and inventory turnover next.

■ Decision Maker

Banker   A company requests a one-year, $200,000 loan for expansion. This company's current ratio is 4:1, with current assets of $160,000. Key competitors carry a current ratio of about 1.9:1. Using this information, do you approve the loan application? Does your decision change if the application is for a 10-year loan? ■ [Answers follow the chapter's Summary.]

Acid-Test Ratio   Quick assets are cash, short-term investments, and current receivables. These are the most liquid types of current assets. The *acid-test ratio,* also called *quick ratio* and introduced in Chapter 4, reflects on a company's short-term liquidity.

$$\text{Acid-test ratio} = \frac{\text{Cash} + \text{Short-term investments} + \text{Current receivables}}{\text{Current liabilities}}$$

Apple's acid-test ratio is computed in Exhibit 13.15. Apple's 2014 acid-test ratio (0.67) is lower than those for Google (4.44) and Samsung (1.73), as well as lower than the 1:1 common guideline for an acceptable acid-test ratio. The ratio for Apple is also less than the 0.9 industry norm; thus, it raises some concern. As with analysis of the current ratio, we need to consider other factors. For instance, the frequency with which a company converts its current assets into cash affects its working capital requirements. This implies that analysis of short-term liquidity should also include an analysis of receivables and inventories, which we consider next.

$ millions	2014	2013
Cash and equivalents	$13,844	$14,259
Short-term securities	11,233	26,287
Current receivables	17,460	13,102
Total quick assets	$42,537	$53,648
Current liabilities	$63,448	$43,658
Acid-test ratio		
$42,537/$63,448	0.67 to 1	
$53,648/$43,658		1.23 to 1

EXHIBIT 13.15

Acid-Test Ratio

Acid-test ratio
Google = 4.44
Samsung = 1.73
Industry = 0.9

Global: Ratio analysis helps overcome currency translation problems, but it does *not* overcome differences in accounting principles.

Accounts Receivable Turnover   We can measure how frequently a company converts its receivables into cash by computing the *accounts receivable turnover*. This ratio is defined as follows (see Chapter 7 for additional explanation).

$$\text{Accounts receivable turnover} = \frac{\text{Net sales}}{\text{Average accounts receivable, net}}$$

Short-term receivables from customers are often included in the denominator along with accounts receivable. Also, accounts receivable turnover is more precise if credit sales are used for the numerator, but external users generally use net sales (or net revenues) because information about credit sales is typically not reported. Apple's 2014 accounts receivable turnover is computed as follows ($ millions).

$$\frac{\$182,795}{(\$13,102 + \$17,460)/2} = 12.0 \text{ times}$$

Apple's value of 12.0 exceeds Google's 7.2 and Samsung's 7.4 values. Accounts receivable turnover is high when accounts receivable are quickly collected. A high turnover is favorable because it means the company need not commit large amounts of funds to accounts receivable. However, an accounts receivable turnover can be too high; this can occur when credit terms are so restrictive that they negatively affect sales volume.

Point: Some users prefer using gross accounts receivable (before subtracting the allowance for doubtful accounts) to avoid the influence of a manager's bad debts estimate.

Accounts receivable turnover
Google = 7.2
Samsung = 7.4
Industry = 5.0

Point: Ending accounts receivable can be substituted for the average balance in computing accounts receivable turnover if the difference between ending and average receivables is small.

Inventory Turnover   How long a company holds inventory before selling it will affect working capital requirements. One measure of this effect is *inventory turnover,* also called *merchandise turnover* or *merchandise inventory turnover,* which is defined as follows (see Chapter 5 for additional explanation).

$$\text{Inventory turnover} = \frac{\text{Cost of goods sold}}{\text{Average inventory}}$$

Using Apple's cost of goods sold and inventories information, we compute its inventory turnover for 2014 as follows (if the beginning and ending inventories for the year do not represent the usual inventory amount, an average of quarterly or monthly inventories can be used).

Inventory turnover
Google = n.a.
Samsung = 7.04
Industry = 7.0

$$\frac{\$112,258}{(\$1,764 + \$2,111)/2} = 57.94 \text{ times}$$

Apple's inventory turnover of 57.94 is higher than Samsung's 7.04 and the industry's 7.0. A company with a high turnover requires a smaller investment in inventory than one producing the same sales with a lower turnover. Inventory turnover can be too high, however, if the inventory a company keeps is so small that it restricts sales volume.

Days' Sales Uncollected   Accounts receivable turnover provides insight into how frequently a company collects its accounts. Days' sales uncollected is one measure of this activity, which is defined as follows (Chapter 6 provides additional explanation).

Rita Qian/AFP/Getty Images

$$\text{Day's sales uncollected} = \frac{\text{Accounts receivable, net}}{\text{Net sales}} \times 365$$

Any short-term notes receivable from customers are normally included in the numerator. Apple's 2014 days' sales uncollected follows.

Days' sales uncollected
Google = 51.9
Samsung = 50.0

$$\frac{\$17,460}{\$182,795} \times 365 = 34.9 \text{ days}$$

Both Google's days' sales uncollected of 51.9 days and Samsung's 50.0 days are more than the 34.9 days for Apple. Days' sales uncollected is more meaningful if we know company credit terms. A rough guideline states that days' sales uncollected should not exceed 1⅓ times the days in its (1) credit period, *if* discounts are not offered, or (2) discount period, *if* favorable discounts are offered.

Days' Sales in Inventory   *Days' sales in inventory* is a useful measure in evaluating inventory liquidity. Days' sales in inventory is linked to inventory in a way that days' sales uncollected is linked to receivables. We compute days' sales in inventory as follows (Chapter 5 provides additional explanation).

$$\text{Day's sales in inventory} = \frac{\text{Ending inventory}}{\text{Cost of goods sold}} \times 365$$

Apple's days' sales in inventory for 2014 follows.

Days' sales in inventory
Samsung = 49.3
Industry = 35

$$\frac{\$2,111}{\$112,258} \times 365 = 6.9 \text{ days}$$

Point: *Average collection period* is estimated by dividing 365 by the accounts receivable turnover ratio. For example, 365 divided by an accounts receivable turnover of 6.1 indicates a 60-day average collection period.

If the products in Apple's inventory are in demand by customers, this formula estimates that its inventory will be converted into receivables (or cash) in 6.9 days. If all of Apple's sales were credit sales, the conversion of inventory to receivables in 6.9 days *plus* the conversion of receivables to cash in 34.9 days implies that inventory will be converted to cash in about 41.8 days (6.9 + 34.9).

Total Asset Turnover   *Total asset turnover* reflects a company's ability to use its assets to generate sales and is an important indication of operating efficiency. The definition of this ratio follows (Chapter 8 offers additional explanation).

$$\text{Total asset turnover} = \frac{\text{Net sales}}{\text{Average total assets}}$$

Apple's total asset turnover of 0.83 for 2014 follows, which is greater than that for Google (0.55) but less than that for Samsung (0.93).

$$\frac{\$182{,}795}{(\$207{,}000 + \$231{,}839)/2} = 0.83 \text{ times}$$

Total asset turnover
Google = 0.55
Samsung = 0.93
Industry = 1.1

Solvency

Solvency refers to a company's long-run financial viability and its ability to cover long-term obligations. All of a company's business activities—financing, investing, and operating—affect its solvency. Analysis of solvency is long term and uses less precise but more encompassing measures than liquidity. One of the most important components of solvency analysis is the composition of a company's capital structure. *Capital structure* refers to a company's financing sources. It ranges from relatively permanent equity financing to riskier or more temporary short-term financing. Assets represent security for financiers, ranging from loans secured by specific assets to the assets available as general security to unsecured creditors. This section describes the tools of solvency analysis. Our analysis focuses on a company's ability to both meet its obligations and provide security to its creditors *over the long run*. Indicators of this ability include *debt* and *equity* ratios, the relation between *pledged assets and secured liabilities,* and the company's capacity to earn sufficient income to *pay fixed interest charges.*

Debt and Equity Ratios   One element of solvency analysis is to assess the portion of a company's assets contributed by its owners and the portion contributed by creditors. This relation is reflected in the debt ratio (also described in Chapter 2). The *debt ratio* expresses total liabilities as a percent of total assets. The **equity ratio** provides complementary information by expressing total equity as a percent of total assets. **Apple**'s debt and equity ratios follow.

Point: For analysis purposes, noncontrolling interest is usually included in equity.

$ millions	2014	Ratios	
Total liabilities	$120,292	51.9%	[Debt ratio]
Total equity	111,547	48.1	[Equity ratio]
Total liabilities and equity	$231,839	100.0%	

Debt ratio :: Equity ratio
Google = 20.3% :: 79.7%
Samsung = 27.1% :: 72.9%
Industry = 35% :: 65%

Apple's financial statements reveal slightly more debt than equity. A company is considered less risky if its capital structure (equity plus long-term debt) contains more equity. One risk factor is the required payment for interest and principal when debt is outstanding. Another factor is the greater the stockholder financing, the more losses a company can absorb through equity before the assets become inadequate to satisfy creditors' claims. From the stockholders' point of view, if a company earns a return on borrowed capital that is higher than the cost of borrowing, the difference represents increased income to stockholders. The inclusion of debt is described as *financial leverage* because debt can have the effect of increasing the return to stockholders. Companies are said to be highly leveraged if a large portion of their assets is financed by debt.

Point: Bank examiners from the FDIC and other regulatory agencies use debt and equity ratios to monitor compliance with regulatory capital requirements imposed on banks and S&Ls.

Debt-to-Equity Ratio   The ratio of total liabilities to equity is another measure of solvency. We compute the ratio as follows (Chapter 10 offers additional explanation).

$$\text{Debt-to-equity ratio} = \frac{\text{Total liabilities}}{\text{Total equity}}$$

Apple's debt-to-equity ratio for 2014 is

$$\$120{,}292/\$111{,}547 = 1.08$$

Debt-to-equity
Google = 0.25
Samsung = 0.37
Industry = 0.6

Apple's 1.08 debt-to-equity ratio is higher than those of Samsung (0.37) and Google (0.25), and greater than the industry ratio of 0.6. Consistent with our inferences from the debt ratio, Apple's capital structure has only slightly more debt than equity, which helps limit risk. Recall that debt must be repaid with interest, while equity does not. Debt requirements can be burdensome when the industry and/or the economy experience a downturn. A larger debt-to-equity ratio also implies less opportunity to expand through use of debt financing.

Point: The times interest earned ratio and the debt and equity ratios are of special interest to bank lending officers.

Times Interest Earned   The amount of income before deductions for interest expense and income taxes is the amount available to pay interest expense. The following *times interest earned* ratio reflects the creditors' risk of loan repayments with interest (see Chapter 9 for additional explanation).

$$\text{Times interest earned} = \frac{\text{Income before interest expense and income taxes}}{\text{Interest expense}}$$

The larger this ratio, the less risky is the company for creditors. One guideline says that creditors are reasonably safe if the company earns its fixed interest expense two or more times each year. Apple's times interest earned ratio follows. Apple's 140.3 result suggests that its creditors have little risk of nonrepayment.

Times interest earned
Google = 177.0
Samsung = 48.0

$$\frac{\$39,510 + \$384 + \$13,973}{\$384} = 140.3 \text{ times}$$

◼ Decision Insight

Bears and Bulls   A *bear market* is a declining market. The phrase comes from bear-skin jobbers who often sold the skins before the bears were caught. The term *bear* was then used to describe investors who sold shares they did not own in anticipation of a price decline. A *bull market* is a rising market. This phrase comes from the once popular sport of bear and bull baiting. The term *bull* came to mean the opposite of *bear.* ◼

Profitability

We are especially interested in a company's ability to use its assets efficiently to produce profits (and positive cash flows). *Profitability* refers to a company's ability to generate an adequate return on invested capital. Return is judged by assessing earnings relative to the level and sources of financing. Profitability is also relevant to solvency. This section describes key profitability measures and their importance to financial statement analysis.

Profit Margin   A company's operating efficiency and profitability can be expressed by two components. The first is *profit margin,* which reflects a company's ability to earn net income from sales (Chapter 3 offers additional explanation). It is measured by expressing net income as a percent of sales (*sales* and *revenues* are similar terms). Apple's profit margin follows.

Profit margin
Google = 21.9%
Samsung = 11.3%
Industry = 11%

$$\text{Profit margin} = \frac{\text{Net income}}{\text{Net sales}} = \frac{\$39,510}{\$182,795} = 21.6\%$$

To evaluate profit margin, we must consider the industry. For instance, an appliance company might require a profit margin between 10% and 15%, whereas a retail supermarket might require a profit margin of 1% or 2%. Both profit margin and *total asset turnover* make up the two basic components of operating efficiency. These ratios reflect on management because managers are ultimately responsible for operating efficiency. The next section explains how we use both measures to analyze return on total assets.

Return on Total Assets   *Return on total assets* is defined as follows.

$$\text{Return on total assets} = \frac{\text{Net income}}{\text{Average total assets}}$$

Apple's 2014 return on total assets is

$$\frac{\$39,510}{(\$207,000 + \$231,839)/2} = 18.0\%$$

Return on total assets
Google = 11.9%
Samsung = 10.5%
Industry = 9%

Apple's 18.0% return on total assets is higher than that for many businesses and is higher than Google's 11.9%, Samsung's 10.5%, and the industry's 9% return. We also should evaluate any trend in the rate of return.

The following equation shows the important relation between profit margin, total asset turnover, and return on total assets.

Point: Many analysts add back *Interest expense × (1 − Tax rate)* to net income in computing return on total assets.

$$\textbf{Profit margin} \times \textbf{Total asset turnover} = \textbf{Return on total assets}$$

or

$$\frac{\textbf{Net income}}{\textbf{Net sales}} \times \frac{\textbf{Net sales}}{\textbf{Average total assets}} = \frac{\textbf{Net income}}{\textbf{Average total assets}}$$

Both profit margin and total asset turnover contribute to overall operating efficiency, as measured by return on total assets. If we apply this formula to Apple, we get

$$21.6\% \times 0.83 = 18.0\% \text{ (with rounding)}$$

Google: 21.9% × 0.55 ≃ 11.9%
Samsung: 11.3% × 0.93 ≃ 10.5%
(with rounding)

This analysis shows that Apple's superior return on assets versus that of both Google and Samsung is driven by its higher profit in the case of Samsung, but by a better asset turnover in the case of Google.

Return on Common Stockholders' Equity Perhaps the most important goal in operating a company is to earn net income for its owner(s). *Return on common stockholders' equity* measures a company's success in reaching this goal and is defined as follows.

$$\textbf{Return on common stockholders' equity} = \frac{\textbf{Net income} - \textbf{Preferred dividends}}{\textbf{Average common stockholders' equity}}$$

Apple's 2014 return on common stockholders' equity is computed as follows:

$$\frac{\$39,510 - \$0}{(\$123,549 + \$111,547)/2} = 33.6\%$$

Return on common equity
Google = 15.1%
Samsung = 14.5%
Industry = 15%

The denominator in this computation is the book value of common equity (noncontrolling interest is often included in common equity for this ratio). In the numerator, the dividends on cumulative preferred stock are subtracted whether they are declared or are in arrears. If preferred stock is noncumulative, its dividends are subtracted only if declared. Apple's return on common stockholders' equity (33.6%) is superior to Google's 15.1% and Samsung's 14.5%.

▣ Decision Insight

Wall Street *Wall Street* is synonymous with financial markets, but its name comes from the street location of the original New York Stock Exchange. The street's name derives from stockades built by early settlers to protect New York from pirate attacks. ■

Market Prospects

Market measures are useful for analyzing corporations with publicly traded stock. These market measures use stock price, which reflects the market's (public's) expectations for the company. This includes expectations of both company return and risk—as the market perceives it.

Price-Earnings Ratio   Computation of the *price-earnings ratio* follows (Chapter 11 provides additional explanation).

$$\text{Price-earnings ratio} = \frac{\text{Market price per common share}}{\text{Earnings per share}}$$

Predicted earnings per share for the next period is often used in the denominator of this computation. Reported earnings per share for the most recent period is also commonly used. In both cases, the ratio is used as an indicator of the future growth and risk of a company's earnings as perceived by the stock's buyers and sellers.

The market price of Apple's common stock at the start of fiscal year 2015 was $100.75. Using Apple's $6.49 basic earnings per share, we compute its price-earnings ratio as follows (some analysts compute this ratio using the median of the low and high stock prices).

$$\frac{\$100.75}{\$6.49} = 15.5$$

Apple's price-earnings ratio is less than that for Google, but it is higher than that for Samsung and near the norm for this period.

Dividend Yield   *Dividend yield* is used to compare the dividend-paying performance of different investment alternatives. We compute dividend yield as follows (Chapter 11 offers additional explanation).

$$\text{Dividend yield} = \frac{\text{Annual cash dividends per share}}{\text{Market price per share}}$$

Apple's dividend yield, based on its fiscal year-end market price per share of $100.75 and its $1.82 cash dividends per share, is computed as follows.

$$\frac{\$1.82}{\$100.75} = 1.8\%$$

Some companies, such as Google, do not declare and pay dividends because they wish to reinvest the cash to grow their businesses in the hope of generating greater future earnings and dividends.

Summary of Ratios

Exhibit 13.16 summarizes the major financial statement analysis ratios illustrated in this chapter and throughout the book. This summary includes each ratio's title, its formula, and the purpose for which it is commonly used.

 Decision Insight

Ticker Prices   *Ticker prices* refer to a band of moving data on a monitor carrying up-to-the-minute stock prices. The phrase comes from *ticker tape,* a 1-inch-wide strip of paper spewing stock prices from a printer that ticked as it ran. Most of today's investors have never seen actual ticker tape, but the phrase survives. ■

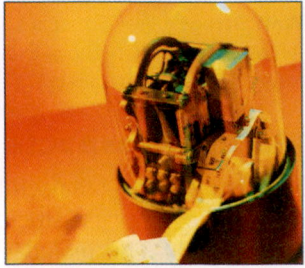

© Comstock Images/Jupiter Images

EXHIBIT 13.16

Financial Statement Analysis Ratios*

Ratio	Formula	Measure of
Liquidity and Efficiency		
Current ratio	$= \dfrac{\text{Current assets}}{\text{Current liabilities}}$	Short-term debt-paying ability
Acid-test ratio	$= \dfrac{\text{Cash + Short-term investments + Current receivables}}{\text{Current liabilities}}$	Immediate short-term debt-paying ability
Accounts receivable turnover	$= \dfrac{\text{Net sales}}{\text{Average accounts receivable, net}}$	Efficiency of collection
Inventory turnover	$= \dfrac{\text{Cost of goods sold}}{\text{Average inventory}}$	Efficiency of inventory management
Days' sales uncollected	$= \dfrac{\text{Accounts receivable, net}}{\text{Net sales}} \times 365$	Liquidity of receivables
Days' sales in inventory	$= \dfrac{\text{Ending inventory}}{\text{Cost of goods sold}} \times 365$	Liquidity of inventory
Total asset turnover	$= \dfrac{\text{Net sales}}{\text{Average total assets}}$	Efficiency of assets in producing sales
Solvency		
Debt ratio	$= \dfrac{\text{Total liabilities}}{\text{Total assets}}$	Creditor financing and leverage
Equity ratio	$= \dfrac{\text{Total equity}}{\text{Total assets}}$	Owner financing
Debt-to-equity ratio	$= \dfrac{\text{Total liabilities}}{\text{Total equity}}$	Debt versus equity financing
Times interest earned	$= \dfrac{\text{Income before interest expense and income taxes}}{\text{Interest expense}}$	Protection in meeting interest payments
Profitability		
Profit margin ratio	$= \dfrac{\text{Net income}}{\text{Net sales}}$	Net income in each sales dollar
Gross margin ratio	$= \dfrac{\text{Net sales} - \text{Cost of goods sold}}{\text{Net sales}}$	Gross margin in each sales dollar
Return on total assets	$= \dfrac{\text{Net income}}{\text{Average total assets}}$	Overall profitability of assets
Return on common stockholders' equity	$= \dfrac{\text{Net income} - \text{Preferred dividends}}{\text{Average common stockholders' equity}}$	Profitability of owner investment
Book value per common share	$= \dfrac{\text{Shareholders' equity applicable to common shares}}{\text{Number of common shares outstanding}}$	Liquidation at reported amounts
Basic earnings per share	$= \dfrac{\text{Net income} - \text{Preferred dividends}}{\text{Weighted-average common shares outstanding}}$	Net income per common share
Market Prospects		
Price-earnings ratio	$= \dfrac{\text{Market price per common share}}{\text{Earnings per share}}$	Market value relative to earnings
Dividend yield	$= \dfrac{\text{Annual cash dividends per share}}{\text{Market price per share}}$	Cash return per common share

* Additional ratios also examined in previous chapters included credit risk ratio; plant asset useful life; plant asset age; days' cash expense coverage; cash coverage of growth; cash coverage of debt; free cash flow; cash flow on total assets; and payout ratio.

NEED-TO-KNOW 13-3

Ratio Analysis

P3

For each ratio listed, identify whether the change in ratio value from 2015 to 2016 is regarded as favorable or unfavorable.

Ratio	2016	2015	Ratio	2016	2015
1. Profit margin	6%	8%	4. Accounts receivable turnover	8.8	9.4
2. Debt ratio	50%	70%	5. Basic earnings per share	$2.10	$2.00
3. Gross margin	40%	36%	6. Inventory turnover	3.6	4.0

Solution

Ratio	2016	2015	Change
1. Profit margin ratio.................	6%	8%	Unfavorable
2. Debt ratio.......................	50%	70%	Favorable
3. Gross margin ratio	40%	36%	Favorable
4. Accounts receivable turnover.........	8.8	9.4	Unfavorable
5. Basic earnings per share	$2.10	$2.00	Favorable
6. Inventory turnover	3.6	4.0	Unfavorable

Do More: QS 13-6, E 13-7, E 13-8, E 13-9, E 13-10, E 13-11, P 13-4

GLOBAL VIEW

The analysis and interpretation of financial statements are, of course, impacted by the accounting system in effect. This section discusses similarities and differences for analysis of financial statements when prepared under U.S. GAAP vis-à-vis IFRS.

Horizontal and Vertical Analyses   Horizontal and vertical analyses help eliminate many differences between U.S. GAAP and IFRS when analyzing and interpreting financial statements. Financial numbers are converted to percentages that are, in the best-case scenario, consistently applied across and within periods. This enables users to effectively compare companies across reporting regimes. However, when fundamental differences in reporting regimes impact financial statements, such as with certain recognition rule differences, the user must exercise caution when drawing conclusions. Some users will reformulate one set of numbers to be more consistent with the other system to enable comparative analysis. This reformulation process is covered in advanced courses. The important point is that horizontal and vertical analyses help strip away differences between the reporting regimes, but several key differences sometimes remain and require adjustment of the numbers.

Ratio Analysis   Ratio analysis of financial statement numbers has many of the advantages and disadvantages of horizontal and vertical analyses discussed above. Importantly, ratio analysis is useful for business decisions, with some possible changes in interpretation depending on what is and what is not included in accounting measures across U.S. GAAP and IFRS. Still, we must take care in drawing inferences from a comparison of ratios across reporting regimes because what a number measures can differ across regimes. **Piaggio**, which manufactures two-, three-, and four-wheel vehicles and is Europe's leading manufacturer of motorcycles and scooters, offers the following example of its own ratio analysis applied to its financing objectives: "The object of capital management . . . , [and] consistent with others in the industry, the Company monitors capital on the basis of a total liabilities to equity ratio. This ratio is calculated as total liabilities divided by equity."

Sustainability and Accounting   **Morgan Stanley**'s sustainability initiative is focused on reducing its environmental impact and investing in sustainable projects. James Gorman, CEO of Morgan Stanley, has made reducing his company's carbon footprint a key priority. Gorman proclaims, "We achieved LEED Gold certification for our New York City headquarters . . . and we have set a new goal of cutting the greenhouse gas intensity of our building operations by 15 percent by 2017. This is on top of the 26 percent reduction we achieved over the previous six years." Morgan Stanley's sustainability report says the company has earned several awards for its work on sustainability. This includes being one of three finalists for Sustainable Global Bank of the Year, S&P 500 Carbon Performance Leadership, and Global 500 Carbon Performance Leadership.

Morgan Stanley has also been a leader in sustainable investments. It launched the Morgan Stanley Institute for Sustainable Investing. Morgan Stanley's sustainability report outlines three core initiatives for the Institute:

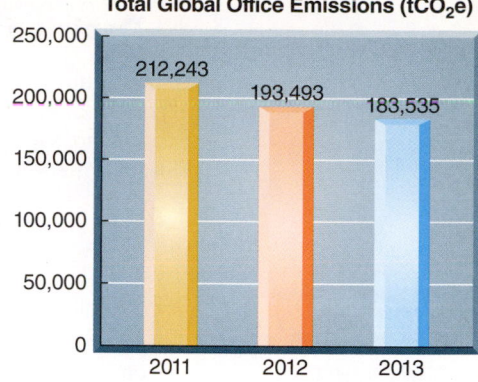

Total Global Office Emissions (tCO₂e)

- By 2018, $10 billion in total client assets invested through the Investing with Impact Platform, which enables clients to choose investments that seek to deliver market-rate returns and positive environmental or social impact.
- Investing $1 billion in a sustainable communities initiative to provide rapid access to capital to low- and moderate-income households.
- Establishing a Sustainable Investing Fellowship with Columbia Business School to develop a cadre of emerging leaders in sustainable finance.

James Gorman believes the Morgan Stanley Institute "is the most effective pathway to a global economy that safeguards scarce resources and invests wisely for the future."

Source: Morgan Stanley website

Fraud

All Else Being Equal Financial regulation has several goals. Two of them are to ensure adequate accounting disclosure and to strengthen corporate governance. For disclosure purposes, companies must now provide details of related-party transactions and material off-balance-sheet agreements. This is motivated by several major frauds. For corporate governance, the CEO and CFO must now certify the fairness of financial statements and the effectiveness of internal controls. Yet, concerns remain. A study reports that 30% of management and administrative employees observed activities that posed a conflict of interest in the past year (KPMG 2013). Another 24% witnessed the falsifying or manipulating of accounting information. The bottom line: All financial statements are *not* of equal quality.

Analysis Reporting **Decision Analysis**

Understanding the purpose of financial statement analysis is crucial to the usefulness of any analysis. This understanding leads to efficiency of effort, effectiveness in application, and relevance in focus. The purpose of most financial statement analyses is to reduce uncertainty in business decisions through a rigorous and sound evaluation. A *financial statement analysis report* helps by directly addressing the building blocks of analysis and by identifying weaknesses in inference by requiring explanation: It forces us to organize our reasoning and to verify its flow and logic. A report also serves as a communication link with readers, and the writing process reinforces our judgments and vice versa. Finally, the report helps us (re)evaluate evidence and refine conclusions on key building blocks. A good analysis report usually consists of six sections:

A1

Summarize and report results of analysis.

1. **Executive summary**—brief focus on important analysis results and conclusions.
2. **Analysis overview**—background on the company, its industry, and its economic setting.
3. **Evidential matter**—financial statements and information used in the analysis, including ratios, trends, comparisons, statistics, and all analytical measures assembled; often organized under the building blocks of analysis.
4. **Assumptions**—identification of important assumptions regarding a company's industry and economic environment, and other important assumptions for estimates.
5. **Key factors**—list of important favorable and unfavorable factors, both quantitative and qualitative, for company performance; usually organized by areas of analysis.
6. **Inferences**—forecasts, estimates, interpretations, and conclusions drawing on all sections of the report.

We must remember that the user dictates relevance, meaning that the analysis report should include a brief table of contents to help readers focus on those areas most relevant to their decisions. All irrelevant matter must be eliminated. For example, decades-old details of obscure transactions and detailed miscues of the analysis are irrelevant. Ambiguities and qualifications to avoid responsibility or hedging inferences must be eliminated. Finally, writing is important. Mistakes in grammar and errors of fact compromise the report's credibility.

Decision Insight

Short Selling *Short selling* refers to selling stock before you buy it. Here's an example: You borrow 100 shares of Nike stock, sell them at $40 each, and receive money from their sale. You then wait. You hope that Nike's stock price falls to, say, $35 each and you can replace the borrowed stock for less than you sold it, reaping a profit of $5 each less any transaction costs. ■

NEED-TO-KNOW 13-4

COMPREHENSIVE

Use the following financial statements of Precision Co. to complete these requirements.

1. Prepare comparative income statements showing the percent increase or decrease for year 2016 in comparison to year 2015.
2. Prepare common-size comparative balance sheets for years 2016 and 2015.
3. Compute the following ratios as of December 31, 2016, or for the year ended December 31, 2016, and identify its building block category for financial statement analysis.

a. Current ratio
b. Acid-test ratio
c. Accounts receivable turnover
d. Days' sales uncollected
e. Inventory turnover
f. Debt ratio

g. Debt-to-equity ratio
h. Times interest earned
i. Profit margin ratio
j. Total asset turnover
k. Return on total assets
l. Return on common stockholders' equity

PRECISION COMPANY
Comparative Income Statements
For Years Ended December 31, 2016 and 2015

	2016	2015
Sales	$2,486,000	$2,075,000
Cost of goods sold	1,523,000	1,222,000
Gross profit	963,000	853,000
Operating expenses		
Advertising expense	145,000	100,000
Sales salaries expense	240,000	280,000
Office salaries expense	165,000	200,000
Insurance expense	100,000	45,000
Supplies expense	26,000	35,000
Depreciation expense	85,000	75,000
Miscellaneous expenses	17,000	15,000
Total operating expenses	778,000	750,000
Operating income	185,000	103,000
Interest expense	44,000	46,000
Income before taxes	141,000	57,000
Income taxes	47,000	19,000
Net income	$ 94,000	$ 38,000
Earnings per share	$ 0.99	$ 0.40

PRECISION COMPANY
Comparative Balance Sheets
December 31, 2016 and 2015

	2016	2015
Assets		
Current assets		
Cash	$ 79,000	$ 42,000
Short-term investments	65,000	96,000
Accounts receivable, net	120,000	100,000
Merchandise inventory	250,000	265,000
Total current assets	514,000	503,000
Plant assets		
Store equipment, net	400,000	350,000
Office equipment, net	45,000	50,000
Buildings, net	625,000	675,000
Land	100,000	100,000
Total plant assets	1,170,000	1,175,000
Total assets	$1,684,000	$1,678,000
Liabilities		
Current liabilities		
Accounts payable	$ 164,000	$ 190,000
Short-term notes payable	75,000	90,000
Taxes payable	26,000	12,000
Total current liabilities	265,000	292,000
Long-term liabilities		
Notes payable (secured by mortgage on buildings)	400,000	420,000
Total liabilities	665,000	712,000
Stockholders' Equity		
Common stock, $5 par value	475,000	475,000
Retained earnings	544,000	491,000
Total stockholders' equity	1,019,000	966,000
Total liabilities and equity	$1,684,000	$1,678,000

PLANNING THE SOLUTION

- Set up a four-column income statement; enter the 2016 and 2015 amounts in the first two columns and then enter the dollar change in the third column and the percent change from 2015 in the fourth column.
- Set up a four-column balance sheet; enter the 2016 and 2015 year-end amounts in the first two columns and then compute and enter the amount of each item as a percent of total assets.
- Compute the required ratios using the data provided. Use the average of beginning and ending amounts when appropriate (see Exhibit 13.16 for definitions).

SOLUTION

1.

PRECISION COMPANY
Comparative Income Statements
For Years Ended December 31, 2016 and 2015

	2016	2015	Increase (Decrease) in 2016 Amount	Increase (Decrease) in 2016 Percent
Sales	$2,486,000	$2,075,000	$411,000	19.8%
Cost of goods sold.	1,523,000	1,222,000	301,000	24.6
Gross profit	963,000	853,000	110,000	12.9
Operating expenses				
Advertising expense.	145,000	100,000	45,000	45.0
Sales salaries expense.	240,000	280,000	(40,000)	(14.3)
Office salaries expense.	165,000	200,000	(35,000)	(17.5)
Insurance expense	100,000	45,000	55,000	122.2
Supplies expense	26,000	35,000	(9,000)	(25.7)
Depreciation expense	85,000	75,000	10,000	13.3
Miscellaneous expenses	17,000	15,000	2,000	13.3
Total operating expenses.	778,000	750,000	28,000	3.7
Operating income	185,000	103,000	82,000	79.6
Interest expense.	44,000	46,000	(2,000)	(4.3)
Income before taxes.	141,000	57,000	84,000	147.4
Income taxes	47,000	19,000	28,000	147.4
Net income.	$ 94,000	$ 38,000	$ 56,000	147.4
Earnings per share	$ 0.99	$ 0.40	$ 0.59	147.5

2.

PRECISION COMPANY
Common-Size Comparative Balance Sheets
December 31, 2016 and 2015

	December 31 2016	December 31 2015	Common-Size Percents 2016*	Common-Size Percents 2015*
Assets				
Current assets				
Cash.	$ 79,000	$ 42,000	4.7%	2.5%
Short-term investments	65,000	96,000	3.9	5.7
Accounts receivable, net.	120,000	100,000	7.1	6.0
Merchandise inventory	250,000	265,000	14.8	15.8
Total current assets.	514,000	503,000	30.5	30.0
Plant assets				
Store equipment, net.	400,000	350,000	23.8	20.9
Office equipment, net	45,000	50,000	2.7	3.0
Buildings, net	625,000	675,000	37.1	40.2
Land	100,000	100,000	5.9	6.0
Total plant assets.	1,170,000	1,175,000	69.5	70.0
Total assets	$1,684,000	$1,678,000	100.0	100.0

[continued on next page]

[continued from previous page]

Liabilities				
Current liabilities				
Accounts payable..................	$ 164,000	$ 190,000	**9.7%**	**11.3%**
Short-term notes payable	75,000	90,000	**4.5**	**5.4**
Taxes payable.....................	26,000	12,000	**1.5**	**0.7**
Total current liabilities.............	265,000	292,000	**15.7**	**17.4**
Long-term liabilities				
Notes payable (secured by				
mortgage on buildings)	400,000	420,000	**23.8**	**25.0**
Total liabilities	665,000	712,000	**39.5**	**42.4**
Stockholders' Equity				
Common stock, $5 par value	475,000	475,000	**28.2**	**28.3**
Retained earnings..................	544,000	491,000	**32.3**	**29.3**
Total stockholders' equity............	1,019,000	966,000	**60.5**	**57.6**
Total liabilities and equity	$1,684,000	$1,678,000	**100.0**	**100.0**

* Columns do not always exactly add to 100 due to rounding.

3. Ratios for 2016:

 a. Current ratio: $514,000/$265,000 = 1.9:1 (liquidity and efficiency)

 b. Acid-test ratio: ($79,000 + $65,000 + $120,000)/$265,000 = 1.0:1 (liquidity and efficiency)

 c. Average receivables: ($120,000 + $100,000)/2 = $110,000

    Accounts receivable turnover: $2,486,000/$110,000 = 22.6 times (liquidity and efficiency)

 d. Days' sales uncollected: ($120,000/$2,486,000) × 365 = 17.6 days (liquidity and efficiency)

 e. Average inventory: ($250,000 + $265,000)/2 = $257,500

    Inventory turnover: $1,523,000/$257,500 = 5.9 times (liquidity and efficiency)

 f. Debt ratio: $665,000/$1,684,000 = 39.5% (solvency)

 g. Debt-to-equity ratio: $665,000/$1,019,000 = 0.65 (solvency)

 h. Times interest earned: $185,000/$44,000 = 4.2 times (solvency)

 i. Profit margin ratio: $94,000/$2,486,000 = 3.8% (profitability)

 j. Average total assets: ($1,684,000 + $1,678,000)/2 = $1,681,000

    Total asset turnover: $2,486,000/$1,681,000 = 1.48 times (liquidity and efficiency)

 k. Return on total assets: $94,000/$1,681,000 = 5.6% or 3.8% × 1.48 = 5.6% (profitability)

 l. Average total common equity: ($1,019,000 + $966,000)/2 = $992,500

    Return on common stockholders' equity: $94,000/$992,500 = 9.5% (profitability)

13A

Sustainable Income

A2

Explain the form and assess the content of a complete income statement.

When a company's revenue and expense transactions are from normal, continuing operations, a simple income statement is usually adequate. When a company's activities include income-related events not part of its normal, continuing operations, it must disclose information to help users understand these events and predict future performance. To meet these objectives, companies separate the income statement into continuing operations, discontinued segments, comprehensive income, and earnings per share. For illustration, Exhibit 13A.1 shows such an income statement for ComUS. These separate distinctions help us measure *sustainable income,* which is the income level most likely to continue into the future. Sustainable income is commonly used in PE ratios and other market-based measures of performance.

Continuing Operations   The first major section (①) shows the revenues, expenses, and income from continuing operations. Users especially rely on this information to predict future operations. Many

ComUS Income Statement For Year Ended December 31, 2015		
Net sales		$8,478,000
Operating expenses		
Cost of goods sold	$5,950,000	
Depreciation expense	35,000	
Other selling, general, and administrative expenses	515,000	
Interest expense	20,000	
① Total operating expenses		(6,520,000)
Other unusual and/or infrequent gains (losses)		
Loss on plant relocation		(45,000)
Gain on sale of surplus land		72,000
Income from continuing operations before taxes		1,985,000
Income taxes expense		(595,500)
Income from continuing operations		1,389,500
Discontinued segment		
② Income from operating Division A (net of $180,000 taxes)	420,000	
Loss on disposal of Division A (net of $66,000 tax benefit)	(154,000)	266,000
Net income		1,655,500
Earnings per common share (200,000 outstanding shares)		
③ Income from continuing operations		$ 6.95
Discontinued operations		1.33
Net income (basic earnings per share)		$ 8.28

EXHIBIT 13A.1

Income Statement (all-inclusive) for a Corporation

users view this section as the most important. Earlier chapters explained the items comprising income from continuing operations.

Gains and losses that are neither unusual nor infrequent are reported as part of continuing operations. Gains and losses that are either unusual and/or infrequent are reported as part of continuing operations *but after* the normal revenues and expenses. Items typically considered unusual and/or infrequent include (1) expropriation (taking away) of property by a foreign government, (2) condemning of property by a domestic government body, (3) prohibition against using an asset by a newly enacted law, (4) losses and gains from an unusual and infrequent calamity ("act of God"), (5) write-downs of inventories and write-offs of receivables, (6) gains and losses from disposing of segments, and (7) financial effects of labor strikes. (At one time, the FASB identified *extraordinary items*; that is no longer the case.)

Discontinued Segments A **business segment** is a part of a company's operations that serves a particular line of business or class of customers. A segment has assets, liabilities, and financial results of operations that can be distinguished from those of other parts of the company. A company's gain or loss from selling or closing down a segment is separately reported. Section ② of Exhibit 13A.1 reports both (1) income from operating the discontinued segment for the current period prior to its disposal and (2) the loss from disposing of the segment's net assets. The income tax effects of each are reported separately from the income taxes expense in section ①.

Decision Maker

Small Business Owner You own an orange grove near Jacksonville, Florida. A bad frost destroys about one-half of your oranges. You are currently preparing an income statement for a bank loan. Where on the income statement do you report the loss of oranges? ■ [Answers follow the chapter's Summary.]

Earnings per Share The final section ③ of the income statement in Exhibit 13A.1 reports earnings per share for each of the two subcategories of income (continuing operations and discontinued segments) when they both exist. Earnings per share is discussed in Chapter 11.

Changes in Accounting Principles The *consistency concept* directs a company to apply the same accounting principles across periods. Yet a company can change from one acceptable accounting

Point: Changes in principles are sometimes required when new accounting standards are issued.

principle (such as FIFO, LIFO, or weighted-average) to another as long as the change improves the usefulness of information in its financial statements. A footnote would describe the accounting change and why it is an improvement.

Changes in accounting principles require retrospective application to prior periods' financial statements. *Retrospective application* involves applying a different accounting principle to prior periods as if that principle had always been used. Retrospective application enhances the consistency of financial information between periods, which improves the usefulness of information, especially with comparative analyses. Accounting standards also require that *a change in depreciation, amortization, or depletion method for long-term operating assets is accounted for as a change in accounting estimate*—that is, prospectively over current and future periods. This reflects the notion that an entity should change its depreciation, amortization, or depletion method only with changes in estimated asset benefits, the pattern of benefit usage, or information about those benefits.

Summary

C1 Explain the purpose and identify the building blocks of analysis. The purpose of financial statement analysis is to help users make better business decisions. Internal users want information to improve company efficiency and effectiveness in providing products and services. External users want information to make better and more informed decisions in pursuing their goals. The common goals of all users are to evaluate a company's (1) past and current performance, (2) current financial position, and (3) future performance and risk. Financial statement analysis focuses on four "building blocks" of analysis: (1) liquidity and efficiency—ability to meet short-term obligations and efficiently generate revenues; (2) solvency—ability to generate future revenues and meet long-term obligations; (3) profitability—ability to provide financial rewards sufficient to attract and retain financing; and (4) market prospects—ability to generate positive market expectations.

C2 Describe standards for comparisons in analysis. Standards for comparisons include (1) intracompany—prior performance and relations between financial items for the company under analysis; (2) competitor—one or more direct competitors of the company; (3) industry—industry statistics; and (4) guidelines (rules of thumb)—general standards developed from past experiences and personal judgments.

A1 Summarize and report results of analysis. A financial statement analysis report is often organized around the building blocks of analysis. A good report separates interpretations and conclusions of analysis from the information underlying them. An analysis report often consists of six sections: (1) executive summary, (2) analysis overview, (3) evidential matter, (4) assumptions, (5) key factors, and (6) inferences.

A2ᴬ Explain the form and assess the content of a complete income statement. An income statement has three sections: (1) continuing operations, (2) discontinued segments—provided any exist, and (3) earnings per share.

P1 Explain and apply methods of horizontal analysis. Horizontal analysis is a tool to evaluate changes in data across time. Two important tools of horizontal analysis are comparative statements and trend analysis. Comparative statements show amounts for two or more successive periods, often with changes disclosed in both absolute and percent terms. Trend analysis is used to reveal important changes occurring from one period to the next.

P2 Describe and apply methods of vertical analysis. Vertical analysis is a tool to evaluate each financial statement item or group of items in terms of a base amount. Two tools of vertical analysis are common-size statements and graphical analyses. Each item in common-size statements is expressed as a percent of a base amount. For the balance sheet, the base amount is usually total assets, and for the income statement, it is usually sales.

P3 Define and apply ratio analysis. Ratio analysis provides clues to and symptoms of underlying conditions. Ratios, properly interpreted, identify areas requiring further investigation. A ratio expresses a mathematical relation between two quantities such as a percent, rate, or proportion. Ratios can be organized into the building blocks of analysis: (1) liquidity and efficiency, (2) solvency, (3) profitability, and (4) market prospects.

Guidance Answers to Decision Maker

Auditor The *joint relation* referred to is the combined increase in sales and the decrease in expenses yielding more than a 5% increase in income. Both *individual* accounts (sales and expenses) yield percent changes within the ±5% acceptable range. However, a joint analysis suggests a different picture. For example, consider a joint analysis using the profit margin ratio. The client's profit margin is 11.46% ($206,000 − $182,400/$206,000) for the current year compared with 5.0%

($200,000 − $190,000/$200,000) for the prior year—yielding a 129% increase in profit margin! This is what concerns the partner, and it suggests expanding audit tests to verify or refute the client's figures.

Banker Your decision on the loan application is positive for at least two reasons. First, the current ratio suggests a strong ability to meet short-term obligations. Second, current assets of $160,000 and a current ratio of 4:1 imply current liabilities of $40,000 (one-fourth of current assets) and a working capital excess of $120,000. This working capital excess is 60% of the loan amount. However, if the application is for a 10-year loan, our decision is less optimistic. The current ratio and working capital suggest a good safety margin, but indications of inefficiency in operations exist. In particular, a 4:1 current ratio is more than double its key competitors' ratio. This is characteristic of inefficient asset use.

Small Business Owner The frost loss is probably unusual in nature, meaning that while it is reported as part of continuing operations, it is in the nonrecurring section. Management would want to highlight the frost loss apart from the ongoing, normal operating results, and hope the bank views this uncommon event separately from normal operations.

Key Terms

Business segment

Common-size financial statement

Comparative financial statement

Efficiency

Equity ratio

Financial reporting

Financial statement analysis

General-purpose financial statements

Horizontal analysis

Liquidity

Market prospects

Profitability

Ratio analysis

Solvency

Vertical analysis

Working capital

Multiple Choice Quiz   Answers at end of chapter

1. A company's sales in 2015 were $300,000 and in 2016 were $351,000. Using 2015 as the base year, the sales trend percent for 2016 is:

  a. 17%   **c.** 100%   **e.** 48%
  b. 85%   **d.** 117%

Use the following information for questions 2 through 5.

ELLA COMPANY
Balance Sheet
December 31, 2016

Assets

Cash	$ 86,000
Accounts receivable	76,000
Merchandise inventory	122,000
Prepaid insurance	12,000
Long-term investments	98,000
Plant assets, net	436,000
Total assets	$830,000

Liabilities and Equity

Current liabilities	$124,000
Long-term liabilities	90,000
Common stock	300,000
Retained earnings	316,000
Total liabilities and equity	$830,000

2. What is Ella Company's current ratio?
  a. 0.69
  b. 1.31
  c. 3.88
  d. 6.69
  e. 2.39

3. What is Ella Company's acid-test ratio?
  a. 2.39
  b. 0.69
  c. 1.31
  d. 6.69
  e. 3.88

4. What is Ella Company's debt ratio?
  a. 25.78%
  b. 100.00%
  c. 74.22%
  d. 137.78%
  e. 34.74%

5. What is Ella Company's equity ratio?
  a. 25.78%
  b. 100.00%
  c. 34.74%
  d. 74.22%
  e. 137.78%

^A *Superscript letter A denotes assignments based on Appendix 13A.*

[i] Icon denotes assignments that involve decision making.

Discussion Questions

1. Explain the difference between financial reporting and financial statements.

2. What is the difference between comparative financial statements and common-size comparative statements?

3. Which items are usually assigned a 100% value on (a) a common-size balance sheet and (b) a common-size income statement?

4. [i] What three factors would influence your evaluation as to whether a company's current ratio is good or bad?

5. [i] Suggest several reasons why a 2:1 current ratio might not be adequate for a particular company.

6. [i] Why is working capital given special attention in the process of analyzing balance sheets?

7. [i] What does the number of days' sales uncollected indicate?

8. [i] What does a relatively high accounts receivable turnover indicate about a company's short-term liquidity?

9. [i] Why is a company's capital structure, as measured by debt and equity ratios, important to financial statement analysts?

10. [i] How does inventory turnover provide information about a company's short-term liquidity?

11. [i] What ratios would you compute to evaluate management performance?

12. [i] Why would a company's return on total assets be different from its return on common stockholders' equity?

13. Where on the income statement does a company report an unusual gain not expected to occur more often than once every two years or so?

14. Refer to **Apple**'s financial statements in Appendix A. Compute its profit margin for the years ended September 27, 2014, and September 28, 2013.   **APPLE**

15. Refer to **Google**'s financial statements in Appendix A to compute its equity ratio as of December 31, 2014, and December 31, 2013.   **GOOGLE**

16. Refer to **Samsung**'s financial statements in Appendix A. Compute its debt ratio as of December 31, 2014, and December 31, 2013.   **Samsung**

17. Use **Samsung**'s financial statements in Appendix A to compute its return on total assets for fiscal year ended December 31, 2014.   **Samsung**

Mc Graw Hill Education **connect**

QUICK STUDY

QS 13-1

Financial reporting

C1

Which of the following items *a* through *i* are part of financial reporting but are *not* included as part of general-purpose financial statements?

_____ **a.** Income statement

_____ **b.** Balance sheet

_____ **c.** Prospectus

_____ **d.** Financial statement notes

_____ **e.** Company news releases

_____ **f.** Statement of cash flows

_____ **g.** Stock price information and analysis

_____ **h.** Statement of shareholders' equity

_____ **i.** Management discussion and analysis of financial performance

---

QS 13-2

Standard of comparison

C2

Identify which standard of comparison, (a) intracompany, (b) competitor, (c) industry, or (d) guidelines, is best described by each of the following.

_____ **1.** Is often viewed as the best standard of comparison.

_____ **2.** Rules of thumb developed from past experiences.

_____ **3.** Provides analysis based on a company's prior performance.

_____ **4.** Compares a company against industry statistics.

QS 13-3

Horizontal analysis

P1

Compute the annual dollar changes and percent changes for each of the following accounts.

	2016	2015
Short-term investments.........	$374,634	$234,000
Accounts receivable...........	97,364	101,000
Notes payable	0	88,000

Use the following information for Topps Corporation to determine the 2015 and 2016 trend percents for net sales using 2015 as the base year.

$ thousands	2016	2015
Net sales	$801,810	$453,000
Cost of goods sold.	392,887	134,088

QS 13-4
Trend percents
P1

Refer to the information in QS 13-4. Use that information for Topps Corporation to determine the 2015 and 2016 common-size percents for cost of goods sold using net sales as the base.

QS 13-5
Common-size analysis **P2**

For each ratio listed, identify whether the change in ratio value from 2015 to 2016 is usually regarded as favorable or unfavorable.

QS 13-6
Ratio interpretation
P3

Ratio	2016	2015	Ratio	2016	2015
_____ 1. Profit margin	9%	8%	_____ 5. Accounts receivable turnover. . . .	5.5	6.7
_____ 2. Debt ratio	47%	42%	_____ 6. Basic earnings per share	$1.25	$1.10
_____ 3. Gross margin. . . .	34%	46%	_____ 7. Inventory turnover	3.6	3.4
_____ 4. Acid-test ratio. . .	1.00	1.15	_____ 8. Dividend yield	2.0%	1.2%

The following information is available for Edison Company and Tesla Company, similar firms operating in the same industry. Write a half-page report comparing Edison and Tesla using the available information. Your discussion should include their ability to meet current obligations and to use current assets efficiently.

QS 13-7
Analysis of short-term financial condition
A1

	A	B	C	D	E	F	G	H
1			Edison				Tesla	
2		2016	2015	2014		2016	2015	2014
3	Current ratio	1.7	1.6	2.1		3.2	2.7	1.9
4	Acid-test ratio	1.0	1.1	1.2		2.8	2.5	1.6
5	Accounts receivable turnover	30.5	25.2	29.2		16.4	15.2	16.0
6	Merchandise inventory turnover	24.2	21.9	17.1		14.5	13.0	12.6
7	Working capital	$70,000	$58,000	$52,000		$131,000	$103,000	$78,000
8								

Team Project: Assume that the two companies apply for a one-year loan from the team. Identify additional information the companies must provide before the team can make a loan decision.

A review of the notes payable files discovers that three years ago the company reported the entire $1,000 cash payment (consisting of $800 principal and $200 interest) toward an installment note payable as interest expense. This mistake had a material effect on the amount of income in that year. How should the correction be reported in the current-year financial statements?

QS 13-8^A
Error adjustments
A2

Answer each of the following related to international accounting and analysis.

a. Identify a limitation to using ratio analysis when examining companies reporting under different accounting systems such as IFRS versus U.S. GAAP.

b. Identify an advantage to using horizontal and vertical analyses when examining companies reporting under different currencies.

QS 13-9
International ratio analysis
C2

---

connect

Match the ratio to the building block of financial statement analysis to which it best relates.

A. Liquidity and efficiency   **B.** Solvency   **C.** Profitability   **D.** Market prospects

_____ 1. Equity ratio	_____ 6. Accounts receivable turnover
_____ 2. Return on total assets	_____ 7. Debt-to-equity
_____ 3. Dividend yield	_____ 8. Times interest earned
_____ 4. Book value per common share	_____ 9. Gross margin ratio
_____ 5. Days' sales in inventory	_____ 10. Acid-test ratio

EXERCISES

Exercise 13-1
Building blocks of analysis
C1

Exercise 13-2
Identifying financial
ratios

C2

Identify which of the following six metrics *a* through *f* best completes questions *1* through *3* below.

  a. Days' sales uncollected
  b. Accounts receivable turnover
  c. Working capital
  d. Return on total assets
  e. Total asset turnover
  f. Profit margin

  1. Which two ratios are key components in measuring a company's operating efficiency? _____ _____
     Which ratio summarizes these two components? _____
  2. What measure reflects the difference between current assets and current liabilities? _____
  3. Which two short-term liquidity ratios measure how frequently a company collects its accounts?
     _____ _____

Exercise 13-3
Computation and
analysis of trend
percents

P1

Compute trend percents for the following accounts, using 2012 as the base year (round percents to whole numbers). State whether the situation as revealed by the trends appears to be favorable or unfavorable for each account.

	2016	2015	2014	2013	2012
Sales	$282,880	$270,800	$252,600	$234,560	$150,000
Cost of goods sold.	128,200	122,080	115,280	106,440	67,000
Accounts receivable.	18,100	17,300	16,400	15,200	9,000

Exercise 13-4
Common-size percent
computation and
interpretation

P2

Express the following comparative income statements in common-size percents and assess whether or not this company's situation has improved in the most recent year (round the percents to one decimal).

GOMEZ CORPORATION		
Comparative Income Statements		
For Years Ended December 31, 2016 and 2015		
	2016	2015
Sales	$740,000	$625,000
Cost of goods sold.	560,300	290,800
Gross profit	179,700	334,200
Operating expenses.	128,200	218,500
Net income	$ 51,500	$115,700

Exercise 13-5
Determination of income
effects from common-
size and trend percents

P1   P2

Common-size and trend percents for Rustic Company's sales, cost of goods sold, and expenses follow. Determine whether net income increased, decreased, or remained unchanged in this three-year period.

	Common-Size Percents			Trend Percents		
	2016	2015	2014	2016	2015	2014
Sales.	100.0%	100.0%	100.0%	105.4%	104.2%	100.0%
Cost of goods sold	63.4	61.9	59.1	113.1	109.1	100.0
Total expenses	15.3	14.8	15.1	106.8	102.1	100.0

Simon Company's year-end balance sheets follow. Express the balance sheets in common-size percents. Round amounts to the nearest one-tenth of a percent. Analyze and comment on the results.

Exercise 13-6
Common-size percents
P2

At December 31	2016	2015	2014
Assets			
Cash.	$ 31,800	$ 35,625	$ 37,800
Accounts receivable, net	89,500	62,500	50,200
Merchandise inventory.	112,500	82,500	54,000
Prepaid expenses	10,700	9,375	5,000
Plant assets, net	278,500	255,000	230,500
Total assets.	$523,000	$445,000	$377,500
Liabilities and Equity			
Accounts payable.	$129,900	$ 75,250	$ 51,250
Long-term notes payable secured by			
mortgages on plant assets	98,500	101,500	83,500
Common stock, $10 par value	163,500	163,500	163,500
Retained earnings.	131,100	104,750	79,250
Total liabilities and equity	$523,000	$445,000	$377,500

Refer to Simon Company's balance sheets in Exercise 13-6. Analyze its year-end short-term liquidity position at the end of 2016, 2015, and 2014 by computing (1) the current ratio and (2) the acid-test ratio. Comment on the ratio results. (Round ratio amounts to two decimals.)

Exercise 13-7
Liquidity analysis
P3

Refer to the Simon Company information in Exercise 13-6. The company's income statements for the years ended December 31, 2016 and 2015, follow. Assume that all sales are on credit and then compute: (1) days' sales uncollected, (2) accounts receivable turnover, (3) inventory turnover, and (4) days' sales in inventory. Comment on the changes in the ratios from 2015 to 2016. (Round amounts to one decimal.)

Exercise 13-8
Liquidity analysis and interpretation
P3

For Year Ended December 31	2016		2015	
Sales		$673,500		$532,000
Cost of goods sold.	$411,225		$345,500	
Other operating expenses.	209,550		134,980	
Interest expense.	12,100		13,300	
Income taxes	9,525		8,845	
Total costs and expenses.		642,400		502,625
Net income		$ 31,100		$ 29,375
Earnings per share		$ 1.90		$ 1.80

Refer to the Simon Company information in Exercises 13-6 and 13-8. Compare the company's long-term risk and capital structure positions at the end of 2016 and 2015 by computing these ratios: (1) debt and equity ratios—percent rounded to one decimal, (2) debt-to-equity ratio—rounded to two decimals, and (3) times interest earned—rounded to one decimal. Comment on these ratio results.

Exercise 13-9
Risk and capital structure analysis
P3

Refer to Simon Company's financial information in Exercises 13-6 and 13-8. Evaluate the company's efficiency and profitability by computing the following for 2016 and 2015: (1) profit margin ratio—percent rounded to one decimal, (2) total asset turnover—rounded to one decimal, and (3) return on total assets—percent rounded to one decimal. Comment on these ratio results.

Exercise 13-10
Efficiency and profitability analysis
P3

Exercise 13-11
Profitability analysis
P3

Refer to Simon Company's financial information in Exercises 13-6 and 13-8. Additional information about the company follows. To help evaluate the company's profitability, compute and interpret the following ratios for 2016 and 2015: (1) return on common stockholders' equity—percent rounded to one decimal, (2) price-earnings ratio on December 31—rounded to one decimal, and (3) dividend yield—percent rounded to one decimal.

Common stock market price, December 31, 2016	$30.00
Common stock market price, December 31, 2015	28.00
Annual cash dividends per share in 2016	0.29
Annual cash dividends per share in 2015	0.24

Exercise 13-12
Analysis of efficiency and financial leverage
A1

Bud Company and Miller Company are similar firms that operate in the same industry. Miller began operations in 2014 and Bud in 2011. In 2016, both companies pay 7% interest on their debt to creditors. The following additional information is available.

	Bud Company			Miller Company		
	2016	2015	2014	2016	2015	2014
Total asset turnover	3.1	2.8	3.0	1.7	1.5	1.1
Return on total assets	9.0%	9.6%	8.8%	5.9%	5.6%	5.3%
Profit margin ratio	2.4%	2.5%	2.3%	2.8%	3.0%	2.9%
Sales	$410,000	$380,000	$396,000	$210,000	$170,000	$110,000

Write a half-page report comparing Bud and Miller using the available information. Your analysis should include their ability to use assets efficiently to produce profits. Also comment on their success in employing financial leverage in 2016.

Exercise 13-13[A]
Income statement categories

A2

In 2016, Randa Merchandising, Inc., sold its interest in a chain of wholesale outlets, taking the company completely out of the wholesaling business. The company still operates its retail outlets. A listing of some major sections of an income statement follows:

A. Net sales less operating expense section

B. Other unusual and/or infrequent gains (losses)

C. Taxes reported on income (loss) from continuing operations

D. Income (loss) from operating a discontinued segment, or gain (loss) from its disposal

Indicate where each of the following income-related items for this company appears on its 2016 income statement by writing the letter of the appropriate section in the blank beside each item.

Section	Item	Debit	Credit
_____	1. Net sales		$2,900,000
_____	2. Gain on state's condemnation of company property, net of tax		230,000
_____	3. Cost of goods sold	$1,480,000	
_____	4. Income taxes expense	217,000	
_____	5. Depreciation expense.......................	232,000	
_____	6. Gain on sale of wholesale business segment (net of tax)........................		775,000
_____	7. Loss from operating wholesale business segment (net of tax)	444,000	
_____	8. Loss of assets from meteor strike, net of tax	640,000	

Exercise 13-14[A]
Income statement presentation   A2

Use the financial data for Randa Merchandising, Inc., in Exercise 13-13 to prepare its income statement for calendar year 2016. (Ignore the earnings per share section.)

Nintendo Company, Ltd., reports the following financial information as of, or for the year ended, March 31, 2015. Key Nintendo financial results in both Japanese yen and U.S. dollars follow (amounts in millions).

Current assets	¥1,097,597	$ 9,110
Total assets.	1,352,944	11,229
Current liabilities	144,232	1,197
Net sales	549,780	4,562
Net income	41,843	347

Exercise 13-15
Ratio analysis under different currencies

P3

1. Compute Nintendo's current ratio, net profit margin percent, and sales-to-total-assets ratio using the financial information reported in (*a*) yen and (*b*) dollars. Round amounts to two decimals.
2. What can we conclude from a review of the results for part 1?

connect

Selected comparative financial statements of Haroun Company follow.

PROBLEM SET A

Problem 13-1A
Calculation and analysis of trend percents

A1   P1

HAROUN COMPANY							
Comparative Income Statements							
For Years Ended December 31, 2016–2010							
$ thousands	2016	2015	2014	2013	2012	2011	2010
Sales	$1,694	$1,496	$1,370	$1,264	$1,186	$1,110	$928
Cost of goods sold.	1,246	1,032	902	802	752	710	586
Gross profit	448	464	468	462	434	400	342
Operating expenses.	330	256	234	170	146	144	118
Net income	$ 118	$ 208	$ 234	$ 292	$ 288	$ 256	$224

HAROUN COMPANY							
Comparative Balance Sheets							
December 31, 2016–2010							
$ thousands	2016	2015	2014	2013	2012	2011	2010
Assets							
Cash	$ 58	$ 78	$ 82	$ 84	$ 88	$ 86	$ 89
Accounts receivable, net	490	514	466	360	318	302	216
Merchandise inventory	1,838	1,364	1,204	1,032	936	810	615
Other current assets	36	32	14	34	28	28	9
Long-term investments.	0	0	0	146	146	146	146
Plant assets, net	2,020	2,014	1,752	944	978	860	725
Total assets	$4,442	$4,002	$3,518	$2,600	$2,494	$2,232	$1,800
Liabilities and Equity							
Current liabilities	$1,220	$1,042	$ 718	$ 614	$ 546	$ 522	$ 282
Long-term liabilities	1,294	1,140	1,112	570	580	620	400
Common stock.	1,000	1,000	1,000	850	850	650	650
Other paid-in capital.	250	250	250	170	170	150	150
Retained earnings	678	570	438	396	348	290	318
Total liabilities and equity	$4,442	$4,002	$3,518	$2,600	$2,494	$2,232	$1,800

Required

1. Compute trend percents for all components of both statements using 2010 as the base year. (Round percents to one decimal.)

Check (1) 2016, Total assets trend, 246.8%

Analysis Component

2. Analyze and comment on the financial statements and trend percents from part 1.

Problem 13-2A

Ratios, common-size
statements, and trend
percents

P1 P2 P3

Selected comparative financial statements of Korbin Company follow.

KORBIN COMPANY
Comparative Income Statements
For Years Ended December 31, 2016, 2015, and 2014

	2016	2015	2014
Sales	$555,000	$340,000	$278,000
Cost of goods sold..............	283,500	212,500	153,900
Gross profit	271,500	127,500	124,100
Selling expenses	102,900	46,920	50,800
Administrative expenses	50,668	29,920	22,800
Total expenses..................	153,568	76,840	73,600
Income before taxes	117,932	50,660	50,500
Income taxes	40,800	10,370	15,670
Net income	$ 77,132	$ 40,290	$ 34,830

KORBIN COMPANY
Comparative Balance Sheets
December 31, 2016, 2015, and 2014

	2016	2015	2014
Assets			
Current assets	$ 52,390	$ 37,924	$ 51,748
Long-term investments	0	500	3,950
Plant assets, net................	100,000	96,000	60,000
Total assets.....................	$152,390	$134,424	$115,698
Liabilities and Equity			
Current liabilities	$ 22,800	$ 19,960	$ 20,300
Common stock	72,000	72,000	60,000
Other paid-in capital	9,000	9,000	6,000
Retained earnings................	48,590	33,464	29,398
Total liabilities and equity	$152,390	$134,424	$115,698

Required

1. Compute each year's current ratio. (Round ratio amounts to one decimal.)
2. Express the income statement data in common-size percents. (Round percents to two decimals.)

Check (3) 2016, Total
assets trend, 131.71%

3. Express the balance sheet data in trend percents with 2014 as the base year. (Round percents to two decimals.)

Analysis Component

4. Comment on any notable relations revealed by the ratios and percents computed.

Problem 13-3A

Transactions, working
capital, and liquidity
ratios

P3

Plum Corporation began the month of May with $700,000 of current assets, a current ratio of 2.50:1, and an acid-test ratio of 1.10:1. During the month, it completed the following transactions (the company uses a perpetual inventory system).

May	2	Purchased $50,000 of merchandise inventory on credit.
	8	Sold merchandise inventory that cost $55,000 for $110,000 cash.
	10	Collected $20,000 cash on an account receivable.
	15	Paid $22,000 cash to settle an account payable.
	17	Wrote off a $5,000 bad debt against the Allowance for Doubtful Accounts account.
	22	Declared a $1 per share cash dividend on its 50,000 shares of outstanding common stock.

Check May 22: Current
ratio, 2.19; Acid-test ratio, 1.11

26   Paid the dividend declared on May 22.
27   Borrowed $100,000 cash by giving the bank a 30-day, 10% note.
28   Borrowed $80,000 cash by signing a long-term secured note.
29   Used the $180,000 cash proceeds from the notes to buy new machinery.

May 29: Current ratio, 1.80; Working capital, $325,000

Required

Prepare a table, similar to the following, showing Plum's (1) current ratio, (2) acid-test ratio, and (3) working capital after each transaction. Round ratios to two decimals.

Transaction	Current Assets	Quick Assets	Current Liabilities	Current Ratio	Acid-Test Ratio	Working Capital
Beginning	$700,000	—	—	2.50	1.10	—

Selected year-end financial statements of Cabot Corporation follow. (All sales were on credit; selected balance sheet amounts at December 31, 2015, were inventory, $48,900; total assets, $189,400; common stock, $90,000; and retained earnings, $22,748.)

Problem 13-4A
Calculation of financial statement ratios
P3

| CABOT CORPORATION |
| Income Statement |
| For Year Ended December 31, 2016 |

Sales	$448,600
Cost of goods sold.	297,250
Gross profit	151,350
Operating expenses.	98,600
Interest expense.	4,100
Income before taxes	48,650
Income taxes	19,598
Net income	$ 29,052

| CABOT CORPORATION |
| Balance Sheet |
| December 31, 2016 |

Assets		Liabilities and Equity	
Cash	$ 10,000	Accounts payable	$ 17,500
Short-term investments.	8,400	Accrued wages payable	3,200
Accounts receivable, net	29,200	Income taxes payable.	3,300
Notes receivable (trade)*	4,500	Long-term note payable, secured by	
Merchandise inventory.	32,150	mortgage on plant assets.	63,400
Prepaid expenses	2,650	Common stock	90,000
Plant assets, net	153,300	Retained earnings.	62,800
Total assets.	$240,200	Total liabilities and equity.	$240,200

* These are short-term notes receivable arising from customer (trade) sales.

Required

Compute the following: (1) current ratio, (2) acid-test ratio, (3) days' sales uncollected, (4) inventory turnover, (5) days' sales in inventory, (6) debt-to-equity ratio, (7) times interest earned, (8) profit margin ratio, (9) total asset turnover, (10) return on total assets, and (11) return on common stockholders' equity. Round to one decimal place; for part 6, round to two decimals.

Check   Acid-test ratio, 2.2 to 1; Inventory turnover, 7.3

Summary information from the financial statements of two companies competing in the same industry follows.

Problem 13-5A
Comparative ratio analysis   **A1**   **P3**

	Fender Company	Gibson Company		Fender Company	Gibson Company
Data from the current year-end balance sheets			**Data from the current year's income statement**		
Assets			Sales	$770,000	$880,200
Cash	$ 19,500	$ 34,000	Cost of goods sold...............	585,100	632,500
Accounts receivable, net	37,400	57,400	Interest expense..................	7,900	13,000
Current notes receivable (trade)....	9,100	7,200	Income tax expense..............	14,800	24,300
Merchandise inventory............	84,440	132,500	Net income	162,200	210,400
Prepaid expenses	5,000	6,950	Basic earnings per share...........	4.51	5.11
Plant assets, net	290,000	304,400	Cash dividends per share..........	3.81	3.93
Total assets....................	$445,440	$542,450			
			Beginning-of-year balance sheet data		
Liabilities and Equity			Accounts receivable, net	$ 29,800	$ 54,200
Current liabilities	$ 61,340	$ 93,300	Current notes receivable (trade)....	0	0
Long-term notes payable	80,800	101,000	Merchandise inventory............	55,600	107,400
Common stock, $5 par value.......	180,000	206,000	Total assets....................	398,000	382,500
Retained earnings...............	123,300	142,150	Common stock, $5 par value	180,000	206,000
Total liabilities and equity..........	$445,440	$542,450	Retained earnings................	98,260	93,666

Required

Check   (1) Gibson:
Accounts receivable turnover,
14.8; Inventory turnover, 5.3

(2) Fender: Profit
margin, 21.1%; PE, 16.6

1. For both companies compute the (*a*) current ratio, (*b*) acid-test ratio, (*c*) accounts (including notes) receivable turnover, (*d*) inventory turnover, (*e*) days' sales in inventory, and (*f*) days' sales uncollected. Identify the company you consider to be the better short-term credit risk and explain why. Round to one decimal place.

2. For both companies compute the (*a*) profit margin ratio, (*b*) total asset turnover, (*c*) return on total assets, and (*d*) return on common stockholders' equity. Assuming that each company's stock can be purchased at $75 per share, compute their (*e*) price-earnings ratios and (*f*) dividend yields. Round to one decimal place. Identify which company's stock you would recommend as the better investment and explain why.

Problem 13-6A^A
Income statement
computations and format

A2

Selected account balances from the adjusted trial balance for Olinda Corporation as of its calendar year-end December 31, 2016, follow.

	Debit	Credit
a. Interest revenue.....................................		$ 14,000
b. Depreciation expense—Equipment........................	$ 34,000	
c. Loss on sale of equipment.............................	25,850	
d. Accounts payable		44,000
e. Other operating expenses.............................	106,400	
f. Accumulated depreciation—Equipment		71,600
g. Gain from settlement of lawsuit		44,000
h. Accumulated depreciation—Buildings......................		174,500
i. Loss from operating a discontinued segment (pretax).........	18,250	
j. Gain on insurance recovery of tornado damage.............		20,000
k. Net sales...		998,000
l. Depreciation expense—Buildings	52,000	
m. Correction of overstatement of prior year's sales (pretax)......	16,000	
n. Gain on sale of discontinued segment's assets (pretax).........		34,000
o. Loss from settlement of lawsuit	23,250	
p. Income taxes expense	?	
q. Cost of goods sold..................................	482,500	

Required

Answer each of the following questions by providing supporting computations.

1. Assume that the company's income tax rate is 30% for all items. Identify the tax effects and after-tax amounts of the three items labeled pretax.

2. Compute the amount of income from continuing operations before income taxes. What is the amount of the income taxes expense? What is the amount of income from continuing operations?

3. What is the total amount of after-tax income (loss) associated with the discontinued segment?

4. What is the amount of net income for the year?

Check (3) $11,025

(4) $257,425

Selected comparative financial statements of Tripoly Company follow.

PROBLEM SET B

Problem 13-1B
Calculation and analysis
of trend percents

A1 P1

TRIPOLY COMPANY Comparative Income Statements For Years Ended December 31, 2016–2010							
$ thousands	2016	2015	2014	2013	2012	2011	2010
Sales	$560	$610	$630	$680	$740	$770	$860
Cost of goods sold.	276	290	294	314	340	350	380
Gross profit	284	320	336	366	400	420	480
Operating expenses.	84	104	112	126	140	144	150
Net income	$200	$216	$224	$240	$260	$276	$330

TRIPOLY COMPANY Comparative Balance Sheets December 31, 2016–2010							
$ thousands	2016	2015	2014	2013	2012	2011	2010
Assets							
Cash	$ 44	$ 46	$ 52	$ 54	$ 60	$ 62	$ 68
Accounts receivable, net	130	136	140	144	150	154	160
Merchandise inventory.	166	172	178	180	186	190	208
Other current assets	34	34	36	38	38	40	40
Long-term investments	36	30	26	110	110	110	110
Plant assets, net	510	514	520	412	420	428	454
Total assets.	$920	$932	$952	$938	$964	$984	$1,040
Liabilities and Equity							
Current liabilities	$148	$156	$186	$190	$210	$260	$ 280
Long-term liabilities	92	120	142	148	194	214	260
Common stock	160	160	160	160	160	160	160
Other paid-in capital	70	70	70	70	70	70	70
Retained earnings.	450	426	394	370	330	280	270
Total liabilities and equity	$920	$932	$952	$938	$964	$984	$1,040

Required

1. Compute trend percents for all components of both statements using 2010 as the base year. (Round percents to one decimal.)

Analysis Component

2. Analyze and comment on the financial statements and trend percents from part 1.

Check (1) 2016, Total assets trend, 88.5%

Problem 13-2B

Ratios, common-size statements, and trend percents

P1 P2 P3

Selected comparative financial statement information of Bluegrass Corporation follows.

BLUEGRASS CORPORATION Comparative Income Statements For Years Ended December 31, 2016, 2015, and 2014			
	2016	**2015**	**2014**
Sales	$198,800	$166,000	$143,800
Cost of goods sold.	108,890	86,175	66,200
Gross profit	89,910	79,825	77,600
Selling expenses	22,680	19,790	18,000
Administrative expenses	16,760	14,610	15,700
Total expenses	39,440	34,400	33,700
Income before taxes	50,470	45,425	43,900
Income taxes	6,050	5,910	5,300
Net income	$ 44,420	$ 39,515	$ 38,600

BLUEGRASS CORPORATION Comparative Balance Sheets December 31, 2016, 2015, and 2014			
	2016	**2015**	**2014**
Assets			
Current assets	$ 54,860	$ 32,660	$ 36,300
Long-term investments	0	1,700	10,600
Plant assets, net	112,810	113,660	79,000
Total assets.	$167,670	$148,020	$125,900
Liabilities and Equity			
Current liabilities	$ 22,370	$ 19,180	$ 16,500
Common stock	46,500	46,500	37,000
Other paid-in capital	13,850	13,850	11,300
Retained earnings.	84,950	68,490	61,100
Total liabilities and equity	$167,670	$148,020	$125,900

Required

1. Compute each year's current ratio. (Round ratio amounts to one decimal.)

2. Express the income statement data in common-size percents. (Round percents to two decimals.)

Check (3) 2016, Total assets trend, 133.18%

3. Express the balance sheet data in trend percents with 2014 as the base year. (Round percents to two decimals.)

Analysis Component

4. Comment on any notable relations revealed by the ratios and percents computed.

Problem 13-3B

Transactions, working capital, and liquidity ratios P3

Koto Corporation began the month of June with $300,000 of current assets, a current ratio of 2.5:1, and an acid-test ratio of 1.4:1. During the month, it completed the following transactions (the company uses a perpetual inventory system).

Check June 3: Current ratio, 2.88; Acid-test ratio, 2.40

June	1	Sold merchandise inventory that cost $75,000 for $120,000 cash.
	3	Collected $88,000 cash on an account receivable.
	5	Purchased $150,000 of merchandise inventory on credit.
	7	Borrowed $100,000 cash by giving the bank a 60-day, 10% note.

10 Borrowed $120,000 cash by signing a long-term secured note.
12 Purchased machinery for $275,000 cash.
15 Declared a $1 per share cash dividend on its 80,000 shares of outstanding common stock.
19 Wrote off a $5,000 bad debt against the Allowance for Doubtful Accounts account.
22 Paid $12,000 cash to settle an account payable.
30 Paid the dividend declared on June 15.

June 30: Working capital, $(10,000); Current ratio, 0.97

Required

Prepare a table, similar to the following, showing the company's (1) current ratio, (2) acid-test ratio, and (3) working capital after each transaction. Round ratios to two decimals.

Transaction	Current Assets	Quick Assets	Current Liabilities	Current Ratio	Acid-Test Ratio	Working Capital
Beginning	$300,000	—	—	2.50	1.40	—

Selected year-end financial statements of Overton Corporation follow. (All sales were on credit; selected balance sheet amounts at December 31, 2015, were inventory, $17,400; total assets, $94,900; common stock, $35,500; and retained earnings, $18,800.)

Problem 13-4B
Calculation of financial statement ratios
P3

OVERTON CORPORATION
Income Statement
For Year Ended December 31, 2016

Sales	$315,500
Cost of goods sold	236,100
Gross profit	79,400
Operating expenses	49,200
Interest expense	2,200
Income before taxes	28,000
Income taxes	4,200
Net income	$ 23,800

OVERTON CORPORATION
Balance Sheet
December 31, 2016

Assets		Liabilities and Equity	
Cash	$ 6,100	Accounts payable	$ 11,500
Short-term investments	6,900	Accrued wages payable	3,300
Accounts receivable, net	12,100	Income taxes payable	2,600
Notes receivable (trade)*	3,000	Long-term note payable, secured	
Merchandise inventory	13,500	by mortgage on plant assets	30,000
Prepaid expenses	2,000	Common stock, $5 par value	35,000
Plant assets, net	73,900	Retained earnings	35,100
Total assets	$117,500	Total liabilities and equity	$117,500

* These are short-term notes receivable arising from customer (trade) sales.

Required

Compute the following: (1) current ratio, (2) acid-test ratio, (3) days' sales uncollected, (4) inventory turnover, (5) days' sales in inventory, (6) debt-to-equity ratio, (7) times interest earned, (8) profit margin ratio, (9) total asset turnover, (10) return on total assets, and (11) return on common stockholders' equity. Round to one decimal place; for part 6, round to two decimals.

Check   Acid-test ratio, 1.6 to 1; Inventory turnover, 15.3

Problem 13-5B

Comparative ratio analysis **A1 P3**

Summary information from the financial statements of two companies competing in the same industry follows.

	Nikon Company	Canon Company		Nikon Company	Canon Company
Data from the current year-end balance sheets			**Data from the current year's income statement**		
Assets			Sales	$393,600	$667,500
Cash	$ 20,000	$ 36,500	Cost of goods sold...............	290,600	480,000
Accounts receivable, net	77,100	70,500	Interest expense.................	5,900	12,300
Current notes receivable (trade)....	11,600	9,000	Income tax expense..............	5,700	12,300
Merchandise inventory............	86,800	82,000	Net income	33,850	61,700
Prepaid expenses	9,700	10,100	Basic earnings per share...........	1.27	2.19
Plant assets, net	176,900	252,300			
Total assets.....................	$382,100	$460,400			
			Beginning-of-year balance sheet data		
Liabilities and Equity			Accounts receivable, net	$ 72,200	$ 73,300
Current liabilities	$ 90,500	$ 97,000	Current notes receivable (trade)....	0	0
Long-term notes payable	93,000	93,300	Merchandise inventory............	105,100	80,500
Common stock, $5 par value.......	133,000	141,000	Total assets.....................	383,400	443,000
Retained earnings................	65,600	129,100	Common stock, $5 par value	133,000	141,000
Total liabilities and equity..........	$382,100	$460,400	Retained earnings................	49,100	109,700

Required

1. For both companies compute the (*a*) current ratio, (*b*) acid-test ratio, (*c*) accounts (including notes) receivable turnover, (*d*) inventory turnover, (*e*) days' sales in inventory, and (*f*) days' sales uncollected. Identify the company you consider to be the better short-term credit risk and explain why. Round to one decimal place.

2. For both companies compute the (*a*) profit margin ratio, (*b*) total asset turnover, (*c*) return on total assets, and (*d*) return on common stockholders' equity. Assuming that each company paid cash dividends of $1.50 per share and each company's stock can be purchased at $25 per share, compute their (*e*) price-earnings ratios and (*f*) dividend yields. Round to one decimal place; for part *b*, round to two decimals. Identify which company's stock you would recommend as the better investment and explain why.

Problem 13-6B^A

Income statement computations and format

A2

Selected account balances from the adjusted trial balance for Harbor Corp. as of its calendar year-end December 31, 2016, follow.

	Debit	Credit
a. Accumulated depreciation—Buildings............................		$ 400,000
b. Interest revenue...		20,000
c. Net sales		2,640,000
d. Income taxes expense..	$?	
e. Loss on hurricane damage.......................................	48,000	
f. Accumulated depreciation—Equipment		220,000
g. Other operating expenses..	328,000	
h. Depreciation expense—Equipment..............................	100,000	
i. Loss from settlement of lawsuit	36,000	
j. Gain from settlement of lawsuit		68,000
k. Loss on sale of equipment.......................................	24,000	
l. Loss from operating a discontinued segment (pretax)	120,000	
m. Depreciation expense—Buildings	156,000	
n. Correction of overstatement of prior year's expense (pretax).........		48,000
o. Cost of goods sold	1,040,000	
p. Loss on sale of discontinued segment's assets (pretax)..............	180,000	
q. Accounts payable..		132,000

Required

Answer each of the following questions by providing supporting computations.

1. Assume that the company's income tax rate is 25% for all items. Identify the tax effects and after-tax amounts of the three items labeled pretax.

2. What is the amount of income from continuing operations before income taxes? What is the amount of income taxes expense? What is the amount of income from continuing operations?

3. What is the total amount of after-tax income (loss) associated with the discontinued segment?

4. What is the amount of net income for the year?

Check   (3) $(225,000)

(4) $522,000

(This serial problem began in Chapter 1 and continues through most of the book. If previous chapter segments were not completed, the serial problem can begin at this point. It is helpful, but not necessary, to use the Working Papers that accompany the book.)

SERIAL PROBLEM
Business Solutions

P3

SP 13   Assume the following selected data from Business Solutions's income statement for the three months ended March 31, 2017, and from its March 31, 2017, balance sheet to complete the requirements below: computer services revenue, $25,307; net sales (of goods), $18,693; total sales and revenue, $44,000; cost of goods sold, $14,052; net income, $18,833; quick assets, $90,924; current assets, $95,568; total assets, $120,268; current liabilities, $875; total liabilities, $875; and total equity, $119,393.

Required

1. Compute the gross margin ratio (both with and without services revenue) and net profit margin ratio (round the percent to one decimal).

2. Compute the current ratio and acid-test ratio (round to one decimal).

3. Compute the debt ratio and equity ratio (round the percent to one decimal).

4. What percent of its assets are current? What percent are long term (round the percent to one decimal)?

Beyond the Numbers

BTN 13-1   Refer to **Apple**'s financial statements in Appendix A to answer the following.

1. Using fiscal 2012 as the base year, compute trend percents for fiscal years 2012, 2013, and 2014 for net sales, cost of sales, operating income, other income (expense) net, provision for income taxes, and net income. (Round percents to one decimal.)

2. Compute common-size percents for fiscal years 2013 and 2014 for the following categories of assets: (*a*) total current assets; (*b*) property, plant and equipment, net; and (*c*) goodwill plus acquired intangible assets, net. (Round percents to one decimal.)

3. Comment on any notable changes across the years for the income statement trends computed in part 1 and the balance sheet percents computed in part 2.

REPORTING IN ACTION

A1 P1 P2

APPLE

Fast Forward

4. Access Apple's financial statements for fiscal years ending after September 27, 2014, from its website (**Apple.com**) or the SEC database (**www.SEC.gov**). Update your work for parts 1, 2, and 3 using the new information accessed.

BTN 13-2   Key figures for **Apple** and **Google** follow.

COMPARATIVE ANALYSIS

C2 P2

APPLE
GOOGLE

$ millions	Apple	Google
Cash and equivalents	$ 13,844	$ 18,347
Accounts receivable, net	17,460	9,383
Inventories	2,111	0
Retained earnings	87,152	75,706
Cost of sales	112,258	25,691
Revenues	182,795	66,001
Total assets.	231,839	131,133

Required

1. Compute common-size percents for each of the companies using the data provided. (Round percents to one decimal.)
2. Which company retains a higher portion of cumulative net income in the company?
3. Which company has a higher gross margin ratio on sales?
4. Which company holds a higher percent of its total assets as inventory?

ETHICS CHALLENGE

A1

BTN 13-3   As Beacon Company controller, you are responsible for informing the board of directors about its financial activities. At the board meeting, you present the following information.

	2016	2015	2014
Sales trend percent	147.0%	135.0%	100.0%
Selling expenses to sales	10.1%	14.0%	15.6%
Sales to plant assets ratio	3.8 to 1	3.6 to 1	3.3 to 1
Current ratio	2.9 to 1	2.7 to 1	2.4 to 1
Acid-test ratio	1.1 to 1	1.4 to 1	1.5 to 1
Inventory turnover.	7.8 times	9.0 times	10.2 times
Accounts receivable turnover	7.0 times	7.7 times	8.5 times
Total asset turnover.	2.9 times	2.9 times	3.3 times
Return on total assets	10.4%	11.0%	13.2%
Return on stockholders' equity.	10.7%	11.5%	14.1%
Profit margin ratio	3.6%	3.8%	4.0%

After the meeting, the company's CEO holds a press conference with analysts in which she mentions the following ratios.

	2016	2015	2014
Sales trend percent	147.0%	135.0%	100.0%
Selling expenses to sales	10.1%	14.0%	15.6%
Sales to plant assets ratio	3.8 to 1	3.6 to 1	3.3 to 1
Current ratio	2.9 to 1	2.7 to 1	2.4 to 1

Required

1. Why do you think the CEO decided to report 4 ratios instead of the 11 prepared?
2. Comment on the possible consequences of the CEO's reporting of the ratios selected.

COMMUNICATING IN PRACTICE

A1   P3

BTN 13-4   Each team is to select a different industry, and each team member is to select a different company in that industry and acquire its financial statements. Use those statements to analyze the company, including at least one ratio from each of the four building blocks of analysis. When necessary, use the financial press to determine the market price of its stock. Communicate with teammates via a meeting, e-mail, or telephone to discuss how different companies compare to each other and to industry norms. The team is to prepare a single one-page memorandum reporting on its analysis and the conclusions reached.

TAKING IT TO THE NET

P3

BTN 13-5   Access the February 20, 2015, filing of the December 31, 2014, 10-K report of **The Hershey Company** (ticker HSY) at **www.SEC.gov** and complete the following requirements.

Required

Compute or identify the following profitability ratios of Hershey for its years ending December 31, 2014, *and* December 31, 2013. Interpret its profitability using the results obtained for these two years.

1. Profit margin ratio (round the percent to one decimal).
2. Gross profit ratio (round the percent to one decimal).
3. Return on total assets (round the percent to one decimal). (Total assets at year-end 2012 were $4,754,839 in thousands.)
4. Return on common stockholders' equity (round the percent to one decimal). (Total shareholders' equity at year-end 2012 was $1,048,373 in thousands.)
5. Basic net income per common share (round to the nearest cent).

BTN 13-6   A team approach to learning financial statement analysis is often useful.

Required

1. Each team should write a description of horizontal and vertical analysis that all team members agree with and understand. Illustrate each description with an example.

2. *Each* member of the team is to select *one* of the following categories of ratio analysis. Explain what the ratios in that category measure. Choose one ratio from the category selected, present its formula, and explain what it measures.

    a. Liquidity and efficiency   **c.** Profitability

    b. Solvency   **d.** Market prospects

3. Each team member is to present his or her notes from part 2 to teammates. Team members are to confirm or correct other teammates' presentations.

TEAMWORK IN ACTION

P1 P2 P3

Hint: Pairing within teams may be necessary for part 2. Use as an in-class activity or as an assignment. Consider presentations to the entire class using team rotation with slides.

BTN 13-7   Assume that James Gorman of **Morgan Stanley** (**MorganStanley.com**) has impressed you with the company's success and its commitment to ethical behavior. You learn of a staff opening at Morgan Stanley and decide to apply for it. Your resume is successfully screened from the thousands received and you advance to the interview process. You learn that the interview consists of analyzing the following financial facts and answering analysis questions below. (The data are taken from a small merchandiser in outdoor recreational equipment.)

ENTREPRENEURIAL DECISION

A1 P1 P2 P3

	2016	2015	2014
Sales trend percents.	137.0%	125.0%	100.0%
Selling expenses to sales	9.8%	13.7%	15.3%
Sales to plant assets ratio	3.5 to 1	3.3 to 1	3.0 to 1
Current ratio	2.6 to 1	2.4 to 1	2.1 to 1
Acid-test ratio	0.8 to 1	1.1 to 1	1.2 to 1
Merchandise inventory turnover	7.5 times	8.7 times	9.9 times
Accounts receivable turnover	6.7 times	7.4 times	8.2 times
Total asset turnover.	2.6 times	2.6 times	3.0 times
Return on total assets	8.8%	9.4%	11.1%
Return on equity	9.75%	11.50%	12.25%
Profit margin ratio	3.3%	3.5%	3.7%

Required

Use these data to answer each of the following questions with explanations.

1. Is it becoming easier for the company to meet its current liabilities on time and to take advantage of any available cash discounts? Explain.

2. Is the company collecting its accounts receivable more rapidly? Explain.

3. Is the company's investment in accounts receivable decreasing? Explain.

4. Is the company's investment in plant assets increasing? Explain.

5. Is the owner's investment becoming more profitable? Explain.

6. Did the dollar amount of selling expenses decrease during the three-year period? Explain.

BTN 13-8   You are to devise an investment strategy to enable you to accumulate $1,000,000 by age 65. Start by making some assumptions about your salary. Next compute the percent of your salary that you will be able to save each year. If you will receive any lump-sum monies, include those amounts in your calculations. Historically, stocks have delivered average annual returns of around 10%. Given this history, you should probably not assume that you will earn above 10% on the money you invest. It is not necessary to specify exactly what types of assets you will buy for your investments; just assume a rate you expect to earn. Use the future value tables in Appendix B to calculate how your savings will grow. Experiment a bit with your figures to see how much less you have to save if you start at, for example, age 25 versus age 35 or 40. (For this assignment, do not include inflation in your calculations.)

HITTING THE ROAD

C1 P3

GLOBAL DECISION

A1

Samsung

APPLE

GOOGLE

BTN 13-9 **Samsung** (www.Samsung.com), which is a leading manufacturer of consumer electronic products, along with **Apple** and **Google**, are competitors in the global marketplace. Key figures for Samsung follow (in KRW millions).

Cash and equivalents	₩ 16,840,766	Cost of sales	₩128,278,800
Accounts receivable, net	28,234,485	Revenues	206,205,987
Inventories	17,317,504	Total assets.	230,422,958
Retained earnings.	169,529,604		

Required

1. Compute common-size percents for Samsung using the data provided. (Round percents to one decimal.)

2. Compare the results with Apple and Google from BTN 13-2.

ANSWERS TO MULTIPLE CHOICE QUIZ

1. d; ($351,000/$300,000) × 100 = 117%

2. e; ($86,000 + $76,000 + $122,000 + $12,000)/$124,000 = 2.39

3. c; ($86,000 + $76,000)/$124,000 = 1.31

4. a; ($124,000 + $90,000)/$830,000 = 25.78%

5. d; ($300,000 + $316,000)/$830,000 = 74.22%

Financial Statement Information

This appendix includes financial information for (1) **Apple**, (2) **Google**, and (3) **Samsung**. Apple states that it designs, manufactures, and markets mobile communication and media devices, personal computers, and portable digital music players, and sells a variety of related software, services, peripherals, networking solutions, and third-party digital content and applications; it competes with both Google and Samsung in the United States and globally. The information in this appendix is taken from their annual 10-K reports (or annual report for Samsung) filed with the SEC or other regulatory agency. An **annual report** is a summary of a company's financial results for the year along with its current financial condition and future plans. This report is directed to external users of financial information, but it also affects the actions and decisions of internal users.

A company often uses an annual report to showcase itself and its products. Many annual reports include photos, diagrams, and illustrations related to the company. The primary objective of annual reports, however, is the financial section, which communicates much information about a company, with most data drawn from the accounting information system. The layout of an annual report's financial section is fairly established and typically includes the following:

- Letter to Shareholders
- Financial History and Highlights
- Management Discussion and Analysis
- Management's Report on Financial Statements and on Internal Controls
- Report of Independent Accountants (Auditor's Report) and on Internal Controls
- Financial Statements
- Notes to Financial Statements
- List of Directors and Officers

This appendix provides the financial statements for Apple (plus selected notes), Google, and Samsung. The appendix is organized as follows:

- **Apple** **A-2** through **A-9**
- **Google** **A-10** through **A-13**
- **Samsung** **A-14** through **A-17**

Many assignments at the end of each chapter refer to information in this appendix. We encourage readers to spend time with these assignments; they are especially useful in showing the relevance and diversity of financial accounting and reporting.

APPLE
GOOGLE
Samsung

> *Special note:* The SEC maintains the EDGAR (**E**lectronic **D**ata **G**athering, **A**nalysis, and **R**etrieval) database at **www.SEC.gov** for U.S. filers. The **Form 10-K** is the annual report form for most companies. It provides electronically accessible information. The **Form 10-KSB** is the annual report form filed by small businesses. It requires slightly less information than the Form 10-K. One of these forms must be filed within 90 days after the company's fiscal year-end. (Forms 10-K405, 10-KT, 10-KT405, and 10-KSB405 are slight variations of the usual form due to certain regulations or rules.)

Apple Inc.
CONSOLIDATED BALANCE SHEETS
(In millions, except number of shares which are reflected in thousands and par value)

	September 27, 2014	September 28, 2013
ASSETS:		
Current assets:		
Cash and cash equivalents	$ 13,844	$ 14,259
Short-term marketable securities	11,233	26,287
Accounts receivable, less allowances of $86 and $99, respectively	17,460	13,102
Inventories	2,111	1,764
Deferred tax assets	4,318	3,453
Vendor non-trade receivables	9,759	7,539
Other current assets	9,806	6,882
Total current assets	68,531	73,286
Long-term marketable securities	130,162	106,215
Property, plant and equipment, net	20,624	16,597
Goodwill	4,616	1,577
Acquired intangible assets, net	4,142	4,179
Other assets	3,764	5,146
Total assets	$ 231,839	$ 207,000
LIABILITIES AND SHAREHOLDERS' EQUITY:		
Current liabilities:		
Accounts payable	$ 30,196	$ 22,367
Accrued expenses	18,453	13,856
Deferred revenue	8,491	7,435
Commercial paper	6,308	0
Total current liabilities	63,448	43,658
Deferred revenue – non-current	3,031	2,625
Long-term debt	28,987	16,960
Other non-current liabilities	24,826	20,208
Total liabilities	120,292	83,451
Commitments and contingencies		
Shareholders' equity:		
Common stock and additional paid-in capital, $0.00001 par value; 12,600,000 shares authorized;		
5,866,161 and 6,294,494 shares issued and outstanding, respectively	23,313	19,764
Retained earnings	87,152	104,256
Accumulated other comprehensive income/(loss)	1,082	(471)
Total shareholders' equity	111,547	123,549
Total liabilities and shareholders' equity	$ 231,839	$ 207,000

See accompanying Notes to Consolidated Financial Statements.

Apple Inc.
CONSOLIDATED STATEMENTS OF OPERATIONS
(In millions, except number of shares which are reflected in thousands and per share amounts)

Years ended	September 27, 2014	September 28, 2013	September 29, 2012
Net sales	$ 182,795	$ 170,910	$ 156,508
Cost of sales	112,258	106,606	87,846
Gross margin	70,537	64,304	68,662
Operating expenses:			
Research and development	6,041	4,475	3,381
Selling, general and administrative	11,993	10,830	10,040
Total operating expenses	18,034	15,305	13,421
Operating income	52,503	48,999	55,241
Other income, net	980	1,156	522
Income before provision for income taxes	53,483	50,155	55,763
Provision for income taxes	13,973	13,118	14,030
Net income	$ 39,510	$ 37,037	$ 41,733
Earnings per share:			
Basic	$ 6.49	$ 5.72	$ 6.38
Diluted	$ 6.45	$ 5.68	$ 6.31
Shares used in computing earnings per share:			
Basic	6,085,572	6,477,320	6,543,726
Diluted	6,122,663	6,521,634	6,617,483
Cash dividends declared per common share	$ 1.82	$ 1.64	$ 0.38

See accompanying Notes to Consolidated Financial Statements.

Apple Inc.
CONSOLIDATED STATEMENTS OF COMPREHENSIVE INCOME
(In millions)

Years ended	September 27, 2014	September 28, 2013	September 29, 2012
Net income	$ 39,510	$ 37,037	$ 41,733
Other comprehensive income/(loss):			
Change in foreign currency translation, net of tax effects of $50, $35 and $13, respectively	(137)	(112)	(15)
Change in unrecognized gains/losses on derivative instruments:			
Change in fair value of derivatives, net of tax benefit/(expense) of $(297), $(351) and $73, respectively	1,390	522	(131)
Adjustment for net losses/(gains) realized and included in net income, net of tax expense/(benefit) of $(36), $255 and $220, respectively	149	(458)	(399)
Total change in unrecognized gains/losses on derivative instruments, net of tax	1,539	64	(530)
Change in unrealized gains/losses on marketable securities:			
Change in fair value of marketable securities, net of tax benefit/ (expense) of $(153), $458 and $(421), respectively	285	(791)	715
Adjustment for net losses/(gains) realized and included in net income, net of tax expense/(benefit) of $71, $82 and $68, respectively	(134)	(131)	(114)
Total change in unrealized gains/losses on marketable securities, net of tax	151	(922)	601
Total other comprehensive income/(loss)	1,553	(970)	56
Total comprehensive income	$ 41,063	$ 36,067	$ 41,789

See accompanying Notes to Consolidated Financial Statements.

Apple Inc.
CONSOLIDATED STATEMENTS OF SHAREHOLDERS' EQUITY
(In millions, except number of shares which are reflected in thousands)

	Common Stock and Additional Paid-In Capital		Retained Earnings	Accumulated Other Comprehensive Income/(Loss)	Total Shareholders' Equity
	Shares	Amount			
Balances as of September 24, 2011	6,504,937	$ 13,331	$ 62,841	$ 443	$ 76,615
Net income	0	0	41,733	0	41,733
Other comprehensive income/(loss)	0	0	0	56	56
Dividends and dividend equivalents declared	0	0	(2,523)	0	(2,523)
Share-based compensation	0	1,740	0	0	1,740
Common stock issued, net of shares withheld for employee taxes	69,521	200	(762)	0	(562)
Tax benefit from equity awards, including transfer pricing adjustments	0	1,151	0	0	1,151
Balances as of September 29, 2012	6,574,458	16,422	101,289	499	118,210
Net income	0	0	37,037	0	37,037
Other comprehensive income/(loss)	0	0	0	(970)	(970)
Dividends and dividend equivalents declared	0	0	(10,676)	0	(10,676)
Repurchase of common stock	(328,837)	0	(22,950)	0	(22,950)
Share-based compensation	0	2,253	0	0	2,253
Common stock issued, net of shares withheld for employee taxes	48,873	(143)	(444)	0	(587)
Tax benefit from equity awards, including transfer pricing adjustments	0	1,232	0	0	1,232
Balances as of September 28, 2013	6,294,494	19,764	104,256	(471)	123,549
Net income	0	0	39,510	0	39,510
Other comprehensive income/(loss)	0	0	0	1,553	1,553
Dividends and dividend equivalents declared	0	0	(11,215)	0	(11,215)
Repurchase of common stock	(488,677)	0	(45,000)	0	(45,000)
Share-based compensation	0	2,863	0	0	2,863
Common stock issued, net of shares withheld for employee taxes	60,344	(49)	(399)	0	(448)
Tax benefit from equity awards, including transfer pricing adjustments	0	735	0	0	735
Balances as of September 27, 2014	5,866,161	$ 23,313	$ 87,152	$ 1,082	$ 111,547

See accompanying Notes to Consolidated Financial Statements.

Apple Inc.
CONSOLIDATED STATEMENTS OF CASH FLOWS
(In millions)

Years ended	September 27, 2014	September 28, 2013	September 29, 2012
Cash and cash equivalents, beginning of the year	$ 14,259	$ 10,746	$ 9,815
Operating activities:			
Net income	39,510	37,037	41,733
Adjustments to reconcile net income to cash generated by operating activities:			
Depreciation and amortization	7,946	6,757	3,277
Share-based compensation expense	2,863	2,253	1,740
Deferred income tax expense	2,347	1,141	4,405
Changes in operating assets and liabilities:			
Accounts receivable, net	(4,232)	(2,172)	(5,551)
Inventories	(76)	(973)	(15)
Vendor non-trade receivables	(2,220)	223	(1,414)
Other current and non-current assets	167	1,080	(3,162)
Accounts payable	5,938	2,340	4,467
Deferred revenue	1,460	1,459	2,824
Other current and non-current liabilities	6,010	4,521	2,552
Cash generated by operating activities	59,713	53,666	50,856
Investing activities:			
Purchases of marketable securities	(217,128)	(148,489)	(151,232)
Proceeds from maturities of marketable securities	18,810	20,317	13,035
Proceeds from sales of marketable securities	189,301	104,130	99,770
Payments made in connection with business acquisitions, net	(3,765)	(496)	(350)
Payments for acquisition of property, plant and equipment	(9,571)	(8,165)	(8,295)
Payments for acquisition of intangible assets	(242)	(911)	(1,107)
Other	16	(160)	(48)
Cash used in investing activities	(22,579)	(33,774)	(48,227)
Financing activities:			
Proceeds from issuance of common stock	730	530	665
Excess tax benefits from equity awards	739	701	1,351
Taxes paid related to net share settlement of equity awards	(1,158)	(1,082)	(1,226)
Dividends and dividend equivalents paid	(11,126)	(10,564)	(2,488)
Repurchase of common stock	(45,000)	(22,860)	0
Proceeds from issuance of long-term debt, net	11,960	16,896	0
Proceeds from issuance of commercial paper, net	6,306	0	0
Cash used in financing activities	(37,549)	(16,379)	(1,698)
Increase/(decrease) in cash and cash equivalents	(415)	3,513	931
Cash and cash equivalents, end of the year	$ 13,844	$ 14,259	$ 10,746
Supplemental cash flow disclosure:			
Cash paid for income taxes, net	$ 10,026	$ 9,128	$ 7,682
Cash paid for interest	$ 339	$ 0	$ 0

See accompanying Notes to Consolidated Financial Statements.

APPLE

APPLE INC.
SELECTED NOTES TO CONSOLIDATED FINANCIAL STATEMENTS

Basis of Presentation and Preparation

The Company's fiscal year is the 52- or 53-week period that ends on the last Saturday of September. The Company's fiscal years 2014, 2013 and 2012 ended on September 27, 2014, September 28, 2013 and September 29, 2012, respectively. An additional week is included in the first fiscal quarter approximately every six years to realign fiscal quarters with calendar quarters. Fiscal years 2014 and 2013 spanned 52 weeks each. Fiscal year 2012 spanned 53 weeks, with a 14th week included in the first quarter of 2012. Unless otherwise stated, references to particular years, quarters, months and periods refer to the Company's fiscal years ended in September and the associated quarters, months and periods of those fiscal years.

Common Stock Split

On June 6, 2014, the Company effected a seven-for-one stock split to shareholders of record as of June 2, 2014. All share and per share information has been retroactively adjusted to reflect the stock split.

Revenue Recognition

Net sales consist primarily of revenue from the sale of hardware, software, digital content and applications, accessories and service and support contracts. The Company recognizes revenue when persuasive evidence of an arrangement exists, delivery has occurred, the sales price is fixed or determinable and collection is probable. Product is considered delivered to the customer once it has been shipped and title, risk of loss and rewards of ownership have been transferred. For most of the Company's product sales, these criteria are met at the time the product is shipped. For online sales to individuals, for some sales to education customers in the U.S., and for certain other sales, the Company defers revenue until the customer receives the product because the Company retains a portion of the risk of loss on these sales during transit. The Company recognizes revenue from the sale of hardware products, software bundled with hardware that is essential to the functionality of the hardware, and third-party digital content sold on the iTunes Store in accordance with general revenue recognition accounting guidance. The Company recognizes revenue in accordance with industry specific software accounting guidance for the following types of sales transactions: (i) standalone sales of software products, (ii) sales of software upgrades and (iii) sales of software bundled with hardware not essential to the functionality of the hardware.

For the sale of most third-party products, the Company recognizes revenue based on the gross amount billed to customers because the Company establishes its own pricing for such products, retains related inventory risk for physical products, is the primary obligor to the customer and assumes the credit risk for amounts billed to its customers. For third-party applications sold through the App Store and Mac App Store and certain digital content sold through the iTunes Store, the Company does not determine the selling price of the products and is not the primary obligor to the customer. Therefore, the Company accounts for such sales on a net basis by recognizing in net sales only the commission it retains from each sale. The portion of the gross amount billed to customers that is remitted by the Company to third-party app developers and certain digital content owners is not reflected in the Company's Consolidated Statements of Operations.

The Company records deferred revenue when it receives payments in advance of the delivery of products or the performance of services. This includes amounts that have been deferred for unspecified and specified software upgrade rights and non-software services that are attached to hardware and software products. The Company sells gift cards redeemable at its retail and online stores, and also sells gift cards redeemable on the iTunes Store for the purchase of digital content and software. The Company records deferred revenue upon the sale of the card, which is relieved upon redemption of the card by the customer. Revenue from AppleCare service and support contracts is deferred and recognized over the service coverage periods. AppleCare service and support contracts typically include extended phone support, repair services, web-based support resources and diagnostic tools offered under the Company's standard limited warranty.

The Company records reductions to revenue for estimated commitments related to price protection and other customer incentive programs. For transactions involving price protection, the Company recognizes revenue net of the estimated amount to be refunded. For the Company's other customer incentive programs, the estimated cost of these programs is recognized at the later of the date at which the Company has sold the product or the date at which the program is offered. The Company also records reductions to revenue for expected future product returns based on the Company's historical experience. Revenue is recorded net of taxes collected from customers that are remitted to governmental authorities, with the collected taxes recorded as current liabilities until remitted to the relevant government authority.

Shipping Costs

For all periods presented, amounts billed to customers related to shipping and handling are classified as revenue, and

Apple Inc. Notes—continued

the Company's shipping and handling costs are included in cost of sales.

Warranty Costs

The Company generally provides for the estimated cost of hardware and software warranties at the time the related revenue is recognized. The Company assesses the adequacy of its pre-existing warranty liabilities and adjusts the amounts as necessary based on actual experience and changes in future estimates.

Software Development Costs

Research and development ("R&D") costs are expensed as incurred. Development costs of computer software to be sold, leased, or otherwise marketed are subject to capitalization beginning when a product's technological feasibility has been established and ending when a product is available for general release to customers. In most instances, the Company's products are released soon after technological feasibility has been established. Costs incurred subsequent to achievement of technological feasibility were not significant, and software development costs were expensed as incurred during 2014, 2013 and 2012.

Advertising Costs

Advertising costs are expensed as incurred and included in selling, general and administrative expenses. Advertising expense was $1.2 billion, $1.1 billion and $1.0 billion for 2014, 2013 and 2012, respectively.

Accrued Expenses

	2014	2013
Accrued warranty and related costs	$ 4,159	$ 2,967
Accrued marketing and selling expenses	2,321	1,291
Accrued taxes	1,209	1,200
Accrued compensation and employee benefits	1,209	959
Deferred margin on component sales	1,057	1,262
Other current liabilities	8,498	6,177
Total accrued expenses	$ 18,453	$ 13,856

Other Income and Expense

	2014	2013
Interest and dividend income	$ 1,795	$ 1,616
Interest expense	(384)	(136)
Other expense, net	(431)	(324)
Total other income/(expense), net	$ 980	$ 1,156

Earnings Per Share

Basic earnings per share is computed by dividing income available to common shareholders by the weighted-average number of shares of common stock outstanding during the period. Diluted earnings per share is computed by dividing income available to common shareholders by the weighted-average number of shares of common stock outstanding during the period increased to include the number of additional shares of common stock that would have been outstanding if the potentially dilutive securities had been issued.

Cash Equivalents and Marketable Securities

All highly liquid investments with maturities of three months or less at the date of purchase are classified as cash equivalents. The Company's marketable debt and equity securities have been classified and accounted for as available-for-sale. Management determines the appropriate classification of its investments at the time of purchase and reevaluates the designations at each balance sheet date. The Company classifies its marketable debt securities as either short-term or long-term based on each instrument's underlying contractual maturity date. Marketable debt securities with maturities of 12 months or less are classified as short-term and marketable debt securities with maturities greater than 12 months are classified as long-term. The Company classifies its marketable equity securities, including mutual funds, as either short-term or long-term based on the nature of each security and its availability for use in current operations. The Company's marketable debt and equity securities are carried at fair value, with the unrealized gains and losses, net of taxes, reported as a component of shareholders' equity. The cost of securities sold is based upon the specific identification method.

Accounts Receivable (Trade Receivables)

The Company has considerable trade receivables outstanding with its third-party cellular network carriers, wholesalers, retailers, value-added resellers, small and mid-sized businesses, and education, enterprise and government customers.

As of September 27, 2014, the Company had two customers that represented 10% or more of total trade receivables, one of which accounted for 16% and the other 13%. The Company's cellular network carriers accounted for 72% and 68% of trade receivables as of September 27, 2014 and September 28, 2013, respectively. The additions and write-offs to the Company's allowance for doubtful accounts during 2014, 2013 and 2012 were not significant.

Allowance for Doubtful Accounts

The Company records its allowance for doubtful accounts based upon its assessment of various factors. The Company considers historical experience, the age of the accounts receivable balances, credit quality of the Company's customers, current economic conditions and other factors that may affect customers' ability to pay.

Apple Inc. Notes—continued

Inventories

Inventories are stated at the lower of cost, computed using the first-in, first-out method, or market. If the cost of the inventories exceeds their market value, provisions are made currently for the difference between the cost and the market value.

Inventories	2014	2013
Components	$ 471	$ 683
Finished goods	1,640	1,081
Total inventories	$ 2,111	$ 1,764

Property, Plant and Equipment

Property, plant and equipment are stated at cost. Depreciation is computed by use of the straight-line method over the estimated useful lives of the assets, which for buildings is the lesser of 30 years or the remaining life of the underlying building; between two to five years for machinery and equipment, including product tooling and manufacturing process equipment; and the shorter of lease terms or ten years for leasehold improvements. The Company capitalizes eligible costs to acquire or develop internal-use software that are incurred subsequent to the preliminary project stage. Capitalized costs related to internal-use software are amortized using the straight-line method over the estimated useful lives of the assets, which range from three to five years. Depreciation and amortization expense on property and equipment was $6.9 billion, $5.8 billion and $2.6 billion during 2014, 2013 and 2012, respectively.

Property, Plant and Equipment	2014	2013
Land and buildings	$ 4,863	$ 3,309
Machinery, equipment and internal-use software	29,639	21,242
Leasehold improvements	4,513	3,968
Gross property, plant and equipment	39,015	28,519
Accumulated depreciation and amortization	(18,391)	(11,922)
Net property, plant and equipment	$ 20,624	$ 16,597

Long-Lived Assets Including Goodwill and Other Acquired Intangible Assets

The Company reviews property, plant and equipment, inventory component prepayments and certain identifiable intangibles, excluding goodwill, for impairment. Long-lived assets are reviewed for impairment whenever events or changes in circumstances indicate the carrying amount of an asset may not be recoverable. Recoverability of these assets is measured by comparison of their carrying amounts to future undiscounted cash flows the assets are expected to generate. If property, plant and equipment, inventory component prepayments and certain identifiable intangibles are considered to be impaired, the impairment to be recognized equals the amount by which the carrying value of the assets exceeds its fair value. The Company did not record any significant impairments during 2014, 2013 and 2012.

The Company does not amortize goodwill and intangible assets with indefinite useful lives, rather such assets are required to be tested for impairment at least annually or sooner whenever events or changes in circumstances indicate that the assets may be impaired. The Company performs its goodwill and intangible asset impairment tests in the fourth quarter of each year. The Company did not recognize any impairment charges related to goodwill or indefinite lived intangible assets during 2014, 2013 and 2012. The Company established reporting units based on its current reporting structure. For purposes of testing goodwill for impairment, goodwill has been allocated to these reporting units to the extent it relates to each reporting unit. In 2014 and 2013, the Company's goodwill was allocated to the Americas and Europe reportable operating segments.

The Company amortizes its intangible assets with definite useful lives over their estimated useful lives and reviews these assets for impairment. The Company typically amortizes its acquired intangible assets with definite useful lives over periods from three to seven years.

Goodwill and Other Intangible Assets

On July 31, 2014, the Company completed the acquisitions of Beats Music, LLC, which offers a subscription streaming music service, and Beats Electronics, LLC, which makes Beats® headphones, speakers and audio software (collectively, "Beats"). The total purchase price consideration for these acquisitions was $2.6 billion, which consisted primarily of cash, of which $2.2 billion was allocated to goodwill, $636 million to acquired intangible assets and $258 million to net liabilities assumed. The Company also completed various other business acquisitions during 2014 for an aggregate cash consideration, net of cash acquired, of $957 million, of which $828 million was allocated to goodwill, $257 million to acquired intangible assets and $128 million to net liabilities assumed. The Company's gross carrying amount of goodwill was $4.6 billion as of September 27, 2014. The following table summarizes the components of gross and net intangible asset balances as of September 27, 2014 (in millions):

	2014		
	Gross Carrying Amount	Accumulated Amortization	Net Carrying Amount
Definite-lived and amortizable acquired intangible assets	$ 7,127	$ (3,085)	$ 4,042
Indefinite-lived and non-amortizable acquired intangible assets	100	0	100
Total acquired intangible assets	$ 7,227	$ (3,085)	$ 4,142

Apple Inc. Notes—continued

Fair Value Measurements

The Company applies fair value accounting for all financial assets and liabilities and non-financial assets and liabilities that are recognized or disclosed at fair value in the financial statements on a recurring basis. The Company defines fair value as the price that would be received from selling an asset or paid to transfer a liability in an orderly transaction between market participants at the measurement date. When determining the fair value measurements for assets and liabilities, which are required to be recorded at fair value, the Company considers the principal or most advantageous market in which the Company would transact and the market-based risk measurements or assumptions that market participants would use in pricing the asset or liability, such as risks inherent in valuation techniques, transfer restrictions and credit risk. Fair value is estimated by applying the following hierarchy, which prioritizes the inputs used to measure fair value into three levels and bases the categorization within the hierarchy upon the lowest level of input that is available and significant to the fair value measurement:

Level 1—Quoted prices in active markets for identical assets or liabilities.

Level 2—Observable inputs other than quoted prices in active markets for identical assets and liabilities, quoted prices for identical or similar assets or liabilities in inactive markets, or other inputs that are observable or can be corroborated by observable market data for substantially the full term of the assets or liabilities.

Level 3—Inputs that are generally unobservable and typically reflect management's estimate of assumptions that market participants would use in pricing the asset or liability.

The Company's valuation techniques used to measure the fair value of money market funds and certain marketable equity securities were derived from quoted prices in active markets for identical assets or liabilities. The valuation techniques used to measure the fair value of the Company's debt instruments and all other financial instruments, all of which have counterparties with high credit ratings, were valued based on quoted market prices or model driven valuations using significant inputs derived from or corroborated by observable market data.

In accordance with the fair value accounting requirements, companies may choose to measure eligible financial instruments and certain other items at fair value. The Company has not elected the fair value option for any eligible financial instruments.

Accrued Warranty and Indemnification

The Company offers a basic limited parts and labor warranty on its hardware products. The basic warranty period for hardware products is typically one year from the date of purchase by the end-user. The Company also offers a 90-day basic warranty for its service parts used to repair the Company's hardware products. The Company provides currently for the estimated cost that may be incurred under its basic limited product warranties at the time related revenue is recognized. Factors considered in determining appropriate accruals for

product warranty obligations include the size of the installed base of products subject to warranty protection, historical and projected warranty claim rates, historical and projected cost-per-claim and knowledge of specific product failures that are outside of the Company's typical experience. The Company assesses the adequacy of its pre-existing warranty liabilities and adjusts the amounts as necessary based on actual experience and changes in future estimates. The following table shows changes in the Company's accrued warranties and related costs for 2014 and 2013 (in millions):

	2014	2013
Beginning accrued warranty and related costs	$ 2,967	$ 1,638
Cost of warranty claims	(3,760)	(3,703)
Accruals for product warranty	4,952	5,032
Ending accrued warranty and related costs	$ 4,159	$ 2,967

Long-Term Debt

In the third quarter of 2014 and 2013, the Company issued $12.0 billion and $17.0 billion of long-term debt, respectively. The debt issuances included floating- and fixed-rate notes with varying maturities for an aggregate principal amount of $29.0 billion (collectively the "Notes"). The Notes are senior unsecured obligations, and interest is payable in arrears, quarterly for the floating-rate notes and semi-annually for the fixed-rate notes. The Company recognized $381 million and $136 million of interest expense on its long-term debt for the years ended September 27, 2014 and September 28, 2013, respectively. The Company did not have any long-term debt in 2012. As of September 27, 2014 and September 28, 2013, the fair value of the Company's Notes, based on Level 2 inputs, was $28.5 billion and $15.9 billion, respectively.

Segment Information and Geographic Data

The following table shows information by operating segment for 2014, 2013 and 2012 (in millions):

	2014	2013	2012
Americas:			
Net sales	$65,232	$62,739	$57,512
Operating income	$24,316	$22,817	$23,414
Europe:			
Net sales	$40,929	$37,883	$36,323
Operating income	$14,771	$13,025	$14,869
Greater China:			
Net sales	$29,846	$25,417	$22,533
Operating income	$11,016	$ 8,541	$ 9,843
Japan:			
Net sales	$14,982	$13,462	$10,571
Operating income	$ 7,183	$ 6,819	$ 5,861
Rest of Asia Pacific:			
Net sales	$10,344	$11,181	$10,741
Operating income	$ 3,636	$ 3,753	$ 4,253
Retail:			
Net sales	$21,462	$20,228	$18,828
Operating income	$ 4,575	$ 4,025	$ 4,613

Google Inc.
CONSOLIDATED BALANCE SHEETS
(In millions, except share and par value amounts which are reflected in thousands, and par value per share amounts)

As of December 31	2013	2014
Assets		
Current assets:		
Cash and cash equivalents	$ 18,898	$ 18,347
Marketable securities	39,819	46,048
Total cash, cash equivalents, and marketable securities (including securities loaned of $5,059 and $4,058)	58,717	64,395
Accounts receivable, net of allowance of $631 and $225	8,882	9,383
Receivable under reverse repurchase agreements	100	875
Deferred income taxes, net	1,526	1,322
Income taxes receivable, net	408	1,298
Prepaid revenue share, expenses and other assets	3,253	3,412
Total current assets	72,886	80,685
Prepaid revenue share, expenses and other assets, non-current	1,976	3,280
Non-marketable equity investments	1,976	3,079
Property and equipment, net	16,524	23,883
Intangible assets, net	6,066	4,607
Goodwill	11,492	15,599
Total assets	$ 110,920	$ 131,133
Liabilities and Stockholders' Equity		
Current liabilities:		
Accounts payable	$ 2,453	$ 1,715
Short-term debt	3,009	2,009
Accrued compensation and benefits	2,502	3,069
Accrued expenses and other current liabilities	3,755	4,434
Accrued revenue share	1,729	1,952
Securities lending payable	1,374	2,778
Deferred revenue	1,062	752
Income taxes payable, net	24	96
Total current liabilities	15,908	16,805
Long-term debt	2,236	3,228
Deferred revenue, non-current	139	104
Income taxes payable, non-current	2,638	3,407
Deferred income taxes, net, non-current	1,947	1,971
Other long-term liabilities	743	1,118
Stockholders' equity:		
Convertible preferred stock, $0.001 par value per share, 100,000 shares authorized; no shares issued and outstanding	0	0
Class A and Class B common stock, and Class C capital stock and additional paid-in capital, $0.001 par value per share: 15,000,000 shares authorized (Class A 9,000,000, Class B 3,000,000, Class C 3,000,000); 671,664 (Class A 279,325, Class B 56,507, Class C 335,832) and par value of $672 (Class A $279, Class B $57, Class C $336) and 680,172 (Class A 286,560, Class B 53,213, Class C 340,399) and par value of $680 (Class A $287, Class B $53, Class C $340) shares issued and outstanding	25,922	28,767
Accumulated other comprehensive income	125	27
Retained earnings	61,262	75,706
Total stockholders' equity	87,309	104,500
Total liabilities and stockholders' equity	$ 110,920	$ 131,133

Google Inc.
CONSOLIDATED STATEMENTS OF INCOME
(In millions, except share amounts which are reflected in thousands and per share amounts)

Year Ended December 31	2012	2013	2014
Revenues	$ 46,039	$ 55,519	$ 66,001
Costs and expenses:			
Cost of revenues [1]	17,176	21,993	25,691
Research and development [1]	6,083	7,137	9,832
Sales and marketing [1]	5,465	6,554	8,131
General and administrative [1]	3,481	4,432	5,851
Total costs and expenses	32,205	40,116	49,505
Income from operations	13,834	15,403	16,496
Interest and other income, net	635	496	763
Income from continuing operations before income taxes	14,469	15,899	17,259
Provision for income taxes	2,916	2,552	3,331
Net income from continuing operations	$ 11,553	$ 13,347	$ 13,928
Net income (loss) from discontinued operations	(816)	(427)	516
Net income	$ 10,737	$ 12,920	$ 14,444
Net income (loss) per share - basic:			
Continuing operations	$ 17.66	$ 20.05	$ 20.61
Discontinued operations	(1.25)	(0.64)	0.76
Net income (loss) per share - basic	$ 16.41	$ 19.41	$ 21.37
Net income (loss) per share - diluted:			
Continuing operations	$ 17.39	$ 19.70	$ 20.27
Discontinued operations	(1.23)	(0.63)	0.75
Net income (loss) per share - diluted	$ 16.16	$ 19.07	$ 21.02
Shares used in per share calculation - basic	654,426	665,692	675,935
Shares used in per share calculation - diluted	664,610	677,618	687,070
(1) Includes stock-based compensation expense as follows:			
Cost of revenues	$ 359	$ 469	$ 535
Research and development	1,274	1,641	2,200
Sales and marketing	449	552	715
General and administrative	391	465	725
Discontinued operations	219	216	104
Total stock-based compensation expense	$ 2,692	$ 3,343	$ 4,279

GOOGLE

Google Inc.
CONSOLIDATED STATEMENTS OF COMPREHENSIVE INCOME
(In millions)

Year Ended December 31	2012	2013	2014
Net income	$ 10,737	$ 12,920	$ 14,444
Other comprehensive income (loss):			
Change in foreign currency translation adjustment	75	89	(996)
Available-for-sale investments:			
Change in net unrealized gains (losses)	493	(392)	505
Less: reclassification adjustment for net gains included in net income	(216)	(162)	(134)
Net change (net of tax effect of $68, $212, $60)	277	(554)	371
Cash flow hedges:			
Change in unrealized gains	47	112	651
Less: reclassification adjustment for gains included in net income	(137)	(60)	(124)
Net change (net of tax effect of $53, $30, $196)	(90)	52	527
Other comprehensive income (loss)	262	(413)	(98)
Comprehensive income	$ 10,999	$ 12,507	$ 14,346

Google Inc.
CONSOLIDATED STATEMENTS OF STOCKHOLDERS' EQUITY
(In millions, except for share amounts which are reflected in thousands)

	Class A and Class B Common Stock, Class C Capital Stock and Additional Paid-In Capital		Accumulated Other Comprehensive Income	Retained Earnings	Total Stockholders' Equity
	Shares	Amount			
Balance at December 31, 2011	649,790	$ 20,264	$ 276	$ 37,605	$ 58,145
Common stock issued	10,168	736	0	0	736
Stock-based compensation expense		2,692	0	0	2,692
Stock-based compensation tax benefits		166	0	0	166
Tax withholding related to vesting of restricted stock units		(1,023)	0	0	(1,023)
Net income		0	0	10,737	10,737
Other comprehensive income		0	262	0	262
Balance at December 31, 2012	659,958	22,835	538	48,342	71,715
Common stock issued	11,706	1,174	0	0	1,174
Stock-based compensation expense		3,343	0	0	3,343
Stock-based compensation tax benefits		449	0	0	449
Tax withholding related to vesting of restricted stock units		(1,879)	0	0	(1,879)
Net income		0	0	12,920	12,920
Other comprehensive income		0	(413)	0	(413)
Balance at December 31, 2013	671,664	25,922	125	61,262	87,309
Common and capital stock issued	8,508	465	0	0	465
Stock-based compensation expense		4,279	0	0	4,279
Stock-based compensation tax benefits		625	0	0	625
Tax withholding related to vesting of restricted stock units		(2,524)	0	0	(2,524)
Net income		0	0	14,444	14,444
Other comprehensive income		0	(98)	0	(98)
Balance at December 31, 2014	680,172	$ 28,767	$ 27	$ 75,706	$ 104,500

GOOGLE

Google Inc.
CONSOLIDATED STATEMENTS OF CASH FLOWS
(In millions)

Year Ended December 31	2012	2013	2014
Operating activities			
Net income	$ 10,737	$ 12,920	$ 14,444
Adjustments:			
Depreciation expense and loss on disposal of property and equipment	1,988	2,781	3,523
Amortization and impairment of intangible and other assets	974	1,158	1,456
Stock-based compensation expense	2,692	3,343	4,279
Excess tax benefits from stock-based award activities	(188)	(481)	(648)
Deferred income taxes	(266)	(437)	(104)
Gain on divestiture of businesses	(188)	(700)	(740)
Gain on equity interest	0	0	(126)
Gain on sale of non-marketable equity investments	0	0	(159)
Other	(28)	106	87
Changes in assets and liabilities, net of effects of acquisitions:			
Accounts receivable	(787)	(1,307)	(1,641)
Income taxes, net	1,492	401	283
Prepaid revenue share, expenses and other assets	(532)	(930)	459
Accounts payable	(499)	605	436
Accrued expenses and other liabilities	762	713	757
Accrued revenue share	299	254	245
Deferred revenue	163	233	(175)
Net cash provided by operating activities	16,619	18,659	22,376
Investing activities			
Purchases of property and equipment	(3,273)	(7,358)	(10,959)
Purchases of marketable securities	(33,410)	(45,444)	(56,310)
Maturities and sales of marketable securities	35,180	38,314	51,315
Investments in non-marketable equity investments	(696)	(569)	(1,227)
Cash collateral related to securities lending	(334)	(299)	1,403
Investments in reverse repurchase agreements	45	600	(775)
Proceeds from divestiture of businesses	0	2,525	386
Acquisitions, net of cash acquired, and purchases of intangibles and other assets	(10,568)	(1,448)	(4,888)
Net cash used in investing activities	(13,056)	(13,679)	(21,055)
Financing activities			
Net payments related to stock-based award activities	(287)	(781)	(2,069)
Excess tax benefits from stock-based award activities	188	481	648
Proceeds from issuance of debt, net of costs	16,109	10,768	11,625
Repayments of debt	(14,781)	(11,325)	(11,643)
Net cash provided by (used in) financing activities	1,229	(857)	(1,439)
Effect of exchange rate changes on cash and cash equivalents	3	(3)	(433)
Net increase (decrease) in cash and cash equivalents	4,795	4,120	(551)
Cash and cash equivalents at beginning of period	9,983	14,778	18,898
Cash and cash equivalents at end of period	$ 14,778	$ 18,898	$ 18,347
Supplemental disclosures of cash flow information			
Cash paid for taxes	$ 2,034	$ 1,932	$ 2,819
Cash paid for interest	$ 74	$ 72	$ 86
Non-cash investing and financing activities:			
Receipt of notes receivable in connection with the divestiture of Motorola Mobile	$ 0	$ 0	$ 1,314
Receipt of Lenovo shares in connection with the divestiture of Motorola Mobile	$ 0	$ 0	$ 750
Receipt of Arris shares in connection with the divestiture of Motorola Home	$ 0	$ 175	$ 0
Fair value of stock-based awards assumed in connection with the acquisition of Motorola	$ 41	$ 0	$ 0
Leases recorded on the balance sheet during the period	$ 0	$ 258	$ 250

GOOGLE

Samsung Electronics Co., Ltd. and its subsidiaries
CONSOLIDATED STATEMENTS OF FINANCIAL POSITION

(In millions of Korean won)	December 31, 2014	December 31, 2013
	KRW	KRW
Assets		
Current assets		
Cash and cash equivalents	16,840,766	16,284,780
Short-term financial instruments	41,689,776	36,722,702
Available-for-sale financial assets	3,286,798	1,488,527
Trade receivables	24,694,610	24,988,532
Non-trade receivables	3,539,875	2,887,402
Advances	1,989,470	1,928,188
Prepaid expenses	3,346,593	2,472,950
Inventories	17,317,504	19,134,868
Other current assets	1,795,143	2,135,589
Assets held for sale	645,491	2,716,733
Total current assets	115,146,026	110,760,271
Non-current assets		
Available-for-sale financial assets	12,667,509	6,238,380
Associates and joint ventures	5,232,461	6,422,292
Property, plant and equipment	80,872,950	75,496,388
Intangible assets	4,785,473	3,980,600
Long-term prepaid expenses	4,857,126	3,465,783
Deferred income tax assets	4,526,595	4,621,780
Other non-current assets	2,334,818	3,089,524
Total assets	230,422,958	214,075,018
Liabilities and Equity		
Current liabilities		
Trade and other payables	7,914,704	8,437,139
Short-term borrowings	8,029,299	6,438,517
Other payables	10,318,407	9,196,566
Advances received	1,427,230	1,706,313
Withholdings	1,161,635	1,176,046
Accrued expenses	12,876,777	11,344,530
Income tax payable	2,161,109	3,386,018
Current portion of long-term borrowings and debentures	1,778,667	2,425,831
Provisions	5,991,510	6,736,476
Other current liabilities	326,259	467,973
Liabilities held for sale	28,316	–
Total current liabilities	52,013,913	51,315,409
Non-current liabilities		
Debentures	1,355,882	1,311,068
Long-term borrowings	101,671	985,117
Long-term other payables	2,562,271	1,053,756
Net defined benefit liabilities	201,342	1,854,902
Deferred income tax liabilities	4,097,811	6,012,371
Provisions	499,290	460,924
Other non-current liabilities	1,502,590	1,065,461
Total liabilities	62,334,770	64,059,008
Equity attributable to owners of the parent		
Preferred stock	119,467	119,467
Common stock	778,047	778,047
Share premium	4,403,893	4,403,893
Retained earnings	169,529,604	148,600,282
Other components of equity	(12,729,387)	(9,459,073)
Accumulated other comprehensive income attributable to assets held for sale	80,101	–
	162,181,725	144,442,616
Non-controlling interests	5,906,463	5,573,394
Total equity	168,088,188	150,016,010
Total liabilities and equity	230,422,958	214,075,018

Samsung Electronics Co., Ltd. and its subsidiaries
CONSOLIDATED STATEMENTS OF INCOME

(In millions of Korean won)

For the year ended December 31	2014	2013
	KRW	KRW
Revenue	206,205,987	228,692,667
Cost of sales	128,278,800	137,696,309
Gross profit	77,927,187	90,996,358
Selling and administrative expenses	52,902,116	54,211,345
Operating profit	**25,025,071**	**36,785,013**
Other non-operating income	3,801,357	2,429,551
Other non-operating expense	2,259,737	1,614,048
Share of profit of associates and joint ventures	342,516	504,063
Finance income	8,259,829	8,014,672
Finance costs	7,294,002	7,754,972
Profit before income tax	27,875,034	38,364,279
Income tax expense	4,480,676	7,889,515
Profit for the year	23,394,358	30,474,764
Profit attributable to owners of the parent	23,082,499	29,821,215
Profit attributable to non-controlling interests	311,859	653,549
Earnings per share for profit attributable to owners of the parent (in Korean Won)		
–Basic	153,105	197,841
–Diluted	153,096	197,800

Samsung Electronics Co., Ltd. and its subsidiaries
CONSOLIDATED STATEMENTS OF COMPREHENSIVE INCOME

(In millions of Korean won)

For the year ended December 31	2014	2013
	KRW	KRW
Profit for the year	23,394,358	30,474,764
Other comprehensive loss		
Items not to be reclassified subsequently to profit or loss:		
Remeasurement of net defined benefit liabilities, net of tax	(710,318)	(213,113)
Items to be reclassified subsequently to profit or loss:		
Changes in value of available-for-sale financial assets, net of tax	(232,105)	186,480
Share of other comprehensive income (loss) of associates and joint ventures, net of tax	(128,932)	20,756
Foreign currency translation, net of tax	(922,059)	(1,000,961)
Other comprehensive loss for the year, net of tax	(1,993,414)	(1,006,838)
Total comprehensive income for the year	21,400,944	29,467,926
Comprehensive income attributable to:		
Owners of the parent	20,990,732	28,837,590
Non-controlling interests	410,212	630,336

SAMSUNG

Samsung Electronics Co., Ltd. and its subsidiaries
CONSOLIDATED STATEMENTS OF CHANGES IN EQUITY

(In millions of Korean won)	Preferred stock	Common stock	Share premium	Retained earnings	Other components of equity	Accumulated other comprehensive income attributable to assets held for sale	Equity attributable to owners of the parent	Noncontrolling interests	Total
Balance as of January 1, 2013	119,467	778,047	4,403,893	119,985,689	(8,193,044)	–	117,094,052	4,386,154	121,480,206
Profit for the year	–	–	–	29,821,215	–	–	29,821,215	653,549	30,474,764
Changes in value of available-for-sale financial assets, net of tax	–	–	–	–	187,477	–	187,477	(997)	186,480
Share of other comprehensive income(loss) of associates and joint ventures, net of tax	–	–	–	–	20,949	–	20,949	(193)	20,756
Foreign currency translation, net of tax	–	–	–	–	(986,691)	–	(986,691)	(14,270)	(1,000,961)
Remeasurement of net defined benefit liabilities, net of tax	–	–	–	–	(205,360)	–	(205,360)	(7,753)	(213,113)
Total comprehensive income (loss)	–	–	–	29,821,215	(983,625)	–	28,837,590	630,336	29,467,926
Dividends	–	–	–	(1,206,622)	–	–	(1,206,622)	(42,155)	(1,248,777)
Capital transaction under common control	–	–	–	–	(312,959)	–	(312,959)	600,042	287,083
Changes in consolidated entities	–	–	–	–	–	–	–	(918)	(918)
Disposal of treasury stock	–	–	–	–	41,817	–	41,817	–	41,817
Stock option activities	–	–	–	–	(11,999)	–	(11,999)	–	(11,999)
Others	–	–	–	–	737	–	737	(65)	672
Total transactions with owners	–	–	–	(1,206,622)	(282,404)	–	(1,489,026)	556,904	(932,122)
Balance as of December 31, 2013	119,467	778,047	4,403,893	148,600,282	(9,459,073)	–	144,442,616	5,573,394	150,016,010
Profit for the year	–	–	–	23,082,499	–	–	23,082,499	311,859	23,394,358
Changes in value of available-for-sale financial assets, net of tax	–	–	–	–	(314,069)	–	(314,069)	81,964	(232,105)
Share of other comprehensive income(loss) of associates and joint ventures, net of tax	–	–	–	–	(128,495)	–	(128,495)	(437)	(128,932)
Foreign currency translation, net of tax	–	–	–	–	(954,999)	–	(954,999)	32,940	(922,059)
Remeasurement of net defined benefit liabilities, net of tax	–	–	–	–	(694,204)	–	(694,204)	(16,114)	(710,318)
Classified as held for sale	–	–	–	–	(80,101)	80,101	–	–	–
Total comprehensive income (loss)	–	–	–	23,082,499	(2,171,868)	80,101	20,990,732	410,212	21,400,944
Dividends	–	–	–	(2,157,011)	–	–	(2,157,011)	(74,216)	(2,231,227)
Capital transaction under common control	–	–	–	–	(158)	–	(158)	244	86
Changes in consolidated entities	–	–	–	–	–	–	–	569	569
Acquisition of treasury stock	–	–	–	–	(1,125,322)	–	(1,125,322)	–	(1,125,322)
Disposal of treasury stock	–	–	–	–	32,764	–	32,764	–	32,764
Stock option activities	–	–	–	–	(9,436)	–	(9,436)	–	(9,436)
Others	–	–	–	3,834	3,706	–	7,540	(3,740)	3,800
Total transactions with owners	–	–	—	(2,153,177)	(1,098,446)	–	(3,251,623)	(77,143)	(3,328,766)
Balance as of December 31, 2014	119,467	778,047	4,403,893	169,529,604	(12,729,387)	80,101	162,181,725	5,906,463	168,088,188

Samsung Electronics Co., Ltd. and its subsidiaries
CONSOLIDATED STATEMENTS OF CASH FLOWS

(In millions of Korean won)

For the year ended December 31	2014	2013
	KRW	KRW
Cash flows from operating activities		
Profit for the year	23,394,358	30,474,764
Adjustments	22,323,765	23,804,832
Changes in operating assets and liabilities	(3,837,136)	(1,313,245)
Cash flows from operating activities	41,880,987	52,966,351
Interest received	1,555,373	1,034,074
Interest paid	(463,740)	(434,857)
Dividend received	1,495,658	592,217
Income tax paid	(7,492,889)	(7,450,345)
Net cash generated from operating activities	36,975,389	46,707,440
Cash flows from investing activities		
Net increase in short-term financial instruments	(1,110,842)	(19,391,643)
Net decrease (increase) in short-term available-for-sale financial assets	(713,452)	33,663
Proceeds from disposal of long-term available-for-sale financial assets	202,904	1,691,463
Acquisition of long-term available-for-sale financial assets	(6,212,102)	(1,531,356)
Proceeds from disposal of associates and joint ventures	2,014,430	240
Acquisition of associates and joint ventures	(719,800)	(181,307)
Disposal of property, plant and equipment	385,610	377,445
Purchases of property, plant and equipment	(22,042,943)	(23,157,587)
Disposal of intangible assets	31,731	4,562
Purchases of intangible assets	(1,324,307)	(934,743)
Cash outflows from business combination	(176,625)	(167,155)
Others	(3,141,012)	(1,490,601)
Net cash used in investing activities	(32,806,408)	(44,747,019)
Cash flows from financing activities		
Net increase (decrease) in short-term borrowings	1,833,419	(1,861,536)
Acquisition of treasury stock	(1,125,322)	–
Disposal of treasury stock	27,582	34,390
Proceeds from long-term borrowings and debentures	1,740,573	26,672
Repayment of long-term borrowings and debentures	(3,299,595)	(1,368,436)
Payment of dividends	(2,233,905)	(1,249,672)
Net increase in non-controlling interests	139	281,551
Net cash used in financing activities	(3,057,109)	(4,137,031)
Effect of exchange rate changes on cash and cash equivalents	(555,886)	(330,070)
Net increase (decrease) in cash and cash equivalents	555,986	(2,506,680)
Cash and cash equivalents		
Beginning of the year	16,284,780	18,791,460
End of the year	16,840,766	16,284,780

Applying Present and Future Values

Appendix Preview

PRESENT AND FUTURE VALUE CONCEPTS	VALUE OF A SINGLE AMOUNT	VALUE OF AN ANNUITY
C1 Time is money and the concept of interest	**P1** Present value of a single amount **P2** Future value of a single amount	**P3** Present value of an annuity **P4** Future value of an annuity

Learning Objectives

CONCEPTUAL

C1 Describe the earning of interest and the concepts of present and future values.

PROCEDURAL

P1 Apply present value concepts to a single amount by using interest tables.

P2 Apply future value concepts to a single amount by using interest tables.

P3 Apply present value concepts to an annuity by using interest tables.

P4 Apply future value concepts to an annuity by using interest tables.

PRESENT AND FUTURE VALUE CONCEPTS

The old saying "Time is money" reflects the notion that as time passes, the values of our assets and liabilities change. This change is due to *interest*, which is a borrower's payment to the owner of an asset for its use. The most common example of interest is a savings account asset. As we keep a balance of cash in the account, it earns interest that the financial institution pays us. An example of a liability is a car loan. As we carry the balance of the loan, we accumulate interest costs on it. We must ultimately repay this loan with interest.

Present and future value computations enable us to measure or estimate the interest component of holding assets or liabilities over time. The present value computation is important when we want to know the value of future-day assets *today*. The future value computation is important when we want to know the value of present-day assets *at a future date*. The first section focuses on the present value of a single amount. The second section focuses on the future value of a single amount. Then both the present and future values of a series of amounts (called an *annuity*) are defined and explained.

C1

Describe the earning of interest and the concepts of present and future values.

■ **Decision Insight**

What's Five Million Worth?   A maintenance worker duped out of a $5 million scratch-off ticket got his winnings seven years later. Robert Miles bought the ticket in 2006 at a convenience store where the owner and his two sons convinced Miles the ticket was worth $5,000 and paid him $4,000 for it. The brothers waited until 2012 to claim the jackpot, prompting an investigation, which uncovered the fraud. The $5 million will be paid to Miles as a $250,000 annuity over 20 years or as a lump-sum payment of $3,210,000, which equals about $2,124,378 after taxes. ■

PRESENT VALUE OF A SINGLE AMOUNT

We graphically express the present value, called *p*, of a single future amount, called *f*, that is received or paid at a future date in Exhibit B.1.

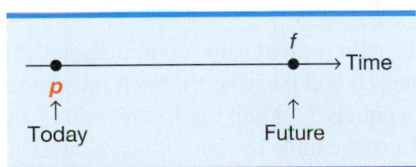

EXHIBIT B.1

Present Value of a Single Amount Diagram

P1

Apply present value concepts to a single amount by using interest tables.

The formula to compute the present value of a single amount is shown in Exhibit B.2, where *p* = present value (PV); *f* = future value (FV); *i* = rate of interest per period; and *n* = number of periods. (Interest is also called the *discount,* and an interest rate is also called the *discount rate.*)

$$p = \frac{f}{(1 + i)^n}$$

EXHIBIT B.2

Present Value of a Single Amount Formula

To illustrate present value concepts, assume that we need $220 one period from today. We want to know how much we must invest now, for one period, at an interest rate of 10% to provide for this $220. For this illustration, the *p*, or present value, is the unknown amount—the specifics are shown graphically as follows:

Conceptually, we know *p* must be less than $220. This is obvious from the answer to this question: Would we rather have $220 today or $220 at some future date? If we had $220 today, we could invest it and see it grow to something more than $220 in the future. Therefore, we would prefer the $220 today. This means that if we were promised $220 in the future, we would take less than $220 today. But how much less? To answer that question, we compute an estimate of the present value of the $220 to be received one period from now using the formula in Exhibit B.2 as follows:

$$p = \frac{f}{(1 + i)^n} = \frac{\$220}{(1 + 0.10)^1} = \$200$$

Point: The FV factor when $n = 2$ and $i = 10\%$, is 1.2100. Its reciprocal, 0.8264, is the PV factor when $n = 2$ and $i = 10\%$.

We interpret this result to say that given an interest rate of 10%, we are indifferent between $200 today or $220 at the end of one period.

We can also use this formula to compute the present value for *any number of periods*. To illustrate, consider a payment of $242 at the end of two periods at 10% interest. The present value of this $242 to be received two periods from now is computed as follows:

$$p = \frac{f}{(1 + i)^n} = \frac{\$242}{(1 + 0.10)^2} = \$200$$

Together, these results tell us we are indifferent between $200 today, or $220 one period from today, or $242 two periods from today given a 10% interest rate per period.

The number of periods (n) in the present value formula does not have to be expressed in years. Any period of time such as a day, a month, a quarter, or a year can be used. Whatever period is used, the interest rate (i) must be compounded for the same period. This means that if a situation expresses n in months and i equals 12% per year, then i is transformed into interest earned per month (or 1%). In this case, interest is said to be *compounded monthly.* For example, the present value of $1 when n is 12 months and i is 12% compounded monthly follows:

$$p = \frac{1}{(1 + 0.01)^{12}} = \$0.8874$$

A present value table helps us with present value computations. It gives us present values (factors) for a variety of both interest rates (i) and periods (n). Each present value in a present value table assumes that the future value (f) equals 1. When the future value (f) is different from 1, we simply multiply the present value (p) from the table by that future value to give us the estimate. The formula used to construct a table of present values for a single future amount of 1 is shown in Exhibit B.3.

EXHIBIT B.3

Present Value of 1 Formula

$$p = \frac{1}{(1 + i)^n}$$

This formula is identical to that in Exhibit B.2 except that f equals 1. Table B.1 at the end of this appendix is such a present value table. It is often called a **present value of 1 table**. A present value table involves three factors: p, i, and n. Knowing two of these three factors allows us to compute the third. (A fourth is f, but as already explained, we need only multiply the 1 used in the formula by f.) To illustrate the use of a present value table, consider three cases.

Case 1   Solve for p when knowing i and n. To show how we use a present value table, let's look again at how we estimate the present value of $220 (the f value) at the end of one period ($n = 1$) where the interest rate (i) is 10%. To solve this case, we go to the present value table (Table B.1) and look in the row for 1 period and in the column for 10% interest. Here we find a present value (p) of 0.9091 based on a future value of 1. This means, for instance, that $1 to be received one period from today at 10% interest is worth $0.9091 today. Since the future value in this case is not $1 but $220, we multiply the 0.9091 by $220 to get an answer of $200.

Case 2   Solve for n when knowing p and i. To illustrate, assume a $100,000 future value ($f$) that is worth $13,000 today ($p$) using an interest rate of 12% (i) but where n is unknown. In particular, we want to know how many periods (n) there are between the present value and the future value. To put this in context, it would fit a situation in which we want to retire with $100,000 but currently have only $13,000 that is earning a 12% return and we will be unable to save any additional money. How long will it be before we can retire? To answer this, we go to Table B.1 and look in the 12% interest column. Here we find a column of present values (p) based on a future value of 1. To use the present value table for this solution, we must divide $13,000 ($p$) by $100,000 ($f$), which equals 0.1300. This is necessary because *a present value table defines* f *equal to 1, and* p *as a fraction of 1.* We look for a value nearest to 0.1300 (p), which we find in the row for 18 periods (n). This means that the present value of $100,000 at the end of 18 periods at 12% interest is $13,000; alternatively stated, we must work 18 more years.

Case 3   Solve for i when knowing p and n. In this case, we have, say, a $120,000 future value ($f$) worth $60,000 today ($p$) when there are nine periods (n) between the present and future values, but the interest rate is unknown. As an example, suppose we want to retire with $120,000 in nine years, but we have only $60,000 and we will be unable to save any additional money. What interest rate must we earn to retire with $120,000 in nine years? To answer this, we go to the present value table (Table B.1) and look in the row for nine periods. To use the present value table, we must divide $60,000 ($p$) by $120,000 ($f$), which equals 0.5000. Recall that this step is necessary because a present value table defines f equal to 1 and p as a fraction of 1. We look for a value in the row for nine periods that is nearest to 0.5000 (p), which we find in the column for 8% interest (i). This means that the present value of $120,000 at the end of nine periods at 8% interest is $60,000 or, in our example, we must earn 8% annual interest to retire in nine years.

A company is considering an investment expected to yield $70,000 after six years. If this company demands an 8% return, how much is it willing to pay for this investment today?

NEED-TO-KNOW **B-1**

Present Value of Single Amount

Solution

P1

$70,000 × 0.6302 = $44,114 (using PV factor from Table B.1, $i = 8\%$, $n = 6$)

FUTURE VALUE OF A SINGLE AMOUNT

We must modify the formula for the present value of a single amount to obtain the formula for the future value of a single amount. In particular, we multiply both sides of the equation in Exhibit B.2 by $(1 + i)^n$ to get the result shown in Exhibit B.4.

P2

Apply future value concepts to a single amount by using interest tables.

$$f = p \times (1 + i)^n$$

EXHIBIT B.4

Future Value of a Single Amount Formula

The future value (f) is defined in terms of p, i, and n. We can use this formula to determine that $200 ($p$) invested for 1 ($n$) period at an interest rate of 10% (i) yields a future value of $220 as follows:

$$
\begin{aligned}
f &= p \times (1 + i)^n \\
&= \$200 \times (1 + 0.10)^1 \\
&= \$220
\end{aligned}
$$

This formula can also be used to compute the future value of an amount for *any number of periods* into the future. To illustrate, assume that $200 is invested for three periods at 10%. The future value of this $200 is $266.20, computed as follows:

$$
\begin{aligned}
f &= p \times (1 + i)^n \\
&= \$200 \times (1 + 0.10)^3 \\
&= \$200 \times 1.3310 \\
&= \$266.20
\end{aligned}
$$

Point: The FV factor in Table B.2 when $n = 3$ and $i = 10\%$ is 1.3310.

A future value table makes it easier for us to compute future values (f) for many different combinations of interest rates (i) and time periods (n). Each future value in a future value table assumes the present value (p) is 1. As with a present value table, if the future amount is something other than 1, we simply multiply our answer by that amount. The formula used to construct a table of future values (factors) for a single amount of 1 is in Exhibit B.5.

EXHIBIT B.5

Future Value of 1 Formula

$$f = (1 + i)^n$$

Point:
1/PV factor = FV factor.
1/FV factor = PV factor.

Table B.2 at the end of this appendix shows a table of future values for a current amount of 1. This type of table is called a **future value of 1 table**.

There are some important relations between Tables B.1 and B.2. In Table B.2, for the row where $n = 0$, the future value is 1 for each interest rate. This is so because no interest is earned when time does not pass. We also see that Tables B.1 and B.2 report the same information but in a different manner. In particular, one table is simply the *reciprocal* of the other. To illustrate this inverse relation, let's say we invest $100 for a period of five years at 12% per year. How much do we expect to have after five years? We can answer this question using Table B.2 by finding the future value (f) of 1, for five periods from now, compounded at 12%. From that table we find $f = 1.7623$. If we start with $100, the amount it accumulates to after five years is $176.23 ($100 × 1.7623). We can alternatively use Table B.1. Here we find that the present value (p) of 1, discounted five periods at 12%, is 0.5674. Recall the inverse relation between present value and future value. This means that $p = 1/f$ (or equivalently, $f = 1/p$). We can compute the future value of $100 invested for five periods at 12% as follows: $f = $100 × (1/0.5674) = $176.24 (which equals the $176.23 just computed, except for a 1 cent rounding difference).

A future value table involves three factors: f, i, and n. Knowing two of these three factors allows us to compute the third. To illustrate, consider these three possible cases.

Case 1   Solve for f when knowing i and n. Our preceding example fits this case. We found that $100 invested for five periods at 12% interest accumulates to $176.24.

Case 2   Solve for n when knowing f and i. In this case, we have, say, $2,000 ($p$) and we want to know how many periods (n) it will take to accumulate to $3,000 ($f$) at 7% interest ($i$). To answer this, we go to the future value table (Table B.2) and look in the 7% interest column. Here we find a column of future values (f) based on a present value of 1. To use a future value table, we must divide $3,000 ($f$) by $2,000 ($p$), which equals 1.500. This is necessary because *a future value table defines* p *equal to 1, and* f *as a multiple of 1.* We look for a value nearest to 1.50 (f), which we find in the row for six periods (n). This means that $2,000 invested for six periods at 7% interest accumulates to $3,000.

Case 3   Solve for i when knowing f and n. In this case, we have, say, $2,001 ($p$), and in nine years ($n$) we want to have $4,000 ($f$). What rate of interest must we earn to accomplish this? To answer that, we go to Table B.2 and search in the row for nine periods. To use a future value table, we must divide $4,000 ($f$) by $2,001 ($p$), which equals 1.9990. Recall that this is necessary because a future value table defines p equal to 1 and f as a multiple of 1. We look for a value nearest to 1.9990 (f), which we find in the column for 8% interest (i). This means that $2,001 invested for nine periods at 8% interest accumulates to $4,000.

NEED-TO-KNOW   B-2

Future Value of Single Amount

P2

Assume that you win a $150,000 cash sweepstakes today. You decide to deposit this cash in an account earning 8% annual interest, and you plan to quit your job when the account equals $555,000. How many years will it be before you can quit working?

Solution

$555,000/$150,000 = 3.7000 (the future value factor)

Table B.2 shows this value is not achieved until reaching <u>17 years</u> at 8% interest.

PRESENT VALUE OF AN ANNUITY

An *annuity* is a series of equal payments occurring at equal intervals. One example is a series of three annual payments of $100 each. An *ordinary annuity* is defined as equal end-of-period payments at equal intervals. An ordinary annuity of $100 for three periods and its present value (*p*) are illustrated in Exhibit B.6.

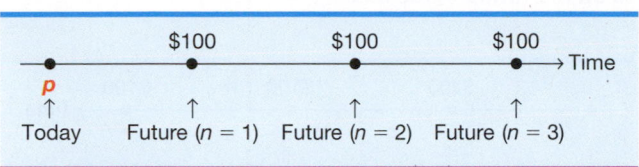

P3_____

Apply present value concepts to an annuity by using interest tables.

EXHIBIT B.6

Present Value of an Ordinary Annuity Diagram

One way to compute the present value of an ordinary annuity is to find the present value of each payment using our present value formula from Exhibit B.3. We then add each of the three present values. To illustrate, let's look at three $100 payments at the end of each of the next three periods with an interest rate of 15%. Our present value computations are

$$p = \frac{\$100}{(1 + 0.15)^1} + \frac{\$100}{(1 + 0.15)^2} + \frac{\$100}{(1 + 0.15)^3} = \$228.32$$

This computation is identical to computing the present value of each payment (from Table B.1) and taking their sum or, alternatively, adding the values from Table B.1 for each of the three payments and multiplying their sum by the $100 annuity payment.

A more direct way is to use a present value of annuity table. Table B.3 at the end of this appendix is one such table. This table is called a **present value of an annuity of 1 table**. If we look at Table B.3 where $n = 3$ and $i = 15\%$, we see the present value is 2.2832. This means that the present value of an annuity of 1 for three periods, with a 15% interest rate, equals 2.2832.

A present value of an annuity formula is used to construct Table B.3. It can also be constructed by adding the amounts in a present value of 1 table. To illustrate, we use Tables B.1 and B.3 to confirm this relation for the prior example:

From Table B.1		From Table B.3	
$i = 15\%, n = 1$	0.8696		
$i = 15\%, n = 2$	0.7561		
$i = 15\%, n = 3$	0.6575		
Total	2.2832	$i = 15\%, n = 3$	2.2832

Point: Excel functions follow:

= −PV (rate, periods, payment)
= −PV (0.15, 3, 100)
= $228.32

We can also use business calculators or spreadsheet programs to find the present value of an annuity.

 Decision Insight ━━━━━━━━━━━━━━━━━━━━━━━━━━━━━━ ♛

Count Your Blessings "I don't have good luck—I'm blessed," proclaimed Andrew "Jack" Whittaker, a sewage treatment contractor, after winning the largest ever undivided jackpot in a U.S. lottery. Whittaker had to choose between $315 million in 30 annual installments or $170 million in one lump sum ($112 million after-tax). ∎

A company is considering an investment that would produce payments of $10,000 every six months for three years. The first payment would be received in six months. If this company requires an 8% annual return, what is the maximum amount it is willing to pay for this investment today?

NEED-TO-KNOW B-3

Present Value of an Annuity

P3

Solution

$10,000 × 5.2421 = $52,421 is the maximum (using PV of annuity factor from Table B.3, $i = 4\%, n = 6$)

FUTURE VALUE OF AN ANNUITY

P4
_____

Apply future value concepts to an annuity by using interest tables.

The future value of an _ordinary annuity_ is the accumulated value of each annuity payment with interest as of the date of the final payment. To illustrate, let's consider the earlier annuity of three annual payments of $100. Exhibit B.7 shows the point in time for the future value (f). The first payment is made two periods prior to the point when future value is determined, and the final payment occurs on the future value date.

EXHIBIT B.7

Future Value of an Ordinary Annuity Diagram

Point: An ordinary annuity is a series of equal cash flows, with the payment at the _end_ of each period.

One way to compute the future value of an annuity is to use the formula to find the future value of _each_ payment and add them. If we assume an interest rate of 15%, our calculation is

$$f = \$100 \times (1 + 0.15)^2 + \$100 \times (1 + 0.15)^1 + \$100 \times (1 + 0.15)^0 = \$347.25$$

This is identical to using Table B.2 and summing the future values of each payment, or adding the future values of the three payments of 1 and multiplying the sum by $100.

A more direct way is to use a table showing future values of annuities. Such a table is called a **future value of an annuity of 1 table**. Table B.4 at the end of this appendix is one such table. Note that in Table B.4 when $n = 1$, the future values equal 1 ($f = 1$) for all rates of interest. This is so because such an annuity consists of only one payment and the future value is determined on the date of that payment—no time passes between the payment and its future value. The future value of an annuity formula is used to construct Table B.4. We can also construct it by adding the amounts from a future value of 1 table. To illustrate, we use Tables B.2 and B.4 to confirm this relation for the prior example:

Point: Excel functions follow:

= −FV (rate, periods, payment)
= −FV (0.15, 3, 100)
= $347.25

From Table B.2		From Table B.4	
$i = 15\%, n = 0$	1.0000		
$i = 15\%, n = 1$	1.1500		
$i = 15\%, n = 2$	1.3225		
Total	3.4725	$i = 15\%, n = 3$	3.4725

Note that the future value in Table B.2 is 1.0000 when $n = 0$, but the future value in Table B.4 is 1.0000 when $n = 1$. Is this a contradiction? No. When $n = 0$ in Table B.2, the future value is determined on the date when a single payment occurs. This means that no interest is earned because no time has passed, and the future value equals the payment. Table B.4 describes annuities with equal payments occurring at the end of each period. When $n = 1$, the annuity has one payment, and its future value equals 1 on the date of its final and only payment. Again, no time passes between the payment and its future value date.

NEED-TO-KNOW   B-4

Future Value of an Annuity

P4

A company invests $45,000 per year for five years at 12% annual interest. Compute the value of this annuity investment at the end of five years.

Solution

$45,000 × 6.3528 = $285,876 (using the FV of annuity factor from Table B.4, $i = 12\%, n = 5$)

Summary

C1 **Describe the earning of interest and the concepts of present and future values.** Interest is payment by a borrower to the owner of an asset for its use. Present and future value computations are a way for us to estimate the interest component of holding assets or liabilities over a period of time.

P1 **Apply present value concepts to a single amount by using interest tables.** The present value of a single amount received at a future date is the amount that can be invested now at the specified interest rate to yield that future value.

P2 **Apply future value concepts to a single amount by using interest tables.** The future value of a single amount invested at a specified rate of interest is the amount that would accumulate by the future date.

P3 **Apply present value concepts to an annuity by using interest tables.** The present value of an annuity is the amount that can be invested now at the specified interest rate to yield that series of equal periodic payments.

P4 **Apply future value concepts to an annuity by using interest tables.** The future value of an annuity invested at a specific rate of interest is the amount that would accumulate by the date of the final payment.

connect

Assume that you must make two-year-ahead future value estimates using the *future value of 1 table* (Table B.2). Which interest rate column *and* number-of-periods row do you use when working with the following rates?

1. 8% annual rate, compounded quarterly

2. 12% annual rate, compounded annually

3. 6% annual rate, compounded semiannually

4. 12% annual rate, compounded monthly (the answer for number-of-periods in part 4 is not shown in Table B.2)

QUICK STUDY

QS B-1
Identifying interest rates in tables
C1

Ken Francis is offered the possibility of investing $2,745 today; in return, he would receive $10,000 after 15 years. What is the annual rate of interest for this investment? (Use Table B.1.)

QS B-2
Interest rate on an investment P1

Megan Brink is offered the possibility of investing $6,651 today at 6% interest per year in a desire to accumulate $10,000. How many years must Brink wait to accumulate $10,000? (Use Table B.1.)

QS B-3
Number of periods of an investment P1

Flaherty is considering an investment that, if paid for immediately, is expected to return $140,000 five years from now. If Flaherty demands a 9% return, how much is she willing to pay for this investment?

QS B-4
Present value of an amount P1

CII, Inc., invests $630,000 in a project expected to earn a 12% annual rate of return. The earnings will be reinvested in the project each year until the entire investment is liquidated 10 years later. What will the cash proceeds be when the project is liquidated?

QS B-5
Future value of an amount P2

Beene Distributing is considering a project that will return $150,000 annually at the end of each year for the next six years. If Beene demands an annual return of 7% and pays for the project immediately, how much is it willing to pay for the project?

QS B-6
Present value of an annuity P3

Claire Fitch is planning to begin an individual retirement program in which she will invest $1,500 at the end of each year. Fitch plans to retire after making 30 annual investments in the program earning a return of 10%. What is the value of the program on the date of the last payment (30 years from the present)?

QS B-7
Future value of an annuity P4

EXERCISES

Exercise B-1
Present value of an
amount **P1**

Mike Derr Company expects to earn 10% per year on an investment that will pay $606,773 six years from now. Use Table B.1 to compute the present value of this investment. (Round the amount to the nearest dollar.)

Exercise B-2
Present value of an
amount **P1**

On January 1, 2016, a company agrees to pay $20,000 in three years. If the annual interest rate is 10%, determine how much cash the company can borrow with this agreement.

Exercise B-3
Number of periods of an
investment **P2**

Tom Thompson expects to invest $10,000 at 12% and, at the end of a certain period, receive $96,463. How many years will it be before Thompson receives the payment? (Use Table B.2.)

Exercise B-4
Interest rate on an
investment **P2**

Bill Padley expects to invest $10,000 for 25 years, after which he wants to receive $108,347. What rate of interest must Padley earn? (Use Table B.2.)

Exercise B-5
Future value of an
amount **P2**

Mark Welsch deposits $7,200 in an account that earns interest at an annual rate of 8%, compounded quarterly. The $7,200 plus earned interest must remain in the account 10 years before it can be withdrawn. How much money will be in the account at the end of 10 years?

Exercise B-6
Future value of an
amount **P2**

Catten, Inc., invests $163,170 today earning 7% per year for nine years. Use Table B.2 to compute the future value of the investment nine years from now. (Round the amount to the nearest dollar.)

Exercise B-7
Interest rate on an
investment **P3**

Jones expects an immediate investment of $57,466 to return $10,000 annually for eight years, with the first payment to be received one year from now. What rate of interest must Jones earn? (Use Table B.3.)

Exercise B-8
Number of periods of an
investment **P3**

Keith Riggins expects an investment of $82,014 to return $10,000 annually for several years. If Riggins earns a return of 10%, how many annual payments will he receive? (Use Table B.3.)

Exercise B-9
Present value of an
annuity **P3**

Dave Krug finances a new automobile by paying $6,500 cash and agreeing to make 40 monthly payments of $500 each, the first payment to be made one month after the purchase. The loan bears interest at an annual rate of 12%. What is the cost of the automobile?

Exercise B-10
Present values of
annuities

P3

C&H Ski Club recently borrowed money and agreed to pay it back with a series of six annual payments of $5,000 each. C&H subsequently borrows more money and agrees to pay it back with a series of four annual payments of $7,500 each. The annual interest rate for both loans is 6%.

1. Use Table B.1 to find the present value of these two separate annuities. (Round amounts to the nearest dollar.)

2. Use Table B.3 to find the present value of these two separate annuities. (Round amounts to the nearest dollar.)

Exercise B-11
Present value with
semiannual
compounding

C1   P3

Otto Co. borrows money on April 30, 2016, by promising to make four payments of $13,000 each on November 1, 2016; May 1, 2017; November 1, 2017; and May 1, 2018.

1. How much money is Otto able to borrow if the interest rate is 8%, compounded semiannually?

2. How much money is Otto able to borrow if the interest rate is 12%, compounded semiannually?

3. How much money is Otto able to borrow if the interest rate is 16%, compounded semiannually?

Exercise B-12
Present value of bonds

P1   P3

Spiller Corp. plans to issue 10%, 15-year, $500,000 par value bonds payable that pay interest semiannually on June 30 and December 31. The bonds are dated December 31, 2016, and are issued on that date. If the market rate of interest for the bonds is 8% on the date of issue, what will be the total cash proceeds from the bond issue?

Compute the amount that can be borrowed under each of the following circumstances:

1. A promise to repay $90,000 seven years from now at an interest rate of 6%.

2. An agreement made on February 1, 2016, to make three separate payments of $20,000 on February 1 of 2017, 2018, and 2019. The annual interest rate is 10%.

Exercise B-13
Present value of an amount and of an annuity   **P1 P3**

Algoe expects to invest $1,000 annually for 40 years to yield an accumulated value of $154,762 on the date of the last investment. For this to occur, what rate of interest must Algoe earn? (Use Table B.4.)

Exercise B-14
Interest rate on an investment   **P4**

Steffi Derr expects to invest $10,000 annually that will earn 8%. How many annual investments must Derr make to accumulate $303,243 on the date of the last investment? (Use Table B.4.)

Exercise B-15
Number of periods of an investment   **P4**

Kelly Malone plans to have $50 withheld from her monthly paycheck and deposited in a savings account that earns 12% annually, compounded monthly. If Malone continues with her plan for two and one-half years, how much will be accumulated in the account on the date of the last deposit?

Exercise B-16
Future value of an annuity   **P4**

Starr Company decides to establish a fund that it will use 10 years from now to replace an aging production facility. The company will make a $100,000 initial contribution to the fund and plans to make quarterly contributions of $50,000 beginning in three months. The fund earns 12%, compounded quarterly. What will be the value of the fund 10 years from now?

Exercise B-17
Future value of an amount plus an annuity

P2 P4

---

a. How much would you have to deposit today if you wanted to have $60,000 in four years? Annual interest rate is 9%.

b. Assume that you are saving up for a trip around the world when you graduate in two years. If you can earn 8% on your investments, how much would you have to deposit today to have $15,000 when you graduate?

c. Would you rather have $463 now or $1,000 ten years from now? Assume that you can earn 9% on your investments.

d. Assume that a college parking sticker today costs $90. If the cost of parking is increasing at the rate of 5% per year, how much will the college parking sticker cost in eight years?

e. Assume that the average price of a new home is $158,500. If new homes are increasing at a rate of 10% per year, how much will a new home cost in eight years?

f. An investment will pay you $10,000 in 10 years, and it will also pay you $400 at the end of *each* of the next 10 years (years 1 thru 10). If the annual interest rate is 6%, how much would you be willing to pay today for this type of investment?

g. A college student is reported in the newspaper as having won $10,000,000 in the Kansas State Lottery. However, as is often the custom with lotteries, she does *not* actually receive the entire $10 million now. Instead she will receive $500,000 at the end of the year for *each* of the next 20 years. If the annual interest rate is 6%, what is the present value (today's amount) that she won? (Ignore taxes.)

Exercise B-18
Practical applications of the time value of money

P1   P2   P3   P4

For each of the following situations, identify (1) the case as either (*a*) a present or a future value and (*b*) a single amount or an annuity, (2) the table you would use in your computations (but do not solve the problem), and (3) the interest rate and time periods you would use.

a. You need to accumulate $10,000 for a trip you wish to take in four years. You are able to earn 8% compounded semiannually on your savings. You plan to make only one deposit and let the money accumulate for four years. How would you determine the amount of the one-time deposit?

b. Assume the same facts as in part (*a*) except that you will make semiannual deposits to your savings account.

c. You want to retire after working 40 years with savings in excess of $1,000,000. You expect to save $4,000 a year for 40 years and earn an annual rate of interest of 8%. Will you be able to retire with more than $1,000,000 in 40 years? Explain.

d. A sweepstakes agency names you a grand prize winner. You can take $225,000 immediately or elect to receive annual installments of $30,000 for 20 years. You can earn 10% annually on any investments you make. Which prize do you choose to receive?

Exercise B-19
Using present and future value tables

C1   P1   P2   P3   P4

TABLE B.1*

Present Value of 1

$$p = 1/(1+i)^n$$

Periods	1%	2%	3%	4%	5%	6%	7%	8%	9%	10%	12%	15%
1	0.9901	0.9804	0.9709	0.9615	0.9524	0.9434	0.9346	0.9259	0.9174	0.9091	0.8929	0.8696
2	0.9803	0.9612	0.9426	0.9246	0.9070	0.8900	0.8734	0.8573	0.8417	0.8264	0.7972	0.7561
3	0.9706	0.9423	0.9151	0.8890	0.8638	0.8396	0.8163	0.7938	0.7722	0.7513	0.7118	0.6575
4	0.9610	0.9238	0.8885	0.8548	0.8227	0.7921	0.7629	0.7350	0.7084	0.6830	0.6355	0.5718
5	0.9515	0.9057	0.8626	0.8219	0.7835	0.7473	0.7130	0.6806	0.6499	0.6209	0.5674	0.4972
6	0.9420	0.8880	0.8375	0.7903	0.7462	0.7050	0.6663	0.6302	0.5963	0.5645	0.5066	0.4323
7	0.9327	0.8706	0.8131	0.7599	0.7107	0.6651	0.6227	0.5835	0.5470	0.5132	0.4523	0.3759
8	0.9235	0.8535	0.7894	0.7307	0.6768	0.6274	0.5820	0.5403	0.5019	0.4665	0.4039	0.3269
9	0.9143	0.8368	0.7664	0.7026	0.6446	0.5919	0.5439	0.5002	0.4604	0.4241	0.3606	0.2843
10	0.9053	0.8203	0.7441	0.6756	0.6139	0.5584	0.5083	0.4632	0.4224	0.3855	0.3220	0.2472
11	0.8963	0.8043	0.7224	0.6496	0.5847	0.5268	0.4751	0.4289	0.3875	0.3505	0.2875	0.2149
12	0.8874	0.7885	0.7014	0.6246	0.5568	0.4970	0.4440	0.3971	0.3555	0.3186	0.2567	0.1869
13	0.8787	0.7730	0.6810	0.6006	0.5303	0.4688	0.4150	0.3677	0.3262	0.2897	0.2292	0.1625
14	0.8700	0.7579	0.6611	0.5775	0.5051	0.4423	0.3878	0.3405	0.2992	0.2633	0.2046	0.1413
15	0.8613	0.7430	0.6419	0.5553	0.4810	0.4173	0.3624	0.3152	0.2745	0.2394	0.1827	0.1229
16	0.8528	0.7284	0.6232	0.5339	0.4581	0.3936	0.3387	0.2919	0.2519	0.2176	0.1631	0.1069
17	0.8444	0.7142	0.6050	0.5134	0.4363	0.3714	0.3166	0.2703	0.2311	0.1978	0.1456	0.0929
18	0.8360	0.7002	0.5874	0.4936	0.4155	0.3503	0.2959	0.2502	0.2120	0.1799	0.1300	0.0808
19	0.8277	0.6864	0.5703	0.4746	0.3957	0.3305	0.2765	0.2317	0.1945	0.1635	0.1161	0.0703
20	0.8195	0.6730	0.5537	0.4564	0.3769	0.3118	0.2584	0.2145	0.1784	0.1486	0.1037	0.0611
25	0.7798	0.6095	0.4776	0.3751	0.2953	0.2330	0.1842	0.1460	0.1160	0.0923	0.0588	0.0304
30	0.7419	0.5521	0.4120	0.3083	0.2314	0.1741	0.1314	0.0994	0.0754	0.0573	0.0334	0.0151
35	0.7059	0.5000	0.3554	0.2534	0.1813	0.1301	0.0937	0.0676	0.0490	0.0356	0.0189	0.0075
40	0.6717	0.4529	0.3066	0.2083	0.1420	0.0972	0.0668	0.0460	0.0318	0.0221	0.0107	0.0037

* Used to compute the present value of a known future amount. For example: How much would you need to invest today at 10% compounded semiannually to accumulate $5,000 in 6 years from today? Using the factors of $n = 12$ and $i = 5\%$ (12 semiannual periods and a semiannual rate of 5%), the factor is 0.5568. You would need to invest $2,784 today ($5,000 × 0.5568).

TABLE B.2†

Future Value of 1

$$f = (1+i)^n$$

Periods	1%	2%	3%	4%	5%	6%	7%	8%	9%	10%	12%	15%
0	1.0000	1.0000	1.0000	1.0000	1.0000	1.0000	1.0000	1.0000	1.0000	1.0000	1.0000	1.0000
1	1.0100	1.0200	1.0300	1.0400	1.0500	1.0600	1.0700	1.0800	1.0900	1.1000	1.1200	1.1500
2	1.0201	1.0404	1.0609	1.0816	1.1025	1.1236	1.1449	1.1664	1.1881	1.2100	1.2544	1.3225
3	1.0303	1.0612	1.0927	1.1249	1.1576	1.1910	1.2250	1.2597	1.2950	1.3310	1.4049	1.5209
4	1.0406	1.0824	1.1255	1.1699	1.2155	1.2625	1.3108	1.3605	1.4116	1.4641	1.5735	1.7490
5	1.0510	1.1041	1.1593	1.2167	1.2763	1.3382	1.4026	1.4693	1.5386	1.6105	1.7623	2.0114
6	1.0615	1.1262	1.1941	1.2653	1.3401	1.4185	1.5007	1.5869	1.6771	1.7716	1.9738	2.3131
7	1.0721	1.1487	1.2299	1.3159	1.4071	1.5036	1.6058	1.7138	1.8280	1.9487	2.2107	2.6600
8	1.0829	1.1717	1.2668	1.3686	1.4775	1.5938	1.7182	1.8509	1.9926	2.1436	2.4760	3.0590
9	1.0937	1.1951	1.3048	1.4233	1.5513	1.6895	1.8385	1.9990	2.1719	2.3579	2.7731	3.5179
10	1.1046	1.2190	1.3439	1.4802	1.6289	1.7908	1.9672	2.1589	2.3674	2.5937	3.1058	4.0456
11	1.1157	1.2434	1.3842	1.5395	1.7103	1.8983	2.1049	2.3316	2.5804	2.8531	3.4785	4.6524
12	1.1268	1.2682	1.4258	1.6010	1.7959	2.0122	2.2522	2.5182	2.8127	3.1384	3.8960	5.3503
13	1.1381	1.2936	1.4685	1.6651	1.8856	2.1329	2.4098	2.7196	3.0658	3.4523	4.3635	6.1528
14	1.1495	1.3195	1.5126	1.7317	1.9799	2.2609	2.5785	2.9372	3.3417	3.7975	4.8871	7.0757
15	1.1610	1.3459	1.5580	1.8009	2.0789	2.3966	2.7590	3.1722	3.6425	4.1772	5.4736	8.1371
16	1.1726	1.3728	1.6047	1.8730	2.1829	2.5404	2.9522	3.4259	3.9703	4.5950	6.1304	9.3576
17	1.1843	1.4002	1.6528	1.9479	2.2920	2.6928	3.1588	3.7000	4.3276	5.0545	6.8660	10.7613
18	1.1961	1.4282	1.7024	2.0258	2.4066	2.8543	3.3799	3.9960	4.7171	5.5599	7.6900	12.3755
19	1.2081	1.4568	1.7535	2.1068	2.5270	3.0256	3.6165	4.3157	5.1417	6.1159	8.6128	14.2318
20	1.2202	1.4859	1.8061	2.1911	2.6533	3.2071	3.8697	4.6610	5.6044	6.7275	9.6463	16.3665
25	1.2824	1.6406	2.0938	2.6658	3.3864	4.2919	5.4274	6.8485	8.6231	10.8347	17.0001	32.9190
30	1.3478	1.8114	2.4273	3.2434	4.3219	5.7435	7.6123	10.0627	13.2677	17.4494	29.9599	66.2118
35	1.4166	1.9999	2.8139	3.9461	5.5160	7.6861	10.6766	14.7853	20.4140	28.1024	52.7996	133.1755
40	1.4889	2.2080	3.2620	4.8010	7.0400	10.2857	14.9745	21.7245	31.4094	45.2593	93.0510	267.8635

† Used to compute the future value of a known present amount. For example: What is the accumulated value of $3,000 invested today at 8% compounded quarterly for 5 years? Using the factors of $n = 20$ and $i = 2\%$ (20 quarterly periods and a quarterly interest rate of 2%), the factor is 1.4859. The accumulated value is $4,457.70 ($3,000 × 1.4859).

$$p = \left[1 - \frac{1}{(1+i)^n}\right]/i$$

TABLE B.3‡

Present Value of an Annuity of 1

Periods	\multicolumn{12}{c}{Rate}
	1%	2%	3%	4%	5%	6%	7%	8%	9%	10%	12%	15%
1	0.9901	0.9804	0.9709	0.9615	0.9524	0.9434	0.9346	0.9259	0.9174	0.9091	0.8929	0.8696
2	1.9704	1.9416	1.9135	1.8861	1.8594	1.8334	1.8080	1.7833	1.7591	1.7355	1.6901	1.6257
3	2.9410	2.8839	2.8286	2.7751	2.7232	2.6730	2.6243	2.5771	2.5313	2.4869	2.4018	2.2832
4	3.9020	3.8077	3.7171	3.6299	3.5460	3.4651	3.3872	3.3121	3.2397	3.1699	3.0373	2.8550
5	4.8534	4.7135	4.5797	4.4518	4.3295	4.2124	4.1002	3.9927	3.8897	3.7908	3.6048	3.3522
6	5.7955	5.6014	5.4172	5.2421	5.0757	4.9173	4.7665	4.6229	4.4859	4.3553	4.1114	3.7845
7	6.7282	6.4720	6.2303	6.0021	5.7864	5.5824	5.3893	5.2064	5.0330	4.8684	4.5638	4.1604
8	7.6517	7.3255	7.0197	6.7327	6.4632	6.2098	5.9713	5.7466	5.5348	5.3349	4.9676	4.4873
9	8.5660	8.1622	7.7861	7.4353	7.1078	6.8017	6.5152	6.2469	5.9952	5.7590	5.3282	4.7716
10	9.4713	8.9826	8.5302	8.1109	7.7217	7.3601	7.0236	6.7101	6.4177	6.1446	5.6502	5.0188
11	10.3676	9.7868	9.2526	8.7605	8.3064	7.8869	7.4987	7.1390	6.8052	6.4951	5.9377	5.2337
12	11.2551	10.5753	9.9540	9.3851	8.8633	8.3838	7.9427	7.5361	7.1607	6.8137	6.1944	5.4206
13	12.1337	11.3484	10.6350	9.9856	9.3936	8.8527	8.3577	7.9038	7.4869	7.1034	6.4235	5.5831
14	13.0037	12.1062	11.2961	10.5631	9.8986	9.2950	8.7455	8.2442	7.7862	7.3667	6.6282	5.7245
15	13.8651	12.8493	11.9379	11.1184	10.3797	9.7122	9.1079	8.5595	8.0607	7.6061	6.8109	5.8474
16	14.7179	13.5777	12.5611	11.6523	10.8378	10.1059	9.4466	8.8514	8.3126	7.8237	6.9740	5.9542
17	15.5623	14.2919	13.1661	12.1657	11.2741	10.4773	9.7632	9.1216	8.5436	8.0216	7.1196	6.0472
18	16.3983	14.9920	13.7535	12.6593	11.6896	10.8276	10.0591	9.3719	8.7556	8.2014	7.2497	6.1280
19	17.2260	15.6785	14.3238	13.1339	12.0853	11.1581	10.3356	9.6036	8.9501	8.3649	7.3658	6.1982
20	18.0456	16.3514	14.8775	13.5903	12.4622	11.4699	10.5940	9.8181	9.1285	8.5136	7.4694	6.2593
25	22.0232	19.5235	17.4131	15.6221	14.0939	12.7834	11.6536	10.6748	9.8226	9.0770	7.8431	6.4641
30	25.8077	22.3965	19.6004	17.2920	15.3725	13.7648	12.4090	11.2578	10.2737	9.4269	8.0552	6.5660
35	29.4086	24.9986	21.4872	18.6646	16.3742	14.4982	12.9477	11.6546	10.5668	9.6442	8.1755	6.6166
40	32.8347	27.3555	23.1148	19.7928	17.1591	15.0463	13.3317	11.9246	10.7574	9.7791	8.2438	6.6418

‡ Used to calculate the present value of a series of equal payments made at the end of each period. For example: What is the present value of $2,000 per year for 10 years assuming an annual interest rate of 9%. For (n = 10, i = 9%), the PV factor is 6.4177. $2,000 per year for 10 years is the equivalent of $12,835 today ($2,000 × 6.4177).

TABLE B.4§

Future Value of an Annuity of 1

$$f = [(1+i)^n - 1]/i$$

Periods	\multicolumn{12}{c}{Rate}
	1%	2%	3%	4%	5%	6%	7%	8%	9%	10%	12%	15%
1	1.0000	1.0000	1.0000	1.0000	1.0000	1.0000	1.0000	1.0000	1.0000	1.0000	1.0000	1.0000
2	2.0100	2.0200	2.0300	2.0400	2.0500	2.0600	2.0700	2.0800	2.0900	2.1000	2.1200	2.1500
3	3.0301	3.0604	3.0909	3.1216	3.1525	3.1836	3.2149	3.2464	3.2781	3.3100	3.3744	3.4725
4	4.0604	4.1216	4.1836	4.2465	4.3101	4.3746	4.4399	4.5061	4.5731	4.6410	4.7793	4.9934
5	5.1010	5.2040	5.3091	5.4163	5.5256	5.6371	5.7507	5.8666	5.9847	6.1051	6.3528	6.7424
6	6.1520	6.3081	6.4684	6.6330	6.8019	6.9753	7.1533	7.3359	7.5233	7.7156	8.1152	8.7537
7	7.2135	7.4343	7.6625	7.8983	8.1420	8.3938	8.6540	8.9228	9.2004	9.4872	10.0890	11.0668
8	8.2857	8.5830	8.8923	9.2142	9.5491	9.8975	10.2598	10.6366	11.0285	11.4359	12.2997	13.7268
9	9.3685	9.7546	10.1591	10.5828	11.0266	11.4913	11.9780	12.4876	13.0210	13.5795	14.7757	16.7858
10	10.4622	10.9497	11.4639	12.0061	12.5779	13.1808	13.8164	14.4866	15.1929	15.9374	17.5487	20.3037
11	11.5668	12.1687	12.8078	13.4864	14.2068	14.9716	15.7836	16.6455	17.5603	18.5312	20.6546	24.3493
12	12.6825	13.4121	14.1920	15.0258	15.9171	16.8699	17.8885	18.9771	20.1407	21.3843	24.1331	29.0017
13	13.8093	14.6803	15.6178	16.6268	17.7130	18.8821	20.1406	21.4953	22.9534	24.5227	28.0291	34.3519
14	14.9474	15.9739	17.0863	18.2919	19.5986	21.0151	22.5505	24.2149	26.0192	27.9750	32.3926	40.5047
15	16.0969	17.2934	18.5989	20.0236	21.5786	23.2760	25.1290	27.1521	29.3609	31.7725	37.2797	47.5804
16	17.2579	18.6393	20.1569	21.8245	23.6575	25.6725	27.8881	30.3243	33.0034	35.9497	42.7533	55.7175
17	18.4304	20.0121	21.7616	23.6975	25.8404	28.2129	30.8402	33.7502	36.9737	40.5447	48.8837	65.0751
18	19.6147	21.4123	23.4144	25.6454	28.1324	30.9057	33.9990	37.4502	41.3013	45.5992	55.7497	75.8364
19	20.8109	22.8406	25.1169	27.6712	30.5390	33.7600	37.3790	41.4463	46.0185	51.1591	63.4397	88.2118
20	22.0190	24.2974	26.8704	29.7781	33.0660	36.7856	40.9955	45.7620	51.1601	57.2750	72.0524	102.4436
25	28.2432	32.0303	36.4593	41.6459	47.7271	54.8645	63.2490	73.1059	84.7009	98.3471	133.3339	212.7930
30	34.7849	40.5681	47.5754	56.0849	66.4388	79.0582	94.4608	113.2832	136.3075	164.4940	241.3327	434.7451
35	41.6603	49.9945	60.4621	73.6522	90.3203	111.4348	138.2369	172.3168	215.7108	271.0244	431.6635	881.1702
40	48.8864	60.4020	75.4013	95.0255	120.7998	154.7620	199.6351	259.0565	337.8824	442.5926	767.0914	1,779.0903

§ Used to calculate the future value of a series of equal payments made at the end of each period. For example: What is the future value of $4,000 per year for 6 years assuming an annual interest rate of 8%. For (n = 6, i = 8%), the FV factor is 7.3359. $4,000 per year for 6 years accumulates to $29,343.60 ($4,000 × 7.3359).

C appendix

Investments and International Operations

Appendix Preview

BASICS OF INVESTMENTS

C1 Motivation for investments

Short-term versus long-term

Classification and reporting

Accounting basics

NONINFLUENTIAL INVESTMENTS

P1 Trading securities

P2 Held-to-maturity securities

P3 Available-for-sale securities

INFLUENTIAL INVESTMENTS

P4 Securities with significant influence

C2 Securities with controlling influence

A1 Analyze components of return on assets

Learning Objectives

CONCEPTUAL

C1 Distinguish between debt and equity securities and between short-term and long-term investments.

C2 Describe how to report equity securities with controlling influence.

C3 *Appendix C-A*—Explain foreign exchange rates and record transactions listed in a foreign currency.

ANALYTICAL

A1 Compute and analyze the components of return on total assets.

PROCEDURAL

P1 Account for trading securities.

P2 Account for held-to-maturity securities.

P3 Account for available-for-sale securities.

P4 Account for equity securities with significant influence.

BASICS OF INVESTMENTS

In prior chapters we discussed the reporting of both equity (common and preferred stock) and debt (bonds and notes) from the seller's (also called *issuer* or *investee*) standpoint. This appendix explains the reporting of both equity and debt from the buyer's (also called *investor*) standpoint. The first section of this appendix describes the motivation for investments, the distinction between short- and long-term investments, and the different classes of investments.

C1

Distinguish between debt and equity securities and between short-term and long-term investments.

Motivation for Investments

Companies make investments for at least three reasons. First, companies transfer *excess cash* into investments to produce higher income. Second, some entities, such as mutual funds and pension funds, are set up to produce income from investments. Third, companies make investments for strategic reasons. Examples are investments in competitors, suppliers, and even customers. Exhibit C.1 shows short-term (S-T) and long-term (L-T) investments as a percent of total assets for several companies.

Short-Term Investments   Cash equivalents are investments that both are readily converted to known amounts of cash and mature within three months. Many investments, however, mature between 3 and 12 months. These investments are **short-term investments**, also called *temporary investments* and *marketable securities*. Specifically, short-term investments are securities that (1) management intends to convert to cash

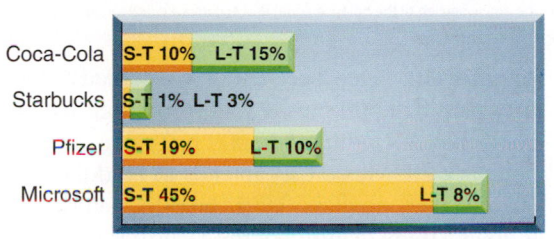

Coca-Cola S-T 10% L-T 15%
Starbucks S-T 1% L-T 3%
Pfizer S-T 19% L-T 10%
Microsoft S-T 45% L-T 8%

Percent of total assets

EXHIBIT C.1

Investments of Selected Companies

within one year or the operating cycle, whichever is longer, and (2) are readily convertible to cash. Short-term investments are reported under current assets and serve a purpose similar to cash equivalents.

Long-Term Investments   **Long-term investments** in securities are defined as those securities that are not readily convertible to cash or are not intended to be converted into cash in the short term. Long-term investments can also include funds earmarked for a special purpose, such as bond sinking funds and investments in land or other assets not used in the company's operations. Long-term investments are reported in the noncurrent section of the balance sheet, often in its own separate line titled *Long-Term Investments*.

Investee's Balance Sheet
Liabilities
  Notes Payable
  Bonds Payable
Equity
  Common Stock
  Preferred Stock

Investor's Balance Sheet
Assets
  Investment in Debt Securities
  Investment in Equity Securities

Debt Securities versus Equity Securities   Investments in securities can include both debt and equity securities. *Debt securities* reflect a creditor relationship such as investments in notes, bonds, and certificates of deposit; they are issued by governments, companies, and individuals. *Equity securities* reflect an owner relationship such as shares of stock issued by companies.

Classification and Reporting

Accounting for investments in securities depends on three factors: (1) security type, either debt or equity; (2) the company's intent to hold the security either short term or long term; and (3) the company's (investor's) percentage of ownership in the other company's (investee's) equity securities. Exhibit C.2 identifies five classes of securities using these three factors. It describes each of these five classes of securities and the standard reporting required under each class.

Debt Securities: Accounting Basics

This section explains the accounting basics for *debt securities,* including that for acquisition, disposition, and any interest.

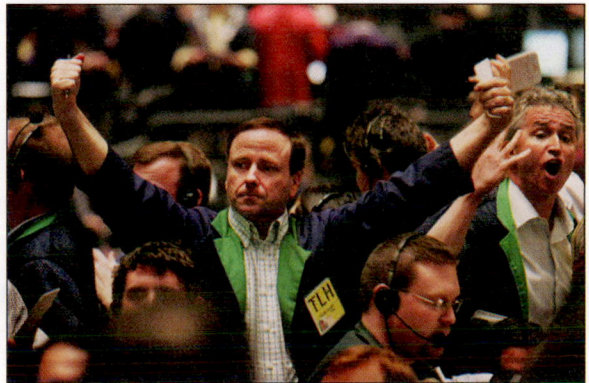

Scott Olson/Getty Images

EXHIBIT C.2

Investments in Securities

a Holding less than 20% of voting stock (equity securities only).   b Holding 20% or more, but not more than 50%, of voting stock.   c Holding more than 50% of voting stock.
* Unrealized gains and losses reported on the income statement.
** Unrealized gains and losses reported in the equity section of the balance sheet and in comprehensive income.

Acquisition   Debt securities are recorded at cost when purchased. To illustrate, assume that Music City paid $29,500 plus a $500 brokerage fee on September 1, 2015, to buy Dell's 7%, two-year bonds payable with a $30,000 par value. The bonds pay interest semiannually on August 31 and February 28. Music City intends to hold the bonds until they mature on August 31, 2017; consequently, they are classified as held-to-maturity (HTM) securities. The entry to record this purchase follows. (If the maturity of the securities was short term, and management's intent was to hold them until they mature, then they would be recorded in the Short-Term Investments—HTM account.)

Assets = Liabilities + Equity
+30,000
−30,000

	2015			
	Sept. 1	Long-Term Investments—HTM (Dell)	30,000	
		Cash		30,000
		Purchased bonds to be held to maturity.		

Interest Earned   Interest revenue for investments in debt securities is recorded when earned. To illustrate, on December 31, 2015, at the end of its accounting period, Music City accrues interest receivable as follows.

Assets = Liabilities + Equity
+700   +700

	Dec. 31	Interest Receivable................................	700	
		Interest Revenue............................		700
		Accrued interest earned ($30,000 × 7% × 1/12).		

The $700 interest earned from September 1 to December 31 is computed as "Principal × Annual rate × Fraction of year" (shown above), which also equals 4/6 of the semiannual cash receipt of interest. Music City's financial statements at December 31, 2015, report the interest revenue and the investment as shown in Exhibit C.3.

EXHIBIT C.3

Financial Statement Presentation of Debt Securities

On the income statement for year 2015:	
Interest revenue	**$ 700**
On the December 31, 2015, balance sheet:	
Long-term investments—Held-to-maturity securities (at amortized cost)	**$30,000**

On February 28, 2016, Music City records receipt of semiannual interest.

Assets = Liabilities + Equity
+1,050   +350
−700

Point: Feb. 28 entry reflects 4 months' interest earned and accrued in 2015 and 2 months earned in 2016.

	Feb. 28	Cash	1,050	
		Interest Receivable*.........................		700
		Interest Revenue†...........................		350
		Received six months' interest on Dell bonds.		

* $30,000 × 7% × 4/12   † $30,000 × 7% × 2/12

Disposition When the bonds mature, the proceeds (not including the interest entry) are recorded as:

2017			
Aug. 31	Cash	30,000	
	Long-Term Investments—HTM (Dell).		30,000
	Received cash from matured bonds.		

Assets = Liabilities + Equity
+30,000
−30,000

The cost of a debt security can be either higher or lower than its maturity value. When the investment is long term, the difference between cost and maturity value is amortized over the remaining life of the security. We assume for ease of computations that the cost of a long-term debt security equals its maturity value.

Example: What is cost per share? *Answer:* Cost per share is the total cost of acquisition, including broker fees, divided by number of shares acquired.

Equity Securities: Accounting Basics

This section explains the accounting basics for *equity securities,* including those for acquisition, dividends, and disposition.

Acquisition Equity securities are recorded at cost when acquired, including commissions or brokerage fees paid. To illustrate, assume that Music City purchases 1,000 shares of Intex common stock at par value for $86,000 on October 10, 2015. It records this purchase of available-for-sale (AFS) securities as follows.

Oct. 10	Long-Term Investments—AFS (Intex)...............	86,000	
	Cash		86,000
	Purchased 1,000 shares of Intex.		

Assets = Liabilities + Equity
+86,000
−86,000

Dividend Earned Any cash dividends received are credited to Dividend Revenue and reported in the income statement. To illustrate, on November 2, Music City receives a $1,720 quarterly cash dividend on the Intex shares, which it records as:

Nov. 2	Cash	1,720	
	Dividend Revenue.		1,720
	Received dividend of $1.72 per share.		

Assets = Liabilities + Equity
+1,720   +1,720

Disposition When the securities are sold, sale proceeds are compared with the cost, and any gain or loss is recorded. To illustrate, on December 20, Music City sells 500 of the Intex shares for $45,000 cash and records this sale as:

Dec. 20	Cash	45,000	
	Long-Term Investments—AFS (Intex)...........		43,000
	Gain on Sale of Long-Term Investments		2,000
	Sold 500 Intex shares ($86,000 × 500/1,000).		

Assets = Liabilities + Equity
+45,000   +2,000
−43,000

REPORTING OF NONINFLUENTIAL INVESTMENTS

Companies must value and report most noninfluential investments at *fair value.* The exact reporting requirements depend on whether the investments are classified as (1) trading, (2) held-to-maturity, or (3) available-for-sale.

Trading Securities

Trading securities are *debt and equity securities* that the company intends to actively manage and trade for profit. Frequent purchases and sales are expected and are made to earn profits on short-term price changes. Trading securities are *always* reported as current assets.

P1

Account for trading securities.

Valuing and Reporting Trading Securities   The entire portfolio of trading securities is reported at its fair value; this requires a "fair value adjustment" from the cost of the portfolio. The term *portfolio* refers to a group of securities. **Any unrealized gain (or loss) from a change in the fair value of the portfolio of trading securities is reported on the income statement.** Most users believe accounting reports are more useful when changes in fair value for trading securities are reported in income.

Point: *Unrealized gain (or loss) refers to a change in fair value that is not yet realized through actual sale.*

To illustrate, TechCom's portfolio of trading securities had a total cost of $11,500 and a fair value of $13,000 on December 31, 2015, the first year it held trading securities. The difference between the $11,500 cost and the $13,000 fair value reflects a $1,500 gain. It is an unrealized gain because it is not yet confirmed by actual sales. The fair value adjustment for trading securities is recorded with an adjusting entry at the end of each period to equal the difference between the portfolio's cost and its fair value. TechCom records this gain as follows.

Point: Fair Value Adj. is a balance sheet account with either a debit balance (Fair value > Cost) or credit balance (Fair value < Cost).

Assets = Liabilities + Equity
+1,500   +1,500

Dec. 31	Fair Value Adjustment—Trading	1,500	
	Unrealized Gain—Income		1,500
	Record an unrealized gain in fair values		
	of trading securities.		

This adjustment can also be determined using our "three-step adjusting process" from Chapter 3.

Unadj. bal. is rarely $0; it is $0 here because it's the first year.

Step 1: Determine what unadjusted balance equals: Fair Value Adj—Trading = $0.

Step 2: Determine what adjusted balance should equal: Fair Value Adj—Trading = $1,500 Dr.
Explanation: $13,000 fair value > $11,500 cost, thus the Fair Value Adj—Trading requires a $1,500 debit so securities are at fair value.

Step 3: Record the $1,500 adjusting entry to get from Step 1 to Step 2.
Explanation: This implies a $1,500 debit to Fair Value Adj—Trading (and the Unrealized Gain).

Example: If TechCom's trading securities have a cost of $14,800 and a fair value of $16,100 at Dec. 31, 2016, its adjusting entry is
Unreal. Loss—Income . . 200
  FV Adj.—Trading   200
This is computed as:
$1,500 Beg. Dr. bal. + $200 Cr. = $1,300 End. Dr. bal.

The **unrealized gain (or loss)** is reported in the Other Revenues and Gains (or Expenses and Losses) section on the income statement. Unrealized Gain (or Loss)—Income is a *temporary* account that is closed to Income Summary at the end of each period. Fair Value Adjustment—Trading is a *permanent* account, which adjusts the reported value of the trading securities portfolio from its prior period fair value to the current period fair value. The total cost of the trading securities portfolio is maintained in one account, and the fair value adjustment is recorded in a separate account. For example, TechCom's investment in trading securities is reported in the current assets section of its balance sheet as follows.

ST Investments–Trading

1/1/2015	0	
Purch.	11,500	
12/31/2015	11,500	

Fair Value Adj.–Trading

1/1/2015	0	
Adj.	**1,500**	
12/31/2015	1,500	

Current Assets

Short-term investments—Trading (at cost)	$11,500	
Fair value adjustment—Trading.	1,500	
Short-term investments—Trading (at fair value)		$13,000

or simply

Short-term investments—Trading (at fair value; cost is $11,500)		$13,000

Selling Trading Securities   When individual trading securities are sold, the difference between the net proceeds (sale price less fees) and the cost of the individual trading securities that are sold is recognized as a gain or a loss. **Any prior period fair value adjustment to the portfolio is *not* used to compute the gain or loss from the sale of individual trading securities.** This is because the balance in the Fair Value Adjustment account is for the entire portfolio, not individual securities. For example, if TechCom sold some of its trading securities that had cost $1,000 for $1,200 cash on January 9, 2016, it would record the following.

Point: Reporting securities at fair value is referred to as *mark-to-market* accounting.

Assets = Liabilities + Equity
+1,200   +200
−1,000

Jan. 9	Cash	1,200	
	Short-Term Investments—Trading		1,000
	Gain on Sale of Short-Term Investments		200
	Sold trading securities costing $1,000 for $1,200 cash.		

A gain is reported in the Other Revenues and Gains section on the income statement, whereas a loss is shown in Other Expenses and Losses. When the period-end fair value adjustment for the portfolio of trading securities is computed, it excludes the cost and fair value of any securities sold.

Berkshire Co. purchases investments in trading securities at a cost of $130 on December 15, 2016. (This is its first and only purchase of such securities.) On December 28, Berkshire received a $15 cash dividend from the stock purchased on December 15. At December 31, 2016, the trading securities had a fair value of $140.

a. Prepare the December 15 acquisition entry for the trading securities' portfolio.

b. Prepare the December 28 receipt of cash dividends entry for the trading securities' portfolio.

c. Prepare the December 31 year-end adjusting entry for the trading securities' portfolio.

d. Explain how each account in entry *c* is reported in financial statements.

e. Prepare the January 3, 2017, entry when a portion of its trading securities (that had originally cost $33) is sold for $36.

> **NEED-TO-KNOW C-1**
>
> Trading Securities
>
> P1

Solution

a.

Dec. 15	Short-Term Investments—Trading	130	
	Cash		130
	Record purchase of trading securities.		

b.

Dec. 28	Cash	15	
	Dividend Revenue......................		15
	Record dividend received on trading securities.		

c.

Dec. 31	Fair Value Adjustment—Trading	10	
	Unrealized Gain—Income		10
	Record unrealized gain in fair value of trading securities.		

Fair Value Adj.–Trading		
Unadj.	0	
Adj.	10	
12/31/2016	10	

d. (i) The $10 debit in the Fair Value Adjustment—Trading account is an adjunct asset account in the balance sheet. It increases the $130 balance of the Short-Term Investment—Trading account to its $140 fair value.

(ii) The $10 credit for Unrealized Gain is reported in the Other Revenues and Gains section of the income statement.

e.

Jan. 3	Cash	36	
	Gain on Sale of Short-Term Investments		3
	Short-Term Investments—Trading		33
	Record sale of trading securities.		

> Do More: QS C-3, QS C-4, QS C-5, E C-2, E C-3

Held-to-Maturity Securities

Held-to-maturity (HTM) securities are *debt* securities a company intends and is able to hold until maturity. They are reported in current assets if their maturity dates are within one year or the operating cycle, whichever is longer. HTM securities are reported in long-term assets when the maturity dates extend beyond one year or the operating cycle, whichever is longer. All HTM securities are recorded at cost when purchased, and interest revenue is recorded when earned.

The portfolio of HTM securities is usually reported at (amortized) cost, which is explained in advanced courses. There is no fair value adjustment to the portfolio of HTM securities—neither to the short-term nor long-term portfolios. The basics of accounting for HTM securities were described earlier in this appendix.

P2

Account for held-to-maturity securities.

Point: Only debt securities can be classified as *held-to-maturity*; equity securities have no maturity date.

 Decision Maker

Money Manager You expect interest rates to sharply fall within a few weeks and remain at this lower rate. What is your strategy for holding investments in fixed-rate bonds and notes? ■ [Answers follow the appendix's Summary.]

C-2

Held-to-Maturity Securities

P2

Prepare journal entries to record the following transactions involving the short-term securities investments of LA Life.

a. On May 15, paid $100 cash to purchase Muni's 120-day short-term debt securities ($100 principal), dated May 15, that pay 6% interest (categorized as held-to-maturity securities).

b. On September 13, received a check from Muni in payment of the principal and 120 days' interest on the debt securities purchased in transaction *a*.

Solution

a.

May 15	Short-Term Investments—HTM (Muni)............	100	
	Cash....................................		100
	Purchased 120-day, 6% debt securities.		

b.

Sep. 13	Cash......................................	102	
	Short-Term Investments—HTM (Muni)........		100
	Interest Revenue..........................		2
	Collected $100 principal plus interest of $100 × 6% × 120/360.		

Do More: QS C-6, E C-4

Available-for-Sale Securities

P3

Account for available-for-sale securities.

Available-for-sale (AFS) securities are *debt and equity securities* not classified as trading or held-to-maturity securities. AFS securities are purchased to yield interest, dividends, or increases in fair value. They are not actively managed like trading securities. If the intent is to sell AFS securities within the longer of one year or the operating cycle, they are classified as short-term investments. Otherwise, they are classified as long-term investments.

Valuing and Reporting Available-for-Sale Securities   As with trading securities, companies adjust the cost of the portfolio of AFS securities to reflect changes in fair value. This is done with a fair value adjustment to its total portfolio cost. However, **any unrealized gain or loss for the portfolio of AFS securities is *not* reported on the income statement.** Instead, it is reported in the equity section of the balance sheet (and is part of *comprehensive income,* explained later). To illustrate, assume that Music City had no prior period investments in available-for-sale securities other than those purchased in the current period. Exhibit C.4 shows both the cost and fair value of those investments on December 31, 2015, the end of its reporting period.

EXHIBIT C.4

Cost and Fair Value of Available-for-Sale Securities

Example: If fair value in Exhibit C.4 is $70,000 (instead of $74,550), what entry is made? *Answer:*
Unreal. Loss—Equity. . 3,000
    FV Adj.—AFS. . .   3,000

	Cost	Fair Value	Unrealized Gain (Loss)
Improv bonds	$30,000	$29,050	$ (950)
Intex common stock, 500 shares.........	43,000	45,500	2,500
Total	$73,000	$74,550	$1,550

The year-end adjusting entry to record the fair value of these investments follows.

Assets = Liabilities + Equity
+1,550   +1,550

Dec. 31	Fair Value Adjustment—Available-for-Sale (LT)........	1,550	
	Unrealized Gain—Equity		1,550
	Record adjustment to fair value of		
	available-for-sale securities.		

Point: Unrealized Loss—Equity and Unrealized Gain—Equity are *permanent* (balance sheet) equity *accounts.*

Exhibit C.5 shows the December 31, 2015, balance sheet presentation—it assumes these investments are long term, but they can also be short term. It is also common to combine the cost of investments with the balance in the Fair Value Adjustment account and report the net as a single amount.

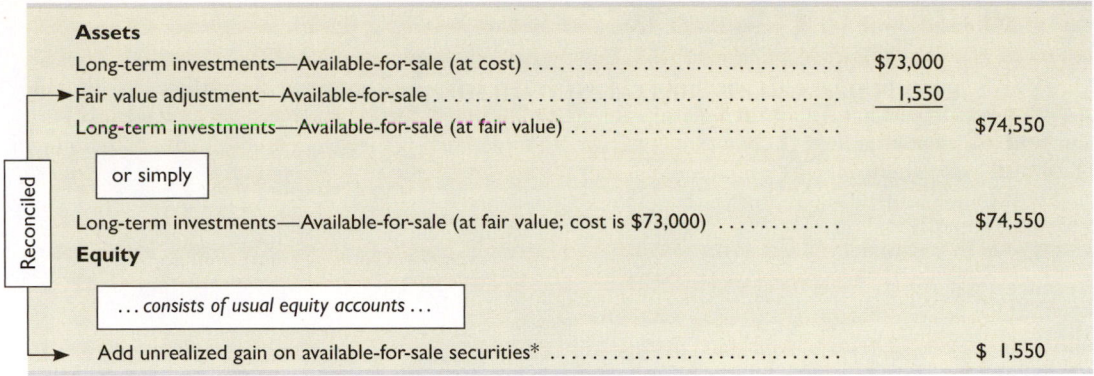

Assets

Long-term investments—Available-for-sale (at cost)	$73,000
Fair value adjustment—Available-for-sale	1,550
Long-term investments—Available-for-sale (at fair value)	$74,550

or simply

Long-term investments—Available-for-sale (at fair value; cost is $73,000)	$74,550

Equity

... consists of usual equity accounts ...

Add unrealized gain on available-for-sale securities*	$ 1,550

Reconciled

* Often included under the caption Accumulated Other Comprehensive Income.

EXHIBIT C.5

Balance Sheet Presentation of Available-for-Sale Securities

LT Investments–AFS

1/1/2015	0	
Purch.	73,000	
12/31/2015	73,000	

Fair Value Adj.–AFS (LT)

1/1/2015	0	
Adj.	**1,550**	
12/31/2015	1,550	

Point: Income is increased by selling AFS securities with unrealized gains; income is reduced by selling those with unrealized losses.

Let's extend this illustration and assume that at the end of its next calendar year (December 31, 2016), Music City's portfolio of long-term AFS securities has an $81,000 cost and an $82,000 fair value. It records the adjustment to fair value as follows.

Assets = Liabilities + Equity
−550   −550

Dec. 31	Unrealized Gain—Equity	550	
	Fair Value Adjustment—Available-for-Sale (LT)		550
	To record adjustment to fair value of		
	available-for-sale securities.		

Example: If cost is $83,000 and fair value is $82,000 at Dec. 31, 2016, it records the following adjustment:
Unreal. Gain—Equity 1,550
Unreal. Loss—Equity 1,000
    FV Adj.—AFS   2,550

The effects of the 2015 and 2016 securities transactions are reflected in the following T-accounts.

Unrealized Gain—Equity

| Adj. 12/31/16 | 550 | Bal. 12/31/15 | 1,550 |
| | | **Bal. 12/31/16** | **1,000** |

Fair Value Adjustment—Available-for-Sale (LT)

| Bal. 12/31/15 | 1,550 | Adj. 12/31/16 | 550 |
| **Bal. 12/31/16** | **1,000** | | |

Amounts reconcile.

This adjustment can also be determined using our three-step adjusting process.

Step 1: Determine what unadjusted balance equals: Fair Value Adj.—AFS = $1,550 Dr.

Step 2: Determine what adjusted balance should equal: Fair Value Adj.—AFS = $1,000 Dr.
Explanation: $82,000 fair value > $81,000 cost, thus Fair Value Adj.—Trading requires a $1,000 debit so securities are at fair value.

Step 3: Record the $550 adjusting entry to get from step 1 to step 2.
Explanation: This implies a $550 credit to Fair Value Adj.—AFS (and reduction of Unrealized Gain).

Selling Available-for-Sale Securities   Accounting for the sale of individual AFS securities is identical to that described for the sale of trading securities. When individual AFS securities are sold, the difference between the cost of the individual securities sold and the net proceeds (sale price less fees) is recognized as a gain or loss.

Point: Fair Value Adj.—AFS is a permanent account, shown as a deduction or addition to the investment account.

Alert: Both U.S. GAAP (and IFRS) permit companies to use fair value in reporting financial assets (referred to as the fair value option). This option allows companies to report any financial asset at fair value and recognize value changes in income. This method was previously reserved only for trading securities, but is now an option for available-for-sale and held-to-maturity securities (and other "financial assets and liabilities" such as accounts and notes receivable, accounts and notes payable, and bonds). U.S. standards also set a three-level system to determine fair value:
—Level 1: Use quoted market values.
—Level 2: Use observable values from related assets or liabilities.
—Level 3: Use unobservable values from estimates or assumptions.
To date, a fairly small set of companies has chosen to broadly apply the fair value option—but we continue to monitor its use.

Available-for-Sale Securities

P3

Gard Company completes the following selected transactions related to its short-term investments.

May 8   Purchased 300 shares of FedEx stock as a short-term investment in available-for-sale securities at $40 per share plus $975 in broker fees.

Sept. 2   Sold 100 shares of its investment in FedEx stock at $47 per share and held the remaining 200 shares; broker's commission was $225.

Oct. 2   Purchased 400 shares of Ajay stock for $60 per share plus $1,600 in commissions. The stock is held as a short-term investment in available-for-sale securities.

Required

1. Prepare journal entries for the above transactions.

2. Prepare a year-end adjusting journal entry as of December 31 if the fair values of the equity securities held by Gard are $48 per share for FedEx and $55 per share for Ajay. (This year is the first year Gard Company acquired short-term investments.)

Solution

1.

May 8	Short-Term Investments—AFS (FedEx)	12,975	
	Cash		12,975
	Purchased FedEx stock; (300 sh. × $40) + $975.		
Sept. 2	Cash	4,475	
	Gain on Sale of Short-Term Investment		150
	Short-Term Investments—AFS (FedEx)		4,325
	Sold FedEx shares; original cost is ($12,975 × 100/300)		
Oct. 2	Short-Term Investments—AFS (Ajay)	25,600	
	Cash		25,600
	Purchased Ajay shares; (400 sh. × $60) + $1,600.		

ST Investments–AFS

Jan. 1	0		
May 8	12,975		
		Sept. 2	4,325
Oct. 2	25,600		
Dec. 31 bal.	34,250		

2. Computation of unrealized gain or loss follows.

Short-Term Investments in Available-for-Sale Securities	Shares	Cost per Share	Total Cost	Fair Value per Share	Total Fair Value	Unrealized Gain (Loss)
FedEx	200	$43.25	$ 8,650	$48.00	$ 9,600	
Ajay..........................	400	64.00	25,600	55.00	22,000	
Totals			$34,250		$31,600	$(2,650)

Fair Value Adj.–AFS (ST)

Jan. 1	0		
		Dec. 31 adj.	**2,650**
		Dec. 31 bal.	2,650

The adjusting entry follows:

Dec. 31	Unrealized Loss—Equity	2,650	
	Fair Value Adjustment—Available-for-Sale (ST)		2,650
	Record an unrealized loss in fair values.		

Do More: QS C-7, QS C-8, QS C-9, QS C-10, E C-5, E C-7, E C-8, E C-10

REPORTING OF INFLUENTIAL INVESTMENTS

Investment in Securities with Significant Influence

P4

Account for equity securities with significant influence.

A long-term investment classified as **equity securities with significant influence** implies that the investor can exert significant influence over the investee. An investor that owns 20% or more (but not more than 50%) of a company's voting stock is usually presumed to have a significant influence over the investee. In some cases, however, the 20% test of significant influence is overruled by other, more persuasive, evidence. This evidence can either lower the 20% requirement or increase it. The **equity method** of accounting and reporting is used for long-term investments in equity securities with significant influence, which is explained in this section.

Long-term investments in equity securities with significant influence are recorded at cost when acquired. To illustrate, Micron Co. records the purchase of 3,000 shares (30%) of Star Co. common stock at a total cost of $70,650 on January 1, 2015, as follows.

Jan. 1	Long-Term Investments—Star....................	70,650	
	Cash		70,650
	Record purchase of 3,000 Star shares.		

Assets = Liabilities + Equity
+70,650
−70,650

The investee's (Star) earnings increase both its net assets and the claim of the investor (Micron) on the investee's net assets. Thus, when the investee reports its earnings, the investor records its share of those earnings in its investment account. To illustrate, assume that Star reports net income of $20,000 for 2015. Micron then records its 30% share of those earnings as follows.

Dec. 31	Long-Term Investments—Star....................	6,000	
	Earnings from Long-Term Investment...........		6,000
	Record 30% equity in investee earnings.		

Assets = Liabilities + Equity
+6,000   +6,000

The debit reflects the increase in Micron's equity in Star. The credit reflects 30% of Star's net income. Earnings from Long-Term Investment is a *temporary* account (closed to Income Summary at each period-end) and is reported on the investor's (Micron's) income statement. If the investee incurs a net loss instead of a net income, the investor records its share of the loss and reduces (credits) its investment account. The investor closes this earnings or loss account to Income Summary.

The receipt of cash dividends is not revenue under the equity method because the investor has already recorded its share of the investee's earnings. Instead, cash dividends received by an investor from an investee are viewed as a conversion of one asset to another; that is, dividends reduce the balance of the investment account. To illustrate, Star declares and pays $10,000 in cash dividends on its common stock. Micron records its 30% share of these dividends received on January 9, 2016, as:

Jan. 9	Cash	3,000	
	Long-Term Investments—Star.................		3,000
	Record share of dividend paid by Star.		

Assets = Liabilities + Equity
+3,000
−3,000

The book value of an investment under the equity method equals the cost of the investment plus (minus) the investor's equity in the *undistributed (distributed)* earnings of the investee. Once Micron records these transactions, its Long-Term Investments account appears as in Exhibit C.6.

EXHIBIT C.6

Investment in Star Common Stock (Ledger Account)

Long-Term Investment—Star			
1/1/2015 Investment acquisition	70,650		
12/31/2015 Share of earnings	6,000		
12/31/2015 Balance	76,650		
		1/9/2016 Share of dividend	3,000
1/9/2016 Balance	73,650		

Micron's account balance on January 9, 2016, for its investment in Star is $73,650. This is the investment's cost *plus* Micron's equity in Star's earnings since its purchase *less* Micron's equity in Star's cash dividends since its purchase. When an investment in equity securities is sold, the gain or loss is computed by comparing proceeds from the sale with the book value of

Point: Security prices are sometimes listed in fractions. For example, a debt security with a price of $22\frac{1}{4}$ is the same as $22.25.

the investment on the date of sale. If Micron sells its Star stock for $80,000 on January 10, 2016, it records the sale as:

Assets = Liabilities + Equity
+80,000   +6,350
−73,650

Jan. 10	Cash	80,000	
	Long-Term Investments—Star		73,650
	Gain on Sale of Investment		6,350
	Sold 3,000 shares of stock for $80,000.		

Investment in Securities with Controlling Influence

C2

Describe how to report equity securities with controlling influence.

A long-term investment classified as **equity securities with controlling influence** implies that the investor can exert a controlling influence over the investee. An investor who owns more than 50% of a company's voting stock has control over the investee. This investor can dominate all other shareholders in electing the corporation's board of directors and has control over the investee's management. In some cases, controlling influence can extend to situations of less than 50% ownership. Exhibit C.7 summarizes the accounting for investments in equity securities based on an investor's ownership in the stock.

EXHIBIT C.7

Accounting for Equity Investments by Percent of Ownership

Fair value method (under 20%) | Equity method (20% to 50%) | Equity method with consolidation (more than 50%)

0%   20%   50%   100%

Investor's percent ownership of a company's stock

The *equity method with consolidation* is used to account for long-term investments in equity securities with controlling influence. The investor reports *consolidated financial statements* when owning such securities. The controlling investor is called the **parent,** and the investee is called the **subsidiary.** Many companies are parents with subsidiaries. Examples are (1) **Gap Inc.**, the parent of Gap, Old Navy, and Banana Republic; and (2) **Whole Foods Market, Inc.**, the parent of Allegro Coffee, Mrs. Gooch's Natural Food Markets, and other subsidiaries. A company owning all the outstanding stock of a subsidiary can, if it desires, take over the subsidiary's assets, retire the subsidiary's stock, and merge the subsidiary into the parent. However, there often are financial, legal, and tax advantages if a business operates as a parent controlling one or more subsidiaries. When a company operates as a parent with subsidiaries, each entity maintains separate accounting records. From a legal viewpoint, the parent and each subsidiary are separate entities with all rights, duties, and responsibilities of individual companies.

Tim Greenway/Portland Press Herald/Getty Images

Consolidated financial statements show the financial position, results of operations, and cash flows of all entities under the parent's control, including all subsidiaries. These statements are prepared as if the business were organized as one entity. The parent uses the equity method in its accounts, but the investment account is *not* reported on the parent's financial statements. Instead, the individual assets and liabilities of the parent and its subsidiaries are combined on one balance sheet. Their revenues and expenses also are combined on one income statement, and their cash flows are combined on one statement of cash flows. The procedures for preparing consolidated financial statements are in advanced courses.

 IFRS ───

Unlike U.S. GAAP, IFRS requires uniform accounting policies be used throughout the group of consolidated subsidiaries. Also, unlike U.S. GAAP, IFRS offers no detailed guidance on valuation procedures. ■

Accounting Summary for Investments in Securities

Exhibit C.8 summarizes the standard accounting for investments in securities. Recall that many investment securities are classified as either short term or long term depending on management's intent and ability to convert them in the future. Understanding the accounting for these investments enables us to draw better conclusions from financial statements in making business decisions.

EXHIBIT C.8

Accounting for Investments in Securities

Classification	Accounting
Short-Term Investment in Securities	
Held-to-maturity (debt) securities	**Cost** (without any discount or premium amortization)
Trading (debt and equity) securities	**Fair value** (with fair value adjustment to income)
Available-for-sale (debt and equity) securities.	**Fair value** (with fair value adjustment to equity)
Long-Term Investment in Securities	
Held-to-maturity (debt) securities	**Cost** (with any discount or premium amortization)
Available-for-sale (debt and equity) securities.	**Fair value** (with fair value adjustment to equity)
Equity securities with significant influence	Equity method
Equity securities with controlling influence	Equity method (with consolidation)

Comprehensive Income   Comprehensive income is defined as all changes in equity during a period except those from owners' investments and dividends. Specifically, comprehensive income is computed by adding or subtracting *other comprehensive income* to net income:

Net income	$ #
Other comprehensive income.	#
Comprehensive income.	$ #

Other comprehensive income includes unrealized gains and losses on available-for-sale securities, foreign currency translation adjustments, and certain pension adjustments. (*Accumulated other comprehensive income* is defined as the cumulative impact of *other comprehensive income.*)

Comprehensive income is reported in financial statements in one of two ways (which reflects new FASB guidance):

1. On a separate *statement of comprehensive income* that immediately follows the income statement.
2. On the lower section of the income statement (as a single continuous *statement of income and comprehensive income*).

Option 1 is the most common. Google, for example, reports a statement of comprehensive income following its income statement. Shown here is an abbreviated version of the Google statement:

GOOGLE

Net income	**$14,444**
Available-for-sale investments, net of tax	371
Foreign currency translation from consolidation	(996)
Cash flow hedges, net of tax.	527
Other comprehensive income	(98)
Total comprehensive income.	**$14,346**

Other comprehensive income

Option 2 adds the components of other comprehensive income to net income on the bottom of the income statement to compute a continuous statement of income and comprehensive income. There is no difference in the numbers; it is simply a matter of how those numbers are presented. A third option, which is no longer generally acceptable by itself, was to include the components of other comprehensive income and its total along with the total of comprehensive income in the statement of equity.

GLOBAL VIEW

This section discusses similarities and differences for the accounting and reporting of investments when financial statements are prepared under U.S. GAAP vis-à-vis IFRS.

Accounting for Noninfluential Securities   The accounting for noninfluential securities is broadly similar between U.S. GAAP and IFRS. *Trading securities* are accounted for using fair values with unrealized gains and losses reported in net income as fair values change. *Available-for-sale* *securities* are accounted for using fair values with unrealized gains and losses reported in other comprehensive income as fair values change (and later in net income when realized). *Held-to-maturity securities* are accounted for using amortized cost. Similarly, companies have the option under both systems to apply the fair value option for available-for-sale and held-to-maturity securities. Also, both systems review held-to-maturity securities for impairment. There are some differences in terminology under IFRS: (1) trading securities are commonly referred to as *financial assets at fair value through profit and loss* and (2) available-for-sale securities are commonly referred to as *available-for-sale financial assets.* NOKIA reports the following categories for noninfluential securities: (1) **Financial assets at fair value through profit or loss,** consisting of financial assets held for trading and financial assets designated upon initial recognition as at fair value through profit or loss, and (2) **Available-for-sale financial assets,** which are measured at fair value.

Accounting for Influential Securities

The accounting for influential securities is broadly similar across U.S. GAAP and IFRS. Specifically, under the *equity method,* the share of investee's net income is reported in the investor's income in the same period the investee earns that income; also, the investment account equals the acquisition cost plus the share of investee income less the share of investee dividends (minus amortization of excess on purchase price above fair value of identifiable, limited-life assets). Under the *consolidation method,* investee and investor revenues and expenses are combined, absent intercompany transactions, and subtracting noncontrolling interests. Also, nonintercompany assets and liabilities are similarly combined (eliminating the need for an investment account), and noncontrolling interests are subtracted from equity. There are some differences in terminology: (1) U.S. GAAP companies commonly refer to earnings from long-term investments as *equity in earnings of affiliates* whereas IFRS companies commonly use *equity in earnings of associated (or associate) companies* and (2) U.S. GAAP companies commonly refer to noncontrolling interests in consolidated subsidiaries as *minority interests* whereas IFRS companies commonly use *noncontrolling interests.*

 Decision Analysis 🟩🟨🟥   **Components of Return on Total Assets**

A1
Compute and analyze the components of return on total assets.

A company's **return on total assets** (or simply *return on assets*) is important in assessing financial performance. The return on total assets can be separated into two components, profit margin and total asset turnover, for additional analyses. Exhibit C.9 shows how these two components determine return on total assets.

EXHIBIT C.9

Components of Return on Total Assets

$$\text{Return on total assets} = \text{Profit margin} \times \text{Total asset turnover}$$

$$\frac{\text{Net income}}{\text{Average total assets}} = \frac{\text{Net income}}{\text{Net sales}} \times \frac{\text{Net sales}}{\text{Average total assets}}$$

Profit margin reflects the percent of net income in each dollar of net sales. Total asset turnover reflects a company's ability to produce net sales from total assets. All companies desire a high return on total assets. By considering these two components, we can often discover strengths and weaknesses not revealed by return on total assets alone. This improves our ability to assess future performance and company strategy.

To illustrate, consider return on total assets and its components for **Gap, Inc.**, in Exhibit C.10.

EXHIBIT C.10

Gap's Components of Return on Total Assets

Fiscal Year	Return on Total Assets	=	Profit Margin	×	Total Asset Turnover
2015	16.3%	=	7.7%	×	2.12
2014	16.7	=	7.9	×	2.11
2013*	15.0	=	7.3	×	2.06
2012	11.5	=	5.7	×	2.01
2011	16.0	=	8.2	×	1.95

* 2013 sales and income data scaled by 52/53 due to the 53-week year.

At least three findings emerge. First, Gap's return on total assets improved over the past few years from 11.5% in 2012 to 16.3% in 2015. Second, total asset turnover has improved over this period, from 1.95 to 2.12. Third, Gap's profit margin dipped in 2012, but it has otherwise stayed between 7.3% and 8.2%. These components reveal the dual role of profit margin and total asset turnover in determining return on total assets. They also reveal that the drivers of Gap's recent improvement in return on total assets are both total asset turnover and profit margin.

Generally, if a company is to maintain or improve its return on total assets, it must meet any decline in either profit margin or total asset turnover with an increase in the other. If not, return on assets will decline. Companies consider these components in planning strategies. A component analysis can also reveal where a company is weak and where changes are needed, especially in a competitor analysis. If asset turnover is lower than the industry norm, for instance, a company should focus on raising asset turnover at least to the norm. The same applies to profit margin.

■ Decision Maker

Retailer You are an entrepreneur and owner of a retail sporting goods store. The store's recent annual performance reveals (industry norms in parentheses): return on total assets = 11% (11.2%); profit margin = 4.4% (3.5%); and total asset turnover = 2.5 (3.2). What does your analysis of these figures reveal? ■ [Answers follow the appendix's Summary.]

The following transactions relate to Brown Company's long-term investments. Brown did not own any long-term investments prior to these transactions. Show (1) the necessary journal entries and (2) the relevant portions of each year's balance sheet and income statement that reflect these transactions for both years.

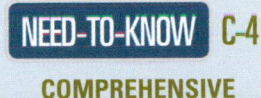

NEED-TO-KNOW C-4

COMPREHENSIVE

2015

Sept. 9 Purchased 1,000 shares of Packard, Inc., common stock for $80,000 cash. These shares represent 30% of Packard's outstanding shares.

Oct. 2 Purchased 2,000 shares of AT&T common stock for $60,000 cash as a long-term investment. These shares represent less than a 1% ownership in AT&T.

17 Purchased as a long-term investment 1,000 shares of Apple Computer common stock for $40,000 cash. These shares are less than 1% of Apple's outstanding shares.

Nov. 1 Received $5,000 cash dividend from Packard.

30 Received $3,000 cash dividend from AT&T.

Dec. 15 Received $1,400 cash dividend from Apple.

31 Packard's net income for this year is $70,000.

31 Fair values for the investments in equity securities are Packard, $84,000; AT&T, $48,000; and Apple Computer, $45,000.

31 For preparing financial statements, note the following post-closing account balances: Common Stock, $500,000, and Retained Earnings, $350,000.

2016

Jan. 1 Sold Packard, Inc., shares for $108,000 cash.

May 30 Received $3,100 cash dividend from AT&T.

June 15 Received $1,600 cash dividend from Apple.

Aug. 17 Sold the AT&T stock for $52,000 cash.

19 Purchased 2,000 shares of Coca-Cola common stock for $50,000 cash as a long-term investment. The stock represents less than a 5% ownership in Coca-Cola.

Dec. 15 Received $1,800 cash dividend from Apple.

31 Fair values of the investments in equity securities are Apple, $39,000, and Coca-Cola, $48,000.

31 For preparing financial statements, note the following post-closing account balances: Common Stock, $500,000, and Retained Earnings, $410,000.

PLANNING THE SOLUTION

● Account for the investment in Packard under the equity method.

● Account for the investments in AT&T, Apple, and Coca-Cola as long-term investments in available-for-sale securities.

- Prepare the information for the two years' balance sheets by including the relevant asset and equity accounts, and the two years' income statements by identifying the relevant revenues, earnings, gains, and losses.

SOLUTION

1. Journal entries for 2015.

Sept. 9	Long-Term Investments—Packard.................	80,000	
	Cash		80,000
	Acquired 1,000 shares, representing a 30% equity in Packard.		
Oct. 2	Long-Term Investments—AFS (AT&T)	60,000	
	Cash		60,000
	Acquired 2,000 shares as a long-term investment in available-for-sale securities.		
Oct. 17	Long-Term Investments—AFS (Apple)	40,000	
	Cash		40,000
	Acquired 1,000 shares as a long-term investment in available-for-sale securities.		
Nov. 1	Cash	5,000	
	Long-Term Investments—Packard.............		5,000
	Received dividend from Packard.		
Nov. 30	Cash	3,000	
	Dividend Revenue......................		3,000
	Received dividend from AT&T.		
Dec. 15	Cash	1,400	
	Dividend Revenue......................		1,400
	Received dividend from Apple.		
Dec. 31	Long-Term Investments—Packard.................	21,000	
	Earnings from Investment (Packard)		21,000
	Record 30% share of Packard's annual earnings of $70,000.		
Dec. 31	Unrealized Loss—Equity	7,000	
	Fair Value Adjustment—Available-for-Sale (LT)*....		7,000
	Record change in fair value of long-term available-for-sale securities.		

LT Investments–AFS

1/1/2015	0
10/2/2015	60,000
10/17/2015	40,000
12/31/2015	100,000

Fair Value Adj.–AFS (LT)

1/1/2015	0
Adj.	**7,000**
12/31/2015	7,000

* Fair value adjustment computations:

	Cost	Fair Value	Unrealized Gain (Loss)
AT&T	$ 60,000	$48,000	$(12,000)
Apple	40,000	45,000	5,000
Total	$100,000	$93,000	$ (7,000)

Required balance of the Fair Value Adjustment—Available-for-Sale (LT) account (credit)	$(7,000)
Existing balance	0
Necessary adjustment (credit)	$(7,000)

2. The December 31, 2015, selected balance sheet items appear as follows.

Assets	
Long-term investments	
Available-for-sale securities (at fair value; cost is $100,000)	$ 93,000
Investment in equity securities	96,000
Total long-term investments.................................	189,000
Stockholders' Equity	
Common stock	500,000
Retained earnings...	350,000
Unrealized loss—Equity	(7,000)

The relevant income statement items for the year ended December 31, 2015, follow.

Dividend revenue..	$ 4,400
Earnings from investment	21,000

1. Journal entries for 2016.

Date	Account	Debit	Credit
Jan. 1	Cash	108,000	
	Long-Term Investments—Packard..............		96,000
	Gain on Sale of Long-Term Investments		12,000
	Sold 1,000 shares for cash.		
May 30	Cash	3,100	
	Dividend Revenue..........................		3,100
	Received dividend from AT&T.		
June 15	Cash	1,600	
	Dividend Revenue..........................		1,600
	Received dividend from Apple.		
Aug. 17	Cash	52,000	
	Loss on Sale of Long-Term Investments	8,000	
	Long-Term Investments—AFS (AT&T)		60,000
	Sold 2,000 shares for cash.		
Aug. 19	Long-Term Investments—AFS (Coca-Cola)	50,000	
	Cash		50,000
	Acquired 2,000 shares as a long-term investment in available-for-sale securities.		
Dec. 15	Cash	1,800	
	Dividend Revenue..........................		1,800
	Received dividend from Apple.		
Dec. 31	Fair Value Adjustment—Available-for-Sale (LT)*........	4,000	
	Unrealized Loss—Equity		4,000
	Record change in fair value of long-term available-for-sale securities.		

LT Investments–AFS

1/1/2016	100,000		
		8/17/2016	60,000
8/19/2016	50,000		
12/31/2016	90,000		

Fair Value Adj.–AFS (LT)

		1/1/2016	7,000
Adj.	**4,000**		
		12/31/2016	3,000

* Fair value adjustment computations:

	Cost	Fair Value	Unrealized Gain (Loss)
Apple	$40,000	$39,000	$(1,000)
Coca-Cola	50,000	48,000	(2,000)
Total	$90,000	$87,000	$(3,000)

Required balance of the Fair Value Adjustment—Available-for-Sale (LT) account (credit)	$(3,000)
Existing balance (credit)	(7,000)
Necessary adjustment (debit)	$ 4,000

2. The December 31, 2016, balance sheet items appear as follows.

Assets	
Long-term investments	
Available-for-sale securities (at fair value; cost is $90,000)	$ 87,000
Stockholders' Equity	
Common stock	500,000
Retained earnings	410,000
Unrealized loss—Equity	(3,000)

The relevant income statement items for the year ended December 31, 2016, follow.

Dividend revenue..	$ 6,500
Gain on sale of long-term investments........................	12,000
Loss on sale of long-term investments........................	(8,000)

C-A   Investments in International Operations

Many entities from small entrepreneurs to large corporations conduct business internationally. Some entities' operations occur in so many different countries that the companies are called **multinationals.** Many of us think of **Coca-Cola** and **McDonald's,** for example, as primarily U.S. companies, but most of their sales occur outside the United States. Exhibit C-A.1 shows the percent of international sales and income for selected U.S. companies. Managing and accounting for multinationals present challenges. This section describes some of these challenges and how to account for and report these activities.

Two major accounting challenges that arise when companies have international operations relate to transactions that involve more than one currency. The first is to account for sales and purchases listed in a foreign currency. The second is to prepare consolidated financial statements with international subsidiaries. For ease in this discussion, we use companies with a U.S. base of operations and assume the need to prepare financial statements in U.S. dollars. This means the *reporting currency* of these companies is the U.S. dollar.

EXHIBIT C-A.1

International Sales and Income as a Percent of Their Totals

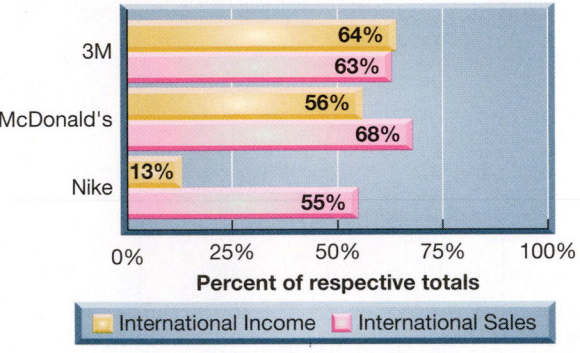

Point: Transactions *listed* or *stated* in a foreign currency are said to be *denominated* in that currency.

C3

Explain foreign exchange rates and record transactions listed in a foreign currency.

Point: To convert currency, see XE.com.

Exchange Rates between Currencies   Markets for the purchase and sale of foreign currencies exist all over the world. In these markets, U.S. dollars can be exchanged for Canadian dollars, British pounds, Japanese yen, euros, or any other legal currencies. The price of one currency stated in terms of another currency is called a **foreign exchange rate.** Exhibit C-A.2 lists recent exchange rates for selected currencies. The exchange rate for British pounds and U.S. dollars is $1.5506, meaning 1 British pound could be purchased for $1.5506. On that same day, the exchange rate between Mexican pesos and U.S. dollars is $0.0615, meaning 1 Mexican peso can be purchased for $0.0615. Exchange rates fluctuate due to changing economic and political conditions, including the supply and demand for currencies and expectations about future events.

EXHIBIT C-A.2

Foreign Exchange Rates for Selected Currencies*

Source (unit)	Price in $U.S.	Source (unit)	Price in $U.S.
Britain (pound)	$1.5506	Canada (dollar).........	$0.7653
Mexico (peso)	0.0615	Japan (yen)	0.0081
Taiwan (dollar).........	0.0318	Europe (euro)..........	1.0977

* Rates will vary over time based on economic, political, and other changes.

Decision Insight

Greek Haircut   Investors in government debt securities in the eurozone are wary of the heightened default risk with securities issued by certain eurozone member nations. For example, buyers of certain Greek bonds were repaid only 30% of principal because of the government's inability to honor its full obligation on the bonds. ■

Glow Images

Sales and Purchases Listed in a Foreign Currency   When a U.S. company makes a credit sale to an international customer, accounting for the sale and the account receivable is straightforward if sales terms require the international customer's payment in U.S. dollars. If sale terms require (or allow) payment in a foreign currency, however, the U.S. company must account for the sale and the account receivable in a different manner.

Sales in a Foreign Currency   To illustrate, consider the case of the U.S.-based manufacturer Boston Company, which makes credit sales to London Outfitters, a British retail company. A sale occurs on December 12, 2015, for a price of £10,000 with payment due on February 10, 2016. Boston Company keeps its accounting records in U.S. dollars. To record the sale, Boston Company must translate the sales price from pounds to dollars. This is done using the exchange rate on the date of the sale. Assuming the exchange rate on December 12, 2015, is $1.80, Boston records this sale as follows.

Dec. 12	Accounts Receivable—London Outfitters	18,000	
	Sales*		18,000
	*Record a sale at £10,000 when the exchange rate equals $1.80. * (£10,000 × $1.80/£)*		

Assets = Liabilities + Equity
+18,000   +18,000

When Boston Company prepares its annual financial statements on December 31, 2015, the current exchange rate is $1.84. Thus, the current dollar value of Boston Company's receivable is $18,400 (£10,000 × $1.84/£). This amount is $400 higher than the amount recorded on December 12. Accounting principles require a receivable to be reported in the balance sheet at its current dollar value. Thus, Boston Company must make the following entry to record the increase in the dollar value of this receivable at year-end.

Dec. 31	Accounts Receivable—London Outfitters	400	
	Foreign Exchange Gain.......................		400
	Record increased value of British pound for the receivable.		

Assets = Liabilities + Equity
+400   +400

On February 10, 2016, Boston Company receives London Outfitters's payment of £10,000. It immediately exchanges the pounds for U.S. dollars. On this date, the exchange rate for pounds is $1.78. Thus, Boston Company receives only $17,800 (£10,000 × $1.78/£). It records the cash receipt and the loss associated with the decline in the exchange rate as follows.

Point: Foreign exchange gains are credits, and foreign exchange losses are debits.

Feb. 10	Cash	17,800	
	Foreign Exchange Loss...........................	600	
	Accounts Receivable—London Outfitters		18,400
	Received foreign currency payment of an account and converted it to dollars.		

Assets = Liabilities + Equity
+17,800   −600
−18,400

Gains and losses from foreign exchange transactions are accumulated in the Foreign Exchange Gain (or Loss) account. After year-end adjustments, the balance in the Foreign Exchange Gain (or Loss) account is reported on the income statement and closed to the Income Summary account.

Purchases in a Foreign Currency   Accounting for credit purchases from an international seller is similar to the case of a credit sale to an international customer. In particular, if the U.S. company is required to make payment in a foreign currency, the account payable must be translated into dollars before the U.S. company can record it. If the exchange rate is different when preparing financial statements and when paying for the purchase, the U.S. company must recognize a foreign exchange gain or loss at those dates. To illustrate, assume NC Imports, a U.S. company, purchases products costing €20,000 (euros) from Hamburg Brewing on January 15, when the exchange rate is $1.20 per euro. NC records this transaction as follows.

Example: Assume that a U.S. company makes a credit purchase from a British company for £10,000 when the exchange rate is $1.62. At the balance sheet date, this rate is $1.72. Does this imply a gain or loss for the U.S. company? *Answer:* A loss.

Jan. 15	Inventory	24,000	
	Accounts Payable—Hamburg Brewing		24,000
	Record a €20,000 purchase when exchange rate is $1.20 (€20,000 × $1.20/€).		

Assets = Liabilities + Equity
+24,000   +24,000

NC Imports makes payment in full on February 14 when the exchange rate is $1.25 per euro, which is recorded as follows.

Feb. 14	Accounts Payable—Hamburg Brewing	24,000	
	Foreign Exchange Loss.........................	1,000	
	Cash		25,000
	Record cash payment toward €20,000 account when exchange rate is $1.25 (€20,000 × $1.25/€).		

Assets = Liabilities + Equity
−25,000   −24,000   −1,000

▮ Decision Insight

Global Greenback   What do changes in foreign exchange rates mean? A decline in the price of the U.S. dollar against other currencies usually yields increased international sales for U.S. companies, without hiking prices or cutting costs, and puts them on a stronger competitive footing abroad. At home, they can raise prices without fear that foreign rivals will undercut them. ▪

Consolidated Statements with International Subsidiaries

A second challenge in accounting for international operations involves preparing consolidated financial statements when the parent company has one or more international subsidiaries. Consider a U.S.-based company that owns a controlling interest in a French subsidiary. The reporting currency of the U.S. parent is the dollar. The French subsidiary maintains its financial records in euros. Before preparing consolidated statements, the parent must translate financial statements of the French company into U.S. dollars. After this translation is complete (including that for accounting differences), it prepares consolidated statements the same as for domestic subsidiaries. Procedures for translating an international subsidiary's account balances depend on the nature of the subsidiary's operations. The process requires the parent company to select appropriate foreign exchange rates and to apply those rates to the foreign subsidiary's account balances, and report the change as a component of other comprehensive income. This is described in advanced courses.

▮ Decision Maker

Entrepreneur   Assume that **Ben & Jerry's** purchases milk from dairies in both the U.S. and Canada. The price of the Canadian dollar in terms of the U.S. dollar jumps from US$0.70 to US$0.80. Is the ice cream maker now more or less likely to buy milk from Canadian or U.S. suppliers? ▪   [Answers follow the appendix's Summary.]

Summary

C1   Distinguish between debt and equity securities and between short-term and long-term investments. *Debt securities* reflect a creditor relationship and include investments in notes, bonds, and certificates of deposit. *Equity securities* reflect an owner relationship and include shares of stock issued by other companies. Short-term investments in securities are current assets that meet two criteria: (1) They are expected to be converted into cash within one year or the current operating cycle of the business, whichever is longer, and (2) they are readily convertible to cash, or *marketable*. All other investments in securities are long term. Long-term investments also include assets not used in operations and those held for special purposes, such as land for expansion. Investments in securities are classified into one of five groups: (1) trading securities, which are always short-term; (2) debt securities held-to-maturity; (3) debt and equity securities available-for-sale; (4) equity securities in which an investor has a significant influence over the investee; and (5) equity securities in which an investor has a controlling influence over the investee.

C2   Describe how to report equity securities with controlling influence. If an investor owns more than 50% of another company's voting stock and controls the investee, the investor's financial reports are prepared on a consolidated basis. These reports are prepared as if the company were organized as one entity.

C3ᴬ   Explain foreign exchange rates and record transactions listed in a foreign currency. A foreign exchange rate is the price of one currency stated in terms of another. An entity with transactions in a foreign currency when the exchange rate changes between the transaction dates and their settlement will experience exchange gains or losses. When a company makes a

credit sale to a foreign customer and sales terms call for payment in a foreign currency, the company must translate the foreign currency into dollars to record the receivable. If the exchange rate changes before payment is received, exchange gains or losses are recognized in the year they occur. The same treatment is used when a company makes a credit purchase from a foreign supplier and is required to make payment in a foreign currency.

A1   Compute and analyze the components of return on total assets. Return on total assets has two components: profit margin and total asset turnover. A decline in one component must be met with an increase in another if return on assets is to be maintained. Component analysis is helpful in assessing company performance compared to that of competitors and its own past.

P1   Account for trading securities. Investments are initially recorded at cost, and any dividend or interest from these investments is recorded in the income statement. Investments classified as trading securities are reported at fair value. Unrealized gains and losses on trading securities are reported in income. When investments are sold, the difference between the net proceeds from the sale and the cost of the securities is recognized as a gain or loss.

P2   Account for held-to-maturity securities. Debt securities held-to-maturity are reported at cost when purchased. Interest revenue is recorded as it accrues. The cost of long-term held-to-maturity securities is adjusted for the amortization of any difference between cost and maturity value.

P3   Account for available-for-sale securities. Debt and equity securities available-for-sale are recorded at cost when purchased. Available-for-sale securities are reported at their fair values on the balance sheet with unrealized gains or losses shown in the equity section. Gains and losses realized on the sale of these investments are reported in the income statement.

P4   **Account for equity securities with significant influence.**
The equity method is used when an investor has a significant influence over an investee. This usually exists when an

investor owns 20% or more of the investee's voting stock but not more than 50%. The equity method means an investor records its share of investee earnings with a debit to the investment account and a credit to a revenue account. Dividends received reduce the investment account balance.

Guidance Answers to Decision Maker

Money Manager   If you have investments in fixed-rate bonds and notes when interest rates fall, the value of your investments increases. This is so because the bonds and notes you hold continue to pay the same (high) rate while the market is demanding a new lower interest rate. Your strategy is to continue holding your investments in bonds and notes, and, potentially, to increase these holdings through additional purchases.

Retailer   Your store's return on assets is 11%, which is similar to the industry norm of 11.2%. However, disaggregation of return on assets reveals that your store's profit margin of 4.4% is much higher than the norm of 3.5%, but your total asset turnover of 2.5 is much lower than the norm of 3.2. These results suggest that, as compared with competitors, you are less efficient in using assets.

You need to focus on increasing sales or reducing assets. You might consider reducing prices to increase sales, provided such a strategy does not reduce your return on assets. For instance, you could reduce your profit margin to 4% to increase sales. If total asset turnover increases to more than 2.75 when profit margin is lowered to 4%, your overall return on assets is improved.

Entrepreneur   You are now less likely to buy Canadian milk products because it takes more U.S. money to buy a Canadian dollar (and milk). For instance, the purchase of milk from a Canadian dairy with a $1,000 (Canadian dollars) price would have cost the U.S. company $700 (U.S. dollars, computed as C$1,000 × US$0.70) before the rate change, and $800 (U.S. dollars, computed as C$1,000 × US$0.80) after the rate change.

Key Terms

Available-for-sale (AFS) securities	Equity securities with significant influence	Parent
Comprehensive income	Foreign exchange rate	Return on total assets
Consolidated financial statements	Held-to-maturity (HTM) securities	Short-term investments
Equity method	Long-term investments	Subsidiary
Equity securities with controlling influence	Multinational	Trading securities
	Other comprehensive income	Unrealized gain (loss)

Multiple Choice Quiz   Answers at end of appendix

1. A company purchased $30,000 of 5% bonds for investment purposes on May 1. The bonds pay interest on February 1 and August 1. The amount of interest revenue accrued at December 31 (the company's year-end) is:
   a. $1,500   **c.** $1,000   **e.** $300
   b. $1,375   **d.** $625

2. Earlier this period, Amadeus Co. purchased its only available-for-sale investment in the stock of Bach Co. for $83,000. The period-end fair value of this stock is $84,500. Amadeus records a:
   a. Credit to Unrealized Gain—Equity for $1,500.
   b. Debit to Unrealized Loss—Equity for $1,500.
   c. Debit to Investment Revenue for $1,500.
   d. Credit to Fair Value Adjustment—Available-for-Sale for $3,500.
   e. Credit to Cash for $1,500.

3. Mozart Co. owns 35% of Melody Inc. Melody pays $50,000 in cash dividends to its shareholders for the period. Mozart's entry to record the Melody dividend includes a:
   a. Credit to Investment Revenue for $50,000.
   b. Credit to Long-Term Investments for $17,500.

   c. Credit to Cash for $17,500.
   d. Debit to Long-Term Investments for $17,500.
   e. Debit to Cash for $50,000.

4. A company has net income of $300,000, net sales of $2,500,000, and total assets of $2,000,000. Its return on total assets equals:
   a. 6.7%   **c.** 8.3%   **e.** 15.0%
   b. 12.0%   **d.** 80.0%

5. A company had net income of $80,000, net sales of $600,000, and total assets of $400,000. Its profit margin and total asset turnover are:

	Profit Margin	Total Asset Turnover
a.	1.5%	13.3
b.	13.3%	1.5
c.	13.3%	0.7
d.	7.0%	13.3
e.	10.0%	26.7

^A *Superscript A denotes assignments based on Appendix C-A.*

Icon denotes assignments that involve decision making.

Discussion Questions

1. Under what two conditions should investments be classified as current assets?

2. On a balance sheet, what valuation must be reported for short-term investments in trading securities?

3. If a short-term investment in available-for-sale securities costs $10,000 and is sold for $12,000, how should the difference between these two amounts be recorded?

4. Identify the three classes of noninfluential and two classes of influential investments in securities.

5. Under what conditions should investments be classified as current assets? As long-term assets?

6. For investments in available-for-sale securities, how are unrealized (holding) gains and losses reported?

7. If a company purchases its only long-term investments in available-for-sale debt securities this period and their fair value is below cost at the balance sheet date, what entry is required to recognize this unrealized loss?

8. On a balance sheet, what valuation must be reported for debt securities classified as available-for-sale?

9. Under what circumstances are long-term investments in debt securities reported at cost and adjusted for amortization of any difference between cost and maturity value?

10. In accounting for investments in equity securities, when should the equity method be used?

11. Under what circumstances does a company prepare consolidated financial statements?

12.^A Assume a U.S. company makes a credit sale to a foreign customer that is required to make payment in its foreign currency. In the current period, the exchange rate is $1.40 on the date of the sale and $1.30 on the date the customer pays the receivable. Will the U.S. company record an exchange gain or loss?

13.^A What are two major challenges in accounting for international operations?

14.^A If a U.S. company makes a credit sale to a foreign customer required to make payment in U.S. dollars, can the U.S. company have an exchange gain or loss on this sale?

15. Refer to **Apple**'s statement of comprehensive income in Appendix A. What is the amount of foreign currency translation adjustment for the year ended September 27, 2014? Is this adjustment an unrealized gain or an unrealized loss? **APPLE**

16. Refer to **Google**'s statement of comprehensive income in Appendix A. What was the amount of its 2014 *change in net unrealized gains* for its AFS investments? **GOOGLE**

17. Refer to the income statement of **Samsung** in Appendix A. How can you tell that it uses the consolidated method of accounting? **Samsung**

connect

QUICK STUDY

QS C-1

Distinguishing between short- and long-term investments

C1

Which of the following statements *a* through *g* are true of long-term investments?

_____ **a.** They are held as an investment of cash available for current operations.

_____ **b.** They can include funds earmarked for a special purpose, such as bond sinking funds.

_____ **c.** They can include investments in trading securities.

_____ **d.** They can include debt securities held-to-maturity.

_____ **e.** They are always easily sold and therefore qualify as being marketable.

_____ **f.** They can include debt and equity securities available-for-sale.

_____ **g.** They can include bonds and stocks not intended to serve as a ready source of cash.

QS C-2

Distinguishing between debt and equity securities

C1

A solar company invests in the following securities. Identify those investments as an investment in either debt (D) securities or equity (E) securities.

_____ **a.** U.S. treasury bonds   _____ **e.** IBM corporate notes   _____ **i.** Chicago municipal bonds

_____ **b.** Google stock   _____ **f.** German government bonds   _____ **j.** Apple stock

_____ **c.** Certificate of deposit   _____ **g.** Amazon stock   _____ **k.** David Bowie bonds

_____ **d.** Apple bonds   _____ **h.** Costco corporate notes   _____ **l.** Facebook stock

QS C-3

Short-term equity investments   P1

On April 18, Riley Co. made a short-term investment in 300 common shares of XLT Co. The purchase price is $42 per share and the broker's fee is $250. The intent is to actively manage these shares for profit. On May 30, Riley Co. receives $1 per share from XLT in dividends. Prepare the April 18 and May 30 journal entries to record these transactions.

Prepare Hertog Company's journal entries to reflect the following transactions for the current year.

May 7   Purchases 200 shares of Kraft stock as a short-term investment in trading securities at a cost of $50 per share plus $300 in broker fees.

June 6   Sells 200 shares of its investment in Kraft stock at $56 per share. The broker's commission on this sale is $150.

QS C-4
Recording trading securities
P1

Kitty Company began operations in 2015 and maintains short-term investments in trading securities. The year-end cost and fair values for its portfolio of these investments follow. Prepare journal entries to record each December 31 year-end fair value adjustment for these securities.

Portfolio of Trading Securities	Cost	Fair Value
December 31, 2015.....................	$37	$35
December 31, 2016.....................	42	46
December 31, 2017.....................	60	69
December 31, 2018.....................	56	55

QS C-5
Multiyear fair value adjustments to trading securities
P1

On February 1, 2016, Garzon purchased 6% bonds issued by PBS Utilities at a cost of $40,000, which is their par value. The bonds pay interest semiannually on July 31 and January 31. For 2016, prepare entries to record Garzon's July 31 receipt of interest and its December 31 year-end interest accrual.

QS C-6
Debt securities transactions   **P2**

Derr Co. purchased short-term investments in available-for-sale securities at a cost of $50,000 on November 25, 2016. At December 31, 2016, these securities had a fair value of $47,000. This is the first and only time the company has purchased such securities.

1. Prepare the December 31, 2016, year-end adjusting entry for the securities' portfolio.
2. For each account in the entry for part 1, explain how it is reported in financial statements.
3. Prepare the April 6, 2017, entry when Derr sells one-half of these securities for $26,000.

QS C-7
Available-for-sale securities
P3

Riker Company completes the following transactions during the current year. Prepare the May 9 and June 2 journal entries and the December 31 adjusting entry. This is the first and only time the company purchased such securities.

May 9   Purchases 200 shares of Higo stock as a short-term investment in available-for-sale securities at a cost of $25 per share plus $150 in broker fees.

June 2   Sells 100 shares of its investment in Higo stock at $28 per share. The broker's commission on this sale is $90.

Dec. 31   The closing market price (fair value) of the Higo stock is $23 per share.

QS C-8
Available-for-sale securities
P3

During the current year, Reed Consulting Group acquired long-term available-for-sale securities at a $70,000 cost. At its December 31 year-end, these securities had a fair value of $58,000. This is the first and only time the company purchased such securities.

1. Prepare the necessary year-end adjusting entry related to these securities.
2. Explain how each account used in part 1 is reported in the financial statements.

QS C-9
Recording fair value adjustment for securities
P3

On May 20, 2016, Monte Co. paid $1,000,000 to acquire 25,000 common shares (10%) of ORD Corp. as a long-term investment. On August 5, 2017, Monte sold one-half of these shares for $625,000. What valuation method should be used to account for this stock investment? Prepare entries to record both the acquisition and the sale of these shares.

QS C-10
Recording long-term equity securities   **P3**

Monte Co. holds 100,000 common shares (40%) of ORD Corp. as a long-term investment. ORD Corp. paid a $100,000 dividend on November 1, 2016, and reported a net income of $700,000 for 2016. Prepare Monte's entries to record (a) the receipt of the dividend and (b) the December 31, 2016, year-end adjustment required for the investment account.

QS C-11
Equity method transactions   **P4**

QS C-12

Describing investments
in securities

C2

Complete the following descriptions by filling in the blanks.

1. Equity securities giving an investor significant influence are accounted for using the _____ _____.

2. Available-for-sale debt securities are reported on the balance sheet at _____ _____.

3. Trading securities are classified as _____ assets.

4. Accrual of interest on bonds held as long-term investments requires a credit to _____.

5. The controlling investor (more than 50% ownership) is called the _____, and the investee company is called the _____.

QS C-13

Equity securities with
controlling influence

C2

Complete the following descriptions by filling in the blanks.

1. The controlling investor is called the _____, and the investee is called the _____.

2. A long-term investment classified as equity securities with controlling influence implies that the investor can exert a _____ influence over the investee.

QS C-14

Return on total assets

A1

The return on total assets is the focus of analysts, creditors, and other users of financial statements.

1. How is the return on total assets computed?

2. What does this important ratio reflect?

QS C-15

Component return on
total assets   **A1**

Return on total assets can be separated into two important components.

1. Write the formula to separate the return on total assets into its two basic components.

2. Explain how these components of the return on total assets are helpful to financial statement users for business decisions.

QS C-16^A

Foreign currency
transactions   **C3**

A U.S. company sells a product to a British company with the transaction listed in British pounds. On the date of the sale, the transaction total of $14,500 is billed as £10,000, reflecting an exchange rate of 1.45 (that is, $1.45 per pound). Prepare the U.S. company's entry to record (1) the sale and (2) the receipt of payment in pounds when the exchange rate is 1.35.

QS C-17^A

Foreign currency
transactions   **C3**

On March 1, 2016, a U.S. company made a credit sale requiring payment in 30 days from a Malaysian company, Hamac Sdn. Bhd., of 20,000 Malaysian ringgits. Assuming the exchange rate between Malaysian ringgits and U.S. dollars is $0.4538 on March 1 and $0.4899 on March 31, prepare the U.S. company's entries to record the sale on March 1 and the cash receipt on March 31.

QS C-18

International accounting
for investments

P1

The **Carrefour Group** reports the following description of its trading securities (titled "financial assets reported at fair value in the income statement").

> These are financial assets held by the Group in order to make a short-term profit on the sale. These assets are valued at their fair value with variations in value recognized in the income statement.

Carrefour's financial statements report €7 million in unrealized gains and €26 million in unrealized losses, both included in the fair value of those financial assets held for trading. What amount of these unrealized gains and unrealized losses, if any, are reported in its income statement? Explain.

Mc Graw Hill connect®

EXERCISES

Exercise C-1

Debt and equity
securities and short- and
long-term investments

C1

Complete the following descriptions by filling in the blanks.

1. Debt securities reflect a _____ relationship such as investments in notes, bonds, and certificates of deposit.

2. Equity securities reflect an _____ relationship such as shares of stock issued by companies.

3. Short-term investments are securities that (1) management intends to convert to cash within _____ or the _____, whichever is longer, and (2) are readily convertible to _____.

4. Long-term investments in securities are defined as those securities that are _____ convertible to cash or are _____ to be converted into cash in the short term.

Prepare journal entries to record the following transactions involving the short-term securities investments of Duke Co., all of which occurred during year 2016.

a. On March 22, purchased 1,000 shares of RIP Company stock at $10 per share plus an $80 brokerage fee. These shares are categorized as trading securities.

b. On September 1, received a $1.00 per share cash dividend on the RIP Company stock purchased in transaction *a*.

c. On October 8, sold 500 shares of RIP Co. stock for $15 per share, less a $50 brokerage fee.

Exercise C-2
Accounting for short-term trading securities
P1

(c) Dr. Cash $7,450

Brooks Co. purchases various investments in trading securities at a cost of $66,000 on December 27, 2016. (This is its first and only purchase of such securities.) At December 31, 2016, these securities had a fair value of $72,000.

1. Prepare the December 31, 2016, year-end adjusting entry for the trading securities' portfolio.

2. Explain how each account in the entry of part 1 is reported in financial statements.

3. Prepare the January 3, 2017, entry when Brooks sells a portion of its trading securities (that had originally cost $33,000) for $35,000.

Exercise C-3
Accounting for trading securities
P1

Check   (3) Gain, $2,000

Prepare journal entries to record the following transactions involving the short-term securities investments of Natura Co., all of which occurred during year 2016.

a. On June 15, paid $1,000,000 cash to purchase Remedy's 90-day short-term debt securities ($1,000,000 principal), dated June 15, that pay 10% interest (categorized as held-to-maturity securities).

b. On September 16, received a check from Remedy in payment of the principal and 90 days' interest on the debt securities purchased in transaction *a*.

Exercise C-4
Accounting for short-term held-to-maturity securities
P2

Prepare journal entries to record the following transactions involving the short-term securities investments of Krum Co., all of which occurred during year 2016.

a. On August 1, paid $450,000 cash to purchase Houtte's 9% debt securities ($450,000 principal), dated July 30, 2016, and maturing January 30, 2017 (categorized as available-for-sale securities).

b. On October 30, received a check from Houtte for 90 days' interest on the debt securities purchased in transaction *a*.

Exercise C-5
Accounting for short-term available-for-sale securities
P3

Prepare journal entries to record the following transactions involving both the short-term and long-term investments of Cancun Corp., all of which occurred during calendar-year 2016. Use the account Short-Term Investments for any transactions that you determine are short term.

a. On February 15, paid $160,000 cash to purchase AG's 90-day short-term notes at par, which are dated February 15 and pay 10% interest (classified as held-to-maturity).

b. On March 22, bought 700 shares of Fran Industries common stock at $51 cash per share plus a $150 brokerage fee (classified as long-term available-for-sale securities).

c. On May 15, received a check from AG in payment of the principal and 90 days' interest on the notes purchased in transaction *a*.

d. On July 30, paid $100,000 cash to purchase MP3 Electronics's 8% notes at par, dated July 30, 2016, and maturing on January 30, 2017 (classified as trading securities).

e. On September 1, received a $1.00 per share cash dividend on the Fran Industries common stock purchased in transaction *b*.

f. On October 8, sold 350 shares of Fran Industries common stock for $64 cash per share, less a $125 brokerage fee.

g. On October 30, received a check from MP3 Electronics for three months' interest on the notes purchased in transaction *d*.

Exercise C-6
Transactions in short-term and long-term investments
P1   P2   P3

On December 31, 2016, Reggit Company held the following short-term investments in its portfolio of available-for-sale securities. Reggit had no short-term investments in its prior accounting periods. Prepare the December 31, 2016, adjusting entry to report these investments at fair value.

Exercise C-7
Adjusting available-for-sale securities to fair value
P3

Available-for-Sale Securities	Cost	Fair Value
Verrizano Corporation bonds payable	$89,600	$91,600
Preble Corporation notes payable	70,600	62,900
Lucerne Company common stock	86,500	83,100

Check   Unrealized loss, $9,100

Exercise C-8

Fair value adjustment
to available-for-sale
securities

P3

On December 31, 2016, Lujack Co. held the following short-term available-for-sale securities. Lujack had no short-term investments prior to the current period. Prepare the December 31, 2016, year-end adjusting entry to record the fair value adjustment for these securities.

Available-for-Sale Securities	Cost	Fair Value
Nintendo Co. common stock	$44,450	$48,900
Atlantic bonds payable	49,000	47,000
Kellogg Co. notes payable	25,000	23,200
McDonald's Corp. common stock	46,300	44,800

Exercise C-9

Fair value adjustment
to available-for-sale
securities

P3

Prescrip Co. began operations in 2015. The costs and fair values for its long-term investments portfolio in available-for-sale securities are shown below. Prepare Prescrip's December 31, 2016, adjusting entry to reflect any necessary fair value adjustment for these investments.

Portfolio of Available-for-Sale Securities	Cost	Fair Value
December 31, 2015	$120,483	$118,556
December 31, 2016	60,120	90,271

Exercise C-10

Multiyear fair value
adjustments to available-
for-sale securities

P3

Ticker Services began operations in 2014 and maintains long-term investments in available-for-sale securities. The year-end costs and fair values for its portfolio of these investments follow. Prepare journal entries to record each year-end fair value adjustment for these securities.

Portfolio of Available-for-Sale Securities	Cost	Fair Value
December 31, 2014	$372,000	$360,860
December 31, 2015	428,500	455,800
December 31, 2016	600,200	700,500
December 31, 2017	876,900	780,200

Exercise C-11

Classifying investments
in securities; recording
fair values

C1 P2 P3 P4

Information regarding Carperk Company's individual investments in securities during its calendar-year 2016, along with the December 31, 2016, fair values, follows.

a. Investment in Brava Company bonds: $420,500 cost, $457,000 fair value. Carperk intends to hold these bonds until they mature in 2021.

b. Investment in Baybridge common stock: 29,500 shares; $362,450 cost; $391,375 fair value. Carperk owns 32% of Baybridge's voting stock and has a significant influence over Baybridge.

c. Investment in Buffa common stock: 12,000 shares; $165,500 cost; $178,000 fair value. This investment amounts to 3% of Buffa's outstanding shares, and Carperk's goal with this investment is to earn dividends over the next few years.

d. Investment in Newton common stock: 3,500 shares; $90,300 cost; $88,625 fair value. Carperk's goal with this investment is to reap an increase in fair value of the stock over the next three to five years. Newton has 30,000 common shares outstanding.

e. Investment in Farmers common stock: 16,300 shares; $100,860 cost; $111,210 fair value. This stock is marketable and is held as an investment of cash available for operations.

Required

1. Identify whether each investment should be classified as a short-term or long-term investment. For each long-term investment, indicate in which of the long-term investment classifications it should be placed.

Check (2) Unrealized gain, $10,825

2. Prepare a journal entry dated December 31, 2016, to record the fair value adjustment of the long-term investments in available-for-sale securities. Carperk had no long-term investments prior to year 2016.

Prepare journal entries to record the following transactions and events of Kodax Company.

2016

Jan.   2   Purchased 30,000 shares of Grecco Co. common stock for $408,000 cash plus a broker's fee of $3,000 cash. Grecco has 90,000 shares of common stock outstanding and its policies will be significantly influenced by Kodax.
Sept. 1   Grecco declared and paid a cash dividend of $1.50 per share.
Dec. 31   Grecco announced that net income for the year is $486,900.

2017

June 1   Grecco declared and paid a cash dividend of $2.10 per share.
Dec. 31   Grecco announced that net income for the year is $702,750.
Dec. 31   Kodax sold 10,000 shares of Grecco for $320,000 cash.

Exercise C-12
Securities transactions; equity method
P4

Complete the following descriptions by filling in the blanks.

1. Consolidated _____ show the financial position, results of operations, and cash flows of all entities under the parent's control, including all subsidiaries.

2. The equity method with _____ is used to account for long-term investments in equity securities with controlling influence.

Exercise C-13
Equity securities with controlling influence
C2

The following information is available from the financial statements of Regae Industries. Compute Regae's return on total assets for 2016 and 2017. (Round returns to one-tenth of a percent.) Comment on the company's efficiency in using its assets in 2016 and 2017.

Exercise C-14
Return on total assets
A1

	A	B	C	D
1		**2015**	**2016**	**2017**
2	Total assets, December 31	$210,000	$340,000	$770,000
3	Net income	30,200	38,400	60,300
4				

Leigh of New York sells its products to customers in the United States and the United Kingdom. On December 16, 2016, Leigh sold merchandise on credit to Bronson Ltd. of London at a price of 17,000 pounds. The exchange rate on that day for £1 was $1.4583. On December 31, 2016, when Leigh prepared its financial statements, the rate was £1 for $1.4382. Bronson paid its bill in full on January 15, 2017, at which time the exchange rate was £1 for $1.4482. Leigh immediately exchanged the 17,000 pounds for U.S. dollars. Prepare Leigh's journal entries on December 16, December 31, and January 15 (round to the nearest dollar).

Exercise C-15ᴬ
Foreign currency transactions
C3

On May 8, 2016, Jett Company (a U.S. company) made a credit sale to Lopez (a Mexican company). The terms of the sale required Lopez to pay 800,000 pesos on February 10, 2017. Jett prepares quarterly financial statements on March 31, June 30, September 30, and December 31. The exchange rates for pesos during the time the receivable is outstanding follow.

Exercise C-16ᴬ
Computing foreign exchange gains and losses on receivables
C3

May 8, 2016	$0.1323
June 30, 2016	0.1352
September 30, 2016	0.1368
December 31, 2016	0.1335
February 10, 2017	0.1386

Compute the foreign exchange gain or loss that Jett should report on each of its quarterly income statements for the last three quarters of 2016 and the first quarter of 2017. Also compute the amount reported on Jett's balance sheets at the end of each of its last three quarters of 2016.

Exercise C-17
International accounting
for investments

P3

The **Carrefour Group** reports the following description of its financial assets available-for-sale.

> Assets available for sale are . . . valued at fair value. Unrealized . . . gains or losses are recorded as shareholders' equity until they are sold.

Carrefour's financial statements report €18 million in *net* unrealized losses (net of unrealized gains), which are included in the fair value of its available-for-sale securities reported on the balance sheet.

1. What amount of the €18 million net unrealized losses, if any, is reported in the income statement? Explain.

2. If the €18 million net unrealized losses are not reported in the income statement, in which statement are they reported, if any? Explain.

PROBLEM SET A

Problem C-1A
Recording transactions
and fair value
adjustments for trading
securities

P1

Carlsville Company, which began operations in 2016, invests its idle cash in trading securities. The following transactions are from its short-term investments in trading securities.

2016

Jan. 20	Purchased 800 shares of Ford Motor Co. at $26 per share plus a $125 commission.
Feb. 9	Purchased 2,200 shares of Loews at $44.25 per share plus a $578 commission.
Oct. 12	Purchased 750 shares of Z-Seven at $7.50 per share plus a $200 commission.
Dec. 31	Fair value of the short-term investments in trading securities is $130,000.

2017

Apr. 15	Sold 800 shares of Ford Motor Co. at $29 per share less a $285 commission.
July 5	Sold 750 shares of Z-Seven at $10.25 per share less a $102.50 commission.
July 22	Purchased 1,600 shares of Hunt Corp. at $30 per share plus a $444 commission.
Aug. 19	Purchased 1,800 shares of Donna Karan at $18.25 per share plus a $290 commission.
Dec. 31	Fair value of the short-term investments in trading securities is $160,000.

2018

Feb. 27	Purchased 3,400 shares of HCA at $34 per share plus a $420 commission.
Mar. 3	Sold 1,600 shares of Hunt at $25 per share less a $250 commission.
June 21	Sold 2,200 shares of Loews at $42 per share less a $420 commission.
June 30	Purchased 1,200 shares of Black & Decker at $47.50 per share plus a $595 commission.
Nov. 1	Sold 1,800 shares of Donna Karan at $18.25 per share less a $309 commission.
Dec. 31	Fair value of the short-term investments in trading securities is $180,000.

Required

Check Dec. 31, 2017
Cr. Fair Value Adjustment—
Trading $24,834

Prepare journal entries to record these short-term investment activities for the years shown. On December 31 of each year, prepare the adjusting entry to record any necessary fair value adjustment for the portfolio of trading securities.

Problem C-2A
Recording, adjusting,
and reporting short-term
available-for-sale
securities

P3

Rose Company had no short-term investments prior to year 2016. It had the following transactions involving short-term investments in available-for-sale securities during 2016.

Apr. 16	Purchased 4,000 shares of Gem Co. stock at $24.25 per share plus a $180 brokerage fee.
May 1	Paid $100,000 to buy 13-week U.S. Treasury bills (debt securities): $100,000 principal amount, 6% interest, securities dated May 1 and maturing July 31 with $1,500 in interest revenue.
July 7	Purchased 2,000 shares of PepsiCo stock at $49.25 per share plus a $175 brokerage fee.
20	Purchased 1,000 shares of Xerox stock at $16.75 per share plus a $205 brokerage fee.
31	Received a check for principal and accrued interest on the U.S. Treasury bills that matured on July 31.
Aug. 15	Received an $0.85 per share cash dividend on the Gem Co. stock.
28	Sold 2,000 shares of Gem Co. stock at $30 per share less a $225 brokerage fee.
Oct. 1	Received a $1.90 per share cash dividend on the PepsiCo shares.
Dec. 15	Received a $1.05 per share cash dividend on the remaining Gem Co. shares.
31	Received a $1.30 per share cash dividend on the PepsiCo shares.

Required

1. Prepare journal entries to record the preceding transactions and events.
2. Prepare a table to compare the year-end cost and fair values of Rose's short-term investments in available-for-sale securities. The year-end fair values per share are: Gem Co., $26.50; PepsiCo, $46.50; and Xerox, $13.75.
3. Prepare an adjusting entry, if necessary, to record the year-end fair value adjustment for the portfolio of short-term investments in available-for-sale securities.

Check   (2) Cost = $164,220

(3) Dr. Unrealized Loss—Equity $4,470

Analysis Component

4. Explain the balance sheet presentation of the fair value adjustment for Rose's short-term investments.
5. How do these short-term investments affect Rose's (*a*) income statement for year 2016 and (*b*) equity section of its balance sheet at year-end 2016?

Grass Security, which began operations in 2016, invests in long-term available-for-sale securities. Following is a series of transactions and events determining its long-term investment activity.

Problem C-3A
Recording, adjusting, and reporting long-term available-for-sale securities
P3

2016

Jan. 20   Purchased 1,000 shares of Johnson & Johnson at $20.50 per share plus a $240 commission.
Feb. 9   Purchased 1,200 shares of Sony at $46.20 per share plus a $225 commission.
June 12   Purchased 1,500 shares of Mattel at $27.00 per share plus a $195 commission.
Dec. 31   Per share fair values for stocks in the portfolio are: Johnson & Johnson, $21.50; Mattel, $30.90; Sony, $38.00.

2017

Apr. 15   Sold 1,000 shares of Johnson & Johnson at $23.50 per share less a $525 commission.
July 5   Sold 1,500 shares of Mattel at $23.90 per share less a $235 commission.
July 22   Purchased 600 shares of Sara Lee at $22.50 per share plus a $480 commission.
Aug. 19   Purchased 900 shares of Eastman Kodak at $17.00 per share plus a $198 commission.
Dec. 31   Per share fair values for stocks in the portfolio are: Kodak, $19.25; Sara Lee, $20.00; Sony, $35.00.

2018

Feb. 27   Purchased 2,400 shares of Microsoft at $67.00 per share plus a $525 commission.
June 21   Sold 1,200 shares of Sony at $48.00 per share less an $880 commission.
June 30   Purchased 1,400 shares of Black & Decker at $36.00 per share plus a $435 commission.
Aug. 3   Sold 600 shares of Sara Lee at $16.25 per share less a $435 commission.
Nov. 1   Sold 900 shares of Eastman Kodak at $22.75 per share less a $625 commission.
Dec. 31   Per share fair values for stocks in the portfolio are: Black & Decker, $39.00; Microsoft, $69.00.

Required

1. Prepare journal entries to record these transactions and events and any year-end fair value adjustments to the portfolio of long-term available-for-sale securities.
2. Prepare a table that summarizes the (*a*) total cost, (*b*) total fair value adjustment, and (*c*) total fair value of the portfolio of long-term available-for-sale securities at each year-end.
3. Prepare a table that summarizes (*a*) the realized gains and losses and (*b*) the unrealized gains or losses for the portfolio of long-term available-for-sale securities at each year-end.

Check   (2b) Fair Value Adj. bal.: 12/31/16, $3,650 Cr.; 12/31/17; $13,818 Cr.

(3b) Unrealized Gain at 12/31/2018, $8,040

Selk Steel Co., which began operations on January 4, 2016, had the following subsequent transactions and events in its long-term investments.

Problem C-4A
Accounting for long-term investments in securities; with and without significant influence
P3   P4

2016

Jan. 5   Selk purchased 60,000 shares (20% of total) of Kildaire's common stock for $1,560,000.
Oct. 23   Kildaire declared and paid a cash dividend of $3.20 per share.
Dec. 31   Kildaire's net income for 2016 is $1,164,000, and the fair value of its stock at December 31 is $30.00 per share.

2017

Oct. 15   Kildaire declared and paid a cash dividend of $2.60 per share.
Dec. 31   Kildaire's net income for 2017 is $1,476,000, and the fair value of its stock at December 31 is $32.00 per share.

2018

Jan.   2   Selk sold all of its investment in Kildaire for $1,894,000 cash.

Part 1

Assume that Selk has a significant influence over Kildaire with its 20% share of stock.

Required

1. Prepare journal entries to record these transactions and events for Selk.

Check   (2) Carrying value per share, $29

2. Compute the carrying (book) value per share of Selk's investment in Kildaire common stock as reflected in the investment account on January 1, 2018.

3. Compute the net increase or decrease in Selk's equity from January 5, 2016, through January 2, 2018, resulting from its investment in Kildaire.

Part 2

Assume that although Selk owns 20% of Kildaire's outstanding stock, circumstances indicate that it does not have a significant influence over the investee and that it is classified as an available-for-sale security investment.

Required

(1) 1/2/2018 Dr. Unrealized Gain—Equity, $360,000

1. Prepare journal entries to record the preceding transactions and events for Selk. Also prepare an entry dated January 2, 2018, to remove any balance related to the fair value adjustment.

2. Compute the cost per share of Selk's investment in Kildaire common stock as reflected in the investment account on January 1, 2018.

(3) Net increase, $682,000

3. Compute the net increase or decrease in Selk's equity from January 5, 2016, through January 2, 2018, resulting from its investment in Kildaire.

Problem C-5A

Long-term investment transactions; unrealized and realized gains and losses

C2   P3   P4

Stoll Co.'s long-term available-for-sale portfolio at December 31, 2015, consists of the following.

Available-for-Sale Securities	Cost	FairValue
40,000 shares of Company A common stock..........	$535,300	$490,000
7,000 shares of Company B common stock...........	159,380	154,000
17,500 shares of Company C common stock.........	662,750	640,938

Stoll enters into the following long-term investment transactions during year 2016.

Jan. 29   Sold 3,500 shares of Company B common stock for $79,188 less a brokerage fee of $1,500.
Apr. 17   Purchased 10,000 shares of Company W common stock for $197,500 plus a brokerage fee of $2,400. The shares represent a 30% ownership in Company W.
July   6   Purchased 4,500 shares of Company X common stock for $126,562 plus a brokerage fee of $1,750. The shares represent a 10% ownership in Company X.
Aug. 22   Purchased 50,000 shares of Company Y common stock for $375,000 plus a brokerage fee of $1,200. The shares represent a 51% ownership in Company Y.
Nov. 13   Purchased 8,500 shares of Company Z common stock for $267,900 plus a brokerage fee of $2,450. The shares represent a 5% ownership in Company Z.
Dec.   9   Sold 40,000 shares of Company A common stock for $515,000 less a brokerage fee of $4,100.

The fair values of its investments at December 31, 2016, are: B, $81,375; C, $610,312; W, $191,250; X, $118,125; Y, $531,250; and Z, $278,800.

Required

1. Determine the amount Stoll should report on its December 31, 2016, balance sheet for its long-term investments in available-for-sale securities.

Check   (2) Cr. Unrealized Loss—Equity, $20,002

2. Prepare any necessary December 31, 2016, adjusting entry to record the fair value adjustment for the long-term investments in available-for-sale securities.

3. What amount of gains or losses on transactions relating to long-term investments in available-for-sale securities should Stoll report on its December 31, 2016, income statement?

Doering Company, a U.S. corporation with customers in several foreign countries, had the following selected transactions for 2016 and 2017.

Problem C-6A
Foreign currency transactions
C3

2016

Apr.   8   Sold merchandise to Salinas & Sons of Mexico for $5,938 cash. The exchange rate for pesos is $0.1043 on this day.

July 21   Sold merchandise on credit to Sumito Corp. in Japan. The price of 1.5 million yen is to be paid 120 days from the date of sale. The exchange rate for yen is $0.0094 on this day.

Oct. 14   Sold merchandise for 19,000 pounds to Smithers Ltd. of Great Britain, payment in full to be received in 90 days. The exchange rate for pounds is $1.4566 on this day.

Nov. 18   Received Sumito's payment in yen for its July 21 purchase and immediately exchanged the yen for dollars. The exchange rate for yen is $0.0092 on this day.

Dec. 20   Sold merchandise for 17,000 ringgits to Hamid Albar of Malaysia, payment in full to be received in 30 days. On this day, the exchange rate for ringgits is $0.4501.

Dec. 31   Recorded adjusting entries to recognize exchange gains or losses on Doering's annual financial statements. Rates for exchanging foreign currencies on this day follow.

| Pesos (Mexico).......... | $0.1055 | Pounds (Britain).......... | $1.4620 |
| Yen (Japan)............. | 0.0093 | Ringgits (Malaysia) .... | 0.4456 |

2017

Jan. 12   Received full payment in pounds from Smithers for the October 14 sale and immediately exchanged the pounds for dollars. The exchange rate for pounds is $1.4699 on this day.

Jan. 19   Received Hamid Albar's full payment in ringgits for the December 20 sale and immediately exchanged the ringgits for dollars. The exchange rate for ringgits is $0.4420 on this day.

Required

1. Prepare journal entries for the Doering transactions and adjusting entries (round amounts to the nearest dollar).

2. Compute the foreign exchange gain or loss to be reported on Doering's 2016 income statement.

Check   (2) 2016 total foreign exchange loss, $274

Analysis Component

3. What actions might Doering consider to reduce its risk of foreign exchange gains or losses?

Harris Company, which began operations in 2016, invests its idle cash in trading securities. The following transactions relate to its short-term investments in its trading securities.

PROBLEM SET B

Problem C-1B
Recording transactions and fair value adjustments for trading securities
P1

2016

Mar. 10   Purchased 2,400 shares of AOL at $59.15 per share plus a $1,545 commission.
May   7   Purchased 5,000 shares of MTV at $36.25 per share plus a $2,855 commission.
Sept. 1   Purchased 1,200 shares of UPS at $57.25 per share plus a $1,250 commission.
Dec. 31   Fair value of the short-term investments in trading securities is $380,000.

2017

Apr. 26   Sold 5,000 shares of MTV at $34.50 per share less a $2,050 commission.
Apr. 27   Sold 1,200 shares of UPS at $60.50 per share less a $1,788 commission.
June   2   Purchased 3,600 shares of SPW at $172 per share plus a $3,250 commission.
June 14   Purchased 900 shares of Walmart at $50.25 per share plus a $1,082 commission.
Dec. 31   Fair value of the short-term investments in trading securities is $828,000.

2018

Jan. 28   Purchased 2,000 shares of PepsiCo at $43 per share plus a $2,890 commission.
Jan. 31   Sold 3,600 shares of SPW at $168 per share less a $2,040 commission.
Aug. 22   Sold 2,400 shares of AOL at $56.75 per share less a $2,480 commission.
Sept. 3   Purchased 1,500 shares of Vodaphone at $40.50 per share plus a $1,680 commission.
Oct.   9   Sold 900 shares of Walmart at $53.75 per share less a $1,220 commission.
Dec. 31   Fair value of the short-term investments in trading securities is $140,000.

Required

Prepare journal entries to record these short-term investment activities for the years shown. On December 31 of each year, prepare the adjusting entry to record any necessary fair value adjustment for the portfolio of trading securities.

Problem C-2B

Recording, adjusting, and reporting short-term available-for-sale securities

P3

Slip Systems had no short-term investments prior to 2016. It had the following transactions involving short-term investments in available-for-sale securities during 2016.

Feb.	6	Purchased 3,400 shares of Nokia stock at $41.25 per share plus a $3,000 brokerage fee.
	15	Paid $20,000 to buy six-month U.S. Treasury bills (debt securities): $20,000 principal amount, 6% interest, securities dated February 15.
Apr.	7	Purchased 1,200 shares of Dell Co. stock at $39.50 per share plus a $1,255 brokerage fee.
June	2	Purchased 2,500 shares of Merck stock at $72.50 per share plus a $2,890 brokerage fee.
	30	Received a $0.19 per share cash dividend on the Nokia shares.
Aug.	11	Sold 850 shares of Nokia stock at $46 per share less a $1,050 brokerage fee.
	16	Received a check for principal and accrued interest on the U.S. Treasury bills purchased February 15.
	24	Received a $0.10 per share cash dividend on the Dell shares.
Nov.	9	Received a $0.20 per share cash dividend on the remaining Nokia shares.
Dec.	18	Received a $0.15 per share cash dividend on the Dell shares.

Required

1. Prepare journal entries to record the preceding transactions and events.

2. Prepare a table to compare the year-end cost and fair values of the short-term investments in available-for-sale securities. The year-end fair values per share are: Nokia, $40.25; Dell, $40.50; and Merck, $59.

3. Prepare an adjusting entry, if necessary, to record the year-end fair value adjustment for the portfolio of short-term investments in available-for-sale securities.

Analysis Component

4. Explain the balance sheet presentation of the fair value adjustment to Slip's short-term investments.

5. How do these short-term investments affect (*a*) its income statement for year 2016 and (*b*) the equity section of its balance sheet at the 2016 year-end?

Problem C-3B

Recording, adjusting, and reporting long-term available-for-sale securities

P3

Paris Enterprises, which began operations in 2016, invests in long-term available-for-sale securities. Following is a series of transactions and events involving its long-term investment activity.

2016

Mar.	10	Purchased 1,200 shares of Apple at $25.50 per share plus $800 commission.
Apr.	7	Purchased 2,500 shares of Ford at $22.50 per share plus $1,033 commission.
Sept.	1	Purchased 600 shares of Polaroid at $47.00 per share plus $890 commission.
Dec.	31	Per share fair values for stocks in the portfolio are: Apple, $27.50; Ford, $21.00; Polaroid, $49.00.

2017

Apr.	26	Sold 2,500 shares of Ford at $20.50 per share less a $1,207 commission.
June	2	Purchased 1,800 shares of Duracell at $19.25 per share plus a $1,050 commission.
June	14	Purchased 1,200 shares of Sears at $21 per share plus a $280 commission.
Nov.	27	Sold 600 shares of Polaroid at $51 per share less an $845 commission.
Dec.	31	Per share fair values for stocks in the portfolio are: Apple, $29.00; Duracell, $18.00; Sears, $23.00.

2018

Jan.	28	Purchased 1,000 shares of Coca-Cola Co. at $40 per share plus a $1,480 commission.
Aug.	22	Sold 1,200 shares of Apple at $21.50 per share less a $1,850 commission.
Sept.	3	Purchased 3,000 shares of Motorola at $28 per share plus a $780 commission.
Oct.	9	Sold 1,200 shares of Sears at $24.00 per share less a $599 commission.
Oct.	31	Sold 1,800 shares of Duracell at $15.00 per share less an $898 commission.
Dec.	31	Per share fair values for stocks in the portfolio are: Coca-Cola, $48.00; Motorola, $24.00.

Required

1. Prepare journal entries to record these transactions and events and any year-end fair value adjustments to the portfolio of long-term available-for-sale securities.

2. Prepare a table that summarizes the (*a*) total cost, (*b*) total fair value adjustment, and (*c*) total fair value for the portfolio of long-term available-for-sale securities at each year-end.

3. Prepare a table that summarizes (*a*) the realized gains and losses and (*b*) the unrealized gains or losses for the portfolio of long-term available-for-sale securities at each year-end.

Check   (2b) Fair Value Adj. bal.: 12/31/16, $2,873 Cr.; 12/31/17, $2,220 Dr.

(3b) Unrealized Loss at 12/31/2018, $6,260

Brinkley Company, which began operations on January 3, 2016, had the following subsequent transactions and events in its long-term investments.

Problem C-4B
Accounting for long-term investments in securities; with and without significant influence
P3   P4

2016

Jan.   5   Brinkley purchased 20,000 shares (25% of total) of Bloch's common stock for $200,500.
Aug.   1   Bloch declared and paid a cash dividend of $1.05 per share.
Dec. 31   Bloch's net income for 2016 is $82,000, and the fair value of its stock is $11.90 per share.

2017

Aug.   1   Bloch declared and paid a cash dividend of $1.35 per share.
Dec. 31   Bloch's net income for 2017 is $78,000, and the fair value of its stock is $13.65 per share.

2018

Jan.   8   Brinkley sold all of its investment in Bloch for $375,000 cash.

Part 1
Assume that Brinkley has a significant influence over Bloch with its 25% share.

Required

1. Prepare journal entries to record these transactions and events for Brinkley.

2. Compute the carrying (book) value per share of Brinkley's investment in Bloch common stock as reflected in the investment account on January 7, 2018.

3. Compute the net increase or decrease in Brinkley's equity from January 5, 2016, through January 8, 2018, resulting from its investment in Bloch.

Check   (2) Carrying value per share, $9.63

Part 2
Assume that although Brinkley owns 25% of Bloch's outstanding stock, circumstances indicate that it does not have a significant influence over the investee and that it is classified as an available-for-sale security investment.

Required

1. Prepare journal entries to record these transactions and events for Brinkley. Also prepare an entry dated January 8, 2018, to remove any balance related to the fair value adjustment.

2. Compute the cost per share of Brinkley's investment in Bloch common stock as reflected in the investment account on January 7, 2018.

3. Compute the net increase or decrease in Brinkley's equity from January 5, 2016, through January 8, 2018, resulting from its investment in Bloch.

(1) 1/8/2018 Dr. Unrealized Gain—Equity, $72,500

(3) Net increase, $222,500

Troyer's long-term available-for-sale portfolio at December 31, 2015, consists of the following.

Problem C-5B
Long-term investment transactions; unrealized and realized gains and losses
C2   P3   P4

Available-for-Sale Securities	Cost	Fair Value
27,500 shares of Company R common stock..........	$559,125	$599,063
8,500 shares of Company S common stock	308,380	293,250
11,000 shares of Company T common stock..........	147,295	151,800

Troyer enters into the following long-term investment transactions during year 2016.

Jan. 13 Sold 2,125 shares of Company S stock for $72,250 less a brokerage fee of $1,195.

Mar. 24 Purchased 15,500 shares of Company U common stock for $282,875 plus a brokerage fee of $1,980. The shares represent a 62% ownership interest in Company U.

Apr. 5 Purchased 42,500 shares of Company V common stock for $133,875 plus a brokerage fee of $1,125. The shares represent a 10% ownership in Company V.

Sept. 2 Sold 11,000 shares of Company T common stock for $156,750 less a brokerage fee of $2,700.

Sept. 27 Purchased 2,500 shares of Company W common stock for $50,500 plus a brokerage fee of $1,050. The shares represent a 25% ownership interest in Company W.

Oct. 30 Purchased 5,000 shares of Company X common stock for $48,750 plus a brokerage fee of $1,170. The shares represent a 13% ownership interest in Company X.

The fair values of its investments at December 31, 2016, are: R, $568,125; S, $210,375; U, $272,800; V, $134,938; W, $54,689; and X, $45,625.

Required

Check (2) Dr. Unrealized Loss—Equity, $16,267; Cr. Fair Value Adjustment—AFS (LT), $45,580

1. Determine the amount Troyer should report on its December 31, 2016, balance sheet for its long-term investments in available-for-sale securities.

2. Prepare any necessary December 31, 2016, adjusting entry to record the fair value adjustment of the long-term investments in available-for-sale securities.

3. What amount of gains or losses on transactions relating to long-term investments in available-for-sale securities should Troyer report on its December 31, 2016, income statement?

Problem C-6B[A]
Foreign currency transactions

C3

Datamix, a U.S. corporation with customers in several foreign countries, had the following selected transactions for 2016 and 2017.

2016

May 26 Sold merchandise for 6.5 million yen to Fuji Company of Japan, payment in full to be received in 60 days. On this day, the exchange rate for yen is $0.0093.

June 1 Sold merchandise to Fordham Ltd. of Great Britain for $64,800 cash. The exchange rate for pounds is $1.4498 on this day.

July 25 Received Fuji's payment in yen for its May 26 purchase and immediately exchanged the yen for dollars. The exchange rate for yen is $0.0092 on this day.

Oct. 15 Sold merchandise on credit to Martinez Brothers of Mexico. The price of 378,000 pesos is to be paid 90 days from the date of sale. On this day, the exchange rate for pesos is $0.1020.

Dec. 6 Sold merchandise for 250,000 yuans to Chi-Ying Company of China, payment in full to be received in 30 days. The exchange rate for yuans is $0.1439 on this day.

Dec. 31 Recorded adjusting entries to recognize exchange gains or losses on Datamix's annual financial statements. Rates of exchanging foreign currencies on this day follow.

Yen (Japan)	$0.0094	Pesos (Mexico)	$0.1060
Pounds (Britain)	1.4580	Yuans (China)	0.1450

2017

Jan. 5 Received Chi-Ying's full payment in yuans for the December 6 sale and immediately exchanged the yuans for dollars. The exchange rate for yuans is $0.1580 on this day.

Jan. 13 Received full payment in pesos from Martinez for the October 15 sale and immediately exchanged the pesos for dollars. The exchange rate for pesos is $0.1039 on this day.

Required

1. Prepare journal entries for the Datamix transactions and adjusting entries.

Check (2) 2016 total foreign exchange gain, $1,137

2. Compute the foreign exchange gain or loss to be reported on Datamix's 2016 income statement.

Analysis Component

3. What actions might Datamix consider to reduce its risk of foreign exchange gains or losses?

(This serial problem began in Chapter 1 and continues through most of the book. If previous chapter segments were not completed, the serial problem can begin at this point. It is helpful, but not necessary, to use the Working Papers that accompany the book.)

SP C While reviewing the March 31, 2017, balance sheet of Business Solutions, Santana Rey notes that the business has built a large cash balance. Its most recent bank money market statement shows that the funds are earning an annualized return of 0.75%. Santana decides to make several investments with the desire to earn a higher return on the idle cash balance. Accordingly, in April 2017, Business Solutions makes the following investments in trading securities:

Apr. 16   Purchases 400 shares of Johnson & Johnson stock at $50 per share plus a $300 commission.
Apr. 30   Purchases 200 shares of Starbucks Corporation at $22 per share plus a $250 commission.

On June 30, 2017, the per share market price (fair value) of the Johnson & Johnson shares is $55 and the Starbucks shares is $19.

Required

1. Prepare journal entries to record the April purchases of trading securities by Business Solutions.
2. On June 30, 2017, prepare the adjusting entry to record any necessary fair value adjustment to its portfolio of trading securities.

GENERAL LEDGER PROBLEMS

Available in Connect

The following General Ledger assignments focus on the accounting for investments in available-for-sale securities and equity method investments.

GL C-1   General Ledger assignment C-1 is adapted from Problem C-2A. Prepare journal entries related to short-term investments in available-for-sale securities, including the adjustment to fair value, if necessary.

GL C-2   General Ledger assignment C-2 is adapted from Problem C-5A. Prepare journal entries related to long-term investment transactions and the related realized and unrealized gains.

Beyond the Numbers

BTN C-1   Refer to **Apple**'s financial statements in Appendix A to answer the following.
1. Are its financial statements consolidated? How can you tell?
2. What is the amount of *comprehensive income* for the year ended September 27, 2014?
3. Does it have any foreign operations? How can you tell?
4. Compute its return on total assets for the year ended September 27, 2014.

Fast Forward

5. Access Apple's annual report for a fiscal year ending after September 27, 2014, from either its website (**Apple.com**) or the SEC's database (**www.SEC.gov**). Recompute its return on total assets for the years subsequent to September 27, 2014.

BTN C-2   Key figures for **Apple** and **Google** follow.

$ millions	Apple			Google		
	Current Year	1 Year Prior	2 Years Prior	Current Year	1 Year Prior	2 Years Prior
Net income	$ 39,510	$ 37,037	$ 41,733	$ 14,444	$ 12,920	$10,737
Net sales	182,795	170,910	156,508	66,001	55,519	46,039
Total assets.........	231,839	207,000	176,064	131,133	110,920	93,798

Required

1. Compute return on total assets for Apple and Google for the two most recent years.
2. Separate the return on total assets computed in part 1 into its components for both companies and both years according to the formula in Exhibit C.9.
3. Which company has the highest total return on assets? The highest profit margin? The highest total asset turnover? What does this comparative analysis reveal? (Assume an industry average of 10.0% for return on assets.)

ETHICS CHALLENGE

P2   P3

BTN C-3   Kasey Hartman is the controller for Wholemart Company, which has numerous long-term investments in debt securities. Wholemart's investments are mainly in five-year bonds. Hartman is preparing its year-end financial statements. In accounting for long-term debt securities, she knows that each long-term investment must be designated as a held-to-maturity or an available-for-sale security. Interest rates rose sharply this past year, causing the portfolio's fair value to substantially decline. The company does not intend to hold the bonds for the entire five years. Hartman also earns a bonus each year, which is computed as a percent of net income.

Required

1. Will Hartman's bonus depend in any way on the classification of the debt securities? Explain.
2. What criteria must Hartman use to classify the securities as held-to-maturity or available-for-sale?
3. Is there likely any company oversight of Hartman's classification of the securities? Explain.

COMMUNICATING IN PRACTICE

P4

BTN C-4   Assume that you are Jolee Company's accountant. Company owner Mary Jolee has reviewed the 2016 financial statements you prepared and questions the $6,000 loss reported on the sale of its investment in Kemper Co. common stock. Jolee acquired 50,000 shares of Kemper's common stock on December 31, 2014, at a cost of $500,000. This stock purchase represented a 40% interest in Kemper. The 2015 income statement reported that earnings from all investments were $126,000. On January 3, 2016, Jolee Company sold the Kemper stock for $575,000. Kemper did not pay any dividends during 2015 but reported a net income of $202,500 for that year. Mary Jolee believes that because the Kemper stock purchase price was $500,000 and was sold for $575,000, the 2016 income statement should report a $75,000 gain on the sale.

Required

Draft a half-page memorandum to Mary Jolee explaining why the $6,000 loss on sale of Kemper stock is correctly reported.

TAKING IT TO THE NET

C1

BTN C-5   Access the July 31, 2014, 10-K filing (for year-end June 30, 2014) of **Microsoft** (MSFT) at www.SEC.gov. Review its note 4, "Investments."

Required

1. How does the "cost-basis" total amount for its investments as of June 30, 2014, compare to the prior year-end amount?
2. Identify at least eight types of short-term investments held by Microsoft as of June 30, 2014.
3. What were Microsoft's unrealized gains and its unrealized losses from its investments for 2014?
4. Was the cost or fair value ("recorded basis") of the investments higher as of June 30, 2014?

BTN C-6   Each team member is to become an expert on a specific classification of long-term investments. This expertise will be used to facilitate other teammates' understanding of the concepts and procedures relevant to the classification chosen.

TEAMWORK IN ACTION

C1 C2 P1 P2 P3 P4

1. Each team member must select an area for expertise by choosing one of the following classifications of long-term investments.

  a. Held-to-maturity debt securities

  b. Available-for-sale debt and equity securities

  c. Equity securities with significant influence

  d. Equity securities with controlling influence

2. Learning teams are to disburse and expert teams are to be formed. Expert teams are made up of those who select the same area of expertise. The instructor will identify the location where each expert team will meet.

3. Expert teams will collaborate to develop a presentation based on the following requirements. Students must write the presentation in a format they can show to their learning teams in part 4.

Requirements for Expert Presentation

  a. Write a transaction for the acquisition of this type of investment security. The transaction description is to include all necessary data to reflect the chosen classification.

  b. Prepare the journal entry to record the acquisition.

  [*Note:* The expert team on equity securities with controlling influence will substitute requirements (*d*) and (*e*) with a discussion of the reporting of these investments.]

  c. Identify information necessary to complete the end-of-period adjustment for this investment.

  d. Assuming that this is the only investment owned, prepare any necessary year-end entries.

  e. Present the relevant balance sheet section(s).

4. Re-form learning teams. In rotation, experts are to present to their teams the presentations they developed in part 3. Experts are to encourage and respond to questions.

BTN C-7ᴬ   Assume that a company desires to acquire the Japanese rights to a website, which will then be branded with its products for sale in Japan. Assume the company acquires those rights on January 1, 2016, from a Japanese distributor and agrees to pay 12,000,000 yen per year for those rights. Quarterly payments are due March 31, June 30, September 30, and December 31 each year. On January 1, 2016, assume the yen is worth $0.00891.

ENTREPRENEURIAL DECISION

C3

Required

1. Prepare the journal entry to record the Internet rights purchased on January 1, 2016.

2. Prepare the journal entries to record the payments on March 31, June 30, September 30, and December 31, 2016. The value of the yen on those dates follows.

March 31	$0.00893
June 30	0.00901
September 30	0.00902
December 31	0.00897

3. How can the company protect itself from unanticipated gains and losses from currency translation if all of the payments are specified to be paid in yen?

BTN C-8ᴬ   Assume that you are planning a spring break trip to Europe. Identify three locations where you can find exchange rates for the dollar relative to the euro or other currencies.

HITTING THE ROAD

C3

GLOBAL DECISION

A1

Samsung
APPLE
GOOGLE

BTN C-9 **Samsung**, **Apple**, and **Google** are competitors in the global marketplace. Following are selected data from each company.

Key Figure	Samsung (Korean won millions) Current Year	One Year Prior	Two Years Prior	Apple Current Year	Apple Prior Year	Google Current Year	Google Prior Year
Net income	₩ 23,394,358	₩ 30,474,764	₩ 23,845,285	—	—	—	—
Net sales	206,205,987	228,692,667	201,103,613	—	—	—	—
Total assets	230,422,958	214,075,018	181,071,570	—	—	—	—
Profit margin	?	?	—	21.6%	21.7%	21.9%	21.6%
Total asset turnover	?	?	—	0.83	0.89	0.54	0.58

Required

1. Compute Samsung's return on total assets, and its components of profit margin and total asset turnover, for the most recent two years using the data provided.

2. Which of these three companies has the highest return on total assets? Highest profit margin? Highest total asset turnover? Interpret these results for the (*a*) current year and (*b*) prior year.

ANSWERS TO MULTIPLE CHOICE QUIZ

1. d; $30,000 × 5% × 5/12 = $625
2. a; Unrealized gain = $84,500 − $83,000 = $1,500
3. b; $50,000 × 35% = $17,500
4. e; $300,000/$2,000,000 = 15%
5. b; Profit margin = $80,000/$600,000 = 13.3%
   Total asset turnover = $600,000/$400,000 = 1.5

Chart of Accounts

Following is a typical chart of accounts, which is used in several assignments. Each company has its own unique set of accounts and numbering system. *An asterisk denotes a contra account.

Assets

Current Assets

101 Cash
102 Petty cash
103 Cash equivalents
104 Short-term investments
105 Fair value adjustment, _____ securities (S-T)
106 Accounts receivable
107 Allowance for doubtful accounts*
108 Allowance for sales discounts*
109 Interest receivable
110 Rent receivable
111 Notes receivable
112 Legal fees receivable
119 Merchandise inventory (or Inventory)
120 _____ inventory
121 Inventory returns estimated
124 Office supplies
125 Store supplies
126 _____ supplies
128 Prepaid insurance
129 Prepaid interest
131 Prepaid rent
132 Raw materials inventory
133 Work in process inventory, _____
134 Work in process inventory, _____
135 Finished goods inventory

Long-Term Investments

141 Long-term investments
142 Fair value adjustment, _____ securities (L-T)
144 Investment in _____
145 Bond sinking fund

Plant Assets

151 Automobiles
152 Accumulated depreciation—Automobiles*
153 Trucks
154 Accumulated depreciation—Trucks*
155 Boats
156 Accumulated depreciation—Boats*
157 Professional library
158 Accumulated depreciation—Professional library*
159 Law library
160 Accumulated depreciation—Law library*
161 Furniture
162 Accumulated depreciation—Furniture*
163 Office equipment
164 Accumulated depreciation—Office equipment*
165 Store equipment
166 Accumulated depreciation—Store equipment*
167 _____ equipment
168 Accumulated depreciation—_____ equipment*
169 Machinery
170 Accumulated depreciation—Machinery*
173 Building _____
174 Accumulated depreciation—Building _____*
175 Building _____
176 Accumulated depreciation—Building _____*
179 Land improvements _____
180 Accumulated depreciation—Land improvements _____*
181 Land improvements _____
182 Accumulated depreciation—Land improvements _____*
183 Land

Natural Resources

185 Mineral deposit
186 Accumulated depletion—Mineral deposit*

Intangible Assets

191 Patents
192 Leasehold
193 Franchise
194 Copyrights
195 Leasehold improvements
196 Licenses
197 Accumulated amortization—_____*

Liabilities

Current Liabilities

201 Accounts payable
202 Insurance payable
203 Interest payable
204 Legal fees payable
207 Office salaries payable
208 Rent payable
209 Salaries payable
210 Wages payable
211 Accrued payroll payable
212 Factory payroll payable
214 Estimated warranty liability
215 Income taxes payable
216 Common dividend payable
217 Preferred dividend payable
218 State unemployment taxes payable
219 Employee federal income taxes payable
221 Employee medical insurance payable
222 Employee retirement program payable
223 Employee union dues payable
224 Federal unemployment taxes payable
225 FICA taxes payable
226 Estimated vacation pay liability
227 Sales refund payable

Unearned Revenues

230 Unearned consulting fees
231 Unearned legal fees
232 Unearned property management fees
233 Unearned _____ fees
234 Unearned _____ fees
235 Unearned janitorial revenue
236 Unearned _____ revenue
238 Unearned rent

Notes Payable

240 Short-term notes payable
241 Discount on short-term notes payable*
245 Notes payable
251 Long-term notes payable
252 Discount on long-term notes payable*

Long-Term Liabilities

253 Long-term lease liability
255 Bonds payable
256 Discount on bonds payable*
257 Premium on bonds payable
258 Deferred income tax liability

Equity

Owner's Equity

301 _____, Capital
302 _____, Withdrawals
303 _____, Capital
304 _____, Withdrawals
305 _____, Capital
306 _____, Withdrawals

Paid-In Capital

307 Common stock, $ _____ par value
308 Common stock, no-par value
309 Common stock, $ _____ stated value
310 Common stock dividend distributable
311 Paid-in capital in excess of par value, Common stock

312 Paid-in capital in excess of stated value, No-par common stock
313 Paid-in capital from retirement of common stock
314 Paid-in capital, Treasury stock
315 Preferred stock
316 Paid-in capital in excess of par value, Preferred stock

Retained Earnings

318 Retained earnings
319 Cash dividends (or Dividends)
320 Stock dividends

Other Equity Accounts

321 Treasury stock, Common*
322 Unrealized gain—Equity
323 Unrealized loss—Equity

Revenues

401 _____ fees earned
402 _____ fees earned
403 _____ revenues
404 Revenues
405 Commissions earned
406 Rent revenue (or Rent earned)
407 Dividends revenue (or Dividends earned)
408 Earnings from investment in _____
409 Interest revenue (or Interest earned)
410 Sinking fund earnings
413 Sales
414 Sales returns and allowances*
415 Sales discounts*

Cost of Sales

Cost of Goods Sold

502 Cost of goods sold
505 Purchases
506 Purchases returns and allowances*
507 Purchases discounts*
508 Transportation-in

Manufacturing

520 Raw materials purchases
521 Freight-in on raw materials
530 Direct labor
540 Factory overhead
541 Indirect materials
542 Indirect labor
543 Factory insurance expired
544 Factory supervision
545 Factory supplies used
546 Factory utilities
547 Miscellaneous production costs
548 Property taxes on factory building
549 Property taxes on factory equipment
550 Rent on factory building
551 Repairs, factory equipment
552 Small tools written off
560 Depreciation of factory equipment
561 Depreciation of factory building

Standard Cost Variances

580 Direct material quantity variance
581 Direct material price variance
582 Direct labor quantity variance
583 Direct labor price variance
584 Factory overhead volume variance
585 Factory overhead controllable variance

Expenses

Amortization, Depletion, and Depreciation

601 Amortization expense—_____
602 Amortization expense—_____
603 Depletion expense—_____
604 Depreciation expense—Boats
605 Depreciation expense—Automobiles
606 Depreciation expense—Building _____
607 Depreciation expense—Building _____
608 Depreciation expense—Land improvements _____
609 Depreciation expense—Land improvements _____
610 Depreciation expense—Law library
611 Depreciation expense—Trucks
612 Depreciation expense—_____ equipment
613 Depreciation expense—_____ equipment
614 Depreciation expense—_____
615 Depreciation expense—_____

Employee-Related Expenses

620 Office salaries expense
621 Sales salaries expense
622 Salaries expense
623 _____ wages expense
624 Employees' benefits expense
625 Payroll taxes expense

Financial Expenses

630 Cash over and short
631 Discounts lost
632 Factoring fee expense
633 Interest expense

Insurance Expenses

635 Insurance expense—Delivery equipment
636 Insurance expense—Office equipment
637 Insurance expense—_____

Rental Expenses

640 Rent expense
641 Rent expense—Office space
642 Rent expense—Selling space
643 Press rental expense
644 Truck rental expense
645 _____ rental expense

Supplies Expenses

650 Office supplies expense
651 Store supplies expense
652 _____ supplies expense
653 _____ supplies expense

Miscellaneous Expenses

655 Advertising expense
656 Bad debts expense
657 Blueprinting expense
658 Boat expense
659 Collection expense
661 Concessions expense
662 Credit card expense
663 Delivery expense
664 Dumping expense
667 Equipment expense
668 Food and drinks expense
671 Gas and oil expense
672 General and administrative expense
673 Janitorial expense
674 Legal fees expense
676 Mileage expense
677 Miscellaneous expenses
678 Mower and tools expense
679 Operating expense
680 Organization expense
681 Permits expense
682 Postage expense
683 Property taxes expense
684 Repairs expense—_____
685 Repairs expense—_____
687 Selling expense
688 Telephone expense
689 Travel and entertainment expense
690 Utilities expense
691 Warranty expense
692 _____ expense
695 Income taxes expense

Gains and Losses

701 Gain on retirement of bonds
702 Gain on sale of machinery
703 Gain on sale of investments
704 Gain on sale of trucks
705 Gain on _____
706 Foreign exchange gain or loss
801 Loss on disposal of machinery
802 Loss on exchange of equipment
803 Loss on exchange of _____
804 Loss on sale of notes
805 Loss on retirement of bonds
806 Loss on sale of investments
807 Loss on sale of machinery
808 Loss on _____
809 Unrealized gain—Income
810 Unrealized loss—Income
811 Impairment gain
812 Impairment loss

Clearing Accounts

901 Income summary
902 Manufacturing summary

Income Statement*
For *period* Ended *date*

Net sales (revenues)		$ #
Cost of goods sold (cost of sales)		#
Gross margin (gross profit)		#
Operating expenses		
Examples: depreciation, salaries, wages, rent, utilities, ...	$ #	
interest, amortization, advertising, ...	#	
taxes, selling, general and administrative.	#	
Total operating expenses.		#
Nonoperating gains and losses (unusual and/or infrequent).		#
Net income (net profit or earnings)		$ #

* A typical chart of accounts is at the end of the book and classifies all accounts by financial statement categories.

Balance Sheet
Date

ASSETS

Current assets

Examples: cash, cash equivalents, short-term investments, ...	$ #	
accounts receivable, current portion of notes receivable, ...	#	
inventory, inventory returns estimated, prepaid expenses	#	
Total current assets		$ #

Long-term investments

Examples: investment in stock, investment in bonds, ...	#	
land for expansion	#	
Total long-term investments		#

Plant assets

Examples: equipment, machinery, buildings, land	#	
Total plant assets, net of depreciation		#

Intangible assets

Examples: patent, trademark, copyright, license, goodwill	#	
Total intangible assets, net of amortization		#
Total assets.		$ #

LIABILITIES AND EQUITY

Current liabilities

Examples: accounts payable, wages payable, salaries payable, ...	$ #	
current notes payable, taxes payable, interest payable, ...	#	
unearned revenues, current portion of debt, sales refund payable . .	#	
Total current liabilities.		$ #

Long-term liabilities

Examples: notes payable, bonds payable, lease liability	#	
Total long-term liabilities.		#
Total liabilities		#

Equity

Common stock		#
Paid-in capital in excess of par or stated value		#
Retained earnings.		#
Less treasury stock		(#)
Total liabilities and equity		$ #

Statement of Cash Flows
For *period* Ended *date*

Cash flows from operating activities		
[Prepared using the indirect (see below)† or direct method]		
Net cash provided (used) by operating activities.		$ #
Cash flows from investing activities		
[List of individual investing inflows and outflows]		
Net cash provided (used) by investing activities.		#
Cash flows from financing activities		
[List of individual financing inflows and outflows]		
Net cash provided (used) by financing activities.		#
Net increase (decrease) in cash		$ #
Cash (and equivalents) balance at beginning of period		#
Cash (and equivalents) balance at end of period		$ #

Attach separate schedule or note disclosure of "Noncash investing and financing transactions."

†Indirect Method: Cash Flows from Operating Activities

Cash flows from operating activities		
Net income		$ #
Adjustments for operating items not providing or using cash		
+Noncash expenses and losses	$ #	
Examples: Expenses for depreciation, depletion, and amortization;		
losses from disposal of long-term assets and from retirement of debt		
−Noncash revenues and gains.	#	
Examples: Earnings from equity-method investments; gains from		
disposal of long-term assets and from retirement of debt		
Adjustments for changes in current assets and current liabilities		
+Decrease in noncash current operating asset	#	
−Increase in noncash current operating asset	#	
+Increase in current operating liability	#	
−Decrease in current operating liability	#	
Net cash provided (used) by operating activities.		$ #

Statement of Retained Earnings
For *period* Ended *date*

Retained earnings, beginning	$ #	
Add: Net income	#	
	#	
Less: Dividends declared	#	
Net loss (if exists)	#	
Retained earnings, ending	$ #	

Statement of Stockholders' Equity†
For *period* Ended *date*

	Common Stock	Capital in Excess of Par	Retained Earnings	Treasury Stock	Total
Balances, beginning.	$ #	$ #	$ #	$ #	$ #
Net income					
Cash dividends.					
Stock issuance					
Treasury stock purchase					
Treasury stock reissuance.					
Other					
Balances, ending.	$ #	$ #	$ #	$ #	$ #

† Additional columns and account titles commonly include number of shares, preferred stock, unrealized gains and losses on available-for-sale securities, foreign currency translation, and comprehensive income.

Premium Bond Amortization (Straight-Line) Table†

Semiannual Period-End	Unamortized Bond Premium*	Bond Carrying Value**
Bond life-start	$ #	$ #
. . . .		
. . . .		
Bond life-end	0	par

† Bond carrying value is adjusted downward to par and its amortized premium downward to zero over the bond life (note: carrying value less unamortized bond premium equals par).
* Equals total bond premium less its accumulated amortization.
** Equals bond par value <u>plus</u> its unamortized bond premium.

Discount Bond Amortization (Straight-Line) Table†

Semiannual Period-End	Unamortized Bond Discount*	Bond Carrying Value**
Bond life-start	$ #	$ #
. . . .		
. . . .		
Bond life-end	0	par

† Bond carrying value is adjusted upward to par and its amortized discount downward to zero over the bond life (note: unamortized bond discount plus carrying value equals par).
* Equals total bond discount less its accumulated amortization.
** Equals bond par value <u>less</u> its unamortized bond discount.

Effective Interest Amortization Table for Bonds with Semiannual Interest Payment

Semiannual Interest Period-End	Cash Interest Paid[A]	Bond Interest Expense[B]	Discount or Premium Amortization[C]	Unamortized Discount or Premium[D]	Carrying Value[E]
#	#	#	#	#	#
⋮	⋮	⋮	⋮	⋮	⋮

[A] Par value multiplied by the semiannual contract rate.
[B] Prior period's carrying value multiplied by the semiannual market rate.
[C] The difference between interest paid and bond interest expense.
[D] Prior period's unamortized discount or premium less the current period's discount or premium amortization.
[E] Par value less unamortized discount or plus unamortized premium.

Installment Notes Payment Table

Period Ending Date	Beginning Balance	Debit Interest Expense	+	Debit Notes Payable	=	Credit Cash	Ending Balance
#	#	#		#		#	#
⋮	⋮	⋮		⋮		⋮	⋮

Bank Reconciliation
Date

Bank statement balance.	$#	Book balance.		$#
Add: Unrecorded deposits	#	Add: Unrecorded bank credit		
		memoranda		#
Bank errors understating		Book errors understating		
the balance	#	the balance.		#
	#			#
Less: Outstanding checks	#	Less: Unrecorded bank debit		
		memoranda		#
Bank errors overstating		Book errors overstating		
the balance	#	the balance.		#
Adjusted bank balance.	**$#**	**Adjusted book balance**		**$#**

Balances are equal (reconciled)

BRIEF REVIEW: SELECTED TRANSACTIONS AND RELATIONS

① Merchandising Transactions Summary—Perpetual Inventory System

	Merchandising Transactions	Merchandising Entries	Dr.	Cr.
Purchases	Purchasing merchandise for resale.	Merchandise Inventory	#	
		Cash or Accounts Payable.		#
	Paying freight costs on purchases; FOB shipping point.	Merchandise Inventory	#	
		Cash		#
	Paying within discount period.	Accounts Payable.	#	
		Merchandise Inventory		#
		Cash		#
	Paying outside discount period.	Accounts Payable.	#	
		Cash		#
	Recording purchase returns or allowances.	Cash or Accounts Payable.	#	
		Merchandise Inventory		#
Sales	Selling merchandise.	Cash or Accounts Receivable	#	
		Sales		#
		Cost of Goods Sold.	#	
		Merchandise Inventory		#
	Receiving payment within discount period.	Cash	#	
		Sales Discounts	#	
		Accounts Receivable		#
	Receiving payment outside discount period.	Cash	#	
		Accounts Receivable		#
	Receiving sales returns of nondefective inventory	Sales Returns and Allowances	#	
		Cash or Accounts Receivable		#
		Merchandise Inventory	#	
		Cost of Goods Sold.		#
	Recognizing sales allowances.	Sales Returns and Allowances	#	
		Cash or Accounts Receivable		#
	Paying freight costs on sales; FOB destination.	Delivery Expense	#	
		Cash		#

	Merchandising Events	Adjusting and Closing Entries		
Adjusting	Adjustment for shrinkage (occurs when recorded amount larger than physical inventory).	Cost of Goods Sold.	#	
		Merchandise Inventory		#
	Period-end adjustment for expected sales discounts.*	Sales Discounts	#	
		Allowance for Sales Discounts		#
	Period-end adjustment for expected returns—both revenue-side and cost-side.*	Sales Returns and Allowances	#	
		Sales Refund Payable		#
		Inventory Returns Estimated.	#	
		Cost of Goods Sold.		#
Closing	Closing temporary accounts with credit balances.	Sales	#	
		Income Summary		#
	Closing temporary accounts with debit balances.	Income Summary	#	
		Sales Returns and Allowances		#
		Sales Discounts		#
		Cost of Goods Sold.		#
		Delivery Expense		#
		"Other Expenses"		#

* Period-end adjustments depend on unadjusted balances, which can reverse the adjusting entries shown.

⑥ Stock Transactions Summary

	Stock Transactions	Stock Entries	Dr.	Cr.
Issue Common Stock	Issue par value common stock at par (par stock recorded at par).	Cash	#	
		Common Stock.		#
	Issue par value common stock at premium (par stock recorded at par).	Cash	#	
		Common Stock.		#
		Paid-In Capital in Excess of Par Value, Common Stock		#
	Issue no-par value common stock (no-par stock recorded at amount received).	Cash	#	
		Common Stock.		#
	Issue stated value common stock at stated value (stated stock recorded at stated value).	Cash	#	
		Common stock		#
	Issue stated value common stock at premium (stated stock recorded at stated value).	Cash	#	
		Common stock		#
		Paid-In Capital in Excess of Stated Value, Common Stock. . . .		#
Issue Preferred Stock	Issue par value preferred stock at par (par stock recorded at par).	Cash	#	
		Preferred Stock.		#
	Issue par value preferred stock at premium (par stock recorded at par).	Cash	#	
		Preferred Stock.		#
		Paid-In Capital in Excess of Par Value, Preferred Stock		#
Reacquire Common Stock	Reacquire its own common stock (treasury stock recorded at cost).	Treasury Stock, Common	#	
		Cash		#
Reissue Common Stock	Reissue its treasury stock at cost (treasury stock removed at cost).	Cash	#	
		Treasury Stock, Common		#
	Reissue its treasury stock above cost (treasury stock removed at cost).	Cash	#	
		Treasury Stock, Common		#
		Paid-In Capital, Treasury.		#
	Reissue its treasury stock below cost (treasury stock removed at cost; if paid-in capital is insufficient to cover amount below cost, retained earnings is debited for remainder).	Cash	#	
		Paid-In Capital, Treasury	#	
		Retained Earnings (if necessary)	#	
		Treasury Stock, Common		#

② Merchandising Cash Flows

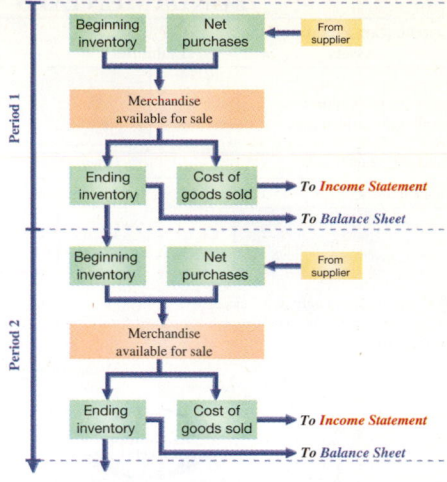

③ Credit Terms and Amounts

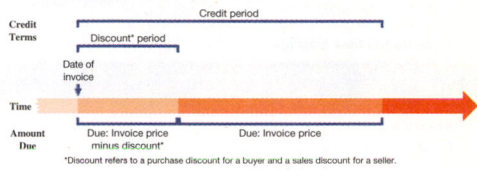

*Discount refers to a purchase discount for a buyer and a sales discount for a seller.

④ Bad Debts Estimation

⑤ Bond Valuation

⑦ Dividend Transactions

Account Affected	Type of Dividend		
	Cash Dividend	Stock Dividend	Stock Split
Cash	Decrease	—	—
Common Stock	—	Increase	—
Retained Earnings . . .	Decrease	Decrease	—

⑧ A Rose by Any Other Name
The same financial statement sometimes receives different titles. Following are some of the more common aliases.*

Balance Sheet	Statement of Financial Position Statement of Financial Condition
Income Statement	Statement of Income Operating Statement Statement of Operations Statement of Operating Activity Earnings Statement Statement of Earnings Profit and Loss (P&L) Statement
Statement of Cash Flows	Statement of Cash Flow Cash Flows Statement Statement of Changes in Cash Position Statement of Changes in Financial Position
Statement of Stockholders' Equity	Statement of Shareholders' Equity Statement of Changes in Shareholders' Equity Statement of Stockholders' Equity and Comprehensive Income Statement of Changes in Owner's Equity Statement of Changes in Owner's Capital Statement of Changes in Capital Accounts

* The term **Consolidated** often precedes or follows these statement titles to reflect the combination of different entities, such as a parent company and its subsidiaries.

FUNDAMENTALS

① Accounting Equation

Assets = Liabilities + Equity

| Debit for increases ↑ | Credit for decreases ↓ | Debit for decreases ↓ | Credit for increases ↑ | Debit for decreases ↓ | Credit for increases ↑ |

Equity = Contributed Capital* + Retained Earnings

Contributed Capital* + Retained Earnings

Common Stock − Dividends + Revenues − Expenses

| Dr. for decreases | Cr. for increases | Dr. for increases | Cr. for decreases | Dr. for decreases | Cr. for increases | Dr. for increases | Cr. for decreases |

Indicates normal balance.
*Includes common stock and any preferred stock.

② Accounting Cycle

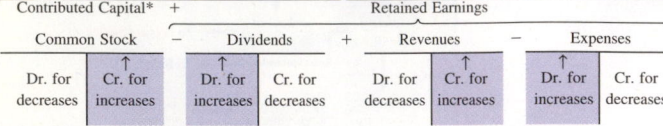

1. Analyze transactions
2. Journalize
3. Post
4. Prepare unadjusted trial balance
5. Adjust
6. Prepare adjusted trial balance
7. Prepare statements
8. Close
9. Prepare post-closing trial balance
10. Reverse (Optional)

Accounting Cycle

③ Adjustments and Entries

Type	Adjusting Entry	
Prepaid Expenses	Dr. Expense	Cr. Asset*
Unearned Revenues	Dr. Liability	Cr. Revenue
Accrued Expenses	Dr. Expense	Cr. Liability
Accrued Revenues	Dr. Asset	Cr. Revenue

* For depreciation, credit Accumulated Depreciation (contra asset).

④ Four-Step Closing Process
1. Transfer revenue and gain account balances to Income Summary.
2. Transfer expense and loss account balances to Income Summary.
3. Transfer Income Summary balance to Retained Earnings.
4. Transfer Dividends balance to Retained Earnings.

⑤ Accounting Concepts

Characteristics	Assumptions	Principles	Constraints
Relevance	Business entity	Measurement (historical cost)	Cost-benefit
Reliability	Going concern	Revenue recognition	Materiality
Comparability	Monetary unit	Expense recognition	Industry practice
Consistency	Periodicity	Full disclosure	Conservatism

⑥ Ownership of Inventory

Shipping Terms	Ownership Transfers at	Goods in Transit Owned by	Transportation Costs Paid by
FOB shipping point	Shipping point	Buyer	**Buyer** — Merchandise Inventory ... # / Cash ... #
FOB destination	Destination	Seller	**Seller** — Delivery Expense ... # / Cash ... #

⑦ Inventory Costing Methods
- Specific identification
- First-in, first-out (FIFO)
- Weighted-average
- Last-in, first-out (LIFO)

⑧ Depreciation and Depletion

Straight-line: $\dfrac{\text{Cost} - \text{Salvage value}}{\text{Useful life in periods}}$

Units-of-production: $\dfrac{\text{Cost} - \text{Salvage value}}{\text{Useful life in units}} \times \text{Units produced in current period}$

Declining-balance: Rate* × Beginning-of-period book value
* Rate is often double the straight-line rate, or 2 × (1/Useful life)

Depletion: $\dfrac{\text{Cost} - \text{Salvage value}}{\text{Total capacity in units}} \times \text{Units extracted in current period}$

⑨ Interest Computation
Interest = Principal (face) × Rate × Time

⑩ Accounting for Investment Securities

Classification*	Accounting
Short-Term Investment in Securities	
Held-to-maturity (debt) securities	**Cost** (without any discount or premium amortization)
Trading (debt and equity) securities	**Fair value** (with fair value adjustment to income)
Available-for-sale (debt and equity) securities	**Fair value** (with fair value adjustment to equity)
Long-Term Investment in Securities	
Held-to-maturity (debt) securities	**Cost** (with any discount or premium amortization)
Available-for-sale (debt and equity) securities	**Fair value** (with fair value adjustment to equity)
Equity securities with significant influence	Equity method
Equity securities with controlling influence	Equity method (with consolidation)

* A *fair value option* allows companies to report HTM and AFS securities much like trading securities.

ANALYSES

① Liquidity and Efficiency

Current ratio $= \dfrac{\text{Current assets}}{\text{Current liabilities}}$ — pp. 125 & 604

Working capital = Current assets − Current liabilities — p. 603

Acid-test ratio $= \dfrac{\text{Cash} + \text{Short-term investments} + \text{Current receivables}}{\text{Current liabilities}}$ — pp. 187 & 605

Accounts receivable turnover $= \dfrac{\text{Net sales}}{\text{Average accounts receivable, net}}$ — pp. 335 & 605

Credit risk ratio $= \dfrac{\text{Allowance for doubtful accounts}}{\text{Accounts receivable, net}}$ — p. 335

Inventory turnover $= \dfrac{\text{Cost of goods sold}}{\text{Average inventory}}$ — pp. 236 & 605

Days' sales uncollected $= \dfrac{\text{Accounts receivable, net}}{\text{Net sales}} \times 365^*$ — pp. 296 & 606

Days' sales in inventory $= \dfrac{\text{Ending inventory}}{\text{Cost of goods sold}} \times 365^*$ — pp. 236 & 606

Total asset turnover $= \dfrac{\text{Net sales}}{\text{Average total assets}}$ — pp. 375 & 606

Plant asset useful life $= \dfrac{\text{Plant asset cost}}{\text{Depreciation expense}}$ — p. 376

Plant asset age $= \dfrac{\text{Accumulated depreciation}}{\text{Depreciation expense}}$ — p. 376

Days' cash expense coverage $= \dfrac{\text{Cash and cash equivalents}}{\text{Average daily cash expenses}}$ — p. 280

* 360 days is also commonly used.

② Solvency

Debt ratio $= \dfrac{\text{Total liabilities}}{\text{Total assets}}$ — Equity ratio $= \dfrac{\text{Total equity}}{\text{Total assets}}$ — pp. 75 & 607

Debt-to-equity $= \dfrac{\text{Total liabilities}}{\text{Total equity}}$ — pp. 460 & 607

Times interest earned $= \dfrac{\text{Income before interest expense and income taxes}}{\text{Interest expense}}$ — pp. 414 & 608

Cash coverage of growth $= \dfrac{\text{Cash flow from operations}}{\text{Cash outflow for plant assets}}$ — p. 556

Cash coverage of debt $= \dfrac{\text{Cash flow from operations}}{\text{Total noncurrent liabilities}}$ — p. 556

③ Profitability

Profit margin ratio $= \dfrac{\text{Net income}}{\text{Net sales}}$ — pp. 125 & 608

Gross margin ratio $= \dfrac{\text{Net sales} - \text{Cost of goods sold}}{\text{Net sales}}$ — p. 188

Return on total assets $= \dfrac{\text{Net income}}{\text{Average total assets}}$ — pp. 24 & 608

$= \text{Profit margin ratio} \times \text{Total asset turnover}$ — p. 609

Return on common stockholders' equity $= \dfrac{\text{Net income} - \text{Preferred dividends}}{\text{Average common stockholders' equity}}$ — p. 611

Book value per common share $= \dfrac{\text{Stockholders' equity applicable to common shares}}{\text{Number of common shares outstanding}}$ — p. 512

Basic earnings per share $= \dfrac{\text{Net income} - \text{Preferred dividends}}{\text{Weighted-average common shares outstanding}}$ — p. 510

Cash flow on total assets $= \dfrac{\text{Cash flow from operations}}{\text{Average total assets}}$ — p. 555

Payout ratio $= \dfrac{\text{Cash dividends declared on common stock}}{\text{Net income}}$ — p. 511

④ Market

Price-earnings ratio $= \dfrac{\text{Market value (price) per share}}{\text{Earnings per share}}$ — pp. 511 & 610

Dividend yield $= \dfrac{\text{Annual cash dividends per share}}{\text{Market price per share}}$ — pp. 511 & 610

Residual income = Income − Target income